Lotus Notes® and Domino™ R5 Development

Debbie Lynd
Steve Kern

SAMS

A Division of Macmillan USA

201 West 103rd Street, Indianapolis, Indiana 46290

Unleashed

Lotus Notes® and Domino™ R5 Development Unleashed

Copyright ©2000 by Sams Publishing

All rights reserved. No part of this book shall be reproduced, stored in a retrieval system, or transmitted by any means, electronic, mechanical, photocopying, recording, or otherwise, without written permission from the publisher. No patent liability is assumed with respect to the use of the information contained herein. Although every precaution has been taken in the preparation of this book, the publisher and author assume no responsibility for errors or omissions. Neither is any liability assumed for damages resulting from the use of the information contained herein.

International Standard Book Number: 0-672-31414-2

Library of Congress Catalog Card Number: 98-86483

Printed in the United States of America

First Printing: November 1999

01   00   4   3   2

Trademarks

All terms mentioned in this book that are known to be trademarks or service marks have been appropriately capitalized. Sams Publishing cannot attest to the accuracy of this information. Use of a term in this book should not be regarded as affecting the validity of any trademark or service mark.

Lotus Notes is a registered trademark of Lotus Development Corporation.

Domino is a trademark of Lotus Development Corporation.

Warning and Disclaimer

Every effort has been made to make this book as complete and as accurate as possible, but no warranty or fitness is implied. The information provided is on an "as is" basis. The authors and the publisher shall have neither liability nor responsibility to any person or entity with respect to any loss or damages arising from the information contained in this book or from the use of the CD or programs accompanying it.

PUBLISHER
Dean Miller

DEVELOPMENT EDITOR
Brad Miser

MANAGING EDITOR
Lisa Wilson

SENIOR EDITOR
Susan Ross Moore

COPY EDITOR
Michael Dietsch

INDEXER
Larry Sweazy

PROOFREADER
Billy Fields

TECHNICAL EDITOR
Victor Mascari

TEAM COORDINATOR
Cindy Teeters

MEDIA DEVELOPER
John Warriner

INTERIOR DESIGN
Gary Adair

COVER DESIGN
Aren Howell

COPY WRITER
Eric Borgert

PRODUCTION
Dan Harris
Staci Somers
Mark Walche

From the Series Editor:

Macmillan USA is excited and proud to announce that *Lotus Notes and Domino R5 Development Unleashed* is part of our new integrated series of books on Lotus Notes and Domino R5.

As illustrated in the User Pyramid (see facing page) this series is not merely a collection of books but a carefully planned succession of tutorials and reference material. Our building block approach to Lotus Notes and Domino R5 gives corporations the ability to identify the right book for each of their users. Individuals "graduate" to the next level of proficiency with confidence that the topics and depth of coverage are appropriately expanded and enhanced.

The lead authors in our series are Certified Lotus Notes Professionals (CLP) and/or Certified Lotus Notes Instructors (CLI) with real-world product experience. They represent the professional Lotus Notes and Domino community, and they understand your need to augment skills commensurate with new product releases and evolving user community needs.

I hope you enjoy our series of R5 books as much as we have enjoyed our collaborative efforts to deliver them to you. Thank you.

Sincerely,

Jane Calabria

Series Editor

Contents at a Glance

Contents

About the Authors

Debbie Lynd is a Principal Certified Lotus Professional for Release 5 in both Application Development and System Administration and a Certified Lotus Instructor. She is the president of Technology Alliance Partners, a training and consulting firm located just outside of Philadelphia. Debbie has been working with computers since 1979, when she fell in love with a Vector Graphics CPM computer and wrote her first application.

Debbie lives in the suburbs of Philadelphia with her husband, three sons (when they come home from college), and a Lhasa apso named Gretchen. Also living on the property are some fish, frogs, and a snake that has taken up residence because of the tasty fish and frogs.

Steve Kern is a Certified Lotus Professional and is the senior manager of the Lotus Notes and Domino practice for Computer Associates in Columbus, Ohio. Before becoming a consultant, Steve spent 15 years in business management. Steve has been working with PCs and writing applications since the early 1980s.

Steve was the lead author for Sams' *Lotus Notes and Domino 4.5 Developer's Guide* and has contributed chapters to other Macmillan publications. He has also written numerous magazine articles and was a columnist for *Enterprise Solutions for Lotus Notes and Domino*. Steve has also served as technical editor for many Notes books, including *Lotus Notes 4 Unleashed* and *Lotus Notes and Domino Server 4.5 Unleashed* for Sams, as well as Que's *Special Edition Using Lotus Notes and Domino 4.5*, *Special Edition Using Lotus Notes and Domino 4.6*, *Professional Developer's Guide to Domino*, and *Easy Lotus Notes 4.5*.

He received a bachelor of science in Agriculture from The Ohio State University and lives in Columbus, Ohio with his wife and two daughters, four fish tanks, and a golden retriever.

Timothy Falconer is a software developer and Lotus expatriate who worked on several new administration features in Notes and Domino R5. He left Lotus to start Immuexa Corporation, a company that makes distributed Java apps and e-commerce sites for budding Internet entrepreneurs.

He has a degree from Lehigh University rolled up somewhere in the attic and nineteen years of pizza and programming experience under his belt. Most days, you'll find him working at home with his feline co-workers, Ishtar and Chloe. He spends nearly all his free time with his wonderful wife, Paula Zerkle.

Jonathan Kern is the president of Lightship, Inc. (`jkern@LightshipInc.com`), a software engineering solutions firm. Lightship provides advanced, object-oriented, multitier solutions using best-practice software development methods. From 1995 to 1998, Jonathan was the chief architect and object modeler for IBM's commercial Manufacturing Execution Software system. He has also designed an object-oriented solution to replace a legacy, DOS-based engineering product configurator and proposal generation system for Ingersoll-Dresser Pump. He is also working on an advanced design to create a distributed pump inspection application. Jonathan provides training in object modeling and Java and provides mentoring services to small teams of developers. Kern is also a co-author on Prentice-Hall's *Java Design: Building Better Apps and Applets, Second Edition* with Peter Coad, and is currently writing *Distributed Java Design* with Peter Coad (due in early 2001).

Dedication

I dedicate this book to my husband, Harry, who has never asked me to be anything other than what I am, and who always provides me with the support and encouragement I need. And to my children, who have put up with a lot so that I might succeed. May your lives be as blessed as you've made mine. I love you guys.

Debbie Lynd

I dedicate this book to the memory of my father who passed away during its writing. To my wife and children—thanks for putting up with all this craziness! I love you.

Steve Kern

Acknowledgments

There are many people to thank in the journey of this, my first book. I would be remiss if I didn't thank Jane Calabria; without her, I would never have taken on this project. And without the guidance of my co-author, Steve Kern, I may just have given up! Thanks, Steve, for being there and knowing how and when I needed the help most. Of course I'd like to thank the contributing authors without whom this book would be incomplete and specifically Doug Faulkner, who jumped in and helped wherever he could. A special thanks to everyone at Macmillan and, in particular, Susan Moore for her patience and understanding and Brad Miser, who kept me on track and provided the much-needed humor.

On a more personal note, I would like to thank my parents who taught me to strive to learn something new every day. I hope I always will! Thanks to my husband Harry, who keeps me centered and who has taught me that I can do anything if I really want to. And to my business partner Valerie Freund, who provides me with insight and humor and puts up with me no matter what. To my children, who are the reason I became brave enough to try anything once. And a special thanks to Gary and Diane Sullivan, without whom Friday nights would just be another work night. And to the "I AM," for helping me to understand that I am whatever I believe I am.

Debbie Lynd
September 1999

A glimpse at the Credits page in this book indicates just how many people it takes to produce a book! Thanks to my co-author, Debbie Lynd, and to all the other authors who have contributed to this book. Thanks to Jonathan Kern, who provided chapters about project management and business process analysis; thanks to Timothy Falconer, who wrote the chapters on Java; and to Doug Faulkner who contributed the chapter on JavaScript. Thanks also to the folks at Macmillan USA for their hard work. Thanks in particular to our development editor, Brad Miser, without whose skill this book wouldn't be what it is today. His wit and humor kept us going when things were tough. Thanks also to Victor Mascari, the technical editor for this book, who helped ensure the accuracy of the material in this book. This book would not be what it is today without the hard work of my colleagues!

I am the sum of what I learn, and I pray that I always remain teachable. I have learned many technical things over the years, but perhaps the most important lessons have come from other teachings. I have had many teachers along the way. From my parents I learned perseverance, dedication, and an insatiable thirst for knowledge. Without their teaching and guidance, I would not be where I am today! Although my father did not live to see this book, I am sure he would be proud.

To my good friend Gunner Riley, who reminds me that there are still greater things to come and that I frequently miss the obvious <g>, my humble thanks. My life *is* beyond my wildest dreams! Thanks to my good friend Gus Brunsman, who believed in me and who supported and encouraged me when I chose this career. Thanks to all the guys on Saturday mornings who help me keep my sanity. When things are craziest, you remind me that life is perfect the way it is—as long as I stay in the moment.

Thanks to my family who put up with me during this lengthy project. Thanks to Cate Richards, who believed in me and helped me get started in publishing many years ago. Thanks also to the people at Computer Associates (formerly LDA Systems) from whom I've learned a lot about the business of consulting.

Steve Kern
September 1999

Tell Us What You Think!

As the reader of this book, *you* are our most important critic and commentator. We value your opinion and want to know what we're doing right, what we could do better, what areas you'd like to see us publish in, and any other words of wisdom you're willing to pass our way.

As a publisher for Sams Publishing, I welcome your comments. You can fax, email, or write me directly to let me know what you did or didn't like about this book—as well as what we can do to make our books stronger.

Please note that I cannot help you with technical problems related to the topic of this book, and that due to the high volume of mail I receive, I might not be able to reply to every message.

When you write, please be sure to include this book's title and authors as well as your name and phone or fax number. I will carefully review your comments and share them with the author and editors who worked on the book.

Fax: (317) 581-4770
Email: opsys@mcp.com
Mail: Publisher
         Sams Publishing
         201 W. 103rd Street
         Indianapolis, IN 46290

Introduction

Lotus Notes has been available since 1989 but did not come into prominence until a few years ago. The momentum began to build with Release 3 in 1994 and exploded with Release 4.5 in 1996. Notes and Domino R5 continues the momentum with the addition of a large number of powerful new features. There isn't much that needs to be said about how hot Lotus Notes is! The 10,000 attendees at Lotusphere—the annual conference in Orlando, Florida—attest to that fact. Lotus Notes is the undisputed leader of groupware applications. No other application development platform even comes close to being able to do what Notes and Domino can do.

Lotus released its much-awaited R5 in March 1999.

From the development side, this latest release extends the integration of Domino and Notes to Web clients. It also extends the reach of JavaScript and Java into the Domino Designer. R5 also introduces several new and powerful programming objects: pages, outlines, and framesets. There are numerous new enhancements to existing programmable objects, new field types, new ways to link objects to forms and pages, and so on.

Who Should Read This Book

Many Notes and Domino books attempt to cover the broad spectrum of the Lotus Notes universe. Their audience is generally made up of end users, technical users, and beginning application developers. Few are dedicated specifically to advanced applications development. This book is one of those few. Topics such as systems administration are covered only where they pertain to applications development. A basic knowledge of the Lotus Notes client interface is required because it will not be covered in depth. This book is written for the intermediate-to-expert applications developer, although a beginner will benefit from it as well because brief coverage is provided for basic tasks.

This book is intended as a hands-on manual and includes tips, techniques, practical step-by-step instructions, and examples. The intent is not only to present the various aspects of application design, but also to educate the reader in a practical approach to Notes application development.

How This Book Is Organized

Five parts will lead you through all the aspects of application development. Part I introduces Lotus Notes and Domino, covers what's new in R5, and presents a methodology for project management and analysis. Part II presents the basics of application design, covering design objects such as views, forms, pages, and outlines. Part III covers each of the five programming languages you can use to design Domino applications in detail. Part IV presents advanced design topics, and Part V covers other development tools. The appendixes contain a wealth of reference material.

Part I: Introduction to Application Design

The chapters in this section are devoted to topics you need to consider before beginning development of an application. Chapter 1 begins with an introduction to Lotus Notes, followed by a discussion of how Notes can solve business problems. Chapter 2 covers many new features available in the R5 Domino Designer.

Chapters 3, 4, and 5 strive to provide a foundation for how to approach application development using *Object-Oriented Analysis* (OOA) techniques. Chapter 3 covers some of the standard development methods and their pros and cons and then describes the preferred phased, incremental development approach. It also discusses some project management techniques. Chapter 4 provides the details behind the preferred approach and presents a concept for maintaining critical project information in a virtual project notebook. This chapter also details requirements definition, application development, and software quality assurance, testing, and deployment. Chapter 5 presents a brief look at how to perform a detailed analysis of a business process using OOA techniques. These techniques implement the approach as outlined in Chapter 4, only this time you'll look at some diagramming techniques (using the *de facto* standard *Unified Modeling Language*, or UML) and some helpful strategies to quickly get the answers you need. The emphasis is on engendering good up-front design habits that can help you succeed in developing robust Notes applications that not only answer today's demanding needs, but provide a flexible solution to adapt gracefully (and cost-effectively) to tomorrow's changing requirements.

Part II: Foundations of Application Design

This section describes in detail the various design elements of a Lotus Notes application. It begins in Chapter 6 with a discussion of some basic principles of design, such as naming conventions, reusability, and interface design standards. Chapter 7 covers the R5 Object Store (databases), and Chapter 8 discusses the IDE—Integrated Development Environment—of the Domino Designer and shows you how to take full advantage of this powerful feature. Chapter 9 discusses basic form design, and Chapter 10 expands on that knowledge and presents more advanced topics related to form design. Chapter 11 shows how to present data using Notes views and folders. Chapters 12, 13, and 14 cover design features new to R5: resources, outlines, and pages, respectively. Chapter 15 covers techniques for providing help to users of applications. Chapter 16 discusses two ways to analyze your databases, using the Domino Designer Database Analysis and Ives's TeamStudio Analyzer.

Part III: Domino Programming Languages

This part covers each of the five programming languages, the Formula language, HTML, LotusScript, JavaScript, and Java in detail.

Chapter 17 introduces Part III, covering ways to determine which language to use.

Chapters 18, 19, and 20 cover the Formula language. The Formula language was the first, and for a long time the only, language that could program applications in Notes. In many places, only the Formula language can be used, and many times, it is the best choice for a programming task. The Formula language is a very powerful language in its own right and includes list-processing capabilities that are unsurpassed in any language. Chapter 18 introduces the Formula language. Chapter 19 covers the types of formulas that can be written in the language, and Chapter 20 covers writing formulas.

There are many ways to enhance applications with HTML for use with Web clients, and these are covered in Chapter 21.

Chapters 22, 23, and 24 cover LotusScript, the object-oriented, event-driven, and BASIC-compatible scripting language added to Lotus Notes in Release 4. LotusScript significantly extends the capability of Lotus Notes by providing the developer with access to Notes objects at a deeper level than the Formula language, with greater control and flexibility. Chapter 22 introduces LotusScript, covering the basics of the language and how LotusScript fits into the Notes development environment. Chapter 23 builds a foundation of knowledge and techniques for manipulating Notes objects via LotusScript. Chapter 24 presents examples of LotusScript built into various pieces of Notes applications, from simple button scripts to database scripts to automation agents, concluding with even more complex scripts that show you how to access data contained in non-Notes sources.

Chapter 25 covers JavaScript. In prior releases of Notes and Domino, JavaScript could be used only with Web clients. In R5, JavaScript works for both Web and Notes clients. Because the Document Object Model for JavaScript is so extensive and the number of programmable events is significant, JavaScript is one of the most powerful languages available to developers. JavaScript is introduced, discussing the background and direction of the language and presenting the object hierarchy.

Chapters 26, 27, and 28 cover the use of Java in Notes and Domino R5. Although you could create Java agents in R4.6, you had to build them outside of Notes and import their class files manually. Domino Designer R4.6 also lacked any debug support for Java agents. In R5, you can create Java agents right in Designer and debug them using your favorite Java IDE with help from the AgentRunner database. R5 also includes expanded Java support for the Notes Object Interface (NOI), Java server add-ins using the runjava task, and remote access from Web browsers to servers using Java and CORBA. Chapter 26 is a crash course in Java fundamentals, which serves as a foundation for the next two chapters. Chapter 27 discusses how to get the different kinds of Java programmatic entities—agents, applets, applications, add-in tasks, and servlets—wired right, and why you'd choose one over the other. The Java binding of the NOI is also covered briefly, with emphasis on the idiosyncrasies of the Java interface. Chapter 28 covers debugging with AgentRunner, multithreading, and the use of CORBA to access Domino objects remotely.

Part IV: Advanced Design Topics

This section discusses advanced topics, including framesets, agents, security, workflow applications, and templates. Although these topics are under the umbrella of advanced design, by no means should beginning or intermediate applications developers skip over or ignore this section! Chapter 29 discusses how to use framesets to polish your applications. Chapter 30 shows you how to automate your applications using agents. Chapter 31 discusses an extremely important topic—security—as it relates to application design. Chapter 32 discusses creating workflow applications, a typical use of Notes and Domino. Chapter 33 discusses an important reusable design element, Notes templates.

Part V: Other Development Tools

As is true for any mature application, Lotus Notes and Domino enables you to use a number of other tools to develop applications. Chapter 34 covers the Domino Global Workbench, which is used to "internationalize" Domino applications. Chapter 35 discusses DECS, which enables developers to access enterprise data sources such as Oracle, Sybase, and SQL Server. Chapter 36 covers NetObjects BeanBuilder, formerly the Lotus BeanMachine. BeanBuilder quickly creates Java Beans that you can plug into your applications. Chapter 37 covers Lotus Components and ActiveX technology for use with 32-bit Windows PCs, which lets you quickly create fast, reusable applets. Chapter 38 covers creating reports. Because the reporting facilities native to Notes and Domino are limited, this chapter covers using other tools such as Lotus Approach and Microsoft Access.

Part VI: Appendixes

Included in this book are seven appendixes that you can use for reference. The first three appendixes cover LotusScript and Java classes and JavaScript objects. Appendix D contains a reference of useful HTML commands. NotesPeek, a handy tool for examining Domino databases, is covered in Appendix E. Appendix F covers Domino URLs, and Appendix G is a glossary of Notes and Domino terms.

Conventions Used in This Book

New terms and placeholders appear in *italics*.

Menu choices are separated by a comma, as in File, Tools, User Preferences.

Lines of code and syntax are printed in this special `monospaced` font.

Caution

Cautions appear in the text, warning you of possible difficulties.

Tip

Tips aid you in performing tasks more expediently.

Note

Notes provide additional pertinent information on the topic being discussed.

Introduction to Application Design

PART

I

Introducing Lotus Notes and Domino

by Steve Kern

CHAPTER 1

IN THIS CHAPTER

This chapter introduces one of the hottest software products on the market today, Lotus Notes and Domino. Notes has survived the doomsayers, the naysayers, market vagaries, and Internet explosions and has grown beyond the expectations of Lotus Development Corporation itself. It has attracted the attention of one of the industry giants, IBM, who purchased Lotus in 1996 for about 1.8 billion dollars. The discussion in this introductory chapter is at a fairly high level and attempts to illustrate what Notes and Domino can do for a business. Notes and Domino is a very large product, so it would be difficult to summarize its capabilities in a book, let alone a single chapter.

A Brief History of Lotus Notes

When PCs were introduced in the early 1980s, there were no networks and software was limited, as was processing power. Today, PCs are emerging as perhaps the most dominant market force of the information age, especially with the advent of inexpensive and high-bandwidth connections to the Internet. The processing power of today's typical PC dwarfs that of the early introductions. The first PCs proudly boasted 64KB of RAM; today, most new desktops ship with a minimum of 64MB of RAM. CPUs have grown from 4,000 transistors to more than 4 million, with corresponding increases in processing power and speed. Early PCs had little storage, with one or two 5-1/4" floppy disk drives. The first hard drives introduced with 5MB of storage cost nearly twice what a desktop PC costs today. Today, desktops come with 6–20GB hard drives.

Many people in the IT world viewed these early PCs as little more than toys on which to play games. Business software was limited to very simple (by today's standards) word processors, spreadsheets, and databases. The only way to share information was to print it or exchange files via floppy disks. A PC was a stand-alone system. Networks were later developed to link PCs together, and the IT (information technology) world began to see and use the potential of PCs. Applications were developed to take advantage of networks, and the information age advanced to a new plateau. Users could now share files and applications. With the growth of processing power, the development of more powerful applications, and the introduction of networks and the extension of the enterprise to the Internet, PCs were no longer toys but an integral part of business. Computing power that used to be available only to large companies that could afford mainframes is now available for small businesses.

The Growth of Notes

Lotus Development Corporation has been developing software for PCs since the introduction of Lotus 1-2-3. Lotus Notes was released in 1989, and was primarily a distributed document management system. Notes servers (now called Domino servers) ran only under OS/2, and the cost of ownership for a 10-user installation was in the $60,000 dollar range. By the time Release 3 was introduced in 1994, there were still only approximately 1 million users. In 1996, Lotus sold nearly 10 million seats worldwide, almost doubling the installed base from the prior year. By the end of 1998, the number of licenses has grown to over 30 million. Calling this growth "explosive" is an understatement; it is nothing short of miraculous. What are some of the reasons for this growth?

The cost of ownership for the same 10-user system has dropped dramatically. The list price for Notes clients is under $70 U.S. and the Domino Designer is around $400. Although server licensing has changed from the earlier flat pricing structure to one where licenses for the more powerful processors cost more, server licenses are still relatively inexpensive. Hardware is an additional expense, but, as pointed out earlier in this chapter, the cost of hardware has dropped quite dramatically as processing power has increased dramatically. Today, licenses for 10 users and a Domino Designer license would cost around $6,000. You could purchase an adequate server for 10 users for well under $10,000, in the $5,000–8,000 price range. As you can see, there have been dramatic improvements in power and capability, at a significantly lower price.

Today, Notes and Domino is platform-independent with servers and clients available on nearly all major operating systems. Server platforms exist for OS/2, NetWare, Windows 95, Windows NT, UNIX (Solaris, HP-UX, and AIX), DEC Alphas, S/390, and the AS/400. Clients are available for most of these operating systems as well (with the exception of NetWare, OS/2, and UNIX). Domino servers also support Web clients, and Notes clients are server-independent. The power of Domino servers has grown significantly. Release 3.x Notes servers typically supported about 100 users; new multiprocessor Release 5.x servers can support upwards of 1000; UNIX boxes can support even more, and in benchmark tests a single AS/400 box can support about 27,000 users!

When the HTTP service was added to the server, Notes and Domino became the first true applications server for the Internet. When Notes and Domino 4.5 was released, the name changed from Notes Servers to Domino Servers. This was to underscore the shift in emphasis to the Internet. Release 4.6 and Release 5 have increased support for Internet protocols, and the server now supports HTTP, POP3, IMAP, NNTP, and more. With the increase in power of the servers, the size of a Domino database that can be supported has increased also. A few years ago, the rule of thumb was that a Domino database should not exceed 100MB, at which point performance would be unacceptable. The actual maximum size limit in R3 was 1GB, and in R4, the maximum size limit was increased to 4GB. Today, especially with powerful 64-bit server platforms such as the AS/400, a database could easily grow well beyond 1GB and still have acceptable performance. In fact, the current limit (if you want to call it that!) for a database is 64GB for Windows and UNIX, and 32GB for OS/2.

The Notes Clients

The Notes client has been split into the Notes client, the Admin client, and the Domino Designer in R5. Although the client is still called a Notes client, it has become "server agnostic," meaning that it can access servers other than Domino servers, such as POP3 and IMAP for mail and Web servers on the Internet/intranet. One of Lotus's goals was to create a "best of breed" messaging and Internet client. Chapter 2, "What's New in Release 5?" discusses the new features of Notes clients and Domino servers in more detail.

A Notes client presents a very similar appearance from one platform to the next. Applications, which can consist of single or multiple databases in Notes, execute seamlessly from one platform to the next. In other words, as a developer, you can create an application that runs as well on the AS/400 as it does on the Solaris. More importantly, it will look nearly identical. No other application development system can boast this degree of cross-platform support.

Further extending this concept, Notes and Domino can stage multiple applications. After a user understands the Notes client interface, learning new applications is very simple. A user doesn't have to learn Notes all over again, just the new application. The reduction in training costs over time can pay for the initial expense of Notes. Contrast this with a typical applications development system such as one that is based on Oracle, or Sybase, where each application is developed independently and has its own interface built from the ground up. Each time a new application is introduced to the user, he or she must be trained in the interface as well as the application itself. Each time a user wants to switch applications, he has to launch a new executable file. In Notes, the user simply double-clicks a different icon in the Notes client.

Domino Connectivity

One of Notes and Domino's greatest strengths is its capability to transfer information over LANs, WANs, the Internet, and telephone lines. Domino servers communicate with each other, transferring email and synchronizing databases. Similarly, a user can use the Notes client to dial the Domino server, receive email, and exchange database information with the click of a single button. The process of exchanging database information is known as *replication*. No other product on the market today does this as powerfully, as quickly, or as well as Notes and Domino.

Two years ago, the doomsayers were prophesying the downfall of Notes and were stating that the Internet and intranets would kill it off, which has turned out to be absolutely incorrect. Today, Notes is more tightly integrated with the Internet than any other product. In the middle of 1996, Lotus introduced the world's first I-Net applications server—Domino—to industry-wide acclaim. The term *I-Net* either refers to an intranet serving HTML content over HTTP or refers to the Internet. An entire new industry has been built up around hosting applications for customers on the Web using this new technology. Along with the Domino Web Server in R4, Lotus also introduced a technology to send and receive Internet mail in your Notes mailbox: the SMTP MTA, or Simple Message Transfer Protocol Message Transfer Agent. In R5, the Domino mail router handles both Notes mail and SMTP mail natively. In addition, a whole family of products has been developed based on the Internet, including Domino.Merchant, Domino.Broadcast, and eSuite.

Third-Party Support for Notes and Domino

A very rich and vibrant community has grown up around Notes. This community consists of application developers, systems administrators, consulting companies, third-party tools, shrink-wrapped software, and a Lotus Business Partner community in excess of 18,000 members. Lotus has developed a Business Partner program and a certification program for consultants, developers, and administrators. The intent of the certification program is to raise the knowledge level of developers and administrators. Lotusphere, which started in 1994 with about 2,000 attendees, has grown to over 10,000. Forums on CompuServe and many Internet newsgroups are dedicated to Notes. Lotus itself supports many forums for discussions related to Notes and Domino on Notes.Net. Many major publishers of computer literature have created entire lines of Notes books ranging from end-user books to books on applications development and systems administration.

A Mature Product

In short, Notes is a very mature and powerful product. No other product has the capabilities of Notes and Domino. Even the competition, of which there is very little, has a very long way to go to catch up. According to a recent IDC report, it will take Exchange until the year 2004 to catch up to Notes and Domino. Who knows how much further ahead Notes and Domino will be by then? In 1996, IBM acquired Lotus for one principal reason: Notes and Domino. More than any other product, Notes has helped define and drive the groupware market.

What does this mean to developers? Notes and Domino is very, very hot right now, and if Lotus continues its aggressive development pace and keeps finding innovative approaches, for the foreseeable future, work will be available!

The Evolution of Groupware

At the heart of the information age, or information revolution, is knowledge. A business lives and dies by its capability to use, manage, and share information. It is important to note that data is not information. Application developers are charged with turning raw data into knowledge—useful information. The term *groupware* (group information management software) is a loosely defined concept that refers to a type of application that enables groups of people to collaborate together to create, share, and use information more effectively. Note that you might see other definitions of groupware. The most recent buzz word associated with this is Knowledge Management, or *KM*. The concepts driving the evolution of KM are derived from groupware.

Prior to network-based applications, as pointed out earlier, information could be shared only by physical transfers of files from one individual to another (also known as a *sneaker net*) or by printing reports and sharing them with others. In many respects, this type of information was private and stand-alone; it only became public when printed and distributed. Sometimes, the individuals responsible for the acquisition and dissemination of knowledge would jealously guard such information.

On the other hand, groupware relies heavily on networks for the transfer of information among individuals and organizations. Groupware promotes working together in teams. This fits in well with today's business climate, where teams are promoted and heavily emphasized in almost every sector of business. Groupware evolved from two basic models: the *share* model and the *send* model.

The Share Model

Applications that work in a networking environment enable people to share data. Examples of this include applications written in a wide variety of languages and database engines, such as C, dBASE, FoxPro, Sybase, Oracle, and PowerBuilder. Some of the newer word processing and spreadsheet software, such as Lotus WordPro, Lotus 1-2-3, and Microsoft Word, enable groups of people to collaborate on a single document or spreadsheet. The author of the document can lock out subsequent editors from certain types of changes and certain areas of the documents and can support version control.

The share model relies on the document or database application being in an area accessible to all users—that is, shared—typically on a file server. If all users have access to the directory on the file server where the file exists, they can all work on the file. Most database applications do not support concurrent access of specific records but do support concurrent access to files. This is referred to as the *share model*.

In this model, a user must go to the file on the server and open the application to add, modify, and view the data. This is perhaps the most widely used architecture today. Examples of this kind of application abound in most organizations and can include accounting applications, inventory applications, and other types of business applications. An application of this type is passive; it does nothing in and of itself. Users must go to it to get any information. This can be a significant drawback because you must rely on the user to perform an action, say approval of a requisition, in a timely fashion and of their own volition. In fact, unless a user visits the database, he or she won't even be aware of the requisition in the first place. Although a central repository of all documents exists, the application is not capable of taking any actions based on a change in status.

Possibly as a response to the success of Notes and Domino, groupware features have been added to word processors such as Microsoft Word, and even to spreadsheet applications. Collaborative features such as master documents and version control were added to an existing product that was previously stand-alone. On the other hand, Notes and Domino was *designed* to enable groups of people to work together.

The Send Model

In the send model, information is pushed, or sent, to the user. This typically involves email. Examples of this type of application are forms routing, requisitions, and document approval. Using email to route forms closely mimics that of a paper document in an office. In a typical scenario, you might fill out a requisition form for a new PC and send it to your boss. He then approves it, but because you want a $5,000 laptop and it's over his approval ceiling, the form then gets routed to the branch manager, exactly like a paper-routing flow.

The problem with this model (and its paper-based cousin) is that there is no convenient way to determine the status of your requisition or even who has it. There is no central place for you to look, and there is no shared database containing the requisition. This lack of a central repository for requisitions also means that there is no way to keep and track the history of requisitions. After the requisition is purged from the last mailbox, it's gone for good. In other words, there is no document management.

Workflow: The Integrated Model

Lotus Notes and Domino solves the problems inherent in both the send and share models by merging a shared database with an email engine. In addition, the server has the capability to schedule agents to run at certain times and take actions based on certain conditions independent of any user involvement. A Requisitions process is a typical workflow solution. Enabling workflow involves creating *mail-enabled databases*. Chapter 34, "Creating Workflow Applications," discusses this in detail.

In a workflow solution, after a requisition is composed and saved in the database, the application determines the approver and then notifies the approver of the requisition. The notification usually includes a document link that can be clicked to open the document. The approver assesses the requisition and can approve it on the spot. An Agent runs nightly on the server sending tardy notifications to ensure timely responses.

Although this example has only touched the surface of workflow applications, it is quite apparent that this type of solution can save a lot of administrative headaches and significantly reduce the amount of time to complete a process. If this had been simply a shared database, none of the email notifications or the agents would have been present. A send model would not allow the originator or the administrator to determine the status of a requisition. There would be no automatic monitoring of the process. Another very important point is that not only does the process work better, the company now has a history of requisitions that can be easily researched. Because Notes and Domino very successfully combines the share and send model and is also a RAD (Rapid Application Development) tool, analysts and developers can spend more time solving business problems.

The Three Cs of Workflow

The three *C*s of Workflow are communication, collaboration, and coordination. *Communication* is messaging, or the send model; *collaboration* is the share model; *coordination* is people working together to meet specific business objectives. *Communication* and c*ollaboration* support *coordination*. This is the essence of groupware. The three *C*s are illustrated in Figure 1.1.

Communication was achieved in the Requisitions example mentioned earlier by emailing the approvers when a new requisition was added to the database. Collaboration was achieved with the shared database and the knowledge contained within. Coordination occurred when the shared database and messaging combined to send email notices to tardy approvers. The application actively manages the associated workflow—freeing the time spent by administrators on a manual process.

You will often hear the term *workflow* used in conjunction with Notes and Domino. What is workflow? Simply defined, it is how an enterprise accomplishes a specific business process. In your job, you might need a book or some software to help on a particular assignment. To get that material, you have to send a requisition to your manager, who then forwards it to the branch manager for final approval. This describes the flow of work of the requisition process, or workflow. Notes and Domino is uniquely suited to designing a workflow application because it is capable of uniting messaging and shared databases, overcoming the limitations of the share and send models. Chapter 5, "Business Process Analysis," discusses business process analyses (such as a workflow analysis) in more detail. Chapter 5 examines the basic elements of workflow, which are listed in Table 1.1.

FIGURE 1.1

The confluence of communication, collaboration, and coordination is groupware.

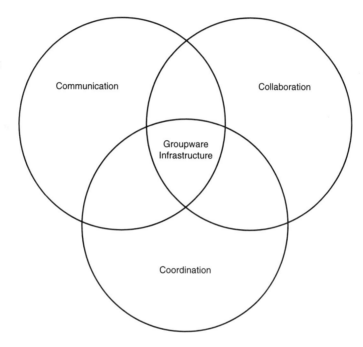

TABLE 1.1   Workflow Elements

Element	Definition
Actors	People or processes that take actions. In Notes, actors can be users or agents.
Information	The data items being captured.
Events	Changes in status or other things that cause work to flow.

Major Features of Lotus Notes

So far, this chapter has described some of the strengths behind Notes and Domino. Now, you'll read about how Notes Clients interact with Domino Servers, Domino databases, replication, and security. You'll also learn about how Notes and Domino integrates email, calendaring and scheduling, and remote access. I also discuss the Domino Web server, Internet Protocols, and the Personal Web Navigator. Finally, I cover two products that enable developers to create small, fast reusable applets: eSuite and Lotus Components.

Notes Clients and Domino Servers

Notes and Domino is a true distributed client/server application. There has been a lot of discussion over the last several years about client/server applications. Some IT departments have successfully replaced mainframes with PC-based client/server applications. A client/server system has two basic pieces: the client, which requests services, and the server, which supplies those services. Typical client/server systems exist on LANs or WANs and take advantage of the available network protocols to transfer information. Figure 1.2 shows a typical client/server LAN architecture.

FIGURE 1.2

A typical LAN configuration illustrates the idea behind client/server architecture.

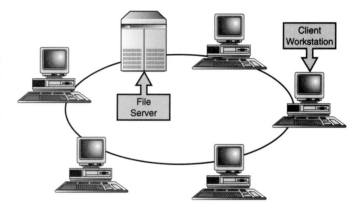

Domino applications are or can be *distributed*; more than one copy of a database or application can be distributed to more than one client or server. Figure 1.3 shows a Notes client/server topology that illustrates how a database can be distributed.

Although this is not a book about system administration, it is important to understand how a Notes system fits together. In Figure 1.3, notice that there are two types of Domino servers: hub servers and spoke servers. This topology is called *hub and spoke* and is most frequently used in a large Notes installation. It is called *hub and spoke* because of the similarity to a wagon wheel, as illustrated in Figure 1.4. The hub server contains all the databases that are used by the spoke servers. Replication (described later) can be initiated by the hub server or spoke servers, and it always takes place between the hub and a spoke but never between spokes. Typically, users are never attached directly to a hub server but are attached only to spoke servers.

FIGURE 1.3

This topology illustrates a multi-server Notes environment. Replica copies of a database application can be distributed across all or some of the servers.

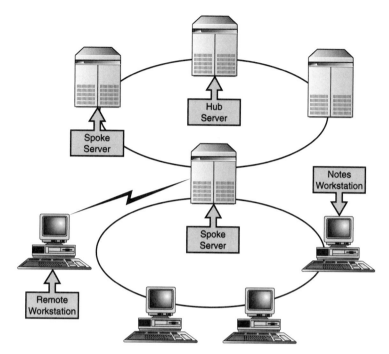

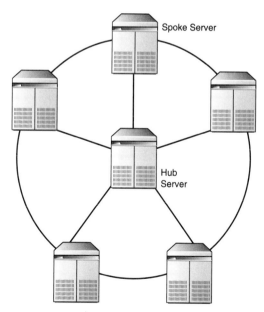

FIGURE 1.4

You can see why hub and spoke topology was named after a wagon wheel.

This is not the only way to put a Notes system together. Small organizations often have only a single Notes server. Some organizations, even though they are small, might have servers distributed geographically to offices in different cities. A WAN, modems, or a combination of the two can connect these servers.

Servers and users exchange information using available network protocols. As database designers, you should never have to deal directly with this part of Notes and Domino, but you should have at least a minimum understanding of it. Perhaps the most frequently used protocols are TCP/IP and NetWare SPX, but Domino can also use AppleTalk, Banyan Vines, and NetBIOS. These protocols are seamless to the user and to a Notes application. Servers and users typically communicate across a LAN or a WAN, or via a modem. Servers can now communicate over the Internet using Notes *RPCs* (Remote Procedure Calls), and Web clients can communicate with Domino servers running the HTTP service. Note that for Domino to act as a Web server, it must run TCP/IP.

The Domino Directory

Domino servers and Notes clients exist within domains. A business enterprise can have a single domain or multiple domains. A single public directory defines a domain and contains documents for the users, groups, and servers. The mail router uses the public directory to deliver mail and to authenticate users. If a message is destined for a different domain or the Internet, the router determines a path to reach the correct mailbox on the correct server or delivers the message to an Internet server. Server documents contain information that configures the server, including items such as the name, the domain, who can access the server, and who can create databases on the server. A server document is illustrated in Figure 1.5.

Connection documents control how and when Notes servers connect with each other to exchange mail and replicate databases (see Figure 1.6).

Person documents contain information such as the name of the person, mailbox file, and the license type. Figure 1.7 shows a person document.

Domino Databases

A Domino database is a container for data within Notes and Domino and is also referred to as an *Object Store*. Data is represented by fields contained within documents, so a general definition of a Domino database is a collection of related documents. This is quite different from a relational database, which can be defined as a collection of related tables and reflects Domino's origins as a document-driven database. This is an important distinction, especially if you are familiar with relational databases. A database table contains records, which loosely correspond to documents in Domino. Chapter 7, "The

Release 5 Object Store," discusses Domino Databases in detail. Records in a relational database such as Oracle or Sybase are structured and defined by tables and have fixed field definitions. Domino does not have fixed field definitions for documents and is therefore unstructured. Similarly, fields are unstructured; for example, a text field has no property to set its width. A Domino database is also unique because it can store and link many different types of objects.

FIGURE 1.5

The Basics section of the server document includes information such as the server and domain name.

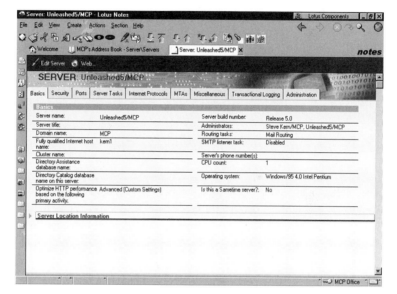

FIGURE 1.6

This connection document connects two servers for mail routing via a local area network (LAN) connection.

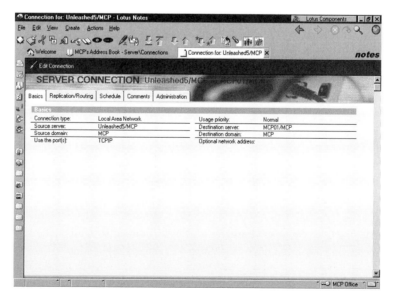

FIGURE 1.7

*The Basics tab
of the person
document from a
public directory
contains informa-
tion about the
person's name.
The Internet pass-
word is encrypted
and is not visible
in read mode.*

The extension applied to a Domino database is `.NSF` and stands for Notes Storage
Facility. In this storage facility are special fields called rich-text fields. These fields can
contain entire files, bitmaps, OLE objects, and different fonts and formatting. In effect,
Domino databases are *bit buckets* that can contain just about any data structure or pointer. The document links described previously are examples of how to link a database document in another database store to an email message. Such links are similar to hypertext
links on the Web. Email is a specially designed Domino database and is discussed in the
next section.

Replication

One of the key features of a Domino database is that you can distribute copies of it to
Notes clients (not Web clients) and other servers. Through a process called *replication*,
Notes clients and servers keep the information synchronized. A replica copy of a database is a special type of copy. Every Domino database has a replica ID that identifies it
to Notes clients and Domino servers. When two databases have the same replica ID, they
are *replica copies*. Servers and clients can then replicate the two copies, which synchronize the databases so that when complete, they contain essentially the same information.
This process compares all elements of the database, including design elements, and
checks for modifications, deletions, and additions. In Release 3, this was done on a
document-by-document basis; in Release 4, comparisons are made at the field level,
increasing the speed with which Notes completes replication.

Replication can occur between Domino servers or between Domino servers and Notes clients. Replication can be controlled by formulas, which limit the data exchanged between the replica copies of the database. For example, a salesperson might want to see only documents that relate to his or her sales territory; a replication formula can be created to limit the documents replicated to the Notes client. This permits the user to work more efficiently. Similarly, you can limit the documents sent between replica copies on servers. This is an absolutely terrific way of distributing information! It has proved so powerful and popular that many other database systems such as Sybase are beginning to incorporate this approach.

It is important to note that not all copies of the database are in synch at the same time. Over time, however, all the replicas will be synchronized. This has an impact on the type of applications that are suitable for Notes. If you depended on and absolutely had to know the precise number of items in stock, you could not use a distributed database with multiple replicas and expect that level of precision. The scenario shown in Table 1.2 should help you better understand this; for the purposes of this illustration, assume that each user is working on a local replica of the database and that the database resides on only one server.

TABLE 1.2   The Effects of Replication on a Database

User	Action	Server	User A	User B	User C
A	Creates document A1	None	A1	None	None
B	Creates document B1	None	A1	B1	None
B	Replicates with the server	B1	A1	B1	None
C	Creates Doc C1; replicates	B1, C1	A1	B1	B1, C1
A	Replicates with the server	B1, C1, A1	A1, B1, C1	B1	B1, C1
B	Replicates with the server	B1, C1, A1	A1, B1, C1	B1, C1 A1	B1, C1
C	Replicates with the server	B1, C1, A1	A1, B1, C1	B1, C1 A1	B1, C1 A1

It is only when user C performs the last replication that all the replicas of the database are finally in synch. Typically, this is not a real problem, and the illustration is a little contrived, but you must understand this concept not only to design effective applications but also to avoid using Notes inappropriately.

Security

With the power of this database access technology at a user's fingertips, there must be some security associated with it. The security used by Notes uses RSA encryption, arguably the most secure and advanced encryption scheme available today. *RSA* are the initials of the three founders of RSA Data Security—Rivest, Shamir, and Adelman. Developed in 1977, RSA encryption is based on a dual-key system of public and private keys. It is so secure that it is under export control and the most secure versions cannot be exported outside the U.S. and Canada. Currently there are two versions of Notes and Domino: the North American and the international. Even the CIA uses this technology for encryption. It is rumored that it would take a roomful of mathematicians and a super-computer thousands of years to break the encryption.

The encryption scheme uses two mathematically related keys: public and private. These keys are issued whenever an ID is generated for users and servers. In order for a user to connect with a server or for a server to connect to another server, a test called authentica-tion must be passed. After it is determined that the user or server is who or what they say they are (or *authentic),* then and only then is any information exchanged.

There are seven levels of database security in Notes. These are listed in Table 1.3. There are additional security features that further restrict access. Security, as it pertains to application development, is further discussed in Chapter 33, "Security and Domino Applications."

TABLE 1.3 Notes Security Levels

Level	Privilege
No Access	None
Depositor	Allowed to author a document, but not read or edit documents—not even one the user authored
Reader	Able to read documents but not add or edit
Author	Allowed to author and (usually) edit their own documents; can also read other documents
Editor	Can create new documents and edit documents, even those authored by others
Designer	All privileges listed previously but also can design databases
Manager	All privileges listed previously and in addition can change the Access Control List

After access to the server is granted, access to databases is limited by the Access Control List mentioned in the last item in Table 1.3. This list can contain servers, individuals, groups of servers, groups of individuals, and mixed groups of both servers and individuals. Figure 1.8 shows a typical Access Control List.

FIGURE 1.8

The Default entry in the ACL of a public directory is set to Author.

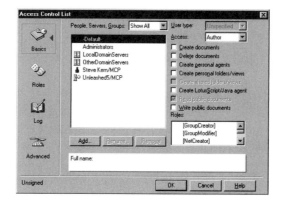

Integrated Email

Email has gone through several phases of growth, starting with simple text messages on mainframes and online services. Next came file attachments and embedded graphics, and finally pointers to objects in other data stores. In Notes and Domino, this is embodied in a document link. Release 4 introduced three levels of links: database, view, and document. Double-clicking the doclink (short for document link) icon can open each link. The highest level is a database link. Double-clicking the database link opens the database to the default view. The next level is a view link; double-clicking that link opens the database to the specific view. The lowest level is a document link. Double-clicking a document link displays an actual document. Table 1.4 illustrates the icons for the three levels.

TABLE 1.4   Document Links in Notes

Icon	Link
	Database link
	View link
	Document link
	Anchor link

Note

These links are similar to links on the Web; you click them, and they take you somewhere. Release 4.6 introduced a popular Web construct, anchor links, which extends the reach of links from the document level to enable document authors to link to specific parts of a document.

Figure 1.9 is an example of Notes email illustrating an attached Word document.

FIGURE 1.9

This is an example of the rich messaging available with Notes email.

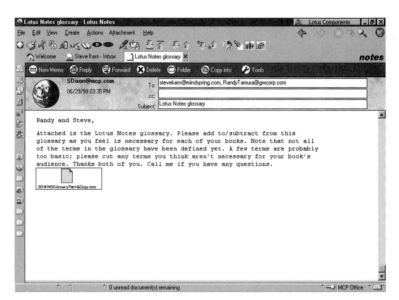

Because you can easily attach files and embed images, Notes email is perfect for communicating with clients and coworkers. On a systems level, it is one of the most reliable and complete transport mechanisms for messaging available today. Notes mail can be connected to email from different systems, such as cc:Mail, Internet mail, and Exchange. Domino servers support Notes mail, POP3, and IMAP mail. Today, you can seamlessly receive Internet mail, faxes, voice mail messages, and cc:Mail directly in your Notes mailbox. You can even set up the Pager Gateway to page you when messages arrive in your mailbox, and listen to your messages over the telephone. In R4.5, a Web mail client was introduced, which was enhanced in R4.6 and even further enhanced in R5.

Calendaring and Scheduling

Release 4.5 introduced calendaring and scheduling to Notes. R5 has many new enhancements, including calendaring and scheduling for groups and a new look and feel. Figure 1.10 shows the default one-week view of the calendar.

FIGURE 1.10

The one-week calendar view showing a number of entries. The interface is intuitive and easy to master.

Because Calendaring & Scheduling is a part of your email database, it can be replicated, and you can take it wherever you go. Calendaring & Scheduling is convenient to use and is truly powerful, especially with the addition of Group calendars. It is awfully convenient to have access to your calendar and schedule meetings right from within Notes and Domino. The meeting scheduler is quite powerful and is seamlessly integrated with Notes and Domino. The members of a workgroup can share calendars with each other so that they can see where the other team members are and easily schedule meetings at a convenient time.

Remote Access

A natural extension of the replication strategy and email is remote access. Notes supports dial-up connections via modems from both servers and clients. It is also possible to connect to servers across the Internet.

This is a powerful tool for most organizations, particularly if their staff and offices are geographically dispersed. It is ideal for multinational corporations because Domino can schedule connections between servers at times when the telephone rates are inexpensive. It is ideal for users who travel. A salesperson might dial his or her Domino server in the morning for the latest prices and retrieve email, and later in the day when all the sales calls are complete, replicate with the server to transfer all those big dollar orders taken because information was delivered in a timely fashion! A CEO might decide to schedule a meeting while in the air from New York to Paris and turn on his or her laptop, schedule the meeting, and dial the server from the air. When the laptop connects to the server, meeting invitations are automatically sent to the invitees.

Although Notes and Domino provides outstanding mobile support, using the same technology, it also provides support for remotely connected users. For example, by using remote access, you can work directly on a client's server from your office or from your home office. You can also work at home on projects. One of my clients is taking advantage of this technology by contracting with an answering service to take phone calls. These calls are then entered into a Domino database and replicated from a server at the answering service's offices to the client's server.

Of course, if your Domino server is on the Internet, you can access it using a Web browser and interact with databases and even your Notes mail.

The Domino Web Server

With the addition of graphics to the Internet several years ago, the number of companies and individuals using the World Wide Web has exploded. Current estimates are that over 50 million people are using the Web today. Companies advertise and sell products and offer support services in record numbers. This shows no sign of abating any time soon. The opportunities for businesses to profit on and from the Web are abundant, from creating and managing Web Sites to selling products and services on the Web.

You can extend the powerful security built into Notes and Domino to the Web by registering Web clients on your Domino server. This is a significant advance because the Internet isn't entirely safe. As an ad campaign for Domino stated, "There are 50 million people on the Internet and not all of them are nice!"

By extending Domino databases to the Web, Lotus makes it very easy to provide dynamic content for your Web site. Web sites that don't change much don't get visited much. This incorporates one of Domino's most powerful features: collaboration. Many people can contribute to a database published on the Web, both Notes clients and Web clients, and a user doesn't have to be a programmer or understand HTML (Hypertext Markup Language) to publish a document on the Web. Documents created are available as soon as they are saved, whether it comes from the Web or from Notes. For those of you who are familiar with Notes and its full-text search capability, you'll be happy to know that this has been extended to the Web. You can also set up site searches such as those provided on some Web pages.

With Domino, Lotus has created an exciting new technology, an applications server for the Web. It is simple to set up and maintain. Domino provides a powerful method of extending the enterprise to a great new frontier—the Internet.

Internet Protocols

Notes and Domino 5 is even more tightly integrated with the Internet, and embrace even more protocols than 4.5 and 4.6. This section only discusses this briefly to give you a glimpse of the capabilities of a Domino server because this is a book about applications development, and not about Domino Server administration. Domino 5 servers support Lightweight Directory Access Protocol (LDAP), Network News Transfer Protocol (NNTP), and Multipurpose Internet Mail Extensions (MIME) in addition to HTTP, POP3, and IMAP. More important perhaps to developers is that there is now support for hidden fields in HTML, which permits Web clients to act more like Notes clients. MIME is now a native data type, and you can choose to store rich-text fields in MIME format. The list of Web based enhancements is lengthy and beyond the scope of this discussion. To learn more about the changes to Domino databases, please read Chapters 2 and 7. To learn more about the Domino Server, please see Que's *Special Edition Using Lotus Notes and Domino 5* by Randy Tamura.

Personal Web Navigator

Notes 5 comes with a special database, the Personal Web Navigator. With this database, you can access the Internet from your own workstation. It is relatively easy to set up and has fairly extensive help available. Access to the Internet can be through a proxy server or a dial-up connection from your workstation. The two previous iterations of the Personal Web Navigator did not handle framed Web sites, and because many Web sites now use frames, the versions released in 4.5 and 4.6 were disappointing to many. The R5 version is much faster and much improved—and it handles framed Web sites!

The Personal Web Navigator looks and feels much like other navigators, such as Netscape Navigator or Microsoft Internet Explorer (see Figure 1.11). On the plus side, it does a very fine job of storing Web pages; after all, it is a database. Also, a feature called Page Minder automatically updates Web pages that you specify on a schedule you determine. Web Ahead downloads linked pages to a depth you specify. Imagine arriving at work in the morning and while you're having coffee reviewing the competition's Web pages that Notes has conveniently retrieved in the wee hours.

FIGURE **1.11**

*The Notes
Personal Web
Navigator works
just like other
browsers.*

Components

Lotus components are small, fast software applets. Unfortunately, they run only on 32-bit Windows platforms, so they are unavailable for older versions of Windows. There are six components: spreadsheet, chart, drawing component, project scheduling, comment, and a file viewer.

The basic idea once again is to put everything the user needs in one place, the Lotus Notes desktop. Lotus has added calendaring, scheduling, and a Web browser to email and database access. Components add even more functionality to the Notes workspace. Components can be used directly by end users and programmed and distributed by developers. For more information, see Chapter 39, "Lotus Components." The last version of Components is due out soon, and the product will be discontinued in favor of eSuite.

eSuite

Similar to Lotus Components, eSuite is designed to replace huge office suites such as Microsoft Office and Lotus SmartSuite with small, fast, focused productivity applets. Because it is written in Java, the applets can be used on the Internet by Web clients using a browser that supports the Java Virtual Machine (JVM). eSuite also works on network computers (also known as NCs or thin clients). There are two products in the eSuite line: the eSuite WorkPlace and the eSuite DevPack. The eSuite WorkPlace is a set of productivity applets that are fast, focused, and easy to use, and the DevPack enables developers

to customize the applications. Designed for use on the Web, eSuite promises to reduce development costs, support costs, and user training costs.

Extending Notes with Add-ons and Third-Party Software

As mentioned earlier, a very robust industry has grown up around Lotus Notes. A large number of third-party products and some noteworthy add-ons are available from Notes. API libraries and other tools are also available.

The Notes Universe

Add-ons fall into these general areas: connectivity to other email systems, enhancement of data storage, telephony and fax interfaces, ODBC drivers, and data integration. This should illustrate that Notes and Domino is not only a database system with email attached.

Lotus Products

There are numerous products in the Notes family. These products fall into several distinct areas: messaging, data storage and access, developer tools, administration tools, and end-user tools and software.

Lotus offers a very complete messaging solution. Various *MTAs* (Message Transfer Agents) such as the cc:Mail and X.500 MTAs, bring messages in from other mail servers. The Domino Fax server enables users to send and receive faxes from Lotus Notes. The Lotus Pager gateway can initiate telephone pages and VideoNotes can handle video conferencing.

Although some of the following are not Lotus Products, strictly speaking, accessing data in other applications can be handled via ODBC and Notes/FX (Notes Field Exchange) directly from within Notes. The LotusScript Data Object (LS:DO) is yet another method of accessing external data from Notes. On the other hand, Lotus NotesPump provides a server-based method of batch-processing external data. NotesSQL reverses this by allowing other applications to access Domino data. Introduced in R4.6.3, DECS (Domino Enterprise Connectivity Services) brings connectivity to back-end databases to the server and client without incurring the expense and overhead of a product such as NotesPump. Domino.Doc provides an "out-of-the-box" solution for Document management. Lotus provides some developer-oriented tools, such as the API toolkits available, the C API, the C++ API, and a high-level C API called HiTest. SmartSuite is pretty tightly integrated with Notes and Domino, and you can use Lotus Approach to report on Domino databases. Both Approach and the Notes Reporter enables developers and sophisticated end users to create reports and mailing labels. The Notes Reporter is "borrowed" from Lotus Approach, and naturally shares many similarities. Both Approach and the Reporter honor the security of Notes and Domino. Lotus SmartSuite features Lotus 1-2-3, WordPro, Freelance Graphics, Organizer, FastSite and Approach. You can even write LotusScript in SmartSuite applications.

Third-Party Products

There are so many third-party products that it would be impossible to list them all. At Lotusphere 99, there were more than 100 exhibitors at the Product showcase. Products fell into the same general categories for Lotus Products, but in addition there were shrink-wrapped and near shrink-wrapped software solutions available, such as GWI's Help!, Project Gateway from Marin Research, QSI's System 9000 for ISO9000 and QS9000 compliance, and a wide variety of other products. There are also training applications, such as CBT Systems courseware for Notes and ReCor Notes Training.

Table 1.5 lists some of the developer tools available.

TABLE 1.5 Developer Tools

Company	Tool	Usage
Cambridge Software	Formula Editor	Enhanced formula editor
	Application Outliner	Design analysis
Casahl Technology, Inc.	ReplicAction	Data Integration
IT Factory	ITF Development Kit	Design Library
Ives Development	TeamStudio Analyzer	Design analysis
	TeamStudio Ciao	Project management
	TeamStudio Librarian	Design Library
Percussion Software	PowerFlow	Workflow Design
	Notrix	Data Integration
Trilog Group	FlowBuilder	Workflow Design

By no means is this an exhaustive listing of application development tools, but it is a representative sampling.

Types of Applications

There are five general application types:

- **Workflow**—Applications in this category include requisitions, document approval, and so on, as described earlier in this chapter. Most often, these applications rely heavily on messaging and agents to perform actions associated with the business processes that they support.

- **Discussion**—These applications are often the first introduced in a new Notes deployment. They are easy to use, and the Discussion template that comes with Notes is very well-designed. For those of you familiar with online services such as CompuServe, these databases are similar to forums; they are also similar to newsgroups on the Internet. In effect, they are virtual meetings where not all participants need be present at the same time. You can find examples of discussion databases on Notes Net at `http://www.Notes.net`.

- **Tracking**—As is evident from the name, these applications keep track of items. These items can be schedules, data items of interest to the enterprise, surveys, and so on.

- **Reference**—A reference application contains items that are typically not changed often; the Help database in Notes is an example of this type of application, and a Company Policy database is another. Database libraries of either books or other databases is another example.

- **Broadcast**—Broadcast applications provide news to users that is often transferred via email.

In practice, applications often are a blend of the different types. For example, in a discussion database, to keep the participants aware of changes and to encourage active participation, you can include a newsletter agent that sends an email containing document links to all the new and changed documents in the database. A reference application for a corporate policy database would almost certainly have an approval process connected with it. A workflow application that handled requisitions might include a discussion component to provide a forum for appeal of a denied requisition. These are merely a few examples illustrating the rich applications that can be created when the different types are blended together into a solution.

Notes can also provide a front end to a legacy system. In other words, through ODBC or one of the data integration tools such as NotesPump, DECS, or IBM's MQSeries, Notes users not only read data in other databases but also enter and modify it as well. Some integrators can provide a two-way exchange of information, such as MQSeries and

NotesPump; others provide batch updates. DECS is covered in Chapter 37, "Real-Time Access to Enterprise Data."

Despite all this impressive power, Notes and Domino simply isn't suited for some types of applications. Applications that have high-transaction volume such as a telephone call center that takes hundreds of calls an hour might not be a good candidate for Notes. Likewise, if you need complete accuracy and real-time updates of stock in a warehouse, Notes probably shouldn't be your first choice, although it is conceivable that you could interface with a back-end database such as Oracle to provide accurate up-to-the-minute information. Writing an accounting application in Notes is not something you should try, although you could consider interfacing with one. As a general rule of thumb, if the application's data model more closely matches a relational model, use a relational database and not Notes and Domino. In each of these examples, you could possibly find ways to design around the limitations of Notes; however, it is best to find an appropriate tool to solve the business problem rather than force the tool to fit the problem. Here are some rules of thumb you can use to weed out unlikely candidates. Remember not to take these literally, and use a good dosage of common sense! In general, avoid Applications that do the following:

- Require real-time updates and access to data (except where a back-end data source stores the data)
- Have high transaction volumes
- Need sophisticated reporting or a high level of statistical analysis

Summary

This chapter has given you some insight into the maturity and depth of Lotus Notes. This incredibly rich and fascinating product is predominant in the messaging and groupware software markets globally today. Between cc:Mail and Notes, Lotus has by far the largest market share of corporate email, dwarfing the competition. The integration of the send and share models makes it ideal for many applications, not only workflow. The new Design client is a significant improvement over R4 and is covered in Chapter 2.

What's New in Release 5?

by Debbie Lynd

CHAPTER 2

Release 5 provides significant enhancements for developers. Internet development is improved with the addition of pages, JavaScript events, and applets for views and rich text. Tables are enhanced with the capability to create both tabbed tables and tables within tables.

This chapter serves as a brief overview of what's new, whereas the rest of this book gives an in-depth look at ways to implement the features of R5.

What Is Domino Designer?

Domino Designer is the new development environment for Release 5. It is new in that it is separate from the Notes client and actually launches a separate development client. Until now, all database development has been done within the Notes client.

The individuality of Designer provides an obvious separation between the design environment and the client environment, which is intentional on the part of Lotus. This difference serves to help accentuate that, in Release 5, development is done with a Designer client, whereas database access can be accomplished with any Web client, including Notes.

The Designer provides the capability to test and preview applications using a Notes client, Netscape Navigator, or Internet Explorer. The preview options available to you are based on which of those applications you have installed.

The purpose of the Designer is to provide an integrated development environment that provides a place for all code to be entered and tested. In Release 4.6, Java agents and JavaScript was introduced and supported but not embraced in the design environment as it is in Release 5.

The way applications are developed in Release 5 is similar to how they were developed in Release 4. The Integrated Development Environment (IDE), however, has changed somewhat and there are quite a few new objects and design elements that make Release 5 a stellar development environment for any Web developer. To those of us who have been with Notes forever, it's all still there and then some. To those of you coming from other Web development environments, you will find that Domino Designer gives you all the tools you've always used and much more. The IDE is covered in detail in Chapter 8, "The Integrated Development Environment."

Enhancements to the IDE

There are quite a few enhancements in the Integrated Development Environment, which is more commonly referred to as the IDE. These are covered in detail in Chapter 8. Highlights include the following:

- Recent Databases pane lists the last five databases used
- Browser pane replaced with tabbed Objects List and Reference List
- Ability to place tabs in design pane
- Auto-indent LotusScript
- Auto-Wrap Formulas
- Column/row numbers displayed in design pane
- Setting of fonts and color coding for actions, formulas, and other languages
- AgentRunner debugger for Java agents
- Improved error messages
- Ability to do Find/Replace in design pane
- Import and Export code in design pane
- Print code from design pane
- Enhanced Ruler which enables use of left, right, decimal, and center tabs

New Database Properties

Some new properties that improve database performance and others improve server performance. Still others help reduce the size of a database. All these properties are covered in detail in Chapter 7, "The Release 5 Object Store." The new properties include the following:

- Don't maintain unread marks
- Document table bitmap optimization
- Don't overwrite free space
- Maintain `LastAccessed` property
- Disable Transaction Logging
- Don't allow headline monitoring
- Limit entries in `$UpdatedBy` fields
- Limit entries in `$Revisions` fields

- $Undelete Expire Time
- Allow soft deletions
- Don't support specialized response hierarchy
- Default Language
- Default Region
- Default sort order
- Launch Option - Open Designated Frameset

Support for HTML 4 Attributes

There are now many HTML attributes available from the properties box. Importing and copy/paste is supported for HTML pages. These pages can be placed in a form, page, or rich-text field. This provides easy reuse of existing pages, prototyping, or page creation in an HTML editor of your choice and easily bringing the page into Designer. Chapter 21, "Enhancing Domino Applications with HTML," covers HTML in detail.

Embedded Elements

With Release 4.6, the capability to embed views, folders, navigators, and a File Upload Control in a form was introduced for use in Web clients. In R5, this has been expanded to include new embedded objects and the capability to manipulate the objects in ways that were unavailable in 4.6. Embedded elements are discussed in more detail in Chapter 10, "Advanced Form Design." The new embedded elements include the following:

- Calendar Control, which can be used only by Notes clients
- Outline which is available to all clients
- Group Scheduling Control which can only be used by Notes clients

New Design Elements

New design elements in Domino provide additional support for building robust Web applications. The Navigator, which was so exciting and hard to work with, can be ignored now that you have an outliner, pages, and framesets. And the capability to create hotspots on images certainly makes it less attractive to use the old kludge, Navigator. This section describes the new objects that make your life as a developer much easier.

Outline Designer

The Outliner is a new design element that provides the developer with the capability to create a layout of the navigational structure of the application. By defining an outline, entries can be made in the outline that set the hierarchy and define the relationships of the outline entries. The embedded outline control provides a quick and easy method of placing an outline or navigational tool for the application in a frameset. Properties associated with the outline provide the capability to customize the look and feel of the outline. Outlines are covered in detail in Chapter 13, "Creating Outlines." Some highlights of this new design element include capabilities to

- Set the name, link, and target frame for an outline entry
- Create programmable outline content
- Provide a top-level view of the structure of an application
- Match the style for the outline to the site style
- Place an action, link, named element, or URL in an Outline entry

Framesets

Framesets were first introduced in Release 4, but they were quite difficult to create. There weren't separate design elements to represent frames as there are in Release 5.

In R5, framesets are a design element that enables you to create multiple panes, frames within a window, or framesets in an easy-to-use manner. Each pane is independently scrollable and can contain a page, form, document, view, navigator, URL, or another frameset. Framesets are covered in detail in Chapter 31, "Adding Framesets to Domino Applications." Some highlights of this new design element are

- Creating multiple frames within one window
- Placing a link to a view, document, or anchor in a frame
- Placing a named element such as a page, form, frameset, view, folder, or navigator in a frame
- Targeting a specific frame for data display

Page Designer

Pages are a new design element that provides Web developers quick access to a familiar environment in which they can create Web pages using HTML and JavaScript. Pages are covered in detail in Chapter 14, "Using the Page Designer."

The elements available in pages are

- Text
- Tables
- Horizontal rules
- Sections
- Graphics
- Links
- Attachments
- Imagemaps
- Applets
- Actions
- HTML
- Embedded elements
- OLE objects and custom controls

Design Elements in Pages

Pages cannot contain fields, subforms, or layout regions.

Shared Resources

In Release 3, sharing was first introduced with shared fields and subforms. In Release 4, script libraries were added as an additional place to store shared code. In Release 5, shared resources offer a place to keep shared fields and script libraries as well as quite a few other shared elements. Some of these elements have also been available for some time. All elements are discussed in detail in Chapter 12, "Using Resources in Domino Applications." Those that are new are listed here:

- Shared images
- Shared applets
- Shared actions

Tables

Tables have been greatly enhanced. Anyone who has struggled through the versions of tables in Releases 3 and 4 will be very happy to see that the struggle is over and many of the wished-for capabilities are now here. Tables are covered in detail in Chapter 10. Some features that you've been waiting for are

- Nesting of tables
- Fixed width columns
- Table alignment
- Cell alignment
- Minimum row height
- Margins set in percentage, inches, or centimeters
- Gradient cell backgrounds
- Image cell backgrounds
- Shading templates
- Named tables
- Display of table rows via formulas
- Auto smart resize
- Flow text in all table rows
- Tabbed tables
- Row discovery based on tabs, which includes advance on click or advance on interval with transition
- Enhanced border attributes and additional border types

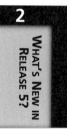

Color and Image Enhancements

In R5, there is an option to use the Web Palette as opposed to the Lotus color palette that provides better color fidelity on the Web. New colors are available, as is the capability to generate custom colors. These are covered in Chapter 9, "Review of Basic Forms Design."

Images are defined as any picture that appears on a page or form. The new functions of images include image properties and JavaScript programmability. Images are covered in detail in Chapter 12, and JavaScript is covered in Chapters 25, "Introduction to JavaScript," 26, "Basic JavaScript," and 27, "Using JavaScript in Domino Applications."

Highlights of the image enhancements include

- Storing images in native format
- Wrapping text around an image

- Scaling images
- Providing alternative text in place of image
- Including captions for an image
- Placing hotspots on an image
- Setting image borders, style, color, and thickness
- Aligning and space images
- Setting HTML tags for images

UI Applets

With enhanced Web capabilities come four Java applets that can be optionally downloaded to the Web browser when selected by the developer. These applets provide additional capability to emulate Notes functionality when using another client through Java. Each of these is described in the following sections.

Outline Applet

Outlines are new to R5 and are an additional way to provide navigation in your application. This is described earlier in this chapter and covered fully in Chapter 13. You will probably use outlines extensively for navigational purposes within your applications. Outline entries can represent links to views, databases, documents, and actions. The Outline applet can be selected for Web viewing and can improve the appearance of an outline, provide background images, and enable mouse over changes such as change of color in the item selected.

Action Bar Applet

Actions were first introduced in Release 4 to provide a developer with programmable buttons on a static Action Bar, as opposed to placing a button on a form which could cause the button to scroll out of the viewable range. These actions were available for Web browsers. In Release 5, choosing to use the Action Bar applet enables scrolling of the Action Bar from a Web browser as well as the capability to access pull-down lists from an action. Actions are covered in detail in Chapter 11, "View Design."

Editor Applet

The Editor applet enables you to work with rich-text fields on the Web. Enabling the Editor applet for a rich-text field provides a Web client with the capability to change the font to the JDK 1.0.2 supported font set, change the size and color of text, set bold text, and underline and italicize text. It also provides paragraph alignment; bulleted and numbered lists; cutting, copying, and pasting text within the field; and creating links. The Editor applet is covered in Chapter 10.

View Applet

The View applet causes a Notes view to have the same functionality in a Web browser as it does in a Notes client.

In Release 4, when a standard or embedded view is displayed to a Web browser, it is displayed using standard HTML. In R5, by enabling a View applet, you can additionally resize columns, select multiple documents, and scroll through the view. It also provides a set of programmable functions through the @Command language. Also new is the capability to mark documents for deletion and use the F9 key to refresh the view; that is a great function to use in dynamic discussion databases on the Web. The new functions of View applets are all covered in Chapter 11.

Languages

There is additional support for Java, JavaScript, and HTML in R5. HTML is covered in detail in Chapter 21. Java is covered in Chapters 28, "Introduction to Java, 29, "Basic Java," and 30, "Using Java in Domino Applications." JavaScript is covered in Chapters 25, 26, and 27. This section covers the enhancements to the Formula language and LotusScript.

Additions and Enhancements to the Formula Language

Many new @Functions have been added to support many of the new design elements. Formulas are covered in detail in Chapters 18, "The Formula Language," 19, "Formula Types," and 20, "Writing Formulas." Additional @Commands have been added for use in the View applet for the capability to manipulate a view from the applet. The new and enhanced functions are listed in Tables 2.1 and 2.2:

TABLE 2.1   New @Commands and @Functions

@Command/@Function	*Description*
@AddToFolder	Enables programmatic addition of the current document to a specified folder. Can be used in SmartIcons, Buttons, and Agents.

continues

TABLE 2.1 continued

@*Command/*@*Function*	*Description*
@BrowserInfo	Returns specific information about a browser or Notes client based on the browser property requested.
@Command([OpenFrameset])	Opens the specified frameset in the current database.
@Command([OpenHelpDocument])	Opens a specific document from a view. Very similar to using a DBLookup; however, instead of returning a value, it returns a document.
@Command([OpenPage])	Opens the specified page.
@Command([RefreshParentNote])	Sends the values from a dialog box to the parent document. Only used in a dialog box.
@FontList	Returns a list of available fonts.
@HardDeleteDoc	Physically deletes a document from a database. @Deletedoc will now be used for a soft delete.
@LanguagePreference	Returns the users' preferred language, in order to determine which language to display specific data in. Works only for Notes users because it looks up the $Language variable from the Notes.INI file on the user's workstation.
@Locale	Returns the alternative name of a user if identified. Parameters determine what is actually returned. This is available only for Notes users.
@NameLookup	Enables a lookup in the Domino Directory to a specific person document in order to return the value of a field in that document.
@Narrow	Converts full-pitch characters to half-pitch. Available for Japanese, Korean, simplified Chinese, and traditional Chinese.
@SetTargetFrame	Used in action and hotspot formulas to set the frame that an open command for a form, view, and so on will be displayed in.
@UndeleteDocument	If a document has been set for a soft delete, this command removes the delete flag on the document.
@UserNameLanguage	Returns the language used for your alternative name, if used.
@UserNamesList	Returns a list of the Groups and Roles that the current user belongs to within the database ACL. Also returns the actual username.

@*Command/@Function*	*Description*
@ValidateInternetAddress	Checks an Internet address for RFC 822 or RFC 821 compliance.
@Wide	Converts half-pitch characters to full-pitch. Available for Japanese, Korean, simplified Chinese, and traditional Chinese.

TABLE 2.2   Enhanced @Commands and @Functions

@*Command/@Function*	*Description*
@Command([CalendarFormat])	Can now specify a one day format.
@Name	New parameters include options to display specific parts of an Internet address and the capability to return a hierarchical Notes name without the common name portion.
@Picklist	New parameters include enabling a Replica ID to be used in the place of a server and filename, returning a list of all folder names in a database or on the desktop, and selecting rooms and resources from the Domino Directory.
@UserName	Can now return an alternative name or actual username. Can also return any of the available server names.

Additions to the LotusScript Language

In support of the new design elements, there are also new LotusScript classes. The new classes are covered in detail in Chapter 24, "Writing LotusScript." The Notes ACL class has also been enhanced to support the Internet level of the ACL and the ACLEntry class has been enhanced to support additional entry properties. There are more new properties and methods for many of the existing classes that can be found in the release notes for R5. A few interesting new functions include Array append and ArrayReplace, which are also covered in Chapter 24.

In addition, there are additional classes for rich-text support and views as well as a new class for replication. These new classes are listed here.

- NotesOutline
- NotesOutlineEntry
- NotesReplication
- NotesRichTextParagraphStyle

- NotesRichTextTab
- NotesViewEntry
- NotesViewEntryCollection
- NotesViewNavigator

Summary

This chapter provided a brief overview of some of the new capabilities available in Release 5 as well as references to additional information for each of the new features.

Project Management

by Jonathan Kern

IN THIS CHAPTER

The term *software development project management* is arguably an oxymoron to many in our industry. Indeed, the industry as a whole has a reputation for delivering software products that are late and over budget, while missing the target. What's worse, this is at a time when the demand for software production (paralleling the shrinking business cycle) is continuing to rise at a seemingly, unchecked rate—coined "The Software Crisis."

According to the Standish group (1998), the average project exceeds its budget by 90% and schedule by 120%. Why is that? Is it because developers are poor performers? Is it because we lack high-productivity tools with good development environments? Or is it a result of not applying good development practices?

The Software Crisis

Over the past 5 years, the need for software development has far surpassed the ability of the industry to deliver the required high-quality, on-time, within-budget, products. In addition, much of the time is spent doing maintenance—or worse, fixing the Y2K bug.

By the way, this isn't a true "bug" because it was done by design, not by accident. Twenty to thirty years ago, when memory/storage was expensive, folks made the (pragmatic) decision to trade off two digits of the date for storage space. I'm sure, in their defense, they never thought these programs would still be in use at the turn of the century.

A study in 1996 on the software projects in the United Kingdom revealed the following information:

- Eighty to ninety percent do not meet performance goals
- About 80% are delivered late and over budget
- Around 40% of projects fail or are abandoned
- Fewer than 40% fully address training and skills requirements
- Fewer than 25% properly integrate technology and business objectives
- Only 10–20% meet all their success criteria

And similarly from the US [Standish Group, 1995]:

- US companies spent $81 billion on canceled software projects
- Thirty-one percent of software projects were canceled
- Fifty-three percent of software projects overran by more than 50%
- Only 9% of software projects for large companies were on time and within budget. The numbers were 16% for medium-sized and 28% for small companies

More and more, the information technology silver bullet is being brought into organizations as a panacea for the woes besetting their bottom line. Providing group ware, Internet, and intranet applications, plus high-level applications to tie across every department and function and low-level applications to improve the communication with equipment and assembly lines—you name it, software is often a major player. Unfortunately, market hype and overblown benefits of the latest faddish software tool can wreak havoc on a development team. Just about the time the team members were getting used to their tools and environment and becoming productive, it's time to switch to the next technology that is certain to save the day.

As software engineers and developers, it is our responsibility to improve the methods by which we construct these software applications. Solid development methods transcend fads and provide a good foundation on which to base application construction. From capturing the user's needs, designing in flexibility to grow the application, and building a robust application that doesn't crash to providing smooth deployment and helpful documentation and tech support—all phases need to be properly approached and managed. The proper methodology will go a long way to ensuring a successful end product and a satisfied client.

Software engineering is a discipline applied to software development—much like aerospace engineering is used for aircraft development. As in many technical disciplines, methods, tools, standard processes, and industry standards all come together to serve the common goal. In software development, these technical disciplines include requirements analysis, design, implementation, software quality assurance, coordinated management control, and so on. Today, the goal of improved software development is aided by software engineers being able to take advantage of ever more powerful third-party tools:

- Project management, planning, and tracking
- Requirements documenting and tracking
- Design tools for object models, databases, and state diagrams
- Automated GUI testing
- Test coverage analysis
- Metrics gathering and analysis
- Documentation and help tools
- Integrated development environments

Because an entire book could be devoted to the subject of software engineering (and this isn't that book), this chapter touches on some of the standard development methods in use today, explain their pros and cons, describe (in a bit more detail) a preferred approach, and discuss the management techniques available.

Common Methodologies

Some of the more popular and common methods for developing software over the past couple of decades include

- Waterfall model
- Modified waterfall model
- Technical and functional specifications
- Ad hoc/ad infinitum development
- Rapid application development
- Phased, feature-based development

The Waterfall Model

The waterfall model was introduced in 1970 by Winston Royce at IEEE WESCON in a paper titled "Managing the Development of Large-Scale Software Systems." What most people have come to know as "the waterfall model" is actually a greatly watered down version from the original treatise based on how it is practiced in the field. Many of the flaws of the waterfall model were in the common practice, not in the actual treatise. Indeed, for being 30 years old, the paper has amazing insight into the process of developing software that remains applicable to today's dilemma!

The waterfall model, as practiced, involves some or all of the steps shown in Figure 3.1. The most obvious aspect of this model for the software development life cycle is the *sequence*: Each activity follows in step. The output of one step serves as the input to the next. In rigorous cases, the activity output is *frozen* at the end of each step. This conventional approach, as you will see, is no longer workable for modern software engineering practices.

FIGURE 3.1

The classic water-fall model as practiced preclud-ed upstream feed-back eddies.

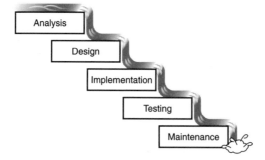

The conventional waterfall model steps shown in Figure 3.1 comprise the following basic components.

Analysis

This step encompasses getting *very* deep into understanding exactly what the application is to do. This typically requires the analyst to work closely with experts in the given problem domain. The system and software requirements feeding into the analysis step must include things such as system functionality, performance constraints, and external system interfaces. This step also exposes the "what"—that is, exactly what information (data) is required to be captured and used within this application to meet the needs of the customer. It is crucial that the requirements are thorough and detailed. The requirements document (often referred to as "Technical and Functional Specifications") is typically signed off by the customer, signaling the start of the next step.

Design

Given the set of fixed requirements provided from the previous step, the design task begins in earnest. Design requires that the textual requirements get translated into specifics meaningful to both the software environment (Notes, C++, Java, Smalltalk, Eiffel, BASIC, FORTRAN, and so on) and the proposed system (hardware, networks, and so on). The primary aspects addressed in program design are

- Software architecture
- Data (storage)
- Timing
- Procedural

3

PROJECT MANAGEMENT

Problems with Requirements "Transformations"

One of the major problems with non–object-oriented analysis and design methods lies in the activity mentioned earlier: "requirements get translated." Within this transformation lies a potential for error. Because the best model of the real world is the real world itself, the OO paradigm proves to be the better approach for software modeling. This is because of the intent of the OO paradigm to closely model the world as it stands, requiring little or no translation from analysis to design to implementation. This is in contrast to attempts to jam a model of the world into structured, data flow diagrams, entity-relationship diagrams, process models, and so on.

You'll see more on this in Chapters 4, "Project Phases," and 5, "Business Process Analysis."

Implementation

When the program design is frozen, developers are assigned various pieces of the effort to complete. Sometimes, design is taken to such granularity that developers have very small, well-defined modules to develop. These are often thought of as a series of units or "black boxes." Meaning, the developer writes code to ensure that output "y" results given an input "x" as specified. In huge waterfall-based projects, hordes of cubical dwellers crunch out their small piece of the pie, sometimes with only a rudimentary knowledge of the overall objective of the software component that they are a part of—the latter being a fault of the management principles at work. Putting all the pieces together makes a complete application to (hopefully) meet the original (long ago frozen) requirements.

Testing

The testing is often broken down into "white box" and "black box" testing. The test team has to work closely with the developers to ensure proper white box testing. Both the logic within each module must be tested, and the overall external logic must be verified. After all, the application hopefully produces results that resemble the needs of the original requirements.

In addition, for large-scale systems that integrate with legacy systems, there is a very crucial system-integration test phase. This involves testing the system interactions, throughput, error handling, and so on.

Following testing, the product is shipped or installed.

Maintenance

This step involves activities to

- Fix defects found in the field
- Accommodate small upgrade requests to enhance the application
- Provide major upgrades
- Develop completely new functionality

For major upgrade efforts, the entire waterfall model is reapplied—analysis, design, implementation, and testing—and can become a project unto itself.

The Waterfall Method in Practice

In practice, the waterfall method was often too rigorous, too stiff. Practitioners found themselves having to go back to previous steps as discoveries were made in the current step that impacted previous frozen information. The modified waterfall model approach does allow some upstream propagation to occur. In other words, if analysis discoveries were made during the design phase, these could be incorporated in the analysis documents.

Advantages and Disadvantages of Waterfall/Modified Waterfall Model

The *advantages* of the waterfall model are in its simplicity! The stepped approach leaves little to the imagination: requirements analysis, design, code, test, ship, and fix. This also makes schedule tracking easy:

"Boss, we are 14 weeks into the 40-week design phase."

The primary *disadvantage* of the waterfall model is the amount of documentation developed—unless you need heat in the winter, or were looking for a good project to try out that Notes Microsoft Office Object Library database and archiving template. Though excessive documentation is often lamented as a government-only curse (those familiar with MIL-STD-498 "Software Development and Documentation" or the older MIL-STD-2167A/B will know what I mean), it can happen on any project. On large projects, requirements analysis consultants are brought in from the "Big 6" to discuss and document the needs of the customer. Often, *in lieu* of tailoring the requirements documents to meet the needs of the designers and developers, a veritable river raft of documents spews forth—after all, this is the first team's only output. Judging on sheer weight alone, the documentation must be worthwhile! Right?

Unfortunately, the design cycle often yields numerous questions that affect requirements. For nontrivial systems, it is ludicrous to think that all requirements can come forth solely during the requirements gathering phase. The mere act of designing—holding the objects in your mind's eye, looking at how the different parts of the system interconnect, thinking through different techniques, examining time-ordered sequences of events, analyzing state changes over time, sketching different GUI concepts—often leads to discoveries in new requirements by both the client and the developers.

The waterfall method requires the project to specify all requirements completely and unambiguously up front in the process. This is a naive goal for nontrivial projects where it takes a great deal of effort to get to the true requirements. Also, the waterfall-style

3

PROJECT MANAGEMENT

requirements often get treated equally in terms of rough scheduling estimates. In reality, it often turns out that about 20% of the requirements actually drive 80% of the design solution (budget and schedule).

If the requirements are frozen, a great deal of inertia (often including contractual obligations), needs to be overcome should a change in requirements be needed. This inertia makes it more difficult to institute change—a dangerous precedent. (Of course, those of you who have experienced customers whose motto is "I'm the King of Requirements Creep" might prefer such inertia.) Nonetheless, unchanging requirements in today's business environment is a rarity. You must design for elegantly adapting your solution to the inevitable changes in requirements. You must design in flexibility.

Other disadvantages involve resource planning. In practice, it is rare for a development organization to have individuals with the requisite roles for each step available at the perfect time to support each phase of the project. Instead, some developers might have become available to the project while the analysts were still working up their details. Not wanting to waste resources, the project manager might assign the developer to start some downstream task ahead of schedule, risking that the effort won't be counterproductive.

And probably harshest of all disadvantages is that the client has to wait long into the development cycle to see even the faintest glimmer of an application. The bulk of the time is spent in up-front analysis, design, and documentation. Some people refer to this as analysis paralysis. Tons of design. Tons of supporting documentation. Nothing tangible as far as a working system. The most serious aspect of this disadvantage is the very real possibility that, when the application is finally done and ready for beta testing, the business has changed and so have the real requirements!

In addition, all those mountains of paper requirements and design documents don't add up to a hill of beans in terms of truly defining the application. The only real, tangible evidence that a requirement was accurately met is in working code. In my opinion, hundreds of use cases and pretty diagrams can still leave room for interpretation, room for being ambiguous.

Another major problem is delaying integration issues until late in the cycle, when the system is much less nimble. If the project does a great deal of up-front work with little attention along the way to the real implementation environment and intended uses, the project is in serious risk of causing late-stage design breakage. On typical waterfall-model projects, integration and test routinely consumed 40% of the software budget!

Technical and Functional Specifications

In this methodology, the development team is handed a complete document outlining exactly what the application is supposed to do. Yeah, right. I remember the first time I was handed a 400-page requirements document. I was elated at the prospect of having so much good information already compiled—until I looked more closely and got further into my own analysis and design.

This is similar to the waterfall model, only that the team picks up after analysis (and sometimes some design) has been performed by someone else, documented, and handed over. Given this requirements specification, design continues and the rest of the cycle progresses using any number of methods (waterfall, spiral, or RAD).

Advantages and Disadvantages of Technical and Functional Specifications

As an offshoot of the waterfall model, being h anded a stack of specifications simply puts you a couple of steps into the waterfall process. In theory, the specs capture the complete set of requirements. Of course this is highly dependent on the accuracy of the specs, their level of detail, and how closely the specification followed the client's needs.

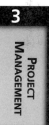

Assuming a well-written spec, the *advantages* are

- Requirements phase has been done elsewhere
- Build only what is specified
- Cost and schedule risks are minimized

The *disadvantages*, along with those mentioned for the waterfall method, include

- Ill-defined requirements
- Lost opportunity for the development team to mentally ramp up during the requirements gathering phase
- The difficulty in scheduling contingencies for correcting ill-formed requirements
- The potential for getting lost in the translation increases dramatically
- Diminished sense of ownership by the development team

The Importance of Developer Ramp-Up

Most of the earlier disadvantages are straightforward; however, the lost ramp-up time deserves some attention. In complex applications, developers need to have a good understanding of the problem domain, how the user expects to interact with the application, how a given subject area impacts other areas in the application, and so on. By not participating in the all-important interviews during requirements gathering, the development team loses many of the nuances—despite best efforts to the contrary.

The risks to the project are significant. The developer can press ahead in implementing the requirements, only to find a misunderstanding when the user finally sits in front of the GUI. Or the savvy developer might recognize the need to first call in the client or domain expert and gather more insight into the requirement.

Bottom line: There's no free lunch. If you must prepare a specification ahead of time independent of the development team, understand the need to transmit the nuances to the development team. This can be done by spending a great deal of extra effort in preparing the specs to include the nuances. Or the development team (at least some of the senior designers/analysts/architects) can participate during the requirements gathering process. Or you can really spend lots of extra resources fixing during integration and testing what actually amounted to a poorly understood requirement.

Ad Hoc/Ad Infinitum Development

Unfortunately, this is one of the more practiced techniques. With little up-front planning, developers barge on ahead and cut code. This is usually because management or the client needs (mistakenly or not) instant results.

The analysis and design activities are either cast aside or given short shrift. After all, it is more glamorous to plunge immediately into implementation. This is especially true given the myriad of GUI-based tools that allow for quick results in the form of a working application.

With a little client education, it isn't too hard to move this development methodology over to the more successful phased, feature-based development methodology described in a subsequent section. This way, you'll be able to avoid the infinite loop shown in Figure 3.2.

FIGURE 3.2

Have you found yourself in the circular traps of ad hoc development?

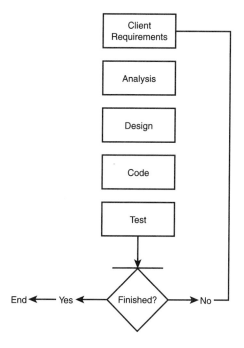

3

PROJECT
MANAGEMENT

Advantages and Disadvantages of Ad Hoc/Ad Infinitum Development

The *advantages* of this method are the ability to get some initial results—and *fast*—and show the customer progress. And to think, you did it all without wasting time planning the project. If the project is to be short-lived, or is a very small effort, or is meant to never be more than a quick-and-dirty prototype, this might be acceptable—even desirable.

The *disadvantages* of this method are many. Rushing into implementation without adequate requirements analysis can result in

- Ill-defined problem statements
- Missing requirements
- Probable lacking of a project plan with clear milestones
- Lack of adequate understanding of the problem domain (from the perspective of the subject matter experts)
- Difficulty in managing complexity (because you don't have it well laid out)

- Poor use of development resources
- Hit or miss quality (quality is a process, not an add-in)
- Customer dissatisfaction
- Inability to judge progress
- Not knowing when the application has met its goals

Because of these problems, the development seems to go on forever without reaching a conclusion. You are always at the 90% point. I'd like to say that these methods are most often employed on small one- or two-person projects, but even large, multimillion-dollar projects fall victim to this approach (until someone in upper management cancels the project about the third time it goes back to the well).

In skipping past the design activity, you also lose by possibly

- Not leveraging previous designs
- Reinventing the proverbial wheel
- Building a point solution versus a more global solution that could be applied to additional projects
- Building a solution to the wrong problem
- Not gaining further insights

Rapid Application Development (RAD)

The RAD method takes many forms:

- Rapid prototyping
- Joint application design (JAD)
- Fourth-generation tools (4GL) to quickly generate apps

In general, the idea to quickly assimilate an initial—often fuzzy—requirements statement into a simple system. Often, the system demonstrates the critical user interfaces and maybe some of the key underlying data structures. In other words, it is a shallow implementation so that the customer can get a look at some functioning code and get a feel for the dynamics of the application. The customer is typically heavily involved through frequent review sessions. As shown in Figure 3.3, evaluation of the prototype often leads to making changes in the requirements.

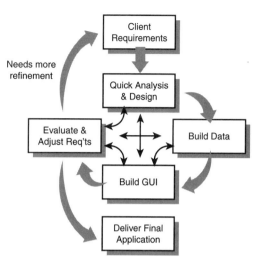

FIGURE 3.3
*In a typical proto-
typing cycle, you
get a little taste of
everything.*

Client
Requirements

Needs more
refinement

Quick Analysis
& Design

Evaluate &
Adjust Req'ts

Build Data

Build GUI

Deliver Final
Application

Rapid prototyping can be an effective tool—even when employed from within another development paradigm. It can be used to explore critical user interface designs, complex algorithms, use of third-party tools, application architecture—or even the whole application itself. For example, you can use it to try out two or three different approaches to present the user with the same information—only in different GUI styles or with different user controls. The user can then try out the working prototypes and provide the development effort with invaluable feedback.

There are many tools available today that serve as very high-level design tools. One can often paint the GUI, data repository, or reports from an easy-to-use interface. These 4GL tools are then able to generate code from the design. Some of these tools work in only one direction—that is, you can generate the code once, but then it will not reverse-engineer existing (changed) code back into the graphical model. More modern tools (especially many graphical IDEs for Java) provide two-way translation between graphically designing and altering source code directly. These types of code generation tools can be a big boon to rapid application development.

Advantages and Disadvantages of RAD

Rapid Application Development does have its place as a viable development methodology, as long as it is applied correctly and under the right circumstances. The key is to understand the following aspects of your current project:

- How well are your requirements defined?
- What does your customer expect of a prototype?
- How well do your current development techniques allow for rapid prototype development?
- Do you have enough standards and procedures in place to ensure quality prototyping?
- Objectively rank your prototyping efforts from (1) throw-away (worse) to (3) keep some, throw some away, to (5) keep all, expand (best).

If you have poorly defined requirements, whipping up some prototypes might be the best near-term solution to getting the project off the ground. You must also educate the customer to understand the meaning of a prototype—that speed is of the essence, not perfection or elegance. Some customers don't quite get it. They have trouble abstracting the overall suggested solution that the prototype has to offer and instead get lost in the morass of minutiae (for example, GUI tweaks). It is important that you can distinguish these types of customers; you might be better off in a phased, feature-based approach, as discussed later in this chapter.

If you have developed a strong set of reusable business objects (libraries, databases, forms, reports, and so on), you might be well-positioned to create a rapid prototype. If these were created on a foundation of tightly crafted and efficient coding, an effective set of standards, and solid quality assurance procedures, so much the better. If the latter positive qualities are in place at your development house, you even stand a chance of developing a prototype that might have a large percentage remain intact for the actual application development cycle. This is always good news.

Phased, Feature-Based Development

This *preferred* method is a blend of many others and honed through the School of Hard Knocks. This method combines the positive traits of the waterfall model, spiral development, rapid prototyping, and so on and strives to eliminate the negatives.

I cannot present a single method as appropriate for all cases, but this one comes closest. The best use of the approach is to apply it to many projects and keep notes—gripes, variations on a theme, feedback from all levels. Continually adjust the method details to suit your environment and customer needs. The size, complexity, level of requirements certainty, and the familiarity of the developers with the development environment, all contribute to determining how you tailor the method.

The phased approach provides comfort for both the customer and the development team. As shown in Figure 3.4, there are two primary phases:

- Phase 1: Requirements definition
- Phase 2: Application development

These are introduced to help address the normal problems associated with providing accurate estimates of time and money. The first phase gets you to a comfort level to make an accurate quote. The next phase is used to complete the development. To the degree to which you can make accurate quotes, the length of the phases are on a sliding scale. The activities are still accomplished, however the duration can vary widely.

During requirements definition, requirements are gathered through sessions spent with the client—examining pertinent aspects of the client's business, their processes, their products, their workflow. To help define the requirements, it might be appropriate to do some form of rapid prototyping. The basic output of this phase in terms of classic requirements is a prioritized features list.

Application development follows the baseball model (based on Coad93; see "Bibliography," later in this chapter). The technique is to concurrently apply analysis, design, implementation, and testing against the prioritized features—hence, a feature-based approach.

One business benefit to this phased approach is to perform the Requirements phase under a time and materials (T&M) contract. The actual development effort can then be a fixed-price bid—theoretically, by anyone, given an adequate documented output of the first phase (remember, it isn't easy to impart in document form all nuances learned through months of requirements definition and discussions with the client). In general, the application development is best performed by the team that did the first phase.

The lofty goal is to mitigate risks of failure through this phased approach:

- Ensure clear understanding of the client's problem domain, needs, priorities, fears, and value-add ranking.
- Start prototyping solutions early on to provide tangible, working solutions. No sense waiting to discover we've misinterpreted a requirement or must overcome some very difficult technical details during integration (for example, database access is too slow or network bandwidth is insufficient).
- Provide a separation of concerns to partition the problem domain solution from the user interface, persistent store, and external system interfaces.
- Providing documentation for the requirements phase captures the changing face of the application needs and provides continuity. Many aspects of the documentation

reflect concrete truths regarding the client's problem domain—although changes can occur within the development environment (third-party tools and libraries, methods, and so on).

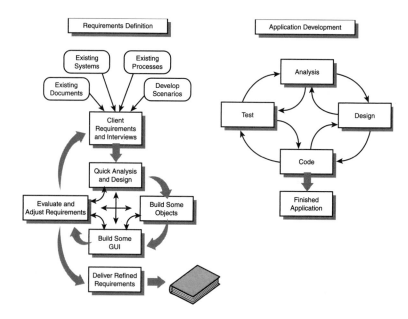

FIGURE 3.4

Use this phased, feature-based development methodology to achieve greater success.

Requirements Definition

At the cornerstone of this methodology is the analysis and design techniques that I've learned primarily from Peter Coad's object-oriented analysis and design books (Coad91, Coad92), applying the techniques described later to numerous applications, working with Peter Coad himself, and helping Pete with his latest *Java Design* book.

The types of applications where I have used these techniques span quite a few varied problem domains—a testament to the robust nature of the process.

The primary product of this requirements definition phase is a reasonably detailed set of requirements and design documents that include

- System Purpose
- System Features
- Use Cases
- Initial Object Model
- Sequence Diagrams
- Sample GUI (sketches or working prototypes)

The goal is to get to a level of detail sufficient to enter into the next phase with a fairly accurate projection of tasks, resources, schedule, and costs. In other words, you and your customer have done enough homework to feel confident that the project is well understood and bounded—this is not to say that it is completely understood; there should still be some room for modifications within the bounding box.

Chapters 4 and 5 discuss this methodology in greater detail.

Application Development

During this phase of development, an incremental approach is taken to continually build up the application functionality to discrete levels. The increments in this methodology refer to functional requirements expressed as features (something useful to the client), as opposed to other components of the application development paradigm (such as documents, objects, tables, or methods). Within each increment, development iterates to a correct solution for implementing a set of discrete features.

The methodology also uses a vertical and horizontal partitioning of the solution space as shown in Figure 3.5. The subjects are used to help break down conceptual areas in the problem domain. This further partitioning of the solution space benefits all involved in terms of creating bite size chunks of the problem that are more digestible than looking at the entire problem as a monolithic whole.

FIGURE 3.5

Two-dimensional partitioning of the solution space is a technique to keep your application organized.

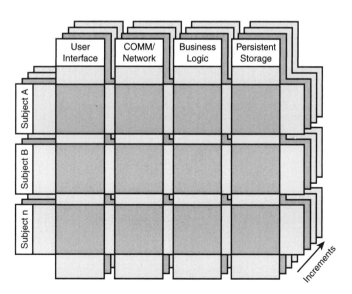

In brief, the vertical partitioning (Coad95) provides insulation from changes in the implementation environment. Depending on what environment you are developing within, you will have more or less need to adhere to this partitioning. For example, in a tightly controlled database GUI development environment, you would likely be forced to a two-tier solution with little chance to separate the problem domain Business Logic from the GUI and the Persistent Storage. In a three-tier system where you are developing a thin client solution, you will be able to develop a solid separation between the GUI presentation layer, the network middleware, the business logic, and the persistent store.

In addition, the number of target hardware platforms and operating systems can play a role in determining how many vertical partitions exist. On the other hand, a single point solution developed in Notes has many of the vertical partitions handled automatically by the tool. In this case, the developer can concentrate more on the application logic and the interface, and less on worrying about how communication or persistence is accomplished.

Regardless of the solution environment, it is imperative to always strive to maintain a separation of concerns to keep the solution as flexible and maintainable as possible. It isn't hard to realize that business logic captured in the code to support a button press is hardly reusable or flexible. If this logic is then unwisely copied to another part of the application, a change in logic requires code changes in multiple places—clearly making maintenance and testing more costly and risky.

The technique is discussed further in Chapters 4 and 5.

The horizontal partitions represent major subject areas of the problem domain, or application. This is useful from an organizational perspective. Examples from a manufacturing application can include

- Product
- Bill of material
- Process plan
- Work position
- Equipment
- Associate/organization
- Order
- Work in process

The concurrent efforts of doing some analysis, some design, and some coding provide the developer the ability to make frequent working (working!) versions of the application. Presenting these frequent alpha releases to the client will provide invaluable feedback along the way. Assumptions can be verified, details cleared up, dynamic scenarios demonstrated, GUIs streamlined, and tangible progress presented to the client.

The technique also provides management with valuable feedback in terms of how long particular aspects of the requirements take to develop—useful if you have established metrics.

Another benefit is to head off at the pass any "showstoppers" that could threaten the success of the application. The architecture of core systems can be designed and tested prior to committing the whole application to the architecture. This is an especially helpful technique when it comes to difficult interfaces to external systems, or if the team is not very experienced with some complex new technology. Sometimes, you need to try one or more solutions and select the most promising. All these work well in this development paradigm, helping to mitigate the risks early on rather than later, when it is costly and so very disruptive to the project.

Circling the Business Target

One big advantage of prototyping is the rapidity by which the customer sees results. When it is difficult to nail down the requirements (or occasionally, it is even hard to get enough face-to-face time with the customer), prototyping can be very effective. Some customers know what they want only when they see it on the screen.

Much like the customer's probably fuzzy requirements, hand-waving, and pie-in-the-sky wishes, your prototyping effort can start off at a very high altitude—getting the big picture. As you gain feedback from the customer, add insights of your own, and learn more about the problem domain, you can continue to enhance the prototype. Eventually, you will either spiral into lower altitudes with greater and greater detail and the final prototype, or you'll crash and burn as you or the customer runs out of time, money, patience, or any combination thereof.

However, if the reason for prototyping is merely to get started, then you might forever be in a holding pattern above the business target.

Notes: an Ideal Prototyping Tool

Due to the rich development environment of Notes, you can quickly put together a prototype system for your customer:

- The ease by which databases can be created from scratch
- The ability to create like databases using a template
- The feature-rich form creation tools

- The ability to easily add advanced field-level extended attributes
- The ease of adding form/field dynamics via logic in scripts
- The ability to inherit template changes
- And many more…

If you have customers in common or identical business areas, the ability to easily clone a database and forms is an extra advantage that Notes provides you.

The Value of Reusable Designs

This makes a strong case to spend the extra time to ensure your designs are relatively generic. By doing so, you can build up a repository of reusable business objects in Notes. With these at your disposal, you can quickly snap together prototypes and even complete working systems. Remember, you gain by being able either to underbid your competition or to get a fixed-price contract that is reasonable from the client's perspective but allows you to increase your profit. No complaints here!

The "We'll Fix It Later" Syndrome

On the down side of prototyping is the risk that the quick-and-dirty prototype you worked up over an all-nighter with *caffe latte* and pretzels is shrink-wrapped and sent to the client!

Well, maybe not quite that dramatic. However, it is quite often the case that the prototyping methodology lures the customer, the manager, and even some developers into thinking "we're done." For trivial applications, I suppose they might be right. However, for complex applications, what wins out in a prototype phase is often not the best implementation, but merely a step along the path of determining what is needed in the solution space.

Given a greater range and depth of requirements analysis, some time to tinker with varying approaches, and a better understanding of where reuse might fit into the application development cycle, the prototyping effort can often be improved with a full-cycle, real development effort.

All too often, the death knell phrase (described later in this chapter) is uttered by dreamy project managers in the hopes of accelerating the making of target completion milestones.

Just get it to work for this build, we'll fix it later in the development plan when
things are a little easier.

—Anonymous (former) Project Manager

Yeah. All the projects I've worked on got easier and had more slack time as they pro-
gressed to completion. (And by the way, I've got some great beachfront property in
Arkansas for a steal!)

Do not forget the rule of thumb that an error in requirements costs 1.5–10 times more to
fix in development, and 60–100 times more to fix in maintenance. Hacking up a solution
early on with the hopes of fixing it later is akin to robbing Peter to pay Paul.

Just say no! Don't get sucked into this approach!

Advantages and Disadvantages of Phased, Feature-Based Development

The *advantages* of this method distinguish it as my favorite:

- Requirements are clearly delineated and understood to a sufficient level of detail
- Important architectural design ideas are validated early on in the project
- Critical user interface issues are handled
- Feedback is available quickly and early in the project
- Concurrent development and continuous integration ensures all areas of the devel-
  opment environment are being exercised, minimizing finding showstoppers late in
  the game
- Concurrent development allows for more resources to be used in an effective,
  largely consistent manner
- Capabilities (functionality, features) are implemented in an order closely aligned
  with the client's priorities
- Frequent, working code releases provide the team (and client/stakeholders) with
  success to build on
- An application is built successfully, one step at a time
- Implementation realities can help to improve design and even architecture—again,
  early on in the project, when it is still inexpensive to make changes (application is
  more nimble)

- Patterns can be easily discerned by looking at the high-level system design across many subject areas—and then applied across the other areas

- The initial requirements definition phase can help provide a detailed initial specification on which to base estimates (cost and schedule) for complete implementation

- Opportunities for reuse can be identified

The *disadvantages* of this methodology are few, if handled properly. The following list provides more of a set of misconceptions that need to be managed, rather than a set of disadvantages:

- Management is more complex because the development progression is much more three-dimensional and nonlinear when compared to the waterfall method. However, tracking now falls to a list of features that should be granular enough to ameliorate this possible disadvantage.

- Due to successive passes at a given subject area to add functionality supporting more detailed requirements, existing code is often perturbed—the ripple effect. But because we are doing continuous integration (hence testing), errors should be caught almost immediately.

- Developers must learn to work in teams of people with the abilities to participate in the concurrent tasks for delivering the current feature (for example, experts in user interface, subject matter, data management, architecture, object modeling, and use case).

- Performing builds becomes more difficult in terms of managing what changed source needs to be included for successive incremental deliveries. However, this can be countered with a management approach that centers on feature-based code changes.

If you are in an organization steeped in a methodology that can stand to benefit from the application of some of the methodologies presented herein, you'll have to hone your marketing skills. Why? As with any paradigm shift, the inertia of management and fellow developers, and even the expectations of your customer base have to be handled carefully.

The Phased, Feature-Based Development Model in Practice

This approach provides a win-win situation for both the client and the consultants.

In addition, the software industry (or at least your team) can begin to gain a reputation for

- Delivering quality products that meet the current needs (features) of the client
- Delivering on time
- Delivering within budget
- Building a system that can embrace change over time
- Achieving overall lower lifecycle costs

The Client's Perspective

Through the *phasing,* the client gains by

- Allowing the project to start even though the initial client-produced requirements statements are minimal
- Having the expertise of the developers assist in requirements gathering, possibly leveraging domain experience gained over many other projects
- Refining the requirements to a point where cost and schedule can be accurately estimated

Through the *feature-based development*, the client gains by

- Having a development cost and schedule predicated on a sound requirements phase (helpful if further reporting is required up the chain)
- Seeing frequent, working prototypes with features added in a client-prioritized manner
- Providing feedback early in the development cycle (avoiding costly late cycle breakage)
- Using the system (depends on the application) when a minimal set of requirements have been met
- Adding new features very quickly
- Reducing the overall life cycle cost
- Seeing the high-priority, high-value items implemented first

The Consultant's Perspective

Through the *phasing,* the consultant gains by

- Participating from the start—this helps to develop a deep understanding of the client's requirements within the consultant(s)
- Able to explore difficult issues—and share findings (good and bad) with the client—without worrying that the fixed price schedule and budget hadn't foreseen

such delays due to complexity (and the oft-applied response—hack a quick and dirty, cheap solution that we'll do right on the next contract with the client)

- Minimizing overall risk by being paid to do the up front effort that yields a more certain development estimate

Through the *feature-based development*, the consultant gains by

- Frequently providing a working version to obtain immediate feedback

- Learning as each small, incremental step is taken to implement features

- Not being overcome by minutiae found in a detailed specification, but rather being able to enjoy the forest view through the trees

- The confidence in developing meaningful, quality software in a timely, cost-effective manner

Bibliography

[Coad91] Coad, Peter, and Yourdon, Edward, *Object-Oriented Analysis*. Prentice Hall, Englewood Cliffs, NJ, 1991

[Coad92] Coad, Peter, and Yourdon, Edward, *Object-Oriented Design*. Prentice Hall, Englewood Cliffs, NJ, 1992

[Coad93] Coad, Peter, and Nicola, Jill, *Object-Oriented Programming*. Prentice Hall, Englewood Cliffs, NJ, 1993

[Coad95] Coad, Peter, North, David, and Mayfield, Mark, *Object Models: Strategies, Patterns, and Applications*. Prentice Hall, Englewood Cliffs, NJ, 1995

Project Phases

by Jonathan Kern

CHAPTER 4

As we learned in the previous chapter, you will be able to achieve a win/win solution with a modern, incremental, phased approach to software development.

Assuming a relatively large project, iterative development by itself can lead to design changes that always seem to be too disruptive. Tackling the project one part (or component) at a time can cause problems due to the incapability to test the system as a whole. If you discover errors as you build and integrate one of the "last" subsystems into the overall system, it is difficult to get corrective changes back into the system without blowing the schedule.

The solution is to apply the following project phases repeatedly to each developmental increment. The first application of these activities is to help define a robust set of requirements—built from the model perspective, from some GUI prototypes, and from discussions with the client. These requirements can take the form of a simple bulleted list of features or as full-fledged use cases. As the project enters full-scale development (the construction phase), the activities can again be applied—only this time, to a greater depth. In addition, if the client adds new requirements, the activities are applied yet again to these requirements.

The next chapter provides a more thorough discussion of the techniques that you can employ to perform an object-oriented analysis and design. The approach to the sample project in the next chapter will use the Unified Modeling Language (UML) notation (refer to www.omg.org or www.rational.com).

Using a Project Notebook

One of the most important aspects of any nontrivial project is the capability to communicate the project details to others. The best way to do this in an integrated team environment is through a logical Project Notebook that you maintain in a central project location. This lets all team members easily access the Notebook. Usually, more than one individual—and often teams—create and update specific sections of the Project Notebook. The Notebook is a place to keep the artifacts of the software development activities during project evolution.

It is important that you approach this Project Notebook in a proactive manner. The Notebook is of little value if it is not up-to-date with the latest direction, changes in requirements, algorithm and behavioral write-ups, and agreed-to schedule changes. By maintaining a current Notebook, it becomes much easier to transition new people through the project. This includes new developers, new customers, new testers, new management, new marketing reps, and so on. The value of the Notebook to members of the extended application development organization (the stakeholders) is tremendous.

Depending on your environment, this logical notebook can take different forms. In many file-based development environments, third-party tools are used to maintain source code and other project documents. An Integrated Team Environment, such as StarBase's StarTeam (see Figure 4.1), grants users full access to the Notebook repository (even through remote login or the Internet).

FIGURE 4.1

Maintain a virtual project notebook in a central repository to keep everyone informed.

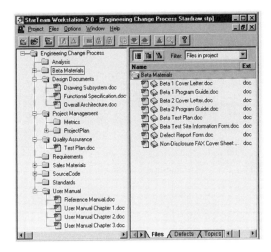

A Project Notebook in Notes

You could also set up a Project Notebook using Notes. You may want to start with the provided Document Library template and extend it to suit your needs. Figure 4.2 shows a sample set of folders.

Figure 4.3 shows how you might extend the default fields of the Document database to accept additional information:

- *Owner*—This can be a drop-down list of names to assign the responsibility of seeing the document through to completion. For example, the Test Scenario document will likely be created by numerous testers; however, the lead tester may have overall ownership of the document to see that it gets finished and is updated as required.

- *Status*—In addition to a notion of review cycle, the document status field can indicate different levels of document state. For example, the document status may transition from Not Started, to Draft, to In Review, to Accepted, to Superceded.

- *Traceability*—Many times, a change to one document requires an update of others. This multivalue field enables the document developer to indicate any number of other documents that should be checked for needed change. This means that the

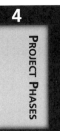

development team is able to more easily conduct impact analyses at the overall document level. From there (and in conjunction with a robust requirements analysis tool), you can gather further impact analysis details.

- *Comments*—As users alter the document, they can keep a running log of information that pertains to the recent modifications.

FIGURE 4.2

You can also maintain a project notebook using a Notes database.

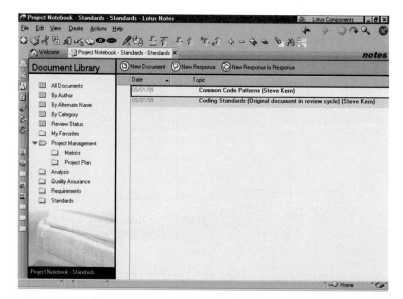

FIGURE 4.3

Make an extension of the Notes document database to add in your own coding standards.

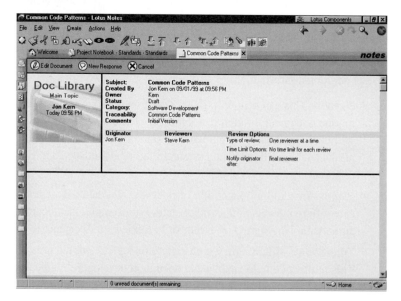

Requirements Management

Use of a requirements management tool can be very valuable, especially for large projects. By cataloging the true list of requirements that are intertwined within the prose of the requirements document, it becomes much easier to see the following information:

- What needs to be done (in list form)
- Relative priority of the requirements
- Traceability between requirements
- The ability to conduct impact analysis studies

Using a tool (such as Requisite Pro, DOORS, a simple outliner tool, a word processor, or even a spreadsheet) to capture the individual requirements, the project manager can always get a snapshot of the up-to-date list of requirements. Such a third-party tool (see Figure 4.4) also makes it possible to maintain additional information about each requirement, such as status, priority, estimated effort, and the responsible individual.

FIGURE 4.4

This sample requirements matrix from Requisite Pro shows the additional fields available.

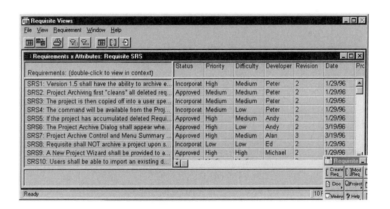

What's in It for Your Client?

The benefits of a Project Notebook to your client are many. By clearly writing down the requirements, you make the project something more concrete than an idea in the customer's mind. With the phased approach to contracting, the Project Notebook following the initial Requirements Definition and Engineering Phases (with initial design and prototyping) can serve both parties in a contractual sense.

Through clear documentation that has been agreed to by both the development team and the client, the project stands a very good chance of success. This is especially true in contrast to a project that has poor or sketchy requirements documents and where the customer was continually revising the requirements. The development team never seems to be able to catch up and complete anything—a symptom of the "moving target" syndrome.

The documentation is also a means of efficiently bringing on new staff or for educating new customers. Instead of continually re-explaining the project to every newcomer (taking up valuable management and developer resources), the document can serve as the tutorial to explain what's going on.

Life Cycle Overview

A modern, incremental, phased approach has evolved in an attempt to combat the following common problems that result in software projects failing to be on time, on the mark, and within budget:

- Analysis paralysis
- Long-winded requirements phase
- Lack of confronting architectural risks early on
- Overemphasis on cutting code before design is complete
- Hacking fast solutions instead of crafting robust solutions
- Mistaking a working GUI prototype for a long-term, elegant design

The two primary software development life cycle phases (shown in Figure 4.5) involve these:

- Engineering the solution
- Producing the solution

FIGURE 4.5

The software development life cycle consists of two major development phases.

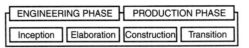

The trick to successful project management is to balance the time spent within each phase. During the Engineering Phase, activities are undertaken to define the requirements, begin the design, hit the risk drivers, and start to build out the overall functionality. By the time you have completed the Engineering Phase, you should be ready to make a firm, fixed-price commitment to your stakeholders on what you'll deliver, by when, and for how much (given a +/- percentage tolerance). The Production Phase is more concerned with in-depth implementation of the required features, handling the details of deployment, ensuring robustness, continuing to keep an eye on real-world performance as testing gathers momentum, and so on.

The Stakeholders

Stakeholders are an important part of the extended project team. These folks often include domain experts, user representatives, customers, marketing personnel, partners, purse holders—anyone who can help the team elicit the true requirements. Stakeholders help the team form the business case and initial requirements early on. They are also part of the periodic review process to ensure that problem areas are being addressed properly, to help gain consensus to change initial requirements, to resolve impacts to budget and schedule, and so on.

Engineering Phase

During the Engineering Phase, you concentrate on the following major subphases:

- Inception Phase
- Elaboration Phase

You can gather requirements through sessions spent with the client, examining pertinent aspects of the client's business, processes, products, and workflow. If you have an opportunity to obtain the services of a mentor, this person will work with the core project team early on to help establish this crucial engineering step.

The Inception Phase strives to achieve the following through meetings held with all stakeholders:

- Develop a refined list of requirements to indicate what the product is intended to be and do—its scope, a concept of operations, critical success metrics, and so on
- Create a list of high-value Use Cases that will stress the architecture and prompt significant design trade-offs
- Prepare a prototype to help prove that at least one architectural approach is viable
- Estimate the cost and schedule for the project—at least through the Engineering Phase
- Highlight potential risks

The Elaboration Phase is just that—the time when you achieve greater depth and breadth of requirements, architecture, design, prototypes, and other factors. The end goal for the Elaboration Phase is to have enough information to put together a fixed-price quotation (cost, schedule, and resource requirements) to execute the project by entering into the Production Phase. (Or, at least, if not actually fixed-price, you generally get to the point where an estimate can be made that is within some agreed-to plus-or-minus percentage, such as within 20%.)

During elaboration, inputs to the requirements definition come in many sizes, shapes, and formats. Example types of requirements inputs include these:

- Existing business procedures
- Forms
- Formal mission statements
- Requirements documents
- Systems in use (maybe ones that are to be replaced)
- Meetings with marketers and problem domain experts

To help refine the requirements, you have to do more than write them down. When I mentor teams or lead my own projects, we concurrently develop lists of requirements, do a little object modeling, and typically do some form of rapid prototyping. We are continually producing tangible, working results—not just pretty pictures or reams of use case documentation. In addition to producing class diagrams, use cases, and sequence diagrams, we also produce working code and runnable GUIs.

In each phase, we are building results with one or more passes through the processes of analysis, design, prototyping, and evaluating. On most nontrivial projects, there is the classic 20% of the issues driving 80% of the effort. It is important that, during elaboration, the prototype designs delve into these high-risk mine fields and see just how troublesome they might be. Remember, when you're done with the elaboration phase, it's time to put forth a credible cost and schedule quote. Doing the easy requirements and avoiding the sticky issues could mean losing your shirt, at best, or abject project failure, at worst (an all too common outcome, unfortunately).

Typically, the process is continually building up the one model, the one body of source code that will eventually be the delivered application. However, there are times when I send out scouts to forge ahead into uncharted territory. This might be for specific new technologies—how to support XML or how to integrate with a legacy system—or simply to explore trade-offs between design and requirements issues. Sometimes these efforts generate throw-away prototypes, but in general we are merely adding—in an evolutionary manner—to our code base of production-quality source.

As shown in Figure 4.6, the end result of these concurrent, iterative exercises is a set of documented requirements backed up by a good deal of effort. Because the effort involves collaboration between the development team and the client, the requirements are consensus-based and not contentious-based.

Tip

Though you may think that you are working on throw-away code, continue to adhere to the same coding standards as for production code. Don't fall into the trap of producing sloppy code: All too often, this prototype code ends up getting shipped (and having to be maintained).

FIGURE 4.6

The Engineering Phase involves iteratively going through the breadth of the application, gaining depth each time.

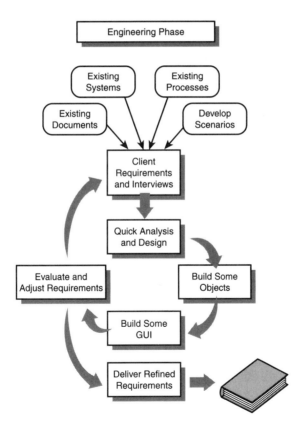

The tasks outlined here, are not so much steps, but rather activities that are done iteratively, in an order that best fits the needs of the current project (or subproject). You will likely revisit some of the activities many times, and in a different order. However, within the confines of this chapter, we'll explore the activities in a singular order.

This approach is tailored after the methods developed by Peter Coad (*Object-Oriented Analysis; Object Models: Strategies, Patterns, and Applications;* and *Java Design*) for doing object-oriented model development. Over the years and across many varied projects, I've refined and applied the techniques that are presented herein.

The approach to developing robust requirements includes these steps:

- Hold frequent sessions with the client and other subject matter experts.
- Do some design:
    - Identify system purpose and features and critical use cases
    - Identify potential classes for the object model (captured in class diagrams)
    - Develop prototype GUI screens
    - Develop sequence diagrams (scenarios) to capture dynamics
- Factor in architecture concepts (keeping in mind any performance requirements)
- Determine initial deployment strategies

In timeline fashion, the project activities might look something like Figure 4.7.

FIGURE 4.7

This shows project increments over time, going from engineering to production.

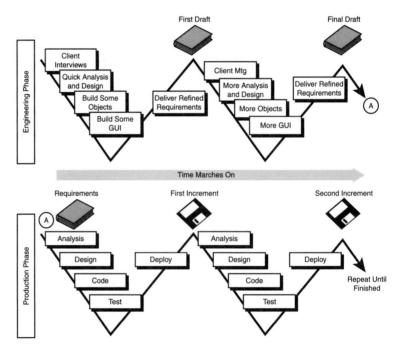

The Engineering/Elaboration Phase iterates through the same activities, continually refining the requirements documents and building working prototypes:

- Developing an initial architecture
- Determining critical drivers
- Determining tools and processes required
- Mapping out a credible cost and schedule for the construction phase

Similarly, the Production/Construction Phase iterates through a set of activities, delivering discrete increments of functionality over time. (These are often referred to as *releases*, implying that alpha or beta code drops are provided to the internal SQA/test teams or beta clients.)

Depending on the size of the project, the major increments can be formalized via a release plan. Each major increment will usually implement a primary set of functionality (a group of major feature sets). Within the major increments, you can develop a series of smaller deliverables. These might serve to increase the depth of the functionality planned for that increment.

Setting the Scope for the Project

During the requirements gathering and initial design, you may discover information that is of interest and importance to the project, yet that lies outside the *scope* of the requirements. We often leave these findings in the project documentation (that is, added it to the features list) and in the object models, but, these are labeled "Not This Time." As Peter Coad (*Object-Oriented Analysis)* notes, this allows us to capture and retain the discoveries during the time when they naturally occur. However, we don't let it bog down the project in doing extra work that wasn't agreed on (at least for this version of the application).

Discovering new features—also known as *feature creep*—is merely the addition of new ideas that are outside the present scope of the project. Knowing what future features may be in the product can sometimes help you adjust the current design to be flexible enough to handle such features down the road. Just be sure not to implement every neat, new feature that you or your client discover, or you will likely jeopardize your contractual obligations (and blow the budget and schedule). In addition, handle the new potential features like any other potential requirement: The client and development teams must be sure to work together through the same process activities as for developing the entire application.

One way to avoid the negative aspects of feature creep is to concentrate on the high-priority use cases and features that provide the most value to the client. As resources permit, you can then concentrate on lower-priority items and even begin to consider

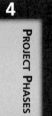

some of the features that were originally designated as out of scope. This is most easily accomplished by maintaining the requirements in the form of a set (list) of prioritized features.

With this feature list, you can begin to tackle estimates on a more granular basis. Feature by feature, using a tool such as MS Project or even a simple spreadsheet, you can break down the features so that there are none with an estimated duration greater than a couple of weeks (even if that means breaking a feature into discrete tasks). This may entail creating subfeatures and subtasks, but the benefits to smaller, bite-size tasks are many, including the following:

- Higher confidence in estimates
- Better ability to track progress
- Rapid sense of accomplishment for developers as features are completed
- More nimble resource scheduling
- Overall increased predictability of making scheduled release dates with the promised levels of functionality

With a feature-driven development schedule, you can assign new features to later releases of the application. You might even think of this as a preplanned product improvement program.

Examining the Business Process

As one of the initial tasks, you will need to work with the client and subject matter experts to gain an understanding and insight into the business process(es) pertinent to the application.

This section introduces analysis techniques that will be amplified and expanded on in the next chapter.

The primary tasks involved with examining the business process include these:

- Identifying the purpose
- Documenting use cases
- Uncovering and prioritizing features
- Selecting classes
- Developing prototype GUIs, if needed
- Establishing responsibilities
- Working out details with sequence diagrams

Purpose

The purpose of the application should describe the business requirements in a short statement—that is, 25 words or less. The purpose is not to describe so much the what, but rather why the application is needed. What is the vision that is driving the need for this application?

Requirements/Use Cases

Requirements can be documented by a set of simple bullets, a large document of detailed, sequentially numbered paragraphs, or by use cases. Quite simply, use cases (*The Object Advantage* by Jacobsen) consist of two elements:

- *Actors*—Users of the system (people or external systems) that play a particular role that relates to the business at hand
- *Use cases*—What the users expect to be able to do with the system

Use cases provide a means to document the high-level functional requirements of the system. In simple form, the use case is capable of clearly stating tangible system behavior. That is, only external views of the system are presented in use cases; the internal workings must remain hidden from view in all use cases. An example of a use case is shown here:

- *Actor*—Salesman
- *Use cases*—Upload a customer order via remote login and refresh local database with the latest product information

When looking at the length of the use case, you may choose to break this up into two parts: uploading and refreshing. A sample use case diagram is shown in Figure 4.8.

FIGURE 4.8

A sample use case diagram.

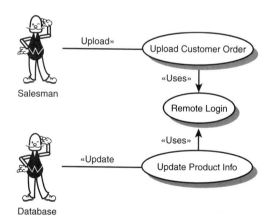

By the way, I use the UML visual modeling tool, Together, from Object International (free download at www.togethersoft.com). Together is good at helping to create and maintain the type of modeling documentation that is presented herein.

In the Project Notebook, you may choose to replace the typical Functional Requirements specification with a listing of all the use cases. At a minimum, including both the functional spec and the us case model will be redundant, requiring a little extra care to keep the two in sync. A tool such as Together is adept at creating a combined textual and graphical documentation of the use case-based requirements.

The importance of the use case model is that it can serve to drive the entire application development process, from analysis forward. You should be able to trace all development activity back to one or more use cases. One of the ways this is accomplished is by having the use cases help drive subsequent tasks, perhaps eliciting features and developing sequence diagrams.

Features

As part of the process of developing requirements, you should document the important features. Features are couched in terms of functionality that is useful to the client. Much like the use case language is independent of implementation, features are similarly non-technical. For example: "Calculate commission for a sales rep."

One of Peter Coad's strategies is to discover features by thinking about them in four different categories:

- Setting up, preparing for business
- Conducting business
- Analyzing results
- Interacting with external systems

When additions are made to the requirements after the initial development cycle, this strategy can be applied again to develop the appropriate features. The list of features is an important stepping stone on the way to developing a comprehensive project plan that includes schedule, resources, and budget. In collaboration with your client, take the list of features and prioritize them—possibly marking some features down for a future version. Then use this prioritized list to know what to tackle first. Break down the feature list to deal with blocks of time that are two weeks or less in duration. You may take the hottest features or the ones with the most technical risk and do a complete work-up through analysis, design, and even prototyping.

Selecting Classes

Much more detail lies behind the methodology for finding classes and objects for the problem domain and likewise for the user interface, data management, and system interaction layers (see Table 4.1). This is expanded on in the next chapter.

Separation of Concerns

A key aspect of this development methodology is what's known as the separation of concerns. Throughout the analysis and design, a distinct separation is maintained between topics such as the problem domain definition and the user interface portion of the project. At any point in the development cycle, different pieces of the model layers can be tackled. The benefit is that the best decisions can be made immediately at the time of discovery. In other words, this methodology supports the ad hoc capture of this information—that's much better than waiting for the proper phase or step.

Given the initial gathering of facts from the features activity (which, by the way, continues throughout the project, albeit at a much lower rate), the enterprise-based object model can be formulated. To do this, the four object model layers (see Table 4.1) are used to provide a means to partition the classes that are developed to support the project at hand.

Table 4.1   The Object Model Layers and Their Purpose

Layer	*Label*	*Purpose*
User interaction	(UI)	Windows, reports, controls required
Problem domain	(PD)	Classes that relate to the systems under study
Data management	(DM)	Databases for providing persistent storage
System interaction	(SI)	Other (external) systems

To develop the objects that are within scope, we use the four model layers (UI, PD, DM, and SI) to help attain a top-level partitioning. Each class/object will fit into just one of these model layers. Unlike many structured approaches, this architecture strives to build very loosely coupled, meaningful subsets of classes. The term *loosely coupled* indicates the degree of interdependence of one software component on another. A functional decomposition/structured approach typically results in modules that have a heavy degree of reliance on one another, resulting in less portable and less maintainable software. This object-oriented approach purposefully keeps a firm distinction between separate objects and allows for greater reusability, a clean interface to the objects, easy maintainability, and cost-effective enhancements.

Problem Domain (PD)

The PD layer is involved with objects that directly correspond to the problem being modeled (for example, a banking system, a document management application, or human resources management). These are implementation- and technology-neutral, and they have little to no knowledge about objects in other layers (UI, DM, or SI). To build in knowledge of, for example, the Notes forms or Windows implementation into a PD layer is to subtly erode what could otherwise be a more stable system and one that could provide reuse to other projects.

Because of the size of some projects, it is often necessary to partition the problem domain of the application into vertical slices that represent subject areas. In a manufacturing arena, for example, subject areas might consist of the following:

- Product (parts you make and parts you consume)
- Bill of material (list of parts for a product you make)
- Shop floor (definition of the manufacturing floor and its resources)
- Process plan (the steps for building the product)
- Claiming (the act of performing steps in the process plan and claiming parts installed)

Most of the vertical partitions can be relatively standalone, making it easy for developers to be partitioned into specific subject areas. Where the subject areas interact, it is critical to form binding contracts, or interfaces. Claiming (work done on the factory floor), for example, needs to interact with nearly all the other subject areas.

In UML terms, these partitions are known as packages. For languages such as Java and C++, packages are represented physically by a directory structure.

User Interaction (UI)

The UI layer contains objects that provide the interface between the computer system(s)/problem domain objects and the users. Typically, these involve windows, reports, and maybe some hardware data-entry keypads. Notes has a feature-rich means to design the UI layers. In general, you would want to code the majority of the business logic in the PD layer, not in the UI layer. To place lots of logic in the UI is to make it difficult to reuse elsewhere or hard to copy the source code to another location where it is needed. The latter results in code that works for a while but that eventually breaks down as multiple identical changes start to be missed and the application starts to behave in an inconsistent manner. Placing the logic in the *one* spot in the PD object model where it makes sense allows for simple maintenance and improved reuse. No matter how many GUIs or reports need to access the business logic, it is all encapsulated into one neat package: the PD class.

Data Management (DM)

The DM layer is responsible for the persistent storage related to the problem domain objects and other implementation-specific needs. Notes provides a simple means for defining the database. If you have other needs for persistent storage, create separate classes to handle just that functionality. This will keep the PD classes that pertain to the persistent storage pure in the sense that they won't have to dirty themselves with the persistent mechanism.

System Interaction (SI)

The SI layer contains objects that provide an interface to external systems or devices. This is where things such as low-level communications protocols are encapsulated, keeping the PD objects "clean" from such implementation-specific details. Other examples might include creating proxy objects to serve as wrappers for legacy systems or other external computers. This is also the place where you would create classes that encompass the behavior of physical devices (for example, sensors, card readers, retinal scanning security devices, or an electronic funds transfer system).

GUI Prototyping

At times, it is handy to use GUI prototyping (either with Notes or just simply a pad of paper) to elicit further requirements and information about the makeup of a class. When GUIs contain things such as a user ID, date, tabular list of items, and so on, there is a good deal of information useful to the process of fleshing out the object model.

Establishing Responsibilities

Every object in the object model has responsibilities based on the following:

- What the object knows about itself (attributes)
- What other objects it knows about (associations)
- What the object does itself (methods)

The intent here is to develop a level of detail about an object sufficient enough for that object to carry out its piece of the overall system's responsibilities.

Specifying Dynamics Using Sequence Diagrams

To capture the all-important dynamics behind modeling real-world systems, we use the concept of specifying sequence diagrams (also known as Coad scenarios or object interaction diagrams). As Peter Coad so aptly describes it, a scenario is nothing more than a time-ordered sequence of events based on using object interactions to meet a required system function (or use case). The sequence diagram depicts all the necessary objects that must interact to carry out the function.

In addition to providing a concrete capture of dynamic requirements, sequence diagrams serve the following purposes as well:

- Help to find missing objects that you had not yet modeled
- Work to distribute and refine the responsibilities associated with each object
- Determine if sufficient navigability of the model exists
- Further the developer's understanding of the system dynamics
- Help assess the completeness of the model
- Provide a means to test an object model

Sequence diagrams are also particularly useful to depict the interaction of a user with the system. For example, you may have a requirement to allow the user to pop up a dialog box to alter an object's characteristics. This sequence may start with the human interface (dialog box/window) and show how the changes wind their way down through the necessary intermediary objects to the actual object's initialization.

Designing a New Process

After discussing the client's requirements, you should have developed a problem statement and a set of preliminary features/use cases to help document the client's needs. From the information gathered during the creation of use cases, sequence diagrams, and the preliminary object model, you may be able to employ some business process reengineering to design a new and improved process. Of course, in deference to your client's way of doing business, do this with the utmost respect—and be certain that you can show clear advantages by presenting a change in business as usual. Many times, a clear, object-oriented model of the system, the participants, and the interactions provide a sound vantage point from which to spot opportunities for improvement.

Security Considerations

The requirements gathering process should yield the client's security requirements. In some applications, the system administrator/manager needs to have the ability to control a user's access rights at various levels.

At times, it is better to create a special user interface to handle project-unique needs. Otherwise, use the built-in security features whenever possible.

In Notes, you have security control from the broadest sense (the Notes Domain, Notes Server, and the database Access Control List) to form-specific, down to field-level. Notes provides many different levels of access, with Author and Reader being the most common for users.

Security is one of those things that can sometimes be added in toward the end of a Notes project without too much disruption. Other times, it should be addressed early in the development phases.

A good time to begin is with consecutive beta releases of the application. With each release, you can add in a bit more of the security needed by the user. Client feedback may help to refine the actual requirements as users try out the beta application and its security. (In general, security is a trade-off among security, user acceptance, and performance.)

Writing a Project Document

For the Engineering Phase, you should add the following documents to the Project Notebook:

- *Problem definition*—This describes the high-level needs of your client in plain, simple language.

- *Use cases*—List the actors who participate with this application, and list the clearly defined functional requirements that describe how the system is to be used. These should be broken down into broad feature components, feature sets, features, and so on.

- *Nonfunctional requirements*—This covers the peripheral requirements such as time constraints, anticipated client usage (number of concurrent users, number of total users, transaction rates, and so on), required interfaces to external systems, and target environment(s) (hardware and operating systems).

- *Acceptance Test Plan*—Used heavily in DoD contracts (and in my company's contracts), this plan outlines the test plan (and expected results), which will verify that the application meets the stated goals.

Except for the Acceptance Test Plan (ATP), the other areas have been covered in the preceding subsections. The ATP is not always an essential part of the Project Notebook, but it may be useful in certain circumstances. In general, it is difficult at best to verify that every requirement in the requirements document is met. Therefore, you may want to spend the extra time and resources to put together a representative test suite in the form of an ATP. The ATP indicates the steps required to conduct each test and the expected results. The ATP can be made part of the contract as a means to get the customer to sign off that the application has been developed to the required level of functionality as dictated contractually. Often, the acceptance of the ATP results triggers the final payment on a contract.

Naturally, if the requirements change during the course of the development process, the ATP must be updated to reflect the changes. Then both parties must renegotiate the ATP.

Depending on the size of the project, there may be one or more physical documents that comprise the Project Notebook, and some of the items may be left out. The important point here is not how the information is documented but rather the "what" that is involved and the simple fact that the information *is* documented.

Creating a Plan for the Next Step

When the Engineering Phase is completed, you and your customer are in a good position to negotiate a fixed-price contract to complete the Production Phase and deliver the application.

Your Project Notebook should serve you well as a starting point to develop a road map for the next step. Depending on how formal your customer requires the Production Phase to be defined (possibly as a formal proposal), you can create some or all of the following documents:

- *Development methods and tools*—Indicates the processes, standards, project management tools, quality assurance methods, development tools, test tools, and so on
- *Project plan*—Contains the schedule of tasks (based on the requirements documents) and a list of resources required (and possibly a resource utilization plan)
- *Quality assurance plan*—Describes how you will implement bug tracking and fixing, possibly your procedures for continuous improvement, code review methods, and so on
- *Test plan*—Documents the method that you will employ to test that the application is meeting the performance specifications (both functional and nonfunctional)
- *Project measurement*—States how and with what metrics you may record to indicate progress and quality

These will be added to the Project Notebook and will be kept up-to-date as the development proceeds.

Production Phase

This phase involves more detailed implementation. Likely, your efforts in the Engineering Phase resulted in requirements documents, an initial object model (class diagrams and sequence diagrams), some initial GUIs, maybe some database details, initial deployment concepts, and a project plan. Remember, the level of detail is based on the comfort level required by both parties to consider that the Engineering Phase has been completed. In a simple, low-risk application, you may enter the Production Phase with a minimal set of requirements documents and up-front design. Conversely, a high-risk project may result in a thorough exploration of the requirements and some detailed object models.

Collaborating with Your Client

Much like you did in the iterative requirements refinement efforts of the previous phase, you should involve your client often through the development process. This is typically accomplished through detailed design reviews and interim application deliverables such as working software.

Your client can help be part of the development process by providing valuable feedback on design issues (specifically user interface, workflow, reports, and other external manifestations of the design) and on installation and other deployment issues. Typically, your incremental application deliverables should begin with breadth, and then fill in depth. This way, your client can begin to get a feel for the entire application. All functionality either should be implemented or should at least indicate to the user that this particular function is stubbed out. As each increment is delivered for the client to work with and review, additional functionality is demonstrated.

Coupling this philosophy with a feature-driven approach goes a long way to increasing the level of confidence of the client and the development team in meeting deliverable deadlines and becoming predictable.

> **Tip**
>
> In general, you should almost never slip a scheduled deliverable. Instead, you should slip functionality to the next release.

This collaboration allows the client to be part of the process and to feel a sense of ownership. A side benefit is that involving the client early and often allows the client to witness difficulties that might arise during the course of development. A proactive client may be willing to alter the requirements in the face of unforeseen difficulties witnessed firsthand.

Ongoing Communication

Throughout the Implementation Subphase, it is important that the project plan be updated as features are completed. This includes updating the schedule, progress metrics, quality metrics, and so on. The feature-driven approach will immediately show the client the

4

PROJECT PHASES

amount of functionality included in any given build. The client must remain well-informed of all project activities—including unforeseen delays. Developing a deep rapport with the client can go a long way toward bringing in additional work and helping to reduce the impact of bad news. In spite of the best plans, software development sometimes does fall behind schedule or go over budget. Communicating this to your client earlier rather than later is a good idea.

Integrating Prototypes with the Design Process

At times, you may use the technique of creating a prototype to help determine the final requirements. This may be integrated into the current application, or it may be done as a standalone application just to serve as a prototype. Regardless of the means of demonstrating the concept being prototyped, the client gets the opportunity to try out the design and provide early feedback.

Zeroing In on the Target

Though the Engineering Phase should have done a fairly complete job of refining the client's needs, it usually is never 100% complete. Therefore, the development process applies the iterative approach to continue to home in on the final design. You still need to apply the good design and development techniques described previously—you don't want this step to go on ad infinitum.

The amount of spiraling in on the target will depend largely on how complete the initial Engineering Phase was. If you spent time zeroing in on the target during the Elaboration Phase, you probably won't have too much iteration to get the design to the point where your customer is satisfied. Often, the iterations deal more with details in a business process or algorithm, cosmetic user interface changes, or usability issues, not in discovering new core requirements.

If the requirements were only cursory, be prepared to involve more of the techniques described in the previous sections—and be sure to have budgeted appropriately.

SQA, Testing, and Deployment

The entire software development process is more a feat of systems engineering than a series of sequential steps. As we'll see in this section, software quality assurance (SQA) is an activity that pervades application development every step of the way.

Unfortunately, testing is rarely given the proper attention it deserves. In today's environment, applications are more complex than ever and are responsible for business-critical functions. In addition, today's applications are being deployed in very complex configurations. From desktop, to workgroup, to client/server, to remote access, to Internet-enabled, to intranet, to integration with legacy mainframe systems, deployment is not trivial.

Given the application and deployment complexity, testing should be high on any project's list of priorities. Don't forget that, even though you may develop and deploy the world's most function-rich application, it won't matter if a bug causes a failure that in turn is very harmful to the client. That bug is what will be remembered most.

This section discusses SQA, test techniques, and deployment concerns.

Software Quality Assurance (SQA)

The reasons for striving to develop a sound software quality assurance program include these:

- You can avoid the publicity of a buggy application.
- Delivering a buggy application makes it harder to get follow-on jobs at the same client site.
- An application built on a shaky quality foundation costs more to maintain and upgrade—sometimes to the point of no return.
- With testers working alongside developers, the development team can be reminded of coding pitfalls to avoid.

If you link SQA activities with the phased, incremental development approach, your end product will more likely achieve the lofty goal of outstanding software quality. Though software quality is difficult to concisely define, here's one definition:

Quality Software

Quality software meets the client's functional and performance requirements, has been developed and documented in adherence with sound standards and practices, is maintainable, and can absorb changes by being flexible.

4

PROJECT PHASES

Hmmm…"meets the client's requirements"…. To judge an application's quality, we first need solid requirements documentation (discussed earlier). It also looks as if we'll need a set of standards for the developers to follow. To achieve flexibility, the application development must be based on a good, solid, object-oriented analysis (discussed in the next chapter).

The moral here?

Good software development is not achieved by a single means. Instead, it is a synergistic blend of numerous methods, processes, standards, and procedures—a variation on classic systems engineering. All pieces interrelate and are an important part of the end goal. Overemphasize one aspect, and you may jeopardize another.

Planning for Change: Structured Testing

A major part of SQA is software testing, which is specified clearly via the test plan document. The plan delineates what is to be tested, how it is to be tested, in what order the tests should occur, and whether any environment-specific tests are needed.

The test plan is jointly developed by the test leader, developers, subject matter experts, GUI experts, and the project manager. Testing in conjunction with an incremental, iterative development approach requires a good bit of coordination among the various parties. The test team must know which functional aspects are to be tested in each increment.

In addition, the test team needs to be testing the overall application as an integrated system, even while specific subsystems may be undergoing tests within their iterative development cycles.

The developers need to participate for a few reasons. First, the developer is in the best position to suggest that certain nonintuitive paths through the logic be tested. In addition, the developer can help the testers understand how the requirements have been implemented (because this effort usually predates specific documentation). Finally, the developers can learn from the testers how to look for problems—this can help the developer learn how to code to avoid these potential pitfalls in the future.

In an incremental and iterative development paradigm, it becomes very important that testing is automated and continuous. Numerous third-party tools exist to help test GUI applications, stress database applications, and push communications bandwidths to their limits. As you build your tests, add them to a reusable test suite—appropriately labeled for ease of identification—that can be invoked with every new increment.

When you employ reuse of libraries built internally, you should have the ability to perform regression testing. Because the reusable component can be used in many different applications, it must be treated almost as if it is a product unto itself. As the component is enhanced over time, your regression testing will ensure that the component still works in the manner that older applications still expect. If you ignore regression testing, you risk breaking older code that relied on inclusion of that component.

If you are employing a third-party package (for example, to generate 3D graphs of mutual fund prices versus the planet locations), be sure to include tests that encompass your use of the package. This will allow you to regression-test that part of your application that relies on the library if the library is erroneously upgraded at some future date.

One of the benefits of testing within the incremental, iterative development paradigm is early feedback of bugs and enhancements. This is far better than getting a list of bugs in one fell swoop at the supposed end of the project.

Planning the Deployment

As part of the nonfunctional requirements, the client typically specifies the target environment. This includes the following:

- Hardware platform(s)
- Operating system(s)
- Windowing system(s)
- Network protocol(s)

Distributed and client/server architectures can complicate specifying the target environment by permitting multiple server architectures distinct from the client platform(s).

With the incremental, iterative development method, you will have early opportunity to test installation and deployment on the required target platforms. With each increment, the installation script can be refined, tested, and tweaked as needed.

When the final application rollout comes, the development team won't be faced with the inevitable bugs that plague initial complex install techniques. Instead, the final increment may have required no changes to the installation procedures, as these were adequately refined and tested through the preceding increments.

Pilot Testing

As part of the test plan, a system test should be conducted at each major increment. For a large application, you may want to solicit the aid of your customer to do a pilot deployment. This system will be installed and functioning within its intended environment. However, it is usually not permitted to make real changes or otherwise impact the company's data. (After all, you wouldn't want to have valuable company assets relying on an application that hasn't been thoroughly tested.)

4

PROJECT PHASES

Workgroup Deployment

During the pilot test, the application can be set up on a standalone workgroup to exhaustively test the interoperability of the application with the client's network. This procedure is also designed to test the installation and configuration features that pertain to workgroup testing: access rights, network availability, and so on.

Often, a group of end users from the client are trained on the new application and assist the development team in testing the application. This "tiger team" core of client users will then serve as internal trainers to the remainder of the company's staff after the application is deemed okay to go live.

Measuring the Success of a Project

An ongoing dilemma of software development is the ability to measure the progress and success of a project. Earlier, we defined software quality to mean that the application meets the functional and performance goals stated in the agreed-to requirements document.

One clear measure of this would be the results of conducting a test suite designed to specifically test the capability of the software to meet the requirements.

Other measures include

- Feature completion
- Project size, for example
    - Number of classes/entities
    - Number of GUI views/forms
    - Number and complexity of use cases/scenarios
    - Number of databases/tables/fields
- Tracking the defect count by, for example
    - Normalized via lines of code
    - Normalized via database fields (or some other size metric)
    - Tallied and compared on an increment-by-increment basis
- Project productivity (how fast project features are built)
- Metrics to record reuse (both internal and external libraries)

If the schedule is granular enough to contain the development of features (and I recommend that it should be), completion of such tasks can be tracked using your favorite project management tool (such as Microsoft Project). In general, the project schedule can be down to the week level, but not much finer. However, you should guard against getting too detailed in the project schedule. Don't let the schedule become a project within a project, taking tremendous resources to keep up-to-date and to change as priorities and requirements change. Instead, use the schedule to accomplish the following:

- Communicate the work required to achieve the goal
- Communicate the work already accomplished
- Communicate differences between planned and actual

If you need greater level of granularity, you can develop a table containing a list of all features and feature sets that need to be developed. By tracking the completion of each required feature, you can keep on top of what has been implemented and what is still pending. And remember, features are what clients want built!

You may instead use a third-party tool that can help integrate all the information requirements that allows project tracking, scheduling, bug tracking, and so on to play together.

Those Who Use Rulers, Rule

Measuring a project before, during, and following completion is an important activity to realizing an overall goal of repeatable, quality software development. As you build up a repository of metrics data, you can begin to influence your bidding/estimation process by factoring in past experience. Because initial design can lead to some of the sizing criteria, you can base estimates on how big the project appears to be. If you know that your initial design is only a percentage of the probable final product, increase your estimate accordingly. Typically, if your requirements are skimpy, you'll need to increase your estimate by a larger factor than when you have, for example, requirements that are 75% comprehensive.

A solid start at getting projects, keeping clients, and expanding business is the reputation won or lost on accuracy of development plans.

Harvesting the Crop

The means by which metrics are gathered can be difficult. Wherever possible, spending resources on automating the metrics collection mechanism is a wise investment. You may be able to find third-party tools or develop some homegrown applications to suit your development environment. The alternative is to rely on developers to collect the metrics—a daunting task even for the best-loved project manager!

As you record and track feature completion, you can simultaneously assess the on-time performance. If you've done a good job at breaking down the development process into granular features and feature sets, and if you've done a good job at meeting the estimated feature completion rates, you have a great start at accurate estimation and timely deliveries. On the other hand, if you typically took longer on each feature, or if you missed many subfeatures required to truly implement the feature, you'll need to change your processes accordingly.

Summary

In this chapter, you learned about maintaining a project notebook throughout the software development life cycle. You also learned about the primary Engineering and Production Phases, and how to get started by breaking down the business process. And, you studied the all-important quality assurance and metrics. Next up: more details on actually performing an object-oriented analysis and design.

Business Process Analysis

by Jonathan Kern

IN THIS CHAPTER

CHAPTER 5

Chapter 3, "Project Management," discusses the pros and cons of different software development methodologies and presents the incremental, phased approach as the preferred paradigm. Chapter 4, "Project Phases," is a bit more detailed with the actual activities associated with requirements definition and application development—in short, the phases associated with the overall software development lifecycle.

This chapter zeros in on the portion of the development that involves *analysis* of the business process. We take the same approach as outlined in Chapter 4 (beginning with the section titled "Examining the Business Process"), but this time we look at some diagramming techniques and some helpful strategies to get the answers you need and get them quickly. The goal here is to spend some time doing up-front analysis and design—not just jumping in right away with building Notes databases and GUIs, which is tempting, I know. The payoffs include building a more flexible solution that allows agility in the marketplace as application needs evolve over time. If you had built a quick-and-dirty "point solution," it is likely that the application wouldn't gracefully adapt to new requirements. The alternative is to continue building on the existing application—but you'll find it gets harder and harder, and tends to cause more breakage as time goes on. Developing a solid design from the outset goes a long way to reducing the overall lifecycle cost of an application.

The methods that I've adopted over the years are largely based on working with Peter Coad's analysis techniques, providing object-oriented (OO) analysis and design mentoring to companies across the nation, using the strategies and patterns that Peter has promulgated over the years, and running my own development company. Through many object-oriented projects, the methods presented herein have been honed through application of other methodologies, blending the best techniques into this repertoire, and through the inevitable discoveries and innovation that result from "just doing it. What works best in one project might not work as well in another. I suggest you take these methods, pluck out the parts that are good and applicable, read about other techniques, and slowly develop your own methodology for the types of work you typically perform.

Peter Coad has developed a handy set of strategies that I use during the analysis process (initially published in *Object Models: Strategies, Patterns, and Applications*). You can download *The Strategies and Patterns Handbook* on the Web (`http://www.oi.com/handbook.htm`), and you can download a hypertext version. The strategies give practical advice on how to develop the object model and how to tease out analysis results; the patterns help define consistent approaches to like problems. For larger-scale business patterns, I worked with Pete on his latest book: *Java Modeling in Color with UML*, which covers 61 different major business problem domains.

The remainder of this chapter provides examples of object-oriented (OO) analysis, presents diagram techniques using the Unified Modeling Language (UML), and shows how OO principles can be applied directly to developing Notes applications. This chapter looks at a fictitious application.

Business Process Analysis—Why Bother?

After the initial requirements are in, it is time to begin an analysis and design phase.

Why, you might ask? Shouldn't we just start coding?

For starters, the requirements are rarely stated in terms sufficient for actual development to begin. It is important to take the time to try to fully understand the reasons behind the project in the first place, to get in the client's shoes, so to speak. This process helps to refine the requirements, get the development team started up the ramp of understanding the Problem Domain, and lay the groundwork for being successful!

> **Note**
>
> The Problem Domain (PD) includes objects that directly correspond to the real world being modeled (often termed the *business objects*). These objects are implementation- and technology-neutral and serve to capture the core business logic. They have little or no knowledge about objects in other portions of the application (such as utility classes, GUI classes, and Internet-enabling classes); the more completely separated from these other layers, the better. To build in knowledge of, for example, the Windows implementation into a PD component is to build an unstable system. Similarly, to build core business logic into visual components (such as a button press) makes it impossible to reuse that logic elsewhere in the app (or a related app).

In addition, the best software designs arise when the subject matter is fully understood by the designers and developers. We've all seen projects in which this *wasn't* the case. By the time the developers were finishing, they had finally achieved a good understanding of the client's business. At this point, the developers are ready to contribute different ideas to the software design—but it is a little late for that. Or the developers find themselves saying that if only we could do a redesign from a clean sheet, given what we know now (at the end of a project that was likely over budget and blew the schedule).

An additional benefit to doing design is to be able to address some of the future requirements. This helps to ensure a flexible design that can grow over time.

If you traditionally don't do much up-front application design, reverse these trends right now—do a thorough analysis of the requirements at the outset of the project. Flesh out the true needs of the client. Analyze the business to uncover the users, the pertinent objects, the dynamic interaction of the objects when the system is being used, and the potential for business process reengineering. You'll be surprised what these techniques uncover when a business is properly modeled using OO techniques.

Note, however, you need to sell your client on the idea that some up-front time is required before coding starts. In every situation I've been involved with, the client was always very happy to see the level of up-front information gathering and participated with zeal. After all, it is only in the client's best interest to invest the time and energy to educate the development team and to strive to get the design right.

I might also add that I am not promoting *analysis paralysis*. Indeed, the requirements gathering process is iterative and involves many forms, as we'll see: features list; use cases; GUI prototypes; object models and sequence diagrams; and frequent, tangible, and working code. All activities form part of the "breadth (across the app) then depth (into each area)" approach I like to take when confronted with a new application design effort.

Major Activities

The analysis and design method consists of the following major activities:

- Identify system purpose and features
- List requirements as use cases and features
- Identify classes
- Sketch prototype GUIs
- Work out object interaction dynamics with sequence diagrams
- Build an object model
- Continually produce working results

These activities are presented in an approximate order that makes sense; however, they are not to be misconstrued as *steps*. It is important to realize that you can work from one activity to the next and back again as you see fit—and as you gain greater understanding.

When you work back and forth among these activities, the overall results are improved. This is because discoveries in one activity can help you discover new information for other activities. No matter when the application information is collected, the model is used to capture the details.

Traceability

An important part of the business analysis activity is providing connectivity between what you design and what the client requires. Figure 5.1 loosely depicts this trail of dependencies.

FIGURE 5.1

It is important to maintain trace-ability from requirements to implementation.

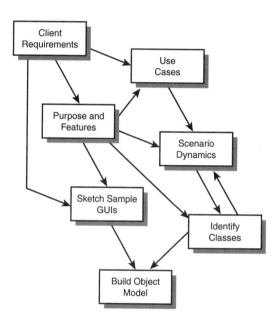

The client's basic requirements are captured in the purpose and features list. As you build the features list (from initial discussions and as subsequent detailed features are discovered), you must strive to group them in a hierarchical manner. For example, you can have major feature groups that serve as a component-scale grouping (for example: Human Resources, Accounting, General Ledger). The feature groups are then broken down into feature sets, which in turn contain a number of individual features. These features must also be prioritized into the "must haves," "nice to haves," and "in your dreams" levels. The prioritization is used to know what is needed to get the first release out the door. This list of features help you develop use cases (which can be thought of as a more formal, graphical way to view a list of features, with the advantage of being able to show "composition" and "generalization" relationships between use cases).

5

BUSINESS PROCESS ANALYSIS

You use the list of features and use cases to help identify sets of objects (that get turned into classes), to expand on the GUI needs, and to identify high-value scenarios to expand into sequence diagrams—a technique to flesh out logic flow, much like visual pseudocode.

Identifying and defining classes increases the detail of the features (by adding attributes and methods), and allows you to create more detailed sequence diagrams for the scenarios. A strong interplay exists between building the object model and refining the sequence diagrams.

Sketching out the GUI—especially with the client—is very beneficial. Often, clients can think in terms of how they would like to view the information or feature on the screen. These GUI sketches usually result in new features and the definition of new classes. After all, the collection of information to support a GUI can be a superset or subset of the problem domain entities.

Detailing the scenarios help you discover new classes, add additional methods and refine the class attributes. The scenarios also feed into the GUI development—pointing out the need for specific UI controls—for example, buttons that invoke actions and the presence of list boxes to indicate iteration over a contained list of references to other objects. This all feeds into the object model, adding to your understanding of how the requirements turn into actual source code implementation.

As these prior activities help make the object model more complete, the object model activity can return the favor. As the model is thought out, you'll often discover additional features, add new classes, adjust a GUI screen, and so on. In addition, you often begin to understand the level of difficulty that might be associated with certain features. Knowing this, you and your client might be able to refine the feature (for example, dropping the requirement to retrieve 100,000 records in less than one second) or change the prioritization. Without taking the time to iteratively work the features and design model up front (with the client involved), it is difficult to make these types of trade-off decisions.

As Coad points out, by treating these activities as interrelated *activities* and not *steps*, you can achieve a synergistic effect of the whole being greater than the sum of its parts. In this case, the "whole" is moving back and forth between the various activities as required, in an ad hoc manner, as opposed to rigidly progressing through a fixed sequence.

The next sections show how to apply some of these techniques to a specific challenge from a hypothetical client.

The Project

The client needs you to develop an interactive electronic catalog to automate tracking the company's book and software resources. In addition, the client wants to tie in a requisition process to allow employees to request resources to be acquired (for example, new books about learning Java design).

Use Cases

As part of the project notebook, you will want to capture the functional requirements in a second model, referred to as the use case model. It is very simple to develop because it involves only the actors and their "uses" of the software system. As a central part of the object-oriented approach outlined herein, it is important to capture the use cases correctly and to have your client in agreement with the use cases and features.

Definition of a Use Case

actors   People who use the system or external systems that need to interface with the system being built

use cases   The activity with the system (what people will do with the system)

As a rule of thumb, use cases are to be used only for external activities or events tied to actors. This implies that they are *observable* from an outside perspective. Don't fall into the trap of documenting what would end up being internalized flowchart-type logic that is subsequent to an event or activity.

Use cases can get as complex as you want. For example, you can add more user roles, a precondition (to allow "entry" into this use case), post-condition (to permit "exit" from the use case), normal flow (the typical events or steps that would occur if all goes well), alternative flows (different way to achieve the same end result), and exceptional flows (what happens if an error in the process occurs).

Some elaborate modeling tools can help capture requirements—including use cases—but the simple nature of use cases doesn't require an elaborate system. At a minimum, maintain the use case model in a simple word processor or spreadsheet document that you might or might not have fed into a requirements management tool (such as Requisite Pro or DOORS). Or choose to maintain the use case model in a simple Notes database; after all, you only need to track actors and their use cases at a minimum and a few more fields if deemed necessary. A report of the use cases can be used to derive a list of functional requirements; this flat list is often useful for providing progress. If you also maintain the functional requirements in Notes, you can have each requirement refer to the appropriate use case.

You might want to model the capturing of actors and use cases as follows:

Actor-descriptive fields

Actor name

Description

Comments

Use case descriptive fields

Use case name

Description

Comments

The bottom line is the ability to document and revise the set of system behavior so that you and your client can agree on what is going to be developed. The tone of the language should be more general than technical. The client, end users, domain experts, and customers should be able to understand each use case.

Large Use Cases Doth Not an Application Get

Do not stray into internal coding logic or implementation details. Stick to defining the "boundary" of the application and how it relates to external interfaces with actors—in other words, how the actor would use the system. You don't want the use case model to define the internal architecture of the solution, algorithms to use to achieve a use case, or other details better left to the analysis and design phases.

Analysis Paralysis?

Remember, avoid analysis paralysis; don't let use cases become a behemoth. Don't let the requirements documents get bogged down in implementation details. The result is documentation that is too big to digest, and too technical for the high-level readers (often with budgetary power!); worse, the documentation might constrain the design.

Pretend that you spent an extended lunch with your client and were able to develop some preliminary use cases. From this informal interview process, you were able to glean a list of actors for the overall system and some high-level use cases.

Table 5.1 shows some representative use cases that you gleaned from your initial meeting:

TABLE 5.1 Sample Use Cases for the Electronic Catalog System

Actor	Use Case
Employee	Search for software or book titles
Employee	Check out a book or software title
Employee	Check in a book or software title
Employee	Enter a requisition for a new book or software title
Manager	Approve a purchase requisition
Librarian	Enter/edit software or book titles
Librarian	Send messages for overdue materials
Librarian	Distribute a listing of "recent entries" to interested subscribers

System Purpose

This activity is designed to succinctly capture the client's needs through a high-level system purpose statement:

> To provide an interactive means for employees to search for and check out resources and to order additional resources.

If you find it difficult to crisply define the system purpose, turn to the next activity—identifying features. Shift gears and develop a features list first; then prioritize those features and incorporate the most important features into an official-sounding system purpose statement.

System Features

Combining the client interviews with the use case model (as it grows), you can glean the needed system feature list. It is important to maintain traceability from the feature to the actual client's need. If you let the development team run hog wild with feature development, you can end up with some really nifty bells and whistles that serve only to extend the schedule, use up resources, drive up costs, and potentially eat into profits.

Some of the features that are required for our library system are represented by the use cases listed earlier and shown in Figure 5.2.

If you can't tie a feature to a legitimate use case, more than likely that feature isn't needed by either the client or the end users of the system. Don't include it on the must-have list; instead, relegate it to a maybe-later list.

5

BUSINESS PROCESS ANALYSIS

FIGURE 5.2
Initial system use cases help to articulate the requirements.

An easy way to spur thought on how to arrive at features is to break down the application into three segments:

- Setting up the system
- Using the system
- Analyzing results

Features for Setting Up the System

Ask yourself what it takes to get the system ready to be useful to end users before they even start the application for the first time. An example of this would be tied to the use cases involving dealing with resource titles (books and software) that the company currently owns. Obviously, the application must have a way to enter and maintain a collection of such resources. Following are a list of some setup-based features:

Manage (create, retrieve, update, and delete) lists of resources (software and books)

Manage lists of users

Provide rights of system usage (requester, approver, and librarian)

Let's jump over to a different activity and do a little object modeling. You've just learned that you need something to cover software titles, books, requesters, approvers, and librarians. These are objects visible to us in the system. They each have different characteristics, rights, and roles in the system.

Before we begin, let's go over some of the basic definitions of a class and the UML notation for classes. Figure 5.3 provides the symbolism and the sidebar discusses the class concept.

FIGURE 5.3

This is the class symbol in UML notation.

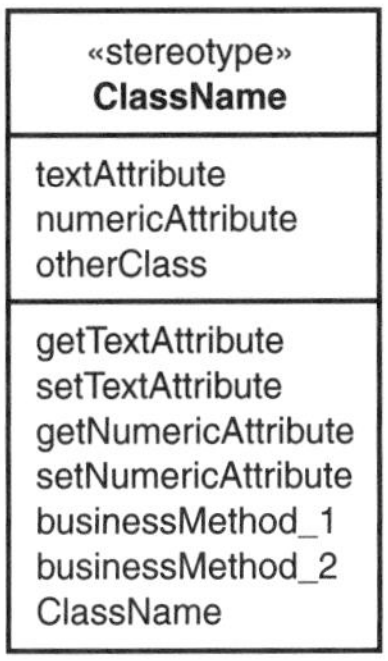

```
        «stereotype»
        ClassName

    textAttribute
    numericAttribute
    otherClass

    getTextAttribute
    setTextAttribute
    getNumericAttribute
    setNumericAttribute
    businessMethod_1
    businessMethod_2
    ClassName
```

Definition of a Class and the UML Notation

A *class* is a common definition for a like number of objects. It embodies one of the fundamental tenets of the object-oriented paradigm—encapsulation. The class is a self-contained unit able to describe its characteristics, or attributes, and able to define its behavior—that is, responsibilities that it can carry out alone or in collaboration with other objects. The class also contains associations to other classes. The symbol used is shown in Figure 5.3.

The top section, or "compartment," is for the name of the class. Optionally, it can also contain a stereotype name (shown within « »). The middle compartment indicates the attributes used to describe the defining characteristics of the class plus any associations to other classes (for example, otherClass). The last compartment is reserved for the methods the class is able to carry out. Some of the more trivial methods include what are loosely termed "sets" and "gets" or

continues

"accessors" and "mutators." The idea is that because attributes are private to the class (encapsulated), methods must be used to allow getting the value of the attribute and setting the value. The accessors/getters allow "reading" the object's attributes; while the mutators/setters allow for changing the value.

From the initial findings, we can abstract the following classes from the objects that we see in the problem domain. Figure 5.4 shows the object model so far (I use the Together UML modeling tool—http://www.togethersoft.com).

FIGURE 5.4

Our application takes shape in the beginnings of an object model.

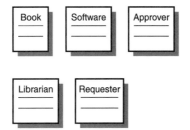

Features for Using the System

Using the system features includes requirements for when we're up and running with the application on the user's desktop. What will the user need to do and see to achieve what he or she wants?

One of the central design concepts is to look for important problem domain items or activities that occur at a moment in time (such as a sale) or over an interval of time (something with a beginning and an ending, such as a lease or a rental). The checkout and check in of a book would represent such a "rental" moment-interval. The cycle of requesting a new title and getting it approved would also be an important item to track in the software system we are building. These will represent two new classes in the problem domain.

Note

For more information about some of these design techniques, to learn more about stereotypical classes and relationships, and to see additional business system components, see *Java Modeling in Color with UML* by Peter Coad (Prentice Hall, 1999).

Features for Analyzing Results

These features support any after-the-fact analysis or output that your client wants. In many cases, these features are the most important to your client, just as a report or graph becomes the ultimate result of using the application.

Select Classes of Objects

From the features exercise, you discovered some of the classes you need:

- Checkout
- Request
- Book
- Software
- Requester
- Approver
- Librarian

To find other objects, you can consult the use case model and get a list of actors. An easy way to think of an *object* is to remember it is usually a person, place, or thing. This sounds like the definition of a noun that we learned in grade school English class, doesn't it? In software design, it's a discrete entity that has a set of values (attributes) and that can do its own thing with its values (a set of behavior).

The high-level description of a collection of like objects is termed a *class*. The class holds the defining characteristics of the objects (its attributes or properties). The class also defines the capabilities of an object—the methods (functions) indicating what the object can do. Certain classes also require class-level methods to work with the collection of all objects in that class (lists of itself, for example). When an object needs to collaborate with other objects to fulfill its duties, you can define object connections (or associations) within a class.

Run Through the Use Cases

Add some knowledge of the attributes and behavior for the classes you've identified based on the use cases:

> **Use case:** Search for software or book titles. Add a `search()` method to... To where? Maybe we could add a class-level method to perform the search across all objects. Or, maybe we could add a `Catalog` class (new discovery) that owns the list of titles, and therefore, the search method.

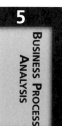

Use case: Check out or check in a book or software title. Add a method to allow each title to do its own checking in and out.

Use case: Enter a requisition for a new book or software title. Add a `request()` method to a new `Requester` class, or somewhere else?

Hmm...You need some sort of additional means for managing lists of requests. Maybe we can add this to the `Catalog` class as well.

Use case: Send messages for overdue materials. We can send this request through the `Catalog` class.

Distribute Functionality

Place as much responsibility as low in the class hierarchy as possible. It is best to have the object that can handle the job do it (for example, let `Software` perform the search) versus some higher-level manager class that merely directs activity. (This adage works in real life too <g>.)

Figure 5.5 shows what the object model looks like now, given the addition of the following:

- A new `Catalog` class and its relationship to `Software` and `Book` titles
- Addition of "description" classes for both `Software` and `Book`
- Methods to support the use cases previously listed
- Four types of users/roles (borrower, librarian, requester, and approver)
- Two moment-intervals: `Borrow` and `Requisition`

Note how `Book` is coupled with `BookDesc`. This is a design technique to couple the need to track individual items (actual books, for example, if you have more than one copy), with the description (details) that go along with defining the item.

Modeling Associations

Some important aspects of OO modeling are identifying and displaying relations between classes. After all, only trivial systems are composed of objects that do everything themselves (or poorly written nontrivial systems!). The way we show that one class knows of (or has) a list of other classes is through the diamond-ended association line signifying aggregation. The empty end of the line indicates the "many" side of the relationship, and the diamond is for the "whole" side. Additional cardinality (such as 1, 0..1, 0..*, or 1..*) can be presented to further the descriptive nature of the diagram.

FIGURE 5.5

The object model is shaping up with a little more meat.

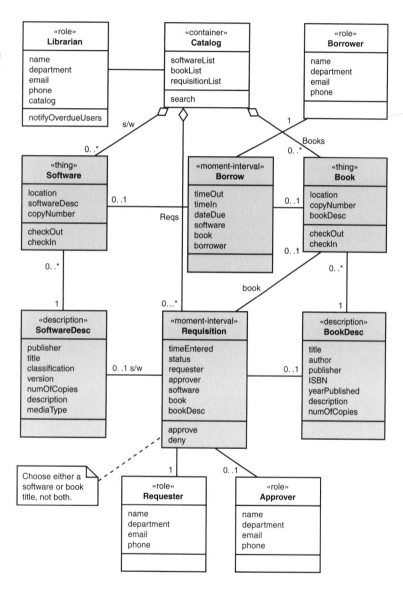

5

Useful Stereotypes

Description: When modeling objects that have catalog-like descriptions (think of a clothing or music catalog), it is best to use a description-type class stereotype. These have typical attributes that are used to describe the entire family of

continues

BUSINESS PROCESS ANALYSIS

items that would be in the "catalog." In other words, you don't need to create zillions of classes to define different objects (for example: shirt, short-sleeve shirt, button-down shirt, shorts, long pants).

```
type
description
itemNumber
defaultValue
```

If you need to know the number of items on hand for a specific object, simply add a "quantity" type of attribute. Examples of description-like classes include: book title, software title, movie title, store products, catalog items, aircraft types (B737, B747, B777, F100, Dash-8, and so on), automobile types (Ford GT90, Audi Avus, Lamborghini Diablo, McLaren F1, Ferrari F50).

Thing: if you need to know about a *specific* item (for example, US Airways B757 Tail Number 17A4392, McLaren VIN #WAUBB74779), you need to create a "Thing" stereotype class. The typical attributes include

```
serial number
name
address
customValue
```

But Wait! Time for Challenging Our Model

Let's look more closely at the class design to see whether we can make some improvements.

The Book and Software classes look very similar. The client had even discussed the potential for this system to eventually encompass training materials, videos, and so on. The Librarian, Approver, Requester, and Borrower classes also look suspiciously similar. The act of modeling with the class diagram has served its purpose—it has clearly shown us what we modeled and has allowed us to think about ways we might rearrange the model to improve the system design. (Had we just jumped in and started coding, we might not have had the perspective to challenge the model.) Now, let's factor in a bit of knowledge about where the client ultimately wants to head with this application.

Take the time to lay the foundation right the first time. You'll reap benefits later when you go to expand the model to adapt to different (but similar) uses. The client will be pleased with the rapid and cost-effective response rate. You'll also be happy by reduced maintenance costs!

Pull out the common features of Book and Software, and specialize the differences in subclasses (a.k.a. child classes or descendant classes—you pick). This "foresight" will undoubtedly build in flexibility to the model, allowing gracious accommodation of new requirements. If we abstract what we are storing and loaning in our library, and we add the fact that new items such as video and CBT might be added, we can come up with a new, more generic, `Title` class.

Looking at the `Librarian`, `Approver`, `Requester`, and `Borrower` classes, we see that these are actually different roles played by various employees at various times. Given the similarity of the attributes, one might be tempted to bring inheritance into play. However, because we have an assortment of roles, we will combine the power of designing a new `Person` class and add multiple roles via the more flexible composition of another new class: `PersonRole`. From the `PersonRole` class, we will use inheritance to define the many roles that the system requires.

After using Together's simple drag-and-drop capability to rearrange the original parts of the model and after adding some new parts, you have the latest class diagram (Figure 5.6).

Note that `BookDesc` and `SoftwareDesc` now inherit from the newly added `TitleDesc` class. The `BookDesc` class holds the attributes that are unique to books, such as author and ISBN. The `SoftwareDesc` class holds classification, version, and media. The root `TitleDesc` class holds all the common attributes to both books and software. Note the parallel modeling pattern of `Title` being associated to `TitleDesc`, and `Book` and `Software` being associated to exactly one `BookDesc` and `SoftwareDesc`, respectively.

Inheritance

Figure 5.6 has introduced a new UML symbol for inheritance. The symbol looks like a large arrowhead pointing from the child to the parent class. For example, `Software` inherits from `Title`.

Sketch a Human Interface

Another way to help flesh out the object model is to sketch out some of the graphical user interface (GUI) screens. This can be another technique to help add content to the classes that participate in the GUI. For system setup or system administration-type GUIs, the screens are often simple. Consider the librarian use case—Enter/edit book or software titles. (See Figure 5.7)

Adding one setup use case for demonstration of how this is done is not a bad idea, but "if you've seen one you've seen 'em all" often applies here. Most clients and developers are familiar with GUIs that need to perform the simple tasks of creating, updating, and deleting objects. You should concentrate on GUIs to satisfy some of the "tougher" required features.

FIGURE 5.6

The object model now reflects the simplification of Book *and* Software *classes, and dealing with various roles.*

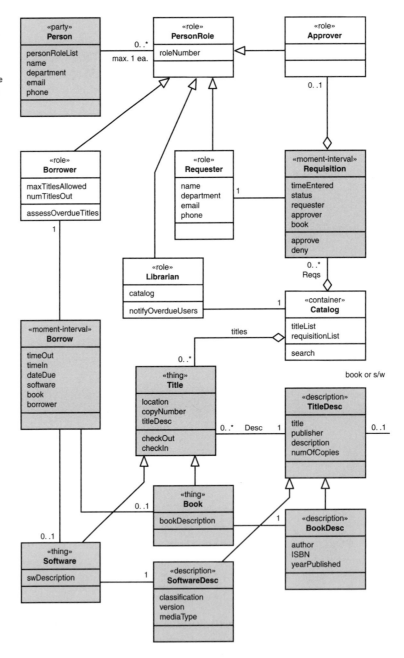

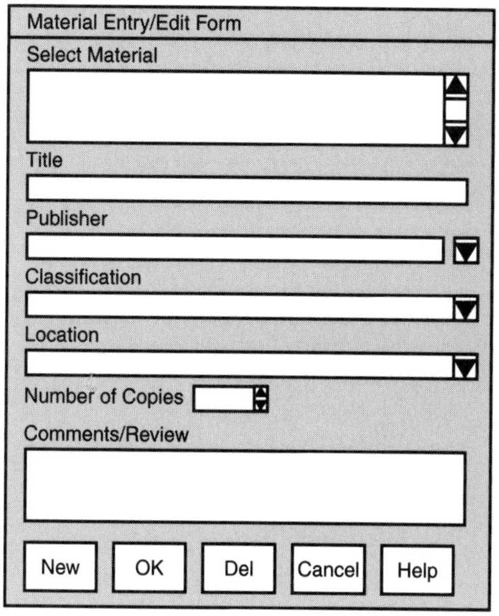

FIGURE 5.7

This simple sketch of catalog entry/edit form can be used to elaborate parts of the model.

When you place New, OK, Search, and Delete buttons on the forms, your object model will need to be able to perform such operations.

You can begin to design many other pieces of the GUI—particularly when using a good GUI development environment such as Notes. You can easily snap together some sample screens and proposed navigation and connection. Although you might not have the details nailed down, the client will be able to get the general feel of the application through these GUI prototypes.

If you prefer to use paper to do your sketching, simply relate the action of clicking a control to the next sketch that shows what would be presented to the user. Sometimes this is actually faster than working with a GUI tool. You can quickly sketch the main screen and show the next level of screens when one of the controls is pressed.

In this library example, the typical Requester user can select from two primary functionality branches:

- Material searching and checking in/out
- Material requisition

The next sketches would show the Material Search form (used for finding information or for checking out and returning materials) and the Requisition form, respectively. A third level for the Search form can show the Check Out / In form. (See Figure 5.8.)

5

BUSINESS PROCESS ANALYSIS

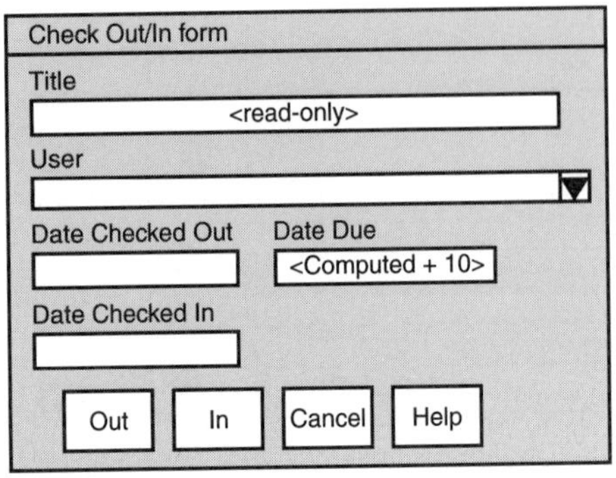

FIGURE 5.8

The sketch of the Check Out / In form begins to tackle a more complex feature.

Build Sequence Diagrams

A UML *sequence diagram* is a powerful means of capturing the dynamics behind an object model. The scenario is a class-based means for showing the time-ordered sequence of method calls—both within classes and between classes. Many developers have experience in creating pseudocode or in charting a function call tree—and this is very similar. The intent is to capture additional details about the object model by asking the system to do something. In many cases, going the extra length to map out some of the harder functionality required of the system will uncover missing elements of the model. These might be methods that need to be added to support the sequence diagram, missing associations between classes to permit calling an object's method, or sometimes finding complete classes that are missing.

Sequence Diagrams for Using the System

"Using the System" sequence diagrams are usually more valuable than the "Setting Up" sequence diagrams because of their worth to meeting the customer's end needs. The logic is often more complex and the interactions between objects more intricate, and often the client interest in these scenarios is greater because it is core business functionality. After all, the use cases that represent using the system get right to the client's main needs; the system is being built to serve a purpose. This is the step wherein you develop these all-important scenarios! Let's try one on for size....

Scenario for Checking Out a Title

Start with a sequence for checking out a title (either software or book). We might first conjure up the general flow of events, and then create the sequence diagram around this list.

1. The GUI needs to be created

2. During initialization, a list of titles needs to be retrieved (likely book *or* software, not both simultaneously)

3. The user can then select one or more titles to check out

4. The system then tries to perform the checkouts, which succeeds when the status can be set to "checked out"

5. If all goes well, a `Borrow` transaction instance is created and due date entered

The sequence diagram, shown in Figure 5.9, has added a notion of the GUI representation of the objects. On the GUI, you have a *pick list* that presents all current titles to select from, and possibly fields to display the values associated with the current highlighted title. The sequence diagram shows the objects across the top with time increasing down the vertical axis. The arrows going from one object to another represent message sends (method calls). When a message hooks back on itself, this implies a "message to self" or "self delegation." This simply means that an internal method was invoked on that object.

FIGURE 5.9

The "check out a title" sequence diagram shows how our objects interact to get the job done.

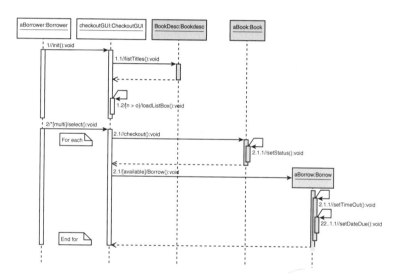

Running through the sequence diagram definition results in discovering additional methods and some other changes to the object model. This is typical (and desirable). By thinking explicitly of the dynamics of how an object model is actually going to carry out some of the methods listed in a given class, we end up spotting areas of the model that need improving. If this step is skipped, it will get done on-the-fly when the developer is building out the functionality. It is better to see the flaws in the object model during design and fix them with a more global model perspective, than when down and dirty in the coding phase.

A New Discovery—A Missing Class, and So On

In the Employee Checkout/in a book or software title use case, we made some key discoveries. The highlights of the changes involved adding methods that didn't exist and changing Title class to being abstract (implying we can only ever really use the Book or Software class).

As you can see, we impacted the object model via this exercise—precisely why we use sequence diagrams. By stressing the dynamics of using the system for specific use cases (features), the sequence diagrams play an important role in furthering the completeness of the overall object model design. The results of factoring in our new discovery to the object model are shown in Figure 5.10.

FIGURE 5.10

The refined object model reflects our latest modifications.

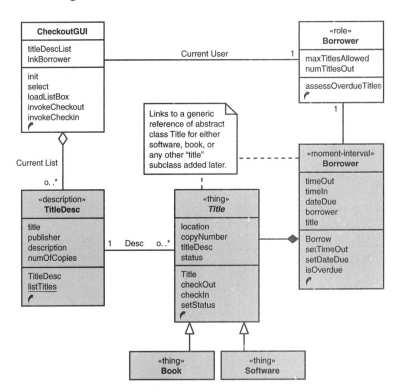

One alternative that Peter Coad and I strongly encourage is to use composition in place of inheritance whenever it makes sense. One of the tests for determining whether composition is better than inheritance is whether a subclass is actually more like a "role played by" the base class versus a true specialization that extends the attributes and methods of the base class. Because librarian, requester, and approver are really just roles played by a user, we used this technique for modeling this aspect of our design. Composition is preferred due to the complexity of inheritance and the inherent weak encapsulation along the inheritance hierarchy. (Changes in base classes can have "downstream" impact on subclasses.) Good software design always strives for loose coupling between entities to keep the system more flexible and less difficult to test, maintain, and extend.

In Peter Coad's words [*Java Design*, 1999]:

> Composition extends the responsibilities of an object by delegating work to additional objects. Composition is *the* major mechanism for extending the responsibilities of an object. Nearly every object in an object model is composed of, knows of, or works with other objects (composition).

Figure 5.11 shows the results of taking the opportunity to model the `Person` class into one that exploits composition.

Working out scenarios for using the system is far more valuable than the setup scenarios. These scenarios get to the heart of the customer's needs. They demonstrate the capability for the design to stand up and deliver the needed content to the user. You'll find that the client's subject matter experts will be very interested in helping you get these scenarios right.

FIGURE 5.11

We choose to model user roles via the more powerful composition technique.

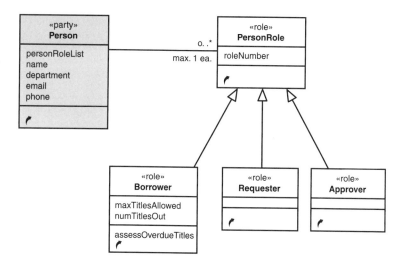

Sequence Diagrams for Analyzing Results

Similar to the sequence diagrams for using the system, the sequence diagrams that concentrate on delivering output to the user can be valuable to the client. These often involve invoking methods that perform computations or comparisons to yield assessing-style results, such as generating a list of overdue material (to send weekly notifications) and a list of new material additions.

Summary

In this chapter, you went through a brief, whirlwind tour of employing a handful of object-oriented modeling tips and principles in analyzing the user's problem domain in the context of the requirements. You jumped back and forth across activities—from object modeling to sequence diagrams to use cases/features. Maybe it seemed a little disjointed, at times, but this is much more in line with the way you really ought to perform your analysis and design activities.

This chapter employed the approach outlined in Chapter 4 (beginning with the section titled "Examining the Business Process"). You looked at some object-model and sequence-diagramming techniques and applied some helpful strategies to get the needed answers. You quickly built up an object model, sketched out some GUI, and developed some pertinent scenarios—refining the object model at every turn. In summary, you did the following:

- Identified system purpose and features
- Listed requirements as use cases
- Identified classes
- Sketched prototype GUIs
- Worked out object-interaction dynamics with sequence diagrams
- Built and refined an object model

The scenarios helped identify classes. The GUI gave some dynamics to work with and also identified classes. Along the way, you would have continually placed your output into the virtual Project Notebook (covered in Chapter 4) for all to use.

The diagramming methods in this chapter were simple enough to communicate the basic intentions of object interactions and relationships—without bogging you down in nitty-gritty detail. If you want a whiteboard style of an OO diagramming tool, there are many to choose from—including my favorite: Together/J, available free from http://www.togethersoft.com. Remember to keep requirements traceability at an all-time high priority and to work with your client to establish meaningful use cases.

Also, remember to make composition do most of your work and use inheritance only when absolutely called for.

Happy modeling.

Foundations of Application Design

PART II

IN THIS PART

Design Guidelines

by Steve Kern

CHAPTER 6

Defining good application design is much more difficult than defining bad design, which is often easy to identify. With a good design, the designer must take into consideration many elements of the user interface of an application before designing and coding. Here are some design elements a user might see when opening a Domino application in a Notes client:

- The Windows desktop interface
- The Notes Start Menu option or desktop shortcut
- The splash screen
- The password dialog box
- The Notes client Welcome page
- The database icon on a bookmark tab

After the database is opened, the user might then see a frameset with an outline embedded on a page to provide navigation, or the standard folders and views navigator, or any one of a wide array of options available to a Domino applications developer. The user has to determine what to do next from the plethora of choices available from both the user interface and the options specific to the application itself. This is a daunting task, especially to a new user. It is up to the developer to make this as easy for the user as possible. If the developer makes it too difficult, the application might not be used, or it might not be used properly.

Although not often considered, good design also holds true for what goes inside an application or under the hood. Writing sloppy and undocumented code often results in another programmer cleaning up after you. Don't forget, that poor programmer doing application maintenance just might be you! What might seem obvious to you when constructing a piece of code might not be so obvious six months later. If you document your code thoroughly and format it attractively so that it is easy to read, it is far easier to maintain.

This chapter is principally about the interface, although other topics pertinent to the discussion are covered.

- User considerations
- Naming conventions
- Interface design

Keeping the User in Mind

Think for a moment about the design of common items—a door, for example. There are many types of doors, but the one that is principally used is a single-hinged door opening to the inside of the room or building. Doors are typically opened with a doorknob. Most doorknobs are round, and when we see one, we almost instinctively know what it does. Without even testing it, we know that it opens the door to which it is attached. Another familiar example is that in the United States, the hot water is always on the left and the cold on the right. We know when we walk into a bathroom or kitchen which faucet to turn without looking at the faucet handles. These and other common designs abound in our daily life. These well-designed utilities give us the luxury of not thinking about everything we do, as well as saving us time. Consider what it would be like to have to think deeply about how to open a door. How many steps would it take? The point is that because we have stored the concept of a doorknob, we don't have to think deeply about opening a door. We walk toward a door and just open it, without consciously thinking about how it happens.

For the same reasons, most well-designed computer applications have a similar menu structure. This was less true some years ago before Windows became the prevalent operating system. Most applications have a menu structure that starts on the left with the following three menu choices: File, Edit, and View. The rightmost menu choice is always the Help menu. This is true of the word processor used to compose this chapter, Microsoft Word, as well as Lotus Notes, Lotus 1-2-3, Lotus Word Pro, Lotus Freelance Graphics, and almost any other professionally produced software. Why? Some years ago, industry professionals adopted these standards for user interface (UI) design.

This standard works well for the same reasons that those for doorknobs work. The user doesn't have to think a lot about where to go to accomplish certain tasks. For example, in all the applications mentioned previously, if you want to print a document you go to the File menu to do so. If you want to cut and paste text, you use the Edit menu. If you want to change the way you look at documents, you go to the View menu. This style of menu design is known as *Common User Access* (CUA). Figures 6.1 through 6.3 illustrate the File menu of Word, the Edit menu of Freelance Graphics, and the View menu of 1-2-3.

Consistency in application design works just as well as consistency in a doorknob design. It is not enough to stop there, however. It is certainly tempting to do so, though, because Lotus Notes attends to the vast majority of the UI, at least as far as the menu is concerned. It is imperative that developers attend to other parts of the user interface as well. This chapter examines those parts.

FIGURE 6.1

The File Menu of Microsoft's Word for Windows is where users go to create, open, save, and print documents.

FIGURE 6.2

The Edit menu of Freelance Graphics enables users to cut, copy, and paste text, and undo changes.

FIGURE 6.3

The View menu of 1-2-3 has menu items affecting the appearance of the open spreadsheet.

References on Interface Design

Here are some interesting references if you want to pursue the topic of user interface design further:

Macintosh Human Interface Guidelines, Apple Computers, Addison-Wesley 1992

The Art of Human-Computer Interface Design, by Brenda Laurel, Addison-Wesley 1990

The Design of Everyday Things, by Donald Norman, Doubleday 1988

TOG on Interface, by Bruce Tognazzini, Addison-Wesley 1992

The consistency of the user interface is one of Notes greatest strengths. Along with Lotus's philosophy of platform independence, Lotus has built a UI that is strikingly similar across all the disparate platforms on which Notes runs. Even the use of color in an application can be helpful. For example, in R5, the Action Bars of many templates are color-coded according to the type of application. Because Notes and Domino can launch multiple applications, unlike any other applications generator on the market, the Notes client portion of the interface doesn't change that much between applications. The parts of the interface that do change from application to application do so in predictable places. After you teach Notes to users, introducing applications subsequently is very easy and requires far less training time. This consistency can quite easily translate into significant dollar savings.

The same consistency often translates into greater user acceptance. There's no place like home! A familiar environment works well because change is disorienting. If you are constantly moving from one application to another and each is different, stress can become a real factor. "Okay, now that I'm in Xyz application, how do I print?" Mistakes in data entry can become more prevalent, and user dissatisfaction can ultimately contribute to greater staff turnover. Just think about how we store addresses:

> Person or company name
>
> Street address
>
> City, state, postal code

What if one out of the four or five applications that the user regularly used turned the order of the fields upside-down? That would surely cause a small riot among those responsible for data entry!

> State
>
> Person or company name
>
> City, postal code
>
> Street address

Keeping It Simple!

It is important to keep things simple when designing applications. All the design elements that the user interfaces directly with need to be simple; this includes items that impact the menu such as forms, views, and agents, as well as the design of forms, subforms, and views. Many Notes applications are designed to replace paper. Workflow applications and tracking applications often trace their origins to a piece of paper. Users often view paper forms as burdensome, and they want Notes to make their lives easier. What is it about these pieces of paper that makes life so difficult for the users of the process? Often, the paper forms are cluttered with boxes, check boxes, and blanks packed so densely that it takes a practiced eye just to read them. The forms can be far from simple, and the associated business rules are often quite complex and nearly impenetrable. It is your job as an applications developer to make some sense of the business rules for an application and to make the application easy to use.

As an example, many companies have forms that are used to grant access to various things, such as doors in buildings, email, LAN based servers, mainframe systems, and specific applications. A paper based form and its electronic equivalent may be fairly similar in appearance, but there the similarity stops. Properly written, the electronic form can provide built in flexibility. A good developer might create a method that would allow a select group of users to add and remove new systems for access. Forms created using this technique are referred to as *data-driven*. In other words, data created by the end-users drives the content in the form. Of course, it could be argued that a simple change to the paper form accomplishes the same thing.

While that may be true, a paper form has no "intelligence," unlike its electronic counterpart. Usually, specific individuals control access to various systems, servers and applications. Similarly, doors to vital areas such as product storage, warehouse areas, the server rooms, and so forth also have people assigned to them who approve their use for individuals. Ultimately, an access request would need to be routed to the managers for each of the areas and systems for approval before granting access. For a new employee, access could be requested for dozens of systems and doors in a large company. It would be tedious at best to include this sort of logic in a paper form! Usually, someone is assigned to monitor and process these requests, an onerous job at best. In the paper shuffle, the big question is "Who has the request?" The time to route the paper form to each of the approvers can be considerable.

In an electronic form, all of this logic would exist in user configurable data items, and the routing takes place electronically. It is much faster and much cleaner. The electronic forms can be streamlined, and if constructed properly, can provide much greater detail, including document history.

Following the Paper Form's Model

Many applications start out mimicking paper forms, but even well-designed paper forms don't often translate well into electronic applications without substantial redesign. Yet, maintaining the familiarity of the paper forms in an application can provide an important bridge for the users. If you are careful about the design, you can significantly ease the transition from paper to Notes and Domino. Many paper forms now use tables to help position text, and electronic forms should make use of tables as well. Tables are an extremely powerful design element. In R5, with the addition of tabbed tables, developers can create forms that pack a lot of information into a single screen, providing a simpler more elegant interface for the user. Tabbed tables are discussed in Chapter 10, "Advanced Form Design."

You can also make life easier for the user by providing default values for fields, which significantly speeds up data entry. A well-designed form also reduces the amount of errors and missed data by supplying appropriate lists and ensuring that the user enters required fields. It is of the utmost importance that you consult with the users. With very little prodding, the users will tell you what's wrong with the current system, whether it is paper-based or electronic, and tell you how to fix it. You just have to listen! Striking an appropriate balance of all the factors is more a matter of artistry and experience than of science or rules.

Designing Consistently

There are some rules that you should follow, however. Paramount among them is keeping a consistent user interface. If you have surfed the Web, you surely have noticed that whenever you click blue underlined text, you are transported elsewhere. You might also have noticed that whenever you position your mouse pointer over certain areas of a Web page, the text in the status bar of the browser changes to a URL; clicking that area (called a *hyperlink* or *hypertext link*) takes you to the linked page. This is exactly like the doorknob mentioned in the introduction to this chapter. Figures 6.4 and 6.5 illustrate this.

The Colors of Links

Blue text is the standard color for an unvisited hypertext link on the Internet. Visited links are often purple, while active links are red. Developers can set the colors of each type of link on a web page, and users can change the colors to suit their own preferences, so the text links that you see might not be these colors.

FIGURE 6.4

This unaltered Domino Web site illustrates hotlinked text. Note the underlined text; clicking the text opens the underlying database.

FIGURE 6.5

The Lotus Web page showing the text of the URL link in the status bar.

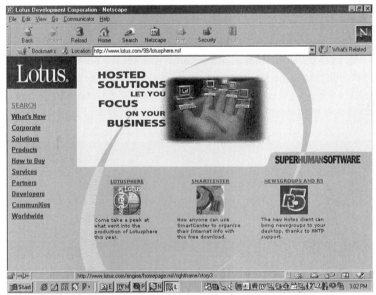

Certainly, one of the most common elements presented to a user is a view. With some exceptions, well-designed views are simple, as are well-designed forms. Naturally, it will be difficult to keep views designed to report on significant amounts of data and forms that have massive quantities of fields simple in their appearance. Even so, a form with a lot of fields doesn't need to be cluttered. Tables can organize information on forms, and white space can keep the appearance uncluttered. New in R5 are tabbed tables that can further reduce onscreen clutter. You can add collapsible sections to organize information on forms. In both views and forms, it is a good idea to limit the use of colors and fonts. Use of color should be consistent; for example, if you choose a light yellow background for a form, you might consider also using light yellow as the alternate row color. Lotus recommends using certain background colors for the Action Bar and navigators to identify the type of application. Action Bars colors for System applications are purple, Client applications (like the mail database) are dark green, and applications such as discussion and document libraries are gold. This provides an element of consistency linking the form and the view in the user's mind.

It is also important to provide help for the user. The Notes client already provides extensive help; there are numerous help and reference files. The file your users see is the standard Notes 5 Client help file. Similarly, the Domino Designer has its own help file, Domino 5 Designer Help. Notes 5 Client help is a good start because it deals with the Notes user interface. Beyond that, you need to provide help that is application-specific. There are several techniques for doing so, which are discussed in Chapter 15, "Providing End-User Help."

Using Naming Conventions

Consistency should not stop at end-user considerations! It is important to be consistent at the programming level as well. The modified Hungarian notation or naming convention is a popular convention for field and variable names. The first character of a field's name indicates the field data type. Table 6.1 illustrates one version of the modified Hungarian field-naming convention.

TABLE 6.1   Modified Hungarian Field-Naming Convention

Letter	Data Type
c	Character
d	Date
l or b	Logical (or Boolean)
m	Memo
n	Numeric

Thus, a field name might be cCustomer or dDate. Variables are named similarly, except that the first character is reserved for the scope of the variable and the second character for the type of the variable. Table 6.2 shows the letters indicating the scope.

TABLE 6.2   Modified Hungarian Variable Scope Naming

Letter	Scope
g	Public
l	Private or local
j	Junk, or local to a procedure or function

Variable names might be lcCustomer or jdDate, for example.

Using Mixed Case

Studies have shown that people find it easier to read mixed case than all lower-case or all uppercase. If you noticed, in the examples of field and variable names, I used mixed case. By convention, the type was in lowercase (c for character or n for numeric), and the next letter of the field or variable was capitalized. Because Notes and Domino support mixed case for field names, it makes good sense to use mixed case for the field names. If you check the designs of the databases that ship with Notes, you'll find that the designers at Lotus also use mixed case.

Picklists and Field Names

One difficulty with this naming convention in Notes is that the field picklists are alphabetical, and only the first character is significant in searches. So if you have numerous fields with the letter c as the first letter, it is not easy to locate the field you want.

Notes currently supports 32-character field names. Although this is convenient, it is certainly not a reason to create field names of that length. Here is what one would look like:

```
thisfieldhasthirty_twocharacters
```

This is not a particularly practical length; it is far better to keep the length around 16 characters, which is easier to read and easier to type. Even typed in mixed case, it is not very readable:

```
ThisFieldhasThirty_TwoCharacters
```

With a greater number of characters, it is possible to create very descriptive field and variable names. The names that you choose should strike a balance between length and clarity.

If you look at some of the database designs that ship with Lotus Notes, you will not find any sort of field-naming convention. Despite this absence, you are encouraged to adopt naming conventions for your own use. You might find it quite useful to know at a glance what type of field you're working with.

Lotus Notes has more and different field types available than those listed in Table 6.1. Table 6.3 lists the field types along with a proposed naming convention for your consideration.

TABLE 6.3   Naming Convention for Domino Data Types

Letter	Data Type
c	Text
d	Time
n	Number
rt	Rich text
an	Authors
nm	Names
rn	Readers
p	Password
f	Formula

In a relational database, it is easy to see what table a field is from because it can be referred to using dot notation: *TableName.FieldName*. In a Notes database application there are no tables (well, technically speaking, there is a single table called the Universal Relation Table). Although fields are associated with a document, documents are not the same as a record in a table. You can add or remove fields in documents without changing the underlying form, something not possible in a relational database table. To make matters even more difficult, the name of the form associated with a document can be changed easily by changing the Form field. I have attempted to differentiate fields from each other by using the form alias as part of the field name. This unfortunately breaks down at too many points. Principally, it is often convenient to use several different forms to view the same document at different stages in its life cycle. It is impractical and inconvenient to rename the field in each successive form. I have therefore abandoned this attempt and have settled for simply distinguishing the field type from the first characters of the name.

It is important to mention here that scripting languages such as LotusScript support different variable types than are available at the database field level. For example, LotusScript supports the *variant* data type. You should consider a naming convention for those types as well, even though the variables have no presence outside the application itself.

For naming forms and views, a large number of characters is available. Form and view names can be 128 characters long but cannot exceed 256 bytes. Both views and forms can have an alias, which is a name that the design element goes by internally. The user doesn't see the alias, but the alias is used to refer to the view or the form in formulas. In addition, if you use an alias, you can change the name of the view or form that the user sees, without having to change any of the formulas that reference the design element. It is important to establish some sort of naming convention; I usually keep aliases down to a few characters and use caps. A form or view called Invoice might have an alias of INV, and a status form might have an alias of SF.

It is also important not to neglect filenames and database titles. As you'll see in Chapter 7, "The Release 5 Object Store," platforms such as NT and Windows 95 that support long filenames match the operating system filename to the database title, including spaces. However, you might want to consider keeping filenames to the standard eight characters plus three characters for the extension. If your application consists of multiple databases, you might consider using a naming scheme that groups them together. For example, XyzSales.nsf, XyzLeads.nsf, and XyzProd.nsf might be databases from an application written for Xyz Corporation. Using a naming scheme such as this groups the databases together in Windows Explorer, whether the sort is by name or by extension (type). A similar naming structure for the database title groups the databases together in the Notes Open Database dialog box, reducing frustration when a user attempts to open databases for the application (see Figure 6.6).

FIGURE 6.6

The three databases for Xyz Corporation are listed together because of their titles.

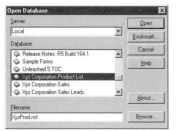

Designing the Interface

The Domino database icon should be indicative in some way of what the database is and does. These icons are not separate files with an `.ico` extension like icons in other applications; nor are they embedded in an application's executable file. Also, tools other than the icon editor supplied in the Domino Designer cannot edit them. However, you can work on them outside of the Designer in a graphics program such as Paint Shop Pro, copy them to the clipboard, and paste them back into the Icon editor. It is important that you take some care when designing database icons. For example, if you use drop shadows, be sure to use them consistently in all the databases associated with your application.

Attention to Detail

Paying attention to detail at all levels of design is important, just as great chefs earn their reputations by paying attention to every detail of the presentation of the meals they create.

You might have noticed that the default font for Notes is Default Sans Serif, which replaces the Helvetica font in earlier versions. Like Helvetica, Default Sans Serif translates well across all platforms. Don't forget that there might not be a way to predict the platform on which the application will function. Establish standards for font, point size, and color use before beginning an application. If you have a group of designers, it is important that all their work looks and feels similar. Pick standards, and stick with them. Figure 6.7 shows a form that is difficult to read.

FIGURE 6.7

This nonstandard form is difficult to read.

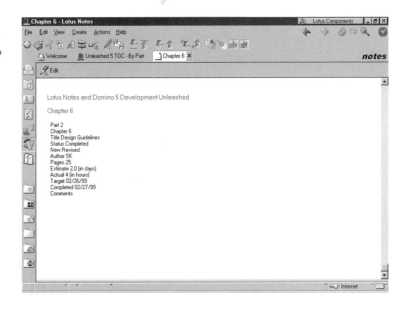

Table 6.4 has some suggested standards for fonts.

TABLE 6.4 Standards for Design Elements

Element	Font	Size	Style	Color
Field label	Default Sans Serif	8	Bold	Black
Field	Default Sans Serif	8	Plain	Black
Database title	Default Sans Serif	12	Plain	Light blue
Form title	Default Sans Serif	10	Bold	Light blue
Form subtitle	Default Sans Serif	8/10	Bold	Magenta
Section	Default Sans Serif	8	Bold	Light blue/dark cyan
Hidden items	Default Sans Serif	8	Plain	Dark cyan
View columns	Default Sans Serif	8	Plain	Black
View category 1	Default Sans Serif	8/10	Bold	Light blue
View category 2	Default Sans Serif	8/10	Bold	Magenta
View Category 3	Default Sans Serif	8/10	Bold	Black

It is important to set and follow standards. Perhaps you will use the ones listed in Table 6.4 or ones of your own devising. There will undoubtedly be times when you will need to vary from those standards; these standards are meant to be guidelines. It is not necessary to follow them slavishly. Figure 6.8 illustrates a form using the standards listed in the Table 6.4. Note that this form is rather plain, and you may consider jazzing up the form with graphics. The form is intended mainly to display how much easier it is to read and understand than the form in Figure 6.7 as well as show the effects of standardizing various elements of form design.

FIGURE 6.8

This simple form is much easier to read.

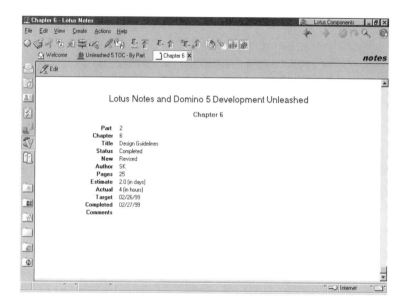

Use radio buttons sparingly. When clicked, they cannot be unclicked. They do not format nicely when printed, necessitating a cumbersome duplicate row for printing and reading. You then use Hide-when formulas to hide the radio buttons when printing and the normal text when editing. When using radio buttons or check boxes, don't use the default 3D style unless you're in a layout region or are using a form with a gray background. Otherwise, the gray background of the 3D radio button set sticks out like a sore thumb on a white or light colored background. Controls without borders look better on most forms (see Figure 6.9).

FIGURE **6.9**

This form uses 3D Radio buttons and text with a drop shadow that makes it hard to read.

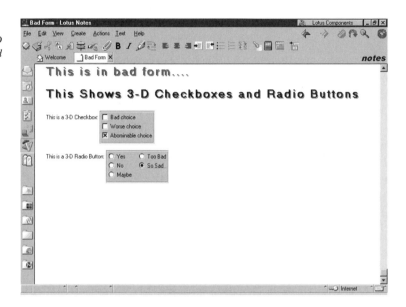

One way to enhance the look and feel of your applications is to use reusable elements, such as Shared actions and Subforms. For example, you can create a subform called `subHeader` that contains a standard form header for your company. On this element, you can place standardized text, graphics, and so on. One way to leverage this element is to assign the name of the form to a hidden field at the top of the form. Include a field in the subform that inherits the name of the form from the hidden field, and the title of the database using `@DbTitle`. Using this technique makes the subform reusable across many databases with a minimum of effort. Figure 6.10 shows the subform in design.

Using Computed for Display Fields

There is no need to store the information in the display fields `cDatabaseTitle` or `cInheritFormTitle`, so make them Computed for Display. You can also create an Image Resource for the graphic, and insert the resource into the subform. Resources are covered in Chapter 12, "Using Resources in Domino Applications."

Standard action buttons such as Save & Close, Delete, and Edit can be created as Shared Actions so that they can be embedded wherever needed. This saves time because the actions don't have to be coded again. You can have an action that is used under several different circumstances; by creating it as a Shared action, you can write the code once and debug it, and whenever you insert it into a form or view, it always works. You can also include standard action in a single subform that is placed at the top of each form. Figure 6.11 illustrates the use of a subform.

FIGURE 6.10

The subform subHeader *is shown in the Domino Designer.*

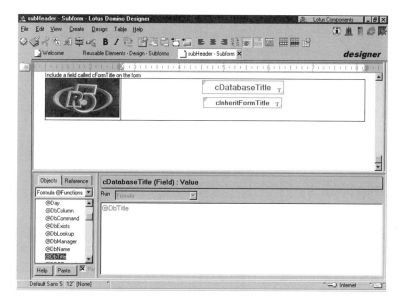

FIGURE 6.11

The subform subHeader *blends in seamlessly with the form.*

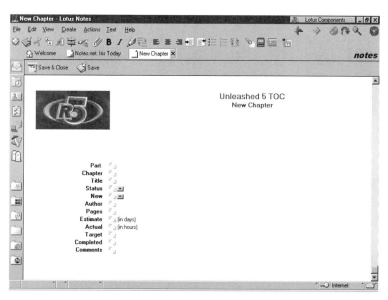

Consistency with Style!

Another method of enforcing consistency is to use the Styles tab of the Text Properties Box. Using it is quite simple. Set up some text in the style you want to create. For example, use hidden text that is dark cyan and Helvetica 8 point. Click the mouse somewhere in the text and open the Text Properties Box. Click the Styles tab and choose Create Style. Name the style, and it is now available whenever you need it. Figure 6.12 shows the Styles tab in use.

FIGURE 6.12

The Styles tab shows a style being created.

When using icons for actions, choose them consistently throughout your applications. Follow the functionality of the toolbar wherever possible or come up with a consistent set to use in all your applications. Figure 6.13 shows the Action Bar button icon palette. Table 6.5 shows some commonly used Action Bar icons.

FIGURE 6.13

The Action Bar icon palette has a large number of choices available for button icons.

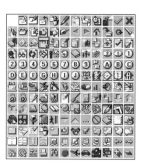

TABLE 6.5   Action Bar Icons

Icon	Usage
	Close
	Edit
	Delete

Enforcing these standards across multiple applications is actually quite easy. If you maintain a template on a central server, each time you design a reusable element, you can save it in this template file. Whenever you need a design element, you can cut and paste it from this template. The Domino Designer even asks you whether you want to preserve the inheritance. If you choose to do so, each improvement to the design element is also made templatesin your applications. A *template* is a design copy of a Domino database. It can store all the forms, views, agents, and other design elements of a database. Templates are covered in Chapter 35, "Tracking Design Changes and Using Templates."

CAUTION

Be careful when you make changes to design elements stored in a central template, since they may significantly affect multiple databases. If you make major or unannounced changes, users might become confused or your application might become unusable. It is important that you consider carefully any changes to this design library and that you restrict access to it or have some sort of approval mechanism in place before an element is changed. It goes without saying than any changes should be backward compatible and thoroughly tested and debugged. "Backward compatible" means that all databases which used the original version of the design element should function flawlessly with the new version.

Standardizing View Design

Table 6.4 listed suggestions for view design standards. Figure 6.14 is an example of a view following those suggestions. A *view category* refers to columns that are sorted and categorized. Choosing colors carefully can help delineate the different categories and visually break up the columns when viewed on screen. Unfortunately, since this is not a color screen shot, you cannot get the full effects from looking at Figure 6.14.

It is important that you not mix many different fonts in views. Keep it simple! Right-justify numbers in columns and left-justify text. Avoid centering the text or numerals in columns.

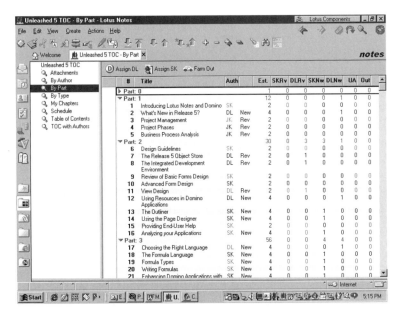

FIGURE **6.14**

View categories such as Part 0 and Part 1 have a twistie to the left. Click twisties to open and close the category.

Displaying Numeric Columns

If you right-justify a numeric column and then right-justify the title accordingly, often the title and the data in the columns butt right up against the next column, especially if the next column is a left-justified text column. To overcome this, include a single-spaced column with a null value (either the word *null* or double-quotes will work) between the two. You can also pad a right-justified column title with a space, which adds a small cushion between the next right-most column title.

Keep Action Bar buttons limited in number. According to Lotus, there should rarely be more than four Action Bar buttons in a view or form. When you do use buttons, either in a view or in a form, be sure to use the Hide-when attributes appropriately. For example, if the button is an Edit button on a form, be sure that it only shows up in read mode. Having an Edit button visible in edit mode makes no sense. Having a Save button that appears in read mode likewise makes no sense. A Close button can show up in either mode, because it typically executes @Command([FileCloseWindow]), which offers to save the document in edit mode and then close the window or simply close the window if in read mode. In R5, the introduction of cascaded actions allows Domino developers to pack more actions into an Action Bar without unnecessarily cluttering the bar. Cascaded actions stack multiple actions into a single Action Bar button. You can read more about cascaded actions in Chapter 10, "Advanced Form Design."

Organizing Views

Views tend to proliferate after the users have used an application for a while. As users begin to work with the database, it is natural that they will come to the developers and ask for different sorts, different column orders, and so on. However, you should attempt to keep the number of views to a minimum. Remember that a view when populated occupies physical disk space, unlike a browse of records in a relational database. Continually adding views is potentially bewildering to a user. Views need to be organized in order for them to be easy to use. You can collect the views into related groups and cascade (or nest) them to accomplish this task. When views are nested, a twistie indicates that they can be expanded or collapsed. Twisties can be displayed in both the standard folder and view navigator, or in an outline. You can also reduce the number of views by allowing columns to be sorted by the user. For example, instead of including a view sorted by date ascending and another by date descending, include a single view and allow the user to sort the view by clicking the column header. The technique to do this is discussed in Chapter 11, "View Design." In R5, a new design element called an Outline has been added. In an outline, views can be selectively added and grouped along with other design elements. The outline is then added to a page, and included in a frameset. This is an ideal way to present views. You can see this at work in Figure 6.14. Chapter 13 covers the Outliner, Chapter 14 covers the Page Designer, and Chapter 31 covers Framesets.

Using Structural Elements in Views

In Release 4.x of Notes and Domino, many improvements were added to views, among them the capability to have multiline titles in view columns and multiple lines per document in view rows. Be sparing in your use of these features, especially multiline titles. If you use multiline rows, be sure to check the Shrink Rows to Content check box and use colors in alternate rows. That makes the view easier to read.

Using Twisties in Rows

Always use twisties to indicate expandable rows. If you're migrating from Release 3 and you have formulas using @IsExpandable to show a + sign indicating that the row is expandable, get rid of the formula in the column and use twisties instead. This is a much more pleasing and useful interface.

Designing Forms

As in designing views, consistency is important when designing forms. Use fonts consistently and use a similar set of Action Bar buttons. Forms look much better when they have lots of white space; it's easier for the user to read than densely packed text, with fields scattered throughout the form. Make sure that your use of capitalization and punctuation is consistent. When using background colors to differentiate form types, be careful which ones you choose. Dark backgrounds make forms difficult to read; choosing fonts that contrast with the background is hard to do. Using graphical backgrounds on forms can look unprofessional, unless carefully chosen, and can slow the form down if the users have minimal hardware.

Using Text in Form Design

Be sparing in your use of special text effects. Figure 6.15 shows the special effects text styles introduced in 4.5—extruded, embossed, and shadowed. In order for the special effects to be effective, they are placed on a form with a gray background.

FIGURE 6.15

Special text effects work well against a gray background.

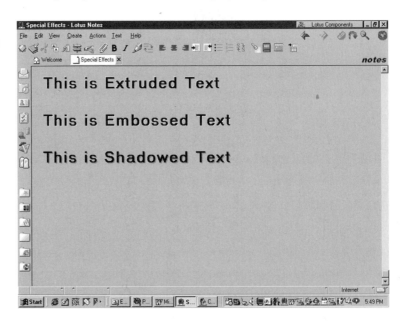

Special text effects also work in a layout region to give a 3D appearance to the form. This has been a popular look lately and can have a pleasing appearance work if used carefully. Special effects can also be used in a table with an appropriate graphic or background color. In any case, be judicious in your use of these text effects.

> **Caution**
>
> There are some issues that affect performance of a form. Layout regions can slow down a form and should be used sparingly. Hide-when conditions also slow down a form because they have to be calculated each time the form is opened or refreshed. Used carefully, Hide-when attributes can significantly enhance the form by selectively hiding form elements based on conditions. Done properly, they can make a form substantially easier to use by removing unnecessary fields from the user's view. This is becoming less of a factor today, with the availability of powerful and inexpensive PCs. If there are any factors that could slow the forms down, you should test them for performance with a workstation configuration that is commonly in use.

Table 6.4 suggests using one setting for field labels, Default Sans Serif 8, bold, and Default Sans Serif 8 plain for the fields themselves. The intent is to differentiate the contents of the fields from the text labels. This makes it easier for data entry because the form flows better visually and is easier to read when completed. In general, it's best to keep the amount of text in field labels down to the minimum required in order to clarify the field's contents. Data-entry operators don't want to read; they just want to enter data. Quickly! Anything you can do to speed up the process for them is appreciated. Lengthy text can be saved for field-level help. Consider this as a field label:

```
Please enter the name of the customer
```

This takes up unnecessary space on the form. With a lot of labels such as this one, the form becomes cluttered and difficult to work with. Here's an alternative; with this shortened field label, the preceding text is placed in the field help:

```
Customer Name
```

Using Tables in Form Design

It is best to use tables to help arrange fields on forms. Tables have certain advantages over a line of text. Hide-when formulas are applied to an entire paragraph (or line, if a carriage return is at the end). Therefore, you cannot conditionally hide different objects on the same line. With a table, each cell is treated as a paragraph, so each cell in a row can have different hide-when formulas. You can also use tables to present graphics in the same line as a text object and conditionally hide or show elements on the same row. With the use of tabbed tables, and tables within tables, you can more effectively present documents using significantly less screen real estate. Tables should be used to position fields and field labels on the form. For example, if you use three columns, the first column can contain the field labels, the second can be a narrow column separating the field label from the field, and the third column can contain the fields. The first column can be right-justified, and the third left-justified(see Figure 6.16).

Spacer column   Fields, left-justified

FIGURE 6.16

Using a table to position fields and field labels is a good design practice!

Field labels, right-justified

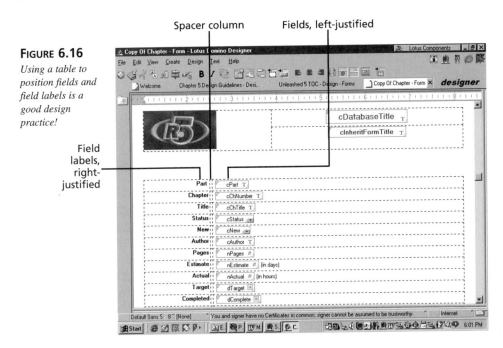

Tables can also be useful for identifying required fields, which presents something of a dilemma. Unfortunately, there is no feature similar to the keyword entry helper button that is native to the Domino Designer which indicates that a field is required. There are several choices if you want to mark required fields, which can be helpful to the data entry operators:

- Use some sort of color coding, such as black for nonrequired fields and red for required.
- Add text such as "REQ:" or "Required:" to the field help.
- Use a graphical object such as a checkmark or round bullet pasted next to the field label. In order to keep the graphical object from printing, add a second line containing the same fields and text, except without the graphical object. Add a hide-when clause to the first line that hides the line when the user prints, opens, or previews the document for reading. Add a hide-when clause to the second line that hides the line in edit mode.
- Place the field label, graphical object, and field in the cells of a table. You don't need to add second lines for printing because the graphical object can have a hide-when printing clause set just for it (because it is in a cell of its own).

None of the first several solutions are particularly attractive. Picking a color is difficult—and if the data entry operator is color blind, the first technique won't succeed. Both the second and third techniques listed are cumbersome to implement—and depending on the number of hide-when clauses, they might cause the form to perform poorly. Remember that large numbers of hide-when formulas can cause significant performance degradation. The fourth technique has gained popularity lately, especially for forms used on the web (although this works equally well for a Notes client). Essentially, this is a variant on the technique discussed above of using a separator column between the text label of a field and the field itself. Simply widen the separator column, and insert a graphic object in the rows next to required fields. You can then hide the graphic objects when printed, since they are in their own cell. You can see how effective a table is in controlling the presentation of objects to a client.

In Release 5, there are many new features added to tables, including tabs. Figure 6.17 shows the server document, which contains a large amount of data. In Release 4.x, even though the server document used collapsible sections, it was still quite lengthy. With the use of tabbed tables and tables within tables in R5, it fits into a single screen (depending on your monitor and screen resolution, of course). The construction of this form is worth digging into to learn some of the techniques discussed in this chapter and other chapters. The Server form has tabbed tables, collapsible sections, and hide-when clauses all working in concert to make data entry easier.

FIGURE 6.17

The R5 Server document uses tabbed tables elegantly.

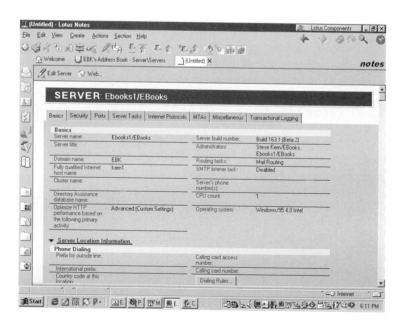

Designing Menus

Why discuss menu design in the Notes client? What menu? Well, design elements such as forms, views, and agents have a presence on the Notes menus that as a designer you need to consider. When creating these design elements, you can optionally place them on the menu. Forms appear on the Create menu and views appear on the View menu. Agents are displayed on the Action menu along with Form and View Actions. The menus can display up to nine items before Notes displays an "Other…" prompt. Both agents and forms display on the menu by default; views do not. The reason views do not display on the menu is simple; they show up in the navigation pane, so there isn't any reason to add clutter to the menu. Consider naming views in the same way you do a menu.

> **Caution**
>
> Designers should avoid the "Other…" menu selection at all costs. It is simple to do. Collect similar forms and views into cascaded menus or view folders. Keep these collections to a small number, perhaps four or five.

There is a reason why telephone numbers have seven digits. Studies show that people can remember seven numbers very easily. It is far more difficult to remember a nine-digit number than a seven-digit number. Similarly, presenting too many elements to users makes it more difficult for them to work. Collecting similar elements into cascaded menus and limiting the number of elements within a grouping will make your application much more useable.

Designing for the Web

Web surfers have grown to expect a lot of snappy design and flashy graphics from Web pages. Form design can be handled by application designers—but unless you're also good at designing graphics, consider having the graphics professionally designed. You can also purchase any one of a number of libraries of graphic designs that you can use or customize for your web site. If you wish to design graphics on your own, there are a number of good graphics packages available, including Paint Shop Pro (a personal favorite) and Corel Draw.

Although in R5, the feature sets available for web and Notes clients are getting closer, many features available to the Notes client work still aren't available to a web client. For example, Web browsers can't display the Notes client menu, so designers have to work around this limitation. One technique is to use Action Bar buttons or hotspots. Most Web sites use a consistent set of hotlinks from page to page; you can enforce this consistency by creating a page containing common links. The page can then be used in a frame within a frameset. A set of common links can also be included in a subform, and the subform can be conditionally added to a form when a document rendered by the form is accessed by a web client.

A Welcome Addition!

One of the most significant improvements in Release 5 is the extensive support for pages and Framesets. Framesets function equally well for both web and Notes clients. Pages are covered in Chapter 14, "Using the Page Designer," and Framesets are discussed in Chapter 31, "Adding Framesets to Your Applications."

As discussed above in the section on using tables in forms, you can and should use tables on forms to enforce a consistent display of objects and fields on the Web. All of the nice formatting that you can apply to a form without tables, using tabs, spaces and interline settings will disappear when viewed with a web client.

Simply putting a field on a form and displaying it on the Web doesn't always work well. The field displays at a default width, which might not be adequate for the length of the data item being entered. Of course, the field scrolls, but that's not desirable. If embedded HTML is on forms, hide it from Notes clients using Pass-Thru HTML. Hide Notes features that are not applicable to the Web from Web clients. You can accomplish this by clicking the appropriate check boxes on the Hide-when tab of the Text Properties Box. This is discussed in Chapter 9, "Review of Basic Forms Design."

Before embedding graphics in forms, consider the user. Keep the files fairly small so the download times are fast. Nobody likes to wait several minutes for a Web page to load. You can improve performance by keeping calculations in fields to a minimum and by either restricting or not using shared fields.

In and of themselves, documents do not refresh on the Web, although there are some techniques which can make them appear to do so. HTML is a static presentation language. This prevents the use of cascaded keyword lookups, unfortunately. By *cascaded lookups,* I mean that the second keyword lookup is dependent on the value in the first. Keyword fields have an option, "Refresh fields on keyword change," which, when checked, forces a refresh. When a selection is made in the first keyword field, after refreshing it is available as a key in the second keyword lookup. When you use `@DbLookup()`, the second keyword field formula can return a list matching the value of the first. This also prevents refreshing hide-when formulas conditionally. You can get around this limitation by using JavaScript.

Summary

One of the most important elements in application design is consistency, especially as it relates to the design of the UI. At the same time, try to design the form as attractively as possible! Your payoff for this effort is increased user satisfaction, ease of use, and ultimately, user productivity.

You have also seen ways in which you, the designer, can be consistent when writing the code for the application itself, and this is equally important. Whether you choose to use the naming conventions presented in this chapter or use your own is not important. What is important is picking a convention and sticking to it. Similarly, documenting the application's code thoroughly is important for future maintenance.

CHAPTER 7

The Release 5 Object Store

by Debbie Lynd

IN THIS CHAPTER

Databases are the primary units of storage in Domino. In simple terms, a Domino database is a collection of unrelated documents stored in a file, usually with the NSF extension (which stands for *Notes Storage Facility*). You can store a Domino database file on a server or on a local hard disk (or both). This chapter is dedicated to furthering your understanding of Domino databases.

Defining a Domino Database

A Domino database is not like a relational database; it is an unstructured, or at best a semistructured, database. Relational databases, on the other hand, are structured. In relational databases, a table is defined by its fields, and each field is structured (with the exception of Memo fields, which are similar to Domino rich-text fields). For example, you might define a customer table in FoxPro as shown in Table 7.1.

TABLE 7.1   Relational Database Table Structure

Field Name	Field Type	Width	Description
cId	Character	9	Internal ID
cCustomer	Character	40	Customer name
cAddr1	Character	40	Address 1
cAddr2	Character	40	Address 2
cCity	Character	25	City
cState	Character	2	State
cZip	Character	10	Zip or postal code
nLimit	Numeric	10,2	Purchasing credit limit

This example of a structured data table has a definable disk presence. The record size is the sum of bytes in the Width column plus 1. In this example, there are eight fields and the record size is 177; so, if you input 100,000 records, the size of the resulting database is 17,700,000 bytes, or roughly 18MB. Additional disk space is consumed by the file header, which has to be added to the total bytes from the records to get the total file size. The point here is that the database is structured, definable, and quantifiable. Each record contains all the fields in the table definition, regardless of whether there is any data present in the fields.

On the other hand, it is difficult to predict the ultimate size of a Domino database, even if you know the number of documents. Databases are collections of documents; documents contain fields, which are the basic units of information in Notes, just as they are the basic units of information in the database described in Table 7.1. However, when you pick a field type in Domino, you don't specify the width. For `cCustomer`, simply choose `Text` as the field type; no option for width exists. A user can type a couple of words or a couple of paragraphs into that field. Therefore, record size cannot be defined in Notes as it is in Table 7.1.

Data Elements in Domino Are Known as Items

Technically speaking, data elements in a Domino database are called *items*; the term *fields* refers to the objects on a form that enable you to create and modify items. However, I generally refer to *fields* rather than *items* to avoid confusion.

Domino doesn't necessarily add disk space when you add a document. If Domino determines that more disk space is needed, it adds space based on an internal algorithm that can accommodate several new documents. When documents are deleted, Domino leaves a deletion stub, but doesn't immediately release the disk space. These document stubs are important in that they are used to properly replicate the deletions to any other replica copies of the database that exist. Then, after a defined period of time (90 days by default), the document stub is deleted. The space left over by the deletion of the document or the deletion stub is referred to as *whitespace*. The whitespace can be reused by documents, or compacting the database can remove the whitespace (which is covered in the "Working with Database Properties" section later in this chapter). Again, the amount of disk space for a given number of documents cannot be accurately calculated.

To further complicate matters, there is no fixed definition of a document like there is a fixed definition of a record in a relational database table. Therefore, different documents can and do have different fields, even though they might all have been created and edited with the same form. You can create fields in a document based on conditions in the underlying form. You can examine the fields in a document by right-clicking the document and choosing Document Properties from the menu. Choose the Fields tab, and you can scroll through the list of fields as shown in Figure 7.1.

FIGURE 7.1

The Fields tab in the Document Properties dialog box provides a window to the field information for each item in a document.

Understanding the Database Structure

Now that I've explained the "record" aspect or non-aspect of a Domino database, I will explore the structure of the NSF file. As mentioned earlier, Domino databases store unstructured data in a semistructured way. Each database is identified by its filename and Replica ID. The Replica ID is unique in each database that is created and is used to identify each replica or identical copy on multiple servers or workstations for the purpose of synchronizing the data. This means that when synchronization occurs through replication, the database Replica IDs are compared before replication occurs. It also means that a replica of a database does not need to be in the same path or have the same filename on each server. However, as a developer, it is not a good practice to change the filename or path for a database. It always pays to be consistent because the path might be hard coded into a formula or script.

When developing an application, there are two ways to reference a database. One way is to reference a database by its filename. The other is to reference it by its Replica ID. If the database is referenced by filename, the reference must also contain the appropriate path, which means that you must store the file in the same place on each server. This is actually better than referencing the Replica ID programmatically; the filename is stored within the file system of the computer as opposed to the Replica ID that is stored inside the database, which is inside the file system which is inside the computer. So what, you ask? Well, if I reference the Replica ID, that means the program must look in each database within the file system to find the ID of the appropriate database, as opposed to finding the filename in the file system. The Replica ID for a database can been seen in the database properties as in Figure 7.2.

FIGURE 7.2

The Replica ID of a database is displayed in the Database Properties dialog box.

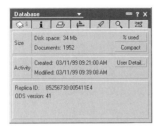

If you were able to peel the wrapper off a Domino database, what you would find inside instead of records would be additional wrappers. Each of these wrappers would, in turn, contain objects or groups of objects, such as a form or a view or a document. In any case, each of the wrappers in the database is considered a note and is the unit of storage assigned to each record in the database.

All types of information can be stored in a note. Unlike relational database systems where there are separate files for tables and programs, Domino stores all the data and all the programming and design elements for a database in one NSF file. This is a self-contained unit that is then very easy to distribute through the replication process.

So, what then is in a Note? The ACL of a database is stored in a Note; each Form created in a database is stored in a note; each view is a note; and so on. Some Notes have only one instance per database, whereas others might have multiple instances. As an example, the ACL note has only one instance, whereas there can and usually are multiple form notes in a database. Every form that is created by a designer is stored as a separate note, whereas there is only one ACL for a database.

Notes are not related to each other in any way, although the "wrapper" of a note does provide a label that defines its contents as being that of a form, view, document, and so on. In other words, Domino databases are not relational databases because not all the notes are related to each other in any way, although relationships can be created programmatically. The identifying component of each Note is the universal ID, also known as the UNID. You can see what a note ID looks like by opening the properties for the design element or document as shown in Figure 7.3.

FIGURE 7.3

Each note is identified by a document UNID.

The most recognizable types of notes that are stored in the database are listed in
Table 7.2.

TABLE 7.2 Note Types

Note Type	Description
Design	Collection of all forms, views, pages, and so on.
Info	This is the database help About Database document.
Icon	The database icon.
Help	The Help – Using Database document.
ACL	The access control list for the database.
Page	Displays information other than fields. The information can be an embedded element, text, graphics, and hotspots.
Form	Used to enter information into a document and to display a document, a form provides a template for the layout of the user interface you will provide for data input and viewing data.
View	Contains a list of documents programmatically selected to display specific information in a columnar format.
Folder	Contains a list of documents selected by the user to display specific information in a columnar format.
Outline	A method for providing a navigational structure to an application, through outline entries which can represent views, documents, other databases, and pages.
Document	A data note or record.
Item	A field Note.
Outline	A note that contains the outline information for providing navigation of the database.
Navigator	Contains an imagemap for navigational purposes.
Frameset	A set of frames or display areas, used to display other design elements and documents, whose contents are changed programmatically.
Agent	A set of instructions or program that performs specific actions in your application based on a triggered event.
Shared Images	A storage facility for image files (GIF, JPEG, BMP) that will be reused in other design elements.
Shared Applets	A storage facility for Java applets that will be reused in multiple places within the database.
Subforms	A portion of a form that can be embedded in multiple forms within a database.
Shared Fields	Field definitions that can be reused in multiple forms and subforms.

Note Type	Description
Script Libraries	Storage facility for LotusScript and Java that will be reused in multiple places within the database.
Shared Actions	Programmable hotspots that appear at the top of a view or form that can be reused in multiple views or forms.
Database Script	Programmable events available at the database level.

From Table 7.2, you can see that almost everything can be considered a Note. How does this affect you as a developer who is looking to provide an application that is optimized for performance? Well, consider the following. I create a shared field which I then use in a subform. Then say that I also use this subform within a form. The net effect of embedding these separate elements within each other is that it will take longer for the form to open than it would if I did not use a shared field within a subform within a form. This is due to the fact that in order to open the form, the subform must be found within the database, based on its note ID as specified in the form. Not only that, but in order to complete loading the subform, the shared field must be found with the database based on its note ID as specified in the subform. Does this mean that you shouldn't use shared objects? Not at all! What it does mean, however, is that you should be cautious of the number of shared elements you place in a form, as well as the levels at which you place the shared elements. The more shared objects, the longer it will take to open the document.

Consider the Number of Shared Elements Applied to a Form

When using shared elements in a form, do not apply too many to the same form because it slows the time it takes to open the form.

So if the database contains a Note for everything that I create, what is in that Note? You can actually view some of that information by looking at the document properties for any document or design element that you have in the database. If I look at the document properties of a form, such as the one shown in Figure 7.4, there are items in the Note that define the contents of the note.

As a developer, you are used to referring to items each time you access the data contained in a field because a field is referred to as an item. This is actually true for all the information stored in a Note. If you look at the Design Document Properties box shown in Figure 7.5, you will see that each of the items in the fields list contain different types of information that described the view and its contents. These are all considered items within the view note.

FIGURE 7.4

In the Design Document Properties box all the items within the form note are displayed.

FIGURE 7.5

In the Design Document Properties box, all the items within the view note are displayed.

Creating a Database

Creating a database in Domino is a fairly simple task. Databases can be created from scratch, from templates, or by copying of another database. The process of creating a database is essentially the same regardless of the method that you choose. By choosing File, Database, New from the menu options at the top of the Notes client or the Domino Designer client, you are presented with the screen displayed in Figure 7.6. You begin by choosing a location for the database, either on your local workstation or on a server. Following that, you assign a name and a title to the database. Next to the filename is a folder icon which enables you to pick the folder or directory in which the database will be stored. The rest of the choices are optional, some of which I'll cover in this section (the Advanced button will be covered later in this chapter).

FIGURE 7.6

When creating a new database, the database proper-ties are set in the New Database dialog box.

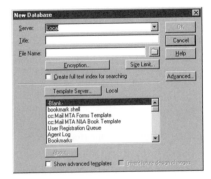

Securing a Local Database Through Encryption

The option for encryption is included to provide security for databases stored on local workstations, particularly laptop computers. The encryption is based on the user ID of the current user or a user ID that you choose. The levels of encryption to apply are simple, medium, or strong encryption, as shown in Figure 7.7. The level chosen affects database access speed, as well as whether the database can be compressed using a compression tool. With simple encryption, access to the database is fast, and the database can be compressed. However, the capability to break the encryption is far easier than with medium or strong encryption. Medium encryption does not allow compression but still provides fast database access. This is the preferred level of encryption for local databases because it provides a harder-to-break code. Strong encryption does not allow compression and is slower to access. This is the hardest code to break, but due to the slower access, it should only be used on databases where the tightest security is required.

FIGURE 7.7

Encryption for databases that will be stored on a laptop can be set from the Local Encryption dialog box.

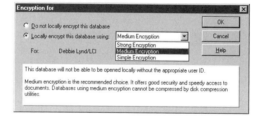

Restricting the Size of the Database

There really is no way to limit the size of a Release 5 database. The size limit property pertains only to databases that have a Release 4 or lower On Disk Structure or (ODS), as shown in Figure 7.8.

FIGURE 7.8

The database size restriction is no longer used in Release 5.

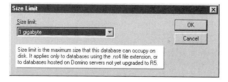

Release 4 databases have a size limitation of 4GB; the default size of a Release 4 database is 1GB. The Release 5 ODS does not impose database size restrictions. If you create a database with an NS4 extension, that database has a Release 4 ODS and can have the size restriction set.

Using Templates

A *template* is a special design copy of a Domino database. Press Ctrl+N or choose File, Database, New from the menu at the top of the Notes client or Domino Designer client. A list box at the bottom of the New Database dialog box contains a list of templates. To see advanced templates, click Show Advanced Templates. To change to another server or a local drive, click the Template Server button.

From the list of templates, you can choose a template to use for the design of your new database. A listing of the templates provided in Release 5 is included in Chapter 35, "Tracking Design Changes and Using Templates." While creating a new database, you can see information describing the purpose of the template by clicking the template name in the list provided within the New Database dialog box and then clicking the About button. This shows the About document for the database as long as one has been provided.

Template files are saved with an extension of .NTF (for *Notes Template Facility*), whereas databases are saved (usually) with the extension .NSF (for *Notes Storage Facility*).

Figure 7.8 shows the New Database dialog box with a template chosen.

To create a Project Discussion database from the Discussion template supplied with Lotus Notes, follow these steps:

1. Choose File, Database, New from the menu bar of the Notes client or the Domino Designer client.
2. In the Server drop-down list, leave Local selected.
3. Enter the title, `Notes Project Discussion`.
4. Enter the filename, `ProjDisc.nsf`, or accept the default. If you type the title first, Notes automatically fills in the filename.
5. Choose the Discussion(R5) template.
6. Click the About button to read a description of the purpose of the database contained in the database's About document, as shown in Figure 7.9.
7. To change the design, uncheck Inherit Future Design Changes. Otherwise, leave it checked.
8. Finally, click the OK button to save your new database.

Templates are special design copies of a database. They do more than provide a basis for your database's design; you can use templates to update the design of the database and propagate design changes throughout your organization.

FIGURE 7.9

The New Database dialog box with the Discussion template chosen. The About button is at the bottom of the window and is selected to show a description of the database and its purpose.

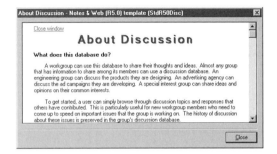

7

THE RELEASE 5
OBJECT STORE

> ## The Design Task Updates the Design of a Database Based on Its Templates Nightly on the Server
>
> If the template for the database exists on the server (all the templates supplied by Notes do by default), a process called Design, which runs on the server, ensures that the design of your databases are kept current. The Design task runs at 1 a.m. by default. If you leave Inherit Future Design Changes checked and if the database is on the server, this process runs on the database every day. If you try to change the design of the database instead of the template, you will be warned that your changes will be overwritten.

You should create a new database on a local hard drive and then create a replica copy on the server when you are ready to test the database. This reduces network traffic and conserves server resources. It is also good to have multiple replica copies of databases for backup. Most of the examples given here show Local as the choice for location of the database. This is the default.

You must have sufficient rights to create either a database or a replica on the server. Your Domino administrator specifies who has these rights in the server document in the Domino Directory. In the Restrictions section of the Server document, you must be either in the Create New Databases field or in a group listed in that field before you can create a new database on the server. Similarly, you must be in the Create Replica Databases field or in a group in that field to create a replica on the server. Typically, application designers in an organization belong to a group that is placed in both of these fields. If you have trouble creating databases on your server, check with your Domino administrator.

If you create copies or replica copies of databases, you must be certain that you have sufficient access privileges to the database you want to copy.

Designers often find it useful to assign roles to groups in the ACL of a database. These roles can be used to further refine the ACL; access to design elements can be restricted using roles. Roles are discussed in Chapter 8, "The Integrated Development Environment."

For these and other reasons, I strongly encourage you to familiarize yourself with system administration. It will help you immensely with application design. This book is not about system administration, but good books are available. Also a database called Domino Administration Help (the filename is Helpadmn.nsf) comes with Domino and is an excellent place to start. If it is not on your local drive, it should be on your server in the \Help subdirectory.

Chapter 33, "Security and Domino Applications," discusses security as it pertains to deploying an application.

Making a Database Copy

Sometimes you can't find a template that suits you, but you can find a database that is exactly what you need. You can easily copy the design elements to a new database by following the procedure outlined here:

1. Click the database icon you want to copy. You don't need to open the database.
2. Choose File, Database, New Copy from the menu bar at the top of the Notes client or Domino Designer client. You will see a dialog box similar to the one shown in Figure 7.10.
3. Leave the Server drop-down list Local.
4. Change the title and filename, and click Database Design Only.
5. Click OK to save your new database.

FIGURE 7.10

The original database name is in quotes in the window title of the Copy Database dialog box.

Now you have a new database that is a completely functional design copy of the original database.

Creating a Replica Copy

Despite the fact that this book is about application design, which of course involves creating new databases, in order to understand this section, you need to understand a special type of database copy called a *replica copy*. Replication is at the very heart of Domino. It is the process by which information is exchanged between servers and users to synchronize the data between replica copies of databases. Each database that is created contains a unique database identifier called the Replica ID. The Replica ID determines whether a database on one server should replicate or be synchronized with a database on another server. This capability is one fundamental aspect of Domino that sets it apart from other database systems. The approach has been so successful that other companies are now adding this feature to their systems.

Domino is a true distributed client/server application. Replica copies of databases can exist on multiple servers and on multiple workstations. There can be replicas of the same database on the same computer. Domino identifies replicas by a Replica ID that is a part of the Domino database file. You can see the Replica ID for a database by clicking the database icon and then choosing File, Database, Properties from the menu, or right-clicking the icon and choosing Database Properties from the menu as discussed earlier in this chapter.

As I mentioned in the previous section, "Making a Database Copy," the new database contains different data and possibly different design changes than the original. It is important that the database be created as a new copy and not a replica copy of the database because a replica copy would contain the same Replica ID as the original. However, because it is not a replica copy, a new Replica ID would be assigned to the database on creation. If the new database had been created as a replica copy, the replication task would cause the two replica copies to be synchronized, meaning that all design changes and documents in the new replica copy would end up in the original database, and vice versa.

Note

Remember that you must have sufficient access privileges to the database to create a replica copy of a server database.

To create a replica copy, follow these steps:

1. Click the database icon from which you want to create a replica copy. You don't have to open it; just click it once.

2. Choose File, Replication, New Replica from the menu.

3. The New Replica dialog box shown in Figure 7.11 is displayed.

FIGURE 7.11

The New Replica dialog box automatically fills in the Local in the Server drop-down list and supplies the database title and filename.

4. Leave Local selected and click the Immediately radio button.

5. You can leave the title and filename as they are (or change them if you want to).

6. Unless you need to change the ACL and know what you are doing, leave Copy Access Control List checked.

7. Click OK.

Use Care in Creating New Filenames

Don't inadvertently overwrite another database when you create a database replica. In particular, if you create a local replica of the Domino Directory, the default filename supplied is Names.nsf. This is also the filename of your personal address book; if you accept the default, you will lose your personal address book! Your Notes client will no longer function properly, and you will have to reinstall Notes. Any person documents you might have stored, any groups you've created, and the location documents in your personal address book will all be lost!

Now that a replica is on your local hard drive, you can replicate with the server, either on demand or on a schedule. Normally, data entry operators work on local copies and have a replication schedule set up. Scheduled replication takes place in the background, with little or no impact on performance.

Designing a Database on a Workstation

Working on a local replica is also a convenient way to work on application design. For reasons outlined earlier, I almost always work on a local replica when I design or change designs. I can then test my work locally, without affecting the server copy of the database. When I'm satisfied with the design, I replicate the changes to the server. Then, I can test the security aspects of my application. I do not normally use scheduled replication on my workstation; otherwise, untested design features might make it to the server copy of the database.

Working with Database Properties

Each database that is created contains properties unique to that database. The Database Properties settings enable you to customize the behavior and performance of the database. They also provide a window into statistics about the database and who is accessing the database, as well as the size and general health of the database.

Database Basics Tab

The Basics tab contains three sections. The first section displays the initial information about the database that was entered when the database was first created and additional information that you can change as indicated in Figure 7.12.

FIGURE 7.12

The title of the database can be modified from the Basics tab of the Database Properties dialog box.

When a database is first created, it is given a filename and a title, both of which are shown in the Basics tab. The title can be changed here, but the filename can't because that is part of the file system, not Notes. The database type can also be set here. Various types of databases can be created, as shown in Table 7.3.

TABLE 7.3 Database Types

Type	*Description*
Standard	The database type for most applications and the default for all new databases that are created.
Library	The Database Library Template is of the Library database type. A database library lists published databases for users to review and add to their workspace. By setting a database with the type Library, you can then publish databases to the library by choosing the database you want to publish and then choosing File, Database, Publish from the menu.
Personal Journal	This database type can be used by a Mail client or a full Notes client and is intended for personal use.
Address Book	The Address Book database type is reserved for the various types of address book templates available in R5.
Light Address Book	The Directory Catalog is based on the Light Address Book, which is an address book with fewer design elements.
Portfolio	The portfolio database template was new in Release 4 and provided a single point of entry into often-used databases for a user.
IMAP Server Proxy	Defines to the server the database type for an IMAP server proxy.
News Server Proxy	Defines to the servers the database type for an NNTP proxy server.
Subscriptions	This is the Headlines database that is part of the R5 interface and provides a way to log subscriptions to databases.
	Subscription databases cannot be replicated.
Mailbox	Identifies a mail database type.

The checkboxes at the bottom of the Basics tab are switches that control various settings. These settings include whether background agents can be enabled from a workstation for this database, when images are loaded, whether JavaScript should be used when generating the page for viewing over the Web, and whether this database requires an SSL connection for access. Another setting determines whether a document can be stored with the associated form embedded in that document. This is used when mailing a document to a Notes user that does not have the form to display the document in the Mail template.

The Settings section of the Basics tab provides access to the replication settings and history of a database, as well as its archive and encryption settings. The Archive settings are new to R5. Archiving was available for mail, discussion, and document library databases in Release 4, and that has now been extended to include all databases.

Archive Settings

The Archive option makes it easy to create and maintain time-based archives of the data that are no longer needed on a day-to-day basis. The basic archive settings are shown in Figure 7.13.

FIGURE 7.13

All databases can now be set up for archiving through the Archive Settings dialog box.

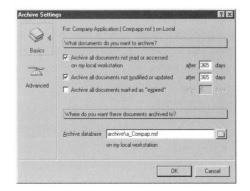

From the Basics screen, the first determination is which documents should be archived. This is time-based, and the options are those documents not read or accessed in the specified timeframe, documents not modified or updated with the specified timeframe, and expired documents. If you are archiving documents that have not been read or accessed, you must also set the Maintain Last Accessed Database property for the Advanced tab to log the document read activity. Expired documents are marked using the Mark/Unmark Document as Expired agent that can be found in the document library or discussion database templates. By including the functionality to mark a document as expired, you are placing the removal of documents through expiry into the hands of the users.

The next step is to determine where the document archive database will be stored and the name that will be given to the file. The folder icon next to the filename is used to pick a folder or directory to store it in. By default, the archive will be stored locally; to store it on a server, you have to choose the Advanced button. This changes the screen options as shown in Figure 7.14. From the Advanced screen, you can choose whether to archive automatically from the server or manually from the local workstation. You can also set whether to delete documents that have responses. If this is set to not delete, you avoid leaving orphaned response documents. You can also set whether to delete the documents without archiving them.

> **Note**
>
> Archiving expired documents can be done on any database. Simply copy the Mark/Unmark Document as Expired agent from the discussion template and add an action to the form or view to run the agent.

FIGURE 7.14

The Advance Archive properties provide settings for not only archiving but automatically deleting documents based on the selected settings.

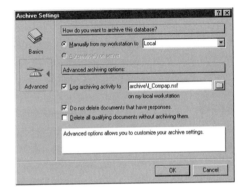

Encryption Settings

The encryption settings are the same as shown in the section "Creating a New Database," earlier in the chapter.

Replication Settings

When designing Domino applications, you need to understand the process of replication to take full advantage of the capabilities of Domino. Typically, mobile and remote users work on replicas of a database on their workstations—adding, updating, and deleting information. When users replicate with their server, their information and the server's information is synchronized. Their server can also replicate with other servers in their organization and with servers outside their organization, perhaps with a customer or a vendor. For example, information the user enters on her workstation might eventually end up at a vendor's server.

The process of replication provides both the sender and the receiver with the same data when completed. Therefore, if a user modifies a document in the database on his workstation and another user modifies the same document in the database on the server, when replication occurs, the two documents are compared for changes. If a setting in the Form that created the document states that changes should be merged, both changes are recorded in the updated document. However, if this has not been set, a replication or save conflict would occur and both documents would be saved to the database with a warning and someone would have to manually resolve the problem.

On a workstation, replication can take place according to a predefined schedule that the user or administrator sets. However, this is usually not done because it would require that the computer be turned on and access to the server be available at the predefined time, which is not always possible. Instead, a user usually invokes manual replication at his discretion. Replication between servers is scheduled by a connection document in the Domino Directory. In either case, you can control which documents are replicated by a replication formula. You can use a replication formula to reduce the number of documents replicated to a particular user, thus enabling the user to see information only from his customers, for example. A replication formula might also be set up between servers, such as sending only East Coast sales leads from the headquarters server to the East Coast server. Understanding this process helps you build better applications.

The space saving replication settings are displayed in Figure 7.15. The first checkbox on this screen is not really a replication setting at all, but one that helps to determine how document deletions are controlled. The setting Remove Documents Not Modified in the Last has two meanings. If the box is checked, this number, 90 days by default, controls when a document that has not been changed in any way is deleted from the database. So for instance, if the box is checked and a document has not been modified for 90 days, that document would be deleted from the database. When the document is deleted, it leaves a deletion stub in its place. The deletion stub is an identifier of the original document used to ensure that the document gets deleted on each replica copy of the database.

The second meaning for this entry is the number of days before the deletion stub is purged from the database. This number is established by dividing the number in the Remove Documents Not Modified in the Last field by 3. For example if I use the default of 90 for the number of days to delete documents, the purge interval would be 30 days.

Therefore, if a document gets deleted today because it is not modified in the last 90 days, that document's deletion stub would then remain in the database for another 30 days before it is purged.

The purge interval is independent of the checkbox for this option and is always one-third the number in the field. So even if I am not checking the box for automatic deletion, any document deleted by a user or through an agent has its deletion stub removed based on the number in that field.

This is important to remember because the purge interval, if set too low, could cause a document to not be deleted in all the replica copies. For example, if I set the number of days for deletion to 3, the purge interval would be one day. Now, if replication of the deletion stub of a document does not occur within that one-day timeframe, the document would not be deleted in the other replica copies.

FIGURE 7.15

Automatic dele-tion of documents can be set in the Space Savers pane of the Replication Settings.

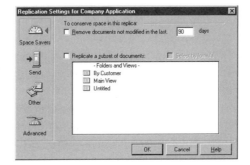

The second setting to replicate a subset of documents replicates a selected set of documents, instead of replicating the entire database. You can choose to replicate based on the contents of a view, folder, or based on a formula. This is good for laptop users who need to see only a subset of the documents in a database when they are on the road. However, this is not to be used as a security measure to guard against a user getting all the data in the database. The user can always change this formula or deselect the selection criteria and get all the documents.

The Send option is displayed in Figure 7.16 and determines three things. The first setting, Do Not Send Deletions Made in This Replica to Other Replicas, determines whether deleted documents are replicated to other replicas. This is useful in very few instances, which include when you want each replica to maintain only those documents that seem important to the users of that replica.

FIGURE 7.16

The Send options for Replication provides the set-tings for limiting what is replicated.

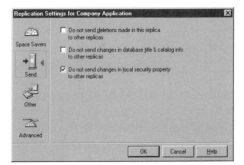

The second checkbox determines whether a change to the title of a database or the catalog information, such as categories, is replicated. This is turned off by default and is usually not replicated. The final checkbox determines whether the Local Encryption properties are replicated. This is off by default and should rarely be used. Local Encryption is used only when a mobile user carries a sensitive database replica on his laptop and wants to ensure that it cannot be read by an unauthorized user.

The Other option displays additional settings for replication as shown in Figure 7.17. Temporarily disabling replication can be useful if there is a problem with replication and someone needs to look into the matter. Scheduling the priority is up to the administrator because he will determine how replication is scheduled. The saved or modified date is automatically incremented and needs to be changed only if databases fall out of synch and a complete replication needs to take place. Again, this is usually something the administrator would do. The CD-ROM publishing date is useful for organizations that distribute a database on CD-ROM for installation on a server or users workstation. The date makes it faster to do the first replication with the company because it scans only for new and modified documents that occur after that date.

FIGURE 7.17

The Other options of the Replication Settings is where replication can be disabled on a specific replica copy of a database.

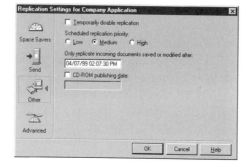

The Advanced tab of the replication settings for a database contains refinements to what can be replicated. Usually, the default settings are sufficient; however, in cases where restricted information should be sent, the options here make it possible to determine what gets sent to whom as indicated in Figure 7.18.

FIGURE 7.18

Further restrictions of replication can be set in the Advanced pane of the Replication Settings dialog box.

Info Tab

The Info tab displays information about the database usage and size, the Replica ID, and the version of the On Disk Structure of the database as indicated in Figure 7.19.

FIGURE 7.19

The Info tab of a database provides information about the Replica ID of a database and the version of the ODS.

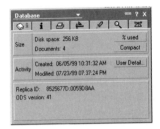

Size

The size section provides data about the physical size of the database file, as well as the number of documents in the database and the percentage of space used in the file. The amount of space used helps determine whether compacting the database is in order. If there is more than 10% free space, it is generally a good idea to compact the database in order to remove the free space and cause the database to operate more efficiently. This is particularly true if the free space is being overwritten, which is the default. If there is free space, Domino will try to reuse that space before writing to new space. This can cause the writing of documents to disk to take longer than it would if all free space were recovered.

The Compact button in this section enables you to manually run the compact utility to clean up the free space. However, your administrator should have Compact set to run from the server on a regular basis to ensure that databases maintain their efficiency.

Activity

The activity section displays information about the dates the database was created and last modified. It also logs activity for all users who have accessed the file. The User Detail button opens a dialog box in which the settings for logging this information is found, as well as the list of people and servers that have accessed the database, as shown in Figure 7.20.

Replica ID

As indicated earlier, the Replica ID is available from the Info tab and provides a good reference when looking at two copies of a database to determine whether they are replicas or copies.

FIGURE 7.20

Reviewing User Activity is helpful when trying to determine how much a database is being used.

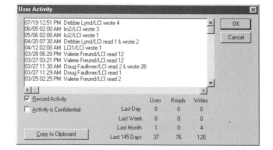

ODS Version

This information is new in the Info tab of the Database Properties dialog box. It provides a visual cue as to the version of a database. If it is a Release 5 ODS, the number displayed is 41. Test build 1 of Release 5 has an ODS of 32, and the Beta Preview has an ODS of 36. The version number determines whether the Notes client can access the database locally. For instance, if an R4 client has an R5 database on its hard drive, it will not be able to access that database because R4 cannot read the R5 ODS. However, if that same database is on an R5 server, the R4 client can access it because the server will do the translation. The ODS versions are shown in Table 7.4.

TABLE 7.4 Version Numbers

Notes Release	ODS Number
1.x	16
2.x	16
3.x	17
4.x	20 or less
5.x	41 or less

Printing Tab

The Printing tab sets the default header and footer information for printing in the database. This property is very rarely used and will probably not be used at all in Release 5 because it has little flexibility in determining what can be placed in these areas. Compared this to Headers and Footers in Forms design that enables you to designate an area for a header that can then contain graphics and the like.

Design Tab

The Design tab controls the properties for template information and availability of a database from a database catalog or the File Database Open dialog box. Database Templates are described in detail in Chapter 35. The options for the Design tab are shown in Figure 7.21. The option Do Not Mark Modified Documents as Unread is useful if you are tracking unread marks but do not want to refresh the marks if the document changes. This can affect performance, so use it with caution.

FIGURE 7.21

The Design tab of the Database Properties dialog box.

Multi database indexing is up to the administrator to invoke because it requires additional steps to be taken. The Multilingual Database option is described in detail in Chapter 36, "Using Domino Global Workbench 5.0."

Launch Tab

The Launch tab is where you get to determine what the user sees when she first opens the database. When Notes was in its infancy, there were no options for what was displayed when opening a database. You were presented with the About document when the database was opened for the first time, and the last view you were accessing when you closed the database on subsequent returns to the database. In Release 4, you were able to choose from many more options than in previous versions, such as opening to a Navigator window. Now in Release 5, the options have been expanded to include opening a frameset. This is the best option yet, and provides a way to manipulate what the user can access by placing only those design elements you want them to see in the frames within a frameset. The full set of options and their descriptions are in Table 7.5.

TABLE 7.5   Launch Options

Option	Description
Restore as Last Viewed by User	This is the default
Open About Database Document	Useful if there are navigational buttons or specific instructions provided on this document that users should see every time they open the database.
Open Designated Frameset	To me, this is the best option because it enables me to creatively place what I want the users to see in multiple frames on the screen. Navigation in one frame, a default view or page in another, and possibly even a third frame with other information.
Open Designated Navigator	A Release 4 addition that will probably not be used much with the advent of pages and outlines in R5. Navigators have always been difficult to work with and unpredictable in appearance.
Open Designated Navigator in Its Own Window	Opens a navigator or imagemap as the full screen.
Launch First Attachment in About Database	If an attachment is placed in an About Document and this option is chosen, the attachment is launched when the database is opened.
Launch First Doclink in About Database	If a doclink is placed in an About Document and this option is chosen, the doclink is launched when the database is opened.

Two checkboxes under the Launch tab are useful. The first, Show About Database Document if Modified is useful for providing new instructional information to the users because it will only show to a user when it is modified.

The second, Show About Database Document when Database Is Opened for the First Time is on by default and is helpful to a new user in that, if the designer has included instructional information here, it is displayed to the user prior to him or her actually entering the database. If the designer does not include information in this document, a blank screen appears, which is not very helpful!

Full-Text Tab

Indexing a database to provide search capabilities is a great feature. However, the index can take a considerable amount of space, and therefore, take care to determine which databases really need a full-text index. When an index is created, it is, by default, automatically kept up-to-date as documents are added. However, the indexing options provide other settings for when updating should occur, as shown in Figure 7.22.

FIGURE 7.22

Manually updating the Full-Text Index can be done from the Indexing tab of the Database Properties.

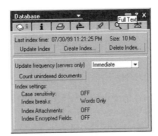

Creating a full-text index provides options for indexing attachments and creating case-sensitive indexes, as shown in Figure 7.23.

FIGURE 7.23

A database index can be created to include the indexing of attachments.

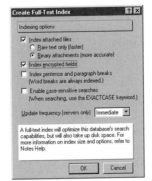

Advanced Tab

The Advanced tab of the database properties is by far the most interesting in that it gives you the ability to control settings that affect performance. These settings are shown in Figure 7.24. Each setting and its impact on performance is discussed in this section.

Don't Maintain Unread Marks

By default, unread marks are maintained for each person accessing a database. You, as the developer, might not use the unread marks in your views, which means this is then an unnecessary task. By removing the unread marks from the database, performance is enhanced by not having to check and store that information for each user. You would definitely not check this option for Mail databases because they make good use of unread marks in that it is very important to users to know which mail they have or have not read; however, in a reference or help database, this is not important and therefore not necessary to track.

FIGURE 7.24

The Advanced database properties provide options for optimizing database performance.

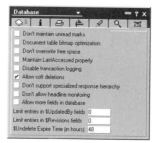

Document Bitmap Table Optimization

I find this particular option to be one of the most interesting because, for me, the option and its description do not seem to have any correlation to one another. However, I am sure that however labeled, the option had a technical reason for doing so. In any case, what this option provides is a way to manage the indexing and opening of views that select documents by form. If a database has a large number of these types of views, this option should be enabled. What will then occur is that the value in the form field for each document will be stored in the view collection, and then when a view is refreshed, indexed, or opened for the first time, the view information will be updated by looking at only those documents that use the forms indicated.

Don't Overwrite Free Space

When a database begins to have document deletions, free space is created and, in turn, reused where possible. In order to reuse free space, a table of the available space must be maintained and checked every time a new note is written to the database. This takes more I/O time to process. If free space is not overwritten, all data is written to the end of the file, and the free space table is not referred to. So, does the freespace ever get reclaimed? Yes, when Compact is run with options, the database is completely rewritten, and all free space is reclaimed.

Maintain Last Accessed Property

Any time a user accesses a document to read or edit, the Last Accessed field on that document is updated if this property is turned on. The only time you should use this is when you have archiving set up for the database based on when documents were last accessed. Otherwise, this is a setting that unnecessarily affects performance because it requires writing to the document each time the document is opened.

Disable Transaction Logging

This option is displayed only if transaction logging is turned on in the server document in the Domino Directory. Transaction Logging provides a vehicle for recovering the document changes, additions, and deletions within a database after a server crash. Prior to R5, when a server crashed, all databases that were open at the time of the crash were recovered by running Fixup on server startup, which literally deletes any document that is corrupted. Not only that, but until Fixup was run on the database, it was unavailable to the users. In R5, with Transaction Logging enabled, all transactions are logged to log files which are stored on a separate hard disk. If there is a server crash, the log file is then used at server start up to apply any transactions that were not written to the database when the crash occurred.

Allow Soft Deletions

Very often, a user complains that she deleted a document or a group of documents that she did not mean to delete. Or more often, she will say that documents have been deleted, and she doesn't know how it happened! Which basically means that she did it; it was a mistake; and she doesn't want to be responsible for it. When this occurs under Release 4, the only recourse is to go to a backup copy of the database, copy the deleted documents, and paste them into the production database. Under Release 5, there is another option. If you enable soft deletions, you can provide a vehicle for users to undelete a document or group of documents that they have deleted. This option requires that you place a time period on the documents that can be recovered. It also requires that you create a view to display deleted documents in order to provide a vehicle for the users to choose the documents that they want to undelete. A special view type supports the view of deleted documents. This is covered in Chapter 8.

Don't Support Specialized Response Hierarchy

If your database does not use view formulas, which include the @AllChildren or @AllDescendants formulas, you can turn on this property. It improves database performance by not storing this information. This has no effect on any views with response columns or any other formulas.

Don't Allow Headline Monitoring

Users can subscribe to databases to monitor the data that is most interesting to them. This can affect the performance of the server if many people decide to monitor a database because the database must be scanned each time documents are added. Consider turning this option on if Headline Monitoring is not a requirement.

Allow More Fields in Database

This is a new property in R5, and when I first saw it, I thought it was a joke. What did they mean, allow more fields? More fields than what, and why? As it turns out, the total number of characters allowed for all field names concatenated in a database by default is 64KB, which is an average of 3000 fields. By turning on this property, this number increases to 64,000 fields. However, there is a catch. By e nabling this property, there can be some problems with full-text indexing the database. So I would suggest choosing smaller field names instead of enabling this property.

Limit Entries in $UpdatedBy Fields

Each document that is created contains a $UpdatedBy field that stores the names of the users or the servers that have edited the document. If this is not a requirement for the database, it is a good idea to limit the number of entries kept to conserve disk space and increase database performance.

Limit Entries in $Revisions Fields

Each document that is created contains a $Revisions field that stores the date and time of an editing session for a document. Domino uses the contents of this field to determine how it should resolve replication and save conflicts. A replication conflict occurs when a document is edited by people accessing the database from two different server replicas of a database, and the database is subsequently replicated. A save conflict occurs when two people edit the same document on the same server at the same time. The number of entries that the $Revisions field stores by default is 500. This can take a considerable amount of space. By limiting the number of entries in the $Revisions field, you can reduce the amount of space consumed by the contents of this field in each document. If the database is not replicated often, do not change this; however, if the database is replicated daily and the number of changes to a particular document is likely to be fairly low, consider changing this to a value of 10 or less because it usually is not important to have any history beyond the last ten edits.

$Undelete Expire Time (Hours)

This property is used in conjunction with the Soft Deletion property discussed earlier and has no meaning alone. Keep in mind that this value is in hours—for example, if you want the undelete capabilities for 2 days, you enter 48 hours.

Summary

This chapter introduced you to the object store of a Domino database and provided you with key information for creating and managing your databases. "Working with Database Properties" explained the ways in which you can optimize the performance of your database using the advanced properties. "Replication Settings" helped you to understand the way that Domino distributes the changes and additions made to replicas of databases. This information has given you a solid base from which to move forward in to the world of development with Domino.

The Integrated Development Environment

by Debbie Lynd

CHAPTER 8

The design interface introduced with Release 4 of Notes was an outstanding interface for application designers, and from the suggestions of people such as you and me, the IDE has changed to be even better in R5. This interface is intuitive to work with and consistent from one design element to the next, in that it provides detailed, context-sensitive help with the programming constructs in all the available languages. For those of you who have worked with Release 4, I am sure you're as pleased with the changes as I am.

There are quite a few changes in Release 5. The Programmer's pane provides a choice of languages for writing and compiling code. You can create Domino Agents using Java. There is also support for JavaScript using the ECMA 262 scripting standard. JavaScript is used in conjunction with a subset of the Document Object Model, which is explained in more detail in Chapter 7, "The Release 5 Object Store." You can also code HTML directly in the page designer and forms designer. All these changes make it easier to work in the IDE.

The programming of a Domino database is done using a variety of languages. Each language has its strengths and weaknesses, and there is some overlap of functionality, which is discussed in Chapter 17, "Choosing the Right Language."

- Formula language
- LotusScript
- JavaScript
- Java
- HTML

Working in the Application Design Environment

In discussing the IDE, I'll start with the application design area of a database. After opening the Designer client, open a database in design mode by highlighting a database icon and choosing View Design from the menu. Or, you can right-click the mouse while selecting the icon and choose Design from the menu. What you will see in the Navigator pane is a list of all the databases defined in your site, and the database you selected will be expanded to expose the design elements list.

On the right, in the view pane will be a list of the forms in the database.

The database illustrated in Figure 8.1 is based on the Team Room template that comes with Release 5. All databases display the same set of design elements, whether or not there are any actual design objects in them. For example, in this database, there are no folders, yet that entry is listed. Table 8.1 lists all the new design elements in Release 5, with a short description of each.

FIGURE 8.1

The design folder is open with each of the forms created for this database available for selection.

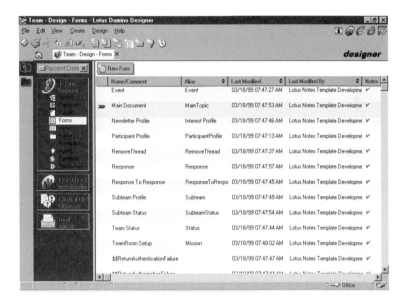

TABLE 8.1   New Release 5 Design Elements

Element	Description
Outline	The outline provides an organizational structure for viewing and navigating through an application.
Page	Like a form, a page is used for displaying information. Unlike a form, a page cannot contain fields or subforms.
Frameset	A frameset is a container for displaying multiple pages at the same time.
Resources - Other - Shared Actions	Actions created and stored in the Other category can be shared with other design elements in the database.
Resources - Images	Image resources are stored as files within the database design. This provides a programmable reference point for images that need to be shared within a database.
Resources - Java	Java applets can be stored within the database to provide a single point of reference for sharing applets between design elements in the database.

If you are unfamiliar with this interface, it will be worthwhile to take a few moments and move around in the design area of the database. Many of the design elements have their own context-sensitive SmartIcon sets, as does the design area itself. The SmartIcon sets appear in the icon bar, which is sometimes referred to as a toolbar.

The right pane lists all the objects that currently exist for the selected design element. This screen is essentially a view of design objects as opposed to a view of document objects. The best part about this pane is the ability to see at a glance additional information about the design element. In most of the views, it will display the name of the design element, the alias name of the design element, the last modified date, and who last modified the design element, as well as whether the design element is Web or Notes enabled. In the agents view, it also displays the owner of the agent and the trigger. In the Script Libraries view, it also displays the Library Type—whether or not the library entry is LotusScript or Java.

First, I want to discuss a common element: the Lotus Notes Properties box. Not only is this common to Lotus Notes objects but it's used throughout the Lotus SmartSuite. The Properties box is where the attributes of a design element are set.

Working with the Properties Box

The Properties box is where you can modify all the attributes belonging to the selected design element in Domino. These elements include workspace pages, databases, view, documents, forms, fields, and so on. Actually, every design element has properties associated with it.

Accessing the Properties Box

To display the Properties box, either click the left-most SmartIcon on the icon bar or right-click the object. When displayed, the Properties box appears with a set of tabs, each of which represents specific properties according to the categories available for that design element as shown in Figure 8.2. In this manner, the Properties box is context sensitive; if you highlight a document in a view and then select the Properties box, you can view the properties for the document. Or, on the other hand, if you right-click in the programmer's pane for a form, you will see the Properties box for the form.

From the drop-down list in the title bar of the Properties box, you can switch context and move to another design element such as document properties or database properties, as illustrated in Figure 8.3.

FIGURE 8.2

The Properties box for a database is chosen by a right-click menu option from the bookmark.

FIGURE 8.3

The drop-down list in the Properties box allows you to select other design elements to view. The options shown are also context sensitive.

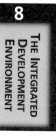

If you examine Figures 8.1 and 8.2 more closely, you'll note that multiple tabs are available. Clicking each tab reveals a new set of properties for the current object. For example, in Figure 8.3 clicking the Printer tab shows the list of available header and footer settings in Figure 8.4.

FIGURE 8.4

The Printer tab shows a list of available header and footer settings.

Different objects have more or fewer tabs on the Properties box, depending on the attributes of the object. The Workspace page Properties box has two tabs, whereas the Database Properties box has seven tabs. The Properties box plays a pivotal role in setting design attributes throughout Domino Designer and consequently will be a theme throughout this book.

The Properties box has some interesting aspects when it comes to the design elements displayed in the design views. While looking at the Forms listed in Form Design, if you highlight a listed form and select the Properties box, you will get a very different Properties box than you will if you open the Form in design mode and select the Form properties. The Properties box you see when in the view provides four tabs, as shown in Figure 8.5. These tabs are consistent for all the design elements highlighted in the view. The first tab is the Info tab that provides information about when the document was created and modified. It also provides information about when and by whom it was last modified. The size of the item is also provided.

FIGURE 8.5

The Info tab of the Design Document Properties box for a form in the Form Design view displays the date and time the database was last modified.

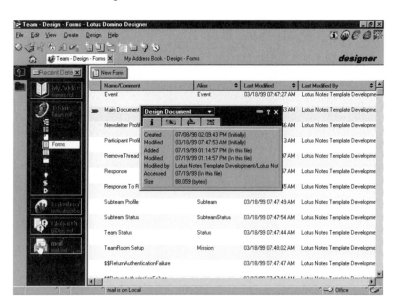

The Fields tab provides a list of all the elements within the form.

You can then choose the Design tab (see Figure 8.6), which displays the properties for design inheritance. This includes the name of the template from which the element should be inherited and prohibits the design element from being replaced. New in R5 is the ability to enable or disable propagation of a design change to other replicas of the database which enables a design element to be changed within one replica and either replicated or not replicated to the other replicas. Other checkboxes on this screen include the following:

- Do Not Allow Design Refresh/Replace to Modify is covered in detail in Chapter 35, "Tracking Design Changes and Using Templates." This is the only checkbox available for Shared Fields, Script Libraries, and all design elements in the Other category.

- Check the box Do Not Show this Design Element in Menus of Notes R4 or Later Clients when there are older design elements that are not forward compatible.

- Hide Design Element from checkboxes allows restrictions to be placed on Web browsers and Notes 4.6 or better clients.

- For agents there is an additional option for Web Access. The checkbox Run Agent as Web User is for testing purposes.

FIGURE 8.6

The Design tab of the Design Properties for a Form in the Form Design View provides various settings for refreshing and replacing the design.

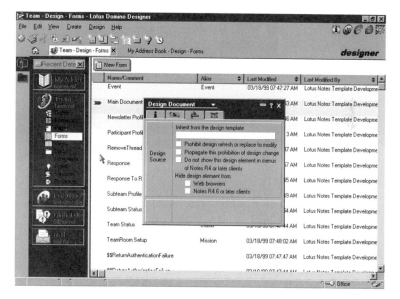

The Fields tab, shown in Figure 8.7, is interesting because it lists the structure of the form itself including a `$UpdatedBy` field with a list of the people who have worked on the design the form. You will find the same sort of information available for all design elements. This can be helpful when multiple people are working on the design of a database and you want to check out the edit history of a design element.

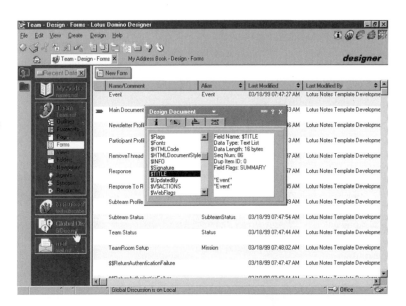

FIGURE 8.7

The Fields tab of the Design Properties for a Form in the Form Design View displays the elements of the Form design in context of a Note.

Design Elements Are Stored as Notes

You'll notice that the heading of the Properties box for the design elements is titled "Design Document" and the Fields tab displays the contents of each of the fields in the Design element. Each design element is stored as a Note in the same way that a document is stored as a Note.

Enabling the Domino Designer Context-Sensitive SmartIcon Sets

Just as the Properties box is context sensitive, so too are the SmartIcons, which appear in the icon bar. In Release 5, context-sensitive SmartIcons are turned off by default. This means that only the Universal SmartIcons are available. Context-sensitive SmartIcons can be turned on through the Preferences menu as indicated in the following list:

1. Choose Preferences from the File Menu.
2. Choose SmartIcons.
3. Check the Show Icon Bar checkbox to enable SmartIcons.

When SmartIcons is turned on, open a database, click the Design folder to expand the category, and select one of the design elements, such as View.

The toolbar changes, as shown in Figure 8.8.

FIGURE 8.8

The Design icon is context sensitive.

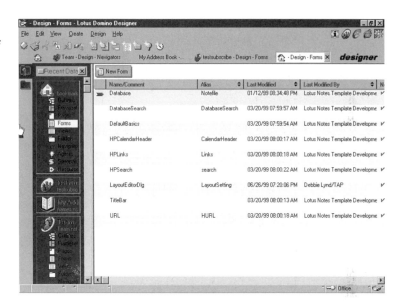

Table 8.2 pairs the SmartIcons in the right-most block of the icon bar, with the design objects that you can create by clicking the SmartIcons.

TABLE 8.2   Design SmartIcons

Icon	Create New
	Forms
	Subforms
	Shared fields
	Views
	Folders
	Agents
	Navigators

Getting Help for SmartIcons

The function of any SmartIcon can be determined by resting the mouse pointer on top of the button and waiting a few moments. Help appears, briefly stating the purpose of the button, such as Create Form or Design View. If you do not see help, check the Context Icons option in the SmartIcons Preferences.

Some design elements do not have specific SmartIcons associated with them. Pages are one such design element. In this case, the design menu will be the way to access the options.

Whenever you are in design mode, an additional menu appears, which is the Design menu. This has context-sensitive items; for example, Form Design offers a choice for creating a field, but no such choice appears in View Design because it doesn't make any sense to allow the creation of fields in a view. Principally, this menu lists choices for properties of design objects in that context. Choices on the Create menu also change with the design type.

The Page, Form, and Subform SmartIcon Bars

The Page, Form, and Subform SmartIcon bars are identical, containing SmartIcons for many functions you'll find useful during design. A form in design mode is shown in Figure 8.9.

FIGURE 8.9

The SmartIcon set for designing a form is context sensitive.

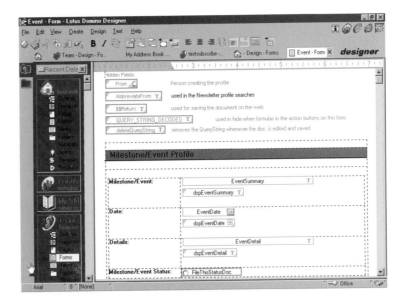

The buttons and their functions are listed in Table 8.3. I've skipped the first group of buttons that remain the same between SmartIcon sets and began the table with the Bold button.

TABLE 8.3   Form Toolbar Buttons

Icon	Function
B	Text Bold
I	Text Italic
	Text Cycle Paragraph Spacing
	Design Form Properties
	Create Field
	Create Insert Shared Field
	Create Layout Region
	Create Hotspot Button
	Text Align Paragraph Left
	Text Align Paragraph Center
	Text Align Paragraph Right
	Text Style Cycle Key
	View Show/Hide Programmer's Pane
	View Show/Hide Action pane
	View Ruler
	Create Table

8

THE INTEGRATED
DEVELOPMENT
ENVIRONMENT

As previously mentioned, when you are in design mode, a Design menu appears. Of particular note on this menu are the final two choices: Preview in Notes and Preview in Web Browser. These are available in multiple design elements as indicated in Table 8.4.

TABLE 8.4   Design Elements with Preview Option

Design Element	Menu Option	Preview in Notes	Preview in Web Browser
Form	Design	X	X
Page	Page	X	X
Frameset	Frame	X	X
View	Design	X	X
Folder	Design	X	X
Navigator	Design	X	X

Previewing Requires That You Save the Design Element

One drawback is the requirement that you save the form before previewing it. Notes will always ask "Do you want to save this form?" before previewing. If you choose No, the prior version is previewed. Personally, I like to see the effect my changes have before saving the design changes.

If you choose to create a table, three new icons are added in a group to the left: Table Insert Row, Table Delete Selected Row(s), and Table Properties. When the cursor is in a table, the Table menu option appears. This menu has many useful actions on it and is worth the time to explore. Tables are discussed in more detail in Chapter 10, "Advanced Form Design."

Figure 8.10 shows a form with a table. Tables can be added to Forms and Pages.

FIGURE 8.10

A form with a new table added displays the SmartIcon set for tables to the right of the icon bar, and a new Table menu is added.

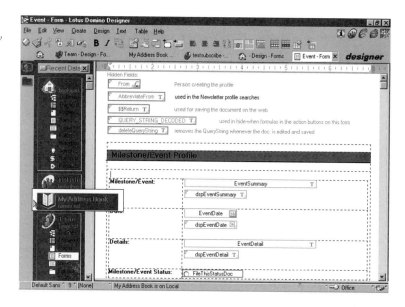

The View and Folder Toolbar

Table 8.5 describes the icons specific to the View Design toolbar shown in Figure 8.11.

FIGURE 8.11

The By Category view from a TeamRoom database in design mode displays the context-sensitive SmartIcons.

8

THE INTEGRATED DEVELOPMENT ENVIRONMENT

TABLE 8.5 The View Design Icon Bar

Icon	Function
	File Database Properties
	File Database Access Control
	Design View Properties

continues

TABLE 8.5   continued

Icon	Function
	Create Insert New Column
	Design View Selection Conditions
	View Show/Hide Programmer's Pane
	View Show/Hide Action Pane

Although there is a button for inserting a new column, you can append a column from the Create menu or by double-clicking the gray title bar of the view in the area after the last defined column. There is no Test option on the menu as there is for forms, but clicking the Refresh icon (the blue circular arrow in the upper-left corner next to the View title bar) will populate the view, as will pressing F9. Unfortunately, the Action Bar buttons do not show up in View Design as they do when testing forms.

The Navigator Icon Bar

This toolbar is quite different from the others in that there are a lot of buttons dealing with graphics. Figure 8.12 shows a navigator in design mode.

FIGURE 8.12

The Team Room navigator in design mode contains additional SmartIcons for graphics options.

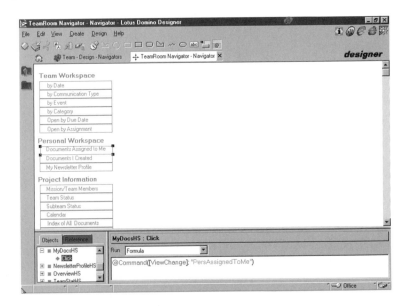

Table 8.6 describes the buttons for the Navigator Design icon bar.

TABLE 8.6 The Navigator Icon Bar

Icon	Function
	Navigator Properties
	Create Hotspot Polygon
	Create Hotspot Circle
	Create Hotspot Rectangle
	Create Rectangle
	Create Rounded Rectangle
	Create Polygon
	Create Polyline
	Create Ellipse
	Create Textbox
	Create Hotspot Button
	View Show/Hide Programmer's Pane

Again, the options on the Create menu change. One option that is available on the menu and not available from the SmartIcon set is Create Graphic Background. The graphic objects all have modifiable properties you can access from the Properties box when the object is selected. The properties for the graphic objects determine relative position and whether an outline should appear based on state.

In this case, the options on the Design menu also change. Figure 8.13 shows the Design menu of a navigator. Besides activating the properties for the navigator and objects, most importantly, from this menu you can test the navigator. When in test mode, clicking the hotspots produces a prompt window indicating the function of the hotspot.

8

THE INTEGRATED
DEVELOPMENT
ENVIRONMENT

FIGURE **8.13**

The navigator Design menu has more than only properties on it.

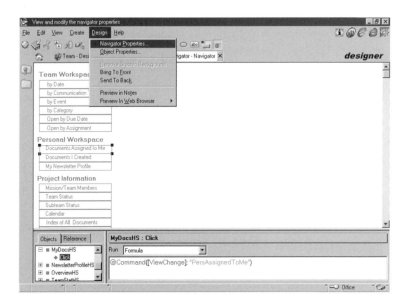

The About and Using Document Toolbars

When writing an About document or Using document, the toolbar is similar to the toolbar you would see if creating a document in a database. You cannot place fields on these documents, but you can place attachments in these documents that will launch a document that contains fields, as shown in Figure 8.14.

FIGURE **8.14**

The About document can include attachments that can be launched when the database is opened.

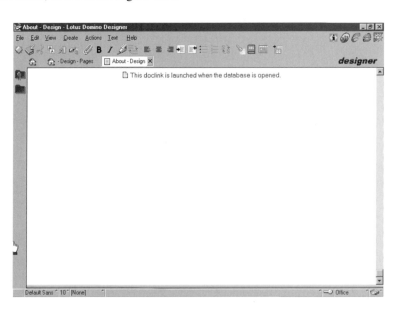

Every database needs to have at least an About document that describes the purpose of the database, as well as who should use it and where to go for help.

TABLE 8.7 The About Document Icon Bar

Icon	Function
	File Attach
	Text Bold
	Text Italic
	Text Permanent Pen
	Text Cycle Paragraph Spacing
	Text Align Paragraph Left
	Text Align Paragraph Center
	Text Align Paragraph Right
	Text Indent
	Text Outdent
	Text Bullets
	Text Numbers
	Text Style Cycle Key
	Edit Find/Replace
	Edit Check Spelling
	View Ruler
	Create Table

8

THE INTEGRATED
DEVELOPMENT
ENVIRONMENT

Working in the Design Screen

Open one of the forms, and you will now see the IDE, as shown in Figure 8.15. The navigator is still visible on the left, but, at this point it is in the way, so you can close it by clicking on the × or Close button.

Figure 8.15

The Main Document Form opened in Design mode with the Navigator pane closed provides more work space.

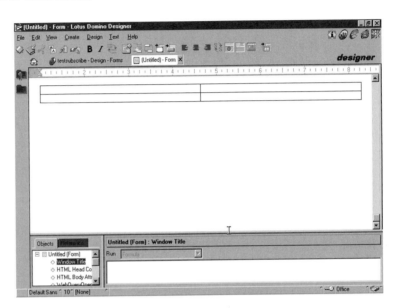

Now that you have taken a look at the toolbars available in the different design elements, take a look at the parts of the design interface itself. Four design panes are available: the Work pane in the upper half (or upper left if the Action pane is open), the Programmer's pane at the bottom right, the Browser pane at the bottom left, and the Action pane in the upper right. Table 8.8 shows which panes are available for each design element.

Table 8.8 Design Window Panes for Design Elements

Element	Work Pane	Programmers Pane	Browser Pane	Action Pane
Outline	Yes	Yes	Yes	
Pages	Yes	Yes	Yes	Yes
Forms	Yes	Yes	Yes	Yes
Subforms	Yes	Yes	Yes	Yes
Views	Yes	Yes	Yes	Yes

Element	Work Pane	Programmers Pane	Browser Pane	Action Pane
Folders	Yes	Yes	Yes	Yes
Shared fields		Yes		
Navigators	Yes	Yes	Yes	
Agents		Yes	Yes	
Script libraries		Yes	Yes	
About document*	Yes			
Using document*	Yes			
Database script		Yes	Yes	
Actions	Yes	Yes	Yes	Yes

There are five design elements not included in Table 8.8 because they do not use the general IDE, but instead have a separate interface. These are

- Framesets
- Database icons
- Image resources
- Java resources
- Design synopsis

Framesets have a one-pane UI with Action buttons for splitting the frames and deleting frames, as well as menu options for working with frames, as shown in Figure 8.16. There are properties for each frame and also for the frameset. Framesets are covered in detail in Chapter 10.

The Database icon has a Design Icon dialog box, shown in Figure 8.17, where you can copy and paste the icon or manually design one. You can create a Database icon from any image that you can copy to the clipboard, but you must size it first to fit the icon box, and you might find that your image leaves a lot to be desired if is becomes too small.

The Image Resource Properties box defines the image file, not an actual UI. The Image Resource is actually a document with a file attachment. The document simply does not appear anywhere. Check it out in the Field tab of the Properties box in Figure 8.18.

FIGURE 8.16

The Frameset UI is different from the other design elements.

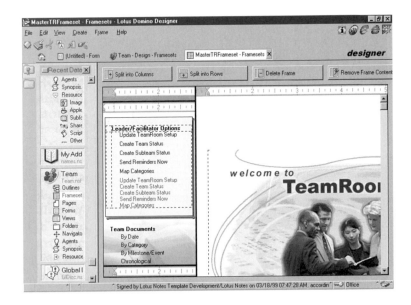

FIGURE 8.17

The Design Icon dialog box provides a palette of tools for creating a custom icon.

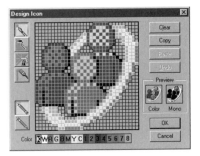

FIGURE 8.18

The field properties for an Image resource displays the contents of the resource document.

Script Libraries provide only the Programmer's pane and the browser pane, as shown in Figure 8.19. Both LotusScript and JavaScript are stored in libraries.

The Database Synopsis displays a dialog box, shown in Figure 8.20, with tabs that allow you to describe which design elements you want to include in the synopsis. A design synopsis provides a report that details all design information for a database. This includes information about the size of the database; the access control list; each of the forms, views, and so on; and all the programming for each design element.

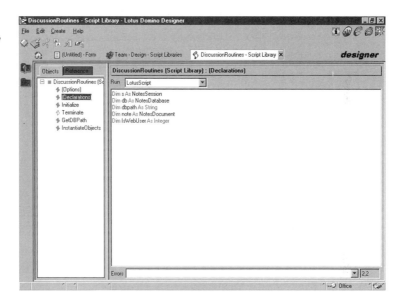

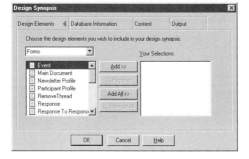

Understanding the Work Pane

Use the Work pane, shown in Figure 8.21, in forms, subforms, views, folders, and navigators to place the design elements such as fields, columns, graphic objects, hotspots, and so on. For a form or subform, this area is exactly like one big rich-text field. When you're designing views and folders, the active area of the Work pane is the title bar of the view. This is where columns are added and modified. By default, if the Work pane is available for the design element, it is displayed.

FIGURE 8.21

The Work pane is where you place and manipulate design elements.

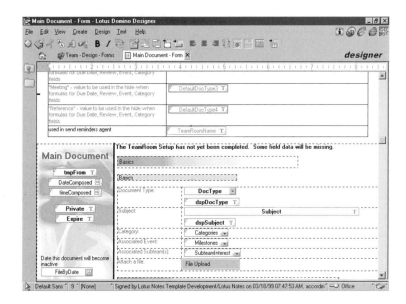

When you design forms, it is sometimes useful to see more than the default half-screen for the Work pane. You can change this view in any of the following ways:

- Click and drag the narrow gray bar that separates the Work pane from the Programmer's pane. Notes resizes the pane accordingly.

- Double-click the separator bar that separates the Work pane from the Programmer's pane. The Programmer's pane collapses completely; double-click again, and it is restored to its original height.

- Uncheck Programmer's Pane from the View menu.

- Click the View Show/Hide Programmer's Pane button on the toolbar.

Right-clicking the Work pane displays a floating submenu (also called the properties menu; see Figure 8.22) that is different for each of the design elements. The top choice on the menu is always Properties of the current object. With forms and subforms, the second choice is Text Properties; for Navigators, it is Object Properties. The remainder of the submenu varies with the object you are designing.

Use the Right Mouse Button to Quickly Access Options

Get in the habit of right-clicking objects and taking advantage of the submenu and the Properties box. This is a convenient shortcut for many menu options.

FIGURE 8.22

The floating sub-menu for a form provides easy access to text attributes.

Using the Programmer's Pane

The Programmer's pane is opened by default in every design element unless that element has a different design tool, as is the case with the icon and the About and Using documents. This pane is where all code is produced for the design elements that support the four-pane UI. Figure 8.23 shows the Programmer's pane.

FIGURE 8.23

The Programmer's pane provides an area to write code for each of the design elements.

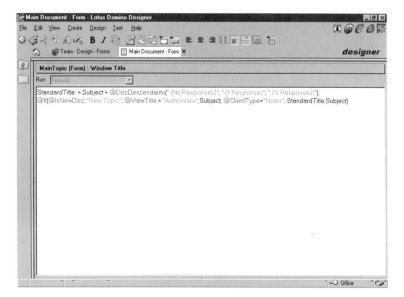

The Programmer's pane displays the name of the Design Element that you are working with and the event that you are programming.

Under the name, you will notice the Run options (shown in Figure 8.24) that describe the type of language being used for the event. The options are

- Simple actions
- Formula
- LotusScript
- JavaScript
- Java

FIGURE 8.24

The Programmer's pane displays the programming options.

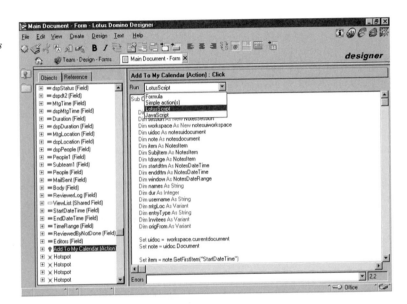

In order to write the code for an object, you must select the object and the event that should trigger the code. When it's selected, you can then choose the language you will use and type your code in the Programmer's pane. Determining the right language for the job is covered in Chapter 17.

There are two ways to select the object that you want to work with. One is to click the object in the Work pane; the second is to select the object from the Object View box, shown in Figure 8.25. If you have selected the object in the Work pane, the object will also be highlighted in the Object View box. Next, you must select the event associated with the object that you want to program. The events that you can program will change based on the object that you select. The list of events for any object is indented under the object name in the Object View. Clicking the plus sign next to the object expands the category so that you can see the list of available events. You can select an event by highlighting it in the Object View box.

You might also have noticed that in the last several figures showing the LotusScript browser, a drop-down field titled Errors is visible below the main LotusScript window.

This is a convenient feature. When script is saved, Notes checks for syntax errors. Those errors appear in this field. More information on LotusScript can be found in Chapters 22, "Introduction to LotusScript," 23, "Basic LotusScript," and 24, "Writing LotusScript."

FIGURE 8.25

Selecting a object to work with can be done in the Object View Browser

8

THE INTEGRATED DEVELOPMENT ENVIRONMENT

Context-Sensitive Help Is Available from the Reference Tab

From this dialog box, you can get help on @Functions and @Commands by pressing the F1 key or clicking the Help button. Help for an @Command is shown in Figure 8.26.

The Agent Design window also has a Programmer's pane. Simple actions, formulas, LotusScript, and Java are available there as well. Agents are discussed in detail in Chapter 32, "Automating Your Application with Agents."

Tips for Writing Code

Take advantage of the formatting features for adding comments and for clarity. Including blank lines after comments separates them from the formulas that follow. Breaking up and indenting portions of complex formulas can significantly improve their readability, thus making code easier to conceptualize and maintain.

FIGURE 8.26

The @Command dialog box with the Help window for the current @Command showing.

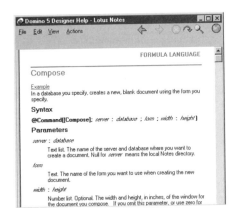

The sample code in Listing 8.1 illustrates the use of blank lines and indentations.

```
REM "If the doc is not being saved, exit " ;

@If(@IsDocBeingSaved ; @Success ; @Return("") ) ;

REM "If the doc is new, use @Name... etc. " ;

@If(@IsNewDoc ¦ cEditors = "" ;
      @Name([CN];@UserName) ;
      @Subset( (@Name([CN]; @UserName) : cEditors) ; 5)
         )
```

Using Menu Options in the Programmer's Pane

Of the four panes in the Design window, the Programmer's pane is the only one with its own set of menu options. To get to the menu options, right-click in the Programmer's pane. The options are far more extensive than they were in Release 4. The options are

- Cut
- Copy
- Paste
- Clear
- Select All
- Deselect All
- Find/Replace
- Import
- Export
- Print

When you are coding LotusScript, the Import, Export, and Print options are available. These options are not available for any other languages. The Print option, shown in Figure 8.27, is new to Release 5 and is a welcome addition to the list. There are many times when it's easier to print the code and review a hard copy than it is to scroll up and down through a screen full of code. The Print option provides an additional dialog box from which you can select printing for the Current selection, Current object, or All objects.

FIGURE 8.27

The LotusScript Print Dialog box provides options to print the code for the current object or all objects.

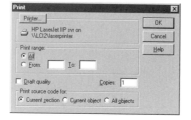

Right-click the Programmer's pane and choose Programmer's Pane Properties. The resulting Properties box is shown in Figure 8.28.

FIGURE 8.28

The Programmer's pane includes a Properties box.

Principally, these properties revolve around fonts. The radio button at the top of the tab has three choices: Script/Java, Formulas, and Simple Actions. In Release 5, each can have its own default font settings and colors set for specific language elements.

The use of color is a very nice feature, cleanly delineating different sections of code. Changes to the properties of the Programmer's pane are immediately made in the Programmer's pane itself.

Understanding the Browser Pane

The Browser pane in Release 4 had to be selected from a button in the Programmer's pane. In Release 5 it is now a permanent window with a slider to adjust the size of the pane. If you change the size of this pane, its settings will be remembered from session to session. The Browser pane has some significant improvements over Release 4. There are now two tabs available which allow you to switch between a list of available objects and the list of available programming help. The Reference window, shown in Figure 8.29, is similar to the LotusScript browser window in Release 4.5 that provided programming help for LotusScript, but this release includes far more information.

FIGURE 8.29

The Reference window is context sensitive.

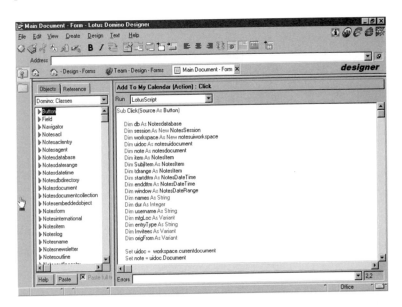

First, the contents of the window will change based on the language you have selected in the Programmer's pane. Second, the languages covered by this new window include

- Formula language
- LotusScript
- JavaScript
- Java

So, in Release 5, if you are editing a Formula, you can check the Reference for help with that formula, or if you're editing JavaScript, you will see the JavaScript classes in the Reference.

The Help Options

The Reference box provides hints to the programming language you are currently working with and the ability to paste a command, formula, or other language element into the Programmer's pane. But maybe you need more than a little memory tweak. Help is available by pressing F1 with the language element in question selected. This will provide you with the ability to check the syntax and view examples of how the command is used. You can also copy and paste the syntax or the example from the help screen into the Programmer's pane.

> Formula language
>> Database Fields
>> Formula @Commands
>> Formula @Functions
> LotusScript
>> LotusScript Language
>> Notes: Classes
>> Notes: Constants
>> Notes: Subs and Functions
>> Notes: Variables
>> OLE Classes
> JavaScript
> Java
>> Core Java
>> Notes Java

The Object View window, shown in Figure 8.30, replaces the define and event drop-down boxes in the Release 4 IDE. This window provides you with the ability to display the available programmable events for the current object and switch to another object. To see the list of available events for an object, expand the category for the object in the Object View window. If you then select an event, the Programmer's pane will display any code that has been written for the event.

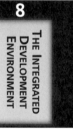

All events that contain code display in the Object View window in a darker color than those that do not contain code! This is a huge improvement for a developer because the only other way to see whether code exists for an event is to look at the event itself or create a Design Synopsis, which, in R4 left a lot to be desired. If you are designing an agent using Java, the Object View tab will become the Class View tab.

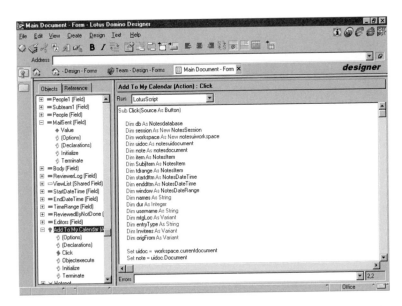

FIGURE 8.30

*The Object View
displays coded
events in a darker
color.*

Understanding the Action Pane

The Action pane is a little different than the other panes in the Design window. First, the pane itself has no properties. However, the Action Bar does have properties.

Second, it contains a list of available actions, some of which are defaults or system actions and cannot be removed. There are six system actions that are common to forms, subforms, views, and folders; these are visible in the Action pane, as shown in Figure 8.31.

All the default actions are system commands and have an asterisk beside them. Although you cannot remove them from the Action list, by default they are turned off, meaning they will not display anywhere. The available system actions are

- Categorize
- Edit Document
- Send Document
- Forward
- Move to Folder
- Remove from Folder

FIGURE 8.31

The default actions for both forms and views are shown in the Action pane in the upper right.

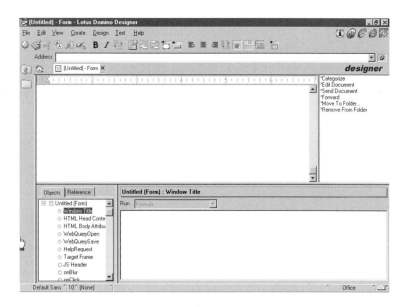

You can turn the system actions on by checking the two display options on the Action Properties box. The display options are

> Include action in Action menu
>
> Include action in button bar

8

THE INTEGRATED
DEVELOPMENT
ENVIRONMENT

> **Caution**
>
> System actions do not display on the Web. If you want to use any of the functionality of the system actions on the Web, you will have to create a new custom action that duplicates the command. Simple actions are also unusable on the Web.

Figure 8.32 shows a new action called Delete that has just been completed. Note that the action—Delete Document—is a simple action and appears with a gray background in the Programmer's pane.

FIGURE 8.32

*You can use many
simple actions
instead of actually
writing a formula.*

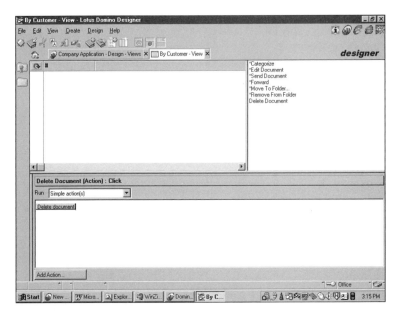

Simple Actions Provide a Quick and Easy Way to Automate Common Tasks

Using simple actions, as in the previous example, is an easy way to accomplish many tasks—in some cases, eliminating the need for writing complex formulas. Simple actions do not work on the Web, and therefore must be replaced with @Commands and @Functions if the application will be used on the Web.

It's also worth noting that any action that will not work on the Web will not display on a Web page!

Summary

In this brief tour of the IDE, I have covered the four principal areas of the Design window: the Work pane, the Programmer's pane, the Browser pane, and the Action pane. I have also discussed the context-sensitive toolbars and the Properties box. A solid understanding of how these tools function and, more importantly, how they function together is essential to designing Notes applications. Now that you have this foundation, I'll move on to discuss the design elements themselves, starting with Outlines, which are a new design element in Release 5.

CHAPTER 9

Review of Basic Forms Design

by Steve Kern

This chapter introduces one of the basic design elements of Domino Applications. Forms are how documents are added, edited, and viewed in Notes databases.

Although it can be argued that you can create a database with an outline and some pages, in general, all databases need to have at least one form and one view. *Forms* are the mechanism by which data gets into Notes databases, and *fields* are what stores data in documents. Fields are the basic building blocks of a Notes form; they can be edited, computed, hidden, or displayed. A Notes form can contain multiple fields.

Without a form and a view, you cannot display, enter, or modify data.

A form is similar to a page, in that you can present content to a user. However, only in a form can you affect the contents—pages are fixed and cannot contain fields. Forms can also contain static text, tables, graphics, actions, hotspots, and other objects. Each form must have a name, contain fields, and have a background color. The default background color is white, but you can change it through the Form Properties box, discussed later in this chapter. Forms can be very simple, consisting of a few fields, to very complex, consisting of many fields with complex formulas, LotusScript, JavaScript, and complex actions. Table 9.1 describes the different objects that can be placed on a Notes form.

For More Information...

For more information about basic form design, see *Sams Teach Yourself Lotus Notes and Domino R5 in 21 Days* by Jane Calabria and Dorothy Burke, or Que's *Special Edition Using Lotus Notes and Domino 5* by Randy Tamura.

Fields or Items?

Technically speaking, data is stored in items in a Notes document, and items are displayed and entered via fields. However, the term *fields* will be used throughout this book. Although the term *items* is technically correct, the term *fields* is commonly used and is therefore far less confusing.

TABLE 9.1 Notes Form Objects

Object	Usage
Static text	Field labels, titles, subtitles, descriptive text.
Graphics	Makes forms more attractive and are sometimes used to indicate status of document. A graphic might indicate a document is locked, and a different image might indicate that it is unlocked.

Object	Usage
Tables	Align fields and text. Table borders can be selectively hidden by position or for the entire table and come in several styles. Table cells can be colored individually, and tables can now exist within tables!
Hotspots	Hotspots can link to Notes documents and Web pages, provide popup help, or execute Notes formulas or Script.
Buttons	Pushbuttons are special types of hotspots that can be added in specific locations on forms to execute simple actions, Notes formulas, or Script.
Actions	Actions can exist on the menu, on the Action Bar as an Action Bar button, or in both places. These are available both for forms and views. Notes formulas, @Commands, and LotusScript can be used. Actions help automate a Notes application. New to Release 5 are Shared Actions which can be created once and added to multiple forms.
Subforms	Subforms can be inserted into forms by formula, or permanently. Subforms are just like forms and usually contain a set of common fields or actions. Subforms are reusable design elements.
Sections	There are two types of sections: access-controlled and standard. Sections provide a way to present, organize, and control information.
Layout regions	Layout regions are special areas on forms that enable the designer to create forms that more easily combine text and graphics. Layout regions can be set to display in 3D format and are often used to gather information in a dialog box.
Computed text	You can use formulas to compute text elements on forms.
Image resources	New to Release 5, you can embed a shared image stored in the database.
Embedded elements	Some of these elements are new to Release 5, and some have been present since Release 4.6. You can now add the following objects: Outline, View, Navigator, Date Picker, Group Scheduler, Folder Pane, Editor Applets for Web clients, and File Upload Controls.
HTML	HTML can be added directly to forms for display in Web browsers.
Java applets	Java applets can be embedded directly on Notes forms. Animated Java applets, such as those created with Bean Machine, now play both in Notes and Web clients.
JavaScript	JavaScript can be directly embedded on forms, just like HTML, for use with Web clients.

continues

9

Review of Basic Forms Design

TABLE 9.1 continued

Object	Usage
Horizontal rules	A Web element that draws a horizontal line on the page when viewed by a Web client. Properties can be set for horizontal rules.
OLE objects	OLE (object linking and embedding) can be used in forms to link to objects created in other applications.

You can think of a form as a window into a document. Although a document in a Domino database is similar to a record in a relational database table, it is by no means the same. For example, you can add or subtract fields from a document, whereas you cannot remove fields in a record. The fields in a relational table's record are fixed by the table that defines it. Sometimes you will create a form that collects and displays data. And sometimes you might need to create a form which displays only data—a special "window" into the document in a different format than that used to collect the data. Often, forms such as this are used as special print documents.

Creating Display-Only Forms

If you do create a special print form or similar form used only to display data in documents, it is a good idea to make all the fields display-only. You can also create a view with a form formula that specifies the print form so that the users don't have to continually choose View, Switch Form from the menu. Whenever they open a document from the view, the form specified in the Form formula will display the document!

What's New in R5?

There are numerous enhancements to forms in R5. There are new field types, new embedded elements, JavaScript for both Web and Notes clients, and form headers. There are two new reusable elements that can be added to forms: Shared Actions and Shared Images. A new tab, the Control tab, has been added to Number and Date/Time fields. There are numerous new display options for Date/Time and Number fields, as well as for fields in general. This short sampling of new features illustrates how much work has been put into the R5 Designer. These and other new features are discussed in this chapter and in Chapter 10, "Advanced Form Design."

For More Information...

For more information about new features in Release 5, see Chapter 2, "What's New in Release 5?"

Designing Forms

Planning the appearance and functions of a form should take place before designing the form begins. Because most database applications consist of more than one form, you should consider the relationships between forms and determine the purpose of the form. Does it simply collect data or does it take actions? What information does the form need to track? Where does the data come from? Do the users enter it, does it come from external data sources, or is it calculated? Are there any security considerations?

Tip

You might find it useful to create a table containing a row for each field on the form. Columns might consist of the following:

Description

Field Name

Field Type

Editable/Computed

Hidden

Required

Default values

Formulas

While designing the forms in a database, you might find that some information is repeated across many forms. Examples of this type of information are author and edit history, which are common to all Notes documents. You might have several forms that need to look up information about employees, such as their name, department, and location. Subforms are an excellent place to store and display such information; they can also help keep the appearance of forms more consistent. Using a subform enables you to enforce consistency in the appearance of the form as well as in the contents of the fields. Subforms are discussed in Chapter 12, "Using Resources in Domino Applications."

Using Shared Fields

Shared Fields can also be used to enforce design consistency. You can define the formula and data type for a Shared Field and reuse it throughout the forms in a database. Shared Fields are discussed in Chapter 10.

When you design the physical appearance of a form, it is sometimes a good idea to sketch it either electronically or on paper. Also, be sure to look for similar forms that might be available in another database that can be used as a starting point for your design.

Understanding Form Types

The default form type is document, but there are actually three types of Notes forms: document, response, and response-to-response. By far, the most common form used is the document type. The Type setting is in the Form Properties box on the Form Info tab, as shown in Figure 9.1.

FIGURE 9.1

Choose the form type from the Form Info tab of the Form Properties box.

The three types of forms are based on a hierarchy of documents. The document form type, also referred to as "main" or "main topic form," is at the top of the hierarchy, followed by the response, and then by the response-to-response form types. The document form type is used to create "main" documents. These documents stand at the top of the hierarchy. Main documents can have multiple response documents associated with it. Similarly, response documents can have multiple response-to-response documents associated with them.

This document hierarchy is used in discussion style databases, but can also be used in data collection applications. For example, you might create a contact management system that collects information about your customers and each contact between your company and theirs. You start by creating a main document form to collect information about your customers, such as company name, address, phone number, fax number, and so on. To create a customer contact form, you could pick the response document type, and include information such as date and time of contact, type of contact, who initiated the contact, and the outcome of the contact including any action items for your company. Because this is a response document, it will always be associated with the main document.

The relationship between documents, response documents, and response-to-response documents is similar to a parent/child relationship in a relational database. A number of @Functions work with this relationship—`@AllChildren`, `@AllDescendants`, `@DocChildren`, and `@DocumentUniqueID`, just to name a few. The relationship between these document types is maintained internally by Notes—the response documents store a reference to the parent document in a field named `$Ref`. This reserved field contains the document ID of the parent.

In a hierarchical view, response documents appear under the main document from which they were composed. Response-to-response documents appear under the response document that was highlighted when they were composed. Hierarchical views automatically indent response and response-to-response documents underneath the parent document. Displaying documents, response documents, and response-to-response documents is useful in discussions but is less useful in forms that principally collect data. (Response hierarchies are discussed in the next section.)

For More Information...

For more information about hierarchical views, see Chapter 11, "View Design."

Understanding Response Hierarchies

To see documents displayed in a hierarchy, open a discussion database. If you don't have a discussion database available, create one based on the Discussion - Notes & Web (R5) template that ships with Domino Designer. After you open the discussion database, you can see the action buttons in the view to create a new main topic (the form type is Document), a response, and a response-to-response document. Create a few documents to get the feel of this functionality. This is also shown in Figure 9.2.

FIGURE 9.2

A response hierar-chy is illustrated in this view from a discussion data-base.

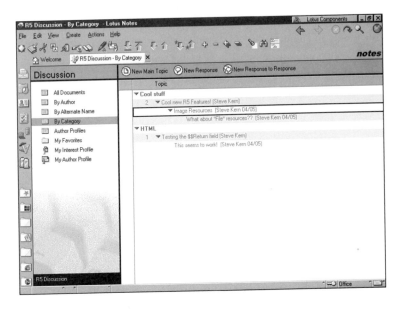

When response documents are listed in a view that enforces the response hierarchy, response documents are indented three spaces underneath the parent. Up to 32 levels are supported. A perfect example of document hierarchies can be found in about any discussion database (see Figure 9.2).

As stated earlier, Domino maintains the relationship between these documents through the use of the document ID. A document ID is shown in the Properties box for a document. Programmatically, it can be accessed with the following formula:

```
@Text(@DocumentUniqueID)
```

Using $Ref in a Document

You can use $Ref in a computed field in a response document as a formula for the Value event. The document will display a doclink icon that can be clicked to open the parent document.

Choosing a Form Type

Choose a form type carefully. In most cases, the form type will be a document. If you come from a relational database development background, it can be tempting to use a response document similar to a child table in a relational database. Domino does not conform well to this model! Because Notes maintains the internal relationship between documents and response documents, response documents can be useful in many situations. Using response documents in a discussion format is obviously a good fit, for example. Another good use of a response document is in a database that tracks projects. The parent document can contain information pertinent to the project itself, whereas response documents can contain information about specific tasks.

> **Caution**
>
> There is a real drawback to using response documents to collect data. Response documents will not total in hierarchical views (views containing both main documents and response documents). Only main documents will total in hierarchical views. If you want to total fields in response or response-to-response documents, you must create a view containing only response-type documents. Consider the reporting needs of the form before deciding to use one of the response types.

Creating a Form

Creating a form is fairly easy. After you have decided what the form should look like, and what items it should contain, create the form in the Domino Designer:

1. Open the Domino Designer.
2. Open the database in the Design Pane.
3. In the Design List, click Forms.
4. In the Work Pane, click the New Form button. See Figure 9.3.
5. Open the Form Properties box, and enter a name and synonym for the form.
6. In the Form Properties box, choose a type for the form, and make any other appropriate selections.
7. Add text, fields, subforms, embedded objects, graphics, and so forth to complete your form.
8. Enter a window title, and add any code to any necessary form events.
9. To close and save the new form, click the Close button (the small *x*) on the form's window tab.

FIGURE 9.3

Click the New Form button in the Forms Design view to create a form.

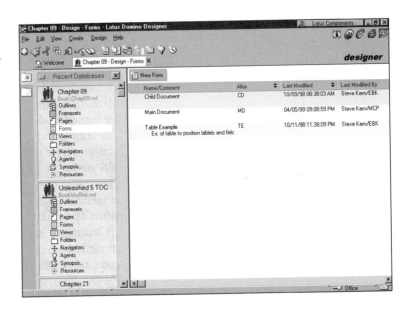

For More Information...

For more information about the Designer IDE, see Chapter 8, "The Integrated Development Environment."

Adding Text, Fields, and Objects to the Form

Adding static text, fields and other objects to a form is very simple. A Notes form is just like one big word processing document or Notes rich-text field. You can enter text, fields, and other objects where you need them simply by positioning the cursor at the desired location. You can add fields and tables from the Create menu (Create, Field), by clicking the Create Field SmartIcon or by right-clicking the form in design and choosing Create Field.

Graphic objects can be copied to the clipboard and pasted into the form, or imported. HTML files can be imported and will display in native format. You can embed any one of a number of Web design elements, Standard and Controlled Access sections, Java Applets, Image Resources, and so on by choosing the appropriate command from the Create menu. Table 9.1 lists some of the available objects that can be used in forms.

Using Transparent GIFs

GIFs are image files that can have a transparent background. If you copy a GIF to the clipboard and then paste it into a form, the background will not be transparent and will retain the background color of the GIF, regardless of the form's background color. This is okay if you are using a GIF with a white background on a form with a white background. If you instead *import* a transparent GIF into a form, the background will remain transparent regardless of the background color of the form. This works for both Web and Notes clients.

Most objects have properties that can be set from Properties boxes. To access the Properties box of any object on the form, simply right-click the object and choose Properties from the floating context menu. For example, to change the properties of a text object, open the Properties box and you will be able to easily change the font, size, color, and attributes of the text. (The Text Properties box is discussed in the "Working with Text Properties" section later in this chapter.)

Testing the Form During Design

Testing the form during design is quite useful and enables the designer to build the form incrementally and test it along the way. Unfortunately, you must save your changes before testing them. Another drawback is that you can test only document forms, not response-type forms. If you attempt to test one of the response forms, Domino Designer will display an error because a response form must be composed while a main document is selected. Because the form is in design, no main document is selected and thus the error message is generated.

Testing Response Forms

A workaround to testing response-type forms is to make the response form a document-type form during design. When design is completed and the appearance and functionality of the form is to your satisfaction, simply change the type back to its original type.

You can test the following four versions of a form:

- **Notes Preview**—Previews the form in the Notes client.
- **Domino Preview**—Previews the form using the Notes Web browser.

- **Internet Explorer Preview**—Previews the form using Internet Explorer.
- **Netscape4 Preview**—Previews the form using Netscape.

Previews are available from the Design, Preview menu option in Notes (Design, Preview in the Web browser), or from one of the Preview buttons in the Designer IDE. The Preview buttons are new to Release 5, as is the capability to test a form using multiple browsers. In earlier versions, when you tested a form with a Web browser, it tested the browser specified in your location document.

Caution

If you are testing a form with one of the Web browsers, the database must be underneath the Notes data directory.

To see how this works, select any document type form, either in design or from the Work Pane, and click one of the Preview buttons. Domino Designer will display the form in the appropriate client. This is a good way to test field formulas such as Input Validation formulas, action buttons and other form objects. You can also check each field for field level help quickly by scrolling through each field and checking the status bar at the bottom of the document.

R5 Field Help

In R3, Field help was an option set on the menu. In R4, the menu option was removed; in R5, it was added again. If you do not see Field help, check the menu option View, Show, Field Help. This menu prompt is a toggle, so you can click it on and off.

Checking the Field Type in Preview

If you display the Properties box when testing a form, each time you navigate to a new field, the Properties box will display the field type, with the exception of rich-text fields. The Properties box in rich-text fields switches to a Text Properties box.

Color-Coded HTML!

When you preview a form for a Web browser, if you choose Domino as the preview browser, you can choose View, Show, HTML Source from the menu to see color-coded HTML source code. This is a feature new to Release 5 of Notes, and is a great way to observe how Domino presents your documents!

Setting Form Properties

As with other Notes objects, forms have properties. The Form Properties box has several tabs that control various settings as listed in Table 9.2.

TABLE 9.2 Form Properties Box Tabs

Tab	Contents
Form Info	Name, Comment, Type, Display, Versions, and Options
Defaults	On Create, On Open, On Close, and On Web Access
Launch	Auto Launch and Auto Frame
Form Background	Color, Graphic or Resource, and Options
Header	Add Header to Form, Size, and Border
Printing	Specify Header or Footer (radio button set), Header/Footer Text, Format, and Options
Security	Read access, Create access, and Encryption keys

Each of these form attributes are discussed in the following sections.

Using the Form Info Tab

The Form Properties box is shown in Figure 9.4. The Form Info tab contains many important settings.

9

REVIEW OF BASIC FORMS DESIGN

Tab Names

You can find the name of a tab on any Properties box if you let the mouse pointer hover over the tab. Floating text will show the name of the tab.

FIGURE 9.4

The Form Info tab is the first tab in the Form Properties box.

First and foremost, every form must have a name. It is also a good idea, as discussed in Chapter 6, "Design Guidelines," to use a synonym. Add a form synonym by placing the pipe symbol (|) next to the form name and following it with the synonym. It is a good idea to limit the length of the synonym to a few characters—a few characters are more recognizable and easier to type. In addition, synonyms are useful when you change the name of the form. Because Domino stores the synonym in the document's form field, you don't lose the connection to documents created with earlier versions. While the form name might be "Supplies Requisition," the synonym might be something like "RQ." The combined name that appears in the name field would be "Supplies Requisition | RQ." The text to the left of the pipe character is what is displayed on the Create menu; if there are multiple synonyms, the leftmost text is used.

If you have a large number of forms, collecting them into categories to display on the menu can be quite useful. Adding text followed by the slash character (\) to the name of the form will cause forms to cascade under the text preceding the slash character in the Create menu. For example, if you have several different types of requisitions, you might include a grouping for hardware requisitions. The following list depicts a series of forms that would cascade under the Create menu as Hardware Requisitions:

> Hardware Requisition\PC
>
> Hardware Requisition\Laptop
>
> Hardware Requisition\Modem

Typing Shortcut!

You don't have to enter the form name followed by a space then the pipe symbol, and then another space followed by the form synonym. The Domino Designer will automatically insert the spaces before and after the pipe symbol.

In other words, you can type a form name like so:

My Form|MF

Domino will correctly insert spaces as in the following:

My Form | MF

You can also use an underscore character preceding a letter in the form's name to create a hotkey for that letter in the form's name.

The complete name of the form, including synonyms, special characters, and cascading menu text cannot be more than 256 bytes. However, as with field names, it is best to keep the name short and user friendly.

The next two fields are the Comment and Type fields. The Comment field can be used to enter a brief comment about the form's purpose. The form type is set in the Type drop-down. As discussed earlier, there are three choices: Document, Response, and Response-to-Response.

In the Display section, the "Include in" settings are both checked by default. The In Menu setting has two choices: Create Menu and Create - Other dialog box. Unless you have an overriding concern, leave it set to Create Menu. This allows new forms to be created from the Create menu. The second Include setting is Search Builder. Leaving Search Builder checked allows the form to be used in a full-text search builder window.

You can establish Version Control by choosing a setting from Versions other than None, which is the default, and making a choice in the Create Versions field. The settings for Version Control are listed in Table 9.3.

TABLE 9.3 Version Control

Field	Option
Versioning	None (default).
	New versions become responses.
	Prior versions become responses.
	New versions become siblings.
Create Versions	(Available when Versioning is changed from None)
	Manual - File, New Version
	Automatic - File, Save

Versioning is useful in applications that involve document approval or collaborative authoring. An example could be a corporate policy library. Most companies have an approval route that corporate policy documents take before becoming official policy. Notes and Domino is ideal for this kind of application because it supports mail routing, and the Corporate Policy database can be mail-enabled to match the corporate routing structure. In this kind of application, it might be useful to allow more than one person to work (collaborate) on a particular document.

With Version Control, each version of the document is saved. Notes controls the manner in which the document's versions are saved with the Versioning and Create versions fields. When a new version becomes a response, the original document remains the main document, and is listed first in the view. The new version is a response document and is indented and listed underneath the original. When a prior version becomes a response, the new version is listed first in the view, and the original is listed as a response underneath the new document. When new versions become siblings, all are saved as main documents with the original listed first in the view.

If Create Versions is automatic, a new version is automatically created whenever the new document is saved. If Version Control is set to Manual, the user can determine whether a new version is created. The latter option is more flexible but less secure.

Caution

Versioning is not available for Web clients.

The bottom of the Form Info tab has a series of checkboxes:

- **Default Database Form**—Domino uses the default database form to display documents with no associated form (the form field is empty).
- **Store Form in Document**—Whenever the document is saved, the form is saved with it.
- **Disable Field Exchange**—Stops documents created with the form from participating in Notes/FX (Notes Field Exchange).
- **Automatically Refresh Fields**—Refreshes all fields whenever a change is made to any field while in Edit.
- **Anonymous Form**—No author information is saved with the document.
- **Merge Replication Conflicts**—Uses field-level replication to help prevent replication conflicts.

Each database should have a default database form. When a form is set as the Default database form, any document that does not have a form designated will be opened with the default form.

Storing the form in documents can be useful in certain circumstances; however, you need to be aware that it can dramatically increase the amount of disk space for the database. To use stored forms, you must also enable Allow Use of Stored Forms in This Database on the Form Info tab of the Database Properties box. Stored forms are available to Web clients as read-only documents—they cannot create a document with a stored form. You can use stored forms to email documents into a database that doesn't contain the form used to create the document. When users open the document in the mail-in database, it will be displayed in its native format. Documents created with stored forms include several reserved fields. $Title contains the original form name, while $Info, $WindowTitle, and $Body contain additional information used to display the document.

Fields can be exchanged with other applications using Notes/FX and OLE. When you Disable Field Exchange, you stop Notes/FX-enabled applications from exchanging information.

Checking Automatically Refresh Fields causes Notes to refresh every field in the document whenever any field is changed. Automatically refreshing the fields can slow performance significantly, although with today's powerful PCs, this is less of a factor than it used to be.

Caution

Automatically Refresh Fields should almost never be used. It can significantly impair the performance of a form because it calculates every formula for every field whenever information in a field is entered or edited. In general, do not use this option, but if you must, ensure that there are few computed field formulas requiring a refresh.

Automatic Refresh and Web Clients

Automatically Refresh Fields does not apply to Web applications because HTML pages are relatively static documents. You can use @Command([ViewRefreshFields]) to refresh the display of fields on a Web document.

The Anonymous Form was introduced in R4. By default, Notes keeps track of the document authors and editors in special fields created internally. If you check Anonymous Form, this tracking does not happen, and a user can enter and save a form anonymously. This is useful for applications such as a Corporate Suggestions application. In this type of application, people might be less than open if they knew their names can be linked to their input. Note that to maintain complete anonymity, you must avoid including any computed fields based on formulas such as @UserName.

When the Merging Replication Conflicts option is checked, Notes will attempt to compare the contents of each field if it detects a replication conflict. Fields as well as forms have an internal sequence number that the Replicator uses to detect a conflict. If no fields conflict with each other, the two documents are merged at the field level and no replication conflict document is created.

Replication Conflicts

Chapter 1, "Introducing Lotus Notes and Domino," introduced the concept of replication. Replication conflicts occur when different users edit the same document and then replicate with the server. Replication conflicts show in views with a black diamond in the margin, and the text "Replication or Save conflict" appears next to the diamond. One of the two documents must be removed eventually. In a well-designed database, this doesn't happen very often.

Using the Defaults Tab

Figure 9.5 shows the settings available on the Defaults tab. There are several sections: On Create, On Open, On Close, and On Web Access.

FIGURE 9.5

The Defaults tab of the Form Properties box has changed considerably from R4.

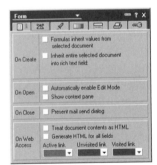

The On Create Section

In the On Create section, you can set up document inheritance from one Notes document to another. Inheritance is a useful tool when designing a Notes application. Because Notes is not a relational database, it is not always easy to get information from other documents. Therefore, if you need information from another document in the current document, you can store it in the current document using inheritance. Duplication of data items among documents (redundancy) is not as significant a consideration when designing Notes forms as it is in relational database design.

Inheritance happens only once—when the document is composed. For Inheritance to work, the new document must be composed while the document from which the information is to be inherited is highlighted in a view or opened. Inheritance is frequently used between main documents and response documents, but it can also occur between two main documents. It is important to note that if information in the parent document changes, the information in the child document will not change automatically.

Using the Document ID

If you store the document ID of the parent document in a field in the child document, you can then update the values of either document using two @Functions: @GetDocField() and @SetDocField(). The syntax requires you to supply the document ID and field name, as in the following:

```
@GetDocField(cParentDocID; "cFullName"
```

In this expression, cParentDocID is created using inheritance from the parent document. The value formula for cParentDocID is @Text(@DocumentUniqueID. Note that if the child document is a response document type, the special field called $Ref can be used to retrieve values from the parent document.

There are two kinds of inheritance. One is field level—individual fields inherit information from a parent document. The fields can have the same name, but don't have to. The default value (or value, if the field isn't editable) formula must be the name of the field to be inherited.

The second type of inheritance inherits the entire document into a rich-text field. When you click this option, two new fields open. The first contains a list of rich-text fields in the document, and the second lists three types of inheritance: Link, Collapsible Rich Text, and Rich Text (see Figure 9.6). If you choose Link, a document link icon appears in the rich-text field. Collapsible rich text places the entire document into a section that can be collapsed or expanded; an example of this type of inheritance is Reply with History form in the Notes Mail database. The Rich Text option simply displays the document as it appears.

FIGURE 9.6

Inheriting documents into rich-text fields allows three choices for the inheritance.

The On Open Section

There are two options in the On Open section: Automatically Enable Edit Mode and Show Context Pane. In some applications, you might want to have certain forms automatically open in Edit mode. This can be a convenience for users. Don't worry about unauthorized access to data—readers will not be able to edit or create a document. Clicking Show Context Pane opens another drop-down list containing two choices: Doclink and Parent. The Show Context Pane can be somewhat obtrusive because the bottom half of the form automatically opens to the linked document, whether you select Doclink or Parent.

The On Close Section

On Close has only one field: Present Mail Send Dialog. This automatically prompts users with the Mail Send dialog box when the document is saved. Note that this will not work for a Web client. (Chapter 34, "Creating Workflow Applications," discusses mail-enabling Notes applications.)

The On Web Access Section

The On Web Access section contains two checkboxes and three color settings for links. The Treat Document Contents as HTML checkbox enables you to paste or enter HTML directly on the form. When the form is opened with a Web client, it will use the HTML. Generate HTML for All Fields allows hidden fields on the form to participate in the Web client session. The three Color Pickers at the bottom are for Active Link (red), Unvisited Link (blue), and Visited Link (purple). This is a great improvement over earlier versions of Domino because you no longer have to use HTML to specify the colors of each link. You can use the color pickers to set the link colors. If you view the HTML source of a document, you'll find a line similar to the following:

```
<BODY TEXT="000000" BGCOLOR="FFFFFF" LINK="0000FF" ALINK="008080"
VLINK="FF00FF">
```

This specifies active links (`ALINK`) as cyan, unvisited links as blue, and visited links as purple. The values are in hexadecimal format.

Working with the Launch Tab

Two settings are available on the Launch tab: Auto Launch and Auto Frame (see Figure 9.7). Numerous choices are available from the Auto Launch drop-down list on the Launch tab. This list is lengthy because of the power available with this setting. You can launch attachments, document links, a wide variety of SmartSuite 9 application objects, Microsoft Office suite objects, Paint Shop Pro 5 images, MIDI sequences, Quick Time movies, and many more. The list is seemingly endless!

Figure 9.7

The Launch tab of the Database Properties box expands when certain Auto Launch options are selected.

New to R5 are the Frameset and Frame choices at the bottom of the Launch tab, shown in Figure 9.8. After you select a frameset in the Auto Frame section of the tab, you can then choose a specific frame in the frameset. Documents created with the form will appear in that frame. (Framesets are discussed in Chapter 31, "Adding Framesets to Your Applications.")

Using the Background Tab

There are three sections on the Background tab: Color, Graphic or Resource, and Options. The Background tab enables you to set the background color of forms and to add images to the background of a form. Various options related to the background of the form can also be set from this tab (see Figures 9.9 and 9.10).

FIGURE 9.8

The Auto Frame section of the Defaults tab launches documents in a specific frame for both Web and Notes clients.

FIGURE 9.9

The Background tab of the Form Properties box has settings for color, images, and options.

FIGURE 9.10

The Background tab of the Form Properties box showing the color palette available for the form's background color.

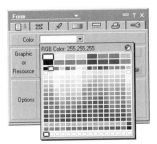

You can use background colors to differentiate forms, as discussed in Chapter 6. The standard Notes color picker is available from the Color field by clicking the drop-down arrow. Although a large number of colors are available, some platforms will not be able to display all those colors, so be careful which colors you choose. It is usually best to choose lighter colors because it can be difficult to read text on a dark background. Having said that, it is worth mentioning that many Web sites employ black backgrounds for their pages!

Using the Notes Color Picker

In previous releases of Notes and Domino, the color picker had a fixed set of colors. Each color had a name assigned such as cyan, red, magenta, 10% gray, or pale yellow. Now, the color picker displays the RGB values of the colors instead, which is somewhat less useful because you don't normally refer to 10% gray as 239,239,239! New to R5 is the capability to customize the color palette. Clicking the small button with the color circle in the upper-right corner of the color picker enables you to build custom colors.

Embedding a graphic in the background is different from pasting or importing it directly on the form. When a graphic is pasted or imported on the form, it is like any other object on the form; it occupies space just as text or fields do. When an image is embedded in the background, other objects can be placed on top of it. You can embed graphics on the background of a form with the Paste Graphic or Import Graphic buttons and remove them with the Remove Graphic button.

To use the Paste button, copy an image to the clipboard and click the Paste Graphic button. Unless the image covers the entire background, it is tiled so that it covers the entire background of the form. You can click the Import Graphic button to import JPEGs or GIFs from the file system. The same rules apply for the effects on the background as those that apply to the Paste Graphic button.

New to R5 is the Image Resource field. If you click the Browse Resources button beside the field, the Designer will open a dialog box from which you can choose and insert a shared image resource. Note that the Image Resource must already exist. You can remove an Image Resource by deleting the filename from the field, or by clicking the Remove button. The Formula button opens a window that enables you to write a formula to insert an image. Figure 9.11 shows the Insert Image dialog box.

For More Information...

For more information about shared resources, see Chapter 12.

9

REVIEW OF BASIC
FORMS DESIGN

FIGURE 9.11

The Insert Image Resource dialog box displays a thumbnail of the image on the right of the dialog box.

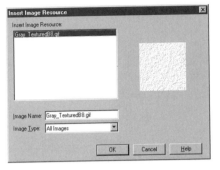

Turning Off Graphics During Development

If you don't want to be bothered with the background during development, click the Hide graphic in design mode. Displaying a background during design can cause your work to go slowly as the Designer refreshes the background image.

The Options section at the bottom of the tab consists of the following:

> Hide Graphic in Design Mode
>
> Hide Graphic on 16 Color Displays
>
> Do Not Tile Graphic
>
> Allow Users to Change These Properties

For the most part, the options are self-explanatory. The Allow Users to Change These Properties option deserves further treatment, however. This option only refers to the settings in the Options setting. If you click one or more of the Options, such as Do Not Tile Graphic and Hide Graphic on 16 Color Displays, users can change them in a document. The Options appear on the Background tab of the Document Properties box. There you can check or uncheck the options as you see fit. For example, you can switch from Do Not Tile Graphic back to a tiled background. When you've created a background color or image, you can add text and fields to the form that will appear in the foreground.

Using Transparent GIFs

Use transparent GIFs where possible. This special image type displays whatever is underneath the background color of the GIF, and works in both Web and Notes clients.

Using the Header Tab

Figure 9.12 shows the Header tab of the Forms Properties box. The Header tab enables you to specify properties for headers for the form. There are three sections: Add Header to Form, Size, and Border. Add Header to Form is simply a checkbox; when checked, the size of the header region can be specified in pixels or by percent. The header region itself remains constant as you scroll through the document.

FIGURE 9.12

The Header tab allows you to set properties for the form header, a nonscrolling region at the top of a document.

You can set scrolling inside the region to Yes, No, or Auto. If the contents of the region exceed the height, scrollbars appear to allow users to scroll through the region. This is similar to scrollbars that appear for frames in framesets in Web browsers.

You can also allow the user to resize the header by clicking Allow Resizing. Note that this setting is available only when a border is specified. To show the border, click the Border spinner to a setting greater than 0 and select a color. 3D shading adds a three-dimensional appearance to the border.

Setting a nonscrolling header region for documents enables you to place certain items such as fields, text, hotspots, and graphics in the header that will remain visible wherever the user happens to be in the document. Any item that a form can contain can be placed in a header. If you want to use a table in the header, you must place a text object before the table. The text object can be a space or an empty line feed.

9

REVIEW OF BASIC FORMS DESIGN

Caution

If you add a header to an existing form, the border will fall wherever you specify. If you have text or fields in that area of the form, they will automatically become part of the header. In the current version, R5.0, if you have a graphic resource used in the background, it will only appear in the header. The form itself will have no background image. Background colors are not affected in the same way.

Caution

Headers only work with Notes clients and can't be used for Web applications.

Setting Print Options

The Printing tab allows you to specify the settings for the header and footer when printing the document (see Figure 9.13). There are four sections: Specify Header or Footer, Header/Footer Text, Format, and Options.

The Specify Header or Footer section enables you to specify whether the settings are for the header or the footer. You can specify different settings for each. After you've clicked the appropriate radio button, you can then create the header or footer in the Header/Footer text window. This window has five buttons below it, which, from left to right, insert the following:

> Page number
>
> Date
>
> Time
>
> Tab
>
> Window title

Except for the Tab button, all the other choices are self-explanatory. There are only three preset tab stops: left, center, and right. The formula for the footer shown in Figure 9.13, `Printed: &D¦¦ Page: &P¦`, places the text "Printed:" plus the date flush left. "Page:" plus the page number is flush right. In the Format section, you can change the font, size, and style of the text for headers and footers. There is only one checkbox in the Options section: Print Header and Footer on First Page. This is checked by default. If you uncheck it, any document that spans multiple pages will not have the header and/or footer on the first page.

Caution

The settings for Header and Footer on the Print tab should not be confused with the settings on the Header tab. These settings affect documents printed with the form, whereas the settings on the Header form affect the visual appearance of the form.

FIGURE 9.13

You can define a formula for a footer on the Print tab of the Form Properties box.

Setting Form Security

The last tab, the Security tab, contains advanced settings for the form. The first two list boxes for read access and create access can be used to enhance author access to the form. Each of these list boxes provides access to the database ACL, from which you can choose specific users, groups or roles to limit read or author access. (These options are covered in more detail in Chapter 33, "Security and Domino Applications.") Figure 9.14 shows the Security tab of the Forms Properties box.

FIGURE 9.14

The Security tab of the Form Properties box enables you to determine reader and author access and set the encryption key.

The Default Encryption Keys field enables you to assign a specific encryption key to a form. If you then place encryptable fields on the form, when the document is saved, the encryption keys are applied to those specific fields.

> **Caution**
>
> Note that although a user might have editor access to the database and the form, if the user does not have the encryption key, he will not be able to save the document created with the form.

9

REVIEW OF BASIC FORMS DESIGN

Specifying Encryption Keys

Users can elect to encrypt a document with any key they possess, as long as there are encryptable fields on the document. However, you can ensure that a specific encryption key is used by adding the reserved field, SecretEncryptionKey, to the form. The field should be computed text, and should evaluate to the name of an encryption key. Whenever a user with the key saves the document, the fields set for encryption will be encrypted using that key. This technique has the same effect as setting a default encryption key, but can offer more flexibility.

For example, you might want to allow a certain class of users to create a document, but not encrypt it. Other users who are editors of the documents can then encrypt the document using a secret encryption key. To accomplish this, you can include a subform that contains unencrypted fields for the first class of users, and another subform for the editors that uses encrypted fields. This second subform should also include the special field, SecretEncryptionKey. Using a computed subform will enable you to display the correct form at the correct time.

There are two checkboxes at the bottom of the Security tab: Disable Printing/Forwarding/Copying to the Clipboard and Available to Public Access Users. Disabling printing and forwarding of the form is not a true security feature, because any reader of the document can access the fields. However, it is a definite deterrent to unauthorized access. Available to Public Access is designed to enable users with No Access or Depositor Access levels to see certain documents, views, or folders in the database. To create a form that is available for Public Access, you must include a field called $PublicAccess with a value of "1."

For More Information...

You can read more about security in Chapter 33.

Working with Text Properties

Now that you have learned about the properties of forms, you need to learn about the properties of various objects on forms. The good news is that although a lot of different objects can be placed on a form, the Properties box for each is common to all. All the settings are in one place, and you don't have to access the menu to change any of them. When you learn how to use the Properties boxes, you will have little trouble with them. They are context sensitive, so as you move from one object to another, the Properties box changes to display the properties for that object.

Perhaps the most common object on a form, except for fields, is text. Text is used to label fields and provide document titles, section titles, and other information. The Text Properties box is used to set text properties—and it is exactly the same Properties box used for text in documents. The Text Properties box has several tabs; from left to right, they are Font, Paragraph Alignment, Paragraph Margins, Paragraph Hide When, and Paragraph Styles. Each of these tabs is discussed in the following sections.

Using Font, Alignment, and Paragraph Margins Settings

The first three tabs enable you to set some basic text properties. The first tab is the Font tab, which is shown in Figure 9.15. On this tab, you can set the font type. The default in R5 has changed from Helv, a variant of the Helvetica text style, to Default Sans Serif. You can also set the text size (the default is 10 points), color (the default is black), and attributes (the default is plain). There is a control that allows you to increment and decrement the font size, or you can enter the font size directly in the field. There is also a button for setting the Permanent Pen font. (Because the Permanent Pen is principally used in documents and is not really a development tool, it will not be discussed here.)

FIGURE 9.15

The Fonts tab of the Text Properties box contains settings for fonts in forms and documents.

All Properties boxes can be moved, but you can also *collapse* the Properties box to reduce the amount of screen space that it occupies. You can do so by double-clicking the title bar or by clicking the Collapse button next to the question mark in the upper-right corner of the title bar. Double-clicking or clicking the Collapse button again restores the Properties box to full size. In R4, the Properties box merely shrank to the height of the title bar, but in R5 certain Properties boxes will display a tool palette when collapsed. This is the case with the Text Properties box (see Figure 9.16).

FIGURE 9.16

When collapsed, the Text Properties box displays a palette of commonly used items.

The collapsed properties box offers a *tool box*, which is a combination of items from the Font and Alignment tabs, plus several other useful options such as buttons to bold, italicize, and underline text; activate and deactivate the Permanent Pen; create tables; attach files; and import objects. There are also buttons to indent text, outdent text, and add bullets and buttons. During form design, you will find this toolbox to be very useful.

Keyboard and Menu Options

Many of these options are available from the menu and the SmartIcons toolbar, and many have corresponding hot keys, such as Ctrl+B to bold text.

The Alignment tab has settings for paragraph alignment, first line, lists, and line spacing. Some of these will be useful for form design, and others are primarily useful when composing and editing pages and documents (see Figure 9.17).

FIGURE 9.17

The Paragraph Alignment tab enables you to set many new List choices.

Significant enhancements have been made to the List types. In earlier releases, there were only bulleted and numbered lists, but now there are the following:

Bullet

Circle

Square

Checkmark

Number

> Alphabet (uppercase)
>
> Alphabet (lowercase)
>
> Roman (uppercase)
>
> Roman (lowercase)

The Paragraph Margins tab, shown in Figure 9.18, has pagination settings that control margins for printing, tab stops, and page breaks. The settings on this tab are used more for text in documents than they are for design.

Use the Ruler!

It is much easier to use the ruler to set tab stops. You can open the ruler from the menu by choosing View, Ruler, or by pressing Ctrl+R. Tab stops can be set by clicking on the ruler.

FIGURE 9.18

The Paragraph Margins tab has three sections: Margins, Tab Stops, and Pagination.

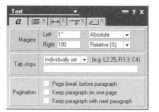

Caution

Tab stops do not work on the Web—HTML ignores tabs, and what appear as neatly formatted documents to a Notes client will wind up a horrible mess!

Using the Paragraph Hide When Tab

The Paragraph Hide When tab (see Figure 9.19) is often used in form design. This tab (also known as the Hide tab) enables you to specify conditions under which to hide objects in a paragraph. You can choose from the available checkboxes, you can use a formula, or you can choose a combination of checkboxes and a formula. For example, you can use the Hide When tab to hide the Action Bar buttons based on the state of the document. It doesn't make much sense to display an Edit action button when the document is already in Edit mode; nor does it make any sense to display a Save action button if the document is in Read mode. You can use the checkboxes to selectively hide such buttons on a form. You can also refine the Hide conditions by using a formula. The following lists each of the Hide conditions:

- Hide Paragraph From
    - Notes R4.6 or Later
    - Web Browsers
- Hide Paragraph When Document Is
    - Previewed for Reading
    - Previewed for Editing
    - Opened for Reading
    - Opened for Editing
    - Printed
    - Copied to the Clipboard
- Hide Paragraph if Formula Is True

Caution

Despite the fact that there is a Hide tab on the Field Properties box and on the Properties boxes for many other objects, hide-when attributes are applied to paragraphs, not to individual objects. For example, you cannot selectively hide objects within a line. If you want to selectively hide objects on the same line, create a table and place the objects in different cells in a table. The only exception to this is in a Layout region. In a Layout region, each object can have its own hide-when attributes.

FIGURE 9.19

The Paragraph Hide When tab is often used in Notes forms to hide objects.

When you write a Hide formula, you must use the Formula language. (The Formula language is discussed in Chapters 18, "The Formula Language," 19, "Formula Types," and 20, "Writing Formulas.") Because the formula must evaluate to True to hide the object, building the formulas can be a little tricky. It is important to remember that when the formula evaluates to true in the Formula language, the object is hidden. At first, this seems backward, and can take some time to understand. Not to belabor this point, but you can hide an object at all times by including a 1 in the formula window (1 is True in the Formula Language), and checking the Hide Paragraph if Formula Is True checkbox.

When you write formulas for this event, it is not always necessary to use @If(). For example, to hide an action when a document is new, which you might do for a button used by approvers for a document used in workflow, you might use the following formula:

```
@If(@IsNewDoc; @True; @False)
```

However, you don't need to go to that much trouble, and can instead use the following:

```
@IsNewDoc
```

This formula returns True, or 1, if the document has just been created, and will effectively hide the action button. To hide a button that might be used only when composing a new document, you can use a formula such as the following:

```
!@IsNewDoc
```

As you probably know, the exclamation point is a logical NOT, so this means "Hide this action button when the document is NOT new," that is, when someone has opened it for editing after it has been created and saved.

You might want to further restrict access to buttons through the use of Roles, which is a typical method in many applications. Perhaps there is a button you want to make available only to application users whom you have designated as the application's manager (not to be confused with manager access). Create a role, perhaps "Admin", and use the following hide formula:

```
!@Contains(@UserRoles; "Admin")
```

This formula hides the button when the user does not have the Admin role.

An earlier paragraph discussed using a combination of a Hide formula and checkboxes. To do this, create a Hide formula and select the appropriate checkboxes. Using the example of a Reviewer button, you might only want it visible during Edit mode. Use a Hide formula such as the following, and click the Previewed for reading and Opened for reading checkboxes:

```
!@Contains(@UserRoles; "Admin")
```

The same ideas can be applied to objects other than actions, such as text, graphics, and HTML code, just to name a few. You might want to hide HTML code from Notes users. To do so, highlight the paragraphs containing the HTML, and click the Notes R4.6 or later checkbox. This allows the HTML to be presented to a Web browser, but not to a Notes client.

As you can see, the artful use of the Hide conditions for objects is of tremendous value to the applications developer.

Using the Style Tab

It is useful to create definitions for frequently used styles in form design. You can define styles for field labels and hidden text, for example. It is very convenient to highlight the text and select a style from the Style tab rather than having to separately apply each element of the style that you want to use. To create a style for hidden text, follow these steps:

1. Format a text selection as Default Sans Serif, 8 points, and plain.

2. Select a color other than black, such as cyan.

3. Launch the Text Properties box and click the Styles tab.

4. Click the Create Style button.

5. Enter the name of the style as Hidden and check Make Style Available for All Documents (see Figure 9.20).

FIGURE 9.20

Creating a new style is very simple.

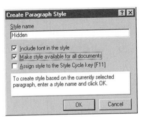

Working with Fields

Fields in Notes and Domino are not like fields in other databases. In a relational database, when you define a field, you pick the data type and then specify a width (with the exception of memo fields, which are similar to rich-text fields, and date fields). If you choose Text as a field data type, you have to specify a certain number of characters for the field. For a zip code field, you might choose 10: 5 for the five character zip code, 1 for the dash, and 4 for the four character "Zip + four" code. You can never enter more than 10 characters in that field.

In Domino, many fields have an indeterminate length—they are unstructured. When you specify Text as a data type, you are not required to set a length for the field. A user can enter a ten-character zip code in a text field or type all the way up to the maximum field size.

The concept of unstructured data extends from fields into documents. A document is unstructured because it does not contain a specific set of fields. Fields can be added and even deleted from a document even though they are not on any form. Different forms can present items in the same document. Contrast this with a structured relational database, which contains a specific set of tables, which in turn contain a specific set of fields. Each record in a table (analogous to a document) has exactly the same set of fields.

Figure 9.21 shows the Field Info tab of the Field Properties box. Before delving into the various attributes of fields, you must first understand some basic information regarding fields. There are two primary kinds of fields: single-use and shared. Single-use fields are the most common. (Shared fields are discussed in in Chapter 12.) Single-use fields can be converted to Shared fields from a menu choice, or you can create a shared field in the Designer. Like any other object, fields have certain attributes. Fields can be either editable or computed, must be a specific data type, and can be single or multivalued. Table 9.4 lists the editable properties of fields.

FIGURE 9.21

The Field Properties box is where you define the attributes of a field—this figure shows the Field Info tab.

TABLE 9.4 Field Types

Editable Properties	*Purpose*
Editable	The default for fields, editable by users and stored in a document. Value can be assigned when the document is first created by writing a formula in the Default event.
Computed	Value created by formula; stored in a document.
Computed for display	Value created by formula; not stored in a document.
Computed when composed	Value created by a formula when a document is first composed. Stored in a document.

> **Caution**
>
> A rich-text field can only be editable or computed.

Regardless of whether the field you create is single-use or shared, multivalued or single-valued, or one of the editable properties, a specific data type must be chosen for each field.

Release 5 has extended the available field types, added several new types to the list, and split up the keywords field type into dialog list, checkbox, and radio button. Listboxes and comboboxes were available in R4 only in Layout regions; in R5, they're field types. In R4, these five types of keyword fields were previously configured in the Options tab, which no longer exists. The default field type is now editable text.

There are several data types in the following list from which you can choose:

Text

Date/Time

Number

Dialog list

Checkbox

Radio button

Listbox

Combobox

Rich text

Authors

Names

Readers

Password

Formula

Multivalued fields are a very powerful feature of Notes that allows a list of values to be stored in a single field. To borrow terminology from other programming languages, Domino is basically storing an array in a field. All types of fields except radio buttons, comboboxes, rich-text, formula, and password fields can be multivalued. In R4, the checkbox was Allow Multi-Values; in R5 it is Allow Multiple Values. To create a multi-value field, just click the Allow Multiple Values checkbox under the Type field. When you do this, additional display options become available on the Control and Advanced tabs of the Field Properties box.

For More Information...

There are many powerful list-processing @Functions available in Notes. For more information, please see Chapter 19.

Time Sliders and Calendar Controls

Prior to Release 5, the time slider and calendar control was only available in layout regions. Now, you can display them in a standard Notes form by clicking Native OS in the Style section of the Field Info tab.

Working with Text Fields

Text fields are the default field type. Text fields in Notes are different from text fields in other databases in that they do not have a fixed width. They can store up to 15KB of data. Text fields can be used in field and view formulas, and can contain numbers, letters, punctuation, and spaces. Text fields cannot be used in numeric calculations, although the function @TextToNumber will convert text values to numbers, which can then be used in calculations. Similarly, text fields can be converted to dates using @TextToTime. Formatting in text fields is fixed at the form level by the developer and cannot be altered by the user.

Working with Date/Time Fields

The name of Date and Time fields has been changed from Time to Date/Time in Release 5. Time fields can contain date and time, date, or time values. Figure 9.22 shows the Control tab of the Properties box for a time field.

FIGURE 9.22

The Control tab for Time fields enables you to set many display options.

The display options for Time fields on the Format tab are far more extensive than in any previous version of Notes and Domino. As you can see from Figure 9.22, there are numerous display rules in the following sections:

- **On Display**—You can Use Preferences From User's Settings or Custom. Selecting Custom displays more options in the Display Date and Display Time sections.
- **Display Date**—When this field is checked, you can use the Show and Special fields to determine the display. Show allows you to specify which date parts to display, whereas Special is primarily for Year 2000 compliance.
- **Display Time**—When this field is checked, you can use the Show and Time Zone fields to determine the display. Show allows you to specify which time parts to display, and Time Zone lets you determine how to handle times from different time zones.
- **On Input**—You can require users to enter four-digit years, which is useful for Year 2000 compliance. You can also require users to enter alphabetic months.
- **Border Style**—This is only available for the Notes style. The setting disappears if Native OS style is chosen on the Field Info tab. Border style consists of a single checkbox: Show Field Delimiters. When checked, the familiar corner brackets appear.

Date and Time Input

Have your users ever been frustrated with Notes's insistence that dates and times be entered in specific formats? In R5, Notes is less restrictive and will attempt to interpret any input in a date/time field. Only when Notes cannot determine a date/time value from the input will the user receive an error message. Now you can type a single number in a date field, such as "9," and Notes will use it to construct a date.

When displaying dates, each of the date parts and separators can be further defined by choosing a Show option. For example, you can set the display to show a date such as Thursday, April 8, 1999 by customizing the date display options.

Each time you change the format options, the Sample field changes to display the effects of your choices.

For example, to display the date in the format Thursday, April 8, 1999, take the following steps:

1. Click the Control tab.

2. Select Custom in the Use Preferences From field.

3. Change the Show field to All.

4. Leave the default Format at WMDY.

5. Add a comma and a space to the first separator field, and leave the other separator boxes as is.

6. Leave the Month box at mm.

7. Leave the Day box at dd.

8. Set the Year box to yyyy.

9. Change the Weekday display box to ww (see Figure 9.23).

FIGURE 9.23

The completed Control tab that causes dates to display in the format: Weekday, Month, Day, and Year.

The Display Time section consists of a Show field, a Time Zone field, and if Custom is chosen, Format and Separator fields. Like the Show field in the Display Date section, the Show field for time enables you to specify which time parts are used. The Time Zone field enables you to determine how Notes interacts with the time zone attribute of a time value. The Format field, new to R5, enables you to switch between 12 and 24 hour formats! Prior versions of Notes did not permit the display of the 24 hour format. The Separator field, also new to R5, defaults to a colon. If you want to change it, type a new character in the box.

Setting Display Options in View Columns

Display options can also be set in view columns. You can also control the display of dates and times with the @Text function. See the section "Converting Time-Date Values" in Chapter 19.

As mentioned earlier in this chapter, prior to Release 5 of Notes and Domino, you could only display calendar controls and time sliders in layout regions. Now you can add them to a regular form by choosing Native OS style on the Field Info tab.

Time sliders created with a multivalued field enable the user to specify a time range; the beginning and ending time control can be moved independently or the entire slider control can be moved as a unit. If you do not specify a multivalued field, the slider will display with a single control allowing the user to select a specific time rather than a range. Figure 9.24 shows a time slider with a time range. To access the Time control, click the Clock button next to the field.

FIGURE 9.24

A multivalued time control lets the users graphically enter start and end times.

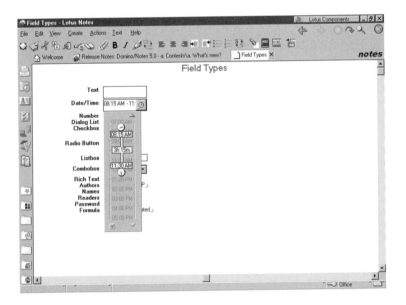

To access the calendar control when the form is in edit, click the Calendar button next to the field. Figure 9.25 shows a calendar control. To create a field that displays a calendar control, click Native OS style on the Form Info tab of the Field Properties box. The control functions easily—the user can click a specific day in the calendar format and can use the arrows to move forward and backward through the months.

FIGURE 9.25

The calendar control presents a visual way to enter a date that is easy to use.

Caution

These controls will work only with a Notes client—they will not be available to a Web client.

Date/Time fields are very frequently used in Domino applications. The numerous display options and the addition of the time and date controls to a regular form are welcome additions to Release 5.

Working with Number Fields

Figure 9.26 shows the Control tab for a number field.

The Control tab for numbers contains the following six sections:

- Number Format
- Preferences for Display Formatting
- Decimal Places
- Additional Display Formatting
- Border Style
- Currency Symbol

FIGURE 9.26

The Control tab has numerous options for numeric fields.

The radio buttons in the Number format section define four numeric types: Decimal, Percent, Scientific, and Currency. Decimal places can be set for Decimal and Percent formats from a control in the Decimal Places section. To enable the Decimal Places spinner, you must deselect the Varying field. Otherwise, the spinner for the Decimal Places is not available.

Similar to display options for a date/time field, you can switch between Custom and User settings in the Use Preferences From field. When Custom is selected, you can determine the decimal symbol and thousands separator. The defaults are a period and a comma respectively. Additional Display Formatting options enclose a number in parentheses when it is negative and punctuate it at thousands. Border style lets you turn field delimiters on and off. Currency Symbol settings are available when the number format is currency and Use Preferences from is set Custom. If Custom is not chosen, the currency symbol defaults to the country that is configured for the user. When custom is chosen, you can choose the country, specify a custom currency character and select Symbol Follows Number (6,000$) or Space Next to Number ($ 6,000).

Number fields can contain the digits 0 through 9, plus the sign (+ or -) and E or e for scientific notation. Number fields are used whenever calculations must be performed on the field. Note that even though telephone numbers and zip codes are numeric, it doesn't make any sense to store them as numbers. Why? You don't need to do any mathematical calculations on zip codes or telephone numbers.

Using Keyword Fields

Keyword fields are special fields that present lists of choices to the users. There are five types of keyword fields: dialog list, checkbox, radio button, listbox, and combobox. Before Release 5, listboxes and comboboxes were available only on Layout regions, but now they are available in standard Notes forms. Keyword used to be a field type, and the five types were display options. In R5, each type of keyword field is listed as a separate field type. Figure 9.27 shows the Control tab of a keyword field.

FIGURE 9.27

You define the contents of a keyword field in the Choices box of the Control tab for a keyword field.

There are three sections to the Control tab, some of which have subsections:

- **Display**—This is available for dialog lists, checkboxes, and radio buttons. In dialog lists, it controls the display of field delimiters; in checkboxes and radio buttons, it controls the border style and number of columns.

- **Choices**—In this field, you define the choices that appear in the field. Choices are the following:

    - **Enter Choices (One per Line)**—This is the default, and it enables the developer to type values directly into the window.

    - **Use Formula for Choices**—This is perhaps the most commonly used choice and allows the developer to use a formula to determine the list of keywords. Typically, the formulas use @DbColumn or @DbLookup. @DbColumn returns a list of values from a column in a view, and @DbLookup also returns a list of values from a view column but allows you to pass a value to filter those values with a key.

    - **Use Address Dialog for Choices**—This presents the familiar Address Book dialog box. If the field is multivalued, you will be able to choose more than one name; if not, only a single name can be chosen. This is similar to @PickList when you specify the [Name] keyword.

    - **Use Access Control List for Choices**—This allows choices to be made from the ACL for the current database.

    - **Use View Dialog for Choices**—When this option is selected, you can select not only a view but also a database from which the view can be chosen! This can be quite useful and is similar in function to @PickList.

9

REVIEW OF BASIC FORMS DESIGN

- **Options**—Some options are always available, and some are conditionally displayed depending on the field type and the setting in Choices. These options are as follows:

    - **Allow Values Not in List**—This option lets the user type a new entry into the field. It is available for dialog lists and comboboxes.

    - **Look Up Names as Each Character Is Entered**—This option is available for dialog lists that use the Address dialog box for choices.

    - **Display Entry Helper Button**—This is available only for Dialog lists. When checked, a small gray button (the entry helper) appears beside the field in Edit mode. Clicking the button opens a dialog box of choices.

    - **Refresh Fields on Keyword Change**—When checked, if the contents of the keyword field change, the document is refreshed. If any field values depend on the value of this field, they will be updated. This is often used in tandem with the next option.

    - **Refresh Choices on Document Refresh**—When checked, if the document is refreshed (perhaps as the result of a change in another keyword field) the choices in the keyword field will be refreshed.

Display Options

The Display section is available for dialog lists, radio buttons, and checkboxes. For dialog lists, you can only turn the border on and off. For radio buttons and checkboxes, you can set the Border style of the field and the number of columns to be displayed. The Border styles are the following:

- **None**   Presents a checkbox or radio button with no background or border.

- **Single**   Presents a checkbox or radio button with a border.

- **Inset**   Displays a standard Windows-style frame with a gray background. This style is useful in layout regions or in forms with a gray background. In R4, this option was called 3D.

The Columns control allows you to display choices horizontally by specifying the number of columns. For example, if you had a keyword field with a Yes or No choice, you would typically use a radio button. By default, the display would be vertical, with Yes appearing above No. To display these two choices in a single line, specify 2 as the number of columns. Note that the Columns option is only available for checkboxes and radio buttons.

> **Radio Buttons or Checkboxes?**
>
> Radio buttons are used when only one choice is possible. If you change the display to a radio button, you will notice that there is no longer a multiple value checkbox available. Checkboxes on the other hand, are used to allow multiple choices. It is important to adhere to this interface standard; in fact, the Domino Designer more or less forces you to.
>
> When you choose display styles, bear in mind that radio buttons and checkboxes are not well suited to lengthy lists.

> **Caution**
>
> When a user has clicked a radio button, it cannot be unclicked. It is sometimes useful to provide a "n/a" or "unknown" choice so that incorrect data is not stored.

Keyword Field Choices

You can create keyword lists by typing them directly into the field, by creating a formula, or by using one of the other dialog choices. Methods of populating keyword lists using @DbLookup, @DbColumn(), @Picklist(), and other formulas are discussed in Chapter 19.

The remaining choices, Use Address Dialog, Use Access Control List, and Use View Dialog all present dialog boxes from which the user can make choices.

Options for Keyword Fields

If you check Allow Values Not in List, you can dynamically build lists of lookup values. In other words, the keyword field can become self-referencing. You do this by building the keyword list with a formula such as @DbLookup() or @DbColumn() against a view that contains the keyword field as the first sorted and categorized column. When a user creates and saves a document with a new value, it automatically adds it to the keyword list. The view should be sorted and categorized so that unique values are returned.

9

REVIEW OF BASIC FORMS DESIGN

Caution

By default, `@DbColumn()` and `@DbLookup()` cache the values returned. This means that a user could add a new value and save the document, but it won't show up in a keyword field. If you specify `NoCache`, the values won't be stored, and the list will be refreshed each time. This causes an impact on performance that depends on the number of documents in the view, so you will have to weigh the application's needs against its performance. The performance impact will be minimal as long as the list remains relatively small, but if the formula returns thousands of items, you will definitely see an impact. The impact will be greater or lesser depending on the server and client hardware.

A workaround to this is to use the Use View dialog box for choices or `@PickList`. However, this doesn't provide a nice, tidy list.

Using Hidden Views

If you elect to build keyword lists from a view with `@DbColumn()` or `@DbLookup()`, use a hidden view as the target. This enables you to build a view consisting of one or more columns that the user doesn't see. Many times views such as this have no real value to an end user, and hiding them is a good idea.

Look Up Names as Each Character Is Entered is available only for dialog lists that use the Address Book. If you check this setting, you can use type-ahead to locate names in the Domino directory.

Display Entry Helper Button is self-explanatory, but the two Refresh options merit further discussion. For example, assume that you have a database of cities, states, and zip codes. Users first select a state, then a city, and last, a postal code. After selecting a state, wouldn't it be nice to display only cities from that state? and after selecting a city, to display only postal codes in that city so that users can more easily pick the right one? This is an example of a *cascaded* lookup. The choices displayed in the city and postal code fields depend on the values in other keyword fields. To accomplish this in Notes (assuming the city database was already created), create a form with the three fields set up as keyword fields. Use `@DbColumn()` to retrieve the list of states, and mark the option Refresh Fields on Keyword Change. For the cities, use `@DbLookup()` with a key of the state field. Mark the options for the city field Refresh Fields on Keyword Change and Refresh Choices on Document Refresh. This will cause the city field to restrict the list of cities to those within the state chosen. The postal code field can be set up with

@DbLookup() using the city as the key. In this case, only Refresh Choices on Document Refresh needs to be set because no other keywords depend on the value of the postal code field. This is a powerful technique!

Workaround for Web Clients

You can imitate this technique for Web documents using JavaScript.

Working with Rich-Text Fields

Rich-text fields are very interesting. They can be thought of as *bit buckets* because you can put nearly anything into them: file attachments, OLE objects, images, and so forth. Unlike other types of fields, the user can change the format of text in a rich-text field. Rich-text fields can contain the following (and this is not even an all-inclusive list!):

- Objects, such as images, cut-and-pasted or imported into them
- Hotspots, whether graphic, pushbutton, or text-added
- Multiple file attachments
- Entire documents (the Reply with History in Notes mail is an example of this)
- Multiple text formatting styles
- OLE objects
- Lotus components
- Java applets
- Embedded objects such as Outlines, Folder Panes, and Navigators
- Sections
- Tables
- Computed text
- HTML

A rich-text field is similar to a word processing document. Rich-text field limits are almost absurdly high; they are limited only by disk space and can be up to 1GB. The maximum size of a single paragraph is 64MB!

Before you decide to use a rich-text field, be aware that you cannot easily access the contents of a rich-text field in a formula, nor can they be directly displayed in a view. Using the Formula language, you can use @Text to return the text content of the field. In LotusScript, you can use the GetFormattedText method of the NotesRichTextItem. You can also access certain properties of a rich-text field with @Functions such as @Attachments, @AttachmentNames, and @AttachmentLength, which return information about any file attachments. You can find out whether the field is available with @IsAvailable. There is extensive support in LotusScript for rich-text fields.

If you are presenting the form to a Web client, you have a very powerful display option at your disposal. On the Field Info tab, there is a section titled On Web Access. Set it to Use Java Applet, and the Editor Applet is enabled, as shown in Figure 9.28. You'll notice that several buttons can be used to control the format of the text and to create links.

FIGURE 9.28

Using a Java applet to display a rich-text field gives a Web client access to powerful formatting options not available with standard HTML.

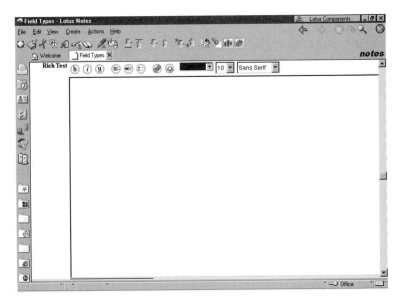

Working with Readers, Authors, and Names Fields

Readers, Authors, and Names fields work with usernames. Readers and Authors fields enable you and the user to control access to documents in conjunction with the ACL. Readers fields limit read access to documents. If the document has a Readers field, and you are not listed in it, you will not even know that the document exists. Authors fields control editor access to documents. Names fields display names as they appear on User IDs, and are used for security.

You can place usernames, groups, or roles in Readers and Authors fields. By controlling the value of Readers and Authors fields, you can control who can read and edit the document. This is a very useful technique in workflow applications, where you might base the value of both Authors and Readers fields on the status of the document.

Readers and Authors fields only *modify* the database ACL; they do not replace it. For example, if you have Reader access to a database, even if you are listed in an Authors field of a document, you cannot edit the document. If you have Editor access to a database, you can edit a document even if you are not listed in an Authors field. However, if you are not listed in the Readers field, even if you have Manager access to the database, you won't be able to see the document.

An Administrative Backdoor!

It is always a good idea to leave yourself a backdoor into a document. You can do this by using a role and placing the role into the Reader or Authors field. By assigning yourself to this role in the database ACL, you can always access any documents. Remember, even if you are a manager of the database and can edit any document, if you are not in the Readers list, you will not even know the document exists! You should also include the LocalDomainServers group in both Readers and Authors fields.

For More Information...

For more information about form security using these field types, see the section titled "Form-Level Security" in Chapter 33.

Working with Password and Formula Fields

These two field types are new to Release 5. Password fields allow you to create a field that accepts alphanumeric entry, but displays only asterisks. However, although a password field can protect a user's entry from prying eyes, if you save the field, it is not secure and can be viewed in the Fields tab of the Document Properties box. As a workaround, you can clear the value of the field before it is saved.

Formula fields are intended for use with database subscriptions. You can add a subscription form to any database. For an example, see the Headlines database $Subscription form. When users subscribe to databases, they are notified when a document that meets their criteria is entered into the database. Essentially, the formula field is a selection statement that the server uses to determine whether a notification is necessary.

Adding Fields to a Form

Adding simple data entry fields to a form is nearly as easy as adding text to the form. To add a field to a form, position the cursor at the desired location. Click the Create Field

SmartIcon on the toolbar or choose Create, Field from the menu. Figure 9.29 shows the Properties box for a new field.

FIGURE 9.29

Fields are named in the Field Info tab of the Field Properties box.

As soon as you create a new field, the Field Properties box is opened to the Field Info tab. Note that a new field is always Untitled (see Figure 9.29) so you must change the name of the field. New fields always default to an editable, single-valued text field. To change the type of field or its editable properties, simply click the Type drop-down list.

You can also insert shared fields from the Create menu (Create, Insert Shared Field) or from the SmartIcons toolbar. After you choose to insert a shared field, you will be presented with a list of shared fields in the database (see Figure 9.30). In this case, you don't have to define the field because the field will be already named and defined. In fact, you cannot change the attributes of a shared field from a form—you must do so from the Resources\Shared Fields view of the Design List. Shared fields can be distinguished from other fields by the thick black border that surrounds the field in design. You can share an existing single use field by choosing Design, Share this field from the menu. (Shared fields are discussed in Chapter 12.)

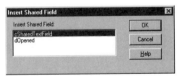

FIGURE 9.30

The Insert Shared Field dialog box lists shared fields available for insertion into the current form.

New to R5 are symbols in the field box in design that identify the type of field. For example, a text field has the letter T on the right whereas a rich-text field has an italicized *T*. Figure 9.31 shows each field type.

FIGURE 9.31

*This form shows
each field type—
note the symbols
in each field box
indicating its type.*

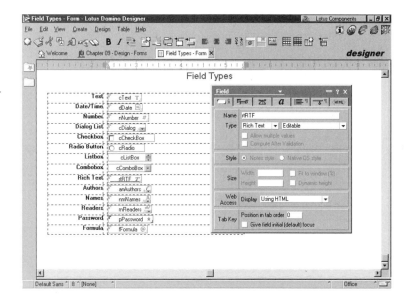

There are several tabs that appear for all fields regardless of type. These are the Field Info, Control, Advanced, Font, Paragraph Alignment, Paragraph Hide When, and the Field Extra HTML tabs.

Using the Field Info Tab

The settings on this tab vary based on the field type. The Field Info tab is used to name a field, choose its type and editable status. There are many features new to Release 5. For example, you can switch between Notes and Native OS style, set the size, determine the display style for rich-text fields to a Web client, and determine the tab order (something that developers have been requesting for some time). Following are the sections on the Field Info tab of the Field Properties box:

- **Name and Type**—Specify the field name and type in this section. Two checkboxes, Allow multiple values and Compute after validation, are enabled based on the field type.

- **Style**—Contains a radio button with two choices: Notes style and Native OS style. For example, clicking Native OS style in a date/time field will display the calendar picker or time slider. When you switch from the default of Notes style to Native OS, the field box enlarges and the symbol changes. This setting is conditionally available.

9

REVIEW OF BASIC
FORMS DESIGN

- **Size**—This is conditionally available for certain field types and styles settings. You can specify width and height and set the width to fit to a percent of the window. You can also set the height to be dynamic.

- **Web Access**—This section is completely blank for all fields except rich-text; the section title does not even appear. You can choose to display rich-text fields Using HTML (the default) or Using Java Applet.

- **Tab Key**—You can enter a number for the tab order in Position in Tab Order. Unfortunately, there is no way to dynamically specify the tab order; you simply have to type a number. When you specify a tab order by entering a number, a number appears in the field on the form. Check Give This Field Initial (Default) Focus if you want the user moved to this field when a document using this form is opened for editing.

Using the Control Tab

The Control tab is illustrated in Figure 9.32. The Control tab contains display and input settings for fields. Many different settings might be present—presenting a comprehensive list of settings that appear on this tab for each field type and style is beyond the scope of this chapter.

FIGURE 9.32

The Control tab changes significantly based on the field type and other settings in the Form Info tab.

Using the Advanced Tab

The Advanced tab has several sections: Help Description, Multi-Value Options, Security Options, and Special Event Options (see Figure 9.33).

Figure 9.33

The Advanced tab lets you specify field-level help, Multi-Value Options, and Security Options; note that Special Event Options appear only for time/date fields.

Field-level help is entered in the Help Description field. Field-level help appears at the bottom of the document window, as long as it is enabled. Multi-Value Options are activated for multivalued fields. They define the way data appears when entered and when it is displayed. Choices for separators are Space, Comma, Semicolon, New Line, and Blank Line. Security Options are the following:

- None
- Sign If Mailed or Saved in Section
- Enable Encryption for This Field
- Must Have at Least Editor Access to Use

Special Event Options only appears for time/date fields when the Native OS style is chosen. This section consists of a single checkbox: Run Exiting Event After Time/Date Change. Code in the Exiting event of the field will execute when the contents change.

Using the Font, Alignment, and Hide When Tabs

These tabs are exactly the same as the tabs for the Text Properties box discussed in earlier sections. For more information on these tabs, please see the sections "Using Font, Alignment, and Paragraph Margins Settings" and "Using the Paragraph Hide When Tab" earlier in this chapter.

Using the Field Extra HTML Tab

This tab has two sections: Name and HTML Tags (see Figure 9.34). The Name section is not available because it makes no sense to rename a field! The HTML Tags section

9

REVIEW OF BASIC FORMS DESIGN

enables you to specify certain HTML attributes for a field. There are five fields on this tab, which are the following:

- ID
- Class
- Style
- Title
- Other

FIGURE 9.34

The Field Extra HTML Tab of the Field Properties box.

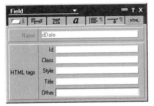

You can use ID to further identify a field to JavaScript or a Cascading Style Sheet. Class and Style are used with Cascading Style Sheets also. Text entered in the Title field appears as a floating text box when the mouse hovers over the field in a Web browser. Currently, the Title feature only works in Internet Explorer. You can enter other tags in the Other field.

For More Information...

For more information using HTML, see Chapter 21, "Enhancing Domino Applications with HTML."

Writing Formulas in Fields

The Design pane at the bottom of the screen has not yet been a part of this discussion because the functionality of this pane is described in Chapter 8. This is where most programming takes place. Not all programming is done in the Design pane; some of it can exist as part of a Keyword field, for example.

If you select Use Formula for Choices on the Form Info tab of a Keyword field, you can enter a formula in the window on the tab or click the Formula Window button. Clicking the Formula Window button causes a new, larger edit window to open in which you can enter more complex formulas. In this case, the formula will populate the keyword list.

For More Information...

For more information about using the Formula language in fields, see Chapters 18, 19, and 20.

Formulas in fields are calculated in a specific order—from left to right and from top to bottom. This calculation takes place when a document is first created, when it is refreshed, when it is opened for editing, and when it is saved. The only exception to this is a Computed when Composed field. Although you can programmatically alter the contents of a Computed when Composed field, the value is never refreshed.

Editable and Computed fields have different events which can be programmed.

Writing Formulas for Editable Fields

Formulas are available for the following types of editable field-level events:

- **Default value**—Formulas in this event determine the initial contents of the field. Default values are assigned only once, when a document is composed.

- **Input Translation**—This event modifies the data entered by the user, adjusting the values in the field or forcing it to conform to a certain formatting. It is executed when a document is saved or refreshed. This event is not available for rich-text fields.

- **Input Validation**—Formulas in this event validate the data entered and are executed when a document is saved or refreshed, after the Input Translation event. This event is not available for rich-text fields.

- **HTML Attributes**—Formulas in this event enable the developer to enter HTML code specific to the field that will be used when displaying documents composed with the form to a Web client.

Writing Formulas for Computed Fields

Computed fields are calculated when a document is composed and when it is saved or refreshed. Computed when Composed fields are only calculated once, when the document is created. Computed fields have a Value formula. If you want to limit the readers of a document, you can include a Readers field as described earlier in the section on Readers, Names, and Authors fields. By making this a computed field, you can very easily control who can see documents created with this form.

Using Other Languages

You don't have to stick to the Formula language to work with fields. You can write LotusScript and JavaScript in field events as well. There are several LotusScript events available for fields. JavaScript is new to R5, and a large number of JavaScript events are available as well.

For More Information...

For more information about LotusScript, see Chapters 22, "Introduction to LotusScript," 23, "Basic LotusScript," and 24, "Writing LotusScript." For more information about JavaScript, see Chapters 25, "Introduction to JavaScript," 26, "Basic JavaScript," and 27, "Using JavaScript in Domino Applications."

Summary

This chapter covered a lot of ground and has provided a solid foundation and reference for form design. You have learned what forms are, what types of forms are available, and how to choose an appropriate form type. You've learned about the different field types as well as the different Properties boxes you are likely to see when designing forms. The information in this chapter is essential to developing Domino applications. The next chapter discusses some of the more advanced features of form design.

On the CD...

The CD-ROM in the back of this book contains a database titled Chapter 09 (Chapt09.nsf) that has several forms used in the screen shots for this chapter.

Advanced Form Design

by Steve Kern

IN THIS CHAPTER

Chapter 9, "Review of Basic Forms Design," covered the basic elements of form design. You learned enough in that chapter to build basic forms that suffice for most purposes. This chapter takes you beyond simple forms and discusses some sophisticated techniques and advanced design elements.

Working with Tables

Tables have been completely revamped in R5, and there are numerous new features. You can use tables in forms as well as in pages and rich-text fields in documents. Tables can help organize and present information in documents and forms.

One advantage of using tables to position elements on a form is that each cell in a table can be treated as a "paragraph." This means that you can apply different paragraph styles in the same row. For example, you can't position a text label for a field in a form by pixels as you can in certain other application designers that treat text as an object. Instead, the text wraps along with the field and any other text in the line. Using a table, you can create a column for field labels and a separate column for the fields and format each column independently. The text labels can be set right-justified, and the fields left-justified to make a neat display.

You might recall from Chapter 9 that Hide-When attributes are applied to paragraphs. This means that you cannot selectively hide objects in a single line. The Hide-When attribute applies to the entire paragraph. In a table, different Hide-When attributes can be applied to individual cells. Text styles and properties can also be applied to each cell. In effect, this allows the conditional display of objects in a single line. All you have to do is selectively apply the attributes to the appropriate cells in a single row. If you then hide the table borders, the row appears as a single "line" in the form.

Applying Changes to Multiple Cells

Ranges of cells can be changed by highlighting rows or columns and making the changes in the appropriate Properties box or through the keyboard. For example, to change the column titles (the topmost row) of a table to bold, highlight the row with the mouse and press Ctrl+B or click the Text Bold SmartIcon.

What's New for Tables in Release 5?

There are so many new features of tables in Release 5 that it is hard to enumerate all of them! Following are some of the more important features:

- The R5 Table Properties box has been expanded to seven tabs. Each will be discussed in the following sections.

- When collapsed, the Table Properties box has several convenient buttons enabling you to add and delete rows and columns, modify cell borders, and more.

- There are now four types of tables: Basic, Tabbed, Animated, and Programmed.

- You can now create recursive tables, or tables within tables.

- There are many enhancements to table formatting including drop shadows for tables, alternate row colors, gradients, colored borders, and more.

- Smart resizing of cells is a new property.

- HTML support has been added for table and cell attributes.

As you read through this section, you will discover how to use many of these exciting new features. Many are purely cosmetic, but remember that although function of a form is of paramount importance, cosmetic enhancements of an application's interface can contribute positively to its usability.

Creating a Table

Creating a table is quite simple; click the Create Table SmartIcon or choose Create, Table from the menu. The resulting Create Table dialog box is completely new and contains settings for Number of Rows, Number of Columns, Table Width, and Table Type. There are now four types of tables: Basic, Tabbed, Animated, and Programmed. The default settings for the Create Table dialog box are two rows and two columns, with a fixed width and a type of basic as shown in Figure 10.1. The Table Width and Table Type fields are also new to R5. After you create a table, you can insert, append, and delete rows and columns.

Creating Tables Within Tables

To include a table within a table, position the cursor in one of the cells, and select Create, Table from the menu or click the Create Table SmartIcon. Specify the number of rows and columns and check or uncheck Fixed Width as appropriate. Tables within other tables are known as Embedded or Recursive tables.

FIGURE 10.1

The Create Table dialog box enables you to specify the number of rows and columns, and to choose the width and type.

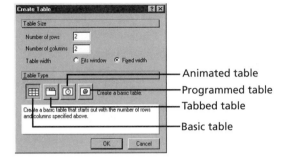

— Animated table
— Programmed table
— Tabbed table
— Basic table

After you create a table, three new SmartIcons appear on the toolbar next to the Create Table SmartIcon. In order from left to right they are

- Table Insert Row
- Table Delete Selected Row(s)
- Table Properties

A new menu, the Table menu, is also added. This menu has the prompts listed in Table 10.1.

TABLE 10.1 Table Menu Prompts

Prompt	Effect
Table Properties	Opens the Table Properties box
Insert Row	Adds a row before the current cell
Insert Column	Adds a column before the current cell
Insert Special	Presents a dialog box with options to insert or append a specific number of rows or columns
Append Row	Adds a row after the current cell
Append Column	Adds a column after the current cell
Delete Selected Row(s)	Deletes the current row or rows if more than one row is highlighted
Delete Selected Column(s)	Deletes the current column or columns if more than one column is highlighted
Delete Special	Presents a dialog box with options to delete a specific number of rows or columns
Merge Cells	Combines two or more cells into a single cell
Split Cells	Splits a merged cell into the constituent cells
Auto Size	Resizes cells based on their contents

Appending Rows the Easy Way!

You can also append rows to tables by positioning the cursor in the cell in the lower-right corner and pressing the Tab key.

Working with Table Properties

The next several sections discuss the expanded Table Properties box. In Release 4.x, there were only three tabs on the Properties box for tables: Borders, Layout, and Colors. See Figure 10.2.

FIGURE 10.2

The Table Properties box from Release 4.6 had only three tabs.

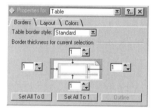

You can open the Table Properties box by clicking Table Properties SmartIcon or choosing Table, Table Properties from the menu when the cursor is within a table. In R5, the Properties box now has seven tabs: Table Layout, Cell Borders, Table/Cell Background, Table Borders, Table Margins, Table Rows, and Table Programming. Many new features for tables are found on these tabs.

Finding Tab Names

To determine the name of a tab in the Properties box, simply momentarily rest the mouse pointer over the tab. A small pop-up window called Hover Help displays the name of the tab. This is particularly useful for those tabs that use a graphic such as the propeller-hat Advanced tabs.

Understanding Table Layouts

The Table Layout tab consists of two sections: Table and Cell. The table settings are global, as are some cell attributes—an asterisk marks those cell attributes that are global. The Table section has two drop-down lists, one for the width and one for the position. There are three choices for width: Fixed Width, Fit to Window, and Fit with Margins (new to R5). The Position setting is new to R5, and you can specify Left (the default), Right, or Center (see Figure 10.3).

FIGURE 10.3

The Table Layout tab contains many global settings for a table—note the ruler along the top of the Form.

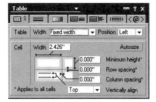

Table 10.2 lists the options that are available in the Cell section of the Table Layout tab.

TABLE 10.2   Table Cell Layout Settings

Setting	Options
Cell Width	Sets the width of cells; affects all cells in a given column.
Autosize	A button which sizes cells to their contents.
Minimum Height	Global; sets minimum cell height.
Row Spacing	Global; specifies the spacing between rows.
Column Spacing	Global; sets the spacing between columns.
Vertically Align	Specific to an individual cell. Choose from Top (the default), Center, and Bottom to position the cell contents within the cell.

When you create a table containing multiple columns, all columns are initially the same width. If you want to have complete control over the width of a table, change the Table Width field to Fixed Width. The width of individual columns can be changed without affecting the remaining cells. With Fit to Window or Fit to Margin set, when an individual cell is changed, the other cells adjust to fill the remaining width. Note that although a value in inches can be typed into the Cell Width field on the Layout tab, it is often far easier to use the ruler to resize the columns. (To turn the ruler on or off, click the View Ruler SmartIcon.) To resize a column of cells using the ruler, click the dark gray drag handle in the ruler for the right column of the cell. A thin black line appears when dragging the cell border and helps visually position the cell borders.

Setting Cell Borders

The Cell Borders tab has two sections: Cell Border Style and Cell Border Thickness. The Style section applies to the entire table.

Global Settings and Embedded Tables

Settings that are global to a table apply to the currently selected table. If a table is embedded within another table, global settings apply to the embedded table if that is the selected table, or to the "parent" table, if the parent table is selected.

You can choose a border style from Solid (the default), Ridge, or Groove. Ridge and Groove are similar to the Extruded and Embossed styles from R4. New to R5 is the ability to specify colors for cell borders. (In R4, you could only apply colors to cell backgrounds.) The standard color picker is available for border color.

On the other hand, the settings for Border thickness can be applied to individual cells, a range of cells, or to the entire table. Cell thickness is controlled buy spinners on all four sides. There are three buttons on the tab: Set All to 0, Set All to 1, and Outline. The two Set All buttons can apply to a single cell, a range of cells, or the entire table. To select a range of cells or the entire table, drag the mouse pointer with the left button held down until the cells you want to affect are highlighted. Release the mouse, and the cells remain highlighted until you click elsewhere. The Outline button is available only when more than one cell is selected. The large spinner buttons on the right side of the tab apply to the current cell selection. If multiple cells are selected, clicking the up or down arrow increases the border thickness for all cells in the selected range. The Cell Borders tab provides a high degree of control over the appearance of the table's borders (see Figure 10.4).

Hiding Table Borders

To make the cell borders of an entire table invisible, highlight all the cells and open the Table Properties box to the Cell Borders tab. Click the Set All to 0 button and the table is now invisible. Using an invisible table allows the text and fields to be tightly formatted without the extra clutter of cell borders.

10

ADVANCED FORM
DESIGN

FIGURE 10.4

The Cell Borders tab of the Table Properties box has settings for the style and thickness of the cell borders.

Using the Table/Cell Background Tab

Colors of individual cells or of the entire table can be set from the Color tab shown in Figure 10.5. Many new features have been added to this tab in R5. In Release 4.x, there was simply a Background Color field for cells, and the Apply to Entire Table and Make Transparent buttons. There are three sections on this tab: Table Color, Cell Color, and Cell Image.

FIGURE 10.5

The Table/Cell Background tab is much more powerful than its R4 predecessor.

The Table Color section has a drop-down list of Table style settings that apply color schemes to the entire table. When you select a scheme other than the default of None, one or two color picker boxes appear in the Table Color section. If you choose a solid color, a single color picker will appear. If you choose a horizontal or vertical gradient, two color pickers appear, and the gradient will range between the two colors you choose.

The default color choices for a two-color scheme are dark gray and gray, but you can change them with the standard Domino color picker (see Figure 10.6). Following are the choices for Table styles:

- None (the default): no color style applied.
- Solid: all cells have the same color.
- Alternating Rows: each row alternates between the two color choices.
- Alternating Columns: each column alternates between the two color choices.
- Left and Top: the leftmost column and the top row are set to one color, and the remaining cells are set to the other color.

- Left: the leftmost column is set to one color, the remaining cells are set to the other color.

- Right and Top: the rightmost column and the top row are set to one color, and the remaining cells are set to the other color.

- Right: the rightmost column is set to one color, the remaining cells are set to the other color.

- Top: the top row is set to one color, the remaining cells are set to the other color.

FIGURE 10.6

When Table styles other than None or Solid are chosen, two color pickers appear.

The Cell Color section can apply to a single cell, a range of cells or when the Apply to All button is clicked, to the entire table. Initially, the style is solid, and only one color picker is available. If you switch from solid to horizontal or vertical gradient, a second color picker appears. The second color picker is labeled "To" (see Figure 10.7).

FIGURE 10.7

The To color picker appears when either the vertical or horizontal gradient button is clicked.

"From" color picker

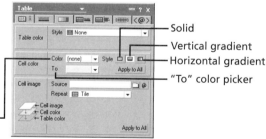

Solid

Vertical gradient

Horizontal gradient

"To" color picker

When you use two different colors and choose one of the two gradient settings, the colors in the range between the From and To colors are displayed in a gradient. The cell gradient is applied only to individual cells. If you click the Apply to All button, the gradient is added to each cell and doesn't apply across all cells. This can make a rather choppy appearance, especially if the vertical gradient is used.

The Cell Image section enables you to select an image resource and to determine how it is displayed. You can click the Browse Image button, or enter a formula to choose an

10

ADVANCED FORM DESIGN

image resource. (For more information about shared image resources, see Chapter 12, "Using Resources in Domino Applications.") There are several Repeat styles available as shown in Figure 10.8.

FIGURE **10.8**

The Cell Image section enables you to choose a Repeat style for the image.

Working with Table Borders

The Table Borders tab (see Figure 10.9) enables you to specify border styles and colors, add a drop shadow, and alter the thickness of the table borders. These settings apply only to the border of the table (the outside edges) and do not affect the cells inside the table.

FIGURE **10.9**

The Table Borders tab is new to R5— note the pleasing drop shadow on the table itself.

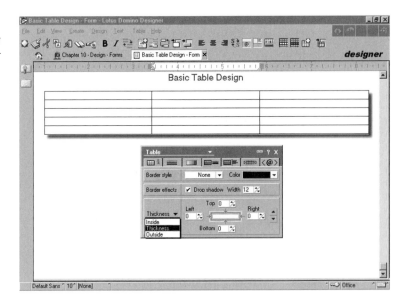

You can choose from the following border styles:

- None
- Inset
- Solid
- Outset
- Double
- Ridge
- Dotted
- Groove
- Dashed

Some of these styles are not readily apparent unless you change the settings for the thickness of the borders in the third section of this tab (discussed in the following section). To see the effects of the border styles, you can switch to a different color for the table borders than is used for the cell borders.

You can add a drop shadow to the table by checking Drop Shadow. The default width for a drop shadow is 12 pixels, but you can change this by clicking the spinner up or down, or by typing a value into the box.

The final section lets you control the width of the table borders. Three settings are available (see Figure 10.9): Inside, Thickness (the default choice), and Outside. Each side of the table border has an individual spinner that sets the property in pixels. You can also click the large spinner control on the right side of the tab to affect all settings. The borders in Figure 10.10 were set uniformly by clicking the up arrow until a thickness setting of 8 pixels was reached.

FIGURE 10.10

This table has a border style of Outset and a thickness of 8.

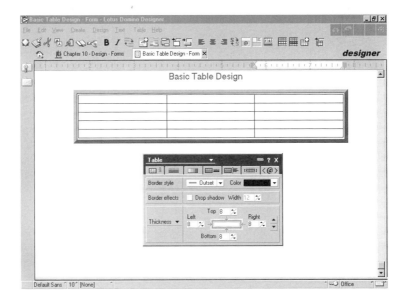

Working with Table Margins

The Table Margins tab is new to R5, and you can set Table Margins, Table Wrap, and R4 compatibility (see Figure 10.11). The left and right margins can be entered in inches or as a percent. The drop-down lists to the right of the settings have two choices: Absolute and Relative (%).

New to R5 is the ability to set word wrap around the table and inside the table. If you check Inside Table, a new field appears, At Height, which allows you to enter a height in inches at which text will wrap from one cell to the next. This is handy for setting up a table in "newspaper column" format. The ability to wrap text in and around tables is a powerful new feature in R5.

FIGURE 10.11

The Table Margin tab allows the right and left margins to be set by a percent or by a specific offset in inches.

Table Rows

All the settings on this tab are completely new to tables in Release 5. The Table Rows tab enables you to switch between the four table styles:

- **Basic** Show All Table Rows.
- **Tabbed** Show Only One Row at a Time, plus Users Pick Row via Tab Buttons in the Which Row to Display section.
- **Animated** Show Only One Row at a Time, plus Switch Row Every *n* Milliseconds in the Which Row to Display section.
- **Programmed** Show Only One Row at a Time, plus Switch Rows Programmatically in the Which Row to Display section.

Some of these styles are useful when designing forms, but others are more useful for documents or pages. For example, animating a table is not as useful for a form as it would be for a document or a page. A tabbed table, on the other hand, is very useful for form design. Using a tabbed table, you can reduce the length of a form significantly, displaying it on a single screen so that the users don't have to page down through line after line of information. Figure 10.12 shows a tabbed table under construction.

FIGURE 10.12

You can label the tab buttons in the last field on the Properties box.

A good example of a tabbed table can be found in the design of the Location document for your personal directory (see Figure 10.13). Each of the table rows has labels such as Basics, Servers, and Ports. Through the artful use of tabbed rows and tables within tables, this document can be presented in a visually appealing and much shorter format, reducing the need to scroll through a lengthy document to locate a setting.

FIGURE 10.13

The tabbed table of the Location document shows how a lengthy document can be condensed to a more usable size.

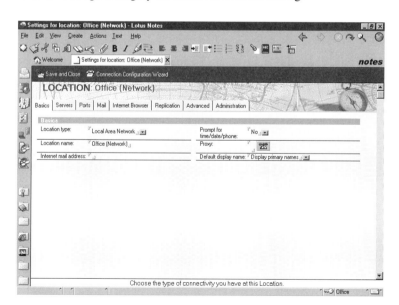

10

ADVANCED FORM DESIGN

Tabbed Tables on the Web!

Tabbed tables do function on the Web. Each of the tabs becomes a hotspot, "opening" the row as a new HTML document.

Using the Table Programming Tab

The Table Programming tab contains HTML settings for the entire table, and settings for individual cells. You can also add tags for each row. With the exception of the Other fields and the Row Tags field all settings are for use with cascading style sheets. The table row container tag <TR> in HTML can take the following attributes: ALIGN, BGCOLOR, and VALIGN (horizontal alignment, background color, and vertical alignment respectively; see Figure 10.14).

FIGURE 10.14

The Table Programming tab contains HTML attributes for the table and for rows and cells.

Using the Collapsed Table Properties Box

As with the Text Properties box, when the table Properties box is collapsed, it displays several buttons enabling you to change certain settings without fully expanding the Properties box (see Figure 10.15). Table 10.3 lists the available buttons on the Collapsed Properties box from left to right.

TABLE 10.3 The Collapsed Table Properties Box

Button	*Effect*
Cell Color Picker	Displays the color picker for the current cell or selection
Cell Borders On	Turns borders on for the current cell or selection

Button	Effect
Cell Borders Off	Turns borders off for the current cell or selection
Split Cells	Splits cells; available only for merged cells
Merge Cells	Merges two or more selected cells
Insert Column	Inserts a column prior to the current column
Delete Column	Deletes the current column
Append Column	Appends a column to the table
Insert Row	Inserts a row prior to the current row
Delete Row	Deletes the current row
Append Row	Appends a row to the table

FIGURE 10.15

The Collapsed Table Properties box allows access to commonly used functions for designing tables.

Merging and Splitting Cells

Merging and splitting cells is available from the Table menu or from the collapsed Table Properties box. To merge cells, highlight the cells with the mouse, and choose Table, Merge Cells; or click the Merge Cells button on the collapsed Table Properties box. To split cells that have been merged, position the cursor in the cell and choose Table, Split Cells from the menu or click the Split Cells button. You can use this technique to create a multiple-column table that contains fields or labels of different widths. Figure 10.16 illustrates the use of merged cells in a data entry form.

Using Tabbed Tables

Rather than use merged cells in a row to label blocks of information in a table, you can use a tabbed table, and label the row tabs instead.

10

ADVANCED FORM DESIGN

FIGURE **10.16**

A data entry form that uses multiple columns and merged cells to accurately position data items and text labels.

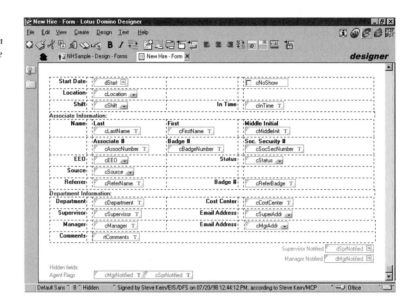

Using Tables To Format Data Entry

In a form, tabs can be set to present information, but fields can easily spill over the next tab stop and ruin the presentation. If the form is presented to a Web client, any spaces or tabs basically vanish. Tables eliminate these problems by confining objects, text, and fields to cells. The width of these cells is set, and if the length of the field contents is greater than the width of the cell, the contents spill to the next line but remain within the cell borders.

Because the contents of each cell can be controlled individually, advanced formatting can be applied to form design. One design standard places field labels flush right and fields flush left with a set space in between.

With Notes, it is very difficult to control the position of text on a form. Creating a Notes form is much like creating a word processing document—except for layout regions, text is not a discrete object. You can get around this limitation by placing fields and field labels within a table in separate columns. Simply highlight the column for the field labels and change the alignment to flush right. Unless the alignment for the column containing the fields has been changed, it will already be flush left. By including a narrow separator column in between the field labels and the fields themselves, you can then hide the table borders and the form presents a very polished appearance. You can change the alignment of a column by highlighting all the cells in the column, and choosing the desired alignment from the appropriate Alignment SmartIcon, or by making a selection in the Paragraph tab of a Text Properties box, or by choosing Text, Align Paragraph from the menu. A sample Contacts form is shown in Figure 10.17. Although the borders of rows containing fields and field labels have been made invisible, you can still see them in design mode.

FIGURE 10.17

This form uses a table to align the text labels flush right and the fields flush left—the cell borders are invisible.

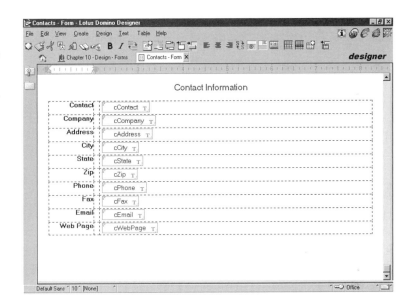

Using Tables with Web Forms

Because tables are supported on the Domino Server, they are quite useful for presenting documents to Web browsers. Tables are, in fact, the preferred method of presenting information and fields to users of both Notes and Web clients. In general, the properties of a table are all taken from the first cell of the table. For example, if that cell has no border, all the cells in the table have no border. HTML doesn't support items such as tabs, indents, and outdents, but a table can be used to simulate the effects by controlling the alignment of objects on the form. Figure 10.18 shows the Contact Information form in Figure 10.17 presented to a Web client.

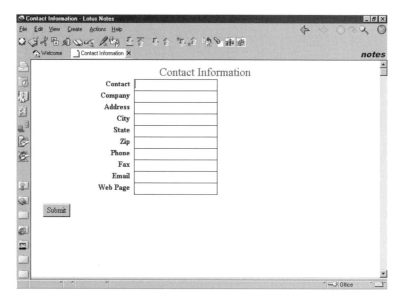

FIGURE 10.18

The Contact Information form as it would appear presented to a Web client.

Using Graphic Objects in Tables

Graphic objects can be embedded in a table's cells. This allows graphics and text to be placed alongside each other; a feat that cannot be accomplished any other way, except in a layout region (Layout Regions are discussed later, in the section "Using Layout Regions"). There are a number of methods for placing graphics into the cells of a table. You can import a graphic image such as a .GIF or .JPG into a cell. You can also copy the image to the clipboard, place the cursor in a cell of the table and press Ctrl+V to paste it into the cell.

Understanding Graphic Files

Two commonly used formats for graphics are JPEG and GIF. *JPEG* is short for Joint Photographic Experts Group, and *GIF* stands for Graphical Interchange Format. Both of these are in widespread use on the Web because they compress well. In graphics terms, *compress* means to reduce the size of the image file; these two formats do that quite well without significant loss of image fidelity. Alternatively, a Windows bitmap (.BMP) generally has a higher image quality, but is also significantly larger. In general, the larger the image, the longer it takes a client—either a Notes or a Web client—to load.

You can also use a shared image resource. Shared image resources can be added through the menu, using Create, Image Resource. You can also add an image through the Table/Cell Background tab. When you add an image to a table through the Properties box, it is a background object. As a result, although you have control over how the image repeats, you lose a lot of control over the image in other areas. You cannot resize it, wrap text, or attach hotspots to a background image. You can, however, add text atop the image.

Using Graphic Objects on Forms

In addition to adding graphics to tables on a form or to creating a graphic background for the form, graphic objects can be added to forms in three ways. You can copy the object to the clipboard and paste it into a form, you can import the image file, or you can create and use a shared image resource. In general, it is best to import the file or use a shared image resource. When the graphic object is stored on the form, you can manipulate it using the Picture menu. You can also resize these embedded graphic objects.

Importing Transparent GIFs

It is often better to import a GIF file than to copy it to the clipboard and paste it in place. GIF supports transparent backgrounds, and if your image is saved in that format, when you paste it into a form, you will lose the transparency. Importing it preserves the transparent background.

To import an image, position the cursor at the desired location, and choose File, Import from the menu. Select the image type and the image, and click Import. To use a shared image, choose Create, Image Resource from the menu. When you have added the image to a form, you can work with it in either the Picture menu or the Picture Properties box (see Figure 10.19).

When you import or paste an image into your form and subsequently select the image, a menu called Picture is added. This menu has several prompts as shown in Table 10.4.

TABLE 10.4 Picture Menu Prompts

Prompt	Effect
Picture Properties	Displays the Picture Properties box
Replace Picture	Displays the Import Picture dialog box, allowing you to replace the image

continues

TABLE 10.4 continued

Prompt	Effect
Add Hotspot Rectangle	Adds a rectangular hotspot area
Add Hotspot Circle	Adds a circular hotspot area
Add Hotspot Polygon	Adds an irregularly shaped hotspot area
Add Default Hotspot	Adds a default hotspot which is the entire image area
Hotspot Properties	Presents the Hotspot Properties box
Delete Selected Hotspot	Removes the selected hotspot

FIGURE 10.19

You can enter alternative text for deferred and Web loading in the Picture Properties box. Note the caption "Earth."

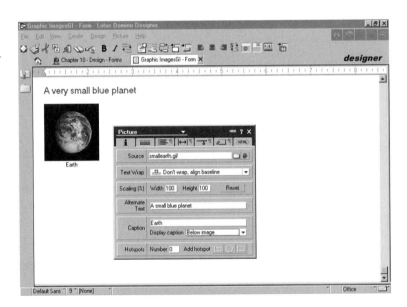

All the choices except Picture Properties are new to Release 5. The extensive support for hotspots enables you to build forms and pages that can be used as imagemaps in Web applications. (For more information on creating hotspots and imagemaps, see Chapter 14, "Using the Page Designer.")

The Picture Properties box has tabs for Picture Info and Picture Border in addition to the standard Paragraph Alignment, Paragraph Margins, Paragraph Hide-When, and Paragraph Styles. The last tab is labeled Picture Extra HTML, but is the standard HTML tab dialog box.

The Picture Info tab has settings for Source (click the Browse or Formula buttons to use shared resources), Text Wrap, Alternate Text, Caption, and Hotspots. For text wrap, you can choose from the following settings:

- Wrap, float image left
- Wrap, float image right
- Wrap around image
- Don't wrap, align top
- Don't wrap, align middle
- Don't wrap, align bottom
- Don't wrap, align baseline (the default)

> **Caution**
>
> You must set the text wrap property before adding the text!

To resize the picture, you can either click the image and use the drag handle in the lower-right corner of the image to size the image, or you can type values directly into the Width and Height fields in the Scaling (%) section. (Note that these values are in percentages, not in pixels.) The percentage is in relationship to the original image size as stored either in a Shared Image Resource or the file system. If you decide that you don't like the new size, you can revert to the original size by clicking the Reset button.

You can add alternative text and captions to images. Any text entered in the Alternate Text field is shown when the browser can't load the image. When text is entered in the Caption field, an additional field appears specifying where the caption is to appear. Captions can be placed below image or centered on image.

Hotspots can be added to the image, and programmed. A hotspot can be a part of the image, or the entire image. (You can read more about adding hotspots in Chapter 14.)

The Picture Border tab lets you choose a Border Style, add a drop shadow, and change the inside, thickness, and outside border widths. The Picture Border tab operates just like the Table Border tab described earlier in the section "Working with Table Borders."

10

ADVANCED FORM DESIGN

Working with Form and Field Level Events

In Release 3, the only way to program Notes was through the Formula language, and there were a limited number of events that could be programmed. An editable field had three events that could be programmed: Default, Input Translation, and Input Validation. There were no form-level events available, except for Window Title. With the addition of LotusScript, an object-oriented programming language, in Release 4 many more events have opened up to the developer. Similarly, in R5, JavaScript events have been added to fields and forms. Form and field events appear in the Objects tab of the Design pane. The number of form and field level events has grown so numerous with the addition of the JavaScript events that space doesn't permit a complete listing. You can find a lengthy document in the Designer Help database titled Event Sequencing that lists the events for databases, forms, fields, views, and their timing.

You can find additional information about programming Formula language events in Chapters 18, "The Formula Language," 19, "Formula Language Basics," and 20, "Writing Formulas." HTML is covered in Chapter 21, "Enhancing Domino Applications with HTML." LotusScript events are covered in Chapters 22, "Introduction to LotusScript," 23, "Basic LotusScript," and 24, "Writing LotusScript," and information about programming JavaScript events is found in the Chapters 25, "Introduction to JavaScript," 26, "Introduction to Java," and 27, "Basic Java."

Using Form Actions

When Actions are added to a form, they appear in the Form Action Bar at the top of a form. The Action Bar remains fixed as the user scrolls through the form, so the buttons are always available, no matter where the user is in the form. Buttons can still be added if they are needed in a specific location.

You can now program an Action using Simple Actions, the Formula language, LotusScript, or JavaScript. Shared Actions are stored in the Resources, Other section of the Design list, and are covered in Chapter 12

Version History

Actions were not available in R3 for either views or forms. In R3, buttons could be added to a form and programmed with the Formula language to accomplish a task such as saving and closing the form. However, the button had a fixed position on the form, and if the form were lengthy, eventually it would scroll up and disappear from the user's screen. Form and view Actions were added in R4. Actions could be programmed with the Formula language, Simple Actions, and LotusScript. R5 added JavaScript for programming and Shared Actions.

Do Actions Print?

Unlike pushbuttons, Action buttons do not print with the rest of the document. Pushbuttons will print, unless the Hide-When printed property has been selected for the paragraph in which the pushbutton resides.

Shared Actions can be created in the Resources, Other Design list area. When you are in the Shared Action design area, you can choose Create, Shared Action from the menu. Shared Actions are programmed in exactly the same way that an Action is programmed. Shared Actions can be inserted into a form by choosing Create, Insert Shared Action. You can use a Shared Action in either a view or a form, and as long as the context for the Action is appropriate, it will work equally well. For example, you might want to create an Edit Shared Action. True, there is a default Edit Document Action, but it won't work for Web clients. You can create a Shared Action and use @Command([EditDocument]) which will work for both Web and Notes clients. This Shared Action will work both in views and in documents!

When a form is in design, Actions can be viewed in the Action Pane. To open the Action Pane, click the View Show/Hide Action Pane, or choose View, Action Pane from the menu. New Actions can be added by choosing Create, Action from the menu. The Action Properties box is displayed, and the new Action is listed as (Untitled). If the Action Pane isn't open, creating a new Action opens it for you. Figure 10.20 shows a new Action added to a form. In the Design pane, the Run drop-down list has choices for Formula, Simple Action(s), LotusScript, and JavaScript.

10

ADVANCED FORM DESIGN

FIGURE 10.20

A new Action displays the Properties box opened to the Action Info tab.

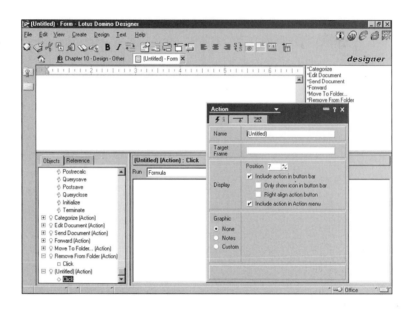

Except for the default Actions, Actions can be deleted by highlighting the Action in the Action Pane and pressing the Delete key or choosing Edit, Clear from the menu.

R5 has some exciting new features available for Actions, which will be covered in the next several sections. First, you will learn about Default Actions and Simple Actions.

Working with Default Actions

Each form has six Default or System Actions that cannot be removed. They are listed in Table 10.5 and appear in the Action menu when a form is opened. By default, these Actions do not appear in the Form Action Bar, but can be set to do so from the Action Properties box Basics tab.

TABLE 10.5 Default Form Actions

Action	Usage
Categorize	If the form has a field called categories, allows the user to modify the value in single or multiple documents. Designers can then sort and categorize the documents in views.
Edit Document	Opens the document in edit mode.
Send Document	Sends the document to a user or mail-in database. A SendTo field must be present for this to work.

Action	Usage
Forward	Forwards the document or documents to users or mail-in databases in a mail message.
Move to Folder	Moves the documents to a folder. Users can create new folders on-the-fly.
Remove from Folder	Removes the document from a folder. Note that this does not delete the document.

Understanding Simple Actions

Simple Actions are also used for agents and views, so some won't be very useful for forms. For example, marking a document as Read doesn't make much sense because the Action Bar doesn't appear unless the document is being read. The following are the Simple Actions available for forms:

- Copy to Database
- Copy to Folder
- Delete from Database
- Mark Document Read
- Mark Document Unread
- Modify Field
- Modify Fields by Form
- Move to Folder
- Remove from Folder
- Reply to Sender
- Run Agent
- Send Document
- Send Mail Message
- Send Newsletter Summary
- @Function Formula

Caution

Simple Actions do not function on the Web. You'll have to substitute @Commands, formulas, LotusScript or JavaScript if Web clients will use the database.

10

ADVANCED FORM DESIGN

You can string together several Simple Actions in the same Action. For example, you can modify a couple of fields, and then send the document. The form in Figure 10.21 has three Actions strung together. The first sets the value of the SendTo field to a legitimate email address using the Modify Field Simple Action. The second uses the Send Document Simple Action to mail the document to the address in the SendTo field. The final is an @Function Formula that combines @Command([FileSave]) and @Command([FileCloseWindow]).

FIGURE 10.21

Several Simple Actions are combined in this Form Action; this technique also works for agents and View Actions.

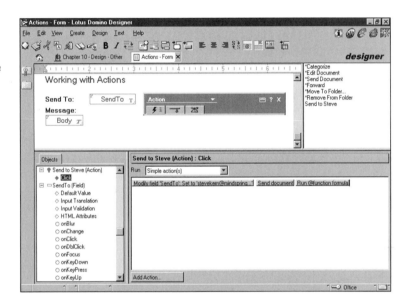

Programming Actions

Despite the ease and power of the Simple Actions, most often, you will use one of the scripting languages (the Formula language, LotusScript, or JavaScript) to program an Action. There is only one event available for programming with the Formula language, the Click event. This event is also available for LotusScript; the equivalent event in JavaScript is the onClick event. The majority of the time, you will use the Click or onClick event to script an Action button.

Choosing which language to use will depend largely on what you're trying to accomplish. (Chapter 17, "Choosing the Right Language," has some pointers that will help you make your decision.) In general, anything programmed with the Formula language executes faster, but is less powerful because the Formula language is somewhat limited, especially when it comes to looping and logic. You also need to consider which client will be using the application. If a Web client will be using it, you can't program the

Action with LotusScript because Web clients can't execute LotusScript. You can work around this by creating an agent, and then calling the agent from the Action. On the other hand, JavaScript works for both Web and Notes clients.

Naming Actions

When you've created an Action, you'll of course want to name it. It is a good idea to keep the names short and to the point, especially if there are multiple Actions on the form. One terrific new feature of R5 is the ability to cascade Actions. When you do so, a drop-down menu appears in the Action button. The Reply button in the Inbox view of the mail database is a good example of this. It combines the following four Shared Actions:

Reply

Reply with History

Reply to All

Reply to All with History

Of course, you can immediately see the power behind a cascaded Action: you can stack more Actions on the Action Bar than ever before! Further, because Actions are available to both Notes and Web clients, cascaded Actions can help replace the menu available to Notes clients but not to Web clients. To cascade an Action, simply place a backslash after the common name for the button. For example, you could create a cascaded Document Action button by naming several Actions like so:

Document\Edit

Document\New

Document\Delete

Whenever you create a cascaded Action, you can also include a graphic image that shows in the Action button. To do so, add the image to the first cascaded Action. Naming an Action is done in the Name section on the Action Info tab of the Action Properties box.

Working with Action Properties

Like most other objects in Notes, a Properties box is available for Actions. There are three tabs available: Action Info, Action Hide-When, and Advanced. To quickly display the Action Properties box, open the Action Pane and double-click the Action.

The Action Info Tab

The Action Info tab is shown in Figure 10.22. On this tab, you specify the name of the Action, a target frame, determine the display properties of the Action and choose a graphic. Because naming has already been covered, this section will discuss the Display and Graphic sections of the Action Info Tab.

FIGURE **10.22**

*The Action Info
tab has been
enhanced in R5—
note the image
chosen for the
cascaded Action.*

Four checkboxes in the Display section control whether the Action appears in the Action Bar, in the Action menu, or in both. If you check Include in Button Bar (the default for a new Action), you can also check Only Show Icon in Button Bar and Right Align Action Button. The first causes only the icon to appear, even if a name has been specified for the Action. When you right align an Action button, it appears on the right hand side of the Action Bar. You can mix right- and left-aligned Actions in the same form. The last checkbox, Include Action in Action Menu is also checked by default. In general, it is a good idea to leave it checked so those Notes users who prefer using the keyboard to the mouse also have access to the Action.

Removing Default Actions

You cannot remove any of the six default Actions, but you can disable them by unchecking both of the Include Action In... checkboxes.

The Display section includes a spinner that enables you to change the order in which the Actions appear. The order is the same in the menu and the Action Bar. When deciding on the position of each Action, consider adopting a standard placement for frequently used Actions. For example, in a view, you might place the New Document button first, followed by the Edit and Delete buttons. Similarly, in a form, you might place the Edit button first, followed by a Close button. Placing design elements in the same location makes your applications easier to use because users know where to find the Actions.

Graphics can be included in Action buttons. The Graphic section has three radio buttons that determine the graphic content: None (no graphics), Notes, and Custom. When you switch from None to Notes or Custom, an Image field appears. If you select Notes, clicking the Image field exposes the Icon palette shown in Figure 10.23.

FIGURE 10.23

The Notes Icon palette contains 155 icons.

New to R5 is the ability to include custom graphics! To include a custom graphic, you must first create it in a graphics program and then include it as a Shared Image Resource. To use the image, click the Custom radio button; next to the Image field appear the Browse and Formula buttons. Either use the Browse button to choose the resource or click the Formula button and write a formula specifying the resource (see Figure 10.24).

Using Transparent Backgrounds

Be sure to use an image with a transparent background so that you can switch colors for the Action Bar and have only the image appear, not the image background.

FIGURE 10.24

Using a custom image is new to R5 and is a welcome addition.

The Hide-When Tab

Hide-When formulas are a powerful way to work with Actions (see Figure 10.25). There are many reasons to hide Actions. For example, it doesn't make any sense to have an Edit

Action appear when the document is already in edit mode; similarly, if the document is in read mode, there's no reason to display a Save Action. You can also hide buttons from users based on their role in the database, the client type, their username, the status of the document, or any one of a number of different reasons. Having Actions that appear only when they are needed helps reduce confusion and clutter on forms.

FIGURE 10.25

The Hide-When tab has remained unchanged since R4.6.

For example, if you want to include some commonly used Actions such as Edit and Save & Close, you can create Shared Actions. As pointed out earlier, both shouldn't be visible at the same time. To make this work, hide the Save & Close Action when the document is previewed or opened for reading. Hide the Edit Action when the document is previewed or opened for editing. You can see these two examples in the chapter database, Chapt10.nsf, under Resources, Other, Shared Actions.

Beyond these simple settings is myriad of possibilities available by using a formula. The Hide-When formula must be in the Formula language and not in LotusScript. It has to evaluate to true or false. This makes writing the formula somewhat tricky, so be careful! Typically, this formula is a simple equality test based on a field or fields in the form. Note that you don't always need to use `@If(condition = value; @True, @False)`; the formula will work with the simpler, more direct statement `condition = value`. For example, you can hide a button that a supervisor uses to approve a document with the following formula (assume that the supervisor's name is stored in a field `cSupervisor`):

```
cSupervisor = @Name([CN]; @UserName)
```

In some cases, you want a group of people to be able to perform a certain type of Action. Perhaps you have an awards process that requires a group of people to review nominations for a given award. You can set up a group in the public directory, add the group to the ACL of the database, and assign a role to the group, `[Reviewers]`, for example. The following formula could be used to hide a Review button from everyone except the reviewers:

```
(@IsNewDoc ¦ !@Contains(@UserRoles; "Reviewer")) ¦ !cStatus =
➥"Released"
```

Note that in this formula, the test for the users' roles is combined with other aspects of the document. First, you wouldn't want a review to be available for a new document, so the function @IsNewDoc is used. If the document is new, it returns True, and the Action isn't visible. In the case of this application, the client needed to approve the nomination before it was released to the reviewers, so a test for a status of Released is also included. Note that each argument is connected by an or so that if any of these conditions were true, the Action would not display.

As a way of further limiting access to the Review document, the form property Include in Menu was deselected. Because it didn't show up on any menu, clicking the Action button was the only way to create a review. As these last few examples have shown, combining the Hide-When tab with Actions is a very powerful way of controlling your application.

The NotesFlow Publishing Tab

NotesFlow publishing is set up on the Advanced tab of the Action Properties box (see Figure 10.26). Settings on this tab allow the developer to work with other applications that support OLE and share information between them. This can be a very powerful tool; Actions that are published are available to other NotesFlow-enabled applications such as Lotus 1-2-3, Freelance Graphics, WordPro, or Microsoft Word.

FIGURE 10.26

The Advanced tab of the Action Properties box enables you to publish the Action to NotesFlow-enabled applications.

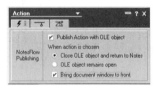

If you create an OLE object such as a Lotus WordPro or Microsoft Word document in a form, you can use NotesFlow to publish Actions. When the Action is published, it appears on the OLE application's menu. As you can see from Figure 10.26, you can control what happens when the Action is chosen from the OLE application's menu system.

Publish Action with OLE Object is what places the Action on the OLE application's Action menu. Close OLE Object and Return to Notes and OLE Object Remains Open is a radio button set that determines what happens when the Action is chosen from the OLE application's menu. The last option is a checkbox and is available for all choices on the Advanced tab. This option makes the OLE document window the active window.

10

ADVANCED FORM DESIGN

Understanding Action Bar Properties

The Action Bar itself has properties also. To open the Action Bar Properties box, you must have the Action Pane open. Select Design, Action Bar Properties from the menu, or choose it from the drop-down list in the title bar of the Properties box. There are three tabs on the Action Bar Properties box: Action Bar Info, Button Background, and Button Font (see Figure 10.27).

FIGURE 10.27

The Action Bar Info tab has settings that apply to the button bar itself.

Working with the Action Bar Info Tab

There are four sections on the Action Bar Info tab: Alignment, Background, Bottom Border, and Web Access. Settings in these four sections control the appearance and function of the Action Bar.

The Alignment section has a single drop-down list with two choices: Buttons Start at Left (the default) and Buttons Start at Right. If you select Buttons Start at Right, the order is reversed. The first Action appears in the rightmost position, the second to the left of the first, and so forth.

In the Background section, the standard color picker is available from the Color field. You can choose from the standard palette, click the RGB button, and mix your own colors, or click the System icon to return to the default gray system color.

The Bottom border gives you substantial control over the appearance of the button bar's border in the form. You can choose from several widths: None, Fit to window (the default), Fixed Width, and Under Buttons Only. You can also choose a color for the border in the Color field. The last setting in the Bottom Border section lets you choose a line style from One Pixel, Two Pixels, Three Pixels, or Double. Adding a border to the button bar further delineates it from the form itself.

The last section, Web Access, has two Display choices: Using HTML and Using Java Applet. In general, it's best to select Using Java Applet because the function is better. Note that if the database property Web Access: Use JavaScript When Generating Pages is not set, you'll be prompted to set it when you choose Using Java Applet.

Working with the Button Background Tab

Sections on the Button Background tab control the background of the buttons themselves, distinct from the Action Bar. The settings on this tab are new to R5, and you can control the size of the buttons, when the border displays, and the background of the buttons (see Figure 10.28).

FIGURE **10.28**

The Button Background tab is new to R5.

You can modify the height, width, and margin sizes of buttons on the Action Bar in the Button Size section. Settings on this tab apply universally to all buttons on the button bar. You can choose from four settings for the height: Default, Minimum Size, Fixed Size, and Background Size. Only the Fixed size lets you specify the height in pixels by opening a spinner at 8 pixels. The Width setting has only two choices: Default and Background Size. The Margin setting also has two choices: Default and Fixed Size. As with the Height Fixed size setting, a spinner is opened at 2 pixels.

The default for the Button Border display is On Mouse Over, but you can also choose Always or Never. In R4, the buttons always displayed a border; so this is new to R5.

You can change the color of the buttons independently of the Action Bar in the Button Background section, or you can select an image from the Shared Image Resources. Any images attached to specific Actions that appear in the Action Bar will display over top the Button Background image, so be careful what sort of image you use. If the image used for the background is a different size than the default button bar, and if you choose Background size for Height or Width, the button size will match the size of the image.

Working with the Button Font Tab

The Button Font tab is a very straightforward tab. You can choose the font, size, style, and color just as you would for any other text object (see Figure 10.29).

10

ADVANCED FORM DESIGN

FIGURE 10.29

The Font tab of the Action Bar Properties box functions just like the Font tab of the Text Properties box.

Working with Hotspots

There are a number of different types of Hotspots available from the Create, Hotspot menu prompt. You can create Links, Buttons, Pop-ups, and Action Hotspots. These can be placed directly on the form wherever the design requires them. These can be quite useful, but be careful not to overdo it and wind up with a cluttered form. Table 10.6 lists the various types of hotspots. In all cases, except for a button, the text or object you want to make into a hotspot must be selected first. Hotspots and buttons can also be added to Notes documents and pages.

TABLE 10.6 Links, Buttons, and Hotspots

Hotspots	*Behavior*
Link Hotspot	Links to other Notes documents, pages, views, databases, URLs, and so on.
Text Pop-up	Displays a text box with a drop shadow containing the text entered.
Button	Performs programmed Action when clicked.
Formula Pop-up	Displays a text box with a drop shadow when clicked. The text in the box is result of the formula.
Action Hotspot	Performs programmed Action when clicked.

Working with Links

There are two ways to create a Link hotspot. First, you can create a link to another Domino object and return to the form, select the hotspot object, and then paste the link onto the object. To create a link, you can select the Domino object, and choose Edit, Copy as Link, Link Type from the menu. This copies a link to the object onto the clipboard. You can copy links to Domino Design objects from the Design Work Pane without opening the object; simply select the object in the Work pane, and choose Edit, Copy as

Link, Named Element. You can also copy anchor, document, view, and database links to the clipboard. There are two ways to paste links onto an object. After selecting the text or object on the form, you can type Ctrl+V to paste the link. You can also choose Create, Hotspot, Link Hotspot, and from the Properties box that opens, click the Paste button.

In the second way to create a link hotspot, you can select the object and choose Create, Hotspot, Link Hotspot from the menu without a link copied to the clipboard. From the Hotspot Resource Link Properties box, you can create a link. There are three types of links available: Link, Named Element, and URL (the default). You've already seen how to work with a Link. URLs can be typed into the Value field or else copied to the clipboard from a browser and pasted into the Value field with the Paste button. Perhaps the most powerful addition to links in R5 is the Named Element link (see Figure 10.30).

FIGURE 10.30

The Hotspot Resources Link Properties box is opened to the Hotspot Info tab with Named Element selected as the Type.

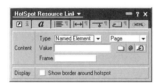

When set to Named Element, all three buttons are available. Table 10.7 lists the buttons and their functions.

TABLE 10.7   Hotspot Resource Link Buttons

Button	Name	Function
🗀	Browse	Browses a listing of the named design elements. Only available for the Named Element type.
@	Formula	Opens the Formula window. Available for Named Elements and URLs.
🔛	Paste	Pastes objects stored on the clipboard. Available for all types except Link.

The following Named Elements are available from the drop-down list:

- Page (the default)
- Form
- Frameset

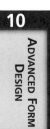

10

ADVANCED FORM DESIGN

- View

- Folder

- Navigator

To choose a Named Element, first select Named Element as the Type, and then click the Browse button. You can also select the type of Named element from the new drop-down list that appears next to the Type field, and then enter a formula or the name of the element directly in the value field. To enter a formula, click the Formula button. When you click the Browse button, the Locate Object dialog box opens (see Figure 10.31).

FIGURE 10.31

The Locate Object dialog box lets you choose from the Named Element type, the database, and the actual element.

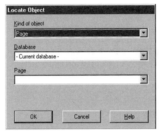

When you've created the link, you can specify a Target frame for the link. When you do so, the link launches into the specified frame in its frameset. (For more information about framesets, please see Chapter 29, "Adding Framesets to Domino Applications.") The last element on the Hotspot Info tab is Show Border Around Hotspot. (In R4, this was checked by default. When it is checked, a thin green rectangular border appears around the text or object.) In R5, it is not checked, and instead, if text is used for the hotspot, the text appears in a blue system color. This brings the usage of hotspots closer to the standard usage on the Web.

There are a number of tabs available in the Hotspot Resources Link Properties box in addition to the Hotspot Info tab already covered: Font, Paragraph Alignment, Paragraph Margins, Paragraph Hide-When, Paragraph Styles, and Hotspot Extra HTML. The color picker on the Font tab has a System button next to the RGB color button in the upper-right corner. Otherwise, each of these tabs function as they do elsewhere in the Domino Designer.

Creating Buttons

Similar to Actions and Action hotspots, buttons allow the use of Simple Actions, formulas, JavaScript, and LotusScript. To create a button, you can choose Create, Hotspot, Button from the menu, or click the Create Hotspot Button SmartIcon (see Figure 10.32). Buttons can be labeled or left blank and are programmed in the Script area. When a button is added, instead of the Hotspot menu, a Button menu is added with two prompts: Button Properties and Edit Button. Buttons can also be added to documents and pages.

FIGURE 10.32

A button hotspot has a typical gray Windows pushbutton appearance.

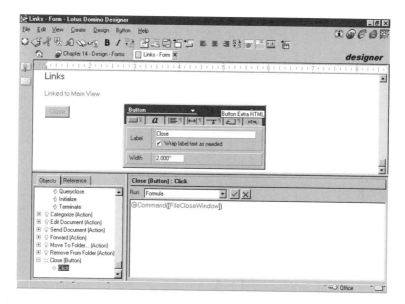

The Button Info tab shown in Figure 10.32 contains entries for the label name and a checkbox to allow text to wrap. You can also specify the size of the button. There are other tabs on the Properties box for Font, Paragraph Alignment, Paragraph Margins, Paragraph Hide-When, Paragraph Styles, and Button Extra HTML. Again, these are the same tabs that you see in a Text Properties box. Remember, as with the Text Properties box, the Hide-When settings apply to the entire paragraph, and not just to the button.

Buttons are usually created when you need to perform some function that is very specific to a location on a form. For example, you might have a lengthy form, and have two entries for a patient's weight: one for weight in pounds, and the other in kilograms. A button to convert one to the other would not make that much sense in the Action Bar but would make sense on the form itself next to the weight fields. After creating the button, add a formula to convert from pounds to kilos or vice versa.

Using Tables

This is a perfect time to use a table! Placing the button and fields in the same row, but in different cells, allows you to turn off printing for the cell containing the button. Obviously, there isn't much need for the button to appear in print, but you do want the data to appear.

10

ADVANCED FORM DESIGN

Using Pop-ups to Inform Users

There are two kinds of pop-ups: Text Pop-ups and Formula Pop-ups. The text displayed by Text Pop-ups is entered into the Popup Text field in the Hotspot Pop-up Properties box. You can control how and when the text is displayed through choices you make in the Hotspot Info tab (see Figure 10.33). As you can see, you no longer have to click the hotspot to activate it—you can set the display to Show Popup On Mouse Over, which is the new default. (In R4, you had to click the hotspot to see the text pop up.) Also new is the Highlight the Text hotspot style. When you choose this option, the text object displays with a yellow background similar to the highlight function available on word processors such as Microsoft Word or Lotus WordPro.

FIGURE 10.33

The Hotspot Popup Info tab has many new features in R5.

Pop-ups can also be created with a Formula Pop-up. To create a Formula Pop-up, select the object, and choose Create, Hotspot, Formula Pop-up from the menu. The Script area opens and the formula to produce the text can be entered (see Figure 10.34). Only the Formula language can be used to program this type of pop-up. The display options for a Formula Pop-up are the same as those for a Text Pop-up.

In R4, pop-ups appeared in a window enclosing the text with a drop shadow. In R5, this has been changed and the drop shadow has been removed. The text box is a simple bordered box with a light off-white background (see Figure 10.35).

FIGURE 10.34

A formula for the popup is written in the script area—note the Display options for the pop-up.

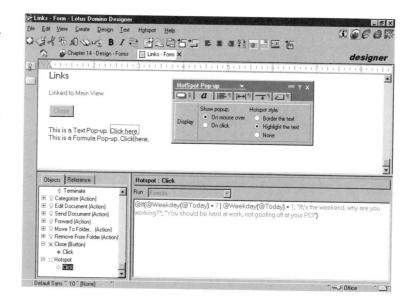

FIGURE 10.35

The text popup produced by the formula shown in Figure 10.34—note the highlight around the text "Click here."

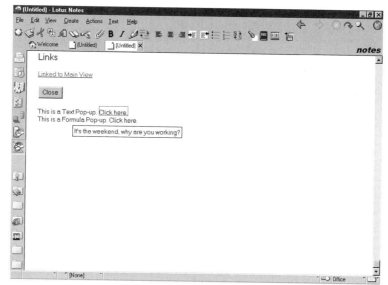

Programming Action Hotspots

An Action Hotspot allows the use of Formulas, Simple Actions, LotusScript, or JavaScript. You can attach an Action Hotspot to text or other objects on the form and program it just like you would a button. To create an Action hotspot, select the hotspot with the mouse and choose Create, Hotspot, Action Hotspot from the menu. The Action Hotspot Properties box opens to the Hotspot Info tab. This tab is simple and consists of a field for a Frame and a single checkbox for displaying a border (see Figure 10.36).

FIGURE 10.36

The Hotspot Info tab of the Action Hotspot Properties box has few selections compared to the other hotspots.

Understanding Sections and Section Properties

Sections can be added to Notes documents, pages, subforms, and forms. On a form, sections are collapsible areas that can contain fields, text, graphics, and so on. Sections are especially useful for forms that contain a large amount of data because they can be used to streamline the form's appearance by collecting similar information and collapsing it. When the users need to view the data, clicking the twistie beside the section title opens the section and displays the data within.

There are two types of sections: Standard and Controlled Access. Standard sections simply collect the text and fields into a collapsible area on the form. Controlled Access sections, however, can limit access to the fields and information within the section.

Using Standard Sections

To create a standard section, highlight the area containing the text and fields and choose Create, Section, Standard from the menu. If there is static text at or near the beginning of the section when it is created, it becomes the default title of the section. When the section is created or when the cursor is on the section title, a new menu is added titled Section (see Figure 10.37). The Section menu has prompts for Properties, Expand, Collapse, and Remove Section. As with the Remove Hotspot prompt, removing a section does not disturb the underlying fields and text; only the section is removed.

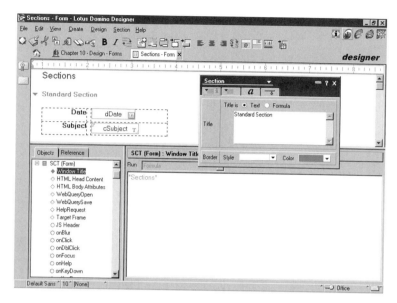

FIGURE 10.37

This standard section contains a table with text and fields—note the Section Properties box.

The Section Properties box, unchanged from R4, has four tabs: Section Title and Border (see Figure 10.37), Expand/Collapse, Font, and Hide-When. Both the Font and Hide-When tab settings apply to the section title only, not to the entire section.

The two most important tabs are the Section Title and Border and the Expand/Collapse tabs. The Section Title and Border tab has a window for the title. A title can be entered as text or a formula can be used. Clicking the Formula radio button adds a button for a formula window. Clicking that button displays the Formula window. Only the Formula language can be used in a Section Title formula. The Title tab also has settings for the style of the section's border and its color.

The Expand/Collapse tab allows the developer to enter rules for expanding and collapsing the section based on the mode of the document. Rules can be set for when the document is previewed, opened for reading, opened for editing, or printed. There are three possible settings:

- Don't auto expand or collapse (the default)
- Auto-expand section
- Auto-collapse section

This tab also has two checkboxes: Hide Title When Expanded, and Show as Text When Not Previewing. When you select the first, the title is hidden when the section is expanded, but visible when the section is collapsed. The Show as Text checkbox displays

10

ADVANCED FORM DESIGN

the section in preview. The contents of the section are visible as text in other modes, and the section itself is absent. Figure 10.38 shows this tab.

FIGURE 10.38

The Expand/Collapse tab of a standard section sets the rules for displaying the section.

Securing Content with Controlled Sections

To create a Controlled Access section, highlight the area containing the text and fields and choose Create, Section, Controlled Access from the menu. Figure 10.39 shows the Controlled Access Section Properties box. The Section Title and Border tab shown in Figure 10.39 allows only the entry of text for the title. You can also specify a section field name, but that is generally not required.

FIGURE 10.39

The Title tab of a Controlled Access section has an entry for the title and also for a section field name.

The expand/collapse tab has two buttons. The first lets you switch between Editors and Non-Editors, and the second lets you apply the settings created for one group to the other (see Figure 10.40).

FIGURE 10.40

In R5, the Expand/Collapse tab contains settings for both Editors and Non-Editors.

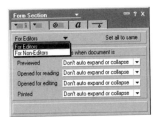

The Formula tab shown in Figure 10.41 lets you enter an access formula. The access formula can be Editable, Computed, Computed When Composed, or Computed for Display. Selecting anything other than Editable forces entry of a formula before the form can be saved. If the access formula is editable, users who have access to the section can modify the Access list.

FIGURE **10.41**

The Formula tab of a Controlled Access section controls who can edit the contents of the section— note the Type drop-down list.

The Font and Hide-When tabs for a Controlled Access section are just like those for the Standard section.

Controlled Access sections have an additional prompt on the Section menu for sections with editable access formulas: Define Editors. Clicking Define Editors displays the Edit Section dialog box, and allows users to specify editors for the section. Changing the radio button to Only the Following Users and clicking the Add button launches the Address Book dialog box.

Although Access Controlled sections are not a true security measure because the contents of the fields can still be accessed through views or the Field dialog box of the Document Properties box, they are still useful in workflow applications. The editors of the sections can be determined by a formula; usernames, groups, and roles can be added to the list of editors. If you set a field's Security Options property to Sign If Mailed or Saved in Section, when an authorized editor works with the document, the document is signed. The signature appears in the Section title with a time stamp in the following format:

```
Section Title - Signed by User Name/Certifier on date and time,
③according to Certifier.
```

Using Layout Regions

Layout regions were introduced in R4 of Notes and provide a means to add elements to Notes forms and subforms that are not otherwise available. Layout regions also have more display options than regular forms. These options enable the designer to create a

10

ADVANCED FORM
DESIGN

more "typical" Windows GUI interface. Layout regions are fixed in size and can be added to both forms and subforms by choosing Create, Layout Region, New Layout Region from the menu. Layout regions can contain fields of all types except rich text. You can also add graphics, static text, graphic buttons, pushbuttons, and more to layout regions. Layout regions can be transparent on the form and they can be 3D. By default, layout regions have a border, but you can turn the border off.

Essentially, a layout region is an enhanced section on a form. In R4, Comboboxes, Listboxes, time sliders, date pickers and tab order were only available in layout regions, but as you know by now, all these features are available in R5 on a standard form or subform. A typical use of a form with a layout region is to create refined data input screens for use with @DialogBox.

There are some drawbacks to using layout regions. First, and possibly foremost, layout regions are not supported on the Web. Second, the design interface in layout regions is somewhat crude in comparison to other Windows applications development systems. For example, there are no alignment tools. You cannot select a group of objects and click an icon or make a choice from the menu that aligns the objects on center or on the bottom, top, or sides. When new objects are added, by default they appear in the center of the layout region and must be moved. Moving and aligning static text and fields is problematic. Last, rich-text fields cannot be used, and layout regions cannot contain subforms or shared fields.

Working with layout regions is different from working with standard form areas. The default size for a layout region is 6"×1.5" starting at a 1" margin. It is transparent and has a border. After the layout region is created and the cursor is in the layout region, the toolbar changes and several new SmartIcons are added: Create TextBox, Create Graphic Button, Design Bring to Front, and Design Send to Back. In addition, there are three prompts available from the Create, Layout Region submenu: Text, Graphic, and Graphic Button.

Fields are added by clicking the Create Field SmartIcon or from the menu. Fields are called *controls* and are added in the center of the region.

Text cannot be added as you would in a standard form area by simply typing in text, but must be added from the menu by choosing Create, Layout Region, Text or by clicking the Create Textbox SmartIcon. As with fields, the textbox is initially placed in the center of the layout region and must be moved.

A Graphic button is similar to a hotspot—you can copy a graphic image to the clipboard, and paste it onto a layout region. You can then program the button. In layout regions, you can stack images and other objects on top of each other. You can control the order of their appearance with the Design Bring to Front and Design Send to Back buttons.

Using the Layout Region Properties Box

As you would expect, layout regions and all objects in a layout region have Properties boxes. The Layout Region Properties box is shown in Figure 10.42. There are two tabs: Layout Info and Layout Hide-When. The Layout Hide-When tab (not shown) is exactly like any other Hide-When tab.

FIGURE 10.42

The Properties box of a layout region has two tabs: Layout Info and Hide-When.

The Layout Info tab is where the style and size of the layout region can be modified. There are three sections: Position, Display, and Grid. The size can be changed in the Position section by typing in new values or by dragging one of the grab handles (small square boxes at the corners and sides of the region) and resizing the region. The Display options are Show border, 3D style, and Don't Wrap Text Around Region. The Grid section has checkboxes for Show Grid and Snap to Grid. The default Grid size is .050″ and can be changed. The grid control features are ones you might be familiar with from other Windows applications. Turning on the grid displays a background of dots to help align controls. Snap to Grid aligns all objects in the layout region with the grid.

Using Layout Regions with Dialog Boxes

Possibly the best use of layout regions is with @DialogBox. @DialogBox displays the form (or subform) specified in a dialog box. @DialogBox displays the first layout region on the form, if one is available. The syntax of @DialogBox is as follows:

```
@DialogBox( form ; [AutoHorzFit] : [AutoVertFit] : [NoCancel] :
③[NoNewFields] : [NoFieldUpdate] : [ReadOnly] ; SizeToTable ;
③NoOkCancel ; title )
```

R5 has added two new options to @DialogBox: SizeToTable and NoOkCancel. Both are optional, and both are Boolean. If SizeToTable is set to True, a table on the form specified in the first argument is scaled to fit the dialog box. If NoOkCancel is set to True, the OK and Cancel buttons will not appear.

The contents of fields that have the same names in the underlying form and the form used with @DialogBox will be transferred to the underlying form if the user presses the OK button. @DialogBox returns a 1 if OK is pressed and 0 if Cancel is pressed. Figure 10.43 illustrates the appearance of the dialog box.

10

ADVANCED FORM DESIGN

FIGURE 10.43

This dialog box displays the history of a document.

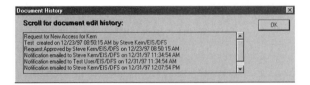

Using Layout Regions with Subforms

You can also place a layout region on a subform and call it using @DialogBox or the LotusScript DialogBox method.

The same function can also be called from LotusScript using the DialogBox method. A sample script is the following:

```
Sub Click(Source As Button)
 Dim uiWorkspace As New NotesUIWorkspace
 Dim uiDoc As NotesUIDocument
 Set uiDoc = uiWorkspace.CurrentDocument
 Call uidoc.FieldSetText("StartTime","")
 Call uidoc.FieldSetText("EndTime","")
 Call uidoc.FieldSetText("Appointment","")
 Call uidoc.FieldSetText("ReturnValue","")
 Call uidoc.Refresh

 If UIWorkspace.Dialogbox("AP",True,True) Then
   Call uiDoc.Refresh
   If uidoc.FieldGetText("ReturnValue") > "" Then
     Call uiDoc.FieldAppendText("MtgDay_1",uidoc.FieldGetText
     ③("ReturnValue") &Chr(10))
   End If
 End If
 Call uiDoc.Refresh
End Sub
```

Working with Special Forms

There are several types of special forms that can be created for specific purposes. You can use a form to create database and user Profile documents, and you can create Search forms and Results forms.

> **Reserved Form Names**
>
> In R4, there were a number of reserved form names for use in Web applications. For the most part, these are no longer necessary with the introduction of pages. Each reserved form name began with $$ and was used to present Domino views and navigators. Here is a list: $$ViewTemplateDefault, $$NavigatorTemplateDefault, $$ViewTemplate for *viewname*, and $$NavigatorTemplate for *navigatorname*.

Working with Profile Documents

Profile documents are created from a Document-type form. Documents created with a profile form have no presence in views and aren't included in the total document count. Profile documents can be global to the database, or they can be specific to individual users of the database. Profile documents are a great place to store information that will be referenced elsewhere in the database. For example, you might store the replica ID of a database that is used for lookups. Of course, you could also place a replica ID in a shared field, but that would require a database designer to modify the field contents, should the lookup database change. When stored in a profile document, users who can create the document can modify the field storing the replica ID. You can also store user specific information in a Profile document that stores default settings for fields, or criteria for email notification when documents are created or modified in the database.

The difference between the two types of Profile documents isn't determined by a setting on the form, but in the way the document is created from the form. If you are creating a database profile document, you call it with the following formula:

```
(@Command([EditProfile]; profileform)
```

To create a user specific profile document, use the following formula:

```
(@Command([EditProfile]; profileform; username)
```

If you are creating a database profile document, you must have at least designer access. After it has been created, anyone with the appropriate permission can modify the profile document.

It is usually a good idea to limit access to a global profile document. You can do so through the use of a Role. You should also keep the profile document off the Create menu, hide it by enclosing the name in parentheses, and provide access to it through an agent.

10

ADVANCED FORM DESIGN

The following code is from a shared agent set to run manually from the Actions menu and to run once (@Commands can be used):

```
@If(@Contains(@UserRoles; "Profile");
        @Do(@Command([EditProfile]; "GPF")) ;
    @Return(@Do(@Prompt([OK]; "Warning!"; "You are not authorized to
③edit this database\'s profile!")) ) )
```

This agent is called Set Global Profile and is in the sample database for this chapter. This agent checks the user's access privilege, and if they have the Profile Role, it permits them to edit the profile document.

When you've created the profile document, you'll need to access the data stored in its fields. You can read the data using @GetProfileField and write data using @SetProfileField. For example, say you've stored a list of categories for a keyword field in a global profile document. You could read it into a keyword field using the following formula:

```
@GetProfileField("GPF"; "cCategories")
```

If you wanted to retrieve values from a user specific profile document, you simply add the username as an argument as in the following example:

```
@GetProfileField("GPF"; "cCategories"; username)
```

All in all, Profile documents are a very welcome addition to the Domino Designer's toolkit. You can find a use for a profile document in almost any database you create.

Customizing Search and Result Forms

The Catalog (5.0) template (catalog.ntf) installed with the Domino server contains several forms, used to search and display search results and which can be customized. There are four forms: Search Form, SearchResults, ResultEntry, and DetailedResultEntry. These forms are functional as is, but you can add corporate logos, instructions, and whatever else you need to the form. These forms are designed to search the database catalog and file system, but you can also customize them to search the Web.

About the Domain Catalog

When the first Domino server is installed and configured, a Domain catalog is created from the catalog.ntf template file, and named Catalog.nsf. The Catalog server task, which runs by default at 1 a.m., populates the catalog with the databases available on the server. You can also set up a server to be a Domain wide Indexer by opening the server document and filling out the Domain Indexer tab in the Server Tasks section.

If you want users to be able to search the file system (something you might do if you stored HTML files on the Domino Server), you must create a File System document in the Catalog. The HTTP task must be running on the Catalog server so that links can be returned to either Notes or Web clients.

There is extensive documentation in the Designer Help database that describes how to customize these search forms. You can find this information in the document titled "Customizing Search Forms." When you have modified the search forms, you can simply add them to the Domain Catalog.

Creating Reusable Design Objects

One fundamental goal of object-oriented programming is to create reusable design elements. Perhaps the single most compelling reason for creating reusable elements is that after the object or reusable element is designed, debugged, and working well, it can be inserted wherever it's needed—without worrying whether it will work or having to rewrite it. This saves a tremendous amount of time, as I'm sure you can imagine! Prior to Release 4 of Notes, there was only a single reusable design object: the shared field. Release 4 introduced subforms and Script libraries. R5 introduced Shared Actions, Image Resources, and applets. All the shared design elements are now collected in the Resources category in the Design list.

Creating and Using Subforms

Subforms are designed exactly like forms and can contain text, fields, graphics, layout regions, buttons, Actions, and so on. Subforms contain common data elements, Actions, and scripts. Deciding what data items are candidates for subforms can be done by following good design principles and by comparing the data items among all the forms.

When comparing the data items, look for repeating elements. The rule of thumb to use when determining whether a subform should be created is this: Will this group of fields, Actions, and so on be used in more than one form? If the answer is yes, a subform should be created. If the subform will be used in more than one database, it gets added to a Design library.

Subforms can also be used to present data on the same document to different users in a different manner. You can do this by conditionally inserting the subform.

A subform is designed exactly like a form. To create a new subform, open the Resources category in the design list, and click Subforms. Click the New Subform button. Figure 10.44 shows a subform in design that can be used to provide a common header for all forms in a database.

FIGURE 10.44

A subform can be used to provide a common appearance to all forms in a database.

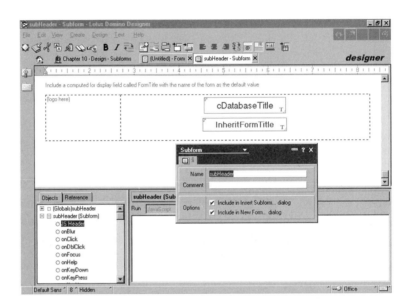

The Subform Properties box shown in Figure 10.44 has only one tab, the Subform Info tab. On this tab, name the subform and add a comment if appropriate. Because there is no alias field, add one by using the pipe symbol (|) after the name of the subform, followed by the alias of the subform. Two checkboxes at the bottom of the tab determine how the subform can be inserted: Include in Insert Subform... dialog and Include in New Form... dialog. If the latter is checked, whenever a new form is created, a dialog box opens displaying any subform with that property.

You can also insert subforms at design time by choosing Create, Insert Subform from the menu. The Insert Subform dialog box displays with a list of available subforms (see Figure 10.45).

Subforms can also be inserted based on a formula. In that case, check the Insert Subform Based on Formula checkbox. The formula must evaluate to the name or alias of a subform.

FIGURE 10.45

The Insert Subform dialog box allows the choice of a sub-form or to insert a subform based on a formula.

Using Shared Fields

Shared fields are stored in the Resources, Shared Field design list. Only the field definition is shared, not the data. To create a shared field:

1. Open the Shared Field design list.
2. Click the New Shared Field button, or click the Create Shared Field SmartIcon.
3. Give the field a name, and set the remaining properties as appropriate.

Converting a Single-Use Field to a Shared Field

A single-use field on a database can be converted to a shared field by selecting the field and choosing Design, Share This Field from the menu.

Shared fields can be added to forms and subforms by clicking the Insert Shared Field SmartIcon or by choosing Create, Insert Shared Field from the menu. A dialog box similar to the Insert Subform dialog box appears, displaying the available shared fields.

To edit a shared field, go to the Shared Fields Design list and double-click the shared field entry. Figure 10.46 shows the Shared Field design window that occupies the entire design area.

Shared fields can be quickly identified on a form by the double-thick outline around the field name.

10

ADVANCED FORM DESIGN

FIGURE **10.46**

A shared field in the design window is showing the Design pane and the Properties box.

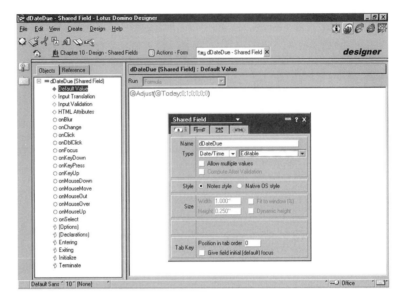

Using Embedded Elements

You can add a number of embedded elements to a form by choosing Create, Embedded Element, Element. Many of these are the same elements that can be embedded on a page, and many times, a page is a better choice for an embedded element than a form. You can embed the following elements on a form:

- Outline
- View
- Navigator
- Import Navigator
- Date Picker
- Group Scheduler
- Folder Pane
- File Upload Control

All but the Group Scheduler and File Upload control can be added to a page, and are covered in Chapter 14, "Using the Page Designer."

Using a File Upload Control

A File Upload Control allows Web clients to attach files to a document. To create an upload control, choose Create, Embedded Element, File Upload Control from the menu. A gray rectangular button is inserted into the form at the cursor's location labeled File Upload. The File Upload has a Properties box, and the tabs are the standard Paragraph Alignment, Paragraph Margins, Paragraph Hide-When, Paragraph Styles, and Upload Extra HTML. Of course, this design element is not needed for a Notes client, so you'll want to hide it from Notes clients by checking Hide Paragraph from Notes R4.6 or later on the Paragraph Hide-When tab. In order for the File Upload Control to work, you must have a temp directory specified on the Domino server (see Figure 10.47).

FIGURE 10.47

The file upload control should be hidden from Notes users because it only functions for Web clients—note the setting in the Properties box.

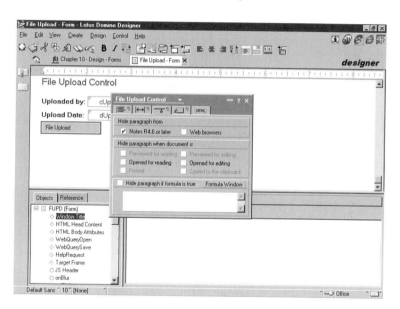

Working with the Group Scheduler

The Group Scheduler can only be embedded in Forms and Subforms. You cannot embed it on a page because the Group Scheduler requires three pieces of information from the underlying document. The Group Scheduler requires three fields to function: one to contain the members of the group, the second to store the starting time of the schedule (as in 8:00 a.m.), and the third field to store the duration of the schedule (as in 9 hours). There are also two reserved fields that you can use to modify the way the Group scheduler works. $GroupScheduleRefreshMode can be set to 0 or 1. 0 is a partial refresh, and 1 is a full refresh of the schedule. $GroupScheduleShowLegend turns the legend on (1) or off (0). Only one Group Scheduler can be added to a form.

10

ADVANCED FORM DESIGN

Creating a form to contain a group scheduler is pretty simple. You can look at the `GroupCalendar` form in the R5 mail database as a starting point. First, add the three fields mentioned in the preceding paragraph. Next, add the Group Scheduler by choosing Create, Embedded Element, Group Scheduler from the menu (see Figure 10.48).

FIGURE 10.48

The Group Scheduler has just three events—note the legend at the bottom of the window.

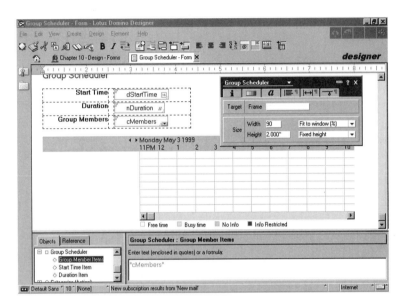

When the Group Scheduler is embedded, open the Properties box for the element, and you'll notice that there are three events. Group Member Items, Start Time Item, and Duration Item. All three need to have the name of the corresponding field entered in the Script area. Use quotes to surround the field names as in Figure 10.48.

The Group Scheduler Properties box has several tabs: Info, Background, Font, and the three familiar Paragraph tabs. The Info tab shown in Figure 10.48 has settings for a Target Frame, and the width and height. Width can be expressed in Fit to Window (%) or a Fixed Width in inches. Height can be expressed as Fit to Content or Fixed Height. Because the default group scheduler is not very high, you can set the height to Fixed and enter a number of inches. The example in Figure 10.48 is set to 2 inches. To keep the edge of the scheduler from going out too far to the right, use the Fit to Window (%) and set it to something less than 100%.

The Background tab contains settings for the colors of the control itself (foreground and background) and settings for each data element type: Busy time, Free time, Unavailable, and Restricted. These colors can be seen in the legend also (see Figure 10.49).

FIGURE 10.49

The Background tab has settings for the colors of the control as well as the data elements.

The Font tab looks basically like any other font tab, and isn't shown here. Settings on this tab apply to the Group Scheduler.

It is important to note that the Group Scheduler must be manually refreshed. Either the user has to press F9 or choose View, Refresh from the menu or else you will have to program an Action that refreshes the contents of the Group schedule. By letting users change the value of the reserved fields, you can give them more control over the behavior of the scheduler.

Using the Form Design Document

Each design object has an associated Design Document. You can view the properties of a Design Document through a Properties box. To open the Properties box for a design object, select the object in the Design work pane and choose Design, Design Properties from the menu. There are four tabs: Info, Fields, Design, and IDs. All tabs except the Design tab are strictly informational. The Info tab displays when the design object was created, modified, and accessed and who last modified it. The Fields tab lists all the fields for the Design document, and the IDs tab lists the Document ID and the NoteID. The Design tab, however, allows you to modify how inheritance and design refresh functions with the form (see Figure 10.50).

FIGURE 10.50

The Design Document Properties box showing the Design tab.

Summary

This chapter discussed many important and powerful form design elements. In many ways, this chapter just scratched the serface, but you should have enough information to begin designing sophisticated forms on your own.

View Design

by Debbie Lynd

CHAPTER 11

Chapter 7, "The Release 5 Object Store," described views as the means by which documents are listed and presented for access in a Domino database. This chapter explores this important design element in depth. All databases have at least one view; when a new database is created, a default untitled view is also created. You will find this default view to be pretty much useless because it displays a number for each document that is based on the order in which the documents were entered. The views that a designer creates are far more informative. A view lists documents in a tabular format similar in appearance to a spreadsheet or a database Browse listing. It is up to developers to determine what documents appear in each view and what each column displays.

Defining the Elements of a View

Views consist of three major presentation areas: the Navigation pane, the View pane, and the optional Preview pane. The Navigation pane and the View pane are always visible; the Preview pane can be turned on and off by the end user. The Preview pane can be toggled by clicking the View Show/Hide Preview pane SmartIcon or by choosing View and then Document Preview from the menu. The default location of each of the display panes is a database property that you can set in the Properties Box. The locations can also be changed by choosing View, Document Preview, Arrange Preview from the menu. Only the Navigation and View panes contain elements that can be affected by the developer. The Preview pane simply previews the document. Table 11.1 lists the display and design elements of a view; Figure 11.1 shows a typical view with the Preview pane displayed on the bottom.

TABLE 11.1 View Elements

Element	*Contents*
	Display
View pane	Documents displayed in rows and columns, each column representing a developer defined set of data, and each row representing one document
Navigation pane	Views and folders or custom navigator
Preview pane	Documents
	Design
Column Object	Simple functions, fields, or formulas that define a set of data displayed
Form Formula	View property that allows a formula entry to determine what forms display any selected document in the view

Element	Contents
	Design
Action Bar buttons	Simple actions, formulas, or LotusScript used to determine what action will occur when the action is selected

FIGURE 11.1

The display areas of a database include the Preview pane in its default location at the bottom of the screen.

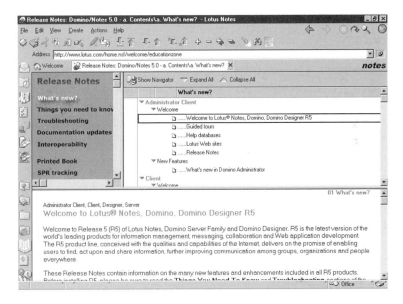

This chapter deals principally with the elements in the View pane. Just as all databases must have at least one view, all views must have at least one column. Columns control what is displayed in the rows. Selection formulas control which documents are displayed in the view. The default selection formula is SELECT @All, which displays all documents in the database. A Form formula is used to determine what Form(s) to use to display the documents in the view. The last item in Table 11.1 is Action Bar buttons. By now, you should be familiar with these; they are also available for forms. Each of these items is discussed in this chapter.

The Navigation pane has a default navigator of views and folders; Figure 11.1 shows an example of a view in a database. Designing views and folders impacts this area through the names chosen by the developer. As long as a view is not hidden and the user has access to the view, it will appear in this default navigator. Consequently, if you intend to use the default navigator, be careful when naming views. Naming views is discussed later in this chapter in the section on the Basics tab of the View Properties Box. However, with the advent of Outlines in R5, it is unlikely that you will use views for navigation purposes as often as was done in the past.

Creating a View

Of all the major design elements, views are perhaps the easiest to create. I don't mean to imply that all views will be simple; indeed, some views can take a considerable amount of time to create. A simple view can be constructed in a relatively short period of time and be demonstrated presently.

There are essentially six types of views:

1. Shared

2. Shared, contains documents not in any folders

3. Shared, contains deleted documents

4. Shared, private on first use

5. Shared, desktop private on first use

6. Private

Private was the default in Release 4. In Release 5 however, Shared is the default. Users with Reader access to the database can create their own private views if given the access through the Create Private Folders/Views option in the Access Control List (ACL) for the database. Users with editor access and above can create shared views as long as Create Shared Folders/Views is checked in the ACL for that user. For designers and managers, it is checked by default. To create a shared view, select Shared from the drop-down box at the top of the Create View dialog box.

Figure 11.2

The default view type from the Create View dialog box is Shared in Release 5.

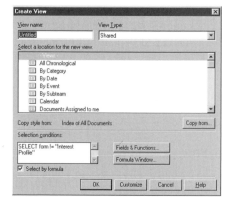

This is the most commonly used view type. The second view type, "Shared, contains documents not in any folder," speaks for itself. The third view type, "Shared, contains deleted documents," is quite useful for reviewing documents that are marked for deletion prior to actually deleting them. To use this properly, you must also set the database property for Allow Soft Deletions as shown in Figure 11.3. This setting determines how long deleted documents can be recovered. When this option is set, any document in the deleted view can be undeleted by dragging it to another folder. The fourth, "Shared, private on first use," and the fifth, "Shared, desktop private on first use," are useful for displaying a subset of documents unique to individual users. Essentially, it is a design that is shared in the sense that it appears to all users—but when it is first used, it becomes personal to the user. In a contact-management database, a view such as this could be used to display accounts specific to a salesperson. The difference between these two views, is that one is stored with the database, and the other is stored on the user's desktop. Of the six views available, the type you will create most often will be shared.

FIGURE 11.3

Enabling soft deletions in the database properties requires a view to support that option.

Navigating the Create View Dialog Box

Quite a few decisions must be made when first creating the database, as you can see from Figure 11.2. Selecting the view type is just one of them. The Create View dialog box in Release 5 is different from Release 4. It is actually far better and much easier to work with.

Naming a view is the first step. In selecting a name for a view, choose one that's descriptive and that reflects the contents of the view. In earlier versions of Notes and Domino, the view name was used as the link to accessing the view from the UI and therefore it was necessary to make the name something that would make sense to the user. However, with all the changes in Release 5, it's easy to customize the label displayed to the user through the use of Navigators, which were available in Release 4, and Outlines, which are new to Release 5. Therefore, the name can be a bit less wordy and still be meaningful to you without having to worry about the UI.

Selecting a location for the view is worth setting up properly because the hierarchical structure that you create can then be used to automatically generate an Outline.

You might notice that the Copy Style From: field already contains a view name. If this is true, it is coming from the view in the database that is set as the Default view for that database. In any case, use the Copy From button to select a view design that is similar to a view that already exists, or select -Blank- if you want to create a view from scratch. In using an already-existing view design, you will avoid having to re-create all those columns and you can cut any columns that you won't need.

I'll skip the Selection conditions for now and come back to them later in this chapter. For now, simply be aware that you can write your selection formula up front rather than waiting to enter the IDE.

If you are not going to actually work on the design of the view at this time, choose the OK button to save your new view without taking you into design mode. However, most of the time you should choose the Customize button so that you can get into design mode and create your new view.

It *almost* goes without saying that it is a good idea to put some thought into what you are about to create. At minimum, you need to determine the following:

- What documents will be displayed (View selection)
- How those documents will be sorted and categorized
- What fields (items) should be displayed in the columns

There are, of course, many other elements for you to consider; I'll discuss those in the coming pages.

Creating a View Design Checklist

You might find it useful to create a view design checklist. When complete, the checklist can become part of the project documentation. This list in Table 11.2 is not necessarily complete, and not all the items are necessary for all views.

TABLE 11.2 View Design Checklist

Item	Description
View Name	Name of the view.
View Alias	Alias of the view.
Description	What will the view be used for and who will use it.
View Contents	A simple description of which documents will appear in the view.
View Type	Shared, private, and so on.
View Selection	Which documents should appear in the view?

Item	Description
View Access	General availability, or secured.
View Hierarchy	Will there be response documents? Should they be indented under the parent?
Form property	Will a special form formula be used to display the documents?
Column 1 . . . *xx*	Describe contents of columns; include sort and categorize settings. Column formula.

Setting View Properties

Before you add columns or other elements to the view, I want to take a moment to discuss the five tabs of the View Properties Box:

- View Info
- Options
- Styles
- Advanced
- Security

The View Properties Box provides options for setting view wide colors and styles as well as indexing options. This is where you also enter the name of the view and the alias for a view name.

Setting View Info Properties

The View Info tab (see Figure 11.4) is where you name views and create aliases. It is always a good idea to create a view alias, just as it is a good idea to create a form alias. Views can be referred to in formulas just as forms can. Using a view alias in formulas allows the view name to be changed without affecting the formulas. When you design a database, changes in view names happen fairly frequently. As the number of views grows, you will probably want to collect them into folders. This involves changing the name; if you have been careful to use a view alias and to use that alias in formulas referencing the view, no formulas have to be changed.

And some views are actually hidden from users. These views appear in the View Design folder with parentheses around them. Including parentheses in a view's title will hide the title.

FIGURE **11.4**

The View Info tab of the View Properties dialog box includes a field for defining the alias.

The ($All) View Includes All Documents in the Database and Is Not Hidden

Although you can hide a view by enclosing the name in parentheses, there is an exception. A view with the title of ($All) will not be hidden, but will appear above the Folders titled All Documents. $All is a reserved word in Notes. There is an ($All) view in the Release Notes database as shown in Figure 11.5. I have noticed that this view does not appear immediately after it is created. Close the database and open it again. The new All Documents view will now display.

Note

Hidden views can be useful. I often use a hidden view for populating keyword fields in a form by using @DbLookup() and @DbColumn() formulas to access the data in the view. To distinguish this type of hidden view from other hidden views, I use LU for "look up" as the first two letters of the name. (LUDept) and (LUCustomer) are typical examples. I try to avoid using regular views for lookup purposes, because if users want a change to the view, it's easy to forget that it's a lookup view and make changes that cause the lookups to fail.

You can collect views into folders and cascade them by naming them with the back slash (\). Everything to the right of the slash appears either inside a folder or cascaded on the menu. This allows the designer to collect related views together easily. Figure 11.5 shows the Release Notes database with the View Design folder open. Note how the views are named (a. Contents\. . .) and how this affects the display in the Navigation pane.

Up to 200 cascading views can be added to a database—a limit that, in practice, you'll never reach. If the views are included on the View menu, there is a limit of nine views per level, after which Other appears on the menu. Clicking Other produces a dialog box that displays all the views. In my opinion, it is best to leave the views completely off the View menu, avoiding the Other window altogether. Another reason to keep views from the View menu is that users are accustomed to working with the Navigation pane, not the

View menu, to navigate the database. Users typically won't look at the View menu to navigate. If for some reason, however, the design calls for the views to be on the View menu, take all possible precautions to keep the levels to nine or fewer.

FIGURE 11.5

Hidden views parenthesized in the view list as shown in the Release Notes database.

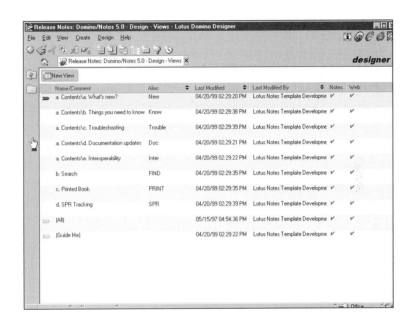

A field called Comment can be used for a simple description of the view. Although the text scrolls in the field, it is impossible to view the complete comment. Practically speaking, the comment is limited to the visible area of the field. Oddly enough, the comment does not even appear in the design synopsis of the view.

Version History

The last field on the Basics tab is the Style field. Not to be confused with the Style tab, this field has two selections: Standard Outline (the default) and Calendar. This was new to Release 4.5, with the addition of calendaring and scheduling. Most views are in the standard outline style; the calendar style creates a view similar to the Calendar view in your mail database.

Setting View Options Properties

Many of the choices on the Options tab are self-explanatory (see Figure 11.6). I mentioned earlier that a Default view will automatically be chosen as the template for all new views that are created. It is important that you as the designer specify a view as the default in each database that you create because this is the template for any Shared/Private view or Folder that a user can create.

The Default View Should Include All Documents

Make sure that the view you specify as Default does not exclude any documents, because this is the view that all new views and folders will be based on.

If the view includes sorted and categorized columns, documents appear under the categories. Choosing Collapse All causes only the top-level categories to appear. Show Response Documents in a Hierarchy is chosen by default; this selection causes response documents to be indented under the parent document. This is commonly used in discussion databases. The Show in View menu was discussed previously, and the last two options are drop-down lists.

FIGURE 11.6

The Options tab of the View Properties Box is where the default view for the database is selected.

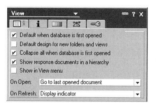

Showing Document Hierarchy

Due to the limitations of displaying response documents in views, you might choose to use all main documents as the form type, even though a parent/child relationship exists between the documents. To create a custom view that displays response hierarchy without the limitation of one column for the response information you can simulate indenting the child documents under the parent by padding the first column with spaces. A formula that accomplishes this might look similar to this:

```
@Repeat(" "; 6) + <fieldname>.
```

On Open has three choices: Go to Last Opened Document (the default), Go to Top Row, and Go to Bottom Row. The last two choices are useful if the documents are sorted by date, for example. If the first column in the view is sorted by date descending, Go to Top Row moves the document highlight to the most recent entry.

On Refresh has four choices: Display Indicator, Refresh Display, Refresh Display from Top Row, and Refresh Display from Bottom Row. In my experience, these settings are rarely used; I prefer to leave this field set at the default. The display indicator is visible in Figure 11.7 and is a small blue circular arrow in the area to the left of the title bar. This visual cue lets the user know that the view needs to be refreshed; clicking the display indicator refreshes the view. Visual cues are an important facet of UI design, and you should use them when they're available.

FIGURE 11.7

The view refresh indicator displays whenever a new document has been added to the database but not your display.

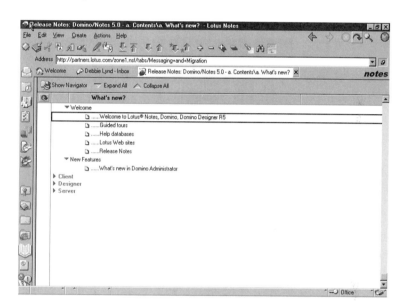

Setting Style Properties

The numerous settings on the Style tab (see Figure 11.8) fall into four categories: color, column headings, row settings, and general settings. You can set color for the view background, column totals, unread rows, and alternate rows. The settings for column headings were new to Release 4. You can turn column headings off and choose to display beveled headings (the default gray title bar) and simple headings. Up to five lines can be used for the column header. In practice, I suggest keeping the number to two or three. Similar to columns, rows can now display up to nine lines. This is useful when stacking lists stored in multivalued fields or displaying text fields that are longer than will fit in a standard single row. If you do use multiline rows, it is a good idea to also choose an alternate row color and to select Shrink Rows to Content, which displays all lines only if necessary to include the entire contents of the columns. If that option is not chosen, the number of lines in the display is fixed, regardless of the amount of data. There are three general settings: Show Selection Margin, Row Spacing, and Extend Last Column to Window Width. Show Selection Margin is checked by default. The selection margin is the area to the left of the view display and is separated from the columns by a thin line. This area displays checkmarks for selected documents, stars for unread documents (when the appropriate settings are made), and the delete icon. Row spacing can be used in conjunction with multiline rows to provide separation between the documents. For many views, the default settings are adequate. By far, the most useful settings on this tab are the multiline rows and color settings.

FIGURE 11.8

The Style tab of the View Properties Box has many settings for the developer.

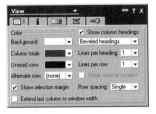

Setting Advanced Properties

For most views, none of the options in the Advanced tab will need to be changed (see Figure 11.9). The Refresh Index options can be changed from automatic to one of the other choices to improve performance. If a column formula is based on @Now or another time-dependent function (as might be used to "age" documents), the refresh indicator displays constantly. To eliminate this, you can either turn off the display indicator or change the Refresh Index options to Manual or Auto, at most every *XX* hours. Changing the Discard Index options from the default of Never can be used to conserve disk space. If the index is discarded, displaying it subsequently can be very time-consuming.

FIGURE 11.9

The Advanced "propeller beanie" tab has choices for indexing, unread documents, form formula, ODBC access, Web access, and categories.

I am sure you have seen how unread documents are displayed in your mail database—in red with a star in the view margin. The Unread Marks field controls this display. In Release 5 storing unread marks is optional and is selected from the Advanced Database

Properties when the database is first created. If you are using unread marks in your database, there are three options for using them in each view you create:

- None (default)
- Unread documents only
- Standard (compute in hierarchy)

The choices are in order of speed of display, from fastest to slowest, and in reverse order of least information to most information. In other words, the faster the display, the less information. Displaying no marks is the fastest display; the slowest is the last because Notes calculates and displays unread marks at all levels. Unread Documents Only does not display unread marks for a collapsed category that contains unread documents, unlike the Standard option. Users have to open the category to see the unread marks.

The Generate Unique Keys in Index checkbox is useful if the view is used in conjunction with an ODBC driver, perhaps to create reports on the underlying documents in a relational database.

The two Web options are Treat View Contents as HTML, which enables you to fill contents of the columns with HTML, and Use Applet in the Browser, which enables the view to run as an applet when a browser is accessing the view.

The view applet provides Web clients with the following abilities for manipulating a view from the Web:

- Resizing columns
- Collapsing and expanding views without a page refresh
- Vertical scroll bar
- Refreshing view with F9
- Multiple document selection
- Mark documents for deletion

The three-color options determine what colors display for the links column in a view.

Up until Release 5, there was a problem with views that contained documents with Reader fields in them. If you did not have access to all the documents in one of the categories in a view, you could still see the category. The option to not show categories having zero documents now takes care of that.

The checkbox under the heading For Web Access: in Figure 11.20 is a welcome addition to Release 5. This option means that the view will have the same functionality as a Notes view when displayed with a browser.

Setting Security Properties

The Security tab (see Figure 11.10) controls access to the view. Access is normally set to readers and above, but by deselecting this, you can restrict the users of a view. The window is scrollable and displays the users and groups in the ACL, as well as the roles for the database. The button to the right of the window allows access to the Public NAB. Using roles in conjunction with author access is a powerful way to extend editing privileges to certain documents without giving the user editor access. You can further extend this control by not allowing certain forms to appear on the Create menu and using a view with limited access to display the forms. Putting an Action Bar button on that view or views to create documents using that form effectively restricts create access to those documents.

FIGURE 11.10

The Security tab (the key icon) controls view access.

Creating Advanced View Selections

View selection formulas restrict the documents that appear in a view. LotusScript cannot be used for this formula. There are two Run options: Easy and Formula. You can access view selection by clicking the Define drop-down list or by clicking the Design View Selection Conditions icon. Clicking Easy and then the Add Condition button at the bottom of the View Design pane displays the Search Builder window. The Search builder is shown in Figure 11.11. Multiple "easy" conditions can be strung together to create a fairly complex view selection criteria. If you examine the View Design pane in Figure 11.11, you will notice that there are two groups of words with a gray background separated by a Boolean AND. You can edit the condition by double-clicking the text. The first condition is By Field, which is displayed in the Search Builder window. The Version History form is selected.

11

VIEW DESIGN

Figure 11.11

The By Field condition in the Search Builder window shows the Body field selected.

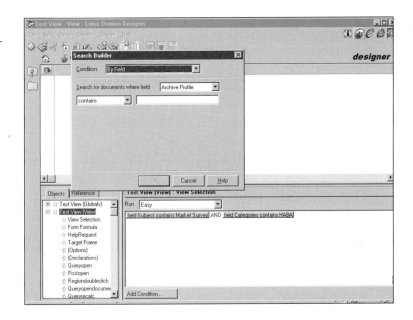

View selection conditions can also be built by using the Notes Formula language. In fact, you can see the formula equivalents to the Easy View selection conditions by clicking the Formula radio button. Take the following steps to create the selection condition:

1. Open the view in design. Go to the View selection condition and choose Easy.

2. Click the Add condition button and choose By Form Used in the Condition dropdown.

3. Click the form that you want to use in the window that appears. Click OK.

To see the formula, click the Formula radio button. Notes displays the following formula:

```
SELECT ((Form = "form name") ¦ (Form = "FN"))
```

The Default selection condition is SELECT @All, which selects all documents in the database. You can build more sophisticated selection conditions with the Formula language than with the Search Builder. The Search Builder is multipurpose and is used in many different places in Notes. Because the Search Builder is general purpose, some of the conditions are not very useful for view selection conditions. By Date and By Form used are two examples. These are better suited to creating full-text queries than to designing selection conditions. Nevertheless, building selection conditions with the Search Builder will work in most instances.

Be Careful Using @today in a Selection Formula

Using a selection formula that compares dates with today's date using @today causes the Refresh icon to be constantly displayed as the value of @today is constantly changing. To get around this use @texttotime(Today) instead.

Adding and Editing View Columns

You can add new columns to the view in several ways. Double-clicking the gray title bar in an area without a column adds a column. Clicking the Create Insert New Column SmartIcon inserts a new column to the left of the currently selected column. You can insert or append columns from the Create menu. You can also remove columns by highlighting the column and pressing the Delete key; choosing Edit, Clear from the menu; or pressing Ctrl+X.

Cut-and-Paste Works for Moving Columns

You can move columns by highlighting the column in the title bar and then pressing Ctrl+X. Position the highlight to the right of the location to which you want to move the column and press Ctrl+V. The column is inserted to the left of the highlight.

Although columns can be hidden, they typically display data in views. Columns are defined in the Design pane. There are three choices: Simple Function, Formula, and Field. LotusScript is not allowed in column definitions. Simple functions are listed in Table 11.2 and are convenient for displaying document statistics and file attachment information. Formulas are the most powerful and flexible way to determine what appears in a column. You will often use formulas when constructing views. The last choice is Field. Please note that view columns cannot display rich-text fields or encrypted data. Although you cannot directly display the contents of a rich-text field, you can use simple functions to indicate whether the document has a file attachment in a rich-text field.

TABLE 11.2   Simple Functions for View Column Definitions

Simple Function	Returns
Attachment Lengths	Number list attachments
Attachment Names	Text list of attachment's filenames
Attachments	Number of files attached

Simple Function	*Returns*
Authors(Dist. Names)	The distinguished name of the author—for example, Henry Henke/Acme
Authors(Simple Names)	The simple name of the author—for example, Henry Henke
Collapse/Expand (+/-)	Uses a + or a - sign to indicate whether a column is expandable
Creation Date	Uses @Created to return the date the document was created
Last Modified	Uses @Modified to return the date the document was last modified
Last Read or Edited	Uses @Accessed to return the date the document was last read or edited
Size	The size of the document in bytes
# in View (such as 2.1.2)	The position of the document in the view
# of Responses(1 level)	The number of direct descendants to the document or next-level subcategories for a category
#of Responses(all levels)	The total number of descendants (both response and response to response docs) for a document or subcategories for a category

Simple functions are also termed *view statistics* for reasons that are apparent by glancing at the list. Some of these are quite useful when building views. For example, because the version history will have attachments, the three attachment functions will be very useful. Choosing Attachments for a column and setting the column to Display as Icons (on the Basics tab) displays an icon if there is a file attachment. This is equivalent to the @Function @Attachments. Some simple functions have no @Function equivalent; Attachment Names is one example. As mentioned earlier, # in view is the default for newly created columns. When you switch from simple functions to a field, a prompt box appears stating "Existing action data will be lost. Do you want to continue?" Switching to a formula does not produce this; but switching from a formula back to simple function does. Unfortunately, this can be rather annoying. Although they're somewhat limited, the simple functions can be quite useful in many situations.

Fields are simple enough to understand; simply choose the field you want to display from the list in the Design pane, and you're finished.

Typing the Name of the Field Might Be Faster

If you know the name of the field, you can switch directly to the formula and type the field name into the Design pane. This will avoid the annoying action data prompt.

Formulas allow you to use @Functions to manipulate the display of columns. The possibilities here are virtually endless and include returning a numeric value to be evaluated as an icon, returning numeric values to total or average, and returning numerous string and time/date functions.

It is also possible to add HTML in a column to display an image instead of the contents of a field or the result of a formula. An HTML column is often used on the Web to display an image as the result of a formula. For instance, if I want to show new entries with a special image and older entries without, I can create a formula such as this one which displays a GIF image if the document was added to the database in the last 14 days.

```
@IF (@NOW > @ADJUST(@CREATED; 0; 0; 14; 0; 0; 0); "";
"[<img src=/gifs/new.gif border=0>]")
```

Reviewing Column Properties

Whenever a new column is added to the view, Notes automatically opens the Column Properties Box. You can open this Properties Box for existing columns by double-clicking the column header in the title bar or by highlighting the header (click once) and choosing Design, Column Properties from the menu. The Column Properties Box for the first column in a new view is shown in Figure 11.12. New columns default to a width of 10 characters and a Notes Simple function of # in View.

FIGURE 11.12

Column properties for the default first column include a default column width of 10.

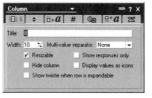

The default column definition is shown with the default width of 10 characters. Notes also adds # as the column title of the default column of a new view.

Working with the Column Info Properties

The Column Info tab illustrated in Figure 11.13 has settings listed in Table 11.3.

FIGURE 11.13

Column Info tab settings include a label for the column heading.

TABLE 11.3 Column Info Tab Settings

Setting	Description
Title	Text that appears in the Column header; defaults to #
Width	Width of the column; defaults to 10
Multivalue separator	The type of separator for multivalued columns; the default is none
Resizable	Allows the user to change the width of the column
Show Responses only	Used to show response and response-to-response documents
Hide column	Hides the column
Display values as icon	Displays icons instead of column values
Show twistie when row is expandable	Displays a small triangle for sorted, categorized rows that are expandable

Title and Width are self-explanatory. A multivalue separator controls the display of columns that store lists. Those lists can originate in a single field, the result of combining fields, or the result of a formula. It is sometimes useful to combine multiline rows with a multivalue field with New Line as a separator. This "stacks" the list in the column. Because the number of lines per row is limited to nine, you might be unable to display all the items in the field, but it is still a valuable technique. I often use a document to store lists that are used in multiple keyword fields on multiple forms. I use this technique to display the list fields of the document in the view. There can be only one Show Responses Only column in a view. This is used to display information in response documents. If you need to show more than a single field, you'll have to combine the fields. When you do this, the values must evaluate to the same data type (that is, string, numeric, or time).

Hiding a column is useful. For example, you might want to sort a view of personnel documents by the last name of the employee, but in the view show the employee's full name, given name first. To do this, create a hidden column with a width of 1 that contains the field for the employee's last name. Sort this field ascending on the Sorting tab and mark it hidden. The next column can contain the employee's name with a formula of

```
cFirstName + " " + cLastName
```

The view presents the employee's full name but is sorted by the employee's last name.

Displaying icons is a good technique to use; a visual cue is presented to the user and can indicate many things such as the status of a document, the type of a document, whether or not there are file attachments, and so on. Over 100 icons can be displayed, as shown in Figure 11.14. To display an icon in a column, make the width 1 and create a formula that evaluates to the number of the icon you want to display.

FIGURE 11.14

The View Icon display palette can be seen from the Help database.

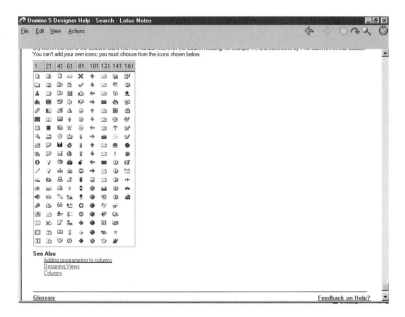

The Resizable and Show twistie settings were new to Release 4. In earlier releases, column widths were fixed. This means users can grab the column separator with the mouse pointer and drag it larger or smaller. Twisties are a very nice addition to views. When a column is sorted and categorized, the documents appear underneath the category. A *twistie* is a dark cyan triangle that indicates expandability when the twistie points to the right. When the category is expanded, the twistie points downward and the categories or documents within the category are displayed.

Working with the Sorting Properties

The sort options are None, Ascending, and Descending. See Figure 11.15. If either Ascending or Descending is chosen, the type can be set to Standard or Categorized. Categorizing documents in a view is a powerful display feature. Multiple categorized columns can be included in a view that can nest documents. With each category opening, other categories become available. Case-sensitive sorting sorts lowercase characters before uppercase. Accent-sensitive sorting sorts accented characters after unaccented characters.

If the column contains a multivalued field, unless Show Multiple Values as Separate Entities is checked, Notes displays the entire field as a single entry.

The option Categorized Is Flat Version 5 or Greater is useful for a categorized column in a hidden view used for lookups. It provides an optimized view with the category shown on each line, so it's not pretty, but it is far faster on lookups.

Checking Click on Column Header to Sort gives the user the capability to change the sort order of a display. Four options are available from the drop-down list next to the checkbox: Ascending, Descending, Both, and Change to View. Of the first three options, Both is the most frequently used. For all three, clicking the column header toggles the sort order of the view. The fourth option causes an entirely different view to be displayed when the header is clicked. When Change to View is selected, a new field appears, in which you choose the name of the view from a drop-down list of available views.

When Click on Column Header to Sort is checked, another checkbox appears for a secondary sort column. If this checkbox is selected, a drop-down list of additional columns appears and another drop-down list appears for the sort order, ascending or descending.

The last item on this tab is the Totals field. There are options here for None, Total, Averages, and Percent. After a selection other than None is made, the Hide Detail Rows checkbox is enabled. Using this checkbox suppresses the display of values for the rows (or detail) and displays only the totals for categories. One drawback when using totals is that response documents cannot be included in totals. This is a design limitation that is probably related to the fact that there can be no more than a single responses-only column. If you need to total values in documents, you have to put the values into a document or main form or figure out a way to add the values to the parent document.

Setting the Font Properties

The Font tab has already been discussed in earlier chapters, but in views there are two additional features, which you can see in Figure 11.16. The justification for a column can be set to left, center, or right. The standard is for text and time values to be justified left and numbers to be justified right. A button at the bottom of the tab labeled Apply to All copies the font settings for the current column to all other columns. There is also a second Font tab for setting fonts in the column titles.

FIGURE 11.16

The Font tab of a view column has two additional settings: Justification and Apply to All.

Font Size Affects the View Display

Notes defaults to a 10-point Helvetica font for view columns. I often prefer to use 8-point Helvetica, especially if a lot of columns are in the view. Using a smaller point size increases the amount of information that can be displayed particularly for Notes users, where real estate is at a premium. Rather than changing the font in each new column, you can create all columns and change a single column to 8-point. When the Apply to All button is clicked, all the other columns will be changed.

Caution

The Apply to All button is not selective! If the column you are on has red, bold, italic, Helvetica 8-point with strikethrough for a text setting, after clicking the Apply to All button, all the other columns will be red, bold, italic, and so on.

Setting the Number and Time Format

Figures 11.17 and 11.18 illustrate the Number and Time format tabs, respectively. Both tabs are self-explanatory. The only real change in R5 is the ability to show a date field with a four-digit year.

FIGURE 11.17

The Number tab controls the display of numeric values in the column.

FIGURE 11.18

The Time tab controls the display of time values in the column.

Setting the Title

The Title tab (see Figure 11.19) is similar to the Font tab. The font of the column and the title can be controlled independently of each other. In fact, the only thing that seems to transfer from the Column font tab to the Title font tab is the point size. Generally speaking, the column and the title justification should be the same. If the column is justified right, the title should be justified right as well. Right-justified column titles often appear as though they are jammed against the next column title. To avoid this, embed a single space to the right of the title.

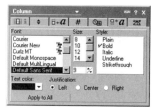

FIGURE 11.19

The Title tab has the same settings as the Font tab.

Working with the Advanced Properties

The Advanced tab (see Figure 11.20) has a field used for programmatic access. The name of the field displayed in the first column appears here. If the column contains a formula, Notes names the column internally. Figure 11.20 illustrates this showing a name of $0. The $ (dollar sign) appears in front of reserved field names in Notes.

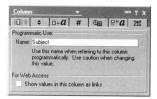

FIGURE 11.20

The Advanced tab shows the internally assigned name ($0) of the column.

The checkbox under the heading For Web Access: in Figure 11.20 is a welcome addition to Release 5. This option, Show Values in This Column as Links, removes the Release 4 restriction on having to use the first sorted column in the view as the link to the document.

> ### Set the Column to Display as the Link to a Document From the Web
>
> You can set the view column, which will be used as the link to the actual document from the Advanced tab. The default is to have the first column in the view as the link to the underlying document; however, this is not always the most sensible column to use.

Adding Actions to a View

Many tasks can be accomplished from a View Action Bar button, including creating new documents, editing documents, deleting documents, and changing the status of a document without opening it. To display the actions, click the View Show/Hide Action pane, drag the Action pane into view with the mouse by grabbing the separator bar, or click View, Action pane. Double-clicking the separator bar also shows or hides the Action pane. Figure 11.21 shows the Action pane for the ($All) view.

FIGURE 11.21

The Action pane of the ($All) view. The actions with asterisks on the left are default actions and cannot be deleted.

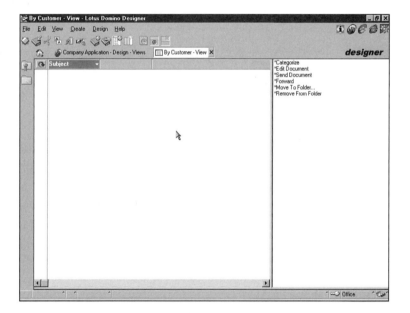

There are six default actions that cannot be removed from the pane but can be disabled. To disable an action, take the following steps:

1. Double-click the action to be disabled. Do this for the Categorize action, because it won't be needed. Notes displays the Action Properties Box.

2. In the center of the Basics tab are two checkboxes, Include Action in Action Menu and Include Action in Button Bar. Deselect both of these, and the action is disabled.

Choose Create Action from the View menu. The Properties Box should look like the one in Figure 11.22. Here is where you can name an action. In general, keep the names short and simple. When an action is displayed on the button bar, you can select an icon from the palette, as you can in forms. An action can be a simple action, a formula using @Commands or the @Function language, or LotusScript. This particular action simply has @Command([Compose]), which functions as is, even though no form is specified. With no form specified, Notes displays a window of available forms from which the user can choose. Creating a formula to provide the appropriate form to the user requires naming that form in the formula. The best way to deal with this is to use the alias name for the form in quotes, rather than using the full name of the form. For instance if the name of the form is "Request for Information" and the alias is "RI," the formula would look like this:

```
@Command([Compose]; "RI")
```

FIGURE 11.22

The Action Properties Box Basics tab, where you choose where the action displays and the icon, if any.

In order for the action to appear on the button bar, make sure that the Include Action in Button Bar option is checked. Actions can be positioned with the spinner at the bottom of the tab.

If you want to share this action with other views, select the checkbox for Share This Action. If this is a shared action, it cannot be modified from the view—you must go to Shared Actions under Resources in order to modify a shared action.

Using Hide-When Attributes with View Actions

Unlike form actions, which have preset conditions to hide Action Bar buttons, the view action buttons can only be hidden using formulas created with Notes' @Function Formula language, as shown in Figure 11.23. To use a formula, click the Hide Action if Formula Is True checkbox and enter a formula. For example, you might want to keep the new action from the view if the user is not a known user. In that case, the following formula would work:

```
@IsNotMember("[<RoleName>]";@UserRoles)
```

FIGURE 11.23

The Hide-When tab of the Action Properties Box allows formulas only.

Publishing Actions to Other Applications

Another tab in the Action Properties Box is the NotesFlow Publishing tab. NotesFlow Publishing is covered in Chapter 10, "Advanced Form Design."

Working with the Action Bar Properties

The Action Bar has display properties that you can set. Figure 11.24 shows the Action Bar Properties Box, Info tab. This is available only if the Action pane is visible and can be accessed by clicking Design, Action Bar Properties from the menu or by choosing Action Bar from the drop-down list in the Properties Box.

FIGURE 11.24

The Action Bar Properties Box controls the style of the Action Bar.

You can set the location of the buttons starting from the left or right with the alignment option. You can change the default gray background color from the Color drop-down. The Use System Color if Customized checkbox is checked by default. If unchecked, the color remains at the color chosen, regardless of the system colors. The Action Bar has a default black line of single thickness that extends to the width of the window. The Bottom Border radio button has four choices: None, Fit to Window (the default), Under Buttons Only, and Fixed Width. You can set the color of the line with the style of the line from the drop-down lists on the right. I have found it unnecessary to change the default settings because they are aesthetically pleasing enough.

Web access settings are available to determine whether to use the Domino view applet to display to Web users or not. With this enabled, Web clients can scroll the Action Bar, and use pull-down lists. An example of an Action Bar viewed through the applet is displayed in Figure 11.25, and the Action Bar displayed with standard HTML is shown in Figure 11.26.

FIGURE 11.25

The Action Bar in a view displayed through a Java applet looks better than through HTML.

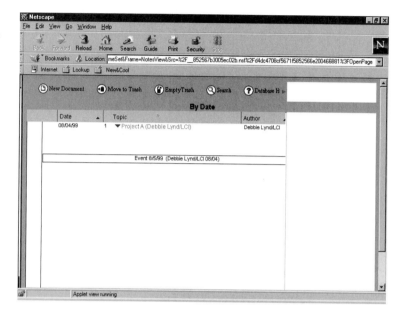

FIGURE 11.26

An Action Bar in a view displayed via HTML does not have the same appearance.

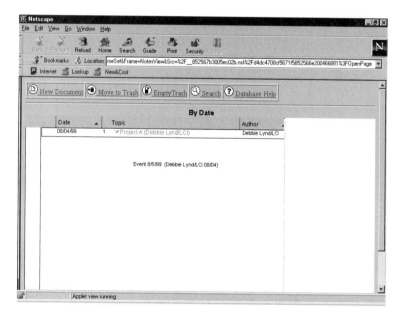

The second tab affects the way the background of a button is displayed. This includes the size of buttons, when the button border is displayed, and whether to use an image or color for the background. The last tab allows setting the fonts for the buttons.

Testing the View with Refresh

When the view is in design, you can test it by clicking the blue refresh arrow or by pressing F9. The columns are populated so that you can see the results of the design changes. Hidden columns also appear when the view is refreshed in design. When changes are made to a column, the display for that column changes to question marks until the view is tested or refreshed again. Figure 11.27 illustrates this.

FIGURE 11.27

The view preview must be refreshed when changing a view column. Note the question marks in the rows and the refresh arrow.

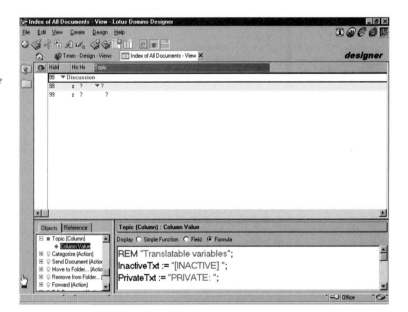

Creating Calendar Views

Calendar views are useful for displaying the contents of a document in a calendar or day-planner format. There are quite a few new features available in R5 for building and working with these views. Calendar views are viewable by Web clients as HTML tables. The restrictions for use by Web clients are that they cannot create new appointments within the view and they cannot scroll through entries for a specific day. These functions will be available in a future release of Domino through the incorporation of the eSuite calendar applet. For now, this means that in order to create a fully functional calendar view which provides the ability to create a new entry or display all the entries for a single day, the view must be embedded in a page or form, and the facility to create the new entry must be outside of the embedded view. And to display all the entries for a specific day, I need to add an action that will display the one day view. Other calendar features that are unavailable on the Web are the Embedded group scheduler, a date picker, and group calendars.

Different view properties are available for a calendar view that are based on the need to display information about a date or an event differently than would be shown in a standard view. The differences are listed later in this chapter.

Color Tab

For calendar views, there are options to define the view background as well as the date background. Colors can also differentiate between busy rows and unread rows. There are colors for non-month background and text, today, and day separators.

Day/Time Tab

This tab determines how the information in the view appears to the user, as indicated in Figure 11.28. The options and their descriptions are explained in Table 11.4.

FIGURE 11.28
Date/Time Properties affect the date format for the calendar view.

TABLE 11.4   Date/Time Tab

Option	*Description*
Enable Time Slots	Determines whether the Start Time, End Time, Duration, and Allow User to Override Times options are enabled or disabled.
Show Daily Bitmaps	Shows dates for the day bitmaps.
Enable Time Grouping	Sets grouping of times by meeting.
Initial Format	Determines which format is shown when the view is opened. Options are -Default- (which means whatever format was last opened), 1 Day, 2 Day, 1 Week, 2 Week, or 1 Month.

continues

TABLE 11.4   Date/Time Tab

Option	Description
Start Time, End Time, and Duration	The default start and end times displayed in the view as well as the default duration. If the Allow User to Override Times option is selected, the user can change these parameters.
Allowed Formats	Determines which formats are available to switch to in this view.
Allow User to Override Times	If selected, users can change the start/end times and duration.

First, change the view display properties on the Style tab to display two lines. Click Shrink Rows to Content and change the alternate row color to light blue to help distinguish between lines). Next, check Extend Last Column to Window Width. See Figure 11.29.

FIGURE 11.29

Changing the view display properties to alternate colored rows and two lines per row.

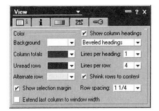

Understanding Folders

Folders are views with user-selectable contents. Documents are placed in folders by an end user or a programmatic process, just as you would place a physical paper document into a folder in a filing cabinet. Users with reader access or above can create personal folders. The manager of a database can determine whether users can create personal views for readers, authors, and editors in the ACL. The steps for creating a folder are identical to those for creating a view except that no selection condition is available.

Folder properties are the same as view properties except for the Security tab. The Security tab is shown in Figure 11.30 and includes an additional section specifying who can update the folder.

Users can move documents into and out of folders, which provides a way to manage documents. For example, the help databases have a Favorites Topics folder. I store help documents that I refer to frequently in that folder for quick and easy access. Documents

can be removed from the folder by choosing Actions, Remove from Folder from the menu. Do not use the Delete key! If you are able to delete documents from the database, the document will not only be removed from the folder, it will be removed from the database. The good news is that in R5, you can implement the soft delete function which enables you to recover a document that is inadvertently deleted.

FIGURE 11.30

The Folder Security tab controls document updates.

Optimizing Views for the Web

All the view options available in the designer are transferable to Web clients, except for the options indicated throughout this chapter. These are summarized in the following list:

- Private folders in outlines
- Private views
- Show in View Menu option—this is specific to a Notes client
- On Open: Go To options and On Refresh options
- Style properties for unread rows, alternate rows, selection margins, and beveled headings
- Index options
- Show Twisties option cannot be turned off

When you have created a view, displaying it on the Web in R5 usually means that you want to display the view in a frame, while displaying the navigator or outline in another frame. Framesets and Outlines are discussed in detail in Chapter 13, "Creating Outlines." In this chapter, I look at embedding a view in a form, in order to explore the functionality of embedded views. By default, a view displayed by a Web browser will be rendered using HTML. In R5, there is an option to display a view using the View Applet, which uses Java to display a view. This provides additional functions to the browser client. View applets and embedded views are covered in the following two sections of this chapter.

View Applets

How a view is displayed and manipulated by a Web browser is determined by the View property displayed in the Advanced tab; choose For Web Access: Use Applet in the Browser. If this is selected, the view displays on the Web with functions similar to that available to the Notes client. A view displayed through the Java applet has functions includingscrolling through the view using arrow keys and expanding and collapsing categories without the page being regenerated from the back end. You can also resize columns, select multiple documents, and use F9 to refresh the view. You can even mark documents for deletion.

However, there are features that are not supported by the View applet:

- Pass-thru HTML
- Horizontal scrollbars
- Calendar views (creates an HTML Calendar view)
- On open: go to last opened document
- On Refresh
- Unread rows color
- Alternate rows color
- Beveled headings
- Lines per heading
- Shrink rows to content
- Row spacing
- Refresh index
- Discard index
- Unread marks
- ODBC access–active link
- ODBC access–unvisited link
- ODBC access–visited link
- Restrict initial index build to designer or manager
- Font properties (limited to subset supported by Java)
- Show values in this column as links

Embedded Views

When views have been created, they can be embedded in a Page or a Form. They can also be placed in a frame of a frameset. Embedding a view in a page or form provides additional display options from the embedded view properties as shown in Figure 11.31. These properties determine the view layout options.

FIGURE 11.31

The Embedded View Properties Box has additional settings for views displayed within a page.

In the Info tab, the target frame for displaying the document selected in a view can be set, as well as directly determining whether the view is to be displayed using the Java applet. If it is displayed using HTML, the number of lines to be displayed can also be set here.

The Display tab provides the ability to determine the size of the view, whether to display column titles, and whether to display scrollbars, as shown in Figure 11.32.

FIGURE 11.32

Embedded View sizing properties in the Display tab allow the size of the view to be changed.

Alignment properties such as spacing and justification are set in the Advanced tab, shown in Figure 11.33. It is also possible to set the rows to display bullets, numbers, or letters at the beginning of each row.

FIGURE 11.33

Embedded View alignment properties includes settings bullets.

The last two tabs provide settings for paragraph, pagination, and hide when settings.

Summary

This chapter presented a thorough look at view design. Design elements, from view selection formulas to column definitions, were covered. This chapter showed you how to create buttons in the View Action Bar. You also designed a new view and learned about adding columns and setting column properties. You should now have enough information to design sophisticated views in your own databases. The last several chapters discussed designing forms, subforms, views, and folders. The next chapter discusses some of the things to consider before releasing the application to users.

Using Resources in Domino Applications

by Debbie Lynd

IN THIS CHAPTER

Shared resources are a good way to maximize the use of design elements throughout the design of the database or multiple databases. These resources are stored with the design of a database; therefore, resources commonly used in multiple databases can be stored in a template and applied to all the databases that need to use them. Most of the design elements stored as resources are those that you share with other design elements. These are images, applets, actions, subforms, script libraries, and fields. There are also a few miscellaneous categories stored here. They are the database icon, the About and Help documents, and the database script. The database script is covered in Chapter 24, "Writing LotusScript."

Sharing Images Within a Database

You often reuse images in the design of a database. For instance, you could place the company logo on multiple forms and pages or on subforms for reuse. In Release 4, many people stored images in a database and referred to them through an @dblookup. Although helpful for providing a central repository for images outside the file system, images that were referenced in this manner were not cached by the browser. This meant that the image had to be retrieved each time a page that referenced the image was opened or refreshed. By creating an image resource in Release 5, the image file is stored within the database, which also enables you to avoid having to make calls out to the file system for the image files. These images are cached, however, which means that subsequent loads are faster. Image resources are used on pages, action buttons, forms, and outline entries. You can also place them as background images on actions, table cells, pages, and forms.

Creating a Shared Image

Create a shared image by storing a GIF or JPEG file within the database. Images are stored as either GIF or JPEG. To create a shared image, you must move to the Images section of Resources in Design (see Figure 12.1).

The New Image action provides the vehicle for adding images. When it's chosen, you can add images from any drive or directory you can access. The images that can be added can be in GIF, JPEG, or BMP format. This is indicated in Figure 12.2. At this point, you can select multiple images, each of which will be separately created as a shared image.

When the images are selected, the shared image is created and listed. Next, you can set the properties for the image. To set properties, double-click the listed image. This displays the Properties box for the image selected as displayed in Figure 12.3.

FIGURE 12.1

Shared images in a discussion database are reused in various design elements.

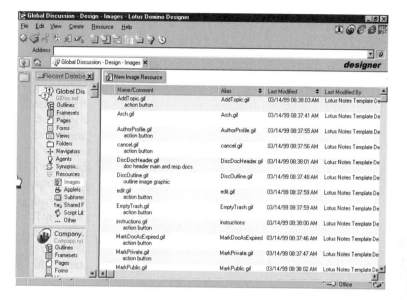

FIGURE 12.2

Multiple image files can be selected to be used as shared images.

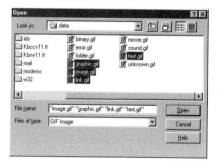

FIGURE 12.3

The Image Resource Properties box provides very few options that you can change.

12

USING RESOURCES IN DOMINO APPLICATIONS

As indicated in Figure 12.3, you can assign the name of the file and an alias to an image. You can then use the name or alias in a formula to specify which image to display based on a condition. The Comment field is useful in providing an explanation of when this image is used in the database. Use the Advanced section of this tab to define an image set. An image set is a graphic file with up to four multiple images that can display each of the four images based on state. If you choose a horizontal image set, by choosing the number of images in the horizontal box, the first image appears by default and each of the other three display based on the mouse-over event, selection, and so on, as shown in Table 12.1. To create a horizontal image set from an image editing program, make four copies of the image horizontally in the same file with one pixel dividing each copy. Then change the image colors to differentiate each image copy. You can also create a vertical image set which you can then use as the database icon that I describe at the end of this chapter.

TABLE 12.1   Horizontal Image Set

Image Number	State
1	Normal
2	Mouse-over
3	Selected
4	Clicked

Take Care Using Multiple Image Files

Horizontal and vertical images do not work on the Web. The multiple image file displays all the images at once on the Web. This function might be included in a future release, but for now, images are handled differently for Notes and Web clients.

Inserting a Shared Image

How you insert an image into a design element depends on the element you choose. The methods are described in Table 12.2.

TABLE 12.2   Inserting a Shared Image

Object	Method
Form	Choose Create, Image Resource from the menu bar
Page	Choose Create, Image Resource from the menu bar
Subform	Choose Create, Image Resource from the menu bar
Outline Entry	Select an image resource from the Properties box
Table Cell	Select the Table Cell Background tab from the Table Properties box
Actions	Choose Custom Graphic from the Info tab of the Actions Properties box

Object	Method
Form background	Choose the image resource from the Form Background Properties box
Page background	Choose the image resource from the Form Background Properties box

You can also reference an image resource with an URL by specifying the filename of the image in the database as follows:

```
http://server/db.nsf/imagefile.gif?OpenImageResource
```

Setting Other Image Properties

The Image Properties box for the image resource also allows you to set the property for not replacing or refreshing the design of the element and propagation of the design element. There are additional image settings that are determined by the design element in which the image is placed.

If an image is placed in a form, page, or subform, the picture properties become available to the embedded image as shown in Figure 12.4. I define these properties in Tables 12.3 and 12.4.

TABLE 12.3   Info Tab

Property	Definition
Source	You can select and change the image from this property. You can also programmatically assign it with a formula specification.
Text Wrap	Define here how text wraps around an image, as shown in Figure 12.4.
Scaling	Sets the size of the image as displayed in this instance.
Alternate Text	In cases where the image will not be displayed, alternative text is displayed instead.
Caption	Text that displays either below the image or centered in the image.

FIGURE 12.4

Text can be wrapped around an image.

12

USING RESOURCES
IN DOMINO
APPLICATIONS

TABLE 12.4   Picture Border Tab

Property	Definition
Border style	Defines the type and color of the border
Border Effects	Defines whether or not a drop shadow is used
Thickness	Defines the thickness of each of the border edges

The remaining picture property tabs define paragraph properties, margins, hide-when, styles, and finally HTML properties.

Adding Hotspots to Images

When adding an image to a page, form, or subform, you can create an imagemap by adding hotspots to the image. To add hotspots, select the image and right-click the mouse to reveal the hotspot options (see Figure 12.5).

FIGURE 12.5

Image hotspot options allow you to select the area where the hotspot will appear.

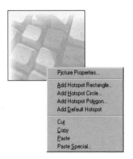

A default hotspot places the hotspot outline around the entire image. All others allow you to select the area where the hotspot will appear by dragging the hotspot around that area. When the hotspot is placed, you can move it by selecting and dragging it to the appropriate place on the image. Figure 12.6 displays an image with a default hotspot and a polygon hotspot.

In the Hotspot Polygon Properties box, you can assign a name to the hotspot for programmatic use. Additional settings determine what occurs when the hotspot is selected. The hotspot can be linked to another object, execute an URL, or open another named element as shown in Figure 12.7. A named element or URL can be programmatically assigned using an @Function formula.

The Advanced tab of the Properties box can be used to define the tab position of the hotspot and alternative text when the image cannot be displayed.

FIGURE 12.6

Image with hotspots including a polygon that segments a portion of the background.

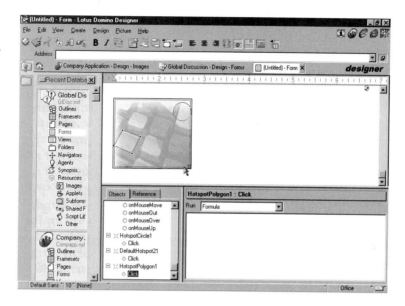

FIGURE 12.7

A hotspot can be set to open another named element.

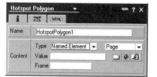

Creating Shared Applets

The shared applet resource provides a storage area within an application for an applet and all its related files. You can then reference the shared applet from multiple agents in the database. It also makes it easy to create applets in a template file and apply those elements to multiple databases.

You can create a shared applet resource from the design pane for applets. The New Applet action provides access to the Locate Java Applet Files dialog box, as shown in Figure 12.8. This dialog box operates in the same way as the Define Java Agent files that is accessed from the Agent design screen when importing a Java applet. This is covered in detail in Chapter 30, "Using Java in Domino Applications." When the files have been selected, a name must be entered for the applet resource. This then creates the entry for the applet resource.

FIGURE 12.8

Files can be selected from the Locate Java Applet Files dialog box.

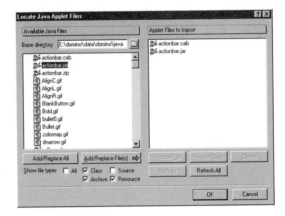

To insert the applet files using the applet resource in a form, page, or rich-text field, choose Create Java Applet from the menu. Choose the Locate button and change from the file system to the shared resource option.

Creating Subforms

Subforms are forms that you can't use on their own, but that you can directly or programmatically insert into a form. This provides a way to create reusable segments of a form that can be used in multiple forms within the application. The process for creating a subform is the same as for creating forms. You can use the same design elements. Apply a subform to a form by opening a form in design mode and placing the cursor where you want the subform to appear. At that point, select the Create Insert Subform option from the menu and choose the appropriate subform to place it in the designated location. Figure 12.9 displays the result of adding a subform directly to a form.

If you add a subform as a computed subform, the subform itself is not displayed, and a placeholder is added instead. By clicking in the placeholder, you can then add the appropriate formula as displayed in Figure 12.10. A computed subform allows you to determine which subform is shown based on who the user is, the role he or she belongs to, the contents of a field, or any other condition you can think of! You can even add the day of the week if you want to.

FIGURE 12.9

The RespBanner *subform added to the Response form for a discussion database can be used over again in other forms.*

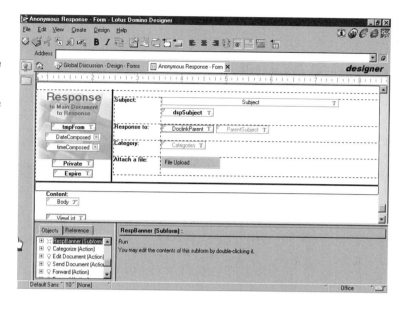

FIGURE 12.10

A computed subform displays a different subform based on the specified condition.

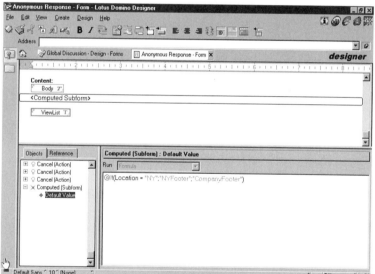

Creating Shared Fields

Shared fields are useful when you anticipate using the same field on multiple forms. When you share a field, it shares the properties and the formulas for the field, not the data! I generally use shared fields if the field has a complicated formula, and it will be used in multiple forms. You can create a shared field from the Design menu, or turn a field that has already been created into a shared field.

To create a shared field from the Design menu, select Shared Fields from Resources and then choose New Shared Field from the Design pane. The Properties box for the field will pop up as usual. When you have defined the field properties, assign the formulas to the appropriate events as you normally would; the only difference is that the Design pane will not appear in the IDE because you are not working in a form (see Figure 12.11).

FIGURE 12.11

A shared-field design looks the same as the design of a single-use field.

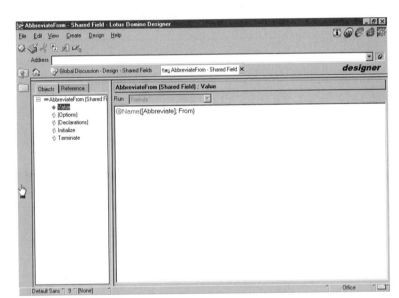

Script Libraries

Storing LotusScript and Java in a script library provides a means for keeping frequently used scripts in one place. When a script is stored, any scriptable object can then use it. When creating a LotusScript library, the only portion of the IDE to be displayed is the Programmers pane and the Browser pane as shown in Figure 12.12.

After you create a library, you can reuse it anywhere within the current database. LotusScript libraries are covered in detail in Chapter 24.

FIGURE 12.12

Reusable LotusScript or Java code is placed in a script library.

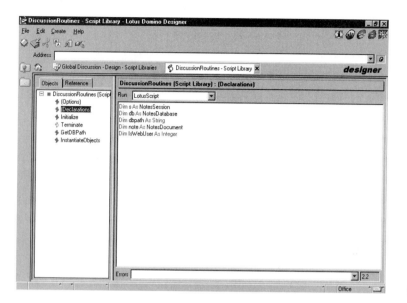

Creating the Database Icon

Adding a database icon to the database defines which icon appears when the database is placed in Bookmarks. There are actually two ways in which you can set the icon for a database. The first way is by choosing the database icon design screen from Resources, Other, as displayed in Figure 12.13. You can draw a database icon directly in the Design Icon dialog box or paste an icon that you've copied to the clipboard.

FIGURE 12.13

You can create a database icon from scratch or paste one from an image on the clipboard.

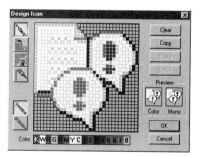

The second way is to right-click the database listed in Bookmarks and choose the option to change icons. This allows you to pick an icon from the list of available image resources in the Bookmarks database as shown in Figure 12.14.

FIGURE 12.14

Change the database icon that displays in Bookmarks from the context menu.

If you create an image resource vertical image set, this is when you would choose that set as the bookmark icon. You cannot create a database icon with mouse-over any other way.

Creating the Using and About Database Documents

The database icon, Using Database document, and About Database document are covered in Chapter 15, "Providing End-User Help." These documents are not shared elements as are the rest because they appear only once in an application and provide additional information to the user. The Using Database document should contain information about the way the database is used. A user can access this document from the Help menu at any time. The About Database document is displayed by default when a user first opens the database, and it should explain the purpose of the database, who should use it, and who can be contacted if there are questions.

Creating Shared Actions

Actions were new in Release 4 and provided a way to create programmable buttons that consistently stayed at the top of the form or view in which they were placed. This was a great advantage to placing a button in a form that would scroll away. Unfortunately, there was no way to create an action and reuse it in multiple forms and views, until now. With Release 5, these actions can now be shared throughout the design of a database. You can place actions in forms, subforms, pages, and views. And you can code an action once and then apply it everywhere. So how does this work? First, you create the action in the Shared Actions area by selecting Shared Action from the Create menu. This then displays the Shared Action Properties box as shown in Figure 12.15. After you enter the name for the Action and select any other properties that you want to use, you can then enter the code for the action in the programming pane.

FIGURE 12.15

Creating a shared action makes the action reusable in any applicable design element.

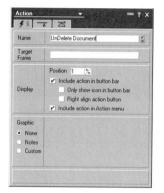

After the action is completed, you can then apply it to the appropriate forms by opening the design element, giving focus to the Action pane, and then choosing Insert Shared Action(s) from the menu, as indicated in Figure 12.16. The key here is to have the focus on the Action pane, otherwise the menu option is unavailable.

FIGURE 12.16

Choosing Insert Shared Action(s) from the menu provides a list of available actions.

Summary

This chapter presented a thorough look at resources. Images, applets, and actions, all new to Release 5, will cut development time significantly. In this chapter, you learned about adding images and actions to multiple design elements. You should now have enough information to optimize the design of your databases.

Creating Outlines

By Steve Kern

Outlines are one of the new design elements of R5 that provide navigation for sites and databases. An Outline is like a combination of a navigator and a folder pane. Like the Table of Contents for this book, an Outline is an element of the UI that not only indicates the various parts of an application or site, but also provides links to those parts. Outlines can contain links to views, forms, framesets, other site databases, and so on. Outlines perform equally well in Web clients as they do in Notes clients.

In R4, you could embed a folder pane in a document or form, but the graphic and text elements were fixed. The only way to add graphics or change the text in R4 was to create Navigators. In R4, you needed multiple Navigators to create a hierarchical effect because a Navigator has a fixed graphic content. Whenever you wanted to open a new element in a Navigator, you had to open a new Navigator with a different graphic image.

In an Outline, you can add graphics to an entry and even change the name. Outlines can be hierarchical like a view, and entries can be expanded and collapsed much like a view category. An Outline can be embedded as an applet in a page or a form, and multiple Outlines can exist in the same database, adding additional flexibility. The choice of design elements to navigate sites and databases is obvious, given the power and flexibility of an Outline compared to a Navigator. Lotus describes Outlines as the "next generation of navigation."

An Outline consists of one or more entries. Each entry in the Outline can link to a database object or an URL, or it can run an Action programmed in the Formula language. After you have created an Outline, you can use it by embedding it in a form, page, or document. Perhaps the most common use is in a page. In fact, if you click the Use Outline button in the work pane, the Domino Designer creates a page for you. After the element is embedded in a page, you can control various display elements. This is discussed this chapter in the section, "Embedding Outlines." Now that the Outline is in a page, you can present it to the user by putting the page into a frameset.

For More Information...

For more information about Pages, see Chapter 14, "Using the Page Designer."
For more information about Framesets, see Chapter 30, "Adding Framesets to Domino Applications."

Creating an Outline

Because Outlines define the structure of your application or site, you can work with them in two ways. First, you can create an Outline before creating any other elements and then add links and Actions as you build the rest of the application. Second, you can add an Outline to a database with elements that already exist. In either case, to create a new Outline, open the Domino Designer, and choose a database in the Design Pane. Click Outlines in the Design list, and click the New Outline button (see Figure 13.1).

FIGURE 13.1

The Work pane of an Outline has several design Action buttons (not visible in this figure is the Outdent Entry button).

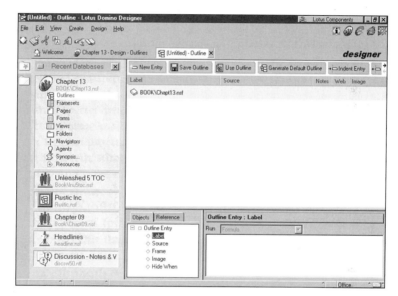

13

CREATING OUTLINES

Scrollable Action Buttons!

When all the Design Action buttons won't fit in the display area, they are scrollable by clicking the arrows on the far right of the Action Bar. The arrows toggle the display to the right or left depending on the state of the Action Bar. This typically happens if you Pin the Bookmarks window.

For More Information...

For more information about the Designer IDE, see Chapter 8, "The Integrated Development Environment."

The Design Action buttons are pretty easy to understand and use. Following is a list of the Action buttons:

- **New Entry**—Creates a new entry immediately after the highlighted Outline entry.
- **Save Outline**—As you might surmise, saves the Outline. If the Outline is new and hasn't been named yet, it prompts you to provide a name.
- **Generate Default Outline**—Creates an Outline based on the views and folders that already exist in the database.
- **Indent Entry**—Moves an entry to the right underneath the entry immediately above. Is used to create a hierarchical Outline.
- **Outdent Entry**—Moves an entry to the left.
- **Scroll arrows**—Move the Action button set to the right or left if not all buttons can fit in the display.

Building an Outline from scratch is actually pretty simple. After you have the Outline created, you simply add the entries necessary to provide a map to your application or site. You must name the Outline in order to save it.

Adding an Entry

After the new Outline has been created, you are presented with the blank work pane as shown in Figure 13.1. To create an entry, click the New Entry button in the Action Bar. As soon as you do so, a new entry is added marked Untitled, and the Entry Properties box opens (see Figure 13.2).

FIGURE 13.2

When you add a new entry, it is positioned immediately after the entry that was highlighted in the Work pane.

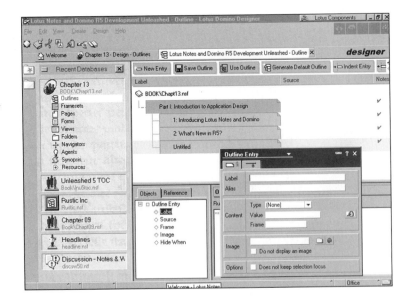

Figure 13.2 shows the beginnings of an Outline for an electronic version of this book. You'll notice that the chapter entries are indented under Part I. You can insert an entry in an existing Outline by appropriately positioning the cursor on the entry before which you want to create the new entry. You can do this to Outlines created from scratch, as this one is, or to Outlines created from the Generate Default Outline button.

After you have created an entry, you need to supply a name and optionally, an alias. There are many more settings available on the Outline Entry Info tab that are discussed this chapter in the section "Working with Outline Entries." In this case, because this Outline is not mapped to any existing objects, a title is all that is needed. Otherwise, you can link it to views, folders, pages, or URLs, create an Action, and so forth. Eventually, you will have to do this for the Outline to be functional. You can also conditionally hide the entry in the Entry Hide When tab, which functions just as a Hide When tab for other objects.

Deleting an Entry

Deleting entries can be accomplished in two ways. The easiest way is to position the cursor on the entry and press the delete key on the keyboard. Domino Designer asks for confirmation, and if you click Yes, the entry is deleted. The other way is to right-click the entry and choose Cut from the context menu. If you cut the entry, it is saved on the clipboard, and you can paste the entry elsewhere in the Outline or even in another Outline.

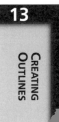

13

CREATING
OUTLINES

Creating a Hierarchical Outline

Figure 13.2 shows a hierarchical Outline—the Chapter entries are indented under the Part entry. Other Parts, Chapters, and subheadings can be added at the appropriate hierarchical level. For example, you might want to create links to subheadings in the chapters. Position the highlight on the appropriate chapter entry, and click the New Entry button. Title the entry, and click the Indent button.

Indenting Multiple Entries

If you have several entries that need to be indented, select them all and then click the Indent button. You can select multiple entries by holding down the Shift or Ctrl key and clicking the entries with the mouse.

When you create a hierarchical Outline, entries that are indented can be expanded and collapsed. Figure 13.3 shows an example of a hierarchical view in design. Note that there are plus and minus signs next to the entries. The entry can be expanded by clicking the plus sign and collapsed by clicking on the minus sign.

FIGURE 13.3

A hierarchical Outline in design mode has plus and minus symbols on which you can click to expand and collapse the entries.

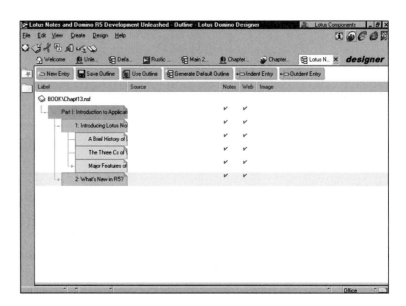

Hierarchical Outlines work much the same as a hierarchical view. Just as views can be nested (or cascaded) in categories, so too can Outline entries. When a hierarchical Outline is embedded in a page or form and presented to the user, the nested entries can be expanded and collapsed with twisties. Figure 13.4 shows the effects of indented entries on an Outline.

If you already have views created that are nested, when you generate a default Outline, a hierarchical Outline will be created similar to the one in Figure 13.4.

Changing Entry Positions

You can change the position of an entry by simply clicking with the left mouse button and dragging it to the desired location. When you click and drag, a small square and a black line appear by the mouse pointer. You can use this graphic symbol to position the entry. Alternatively, you can right-click an entry and choose Cut from the context menu. Right-click the location where you want the entry to appear and choose Paste. The entry will appear after the entry you right-clicked.

FIGURE 13.4

*Note the twisties
beside the Part
and Chapter
entries in this
hierarchical
Outline of a table
of contents.*

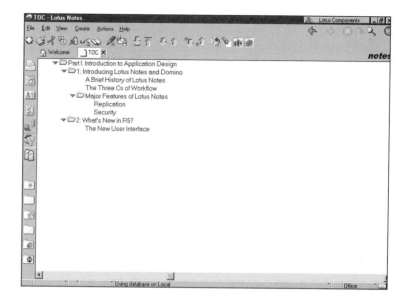

Generating a Default Outline

If you have a database that has already been designed, you can use the Generate Default
Outline button. This builds an Outline from existing views and folders. You can change
the name of the newly created entries, add new entries, and move or delete entries. This
is far easier than constructing an Outline from scratch because all the links are built for
you. If you make changes to the view structures, the Outline won't be refreshed automatically, but if you open the Outline and click the Generate Default Outline button, it will
be refreshed. Of course, any changes you have made to the Outline will be eliminated.

Using an Outline

To use an Outline, you can embed it in a form, page, or document. You can also embed it
in a page directly from the Outline Work pane by clicking the Use Outline button. This
creates a new page with the Outline embedded in the page. You can preview the page to
see how the new Outline appears. Figure 13.5 shows a page with an embedded Outline in
Domino Preview mode.

To use the page, you can attach it to a frameset (you will learn how to do this later in this
chapter). However, you can test the links by clicking the entries. If the entry links to a
view, the view opens to the right of the Outline entries.

13

**CREATING
OUTLINES**

FIGURE 13.5

Generating a default Outline presents all the views and folders in a database— note that the format is similar to the R4 Folder pane.

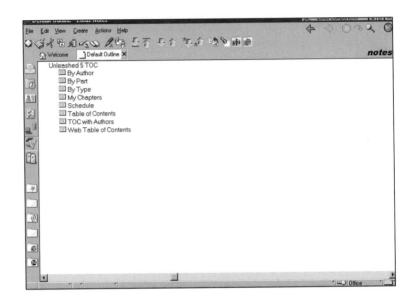

Where's the Rest of the Outline?

Surprised that the embedded Outline shows some but not all of the entries? Check the Info tab of Embedded Outline Properties box. Change the Height setting in the Outline Size section from Fixed height (the default) to Fit to Content.

Working with Outline Properties

There is only one tab in the Properties box for the Outline itself, the Outline Info tab. This tab contains very basic information: Name, Alias, Comment, and Available to Public Access Users. If you click Available to Public Access Users, users with no access to the database will be able to use the Outline to access other elements that are marked for public access. Figure 13.6 shows the Outline Properties box.

FIGURE 13.6

The Outline Properties box has only one tab, the Outline Info tab.

Working with Outline Entries

The heart of an Outline is the *entry*. Entries perform Actions, link to other databases or Web sites, open views and folders, and do much more. You can get fancy with an entry by adding graphics and setting mouse-over properties. As with other design objects, an entry has a Properties box. The Properties box consists of the Entry Info and Entry Hide When tabs. The Entry Info tab has settings for the name, contents, image, and focus.

The Outline Entry Info Tab

The Info tab consists of the following sections (see Figure 13.7):

- **Label and Alias**—Specifies the name and alias of the entry.
- **Content**—Defines the contents of the entry.
- **Image**—Sets the image used for the Outline entry.
- **Options**—Checkbox for selection focus.

FIGURE 13.7

Basic settings for Outline entries are made in the Info tab—note the floating text box help over the Paste button.

Naming an Entry

Label and Alias are self-explanatory: They simply name the entry. If you create a default Outline, the label has the same name as the view. However, unlike the Folders navigator in R4, you can change the entry label to whatever value you want, and the underlying view link will still be in effect. Links to views and other database objects or URLs are set in the Content section.

Working with the Content Tab

The content Tab has a number of options that provide power and flexibility to entries. There are three fields in this section: Type, Value, and Frame. There are also a number of buttons and a drop-down listbox. As you scroll through the choices in the Type field, the items in the Content section of the Info tab change. There are five settings for the Type field, which are the following:

- **None**—Can be used for a placeholder, such as the title of a hierarchical category.
- **Action**—Creates an Action based on @Commands and the Formula language.
- **Link**—Pastes a link previously copied to the clipboard to the entry.
- **Named Element**—A listbox enables you to choose from the following database objects—Page, Form, Frameset, View, Folder, or Navigator.
- **URL**—Enter a valid URL as a link.

There are three buttons in the Content section of the Info tab: Browse, Formula, and Paste. These buttons are conditionally exposed based on the choice made in the Type field. Figure 13.7 shows the buttons, and Table 13.1 describes each button.

TABLE 13.1 Content Buttons

Button	Title	Description
▢	Browse	Browses a listing of the named design elements (see Figure 13.8). Only available for the Named Element type.
@	Formula	Opens the Formula window. Available for Actions, Named Elements, and URL types.
⬚	Paste	Pastes objects stored on the clipboard. Available for all types except Link.

The Outline shown in Figure 13.2 uses None as the type for the Part 1 entry. This entry doesn't need to link to anything; it simply needs to contain the entries listed below it. This is a common and typical use for this entry type.

What's with the Paste Button?

You might have noticed that the entry type None has a Paste button. If you copy an object such as a view link to the clipboard and click the Paste button, the Type field changes to Link, and the Value field changes to the name of the object.

Creating an Action entry gives you access to the Formula language and @Commands. You can use an Action to launch an agent, for example, by using the @Command([ToolsRunMacro]).

Using Form as a Named Element

You don't need to use an Action to create a new document from an entry. Simply select Named Element as the Type and choose Form. Click the Browse button and locate the form. Name the entry appropriately. When a user clicks the entry, a new document is created based on the form you specified!

To create a Link entry, copy a link to the clipboard in Notes. (As you know, a link can be made to a document, view, or database.) Create a new entry or use an existing entry, and set the type to Link. Then click the Paste button. The link will appear in the Value field.

The entry type of Named Element is probably the one you will use the most because it offers access to many different design objects. Choosing Named element and then clicking the Browse button produces the Locate Object dialog box shown in Figure 13.8.

FIGURE 13.8

Clicking the Browse button for Named Elements displays the Locate Object dialog box.

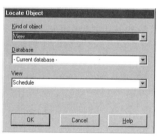

You can choose from the following design objects for Named Elements:

- Page (the default)
- Form
- Frameset
- View
- Folder
- Navigator

You can make the selection for the Named Element in the drop-down list before clicking the Browse button, or you can change the selection in the first drop-down list (Kind of Object) in the Locate Object dialog box. You can also switch databases from the current database to another easily from the Database list in the dialog box. When you are satisfied with your choices, the last field contains the type of object that you selected. Its name changes; for example, in Figure 13.8, it is set to View.

13

CREATING OUTLINES

It is also possible to use a formula to specify a Named Element. You can enter a formula by clicking the Formula button. If you have a link copied to the clipboard, you can click the Paste button. However, whenever you click the Paste button, the Type field changes to Link.

The last item in the Type field is URL. You can enter a URL directly into the field, as in `www.lotus.com` (without quotes), and the link will launch the URL when clicked. You can also use Domino URLs, such as `http://Unleashed5/HomePage.nsf?OpenDatabase`. Figure 13.9 shows an Outline with two entries based on URLs.

FIGURE 13.9

Two entries based on URLs are shown at the bottom of the Work pane.

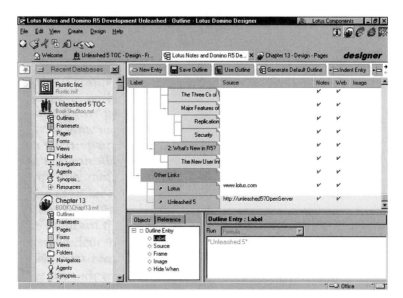

In Figure 13.9, you'll notice that the URLs appear in the Work pane in the Source column. If you look at the Programmer's Pane, you'll see that the Objects tab is open to the Label setting and that the text of the entry's name is in quotes. Similarly, if you open each of the other objects—Source, Frame, Image, and Hide When—you'll see entries there that correspond to the entries in the Properties box. Obviously, because the Programmer's Pane is available, you can write code snippets in here as well as in the Properties box.

Adding Images to an Entry

By default, an entry appears with a folder icon beside it. You can turn this image off by clicking Do Not Display Image, or you can add a custom image to the entry. To use a custom image, first add the image to the Image Resources. You can then choose the image by clicking the Browse Images button or by entering a formula. To use a formula, first click the Formula button, and then enter the formula into the Edit Formula window. The formula must evaluate to the name of an Image Resource.

TABLE 13.2 Image Buttons

Button	Title	Description
☐	Browse Images	Browses Image Resources
@	Formula	Opens the formula window

For More Information...

For more information about creating Image Resources, see Chapter 12, "Using Resources in Domino Applications."

Caution

Regardless of the size of the Image Resource, Domino resizes it to fit the Outline entry. You can change this behavior when you embed an Outline in a page or other design element. For more information, see "Embedding Outlines" later in this chapter.

The last field in the Image section, Do Not Display Image, turns off the display of the image. Obviously, you wouldn't want to add an image and turn off its display, so this is primarily used to turn off the default images that Domino provides for the various elements. For example, if you want to define an image when you embed the element in a page, you could turn off the display of images for the Outline entries. This would turn off the default view icons that appear.

Using Selection Focus

Turning off the selection focus is done in the Options section at the bottom of the Outline Entry Info tab. When you do this, the selection focus remains on the prior Outline entry. You won't notice the effect unless you change the colors of the selections on the Font tab of the Embedded Outline Properties box. This setting is useful if you have an Outline that has an entry that creates a document or takes other Actions. For example, if you've created an entry that uses a form as a Named Element and checked Does Not Keep Selection Focus, when a user clicks the entry that creates a document, the focus will remain on the prior selected entry (a view, perhaps) after the new document is closed. After all, it doesn't make sense to stay on the Action entry, whereas it does make sense to stay on the view entry.

The Entry Hide When Tab

The Entry Hide When tab functions as any other Hide When tab. You can hide the entry from Notes 4.6 or later or Web browsers. Alternatively, you can hide the entry using a formula entered into the formula window.

Embedding Outlines

There are two ways to embed an Outline. First, you can embed it in a page by clicking the Use Outline button from the Outline work pane. Second, to embed it in an existing page, a form, or a document, you can choose Create, Embedded Element, Outline from the menu in Domino Designer. Most often, you will embed an Outline in a page and then use the page in a frameset. This section deals with embedding Outlines in pages because it is the most common use, but the same principles apply to other objects.

The first thing you'll notice when you embed an Outline in a page is that it doesn't necessarily include all the elements in the Outline (see Figure 13.10). To change this effect, you'll need to work with the properties of an embedded Outline. Embedded Outline properties are independent of the Outline design object itself. The Properties box has a number of tabs described in the following sections:

- **Info**—Contains settings that control the appearance of the Outline.
- **Font**—Defines settings for the font of each Outline level.
- **Background**—Controls backgrounds for each Outline level.
- **Layout**—Defines the offsets and other layout properties for each Outline level.
- **Paragraph Alignment**—Standard settings.
- **Paragraph Margins**—Standard settings.
- **Paragraph Hide When**—Standard settings.

The Paragraph Alignment, Paragraph Margins, and Paragraph Hide When tabs should be familiar enough to you by now that they don't need to be covered here.

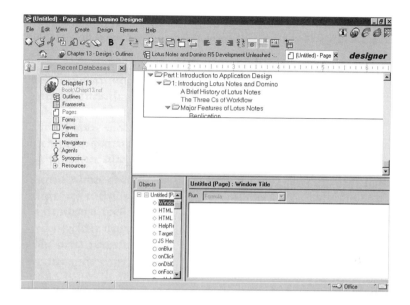

The Info Tab

The Info tab has settings that control the appearance of the Outline (see Figure 13.11). For example, to change the appearance of the Outline in Figure 13.10, you change the Height property. (Embedded Outlines default to a fixed height of one inch.) To change it, choose Fit to Content in the Height field of the Outline Size section of the Properties box.

There are four sections on the Info tab that control the display of the embedded Outline. The first section enables you to name the object and set the type, title, and target frame. The second section specifies a root entry and whether the object is displayed as saved, expanded, or collapsed. The third section enables you to determine the size of the embedded Outline, and the fourth section specifies how the Outline works on the Web.

Embedded Outline Properties

Remember that changing the properties of an embedded Outline in no way affects the Outline design element itself; it just changes this particular use of the Outline.

The Type field has two options: Tree Style (the default) and Flat Style. If you choose Tree Style, the Outline displays in a hierarchical fashion. Figure 13.10 shows an Outline using the Tree Style. When Tree Style is selected, a checkbox is available to turn twisties on or off. A Flat Style Outline only displays the top level of the hierarchy; when you click on an entry that is expandable, the next level rolls out under the entry. Flat Outlines can be displayed either vertically or horizontally. You can make this choice from the drop-down list that replaces the Twisties checkbox when you choose Flat Style. Displaying the Outline horizontally lists the images associated with the entries across the top of the page.

Working with Horizontal Outlines

You can affect the display of a horizontal Outline by working with the Height setting on the Layout tab. The Layout tab is discussed later in this chapter in the section titled "The Layout Tab."

You can choose between Simple and Hide (the default) for the Title setting. If you choose to display the title, you can set various background and font properties on other tabs for the title.

Working with Flat Outlines

If you choose Flat Style, be sure to choose Simple for the Title. If you leave Title at the default (Hide), users will not be able to navigate back up the hierarchy. Setting the Title to Simple displays the next higher level in the hierarchy as the title. Clicking the title navigates up one level.

The last setting in the topmost section is the Target Frame. In this field, you can specify the frame in which the Outline displays when used in a frameset.

The Root Entry section contains a field in which you can enter a category entry in the Outline. Note that you must use the alias of the entry and not the entry label. When you specify a Root Entry, only the entries that fall in or below the root display. The field next to Root Entry lets you determine how a hierarchical view displays. If you choose Flat Style, this field automatically defaults to Collapse All, but if you select Tree style, you can choose from the following options:

- **Expand All**—Expands all entries in the Outline to all levels.
- **Expand First**—Expands only the first-level entries.
- **Display as Saved (the default)**—Displays the Outline as you saved it.
- **Collapse All**—Collapses the Outline to the topmost entries in the hierarchy.

The Outline Size section has settings for the Width, Height, and Show Scroll Bar. Contrary to what you might expect, even if you set a fixed width and height, there is only a vertical scrollbar. For Width, you can choose from the default Fit to Window (%), Fit to Content, and Fixed Width. For Height, you can choose from Fixed Height (the default) and Fit to Content.

The Web Access field consists of two settings: Using HTML (the default) and Using Java Applet. Using the Using Java Applet setting to generate the Outline presents a much snappier interface, including background colors, mouse-over color settings for the Outline entries, and much better graphics. In general, it is preferable to Using HTML.

13

CREATING
OUTLINES

Use JavaScript when Generating Pages

If you choose Using Java Applet, you must have Use JavaScript when generating pages set as a database property. If you don't, when you select Using Java Applet, Domino Designer will prompt you to make the setting.

The Font Tab

The Font tab enables you to specify the fonts for three different levels: Title, Top-Level, and Sub-Level (see Figure 13.12). The Font tab has the standard choices for the font, size, and style. There are additional settings at the bottom of the Properties box for color settings based on the state of the text. The Title setting has two color settings: Normal and Moused. The Level settings have three choices: Normal, Selected, and Moused. Because a title cannot be selected, this setting does not appear.

> **Title Settings**
>
> The Title setting only appears when the Title setting of Simple is made in the Info tab. Also, setting the font style to Shadow, Emboss, or Extrude has no effect on the Web, even if Using Java Applet is enabled.

FIGURE 13.12

The Font tab enables you to set font for three levels—note the three color settings at the bottom of the Properties box.

Clicking any one of these settings opens the Domino color palette. Normal is the color you see when the text is not selected or moused. When you click an Outline entry, the color changes to the choice you made for Selected, and when the mouse passes over the text, the color changes to that selection. Note that these settings don't work on the Web unless you choose Using Java Applet in the Web Access field.

The Background Tab

The Background tab has settings for background colors and images. You can set these properties for the entire control, the title, top-level entries, and sub-level entries. Depending on the element, you can choose background colors for Normal, Selected, and Moused. The control background has just one color choice, but the title background has choices for Normal and Moused, and the top-level and sub-level entries have choices for Normal, Selected, and Moused colors (see Figure 13.13).

FIGURE 13.13

The Background tab has color settings for each level from the entire control to individual entries in the Outline—note the Normal and Moused color palettes available for the Title background setting.

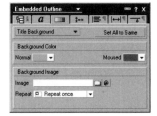

Set All to Same

If you want to use the same settings for the colors (Normal, Selected, and Moused), you can click the Set All to Same button. This button is also available for the Layout tab.

You can also add an image to any one of the levels from Control through Sub-Level. Images must be stored as Image Resources to be used in an embedded Outline. After you add an image to a level, you can set it to display in one of the following modes:

- **Repeat Once**— Displays the image once.
- **Repeat Vertically**—Tiles the image vertically until the viewing area is filled.
- **Repeat Horizontally**—Tiles the image horizontally until the viewing area is filled.
- **Repeat Both Ways**—Tiles the image vertically and horizontally until the viewing area is filled.
- **Size to Fit**—Sizes the image to fit the viewing area.

Entry Images and Background Images

If you apply an image to an entry in the Outline designer, it will still appear in an embedded Outline. The images in the embedded Outline are background images. Any entry image will appear over the background image setting.

The Layout Tab

Settings on the Layout tab determine the positioning of the entry, the entry label and any image associated with the entry. There are three levels that you can affect: the Title Layout, the Top-Level Layout, and the Sub-Level Layout. The Title Layout only has two sections, Entry and Entry Label. The remaining two Layouts have three sections, Entry, Entry Label, and Entry Image (see Figure 13.14).

FIGURE 13.14

The Layout tab is set to the Top-Level Layout, exposing all three sections.

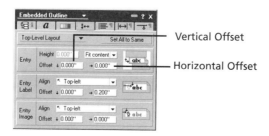

There are two types of settings in each section: Alignment and Offset. In the Entry section, the only alignment that you can affect is the height because the entry section controls the layout of the entire entry as a block. You can control the height by selecting Fit to Content (the default) or Fixed. If you select Fixed, you can specify the height of the entry. The Entry Label and Entry Image sections have extensive Alignment settings available. Each of the three sections has two Offset fields available, Vertical and Horizontal, as shown in Figure 13.14. You can move the Entry, the Entry Label, and the Entry Image around vertically or horizontally with these settings by entering an offset in inches. As the arrows next to the fields indicate, entering a value in the vertical offset pushes the entry down, and entering a value in the horizontal offset pushes the entry to the right.

Controlling the Layout of a Horizontal Flat Outline

If you are using an Outline with a horizontal flat style, you can control the width of the entries with the horizontal offsets.

Adding an Outline to a Frameset

You won't get much use out of a page with an embedded Outline until you add it to a frameset. To add a page to a frameset, first create a frameset or choose an existing one. Take the following steps to finish adding the page:

1. Choose a frame for the page.
2. Open the Frame Properties box, and name the frame.
3. Choose Named Element and Page for the Type, and then click the Browse button (the folder icon next to the Type fields).
4. In the Locate Object dialog box, choose the page you designed, and click OK (see Figure 13.15).
5. Name and save the frameset.

The page is now added to the frame you chose and will appear to both Notes and Web clients.

FIGURE 13.15

To use a page with an embedded Outline in a frameset, choose the page from the Locate Object dialog box.

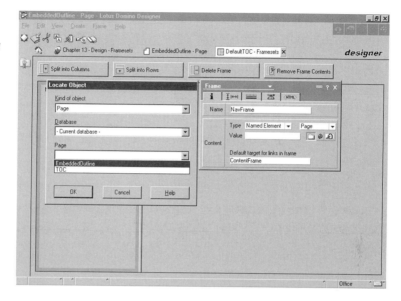

For More Information...

For more information about framesets, see Chapter 31.

Summary

Outlines are a very powerful way to add navigation to your applications. Because Outlines can use images and be embedded in pages, forms, documents, and framesets, there is virtually no need to ever create a navigator again! If you try some of the techniques mentioned in this chapter, you'll see the power first-hand. Outlines are a wonderful addition to the Domino Designer.

CHAPTER 14

Using the Page Designer

by Steve Kern

Pages are new design objects in R5; they add considerable power to Domino applications, especially when you combine them with outlines and framesets. The term *Page* is taken from the world of Internet development, where HTML (*Hypertext Markup Language*) is used to construct "pages" which are displayed to Web browsers.

A Page is similar to a form, but unlike forms, pages are intended not to collect data but rather to display information. Pages can contain text, computed text, and embedded Domino objects such as views, outlines, navigators, folder panes, and a date picker. Pages can also include graphics, imagemaps, HTML, horizontal rules, tables, sections, links, and applets. The only things you cannot place on a page are fields.

Using HTML to Create Input Forms

Despite the fact that you cannot place a field directly on the form as a design object, you can actually use a page to create an HTML Input form that can include fields. You simply have to code the page by hand using HTML that creates a form with FORM METHOD=post and fields with the INPUT tag. Be sure to set the Page property Web Access, Treat page contents as HTML. If you use the Domino URL http://host/database/form?CreateDocument in the HTML, you can actually create and save a document! See the page titled "HTML Input Page" in the database for this chapter, Chap14.nsf, which is on the CD-ROM accompanying this book.

As mentioned in the chapter introduction, Pages have their origins in HTML, and they help bridge the gap between HTML and Domino. Pages are also meant to replace special forms such as $$ViewTemplate used in R4.x to display views and folder panes to Web clients. Embedding elements such as View applets and Outlines on a Page provides not only replaces the functionality in $$ViewTemplate forms, it is more flexible. You can exert greater control over the embedded elements in R5 than was possible in R4.x. In addition, Pages can be viewed in both Notes and Web clients with reasonably consistent display and functioning from one client to the other. The designers of R5 wanted to merge Web and Notes development in R5, and this is one of the fruits of their labor.

Pages are powerful because they combine the best elements of Web and Notes development without the hassle of HTML coding. For example, to add a clickable graphic image using HTML, you have to enter HTML code specifying the reference, URL, and alternative text for a graphic image. In the Page Designer, you simply import or paste the image onto the page, and use the Properties box to set the URL, text wrap, and alternative text for the image! You'll see how that works later in this chapter. For now, envision having to write the following HTML to produce a single image in a Web banner:

```
[<BASE TARGET=_top>]
[<A href="/home.nsf/webOpenMail?OpenAgent&Login">
<img src="/home.nsf/Files/mail9.gif/$FILE/mail9.gif" alt="Web Mail"
border=0></A>]
```

In R4.x, this kind of coding for a frameset was common. This chunk of HTML displays a mailbox GIF (`mail9.gif`) in the banner (or header) frame of a frameset, which when clicked, requests the user to login and runs an agent which then opens the user's mailbox. In the previous code, the first line ensures that the mail doesn't open in a frame contained within this frameset, but in its own window. The second line "opens" (runs) the agent (`?OpenAgent`) and forces the user to login with the `&Login` argument. Next, the image file is referenced (it's stored in a view called Files), and alternative text of "Web Mail" is set.

In R5, you can embed the image from an Image Resource (you can also import or paste an image) and set a few Properties. Remember that Domino generates the HTML on-the-fly for you, so you don't have to endure the HTML code at all!

For More Information...

For more information about HTML and Domino URLs, see Chapter 21, "Enhancing Domino Applications with HTML."

On the CD accompanying this book is a database named Chapter 14 (`Chapt14.nsf`). This database builds on the database created in Chapter 13 (`Chapt13.nsf`).

Working with the Page Properties Box

Before digging into the "how to" of using Pages, it's important to understand the tabs on the Page Properties box. To view the Properties of a Page, either create a new page or open an existing one. Creating a new page is very simple; by now, you should be familiar enough with the IDE to know that you open the database in the Domino Designer and click Pages in the Design list. Clicking New Page in the Designer Action Bar produces a new, completely blank page that looks like a new blank form. Very much like a form, a Page is like a rich-text document into which you can stuff all sorts of objects, except fields. Open the Page properties box, and you'll see the following four tabs:

- **Page Info**—This tab lets you name the page and define Web access and link colors.

- **Background**—This tab lets you choose background colors or graphics for the page.
- **Launch**—This tab lets you define Launch options for the page.
- **Security**—This tab has one checkbox, Available to Public Access Users.

> **Caution**
>
> If you click the Properties SmartIcon or the Display InfoBox button on a page, you'll get the Text Properties box. If you want to open the Page Properties box, choose Design and Page Properties directly from the menu.

The Page Info Tab

When you open the Page Info tab, you'll notice there are three sections (see Figure 14.1).

FIGURE 14.1

The Page Properties box contains settings for the name of the page, Web access, and link colors.

The topmost section enables you to enter a name (which is required) and a comment. The middle section defines how the contents are treated when accessed by a Web client. If you check the Treat Page Contents as HTML checkbox, you can create an entire page from HTML. The last section enables you to define Link colors for Active, Unvisited, and Visited links for Web clients. The defaults are Red, Blue, and Purple respectively. These default colors are fairly standard among Web browsers. If you check your settings for Internet Explorer or Netscape Communicator, you'll see that they both use blue for unvisited links and purple for visited links. Using these buttons opens the color palette and you can change the link colors for the page.

> **Entering an Alias for a Page**
>
> Unlike the Properties boxes for other objects, the Page Properties box doesn't have a field for an alias. However, you can create an alias by entering the pipe symbol (|), followed by the alias. For example, Link Page | Links in the Name

field creates an alias of Links for the page. You can see the aliases in the Pages design view.

The Background Tab

The Background tab also has three sections (see Figure 14.2). You can set the background color, choose an image from a Graphic file or an Image Resource, and set various options.

Figure 14.2

The background tab has several sections that control the display of the background color or image.

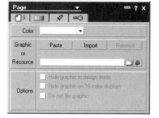

You can enhance your page by setting the background to a color or a graphic image. You set the background color by clicking the Color drop-down, which opens the standard color palette and then choosing a color. There are several methods of using graphic images as backgrounds as well. The choices for graphic image backgrounds are essentially the same as those for a form. You can paste an image that is on the clipboard or import an image from a file (BMP, GIF, JPEG, PCX, or TIFF 5.0). You can also choose an Image Resource by clicking the Browse button next to the Resources field, or by entering a formula by clicking the formula button.

When you have chosen a graphic image for the background, the choices in the Options section are available. Options are not available for colors; they only affect the way images are displayed. The three options are the following:

- **Hide Graphic in Design Mode**—It is sometimes easier to design a page when you hide the graphic in design mode. Graphic images, depending on their appearance, often clutter the design surface.

- **Hide Graphic in 16 Color Displays**—16-color displays often don't render images well, especially those created at resolutions higher than 256 colors.

- **Do Not Tile Graphic**—By default, images are tiled, so if the background image doesn't occupy the entire screen, it is repeated vertically or horizontally until the screen is completely filled. You can change this display by checking Do Not Tile Graphic.

Combining Graphic Images and Background Color

Note that you can combine images and the background color by checking Do Not Tile Graphic. Whatever space the image does not fill will be occupied by the background color.

The Launch Tab

Similar to the Launch tab of a form, there are two sections: Auto Launch and Auto Frame (see Figure 14.3).

FIGURE 14.3

In this figure, the Launch tab has the page launching in a specific frame in a specific frameset.

Auto Launch Settings

The Auto Launch list for a page has a much-reduced list of choices than those for the list for a form (see the following list of choices). Each of the launch types (except for None, of course!) has a page in the accompanying database, Chapter 14 (`Chapt14.nsf`) which is on the CD accompanying this book.

- **None (the default)**—No special launch properties.
- **First Attachment**—Launches the first file attachment on the Page.
- **First Document Link**—Launches the first document link on the Page.
- **First OLE Object**—Launches the first OLE Object on the page.

You can add a file attachment to a page and select First Attachment from the Auto Launch list. When you open the page, the application associated with the attachment launches along with the file itself. For example, if you include a Word document, Word is launched and the attached file is opened. This is like clicking the Launch button on the Attachment Properties box. (See the page Launch Attachment in the database for this chapter.)

If you paste a link to a document, view, or even a database in the page, and set the Auto Launch property to First Document Link, the page will open the Domino object in the doclink. (See the page Launch Doclink in the database for this chapter.)

You can also embed an OLE object that will launch when the page is opened. To embed an OLE object, choose Object from the Create menu. However, as of this writing, while the OLE object launches, you get an error message stating that Changes to Object will not be saved in a Read-only document. Domino treats a page as a Read-only object, so although the OLE application launches, it appears to be less than functional. (See the page Launch OLE in the database for this chapter.)

Auto Frame Settings

In the Auto Frame section, you can choose a frameset and a frame into which to launch the page you are designing. In Figure 14.3, the Auto Frame is set to the frameset Sample, and the frame is set to LinkFrame. You can only choose from framesets that are in the same database as the page. Whenever the page is opened, it opens in the frameset you've chosen. You can test this with the page titled Links. If you preview this page, it will open into the Sample frameset, even though the Sample frameset has no page specified for either the NavFrame or the ContentFrame. See the page Links and the frameset Sample in the database for this chapter.

The Security Tab

The Security tab has only one setting, which is Available to Public Access Users (see Figure 14.4). A Public Access user is someone who either has No Access or Depositor access to the database. In the database ACL, you can add a setting for users such as these that enables them to Read public documents or Write public documents. They otherwise have no access to any of the documents or design objects in the database. You can make this setting for specific pages.

FIGURE 14.4

The Security tab of the Page Properties box only has one setting.

Page

✓ Available to Public Access users

> **Caution**
>
> Because pages are typically displayed in framesets, be sure to make the frame-set in which they appear available to public access users as well. Similarly, if you launch a page from an outline, the outline needs to be available to public access users.

Using the Page Designer

Designing pages is very much like designing forms, except that, as you already know, you can't add any fields. Just like a form, a number of events are available that can be programmed. Some events can be programmed in the Formula language, some in LotusScript, and others in JavaScript. HTML is involved in two events: HTML Head Content and HTML Body Attributes. Table 14.1 lists each event by language.

TABLE 14.1   Page Events by Language

Formula	*JavaScript*	*LotusScript*
Window Title	JS Header	Options
HTML Head Content	onBlur	Declarations
HTML Body Attributes	onClick	QueryOpen
HelpRequest	onDblClick	PostOpen
Target Frame	onFocus	PostRecalc
	onHelp	QueryClose
	onKeyDown	Initialize
	onKeyPress	Terminate
	onKeyUp	
	onLoad	
	onMouseDown	
	onMouseMove	
	onMouseOut	
	onMouseOver	
	onMouseUp	
	onUnload	

For More Information...

For more information about the Formula language, see Chapters 18, "The Formula Language," 19, "Formula Language Basics," and 20, "Writing Formulas." For more information about HTML, see Chapter 21. For more information about LotusScript, see Chapters 22, "Introduction to LotusScript," 23, "Basic LotusScript," and 24, "Writing LotusScript." For more information about JavaScript, see Chapters 25, "Introduction to JavaScript."

As you do with a form, you should always specify a Window Title; the remaining events can be used when needed. You can see some of the events in the Objects tab in Figure 14.5.

FIGURE 14.5

The diamond beside Window Title is filled in the Object tab of the Page Designer when code is present for the event.

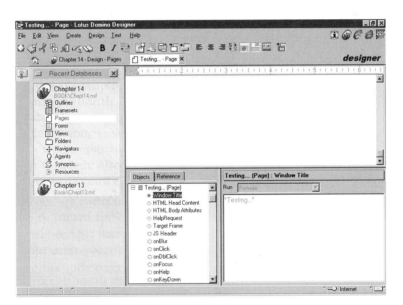

More Information...

For more information about the Designer IDE, see Chapter 8, "The Integrated Development Environment."

Using HTML in Pages

There are two events that are programmed by the Formula language that enable you to add HTML to a page: the HTML Head Content and the HTML Body Attributes events. The HTML Head Content creates HTML between the `<HEAD>` and `</HEAD>` tags of the HTML document. For example, if you want to embed style information or use a cascading style sheet for the page, you include it in the HTML Head Content event using the `<STYLE>` or `<LINK>` tags. Other HTML tags that can be used in the Head Content event include `<BASE>`, `<ISINDEX>`, `<META>`, `<SCRIPT>`, and `<TITLE>`.

For More Information...

For more information about style sheets, see Chapter 21.

Similar to the Head Content event, the HTML Body Attributes event affects the HTML `<BODY>` tag. Unlike the Head Content event, this event is designed to specify the attributes that modify the `<BODY>` tag. Many of these attributes are unnecessary because they can be set more easily from Properties boxes.

In addition to adding HTML to the two HTML page events, there are three ways to add HTML directly to a page. First, you can create the entire page in HTML, and as mentioned earlier in the chapter, set the Web Access property to Treat page contents as HTML. You can create the HTML directly on the page or you can copy the HTML source from an existing HTML page to the clipboard and then paste it into the page.

Second, you can create Pass-Thru HTML directly on the page. To create Pass-Thru HTML, choose Text, Pass-Thru HTML from the menu. You can then add HTML that you can't normally access with Domino, such as the `<H1>` tag, directly to the page.

The third method is to import HTML directly into the page. To do so, choose Import from the File menu, and then choose HTML in the Files of type list. Figure 14.6 shows an HTML document being imported into a page.

When the HTML document is imported, it is rendered on the page itself, as you would see it from a Web browser. In other words, you don't see the HTML source, but the end result (see Figure 14.7).

FIGURE 14.6

Importing HTML is easy in R5!

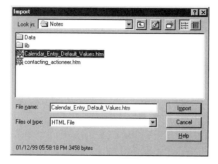

FIGURE 14.7

The Default Calendar Entries HTML page is presented as you would see it in a browser.

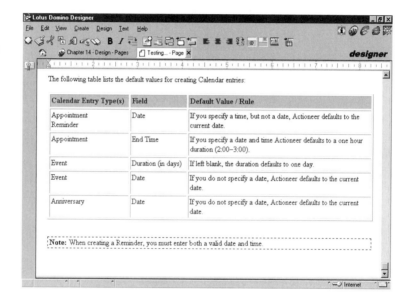

Adding Objects to a Page

By now, you know how similar a page is to a form, so it almost goes without saying that you can add attachments, links, graphics, computed text, horizontal rules, tables, sections, embedded elements, and so forth to a page. If you had to do this coding raw HTML, it would be very time consuming, and in some cases, impossible. The Page Designer makes many of these tasks very easy for you.

Use Tables!

It is a good idea to use tables to present objects in pages. Tables are covered in Chapter 10, "Advanced Form Design."

A page is often used as a means to navigate the various areas of a site. Creating objects on a page that link to other site areas such as databases, views, pages, documents, and even other sites is a common use for a page. Particularly in a framed Web site, one or two pages serve as navigation aides, presenting links to documents and site areas. Graphic images can also lead to other sites or site areas. In a site written strictly in HTML, all these links have to be built by hand—they are not dynamic. The advantage of using Domino is that you can present a view to a Web client, and documents can be dynamically added and deleted from the view and the view is automatically updated. In other words, you don't have to create a single line of HTML to make any of this happen!

Constructing Links

Sometimes you will need to construct links to views, other databases, documents, or pages. Creating a link is simple, and can be done in several ways.

You can copy a link to a Domino object, such as a form, database, document, view, or page to the clipboard, and paste it into your page. To copy a design object such as a page or a view, you can highlight it in the work pane, and from the menu, choose Edit, Copy as Link, Named Element. From the client UI, you can also use the Edit, Copy as Link menu choice, and copy database, view, and document links to the clipboard. When a link is copied to the clipboard, you can return to the page, highlight the text or graphic object that you want to use as the link, and choose Create, Hotspot, Link Hotspot from the menu. Next, click the Paste button, and the object will be pasted into the Hotspot Resource Link box.

For More Information...

For more information about the buttons on the Hotspot Info tab buttons, see Table 13.1 in Chapter 13, "Creating Outlines."

You can also create a link to a design object through the Link Properties box. For example, to create a link from a text item to a view in the database, first highlight the text. Next, choose Create, Hotspot, Link Hotspot from the menu. The Hotspot Resource Link Properties box will open automatically. Specify Named Element in the Type field, and choose View. Click the Browse button, and choose the view. The name of the view is automatically entered in the Value field. Entering the name of a frame in the Frame field will cause the page to launch into a specific frame in a frameset. You can optionally display a border; in R4, displaying a border was turned on by default, but in R5, it is not (see Figure 14.8).

Figure 14.8

Using the Properties box, it is easy to create links.

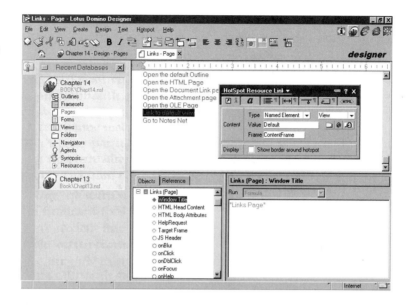

Caution

If you create a link to a Named Element and then change the name of the element, the link will be broken unless the named element has an alias!

If you need to link to a site on the Internet or a corporate Intranet, there are several ways to enter the URL. You can choose URL as the link type and enter the URL directly into the Value field. You can also enter a formula by clicking on the Formula button, which opens the Edit Formula window. You can then enter a formula that evaluates to a URL. If you have a URL on the clipboard, you can paste it into the Value field by clicking on the paste button. You can also use Domino URLs in this field (see Figure 14.9).

Figure 14.9

A URL, such as http://www.notes.net, *can be entered directly into the Value field.*

Adding Graphics

You can also add graphic objects to your pages. You can import graphic images from files, paste them from the clipboard, or use an Image Resource. In general, it is better to

14

Using the Page Designer

import a graphic image or use an Image Resource than it is to paste an image. Importing a GIF preserves any transparency settings for the image, and any colors on the background will show though the image. If you paste a GIF image, it is no longer transparent, and the GIFs background will display.

To create a graphic element using an Image Resource on a page, choose Create, Image Resource from the menu. Figure 14.10 illustrates the use of an Image Resource.

FIGURE **14.10**

This embedded graphics image has the text set to wrap around the image.

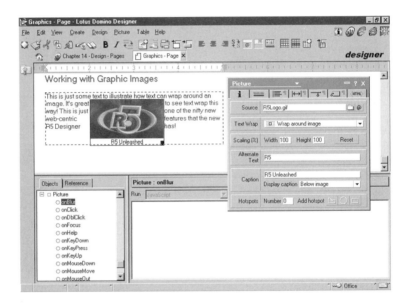

In the Picture Properties box, you have a number of choices for Text Wrap: You can scale the image, and you can enter alternative text and captions.

Setting Text Wrap

If you want the text to wrap around the image, choose the Text Wrap setting, Wrap Around Image, before entering the text. You cannot add an image in the middle of a block of text, or change from one of the other styles and have the text automatically wrap.

When you have made your choices in the Picture Properties box for the image, you can also add a link to the image. To do so, select the image and choose Create, Hotspot, Link Hotspot from the menu. You can then add links as described in the previous section, "Constructing Links." See Figure 14.11 for the finished page.

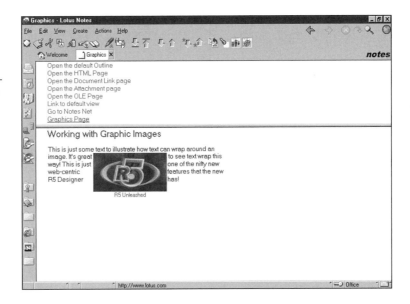

FIGURE 14.11
*The URL to the
Lotus Web site
associated with
the R5 logo is dis-
played in the sta-
tus bar.*

Using Imagemaps

Imagemaps have been around on the Web for some time now. They are used to provide
visual links to site areas. In R5, it is very easy to create an imagemap. In the previous
example, a single URL was associated with the entire image. An imagemap, on the other
hand, is a graphic image with multiple areas that can be clicked. These clickable areas
are called *hotspots* or *hot regions*, and can take you to different site areas.

Creating an imagemap by hand (using HTML) is an extremely arduous process because
you have to specify the exact coordinates of the hotspots using the HTML container tags
<MAP> and </MAP>. Inside the <MAP> tags you use the <AREA> tag to set the shape, coordi-
nates, URL link, alternative text, and target frame. As you can imagine, determining the
coordinates alone is a daunting task. For this reason, tools exist to create imagemaps
graphically. The R5 Domino Designer is such a tool!

It's All in the Client!

Technically speaking, this kind of imagemap is referred to as a *client-side
imagemap* because the client does all the work of locating and loading the
links. Some types of Web servers also permit *server-side imagemaps*. As the
name implies, it is the server that processes the links and serves the pages.
Client-side imagemaps take a lot of the load away from the server, resulting in
better performance.

14

**USING THE PAGE
DESIGNER**

Imagemaps can be created from almost any graphic file type with the exception of files in the .PIC format. Simply add your image to the page in the same manner as described in the section, "Adding Graphics.". After you have added the graphic to your page, you can begin adding hotspots to it.

Three different shapes can be added: Rectangle, Circle, and Polygon; these are available both from the menu and from the Picture Properties box. You can also add a Default hotspot from the menu. Doing so selects the entire image and creates a single hotspot. Figure 14.12 shows an imagemap containing three hotspots.

FIGURE 14.12

This imagemap has two rectangular hotspots and one polygon hotspot.

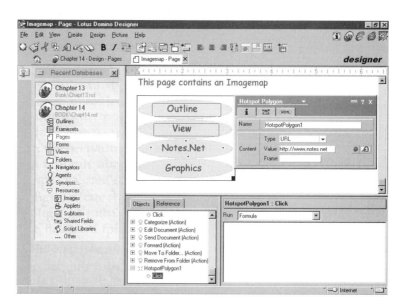

When you've added a hotspot, you can program it just like any other link. You can remove a hotspot by selecting it, and then choosing Picture, Delete Selected Hotspot(s) from the menu. You can also replace the graphic, and the hotspots will remain intact. To do so, choose Picture, Replace Picture from the menu.

In addition to the Hotspot Info tab, there is an Advanced and an HTML tab for the Hotspot Properties box; Figure 14.13 shows the Advanced tab. In the Advanced tab, you can specify the Position in Image Map tab order and alternative text. On the HTML tab, you can set the Class, Style, Title, and Other properties.

FIGURE 14.13

The Advanced Properties tab enables you to specify the tab order.

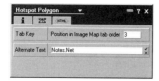

With relatively few clicks of the mouse and a few links built using the Properties box, the imagemap you created replaces the following HTML code:

```
<MAP NAME="n226.$Body.0.27A4">
<AREA SHAPE=rect COORDS="32,15,180,43" ID="HotspotRectangle11"
HREF="/BOOK/Chapt14.nsf/EmbeddedOutline?OpenPage" ALT="Outline"
TARGET="ContentFrame">
<AREA SHAPE=rect COORDS="35,57,176,84" ID="HotspotRectangle12"
HREF="/BOOK/Chapt14.nsf/Default?OpenView" TARGET="ContentFrame">
<AREA SHAPE=polygon COORDS="29,107,104,93,184,107,109,126"
ID="HotspotPolygon1" HREF="http://www.notes.net" ALT="Notes.Net"
TARGET="ContentFrame">
<AREA SHAPE=circle COORDS="99,153,15" ID="HotspotCircle2"
HREF="/BOOK/Chapt14.nsf/Graphics?OpenPage" ALT="Graphics Page"></MAP>
<IMG SRC="/BOOK/Chapt14.nsf/f0c75f686a8571f58525675900101fc5/$Body/
0.CC?OpenElement&FieldElemFormat=jpg" WIDTH=210 HEIGHT=176
USEMAP="#n226.$Body.0.27A4" BORDER=0></FORM>
```

As you can see, coding raw HTML to produce hotspots is not an easy task!

Embedding Elements

As with forms, you can embed Domino design objects into pages by choosing Create, Embedded Element, *element* from the menu. Embedding elements in pages gives you a great deal of flexibility and control in their presentation. When views, outlines, date pickers, and other Domino objects are presented to Web clients, their functionality is very close to that available to a Notes client. This brings you one step closer to designing a single interface that functions equally well for both types of clients. When you embed elements on a page, you can add other elements, such as text and graphics. You can delete an embedded element by selecting the element and choosing Edit, Clear from the menu or by hitting the Delete key.

You can choose from the following list of embedded elements:

- Outlines
- Views
- Folders
- Navigators

14

USING THE PAGE DESIGNER

- Date Pickers
- Folder Panes

Technically Speaking

There are actually two choices on the menu for Navigators. You can choose Navigator or Import Navigator.

On the CD

The embedded elements are all exhibited on pages available from the Embedded Elements Frameset in the database for this chapter, Chapt14.nsf.

Using Outlines in Pages

You've already seen how to embed an outline into a page with the Use Outline button in the Outline Designer (see the section "Using an Outline" in Chapter 13). Of course, you can also create a new page and embed an Outline directly on the page.

Embedding Views and Folders

You can easily embed views and folders into pages. When you choose Create, Embedded Element, View from the menu, you are presented with a dialog box listing available views and folders in the database (see Figure 14.14). You can also check Choose View based on formula, and when you click OK, a blank gray region is added to the page. You can also add an appropriate formula to the programmer's pane. You can also switch back to choosing from the available views by clicking the radio button for the embedded selection event for the embedded element (see Figure 14.15).

FIGURE 14.14

The Insert Embedded View dialog box lists available views and folders—note the selection, Important Documents, which is a folder.

> **Caution**
>
> You can include only one embedded folder or view in a page or a form!

FIGURE 14.15

To determine which view to display, use a formula in the Embedded Selection event; this formula switches views every other day.

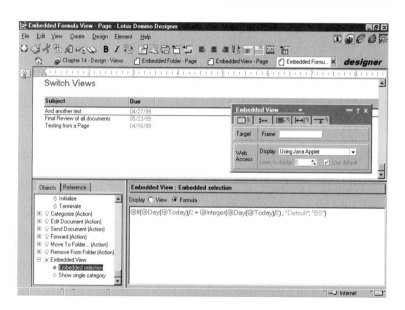

> **Caution**
>
> As of this writing, you cannot use a formula to select a folder. It only works for views, although the Insert Embedded View window permits the selection of folders as well as views.

You can also set up an embedded view to display a single category. This is done in the Show Single Category event of the Embedded View (see Figure 14.16), which restricts the view to the Chapter category. The category is based on the first sorted and categorized column in the view.

The Embedded View Properties box is exactly the same for views and folders. There are five tabs, only two of which will be covered here: the Info and Display tabs. The remaining tabs, Paragraph Alignment, Paragraph Margins, and Paragraph Hide When are covered in the section titled Working with Text Properties in Chapter 9, "Review of Basic Forms Design."

FIGURE 14.16

Setting up a single view category to display on the Page is done in the Show single category event.

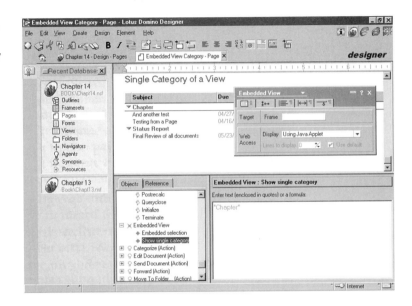

The Info tab contains two sections: Target and Web Access. No doubt you already know what the Target field does—it enables you to set a default frame for the embedded view. The Web Access section consists of a Display drop-down list, a Lines to Display control, and a Use Default checkbox (see Figure 14.17).

FIGURE 14.17

The default setting for the Web Access Display is Using Java Applet—note that the Lines to Display and Use Default checkboxes are disabled.

The Web Access Display field has the following three settings:

- **Using HTML**—This setting enables the Use Default checkbox, which in turn enables the Lines to Display control. The control increases or decreases by 10. For example, if you enter 5 in the control, and click the up arrow, it becomes 15. This setting embeds the View or Folder as an HTML object.

- **Using Java Applet**—This is the default (and usually the best) choice because it offers more features and functions. The Use Default checkbox and the Lines to Display spinner are disabled.

- **Using View's Display Property**—This setting enables the Use Default checkbox, which in turn enables the Lines to Display control.

The default choice, which is Using Java Applet, provides you with the following:

- Twisties are displayed for view categories.
- View categories can be expanded or collapsed without causing the page to refresh.
- View columns can be resized.
- Multiple documents can be selected.
- You can scroll vertically within the applet.
- Documents can be marked for deletion with the Delete key.
- F9 refreshes the view.

With this much power, it is difficult to find a reason to use the other choices! (This is the same display functionality available when you set the view itself to Use Applet in the Browser from the Advanced tab of the View Properties box.) However, although the view applet is a lot nicer than the views available in R4, you still can't do that much with it. You get the view applet with a centered, plain black view title above the applet itself. You don't even get the navigation and search buttons available in R4. However, if you embed a view applet in a page, you can add additional links, graphics, or buttons; jazz up the title; or do whatever is appropriate for your application.

For Backward Compatibility

With the capability to embed a view into a page, set the view as a Java applet, and create other design elements around it, you no longer need to use the R4 $$ViewTemplate forms! However, $$ViewList and $$ViewBody will still function as they did in R4 for backward compatibility.

The setting Using HTML displays the view as you would have seen it from a browser in R4. Unless the column properties are set otherwise, the first column in the view links to the document.

The final choice, Use View's Display Properties, makes the embedded view dependent on whatever display is set in the view design object itself. For example, on the Advanced tab of the View Properties box, you can set the view to Treat View Contents as HTML, in which case it performs as if you set the embedded view to Using HTML.

Table 14.2 lists @Commands that you might find useful for programming hotspots in a page containing an embedded view. These are the same hotspots produced by the R4 views shown on the Web without a $$ViewTemplate. These commands do not work when the view is set to display Using Java Applet. And because the applet scrolls and the twisties work, there is no real need for them.

TABLE 14.2 Programming Hotspots for Views

Action	*@Command*
Expand	@Command(ViewExpandAll])
Collapse	@Command(ViewCollapseAll])
Next	@Command([ViewPageDown])
Previous	@Command([ViewPageUp])
Search	@Command(ViewShowSearchBar])

View Backgrounds

Any background property set in the view or folder will not display in the embedded element.

Working with Navigators

There are two ways to work with Navigators in Pages. You can either embed a navigator or import one. Both are menu choices from the Create, Embedded Element submenu. Figure 14.18 shows an embedded navigator in a page. The Properties box really only has one tab applicable to the navigator, which is the Info tab. Basically, the Info tab identifies the name of the navigator, and if it is a form, whether or not it's used as a Navigator template.

Importing a navigator gives you much greater control over the embedded Navigator object because it is converted to a picture object. In addition, all the hotspots in the navigator are included with the imported navigator. Essentially, the imported navigator is now an imagemap (see Figure 14.19).

For More Information...

For more information about working with Imagemaps, see the section titled "Using Imagemaps."

FIGURE 14.18

*The Embedded
Navigator
Properties box is
pretty simple, and
there are not
many properties
that you can
affect.*

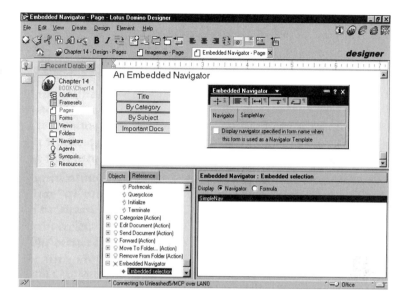

FIGURE 14.19

*Importing a navi-
gator is prefer-
able to embedding
one; as you can
see, the Picture
Properties box is
the same one used
for Imagemaps.*

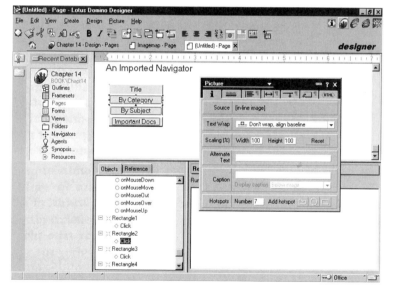

14

**USING THE PAGE
DESIGNER**

Using Date Pickers

A Date Picker looks very much like the calendar available from a date field. If you
embed a date picker in a page and include the page in a frameset, you can target the date
picker to a calendar view appearing in another frame. Clicking a day displays the calendar entries for that day.

Caution

Unfortunately, Date Pickers are *not* available for Web clients!

In order to make what you see in Figure 14.20 work, you need one calendar view, two pages, and one frameset. (To see how this works, you can look at the Date Picker frameset in the database for this chapter.) The page on the left contains the embedded date picker, and the page on the right contains the embedded calendar view. The frame on the left targets the frame on the right. It's easy to construct a frameset like this.

FIGURE 14.20

Clicking a date in the embedded date picker selects the date in the calendar display.

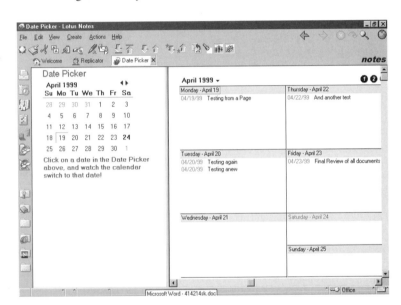

Setting the Calendar View Format

Be sure to choose a setting for the initial format of the calendar view; otherwise, it will default to two days. In this example, the default setting is one week.

For More Information...

For more information about Calendar Views, see Chapter 11, "View Design."

Embedding a Folder Pane

Folder Panes are holdovers from R4, in which there was no way to build an outline. In R4.6, you could include a folder pane and display the standard view and folder navigator to Web clients. Most likely, folder panes exist for backward compatibility. Embedded folder panes do absolutely nothing in the Notes client, but in a Web client, they link to the views and folders available in the database. Figure 14.21 shows a simple frameset (called Folder Pane in the accompanying database).

FIGURE 14.21

The embedded Folder Pane presents a functional but rather plain list of views and folders in the database.

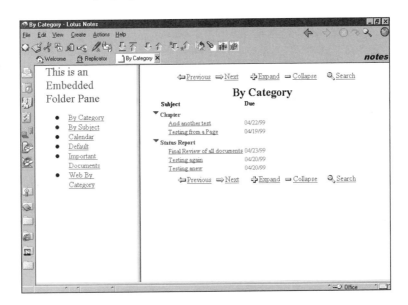

Adding Java Applets

Embedding Java applets is a little more involved than embedding native Domino objects, with the possible exception of imagemaps. However, the process is still relatively simple and has improved considerably from R4. Java applets are principally used to visually jazz up pages with graphics and to display information. In forms, Java applets can also be used to interact with fields in documents. Java applets can be created with tools such as NetObjects BeanBuilder (see Chapter 36, "NetObjects BeanBuilder," for more information).

14

USING THE PAGE
DESIGNER

On the CD

On the CD that accompanies this book is a collection of 40 Java applets from Anfy Java (www.anfyjava.com). Most are written by Fabio Ciucci, and have absolutely stunning visual effects. These applets are shareware, and I encourage you to register them.

The applets from Anfy Java will be used to demonstrate how you can include a Java applet on a page. To set up Anfy Java from the CD, run Setup.exe from the AnfyJava directory on the CD. Follow the instructions in the InstallShield Wizard. You can optionally include a shortcut on your desktop. Double-clicking the shortcut or launching Anfy Java from the menu launches a wizard that lets you preview the applets and then pick the applet to include on your page. Figure 14.22 shows the first page of the Wizard.

FIGURE 14.22

The first page of the Anfy Java Applet Wizard lets you choose from several different categories of applets; you can click the Applet Preview button to see the selected applet.

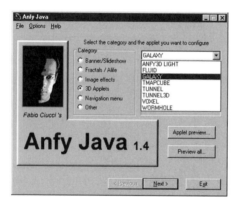

When you're satisfied that you have the applet you want, click Next and choose the parameters for the applet; you can modify the parameters or leave them at the default settings. When you arrive at the final page (see Figure 14.23), you can save the applet to a directory on your hard drive. It is best to save it to its own directory, so you might want to create a directory for Java applets and subdirectories for each applet. When you click the Copy All Files To button, the wizard creates all necessary Java class and JAR files, GIFs, and an HTML document. The HTML document will run the applet on its own, or you can copy the associated code from the HTML document and paste it into your own page or application. There is an easy way to do this in the Domino Designer.

FIGURE 14.23

The final window of the Anfy Java Wizard shows the HTML code necessary to configure the applet.

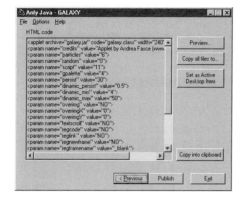

First, you have to add the Java applet to the Applet Resources of your database. (For more information on creating an Applet Resource, please see Chapter 12, "Using Resources in Domino Applications.") Click the New Applet Resource button, and locate the folder in which you stored the applet. Add all the files from that folder to the Applet Resource, and name and save the resource. To embed the Java Applet on a page, choose Create, Java Applet from the menu (see Figure 14.24).

FIGURE 14.24

To use a resource rather than an applet from the file system or another Web server, click the Locate button.

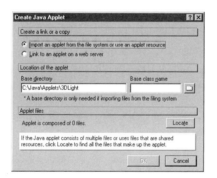

Click the Locate button to use an Applet Resource, and in Locate Java Applet Files, choose Shared Resources in the Browse drop-down menu. Locate your Java applet, and click the Add/Replace All button.

Next, select the Base class from the drop-down menu. You can find the base class if you look at the topmost line in the last page of the wizard (alternatively, you can look in the HTML file). You'll see something like the following:

```
<applet archive="galaxy.jar" code="galaxy.class" width="240"
height="150">
```

14

USING THE PAGE DESIGNER

The base class is found after the `code` tag; in this example, it is `galaxy.class`. Click OK to close the Locate Java Applet Files window, and click OK again to close the Create Java Applet window (see Figure 14.25).

FIGURE 14.25

Adding files from the newly created Applet Resource to the Page is very easy; be sure you are certain of the base class.

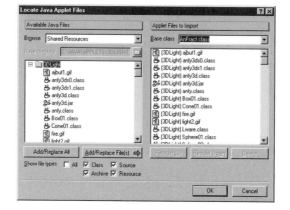

The applet creates a gray rectangular area on the page, and if you right-click it, you can set the properties. You set the width and height on the Java Applet Info tab of the Properties box. The width and height can be obtained from the same line of HTML from which you retrieved the base class. Here's a neat trick: Rather than typing in all the parameters, copy them to the clipboard from the last window of the Wizard! Highlight all the `<param>` tags, and copy them to the clipboard. Return to the Domino Designer, and click the Paste button in the Programmer's pane. All the parameters are neatly created for you (see Figure 14.26).

FIGURE 14.26

An embedded applet is easy to create in the R5 Domino Designer; note the paste button, which is used to paste parameters in from the clipboard.

Enter any alternative text in the Text to Display When Your Applet Is Not Running field, and the applet is ready to go.

The only other tab of interest here is the Applet Files tab immediately to the right of the Info tab. It contains only a list of files related to the applet, however. You can set the background color, if you desire, and now save and preview the page with the embedded applet. There are several such pages in the accompanying database, containing Fractals and Galaxies, both animated Java applets.

> **Troubleshooting**
>
> If you are having problems getting the applet to run, you can select the applet in the page, and choose Java Applet, Refresh from the menu. This opens the Locate Java Applet Files window, and you can go through the steps of adding the files once again. You can also check the parameters, and also the size of the embedded applet.

Summary

In this chapter, you have learned some of the terrific new features of Pages in Domino applications. You've learned how to create pages and embed all kinds of objects and elements, such as links, graphics, embedded elements, and so forth. Lastly, you were shown how to jazz up your applications using Java applets; remember that Java applets work both for Notes and Web clients! This great new design feature in R5 will help you build better applications more quickly that are able to reach a wider segment of users and are easier to use.

Providing End-User Help

by Steve Kern

It's been said that Domino applications are *never* finished, because in many respects, they are easy to change. Finished or not, at some point the application has to be released to the users. It is not enough to simply give the users a bunch of forms and views and wash your hands of the application. Perhaps the most significant task to complete for any application, at least in the eyes of the end user, is online help for the application. No matter how simple or intuitive an application seems to you, the developer, online help for the user is essential to the ultimate success of your application. Several layers of online help are supported by the Notes client and are simple to apply during development.

Other methods are available for use in more complex and demanding applications. Some of the exciting features added to R5 are JavaScript enhancements that enable the designer to create very responsive help systems for your applications. Under Release 5, JavaScript is now available in the IDE and supports both Notes and the Web Client. This enables you to create popup help and field help in either client! R5 of Notes and Domino has also added a terrific, and to some, a long-overdue method of providing help to Notes clients—context-sensitive help that is application-specific and that launches when the user presses the standard F1 Help key. In this chapter, you will learn how to use these help systems in your own applications.

Choosing the Right Approach

Deciding where to place help for an application is an important consideration. A properly constructed help system can improve the usability of the application. Help can be created from the database level all the way down to the field level, and there are a number of ways to present help to the user. Consideration also must be given to the type of client used to access the application. Help can be provided in the following areas:

- About this database document
- Using this database document
- Field-level help descriptions (Notes only)
- Buttons, Actions, Text popups, and Hotspots
- Help documents
- Context-sensitive help
- JavaScript field-level help
- JavaScript popups

At a minimum, help documentation should be placed in the About this database and Using this database documents. All fields that are editable should have field-level help even if they seem self-explanatory to you. This is a basic courtesy to the users of your application. For simple applications, this level of help may be sufficient.

Several techniques for creating field-level help are described in detail in the sections below. The easiest way is to use the Help description property for a field, but unfortunately, help text placed here does not appear in Web browsers. For applications that will support both Notes and Web clients, you should consider using JavaScript to provide field-level help. The good news is that help created with JavaScript in the onFocus event will appear for both Notes and Web clients!

You can also use buttons, actions, and hotspots to create help. This requires more effort during development, but you can provide help at a greater level of detail using these objects. For example, field-level help is limited to the width of the status bar, so only a brief description consisting of one or two short sentences can be entered. However, using a text popup on a field label, you can enter significantly more text, providing the user with detailed instructions for data entry. Unfortunately, text popups only work in Notes clients, but you can use JavaScript to open a separate help window in Web browsers and achieve the same result.

You can create help documents that can be presented to the users in a view. Further, you can use these same documents in the new R5 context-sensitive help. This technique requires creating separate forms and views, plus additional code in various objects to open the correct help document when the F1 key is pressed. Of course, the actual help documents themselves must be created. Since this method of providing help requires significantly more effort than other methods discussed, consider reserving it for more complex applications.

Working with Database-Level Help

As you probably know, two kinds of help documents are available directly from the Help menu for any Domino Database: the "About this Database" document and the "Using this Database" document. These two documents are typically referred to as the *About* and the *Using* documents. These documents can be accessed from the Notes Help menu whenever a database is open.

Creating About this Database Documents

Perhaps the most visible help document in a Domino database is the About document. By default, this document opens the first time a user opens the database, unless the document is empty. As its name implies, this document usually answers the following questions *about* the database:

- Who is the intended audience?

- What is the purpose of the database?
- When should the database be used?

An easy way to get a feel for how this document should be composed is to view the "About this Database" documents for the templates supplied by Lotus. (See Figure 15.1.) When the database is open, or selected on the workspace, choosing Help, About This Database displays the document. When you create a new database from a template, you can open the About document from the New Database dialog box by selecting the template you want and clicking the About button. The About document is displayed in a small dialog box.

FIGURE 15.1

You can use the About database documents supplied by Lotus to see how your own About documents should be structured.

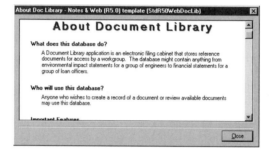

Creating Using this Database Documents

The Using document is available from the Help Menu by choosing Help, Using This Database. This help document should contain information on how to use the database, and it can be fairly detailed, depending on the scope of the application. Again, if you want to see samples, take a look at the Using documents for some of the template applications, such as the Document Library or the Discussion template. Don't be tempted to put all your help documentation into this one document because there are many other ways to provide help. You have to use your own judgment, but anything beyond two or three printed pages is probably too long. Information in this document should provide help to the user for each of the significant elements of the database and at minimum should contain information on the following:

- How to use the database
- How and when to use the forms
- How to accomplish special tasks associated with the application
- A list or description of the views
- Information on other significant database elements such as agents that the user would typically interact with
- Notes to the database administrator

Figure 15.2 shows the Using this Database document from a discussion database.

FIGURE 15.2

The Using this Database document from a discussion database; the first several entries describe how to participate in a discussion.

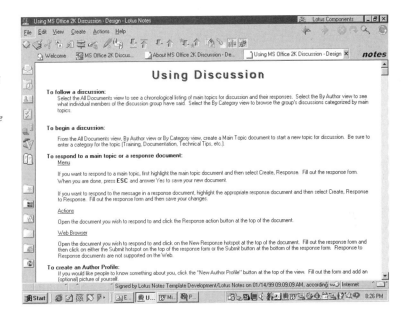

For design, both the Help documents can be accessed from the Domino Designer. When the Designer is open to your database, you can click Resources and choose the Other entry in the Design pane navigator. Double-clicking the design document places it in design mode.

Both of these Help documents are like a rich-text fields. You can place just about anything in them except for fields. In this respect, they are very similar to a Page. You can insert or paste graphic objects and document links (also referred to as *doclinks*) into them; you can also add and format text just about any way that you want to.

Providing Access to Web Clients

If you want to make these documents available to Web clients, you can create a button in a view or form toolbar that uses either @Command([HelpAboutDatabase]) or @Command([HelpUsingDatabase]) to open the About and Using documents respectively. Of course, you can also attach these @Commands to any hotspot.

15

Working with Launch Options for the About Document

As you know from reading Chapter 7, "The Release 5 Object Store," a Domino database has a number of Launch options. These options are found on the Launch tab of the Database Properties box. There are five options that directly involve the About this database document.

- Show "About database" document if modified
- Show "About database" document when database is opened for the first time
- Open the "About database" document
- Launch first attachment in the "About database" document
- Launch first doclink in the "About database" document

Using the "When Opened" Property

The Launch tab of the Database Properties box has two drop-down lists. The first is When Opened in a Notes Client, and the second is When Opened in a Browser. There are quite a number of choices, as you can see in Figure 15.3. Three of the choices are available for Notes clients, and two of those three are available for Web clients.

- **Web and Notes**—Open the "About database" document
- **Notes only**—Launch first attachment in the "About database" document
- **Web and Notes**—Launch first doclink in the "About database" document

FIGURE 15.3

You can choose from a large number of Launch options for both Notes clients and Web browsers.

Disappearing Checkboxes?

Selecting any of the three options that use the About document from the When Opened in the Notes Client drop-down list causes the two Show checkboxes to disappear (the selections in the On Web Open list have no affect on the checkboxes). The two checkboxes are discussed later in this chapter.

The first option, Open "About database" Document, causes the About document to open each time the user opens the database. Because the About document is essentially a rich-text field, URLs and links can be built into the document. In earlier versions of Notes and Domino, the About document was often used as a home page for a Web site. Note that this isn't really necessary any more since Outlines, Pages, and Framesets were added in R5.

The next two options launch attachments and doclinks. Launch First Attachment in "About database" launches a file attachment and is unavailable for Web clients. For example, if you attach a Word document to the About document, Domino launches Word and opens the document when a user clicks the database. Launch First Doclink in "About database" is similar, except that instead of launching a file from another application, Notes switches to the linked document, view, or database.

Using the About Checkboxes

Two checkboxes appear in the center of the Launch tab unless one of the three Launch choices involving the About document is chosen in When Opened in the Notes Client. Selections made in the When Opened in a Browser drop-down list have no effect on the checkboxes. The first checkbox, Show "About document" if Modified causes the About document to open if it has been changed. The second checkbox causes the About document to open the first time a user opens the database. You can click both checkboxes if you need to ensure that the users see the About document the first time, and if it is modified (see Figure 15.4).

FIGURE 15.4

The two check-boxes in the middle of the Database Properties box control the display of the About document.

The first checkbox is useful during development when the designers might be changing things frequently. Entering information about changes to the application into the About document in conjunction with this setting is an excellent method of notifying the users of any recent changes. With this choice, each time you modify the About document to log application changes, the About document automatically displays the next time users access the database.

For applications that use the About document as a source of database help, it is a good idea to check the second checkbox, Show "About database" Document When Database Is First Opened. Users can read about the purpose of the database, its intended audience, and so forth.

Providing Field-Level Help

Field-level help is very simple to add while developing a form. It should be included for most, if not all, editable fields. You add your help text to the Help description field on the Advanced tab of the Field Properties Box (see Figure 15.5). In Release 4.5, the Help description was the only place to store HTML code for the field; R4.6 and R5 both have HTML attributes for fields that can be used for the same purpose. Consequently, you no longer need to use the Help description fields to store HTML formatting instructions.

FIGURE 15.5

You can add help text to a field in the Help description field on the Advanced tab of the Field Properties box.

Field-level help appears at the bottom of the user's screen in a line just above the status bar, as shown in Figure 15.6. Field-level help should be brief and to the point. A user should be able to assimilate it in a glance.

Documenting Fields

You can even add text to the Help description field for non-editable fields. This is a convenient way to document the purpose of the field, as long as you keep it short.

Testing Field-Level Help

When designing forms, you can easily check field-level help by putting the form in test mode. By successively moving through fields and viewing the help at the bottom of the screen, you can check for the help text for accuracy and also for any items for which help is missing.

FIGURE 15.6

FIGURE 15.6

This document shows field-level help at the bottom of the screen.

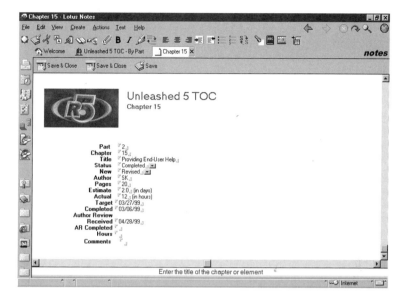

Enter the title of the chapter or element

Caution

If you don't see field-level help, you can turn it on from the menu by choosing View, Show, Field Help. This was an available menu choice in Release 3, but in Release 4, it was removed from the menu. Now, in R5, it has been added back to the menu. Be sure to educate your users about this menu option!

Using Buttons, Hotspots, and Actions to Add Help

There are many different types of hotspots that can be used to provide help. Some ways to provide help are the following:

- Button hotspots
- Graphic buttons (in layout regions only)
- Action Bar buttons
- Text Popups
- Formula Popups
- Link Hotspots

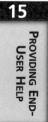

15

PROVIDING END-USER HELP

For More Information...

For a more detailed discussion on the various types of buttons, hotspots, and actions, see Chapter 10, "Advanced Form Design."

Considering the Client

Bear in mind the types of clients that will use your application. Text Popups and Formula Popups don't work on the Web, and for the most part, neither do pushbuttons. Action Bar buttons do work, but the formula used to compose the Action must also work on the Web. For example, you can't put LotusScript into an Action Bar button and expect it to work on the Web. All types of Link Hotspots including database, view, document, and anchor links work for both Notes and Web clients.

With the introduction of context-sensitive help, some of these might not be as useful. In R5, each form, page, view, and folder has a `HelpRequest` event that can be used to display help specific to that object. This removes the need to place a Help button in the Action Bar. However, the `HelpRequest` event, which uses the F1 key to launch the associated help, is unavailable from the Web. Pushing the F1 key while in a browser will launch Help for the browser, not for the application that you developed.

Using Hotspot Buttons and Graphic Buttons

Hotspot buttons, also referred to as pushbuttons, are an easy, visible way to provide help for the user. Hotspot buttons are gray rectangular 3D objects that have a fixed position on the form. Consequently, they scroll with the document. Because they have a fixed position, you can position hotspot buttons anywhere on a form where you think users will need help for a specific area. Hotspot buttons that provide help can have explanatory captions such as "Help" or they can simply be a question mark.

If you are working in a layout region, you can use hotspot buttons or graphic buttons. A graphic button in a layout region uses a custom image rather than the standard 3D gray button. Like their counterparts on a standard form, both graphic buttons and hotspot buttons have a fixed position on layout regions.

Both types of buttons can be programmed with @Commands, the Formula language, Simple Actions, LotusScript, or JavaScript. Figure 15.7 shows a hotspot button programmed with an @Command.

FIGURE 15.7

A simple hotspot button in the form of a question mark can be located anywhere on a form—note the formula uses the new @Command([OpenHe lpDocument];…).

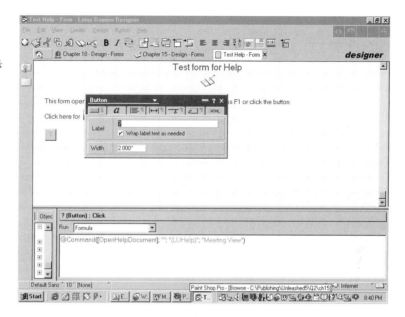

Using Action Buttons

In Release 3, hotspot buttons were the only type of button available. Release 4 changed that with the addition of Action buttons for forms and views; Actions are displayed in the Action Bar for forms and views. Because the Action Bar has a fixed location on the screen rather than on the document, the Action Bar does not scroll with the document. Help can be provided by an Action that is appropriate for the view or form.

Unlike hotspot buttons, Action buttons can display graphic images. R4 had a preset palette of icons available for Actions. In R5, in addition to the icon palette, you can now add a graphic image to an Action button. Graphic images to be used in an Action must be stored in the Image Resources. For example, you can use the standard indicator for help, which is a question mark inside a circle, in an Action. This is available from the Action palette, or you can create one of your own. Figure 15.8 shows an Action using a custom image from the Image Resources.

For More Information...

For more information on creating Image Resources, see Chapter 12, "Using Resources in Domino Applications." For more information on creating Actions, see Chapter 10.

15

PROVIDING END-
USER HELP

Caution

If you create a custom image to use in an Action, be sure to set the background color to transparent. Otherwise, the background of the image displays on the Action button, which might be an effect you don't want.

FIGURE **15.8**

Click the Custom radio button to use an Image Resource.

Display the Graphic Image Only

You can set the button to display only the graphic image by clicking Only show icon in button bar. This enables you to put text in the Name field for the Action to identify it, even though it's not used. In R4.x, if you wanted only the graphic to show, you had to leave the name blank. This made it difficult to tell if an Action was actually present, or what the Actions were, because they were stored in the Action palette as a blank line.

Using Text and Formula Popup Hotspots

If targeted, specific help is necessary, you can accomplish this by using hotspots. Hotspots can be created by highlighting text or graphic objects on the form and selecting Create, Hotspot, *hotspot type* from the menu. You can create text popups, formula pop-ups, and link hotspots. This section focuses on creating text popups, since they are the most useful when providing help.

If you look at the Server document, you'll notice that it has built-in help for fields in the form of text popups. This is handy because there is an awful lot of information in a Server document. Having detailed field help available in this fashion is very convenient (see Figure 15.9).

FIGURE 15.9

The field label can be used to display help in a text popup.

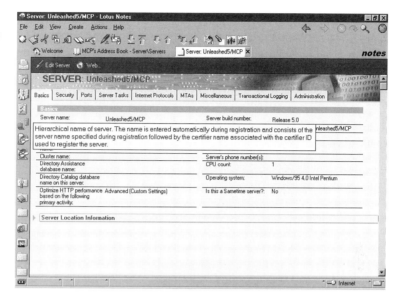

A text popup enables you to enter text that is displayed when the user clicks or mouses over the hotspot. Prior to R5, users had to click on the hotspot to produce the popup. Now, mouse over is the default. Unfortunately, although it seems very much like the JavaScript On mouse over event, mouse over for popups does not work in browsers. Alternatively, you can create a formula hotspot and use the Formula language to create the text. A green border surrounds a hotspot by default, but this can be turned off from the Hotspot Properties box (see Figure 15.10).

FIGURE 15.10

This Text Hotspot Properties box is set to display On mouse over and the border is set to None.

At the bottom of the Hotspot Properties box in the Display section, you will notice two radio button sets. The first set is the Show popup set, in which you can define the display properties. There are two choices for display, On Mouse Over and On Click. The second radio button set is titled Hotspot Style. There are three choices: Border the Text, Highlight the Text, and None. Border the Text displays a green rectangular box around

15

PROVIDING END-
USER HELP

the text as discussed earlier. Highlight the Text displays the text on a light yellow background. None, of course, leaves the text as is. Displaying borders or highlights on all field text labels provides a visual cue to the user that help is available, but overuse can clutter a form. On the other hand, if you are providing help for only a few fields, it might make sense to use borders or highlights. You will have to exercise judgment on this matter.

Using Link Hotspots

You can link to other documents by first copying a link, such as a document link, to the clipboard, and then creating a Link hotspot. The linked documents do not have to reside in the same Domino database, but if they are in another database, that database must be available to the user and the user must have at least reader access to it. If the user cannot access the database, Domino displays an error message. This technique is handy if you create help documents either in the same or in a separate database (see Figure 15.11).

FIGURE 15.11

When you create a Link Hotspot, the Properties box opens to the Hotspot Info tab.

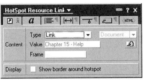

Creating Context-Sensitive Help

Release 5 has introduced a new way of presenting help to the users of your applications. You can now create context-sensitive help that the user can access by pressing the F1 key! This enables developers to produce their own help documents and make them easily accessible to end-users.

To do this, use a combination of the new `HelpRequest` event and `@Command([OpenHelpDocument])` or `@Command([OpenPage])`. The `HelpRequest` event is triggered when the user presses the F1 key, and the `@Command` is used to select the appropriate help document or page. The `HelpRequest` event is available for the following design elements:

- Forms
- Pages
- Views
- Folders

The syntax for @Command([OpenHelpDocument]) is the following:

```
@Command([OpenHelpDocument];"server":"database";"view";"key")
```

You can also use the following syntax, which opens a help document in one of the Notes and Domino Help databases:

```
@Command([OpenHelpDocument];[ClientHelp]¦[DesignerHelp]¦[AdminHelp];"view";"key")
```

Using the first version of @Command([OpenHelpDocument]), you can open a specific help document in a specific. These documents can be located in the same database or another separate database. To open a document in the help database, you specify a sorted view and a key that will locate the document. The second version of @Command([OpenHelpDocument]) opens one of the Notes and Domino help databases—note that there are now three: Client Help, Designer Help, and Admin Help. *View* and *Key* are optional arguments and, if omitted, the database specified simply opens to the default view.

The ability to open specific pages provides a convenient place to store help documents. Simply create and name the pages appropriately, and supply the page name as the argument for the @Command([OpenPage]), and when the user presses F1, the page displays. The syntax is as follows:

```
@Command([OpenPage];"page name"
```

Context-sensitive help is certainly a welcome addition to the application developer's tool kit. You can easily create your own help documents or pages, and when the user presses F1, help specific to the form, page, view, or folder is instantly available.

Creating Help Documents

Notes and Domino ships with a multitude of help and reference databases. You can easily copy the design elements and use them for a help database, with just a little modification. Using the Domino Help database designs can be advantageous because users are already familiar with Notes help. However, you might find it easier to create your own help database, because all you really need is a topic field and a body field; you probably won't need the level of display control and indexing that the Release Notes and other Help databases use.

A help document doesn't need to be a complex form. You can create a simple form such as the one shown in Figure 15.12. Other fields can be added to sort and position the form in a help view. If you plan to use @Command([OpenHelpDocument]), you need to create a sorted view to contain the documents.

FIGURE 15.12

This is a simple help form in design; the field cType at the bottom of the form can be used to sort a help view into help for forms, views, and so on.

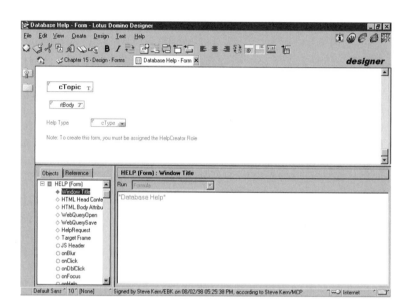

You also need to create a view or views to display the help documents. The view (LUHelp) used in the following formula to retrieve help documents is a hidden view consisting of a single sorted column cTopic:

```
@Command([OpenHelpDocument]; ""; "(LUHelp)"; "document name")
```

"document name" in the previous formula is the value you give the cTopic field when you create the help document. This value retrieves the appropriate help document from the sorted view.

You might also want to present the help documents in a view visible to the end-users. The field cType can be used to sort and categorize the help documents into areas that make sense to you, such as Form, View, General, and so forth. Figure 15.13 shows a Help view in design.

You can find this help document and its associated views on the CD for this book in the database Chapt15.nsf.

FIGURE 15.13

This Help view is sorted and categorized on the cType field.

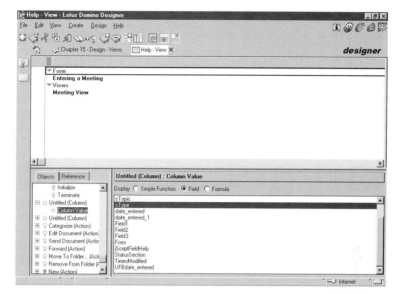

Creating Help Documents within the Same Database

Help documents can be stored in the same database as your application, or they can be stored in an entirely separate database. Most often, you will want to store them in the same database. When help documents are stored in the same database, you can create a help view for the users directly in the database. They are also somewhat easier to access programmatically, and instead of delivering two databases for an application, you only need to deliver one. Keeping the help within the database is simply more intuitive and efficient. However, for applications consisting of multiple databases, using a separate help database is a logical alternative. Using a separate help database is discussed in the next section.

The simple help form shown in Figure 15.12 and the two associated help views, the visible Help view and the Lookup view, can be created easily within the application database. Creating help documents should be restricted to a small group of individuals, perhaps just the developers. Otherwise, you run the risk of destroying the links built in the `HelpRequest` events. To restrict compose and edit access to the help form, use a role and set the Create access for the form to that role. Figure 15.14 shows a form with Create access set to a role called `HelpCreator`.

15

PROVIDING END-
USER HELP

For More Information…

For more information on how to create roles and assign them, see Chapter 31, "Security and Domino Applications."

FIGURE 15.14

You can assign Create access to the form to a user role in the Security tab of the Form Properties Box.

In the Help view visible to the users, you can then create Action Bar buttons to create, edit, and delete help documents. Be sure to hide the action buttons from unauthorized users in the Hide When tab of the Action Properties box with @UserRoles. Consider using the following formula:

```
!@Contains(@UserRoles; "HelpCreator")
```

If you place such a formula in the Hide When property of the Actions, then they will appear only for those users or groups to whom you assign the HelpCreator role. This has the same effect as using a separate database to contain the help documents, and assigning users Author or Editor access in the database ACL.

Once the view is constructed, creating help documents becomes a simple matter of clicking the New Help button, entering a topic and completing the body of the Help text. The topic is then referenced in HelpRequest event as described earlier. Of course, documents can be created that are not used in context help. These documents can have topics such as general help for the application, tips for certain processes, and so on.

Using a Separate Help Database

The advantage of using a separate help database is that you can easily control who can edit and compose documents by assigning Author or Editor access in the ACL. Thus, no roles are required for a separate Help database, although they certainly can be used. You can also consider using a separate help database when an application consists of more than one database.

There are at least two disadvantages to using a separate database for end-user help. First, if users want to look through the help documents, they have to locate and open another database. Second, whenever you distribute an application, you have to remember to include the associated help database as well, or all your HelpRequest lookups will fail.

> **Caution**
>
> Be sure to assign reader access to the separate help database for the end-users, or else they won't be able to access the help documents. You can do this by setting the Default access level of the database ACL to Reader. If for some reason you need to restrict the separate Help database, you can set the Default level to No Access and assign a group Reader access.

Creating a separate help database requires the same number of design elements and the same amount of work as putting the help documentation in the same database as your application. You still have to create a Help form and a hidden lookup view, plus a view displaying the help documents for creating, editing and reading. The @Command([OpenHelpDocument]) formula must reference the separate help database. For example, the following formula opens the Meeting View help document:

```
@Command([OpenHelpDocument]; "server":"database"; "(LUHelp)"; "Meeting View")
```

This works regardless of whether it is called from a button, hotspot, or from the HelpRequest event. The hidden view used to look up the help document has a single sorted column containing the cTopic field, just as it would for help documents contained within the same database.

Accessing Help with @Commands

There are numerous @Commands that display Help. Table 15.1 lists the @Commands available and what they do:

TABLE 15.1 Accessing Help with @Commands

@Command	Usage
Help	Opens the Notes Help database to the Index view
HelpAboutDatabase	Opens the "About this Database" document
HelpAboutNotes	Displays the Notes splash screen

continues

15

PROVIDING END-
USER HELP

TABLE 15.1 Accessing Help with @Commands

@Command	*Usage*
HelpFunctions	Presents a list of @Functions
HelpIndex	Opens Notes help to the Index view
HelpKeyboard	Displays keyboard help
HelpMessages	Shows a list of Notes messages
OpenHelpDocument	Opens specific help documents, used for context-specific help
HelpRelease3MenuFinder	Displays the Release 3 Menu Finder
HelpReleaseNotes	Opens the Release Notes
HelpTableofContents	Opens the Notes Help database to the Table of Contents
HelpUsingDatabase	Displays the Using this Database document

As pointed out earlier in this chapter, you can use these @Commands anywhere you can compose a formula, such as view and form Action Bar buttons, Action hotspots, and pushbuttons.

Providing Help with JavaScript

JavaScript can be an excellent choice for providing help. JavaScript runs from a number of different events, and it works in both Notes and Web Clients. To some extent, you can write your help once and it will run anywhere. For example, it's easy to put field-level help in the Help description field of the field Properties box, but that won't display to a Web client. You can, however, create field-level help in JavaScript that appears in the status bar of a browser. You can also create general help in JavaScript that can be launched from a button or a hotspot in either type of client.

JavaScript is not a particularly difficult language to learn, and it is covered in Chapters 25, "Introduction to JavaScript." There are many places where you can place JavaScript code; however, this section is not intended to be a primer for JavaScript. This is not the place to discuss the ins and outs of the *Domino Object Model* (DOM), syntax, JavaScript's relationship to HTML, and so forth. Instead, I focus on specific scripts that you can use to create help in your own applications. In passing, I give enough explanation so that either you will know where to look for more information or you will understand why the code is written in the way it is.

Like other object-oriented and object-based languages such as C++, Java, and Visual Basic, JavaScript has objects, classes, properties, and methods. As pointed out in chapter 25, JavaScript is quite different from LotusScript. Because HTML is a document presentation language, JavaScript exists in a document or "page." Documents are displayed in Windows, so the two objects you are concerned with are the Window and the Document Object. The JavaScript DOM is much richer than its counterpart in LotusScript. JavaScript can add dynamic elements to your Web pages that you can never do in "straight" HTML.

The Window Object is particularly useful because you can use it to display alerts, simulating the field validation dialog boxes in Notes, or dialog boxes called with @Prompt(). With the Window Object, you can also define the attributes and the size. If you create a new window, it is displayed in a separate window, as you would expect. This gives you a great deal of flexibility. You can also access the browser's status bar from the Window Object as you will see shortly.

To keep the discussion simple, you'll learn about creating a popup Help window and about putting help text into the status bar. Both use the Window object. Fortunately, you can place code in Notes events without learning how to code a JavaScript event in an HTML document!

Creating Field-Level Help in the Status Bar

Using JavaScript, you can mimic the field help available to the Notes Client by creating messages that appear in the bowser status bar. As you might expect, this uses the window.status property available from the Window Object.

Using Frames to Display Help

You can also create a frame at the bottom of the document to display help text. The code required to accomplish this is relatively complex, and is beyond the scope of this chapter.

Creating JavaScript help in the status bar is so simple, presenting it here almost takes the fun away from you discovering it on your own (see Figure 15.15)!. In the onFocus event of a field, place the following code:

```
window.status = "<your field help text goes here>"
```

When the user enters the field, the message is displayed in the status bar of the browser or the Notes client. The message that appears in the status bar does not automatically disappear when you exit the field, as it does when you use the Help description field property. This isn't a problem if all your fields have help, but if one or more doesn't, you will have to explicitly clear the status bar. The following code entered into the `onBlur` event of a field will empty the message in the status bar:

```
window.status = ""
```

FIGURE 15.15

The Help text is displayed in the status bar of a browser; be sure to clear the message in the onBlur event.

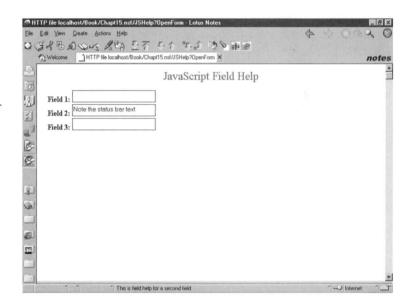

Displaying Field Help

Using the status bar to display messages works in the Domino (Notes) browser whether or not Field help is turned on. It also works in Netscape, but you have to turn the status bar on in Internet Explorer. You must also make sure that JavaScript is enabled in your browser!

Creating Popup Help

Although some might say it is not as easy to create popup help messages in JavaScript as it is in Notes, it is still not difficult. As always, it depends how fancy you want to get! To create popup help in a Web client, you can use the `onClick` event of a button or hotspot. The following code displays a separate help window in a browser:

```
// JavaScriptHelp is a page in this database
jSHandle = window.open('JavaScriptHelp','helpWin','height=250,width=400');
jSHandle.focus();
jSHandle.document.close();
```

This code bears some explanation. Unlike the previous example, which used the window.status property, window.open is a *method*. If you are not familiar with the terminology, a *property* is an attribute of an object, whereas a *method* is an action. The first parameter, JavaScriptHelp, is a the name of a page created in the database. The page contains some help text and a close button (see Figure 15.16). This can be any other URL as well. The second parameter is the name of the new browser window. The last parameter is optional, but in this case, it controls the size of the window as you can easily see from the names height and width.

Using Pages

Using Pages to display help is a great solution for a Web-enabled database! Because you can include a mixture of Notes and HTML constructs on a page, it is easy to build exactly what you want.

Caution

In the current release of R5, the sample code does not open a separate sized window as it does in Netscape and IE 4. It still displays, but it uses a full window.

FIGURE 15.16

The Help window is nicely displayed in Netscape and Internet Explore; be sure to include a close button so the user can easily close the Help dialog box.

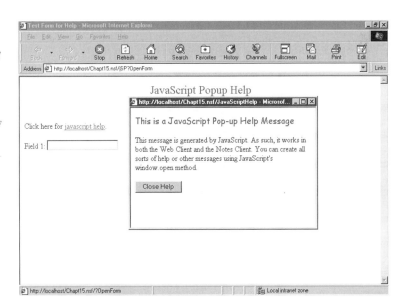

To understand how to create help in a separate window, you need to understand how the methods and properties of a JavaScript `Window` object work. First, you get a handle on the open window, using the `window.open` method. Using the `window.focus` method, navigate to the window you just created and display it to the user. The last line uses the `window.document.close` method to shut the window down.

> **Caution**
>
> If you use `window.close` instead of `window.document.close` in the sample code, your help window will open and then immediately close!

Using JavaScript's `onHelp` Event

The `onHelp` event is available for Forms, Subforms, Pages, and Action Hotspots. Unfortunately, as of this writing, it only functions in Internet Explorer. Since it is quite limited in this regard, its usefulness is questionable. Nevertheless, the functionality might be expanded in the future, so it is worth discussing.

Basically, the `onHelp` event responds to the F1 key in the browser. The event can be coded in exactly the same manner as the `onClick` event described earlier. In practice, however, pressing the F1 key not only launched the JavaScript help window, but Help for Internet Explorer.

Summary

This chapter covers a lot of important ground. It provides a number of different methods of providing end-user help. Most of the techniques are quite simple, from using the About document and Notes field help to JavaScript Field help. You have learned about traditional techniques as well as how to provide context-sensitive help and help using JavaScript. The examples used to illustrate this chapter are available on the CD-ROM that comes with this book in a database specific to this chapter that is called `Chapt15.nsf`.

CHAPTER 16

Analyzing Your Applications

by Steve Kern

IN THIS CHAPTER

The purpose of analyzing your database design is to provide a research and documentation tool that enables developers and administrators to quickly locate information on the various design elements of an application. For example, you might want to find out whether you can eliminate an agent. To do so, you need to make sure that the agent is not launched by other agents or by buttons in views or forms. This chapter discusses two tools that provide the analysis you need: the Design Synopsis available in the Notes clients (both the Notes client and the Domino Designer) and a third-party tool called TeamStudio Analyzer. With these tools, you can create a searchable design synopsis of your applications.

The database Design Synopsis tool is the only method of generating information about the design elements of a database that is native to Lotus Notes and Domino. Earlier versions merely produced a listing of design elements in a window that you could then review, search, print, export, and so on. It was better than nothing, but it was very limited. The Design Synopsis has been significantly enhanced in Release 5. There are many more options for generating information about the design of your applications, and now you can redirect the output of the Synopsis to a document within a database.

While the Design Synopsis is the only tool native to Domino, there is an alternative worthy of consideration, TeamStudio Analyzer from Ives Development. This tool produces a very sophisticated and detailed analysis of databases that is stored in a Domino database. This database has views that drill down from the database level to the object level. More than one database can be included in a single Analyzer database. Like any other database, the Analyzer database can be full-text indexed and searched with ease, and you can even modify the design. You don't have to plod through the database design hoping you can find what you need! As an analysis tool, it simply cannot be beat.

What's New in the Design Synopsis?

Just about everything is new! In Release 4.x, the Design Synopsis enabled you to choose from a limited set of design objects and database information, and directed the output only to the screen. Figure 16.1 shows the Design Synopsis dialog box from Release 4.6. Clicking the checkboxes and clicking beside the design elements in the list boxes and then clicking OK produced a report appearing in a non-modal window. The synopsis could then be searched, reviewed, copied to the clipboard, printed, or exported.

Directing Output to the Screen

If you direct the output to the screen in Release 5 (the default), you can do the same things mentioned in the text: search it with the Find dialog box (Ctrl+F), read through it, copy it to the clipboard, and so on.

Figure 16.1

The Design Synopsis dialog box in Release 4.x is quite limited compared to that in Release 5.

There were a number of problems with the Design Synopsis in Release 4.x. One glaring problem was that LotusScript attached to fields in forms did not appear in the Synopsis. All the forms and subforms were checked by default, which was fine if your database had a limited number of forms. But what if your database had 20, 30, or more forms, and all you wanted was information on a single form? You had to go through and uncheck all the other forms and subforms. It was very tedious. No matter how many or how few design objects you chose, all information was sent to a single window. Not only did this window become extremely lengthy, but on limited machines with large databases, there might not have been enough memory available to complete the operation. Finding the information you wanted was also tedious. A form with many fields and lengthy formulas produced a very long entry in the Synopsis window. You could always use the Find dialog box—if you knew what you were looking for! If you didn't, your only alternative was to scroll through the listing. Despite these limitations, it was the only method from within Notes itself that easily produced information on the design of your database.

The four tabs of the Design Synopsis dialog box are introduced in Table 16.1.

Table 16.1   The Four Tabs of the Design Synopsis

Tab	Contents
Design Elements	A picklist of design objects, such as forms, views, subforms and mover dialog boxes that enable you to choose specific objects
Database Information	General, Space usage, Replication, and ACL information
Content	A picklist of specific items for each type of design object to be included in the Synopsis
Output	Determines whether the output of the Synopsis is to the screen (the default) or to a database. Also enables choice of separators

As you can see from Figure 16.2, there is a lot available from the new Design Synopsis. Not only can you choose which design objects to include from the Design Elements tab, you can pick specific aspects of each type of design object on the Content tab. The

Database Information tab contains nothing new, but the Output tab enables you to define separators for the report and, more importantly, whether the report goes to the screen or to a database. Creating a database that contains design information can be an important tool for both documentation and research. Because you can append analysis documents to the same database, you can create an archive of design changes. As you will see in the section on TeamStudio Analyzer, the database produced from the Design Synopsis tool isn't nearly as detailed as that produced by TeamStudio Analyzer, but it's a step in the right direction.

FIGURE 16.2

The Design Synopsis dialog box in Release 5 has multiple tabs and list boxes; note that two of the three design elements have been moved into the Selections box.

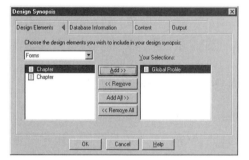

Using the Design Synopsis Dialog Box

There are two ways to launch the Synopsis dialog box. With a database selected or open, you can choose File, Database, Design Synopsis, or you can select Synopsis from the Domino Designer navigation pane. The next few sections cover the new Design Synopsis Dialog box. You will see how each of the tabs contributes to a much more sophisticated, and ultimately more useful, design synopsis.

Using the Design Elements Tab

As you can see from Figures 16.2 and 16.3, the Design Elements tab consists of a drop-down list of design elements and a dialog box. When you choose a design element, a list of design objects of that type appear in the window to the left. A selection window appears to the right. The buttons in the middle offer ways to transfer design objects between the windows. You can choose from the following design objects:

- -All-
- Forms
- Views

- Folders
- Shared Fields
- Subforms
- Navigators
- Script Libraries
- Agents
- Stored Queries
- Pages
- Framesets
- Other

FIGURE 16.3

The Design Elements dialog box uses "mover" windows to add design elements to the report list; note the drop-down list of available elements.

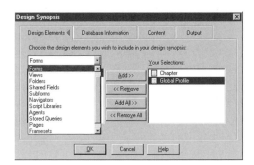

In Figure 16.3, two Form design objects are chosen. In similar fashion, you can continue on to the next class of design objects and make additional selections. Figure 16.4 illustrates the "mix and match" approach Lotus has taken to this new implementation of the Synopsis. This concept extends throughout the remaining tabs.

FIGURE 16.4

You can choose any number of design objects of any type and include them in the Synopsis; each type has a different graphic associated with it.

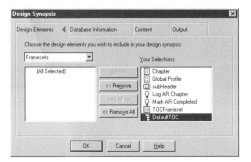

When you complete your selection of design objects, you can move to the next tab.

Using the Database Information Tab

As stated previously, the items on this tab were available in earlier releases. Figure 16.5 shows the Database Information tab. There are only four checkboxes:

- General Information
- Space Usage
- Replication
- Access List

FIGURE 16.5

This tab adds database level information to the Synopsis.

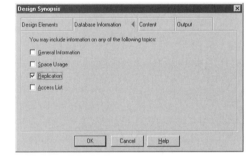

General Information includes items such as path, filename, creation, and modification dates. Space Usage includes file size, number of documents, and information about the white space in the database. Replication is essentially a rehash of the Replication settings of the database, and the Access List is exactly that—a text representation of the ACL. All this information is also available from the Database Properties dialog box, the Replication Settings dialog box, and the Access Control List. However, here you can produce and store this information as a snapshot of the database at a specific moment in time. Although it might not be quite so useful as a listing of the agents, it is useful as a point of reference.

Using the Content Tab

Now *this* is where the fireworks start! Never has there been this level of detail or control over what is produced in the Synopsis. For each design-object type, you can select from a list of specific object properties to include in the Synopsis. Lotus has exposed all the properties for each of the design objects. All the line items are selected by default; if you want to limit what is produced in the report, you will have to deselect specific items.

Using the Deselect All Button

If you want to see only a very limited amount of information, click the Deselect All button under the Line Items window, and then choose the items you want to see (see Figure 16.6).

Notice the checkboxes to the right of Figure 16.6? In earlier releases, you could not get at the LotusScript code in forms and fields. Now you can! You can also get information on JavaScript and Java code. If checked, fields and similar objects appear in the Synopsis.

The line items for each design object are the same properties that are available from the Design Properties boxes and the design interface. For example, Figure 16.6 shows properties for forms that include Alias, Type, Last Modification, Include in Compose Menu, and Include in Query by Form—all of which are available by opening the Forms Properties box. The remaining item that is visible in that figure is Window Title, which is available from the design interface. Of course, there are many more properties of each form available than are visible in the figure, and not all the design objects have quite as many line items available. Contrast the extensive list of items available for Forms with that available for Framesets shown in Figure 16.7.

FIGURE 16.6

The Content Tab showing the drop-down list of design objects; the Forms line items list is fairly extensive.

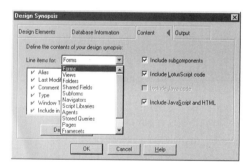

FIGURE 16.7

In contrast to the Forms list, the options under the Framesets design object list are fairly limited.

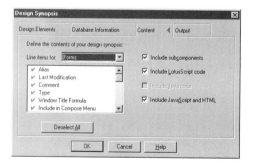

Although you might think that you'll never find a reason to limit the information on the object properties for each element, there are times when you might simply want a listing of the fields on a given form. To accomplish this, click the Deselect All button for the Forms object, and then click Alias. (You don't actually have to click Alias, but if you don't, you won't have any form name attached to the resulting list of fields.) Next, uncheck the checkboxes for LotusScript, JavaScript, and Java. Specify where you want the output to go (covered in the next section), and click OK. You will get a nice output consisting of only the name of the form and the fields on the form. Be sure not to deselect the Subcomponents checkbox, otherwise you will not get a report on the fields.

Using the Output Tab

The Output tab is pretty straightforward, and the items on it are completely new to Release 5. Now you can control how each element is separated and where the output goes. There are two choices for separators, as shown in Figure 16.8: Blank line and Page break. By default, the report goes to the screen in a non-modal tabbed window as in previous releases.

FIGURE 16.8

The Output tab has settings for the report separator and a Write Output to Database checkbox.

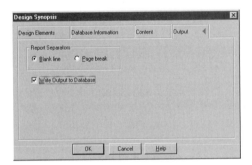

A big improvement is the Write Output to Database checkbox! If you click this checkbox, Domino creates a document based on your choices on the preceding three tabs, and stores the results in a database of your choice. Figure 16.9 shows the dialog box that you'll see when you check Write Output to Database and then click OK. As you can see from Figure 16.9, you can pick a server (including local, of course), choose a title, change the result database filename, and elect to append or overwrite the contents of an existing results database.

FIGURE 16.9

*The Results
Database dialog
box enables you to
choose what hap-
pens when the
Synopsis is written
to a database.*

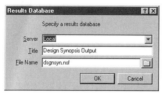

The results database is based on the template file titled "Design Synopsis Template" with
a filename of dsgnsyn.ntf. This database consists of a single form and view, both of
which are very simple. The form contains fields for the database filename, the server on
which it was created, the date of creation, and a field named Body that contains the actual document itself. The view simply displays the date, server, and database filename.

No Page Breaks?

Unfortunately, using the Page Break separator does not produce separate documents in the results database. One lengthy document is produced with page
breaks at the end of the report on each element.

Using the Design Synopsis

The Design Synopsis dialog box is like a wizard dialog box in which you sequentially
step through each tab and make selections. When you're satisfied with your selections,
click OK, and the report is produced using the current selections. If you need a quick look
at a database design object, or just want some quick general information about the database, you can select the items to include, and direct output to the screen. The settings in
the dialog box are not persistent, and the dialog box always opens to the default settings.

Often, you need to use the Replica ID for a particular database. For example, you might
construct a formula such as @DbLookup() and want to use the Replica ID. The Design
Synopsis is a quick and convenient way of obtaining the ID without looking at the
Database Properties box and typing that huge hexadecimal string! To get the Replica ID,
click Replication on the Database Information tab, and click OK (see Figure 16.10).
Then you can highlight the Replica ID and copy it to the clipboard. Now you're able to
paste it wherever you need it in your application. See Figure 16.10.

FIGURE **16.10**

*The Replication
Information cap-
tured to the screen
enables you to
easily copy the
Replica ID to the
clipboard.*

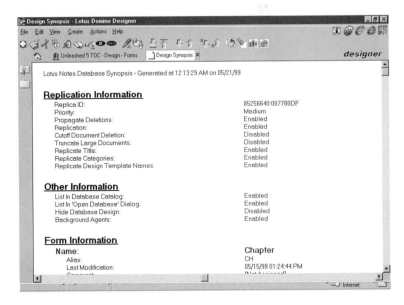

If you want to do a quick search for some specific piece of information, you can direct
output to the screen and then use the Find dialog box to locate instances of that information. Perhaps you need to know where @DbLookup() is being used in a given form.
Sending the results to the screen and using Find to look for occurrences of DbLookup
enables you to locate successive occurrences of the @Function in the form. This is definitely better than laboriously navigating through the field and form-level events of a form
in design, especially if the form has a significant number of fields!

You can also use the Design Synopsis to create historical documentation of application
designs because you can successively append the Design Synopsis to the same database.
To accomplish this, select Append to This Database in the Results Database dialog box,
making sure to select the correct results database. Each time, a new dated document
appears in the results database, as shown in Figure 16.11. Extending this technique to
other databases, you can build a library of application synopses.

When you have created a persistent record of the design of an application, you can use it
as a starting point for technical documentation. It can be as detailed as you need it to be,
as you have seen in the preceding sections. You can copy or export the document into
another format such as Lotus WordPro, or even copy it into another Domino database to
produce documentation that meets your needs or company standards.

FIGURE 16.11

A results database can show Design Synopsis documents from two different databases.

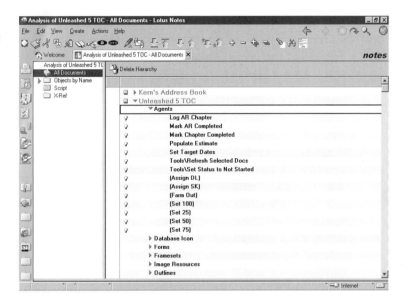

Because the results database is just like any other Domino database, you can full-text index it for more sophisticated searching. This might be useful if you have created a library of application synopses as described in the section titled "Using the Output Tab." For example, you might remember that you used an action button to look up department information in a common lookup database. You can full-text search your application synopsis library for words or phrases that will help you locate the code for the action button. When found, the formula can be copied to the clipboard, and pasted into your new application.

It is this last scenario that illustrates another limitation to the approach that Lotus has taken with the Design Synopsis tool. There is no granularity to the output. Everything is dumped into one gigantic document. Even though you can save it to a database, it is still huge. For a significant database application that can consist of dozens of design objects, this single document is unmanageable. There is no separation of design objects other than the separator you picked in the Output tab. As an alternative, you can use LotusScript to access the design objects, and generate a Design Synopsis that produces a more granular report. You can create a single document for each design object, for example.

TeamStudio Analyzer

Far simpler (and ultimately less expensive) is to purchase a third-party tool called TeamStudio Analyzer, which is a part of the TeamStudio Design System from Ives Development. As one Lotusphere attendee put it "Don't leave home without it!"

The granularity that is not present in results databases produced by the Domino Design Synopsis is present in databases created by Ives TeamStudio Analyzer. Each design element is stored in its own document, and all the objects are stored in what Ives calls a *hierarchy*. You can store multiple database analyses in the same database, and each will occupy its own hierarchy. You can also update the analysis of a database that is already stored in the results database! The tool is simple to install, set up, and run. A sample output database (Analysis.nsf) is available on the CD that accompanies this book. It gives you an idea of just how powerful this tool can be.

On the CD...

A Screen Cam supplied by Ives is also on the CD that you can run. It will show you how Analyzer works. The filename is Analyze1.exe.

Installing Analyzer

To installAnalyzer, copy Install.nsf from the TeamStudio CD that you'll receive when you purchase Analyzer. Make sure that the Read only attribute is turned off, and open the database in the Domino Designer. After you read the copyright document and click the Next button, the TeamStudio Design System Installation document appears. Check TeamStudio Analyzer, and leave the remaining settings as they are. Click the Install button. You have to restart Domino Designer to complete installation. See Figure 16.12.

FIGURE 16.12

Installing TeamStudio Analyzer is very simple.

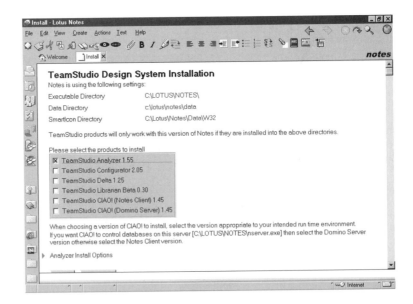

When Domino Designer is restarted, you will notice a new SmartIcon in the toolbar. Figure 16.13 shows the SmartIcon.

FIGURE **16.13**

The TeamStudio Analyzer SmartIcon is loaded automatically by the installation process.

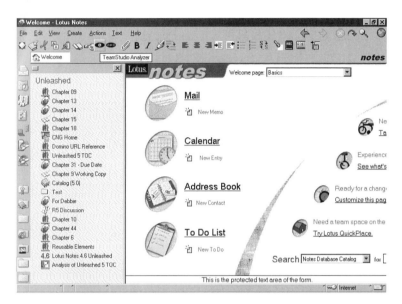

Running Analyzer

Running TeamStudio Analyzer couldn't be simpler. To use Analyzer, select a database and click the SmartIcon. The first time you do this, you are prompted to supply your serial number and activation key to unlock the application. Subsequently, you will not need to reenter the code. The next window is similar to the Results Database dialog box for the Design Synopsis tool. It enables you to choose a server and a database. Clicking the Select button lets you locate an analysis database (see Figure 16.14). The subsequent window enables you to name the output database. The default title is "Analysis of *database title*." Figure 16.15 shows the output database with the hierarchy expanded.

FIGURE **16.14**

This Analyzer window enables you to pick the server and filename for the output database.

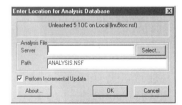

FIGURE **16.15**

*The output data-
base with the hier-
archy expanded
includes the cate-
gories for the
design objects.*

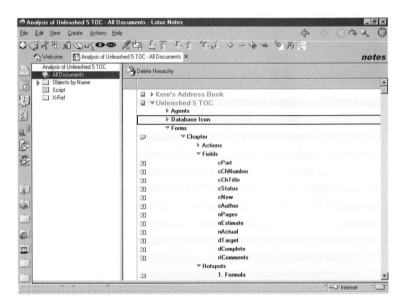

As you can see in Figure 16.14, unlike the Domino Design Synopsis tool, Analyzer offers no opportunity to define the properties of the database or design objects that end up in the report. However, because Analyzer creates database documents for each design object, each class of design object has its own view.

Working with the Output Database

Figure 16.15 shows the granularity of the output database quite clearly. In contrast to the Design Synopsis that produces a single document for an entire database, you can see how TeamStudio Analyzer has produced a document for each design element. This has some significant advantages and some very practical applications, which include the following:

- You can full-text index the analysis database, and search for a specific agent or field and locate all references to it, no matter where they are: in a form, an action button, a field, and so on.

- The analysis database can serve as a very thorough and complete documentation of your application.

- Because you can include multiple applications in a single output database, if you have a suite of databases that work together, you can include them all in the same output database. When you full-text search the database, you can locate instances of the search item in any of the databases.

- Each design element has its own category. Note that in Figure 16.15, the Fields category for a specific form is expanded, listing all the fields for that form.

- Additional views further expose each design type (see Figure 16.16).

FIGURE 16.16

The Output data-base has views for each database design element, including Script.

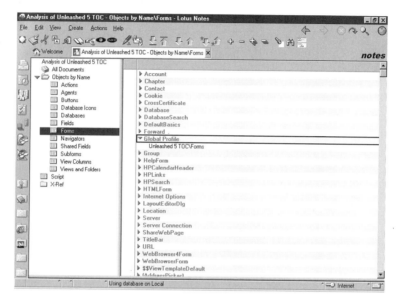

- You can use this database as an aid to enforcing design standards. For example, you can check the fields list and make sure that the field names meet your conventions.

- By going through the list of design elements, you can quickly build a list of features to be tested during acceptance testing.

- By searching for specific names of items in this database, you can decommission design elements that are no longer used easily.

In many ways, this is just the tip of the iceberg for this rich design tool. As you work with it yourself, you will find many more ways to take advantage of the wealth of information stored in the database.

To illustrate how useful this level of granularity can be, consider the following real-life scenario. A very complex, large-scale Domino application had literally dozens of forms and thousands of fields. When deployed to a remote workstation, the application crashed. The offending code could have literally been in any one of the many forms and any one of the fields or Actions. It would have taken hours or perhaps even days to locate this problem. Using Analyzer, the problem was quickly located in less than 15 minutes by searching a full text index. In less than an hour, the problem was fixed. Because of the level of detail, and because Analyzer stores each design element in its own document, when searching the database, specific design elements could be located easily. This alone was ample return on the investment in Analyzer.

Using the Views and Forms in the Output Database

As indicated in the previous section, there are many views available. The view tree is exposed in Figure 16.16. You will quickly note that each design object appears in the main hierarchy and appears in its own view. Each object type has its own form as well. Figure 16.17 shows a document for the Chapter form. You can see that there is a wealth of information available, and that it is easy to read. One particularly nice feature is the list of field names in the middle of the document.

Figure 16.17

The Form Design document uses collapsible sections to organize information.

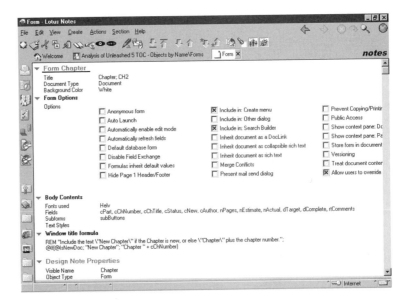

Tweaking Analyzer

Because the analysis database created when you run Analyzer is a Domino database, you can alter the design. You can add new views, forms, agents, and other design objects. Adding a view is a relatively safe and harmless modification because all you are doing is presenting the documents differently.

Adding forms is another matter. You can add forms, but they will not be automatically populated by the Analyzer program. However, you can modify existing forms to change the way they are formatted or how data is presented to suit your needs. You can also create a form to be used when printing or viewing Analyzer documents. This form can be used in a Form Override when printing or in a form formula for a special view.

> **Caution**
>
> Ives recommends that if you do modify the forms and add fields for data entry that you do so only to the design note form types. Examples of design note form types are forms, subforms, navigators, and so on. The Field form also persists, but the remaining subsidiary form types such as Actions and Hotspots are overwritten during a refresh of the output database. Any data you might have added to the subsidiary documents will be lost.

If you do make changes that you want to be permanent, you should make them in Analyzer's output database template. The template name is `IvesDean.ntf`. If you modify the design of this database, each new analysis will use your own design. Make sure that you make a new copy—not a replica copy—of the template and use the same filename. Using a copy ensures that the database template is not accidentally overwritten during replication.

The documentation that ships with TeamStudio Analyzer has several excellent ideas for design modifications. One example is used to locate missing field help by creating a special view restricting the documents to editable fields with blank field help text. Others involve agents to aid testing.

It is also possible to launch Analyzer using LotusScript in an agent. A sample script is included in the documentation accompanying Analyzer, and so is not reproduced here.

A Final Word About TeamStudio Analyzer

Hopefully, this brief look at Analyzer has demonstrated why you shouldn't "leave home without it!" You have seen how detailed the output database is, and how you can work with the database to quickly locate design elements.

There are other tools that come in the TeamStudio suite:

- Configurator—This is a global search and replace tool for database design objects.
- Delta—Delta compares two different versions of a database, and finds the differences between them.

- Librarian—This tool enables a team of developers to work on the same database and not overwrite each other's work by providing version control and check in and check out of database design objects. This is a design library application for developers incorporating repositories for design objects and data dictionaries.

Contacting Ives Development

In North and South America:

Ives Development, Inc., 900 Cummings Center, Suite 326T, Beverly, MA 01915

Tel: 978-232-0145

Fax: 978-232-0146

In the rest of the world:

Ives Development Ltd., PO Box 45, Huntingdon PE17 2NB, UK

Tel: +44 1487 772200

Fax: +44 1487 772211

You can also locate them on the Web at `www.teamstudio.com`.

Summary

It is obviously very important to be able to generate information about the design of your database applications. This chapter has covered two methods of analyzing databases: the native Design Synopsis tool, and a third-party tool, Ives TeamStudio Analyzer. The choice is yours, and this chapter provides you with enough information about each approach to enable you to make an informed decision. This chapter also covered ways to use both analysis tools to make your documentation, research, and debugging easier.

Domino Programming Languages

PART

III

IN THIS PART

Choosing the Right Language

by Debbie Lynd

There are quite a few decisions to make when developing an application. With Domino the decisions include which language you should use. A simple Domino application might use only the Formula language and nothing else. However, an application of any complexity will require additional language considerations. This chapter covers those considerations and provides insight into where each language is most appropriately used.

Within Domino Designer you have at least five language choices. These include the following:

- Simple Actions
- The Formula language
- LotusScript
- JavaScript
- Java
- HTML

These options are pretty awesome when you think about them. What can't be accomplished with one language can usually be done with another. The problem is deciding which to use in specific situations. Actually, Domino makes some of that pretty easy by allowing only certain options for specific events. I'll start each section of this chapter with the areas where you have no choice and then explain what the choices are and how you should decide. But, before I explore the objects and their associated events, it is helpful to know which programming options will be compared.

Comparing the Available Languages in Domino

When determining which language to use, the first thing that must be established is which options you should consider. When programming in Domino, the programmer has the following options:

- Simple actions
- Formula language
- LotusScript
- JavaScript
- Java

Because HTML can be placed almost anywhere and serves a purpose that is not in conflict with the other options, comparisons to it will not be made. For instance, if I need to use HTML for setting a particular header value, I will use it; there really is no other option.

JavaScript can be used anywhere that HTML can be used, which is in forms, views, pages, and fields; and also has many new events of its own. With Release 5, JavaScript becomes pervasive throughout the product, with the ability to manipulate the front end far more effectively than even the Formula language can for a browser client.

Java, on the other hand, is available only in agents and can address only the back-end Notes classes. Java does, however, look like a contender for replacing LotusScript as soon as it reaches LotusScript's maturity in its ability to reach out to all the Domino Objects and their properties, methods, and events.

Coding for Browser Clients

Web browsers are not aware of the Formula language or LotusScript. Therefore, any requests from formulas or LotusScript must be processed in the back end by the Domino server. On the other hand, JavaScript can be processed at the browser.

Events

When you are considering writing code, in many cases you will be writing to an event. However, there are a few places where you can use formulas that are not events and I cover these as well. When you select an event to which to write, you will see in the event viewer that the event will be prefixed with an icon that indicates the primary language used for that event. I say *primary* because there are many events that have multiple languages available, but the primary language is what normally appears there. The icons and their associated values are listed in Table 17.1.

TABLE 17.1   Event Viewer - Language Icons

Icon	*Language*
diamond.gif	Formula language
Lscroll.gif	JavaScript
square.gif	LotusScript (Options or Declarations)
Rscroll.gif	LotusScript

Throughout this chapter, each of the specified languages are explained in context of how they are used (events, properties, or methods), but also where they are used (objects). Where appropriate, comparisons are made between languages.

Using Simple Actions

Simple actions are built-in functions that perform specific tasks. They are available in action buttons, agents, buttons, and hotspots. You'll find that you can create action buttons in views, folders, forms, and subforms. Buttons and hotspots are available in forms, subforms, pages, and navigators. You can perform quite a few tasks with simple actions that would otherwise require lots of code. There is, however, one drawback to using simple actions: They do not translate to the Web. Therefore, unless you are creating a Notes-only application, you will have to use the coding methods available to achieve the simple action results.

Caution

Simple actions do not translate to the Web. Therefore, avoid using them in any application that can be accessed from a Web browser.

Table 17.2 shows a list of tasks that simple actions are available to perform.

TABLE 17.2   Simple Actions

Action	*Description*
Copy to Database	Copies selected documents to a different database
Copy to Folder	Copies selected documents to a named folder
Delete from Database	Deletes selected documents from a database
Mark Document Unread	Marks selected documents as unread
Mark Document Read	Marks selected documents as read
Modify Field	Changes the value of a field in selected documents
Modify Fields by Form	Using the fields available from a particular form, changes the value of a field in selected documents
Move to Folder	Removes selected documents from the current folder and places them in another named folder
Remove from Folder	Removes selected documents for the current folder

Action	Description
Reply to Sender	Initiates the creation of a reply to the sender of the current document
Run Agent	Invokes the running of a named agent
Send Document	Creates a new memo document with a copy of the current document embedded
Send Mail Message	Creates a new memo document
Send Newsletter Summary	Creates a memo with a newsletter summary embedded
@Function Formula	Provides the addition of an @Function formula within a simple action

Using Formulas

The Formula language in Domino provides a quick way to write customized expressions that perform actions from within events. For instance, if I want to create a button that displays a message when clicked, I write a formula in the `click` event.

The places where you can use formulas are actually pretty easy to define. Formula access is pretty much centered around the UI, otherwise known as the front end of Domino. If you examine the design elements, it is pretty easy to point out the places where formulas are used because they all have to do with events.

There are quite a few places where only formulas will work and so no other option is available. The objects that will accept formulas and the events for each are described in Tables 17.3 through 17.8.

TABLE 17.3 Pages

Event	Description
	Window Title
HTMLHeadContent	Combines HTML with formulas in order to provide conditional processing
HTMLBodyAttributes	Combines HTML with formulas in order to provide conditional processing
WebQueryOpen	Executes an agent through an @Command function
WebQuerySave	Executes an agent through an @Command function
OnHelpRequest	Opens the page or document specified, when F1 is selected

continues

TABLE 17.3   continued

Event	Description
	Window Title
ImageResource	Opens the specified image from the shared image resources
Hide Paragraph	Hides the paragraph based on a condition
Section Hide When	Hides a section based on a condition

TABLE 17.4   Outline

Event	Description
Outline Entry	Value property that allows you to write a conditional statement to determine what the outline entry will do when it is selected
Label	The label placed on the Outline entry, which can be a conditional statement
Source	The source of the outline entry, which can be a conditional statement
Frame	The frame for the entry when selected, which can be a conditional statement
Image	The image placed on the outline entry, which can be a conditional statement
HideWhen	A formula that determines when the outline entry is hidden or visible

TABLE 17.5   Fields

Event	Description
Default Value formula	When a document is first created, a formula in the default value event is evaluated.
Input Translation formula	When a document is refreshed or saved, a formula in this event will be evaluated.
Input Validation formula	When a document is refreshed or saved, a formula in this event is evaluated.
Computed formula	The formula is evaluated when the document is refreshed or saved.
Computed when Composed	The formula is only evaluated when the document is first created.

Event	Description
Computed for Display	The formula is computed whenever the document is opened.
Keyword Field formulas	Evaluates and returns a list to the user whenever the document is opened.
Hide-When formulas	Evaluated when the document is opened.

TABLE 17.6   Views and Folders

Event	Description
Selection formula	Determines which documents are displayed in the view
Column formula	Determines which values are displayed in the column
Form formula	Determines which form displays the documents in the view

TABLE 17.7   Forms and Subforms

Event	Description
Window Title	Displays in the title bar for a document
Web Query Open	Executes an agent when the document is opened on the Web
Web Query Save	Executes an agent when the document is saved from the Web
Section Title	Displays in the title of a section on a document
Section Access	Determines who can access a section in a document
Insert Subform	Determines which subform should be displayed based on a condition
Hide Paragraph	Hides the contents of a paragraph based on a condition
Hide/Show Action	Hides or displays an action based on a condition
Image Resource	When an image is added to a form or page, determines when it should be displayed or hidden

TABLE 17.8   Framesets

Event	Description
Frame Value Property	Determines what should be displayed on a frame based on a condition

Using LotusScript

LotusScript provides more than the Formula language in that it gives you the ability to write sophisticated scripts that include branching, looping, and subroutines. LotusScript is written to run based on an event just like formulas are; however, LotusScript can affect far more than the Formula language can. When writing code in LotusScript, I can work in the back end—away from the UI—and manipulate the properties and execute the methods of all the Domino objects, not simply those objects that are currently available to the user. (Details about how to use LotusScript in Domino are provided in Chapters 22, "Introduction to LotusScript;" 23, "Basic LotusScript;" and 24, "Writing LotusScript.")

LotusScript can be written for all objects. The events that are available only for LotusScript are described in Tables 17.9 and 17.10.

TABLE 17.9 Events Available for All Objects

Event	Description
Initialize	Executes when the object is loaded
Terminate	Executes when the object is closed

TABLE 17.10 Fields

Event	Description
Entering	When the user enters a field in edit mode
Exiting	When the user exits a field in edit mode

LotusScript Versus Formulas

When deciding whether to use LotusScript or formulas, it is generally better to use a formula whenever available because the Formula language has been optimized for Domino and usually performs more quickly. The Formula language also usually requires fewer lines of code to accomplish a given task.

So if that's true, why use LotusScript? Well, there are some advantages to using LotusScript over the Formula language. For instance, the Formula language does not possess a way of performing iteration or branching, work with external databases via ODBC, or perform I/O functions.

Following are activities for which the Formula language cannot be used and for which LotusScript is ideal:

- Work with multivalue fields to provide processing of each of the elements in the field
- Make changes to a group of documents based on a user-initiated change to another document
- Attach or import files from the file system into documents based on a condition
- Create new functions and subroutines
- Work with a Domino database without knowing the name of the database
- Modify an ACL
- Manipulate rich-text fields
- Create or delete a database
- Write to the enter and exit field events

The following sections provide some insight into where you might use formulas or LotusScript. I also cover a few places where it is better to use a simple action over both.

Database

The Formula language can actually be used with some of the database events. The usual code for these events is LotusScript. You might think that you can use the Formula language for any of the database events, but, sure enough, if you look at the Database Script option by choosing Resources, Other, Database Script from the menu, you'll find plenty of events where you can place formulas. These are the following:

- `QueryOpen`
- `Postopen`
- `Postdocumentdelete`
- `Queryclose`
- `Querydocumentdelete`
- `Querydocumentundelete`
- `Querydragdrop`
- `Postdragdrop`

Are all these events practical places for formulas just because you can put them there? Not necessarily. To use a formula in a specific event, you first have to think about what occurs during the event and how a formula in that event operates. Some ugly things can happen with formulas stuck in the wrong events. For instance, I wouldn't place the formula from Listing 17.1 into a QueryOpen event because I want a value returned to a field and the field does not exist for a document during QueryOpen. It's not until I get to the PostOpen event that a document is actually available. However, I might place the code in Listing 17.1 in the PostOpen event.

LISTING 17.1   Using an @Prompt Function to Accept Data into a Field

```
@command(EditDocument;1);
FIELD BusinessUnit := @Prompt([okcancellist];"Business Unit";
➥"Select a Business Unit";"";"Repair";Sales";"Manufacturing")
```

Outlines

There are no events in outlines that allow LotusScript to be used. There are, however, hooks to outlines through the following classes:

- NotesOutline
- NotesOutlineEntry

Through these classes, you can use LotusScript to manipulate the entries in an outline by adding, changing, and removing entries. The Formula language cannot be used to manipulate. This is all done in the back end and can be practical in providing customization of an outline based on a specified condition.

Forms and Pages

When opening a form or a page, specific events occur. The following events are shown in the order in which they are executed. Each event accepts both LotusScript and formulas. Most often, LotusScript is used for these events; in some instances, however, the Formula language will do the trick. For instance, if I want to display a message to a user when she opens the document, I can write a formula for the QueryOpen event to do so. In the PostOpen event I can actually write formulas that will populate fields.

- QueryOpen
- PostOpen
- QueryModeChange
- PostModeChange
- PostRecalc
- QuerySave

- PostSave

- QueryClose

Views

View events are available for both LotusScript and the Formula language; however, LotusScript is far more practical because the events are optimized for LotusScript. I can do very little with the Formula language—displaying a message to the user is about it.

- QueryOpen

- PostOpen

- RegionDoubleClick

- QueryOpenDocument

- QueryRecalc

- Queryaddtofolder

- Querypaste

- Postpaste

- Querydragdrop

- Postdragdrop

- Queryclose

However, with script I can do far more. For instance, I could place a script in the QueryOpen event that queries the user for a particular category he is interested in, looks in the view for that category, and returns an error message to the user if the category is not found or displays the category if it does.

Fields

Actually, there are no options for the events provided for fields. They either use Formulas or LotusScript. However, there are some interesting ways to get around the inability to use formulas in the entering or exiting events. For instance, say that I want to have a formula evaluated when the user exits a field. Now, I know that there is an Exiting event available only to LotusScript. However, using LotusScript and the Evaluate statement, I can have the evaluate statement execute a one-line formula, or have it run an agent that executes a multiline formula.

To give you an idea of what I mean, the code in Listing 17.2 runs an agent whose name is defined by the user picking from a keyword list in the current field. When the user exits the field, the agent is kicked off by the Evaluate statement in the Exiting event. The agent then contains the formula that I want to run.

> **Caution**
>
> The Exiting event will not be evaluated by any client other than a Notes client because it runs LotusScript. As stated earlier in the chapter, Web browsers do not know what LotusScript is, so it is ignored by all events that are processed in the UI.

LISTING 17.2 Exiting Event and Execute Statement

```
Sub Entering(Source As Field)
Dim Session as New NotesSession
Dim db as NotesDatabase
Dim Agent as NotesAgent
Set db = session.currentdatabase
Set Agent = db.GetAgent(Source)
If Not(Agent is Nothing) Then
Call Agent.Run
Else
Messagebox "Agent cannot be run. Call the helpdesk"
End If
End Sub
```

One thing to note is that the Evaluate statement cannot be used with any @Function that is designed to run in the UI or front end. Table 17.11 lists these functions. However, keep in mind that some of these functions can run from an agent, and the agent can be called from the Evaluate statement.

TABLE 17.11 @Functions That Cannot Be Used with Evaluate

Function
All @Command functions
@DbLookup
@DbColumn
@DDEInitiate
@DDETerminate
@DDEExecute
@DDEPoke
@MailSend
@Prompt
@PickList
@Dialogbox

If I want to do the same thing with a Web client, I have to use a different event. An example of this is included in the section of this chapter titled "Using JavaScript."

Agents

Agents can be written using formulas or LotusScript. The question as to whether to use one over the other definitely depends on the purpose of the agent. For instance, if I need to run branching or looping, I would write a script because the Formula language cannot do that well.

There are times however, when you can use either a formula or LotusScript to perform the same activity. For instance, if I need an agent that will update documents in a database, whether I use the Formula language or LotusScript depends on the number of documents that I will update and whether or not I need to loop through the documents more than once. This would require LotusScript. If I am updating every document in the database, it would be faster with the Formula language.

Framesets

There are no events for framesets. There are no classes available for frames either.

Using JavaScript

As mentioned earlier, JavaScript can be embedded in HTML and can also be used in many of the events available in Domino objects. Use JavaScript when you code for both Notes clients and browser clients. In Release 5 the Notes client can translate the JavaScript, but the browser clients cannot evaluate formulas and LotusScript. The events shown in the following list are available to JavaScript for forms, pages, and subforms:

- OnBlur
- OnClick
- OnDblClick
- OnFocus
- OnHelp
- OnKeyDown
- OnKeyPress
- OnKeyUp
- OnLoad
- OnMouseDown

- OnMouseMove
- OnMouseOut
- OnMouseOver
- OnMouseUp

JavaScript can also be used in fields and hotspots. (JavaScript is covered in more detail in Chapters 25, "Introduction to JavaScript."

Using JavaScript or LotusScript

How do you know whether to use JavaScript as opposed to LotusScript? Well, for the time being, JavaScript has a more limited use than LotusScript, in that it can only be attributed to the active UI events that a Web client would initiate through the associated events. LotusScript, on the other hand, provides the ability to reach through to the back-end classes, however, only through an agent on the Web. So if I were writing a Web application, I would use JavaScript to handle the UI events from the Web browser, and either a LotusScript or a Java agent to handle the back end through an agent. Table 17.12 includes the JavaScript events available in Release 5.

TABLE 17.12 JavaScript Events

Event	Forms and Pages	Subforms	Fields and Hotspots
JSHeader	X		X
onReset	X		
onSubmit	X (forms only)		
onUnLoad	X		
onClick		X	X
onBlur		X	X
onChange			X
onFocus		X	X

Whether to use the Formula language or JavaScript is another story. If you look at the objects and events that can be compared, there are very few places where they cross over. They are listed in Tables 17.13 and 17.14.

TABLE 17.13   Forms and Pages

Formulas	*JavaScript*
QueryOpen	onLoad
QueryClose	onUnload

Formulas or LotusScript?

Although QueryOpen and QueryClose accept formulas, they have limited functionality in the Formula language. JavaScript provides far more functionality and should be used instead of the Formula language.

TABLE 17.14   Fields

Formulas	*JavaScript*
InputTranslation	onChange
Input Validation	onChange

Evaluating Events

As mentioned earlier in this chapter, events that are strictly used for LotusScript are not evaluated by Web browsers other than the Notes client. Therefore, I can't use the Exiting event to trigger a process from a Web browser. However, I can use a JavaScript event to provide the ability to execute code based on the change of data in a field, which is usually what I am looking to do with the Exiting event. Although there is no Evaluate function in JavaScript, I have the capability in JavaScript of using the onChange event to execute the appropriate JavaScript to evaluate the validity of the data entered. This would be similar to using an Input Validation formula using the Formula language with one difference. The difference is that the Input Validation formula cannot execute until the user saves or submits the form, where the JavaScript can be executed immediately after the data is changed. An example of this is shown in Listing 17.3.

LISTING 17.3   JavaScript in onChange Field Event

```
// this code would go in the JSHeader event of the form

var NewForm
function ValidateField
```

continues

LISTING 17.3 continued

```
{
if(NewForm.FullName.value=="")
{
        alert("You must enter a name to continue!");
        NewForm.FullName.focus;
    }
}


//The following code would go in the onChange event for the field

ValidateField()
```

Field translation is another example of using either JavaScript or the Formula language based on when the change should take place. If the translation does not need to take place until the form is submitted, an Input Translation formula is fine. If the translation should take place prior to submission, JavaScript will do the trick. An example of this is shown in Listing 17.4. In the listing, the form used is called NewForm and the field name is FullName.

LISTING 17.4 JavaScript for Input Translation in onChange Event

```
//This code is placed in the JSHeader event of the NewForm form

var NewForm
function upperMe
{
    inputStr = NewForm.FullName.value;
    NewForm.FullName.value = inputStr.toUpperCase();
}


//This code is placed in the FullName field onChange event

upperMe()
```

Using Java

In Release 5, Java is used in Agents and can access many of the back-end classes of Domino objects. There are no events that Java can use because it does not have access to the UI, but JavaScript takes care of most of that side of things. Should you write your agents in LotusScript or Java? With performance aside, if it can be coded in either Java or LotusScript, use Java. It is more widely supported in the non-Domino world, provides both Core Java classes and Notes Java classes, supports CORBA through the `notes.noi` classes, and will be expanded in future releases of Domino Designer. Okay, with that said, is there anything you can accomplish with LotusScript that you can't accomplish with Java? There are classes that LotusScript can access and Java cannot. These classes are, for the most part, those that have to do with the UI, but in addition, LotusScript has more classes available for handling rich-text items, views, and outlines.

Using HTML

It is not quite so obvious where HTML can be used because it can be embedded in forms, documents, fields, views, columns, and agents, but in an attempt to cover the bases, I list the objects where HTML can be used in Table 17.15. Many of the places where HTML is used are not actually events at all but are properties of an object or of placing the HTML directly into a form or page. It's also worth mentioning that HTML is not a replacement for any of the other languages, but is auxiliary to the other options available. (Chapter 21, "Enhancing Domino Applications with HTML," covers HTML in detail.)

Keep in mind that HTML can also be embedded in JavaScript. A comparison will not be made with HTML because it is used in tandem with the other languages available in Domino.

TABLE 17.15   HTML Usage

Elements	Usage
Forms and Pages	Pass-Thru HTML
	Treat document contents as HTML (Property)
Views	Treat View contents as HTML (Property)
	Columns formulas
Fields	HTML Attributes
	HTML Field Name - Field Contents

Summary

Which language you should use is largely up to you. However, this chapter explained the events that you can code and some of the ways with which you can determine which language you will use.

The Formula Language

by Steve Kern

The Formula language has been around since the inception of Lotus Notes. In some respects, it is an offshoot of Lotus 1-2-3, which, if you'll recall, is loaded with commands prefaced with the @ symbol. The Formula language has three primary constructs—@Functions, @Commands, and five keywords. Although you can program Domino Applications in other languages, there are a number of locations in which you can use only the Formula language.

- About @Functions and how to use them
- About @Commands and how to use them
- About Formula Syntax
- Where to use the Formula language
- About limitations to the Formula language

Overview of the Formula Language

As the name implies, the Formula language constructs formulas. Formulas can range from the extremely simple to the extraordinarily complex (for example, a formula using nested @If() and @Do() commands). Although it may appear to consist of multiple lines, a formula in Lotus Notes equates to a single line of code in a program. Formulas do not iteratively process documents or values. Even an Agent running on all documents can make only one pass through each document that meets the selection criteria. In other words, there is no looping capability equivalent to that built into procedural languages with commands such as Do While or Do Until. Similarly, you can't call one formula from another—there is no branching except within the same formula. This can be a severe limitation. If you need more power and flexibility than that offered by formulas, you can always turn to LotusScript, JavaScript, or Java. Remember that, in general, a process written in the Formula language executes more quickly than an equivalent process written in LotusScript. Also, it is generally much easier to write a formula than to write an equivalent program in LotusScript or Java. On the other hand, JavaScript functions in both Notes and Web clients. See Chapter 17, "Choosing the Right Language," for further discussion on which language to use.

Understanding @Functions and @Commands

The two principal components of the Formula language, @Functions and @Commands, are used to construct formulas that return a result or perform an action. @Functions always return a result. For example, the formula @Name([CN]; @UserName) returns the common name component of the user's name. @Commands work only in the user interface and are based on menu commands. For example, `@Command([FileCloseWindow])` closes the current window, and `@Command([EditDocument])` opens a document in edit mode. The menu equivalents are File, Close and Actions, Edit. Unlike @Functions, @Commands do not necessarily return a value.

> ### @PostedCommand
>
> Because formulas can be a mixture of @Functions and @Commands, an @Command can be literally placed anywhere in the formula. With some exceptions such as `@Command([FileCloseWindow])`, which always executes last, @Commands execute in the order they are entered in the formula. @PostedCommand is a special variation of @Commands. @PostedCommands executes at the end of the formula, similar to the way @Commands functioned in R3.

Working with @Functions

@Functions have a general syntax as follows: `@Function(arguments)`. Not all @Functions require arguments; some merely return a result, such as `@All`. For example, in a view selection formula, `SELECT @All` returns all documents in the database. The command `@SetField("cStatus"; "New")` has two arguments, the name of the document field `cStatus` and the value. This formula sets the value of the `cStatus` field to `"New"`.

Not all @Functions work in all contexts. For example, `@All` works only in view selection, agent selection, and replication formulas. There are many different types of @Functions, including the following listed in Table 18.1.

TABLE 18.1 Formula Types

Type	*Examples*
Arithmetic	`@Abs, @Integer, @Round, @Modulo`
Client Information	`@BrowserInfo, @ClientType`
Data Retrieval	`@DbColumn, @DbLookup, @DbCommand`
Database Information	`@DbTitle, @DbName, @DbManager`
Date and Time	`@Date, @TextToTime, @Time, @Hour, @Year, @Day`
Document Information	`@DocLength, @Attachments, @DocumentUniqueID`
Document Status	`@IsDocBeingSaved, @IsNewDoc, @IsDocBeingEdited`

continues

18

THE FORMULA
LANGUAGE

TABLE 18.1   continued

Type	Examples
Field Values	`@GetDocField, @SetField, @GetProfileField`
List	`@Member, @Elements, @Subset, @Contains, @Trim, @Implode, @Explode`
Logical	`@True, @False, @Success, @IsTime, @IsNumber`
Mail	`@MailSend, @MailDbName, @MailSavePreference`
String	`@Right, @LeftBack, @MiddleBack`
User Information	`@UserName, @UserRoles, @NameLookup, @UserAccess`
User Input	`@Prompt, @DialogBox, @PickList`

Working with @Commands

@Commands have a syntax that is similar to the syntax for @Functions:
`@Command([keyword]; arguments)`. These commands only work in the user interface.
You can use @Commands in Actions, SmartIcons, buttons, and hotspots. You can also
use them in agents that run against the current document. @Commands cannot be used
in scheduled agents, field formulas, or any object that doesn't interact with the user.

Most menu commands have a corresponding @Command. For example, the corresponding @Command for the menu command File, Close is `@Command([FileCloseWindow])`.
Some @Commands have no corresponding counterpart in the menu, such as `@Command`
`([NavigateNext])` and `@Command([NavigatePrev])`. Still others are a holdover from
previous releases of Notes, such as `@Command([ToolsRefreshSelectedDocs])`. The
Tools menu was a Release 3 feature and there is no corresponding menu in Release 4.x
or Release 5.

For example, you can write the following formula for an action button on a form that
would save and close the document. The formula would not work, however, if placed in
an agent that was scheduled on the server to run unattended at 2 a.m.

```
@Command([FileSave]);
@Command([FileCloseWindow])
```

Because @Commands are based on the UI, they will work in *foreground agents*, agents
which are initiated by the user. Because @Commands are based on the Notes client
menu structure (the user interface), many do not work for Web clients because they are
Notes and Domino specific with no counterpart available in a browser. Quite a few do
work on the Web, however, and are very useful. For example, you can use
`@Command([NavigateNext])` in a form action button to enable the user to move to the
next document. Table 18.2 is a list of @Commands that can be used on the Web.

TABLE 18.2 @Commands Supported on the Web

@Command	Function
CalendarFormat	Switches the calendar display specified
CalendarGoTo	Navigates to the specified date
Compose	Creates a new document based on the form specified
EditClear	Deletes a document
EditDocument	Edits a document
EditInsertFileAttachment	Inserts a file into a rich-text field (Note: use the Edit control instead)
FileCloseWindow	Closes the current document
FileOpenDatabase	Opens a database
FileSave	Saves a document
OpenDocument	Opens a document specified by a UNID, in either read or edit mode
NavigateNext	Navigates to the next document in the view
NaviagtePrev	Navigates to the previous document in the view
NavigateNextMain	Navigates to the next main document in the view
NavigatePrevMain	Navigates to the previous main document in the view
OpenNavigator	Opens a specific navigator
OpenView	Opens a specific view
ToolsRunMacro	Runs an agent
ViewChange	Switches to another view
ViewExpandAll	Expands all twisties in a categorized view
ViewCollapseAll	Collapses all twisties in a categorized view
ViewShowSearchBar	Shows the search bar (on the Web, the search form)
FileOpenDBRepID	Opens a database using the Replica ID

18

THE FORMULA
LANGUAGE

Understanding Side Effects

Certain @Commands and @Functions have what are called *side effects*. A *side effect* is an event that occurs outside the scope of the currently executing formula. An example is opening a different database using @DBLookup() or @DBColumn and retrieving a list of values, or displaying a dialog box with @DialogBox() or @Prompt(). Side effects can be quite useful in formulas when you need user input or to create a keyword based on values stored in a field. You will learn more about using @Functions with side effects in Chapter 19, "Formula Language Basics."

Working with Formula Keywords

Keywords are the third component of the Formula language. Keywords are special functions used in formulas. There are five keywords (by convention, they are capitalized), as shown in Table 18.3.

TABLE 18.3   The Formula Language Keywords

Keyword	Function
DEFAULT	If a field does not exist, DEFAULT creates a temporary instance and assigns a value. If the field does exist, the formula uses the current value of the field.
ENVIRONMENT	Assigns a value to an environmental variable stored in the user's preferences file on the Macintosh or in Notes.ini.
FIELD	Assigns a value to a field, creating the field if it doesn't exist.
REM	Sets any text following as non-executing documentation. The text must be in quotes.
SELECT	Used in View Selection formulas, Replication formulas, and Agents to determine whether the current document is included in the document collection.

Keywords are useful in many situations. By far, the most frequently used are REM and SELECT, followed by FIELD. Less frequently used are DEFAULT and ENVIRONMENT. Keywords must be listed first on a line, unlike @Functions.

Commenting Formulas with REM

REM is used to comment your formula. Its syntax is pretty simple: REM *text enclosed in quotes*. If the comment has either a double or a single quote in it, you must preface the quote with the slash character. The following code fragment illustrates the use of REM with an embedded quoted string:

```
REM "Include the text \"New Chapter\" or \"Chapter\" plus the
➥chapter number.";
@If(@IsNewDoc; "New Chapter"; "Chapter " + cChNumber)
```

You can see more examples of the REM keyword in Listing 18.1.

NOTE

You might have noticed by now that a semicolon is used frequently in formulas. The semicolon separates arguments within a function, and it also separates statements in the formula. The semicolon at the end of the REM statement above separates it from the following @If() statement. Inside the @If() statement, semicolons separate the arguments.

Selecting Documents

The SELECT keyword has one argument: a formula that selects documents. As the name implies, SELECT is used to select documents based on the conditions supplied in the argument. The syntax is SELECT *argument*. @All is a frequently used argument and is the default for a new views and agents. If the result of the argument returns a true value for the document, it will be selected. Other examples include the following:

```
SELECT Form = "Main Topic" ¦ @Alldescendants
SELECT (Form = "Main Topic" & Categories = "Applications
Development") ¦ @AllDescendants
SELECT Form = "CHP" ¦ Form = "TTL"
```

If used as a view selection formula, the first formula displays all documents composed with the Main Topic form, and all response and response-to-response documents. The next formula does the same, except that it restricts the view to Main Topic documents with the Categories field set to "Applications Development." The last example selects documents created using two forms with aliases of "CHP" or "TTL." Although this is a fairly straightforward formula, the arguments can be quite complex. For example, consider the following complex SELECT statement:

```
REM "Normally, notify 2 days in advance. On Friday, notify 3 days in
➥advance.";
REM "On Thursday, notify third shift 4 days in advance";
REM "Restrict and offer withdrawn from view. " ;

SELECT (Form = "NH")) & cWithdrawn != "Offer Withdrawn") &
(
  @If(@Weekday(@Today) = 6;
        dStart <= @Adjust(@Today; 0; 0; 3; 0; 0; 0);
        dStart <= @Adjust(@Today; 0; 0; 2; 0; 0; 0))
    ¦
  @If(@Weekday(@Today) > 5 & cShift = "Third" ;
        dStart <= @Adjust(@Today; 0; 0; 4; 0; 0; 0);
        dStart <= @Adjust(@Today; 0; 0; 2; 0; 0; 0))
)
& dStart >= @Adjust(@Today; 0; 0; -2; 0; 0; 0)
```

This view selection formula displays documents created with the "NH" form where the offer is not withdrawn and applies a fairly complex series of date restrictions based on the day of the week.

Setting Field Values with FIELD and DEFAULT

FIELD and DEFAULT are both similar keywords. DEFAULT takes a bit of getting used to because at first glance, it doesn't make that much sense. The syntax is DEFAULT *variablename* := *value*. You use it in a formula when you want to make sure that *variablename* has a value even if the corresponding field doesn't exist. If the field doesn't exist, *variablename* is assigned *value* for the duration of the formula. Remember that the scope of a formula is limited to the execution of the formula itself! If you want to save the variable to a field, you have to use FIELD or @SetField(). The syntax for FIELD is similar: FIELD *fieldname* := *value*. However, if the field exists, its value is overwritten by *value*. This is an important distinction. Many developers use the following formula to ensure that if the field does not exist, that it is initialized for later use in a formula: FIELD *fieldname* := *fieldname*. For example, consider the following code:

```
FIELD cStatus := cStatus
```

This formula ensures that the field cSubject exists and, if it does, that its value is not altered. You might use DEFAULT if you want to make sure that if the field cStatus did not exist, that it was initialized to New. The FIELD keyword could not accomplish that without using a conditional statement. Compare the following three Listings—18.1, 18.2, and 18.3—which evaluate to the same result:

LISTING 18.1 Using the DEFAULT Keyword to Assign a Value

```
REM "Here is how you would use the DEFAULT Keyword:";
REM "If the field cStatus does not exist, create an instance";
REM "of it and assign New to it. If cStatus does exist,";
REM "use the value of the field.";
DEFAULT cStatus := "New"
```

LISTING 18.2 Using FIELD to Assign a Value

```
REM "Here is how you would use the FIELD keyword to accomplish
REM "the same result:";
REM "The first line initializes the field. If it does not exist, ";
REM "it creates it; if it does exist, it sets the value to itself.";
FIELD cStatus := cStatus;
```

LISTING 18.3 Using FIELD and @If() to Conditionally Assign a Value

```
REM "This line checks the value of the field, and if it is empty";
REM "it sets the value to New. Note that if we used ";
REM "FIELD cStatus = \"New\"; the field would be changed";
REM "regardless of the current value. The third argument for";
REM "@If() sets the value of the cStatus field to itself.";
FIELD cStatus := @If(cStatus = ""; "New"; cStatus)
```

Using the ENVIRONMENT Keyword

The keyword ENVIRONMENT sets an environment variable in Notes.ini (or in the preferences file for the Macintosh). ENVIRONMENT is specific to the machine on which it is used. For example, if you want to keep the last navigator used, you can store it to the environment using a formula such as ENVIRONMENT LastNav := *navigatorname* where *navigatorname* is a text value representing the name or alias of the navigator. The value of the variable can be retrieved using @Environment.

@Function Equivalent

@SetEnvironment is the @Function equivalent of ENVIRONMENT. It is an @Function, and can be embedded anywhere inside a formula, unlike a keyword, which must appear first on a line. @SetEnvironment is perhaps more useful than ENVIRONMENT for this reason.

Caution

ENVIRONMENT does not work on the Web, and neither do the related @Environment or @SetEnvironment commands.

Knowing Where to Use @Functions and @Commands

Many events and objects can have LotusScript, JavaScript, Simple Actions, or Formulas written to them. Generally speaking, if an item only allows a Formula to be written in the Formula language, there is a window in which to construct the formula. An example is a formula for a keyword field. (Using the Formula Window is discussed in the next section, "Working with the Formula Window.") If there are multiple ways to program an event or object, you do so in the script area of the Programmer's pane. Objects which can be programmed with Formula language @Functions and @Commands will have Formula as a choice in the Run drop-down.

18

THE FORMULA
LANGUAGE

For More Information...

The Programmer's pane is discussed in the section titled "Writing Formulas in the Script Area." Chapter 8, "The Integrated Development Environment," also covers working in the Programmer's pane.

The Formula language can be used in Agents, Replication Formulas, Views, Forms, and Fields. Table 18.4 lists the various events that can be programmed with the Formula language.

TABLE 18.4 Formula Language Programmable Events

Event	Function
Form Items and Events	
Actions	Appear in the Action bar, take actions such as putting the document in edit mode.
Hide Actions	Conditionally hide actions.
Buttons	Appear in the document; can take various actions when clicked.
Hotspots	Defined areas on the form such as text can be programmed. These then take the action programmed when clicked.
Insert Subform	Conditionally inserts a subform.
OnHelpRequest	Calls a specific help document when the user presses F1.
Section Access	Determines the access list for an access controlled section.
Section Title	Creates the title for a section.
WebQueryOpen	Runs an agent when a Web client opens a document.
WebQuerySave	Runs an agent when a Web client saves a document.
Window Titles	Determines the text that appears in the window title bar.
Field Events	
Default Value	Assigns a value to an editable field when a document is first composed. Has no effect on subsequent values of the field.
Value	Assigns a value to a computed field whenever a document is created, edited or refreshed.
Input Translation	Modifies the value entered into an editable field based on the formula entered.
Input Validation	Validates the entry in an editable field (limited usefulness for Rich Text fields).

Event	Function
Field Events	
Keyword Field Formula	Selects the keyword list for the field. @DBColumn() and @DBLookup() are often used in this context.
Hide paragraph	Conditionally hides the paragraph in which the field lives.
View Items and Events	
Selection	Determines which documents appear in the view.
Form Formula	Determines which form is used to present the documents in the view. This can be other than the form used to compose the document.
Column	Determines what appears in the view column.
Actions	Appear in the Action bar for the view; determines what actions are applied.
Hide Action	Conditionally hides the action.

As you can see, there are many locations where the Formula language can be used. Some of these locations only permit the use of the Formula language whereas others permit the use of the scripting languages as well. Actions, buttons, and hotspots are examples of objects that can be programmed in multiple.

Working with the Formula Window

The Formula window appears in items that are only programmable with the Formula language. Examples are the Hide Action formula and a Keyword Field formula. Two window types are available: One is embedded in the Properties box and the other is a modal window launched from the Formula Window button on the Properties box. See Figure 18.1 for an example of both types.

The space inside the Properties box is quite limited, but if you have a simple formula to enter, it will often suffice. You can see this window in both Figures 18.1 and 18.2.

When you enter a formula directly in the embedded formula window in the Field Properties box, there is a syntax checker available, as shown in Figure 18.2. The syntax checker consists of two buttons, one with a check mark on it and the other with an ×. Whenever you enter or modify a formula, these two buttons appear. Clicking the check mark button tests the syntax of the formula. Clicking the × button restores the syntax to its original state. (This same syntax checker is available in the Design Pane, discussed in the next section.) In any case, you can't save a formula that is not syntactically correct. You can, however, save a formula that has logic errors even though the syntax is correct, so be careful, and test your work! Error trapping is discussed in Chapter 19.

18

THE FORMULA LANGUAGE

FIGURE 18.1

You can compose a keyword field formula in the Properties box or in the larger, modal window; note the formula in the Properties box and the Fields and Functions dialog box.

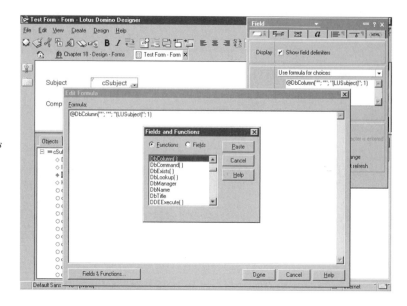

FIGURE 18.2

The syntax checker buttons appear when formulas are modified or created.

Check syntax

Revert to
saved version

Saving Invalid Formulas

To save your work on a formula that is not syntactically correct, enclose the entire formula in quotes and place a REM at the beginning of the line. Be sure to use the slash character if there are embedded quotes in the formula. You can later return to the formula, remove the quotes and continue work.

The second type of window is a modal dialog box. Figure 18.1 shows a keyword formula being constructed in the modal formula window, using @DBColumn(). This larger window is launched from the Formula Window button in the Properties box. In addition to having a larger area in which to work, the formula window also has a Fields & Functions button that launches a picklist for database fields and @Functions. Unfortunately, there is no syntax checker for this window. However, when you click the Done button, the syntax is tested and you can't exit the modal window unless the syntax is correct.

New to Release 5!

In Release 4, one of the unfortunate side effects of the modal Edit Formula window was that you could not press the Enter key and insert a carriage return. Pressing the Enter key terminated the window. This has been fixed in Release 5!

Writing Formulas in the Script Area

The Design Pane is discussed in Chapter 8, "The Integrated Development Environment," and is covered briefly here in the context of writing formulas. Figure 18.3 shows an Input Validation formula for a field. This formula ensures that the user cannot save the document without entering information into the cSubject field.

New to Release 5!

New to Release 5 of Notes is color-coding for the Formula language! This has been available for LotusScript since Release 4, and it is a welcome addition to the Domino Designer. In the Formula language, Keywords, @Functions, and @Commands are in blue, while fields, constants, and other identifiers are in black. Quoted text is in green and errors are in red. The color scheme can be modified in the Design Pane Properties box as discussed in Chapter 8.

To the left of the Script area, you will notice that the Info List is open to the Objects tab and the Input Validation event is selected. This addition to the IDE replaces the Events drop-down list in Release 4 of Notes. The formula in Listing 18.4 is typical of fields with required entry:

FIGURE 18.3

The Script Area is used to construct many types of formulas, including the formula for the Input Validation event.

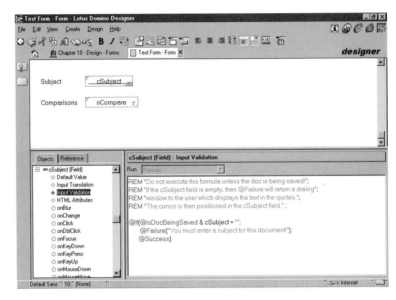

LISTING 18.4   Input Validation for the `cSubject` Field

```
REM "Do not execute this formula unless the doc is being saved!";
REM "If the cSubject field is empty, @Failure returns a ";
REM "window to the user which displays the text in the quotes.";
REM "The cursor is then positioned in the cSubject field." ;

@If(@IsDocBeingSaved & cSubject = "";
    @Failure("You must enter a subject for this document!");
    @Success)
```

If you make a syntax error, Domino Designer catches it when you try to exit the field or save the form. Clicking the syntax checker button also catches any mistakes. An error message appears at the bottom of the design pane; the offending entry is changed to red. Figure 18.4 shows an error condition in the formula listed earlier. However, the syntax checker will not catch mistakes in logic!

Figures 18.3 and 18.4 showed the Objects tab in the Programmer's pane, which lists all of the programmable events for the object. The Reference tab contains extensive help for programming the object. Figure 18.5 shows the Reference tab for the Input Validation event. In the drop-down list, you can choose from Database Fields, Formula @Commands and Formula @Functions. For events that have other scripting languages available, choices appear for those languages as well. Selecting an item in the Reference list and clicking Help opens a separate application window with the appropriate Help document displayed. This is an improvement over R4 because you can leave the Help window open and switch back to the formula. The Paste button can be clicked to copy the field or command into the Script area.

FIGURE 18.4

An extra right parenthesis was placed at the end of the @If() statement to generate an error; the error message is at the bottom of the Script area.

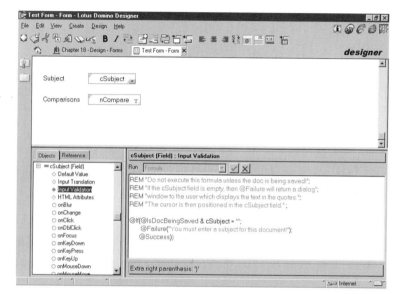

FIGURE 18.5

The Reference tab allows programmers to choose fields and language components to use in the current object.

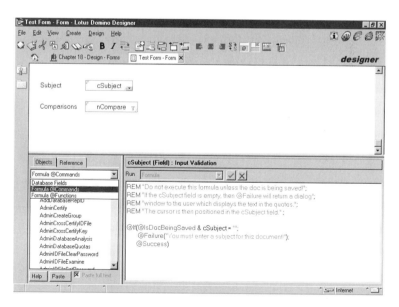

Formula Syntax

Each formula is composed of statements that take actions or evaluate to a result. The @Commands generally take an action, although a few return a result. Most formulas must evaluate to a *main expression*, or a *result*, regardless of the side effects. For example, the following formula for a default value of the cSubject field generates an error.

```
jcSubject := "Formula Syntax"
```

This is because there is no main expression. The formula simply assigns a value to a temporary variable. You can, however, use a *text constant*. A text constant is always enclosed in quotes. For example, "Formula Syntax" could be placed in the default value event which would then be assigned to the field when a document is created. You can also write the following formula, storing the value "Formula Syntax" to a variable and use the variable as the last statement:

```
jcSubject := "Formula Syntax"
jcSubject
```

This has the same effect as the previous formula.

Fields on a form evaluate from left to right and top to bottom. Similarly, formulas always evaluate from left to right and from top to bottom. The only exceptions to the order of execution are @Commands and @PostedCommands. (This was discussed earlier in this chapter in the section titled "Overview of the Formula Language.") Formulas can contain constants, fields, keywords, operators, @Functions, @Commands, and variables.

Working with Constants

A constant is a value that can be assigned during the execution of a formula. There are three types of constants: numeric, text, and time-date. Text constants are enclosed in quotes, numeric constants are simply entered, and time-date constants are enclosed in square brackets. A list can also be a constant. (You can read more about lists in Chapter 19.) The following list shows how each type of constant can be assigned to a field or variable:

```
nNumber := 10.34
cText := "This is a text constant"
dDate := [08/09/98]
dDateTime := [08/09/98 11:30 PM]
```

Operators

Operators typically assign or modify values of variables or fields. A full listing of Operators is available in a Domino Designer Help document titled "Operator Overview and Precedence." You can quickly locate this in the Designer Help Search view by typing in the first few letters of the first word. Domino Help then moves to the document. There are six basic types of operators: arithmetic, assignment, comparison (equality), list concatenation, logical, and unary (positive or negative). Two variables must have an operator between them. Some of these operators are fairly easy to understand; others require more explanation.

Arithmetic operators are just what you expect—they perform mathematical functions. These operators are the commonly used signs +, -, *, /, and so on. You can use these functions to perform permuted operations against lists. You can change the sign of a numeric variable with the + or the - sign.

Comparison operators determine how two values equate to each other. For example, =, >, <, <>, != are all comparison operators. Note that the equal sign (=) does not assign a value—it equates two values. When a comparison operator is used, the return value is a logical value. Because Notes does not have a logical variable type (unfortunately) in the Formula language, numeric 1 is true and 0 is false.

The assignment operator, :=, assigns values to a variable or a `field`. A variable is limited in scope to the currently executing formula. Even if there are several fields in a form, and an event in all the fields has a formula that uses the same variable name, the value of the variable remains with the formula in which it resides—changing it in one field does not affect the value of the variable in another. This is important to understand because in some ways it is quite different from other programming languages. You can use a variable with the same name as a field and if the field has a value, the variable has the same value. You can then modify the value of the variable in the formula. Unless you explicitly save the value using the `FIELD` keyword or `@SetField()`, the value of the variable is discarded when the formula completes execution even though it has the same name as a field. Because the scope of variables is so limited, you should consider developing and using a naming convention. Using j (for junk because it is discarded) as the first letter of a variable is one such convention. Consider Listing 18.5.

LISTING 18.5   Assigning Field Values from an Action Button

```
REM "Look up the departments" ;
jcHRLookupID := @GetProfileField("GP"; "cHRLookupID");

jcDeptList := @DbColumn( ""; jcHRLookupID ; "LUDEPT";1) ;
REM "should add an error trap here..." ;
jcDept := @Prompt([OKCANCELLIST]; "Departments" ; "Choose a department" ;
                  "" ; jcDeptList ) ;
@If(jcDept = ""; @Return(""); @Success) ;

REM "The Department code and description";
REM "are concatenated into a single view column" ;
jcDepartment := @Right(jcDept; " ") ;
REM "The Department code should be the first";
REM "four characters plus 00" ;
jcDeptCode := @Left(jcDept; 4) + "00";

REM "By prefacing the variable name with the letter j" ;
REM "it makes it very easy to use @SetField";
@SetField("cDepartment"; jcDepartment) ;
@SetField("cDeptCode"; jcDeptCode);
```

Using j plus the name of the field—jcDepartment, for example—makes it very easy to read and maintain your code. Using @SetField() is very straightforward because the field name is prominent in the variable.

Lists are concatenated using the colon. In the following example, three lists are created: CTextList, nNumList, and dDateList.

```
cTextList := "Item One" : " Item Two" : " Item Three";
nNumList := 1 : 2 : 3 ;
dDateList := [08/09/98] : @Today : [08/10/98];
```

There are three logical operators: and, not and, or. And is represented by the ampersand, &; not is represented by the exclamation point, !; and or is represented by the pipe, ¦.

Unary operators are the plus sign and the minus sign. These change the sign of a number. By default, all numbers are positive, unless otherwise specified.

All operators can be combined in the same formula under the right circumstances.

Syntax Rules

Many of the syntax rules for the Formula language are similar to those in other programming languages. They are fairly easy to learn, especially because errors are flagged by the syntax checker. Formatting formulas, using semicolons, using case and changing the precedence through the use of parentheses are all discussed in the next several sections.

Formatting Formulas

There are minimal formatting rules for formulas. In Release 3, if you added spaces and line feeds in the formula window, when you saved the object containing the formula, all the formatting disappeared. This made reading and debugging complex formulas extremely frustrating and difficult. In Release 4, white space was allowed in formulas. This meant that you could add line feeds, blank lines, indented lines and spaces. This made formulas easier to read and maintain. You can also change the font used in the Script area with no effect on the code.

Spaces Required!

A space is required only in one condition—after a Keyword such as `FIELD`. For example `FIELDcText` is not correct, but `FIELD cText` is. Although this point might seem rather obvious, it needs to be mentioned, because spaces aren't required elsewhere. Consider the following formula which contains no spaces except the one after the keyword, and those in the text values:

```
FIELD cText:="This is some text created on"+@Today+" by "+
@Name([CN];@UserName);
```

Despite the preceding note, by convention, operators have spaces before and after them to make the formula easier to read.

Using Semicolons

Perhaps one of the most important rules is that each statement in a formula must be separated with the line continuation character that being the semicolon. The semicolon is an extremely important and often-used character. If you look at any one of the formulas in this chapter, you see that rule in effect. If you fail to use a semicolon at the end of any statement except the last, you will receive an error message and you will not be able to save the formula.

All arguments within @Functions and @Commands are separated by semicolons. In the following example, `@SetField("cDeptCode"; jcDeptCode)`, the semicolon separates the first argument, the name of the field, from the second argument, the variable containing its value. In many other languages, LotusScript and Java included, the comma is used as an argument separator. If you are new to Domino applications development, this might take some getting used to!

Using Cases

For the most part, formulas are not case sensitive. Text constants are, of course, case sensitive because TEXT is not the same as text or Text. There are some conventions that are in widespread use also. In particular, keywords are always entered in uppercase. For example, you will see REM, but not Rem, or rem; and FIELD, but not Field. On the other hand, @Functions are usually entered in mixed case, as are variable names. You are probably aware that it is easier to read mixed case than all uppercase or all lowercase words. So, @SetField or, as an even better example, @DocumentUniqueID are much easier to read than @SETFIELD or @documentuniqueid. Particularly in the last example, all the lowercase letters seem to flow together. Arguments specified for @Commands are also entered in mixed case. In Release 4, arguments entered for @Functions such as @Prompt([OkCancelEdit];...) used to be converted to all capitals, as in [OKCANCELEDIT], when the formula was saved. In Release 5, the case you enter is preserved. Used judiciously, case can be an important factor in making the readability and maintenance of your applications easier.

Using Parentheses

The order of operations, as mentioned earlier in this chapter, proceeds from top to bottom and from left to right. You can, however, alter the precedence of logical and arithmetic operators through the use of parentheses. If you are not careful when using parentheses, you can get some rather surprising results! Parentheses can group statements and can be used to great effect in formulas such as those written for SELECT statements and Hide When formulas. Of course, they can be used in many other formulas as well. For example, consider the following view selection formula:

```
SELECT Form = "AD" &! (dDate1 = "" & dDate2 = "" & dDate3 = "")
```

This selection criteria does not display any documents composed with the AD form where the three date fields—dDate1, dDate2, and dDate3—are empty. Without the parentheses around the three date fields, a very different collection of documents would appear. With the parentheses, the &! (AND NOT) applies to the all of the dates. Removing the parentheses causes the view to display documents composed with the AD form where dDate1 is not empty, but dDate2 and dDate3 are empty.

```
SELECT Form = "AD" &! dDate1 = "" & dDate2 = "" & dDate3 = ""
```

To select documents where at least one of the three date fields is not empty, enclose the date fields in parentheses, but separate them with the OR argument, substituting the pipe symbol for the ampersand.

```
SELECT Form = "AD" &! (dDate1 = "" ¦ dDate2 = "" ¦ dDate3 = "")
```

Combining the logical operators, & and ¦, with parentheses to change the order of precedence provides a very powerful method of limiting the documents that appear in views. However, this technique can also be applied in many other areas, such as view column formulas, default value formulas, and so forth.

Parentheses can also be used to alter the order of evaluation in arithmetic statements. As you know, arithmetic operators have a specific order of precedence. For example, multiplication and division take precedence over addition and subtraction. If you wanted to calculate the sales tax of a group of items the following formula would not work:

```
1.99 + 2.89 + 15.99 * .0575
```

Rounded to two decimal places, this formula returns 5.80. The multiplication of 15.99 times the sales tax of .0575 is added to 1.99 and 2.89. The real sales tax is 1.20, which can be returned properly through the use of parentheses:

```
(1.99 + 2.89 + 15.99) * .0575
```

Limitations of the Formula Language

Although the Formula language has similarities to many other programming languages, there are some important differences. The Formula language is great for writing a function quickly because it does not require as much coding as a scripting language that performs the same function. Although the scripting languages generally require more effort, they also have greater capabilities. Despite its ease of use, the Formula language has some rather severe limitations, but by no means should this discourage you from using the Formula language! Not only are there many situations that require the use of the Formula language, there are many reasons to choose the Formula language over a scripting language. Chapter 17, "Choosing the Right Language," discusses how to choose the correct language.

Some of the most limiting factors for the Formula language are the following:

- A formula cannot repeatedly loop through a collection of documents; there is no looping construct in the Formula language.
- There is no way to create subroutines.
- The scope is limited to the formula itself; variables have no persistence beyond the currently executing formula.

- You cannot directly pass a parameter from one formula to another or even to an agent; similarly, you cannot call a formula with a parameter. (You can, however, store a value to an environment variable or a field and retrieve it later to partially work around this limitation.)

- There is no method to transfer control outside the formula itself, perhaps to another formula, although you can stop a formula with `@Return()`. You can get around this to a certain extent by calling an agent.

A number of events must be scripted with another language and cannot have formulas written to them. These events can be found in agents, forms, fields, views, and database scripts. Examples are the `Initialize` event for agents, the `QuerySave` event for forms, and the `Exiting` event for fields.

Summary

Despite the limitations mentioned in the preceding section, the Formula language is a powerful, vital, and useful part of Domino Applications development. You cannot program in Domino without a solid understanding of this language. This chapter provided you with a foundation in the Formula language and discussed @Commands, @Functions, Keywords, syntax, and more. The next two chapters go into more detail and provide more real world examples of formulas.

Formula Language Basics

by Steve Kern

In the previous chapter, you learned about the various components of a formula. These are the building blocks on which you will learn to effectively write formulas in Notes and Domino. This chapter continues with more basics.

> **Caution**
>
> Because there are so many @Functions and @Commands, it is not possible to cover each and every @Function; instead, this chapter concentrates on those which you will frequently use.

Working with Statements

You write formulas for two principal reasons, which are to take an action or to set or get a value (or list of values). Each formula consists of a statement or a series of statements. Statement types are listed in Table 19.1.

TABLE 19.1 Types of Statements Used in the Formula Language

Type	*Examples*
Assignment	`dTarget := @Adjust(dStart; 0; 1; 0; 0; 0; 0)`
	Sets `dTarget` one month past `dStart`
	`@SetField(cStatus; "New")`
	Sets the value of `cStatus` to `"New"`
Comparison	`cStatus = "Completed"`
	Tests whether the value of `cStatus` equals `"Completed"`
	`nRequest > 10000`
	Tests whether the value of `nRequest` is greater than 10,000
Conditional	`@If(cStatus = "Completed"; @Do(...`
	If the value of `cStatus` is `"Completed"`, takes some other action
	`@If(@IsNewDoc & @IsDocBeingSaved; "New"; cStatus)`
	In a computed field value event, if the document is new and is being saved, the value of `cStatus` is set to `"New"`.
Control	`@Return("")`
	Stops execution of the formula
	`@Do()`
	Executes a series of statements
Action	`@MailSend(jcSendTo; jcCC...`
	Sends a memo
	`@Command([FileSave])`
	Saves the current document

Each of the statements or statement fragments in Table 19.1 can be part of a more complex formula; a statement can also be the entire formula. A formula can combine any number of statement types, and in practice, they often do just that.

Assigning Values to Fields and Variables

You often write statements that assign values to variables and fields. There is only one assignment operator, :=, which was discussed in Chapter 18, "The Formula Language." However, there are three other ways to assign values:

- DEFAULT
- FIELD
- @SetField()

Of the three, only DEFAULT can assign a value to a variable. As their names imply, the other two set the values for fields in documents.

Adding and Deleting Fields

Remember that in Domino Applications, you can both add and subtract fields from documents, unlike records in a relational database table. To add a new field, simply use one of the three keywords listed previously and assign a value to the new field. To delete a field, use the following formula:

FIELD *fieldname* := @DeleteField.

Both new and deleted fields are document-specific, meaning that when you create a new instance of a field on a document, it does not exist on any other document. When you delete a field, it is deleted from specific documents.

You can assign values from fields to variables and from variables to fields. A value can be the result of an expression, an @Function, or a constant. By default, any value assigned to a variable is temporary and its scope is limited to the formula. There is no persistence to a value unless you save it in a document field. You can also assign a value to a field in the Value event for a computed field, in the Default Value event for an editable field, or in the Choices event for a keyword field by entering a constant or a formula. In this case, the assignment is implicit and does not require an operator.

In Listing 19.1, examples of assignments are numerous. In the first assignment, the value of the cManager field is assigned to the variable jcSendTo. The variable jcSendTo is later used to send the notification using @MailSend(). Next, jcDocHistory is set using a combination of text constants and @Functions (@Text and @Now). Both jcSendTo and jcDocHistory are variables, and their value will be discarded as soon as the formula is completed. The value of jcDocHistory is stored in the cDocHistory field using @SetField(). The value assigned to jcDocHistory is concatenated with the existing value of cDocHistory, adding to the list of events that happened to the current document.

LISTING 19.1   Code from an Agent Illustrating Assignments to Variables and Fields

```
REM "Send notification to the manager";

SELECT Form = "AR" & cStatus = "New" &! @Contains(cLastAgent;
      "Manager Notification");
REM "Write doc history";

jcSendTo := cManager ;
jcDocHistory := "Notification of New Application Request emailed to "
            + jcSendTo + " on " + @Text(@Now;"S2") ;
@SetField("cDocHistory"; cDocHistory : jcDocHistory) ;

REM "Add agent tracking fields." ;
FIELD dNotified := dNotified ;
@SetField("dNotified"; @If(dNotified = "";
        @Now; dNotified : @Now));
FIELD cLastAgent := cLastAgent ;
jcLastAgent := "Manager Notification" ;
@SetField("cLastAgent"; @If(cLastAgent = ""; jcLastAgent;
        cLastAgent : jcLastAgent));
jcCC := "" ;
jcSubject := "New Application Request # " + cReqNumber ;
jcBody := "A new Application Request has been added to the
➥Applications database. Click the doclink at the bottom of this
➥message, and when you have reviewed the Request, click the Sign
➥button and either approve or deny the Request. Thanks!" ;

@MailSend(jcSendTo; jcCC; ""; jcSubject; jcBody; ""; [IncludeDoclink])
```

Using Comparisons in Formulas

In the following SELECT statement, there are several comparisons.

```
SELECT Form = "AR" & cStatus = "New" &!
➥ @Contains(cLastAgent; "Manager Notification");
```

First, the statement tests the field Form to determine whether it is equal to "AR" and whether the field cStatus is equal to "New". Next, the statement ensures that the field cLastAgent does not contain "Manager Notification" (you don't want to annoy the managers with numerous notifications!). This statement uses the logical operators

& (AND) and ! (NOT) and the @Function, @Contains, to build a collection of documents on which the agent will run. This statement could also be used in an Agent, a View Selection formula, or a replication formula to select a subset of documents.

In addition to comparing values of fields to text or other constants, comparison statements often use conditional @Functions, such as @If(), and logical @Functions, such as @IsDocBeingSaved. For example, you can load the values for a keyword lookup into a computed for display field at the top of a document. Typically, this would involve storing a list in the field using @DbColumn or @DbLookup whenever the document is opened. However, the only time you need this value is when the document is being edited, so there is no sense looking up the value unless you need it. It's simply not efficient. The following statement only retrieves values when the document is new or is being edited:

```
@If(@IsNewDoc ¦ @IsDocBeingEdited;
      @DbColumn( ""; cHRLookupID  ; "LUCost";1);
      "")
```

You can use a comparison statement to determine what appears in view columns, but you can also used it as a counter! Because there is no Boolean data type in Domino, you can take advantage of the fact that a true comparison returns a 1 and a false returns a 0. Setting the column to total produces a count of all documents that meet the comparison! Using the previous example, a view column formula of @Contains(cLastAgent; "Manager Notification") provides a convenient counter by totaling the number of notifications sent to the manager.

Working with Conditional Statements

There is really only one conditional construct in the Formula Language: @If(). The basic form of @If() has three parts: the condition, the true statement, and the false statement. The syntax for this form of @If() is

```
@If(condition; statement if true; statement if false)
```

The statements for the true or false condition can be any type of statement except the assignment statement. Assignments can occur only at the beginning of a statement. An example of this simple form is the following:

```
@If( cType = "Lesson"; "Lesson " + nLesson; "Appendix: " + cAppendix)
```

If used in a view column formula, this displays the word *Lesson* plus the lesson number or the word *Appendix* plus the appendix letter depending on the value of cType.

19

FORMULA
LANGUAGE BASICS

But what if you have more than one value for cType? Perhaps you have three types of documents: introductory documents, lessons, and appendices. The construct @If() can extend the arguments in the following form:

```
@If(1stCondition; 1stTrue; 2ndCondition; 2ndTrue; [...] FalseStatement)
```

If the first condition is not true, the statement evaluation passes to the second condition. If there are more conditional statements, evaluation continues from left to right. The construct @If() must always have an odd number of arguments, no matter how many conditions you have in the statement. In effect, this is like a CASE statement in other languages.

You can also nest @If() statements within @If() statements. For example, you can write the following value formula for a computed field:

```
@If(@IsNewDoc & @IsDocBeingSaved; "Blue";
    @If(cColor = "Green"; "Purple"; "Mauve"))
```

This sets the value to Blue if the document is new and it is being saved. If this isn't the case and the value of cColor is Green, the value of the computed field becomes Purple. If the value of cColor is not Green, the value becomes Mauve. Nesting @If() statements is a very powerful tool, but they can be difficult to write and debug.

Using Control Statements

There might be no way to pass the control of a formula to another formula or to a subroutine, but there are some @Functions that do control a formula to a limited extent. The following three @Functions provide control logic:

- @If()
- @Return()
- @Do()

You learned about @If() in the previous section. The function @Return() stops the execution of a formula and is very useful. You can use @Do() to execute a string of statements from left to right. Both @Return() and @Do() are often combined with @If() statements, which can give your formula a great deal of flexibility. The following code fragment checks to see whether the user really wants to deny the request. If not, it uses @Return("") to stop the execution of the remainder of the formula. If the user decides to proceed, then a dialog box is opened into which the user enters a reason.

```
REM "Deny the request, and enter a reason for the denial.";
jnAreYouSure := @Prompt([YESNO]; "Are you sure?" ;
                "Are you sure you want to deny this request?");
@If(jnAreYouSure; @Success; @Return(""));
```

```
FIELD cDenial := cDenial;
jcDialog := @DialogBox( "dBoxDenial" ;
                       [AutoHorzFit] : [AutoVertFit] ; "Deny TSR" );
@SetField("cDocStatus"; "Denied");
@SetField("nStatusSort"; 99)
```

The @Function, `@Do()`, enables you to execute a series of statements following a conditional statement. In the following example, the user is asked if he wants to release the document. If so, then the value of two fields is set. Ordinarily, there is no way to execute more than one statement in the true condition of an `@If` statement. However, using `@Do` enables you to string together a series of statements, in this case, two `@SetField` statements are used to mark the status of the document.

```
REM "Release to approver";
jnYesNo := @Prompt([YESNO]; "Are you sure?";
                   "Do you want to release this document?");
@If(jnYesNo; @Do(@SetField("cDocStatus"; "Pending");
                 @SetField("nStatusSort"; 4));
       "")
```

Nesting Statements

Writing complex nested statements can be very difficult. The deeper the nesting, the more difficult it is to keep track of the parentheses that you must use. It is often easier to create the statement step-by-step, beginning with the outer @Function, as in the following:

```
@Do()
```

Then add the @Functions inside of the parentheses such as in the following:

```
@Do(@SetField(); @SetField())
```

Continue adding terms until the statement is complete, as in the following example:

```
@Do@SetField("cDocStatus"; "Pending");
              @SetField("nStatusSort"; 4)
```

By adding terms one at a time, you are less likely to miss a closing parenthesis or, worse, to ruin the logic of the statement.

19

FORMULA
LANGUAGE BASICS

Another way to use `@Return` is in combination with `@Success` to stop the execution of a formula at the beginning if a certain condition exists. The @Function, `@Success`, evaluates to true (or 1). You can use it with `@If` to cause the execution of the formula to continue. In the following example, instead of including `@Do` within the `@If`, `@Success` is used in the true condition. When the user answers Yes, the formula continues to execute, saving values to cDocStatus and nStatusSort. If the user answers No, @Return stops the execution of the formula.

```
REM "Release to approver";
jnYesNo := @Prompt([YESNO]; "Are you sure?";
                        "Do you want to release this document?");
@If(jnYesNo; @Success; @Return(""));
@SetField("cDocStatus"; "Pending");
@SetField("nStatusSort"; 4)
```

Although they are few, the control statements are a vital part of the Formula Language. You must learn how to use them in order to write effective formulas.

Using Action Statements in Formulas

Action statements and formulas can have certain side effects or cause some event to occur outside of the formula itself. Side effects are discussed in Chapter 18, "The Formula Language." Action formulas themselves do not return any useful value. For example, @MailSend() is an action statement because it causes mail to be sent. It does have a return value, but it is not important. What is important is that it sends mail, an action which takes place outside of the immediate formula. @Commands often take actions because they are based on the menu structure. For example, @Command([EditProfile]) opens a database profile document, but does not return any value. Action formulas can be written for the following:

- Action Bar buttons, both form and view
- Agents
- Buttons
- Fields (rarely, but it is possible)
- Hotspots
- SmartIcons

For example, agents are often used to mail notifications to users. Typically, the agent will test for the document's status, determine a list of recipients for the notification, and finally create a mail message containing a subject, body text, and a link to the document. The following code fragment illustrates this technique:

```
REM "Send notification of Pending requests to the Approver";
SELECT Form = "SR" & cDocStatus = "Pending"
     &! @Contains(cLastAgent; "Approver Notification");
jcSendTo := @Name([Abbreviate];cApprover);
jcCC := "" ;
```

```
REM "For testing, add a blind carbon copy" ;
jcBCC := "";
jcSubject := "Pending Service Request for "  + cAssociate ;
jcBody := "Click this doclink to open the request —> " ;

@MailSend(jcSendTo; jcCC; jcBCC; jcSubject;
          jcBody; ""; [IncludeDoclink])
```

The last statement, @MailSend, is an action statement within the formula itself. The formula is used to populate the values for the parameters for @MailSend, and the router on the server then sends the mail.

Using Logical @Functions

There are a large number of @Functions that can be classified as logical @Functions. These functions return a Boolean result. Remember that in the Formula Language, true is represented as 1 and false is represented as 0. The return values of these logical @Functions reflect this numeric equivalent of true and false. Table 19.2 lists logical @Functions:

TABLE 19.2   Logical @Functions

@*Function*	*Description*
@IsAgentEnabled	Returns True if the agent is enabled.
@IsAppInstalled	Tests whether Admin or Design client is installed.
@IsAvailable	Tests whether a field exists in a document.
@IsCategory	Returns True if any item in a row of a view is a category.
@IsDocBeingEdited	Returns True if the document is in edit mode.
@IsDocBeingLoaded	Returns True if the document is being opened (loaded).
@IsDocBeingMailed	Returns True if the document is being mailed.
@IsDocBeingRecalculated	Returns True if the documents is being refreshed (recalculated).
@IsDocBeingSaved	Returns True if the document is being saved.
@IsDocTruncated	Returns True if the document is truncated.
@IsError	Returns True if a value has an error condition.
@IsExpandable	Returns True if a row in a view is expandable.
@IsMember	Returns True if a text item or text list is a member of another text list.
@IsModalHelp	Returns True if the document is a modal help document.

19

FORMULA LANGUAGE BASICS

continues

TABLE 19.2 continued

@Function	*Description*
@IsNewDoc	Returns True if the document has just been created.
@IsNotMember	Returns True if a text item or text list is not a member of another text list.
@IsNumber	Returns True if the value is numeric.
@IsResponseDoc	Returns True if the document is a response document.
@IsText	Returns True if the value is text.
@IsTime	Returns True if the value is a time-date value or a time-date list.
@IsUnavailable	Returns True if the field does not exist in the document.
@IsValid	Returns True if all validation formulas are successful.
@False	Returns a False, or 0.
@True	Returns a True, or 1.
@No	Returns a False, or 0.
@Yes	Returns a True, or 1.
@Success	Returns a True, or 1.

The Boolean or logical @Functions in Table 19.2 can be used in many different places. Many of these @Functions are related to the state of a document, such as @IsDocBeingEdited or @IsNewDoc. You can use @Functions like these to hide actions, or to determine whether to populate a field. For example, placing @IsNewDoc in the Hide When of an Action button will hide it when a document is first created. Similarly, if you have a computed for display field that depends on the value of another field in the document, you can populate the value of the display field using @IsNewDoc:

```
@If(@IsNewDoc; "New Service Request"; cStatus)
```

The @Functions @IsAvailable and @IsUnavailable are used to determine whether a field exists in a document. Remember that you can add and delete fields from documents, so you can't always predict whether or not a given document will have a specific field. Rather than have a formula return an error condition because the field doesn't exist, you can test for its existence before executing the formula. Otherwise, the error condition reported by Notes is assigned to the field, variable, or view column. For example, you might want to sort and categorize a view on a date field that exists in some, but not all, documents. If the field containing the date doesn't exist, you want to sort it on the date of the document's creation. The following formula tests whether the date field exists, and uses it if it does; otherwise, it uses @Created.

```
jdDate := @If(@IsAvailable(dCall)
        & dCall != ""; dCall; @Created);
@Date(jdDate)
```

Several other useful @Functions are worth mentioning briefly. Fields and values can have an error condition if the statement that assigns the value produces an error. Using @IsError, you can trap for the error condition, and assign a different value. The @Functions @IsText, @IsNumber, and @IsTime test the data type of a field. @IsMember and @IsNotMember are used with lists to determine whether a value or list does or does not exist within another list.

You might have noticed that @Failure is not in Table 19.2, even though it would seem to be the opposite of @Success. In fact, it is often used in conjunction with @Success. @Success has a return value of 1, but @Failure returns a string value in a dialog box. For example, if you want to alert the user that a value entered in a field is incorrect or that a field with a required entry was left blank, you can use @Failure in a field's Input Validation event as in the following example:

```
@If(cSubject = "";
  @Failure("You must enter a subject
        ➡in order to save this document!");
@Success)
```

The previous formula produces a window containing the text inside the quotes, alerting the user that the document cannot be saved until an appropriate value is entered in the subject field.

Working with Date and Time @Functions

Compared to the amount of work that you have to go through in LotusScript to work with time-date values, it is a pleasure to work with them in the Formula Language! Table 19.3 lists a number of @Functions that you will find useful with time-date values.

TABLE 19.3   Time-Date @Functions

@Function	Usage
@Accessed	The last date a document was accessed
@Adjust()	Modifies a date, adjusting it into the past or the future
@Created	The date a document was created
@Date()	Returns the date component of a time-date value

continues

19

FORMULA LANGUAGE BASICS

TABLE 19.3 continued

@Function	Usage
@Day()	Returns the day of the month of a time-date value
@Hour()	Returns the hour component of a time-date value
@IsTime()	Returns True if the value is a time-date
@Minute()	Returns the minute component of a time-date value
@Modified	A list of dates on which a document was modified
@Month()	Returns the month number of a time-date value
@Now	Returns the current date and time
@Second()	Returns the second component of a time-date value
@Text()	In this context, converts time-date values to text
@TextToTime()	Converts a text representation of a time-date value to a time-date value
@Time()	Returns the time component of a time-date value
@Today	Returns today's date
@Tomorrow	Returns tomorrow's date
@Weekday()	Returns the weekday number of a time-date value
@Year()	Returns the year of a time-date value
@Yesterday	Returns yesterday's date
@Zone	Returns the time zone component of a time-date value

Phew! There are a lot of @Functions aren't there? Believe it or not, you will find good uses for most of them. Three of these @Functions are properties of documents: @Accessed, @Created, and @Modified. These contain the last date and time a document was accessed, when it was created, and the dates and times it was modified, respectively. @Now, @Today, @Tomorrow, and @Yesterday all return specific time-date values, as indicated by their names. You use the other @Functions to manipulate time and date values in formulas.

Time-Date Values

Domino stores both the date and time in Date/Time fields. Similarly, a variable can store both dates and times. A time-date value can contain a date, a time, or a value combining both a date and a time. The function @Date() returns the date component of a time-date value, and @Time returns the time component. The standard format of a time-date value is MM/DD/YYYY HH:MM:SS AM/PM *time zone*. You can also store just a date or time value in a time field or variable. For more information on the Time field, see Chapter 7, "The Release 5 Object Store." Don't forget that in both view column and field properties you can elect to display Date and Time, Date Only, or Time Only. You can also affect the format of the display. View columns are covered in Chapter 11, "View Design." Field properties are discussed in Chapter 9, "Review of Basic Forms Design."

You can work with the values of the document properties @Created, @Accessed, and @Modified, but you can't modify them. You can, however, use these functions to build document histories. An example is in the section titled "Getting Session and User Information," later in this chapter.

Document Properties

If you want to display the date a document was created, you don't need to create a field with document presence, although you can. Simply create a field that is computed for display with a value of @Created! Use the same technique if you want to display the last modification or last access times. There is no reason to take up space in the document with a field to store a value that already exists as a part of the document properties.

Working with Dates

There is not enough space to cover all the @Functions that you can use to work with dates, this section provides some detail on a few of the more useful ones. The function @Adjust() is particularly useful because it enables you to adjust a time-date value into the past or into the future in increments as small as a second. Its syntax is the following:

```
@Adjust(DateTime; Year; Month; Day; Hour; Minute;
➥Second; [InLocalTime] ¦ [InGMT])
```

The first six parameters after the time-date value are all numeric, and all are required. The last parameter is optional and adjusts the date for daylight savings time. For example, to adjust an invoice due date to 30 days in the future, you can use @Adjust(dDue; 0; 0; 30; 0; 0; 0). To adjust it for one month in the future, you can use the following formula: @Adjust(dDue; 0; 1; 0; 0; 0; 0).

Many time-date @Functions can be particularly useful in views in which you want to sort documents by the date of creation or some other date stored in a field. Figure 19.1 illustrates a frequent use for time-date @Functions. In the first column, the `@Function` `@Year()` extracts the year, and the following formula extracts the quarter in the second column:

```
"Quarter " + @Text(@Integer((@Month(@Created)-1) / 3)+1)
```

FIGURE 19.1

This view uses Time-Date @Functions to produce reports categorized by the year and quarter.

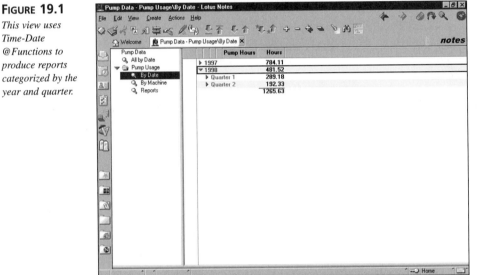

Building on the view shown in Figure 19.1, you can add a month category just underneath the quarter category. To display the text version of the month, you need to work a little harder because there is no function that directly returns *July* or *August*. Even if there were such a function, you couldn't sort on that value because you'd end up with an alpha sort, placing April ahead of January! The function `@Month()` returns the month number, so you can use it to sort the documents by month in a hidden column immediately preceding the alpha month column. Set the `@Month()` column to Ascending (or Descending) sort, and set the alpha month column to sorted and categorized. The following function convert the number of the month to the text equivalent using `@Select`:

```
@Select(@Month(@Created); "January"; "February"; "March"; "April";
        "May"; "June"; "July"; "August"; "September"; "October";
        "November"; "December")
```

An alternative formula uses @Word() instead of @Select(), as in the following:

```
@Word("January February March April May June July August September
➥ October November December"; " "; @Month(@Created));
```

Adding this to the view produces the result shown in Figure 19.2.

FIGURE 19.2

Adding a month category is used frequently to display documents in a date-sorted view.

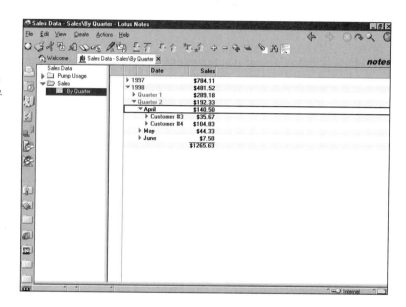

You can control the display format of a field or column that contains a time-date value by using the Control tab of a field properties box and the Date and Time Format tab of a view column properties box. For example, you can display the date component of a view column or field in several different formats such as MM/DD/YY, MM/YY, MM/YYYY, and so on. You can also use the @Date() function to return just the date portion of a time-date value or @Time() to return the time portion. The function @Date() can also be used to convert numeric values to dates. See the section titled "Converting Time-Date Values" a little later in this section for more information.

Working with Time

You can use several @Functions to extract and display the time component. The function @Time(), like its counterpart @Date(), extracts the time component of a time-date value. This is important because Domino can store both dates and times in the same field or variable.

The functions @Hour(), @Minute(), and @Second() return hours, minutes, and seconds respectively, from a time-date value.

The function @Now returns the current time-date of the machine on which the formula is executed; @Now evaluates a complete time-date value accurate to the second. It is useful for storing the time of an operation. For example, an application can have agents that run on a schedule or with a modified trigger. You can track the precise time at which the agent runs and store the value in an agent history or document history field using @Now. The following formula converts the current time to a text value and appends a line to the document history:

```
@SetField("cDocHistory"; cDocHistory: "Notification emailed to "
➥ + jcSendTo + " on " + @Text(@Now; "S2"))
```

Note the colon between cDocHistory and the text constant. This places the text at the end of the document history field, which is a multivalue field. The resulting text might read `Notification emailed to John Smith/IS/MyCompany on 08/16/98 08:48:04 PM`. (The @Text() function is discussed in the next section.)

Converting Time-Date Values

Conversion of time-date values typically involves text values. The @Text() function converts time-date values to text. The function @TextToTime() converts a text value to a time-date value. The functions @Date() and @Time() both convert numeric values to time-date values.

The @Text() function is very versatile, because of the level of control you can exert over the conversion process. The syntax is the following:

```
@Text(time-date; parameters).
```

The parameters are listed in Table 19.4 and control the format of the return value.

TABLE 19.4 Parameters for @Text() Time-Date Conversion

Parameter	Result
General Parameters	
S0	Date only
S1	Time only
S2	Date and time
S3	Date and time, plus Today, Yesterday, or Tomorrow
Sx	Used when the format of the value passed can not be predicted

Parameter	Result
	Date Parameters
D0	Year, month, and day
D1	Month and day, plus year if not the current year
D2	Month and day only
D3	Year and month
	Time Parameters
T0	Hour, minute, and second
T1	Hour and minute only
	Time Zone Parameters
Z0	Converts time to the current time zone
Z1	Displays the zone if not the same as the current time zone
Z2	Always displays the zone

Converting Text to Numbers

`@Text()` can also be used to convert text to numbers. Unlike its counterpart `@TextToNumber()`, `@Text()` enables you to specify the following parameters:

G	General format
F	Fixed
S	Scientific notation
C	Currency
,	Punctuated at thousands
%	Percent
(	Negative numbers in parentheses
n	Digits for precision

Like the format string for Time, these can be combined. For example, `@Text(105001.056; "F2,")` returns 105,001.06.

You will find many uses for the parameters used to convert time to text. For example, the formula `@Text(@Now; "S2")` uses the `format string "S2"`, which returns results such as "05/22/98 04:46:58 PM." If you want to get rid of the seconds component, you can use `@Text(@Now; "S2T1")`, which produces "05/22/98 04:46 PM." Producing just the date can be accomplished as easily with `@Text(@Now; "S0")`. Note that `@Text(@Today)` also works.

19

**FORMULA
LANGUAGE BASICS**

Of course, you are not restricted to using @Text with time-date @Functions like @Now. You can also use them with fields or variables which contain time-date values. @Text(dCall; "D0S0") displays the call date (dCall) using only the date portion.

To convert a text value into a time-date value, you use @TextToTime(*stringvalue*). Note that *stringvalue* must be a legitimate time-date string that matches what Domino expects. It can also be a relative date value such as Tomorrow, Today, or Yesterday. If today is August 15, 1998, @TextToTime("Yesterday") displays 08/14/98. However, @TextToTime("August 15, 1998") fails because the string value is not a recognizable date. The expression @TextToTime("08/15/1998") is the correct format. You can also add a time component to the formula as in the following: @TextToTime("08/15/1998 05:10:10 PM").

> **Caution**
>
> If you fail to include the AM or PM component in a TextToTime() formula or use military time (17:10:10), the time component defaults to AM.

There are several ways to use @Date() and @Time() in addition to the forms of these commands that extract date or time components from an existing time-date value. There are two syntax forms for each function. One is extended and includes all time-date components, while the other is a short form that includes the date part for @Date() and the time part for @Time(). Following is the syntax for each form:

```
@Date( year; month; day )
@Date( year; month; day; hour; minute; second )
@Time( hour; minute; second )
@Time( year; month; day; hour; minute; second )
```

Sometimes you want to convert a date into its "full" version, that is, February 15, 1999. To do so, use the following formula:

```
@Select(@Month(@Today);"January";"February";"March";"April";
        "May";"June";"July";"August";"September";"October";
        "November";"December")+" "+@Text(@Day(@Today))+ ", "
        +@Text(@Year(@Today)
```

Converting a date expressed in this fashion back to a valid time-date value is a little trickier. There are several different techniques; following is one for your review:

```
REM "cCreated is in a text based Month, day, year format";
REM "Trim the value in case the user put extra spaces in there" ;
```

```
jcDate := @Trim(cCreatedDate) ;

REM "Find out which month it is using the short three";
REM "character version of the month.";
jcMonthNumber := @If(@Contains(jcDate; "Jan") ; "01";
        @Contains(jcDate; "Feb") ; "02";
        @Contains(jcDate; "Mar") ; "03";
        @Contains(jcDate; "Apr") ; "04";
        @Contains(jcDate; "May") ; "05";
        @Contains(jcDate; "Jun") ; "06";
        @Contains(jcDate; "Jul") ; "07";
        @Contains(jcDate; "Aug") ; "08";
        @Contains(jcDate; "Sep") ; "09";
        @Contains(jcDate; "Oct") ; "10";
        @Contains(jcDate; "Nov") ; "11";
        @Contains(jcDate; "Dec") ; "12";
        "12") ;
REM "Between the first space and the comma is the day";
REM "of the month; the year is whatever is to the";
REM "right of the comma";
jcDay := @Middle(jcDate; " "; ",");
jcYear := @RightBack(jcDate; ", ");

REM "Put the pieces together in a text string and use";
REM "@TextToTime to create a valid time-date value";
@TextToTime(jcMonthNumber + "/" + jcDay + "/" + jcYear)
```

Working with Date Math

In any programming language, date math can be very tricky. You might expect that
@Today - @Yesterday would return 1 because today and yesterday are 1 day apart.
Instead, it returns 86,400. Remember that number because it is the product of the number
of hours in a day multiplied by the number of minutes per hour and then multiplied by
the number of seconds per minute, or 24 * 60 * 60. All date math is expressed in seconds, so @Tomorrow - @Yesterday returns 172,800. This is an improvement over some
languages that returned seconds past midnight. That made programming date functions
frustrating and tedious.

If you want to know the number of days between two time-date values simply divide the
result by the magic number—86,400. If you need the result in hours, use 3,600, which is
60 minutes * 60 seconds. Remember that when you do date math and divide by 86,400,
the result is the number of days, not the number of days plus the number of hours. For
example, consider the following equation:

```
[02/15/99 05:00 PM] - [02/14/99 05:00 AM]
```

19

Formula Language Basics

The previous equation yields 129,600 seconds, or 1.5 when divided by 86,400. If you just need the number of days and don't want the decimal part of the result, combine your formula with @Integer, as in the following example:

```
@Integer(([02/15/99 05:00:00 PM] - [02/14/99 05:00:00 AM] ) / 86400)
```

The result of the previous expression is 1.

Date math can get more complex if you need to express the result in days plus hours. The following example yields "1 day(s) and 12 hour(s)":

```
@Text(@Integer(
    ➥([02/15/99 05:00:00 PM] - [02/14/99 05:00:00 AM] ) / 86400)
            ➥) +  " day(s) and " +
    ➥@Text((@Modulo(
            ➥([02/15/99 05:00:00 PM] - [02/14/99 05:00:00 AM] );
            ➥86400)) / 3600)
        ➥+ " hour(s)"
```

Working with Strings

You have already seen some examples using string @Functions. The example in the section "Converting Time-Date Values" used @Middle(), @Trim(), and @RightBack(). String functions can locate strings, extract parts of text strings (substrings), trim strings, convert data types to string, compare strings, determine their length, modify strings, and more. Table 19.5 lists some of the commonly used string @Functions.

TABLE 19.5   String @Functions

@Function	*Purpose*
Locating substrings within strings	
@Begins()	Determines whether a string begins with another string
@Contains()	Determines whether a string contains another string
@Ends()	Determines whether a string ends with another string
Extracting substrings from strings	
@Left()	Returns leftmost characters of a string, searching from left to right
@LeftBack()	Returns leftmost characters of a string, searching from right to left
@Middle()	Returns characters from the middle of a string, searching from left to right

@Function	*Purpose*
	Extracting substrings from strings
@MiddleBack()	Returns characters from the middle of a string, searching from right to left
@Right()	Returns rightmost characters of a string, searching from left to right
@RightBack()	Returns rightmost characters of a string, searching from right to left
	Comparing strings
@Like()	Compares two strings; similar to @Match() but is ANSI SQL compliant
@Matches()	Compares two strings
	Manipulating Strings
@Length()	Returns the length of a string
@LowerCase()	Converts a string to lowercase
@ProperCase()	Converts a string to proper case, capitalizing the first letters of words
@UpperCase()	Converts a string to uppercase
@Repeat()	Repeats a string
@ReplaceSubString()	Replaces elements of a string
@Text()	Converts other data types to text strings
@Trim()	Removes leading and trailing blanks

The function for converting dates in the date string format May 22, 1999 the standard Month/Date/Year format 05/22/99 uses several string @Functions. First, the string is trimmed in case the users put extra spaces into the field by jcDate := @Trim(cCreatedDate). Next, using @If(@Contains(jcDate; "Jan") ; "01"..., you obtain the month number. The statement @Middle(jcDate; " "; ",") retrieves the day of the month by extracting the value between the space after the month and the comma. To retrieve the year, @RightBack(jcDate; ", ") was used, extracting anything to the right of the comma and space. You can also use @Right(jcDate; 4) to accomplish the same thing.

Caution

Note that for this formula to work properly the initial value must be entered in the correct format!

Getting Session and User Information

Session information tells you things about the current user such as her name, the type of client she is using to access your application, what roles she has in a database, and what her mail file is. Table 19.6 lists some of these useful session and user information @Functions.

TABLE 19.6 @Functions for Session and User Information

@*Function*	*Result*
@BrowserInfo()	Returns information about the Web browser
@ClientType	Returns the type of client for the user, Notes or Web
@UserName	Returns the username
@Name()	Returns components of the user's name when used in conjunction with @UserName
@MailDBName	Returns the current user's mail server name and path to her mail file
@UserAccess()	Returns the user's access level to a database
@UserRoles	Returns a list of the user's roles in a database

To determine whether a user was a Web or a Notes client before R4.6, you used @UserRoles() in a formula like the following:

```
@Contains(@UserRoles; "$$Web")
```

@ClientType, introduced in R4.6 returns Web or Notes, without resorting to testing @UserRoles(). Nonetheless, @UserRoles() is very useful in its own right. Consider the following example that enables you to take actions based on the user's role assignment in a database:

```
@If(@Contains(@UserRoles; "Profile")...
```

For more information...

For an explanation of roles in a database, see Chapter 31, "Security and Domino Applications."

The @UserName function returns the name of the current user in canonical format if it is a hierarchical user name. A hierarchical name contains components including the full name, the organization, organizational unit, and sometimes the country. Your Notes user ID is a hierarchical name. If the name is nonhierarchical, @UserName displays just the name. A Web user might have a nonhierarchical name, for example. Canonical format displays all the components of a name including common name (CN), organizational unit (OU), organization (O), and country (C). A name displayed in full canonical format would look like the following:

CN=Steve Kern/OU=ISDept/O=MyCompany/C=US

As you can imagine, this isn't something you would want to display to users very often! The function @Name([argument]; *notesname*) can be used to extract various pieces of canonical names. Table 19.7 lists the arguments for @Name().

TABLE 19.7 Arguments for @Name()

Argument	*Return*
[A]	Returns the Administration management domain name
[Abbreviate]	Displays the name in abbreviated format
[C]	Returns the country
[Canonicalize]	Displays an abbreviated name in full canonical format
[CN]	Returns the common name
[G]	Returns the first name
[I]	Returns the initials
[O]	Returns the organization component
[OUN]	Returns the *Nth* organizational component (for example, [OU1], [OU2])
[P]	Returns the private management domain name
[Q]	Returns the generational qualifier
[S]	Returns the last name
[ToKeyword]	Displays the name parts except the common name in reverse order with back slashes instead of forward slashes (C\O\OU)

19

FORMULA LANGUAGE BASICS

Caution

The components [A], [G], [I], [P], [Q], and [S] were designed for use with gateways and other mail systems. They do not function with a Notes name.

The most frequently used arguments are [CN], returning the common name component, and [Abbreviate], which returns the common name plus the organizational unit and organizational certifiers separated by forward slashes. Given the name John Smith, registered under the organizational unit IS of the organization MyCompany, the [CN] argument returns John Smith. [Abbreviate] returns John Smith/IS/MyCompany.

User-Friendly Names

Use [Abbreviate] or [CN] to store names in fields that the users see. This is much friendlier than a canonical name!

You can use @Name and @UserName to build an edit history as shown in Figure 19.3.

FIGURE 19.3

This subform tracks the edit history for a document.

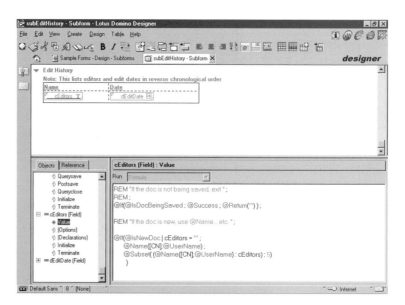

The formula for the cEditors field uses he common name component to build a text list of the last five editors as in the following example:

```
REM "If the doc is not being saved, exit " ;
REM ;
@If(@IsDocBeingSaved ; @Success ; @Return("") ) ;

REM "If the doc is new, use @Name... etc. " ;
```

```
@If(@IsNewDoc ¦ cEditors = "" ;
    @Name([CN];@UserName) ;
    @Subset( (@Name([CN];@UserName) : cEditors) ; 5))
```

The formula for the dEditDate field is the following:

```
REM "If the doc is not being saved, exit " ;

@If(@IsDocBeingSaved ; @Success ; @Return("") ) ;

REM "If the doc is new, or the edit date is blank use @Now" ;

@If(@IsNewDoc ¦ dEditDate = "" ;
    @Now ;
    @Subset( (@Now : dEditDate) ; 5) )
```

Because the fields, cEditors and dEditDate, are placed beside each other in a table, the names of the users who edited the documents are placed right next to the dates on which the edit took place.

Working with Documents

Because Notes originated as a distributed document management system, it is only natural that there are a lot of ways to obtain information about documents. You can obtain information about the document's creation date and last modified date as you saw earlier in the section "Working with Date and Time @Functions." There are also @Functions that tell you the size of the document, the names of any attachments, the lengths of any attachments, and more. Some of these @Functions are available as simple actions in views.

Table 19.8 lists some of the @Functions you can use to display information about documents.

TABLE 19.8 Document @Functions

@Function	Return
General Document Information	
@Accessed	Last date and time the document was accessed
@Attachments	The number of file attachments
@AttachmentNames	Text list of attached filenames
@AttachmentLengths	Text list of attached file sizes
@Author	Text list of document authors

continues

19

FORMULA LANGUAGE BASICS

Table 19.8 continued

@*Function*	*Return*
General Document Information	
@Created	Date the document was created
@DocFields	Text list of document fields
@DocLength	The size of the document in bytes
@DocumentUniqueID	The document's unique ID
@InheritedDocumentUniqueID	The unique ID of the current document's parent document
@Modified	Last modification date and time
@NoteID	"NT" plus the note ID
@Functions used in Views	
@AllChildren	Used in view selection formulas, returns response documents
@AllDescendants	Used in view selection formulas, returns response and response-to-response documents
@Responses	The number of responses to the current document in a view
Logical properties of documents—"Is" functions	
@IsAvailable(*fieldname*)	True if the field is available
@IsDocBeingEdited	True if the document is in edit mode
@IsDocBeingLoaded	True if the document is being loaded into memory
@IsDocBeingMailed	True if the document is being mailed
@IsDocBeingRecalculated	True if the document is being refreshed
@IsDocBeingSaved	True if the document is being saved
@IsNewDoc	True if the document has just been composed and has not been saved
@IsResponseDoc	True if the document is a response document
@IsUnAvailable(*fieldname*)	True if the field is not available
Other useful document properties—special fields	
$Ref	Unique ID of the parent document
$Revisions	List of dates and times the document was edited
$UpdatedBy	List of document authors and editors

You have already seen examples of many of these @Functions scattered throughout the formulas in this chapter. Many document property @Functions are useful in views. For example, if you have a database that serves as a design archive, you can use the

@Functions @Attachments, @AttachmentLengths, and @AttachmentNames to display information about any file attachments. Figure 19.4 shows a view under construction that uses these @Functions.

FIGURE 19.4

This view uses @Functions to display information about the attachments to documents.

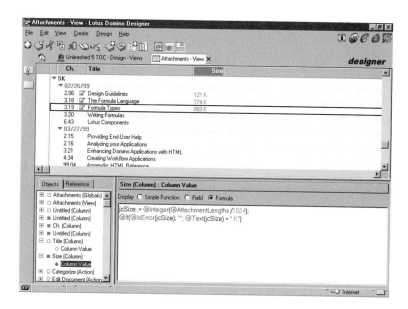

The icon next to the Title column is displayed only when a file attachment exists. To accomplish this, set the view column properties to display icons only, and use the following formula:

```
@If(@Attachments > 0; 58; 0)
```

The number 58 displays a specific view column icon. A grid of view icons is available in Domino Designer Help.

To display the name of the attachment, you can use a simple action or the @Function @AttachmentNames.

To display the size of the attachment, use the @AttachmentLengths @Function. Normally, @AttachmentLengths displays the value in bytes; to display the value in kilobytes, use the following formula:

```
@If(@Attachments > 0;
    @Text(@Integer(@AttachmentLengths / 1024)) + " K"; "")
```

The @Functions related to the document ID can be quite useful. For example, you can update the value of a field on another document as long as you know the unique

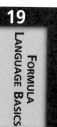

19

FORMULA
LANGUAGE BASICS

document ID. If you want to update the value of the cStatus field on a parent document from a response document you can use a formula such as the following:

```
@SetDocField($Ref; "cStatus"; cRespStatus)
```

Document IDs

Document IDs are unique across all replicas of a database.

The @AllChildren, @AllDescendants, and @IsResponseDoc functions are used in view selection formulas to display main documents and any responses.

Children or Descendants?

It is better to use @AllChildren or @AllDescendants in a view selection formula than @IsResponseDoc. The formula @IsResponseDoc returns all response documents—not just those related to the main documents in the view. Only those response documents that are related to a main document are displayed.

The "Is" @Functions are useful if you need to take certain actions that are dependant on the state of the document. In the edit history example in the section on "Getting Session and User Information," @IsDocBeingSaved was used to make sure that the field values didn't get updated at the wrong time.

The special fields listed at the end of Table 19.8 are not editable, but they can be used in formulas. Of the three, $Ref is used the most frequently; $Ref stores the unique ID of the parent document and provides the link to the document to update the field value. This can be used in @SetDocField() to update a parent document from a response document.

Retrieving Data with @DbColumn and @DbLookup

All database languages have the capability to look up reference or other information, and nearly all applications use this capability at some point. Domino applications frequently use formulas for keyword fields that can look up information within the same database, other Domino databases, or even foreign databases. @DbColumn() and @DbLookup() are the most frequently used @Functions to retrieve data, although @DbCommand() can also be used against ODBC data sources.

The 64K Limit

@DbColumn(), @DbLookup(), and @DbCommand() can return no more than 64KB of data. If you run into this barrier use @PickList().

The function @DbColumn() returns a list of values from the specified column of a view. The view can be in the current database or in another database. The function @DbLookup() also returns a list of values from a specified column in a view. Unlike @DbColumn() that loads whatever is in the column into memory, @DbLookup() enables you to specify a key value. This value is compared against the first sorted column in the view and only values from documents matching the key are retrieved. The following code, which is from an Action button that looks up departments and enables the user to choose a supervisor from a list of supervisors for that department, illustrates the use of @DbColumn() and @DbLookup():

```
REM "Look up the departments" ;
jcHRLookupID := @GetProfileField("GP"; "cHRLookupID");


jcDeptList := @DbColumn( ""; jcHRLookupID ; "LUDEPT";1) ;


jcDept := @Prompt([OKCANCELLIST]; "Departments" ;
     "Choose a department" ; "" ; jcDeptList ) ;
@If(jcDept = ""; @Return(""); @Success) ;


REM "The Department code and description are concatenated";
REM "into a single view column" ;
jcDeptName := @Right(jcDept; " ") ;
REM "The Department code should be the first four characters";
REM "plus 00" ;
jcDeptCode := @Left(jcDept; 4) + "00";


@SetField("cDepartment"; jcDeptName) ;
@SetField("cCostCenter"; jcDeptCode);


REM "Present a list of supervisors from the Cost Center to the user";
jcSuperList := @DbLookup(""; jcHRLookupID; "SDN";
                    cCostCenter; "cSuper");
jcSupervisor := @Prompt([OKCANCELLIST]; "Supervisors";
               "Choose a Supervisor"; ""; jcSuperList );
@SetField("cSupervisor";@If(@IsError(jcSupervisor); "";
     jcSupervisor)) ;
```

The syntax of @DbColumn() and @DbLookup() are quite similar, as you can see in the following:

```
@DbColumn(Class : NoCache ; server : database ;
➥view name; column number)
```

```
@DbLookup(Class : NoCache ; server : database ;
➥view name; key value; column number or field name)
```

Class refers to the database type. You can refer to Notes databases as "Notes" or with double quotes. *NoCache* tells Notes not to store the results in memory (the default). Storing the results of the lookup can provide performance improvements for lookups against data that doesn't change very often. *Server* can be represented by the name of the server or with double quotes indicating the current server. *Database* can be the current database, represented by double quotes, or it can be the replica ID of a database. It can also be the operating system filename. If you choose to use the filename, you must include the path relative to the data directory on the server. The view name can be either the name of a view or its alias. Note that for @DbColumn(), you must specify the column number, whereas with @DbLookup() you can either specify the column number or the name of a document field. The document field does not have to be present in the view.

Using Hidden Views

It is often a good idea to use a hidden view to look up reference information. You can hide a view by enclosing its name in parentheses. You can also indicate the purpose of the view by placing the characters "LU" for "Look up" at the beginning of the view name. This tells other developers about the purpose of the view. The code sample uses a hidden view with the name (LUDept) and an alias of LUDept.

The functions @DbColumn() and @DbLookup() can also be used to perform ODBC lookups. *ODBC* stands for Open Database Connectivity, a standard that supports connectivity between different database sources. For example, you can install an ODBC driver for SQL Server, Sybase, or any one of a number of different databases. When the ODBC source is configured, you can use it to look up information in the foreign database by passing a table name, a key column, and a key value for @DbLookup(), or by specifying a table name and column name for @DbColumn(). For example, if you were to look up the department information in a SQL Server table, you might use the following code:

```
@DbColumn("ODBC" : "NoCache"; "HR Lookup"; skern : nreks;
➥Department; cDeptName; "Distinct" : "Ascending")
```

Using SQL in Notes

For those of you with SQL in your background, you can pass a SQL statement to an ODBC source using @DbCommand.

> **Caution**
>
> There is a risk associated with using ODBC sources in your applications. The users must have appropriate access to the data source. If the user cannot read the ODBC source, the lookup will fail. To get around this problem, you can use DECS or a data integration product such as the Lotus Enterprise Integrator.

Working with Lists

What is arguably one of the most important and powerful aspects of Domino development is the capability to work with lists. A list is similar to an array in other languages; in fact, in LotusScript, you handle lists using arrays. Both fields and variables can contain lists of numbers, time-dates, text, or names. A field that contains a list is called a *multivalue* field. To create a field that accepts multiple values, you set the Allow multiple values property on the Field Info tab of the field properties box.

When you use @DbColumn() or @DbLookup(), Domino returns a list of values. You can perform math on lists, replace specific elements in lists, retrieve specific elements from lists, combine lists, and more. Better yet, you can do so much more easily when compared to array processing in LotusScript. There are a number of @Functions and operators devoted to list processing. Table 19.9 lists the @Functions you are likely to use.

TABLE 19.9 List Processing in Domino

Function	*Returns*
@Contains()	True if the value is in the list
@Elements()	The number of list elements
@Explode()	Creates a list from a text string or date range
@Implode()	Creates a text string from a list
@IsMember()	True if the value is a member of the list
@IsNotMember()	True if the value is not a member of the list
@Member()	The position of a member in a list
@Replace()	Replaces elements of a list
@ReplaceSubString()	Replaces string values with new values
@Subset()	Extracts values from a list; a positive number extracts from left to right and a negative number extracts from right to left
@Sum()	The sum of all the elements of a numeric list
@Trim()	Removes empty elements from a list
@Unique()	A list of unique values

19

FORMULA LANGUAGE BASICS

There are also a number of useful list operators. The most important operator is the list concatenation operator, which is the colon (:). This operator enables you to build lists out of constants or variables as well as fields containing single and multiple values. The only stipulation is that lists must contain like elements. In other words, you cannot mix a time-date value with a text value—you must convert it to a text value first. The following example creates a list of text elements:

```
jcTextList := "Chapter 1" : "Chapter 2" : "Chapter 3" : "Chapter 4"
```

Math can also be performed on lists; the operators you can use include the following: +, -, *, /, >, <, >=, <=, =, and !=. Used alone these operators act in what is called *pair-wise* or parallel fashion. For example, you can use the following to add two text lists together with the + operator:

```
jcTextList1 := "Chapter 1" : "Chapter 1" ;
jcTextList2 := "1" : "2" ;
jcTextList1 + jcTextList2
```

Doing so yields the following result:

```
"Chapter 11"; "Chapter 12"
```

Adding the asterisk to the list operators causes the elements to be *permuted*—all elements are combined with each other. In the previous example, cChange the last line to the following:

```
jcTextList1 *+ jcTextList2
```

The result is the following:

```
"Chapter 11"; "Chapter 12"; "Chapter 11"; "Chapter 12"
```

The following code fragment uses list processing to build several multivalued fields:

```
REM "Write the doc history";
jcApproval := "Approved";
jcAreaMgr := @Name([Abbreviate]; @UserName);
jdAreaMgr := @Text(@Now; "S2");
jcDocHistory := "Request " + jcApproval + " by " + jcAreaMgr +
                " on " + jdAreaMgr ;
jcSignHistory := jcApproval + " by " + jcAreaMgr + " on " +
                @Text(@Today) ;
@SetField("cAreaSign" ;@Trim(cAreaSign : jcSignHistory));

REM "Populate cDocHistory if it is blank";
jcFullName := cFirstName + " " + cInitial + " " + cLastName;
@If(cDocHistory = ""; @SetField("cDocHistory"; "Request " +
    @If(cAccess = "Delete User"; "to "; "for ") + cAccess +
```

```
          " for " + lcFullName + " created on " + jdAreaMgr + " by " +
          jcAreaMgr);
          "") ;

REM "Now add this event to the doc history";
@SetField("cDocHistory" ; cDocHistory : jcDocHistory);

REM "Voting History";
@SetField("cVote"; @Trim(cVote : jcApproval));
@SetField("cVoter"; @Trim(cVoter : @Name([Abbreviate];@UserName)));
@SetField("dVote"; @If(dVote = ""; @Now; dVote : @Now));

REM "Clear the user name from the Approver list";
jcApproverList := @Trim(@Replace(cApproverList ; cVoter; ""));
@SetField("cApproverList"; jcApproverList)
```

This code is from an agent that signs a document. There are multiple signers, stored in a multivalued field, cApproverList. When each signer approves the document, their name is removed from the approvers field, and several fields are modified, tracking the history of this event.

For example, a string is built and added to the field cAreaSign. It is *concatenated* using the concatenation operator (:) and added as the last element in the field cAreaSign. Similarly, document history is stored in the field cDocHistory. Voting history is stored in several fields, cVote, cVoter, and dVote.

To remove the approver from the cApproverList field, @Replace replaces the name of the approver in the field with a null string, and @Trim removes the null string from the list. The resulting list, without the approver's name, is then stored back in the cApproverList field.

As you can see, Domino has extensive support for list processing. It is well worth your time to learn how to work with lists!

Getting User Input

You can use several @Functions to get input from users. The most common is @Prompt(), which has a number of variations from a simple OK dialog box to a multivalue select box. See Table 19.10 for a listing of @Prompt styles. The function @DialogBox() displays any form for user input, but it is most effective when used with a form containing a single layout region. Using @DialogBox() in that fashion enables you to create what appear to be standard Windows dialog boxes. The @Picklist() function displays a view in a dialog box returning the column value specified for the document selected.

19

FORMULA LANGUAGE BASICS

Table 19.10 @Prompt Styles

Argument	Result
[OK]	Displays a simple box with a message and a single OK button
[YesNo]	Displays a box with two buttons, Yes and No
[YesNoCancel]	Presents a box with three buttons, Yes, No, and Cancel
[OkCancelEdit]	Presents an input box with OK and Cancel buttons
[OkCancelList]	Displays a list of choices from which a single value can be selected
[OkCancelCombo]	Displays a list of choices in a drop-down box from which a single value can be selected
[OkCancelEditCombo]	Displays a list of choices in a drop-down box from which a single value can be selected and enables the user to type a new value
[OkCancelListMult]	Displays a list of choices from which more than one value can be selected
[LocalBrowse]	Shows a picklist of files on the local hard drive
[Password]	Enables a user to securely type a password

> **Caution**
>
> Be careful using @Prompt(), @DialogBox(), and @Picklist() in Agents. Agents using the Formula Language operate on one document at a time and do not store values from one document to the next. It is often good practice to restrict an agent using these @Functions to the setting Manually from an Agent List which keeps the agent from appearing in the Action menu. You then launch the agent from a Form Action Bar button. If you enable the user to run the agent from the menu, he can potentially run it on multiple documents—literally, hundreds and hundreds, or worse, all documents in the database. It would be extremely frustrating to the end user to answer an @Prompt([OKCANCELEDIT]...) over and over again!

Following is an example of code from an Agent that runs Manually from Agent List and that is launched by a button in a view titled Done. The following shows you how @Prompt() can be used to obtain user feedback and incorporate that feedback in a document:

```
REM "Find out how many hours it took";
jnHours := @Prompt([OKCANCELEDIT]; "Effort";
        "Please enter the number of hours."; 0);
```

```
@If(jnHours = 0; @Return(""); @Success);
FIELD nActual := jnHours;
FIELD cStatus := "Completed";
FIELD dComplete := @Today
```

Figure 19.5 shows the dialog box displayed by the agent using @Prompt.

FIGURE 19.5

The Prompt box asking for the number of hours is displayed by @Prompt([OKCANCELEDIT...).

Figure 19.6 shows the use of @DialogBox() with a form containing a layout region. The layout region is set to 3D, which gives the dialog box a standard Windows look and feel. When the dialog box is opened, any fields on the form that have corresponding fields in the underlying document are inherited. Similarly, unless you specify otherwise, when you close the dialog box by clicking OK, the values you have entered in the dialog box are saved to the underlying document. This is a most useful @Function!

FIGURE 19.6

Using @DialogBox() *to get user input is a powerful tool.*

In order for the values entered using @DialogBox, the underlying document must be in edit mode. @DialogBox has several parameters that you can use to determine whether it displays information, stores it in the document, or allows new fields to be written to the document. You can also specify a title for the window. The parameters for @DialogBox are as follows:

```
@DialogBox( formname ; [AutoHorzFit] : [AutoVertFit] : [NoCancel] :
[NoNewFields] : [NoFieldUpdate] : [ReadOnly] ; SizeToTable ;
NoOkCancel ; title )
```

If you are using a layout region, it is best to use both [AutoHorzFit] and [AutoVertFit] parameters. If you want to simply display the contents of a field or fields, you can use [ReadOnly]. Including [NoCancel] presents just the OK button on the dialog window. [NoNewFields] and [NoFieldUpdate] control how the dialog box interacts with the fields in the underlying document. [NoNewFields] enables you to use fields on the dialog box that don't exist in the document. When the dialog box is closed, the fields aren't saved to the document. [NoFieldUpdate] stops changes to fields in the dialog box from being written to the underlying document. The parameters SizeToTable and NoOkCancel are new to R5. SizeToTable sizes the table in the dialog box, and NoOkCancel turns off the display of the OK and Cancel buttons. Title should always be used to name the dialog box. If the Title parameter is omitted, Notes displays "Lotus Notes" in the title bar of the dialog window. All parameters are optional except *formname*.

Using a Subform

You don't have to create a full-blown form for @DialogBox. You can create a layout region on a subform, and call it in the same way you call a form. Consider adding a prefix such as dBox to the form or subform name to distinguish it from other forms or subforms. For example, dBoxHistory could be used for a subform used to display document history.

The function @PickList() is a great addition to the Formula Language because it does not have a limitation on the amount of data it can store, as do the @Db functions, and it is extremely fast. Basically, it loads a view into a dialog box with OK and Cancel buttons. Figure 19.7 shows an example. Following is the code that produced the picklist:

```
@PickList( [Custom]; ""; "By Part"; "Select a Chapter";
           "Please select the Chapter to review" ; 2 )
```

FIGURE 19.7

@Picklist produces a dialog box using a view.

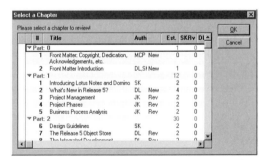

New to R5 is the capability to use a Replica ID in `@PickList()`. This removed a serious limitation in that prior to R5 you had to know the filename and path relative to the data directory to call `@PickList()`. The `@Picklist()` function can also display a lookup into the Domino Directory. Following is the syntax for that lookup:

```
@PickList([Name] : [Single])
```

If you specify Single, Notes displays a list from the Domino Directory that enables you to choose a single name. Otherwise, you get the familiar two-paned mover dialog box that enables the user to select multiple entries from the Domino Directory.

> **Caution**
>
> Each of these @Functions discussed in this section are only available to Notes clients. They will not function on the Web.

Controlling the Flow of a Formula

There are only a couple of methods that you can use to control the flow within a formula; remember that a formula is a lot like a single line of code. You can't pass parameters into or out of a formula. You have no subroutines to which you can pass control. You can, however, stop the execution of a formula with `@Return()`, or cause it to continue with `@Success`. You can also execute a formula sequence with `@Do(statement 1; statement 2; ...)`. You can combine either or both of these with `@If()` to provide a flow control of sorts. In the previous document history example, the execution of the formula was stopped using `@Return()` unless the document was being saved. The code is shown by the following example:

```
@If(@IsDocBeingSaved ; @Success ; @Return("") ) ;
```

Sometimes you might need to execute two different series of statements depending on a certain condition in the document. To accomplish this, you use `@If()` combined with `@Do()` as in the following example:

```
@If(cStatus = "Complete";
   @Do(@SetField("dComplete"; @Today);
       @SetField("cCompletedBy"; @Name([Abbreviate]; @UserName))) ;
   cStatus = "Pending";
   @Do(@SetField("dAssigned"; @Today));
   "")
```

To provide a semblance of control logic can be quite a bit of work using nested @If()
and @Do() statements. As mentioned earlier in this chapter, go slowly and test your logic
at each step of the way.

Trapping Errors in Formulas

While the Domino Designer catches most syntax errors before you save the design
object, there is really only one @Function that will test for an error. It is @IsError().
You can use this @Function to test return values for an error, and substitute the value
with an error with null (double quotes) for example. If you don't make this substitution,
users will see an error message rather than the value you intended. For example, if you
have a view column formula that divides one number with a fixed constant and if that
number is missing, an error shows up in the view column. In the next example, the following formula produces an error for those documents that do not have attachments (see
Figure 19.8):

```
@Text(@Integer(@AttachmentLengths / 1024)) + " K"
```

FIGURE 19.8

*An incorrect state-
ment generates an
error condition
that will be visible
to the user.*

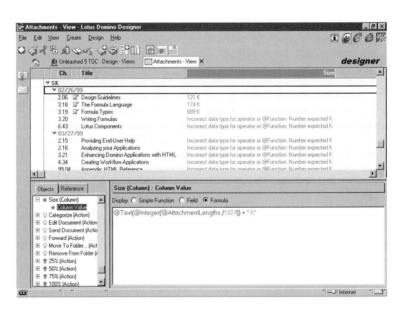

You can rewrite the column formula using @IsError() to trap for an error in the division, and if there is an error, display a blank. The following formula accomplishes this:

```
jcSize := @Integer(@AttachmentLengths / 1024) ;
@If(@IsError(jcSize); ""; @Text(jcSize) + " K")
```

Debugging Complex Formulas

Although your formulas are almost certainly correct syntactically, they can still generate run-time errors and problems. Debugging can be quite tricky with complex formulas. First and foremost, you cannot step through a formula as you can through LotusScript or other languages. Consequently, there are no breakpoints at which you can view the value of a temporary variable or field. You cannot watch how the program logic executes. This can be quite frustrating. There are two ways to work around this limitation.

The first is to create fields in a document to store the values of temporary variables or text statements indicating some event has transpired. This has the drawback of unnecessarily increasing the number of fields on a document. Of course, after you finish you can always create an agent to remove the extra fields using @DeleteField. This approach is appropriate when you are running an agent on multiple documents and need to see what happens for each document.

The second way is to distribute @Prompt([OK]; ...) statements at appropriate intervals which display the values of suspected problem variables or statements that indicate that the execution of the formula reached a certain point. This approach is appropriate for Action button formulas that operate at the document level.

Wishing for a Formula Debugger?

In the current build of R5, there is an undocumented formula debugger. You can launch it by holding down the Ctrl and shift keys when you choose File, Tools, Debug LotusScript. It is very definitely in beta, and is known to crash the Notes client.

Summary

This chapter introduced you to some of the methods that you can use to write formulas in Domino applications. You have covered a lot of ground, from types of formulas and statements to the different groups of @Functions, working with lists, trapping errors, and debugging formulas. The Formula Language is a very rich and mature language, and although this chapter has covered a lot of @Functions, many more @Functions are available. The help available in Domino Designer Help is generally excellent and quite thorough. Better yet, it is available when you are writing formulas! Writing formulas in forms, actions, views, hotspots, and more is discussed in the next chapter.

19

FORMULA
LANGUAGE BASICS

Writing Formulas

by Steve Kern

CHAPTER 20

In this chapter, you will learn about the various places where you can write formulas, and how to write those formulas. In Chapter 18, "The Formula Language," you learned about the components of the Formula language and its syntax. In Chapter 19, "Formula Types," you learned about types of formulas and how to work with the various types of @Functions. This chapter extends that knowledge into specific areas where you can use the Formula language.

Programming Practices

First, it is beneficial to discuss good programming practices. Over time, most developers have adopted practices that help them to write better and more maintainable code. Following are some good rules to start with:

- Keep it simple!
- Keep it readable.
- Build it slowly and *test, test, test*!
- Document your code! You never know who will have to maintain it later; it just might be *you!*

Keeping it Simple

A very wise developer once advised that rather than trying to write a slick program (or formula), it is better to write one that is simple and *works*. Nobody who uses the application ever sees your "slick" code anyway! Keeping your formulas simple is one way to write a formula that works. If you use a lot of nested statements in your routine, it can quickly become a nightmare to debug. Of course, there will be times when you cannot avoid using nested statements that are several layers deep, but for your own mental health, it is a good idea to keep them to a minimum.

Keeping it Readable

Keeping your formulas readable is accomplished in two ways. First, use white space (blank lines and spaces between operators) and REM statements. Second, assign statements to temporary variables. For example, the following code is easy to understand:

```
REM "Get a list of companies" ;
jcCompanyList := @DbColumn(""; ""; (LUCompanies); 1) ;

REM "Set up the @Prompt() statement";
DEFAULT jcDefault := cCompanyName ;
jcPromptTitle := "Company Listing";
```

```
jcPromptText := "Use the drop-down list button to choose a Company or type in a
➡new entry:";
REM "Look up the Company Name";
jcCompany := @Prompt([OKCANCELLIST]; jcPromptTitle; jcPromptText; jcDefault;
➡jcCompanyList);
REM "Store the choice in the cCompanyName field";
FIELD cCompanyName := jcCompany
```

The previous code has temporary variables, REM statements, and blank lines (white space) in the code. The following formula has none and is instead one extremely long complicated line:

```
FIELD cCompanyName := @Prompt([OKCANCELLIST]; "Company Listing"; "Use the drop-
down list button to choose a Company or type in a new entry:";
@If(@IsAvailable(cCompanyName); cCompanyName; ""); @DbColumn(""; "";
(LUCompanies); 1))
```

If you compare this to the previous listing, you will see how much easier it is to read the previous one.

Building it Slowly

In addition, testing debugging in this formula is difficult at best. If you make a mistake, the formula simply won't work and there will be no indication of where it failed. This is particularly important for the Formula language because you cannot step through the code in a debug mode as you can with LotusScript and many other programming languages. The first version of the formula enables you to test at each step. You can first test the @DBColumn() lookup, then test the @Prompt(), and then keep moving until you have tested all of it.

Documenting Your Code

You will also notice that the first version of the formula has several REM statements that tell you what the formula is doing at each step. Not only do these statements break up the code visually and make it more readable, they provide you and other developers with a guide to what the formula is supposed to accomplish. This can be very important at a later date when you need to modify the formula.

Using Formulas in Forms

Chapter 9, "Review of Basic Forms Design," and Chapter 10, "Advanced Form Design," describe what Forms are and how to construct them. This section covers the areas within a Form where formulas can be used.

You can tell where the Formula language can be used in the Object tab of the Info List when the form is in design. Beside each of the Form events, is a small symbol indicating the types of languages that are available. A small cyan diamond indicates that only the Formula language can be used. If code has been written for the event, the symbol is filled. Figure 20.1 shows the Objects tab for Form events.

FIGURE 20.1

The symbols beside the Form events indicate the languages available to program the event.

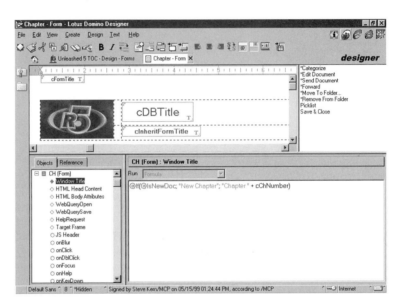

Table 20.1 lists the events that are programmable with the Formula language. The chapters on the other languages, LotusScript, JavaScript and Java cover the events available for those languages.

TABLE 20.1 Form Events Programmable with the Formula Language

Event	Language
Window Title	Formula Language only
HTML Head Content	Formula Language only
HTML Body Attributes	Formula Language only
WebQueryOpen	Formula Language only
WebQuerySave	Formula Language only
HelpRequest	Formula Language only
Target Frame	Formula Language only
QueryOpen	Formula Language and LotusScript

Event	Language
PostOpen	Formula Language and LotusScript
QueryModeChange	Formula Language and LotusScript
PostModeChange	Formula Language and LotusScript
PostRecalc	Formula Language and LotusScript
QuerySave	Formula Language and LotusScript
PostSave	Formula Language and LotusScript
QueryClose	Formula Language and LotusScript

Window Title

Each form can display a title in the Window Title and the task button in the workspace. If you do not specify a Window Title formula, the Notes Client displays "(Untitled)," so it is always a good idea to include this formula, especially for applications intended for use by Notes clients.

Window Titles and Web Clients

Web clients do not display the Window Title, but the value that is returned in the Window Title event is stored in the HTML <TITLE> tag.

Window Title formulas are usually fairly simple, although you have a wide range of @Functions available. The Window Title formula expects a text, which is rendered in the window title bar and task button. Usually, you display the name of the form, and the formula simply evaluates it to a text constant. Frequently, designers test whether the document is a new one, and display "New" as part of the Window Title. Window Title formulas are composed in the Window Title event for a form. To create the Window Title formula that displays "New Chapter" for a new document and "Chapter" plus the number of the chapter for an existing document, use the following steps:

1. Open Domino Designer if you have not done so already, and open the Form you want to work with.

2. Usually, the Window Title event is displayed by default when you open a form. In case it's not, open the Form tree in the Object tab and choose Window Title.

3. Enter the following Window Title formula. You can click the green check mark to check your syntax.

```
@If(@IsNewDoc; "New Chapter"; "Chapter " + cChNumber)
```

As you can see, this is a fairly simple formula. There is really not much reason to create complex formulas here because users rarely look at the Window Title.

HTML Head Content and HTML Body Attributes

If you present your application to Web clients, you can use two Form Events to modify the document using HTML. Both the HTML Head Content and HTML Body Attributes events enable you to define what appears in the corresponding <HEAD> and <BODY> HTML tags when a document is presented a Web client. HTML Head Content is new to R5; HTML Body Attributes is equivalent to the HTML Attributes event available in R4.6.

Both these tags are *container tags*. Container tags must have an opening and closing tag: <BODY> and </BODY>. The opening tag <BODY> turns the effect on, and the slash (/) in the tag </BODY> turns the effect off. These tags can contain other tags and document content. In an HTML document, you might see a construction such as the following:

```
<HEAD>
<TITLE>Web Form</TITLE><!—· This is the HTML Head Content Event —·!>
<META NAME="name" content="Notes">
```

In this example, <HEAD> *contains* two tags, <TITLE> for the page title, and <META> . <META> is used in HTML to specify document level information.

When you add code to these Form events, you do not need to include the <BODY> and <HEAD> tags. Domino automatically generates these tags for documents presented to Web clients. Any code you add simply modifies what Domino places in those tags. For example, in the HTML Head Content event, you can add the following lines:

```
"<META NAME="name" CONTENT="Notes">
```

In R5, there is virtually no point to using the HTML Body Attributes event, because every attribute the <BODY> tag takes can be set on the form itself. Once set on the form, it will overwrite anything you place in the HTML Body Attribute event. The <BODY> tag takes the attributes listed in Table 20.2.

Table 20.2   <BODY> Tag Attributes

Tag	Usage
ALINK	Sets the color of the active link
BACKGROUND	Sets the background image
BGCOLOR	Sets the background color for the document
LINK	Sets the color for unvisited links
TEXT	Sets the color for the body text
VLINK	Sets the color for visited links

Listing 20.1 contains the HTML source of a Notes document presented to a Web client. At the top of the listing, you will find the <HEAD> and <BODY> tags.

LISTING 20.1 HTML—HTML Code Generated by Domino's HTTP Service

```
<HTML>
<! - Lotus-Domino (Release 5.0 - March 30, 1999 on Windows NT/Intel) - >

<HEAD>
<TITLE>Web Form</TITLE><! -- This is the HTML Head Content Event --!> <meta
name="name" content="Notes Geek"></HEAD>
<BODY TEXT="000000" BGCOLOR="FFFFFF" ALINK="cyan" VLINK="Teal">

<FORM METHOD=post
ACTION="/Web46Test.nsf/d74a18e4a8682b498525667e00041b3c?CreateDocument"
NAME="_WS"><CENTER><FONT SIZE=5 COLOR="0000ff">Web Form R5.0</FONT><p>
</CENTER>
<TABLE WIDTH="100%" BORDER=0 CELLSPACING=0 CELLPADDING=0>
<TR VALIGN=top><TD WIDTH="13%"><DIV
ALIGN=right><B>Name</B></DIV></TD><TD></TD><TD WIDTH="85%">
<INPUT NAME="cYourName"></TD></TR>

<TR VALIGN=top><TD WIDTH="13%"><DIV
ALIGN=right><B>Address</B></DIV></TD><TD></TD><TD WIDTH="85%">
<INPUT NAME="cAddress"></TD></TR>
</TABLE>
<BR>
<A HREF="http://www.lotus.com"" TITLE="ggg"><B><U>Lotus Home</U></B></A>
<P>
<INPUT TYPE=submit VALUE="Submit"></FORM>
</BODY>
</HTML>
```

Showing HTML Source in the Notes Browser

New to Release 5 is the capability to show the HTML Source of a document. This is convenient when you are working in design. To show the source, simply preview your form in the Notes Web Browser, and choose View, Show, HTML Source.

The <HEAD> tag can take a number of other tags such as <META> and <TITLE>. The <META> tag has several useful attributes for specifying document variables. Typical document variables are DESCRIPTION, GENERATOR, and KEYWORDS. The attributes you use to specify these variables are NAME and CONTENT. The syntax is the following:

20

WRITING FORMULAS

```
<META NAME=variable name CONTENT= variable content>
```

For example, the following HTML code sets the KEYWORDS attribute:

```
"<META NAME=\"KEYWORDS\" CONTENT=\"Domino Designer, Lotus Notes\">"
```

Keywords are used frequently by search engines on the Web when indexing your site.

> **For More Information...**
>
> For more information about HTML , see Chapter 21, "Enhancing Domino
> Applications with HTML" and Appendix D, "HTML Reference."

WebQueryOpen and WebQuerySave Events

These two events have pre-established formulas. Both events run an agent, and use the
following @Command:

```
@Command([ToolsRunMacro]; "<Your agent goes here>")
```

The WebQueryOpen event runs when the form is opened in a Web browser and the
WebQuerySave event runs when the form is closed. They are functionally equivalent to
the LotusScript QueryOpen and QuerySave events, and also equivalent to adding the
reserved special fields $$QueryOpenAgent and $$QuerySaveAgent fields.

The agents that you run can be any type—Formula, LotusScript, or Java—and they must
be set to one of the Manual options. Because these agents can run on the server, they can
accomplish tasks that a Web client cannot.

Domino Web mail uses this technique to send mail. Because a Web browser can't directly send mail, the agent sends the mail when the document is saved. These agents can also
be used to gather CGI (Common Gateway Interface) variables using the
DocumentContext property of the NotesSession class. This is a great way to gather
information such as the user's name and the type of browser that she is using.

The HelpRequest Event

This event is new to R5, and is discussed in Chapter 15, "Providing End-User Help" in
the section titled, "Creating Context-Sensitive Help." As pointed out in that chapter, this
event, in conjunction with the new @Command([OpenHelpDocument]) enables you to program form-specific help available to end users when they press the F1 key.

Section Formulas

As discussed in Chapter 10, there are two types of sections: Standard and Controlled Access. Sections are collapsible areas on a form that can be opened and closed with a twistie. Form elements such as tables, text, and fields can be included in a section. You can write formulas for the section title of a standard section, and the Section Access formula for a controlled access section.

Section Titles

Both types of sections have a title. If an area of the form containing text is selected when the section is created, the title defaults to the nearest highlighted. If there is no text, the section title defaults to "Untitled Section." You can use the Formula language to create section titles only for Standard access sections. Controlled access sections only allow entry of text. Figure 20.2 shows the Title tab of a Standard access section Properties box, and Figure 20.3 shows the Title tab for a controlled access section.

FIGURE 20.2

The Properties box for a standard access section. Note the radio button selection for Text or Formula.

FIGURE 20.3

The Properties box for a controlled access section. Note that there is no formula available for the title, and that there is also a Section Field Name box.

In the formula box for a standard access section, you can build the section title from fields on the form or standard document fields such as the following:

```
DEFAULT jdModified := @Modified; @Created;
"Last Modified on: " + @Text(jdModified; "S0T0") + " at " +
@Text(jdModified; "S1T1")
```

20

WRITING FORMULAS

This formula produces a section title that indicates when the section was last changed— for example, "Last modified on: 09/13/98 at 3:31 PM." The DEFAULT keyword uses @Modified if it exists, or @Created if it does not. Despite the capability to write section title formulas for standard access sections, most often, you will simply use text. As shown in Figure 20.2, if you click the Text radio button, you can enter text directly into the box without using quotes. The same is true for the section title field for a controlled access section.

Controlled Access Section Formulas

When you create a controlled access section, you must write a formula that determines who can edit the section. You create the formula in the Formula tab of the Section Properties box. You must first choose a type for the formula. Figure 20.4 shows the drop-down list for the type field in the Formula tab.

FIGURE 20.4

The choices for formula type for a controlled access section are the same as for a field.

If you want the document creator to be able to specify the editors, choose Editable. Entering a formula is not required for this type of section access formula, but you must enter a formula for the computed types. However, as a courtesy to your users, you might consider entering @UserName as the formula, which adds the user's name to the section access list. When the document is created, the user can then choose Section, Define Editors and add users or groups to the section access list.

Often, you want to restrict access to the section programmatically— without user intervention. In this case, you can choose Computed or Computed When Composed. The formula must evaluate to a text list of Notes usernames, groups, or roles. In some ways, this can be considered a document level ACL that is specific to an area of the document. It's a good idea to use database roles instead of user names in a section. You can then assign users who need access to a role. A formula that grants access using a role is a simple text constant such as the following:

```
"[Admin]"
```

Selecting Computed When Composed creates a formula that won't change on document conditions. Selecting Computed enables you to use a formula based on the conditions of a document. This can be quite useful in workflow applications, because you can change the edit access easily based on a document field. For example, if you have a field that contains the status of a document, the following formula changes the section access based on the status:

```
@If(cStatus = "New"; @UserName : "[Admin]";
    cStatus = "Review"; "[Reviewers]" : "[Admin]";
    cStatus = "Completed"; "[Admin]";
    "[Admin]")
```

When the document status is New, the user who created the document and anyone who has the Admin role can edit the section. When the status is Review, those with the Reviewers role plus those with the Admin role can edit the section. When complete, or under any other condition, only the users with the Admin role can access the section.

An Administrator's Back Door

A role such as Admin is very useful, because it can provide a "back door" for administrators. This role can be used in many situations other than section editor access formulas; it can be used in Reader and Author fields, hide when formulas, and so forth.

Controlled access sections are very useful because you can include fields within them that have the property Sign If Mailed or Saved in Section set on the Field Properties box Options tab (see Figure 20.5). When a user with access to the section modifies and saves the document, his signature is attached to the document and appears beside the section title. The certifier verifies it so that users can be assured of its authenticity.

Caution

Remember that for a role to function properly, the database must be accessed on a server. Otherwise, you must set Enforce a Consistent Access Control List Across All Replicas of This Database on the Advanced tab of the database ACL.

Insert Subform Formulas

You can write a formula that controls the subform that is inserted at a specific point in a document. This is useful under many circumstances. For example, you might want to have a different set of buttons appear for each client type using your application. The following formula accomplishes this:

```
@If(@ClientType = "Notes"; "subStdButtons"; "subWebButtons")
```

20

WRITING FORMULAS

A more sophisticated approach is illustrated by the following formula:

```
@If(@IsNewDoc ¦ @Contains(@UserRoles;"Admin") ¦
      @Contains(cMgrName; @Name([CN]; @UserName));
    "subEditReq";
    "subReadReq")
```

The subforms involved in this formula, `subEditReq` and `subReadReq` mirror each other, except that one contains editable fields (`subEditReq`) and the other is read-only. When the document is new, or when users with the Admin role or users who are listed as the manager open the document, they are presented with the editable version. Otherwise, the read-only version is displayed. Similarly, you could insert subforms based on other fields or document conditions.

FIGURE 20.5

Setting the Sign if mailed or saved in section property is done on The Options tab of the field properties box.

Writing Field Formulas

Just as there are a variety of programmable events for forms, there are a number of programmable events for fields. There are just a few field events that are programmable with the Formula language. There are no events with mixed languages. Table 20.3 displays those events that are scriptable by the Formula language. Different events are available for the two broad types of fields, computed and editable.

TABLE 20.3 Programmable Field Events

Event	*Field Type*
Default Value	Editable
Value	Computed
Input Translation	Editable
Input Validation	Editable
HTML Body Attributes	Editable and Computed

Default and Value Formulas

The Default value event executes only when a document is composed. If you create an editable field with a default value of @UserName, the name of the user will be stored in that field when the document is first composed. Because it's editable, if the user changes it and saves the document, it contains the new value, not the default value. In other words, when you edit the document again, it will not revert to the default value. A default value formula for an editable field is not required. All computed fields have a similar event, the Value event. However, you must enter a value formula for a computed field before you can save the form.

> ## Switching Forms
>
> Sometimes you might want to create a form that displays the data in a document in a different format than the form used for data entry. For example, you might want to do this for a special printed version of a document. A handy trick for this type of form is to use all Computed for display fields, and then reference the field itself in the Value event. Users can then switch to that form when printing, and there won't be any editable fields. An extension of this technique is to create a view, and specify the print form in the Form formula for the view. If you do this, users don't have to switch forms for printing!

In a typical workflow form, there is usually a field that contains the document's status. Quite often, a view will be created to sort and categorize by this status. If you created a sort on the status field, the view column would be sorted alphabetically, which might not be what you want. In a workflow process, there are specific stages through which a document passes, and the status field reflects those stages. For example, the status might go from New to Pending Approval, and then to Denied or Approved, and finally Completed. A list of possible document status is shown in Table 20.4.

TABLE 20.4   Document Status Sorting

Life-Cycle Sort	Alphabetical Sort
New	Approved
Pending Approval	Completed
Approved	Denied
Completed	New
Denied	Pending Approval

20

WRITING FORMULAS

As you can see from Table 20.4, the alphabetical sort might not be what you want to see in a By Status view. Users can still find the documents, but the sort order doesn't make much sense. It is far better to sort in the order of the life cycle of the document! To accomplish this, create a computed field that is hidden at the bottom of the form that contains numeric values for the sort order of the status. The following code produces values that sort the documents in the same order as the Life-Cycle Sort column of Table 20.4:

```
@If(cDocStatus = "New"; 1;
     cDocStatus = "Pending Approval"; 2;
     cDocStatus = "Approved"; 3;
     cDocStatus = "Completed"; 4;
     cDocStatus = "Denied"; 5;
     99)
```

To create a view sorted and categorized by the document status, add a hidden column in the first position of the view, and set it to the numeric sort field. Set the column to sort ascending. Next, add a sorted and categorized column set to the status field. The status column will be sorted in the proper order because of the hidden column to the left. Note that while you can use text in a sort field, numbers sort more easily.

Input Translation Formulas

Input Translation formulas are used to enforce rules for the format of data in fields. This event executes when the document is being refreshed and when the document is being saved. The Input Translation event executes before the Input Validation event. It is only available for editable fields. Using this event, you can modify the contents of the field after the user has entered data. The result of the Input Translation formula replaces the field's contents.

In some languages, you can enter a mask for a field that ensures that data is entered and displayed in a specific format. In Domino, this is not available as a field property, and you have to write some code to enforce the desired format. This is done in the Input Translation event of the field. For example, it is relatively easy to enforce the case of a field as shown in Table 20.5.

TABLE 20.5 Input Translation Formulas

Purpose	*Formula*
Proper case a city name	`@ProperCase(cCity)`
Uppercase a state name	`@UpperCase(cState)`

However, enforcing more complicated patterns is not always an easy task. Phone numbers are good examples of more difficult formats with which you might have to contend. Usually, you enter a phone number in one of the following commonly used formats (in the United States at least):

999.999.9999

(999) 999-9999

999-999-9999

Because the user can enter the number in many different formats, you have to test for many things, including length to see whether they entered an area code, incorrect length, incorrect characters, what type of separators are used, and so forth. The following example first strips out punctuation such as parentheses, periods, and dashes leaving only numbers. Then it tests for the length; if it is over 7, it assumes that there is an area code, and builds the number accordingly. Otherwise the formula builds a local number. The format it returns is (999) 999-9999 with an area code or 999-9999 without. Bear in mind that the following formula works only with US phone numbers:

```
REM "Get rid of the separators, if any" ;
jcHomePhone1 := @ReplaceSubstring(cHomePhone; "("; "") ;
jcHomePhone2 := @ReplaceSubstring(jcHomePhone1; ")"; "") ;
jcHomePhone3 := @ReplaceSubstring(jcHomePhone2; "-"; "") ;
jcHomePhone := @ReplaceSubstring(jcHomePhone3; "."; "") ;

REM "Determine the length, and if it is over 7, assume an area code.";
REM "If not, assume no area code. Put the pieces together accordingly.";
@If(@Length(jcHomePhone) > 7;
        "(" + @Left(jcHomePhone; 3) + ") " +
                @Middle(jcHomePhone; 3; 3) + "-" +
@Right(jcHomePhone; 4);
        @Length(jcHomePhone) = 7; @Left(jcHomePhone; 3) + "-" +
                @Right(jcHomePhone; 4);
        cHomePhone)
```

Of course, you can get more sophisticated and add code to test for international numbers, but this should serve as a good example of what you can accomplish in the Input Translation event of a field.

Input Validation Formulas

Like Input Translation formulas, the Input Validation event is available only for editable fields. This event also executes when a document is refreshed and when a document is saved. You use this event to make sure that the entered data is valid or to ensure that there actually is data present if the field is required.

The Input Validation event executes after the Input Translation event. If the data entered in the field fails the validity test of this event, an error message can be displayed, and the user (at least in a Notes client) will be returned to the field with the offending entry. In a Web client, an error message is displayed on a separate HTML page.

> ## Enforcing Entry of the Correct Data Type
>
> Notes and Domino ensure that the correct data type is entered. For example, users cannot enter AABC in a numeric or time field. An error message is generated, and the document cannot be saved until an entry of the correct data type is made.

Continuing with the phone number example from the previous section, you might want to ensure that users don't enter characters instead of numbers for the phone number. First, remove any punctuation so that a legitimate phone number won't generate an error, as in the following code:

```
REM "Get rid of the separators, if any" ;
jcHomePhone1 := @ReplaceSubstring(cHomePhone; "("; "") ;
jcHomePhone2 := @ReplaceSubstring(jcHomePhone1; ")"; "") ;
jcHomePhone3 := @ReplaceSubstring(jcHomePhone2; "-"; "") ;
jcHomePhone := @ReplaceSubstring(jcHomePhone3; "."; "") ;


@If(@IsError(@TextToNumber(jcHomePhone)));
    @Failure("Please use the format (999) 999-9999!");
@Success)
```

If the phone number is entered properly, converting the text value to a number should not generate an error, so the test `@If(@IsError...` is used. If an error is generated, a message box is displayed using `@Failure()`. Both the Input Translation and the Input Validation formulas can act in concert as in this case. As the code is written now, if you were to enter ABCDEFGHIJ, you would get the error message contained in the `@Failure()` statement, but the Input Translation formula would be applied anyway, and the field would then look like `(ABC)DEF-GHIJ`! What you need to do is stop the Input Translation formula from executing using `@Return()`, as in the following code:

```
REM "Get rid of the separators, if any" ;
jcHomePhone1 := @ReplaceSubstring(cHomePhone; "("; "") ;
jcHomePhone2 := @ReplaceSubstring(jcHomePhone1; ")"; "") ;
jcHomePhone3 := @ReplaceSubstring(jcHomePhone2; "-"; "") ;
jcHomePhone := @ReplaceSubstring(jcHomePhone3; "."; "") ;

REM "Make sure we have all numbers. If not, stop the execution";
REM "of this formula.";
```

```
@If(@IsError(@TextToNumber(jcHomePhone)));
      @Return(cHomePhone); @Success) ;
REM "Determine the length, and if it is over 7, assume an area code.";
REM "If not, assume no area code. Put the pieces together accordingly.";
@If(@Length(jcHomePhone) > 7;
          "(" + @Left(jcHomePhone; 3) + ") " +
                    @Middle(jcHomePhone; 3; 3) + "-" +
@Right(jcHomePhone; 4);
    @Length(jcHomePhone) = 7; @Left(jcHomePhone; 3) + "-" +
@Right(jcHomePhone; 4);
        cHomePhone)
```

Frequently, you need to require the entry of data in a field. You accomplish this with Input Validation formulas such as the following:

```
REM "Now test for a numeric value, and since this is a required";
REM "field, make sure there is data present.";
@If(cHomePhone = "" ¦ @IsError(@TextToNumber(jcHomePhone));

@Failure("Please use the format (999) 999-9999!")
@Success)
```

This formula builds on the earlier version of the home phone number Input Validation by adding a test for an empty field.

If the user leaves the Home Phone Number field empty and either refreshes or tries to save the document, this formula executes. The Prompt box shown in Figure 20.6 displays. Furthermore, this keeps the user from saving the document. This is truly a very convenient feature, at least for you (although some users might get annoyed when they can't break the rules)!

FIGURE 20.6

The Error window generated by @Failure *displays the message you typed within the quotes.*

Caution

Be careful using Input Validation formulas in forms used on the Web. Remember that the Web is page-based, and when an error condition is generated, there is no dialog box available to alert the user. Instead, a new HTML page is generated as shown in Figure 20.7. This is particularly inconvenient if there are multiple fields with Input Validation tests!

20

WRITING FORMULAS

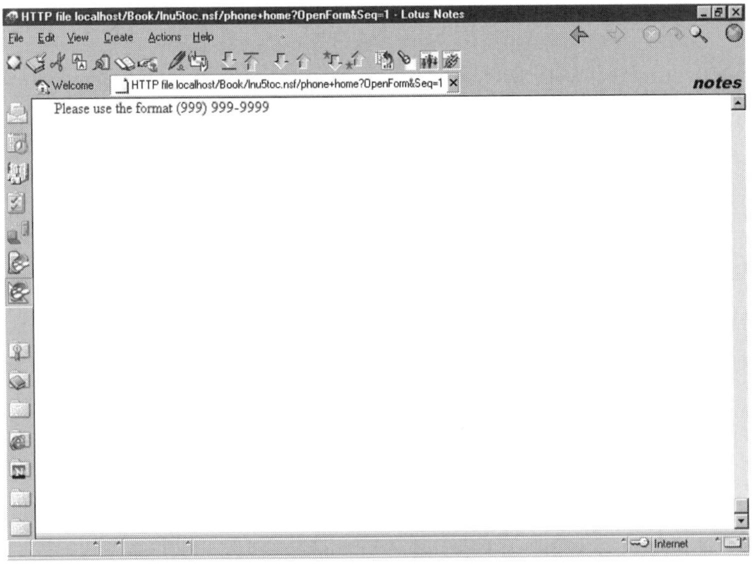

FIGURE 20.7

The same error message in Figure 20.6 appears on the Web in a separate page.

HTML Body Attributes for Fields

The HTML Body Attributes available for fields are based on the HTML form tags `<INPUT>`, `<SELECT>`, and `<TEXTAREA>`. As a Domino developer, you don't have to worry about the tags themselves—the HTTP task generates them for you. These tags are HTML equivalents of data entry fields.

You can modify certain attributes that control the display of fields to Web clients. A Rich Text field is equivalent to a `<TEXTAREA>` in HTML and takes the ROWS and COLS tags. As the names imply, ROWS specifies the number of rows for the field, and COLS specifies the width in columns. For example, `"ROWS=5 COLS=30"` sets up a multiline text area in an HTML document that is 5 rows deep and 30 columns wide. Table 20.6 is a list of commonly used tags.

TABLE 20.6 Field Body Attribute Tags

Attribute	Tag	Effect
SIZE	`<INPUT>`	The display size of the field.
MAXLENGTH	`<INPUT>`	Maximum number of characters the field will accept. If greater than the SIZE, the field will scroll during entry.
ROWS	`<TEXTAREA>`	Number of rows.
COLS	`<TEXTAREA>`	Number of columns.
WRAP	`<TEXTAREA>`	Determines how text flows in a text area. VIRTUAL allows words to wrap within the text box.

To restrict the length of the entry in a standard text field for a Notes client you can use an Input Validation formula to return an error using something like `@If(@Length(cHomePhone) > 14, @Failure(....` The HTML equivalent is to add the following code to the HTML Body Attributes:

```
"SIZE=14 MAXLENGTH=14"
```

Unlike a Notes client, which enables you to continue typing and only alerts you when you refresh or save the document, a Web client does not permit entry beyond 14 characters. The HTML Body Attributes can be very handy for Web forms.

Working with Profile Documents

Profile documents were introduced in Release 4.6. Creating Profile documents is discussed in Chapter 10. Two types of Profile Documents are available: global to the database, and user-specific. Profile documents enable you to store values, such as lists, that can be used in keyword fields, replica IDs for lookup databases, and so forth. Because profile documents do not show up in any views, you use a special @Function, `@GetProfileField()`, to retrieve the values. The syntax is the following:

```
@GetProfileField(profiledocname or alias ; ③profile fieldname [ ; username] )
```

For a global profile, you simply specify the form alias and the field name. For a user-specific profile document, you need to specify the user's name as well.

Profile documents fulfill a great need to enable users to specify values that can be used in many different circumstances. You can create a user-specific profile that stores a user's address and phone number. To retrieve this information into a current document, you simply use a formula like the following:

```
cUserAddress := @GetProfileField("UPF"; "cAddress1"; @UserName)
```

Developers can also include a global profile document that is available to all who can access the database at reader level or above. One use might be to store a list of values that only certain users can edit. These values can be retrieved into a keyword field rather than actually entering the list into the keyword as hard-coded values. This is quite useful for keywords that reference items that can change, such as store or office locations. Set up a multivalue field in a profile document, and retrieve it for use in a keyword field, with a formula such as the following:

```
@GetProfileField("GPF"; "cLocationList")
```

Set the Choices list in the field Properties box to Use Formula for Choices.

20

WRITING FORMULAS

> **Caution**
>
> If you use Depositor access, this formula fails because, even though the user can create and save a document, he can't read any documents—not even a profile document!

There are many other ways to use profile documents as you can easily imagine. Not only can you get the value of a profile field, you can set it as well! The counterpart to `@GetProfileField()` is `@SetProfileField()`. The syntax of this command is the following:

```
@SetProfileField(profile doc name or alias ;
 profile fieldname; new value [ ; username] )
```

You can use this command rather than directly editing the profile document if you want to set the value of a profile field automatically. Usually, however, you allow selected users to edit profile documents using `@Command([EditProfile])`. Creating and editing Profile documents is discussed in Chapter 10.

Writing View Formulas

There are many places where the Formula Language can be used in views. These include Selection formulas, Column formulas, Form formulas and Hide formulas for Actions. As pointed out in Chapter 11, "View Design," Simple Actions are available for Selection and Column formulas, but they are not that sophisticated. Many times, you will turn to the Formula language to accomplish the desired results. The next sections discuss Selection formulas, Column formulas, and Form formulas. Hide formulas are discussed in the section on Hide Formulas. Form formulas are relatively simple, and are covered in Chapter 11, in the section titled "View Selection and Form Formulas."

Creating View Selection Formulas

The default view selection is `SELECT @All` that retrieves all documents in the database. A database can contain several different main forms, and all documents composed with all main forms will be displayed in a view using the default selection formula. What if there are also some response documents and response-to-response documents? To display all of them in a view hierarchy using a responses-only column, you can add an "OR" condition with the @Function `@AllDescendants` to the formula. Remember that the pipe symbolizes a logical `OR`. The formula now becomes the following:

```
SELECT @All ¦ @AllDescendants
```

Selecting Response Documents

There are several other similar @Functions: @AllChildren, which will show immediate responses to main documents, and @IsResponseDoc. @IsResponseDoc used in a view selection formula has the disadvantage of including all response documents in the view index, even though they might not belong to any of the documents in the view itself! In general, use @AllDescendants or @AllChildren instead.

Using the simple actions available from the Easy type of view selection, you can build a reasonably sophisticated selection formula by successively adding simple actions. By default, these are connected with an "AND" as shown in Figure 20.8. The first condition is "By form used" and the second is "By date" using date modified is after 08/01/98. Of course, there is a Formula Language equivalent to this selection criterion that you can examine by switching from Easy to Formula, which is the following:

```
SELECT ((Form = "Chapter") ¦ (Form = "CH")) & (@Modified > [08/01/98])
```

FIGURE 20.8

These two simple conditions are connected by "AND" in the view selection window.

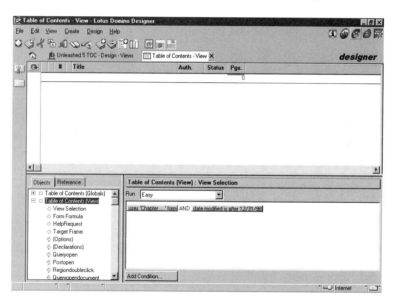

In general, adding "Easy" conditions to the view selection criteria will satisfy most, but not all your needs. However, there are many situations unsuited to the simple actions. For example, there is no way to test for an empty value in a field. The following formula cannot be written using the Search Builder window:

20

WRITING FORMULAS

```
SELECT ((Form = "Chapter") ¦ (Form = "CH")) & @cStatus != ""
```

Similarly, adding @AllDescendants to the selection formula can only be done with the formula language. To add a selection formula, choose Formula in the Run drop-down list in the View Selection window.

> **For More Information...**
>
> For more information about creating and working with views, see Chapter 11.

Writing Column Formulas

View columns can contain simple functions, fields, and formulas. Column formulas can only be written with the Formula language. As with any other type of formula, column formulas can range from the very simple to the extremely sophisticated and complex. The simplest formula is a single field name.

Of course, because fields can be selected from the database fields list, you don't have to enter it in the formula window, although you can. To add a formula to a column, first open the view in design, and then choose the column by clicking the column header. There is only one choice in the Run field, that being Formula, and it is grayed out. There is a set of three radio buttons in the field labeled Display: Simple Function, Field, and Formula. As pointed out in Chapter 11, the simple functions are primarily view statistics such as date created, date last modified, and attachments. Similar to the view selection conditions, you can choose a simple function, and then switch to Formula and see the corresponding @Function. Unlike the simple actions for selection conditions, you cannot add these functions together to build a complex formula. Choosing Field for the display lists all the database fields.

Because a view is the primary reporting tool for a Domino database and a column is the primary vehicle for presenting data items, you will find many occasions to apply your skills with the Formula language! Some typical types of column formulas are the following:

- Counting documents in categories
- Counting documents in categories that meet certain criteria
- Summing field values and subtotaling by category
- Converting field aliases into a text equivalent
- Converting form aliases into a text equivalent
- Displaying dates in the format September 20, 1998 rather than 09/20/98

- Sorting and categorizing by date parts, such as year, month, and quarter
- Displaying an icon instead of a field value

Keeping Views Efficient

In general, it is more efficient to keep column formulas in views simple by limiting the length of the formulas. Since a view is a text representation of the data, the longer and more complex the formula, the longer the view takes to load. Each view column formula must be evaluated against all documents included in the view. To work around this limitation, if you have a complex formula, instead of including it in the view, put it in the form as a field.

Counting and Summing Columns in Views

Counting documents in a view is really quite simple. Just add a column with a formula of 1 (the *number* 1, not the character "1"). Set the column Totals properties on the Sorting tab to Total and you will get a sum in the column for each category in the view and a total at the bottom for all documents. Extending this to conditionally count documents that meet certain criteria, such as a status of Completed, is also fairly simple. Remember that Notes and Domino represent a logical True with the number 1 and a logical False with a 0. A simple equality formula of `cStatus = "Completed"` in a view column will add 1 for completed documents, and 0 for those not marked completed. Title the column appropriately, set it to total, and you instantly have a count of completed documents! This is a relatively simple example; more complex formulas can be built as long as they evaluate to either 0 or 1.

Hiding Detail Rows

When you are creating a column of sums in this manner, consider suppressing the values for the individual documents. You can do so by clicking Hide detail rows next to the Totals list.

Figure 20.9 shows the Sorting tab for a view column. The Totals list on the Sorting tab includes the following:

20

WRITING FORMULAS

FIGURE 20.9

The sorting tab provides several options to total the values in a column.

- Total
- Average per document
- Average per subcategory
- Percent of parent category
- Percent of all documents

To sum the values stored in a field, simply choose the field itself in the view column, and set the totaling option.

Converting Field and Form Aliases into a Text Equivalent

In keyword fields, designers can use an alias. The user sees "Part III" which becomes "3" when the document is saved. Displaying a "3" in a view column is not very informative, so you might want to write a column formula such as the following to enhance the informational value of the data item:

```
@If( cPart = "0"; "Front Matter";
     cPart = "1";
    "Part I: Introduction to Domino Designer Release 5";
cPart = "2";
               "Part II: Foundations of Application Design";
cPart = "3"; "Part III: Domino Programming Languages";
         cPart = "4"; "Part IV: Advanced Design Topics";
         cPart = "5"; "Part V: Integrating External Data";
         cPart = "6"; "Part VI: Other Development Tools";
         cPart = "99"; "Appendices";
"Part: " + cPart)
```

Similarly, if you have documents created from multiple forms displaying in the same view, you might want to differentiate between the forms by creating a column sorted and categorized on the Form field. Unfortunately, the Form field stores the alias, not the descriptive name that you present to the user. "Associate of the Month" becomes "AOM" and "Gold Team" becomes "GT." Needless to say, displaying the Form field in its unadulterated form won't be very informative to the users. Documents can be sorted and categorized on "AOM" and "GT" and whatever other aliases are available. The following formula, which is similar to the previous one, can be employed to compensate for this:

```
@If(Form = "AOM"; "Associate of the Month";
        Form = "GT"; "Gold Team";
        Form = "LA"; "Leadership Award";
        Form)
```

Note that the False statement is the Form field itself. This is used as a catch-all in case new forms have been added. Similarly, for the cPart field, the text constant "Part: " is added to the field cPart. If cPart doesn't match up with one of the prescribed values, the value of the field itself will be displayed. This is useful when creating a new database.

Displaying Dates

Dates in their native format, such as 09/20/98 or 09-20-98, are easily recognizable and generally understood by users, but they are not always display friendly. Quite frequently, you are asked to display the date in its more formal format, as in September 20, 1998. Following is a formula that does just that:

```
REM "Assign the date field to jdDate";
jdDate := dNomDate ;
@Select(@Month(jdDate);
        "January"; "February"; "March"; "April";
        "May"; "June"; "July"; "August"; "September";
        "October"; "November"; "December")
        + " " +@Text(@Day(jdDate))
        + ", " + @Text(@Year(jdDate))
```

Recycle Your Formulas!

Always look for opportunities to reuse code. It is easy to make this formula reusable by adding the line jdDate := *fieldname* as shown in the example. To use this formula in another view column, simply substitute the new date field for *fieldname*!

Your client might want to know how many referrals she received in a given reporting period. Sorting and categorizing by year, quarter, or month is a typical requirement for many date-dependent views. Sorting by year is a simple matter of using @Year(*DateValue*) in a sorted and categorized column. Sorting by month is a little trickier, because @Month()

20

WRITING FORMULAS

returns a number from 1 to 12 for the month. You can convert it to the corresponding text value using the @Select() statement, but sorting on the column containing the name of the months sorts alphabetically. April then comes before January! To solve this problem, include a hidden field with the value @Month(*DateValue*). Sort the hidden column containing the month number, and sort and categorize the column containing the text value for the month. Now the view displays the months in the proper order. Figure 20.10 shows a view sorted and categorized first by the year and then by the month.

FIGURE 20.10

A date-dependent view sorted by the year and the month.

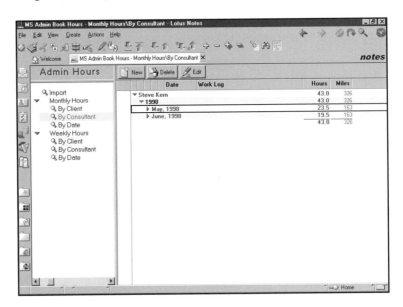

The formula used to create the category "September, 1998" is as follows:

```
REM "Assign the date field to jdDate";
jdDate := dDate ;
@Select(@Month(jdDate);
        "January"; "February" ; "March" ; "April" ;
        "May"; "June" ; "July"; "August"; "September";
        "October"; "November"; "December" )
        + ", " + @Text(@Year(jdDate))
```

A formula for determining the quarter is as follows:

```
REM "Assign the date field to jdDate";
jdDate := dDate;
"Quarter " + @Text(@Integer((@Month(jdDate)-1) / 3)+1)
```

Displaying View Icons

Figure 20.11 shows the use of an icon in a view column. If the status of the chapter is complete, the Notes client displays a green check mark. To have an icon display in a column, set the column property Display values as icons on the Basics tab of the Column properties box as described in Chapter 11. Choose an icon from the table in the Designer Help database. The formulas are generally simple, as is the following formula that displays a green check mark as shown in Figure 20.11:

FIGURE 20.11

The Table of Contents view uses a check mark in the Status column to indicate that a chapter is finished.

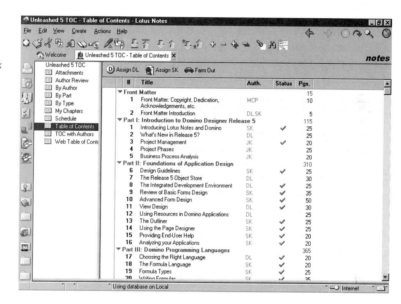

```
@If(cStatus = "Completed"; 82; 0)
```

The following formula displays a note pad and pencil:

```
@If(@Attachments > 0; 58; 0)
```

Using Hide When Formulas

Hide When formulas (also referred to as *hide formulas*) are available for objects including paragraphs, form actions, and view actions. Although you can find a Hide When tab on the Properties Box for fields, buttons, and hotspots, because these objects exist in a paragraph, any entry in that tab applies to the entire paragraph. Hide When formulas can only be written with the Formula language, and can range from the very simple formula @IsNewDoc, which hides the object when the document is new, to formulas that are very complex.

Hide When Properties

There are many hide options available that do not require the use of the Formula language. The Hide tab of the properties box for each object has a number of check boxes, such as Hide from Web Browsers, Previewed for Reading, and Opened for Editing.

Tables and Hide When Formulas

To conditionally hide or display objects, such as fields, on the same line in a form, create a table with the appropriate number of cells for each object. Place each object in its own cell and write the Hide formula. Each cell in a table is treated as a paragraph.

To write a Hide When formula, you click the Hide When tab of the object properties box. Figure 20.12 shows the Hide When tab for a paragraph, and Figure 20.13 shows the Hide When tab for an action. Next, click Hide paragraph (or action) if formula is true, and enter a formula. You can combine these formulas with other Hide attributes such as Previewed for reading. When you enter a formula, if the result evaluates to true, the paragraph or action is hidden. For example, if you want to hide an action when the document is new, include this formula:

```
@IsNewDoc
```

FIGURE 20.12

The Hide tab for a paragraph—note that in reality, a Hide When formula applies to the entire paragraph.

FIGURE 20.13

The Hide tab for an action; you can click the Formula Window button to expand the area in which you compose the formula.

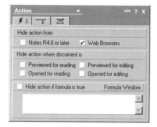

If you want to display a check box stating "Resigned" on the same row as some other information and have it display when the actual value is "Resigned," check Hide paragraph if formula is true and include a formula like the following:

```
cResigned != "Resigned"
```

The effect of this formula is to hide the field if it does not equal "Resigned" and to display it if the value is "Resigned."

Another typical use for hide formulas is to hide actions based on roles assigned to users. If only administrators should access a button, create a role called Admin, and use a formula such as the following:

```
@Contains(@UserRoles; "Admin")
```

Of course, you can combine this with other values. For example, you can create an action button that enables an application administrator to change the status of a document. You might not want anyone outside of the Admin role to use this button, and you also might not want the button displayed when the document is new. The following formula accomplishes this:

```
@IsNewDoc & @Contains(@UserRoles; "Admin")
```

Working with Form, View, and Shared Actions

Whereas Chapters 10 and 11 cover Actions, this section discusses programming Form and View Actions with the Formula language. Action buttons were introduced in R4 of Notes. R5 has introduced Shared Actions, a great improvement that enables you to create code for actions that can be shared between forms and views. The beauty of a shared action is that it is reusable code. Updating the functionality of a shared action updates all instances of it within your application, just like changing any of the other reusable elements such as Shared Fields and Subforms.

"Sharing" an Agent

You can create an agent and set it to run Manually from Agent List. Calling this agent from either View or Form Action buttons simulates a Shared Action. Like a Shared Action, this enables you to write and test your code once. You then call the Agent using `@Command([ToolsRunMacro]; agentname)`.

Another technique of sharing Action buttons that works for Forms is to create a Subform to contain standard form buttons. This Subform can then be inserted into each Form. Standard buttons can include buttons such as those in Table 20.7.

TABLE 20.7 Form Action Buttons

Button Title	Formula	Hide Conditions
Save & Close	`@Command([FileSave]);`	Previewed for Reading
	`@Command([FileCloseWindow])`	Opened for Reading
Close	`@Command([FileCloseWindow])`	Previewed for Editing
		Opened for Editing
Edit	`@Command([EditDocument])`	Previewed for Editing
		Opened for Editing

The button formulas in Table 20.7 are extremely simple. You can develop formulas that perform very complex tasks, including setting document status fields, writing document history, releasing a document for review, and so forth. You can do all this from a View or Form Action button without making the user open the document in Edit mode and manually change the values of the fields. If you place the Action on a form, you effectively limit the scope to a single document. If you place the Action in a View, you can increase the scope to include multiple documents.

Caution

Be careful when placing Action buttons in views that can potentially change the values of fields on multiple documents. For example, it is one thing to enable the user to select multiple documents, and move them to a folder. It is an entirely different proposition to enable them to change the status on a group of documents. If this is the effect you want, you must ensure that your code doesn't change field values inappropriately.

A good example of an action that can be shared between Forms and Views is a button to display document history. Document history usually contains entries that detail the creation of the document, dates and times of email notifications, and status changes. If you store the history of the document in a multivalue text field, you can display it in a dialog box complete with a scrollable text region! To call a dialog box you can use the following code:

```
@DialogBox( "dBoxHistory"; [AutoHorzFit] : [AutoVertFit] :
[NoCancel] : [NoNewFields] : [NoFieldUpdate] : [ReadOnly];
 "Document History" )
```

This use of @DialogBox() does not allow editing and the underlying fields in the document are not changed. Figure 20.14 shows the Document History dialog box. This dialog box consists of a single layout region on a subform that contains a field that is named cDocHistory just as the field on the underlying form. When the dialog box opens, it inherits the value from the underlying document.

FIGURE 20.14

A simple dialog box displaying document history is created with a single layout region on a form.

Typical action buttons in views are ones that create new documents, edit documents, and delete documents. Consider including these in all basic views. Table 20.8 lists formulas for typical buttons.

TABLE 20.8   View Action Buttons

Title	*Formula*
New	@Command([Compose]; *"form alias"*)
Edit	@Command([EditDocument]), or use the default action and make it visible
Delete	@Command([EditClear]), or use a simple action

As mentioned earlier, you can include view action buttons that can alter values in the documents without forcing the user to edit the document and physically change the values of keyword or other fields. With one click, the user can make changes to several different fields. The following sample code marks a chapter as being complete:

```
REM "Find out how many hours it took";
jnHours := @Prompt([OKCANCELEDIT]; "Effort";
        "Please enter the number of hours."; 0) ;
```

```
@If(jnHours = 0; @Return(""); @Success);
FIELD nActual := jnHours;
FIELD cStatus := "Completed";
FIELD dComplete := @Today ;
```

Users love this kind of feature because it saves them a lot of time. As a developer, you can exert more control over the various fields in the document with this technique. If changing the status were done manually by the users, they would first open the document in edit mode. Next, they would have to change the hours field, the date completed field, and the status field. As a developer, you would have to trap for conditions such as marking a document complete without entering any hours or a date of completion. As you can see, this approach is far simpler and less error prone in many respects.

Working with Buttons and Hotspots on Forms

Formulas can be written for buttons and hotspots. Hotspots are defined areas on forms that can be push buttons, text, or images. One difference between hotspots and actions is that actions remain in the action bar at the top of the form, whereas hotspots scroll with the document.

You can write formulas for hotspot buttons, formula pop-ups, and action hotspots. A formula pop-up displays the text that the formula returns. Hotspot buttons and action hotspots can perform other actions, such as composing documents, saving documents, and changing field values.

For More Information...

For more information about Buttons and Hotspots, including examples of formulas, see Chapter 10 "Advanced Form Design."

Summary

The many examples in this chapter of practical, real-world formulas written in the Formula language have given you a glimpse into the power of this language. Despite the limitations of the language, there are many reasons to use it, and many reasons to choose it over an alternative such as LotusScript, JavaScript, or Java. This chapter has demonstrated how to write formulas for forms, views, fields, actions, and hotspots. As you now know, there are many areas where only the Formula language can be used, so the time spent reading Chapters 18, 19, and 20 was a good investment!

CHAPTER 21

Enhancing Domino Applications with HTML

HTML has gained a great deal of publicity and popularity over the last several years. All sorts of applications are now Internet-ready, in that the documents they produce can be converted to HTML. Word processors such as Microsoft Word and Lotus WordPro, spreadsheets such as Lotus 1-2-3 and Excel, and presentation packages like Lotus Freelance Graphics can all produce HTML versions of their documents. As you undoubtedly know, Lotus Notes and Domino have been Internet-ready for several years.

Web servers abound from many companies. All Web servers have at least two components in common: They communicate using *HTTP*, or Hypertext Transfer Protocol, and they share *HTML*, or Hypertext Markup Language, as a common language. The Domino server is unique in that it is capable of transparently presenting a Domino database to either a Web browser or a Notes client. This chapter shows you how to enhance a Domino application with HTML. Even though the Domino server essentially creates HTML for you, a minimal understanding of the language is still important if you want to develop for Web clients.

Understanding the Domino Web Server

Perhaps the hottest feature added to Lotus Notes in all its existence is the Domino Web Server. The Web server has been available in beta form since the summer of 1996 and was finally incorporated into the shipping version of Lotus Notes in Release 4.5. Prior to this, Lotus had released the InterNotes Server, a cumbersome product that met with limited commercial success. On the other hand, the Domino Web server has met with great success because it transparently presents Domino objects to Web clients. The advantages are obvious: You can write one application and make it available to both Web and Notes clients. There has been a steady stream of improvements from the early release of the Domino server, and today, the Domino Designer is very tightly integrated with Web design elements.

Because you can easily present a Domino database to a Web client, it is relatively easy to get content into your Web site. This site might be on the Internet itself, or it might be on a corporate intranet. In either case, the advantage to using the Domino Web Server is that you no longer depend on installing the Notes client. Sure, you lose some functionality by relying solely on a Web browser, but the gain is that you don't have the deployment issues, upgrade issues, and so on because most PCs today are shipped with a Web browser. Because security can be extended to the Web by enforcing user logins, you can easily control who can edit, author, and read documents, regardless of how they access the database.

Enhancing Domino Applications with HTML

CHAPTER 21

585

21

ENHANCING
DOMINO
APPLICATIONS

The network protocol, *TCP/IP* (Transport Control Protocol/Internet Protocol) is the "glue" that holds the Internet together. All Web servers and Web clients must use TCP/IP to communicate with each other. Domino servers are no exception to this, and must likewise run TCP/IP. Web servers use HTTP to serve documents written in HTML to Web browsers, which then interpret the HTML code and present the documents to the user.

Domino servers run a service called HTTP to present Domino content to Web clients. It is this service which translates Domino content to HTML. The HTTP service can be invoked on a Domino server in one of two ways: by typing `load http` at the server console or by adding `http` to the `ServerTasks` line in `Notes.ini`. Adding it to the configuration file causes it to launch when the Domino server starts, as in the following:

```
ServerTasks=Replica,Router,Update,Stats,AMgr,Adminp,Sched,CalConn,
➥Report,http
```

The only other command available from the server console for the HTTP service is `tell http quit`, which causes the HTTP service to stop.

The Java Virtual Machine

The Java Virtual Machine (JVM) is an additional service that can be a part of a Domino Web site. The JVM is what runs Java applets and agents for both Web and Notes clients. However, because this is a chapter on HTML, this isn't covered here.

The HTTP server's job is to service requests from a Web client. These requests can be for Domino objects such as views, forms, pages, documents, HTML documents, CGI (Common Gateway Interface) scripts, and so forth. When a Web client requests a document from the Domino Server, Domino automatically translates it into HTML.

Entire Web sites can, and do, consist of individual HTML documents strung together by hypertext links or URLs. This method of building a site means that all the links between documents (URLs) must be maintained by hand. If you remove one document, you must remove all the links to that document. Notes and Domino make it easy to maintain an entire site in a database or a collection of databases. This way, you can avoid manual tasks such as revising and reorganizing a collection of HTML documents or rewriting the pointers to the documents.

Because Notes is a database applications server, the content of a Domino Web site is stored in documents and pages in Notes databases. The links are maintained internally by Notes itself. When a document is deleted, the links to the document are automatically deleted. Of course, a link to a specific Notes docu ment can be hard-coded in other documents, in which case it would have to be removed manually. Content can be added dynamically from either a Web or a Notes client and is instantly available. No links need to be created. Furthermore, Notes views are presented on the Web as HTML documents. This means that the documents on the Web site can be presented in different sort orders by changing views.

If a database has only four views with different sorts and a document is added, the views are updated automatically. In HTML, each view is a separate HTML document. To re-create what Domino does automatically using HTML would require a tremendous amount of work. For example, you would have to maintain four separate HTML documents containing the code to produce the "views." Adding a single document requires the new document to be inserted into each of the four documents at the appropriate position in the sort order with the appropriate text for each view. Sound like fun? It might not be too bad if there were only a few documents added per month and only a few dozen to maintain. What if the number of documents were in the hundreds or more? Domino is so powerful because it has united a database engine with a Web server, creating what some have called the first, true Internet Applications server.

Because Domino uses HTML to present objects to a Web client, it makes sense to develop a greater understanding of the language. It is also possible to enhance applications using HTML, as you'll soon see.

Understanding the Basics of HTML

HTML is a fairly simple structured language used to display documents to a Web browser. Tim Berners-Lee developed it at CERN, the European Laboratory for Particle Physics in Geneva. HTML grew out of *SGML*, or Standard Generalized Markup Language, a standard for describing markup languages. SGML began as *GML*, or Generalized Markup Language. It was an attempt by IBM in the 1960s to create a standard to port documents across systems. It is *generalized* because it does not define an exact standard to present or format documents. Instead, it defines document types and different kinds of markup languages that define these document types. The term *markup* is inherited from the publishing industry and described the typesetting instructions for formatting a document. GML became SGML in 1986 when it became a standard by the International Standards Organization. The current version of HTML is 4.0, as defined by the World Wide Web Consortium, or W3C.

The HTML language is based on *tags*, which are similar to commands in other languages. Tags define the way elements should be formatted on the screen. Tags consist of

Enhancing Domino Applications with HTML

CHAPTER 21

587

21

ENHANCING
DOMINO
APPLICATIONS

a left angle bracket (<), a tag name, and a right angle bracket (>). HTML is not case sensitive, so the tag <TITLE> is no different from <title>.

There are two kinds of tags: Container and Standalone. A Container tag can contain text or other tags and has a beginning and an ending tag. Container tags are paired (such as <H1> and </H1>) to start and end the tag instruction. The end tag looks exactly like the start tag, except that a slash (/) precedes the text within the brackets. For example, the following line of code centers text:

```
<CENTER> This is centered text! </CENTER>
```

Standalone tags are self-contained. For example, <HR> creates a horizontal line:

```
<HR ALIGN="LEFT" NOSHADE SIZE=5 WIDTH=100%>
```

Tags define and present elements. An *element* is a fundamental component of the structure of a text document. Some examples of elements are heads, tables, paragraphs, and lists. See the section titled "The HTML Document and Document Tags" for additional details.

For More Information...

For more information about HTML Tags, see Appendix D, "HTML Reference." On the CD is a database titled HTML Reference (HTMLRef.nsf), which contains a short list of tags and their descriptions. Many excellent books and a number of resources on the Web are devoted to HTML. The latest HTML 4 specifications can be found at http://www.w3.org/TR/REC-html40.

Whenever you launch a Web browser and point it to a World Wide Web site, you are looking at a document presented with HTML. HTML documents themselves are just plain-text files that you can create using any text editor. Most browsers have a menu choice that lets you view the source of a Web document. If you take a look, you can see the raw HTML source. Even though the language itself is fairly simple, it can be a daunting task to create a Web site or even a single HTML document from scratch. Consequently, plenty of editors are available that can create HTML documents. The Domino Designer is not exactly like other editors for HTML, but coupled with the Domino server it can, in effect, become an HTML editor.

The HTML Document and Document Tags

Several tags are always present in HTML documents that essentially define the document. The first tag is always <HTML> and because it is a container tag the last tag is always `</HTML>`. The `<HEAD>`, `<TITLE>`, and `<BODY>` tags usually follow the `<HTML>` tag. A basic structure for an HTML document might be the following:

```
<HTML>
<HEAD>
<TITLE> document title </TITLE>
... Other tags
</HEAD>
<BODY>
... Document content
</BODY>
</HTML>
```

It is easy to see this structure by viewing the HTML source of a Web document. The database for this chapter, `Chapt21.nsf`, contains a form titled "Simple HTML." It consists of some text at the top, and a single field (see Figure 21.1).

FIGURE 21.1

The Window Title in this simple form appears in the `<TITLE>` tag.

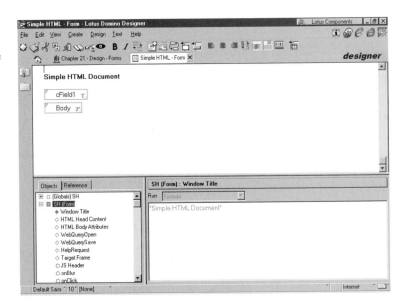

To view the source, first preview the form or a document created with the form in a Web browser. Use the following steps:

1. Open `Chapt21.nsf` in the Domino Designer.

2. Open the Simple HTML form design.

3. Click the Domino Preview icon in the upper-right. Or from the menu, choose Design, Preview in Web Browser, Notes Browser. When the form opens, it is in the Notes Browser.

Enhancing Domino Applications with HTML

CHAPTER 21

589

21

ENHANCING
DOMINO
APPLICATIONS

4. From the menu, choose View, Show, HTML Source.

5. The source displays in its own window (see Listing 21.1).

The nice thing about using Notes to display the source is that it color-codes the HTML, in the same way that LotusScript, JavaScript, and the Formula language are color-coded in the Programmer's pane. Listing 21.1, although not in color, shows the basic elements of an HTML document.

LISTING 21.1 HTML—HTML Source for a Simple HTML Document

```
<HTML>
<!-- Lotus-Domino (Build 165a - March 5, 1999; Windows NT/Intel) -->
<HEAD>
<TITLE>Simple HTML Document</TITLE>
<SCRIPT LANGUAGE="JavaScript">
<!--
document._domino_target = "_self";
function _doClick(v, o, t, h) {
  var form = document._BH;
  if (form.onsubmit) {
     var retVal = form.onsubmit();
     if (typeof retVal == "boolean" && retVal == false)
        return false;
  }
  var target = document._domino_target;
  if (o.href != null) {
    if (o.target != null)
       target = o.target;
  } else {
    if (t != null)
       target = t;
  }
  form.target = target;
  form.__Click.value = v;
  if (h != null)
    form.action += h;
  form.submit();
  return false;
}
// -->
</SCRIPT>
</HEAD>
<BODY TEXT="000000" BGCOLOR="FFFFFF">

<FORM METHOD=post ACTION="/BOOK/Chapt21.nsf/BH?OpenForm&Seq=1"
NAME="_BH">
<INPUT TYPE=hidden NAME="__Click" VALUE="0">
```

continues

LISTING 21.1 continued

```
<B>Simple HTML Document</B><BR>
<BR>

<INPUT NAME="cField1" VALUE=""></FORM>
</BODY>
</HTML>
```

You should quickly notice that Domino has generated all this nice HTML code without any intervention on your part, from a form that took all of a minute or so to create. Typically, you won't have to interact at all with any of these tags; they are generated automatically by Domino for you. Table 21.1 lists commonly used Document-level tags:

TABLE 21.1 Document-Level Tags

Tag	Type	Description
`<HTML>`	Container	Indicates that the document is HTML.
`<HEAD>`	Container	Follows the `<HTML>` tag, and can contain other tags such as `<BASE>`, `<LINK>`, `<META>`, `<SCRIPT>`, `<STYLE>`, and `<TITLE>`.
`<TITLE>`	Container	Creates the document title.
`<META>`	Standalone	Assigns attributes such as NAME, AUTHOR, and KEYWORDS.
`<SCRIPT>`	Container	Defines the script language.
`<STYLE>`	Container	Defines style specifications for the document.
`<BASE>`	Standalone	Sets global "base" values for HREF and TARGET.
`<BODY>`	Container	Follows the `<HTML>` tag. All content and tags for the document body are contained in this tag.
`<LINK>`	Standalone	Links two files.

For More Information...

For more information about Document-level tags, see the section "Document Tags" in Appendix D.

Formatting Tags

Quite a few formatting tags are available in HTML. If you'll look at Listing 21.1, you'll notice the following line of code:

```
<B>Simple HTML Document</B>
```

This is generated because the text Simple HTML Document was created in bold on the form. The container tag <B> instructs the browser to present what's inside the tag in bold. You can nest container tags as in the following line of HTML:

```
<B><CENTER><I>Simple HTML Document</I></CENTER></B>
```

This renders the text Simple HTML Document in bold (<B>), italic (<I>), and centered (<CENTER>).

You can get pretty fancy with formatting in HTML, which includes settings for block quotes, sub- and superscript, and so forth. Table 21.2 lists commonly used formatting tags.

TABLE 21.2   Formatting Tags

Tag	Type	Description
<BASEFONT>	Standalone	Sets size, color, and font face for the body text.
<BIG>	Container	Sets text to a size larger than the default.
<BLOCKQUOTE>	Container	Indents a block of text.
 	Standalone	Creates a linefeed in the text.
<B>	Container	Sets text to bold.
<CENTER>	Container	Centers text.
<FONT>	Container	Sets size, color, and font face contained within the tag.
<H1>...<H6>	Container	Sets the size of the text inside the container to one of the six fonts. <H1> is the largest and <H6> the smallest. All are rendered in bold.
<HR>	Standalone	Creates a horizontal line on the document.
<I>	Container	Sets text to italic.
<nbsp>		Creates a non-breaking space.
<PRE>	Container	Sets the text in the container to a fixed width font.
<P>	Container	Creates a paragraph.
<SMALL>	Container	Sets text to a size smaller than the default.
<SPAN>	Container	Used to apply styles in the STYLE list.
<SUB>	Container	Sets text to subscript.
<SUP>	Container	Sets text to superscript.
<S>	Container	Sets text to strikethrough.
<TT>	Container	Sets text to a fixed width font.
<U>	Container	Sets text to underline.

Again, Domino takes care of most of these tags for you. For example, if you create a form with a line of bold, centered text, Domino renders it as illustrated in the line of HTML immediately before the previous table. However, these tags might prove useful to you if you want to produce your own HTML document. For example, you might want to change the default behavior of Domino when a form is submitted, which is to display the text Form Processed. Not very imaginative or user friendly! You can use the reserved field $$Return to define what is returned to a browser when a form is submitted. Instead of creating a separate form, you can use HTML in this field to produce an HTML document thanking the user for her contribution. See Listing 21.2 for an example of the use of HTML in a $$Return field from the Notes Discussion—Notes & Web R5 database.

LISTING 21.2 HTML—HTML in a $$Return Field

```
REM "This $$Return field returns HTML as a result of the successful
➥form submittal.";
REM;
REM "Warning: Lots of HTML Pass-thru in here...";
REM;
REM  "resource strings..";
PrevDoc := "Previous Document";
AllDoc := "All Documents";
ByCat := "by Category";
ByAltName := "by Alternative Name";
ByAuth := "by Author";
MainTopic := "topic";
Response := "response";
IntProfile := "Interest Profile";
ArcProfile := "Archive Profile";
Message := "message";
ThankYou := "Thank you for your ";

REM "Get the name of this database.";
DB := @ReplaceSubstring(@ReplaceSubstring(@Subset(@DbName; -1);
➥" ";"+");"\\";"/");

REM "Thank the user, personalize based on the first name.";
FormName := @If(Form = "MainTopic"; MainTopic; Form = "Response";
➥Response; Form = "ResponseToResponse";response;form="Interest
➥Profile";IntProfile; @Contains(form;"Archive");ArcProfile;Message);
Thanks := "<h3>" + ThankYou + " " + FormName + ",
➥"+@Name([CN];@UserName) + "! </h3>";

REM "Anchors to discussion views.";
existingdoclink:="<hr><font size=2><a href=/"+db+"/($All)/"+@Text
➥(@DocumentUniqueID )+"?OpenDocument>" + PrevDoc +
➥"</a>   ";
TopicView :=   "<a href=/" + DB + "/($All)?OpenView>" + AllDoc +
```

```
➥"</a>    ";
CategoryView := "<a href=/" + DB + "/by+Category?OpenView>" + ByCat +
➥"</a>    ";
AuthorView := "<a href=/" + DB + "/AuthorView?OpenView>" + ByAuth +
➥"</a>   ";
AltNameView := "<a href=/" + DB + "/by+Alternate+Name?OpenView>" +
➥ByAltName + "</a><hr>    ";

bkgd := "<body bgcolor=\"" + "#ffffff" + "\"+ >";

REM "Assemble the HTML to be returned";
OkMsg :=  bkgd + Thanks + existingdoclink+TopicView +  CategoryView +
➥AuthorView + AltnameView + DateView;
OKMsg
```

If you examine the Formula language code for the $$Return field, you'll see that it produces a message such as, Thank you for your topic, Steve Kern! using the <h3> font container. Next, sandwiched between two horizontal rules are links to the previous document (the one you just composed) and four views (see Figure 21.2).

FIGURE 21.2

The R5 discussion database uses a customized $$Return field to present a "Thank you" page.

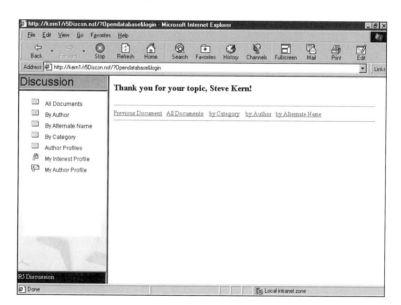

This example demonstrates the use of several formatting tags, including <h3>, <font>, and <hr> to enhance the user's experience with a Domino application. In this case, the designers chose to create $$Return as a shared field so that it could be used in more than one document. Shared fields are discussed in Chapter 10, "Advanced Form Design."

Hyperlinks

If you've used Notes and sent someone a doclink, view link, or database link, you're already familiar with the concept behind hyperlinks. On the Web, hyperlinks are used as a way to jump from one location in a document to another or from document to document, regardless of where the document actually resides. It could be on the same server or on a server halfway around the world. On an intranet Web site, again, the linked document could be on a server in your building or on a server at your corporate headquarters in Switzerland. To the end user, it really doesn't matter!

There is really only one tag that creates a hyperlink: the <A> tag. It is a container tag, and there are two ways of using it. One is with the HREF keyword. You supply a URL, and the hyperlink takes the browser to that URL. Following is the full syntax:

```
<A HREF="url" TARGET="frame" REL="forwardLinkType"
REV="reverselinktype" ACCESSKEY="key" TABINDEX="tabposition"
...hyperlink text or element goes here...
</A>
```

You can see this use of the <A> tag in Listing 21.2. Consider the following example:

```
CategoryView := "<a href=/" + DB + "/by+Category?OpenView>" + ByCat +
➡"</a>    ";
```

This line creates the hyperlink to the By Category view. HREF takes the URL of the hyperlink as the argument.

The second way of using the <A> tag tag;hyperlinks;creating>;creating hyperlinks> tag;creating> is with the NAME keyword. This creates an Anchor link. Anchor links were added to the Domino Designer in Release 4.6 and create a way of jumping from one location in a specific document to another, rather than from one document to another. The syntax for this usage of <A> is the following:

```
<A NAME="anchor"
...text...
</A>
```

Consider the following example:

```
<A NAME="Top"></A>This is at the top<BR>
```

When you've set up your anchor link, you can jump to it by using the following tag:

```
<A HREF="document_url"#"anchor">
```

Following is another example:

```
<A HREF="/BOOK/Chapt21.nsf/2ec261c8271ac0d1852567390004e492/
ec8f9033236391ae8525673b000c871d?OpenDocument#Top">
<FONT COLOR="0000FF">Go to Top</FONT></A>
```

As you can see from this line of HTML, the URL of the document is followed by the # symbol and the name of the anchor—Top.

You don't actually need to use HTML to make this work in Notes. You can easily set up an Anchor link in a Notes document from the menu. To create an Anchor link, position the cursor where you want the link, and from the menu, choose Edit, Copy as Link, Anchor Link. You are prompted to name the link. When you've created an Anchor link, it is on the Notes clipboard, and you can highlight text or an object in your document and create the link from the menu, by choosing Create, Hotspot, Link Hotspot.

> **Caution**
>
> Anchor links can only be created in rich-text fields in a document. In both Notes 4.6 and 5.0, you must save a document and then reopen it before you can create an Anchor link.

The Image Tag

If you want to create a link based on a clickable image, you can use the standalone tag `<IMG>`. This tag enables you to specify the URL to the image file. If you place this inside the container tag `<A>`, you can create an image file as a hyperlink, as in the following example:

```
<A href="/cnghome.nsf/webOpenMail?OpenAgent&Login">
<FONT COLOR="0000ff">Web Mail</FONT></A>]
```

This line of HTML simply places the text Web Mail hyperlinked to the WebOpenMail agent. The following line of HTML uses the `<IMG>` tag to create a hyperlinked image file (mail9.gif) that runs the WebOpenMail agent, logs the user into the server, and opens the mailbox:

```
[<A href="/cnghome.nsf/webOpenMail?OpenAgent&Login">
<img src="/CNGHome.nsf/Files/mail9.gif/$FILE/mail9.gif"
alt="Web Mail" border=0></A>
```

The `<IMG>` tag takes several important attributes as listed in Table 21.3.

TABLE 21.3 <IMG> Tag Attributes

Attribute	Description
ALIGN	Arguments are LEFT, RIGHT, TOP, BOTTOM, and MIDDLE. Determines how text behaves around the image.
ALT	Provides text that appears if the browser has image display turned off.
BORDER	Hyperlinked images appear with a colored border, whereas a standard image has no border by default. This setting controls the width of the border in pixels. To turn off the border use BORDER=0.
HEIGHT	Determines the height of the image in pixels.
HSPACE	Sets the horizontal space around the image in pixels.
ISMAP	Defines the image as part of a server-based imagemap.
SRC	The URL of the file.
USEMAP	Sets the name of the client-based imagemap.
VSPACE	Sets the vertical space around the image in pixels.
WIDTH	Determines the width of the image in pixels.

Frames and Framesets

A frameset splits the viewing area into two or more frames. Each frame can present different content. For example, you can split the window into three frames, presenting a banner page in one, a navigation page in another, and a content page in the third. As with many of the elements discussed in this chapter, you can use the Domino Designer to build frames and framesets. The tools in Domino Designer have come a long way from the frameset template in Release 4.6! This section is included so you can gain an understanding about what is actually created using the Frameset Builder. You might find some of this information useful if you should need to further extend Domino's capabilities.

TABLE 21.4 Frameset Tags

Tag	Type	Description
<FRAME>	Standalone	Sets content in a frame. Takes a number of attributes.
<FRAMESET>	Container	Splits the window into frames.
<IFRAME>	Container	Creates a frame which floats on the page.
<NOFRAME>	Container	Used for browsers which cannot display framesets. Provides alternative content.
_blank	Reserved Name	Opens the content in a new window.

Enhancing Domino Applications with HTML

CHAPTER 21

597

21

ENHANCING
DOMINO
APPLICATIONS

Tag	Type	Description
_parent	Reserved Name	Opens the content in the parent frameset.
_self	Reserved Name	Opens the content in the same frame.
_top	Reserved Name	Opens the content in a full window.

This is a fairly complex topic, and because Domino can build framesets with relative ease, it won't be treated in great detail here. As with an HTML document, there is a specific order in which these tags should be used. Instead of the <BODY> tag, a frameset uses the <FRAMESET> tag. This tag can take one of two attributes: ROWS or COLS. In either case, you can specify the attribute in pixels or percentages or relative to the amount of screen available. Because you are limited to using either a row or column setting, you can only split the first frameset either vertically or horizontally. In order to achieve more complicated layouts, you can nest framesets. In other words, you can first create a vertical frameset, and then split that into a horizontal frameset. This is what the Frameset Builder in the Domino Designer does for you. The syntax of frameset is as follows, where values can be a list of pixels or percentages:

```
<FRAMESET ROWS="values" ¦ COLS="values" >
...
</FRAMESET>
```

A nested frameset example is in Listing 21.3.

LISTING 21.3   HTML—A Simple Nested Frameset Created with the Frameset Builder

```
<HTML>
<FRAMESET ROWS="20%,80%">
  <FRAMESET COLS="20%,80%">
    <FRAME NORESIZE SCROLLING=no NAME="LogoFrame"
     SRC="/BOOK/Chapt21.nsf/LogoPage?OpenPage">
    <FRAME NORESIZE SCROLLING=no NAME="BannerFrame"
     SRC="/BOOK/Chapt21.nsf/BannerPage?OpenPage">
  </FRAMESET>
  <FRAMESET COLS="20%,80%">
    <FRAME NAME="NavFrame" SRC="/BOOK/Chapt21.nsf/
     NavigationPage?OpenPage&BaseTarget=ContentFrame">
    <FRAME NAME="ContentFrame" SRC="/BOOK/Chapt21.nsf/
     ContentPage?OpenPage">
  </FRAMESET>
</FRAMESET>
</HTML>
```

The outer frameset splits the screen in two, with 20% in the top row. The top row is then split into two frames: the LogoFrame and the BannerFrame. Similarly, the bottom row is split into two frames, the `NavFrame` and the `ContentFrame`. The `<FRAME>` tag is used to both name the frames and add content. In this case, the content is four pages in the same Domino database. The syntax of standalone `<FRAME>` tag is the following:

```
<FRAME SRC="url" NAME="name" FRAMEBORDER="0¦1" MARGINWIDTH="pixels"
MARGINHEIGHT="pixels" NORESIZE SCROLLING="Yes¦No¦Auto">
```

The `SRC` attribute in this example is a Domino URL (discussed in the section titled "Adding Power with Domino URLs") that points to a page in the database. The `NAME` attribute is easily understood, containing names for the frames such as `LogoFrame`, `ContentFrame`, and so forth. A `FRAMEBORDER` set to 0 turns off the border for the frame. `MARGINWIDTH` and `MARGINHEIGHT` are the number of pixels for the margin inside the frame borders. `NORESIZE` prevents the user from dragging the border of the frame to a new position, and `SCROLLING` controls the ability of the user to scroll the content within the frame. Figure 21.3 shows the frameset created by Listing 21.3.

FIGURE 21.3

This frameset, from Listing 21.3, splits the window into four frames.

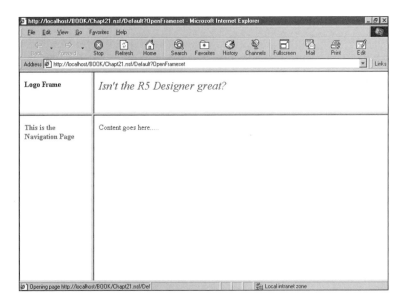

Table 21.4 also listed several reserved names for frames. These reserved names can be used with the `<BASE>` tag in the form `<BASE TARGET="frame">`, or the Domino URL argument `&BaseTarget`. In Listing 21.3, the `NavFrame` points to the `ContentFrame` with the Domino URL argument `&BaseTarget=ContentFrame`. The effect of this is to direct any links in the `NavFrame` to open in the Content Frame. A typical use for this would be to embed a view in the page displayed in the `NavFrame`. The documents would then open in the `ContentFrame`! You can achieve the same effect by placing the HTML `<BASE TARGET="ContentFrame">` into the `NavigationPage`.

This section hopefully provides you with some insight into how framesets are constructed in their native HTML. You might find this information useful as you construct your own framesets, or you might find it helpful in enhancing framesets that you create.

On the CD...

To view this frameset, open the database on the CD titled Chapter 21, or chapt21.nsf. Locate the frameset titled Default.

For more information...

For more information about framesets, see Chapter 29, "Adding Framesets to Domino Applications." For more information about Pages, see Chapter 14, "Using the Page Designer."

Style Sheets

Style sheets can be inline, embedded in the <HEAD> of an HTML document or they can be a separate text file saved with the extension .css. *CSS* stands for Cascading Style Sheet, and is a standard developed by the W3C. The term *cascading* is used because Web browsers follow a set of rules in an ordered sequence to determine document presentation. In a style sheet, you can specify characteristics for the style of text in HTML documents. This is similar in some respects to setting up a named style in Notes, or to using a document template in a word processing program. Style sheets can be created in a text editor or with tools such as Microsoft's FrontPage or Sausage Software's HotDog.

You can apply a style inline by using the STYLE attribute with a tag in an HTML document. Many tags can take the STYLE attribute, ranging from tags such as <BLOCKQUOTE>, <IMG>, and <A> to <P>, <TT>, and <H1>. However, this use of styles is not nearly as useful as either the embedded style sheet or a style sheet in a separate text file. If you create a style sheet using a text file, it can be reused easily. Applying style changes inline requires more work.

To embed a Style sheet in a document, you enclose it in the <STYLE> container tag in the <HEAD> of the HTML document. Following is a short example:

```
<STYLE TYPE="text/css">
   <!--
    a:link {color: blue }
    a:visited {color: red }
```

```
  -->
</STYLE>
```

This sets the color of unvisited links to blue, and the color of visited links to red. The comment tags `<!--` and `-->` are a courtesy to users with browsers that don't read styles. Because the style is enclosed within a comment, it is ignored by such browsers. A style sheet entered like this applies only to the current document, so its scope is somewhat limited.

Storing your styles in a separate text file enables you to reference them from multiple documents. You can control a large number of elements for each tag. To set the style for each tag that you want to control, use the following syntax:

```
TAG {characteristic: value; characteristic: value... }
```

For example, to define the fonts available for the body, you can use the following:

```
BODY {
      background: white;
      font-family: arial, helvetica, sans-serif;
      color: black;
      }
```

Table 21.5 lists some characteristics available in style sheets. Please note that this is not a complete listing but is a listing of the more useful style characteristics.

TABLE 21.5 Style Sheet Characteristics

Characteristic	Description
border	Size of the border in pixels (px), points (pt), inches (in), or centimeters (cm). You can also use thin, medium, or thick.
border-color	Color of the border, set to any of the sixteen colors (red, green, blue, and so on) or an RGB triplet (#FFF, #000, and so on).
border-style	Set to none, dashed, dotted, double, groove, inset, outset, or ridge.
border-bottom-width	Size of the border in pixels (px), points (pt), inches (in), or centimeters (cm). You can also use thin, medium, or thick.
border-left-width	Size of the border in pixels (px), points (pt), inches (in), or centimeters (cm). You can also use thin, medium, or thick.
border-right-width	Size of the border in pixels (px), points (pt), inches (in), or centimeters (cm). You can also use thin, medium, or thick.
border-top-width	Size of the border in pixels (px), points (pt), inches (in), or centimeters (cm). You can also use thin, medium, or thick.
color	Set to any of the sixteen colors (red, green, blue,) or an RGB triplet (#FFF, #000).

Characteristic	*Description*
font-family	List of typefaces.
font-size	Size of the font in pixels (px), points (pt), centimeters (cm), or inches (in). Relative size values can also be set (not covered here).
font-weight	Can be set to Normal, Bold, or relative weights such as Bolder and Lighter.
font-style	Can be Italic, Normal, or Oblique.
line-height	Set to normal or a number of pixels (px), points (pt), inches (in), centimeters (cm), or a percentage of the font size.
margin	Set to a number of pixels (px), points (pt), inches (in), centimeters (cm), or a percentage of the font size.
margin-left	Set to a number of pixels (px), points (pt), inches (in), centimeters (cm), a percentage of the font size, or Auto.
margin-right	Set to a number of pixels (px), points (pt), inches (in), centimeters (cm), a percentage of the font size, or Auto.
margin-top	Set to a number of pixels (px), points (pt), inches (in), centimeters (cm), a percentage of the font size, or Auto.
margin-bottom	Set to a number of pixels (px), points (pt), inches (in), centimeters (cm), a percentage of the font size, or Auto.
text-align	Set to left, right, center, or justify.
text-decoration	Set to none, blink, line-through, overline, or underline.
text-indent	Indents text in pixels (px), points (pt), inches (in), centimeters (cm), or a percentage of the font size.
text-transform	Changes the case of the text: capitalize, lowercase, none, or uppercase.
vertical-align	Set to a percentage of the current line-height, baseline, bottom, sub, super, text-bottom, text-top, or top.

When you have a style sheet created, you can use it by including the <LINK> tag in the head of an HTML document. In Domino Designer, you can place the link in the HTML Head Content event of a form. The following example uses a style sheet called DominoStyles:

```
<LINK REL=STYLESHEET HREF="DominoStyles.css">
```

> ### Using Style Sheets with Domino
>
> The best way to use a style sheet with Domino is to embed the style sheet file in a document. You then use a Domino URL to reference the embedded file. See "Adding Power with Domino URLs" later in this chapter.

Using HTML in the Domino Designer

Now that you've learned a little about HTML itself, it's time to see how you can use it in the Domino Designer. You can add HTML to a number of objects such as hotspots, buttons, fields, views, forms, and pages. Beginning with Release 4.5, the "hooks" for HTML in a Domino database have increased, and in R5, you can now add HTML to documents, pages, forms, fields, views, and many different objects. Some of these objects, such as fields and hotspots, have a new tab, the HTML tab, on the Properties box. This tab is discussed in the next section.

Adding HTML to Fields and Other Objects

There are two places to add HTML to a field. You can add HTML to the field event HTML Attributes or you can add it to the HTML tab for the field.

In the HTML Attributes event, you can control the presentation of text and rich-text fields. In text fields, you can specify SIZE and MAXLENGTH as in the following example:

```
"SIZE=30 MAXLENGTH=80"
```

This sets the initial size of the field to 30 characters and the maximum number of characters that the field accepts to 80. A rich-text field accepts ROWS and COLS, which, as I'm sure you can imagine, define the number of rows (height) and columns (width) that the browser displays. For example, the following sets the number of rows to 20 and the columns to 60 (see Figure 21.4):

```
"ROWS=20 COLS=60"
```

> ### Caution
>
> If you use this technique, be sure to enclose the HTML in quotes!

FIGURE 21.4

The HTML Attributes of text and rich-text fields can be used to control the display of the field to a Web client.

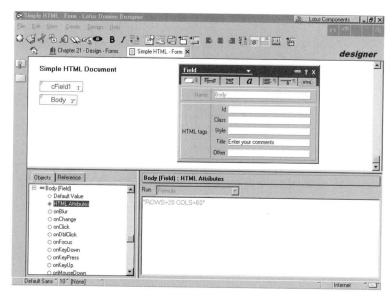

Adding the ROWS and COLS attributes to a rich-text field controls both the width (COLS) and the height (ROWS). Figure 21.5 shows the effects of setting the HTML attributes on text and rich-text fields.

FIGURE 21.5

Setting the HTML Attributes of fields defines the way the field is displayed by the browser.

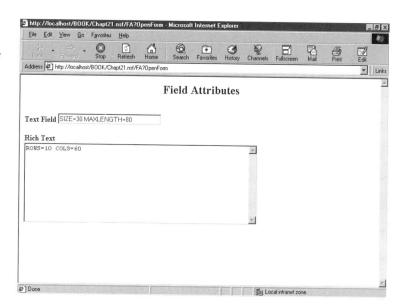

The HTML tab of the Field Properties box is shown in Figure 21.6. This tab enables you to define several different aspects of an object.

FIGURE 21.6

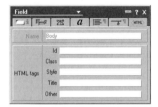

The HTML Tab is new to R5 and available for several objects.

Table 21.6 describes each of the settings on the tab.

TABLE 21.6   The HTML Tab of the Field Properties Box.

Attribute	Description
Name	Names the object, which can be referenced by JavaScript or with a style sheet.
Id	Used to reference the object by JavaScript or with a style sheet.
Class	Used to apply a class from a style sheet.
Style	Applies a specific style to an object from a style sheet.
Title	Used to provide a tip or a prompt to a user.
Other	Adds other attributes (be sure to use quotes) for the object.

The Name attribute is preset for fields, but is available for other objects such as buttons. The Id attribute is similar to the Name attribute, and both are used to reference the object with JavaScript or a Cascading Style Sheet. Class and Style are used to apply styles from a style sheet. The Title attribute, at least in Internet Explorer, provides a little prompt box with the text you include when the mouse passes over the field or object (see Figure 21.7).

Caution

The Title attribute appears to function only in Internet Explorer. It does not work in Netscape 4.51 or in the Notes browser.

You can use the Other property to add additional HTML attributes to objects. For the most part, you can get at all the HTML attributes you'll ever need, so you'll rarely use this property. In the Other field, unlike the remaining fields on this tab, you must use quotation marks and identify the attribute. The syntax is as follows:

```
Attribute = "value"
```

FIGURE 21.7

Adding text (without quotes) to the Title attribute of an object produces a floating box in Internet Explorer—note the box "Rich Text Field."

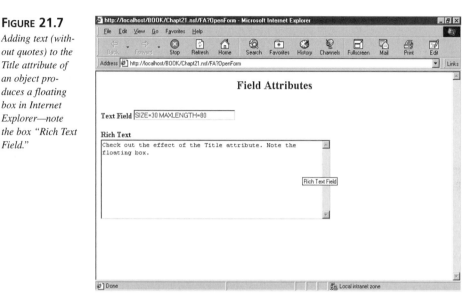

Attributes entered into the HTML tab are incorporated into the document when it is presented to a Web client.

Using Reserved Fields

At present, three fields are reserved for HTML: $$HTMLHead, $$Return, and HTML. $$HTMLHead is a holdover from earlier versions of Notes and Domino. This field enables you to insert tags into the HEAD of an HTML document. It is not really needed any longer because forms and pages contain the HTML Head Content event. As with the HTML Head Content event, $$HTMLHead can take all sorts of tags such as <META>, <SCRIPT>, <STYLE>, and <LINK>. These tags are then inserted into the <HEAD> container of the HTML document. $$Return modifies the default document that Domino sends to the browser when a form is submitted. See Listing 21.2 for an illustration of this field's use.

HTML is a special field. You can create a form with a field on it called HTML, and any HTML you add to this field is passed directly through the Domino server to the Web browser. This can be useful if you are converting a site from HTML documents to a Notes database. Simply create a form with a single field on it called HTML. Copy the contents of an HTML document to the clipboard, and paste it into this field. You can then use the Domino server to present your Web site.

Caution

If you take this approach, remember that you are responsible for maintaining the HTML code itself! For example, you can't rely on Domino to keep track of any links within the HTML stuffed into the field. Therefore, use this approach with care.

Using HTML in Views

Because everything presented to a Web browser must be in HTML by default, the Domino server converts even a view to HTML. Because you don't have to create all those links by yourself, this is very convenient. However, the default view presented by Domino, although very functional, might not have the appearance that you want. There are quite a few things you can do to alter the appearance of a view to the browser.

Using View Applets

Please be sure you consider using a view applet, which adds a great deal more functionality to a view presented to a Web browser. View applets are covered in Chapter 11, "View Design." They are also covered in Chapter 14.

Using a Form to Present a View

You can create a view template form, and name it after the view. On the form, you can place any HTML that is available to you on forms. You can then embed a view applet on the form. The form must be named $$ViewTemplate for *<view name>*. When a Web browser opens the view, it opens with the page set up as in your form.

Both Calendar and Standard views are supported on the Web, but you cannot alter the appearance of a Calendar view. Notes generates an HTML table for Calendar views. You can modify standard views with HTML, however. There are two ways to do this: by marking the view property For Web Access: Treat View Contents as HTML (which can be found on the Advanced tab of the View Properties box); and also by adding pass-thru HTML to a view column.

If you mark the view property Treat View Contents as HTML, then you can enter HTML into a column of the view. You are responsible for creating all the HTML formatting and

Enhancing Domino Applications with HTML

CHAPTER 21

607

21

ENHANCING
DOMINO
APPLICATIONS

links for the view. Because this can be quite laborious, you should use this only as a last resort. HTML is created in the Script area of the Programmer's pane for a view column.

On the other hand, it can be a nice touch to use pass-thru HTML in a view column. With this technique, you can embed images in a view column. For example, if you include a JPEG or GIF file in a view, you can reference it with a Domino URL such as the following:

```
"[<IMG SRC=/BOOK\Chapt21.nsf/(Files)/Hot/$File/Hot.gif?OpenElement>]"
```

Note the use of the square brackets enclosing the URL, which tell Domino to treat what's within the square brackets as HTML. The effect of this can be seen in Figure 21.8.

FIGURE 21.8

Note the italicized word Hot!! in the leftmost view column which is actually a small GIF file created in a graphics program.

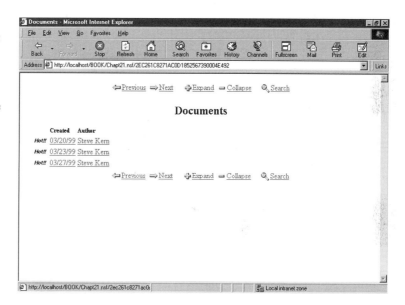

Caution

There is one disadvantage to using this technique. The pass-thru HTML is visible to Notes users. Columns have no Hide attributes, and you cannot use @ClientType in view columns. As a workaround, you can display a view with this type of column formula only to Web browsers.

Using HTML in Forms and Pages

In addition to the objects and reserved fields described in the previous sections, there are other ways to use HTML in forms and pages. On the Advanced tab of the Form

Properties box, there is a setting called Web Access: Treat Document Contents as HTML. Pages have a similar setting for Web Access Treat Page Contents as HTML on the Page Info tab. You can click this setting for either a page or a form, and then you can add HTML to the design object.

There are three ways to add HTML directly to Pages and Forms. First, you can import HTML from an HTML document, in which case Domino renders the Form or Page, translating the HTML. Second, you can copy HTML to the clipboard, and paste it into a form or page. Using either technique, you can quickly create a Web site from a existing HTML documents. Third, you can write HTML directly onto a form.

Of the first two techniques, copying and pasting HTML is pretty straightforward. However, importing HTML needs some elaboration. To import HTML, you need to have HTML documents with an extension of .htm or .html. Create a new form or page, and from the menu, choose File, Import. In the Import dialog box, choose the HTML file, or to filter the file list, change the Files of Type field to HTML File. If you select an HTML file of either extension, the Files of Type field automatically change. Click the Import button. When the import is complete, the HTML is rendered right on the page or form! This is a pretty handy technique.

You can create an entire HTML document by writing HTML directly on the form or page, but that is extremely laborious for a large document. Most often, you'll simply want to add some HTML to enhance the form or page, but not to create the entire design object in HTML. When you're adding HTML like this, don't mark the form or page Treat Contents as HTML. Instead, simply mark the text as Pass-thru HTML from the Text menu.

Pass-thru HTML is much more functional in R5 than it was in R4.6. In R4.6, the setting wasn't very "sticky"—that is, it didn't always stay set to pass-thru HTML; if you modified a form, the setting often disappeared. In R5, the text you've selected for pass-thru HTML shows up with a gray background so you always know when it's set.

> **Caution**
>
> If you try to create an HTML document with <INPUT> and other form tags, Domino produces an error message "Documents treated as HTML cannot be edited."

Because Domino creates all the necessary elements to create a basic HTML document— that is, the <HEAD> tags, <BODY> tags, appropriate JavaScript, and so on—it doesn't make

Enhancing Domino Applications with HTML

CHAPTER 21

609

21

ENHANCING
DOMINO
APPLICATIONS

that much sense to completely re-create an HTML document from scratch within a page or a form.

Writing pass-thru HTML is quite useful. For example, see Figure 21.9. In Figure 21.9, pass-thru HTML was used to create the document title, "Hot Mustard Style," using the <H2> tag. The <BR> tag follows, adding a linefeed below the title. This simple example illustrates how easy it is to combine HTML with Pages and Forms.

FIGURE 21.9
The Hot Mustard page in design showing pass-thru HTML in the title—note the <H2> and <BR> tags and the gray background for the text.

Caution

Similar to pass-thru HTML in views, pass-thru HTML in forms displays to Notes clients. You can, however, open the Text Properties box and click Hide Paragraph from Notes R4.6 or Later on the Paragraph Hide When tab. This hides your pass-thru HTML from a Notes client.

Adding Power with Domino URLs

Domino URLs are a way of extending the power of Domino objects to a Web browser. In its simplest form, the basic syntax of a Domino URL is the following:

```
http://Host/DominoObject?Action&Arguments
```

Typically, you access Domino database objects such as forms, views, pages, and so on, so a more complete version of the syntax is the following:

```
http://Host/Database/DominoObject?Action&Arguments
```

This syntax is pretty straightforward, and it tells the browser what the names of the host, database, and Domino object are and then what action to take. Some actions have arguments, and some arguments can be universally used, such as Login.

Domino URLs cannot have spaces in them and so you must replace any spaces with the + symbol. For example, views and forms often have spaces in their names, so to open them you need to construct the URL such as the following:

```
http://book/lnu5toc.nsf/By+Part?OpenView
```

The parts of a Domino URL are separated by a forward slash. For example, the previous URL refers to a database in the Book subdirectory on the Domino server.

Working with `Host` and `Database`

`Host` can be either a DNS entry or an IP address. `DominoObject` can be any one of a number of server and design elements such as pages, forms, views, and databases. For example, Listing 21.4 uses a Domino URL to access a cascading style sheet stored in a document.

Omitting the `Host` Argument

Domino URLs can be self-referencing. If you need to access an object in the current database, you can safely omit the Host argument. Listing 21.4 uses this technique to build a dynamic Domino URL.

The next several sections elaborate on the various parts of Domino URLs.

LISTING 21.4   Creating a Dynamic Domino URL That Opens a Style Sheet

```
REM "host/database/view/key/$File/stylesheet.css?OpenElement";
cLink := "<LINK REL=STYLESHEET HREF=" ;
cDBName := @Subset(@DbName; -1);
cView := "(StyleSheets)";
cKey := "HotMustard" ;
cFileName := "HotMustard.css";
REM "removed + cServerDB + / ";
cLink + "/" + cDBName + "/" + cView + "/" + cKey + "/$File/" +
➥cFileName + "?OpenElement" + ">"
```

Enhancing Domino Applications with HTML

CHAPTER 21

611

21

ENHANCING
DOMINO
APPLICATIONS

The technique illustrated in Listing 21.4 can be used with all Domino URLs that relate to the same database. In fact, if you need to access other databases on the same host, you can still omit the Host argument and simply use the file name or the replica ID preceded by two underscores. If you need to access a database on a different server, you need to provide that server's host name or IP address. The formula in the Listing 21.4 dynamically obtains the name of the database by the following:

```
cDBName := @Subset(@DbName; -1);
```

`@DbName` returns a text list that contains the server name and the database. To get the database name, use the argument shown in the previous example. You might know that `@Subset(DbName; 1)` produces the name of the server. However, the name of the server and the host name are not the same. The host name is the name associated with the server's IP address in DNS, or the IP address. You can find the name of a Domino server in the HTTP section of the Server document under Internet Protocols. If the entry is blank, it uses the name of the machine on which the server runs.

Using Domino Objects and Actions

When you've determined the host and the database name in a Domino URL, you are ready to work with the objects. An action followed by optional arguments tells the Domino server what to do with the object. Actions are usually preceded by a question mark (?), although an exclamation point (!) is also permissible. The default action is `?Open`, and actions can be explicit or implied. An example of an explicit action is `?EditDocument`, and its implicit counterpart is `?Edit`. Table 21.7 lists the Domino Objects you can access with Domino URLs and their associated actions:

TABLE 21.7   Domino Objects and Actions

Object	*Actions*
Agents	`OpenAgent`
Databases	`OpenDatabase, OpenAbout, OpenHelp, OpenIcon, SearchDomain, SearchSite`
Documents	`OpenDocument, CreateDocument, DeleteDocument, EditDocument,` `SaveDocument`
Forms	`OpenForm, ReadForm, OpenElement`
Framesets	`OpenFrameset`
Navigators	`OpenNavigator`
Pages	`OpenPage`
Server	`OpenServer, Redirect`
Views	`OpenView, SearchView`

For More Information...

For more information and a listing of Domino URLs and their syntax, see Appendix F, "Domino URL Reference."

Referring to Domino Objects

There are a number of ways to refer to Domino Objects. You can refer to them by name or alias. You can also refer to an object by its *universal ID (UNID)* or by the *NoteID*. There are also some special objects that can be referenced in Domino URLs through the use of special identifiers. These identifiers enable you to access objects such as the default view, the About and Using this database documents, and so on. They are listed in a table in Appendix F; that table is repeated in Table 21.8 for your convenience.

TABLE 21.8   Domino Identifiers

Identifier	*Reference*
$defaultView	The default view
$defaultForm	The default form
$defaultNav	The default navigator
$searchForm	A form used to search databases
$file	Used to access a file attachment in a document
$icon	The database icon
$help	The Using this database document
$about	The About this database document
$first	The first document in a view

You can use these identifiers in Domino URLs to perform actions such as opening the Help documents. Following is an example that opens the About document in the database Chapt21.nsf located in the Book subdirectory.

```
http://book/chapt21.nsf/$About?OpenAbout
```

The following example opens the default view:

```
http://book/chapt21.nsf/$defaultview?OpenView
```

Opening Documents by Key

To open documents with a Domino URL, it's pretty apparent that you use the `OpenDocument` Action. So how do you specify a document? You have to reference it with a key value, or the document's UNID or NoteID. It's often much easier to use a key value rather than the UNID or NoteID. The NoteID is an 8-character hexadecimal number, and the UNID is a 32-digit hexadecimal number that Notes generates internally when the document is saved. A *key value* is a string that locates a document in the first sorted column of a view. Because you can specify the field or fields to sort on in the view, it is easy to determine which document to open. For example, Listing 21.4 opens a document based on a key value. The Domino URL that is constructed looks like the following:

```
<LINK REL=STYLESHEET HREF=/BOOK\Chapt21.nsf/(StyleSheets)/HotMustard/
➡$File/HotMustard.css?OpenElement>
```

This URL looks in the hidden view (`StyleSheets`), which is sorted on the first column, for a value of `HotMustard`. The value of the first column is determined using the formula `@Left(@AttachmentNames; ".")`, which returns the name of the attached file without the extension. It then opens the attached file, `HotMustard.css`, using the `OpenElement` argument. Similarly, you can look up any document in any sorted view by supplying the key and the view name.

This is not only easier to code, it is more user-friendly than using either the UNID or NoteID. Domino URLs can appear in the `Address` field (or `Location` field in Netscape Navigator). A URL with a 32-digit hexadecimal number included is not very readable, as you can see from the following example:

```
<LINK REL=STYLESHEET HREF=/Book/Chapt21.nsf/
➡2EC261C8271AC0D1852567390004E492/2357FF89C0B523C005256742000B7EEF
➡/$File/HosMustard.css?OpenElement
```

Working with Domino URL Arguments

Many of the actions listed in Table 21.7 have arguments that can further refine the URL. The arguments for each are listed in the Domino URL reference in Appendix F. Arguments are appended to the Action with the ampersand character (&). Rather than present an exhaustive listing of all arguments, I discuss a few here so that you understand how to use them.

One of the simplest and most common arguments is the `Login` argument. You can append this to almost any Domino URL, and it enforces user authentication. For example, you can provide a login button or hotspot with a Domino URL such as the following:

```
http://MyHome.nsf?OpenDatabase&Login
```

When the user clicks the button or hotspot in the browser, Domino challenges them with a user name and password dialog box.

OpenView has a number of arguments, as you can see in Table 21.9.

TABLE 21.9   OpenView Arguments

Argument	Description
Collapse=n	Where n is the row number. Displays the row in collapsed format.
CollapseView	Displays the view collapsed.
Count=n	Limits the number of rows to display.
Expand=n	Where n is the row number. Expands the view at row n.
ExpandView	Displays the view expanded.
Start=n	Where n is a row number. Starts the display of the view at row n.
StartKey=key	The view must be sorted. Starts the display of the view at the document which matches the key.

To open the default view in the database in collapsed mode, use the following code:

```
http://MyData.nsf/$defaultview/?Openview&CollapseView
```

To open a view and display only 10 rows, use the following code:

```
http://MyData.nsf/$defaultview/?Openview&Count=10
```

Adding arguments to Domino URLs is pretty simple, and can produce some powerful results. In contrast to the simple examples in this section, you can also use arguments to submit requests for SSL certificates or to create sophisticated domain and site searches. Appendix F also lists the arguments for these Domino URLs.

Summary

This chapter has covered a lot of ground fairly quickly, starting with a brief introduction to HTML and HTML document construction. From there you learned about places and ways you can use HTML in Domino applications. Last, the powerful Domino URLs were covered, although they are not technically part of HTML.

Introduction to LotusScript

CHAPTER

22

by Debbie Lynd

IN THIS CHAPTER

You've seen that the formula language available with Domino Designer is pretty powerful. But, there are things that you will want to do that cannot be accomplished with the formula language alone. That's where LotusScript comes in.

You've used many of the events to enter your formulas, and you've probably noticed that some of them will accept only LotusScript. Using LotusScript, an object-oriented, BASIC-compatible language, you can develop Notes applications that go far beyond what can be accomplished only via the formula language. Don't take this to mean that LotusScript is better than or a replacement for the formula language. Both have their strengths and weaknesses, and both have uses for which they are uniquely suited. Your job is to learn which tool is appropriate for the task at hand.

Part III, "Domino Programming Languages," talks all about LotusScript. In this chapter, you'll get a brief overview of the language as a whole and what's new in Release 5.

What Is LotusScript?

LotusScript (commonly called *Script*) is an object-oriented, BASIC-compatible programming language built into Lotus products. LotusScript is supported within several Lotus products, such as Lotus 1-2-3 and Approach. In the latest version of SmartSuite, SmartSuite97, all the products except Organizer support LotusScript. This cross-product language support allows the development of applications, which share data and functionality between different desktop applications.

Because LotusScript is a BASIC-compatible language, the developer gains the use of all the common programming techniques used in more traditional application development, such as looping, iteration, and branching. More importantly, though, you can begin to develop truly reusable code—code that can be shared by multiple objects, applications, and developers.

Using LotusScript, a developer can get access to the objects within an application in ways not possible with the formula language. With Release 5 of Domino, LotusScript 4 is being released.

What's New in LotusScript 4.0

During the year preceding the release of Domino 5.0, rumor on the street was that LotusScript would be replaced with Java. This may become true in Release 6 or 7, but for the next few years LotusScript is here to stay and is still being enhanced to support the new objects in Release 5.

The most important improvement in LotusScript 4.0 is the virtual removal of size limitations that frustrated so many developers. In LotusScript 3, the code size was limited to 64KB, which was a source of frustration when writing agents that reached out to other applications using ODBC connections. In LotusScript 4, the code can grow up to 2GB. Other limitations have been increased as well, as described in Table 22.1.

TABLE 22.1 Other Limitations That Have Increased

Description	Release 3 Limit	Release 4 Limit	Release 5 Limit
Strings	64KB	2GB	Limited by available memory (2 bytes per character)
Arrays	64KB	64KB per array element	Limited by available memory

The code stack size has been increased as well as the size of subroutine data declarations. The storage size for modules is limited by the available memory. The storage size for each class is 64KB, while procedures are 32KB. In Chapter 23, "Basic LotusScript," you will see that new classes have been added and that many new methods have been added to existing classes.

How Does LotusScript Fit into the Domino Environment?

As you've seen throughout the previous chapters, you can do wonderful things with the Notes development environment and the formula language. Where does LotusScript fit into the development landscape? Why should you bother learning LotusScript when the formula language has such rich functionality available?

With the formula language, much of the structuring of a Notes application is molded to fit the way Notes works; the data is organized in such a way that it facilitates the way the functions are evaluated. Developers build an application to fit the desired functionality as defined by the system requirements but structured by the constraints of the formula language.

Sometimes, that means compromise in terms of purity of design—for instance, building in the capability of child documents to be updated with information from the parent when the data changes. This feature is doable, but for some applications it proves more effort than it's worth.

22

INTRODUCTION TO
LOTUSSCRIPT

The addition of LotusScript to your development toolbox opens up vast avenues of additional capabilities in your applications. You gain modularity, iteration, branching, better error handling, the ability to manipulate files external to Notes, and access to more of the hidden features and capabilities of Notes.

The ability to modularize your code into subroutines and functions allows you to write subprograms that can be used and reused throughout any particular application, throughout any number of applications, and even by all the developers in an organization. Some reusability was available before but was limited primarily to fields, field formulas, and agents. It is now possible to create an entire library of routines in Script for commonly used features and to realize significant productivity gains by reusing code.

The addition of *iteration* expands your ability to write code, especially buttons, actions, or agents to iteratively, or repeatedly, process a set of documents. For example, you could write an agent to scan a view containing customer information changes, look up all the documents pertaining to those customers, and change the information in all their documents. Using the formula language, you had no concept of iteration because all the processing had to be completed in one pass through the code. With Script, however, you can run the same code any number of times for a given execution.

Components of LotusScript

As with any programming language, LotusScript has its own set of commands, elements, and rules. This section is not intended to be a detailed introduction to the LotusScript elements, but serves as an overview of the language.

LotusScript is used to write instructions that can be attached to a number of objects inside a Notes application. LotusScripts can be attached to objects such as an action, a button, or a field event (such as exiting). LotusScripts can also be used in an agent or at the form level. A *script* is a series of LotusScript statements or expressions that performs a desired action.

LotusScripts are created by combining the elements of the language to produce a set of instructions that will produce the desired results. The scripts are then compiled and run when an event is triggered. The trigger could be the click of a button or the creation of a new document. All LotusScripts are driven by an event. When a particular event is triggered, such as a button click or the cursor entering or exiting a field, the script associated with that event will execute. LotusScripts are composed of the following language elements:

- Identifiers
- Labels

- Operators
- Keywords
- Constants
- Literals
- Variables

The following sections explore these in greater detail.

Identifiers

Identifiers are the names given to constants, variables, subroutines, types, classes, and functions. Identifiers are defined by the developer. An identifier is a name used to refer to something created by the developer—that "something" can be a variable, constant, object, subroutine, and so on. There are some rules about how an identifier is constructed. For example, identifiers are not case-sensitive; to LotusScript, theVariable is the same identifier as THEVARIABLE. In addition, the first character of the identifier must be a letter. Identifiers can be up to 40 characters long, plus the type suffix if used. Beyond the first character, the remaining characters can be letters, numbers, the underscore, or ANSI character codes above 127. These are keycodes that can be entered via the keyboard by typing Alt+the ANSI code. For example, the yen character, ¥, is entered by holding down the Alt key and typing 0165 on the numeric keypad. Likewise, the copyright symbol, ©, is entered with Alt+0169.

You Can View the ANSI Characters in Windows

In Windows, you can use the Character Map applet to view the full ANSI character map for each font installed on your Windows system. Clicking a character will show you the keystrokes (either direct from the keyboard or the Alt+*nnnn* combination) required to create that character. To get to the Windows Character map in Windows95 or NT4, click Start, Programs, Accessories, Character Map.

On the Macintosh, no built-in applet exists to display character codes, but freeware or shareware applications are available for download from the software archives on the Internet.

Some Lotus products (including Domino) and some OLE classes can contain identifiers, which are illegal in LotusScript. For example, identifiers can start with a dollar sign ($). You can get LotusScript to accept these as valid by putting a tilde (~) in front of the dollar sign as an escape character. Internal Notes fields start with the dollar sign, such as $UpdatedBy, $Body, and $WindowTitle. To access those, use the tilde notation.

Labels

A label can be used to designate where a branching operation is supposed to continue operation. Program flow can be transferred to the statement following a label by using the name of the label in a GoTo or GoSub command (and others). A label is an identifier, too, and shares many of the same rules for constructing a label. Labels can be up to 40 characters long, must begin with a letter, and are followed with a colon. Labels can appear on the same line as another statement, in front of the statement, and with a colon separating them. Labels do not ever have type suffixes appended to them. Listing 22.1 illustrates the use of labels.

Although your code can cause execution to jump to a label, remember that this can be very different from functions and subroutines (discussed shortly). When you transfer program execution to a labeled statement using the GoTo statement, you cannot return to your place in the script. When you transfer control using a GoSub or via a function or subroutine call when the called block of code has finished, you can return to the place from whence you came. See Listing 22.1 for an example of code using labels.

LISTING 22.1   Labels

```
On Error 20 go to myErrorRoutine
.
'generate an error here
Error 20
.
myErrorRoutine:
Print "Error number 20 encountered. Continuing."
Resume Next
```

Standards

By convention, labels usually appear on a line by themselves so that they are clearly evident in the listing.

Operators

Operators determine how the operands in a statement are used to evaluate to a result. An operator can be a unary operator, which means that it acts on a single operand, such as the NOT or the negation operator. Most operators are binary operators and therefore return a result based on the operation specified for its two operands. The operands in an expression must always be the same data type, or an error will be generated.

Table 22.2 shows the LotusScript operators and the types of operations they can be used for. Like their formula language counterparts, LotusScript operators evaluate according to rules of operator precedence. This means that some operators will be evaluated before other operators in the same statement. Table 22.3 lists the LotusScript operators in order of precedence, highest to lowest.

TABLE 22.2 LotusScript Operators

Operator	Operation	Arithmetic	Boolean	String
^	Exponentiation	X		
-	Negation, minus	X		
+	Plus	X		
*	Multiplication	X		
/	Floating-point division	X		
\	Integer division	X		
Mod	Modulo (remainder)	X		
=	Comparison equal	X	X	
=	Assignment	X	X	X
>	Greater than	X		X
<	Less than	X		X
<>, ><	Not equal	X		X
>=, =>	Greater than or equal to	X		X
<=, =<	Less than or equal to	X		X
Not	One's complement	X		
	Logical negation		X	
And	And	X	X	
Or	Or	X	X	
Xor	Exclusive or	X	X	
Eqv	Equivalence	X	X	
Imp	Implication	X	X	X
&, +	Concatenation			X
Like	Contains			X

TABLE 22.3   Precedence of LotusScript Operators

Operator Type	Operator	Operation
Arithmetic	^	Exponentiation
	-	Unary negation, unary minus
	*, /	Multiplication, floating-point division
	\	Integer division
	Mod	Modulo division
	-, +	Subtraction, addition
Concatenation	&	String concatenation
Comparison or	=, <, >,	Numeric or string comparisons
Relational	<>, ><,	Equal, greater/less than,
	<=, =<,	greater/less than, or equal
	>=, =>	
Logical	Not	Negation or one's complement
	And	Boolean or bitwise AND
	Or	Boolean or bitwise OR
	Xor	Boolean or bitwise Exclusive OR
	Eqv	Boolean or bitwise equivalence
	Imp	Boolean or bitwise implication
Object reference	Is	Refers to the same object variable comparison
Assignment	=	Assignment

Keywords

Keywords are the reserved LotusScript words that refer to built-in functions, such as Trim$ or Open#. Both these keywords are functions that perform specific actions and are predefined in the language itself. The meaning of keywords is fixed and cannot be changed by the developer. All keywords are displayed in the color blue.

Constants

Constants are named storage areas in memory that contain a known value and cannot be changed; they are constant, and the value of the constant is known at compile time. Constants and variables are exactly alike except for one small fact: Constants never change their values, and variables are expected to change. Constants can be defined in a number of ways. LotusScript itself contains some constants that are built-in (see Table 22.4). Lotus also supplies files of predefined constants that can be used by the developer by including, for example, the LSCONST.LSS file (see Table 22.5). Including these .LSS constant definition files enables you to write more readable scripts because you can reference (typically numeric) values via a symbolic text name. Lastly, developers can define their own constants. Those Lotus products that support LotusScript might also define product-specific constants in an include file. Lotus includes several definition files that predefine function and error return codes into text values. For example, the error code 101 has been predefined to the variable "ErrOpenFailed." When an error occurs, you can check against the more readable "EffOpenFailed" constant instead of the value 101, as indicated in Listing 22.2

LISTING 22.2   An Error Constant

```
If Err() = ErrOpenFailed Then….
```

> **Note**
>
> Remember to use the predefined constants. Add the directive displayed in Listing 22.2 to the options event of the object.

LISTING 22.3   Adding LSConst.lss to the Options

```
Use "LSConst.lss"
```

TABLE 22.4   LotusScript Built-In Constants

Name	Value
EMPTY	For strings, EMPTY = " "; for numbers, EMPTY = 0. Variant data types have an initial value of EMPTY.
NOTHING	Object reference variables are initially NOTHING until assigned.
NULL	Some functions return NULL, but only variants can be assigned a NULL value. NULL represents unknown or missing data, or the absence of a result.
PI	The ratio of the circumference of a circle to its diameter.
TRUE	Boolean True. Equates to an integer -1.
FALSE	Boolean False. Equates to an integer 0.

TABLE 22.5   LotusScript Constants Include Files

Filename	Usage
lsconst.lss	Defines constants used as arguments or return values from functions and statements
lserr.lss	Defines constants for errors that could be returned by the LotusScript language
lsxbeerr.lss	Defines error constants for back-end methods
lsxuierr.lss	Defines error constants for front-end methods

Literals

A *literal* is a data item whose value doesn't change. This is like a constant, except that a literal doesn't have a name by which to refer to it. Literals can be strings or numbers. In this example, I declare a constant:

```
Const MyConst$ = "Michael"
```

I now have a constant called MyConst that has—and will always have—the string value "Michael". Anytime throughout my script that I need to reference that value, I can do so by using the name MyConst. That's not so for a literal, because a literal doesn't have a name. This statement uses a literal:

```
Dim MyVar as String
MyVar = "Michael"
```

After execution, the variable MyVar contains the text string "Michael". But if I've used that literal in many places and later I decide that I want to recode my script and change the literal to "Marc", I must go through all my code and change each occurrence of "Michael" to "Marc"—a tedious process, at best. By using a constant and then referencing that constant by name throughout my script, I would have to change only the declaration of the constant to effect the "Michael" to "Marc" change throughout my program.

Variables

A *variable* is a named storage area; it's like a constant, but one that can be changed during execution of the program. Variables have a data type that represents the data stored in the variable. The LotusScript data types and range of values are shown in Table 22.6. Variable data types can be represented in one of two ways: either with a type suffix or without, but never in both ways. Also, variables can be explicitly declared with a DIM statement or can be implicitly declared. An implicitly declared variable comes into existence the first time its name is used in an expression. (Remember variables in the formula language? They also can be declared implicitly.) Implicitly declared variables start life as variants, which are the largest type and, consequently, the most wasteful of memory—and they're the slowest type to manipulate, which slows down your application. You're always better off using explicitly declared variables. Even if you know that you'll need a variant type, declare it explicitly for consistency.

A variable can be declared explicitly with a data type, as in this example:

```
Dim loopCounter as Integer
```

Here, the type of the variable named loopCounter has been explicitly declared to be an integer. Alternatively, variable data types can be defined by appending a type suffix to the variable name. Either way is acceptable, but choose one or the other; the same variable cannot be referenced both with and without a type suffix.

```
Dim loopCounter%
```

Use Explicit Typing

I prefer using explicit typing, for a couple of reasons. First, I can't remember what all the type suffixes are. Second, I like seeing the type spelled out in the Declarations section.

Good coding standards require that you use explicit declarations. This takes out any guesswork regarding variables. Many shops require that all variables be explicitly declared, especially those that have been producing code in other languages over the years. To require explicit declarations, use the Option Declare statement in the module.

TABLE 22.6 LotusScript Variable Data Types, Value Ranges, and Type Suffixes

Data Type	*Value Range*	*Type Suffix*
Integer (signed short integer)	−32,768 to +32,767	%
Long (signed long int)	−2,147,483,648 to +2,147,483,647	&
Single (single-precision floating point)	−3.402823E+38 to +3.408823E+38	!
Double (double-precision floating point)	−1.7976931348623158+308 to +1.7976931348623158+308	#
Currency (fixed-point integer with four decimal places)	−922,337,203,685,477.5807 to +922,337,203,685,477.5807	@
String	0 to 32KB characters (0 to 64KB)	$

When entering numbers, you must follow certain rules. When entering a number as a literal, its type is interpreted to be whatever numeric type will hold the number. For example, if I enter the number 1234, LotusScript would interpret this to be an integer because it falls into the range of allowable integers. See Table 22.6 for all the LotusScript numeric value ranges. 235.342 would be interpreted as type double because it is a legal double value. Numbers entered in scientific notation, such as 2.5456E+12, are also typed as double. If you need to enter binary, octal, or hexadecimal values, prefix the number with &B, &O, or &H, as appropriate.

The variable data types listed in Table 22.6 are the scalar data types, types that hold a particular value. LotusScript also supports the other data types and data structures shown in Table 22.7.

TABLE 22.7 LotusScript's Other Data Types

Data Type	*Description*
Array	Named set or collection of elements of the same data type. Up to eight dimensions. Subscript range is –32,768 to +32,767.
List	A one-dimensional array of identically typed elements. Access is via tags instead of subscripts.
Variant	A variable with no declared type. Can hold any other variable type, including arrays, lists, scalar variables, and object references.
User-defined data type	A set of any number or type of variables defined into a single unit.
User-defined class	A user-defined data type expanded to include properties and methods.
Object reference	A pointer or handle to a particular instance of a class object.
Byte	Integer value from 0 to 255
Object	Variant storage to hold an OLE object

When declaring variables, you might want to set some standards, such as deciding that all integer variables will start with the letters I through N. (This is a common one; notice the first two letters of the word *integer*.) You could just enforce this standard with some sort of code review, but that's no fun! Instead, use the Deftype statement. Substitute one of the type abbreviations shown in Table 22.8 for *type*, give a letter range, and, voilá—automatic typing! Letter ranges given in Deftype statements cannot overlap. Deftype statement examples are shown in Listing 22.3.

LISTING 22.3   Using the Deftype Statement

```
DefInt A-D      'all vars that start with a-d are automatically integers!
DefCur E-G      'or Currency
DefDbl H-K, O-R 'here, h-k & o-r will be doubles
```

TABLE 22.8   Deftype Abbreviations

Data Type	Abbreviation
Currency	Cur
Double	Dbl
Integer	Int
Long	Lng
Single	Sng
String	Str
Variant	Var

22

INTRODUCTION TO LOTUSSCRIPT

`Deftype` statements can appear only at the module level and must appear before any other declaration statements except constant declarations. If you have a `Deftype` in effect and then explicitly declare another variable in conflict with the `Deftype`, the explicit declaration takes precedence. See Listing 22.4.

LISTING 22.4   Deftype Versus Explicit Declarations

```
DefInt I-N      'All vars that start with I-n will be integer by default
Dim insideTemp          'an integer variable, as per the DefTYPE
Dim NozzleTemp as Double 'explicitly declared double
Dim motorTemp!          'explicitly declared single
```

Arrays

An *array* is a named set of elements of the same data type. The elements in an array can be scalar values such as strings, integers, and currency variables (discussed previously), or they can be user-defined types, which we'll discuss later. A reference to the name of the array references all elements of the array, not a single element. An individual element in the array is accessed via a *subscript* or *index*. So, if I have a one-dimensional array of 10 string elements and I want to set each element to a text value, I might have something like the example in Listing 22.5.

LISTING 22.5   Array Declaration

```
Dim myArray( 10 ) as String
myArray( 0 ) = "Lotus"
myArray( 1 ) = "Notes"
myArray( 2 ) = "Release"
myArray( 3 ) = "4.5"
myArray( 4 ) = "is"
myArray( 5 ) = "the"
myArray( 6 ) = "best"
myArray( 7 ) = "release"
myArray( 8 ) = "yet!"
myArray( 9 ) = ""
```

Now, each element of the array is set to a text value. Notice that the subscript numbers went from 0 to 9 for my 10 elements. Notes uses zero-based subscripts by default. If I now want to find out what value was in the fifth element in the array, I could reference the fifth element like this:

```
Print myArray( 4 )
```

Changing the Base Subscript Value

If you want your subscripts to start at 1 instead of 0, include `Option Base 1` in the `(Options)` event of your script.

LotusScript arrays can have up to eight dimensions, requiring eight subscripts to reference a particular element—and the subscripts are integers, so they can range from $-32,768$ to $+32,767$. The range of a subscript is known as the *bounds* of the array; an upper-bound and a lower-bound can be used. LotusScript arrays can also be *fixed* or *dynamic*. A fixed array indicates an array for which the number of dimensions and elements is known at compile time. A dynamic array is just the opposite: an array for which the number of dimensions and elements is not known until runtime. At runtime, the dynamic array is *redimensioned* with known parameters. When an array gets redimensioned, you can either preserve its current contents with the `Preserve` keyword, or you can wipe it out and start anew. Arrays can also be declared as `static`, which means that the values in the array are retained between invocations of the procedure in which the array is declared.

Statement Construction

LotusScript statements can be comments, compiler directives, declarations, definitions, block or iterative block statements, or flow control statements. Every line in your LotusScript script must be a complete statement or a continuation statement. LotusScript statements are composed of keywords, identifiers, constants, labels, literals, and operators. You can include blank lines or any spaces (to enhance readability) in your scripts. Each statement needs to be on one line. If you need to break a statement across more than one line, either because of the length of the statement or for formatting aesthetics, you can use the continuation character, the underscore (_), as the last character on the line. There can be nothing on the line following the underscore except line comments or white space.

Two exceptions exist to the one-line-equals-one-statement rule. First, if you must enter more than one statement on a single line, separate the statements with a colon (:). Second, you can enter a multiline text literal into your code by entering it between braces or vertical bars. When entering text into the Programmers pane of the Integrated Design Environment (IDE), you can enter strings surrounded by double quotes (""), vertical bars (¦¦), or braces({ }). Only braces or vertical bars will allow a text string to span multiple lines, as shown in Listing 22.6.

LISTING 22.6 Entering Strings in the IDE

```
Dim s as String
s = "This is an example where" _
& " the text is spread across multiple" _
& "lines quoted, with a continuation character."
s = ¦This is a long line of text
stretching across more than one line
without using the continuation character.¦
s = {Here's another line of text across
multiple lines, this time using the
brace as string delimiters}
```

If you need to include one of the string delimiters (", ¦, or }) inside a string delimited with the same character, enter the character twice. To include the open brace ({) in a brace-delimited string, enter it once. Listing 22.7 illustrates these rules.

LISTING 22.7   Including String Delimiters as Part of the Literal Text

```
Dim stringTwo
stringTwo = "This string includes a "", double quote"
stringTwo = ¦This string includes a ¦¦, vertical bar¦
stringTwo = {This string includes a { and a }}, braces}
```

Use a Vertical Bar as a Delimiter

The easiest and most readable method to add a double quote to a string is to use the vertical bar as the delimiter. The vertical bar will allow the simple use of a double quote without the need for two of them. See Listing 22.8 for an example.

LISTING 22.8   Including Double Quotes Within a Vertical Bar

```
Dim stringthree as string
stringthree = ¦This string uses a "double quote" as a string character.¦
```

There are no other constraints to be aware of when entering text into the IDE.

Comments

Comments, also called *remarks,* serve as inline documentation for your code. Comments are a good thing—use them liberally. Remember that the developer trying to modify this code six months from now just might be you.

LotusScript comments are nonexecutable statements used to document what is happening at a particular point in your code. Comment statements are used in both scripts and formulas. All code should be commented. In general, every block of 5 to 10 statements should have a comment or two describing its function.

Several ways exist by which to enter comments into LotusScript. The first is to do it just exactly as you do when writing formula language comments: Begin the line with REM. The difference in Script is that the actual comment text does not need to be enclosed in quotes. The second way to indicate a comment is with an apostrophe (') anywhere on the line. When the compiler encounters an apostrophe in a statement (not in a quoted string), it considers the rest of the line a comment and ignores it. The third way, which is very useful when writing a block of comments together, is to use the %REM and %END REM compiler directives. (The next section covers compiler directives.) All statements between %REM and %END REM are considered comments and will be ignored by the compiler. The code example in Listing 22.9 illustrates the three ways to indicate comments. The IDE will automatically colorize comment lines to green. You can then assign a different color. This is covered again in the section "Script in the Design Pane," later in this chapter.

LISTING 22.9   Entering Comments into the IDE

```
REM This is all I need for one line of comments
Dim myVar as String
Dim anotherVar as integer
%REM
    This is a long
    block of comments
    within a comment block
%END REM
'This line too is a comment
myVar = "Hello World!"          'everything beyond here is a comment
```

Compiler Directives

Compiler directives are special lines of code that are interpreted only at compile time and that contain special instructions for the compiler. Until you begin writing very sophisticated applications, it's likely that the only compiler directives you'll use will be the %Rem comment directive and the %Include statement to pull in one of the .LSS constant definition files. Directives can go into either the (Options) or (Declarations) section of a script, although usually you'll find them in (Options). See Listing 22.10 for an example of a compiler directive.

LISTING 22.10   Compiler Directives

```
(This would be in the (Options) event of the script)
%Include "lsconst.lss"
%Include "lserr.lss"
```

Flow Control Statements

Statements in LotusScript can serve several different functions. They can be *expressions;* that is, they return the result of a specified operation. Statements can also be *flow control* statements. This type of statement is used to control the order of processing for the script, dependent on other values or conditions. Flow control statements can be block, iteration block, branching, or termination statements. Block statements direct that a series of statements be executed based on a specific condition. Iteration block statements force the execution of a block of statements a number of times, or as long as or until a condition exists. Branching statements redirect program execution, either conditionally or unconditionally. Table 22.8 lists all the flow control statements.

TABLE 22.8 Flow Control Statements

Type	*Statements*
Block	If...Then
	If...Then...Else
	If...Then...ElseIf
	Select Case
Iteration block	Do...Loop
	Do While...Loop
	Do...Loop While
	Do Until...Loop
	Do...Loop Until
	While...Wend
	For-Next
	ForAll-End ForAll
Branching	GoTo
	GoSub
	If...GoTo...Else
	On...GoTo
	On...GoSub
	Return
Termination	End
	Exit

Block Statements

Flow control statements are used to direct the flow of execution through your script. Block statements are used to execute or not execute a set of statements (a block) depending on some condition that is tested. The `If...Then...Else` and the `Select Case` statements are block statements, and their structure is shown in Listing 22.11.

LISTING 22.11 The `If...Then...Else` and the `Select Case` Statements

```
Dim counter as Integer
counter = 1
    .
    .
    .
REM Which block will get executed? It depends on the result of the
REM test on the If line
If counter < 10 Then           'These 3 lines are a block
    Print "The counter is less than 10."
```

```
   Counter = 10
   Print "The counter has now been set to 10."
Else                          'These 2 lines are another block
   Print "The counter was greater than or equal to 10."
   Print "Now continuing..."
End If
.
.
.
Select Case counter
Case < 10
   Print "The counter was less than 10."
Case < 20
   Print "The counter was less than 20."
Case > 50
   Print "The counter was greater than 50."
Case Else
   Print "The counter was between 20 & 50."
End Select
```

Notice that both the If...Then...Else and the Select Case statements are terminated with End statements, the If with an End If, and the Select Case with an End Select statement.

Two other forms of the If...Then...Else statement exist. The first is used only when a single statement will be executed and when the condition tested for that statement is true. In other words, if a condition is true, a single statement is executed; if a condition is false, no statement is executed. In either case, program execution continues with the statement following the If...Then construct. No End If statement is needed with this form of the If...Then.

There is also an If...Then...ElseIf variant of the If statement. This is equivalent to chaining If...Thens together. The If...Then...ElseIf block is terminated with an End If statement.

The Select Case block statement is conceptually like a bunch of Ifs chained together. The Select does look cleaner in code, though. Before starting the Select Case block, you must define the variable used for selection. The Select Case statement then specifies the defined variable; in the previous example, the variable counter is used. Each Case line then lists a condition or conditions that the selected expression is compared against. If one of the Case comparisons returns a true result, the statements listed in that Case block are executed. If none of the Case comparisons evaluate to true, the Case Else block (if there is one) is executed. Program execution then continues with the statement following the End Select statement.

Iteration Block Statements

Iteration block statements are similar to block statements, except that where block statements dictate that a block of statements be executed one time based on a condition, iteration blocks execute the same block of statements many times. These iterative blocks will execute a block of statements a given number of times while a condition exists or until a condition exists. The Do, While, For, and ForAll statements are the iteration block statements. Each controls the execution of a block of statements based upon a condition.

The While statement sits at the top of a block of statements with a Wend at the bottom. The block of statements will be executed as long as the condition specified on the While line is true. If the condition is not true when execution begins at the While statement, the block will not be executed at all. On the other hand, if the condition never goes false, you'll be stuck in an infinite loop. According to the Lotus documentation, the While is a "historical artifact." There's no reason to use the While/Wend in preference to the Do While or Do Until statement. See Listing 22.12 for examples of the While and Do constructs.

The Do loop has several variations. With the Do loop, the controlling condition can be tested either at the beginning or at the end of the loop, and the loop can continue either While or Until the condition is true. Testing the condition at the end of the block statements guarantees that the block statements will be executed at least once; testing the condition at the entry point of the block has no such guarantee. Note that it is possible to purposely create an infinite loop with the Do statement; just don't enter a condition to test for. Use this with caution, however, because you must provide some means for the loop to terminate.

LISTING 22.12 While and Do Statement Constructs

```
'loopControl will be the variable used to control our loop
'although loopcontrol is an integer, concatenating it with & automatically
'converts it to a string for the print function
Dim loopControl as Integer
'A While/Wend loop
loopControl = 0
While loopControl <20
    Print "Loop number: " & loopControl    loopControl = loopControl + 1
Wend
'A Do loop
' This is an infinite loop
Do
    Print "Loop number: " & loopControl    loopControl = loopControl + 1
Loop
'This is a Do While loop
loopControl = 10
```

```
Do While loopControl > 0
    Print "Loop Control = " & loopControl     loopControl = loopControl - 1
Loop
'This is a Do Until loop
loopControl = 10
Do Until loopControl > 20
    Print "Loop Control = " & loopControl
    loopControl = loopControl + 1
Loop
'This is a Do loop - While
'This loop is guaranteed to be executed at least once,
'because execution has to go through the entire
'block before getting to the condition
loopControl = 10
Do
    Print "Loop Control = " & loopControl
    loopControl = loopControl - 1
Loop While loopControl > 0
'This is a Do loop - Until
'This loop also is guaranteed to be executed at least once
loopControl = 10
Do
    Print "Loop Control = " & loopControl     loopControl = loopControl + 1
Loop Until loopControl > 20
```

22

INTRODUCTION TO
LOTUSSCRIPT

The `For` and `ForAll` statements are the last iteration block statements. The `For` statement executes the statement block a specified number of times. The `ForAll` statement executes the statement block once for each of the elements in a specified array or list. The number of times a `For` block will execute is controlled by giving a beginning and ending value for a loop counter and optionally an increment value. The loop counter is initialized at the beginning value, and the block of statements is then executed. At the end of the loop, the loop counter is automatically incremented (by 1 or the specified value), and the block is repeated until the loop counter reaches the specified ending value.

The `ForAll` is similar, except that the number of times the block should be executed is not specified; the block will execute once for each element in the array or list used as the control variable. Listing 22.13 shows examples of both the `For` and the `ForAll` statements.

LISTING 22.13   For and ForAll Statement Constructs

```
'set up the array
Dim theArray( 5 ) as integer
theArray( 0 ) = 10
theArray( 1 ) = 20
```

continues

LISTING 22.13   continued

```
theArray( 2 ) = 30
theArray( 3 ) = 40
theArray( 4 ) = 50
'dim the counter
Dim loopControl as Integer
For loopControl From 0 to 4
    Print "Element number " & CStr( loopControl ) & " = " & _
    CStr( theArray( loopControl ) )
Next loopControl
'Output:
'Element number 1 = 10
'Element number 2 = 20
'Element number 3 = 30
'Element number 4 = 40
'Element number 5 = 50
'create the list
Dim theList List as String
theList( "first" ) = "Adam"
theList( "second" ) = "Bruce"
theList( "third" ) = "Cary"
theList( "fourth") = "Dan"
theList ( "fifth" ) = "Ed"
ForAll X in theList
    Print "List tag: " & X & " contains " & theList( X )
End ForAll
'Output:
'List tag: first contains Adam
'List tag: second contains Bruce
'List tag: third contains Cary
'List tag: fourth contains Dan
'List tag: fifth contains Ed
Next loopControl
```

Branching Statements

The LotusScript branching statements conditionally or unconditionally transfer the flow of execution from its current place in the code to another place. In other languages, the branching statements typically do not allow a return to the point at which the transfer occurred; however, such a return is possible within LotusScript. Branching statements include GoTo, If...GoTo...Else, On...GoTo, On...GoSub, GoSub, and Return.

The GoTo statement unconditionally transfers control to a label somewhere else in your script. There is no return path, except via another GoTo. The If...GoTo...Else is a variation of the If...Then...Else discussed previously. The difference is that when the tested condition is true, program control will transfer to the label named in the GoTo clause. The On...GoTo functions similarly to the If statement. The condition tested in the On statement transfers control to one of the labels listed in the GoTo label list. The On...GoSub functions like the On...GoTo, except that program execution will resume at the statement following the On...GoSub when the end of the called subroutine is reached. The GoSub statement unconditionally transfers execution to the named subroutine, but, unlike the GoTo, program execution will resume at the statement following the GoSub after the called subroutine has completed. The last branching statement, the Return, is the statement that returns program execution to the statement after the one that caused the branch.

> ### Design Guideline
>
> You might have noticed that the GoTo, If...GoTo...Else, On...GoTo, On...GoSub, GoSub, and Return statements didn't receive as much emphasis or explanation on their usage as did the other statement types covered so far. This is not accidental. These statements are really leftovers from before the philosophy of structured code became popular.
>
> When you use statements such as GoTo in your code, it's very easy to turn your structured code into *spaghetti code,* so-called because the GoTos scattered all around send the program execution here, there, and everywhere.
>
> Ideally, you would not use GoTo type statements. I don't subscribe to the notion that you should *never* use them because sometimes they can certainly facilitate your code. However, if you find yourself using them a lot, you should revisit the way you structure your code to do away with most of the GoTos.
>
> Remember, the GoTo police are watching!

Termination Statements

The termination statements, Exit and End, are used to terminate the procedure or Do, For, or ForAll loops prematurely—that is, before the condition specified as the control condition would have terminated the loop or procedure. End is also used to mark the physical end of code for a function or subroutine.

Exit is used to terminate the current block statement, either a Do, For, or ForAll. It is also used to terminate a function, or subroutine. When Exit is executed, control returns to the statement after the end of the Do, For, or ForAll loop, or to the statement after the one that called the function or subroutine. Execution of other lines of code will continue; only the current block, function, or subroutine will exit. The Exit statement should be considered a graceful exit or return. End, on the other hand, is more of a "get the heck out of Dodge right now" kind of exit. It terminates not only the current Do, For, or ForAll function or subroutine, but also the whole darn script. When End executes, that's what it does to script execution: It ends.

Data Definition and Access

Using LotusScript to work with the data contained in a document is quite different from using the formula language to access that data. In the formula language, you simply specify a field name in the formula that is written to respond to an event. In the LotusScript language, you will also refer to fields, but the data is handled differently and you have many more options and freedom to access much more than the limited formula language. In this section, we explore how LotusScript handles various data types and access to those data types, as well as how you can create your own procedures. We also explore where all this stuff is stored.

Fields

Now is a good time to revisit our most basic Notes container, the field. Fields are known as items in LotusScript. When displayed on a form, a field always has a data type as determined by design properties you set for it as the developer. In the macro language, Notes-as-we-know-it-up-till-now form design world, we've always referenced fields by their name, and a reference to a field returned the contents of the field. If the field happened to contain a list, the list was returned. All was good.

Things change a bit when manipulating fields in LotusScript. First, fields don't have a data type in and of themselves. They do take on a data type when a value is placed into them or when displayed in the user interface. Second, all fields are treated as though they were arrays: one-dimensional arrays with an unknown number of elements. (The upper bound of the array is unknown.) If you need to reference the contents of a field, reference the element in location 0 of the field array. To reference all the contents of a field, whether it be a multivalue item or a single element, you can still refer to the field just by its name.

If you need to access a particular element of a field, even if there's only one element in it, you must reference the field as an array. Here's how to do the LotusScript equivalent of this formula:

```
FIELD newField := oldField
```

You must write the previous line like this:

```
doc.newField( 0 ) = doc.oldField( 0 ).
```

If the field that you're referencing has multiple elements in it, such as a multivalue field, use an index to point to a particular element of the field.

> ### Array Subscripts
>
> Remember that, by default, LotusScript array subscripts are zero-based.

Lists

A special kind of array is a *list*. The LotusScript list is a one-dimensional array of similar elements. A list differs from an array in two ways. First, the individual elements in the list are not accessed by using a subscript, but by a *list tag*, which is a string value that indicates the name of each element. Second, the size of the list can shrink or grow without being redimensioned. To access a list value, use its list tag to get the value of the element. Listing 22.14 illustrates the use of lists and list tags.

> ### Note
>
> A list in LotusScript is a very different animal than the multivalue field lists you're used to seeing in Notes fields. Each list value in LotusScript can represent a different field.

LISTING 22.14   LotusScript List and List Tags

```
Dim theList List as String
theList( "Boss" ) = "Jane Doe"
theList( "Secretary" ) = "Fred Flintstone"
theList( "VP Sales" ) = "Mary McCarthy"
theList( "VP Engineering" ) = "Justin Lindstrom"
theList( "Notes Developer" ) = "Michael Hart"
Print theList( "VP Engineering" ) & " is the Vice President of Engineering")
```

In this example, the list variable called `theList` has five string values initialized, with each value having a unique list tag. The `Print` statement uses one of the list tags to recall a specific element from the list and print it, along with some other text.

If you wanted to add another element to the list, set the value into the list by giving another unique identifier. After this statement is executed, there are six elements in the list:

```
theList( "Web Master" ) = "Joey Lieber"
```

Variants

Variants are special data-type variables; they can hold any of the LotusScript data types except user-defined types. Variants can also hold data types that LotusScript doesn't recognize, such as Boolean and date/time. You'll notice that neither Boolean nor date/time are listed anywhere as a LotusScript data type. Booleans can be either true (-1) or false (0), as stated before.

Make It Easy to See Your Variants

Many developers will append a v to their Variant variable names, such as:

```
Dim theDatev as Variant
```

Although I don't like using data type suffixes, this tip makes it easy to remember which variables are variants.

Working with Dates

Although LotusScript doesn't have a built-in date/time data type, it does recognize dates; there are a full set of functions for manipulating date/time values. When manipulating date values in LotusScript, always use Variant data types. The range of allowable date in LotusScript is from 1/1/100 through 12/31/9999. Dates are stored as double floating-point values, with the integer portion of the value representing the date (with 1/1/100 being –657,434, 12/30/1899 being 0, and 2,958,465 being 12/30/9999) and the fractional part of the value representing the time.

As an example, the date 4/20/97 is day number 35540. The formula to determine that value is:

```
Print "Today's number is " & CDbl( Date )
```

It's worth repeating here: When doing date manipulations in LotusScript, use variants.

Similar to variables in the formula language, variants in LotusScript can change their data type depending on what is put into them. This is what makes them useful—and dangerous. It can be very easy to forget what data type is currently in a variant variable and wind up with a runtime error, the infamous Type Mismatch. These types of errors can also be very difficult to track down. Listing 22.15 shows how the variant leopard can change its spots.

Listing 22.15 Changing the Data Type of a Variant

```
Dim leopardv as Variant
leopardv = "a string variable"
Print "The leopard is now " & leopardv
leopardv = 12453
Print "The leopard is now " & leopardv
leopardv = $233,543.353
Print "The leopard is now " & leopardv
```

Functions

A *function* is a named procedure that optionally takes some arguments and returns a value. LotusScript comes with a number of predefined, built-in functions such as Input, Month, and Today. These built-in functions are not changeable by the developer. However, you can write your own functions. Each function takes certain parameters and returns a value. Because the function has a return value, the return value has a data type, so you must be careful when using the value returned from a function. It's easy enough to forget the data type a function returns and wind up with a Type Mismatch error.

Writing your own functions is very simple and requires naming the function in a declaration, defining the arguments it takes, and defining the data type of the returned value. Listing 22.16 shows an example of both a function and a subroutine declaration.

Subroutines

A *subroutine* (also called a *sub*) is a named procedure, like a function, except that a subroutine does not return a value. A sub can take arguments.

Listing 22.16 Function and Subroutine Declarations

```
Dim myVar As String
myVar = "hello there"            'put a value into myVar
' the next line prints the return value from the mySub function
Print "The return value from myFunction is: " & myFunction( myVar )
mySub( myVar )          'this line calls the subroutine which prints
                        'a message

Function myFunction( the_input As String ) As String
    myFunction = Ucase( the_input )
End Function
Sub mySub( the_input As String)
    Print "mySub printed this: " & the_input
End Sub
```

22

INTRODUCTION TO
LOTUSSCRIPT

Objects

In Notes R4.5, everything was an *object*. The database, the ACL, forms, views, agents, buttons, actions, and items (fields) are objects. This is still true in Release 5. Objects, however, are not restricted to those things just mentioned that you can manipulate as a developer. The workspace is an object, as are the workspace pages, the SmartIcons, the database icons, and the Replicator page. Every one of the things just mentioned is an object, something you could point to and describe. Like things in the physical world, Notes objects have properties you can change or examine, and each object has its own list of actions you can perform on or with it.

Let's use a house as a sample object. Our house is a thing; we can point to it, see it, and describe it. It has certain *properties*—number of rooms, exterior finish, color of the roof tiles, floor plan, number of bathrooms, rating of electrical service, and type of heating and air conditioning equipment. There are also things you can do to the house—paint it, enter it, cool or heat it, close the doors, turn on lights, and arm the alarm system. The things you can do to the house are its *methods*.

A very important concept in object-oriented languages is *containment*. To carry our house analogy a little further, you can see that there are other objects within the house—furniture, rooms, pets, people, and clothes. Each of these objects has its own set of properties and methods. Within these objects can be other objects, such as clothes within a dresser. To access the properties of the clothes, you would first have to access the house and then the dresser before you could get to the clothes. You often hear people refer to a Domino database (the .NSF) as an object store. A Domino database is a container for form objects, view objects, document objects, and so on. Each of these objects contains objects. A view object contains a column object. A document object contains an item (field) object.

Not surprisingly, Notes objects are affected by containment. A `NotesDocument` object is contained within a `NotesDatabase` object, which, in turn, is contained within a `NotesSession` object. To manipulate a field object on the `NotesDocument` object, you must access (via object references, to be discussed later) the `NotesSession` object, the `NotesDatabase` object, the `NotesDocument` object, and then the field object. Finally, Notes objects are referenced by declaring *object reference* variables and assigning the object reference equal to an *instance* of the class. In other languages, this is equated to a pointer or handle.

Classes

Classes are the abstract (programmers') definition of objects. Going back to the house analogy, say that your house was at 500 Domino Way. To us, 500 Domino Way is the address of the house; to Domino, it is a reference to an instance of the class *house*. The class house is the definition of what a house should be—what its properties, methods, and so on are. Until the house is actually built at 500 Domino Way—*instantiated*, in OOP terms—it exists only conceptually. After it's instantiated, it's a real thing. 500 Domino Way is the reference—the handle—by which this instantiation of house is manipulated.

Domino classes are broken into two separate groups: the *front-end* classes and the *back-end* classes. Throughout Domino, whenever the front end is mentioned, it refers to something visible in the user interface; you can see it on the screen. Conversely, mention of the back end implies something not visible—behind the scenes, if you will. Domino 4.5 had a total of 21 back-end classes and 7 front-end classes. Domino 5.0 enables us to use 27 back-end classes and 7 front-end classes. The reason for this is that there are just so many things you can display on the screen. The classes are all listed in Appendix A, "Donimo Objects for LotuScript Classes."

Events

Every class describes a thing, such as a class house, dresser, or chair. Each of those things has properties (attributes) and methods (ways to manipulate the object defined by the class). Some classes can also have *events* to which they'll respond. Class `doorbell` has an event, `press`, which it will respond to. As the developer of the `doorbell` class, I've written an event script that makes the buzzer sound when the event `press` happens.

Any particular class can have a set of events to which it will respond. Common events include `Click`, `Entering`, `Exiting`, `Initialize`, `Terminate`, `QueryOpen` and `PostOpen`, and `QuerySave` and `PostSave`. All objects have `Initialize` and `Terminate` events; other objects might also have other scriptable events. Note that just because an object can respond to an event doesn't mean that there is a script written to handle that event. As a developer, you have control over what events an object will choose to respond to. Events are listed in Table 22.17.

TABLE 22.17   Object Events

Event Name	Usage
(Options)	Compiler options that apply to all objects.
(Declarations)	An area to declare variables and types that are available to all events in this object.
Initialize	Every object has an Initialize event that is executed when the object loads.

continues

TABLE 22.17   continued

Event Name	Usage
Terminate	Every object has a Terminate event that is executed when the object is closed.
Query	Executed before the named event is called. There are Query events for Open, ModeChange, Recalc, AddToFolder, Paste, DragDrop, DocumentDelete, DocumentUndelete, Save, and Close.
Post	Executed after the named event is called. There are Post events for Open, Recalc, ModeChange, Paste, and DragDrop.

Scope

Every variable, function, subroutine, or object that you declare (instantiate) in your scripts has a certain *scope,* also called *visibility.* Scope is the context in which your object is known. Within that context, your object is visible and its value is known. Outside that context, however, no other object is aware of your object and consequently cannot act on or respond to your object.

Go back for a minute to your house at 500 Domino Way. Imagine that your electric utility company doesn't exist and that your house has no external power source. However, while tinkering around in your den (the object named YourDen of the class room), you install a power generation and distribution system. The scope (context) of your power system is YourDen. Other objects of the class room—for example, Kitchen—cannot use the power system and don't even know it exists because the power system is not visible to them; it's outside of Kitchens' context. If you had installed your power system into the object 451 Notes Way instead, all the room objects contained in the house object would be capable of using your power system. Because the power system's context is house, the power system would be visible to all the objects within the house.

All analogies aside, scope affects not only the visibility of objects but also that of variables, constants, procedures, functions, and subroutines. If you think of your application as a set of nested boxes, one inside the other inside the other, you begin to get the idea. The outermost box is the module level; in Notes, let's say it's the form object. The next level of boxes is the procedure level. Inside the procedure level boxes are the class and user-defined data type levels. (These three are all contained within the module box.) Anything declared at any level is visible only to its own level and to any other box within it. So, constants and variables (or functions and subroutines) declared at the module level are visible only within that module—and therefore by any procedures, classes, or user-defined data types within that module.

Things declared within one module are not visible to any other module. Things declared within a procedure are not visible to any other procedure within the module or to the module. The exception is that anything created via a declaration can be declared *public* or *private.* By default, everything is declared private. Declaring a variable, constant, function, subroutine, class, or user-defined data type as public means that the object can be seen by every other module and procedure in the application.

See Listing 22.18 for code examples illustrating scope and visibility.

Each identifier has not only a scope but also a *persistence,* or lifetime. Recall how in the formula language a variable exists only during the time that the formula is actually being evaluated. The persistence of the variable is available only during the evaluation of the formula. In LotusScript, the same concept applies. An identifier persists only during the time that its module is loaded. For example, if variable FOO is declared in procedure XYZ of module ABC, then FOO is not in existence until procedure XYZ is called. After this procedure is called, FOO becomes available. As long as procedure XYZ remains active—as long as any code within its scope is executing—FOO is available. After XYZ finishes executing, FOO disappears. At times, you might want a variable to retain its value between calls. When you declare a variable, array, list, function, or procedure as STATIC, the value of the variable (or variables declared with the function or procedure) will not disappear between invocations. In Listing 22.18, the code shows how you would declare variables to be used at the form level. This code will not work in and of itself—it is used only to demonstrate how the variables are assigned.

LISTING 22.18   LotusScript Scope

```
'Declaration section at the form level
Dim FormName as String
'Declaration with a module
Sub Initialize
   Dim moduleVariableOne as String
   Private moduleVariableTwo as String
' funcVariableOne
   Function modFunctionOne as Integer
      Dim funcVariableOne as Integer
   'Variables visible at this level:
   '   moduleVariableOne
   '   funcVariableOne
   End Function
   Sub modSubOne
      Dim subVariableOne as Integer
   'Variables visible at this level:
   '   moduleVariableOne
   '   subVariableOne
```

continues

22

INTRODUCTION TO
LOTUSSCRIPT

Listing 22.18 continued

```
   End Sub
   Sub modSubTwo
      Public subVarPublic as String
   'Variables visible at this level:
   '      moduleVariableOne
   '      subVarPublic
   End Sub
'Variables visible at this level:
'   moduleVariableOne
'   moduleVariableTwo
'   subVarPublic
End Sub
```

Libraries

Despite having all the power and flexibility of object-oriented GUI programmability at
your disposal, you'll find that all is not nirvana. You'll find at times that many objects
within a database might need to share common subroutines or functions. This would
require copying the scripts into each object throughout the database design that required
the script. This isn't a big deal, at first. What happens when you have to change a couple
lines of code? Now you have to search through all the scripts in all the objects to find
where those other seven copies of the script reside. No fun!

You might also discover that many of the scripts you write are usable in other applications. It's possible that you'll even develop a *library* of routines. That is a desirable goal
after all: to develop a base of reusable code. Reusing means not redeveloping, which
means shorter time to completion, which means more successful projects, which means
bigger bonuses and promotions, which lead to fame, fortune, and success! (Note: Your
mileage may vary.) Fortunately, a new design object—the Script Library—in Notes 4.5 is
tailored toward just this goal.

The Notes Script Library acts as a repository for all—or as many as you desire—the
scripts in your database. Many LotusScript developers have begun putting as much script
as possible into the Script Library, for several reasons. First, it consolidates a lot of previously scattered scripts into a single place. This makes it a lot easier to locate a particular
piece of code later. Second, it makes it easier to examine what might be several different
(but similar) routines and to decide that, with just some minor changes, I could make a
single, more generic routine that would replace many others. Third, it's easier to print out
a script. (Are you noticing a common theme here with *easier*?) Lastly, and this is a personal thing, I just like it.

Script in the Design Pane

In Chapter 8, "The Integrated Development Environment," you learned about the IDE and theDesign pane. This section visits the topic again, but it just touches on those additional subjects specific to developing LotusScript via the Design pane and the options in the Object browser.

Properties of the Design Pane

The first thing is to check the Properties for the Design pane. Using the Properties box (see Figure 22.1), you can set different colors to visually distinguish compiler directives, comments, keywords, identifiers, and errors. This is a big help when writing code. The second tab in the Properties box is the Format tab, and this is where you can turn on or off auto indentation of your code.

FIGURE 22.1

The Programmer's Pane Properties Box is where you set the colors for the code in LotusScript statements.

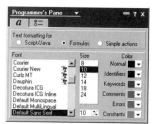

Auto-Indenting Code

The Properties Box for the Programmers Pane shows color settings for simple actions, formulas, and LotusScript (refer to Figure 22.1). The Format tab contains a checkbox for auto-indenting. It is a good idea to enable auto-indent so that you can easily read your code.

You'll notice that just as when writing formulas, there's a Define drop-down listbox that specifies what object it is you're writing script for; there's also an Event drop-down listbox that shows what event script you're putting the script into. Just as when writing formulas, you must be sure that you're writing script into the correct event for the correct object. The events available depend on the object you are in. Refer to Appendix A for a list of events.

The Object Browser

With 34 Notes classes and literally hundreds of properties and methods, remembering what method goes with what class is a tough proposition indeed. Memorization is not the solution. Fortunately, Lotus offers two ways to help developers. As always, the full help file is just an F1 away. As you get more familiar with the classes, though, you'll find you don't need as much detail, and just seeing the listings of properties and methods associated with a class will be enough of a mental nudge in the right direction. Whenever you're in the IDE writing script, you can check the Show Browser checkbox, and up will pop (along the right side of the Design pane) an abbreviated help listing of everything you always wanted to know about LotusScript and the Notes object model.

Selecting LotusScript Language, Notes:Classes, Notes:Constants, Notes:Sub and Functions, Notes:Variables, or OLE Classes from the drop-down listbox at the top of the browser will give you a view-like listing in the rest of the browser of the selected subject. Clicking the *twisties* in the browser will open up the line, just like in a view. The help that you get here won't be detailed, but it will be helpful nevertheless. See Figure 22.2 for an example of viewing a class method in the browser. The Paste button will paste in whatever you have selected in the browser. Also, selecting an item in the browser and pressing the F1 key will open the help file directly to the selected item.

FIGURE 22.2

The Design Pane with the Object Browser pane enabled.

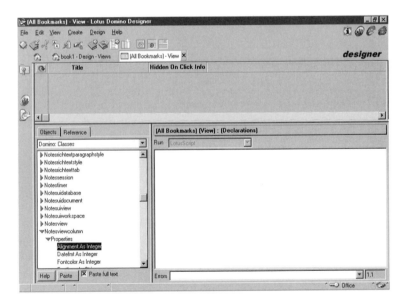

Extending LotusScript

LotusScript is not only a natively powerful and flexible language, but its developers made it extensible via a mechanism called the LSX, which stands for *LotusScript eXtension*. An LSX is essentially a declaration of a dynamic link library (DLL) to your LotusScript program. Loading an LSX via your script enables you to add additional functionality beyond what's available in LotusScript itself. These LSXs can be either custom-written code you develop in C or C++, or they can be commercially available.

Currently, several LSXs are available for Notes. Lotus offers several that are useful. The first Lotus LSX is the LS:DO, or LotusScript:Data Object. This LSX enables LotusScript to connect via Open DataBase Connectivity (ODBC) drivers to any other ODBC data source, such as MS SQL Server, Sybase SQL Server, and dBASE files. Using the properties and methods added via the ODBC LSX, you can query your external data source, get a result set in return, and then use the LS:DO methods to manipulate the returned data or push data updates from your script into the external data source. This single LSX opens up an entire world of corporate data for access by your Notes applications and the LotusScript within them.

Lotus also offers the NotesPump product, which ships with an LSX that enables developers to directly manipulate the NotesPump engine. This then means that NotesPump data movement operations to be scheduled, controlled, monitored, and manipulated from within a script.

For those of you who have SAP AG's R/3 product running in your Information Systems infrastructure, Lotus offers the SAP R/3 LotusScript Extension (LSX) for Domino, which provides the classes, properties, and methods to enable script manipulation of R/3 objects.

IBM has also released an LSX to support the company's popular and very powerful message-queing software, MQSeries. The IBM MQSeries Link for Lotus Notes provides LotusScript access to the MQSeries message transport and queue mechanisms. This allows Notes to act as a sender, receiver, or controller of transaction messages traveling the message queue. This opens up the possibility, for example, of having a mainframe CICS transaction send a message, via the MQSeries transport, to a Notes database that a transaction has just been completed (or started, aborted, and approved, for example) and include data about the transaction. Although this combination doesn't make Notes a real-time system, the guaranteed delivery of the MQSeries message queues does make it very robust and timely.

Lotus provides a NotesLSX for those of you who are developing SmartSuite LotusScript applications and who want to access your Notes data via Script from within a SmartSuite application. Loading the NotesLSX gives full access to the Notes object classes.

The OracleLSX provides insert, update, and delete capabilities from within LotusScript to an Oracle database. The OracleLSX uses Oracle's native SQL*NET network protocols for access to the Oracle databases.

An interesting and little-known LSX is the Lotus GPS LSX, which was developed by Lotus as an internal project allowing integration via LotusScript with the Trimble PCM-CIA GPS (Global Positioning System) mobile receivers. The GPS LSX could come in very handy when you're lost in the woods with only your Notes laptop. This gives you some idea of the capabilities that can be developed into an LSX.

Lastly, Lotus offers the LSX Toolkit for those of you who need to create your own LSX to write some custom functionality into your Notes LotusScript applications (such as the GPS LSX).

With the exception of the LS:DO, which is automatically installed when the Notes client or Domino server software is installed, all the previously mentioned LSXs and the toolkit are available for free download from www.lotus.com/devtools.

LotusScript and the SmartSuite

All the newest versions of the SmartSuite applications—1-2-3, Approach, Freelance, and WordPro—are LotusScript-enabled, as of the release of SmartSuite97 early in 1997. The integration of Script into the SmartSuite products means that a common programming language can now be used to build in automation to each product. Programmer productivity should be enhanced because what makes LotusScript LotusScript—the language elements, the object models, and so on—are very similar throughout the product line.

Each SmartSuite product can also use an included Notes LSX to gain access via LotusScript to the Notes object store and thereby directly access and control Notes databases and documents. The implication here is that, for example, all the freelance presentations that your company creates can be automatically read from and written to a Notes database, thereby ensuring that they are available to everyone with access to that database and that the user then doesn't have to play "where's that dang file?" hide-and-seek. Similarly, an Approach database can be directed to read and write data directly from a 1-2-3 spreadsheet.

This powerful cross-application development toolset, comprised of LotusScript, Notes, and SmartSuite, allows the development of productivity tools for your organization. You'll be a hero!

Summary

LotusScript contains many of the same programming constructs common to most languages: variables, constants, identifiers, keywords, functions, subroutines, arrays, scope, and statements. The objects available in the Domino Object Model can be accessed through the object classes, which include properties, methods, and events.

LotusScript provides the flexibility of branching and looping, which you can't get using the formula language alone. You will see in the next two chapters how to implement LotusScript and use scripting techniques within your Domino Applications.

Basic LotusScript

by Debbie Lynd

CHAPTER 23

Having mastered the concepts and challenges of LotusScript, you're ready to delve into the mysteries and wonders of the Domino Object Model. You might recall from Chapter 22, "Introduction to LotusScript," that everything in Notes is an object and that you manipulate objects using properties and methods. Each object in Notes—whether it's a database, document, view, field, or agent—has properties and methods to determine who can control it.

LotusScript Classes

The Domino classes are broadly divided into front-end and back-end classes and then further divided by object. This chapter covers the objects in a hierarchical fashion—from top-level to bottom—from session to workspace, from database to view, and from document to field. The objects are further divided by type—database, view, and document. You'll see that the distinction between front end and back end is sometimes rather small, and that crossing the line between dealing with a front-end object and a back-end object is sometimes harder to avoid than to do. Likewise, you'll see that there can be multiple ways to access some objects. For instance, in the `NotesDatabase` class, the `GetDocumentByID` method accesses a document by having its `NoteID`. Using a `NotesView` object, the `GetDocumentByKey` method gets a note by using a unique key in a view. Either way, the same document can be retrieved.

The classes, properties, and methods presented here are by no means an exhaustive treatment of the object model. What you'll see throughout this chapter is a representative sample of important and useful code examples to help you write your own LotusScript code to interact with Notes objects.

You'll need to know some general rules before you investigate the classes. There are two steps in creating an object reference variable: declaring it and instantiating the object. The declaration, as with variables, is done with a `Dim` statement—for example, `Dim db as NotesDatabase`. After the object reference has been declared, you now need to set the object reference equal to an object, as in `Set doc = New NotesDocument`. This statement creates an instance of, or *instantiates*, a new `NotesDocument` object and uses the object reference `doc` to point to the document object. Note that `doc` (in this example) doesn't point to any specific existing document but to a new `NotesDocument` object. You could set `doc` to point to an existing document by using `Set doc = db.CurrentDocument`. Assuming `db` is an object reference to a `NotesDatabase` object, the database property `CurrentDocument` points to the current document. Now the object reference `doc` points to a real document in the database. Here's a recap: Create the object reference variable and then assign it to an object.

You can create new Domino objects in a single step by using statements in the format `Dim doc as New NotesDocument( NotesDatabase )`. This creates the object reference and prepares it to point to an object of the `NotesDocument` type but does not actually create the document, which is an important distinction. You now have a document object onto which you can place fields and field values; you can then save it, creating the actual document. You'll see examples of these two methods and other permutations in the sample code listings that follow.

Explicitly Declare Your Variables

As mentioned before, it's good practice to always declare your variables explicitly rather than rely on implicit declarations. The code in Listing 23.1 shows perfectly valid object reference variables being implicitly declared.

Chapter 22, "Introduction to LotusScript," discussed two reasons why you should explicitly declare variables: memory usage and execution speed. The same factors apply when declaring object reference variables.

LISTING 23.1   Implicitly Declared Object Reference Variables

```
Set ws = New notesuiworkspace
Set s = New NotesSession
Set db = s.CurrentDatabase
Set uidoc = ws.CurrentDocument
```

The Front-End Classes

It's worth looking at some of the front-end classes first, because you will want to access the objects that a user is working with in the UI and, at the same time, make changes to the UI that the user can see immediately. The objects that you will need to access are the Workspace, the current database, and the current document. These are covered in this section.

NotesUIWorkspace

The `NotesUIWorkspace` class represents the current workspace, showing in the current window. This can be either the workspace (Notes desktop) or a document that's currently open. Conceptually, a view could be open in the workspace, but access to that would be achieved through the `NotesUIView` class.

If you had an action button in a view that added, changed, or deleted documents in the current view, you could working in the back-end, but you could use the `NotesUIWorkspace` `ViewRefresh` method to make those changes to the view visible to the user. If you didn't use this method, the user would not know that the view had changed. See Listing 23.2 for a view action button script that illustrates the `ViewRefresh` method.

LISTING 23.2   `NotesUIDatabase` `ViewRefresh` Method

```
Sub Click(Source As Button)
    Dim s As New NotesSession
    Dim ws As New notesUIWorkspace
    Dim db As NotesDatabase
    Set db = s.CurrentDatabase

    Dim doc As NotesDocument

Set doc = New NotesDocument( db ) 'creates a new document in the
➥current database

doc.form = "FormOne" 'sets the form field for the new document
    doc.FieldOne = "Created by View Action Script"
    doc.Save True, True

    Messagebox "New doc created, shouldn't be visible yet"

    ws.ViewRefresh

    Messagebox "New doc should now be visible"

End Sub
```

NotesUIDatabase

This object class has two methods: `OpenView` and `OpenNavigator`. One primary use for a `NotesUIDatabase` object is to hang database event scripts onto. Scripts for the `PostOpen`, `QueryDocumentDelete`, `QueryDocumentUnDelete`, `PostDocumentDelete`, and `QueryClose` events can be handled here. So, if you want to write scripts for these events, the `NotesUIDatabase` object is the place to put them. Also, the `NotesUIDatabase` property `Documents` gives a handle to all the documents in the database.

NotesUIDocument

The document currently open and visible on the workspace is a `NotesUIDocument` object. You can manipulate it by moving the cursor, inserting text into a field, getting the contents of a field, refreshing it, or sending it via mail. Properties of the `NotesUIDocument` include `Document` (a reference to the back-end document), `EditMode`, `FieldHelp`, `Ruler`, and `WindowTitle`. Sample methods include `Close`, `DeleteDocument`, `FieldClear`, `FieldGetText`, `Forward`, `GoToNextField`, `Print`, `Refresh`, `Reload`, and `Save`.

You can use the document property of the `NotesUIDocument` class to get a handle on the back-end document (`set doc = uidoc.document`). At this point there is the visible (front-end) representation of an object (`NotesUIDocument` or `uidoc`, in this case) and the back-end representation of the same object (`NotesDocument` or `doc`).

`Refresh` and `Reload` are both important, but are very different methods. The `Refresh` method, available only in the `NotesUIDocument` class, is the LotusScript equivalent of pressing the F9 key: It refreshes the current document, reevaluating all the input translation and validation formulas and the computed field formulas. Until LotusScript Release 4, it was impossible to refresh a `UIDocument` with the values from rich-text fields in the back-end. Now, an optional parameter includes rich-text items. The `Reload` method refreshes the front-end document with changes that have been made to the back-end document. This method is necessary only if the `AutoReload` property of the `NotesUIDocument` is set to `False`. By default, this property is set to `True` so that any changes to the back-end document are automatically visible to the front-end document.

If you make many changes to the back-end document, you can set the `AutoReload` property to `False` and do a `Reload` when all the changes have been made to the back-end document. This optimizes performance of the script.

Listing 23.3 shows a button script that illustrates UI class objects and properties and specifically shows the `Refresh` method with the addition of the `Include RichTextItems` parameter.

LISTING 23.3   NotesUI Classes and the `Refresh` Method

```
Sub Click(Source As Button)
    'this script assumes a field on the form called
    ' ChangeField, which is an editable rich text field, and a default
    ' text value of "Default"
    'instantiate our UI objects
    Dim ws As New NotesUIWorkspace
    Dim uidoc As NotesUIDocument

    Set uidoc = ws.currentdocument

    Dim doc As NotesDocument
```

continues

23

**BASIC
LOTUSSCRIPT**

LISTING 23.3 continued

```
    'This uses the Document property of the UIDoc to get access
    ' to the back end Document object
    Set doc = uidoc.Document

    doc.ChangeField = "New Value"
    Messagebox "Field value has been changed"
    Messagebox "Refreshing now"
    call uidoc.refresh(True)
end Sub
```

NotesSession

The NotesSession class represents the whole Notes environment at the time the script runs—everything that there is to know about Notes' world right now—including who the user is, what the current platform is, the version of Notes that's running, and so on. NotesSession is different than the rest of the classes because there can be one, and never more than one, instance of a NotesSession. You can declare and instantiate as many different NotesSession references as you like during any script, but they'll all point to the same NotesSession. See Listing 23.4 for NotesSession and NotesDatabase examples.

After the NotesSession has been instantiated, you have access to every other object within the session through the front- and back-end classes.

LISTING 23.4 NotesSession and NotesDatabase Examples

```
'This creates the object reference to the current Notes Session
Dim s As New NotesSession

Messagebox "Session Information: " & Chr( 13 ) & _
"Current User Name is: " & s.UserName & Chr( 13 ) & _
"Platform is: " & s.Platform & Chr( 13 ) & _
"NotesVersion is: " & s.NotesVersion

'This is the object reference for the NotesDatabase object
Dim db As NotesDatabase

'Now, set the db object = to the current database
Set db = s.CurrentDatabase

Messagebox "Database Information: " & Chr( 13 ) & _
"Creation Date: " & db.Created & Chr( 13 ) & _
"PerCent Used: " & db.PerCentUsed & Chr( 13 ) & _
"Title: " & db.Title
```

NotesDatabase

The NotesDatabase object represents the back-end or physical database file that is stored on your workstation or on the server. Database objects contain many items, such as ACLs, agents, views, and documents; they have properties such as title, filename, file path, file size, and title. To get to the current database, which is the one that contains the executing script, use the CurrentDatabase property of the NotesSession. Listing 23.5 shows examples of accessing the current database and an existing database and creating a new database from a template file.

LISTING 23.5   Creating a Database Using NotesSession and NotesDatabase

```
'This creates the object reference to the current Notes Session
    Dim s As New NotesSession

    'This is the object reference for the NotesDatabase object
    Dim db As New NotesDatabase ( "", "" )
    'Now, create a new, blank database, on my workstation,
    '    with the filename "myNewDb.nsf", and don't open it
    Call db.Create( "" , "myNewDb.nsf" , False )

    'This statement declares the db2 database object reference
    '   variable, sets it to the log.nsf database on my workstation,
    '   and opens it immediately
    Dim db2 As New NotesDatabase ( "" , "log.nsf" )

    ' This creates a new database from a named template
    '   first, open the template file
    Dim templateDB As New NotesDatabase( "" , "discuss4.ntf" )
    '   now that the template is open, we can use a db method to
    '   create a new database
    Dim newDB As NotesDatabase
    Set newDB = templateDB.CreateFromTemplate ( "" ,
    ➥"bookdisc.nsf" , True )
```

Often, when you're in a NotesDatabase object, you might want to gain access to a particular document or a particular set of documents (called a *collection*). The NotesDatabase methods for gaining access to a particular document require that you know either the NoteID or the universal ID (UNID) of a NotesDocument. To gain access to all the documents in a database, use the collection returned from the NotesDatabase.AllDocuments property. Another collection returns the property called UnprocessedDocuments, which returns a collection of NotesDocuments (considered *unprocessed*) by the current view or the current agent, whichever is appropriate. From a view action script, the unprocessed documents would include any documents selected in the view. For an agent, the definition of unprocessed documents would be based on a combination of the agent setting "Which documents should this agent act on?" and whether or not this agent has acted on the documents before. (See Chapter 30, "Automating Your Application with Agents," for more about agents.)

If your script knows or can get the NoteID or UNID of any document, that document can be accessed using the GetDocumentByID or the GetDocumentByUNID methods. Listing 23.6 shows an example of using GetDocumentByUNID to find the parent of the current document and retrieve some field information from it.

NoteIDs Versus UNIDs

A note on NoteIDs and UNIDs is in order. A *NoteID* is an 8-character hexadecimal number that is automatically generated by Notes and is unique within all replicas of this database. There should never be duplicate NoteIDs within a particular database. A UNID, on the other hand, is a 32-character hexadecimal number, also automatically generated by Notes, which is unique in this universe (maybe not in the whole universe, but close enough!).

What's the difference, and why do you care? Have you ever had a doclink (probably sent to you in an email message) that when clicked gave you a message such as Document cannot be located? That doclink was composed of a NoteID. Because the NoteID contains only the information to locate a document within a database, the linked-to document couldn't be found. When you get a doclink that works from anywhere, that doclink is actually a UNID.

LISTING 23.6   NotesDatabase GetDocumentByUNID Method

```
'These are the back end declarations
    Dim s As New NotesSession
    Dim db As NotesDatabase
    Dim doc As NotesDocument

    'These are the front end declarations
    Dim ws As New NotesUIWorkspace
    Dim uidoc As NotesUIDocument
    Dim myUIParent As NotesUIDocument

    Dim ParentUNID As Variant

    'Here, use the front end doc to get to the back end
    '    of the currently open document
    Set uidoc = ws.CurrentDocument
    Set doc = uidoc.Document
    ' the two lines above could have been written like this:
```

```
'       set note = ws.CurrentDocument.Document

Set db = s.CurrentDatabase

Get the ParentDocumentUNID property of the NotesDocument and
➥display it
ParentUNID = doc.ParentDocumentUNID
Messagebox "My parents' UNID is: " & ParentUNID( 0 )

'use the db method to get the desired doc, change the back end
'   we used before, and move it to be the back end for the newly
'   selected doc. Then, use the edit document method to bring
'   the back end doc into the front end
Set note = db.GetDocumentByUNID ( ParentUNID( 0 ) )
Set myUIParent = ws.EditDocument ( False , note )
```

The example in Listing 23.6 shows how to use the GetDocumentByUNID method. In the real world, however, if you were only trying to get a document's parent, you would most likely leave out the second-to-last line:

```
Set note = db.GetDocumentByUNID ( ParentUNID( 0 ) )
```

and change the last line to read

```
Set myUIParent = ws.EditDocument( False , note.ParentDocumentUNID )
```

NotesDocument

Just as documents are your point of reference when writing formulas, so too will NotesDocument objects likely be your main reference point when writing scripts. You'll get, create, delete, or modify a document. As you might expect, the NotesDocument object is rich with properties and methods. NotesDocument properties enable you to discover all kinds of information about the document, such as its creation date, the values the document shows in view columns (if it was opened from within a view), its embedded objects, whether it is a response doc, whether the front-end doc is open, the number of child docs, its size, and its IDs (NoteID and UNID). Besides being able to get the names of the fields (items) on the document, you can use NotesDocument methods to manipulate any item in the document, create a mail reply, make this document a response, put the doc in or remove it from a folder, mail it, or save it.

NotesDocument Creation

Here are some odds and ends to know about manipulating NotesDocuments. Whenever you create or modify a document, you must save it. If you create a new NotesDocument but don't add any items to it, the document will not be saved, even if you invoke the

Save method. Unlike when you use the Formula language, you can put more than one item (field) with the same name into a document. This could cause you headaches, so be on the alert. Except in rare circumstances, this is probably not something you want to do.

> **Fields Are Items in LotusScript**
>
> In LotusScript, a field is referred to as an item. When a form is created, fields are placed on that form for data input. The form then creates a document through the UI. The client enters information into the fields on the form, and that information is then stored in the document. Along with the data, information about the field is also stored in the document. This data, along with the field information, constitutes an item. Through LotusScript, data can be stored in items within a document, and those items will only be displayed to the user if there is a corresponding field placed on the form used to display the document.

The Form Field

If you create a document using LotusScript and the `NotesDocument` object, set the `Form` field to properly reflect which form should be used when this document is opened by a user, and then save the document, none of the field formulas on the form will evaluate! This is because as the document is being created in the back-end, the form is not opened and the association is not made between the data in the document and the form. Consequently, the document might not show up properly in views. After you open and save the document through the user interface, those field formulas will evaluate. The moral of the story is that if you intend to create documents in the back end, be prepared to programmatically set any fields that need to be computed, or use the `ComputeWithForm` method to force the evaluation of formulas.

> **The Form Field Must Be Set When Creating a Document in LotusScript**
>
> You should always set the form field when creating documents using LotusScript. Notes will not automatically provide the `Form` field like it does when using the formula language. Ways to set the form field include using `doc.form` or `uidoc.setdocfield`.

Listing 23.7 shows common `NotesDocument` properties. Figure 23.1 shows the message box generated from the button script in Listing 23.7.

Listing 23.7 NotesDocument Properties

```
Sub Click(Source As Button)
    Dim s As New notesSession
    Dim ws As New NotesUIWorkspace
    Dim db As NotesDatabase
    Dim doc As NotesDocument
    Dim numResps As Long

    Set db = s.CurrentDatabase
    Set uidoc = ws.CurrentDocument
    Set note = uidoc.Document
    If note.IsResponse Then
        IsRespMsg = "This document IS a response"
    Else
        IsRespMsg = "This document is NOT a response"
    End If
    If note.IsUIDocOpen Then
        IsUIOpenMsg = "This document IS currently open in the UI"
    Else
        IsUIOpenMsg = "This document is NOT currently open in the UI"
    End If
    numResps = note.responses.count
    Messagebox"NotesDocument properties for the current document: " &
    Chr( 13 ) &  _
    "Created on " & note.Created  & Chr( 13 )  & _
    IsRespMsg  & Chr( 13 ) & _
    IsUIOpenMsg  & Chr( 13 )  & _
    "Contains " & Cstr( Ubound( note.Items ) + 1 )& " items" &
    Chr( 13 ) & _
    "Last accessed " & note.LastAccessed & Chr( 13 ) & _
    "Last modified " & note.LastModified & Chr( 13 )  & _
    numResps & " responses "  & Chr( 13 ) & _
    "Size is " &  note.Size

End Sub
```

23

Basic LotusScript

Figure 23.1

The message box shows the results of the LotusScript produced by Listing 23.7.

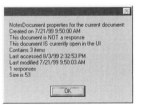

NotesDocument properties for the current document:
Created on 7/21/99 9:50:00 AM
This document is NOT a response
This document IS currently open in the UI
Contains 3 items
Last accessed 8/3/99 2:32:53 PM
Last modified 7/21/99 9:50:03 AM
1 responses
Size is 53

OK

NotesDocument Methods

Now that you've looked at some useful properties, it's time to move on to some of the many methods of the NotesDocument class. Listing 23.8 shows how to create a new document with a specific form. Using the ComputeWithForm method, you can invoke the translation and validation formulas resident in the forms fields. With the Script method, unlike when you compose a form in the user interface, if a validation formula fails, you can still save the document. Of course, the next person who edits the document will have to fix whatever validation formula problem exists before he'll be allowed to save the document. Although this approach is legal, consider the effect it might have on users if they try to save a document and they receive an error in a field that they didn't even change. It could cause some calls to the help desk from confused users.

Listing 23.8 demonstrates the usage of two of the more oft-used methods: Send and Save. As you've surmised by their names, these methods are used to send the specified document via email and to save a specified document, respectively. The Send method requires that at the least a SendTo value be provided. Send also enables you to include the form for the current document, which is handy. Up till now, you've always known that you either did or didn't store the form in the document. With the attachForm argument to the Send method, you can tell Notes to store the form for this document.

The Save method takes up to three arguments: force, createResponse, and markRead. The force argument, a Boolean if True, tells Notes that if someone else has saved this document while you were modifying it, to overwrite their changes with yours. If force is False, the second argument, createResponse, also a Boolean, determines what will happen. With force False, if createResponse is True, the current document becomes a response to the user-edited document. If createResponse is False, your save is canceled. Lastly, the markRead argument determines whether or not the just-saved document will be marked read by the current user.

LISTING 23.8 NotesDocument ComputeWithForm, Send, and Save

```
Dim s As New NotesSession
Dim db As NotesDatabase
Dim note As NotesDocument
Dim MailMsg As NotesDocument
Dim RetCode As Variant


Set db = s.CurrentDatabase

Set note = New NotesDocument( db )
note.Form = "MyForm"
note.Subject = "The LotusScript Project"
note.Department = "Notes Development"

'This will set RetCode false if there are any errors in the xlate
'     or validation formulas, but will still save the document
```

```
'      Since there's a Form field, the document will be computed
'         with the form specified in the Form field
RetCode = note.ComputeWithForm( False , False )

'Save it, forced, no reponse, & mark it read
Call note.Save( True , False , True )

'The document has already been saved. Now set SaveOptions so
'  it won't be saved again. Set the To: and From: fields, then
'  Send it, with the form
note.SaveOptions = "0"
note.SendTo = "All_Developers"
note.From = "Michael Hart/DataSolC"
Call note.Send( True )
```

Illustrated in Listing 23.9 is the usage of the Items property and the GetItemValue methods. These two, along with others, can be used to individually manipulate fields. The code in Listing 23.9 uses Items and GetItemValue to display to the user the values of all the document fields and then deletes the document by using the Remove method. Remove also takes a force argument, which, if True, tells Notes to remove a document even if a user edited it while you were manipulating it in your script.

LISTING 23.9   NotesDocument GetNextItem, GetItemValue, and Remove

```
Dim s As New NotesSession
Dim db As NotesDatabase
Dim collection As NotesDocumentCollection
Dim note As NotesDocument
Dim counter As Integer

Set db = s.CurrentDatabase
Set collection = db.UnprocessedDocuments
Set note = collection.GetFirstDocument
counter = 0

Forall theItems In note.Items
    Messagebox "Item # " & counter & Chr( 13 ) & _
    "Item Name: " & theItems.Name & Chr( 13 ) & _
    "Item Value: " & theItems.Values(0)

    counter = counter + 1

End Forall

Call note.Remove( True )
```

The last method you'll learn about for this class is the MakeResponse method. This is a very handy method to know and use. You might have noticed that so far, every time you created a document via Script, there's no way to tell the document that it is a response document. There is not a document property to set the document as a response, and simply setting the Form field doesn't do it. The $Ref field (which always points to a response document's parent) cannot be set in through a property. The MakeResponse document method does all this for you. To use it (see Listing 23.10), you need two NotesDocument object reference variables, one for the document that will be the parent and another for the document that will be the child. Then you simply call the MakeResponse method, and voilà, you get a hierarchical relationship at its finest.

LISTING 23.10   NotesDocument MakeResponse

```
Dim s As New NotesSession
Dim db As NotesDatabase
Dim note1 As NotesDocument
Dim note2 As NotesDocument

Set db = s.CurrentDatabase

'Create & save the first document
Set notes1 = New NotesDocument( db )
notes1.Form = "MainForm"

Call notes1.Save( True, True, True )

'Create the second document
Set notes2 = New NotesDocument( db )
notes2.Form = "ResponseForm"

'Make the second doc a response to the first
Call notes2.MakeResponse( notes1 )
Call notes2.Save( True , True , True )
```

NotesItem

The fields on a NotesDocument are referred to as *items* in LotusScript. A NotesItem is any data field on a form, rich text included. In fact, a NotesRichTextItem is a *derived* class of NotesItem; that is, it inherits the properties of NotesItem but also has additional properties and methods added.

One important note about NotesItem: If you add a new item to a document, the IsSummary property defaults to False. When an item's IsSummary property is False, the item cannot be displayed in a view (or folder), just as with a rich-text item. Therefore, when you add an item to a document, if you want it to be visible in a view, you must set its IsSummary property to True.

Listing 23.11 contains code showing the usage of NotesItem, NotesRichTextItem, and NotesEmbeddedObject together, so before delving into the code, this section briefly covers the NotesRichTextItem and NotesEmbeddedObject classes.

As mentioned before, the NotesRichTextItem is a class derived from the NotesItem class. By using the NotesItem properties and methods, you can manipulate rich-text fields also. But, because the NotesRichTextItem class contains properties and methods specific to rich-text fields you'll find more functionality there. New classes for rich text have been added in LotusScript 4. These are described in Table 23.1.

TABLE 23.1 New Rich Text Classes

Class	Description
RichTextParagraphStyle	Provides settings for the style properties of a rich-text paragraph. This object is contained in the Session class.
RichTextTab	Provide settings for the tab properties of a rich-text paragraph. This object is contained in the RichTextParagraphStyle class.

The createrichtextparagraphstyle method in NotesSession creates new objects. The code in Listing 23.12 shows how you would use the new rich-text classes.

LISTING 23.11 RichTextParagraph and RichTextTab Classes

```
Dim session As New NotesSession
Dim db As NotesDatabase
Set db = session.CurrentDatabase
Dim doc As New NotesDocument(db)
Call doc.AppendItemValue("Title", "Title of new document")
Call doc.AppendItemValue("Desc", "Description of new document")
Dim pstyle As NotesRichTextParagraphStyle
Set pstyle = session.CreateRichTextParagraphStyle
Dim richText As New NotesRichTextItem(doc, "Body")
pStyle.LeftMargin = RULER_ONE_INCH*.75
Call pStyle.clearalltabs
Call pstyle.settabs(3,Ruler_One_Inch*3,Ruler_One_Inch*2,Tab_Left)
Call richText.AppendParagraphStyle(pStyle)
Call richText.AppendText("Column1")
Call richtext.addtab(1)
Call richText.AppendText("Column2")
Call richtext.addtab(1)
```

continues

23

**BASIC
LOTUSSCRIPT**

LISTING 23.11   continued

```
Call richText.AppendText("Column3")
Call richtext.addtab(1)
Call richText.AppendText("Column4")
Call richText.AppendParagraphStyle(pStyle)
Call richText.AppendText("Item1")
Call richtext.addtab(1)
Call richText.AppendText("Description of Item 1")
Call richtext.addtab(1)
Call richText.AppendText("Cost")
Call richtext.addtab(1)
Call richText.AppendText("Price")
Call doc.Save(True, False)
```

The NotesEmbeddedObject class contains properties for, and methods for manipulating, an object on a document, such as an OLE object, a file attachment, or an embedded document.

LISTING 23.12   NotesItem, NotesRichTextItem, and NotesEmbeddedObject

```
Dim ws As New NotesUIWorkspace
Dim uidoc As NotesUIDocument
Dim doc As NotesDocument
Dim rtitem As Variant

Set uidoc = ws.CurrentDocument
Set doc = uidoc.document
'here's where we actually get the field contents
Set rtitem = doc.GetFirstItem( "FileAttach" )

'loop through all the things in the field, checking each
Forall things In rtitem.EmbeddedObjects
    If things.type = EMBED_ATTACHMENT Then
        Message =  "The object is a file attachment"
    Elseif things.type = EMBED_OBJECT Then
        Message = "The object is an embedded object"
    Else
        Message = "The object is an object link"
    End If
    Messagebox message & Chr( 13 ) & _
    "Name: " & things.name & Chr( 13 ) & _
    "Size: " & things.FileSize

 'now detach the thing (we're assuming it's a file)
    Call things.ExtractFile( "C:\Notes\Data\" & things.Name )

End Forall
```

NotesDocumentCollection

NotesDocumentCollection is a very handy class to know and use. Think of it as a view. However, because the view doesn't exist in the physical database it doesn't need maintaining and doesn't slow down your application. The document collection does not, however, present documents in a hierarchy and you can't sort it. You can create a document collection in several ways—all documents in a database, only the unprocessed documents, the selected documents, or a search or full-text search. You've already seen a document collection in use in the Script version of the agent from Chapter 14. Here, you'll see the NotesDocumentCollection class used in Listing 23.13.

LISTING 23.13   NotesDocumentCollection Class

```
Dim s As New NotesSession
 Dim db As NotesDatabase
 Dim note As NotesDocument
 Dim theDoc As NotesDocument
 Dim collection As NotesDocumentCollection
 Dim dt As NotesDateTime
 Dim rtitem As NotesRichTextItem
 Dim theCount As Integer

 theCount = 0
 Set db = s.CurrentDatabase

 Set dt = New NotesDateTime( "1/1/97" )
 Set collection = db.Search( "@Contains(""Subject"" ; ""Open"" )" ,
➥dt, 100)

 Set note = New NotesDocument( db )
 Set rtitem = New NotesRichTextItem( note , "Body" )

 If collection.Count > 0 Then
     Set theDoc = collection.GetFirstDocument

     Do Until theDoc Is Nothing

         Call rtitem.Appenddoclink( theDoc , "Click here to see
         ➥the document" )
         Call rtitem.AddTab( 1 )
         Call rtitem.AppendText( "This is document number: " &
         ➥theCount )
         Call rtitem.AddNewLine( 2 )
         theCount = theCount + 1
         Set theDoc = collection.GetNextDocument( theDoc )
     Loop
```

continues

23

**BASIC
LOTUSSCRIPT**

LISTING 23.13   continued

```
Else
     Call rtitem.AddNewLine( 1 )
     Call rtitem.AppendText( "These were no documents matching your
     ➥criteria." )
End If
note.Form = "Memo"
note.Subject = "Help documents Requested"
Call note.Send( False, "Requester" )
```

NotesNewsLetter

As you saw in the previous code example, creating a newsletter from scratch is simple. You can create a newsletter with the Send Newsletter simple action in the Agent Builder. Writing your own newsletter agent using LotusScript and the NotesNewsLetter class is almost as easy, as you've just seen, and getting Notes to create one with the NotesNewsLetter class and methods is a piece of cake. Remember that a newsletter is essentially a mail memo with a number of lines, each describing a document and including a doclink to the document being described.

Listing 23.14 shows the creation of a simple newsletter, which you could easily expand to include an almost unlimited amount of information for each document.

LISTING 23.14   NotesNewsLetter

```
Dim s As New NotesSession
Dim db As NotesDatabase
Dim note As NotesDocument
Dim collection As NotesDocumentCollection
Dim dt As NotesDateTime
Dim rtitem As NotesRichTextItem

Set db = s.CurrentDatabase

Set dt = New NotesDateTime( "1/1/97" )
Set collection = db.Search( "Status = ""Open"" : ""Pending"" " ,
➥dt, 100)

If collection.Count > 0 Then
     Set nl = New NotesNewsLetter( collection )
     Set note = nl.FormatMsgWithdoclinks( db )
Else
     Set note = New NotesDocument( db )
     Set rtitem = New NotesRichTextItem( note , "Body" )
     Call rtitem.AddNewLine( 1 )
     Call rtitem.AppendText( "There were no open or pending calls to
```

```
      ➥report today." )
End If
note.Form = "Memo"
note.Subject = "Open Call Listing"
Call note.Send( False, "Call Center Managers" )
```

You've seen quite a few of the object classes, examined some of their properties, and manipulated the objects via their methods. Switch gears now, and look at concepts not directly related to the object model.

Events in LotusScript

Not all objects have events. Those objects that do are affected by an action usually invoked by the user. An example is the click event that occurs when a user clicks on a hotspot or button. The events that are most commonly coded will be discussed in this section.

Database Script

In the ongoing discussion of Notes development, you've considered the actions of the user at a field or form level. The user clicks a button or action, enters data in a field, and so on. Thinking more in terms of the larger picture, there might be some events at the database level that you, as a developer, would like to be able to catch and act on. It should come as no surprise that Lotus has provided the means to write scripts to handle database-level events.

From the Design view, under the Other heading, one of the objects you'll see listed is Database Script. The list shows events that the Database script will handle. As you can tell from looking at the list, these are events that affect the database at the database level. These events can only execute LotusScript; @Functions and @Commands are not allowed in these events.

The following are event that can be scripted in the Database script:

    (Options)
    (Declarations)
    Initialize
    Terminate
    PostOpen
    QueryDragDrop
    PostDragDrop

```
PostDocumentDelete

QueryClose

QueryDocumentDelete

QueryDocumentUnDelete
```

Be Cautious Using the Initialize Event

Lotus documentation states that "you not use [sic] `Initialize` for anything except agents, and not use `Terminate` at all." Although you might be successful going against Lotus' desires, be aware that statements like this are usually made for good reason, perhaps because the results are unpredictable or because of future compatibility. This doesn't mean that there aren't times you'll find putting Script into those events useful.

As an example for understanding database scripts, imagine you have a database with a single line of code in each of the database event scripts (except the `Options` and `Declarations`—because you already know that executable statements don't go there). The code that goes into each database event script is

```
MsgBox "This is from the xxxxxx event"
```

Substitute the name of the actual event for *xxxxxx* in the preceding line, and you're ready to go. Here's the sequence of events that will cause each database event script to execute.

Opening the database will fire the `Initialize` event (because the database is initializing) and then the `PostOpen` event. Now you're at the view level. Creating, opening, or closing documents does not fire one of the database events. Now from the view, select one of your documents and press the Delete key. This fires the `QueryDocumentDelete` event. Note that this event executes before the little trash can symbol shows up in the view margin. Pressing the Delete key again fires the `QueryDocumentUnDelete` event, which, like its sibling, executes before the trash can is removed from the view margin. Pressing Delete again (which again fires off the `QueryDocumentDelete` event and puts the trash can up) and then pressing F9 to finalize the deletion brings up the dialog box that asks "Do you want to permanently delete 1 document from database?" Answering yes to the prompt causes the document to be deleted, immediately after which the `PostDocumentDelete` event fires. Be aware that the `PostDocumentDelete` event fires after the document has been deleted. Now, close the database—using the File, Close menu option or pressing Esc—causes the `QueryClose` and then finally the `Terminate` event scripts to execute.

The Query event scripts have the argument CONTINUE as a parameter. Setting CONTINUE to False for any of the Query event scripts will cause execution to stop. Say, for example, you were trying to determine, in the QueryDocumentDelete event script, whether the user was trying to delete a document, which she should not be allowed to delete. This would be quite easy to do within the QueryDocumentDelete script by returning from that script with CONTINUE set to False based on whatever condition you want to impose; the deletion, then, would not happen. Listing 23.15 shows a simple QueryDocumentDelete event script that does not enable anyone to ever delete a document. The script simply sets the CONTINUE return parameter to False, so the actual deletion (or the displaying of the trash can icon), which would happen after the QueryDocumentDelete event completed, never happens.

LISTING 23.15 QueryDocumentDelete Event Script Prevents All Deletions

```
Sub Querydocumentdelete(Source As Notesuidatabase, Continue As
➥Variant)

    Continue = False

End Sub
```

Now that you know about event scripts, where would you use them? You've seen an example of where you could use an event script to trap the deletion of a document. The database Initialize event could prompt the user to fill out a user profile document if this is the first time he or she has used this database. The database PostOpen event can scan the database for documents that belong to the current user and put up a dialog box informing the user that she has some new documents to view or a number of documents waiting for her approval. Asking the user if she would like to receive a newsletter summary of any documents that have not yet been acted on might be a good QueryClose database event for a workflow/approvals database. You'll find many more useful and interesting opportunities to employ database scripts in your development experiences.

Form-Level Events

As there are events that LotusScript can respond to at the database level, so too are there form-level events to which you can attach scripts. Unlike database scripts, form-level scripts give you the option of using either @Functions and @Commands or LotusScript.

Technical Note

The Initialize and Terminate events only allow LotusScript. Also, neither the database nor the form level events allow simple actions.

Table 23.2 lists the scriptable form-level events.

TABLE 23.2 Form Events

Event	*Occurs when*
Initialize	Immediately before a new or existing document is displayed to the user.
QueryOpen	After the Initialize event has finished but before the document is displayed to the user.
PostOpen	After the document has been displayed to the user and before the user has focus (before the user can enter anything).
QuerySave	Immediately before the document is actually saved.
QueryModeChange	Immediately before the document is changed from edit to read mode or from read to edit mode.
PostModeChange	Immediately after a read-to-edit or edit-to-read mode change has occurred.
PostRecalc	Immediately after all the fields on the form have been recalculated, whether via a user F9, an automatic form refresh, or an @Command-initiated refresh.
PostSave	Immediately after the document is saved.
QueryClose	Immediately before a document is closed and removed from the screen.
Terminate	The document has been closed.

As with database scripts, Query events have the CONTINUE parameter as an argument, and your script can stop the associated event from occurring by returning CONTINUE false from your Query script.

When developing Notes applications, often you'll create hidden computed fields that perform some field-related actions, such as setting a status field, at certain times, like when the document is saved. There's nothing wrong with this practice; it's done all the time and will probably continue to be done this way for a long time to come. As your forms (and databases) get larger, as you have more computed fields, and as you search for ways to speed up your Notes applications, you might become more interested in form-event scripts. As you already know, every computed field on a form evaluates every time the form recalculates. You know this, and you've already taken steps, such as in Listing 23.16, to optimize your computed fields so they evaluate only when they should. Even this type of field formula still takes up CPU cycles though, and given enough computed fields, this area could stand some optimization.

LISTING 23.16   Optimization Technique for Computed Fields

```
REM "This field should only evaluate when the document" ;
REM "is actually being saved";
REM ;
@If(
   @IsDocBeingSaved ;
       @Success ;
   @Return( "" )
);
REM "your code continues from here on";
REM "only when the document is being saved";
```

Using form events instead of some of your computed fields speeds things up a bit. Because the form events are executed only when the event happens, you've saved on unnecessary formula evaluations. Examples of this are when you would put event scripts (either @Functions or LotusScript) into the events for, typically, QuerySave or QueryModeChange.

Field-Level Events

Continuing down the design object hierarchy, you leave database and form events and come to field events. Carry forward everything you've learned about scriptable events and apply it to field events. The scriptable field events are listed in Table 23.3. Note that these events accept only LotusScript. Also, the Entering and Exiting events apply only to editable fields (which makes sense because the cursor never enters or leaves a computed field).

TABLE 23.3   Field-Level Scriptable Events

Event	Occurs when
Initialize	Immediately before the document is displayed to the user.
Entering	The cursor enters the field, via either tabbing or clicking into the field.
Exiting	The cursor leaves the field, via either tabbing or clicking into the field.
Terminate	After the document is closed.

The Entering and Exiting events are the field-level events you'll really be interested in. Using these, you can validate field entries as a user moves the cursor into or out of fields. Contrast that with the formula language, where the only time you can check a field value is when the Input Translation or Input Validation formulas kick off, and only then if the form is being recalculated via an F9, Save, or @Command document refresh. Using the Entering and Exiting events, you can translate and validate field entries as the user enters them.

23

**BASIC
LOTUSSCRIPT**

Order of Events

When writing LotusScript for events, you should be aware of the order in which LotusScript events are processed.

By default, when a database is opened, it opens to a view. Unless you specify in the database launch property that you want to open a Navigator, frameset, or About document, or Launch an object, the view last accessed by the user is what will open for that user. The order in which the opening events are processed is described in Table 23.4. Notice that the order of operation is view events first, followed by database events. If you are opening to a frameset that contains a view in a frame, the order below will still be in effect. If you are opening a frameset that contains a view and a page or document, the order of events depends on which frame the object is in. The frames are processed from top to bottom and left to right. So, if I have two frames and a view is displayed in the first frame, the view events kick off first, but, if the page is first, the form event is kicked off first.

TABLE 23.4   Database Open

Event	*Object Initiating*
Initialize	View
QueryOpen	View
PostOpen	View
Initialize	Page or Form
QueryOpen	Page or Form
PostOpen	Page or Form
Initialize	DB
PostOpen	DB

When closing a database from a view, the view events are processed before the database events, and the same rules are in effect as described earlier for framesets. This is indicated in Table 23.5.

TABLE 23.5   Database Closed

Event	*Object Initiating*
Queryclose	View
QueryClose	Page
Terminate	View

Terminate	Page
QueryClose	DB
Terminate	DB

Creating or editing a document causes events to occur for the form, fields, and other objects within the form. If the document exists and is selected from a view for editing, the QueryOpenDocument event is invoked. If it is a new document, this does not occur.

TABLE 23.6 Creating or Editing a Document

Event	*Object Initiating*
QueryOpenDocument	View
QueryOpen	Form
Initialize	Fields
PostOpen	Form

When a document is opened, and the user decides to switch from read to edit mode or vice versa, there are two events that are invoked. They are QueryModeChange and PostModeChange and they are executed in that order.

When saving a document, there are two events that accept script. They are QuerySave and PostSave and they are executed in that order.

When a document is closed the order of execution is shown in Table 23.7.

TABLE 23.7 Closing a Document

Event	*Object Initiating*
QueryClose	Form
Terminate	Fields
Terminate	Form

When a document is deleted from a view there are two events invoked: QueryDocumentDelete and PostDocumentDelete. They are executed in that order.

Script Libraries

If you've been following the discussion about LotusScript (and I'll assume you have or you wouldn't be here!), you've probably realized that there are roughly a zillion places, give or take a few, wherein you can put Script. This is both good news and bad news. You'll love the flexibility of being able to put Script anywhere you want, but the day will come when you'll want to change a variable name, object reference, or subroutine that you've used in many different places—and it will strike you that you can't remember everywhere you've used it! After you've looked through every procedure of every event of every object to change a variable reference, you'll wish there were a better way.

Guess what? There is, and it's called a script library! Before you get started, let me set the facts straight right here and now: Script libraries will *not* take all the headache out of maintaining Script code. They will, however, substantially ease your burden.

A script library is a special design object that is part of every database. Because it is an object, it has the (Options), (Declarations), Initialize, and Terminate events. What you put into a script library is any and all script code that you want to make accessible to objects anywhere in the database. When a variable, object, constant, function, or subroutine is declared in a script library, it's a very simple matter to make those items available to any scriptable object in your database. By putting a USE statement into the (Options) event of an object, you've referenced and therefore made available every object declared in your script library. Script Libraries are found in the Resources - Other section of the design view.

The Notes R5 Mail template makes extensive use of script libraries. Eleven script libraries—such as DiscussionRoutine, CoreEmailClasses, and Common (see Figure 23.2)—are available. Each of these contains a number of variable declarations, functions, or subroutines that are used throughout the Mail template. See Figure 23.3 for a screenshot showing some of the subroutines declared in the EmailProcessing script library. Rather than make copies of these items in the mail forms or fields where the variables or scripts were required, they were aggregated into script libraries. The picture is not yet complete, however, because the mail forms and fields have not yet been made aware of the existence of the objects in these script libraries.

When you use the LotusScript USE statement, the variables, functions, and subs in a script library can be made known to a form or field. The USE statements syntax is USE *LibraryName*, where *LibraryName* is the name you've given your script library. Where other forms in the Mail template need to use some of the routines in the CoreEmailClasses script library, the line USE CoreEmailClasses is included in the (Options) event for the Form (Globals), as shown in Figure 23.4. Then, in any place you want to use one of the functions or subs contained in the USEd script library, you simply call the procedure as you would call any other procedure. Figure 23.5 shows just such a call to the EmailClose procedure from the QueryClose event of the Memo form.

FIGURE 23.2

The script libraries in the Notes R5 Mail template are reusable in multiple forms.

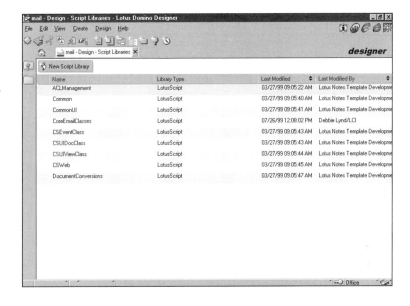

FIGURE 23.3

The Event objects box shows some of the procedures which are defined in the `CoreEmailClasses` *script library in the R5 Mail template.*

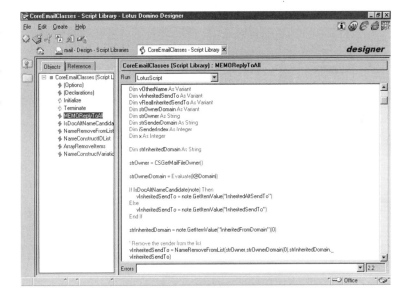

23

BASIC LOTUSSCRIPT

FIGURE 23.4

The Mail Memo in design mode shows the USE CoreEmailClasses *statement in the* Form (Globals) *object definition in the* (Options) *event.*

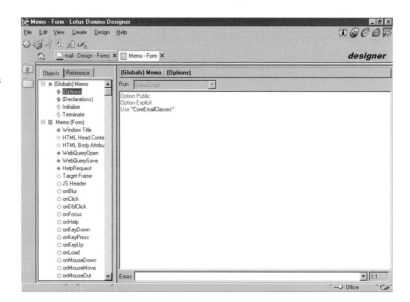

FIGURE 23.5

The Mail Memo QueryClose *event script references a procedure from the* cMemoObject *script library.*

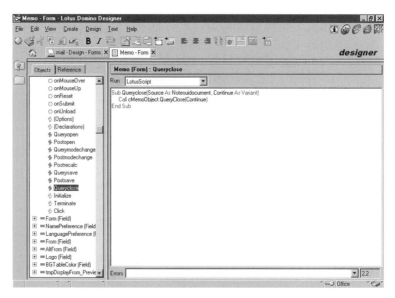

Any time your form objects will reuse the same script routines, you should seriously consider using a script library.

Error Handling

Ah yes, error handling—that thing we curse other developers for not doing well enough, even as you put the minimum error-handling routines into your own code. Such are the foibles of being human! Realistically though, LotusScript does provide a good set of functions that enable you to build robust error handling into any LotusScript you write. Because any script, in any event, could conceivably encounter an error, there should be some kind of error-handling routine in every script you write. C'mon now, stop laughing! This is, of course, impractical. However, you should endeavor to handle at least the likely errors in scripts.

Compile Errors

I need to discuss two types of errors. The first is the compile-time errors, which the compiler detects and alerts us to by providing that annoying dialog box shown in Figure 23.6. You are alerted then and there that a problem lies within your code, and you can either choose to fix it now or abandon any changes you've made since your last successful save. The errors are spelled out for you in the Error List drop-down box at the bottom of the screen and (by default) highlighted in red text. If you click a particular error in the Error List box, the line in question will be highlighted also. Because these compile-time errors must all be resolved before your program can be solved, don't be concerned with running through them.

FIGURE 23.6
The compile-time errors will appear for each line of code that contains an error.

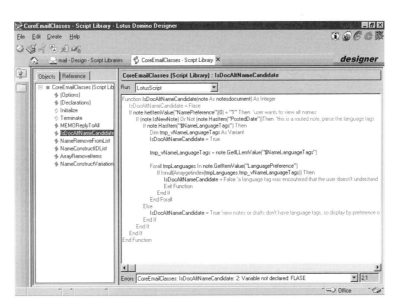

It's the other kind of error, discovered only at runtime, that you're interested in for this section.

Runtime Errors

Runtime errors can run the gamut from the Type Mismatch to Object Reference Not Set to who knows what. The language provides several functions and statements to facilitate the handling of errors. The functions and statements built into the LotusScript language specifically to deal with and handle errors are listed in Table 23.8.

A little information about how LotusScript deals with errors is also called for. When an error is encountered, the current procedure is checked for an On Error statement. If one is found, it is used. If none is found, the procedure that called this procedure (if there was a calling procedure) is checked. If one is found, it is used; otherwise, that procedure's calling procedure is checked, and so on. If no error handler can be found for the current error, the error is presented to the user and the program terminates.

TABLE 23.8   LotusScript Functions and Statements for Error Handling

Command	*Type*	*Usage*
Erl	Function	Returns the line number where the current error occurred
Err	Function	Returns the current error number
Err	Statement	Sets the current error number
Error or Error$	Function	Returns the error message for the current error or a specified error number
Error	Statement	Generates the specified error number and its message
On Error	Statement	Names an error-handling routine or specifies how to handle all or specific errors
Resume	Statement	Directs how execution should continue after an error

The error related commands Err and Error can be used as either functions or statements. The statement form of each is used to set or generate a particular error condition and is most useful when testing your error-handling routines. Use these statements to generate the error your routines are supposed to take care of and see whether they work as intended.

The On Error statement tells LotusScript what to do if a particular error is encountered. You can give an On Error command for a particular error number—for example, error number 13, which is for the Type Mismatch. When an error 13 is encountered, program execution is transferred to the error-handling routine you specified in your On Error command. The On Error statement can also be given with no specified error number, in which case any error encountered (that hasn't been specified in any other On Error statement) will be handled by the routine specified. As you can see, this implies that there can be any number of On Error statements within a given script, each taking care of a specific error number, with another handling everything else. Be aware that if you specify two On Error statements for the same error number, only the last On Error will be honored.

The On Error command has three options for directing program flow in case of an error. The options are GoTo *label*, Resume Next, and GoTo 0. The first directs that the statements following the named *label* be executed on occurrence of the error. Usually, the last statement in the error routine is a Resume statement, which returns execution to the point of the error. The Resume Next option directs that execution should continue with the statement following the one that generated the error—in effect, saying "never mind, continue on." The last option, GoTo 0, directs that the error should not be handled within the current procedure.

The companion to the On Error command is the Resume command. Note that the Resume command is different than the just-discussed Resume Next option to the On Error command. Resume, used exclusively within error-handling routines, directs where program execution should continue. The command has three options: 0, Next, and *label*. Resume 0 indicates that the statement that generated the error is to be executed again. Resume Next says that the statement immediately following the one that generated the error is where execution should be resumed, and Resume *label* directs execution to resume at the named label. Resume also serves another important function: It resets the value of the Erl, Err, and Error functions. When these functions are not set, either there is no error or the most recent error has been handled.

The Erl function returns the line number of the statement that generated the error. This could be useful information to either give to the user in a message box or log to a file. Using Err as a function returns the current error number. Using Error as a function returns the error message for the specified error number, or, when used in the form Error$, returns the error message for the current error. Erl, Err, Error, and Error$ are most often used in an error-handling routine for gathering specific error information and passing it on to the user or logging it.

Having now had your fill of the error-related commands, functions, and statements, see Listing 23.17 for bit of code that illustrates the usage of each statement and shows how to build error-handling routines. One thing to specifically take note of in Listing 23.17 is the Exit Sub before the error-handling routines, which prevents each error-handling routine from being executed unless it's specifically invoked because of an error. The Exit Sub serves to force normal program execution to leave this procedure at this point. If you didn't detour the normal flow of execution around the error-handling routines, the next statement to be executed after the `Error 100` statement would be the first `MessageBox` in the `DivByZero` routine.

LISTING 23.17   Error-Handling Routine Example

```
Sub Initialize
      Const ErrReturnWithoutGoSub  = 3
      Const ErrDivisionByZero = 11

      On Error Goto AnyOtherErrors
      On Error ErrReturnWithoutGoSub Goto NoGoSub
      On Error ErrDivisionByZero Goto DivByZero

      ' This is a Return without a previous sub call
      Return

      'This is a Div by Zero error
      Dim x As Integer
      Dim y As Integer
      y = x / 0

      ' this is a general error
      Error 100 , "My Error!"

      Exit Sub
      'The above Exit Sub statement serves as the end of the
      '  normal executable code in the procedure. Everything below
      '  here is an error handler, and so should only be executed
      '  when there's an error to be handled!
  DivByZero:
      Messagebox "Divide by Zero Error Handler"
      Msgbox "Erl: " & Erl & Chr(13) & "Err: " & Err & Chr( 13 ) &
      "Error: " & Error$
      Resume Next

  NoGoSub:
      Messagebox "No GoSub Handler"
      Msgbox "Erl: " & Erl & Chr(13) & "Err: " & Err & Chr( 13 ) & _
      "Error: " & Error$
      Resume Next

  AnyOtherErrors:
      Messagebox "General Purpose Error Handler"
      Msgbox "Erl: " & Erl & Chr(13) & "Err: " & Err & Chr( 13 ) & _
      "Error: " & Error$
      Resume Next
  End Sub
```

Look at the last On Error statement in Listing 23.17. Notice that the error it is specified to handle is given not as a number but as a symbolic name. Those symbolic names are found by including (via the %Include statements discussed in Chapter 22) the LSERR.LSS, LSXUIERR.LSS, and LSXBEERR.LSS include files. Listing 23.18 includes some sample constant declarations from each file. These are handy to have available, and your code is a lot more readable when you have a statement like this:

```
On Error ErrFileNotFound GoTo GetNewFileName
```

rather than this:

```
On Error 53 GoTo GetNewFileName
```

LISTING 23.18   Sample Include Lines from the *ERR.LSS Files

```
'These are from LSERR.LSS
'    Runtime Errors
Public Const ErrUSER                 = 1
Public Const ErrReturnWithoutGoSub   = 3
Public Const ErrIllegalFunctionCall  = 5
Public Const ErrOverflow             = 6
Public Const ErrOutOfMemory          = 7
Public Const ErrSubscriptOutOfRange  = 9
Public Const ErrDivisionByZero       = 11
Public Const ErrTypeMismatch         = 13
Public Const ErrOutOfStringSpace     = 14
Public Const ErrCantContinue         = 17
Public Const ErrNoResume             = 19
Public Const ErrResumeWithoutError   = 20
Public Const ErrOutOfStackSpace      = 28
Public Const ErrSubOrFunctionNotDefined = 35
Public Const ErrErrorInLoadingDLL    = 48
'
'These are from LSXBEERR.LSS
Public Const lsERR_SYS_OUT_OF_MEMORY = 4001
Public Const lsERR_SYS_LOAD_OUT_OF_MEM = 4002
Public Const lsERR_SYS_FILE_NOT_FOUND = 4003
Public Const lsERR_NOTES_DBOPEN_FAILED = 4043
Public Const lsERR_NOTES_INVALID_FORMULA = 4044
Public Const lsERR_NOTES_DBNOACCESS = 4060
Public Const lsERR_NOTES_UNAME_LOOKUP = 4061
;
;These are from LSXUIERR.LSS
Public Const lsERR_LSXUI_LSBE_DOC_CREATE = 4406
Public Const lsERR_LSXUI_DOC_CMD_NOT_AVAILABLE = 4407
Public Const lsERR_LSXUI_FIELD_CMD_NOT_AVAILABLE = 4408
Public Const lsERR_LSXUI_CMD_NOT_AVAILABLE = 4409
Public Const lsERR_LSXUI_DOC_OBJ_NOT_VALID = 4410
```

23

BASIC LOTUSSCRIPT

continues

LISTING 23.18   continued

```
Public Const lsERR_LSXUI_DOC_SAVE_CANCELLED =   4411
Public Const lsERR_LSXUI_NOTES_ERROR =  4412
Public Const lsERR_LSXUI_INVALID_LSX =  4413
```

The LotusScript Debugger

Although you might never need to know the information in this section, you might have to help someone debug one of his scripts.

The only methods available to assist you in troubleshooting or debugging your formulas are to set intermediate field values, write values to the NOTES.INI file, or use debugging prompts built-in specifically for debugging purposes. It's a limitation all developers learn to live with, like it or not. Fortunately, Lotus has given the LotusScript developer an advanced tool, an integrated LotusScript debugger, to assist in troubleshooting misbehaving scripts. See Figure 23.7 for a view of the Debugger window.

FIGURE 23.7

The Integrated LotusScript Debugger window helps you to inspect and reconcile errors as you run the script.

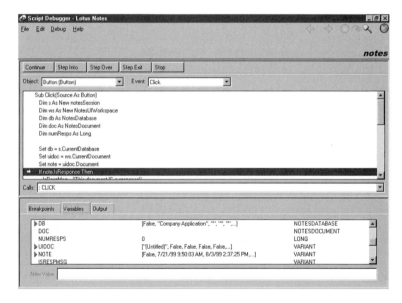

With the script debugger, you can stop execution of your script at specified locations, step through your script a line at a time, inspect or change variables and objects during runtime, or halt execution.

To enable the LotusScript debugger, choose File, Tools, Debug LotusScript. The Debug LotusScript menu choice is a toggle and displays a checkmark next to the choice when it is enabled. Make the menu selection again to toggle the debugger off. There is also an @Command you can use to toggle debug mode on and off, `@Command([DebugLotusScript])`. You can make use of this by placing it into a button or action in your form. Probably the best place for this command would be in a SmartIcon though.

The LotusScript Debugger Can Help You to Learn LotusScript

Turning on the LotusScript debugger turns it on for any script that attempts to run! The debugger has no way to know which scripts you want to debug, so any script that runs will open the Debugger window. You've been warned, so now you'll know why the Debugger window opens up when you open a new mail message.

Turning on the debugger and then stepping through scripts that are encountered in the mail template (or anywhere else for that matter) is a great way to learn Script techniques!

Refer to Figure 23.7. The top half of the window displays your script. The current point of execution is displayed automatically, although you can switch to any part of your script for setting breakpoints or viewing code by using the Event drop-down listbox. The row of buttons directly below the SmartIcons are the execution controls for the debugger. The bottom half of the window contains three tabs. The first is the Breakpoints tab, which lists all the breakpoints set in your script. The Breakpoints tab shows each breakpoint in the format *object:event:line*. The second tab, the Variables tab, shows all the variables, constants, and objects declared in your script and enables you to view and manipulate them. The third tab is the Output tab, which shows all the output generated by your script. In the middle of the screen, actually the bottom part of the code window, is the Calls list. The Calls list shows all the subroutine or function calls in reverse calling order from the main procedure through the current procedure. Each part of the Debugger window is covered in more detail later, starting with the debugger execution buttons. See Table 23.9 for a listing of debugger commands and their keyboard shortcuts.

The Debugger Buttons

The Continue button tells the debugger to continue execution of the script until a STOP command, a breakpoint, or the end of the script is encountered. A STOP command can be placed in your script and invokes the debugger when executed. STOP invokes only the debugger, however, if you've selected File, Tools, Debug LotusScript. STOP has no effect otherwise. Breakpoints are covered later in this section.

The Step Into button tells the debugger to execute only the current line of code. The Step Over button also tells the debugger to execute the current line of code, but with one big difference: If the current line is a function or procedure call, the entire call will be executed and the debugger will stop at the next line of code after the function or procedure call. You would use this if, when stepping through your code, you encounter a subroutine call to a sub that you know is functional. Rather than step into it and watch each statement execute, you could step over it. All the code that is stepped over executes at normal execution speed, so in a flash the debugger is sitting at the next line waiting for you to tell it what to do.

TABLE 23.9 Debugger Commands and Keyboard Shortcuts

Command	*Shortcut*
Continue	F5
Step Into	F8
Step Over	Shift+F8
Step Exit	Control+F8
Set/Clear Breakpoint	F9
Disable Breakpoint	Shift+F9

- **Continue**—Runs the code from the current line through the end of the script without interruption, unless, of course an error is encountered, or you have set a breakpoint.
- **Step Into**—Steps you through the code line by line. This is helpful if you want to take a look at the variables as they are obtaining values to ensure that you are getting what you think you should be getting.
- **Step Exit**—Instructs the debugger to continue execution of the current subroutine or function from the current statement until the statement after the statement that called the current subroutine. An example of the usage of Step Exit would be if you suspected a problem in a section of a particular subroutine, you would step into the sub. Then you step into several lines of code. Satisfied that this sub is not the problem, you click Step Exit to allow the rest of this sub to execute, leaving you back at the calling statement.

As mentioned, you invoke the debugger with File, Tools, Debug LotusScript. When you run any script, by clicking a button or action or running an agent, the Debugger window will pop up. The debugger will have, highlighted in blue and with a yellow arrow in the left column, the first line of your script to be executed (see Figure 23.7). The yellow arrow always points to the next line to be executed. The blue highlight is used as a marker; it doesn't signify anything the debugger is doing. Whenever you click a line, the line becomes highlighted in blue, as a visual aid for keeping your place in the code.

Breakpoints

Breakpoints are interrupts you place in your script to allow execution control to be returned to the debugger. To set a breakpoint, highlight the line where you want execution to be interrupted and then either double-click the line and choose Debug, Set/Clear Breakpoint or double-click the line and press F9. When you set a breakpoint, a red stop sign symbol appears at the left edge of the line. The breakpoint is also listed on the Breakpoints tab in the bottom half of the window. Breakpoints are listed on the Breakpoints tab in the syntax *procedure:event:line*.

Running a Script to the Breakpoint

In the Breakpoints tab, clicking a particular breakpoint reference will take you to the script where the breakpoint is set.

Clicking a breakpoint again disables the breakpoint. It will still be listed on the Breakpoints tab but with a (Disabled) after it, and execution will not stop at that breakpoint. The stop sign symbol will be shown with a yellow "not" sign over it. Clicking the disabled breakpoint again will remove it from the breakpoint listing. You can also clear a breakpoint with the F9 key or disable it with the Shift F9. From the Debug menu, you can also clear, disable, or enable all breakpoints at once. Figure 23.8 shows the full Debug menu.

After you've gotten to a breakpoint and interrupted program execution, you can use the Variables tab to examine objects in your program. The Variables tab lists all the global objects and any local objects that your script is able to see (that are visible to it). Any objects outside the scope of the current script will not be displayed in the Variables tab. The Variables tab shows the name of the objects, any information about the object (such as data type), and the value of the object. Figure 23.9 shows the Variables tab, expanded to take up the entire screen, and various objects.

FIGURE 23.8

Using breakpoints makes it easy to run the script to a specific point.

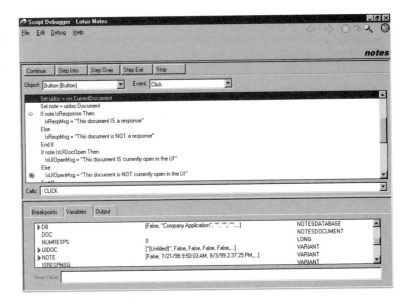

FIGURE 23.9

The Variable tab contains a list of variables and objects that have been defined.

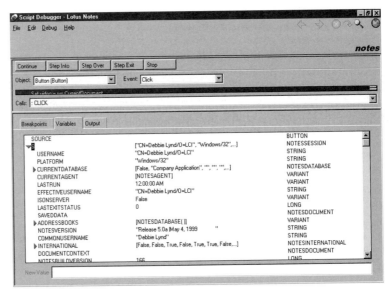

In Figure 23.9, you see that the Variables tab contains listings for the variables defined so far during execution of the script. The lines referencing S, DB, NOTE, and COLLECTION have twisties next to them. As in other places throughout Notes, this indicates that these lines are expandable. The Collection twistie has already been expanded. Below Collection are properties of the Collection object. The properties such as Count,

ISSORTED, and QUERY are scalar values and contain the values listed in the center column of the data type listed in the rightmost column. The property PARENT under COLLECTION also has a twistie next to it, which indicates that it, too, is expandable, and so on.

When you look for a particular item (field) on a document, look for a twistie under the Document object labeled ITEMS—under this will be all the items in the document. Much to your dismay however, they are numbered 0 to whatever, instead of listed with the item name. This makes sense because items are stored in an array, but it doesn't make getting to the field named Status easy when there are 200 items, numbered 0–199.

Notice that the string variable ERRORMESSAGE is highlighted and its value The operation produced an error! shows not only in the center column but also in the New Value box at the bottom of the screen. You could give the highlighted variable a new value by typing it into the New Value box.

Scalar Variable Values Can Be Changed from the Debugger

You can change values for scalar variables only. You can't change Domino objects because there is no way to, for instance, enter a new NotesDocumentCollection into the New Value box.

Reviewing Variables Can Disclose the Problems with a Script

The Variables tab can be a useful tool for helping you discover and fix pesky data errors in your programs. Just about every known piece of information about a particular variable can be found in the Variables tab.

Remember that the Variables tab shows only those objects visible to the script that is showing in the code window of the debugger. If you can't see a particular variable, it's probably because it was defined in some other section of code, and therefore is not visible to this code.

The last part of the Debugger window is the Calls list. Calls is a reverse list of the function and subroutine calls that got you from the main procedure to the current procedure. Perhaps the least valuable of all the tools in the debugger window, it is nonetheless useful in its own way. If you set a breakpoint and then continue execution until that breakpoint is encountered, dropping down the Calls list will show you the execution calling path to the subroutine that contains the breakpoint. See Listing 23.19, which contains sample code.

LISTING 23.19   Call List Sample Script

```
Sub Initialize

    'This is the Main procedure.

    'From here we call the FirstLevelSub routine
    FirstLevelSub

End Sub
Sub FirstLevelSub

    'From here, execution passes, via a call, to the next sub
    SecondLevelSub

End Sub
Sub SecondLevelSub

    'This sub calls two other subroutines

    ThirdLevelA
    ThirdLevelB


End Sub
Sub ThirdLevelA
    'no real code here

End Sub
Sub ThirdLevelB

    'in the Real World, there'd be useful code here!
    'The breakpoint is set at the End Sub line below!

End Sub
```

You can see from the Calls list that the procedures listed are, in reverse order, `Main:ThirdLevelB`, `Main:SecondLevelSub`, `Main:FirstLevelSub`, and `Main:Initialize`. Starting at the top of the list, you can read it like this: `ThirdLevelB` was called by `SecondLevelSub`, which was called by `FirstLevelSub`, which was called by the `Initialize` event of the main procedure. Look again at Listing 23.19, in the `SecondLevelSub` procedure, and you'll see that two subroutine calls are made, `ThirdLevelA` and `ThirdLevelB`. Why isn't `ThirdLevelA` call listed in the Call list? The reason is because the `ThirdLevelA` subroutine has already finished executing when the call to `ThirdLevelB` is made and so therefore is no longer in the chain from current procedure up to the main procedure.

Summary

Now you've learned many of the properties and methods of several of the Notes object model classes and seen them used in working examples. You've explored events at the field, form, and database level, moved toward code reuse with Script Libraries, learned about handling errors in scripts, and been thoroughly introduced to the integrated debugger.

You've covered a lot of ground so far. In this chapter, you combined your knowledge of LotusScript with the Notes object model and seen examples and working code of how to use the classes and their properties and methods to accomplish real-world tasks. What you've seen is by no means all there is! I've only touched the surface—enough to get you off and running on your own. The next chapter continues the LotusScript tour by creating functional buttons, writing event scripts, creating agents for automation, and accessing data in non-Notes applications.

Writing LotusScript

by Debbie Lynd

In This Chapter

CHAPTER 24

So far in Part III, you've learned the basics of LotusScript—including the language elements and the Domino object model—and seen numerous examples of scripts using the LotusScript components to produce results. In this chapter, you'll carry your education farther, putting scripts into context throughout your applications and using scripts tucked into various design elements to manipulate data and interact with the user.

Interacting with the User: MessageBox, InputBox, and DialogBox

Before jumping right into sample scripts, this chapter mentions three LotusScript commands that you've seen in examples but haven't learned about in detail. These commands are `MessageBox`, `InputBox`, and `DialogBox`. `MessageBox` and `InputBox` are functions independent of an object class, whereas `DialogBox` is a method of the `NotesUIWorkspace` class. These are being covered up front because they are three ways to display a message to the user based on a condition as well as providing data entry capabilities from both `InputBox` and `DialogBox`. You will use these very frequently to interact with a user from a script.

`MessageBox`, as you've seen, presents information to the user; `InputBox` gets information from the user; and `DialogBox`, like its Formula language brother the `@DialogBox` command, displays a form or document in a dialog box.

The first thing you should do if you intend to use these three commands is to use `%include "LSCONST.LSS"`. This allows you to use constant names such as `MB_YESNOCANCEL` for arguments rather than numbers such as `3` to represent `MB_YESNOCANCEL`. Not only is this easier to read and understand, it's also easier to remember when writing your code.

Using a `MessageBox` to Display Information

`MessageBox` can also be written as `MsgBox`, which is convenient for us bad typists. The `MessageBox` command can be used as a function or statement. Using `MessageBox` like this:

```
retCode = MessageBox("Do you want to continue?" , MB_YESNOCANCEL)
```

makes it a function call, with the return value from `MessageBox` placed into the `retCode` variable. The return code is a number representing the button the user clicked. Anytime you put up a message box with any buttons other than OK, format the command as a function, because you want to know what button the user clicked. Using `MessageBox` like this:

```
MessageBox "Hello World" , MB_OK
```

is the statement form and does not return a value.

`MessageBox` takes up to three arguments: `message`, `prompt`, and `title`. `message` is whatever text you want displayed in the box, up to 512 characters. `prompt` is actually four arguments combined into one: `buttons`, `icon`, `default`, and `mode`. Each argument is a number (an integer); adding the numbers together determines how the box looks and acts. The `buttons` argument determines what buttons will show up. The options are listed in Table 24.1. The `icon` argument works the same way; icon options are listed in Table 24.2. The `default` argument determines which button will be the default—that is, the one that will be activated if the user presses the spacebar or the Enter key. The `mode` argument determines whether the message box will be application modal or system modal. Application modal stops the current application until the user responds to the dialog box, and system modal stops all applications until the user responds. Last, `title` is a string of up to 128 characters that goes into the title bar of the message box. Tables 24.1, 24.2, 24.3, and 24.4 list the `buttons`, `icon`, `default`, and `mode` options, respectively.

TABLE 24.1   Button Argument Options

Value	Buttons	Constant
0	OK	MB_OK
1	OK, Cancel	MB_OKCANCEL
2	Abort, Retry, Cancel	MB_ABORTRETRYCANCEL
3	Yes, No, Cancel	MB_YESNOCANCEL
4	Yes, No	MB_YESNO
5	Retry, Cancel	MB_RETRYCANCEL

TABLE 24.2   Icon Argument Options

Value	Icon	Constant
16	Stop Sign	MB_ICONSTOP
32	Question Mark	MB_ICONQUESTION
48	Exclamation Point	MB_ICONEXCLAMATION
64	Information	MB_ICONINFORMATION

24

WRITING LOTUSSCRIPT

TABLE 24.3 Default Argument Options

Value	Default Button	Constant
0	First Button	MB_DEFBUTTON1
256	Second Button	MB_DEFBUTTON2
512	Third Button	MB_DEFBUTTON3

TABLE 24.4 Mode Argument Options

Value	Mode	Constant
0	Application	MB_APPLMODAL
4096	System	MB_SYSTEMMODAL

The following example should make clear why you'll want to use the constant names rather than the values, whenever you can. The three following statements shown in Listing 24.1 are equivalent and produce the message box shown in Figure 24.1. Which statement do you like best?

LISTING 24.1 Three Ways to Code a Message Box

```
MessageBox "Would you like to continue?" , 4387 , "Decision Time!"
MessageBox "Would you like to continue?" , 3 + 32 + 256 + 4096 ,
➡"Decision Time!"
MessageBox "Would you like to continue?" , & _
MB_YESNOCANCEL + MB_ICONQUESTION + MB_DEFBUTTON2 + MB_SYSTEMMODAL, & _
"Decision Time!"
```

FIGURE 24.1

Creating a MessageBox *can be done in multiple ways to produce the same result.*

MessageBox, when used as a function, will return an integer value. Just like the arguments listed previously, the return value can be used as a constant. Table 24.5 lists the return values from MessageBox.

TABLE 24.5   MessageBox Return Values

Value	Button	Constant
1	OK	IDOK
2	Cancel	IDCANCEL
3	Abort	IDABORT
4	Retry	IDRETRY
5	Ignore	IDIGNORE
6	Yes	IDYES
7	No	IDNO

Using an `InputBox` for a User Supplied Value

The `InputBox` function allows the user to type a value that is returned to the program. There are two variations of `InputBox`: `InputBox`, which returns a variant data type, and `InputBox$`, which returns a string. `InputBox` takes up to four arguments: `prompt`, `title`, `default`, and `xpos`, `ypos`. `prompt` is a string of up to 128 characters long. `title` is the title of the dialog box, also up to 128 characters. `default` is the value that shows up in the edit field of `InputBox`. `xpos` and `ypos`, which must both be used if either is used, allow you to control where `InputBox` is placed on the screen. The `xpos` and `ypos` arguments specify the distance, in pixels, from the top-left corner of the screen to the top-left corner of `InputBox`, respectively. Figure 24.2 shows the `InputBox` generated from the following statement:

```
retCode = CInt( InputBox( "Please enter your age:" , "How old are
➥you?" , 30 ) )
```

FIGURE 24.2

When using `InputBox`, be sure to convert the return value, a variant, into the proper data type needed.

Using a `DialogBox` to Populate Fields

Last, the `DialogBox` method of the `NotesUIWorkspace` allows you to display a specified form in a dialog box. The information that the user enters in the form is then entered into the fields on the underlying document that have the same names as the fields in the dialog box. It is identical to the @DialogBox function. The main exception is that with this method, you can display either the current document (as with @DialogBox) or any document in the database.

The LotusScript language and the Domino object model provide a rich, full-featured programming environment. Many more functions are available within additional LotusScript commands. I've also talked about many Domino classes and some of the properties and methods associated. There are, however, many more commands, properties, and methods to use. After you've mastered the ones presented in this book, you'll be ready to master the others as well!

Simple Scripts Using Actions or Hotspots

Actions are everywhere. There are actions on the Action Bar and on your forms—the familiar gray buttons or hotspots. Adding LotusScript to actions and hotspots allows you to conceal a tremendous amount of complexity and processing behind a simple click of the mouse. When I discuss actions and hotspot scripts in this chapter, remember that you shouldn't really care which object contains the script. As long as what you're trying to do is within the context of the action or hotspot—it's actually possible—the type of object doesn't matter. I'll look at several action and hotspot scripts—some simple, some not so simple.

Creating an Action to Walk Through the Documents in a Database

Like all objects, actions and hotspots have the (Options), (Declarations), Initialize, and Terminate events. If you'll remember back to your first introduction to LotusScript events, Lotus recommends that the Initialize event is used only in agents. For actions and hotspots, use the Click event as the starting place for all your code.

In the first action example, write a script that walks through a group of documents and displays field information and information about the document itself. The steps to take are these: Get the documents to process, set up a loop to process each document in turn, display the data, move to the next document, and, after all the documents have been processed, display some summary information. I've placed the script in Listing 24.2 in a view action.

Note the first two lines in Listing 24.2. The `Option Public` and the `%Include` `"lsconst.lss"` lines are put into the form scope. `Option Public` is the option that says that all declared variables are public (as opposed to private to the declaring module/procedure) unless explicitly declared private. The `lsconst.lss` file (a file of constants used throughout LotusScript) is to be loaded. The `%include` must be loaded at the form level, because the compiler will not let you declare public constants at the procedure level.

The balance of the code is in the `Click` event of the `action` object. First, declare all the object variables that you'll be using. Next, set the `session` and `db` objects, and then set `collection` to be all the documents in the database by using the `AllDocuments` property of the `NotesDatabase` class. Set `note` to be the first document in the collection, and you're ready to begin looking at the documents themselves.

You could put up a dialog box for each piece of information you want to display, but I find that too tedious; you would be making the user click the OK button too much. What you've done here is to take each piece of information to display and append it to a string variable, `msg`, along with a carriage return (the `Chr( 13 )`), so each piece of information is on its own line. After all the information has been gathered, you put it up in a `MessageBox` with the Info icon showing. After the user clicks OK, you set the note variable to be the next document in the collection, if there is one, and repeat.

LISTING 24.2   Displaying Document Information

```
'These two lines are in the (Globals) for the form,
'in the (Options) event
Option Public
%INCLUDE "lsconst.lss"
Sub Click(Source As Button)
        'declare all the object variables to be used
        Dim ws As New NotesUIWorkspace
        Dim db As NotesDatabase
        Dim s As New NotesSession


        Dim note As NotesDocument
        Dim collection As NotesDocumentCollection
        Dim msg As String
        'set variables & set the note to the first
        'document in the database

        Set db = s.CurrentDatabase
        Set collection = db.AllDocuments
        Set note = collection.GetFirstDocument
```

continues

24

WRITING LOTUSSCRIPT

LISTING 24.2 continued

```
Do until note is nothing
        'gather all info to display into the msg variable
        msg = "Created on : " & note.Created & Chr( 13 )
        If note.IsResponse Then
            msg = msg & "Document is a response document" & Chr( 13 )
        Else
            msg = msg & "Document is a main document" & Chr( 13 )
        End If
        If note.IsSigned Then
            msg = msg & "Document is signed by " & note.Signer &
            ➥Chr( 13 )
        Else
            msg = msg & "Document is not signed" & Chr( 13 )
        End If
        msg = msg & "Last accessed on " & note.LastAccessed & Chr( 13 )
        msg = msg & "Last modified on " & note.LastModified & Chr( 13 )
        msg = msg & "Note ID: " & note.NoteID & Chr( 13 )
        msg = msg & "Universal ID: " & note.UniversalID & Chr( 13 )
        msg = msg & "Form field: " & note.Form( 0 ) & Chr( 13 )
        msg = msg & "Status field: " & note.Status( 0 ) & Chr( 13 )
        'now display the gathered info
        Msgbox msg , MB_OK + MB_ICONINFORMATION , "Document information"
        'move to the next document
        Set note = collection.GetNextDocument( note )
    Loop

End Sub
```

Creating an Action to Mark Completed Documents

For the next action, create another view action that looks through the database for all documents that were marked complete more than 32 days ago and mails them into an archive database. Detailed explanation of the script follows in Listing 24.3.

LISTING 24.3 Archive Button

```
Sub Click(Source As Button)

    'Declare object refs needed    Dim s As New NotesSession
    Dim db As NotesDatabase
    Dim collection As NotesDocumentCollection
    'note will be the current doc being processed
    Dim note As NotesDocument
    'nextNote will be a "placeholder"
```

```
        Dim nextNote As NotesDocument
        'memo will be the new doc we're mailing
        Dim memo As NotesDocument
        'DateTime values for comparison
        Dim item As NotesItem
        Dim compDate As NotesDateTime
        'Set my cutoff date to today - 32
        Dim cutoff As New NotesDateTime ( Now )
        Call cutoff.AdjustDay( -32 )
        Set db = s.CurrentDatabase
        Set collection = db.AllDocuments
        Set note = collection.GetFirstDocument
        'process as long as there's documents
        Do Until note is nothing

            If note.Form( 0 ) = "REQ" Then
                Set item = note.GetFirstItem( "CompletionDate" )
                Set compDate = item.DateTimeValue
                If ( note.Status( 0 ) = "Complete" )
                ➥And ( cutoff.TimeDifference( compDate ) > 0  ) Then
                    Set memo = New NotesDocument( db )
                    Call note.CopyAllItems( memo , True )
                    Call memo.Send( False , "ArchiveDB" )
                    Call DeleteResponses( note )
                    Set nextNote = collection.GetNextDocument( note )
                    note.Remove( True )
                Else
                    Set nextNote = collection.GetNextDocument( note )
                End If
            Else
                Set nextNote = collection.GetNextDocument( note )
            End If
            Set note = nextNote
        Loop
End Sub
Sub deleteResponses( note As NotesDocument )
    Dim respNote As NotesDocument
    Dim respCollection As NotesDocumentCollection
    Dim nextResp As NotesDocument
    Set respCollection = note.Responses
    Set respNote = respCollection.GetFirstDocument
    Do Until respNote is nothing
        Set nextResp = respCollection.GetNextDocument( respNote )
        Call deleteResponses( respNote )
        Call respNote.Remove( True )
        Set respNote = nextResp
    Loop
End Sub
```

The object reference and other variables are declared explicitly at the beginning of the script. Following the declarations, the variable cutoff is set to the `datetime` value of 32 days before today. Next, the object reference variables for the session, database, and document are instantiated. What is left is the processing loop. Because you're going to look at all documents in the database, everything within the loop will be processed for each document encountered in the document collection.

The main loop is controlled by whether any documents in the database are left to process. Within the loop, the first thing you do is to determine whether this document is the proper form; assume, for now, that you will archive documents that use the REQ form. Then, get the `CompletionDate` field from the document and place it into a `NotesItem` variable. Now that it is in the form of a `NotesItem`, you can use the `LocalDateTime` property to get its date value, which is then assigned to `compDate`. Now, the `If` checks for the presence of both conditions, `Status = "Complete"` and `CompletionDate < Today - 32`. If both conditions are true, create a new `NotesDocument` object, `memo`, and copy all the items (fields) from the original document onto the new one. Then send it off. If either of the `If` conditions is not true, you fall through the `If`. Notice that the `memo` object is never saved in this database. After you email it, you no longer need the object. In fact, the next time through the loop, if the `If` conditions are satisfied again, you'll instantiate `memo` as a new `NotesDocument`; the old one will cease to exist.

Now that the memo has been mailed to the archive database, the original can be deleted; after all, it's just been archived. If this document has a response hierarchy, delete all the children first. Otherwise, all those descendants will be orphans clogging up the database. First, test to see whether there are any responses. If not, remove the document. If there are responses, remove all of them. To remove the responses without leaving orphans, navigate down the hierarchy until you're at a response that does not itself have any responses. Because the process is the same, use a recursive subroutine to check and remove responses. A recursive subroutine or function is one that calls itself—a process called *recursion*. In Listing 24.3, the subroutine `DeleteResponses` is a recursive sub; if `note` has responses, `DeleteResponses` calls itself until there are no responses and then deletes `note`.

Recursion Must Be Fully Tested

It is very easy to create a recursive sub that loops infinitely. A recursive sub must include an `exit` clause and be fully tested before implementing. Note also, that many tasks can be accomplished through a typical looping structure that will run faster and use less memory than recursion.

The `DeleteResponses` sub takes a document reference as a parameter; in the listing, the object reference note is passed as the document reference argument. The document argument is the document that you want to check to see whether it has any responses. If it does have a response, set the reference variable to that document and then call the sub again. It appears that you're reusing variable names when `DeleteResponses` recurses. But you're not, because of scope. When one sub or function calls another, the new invocation gets a new memory space. Because `respCollection` and `respNote` are `Dimmed` in the new invocation of the routine, those instances of the variables are the ones visible to the code. The variables of the same name from the calling subroutine are not accessible, because they are *shadowed* by the local variables with those names—and a good thing too, or recursion wouldn't work!

`DeleteResponses` continues recursing until a document has no responses. Then, the current document is deleted. However, if you delete the current document, you'll never get to the next document. So, before you recurse, get the handle to the next document and store it in the `nextResp` variable. That way, after you delete the current document, you know what document to navigate to next.

The last line of the main loop sets the note reference variable to the next document in the collection, if there is one. If there is one, the test at the top of the loop (`While Not ( Doc is Nothing)`) will start the loop again. If the test doesn't pass, the note reference variable no longer points to a document, so you're done.

Working with LotusScript in Forms

Forms, too, can have LotusScript in them. For forms, the scripts you'll write will be either a function or a sub to be shared by any other object on the form declared in the (`Globals`), or an event script to handle one of the form level events listed here:

```
Initialize
QueryOpen
PostOpen
PostRecalc
QuerySave
QueryModeChange
PostModeChange
QueryClose
Terminate
```

The functionality you're used to in Domino formula development can be implemented in LotusScript also—such as default value formulas or computed-when-composed fields.

Using LotusScript in the PostOpen Event

Listing 24.4 shows an example of using the PostOpen event to create default field values. In the example, the Name and Date fields in the form design could be set to be either editable fields, thereby providing default values, or computed fields, providing then its value.

LISTING 24.4 Creating Default Values Using the PostOpen Event

```
Sub Postopen(Source As Notesuidocument)
    Dim s As New NotesSession
    Dim ws As New NotesUIWorkspace

    Dim note As NotesDocument
    Dim theDate As New NotesDateTime( Now )
    Set Source = ws.CurrentDocument
    Set note = Source.Document
    If Source.IsNewDoc Then
        'setting the Name and Date fields to the users' name and
        'the current date/time
        note.Name = s.UserName
        Set note.Date = theDate
        Source.reload
    End If
End Sub
```

All the Query events have Continue as a parameter to the event script, as shown here:

```
Sub Queryopen(Source As Notesuidocument, Mode As Integer, Isnewdoc As
➥Variant, Continue As Variant)
```

The Continue parameter is returned from the event script and used to determine whether the current event should continue to completion. Knowing this, it's easy to trap for the existence of certain conditions and then make a decision about whether the operation should be allowed to continue. For example, you might want to determine whether a user has entered certain combinations of fields and not allow a save to continue if those combinations exist. In the example in Listing 24.5, the user will be alerted and the document will not be saved if the PartsStatus field is In Transit and the user tries to change the WorkStatus field to anything except Awaiting Parts.

LISTING 24.5 Using the Continue Parameter to Control Execution

```
Sub Querysave(Source As Notesuidocument, Continue As Variant)
    If source.FieldGetText( "PartsStatus" ) = "In Transit" Then
        wStat = source.FieldGetText( "WorkStatus" )
        Select Case wStat
        Case "Awaiting Parts"  , ""
            continue = True
        Case Else
            Msgbox "You have an incorrect Work Status value. Save
            ➥cancelled"
            continue = False
        End Select
    End If
End Sub
```

Using LotusScript in the `QueryOpen` Event

Combining the `QueryOpen` event, the `Continue` parameter, and a new `NotesSession` method, `GetEnvironmentString` allows you to build a mechanism that will check the user's `Notes.INI` for a particular value when the user opens a document in the database. If the value is not set (perhaps the user is supposed to run an agent or click a button to do some setup before using the database), the document does not open.

Listing 24.6 starts with the `QueryOpen` event. Having instantiated the session, this listing uses the `GetEnvironmentString` method to get the `DBUserInfo` variable from `Notes.INI`. If the variable isn't set or doesn't exist, setting the `Continue` parameter to `false` will present a `MessageBox` to the user telling what the problem is, and the document won't open. If the value is set, leaving `Continue` alone will continue processing and the document will open.

LISTING 24.6 Using `PostOpen`, `Continue`, and `GetEnvironmentString`

```
Sub Queryopen(Source As Notesuidocument, Mode As Integer, Isnewdoc As
➥Variant, Continue As Variant)
    Dim s As New NotesSession
    Dim iniVar As Variant
    iniVar = s.GetEnvironmentString( "$DBUserInfo" )
    If iniVar = "" Then
        Messagebox "You must click the Register User button before
        ➥viewing any documents!"
        Continue = False
    End If
End Sub
```

24

WRITING
LOTUSSCRIPT

Here's one last interesting example before moving on to fields. Something that many people want to do is to be able to tell how many times a document has been read. Actually, you can't tell how many times users have read a document; the best you can hope for is to know how many times the document has been opened. To accomplish this, use the QueryClose event. In it, you'll test to see whether the document is in edit mode. If it is, you'll just increment the value in a hidden field, and the value will be saved when the document is saved. If the document is not being edited, you'll put it into edit mode, increment the read counter, and then save the document—and the user will never even know anything has happened. See Listing 24.7.

Look closely at the code, and you'll see that it's not really manipulating the front-end document at all, even though you start with it. The very first thing to do is move from the front end into the back end by setting the note object variable to the Document property of source. From now on, everything you do will be in the back end. There are two reasons for this. First (and foremost, if you ask me!), it's easier! Second, because this code is in the QueryClose event, the user is in the process of closing this document. Therefore, you don't have to affect the front end at all; it's already going away. Continuing then, check to see whether this is a new document. If it is, initialize the counter to 0; otherwise, start it at whatever count is in the NumTimesRead field. You might wonder why you shouldn't be concerned with whether the front-end doc was in edit or read mode. Actually, it doesn't matter, because all the changes you're making are to the back end— so, who cares what mode the front end was in? Anyway, now increment the counter variable: Put the new value into the NumTimesRead field, save the back end, and exit. That's it!

LISTING 24.7 Using QueryClose to Track Document Accesses

```
Sub Queryclose(Source As Notesuidocument, Continue As Variant)
     Dim readCounter As Integer
     Dim ntr As Long
     Dim note As NotesDocument
     Set note = source.Document
     If note.IsNewNote Then
          ntr = 0
     Else
          ntr = Clng( note.NumTimesRead( 0 )  )
     End If

     ntr = ntr + 1
     Call note.ReplaceItemValue( "NumTimesRead" , Cstr( ntr ) )
     Call note.Save( True , True )
End Sub
```

Using LotusScript in Fields

The Entering and Exiting field events make it easy to perform some processing when the cursor enters or leaves a field. Listing 24.8 shows Entering and Exiting event scripts for the same field. The Entering script pops an input box if the field is currently empty. If the field has a value, nothing happens. The Exiting script checks to determine whether the value in the field is a number greater than 1000. If so, it puts up a dialog box indicating that the limit is 1000 and clears the field. The Entering event also checks that the value the user enters in the dialog box is numeric.

LISTING 24.8 Entering and Exiting Event Scripts

```
Sub Entering(Source As Field)
    Dim ws As New NotesUIWorkspace
    Dim uidoc As NotesUIDocument
    Set uidoc = ws.CurrentDocument
    If uidoc.FieldGetText( "SomeField" ) = "" Then
        retCode =  Inputbox$ ("Enter a new field value:" )
        If Isnumeric( retCode ) Then
            Call uidoc.FieldSetText( "SomeField" ,  retCode )
        Else
            Msgbox "Sorry, you must enter a numeric value"
            Call uidoc.FieldSetText( "SomeField" , "" )
        End If
    End If
End Sub
Sub Exiting(Source As Field)
    Dim ws As New NotesUIWorkspace
    Dim uidoc As NotesUIDocument
    Set uidoc = ws.CurrentDocument
    temp = uidoc.FieldGetText( "SomeField" )
    If temp <> "" Then
        If Clng( temp ) > 1000 Then
            Msgbox "Sorry, you can only order items up to $1000."
            Call uidoc.FieldSetText( "SomeField" , "" )
        End If
    End If
End Sub
```

24

WRITING LOTUSSCRIPT

Writing LotusScript Agents

Chapter 30, "Automating Your Application with Agents," covers formula agents and an example of a LotusScript agent. Presented in Listing 24.9 is another agent, this one a LotusScript agent, whose purpose in life is to send reminders.

The agent runs on schedule daily in a database that contains REQ forms that have a DueDate field that lists the date the task is due, a Status field to show the status, and a PersonAssigned field to indicate who is responsible for completing the task. Every day, the agent runs and looks at all the documents in the database. If Status is open and DueDate is before today, the person receives a mail memo with a doclink to the task. Detailed discussion of the flow of the LotusScript code follows.

As you've seen in the other code examples, you start by declaring all the object references and variables you're going to need. Then, set the db, collection, and note objects. Next, set up the main processing loop, again in this case, a Do. . .While loop based on whether note points to a document. Inside the loop, first determine whether this document is an REQ form; if it's not, skip right over it. You want to process REQ forms only. If the form is a REQ, apply the main test conditions: Is Status open, and is DueDate before today? Similar to when you tested for the form name, if either of these two conditions is not true, you fall through the If.

If both conditions are true, you have work to do—namely, send the email. Instantiate memo as a new NotesDocument object, and set the Form, SendTo, and Subject fields. In the body of the message, generate a short message telling the recipient what the problem is and include a doclink to the task itself. It's worth looking closely at the creation of the Body field as an example of how to effectively manipulate a rich-text field.

Several methods in the NotesRichTextItem class allow you to easily manipulate rich text. The methods that are useful for building a formatted body field like the agent has done are AddNewLine, AddTab, AppendDocLink, and AppendText. There are a few new methods that enable the additional formatting of text as it is added to the field. Additionally, the AppendRTFile allows you to include a file attachment, AppendRTItem allows you to put the contents of another rich-text field into this one, and EmbedObject allows you to create an embedded object such as a spreadsheet or presentation.

What you've done in the agent to build the Body field is to simply add one thing at a time to the field to get the desired appearance. First, you add the text This is a reminder that you have a task due. Then you add two blank lines and more text, Click this doclink to view the task document ->, followed by a doclink to the task document and pointed to by note. The AppendDocLink method requires one argument, the document to be linked to, but will accept a second, optional, argument as well. The second argument is a string that will be shown in the status bar of the Notes windows when the user moves the cursor over the doclink. Because this is a string, you could just as easily have computed some personalized message instead of Click to see the task.

Having created the memo, send it, move to the next document in the database, and repeat the whole process.

LISTING 24.9 Automation Agent to Send Reminder Mail Messages

```
Sub Initialize
    Dim s As New NotesSession
    Dim db As NotesDatabase
    Dim collection As NotesDocumentCollection
    Dim note As NotesDocument
    Dim memo As NotesDocument
    Dim forWho As NotesName
    Dim item As NotesItem
    Dim rtitem As NotesRichTextItem
    Dim cutoff As New NotesDateTime( Today )
    Dim dueDate As NotesDateTime
    Set db = s.CurrentDatabase
    Set collection = db.AllDocuments
    Set note = collection.GetFirstDocument
    Do Until note is nothing
        If note.Form( 0 ) = "REQ" Then
            Set item = note.GetFirstItem( "CompletionDate" )
            Set dueDate = item.DateTimeValue
            If ( note.Status( 0 ) = "Open" ) And ( cutoff.TimeDifference
            ➥( dueDate ) > 0 ) Then
                Set memo = New NotesDocument( db )
                memo.Form = "Memo"
                memo.SendTo = note.PersonAssigned( 0 )
                memo.Subject = "Overdue Task!"
                Set rtitem = New NotesRichTextItem( memo , "Body" )
                Call rtitem.AppendText( "This is a reminder that you
                ➥have a task due." )
                Call rtitem.AddNewLine( 2 )
                Call rtitem.AppendText( "Click this doclink to view
                ➥the task document -> " )
                Call rtitem.AppendDocLink( note , "Click to see
                ➥the task" )
                Call memo.Send( False )
            End If
        End If
        Set note = collection.GetNextDocument( note )
    Loop
End Sub
```

24

Accessing Non-Domino Data

Getting data into and out of Domino has traditionally been an arduous task—one that has gotten much easier as Domino has matured, to be sure. There are many third-party tools whose sole purpose in life is to move data into and out of Domino. The introduction of LotusScript, coupled with improved and constantly improving ODBC (open database connectivity) drivers, has opened access to all that data stored out there in corporate databases! DECS is another way to access non-Domino data and is covered later in this book. There are also many data movers available on the market (see Table 24.6 for a partial list). Our purpose here is to demonstrate the ease, power, and flexibility of using LotusScript, together with the LS:DO LSX, to gain access to data from non-Domino sources. An LSX is a LotusScript extension, which means that it adds classes, functions, or constants to LotusScript. They are then made available in the browser. Without an LSX you would be forced to use a toolkit such as Hi-Test Visual Basic or Windows SDK, or use either C or C++ to write your code.

Understanding the LotusScript Data Object

The LS:DO is the interface between LotusScript and ODBC. The LS:DO LSX (LotusScript:DataObject) is part of Domino, but as an LSX, it needs to be identified to LotusScript before it is used. The LSX adds three classes to the Domino object model: ODBCConnection, ODBCQuery, and ODBCResultSet. The three components are collectively referred to as the LS:DO—the data object. However, installing and using the LS:DO does not automatically give you access to your external data; the ODBC Data Source must be configured on the machine that you're running from. The configuration of the ODBC Data Source is beyond this discussion, because it is a potentially complex operation.

TABLE 24.6   Other Available LSXes

LSX	Description
DB2	Provides access to DB2 data
MQ	Provides access to MQ Series data
SAP	Provides access to SAP R/3 data
Oracle	Provides access to Oracle data

To look at the data types that you can access, if you're running Windows NT or Windows 95, go to the Control Panel and open the ODBC applet. The Data Sources dialog box shown in Figure 24.3 will be presented, listing all the data sources already configured on your machine. In Figure 24.3, you see that my machine has nine data sources configured. The type of ODBC driver used for each source is listed in parentheses after the name of the driver. The ODBC data sources are named so that when you reference a source in LotusScript (or any other method you use to access to ODBC data), you can use the name of the data source.

FIGURE 24.3

ODBC Data Source Administrator dialog box displays the data sources configured on your machine.

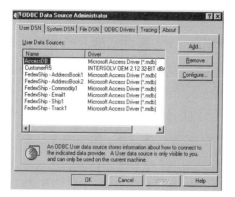

In order to allow LotusScript to use the ODBC data sources, you have to load the LS:DO LSX. To do so, include the line

```
USELSX "*lsxodbc"
```

in the (Options) event of your script. Notice the asterisk in the USE statement. Domino runs on many different platforms, and the .dll and LSX files for each platform are named differently. Files specific to Windows 95 and Windows NT start with an n, and the Windows 3.x–specific files start with an underscore _. The asterisk as the first letter of the USELSX command indicates that the system should check its own Registry to determine what the exact name of the LSX file should be. You should always use the file-names with * to further remove any platform specificity from your code.

To access the ODBC data, you need to make the connection, define a query, execute the query, and then handle the result set. To do this, you'll use, in turn, the ODBCConnection class, ODBCQuery, and ODBCResultSet.

Making a Connection to a Data Object

Establishing the connection is actually quite simple. Declare an object reference variable to hold the connection information, supply a data source name, supply a username and password if the data source requires one, and then make the connection. Test for a return code to handle errors, if they occur, and you're set. See Listing 24.10 for an example of making an ODBC connection.

24

WRITING LOTUSSCRIPT

LISTING 24.10 Creating the ODBC Connection

```
'Declare the variables needed
Dim RetCode as Integer
Dim dataSource as String
Dim userName as String
Dim userPassword as String
Dim ODBCCon as ODBCConnection
'Set my string variables to a value
dataSource = "Employees"
userName = "Doctor Domino"
userPassword = "password"
'Instantiate a new ODBC connection
Set ODBCCon = New ODBCConnection
'print the ODBC LSX version for information
Print "LS:DO LSX Version: " & ODBCCon.GetLSDOMasterRevision
'Attempt the connection, and put the result code into RetCode
'Here we're passing the username and password as arguments, so
'the user won't have to enter them
RetCode = ODBCCon.ConnectTo( dataSource  , userName , userPassword)
'ConnectTo returns true if a successful connection
If RetCode Then
    Print "ODBC Connection to " & dataSource & " opened."
Else
    'if not succeeful, get the error number and text, display them
    MessageBox "The ODBC connection could not be established. Exiting."
    MessageBox "Error number: & ODBCCon.GetError & Chr( 13 ) & _
    "Error message: & ODBCCon.GetExtendedError
    Exit Sub
End If
```

Listing 24.10 makes use of several methods of the ODBCConnection class: ConnectTo, GetLSDOMasterRevision, and two error-related methods, GetError and GetExtendedError. The purpose of ConnectTo is obvious. In Listing 24.11, the user-name and password you would use when opening up the ODBC data source are provided as arguments to the ConnectTo method. You could also leave them out of the command string, and a login-type dialog box would be presented.

Querying the Connection

Now that you have your connection, you need a query to pass—something that tells the data source what data to return. In most cases, this would be an SQL statement, assuming that you were accessing an SQL data source. When you have the connection, you then need to create an ODBCQuery object, point it to the connection previously established, and then set the query statement. In Listing 24.11, you'll see these steps done, added to what you saw in Listing 24.10.

First, you must instantiate an ODBCQuery object. Then you will set the Connection property of the ODBCQuery object to be the ODBCConnection just established. Yes, you're taking an object, ODBCConnection, and putting it into ODBCQuery as a property! One of the properties of the query is where does the data come from?. It comes from whatever the Connection property is set to; therefore, you need to set the Connection property to a real connection. The other property to be concerned with is the SQL property, which is the actual SQL statement being passed to the data source. To do this, take the SQL statement (assume for right now that you're using a known, simple statement such as Select * from LoanDetail) and assign it into the SQL property of the ODBCQuery. That's it; you're ready to roll.

Listing 24.11   Adding ODBCQuery

```
'Declare the variables needed
Dim RetCode as Integer
Dim dataSource as String
Dim userName as String
Dim userPassword as String
Dim ODBCCon as ODBCConnection
'Set my string variables to a value
dataSource = "Employee"
userName = "Doctor Domino"
userPassword = "password"
'Instantiate a new ODBC connection
Set ODBCCon = New ODBCConnection
'print the ODBC LSX version for information
Print "LS:DO LSX Version: " & ODBCCon.GetLSDOMasterRevision
'Attempt the connection, and put the result code into RetCode
'Here we're passing the username and password as arguments, so
'the user won't have to enter them
RetCode = ODBCCon.ConnectTo( dataSource  , userName , userPassword)
'ConnectTo returns true if a successful connection
If RetCode Then
    Print "ODBC Connection to " & dataSource & " opened."
Else
    'if not successful, get the error number and text, display them
    MessageBox "The ODBC connection could not be established. Exiting."
    MessageBox "Error number: & ODBCCon.GetError & Chr( 13 ) & _
    "Error message: & ODBCCon.GetExtendedError
    Exit Sub
End If
'Instantiate the query object and the SQL string
Dim SQLQuery As New odbcquery
Dim theSQL as String
theSQL = "Select * from Employee"
'Set the Connection property
Set SQLQuery.Connection = ODBCCon
'Set the SQL property
SQLQuery.SQL = theSQL
```

Storing the Result Set

Now the stage is set. All you have to do is execute the query. But wait, where will the data go when it's returned? You have to create a place for the data that's returned to be held while you work on it. That place is called a *result set*, and it comes from the ODBCResultSet class. There's just one more step to take before you actually get the data in hand. The ODBCResultSet has a Query property. What do you think goes into the Query property? Right! The ODBCQuery object you just finished creating!

So, you instantiate ODBCResultSet, set its Query property equal to the ODBCQuery object, and then, at long last, call the Execute method of the result set. Assuming there aren't any errors, your result set object now contains the rows for all the data that matched your query. See Listing 24.12 for the last additions to the code. This code follows the code in Listing 24.11.

LISTING 24.12   Creating the Result Set

```
'Instantiate the result set object
Dim ResultSet As New ODBCResultSet
'Set the Query property
Set ResultSet.Query = SQLQuery
'Do it!
ResultSet.Execute
'ResultSet now contains rows or an error
'Test to see which, and act accordingly
If ResultSet.GetError <> DBstsSUCCESS Then
    'oops! An error of some kind
    MessageBox "An error was encountered." & Chr( 13 ) & _
"Error Number: " & ResultSet.GetError & Chr( 13 ) & _
"Error Message: " & ResultSet.GetExtendedError
Else
    MessageBox "Result set retrieved"
End If
```

So, what do you have now? What is this result set thing? A result set is like a spreadsheet in memory. It has columns that represent the column or field values from the data source being queried. It has rows, each of which represents one record from the queried data source. How do you know what the columns are? If you do a simple query such as that in the previous example, Select * from Employee, you'll get back every column from the Employee table and the order of the columns will match the source table. You might need to check with the DBA (database administrator) of the target data source to get the table structure. You can also use the ODBCConnection or ODBCResultSet methods to find out what the columns are. If you used a more specific SQL query, perhaps something like this:

```
SELECT ApplNum, FirstName, LastName, ApplDate, Sex, MaritalStatus, Salary,
⮡ReviewDate, FROM Employee
```

you would already know what columns to expect because you told SQL what to return, and in what order.

Checking ODBC Connections

I use a few simple scripts on a regular basis to help me with ODBC connections. Listing 23.13 lists all the ODBC Data Sources available to me. This is helpful when I can't remember the name of the data source I want to use. Listing 23.14 lists all the tables available in the data source I choose. Listing 23.15 displays a list of all the fields available in the table I request.

LISTING 24.13   Available Data Sources

```
Dim con As New ODBCConnection
    Dim msg As String
    Dim dsnames As Variant
    dsnnames = con.ListDataSources
    For n% = Lbound(dsnnames) To Ubound(dsnnames)
        msg = msg & dsnnames(n%) & Chr(10)
    Next
    Messagebox msg,,"List of DSNs"
```

LISTING 24.14   Tables in Specified Data Source

```
Dim con As New ODBCConnection
    Dim dsn As String
    Dim msg As String
    dsn = Inputbox("ODBC data source name", "DSN")
    con.ConnectTo(dsn)
    If Not con.IsConnected Then
        Messagebox "Could not connect to " & dsn,, "Error"
        Exit Sub
    End If
    tables = con.ListTables(dsn)
    msg = dsn & " contains the following tables:" & Chr(10)
    For n% = Lbound(tables) To Ubound(tables)
        msg = msg & Chr(10) & tables(n%)
    Next
    Messagebox msg,, "Tables for " & dsn
    con.Disconnect
```

LISTING 24.15 Fields Available in Table

```
Dim con As New ODBCConnection
     Dim qry As New ODBCQuery
     Dim result As New ODBCResultSet
     Dim msg As String
     Dim fields As Variant
    Set qry.Connection = con
    Set result.Query = qry

    dsn = "DBase Test Files"
    tables = con.ListTables(dsn)
    num% = Ubound(tables)
    fn = tables(num%)
    fn = Inputbox$("Select Table","TABLE",tables)

    con.ConnectTo(fn)
    fields = con.ListFields(fn)
    msg = fn & " contains the following fields:" & Chr(10)
    For n% = Lbound(fields) To Ubound(fields)
         msg = msg & Chr(10) & fields(n%)
    Next
    Messagebox msg,, "Fields for " & fn
    qry.SQL = "SELECT * FROM " & fn
    result.Execute
    msg = "Items:" & Chr(10)
    If result.IsResultSetAvailable Then

         Do
              result.NextRow
              msg = msg & Chr(10)
              For i = 1 To result.NumColumns
                   msg = msg & "  " & result.GetValue(i)
              Next
         Loop Until result.IsEndOfData
         Messagebox msg,, "Data from " & fn
         result.Close(DB_CLOSE)
    Else
         Messagebox "Cannot get result set for " & fn
         Exit Sub
    End If
    con.Disconnect
```

As you've seen in Domino, there are some things to look out for. First, when the result set is returned, you don't get all the rows right away. By default, a single row at a time is returned, which usually isn't the most efficient way to do it. To enable fetching of more rows at a time, set the result set FetchBatchSize property to a value other than 1. The NumRows property will tell you how many rows were fetched for the result set; however, NumRows will not be valid until all the rows have been fetched. You can use the

IsEndOfData property to determine whether the last row has been fetched. Checking NumRows immediately after executing a query or while in the process of fetching and processing rows will return the constant DB_ROWSUNKNOWN. If there are no rows returned from a query, NumRows will return DB_NORESULT. You can also use the IsResultSetAvailable property to determine whether any rows were actually returned.

You could force the result set to get all rows by one of two methods. After the Execute method is invoked, use the LastRow method. This method forces the result set to fetch rows until the last row is returned and then makes the last row the current row. The second method is to create a small loop that steps through the result set row by row until the last row is reached. Using the FieldName property, you can step through all the columns of the result set and get the name of the SQL field the column is from. Using the FieldNativeDataType, you can also get the type of data in the column. See Listing 24.16 for code examples illustrating these properties and methods.

LISTING 24.16   Examples Using ODBCResultSet Properties and Methods

```
Dim con As New ODBCConnection
Dim query As New ODBCQuery
Dim res As New ODBCResultSet
Dim x As Integer
Dim dt As String
Dim msg As String
retCode = con.ConnectTo( "DSCEXT IP" , "sa" , "lotusnotes" )
query.sql = "Select * from MHTEST"
Set query.connection =  con
Set  res.query = query
Call res.execute
'Use LastRow to navigate to the last row, then get number of rows
res.LastRow
msg = "Number of rows (by LastRow method): " & res.NumRows & Chr( 13 )
'drop this result set, execute the query again
Call res.execute
'use loop to get to last row
Do While Not res.IsEndOfData
    res.NextRow
Loop
'add the results to msg
msg = msg & "Number of rows (by loop method): " & res.NumRows & Chr( 13 )
'get some information about the result set
'column names
For x = 1 To res.NumColumns
    msg = msg & "Column " & x & "'s name is: " & res.FieldName( x )
➥& Chr( 13 )
    Select Case res.FieldNativeDataType( x )
    Case 1
        dt = "SQL_CHAR"
```

continues

24

**WRITING
LOTUSSCRIPT**

LISTING 24.16 continued

```
    Case 2
        dt = "SQL_NUMERIC"
    Case 3
        dt = "SQL_DECIMAL"
    Case 4
        dt = "SQL_INTEGER"
    End Select
    msg = msg & "    Its data type is " & dt & Chr( 13 )
Next
Msgbox msg , MB_OK + MB_ICONINFORMATION , "Result Set Information"
```

After you've gotten the data you want into your result set, you'll want to do something with it. Naturally, methods are available to facilitate your data manipulation. To get column values, use the result set GetValue method. This will return to you a data value from a specified column of the result set. Watch out for NULLs though. If you have a column that could contain NULLs, test for that condition first with IsValueNull. You can walk through your result set in either direction, top down or bottom up, using the FirstRow, LastRow, NextRow, and PrevRow methods. You can also jump directly to a particular row by setting the CurrentRow property to a specific row number.

There will be times when you want to not only read data from another data source, but also update or add data. To do so, you'll need to create a result set as before. For updating a row, navigate to the row to be updated. Make whatever column value changes are required and then invoke the UpdateRow method. Assuming the username you're using for access to the data source has enough privileges to do so, the data row will be updated.

For adding rows, create a result set and then invoke the AddRow method. This will create a new row, with the special row number DB_ADDROW. The new row is not really a part of the existing result set rows; it's a separate area. The new row exists in parallel with the returned rows, and you can switch back and forth between the two by setting CurrentRow to either a row number or DB_ADDROW. Put your new data values into the new row using the SetValue method. Finally, call the UpdateRow method, and the new row will be added to the data source and removed from your result set. If you want the new row to be visible now as part of your result set, you'll have to execute your query again.

What's New in Release 4 of LotusScript

There are new classes, properties, methods, functions, and events in LotusScript Release 4. Many of them will make life a lot easier for us. The new functions for manipulation of strings and text lists finally give the scripting language what the Formula language has always had, and what makes a developer crazy trying to re-create in LotusScript. The new functionality is covered in this section.

New Functions for String and Text List Manipulation

The new functionality for string and text list manipulation makes it easier to search for information in a text string and add or remove data from a text list. The following list explains these new functions.

- STRLeft—Searches a string from left to right for a specified substring and returns all characters to the left of the substring.

- STRLeftBack—Performs the same search as STRLeft, but searches the string from right to left.

- STRRight—Searches a string from right to left for a specified substring, and returns all characters to the right of the substring.

- STRRightBack—Performs the same search as STRRight, but searches the string from right to left.

- ArrayAppend—Saves time by allowing you to append an array to another array, which creates a third array that contains all the elements from both arrays. In the past, this has not been easy to do, and it required extending the upper boundary for an array, and then assigning each value from the second array to the appropriate element in the first array.

- ArrayGetIndex—Allows a comparison between a string and a list of array values, to return the index of the value in the array.

- ArrayReplace—Allows a comparison between two arrays. A third array is then created, based on the following: If the element in array1 does not have a match in array2, the element from array1 is written to array3; if a match is found in array2, the element from array2 is written to array3.

- FullTrim—Removes empty entries from an array, as well as removing duplicate, trailing and leading spaces.

Okay, so there are eight new functions. I consider the number-one function to be the ArrayAppend function because it saves an incredible amount of coding time. To give you an idea of how you can save time with this function, I have two partial listings. The first, Listing 24.17, shows 4.6 code to take the values from one array and append them to the second array. Listing 24.18 shows the same code in 5.0 using the ArrayAppend function. As you can see, you've been able to remove the For loop and use the function instead saving quite a few lines of code.

LISTING 24.17   Does Current Document Already Have Parts Entered? If So, Get These Values – 4.6 Code

```
uidoc.autoreload = False

'get the current field values
oPart = doc.getitemvalue("Part")
    oupper = Ubound(oPart)
    oList = doc.getitemvalue("List")
    oCost = doc.getitemvalue("Cost")
    oQty = doc.getitemvalue("Qty")
    odesc = doc.getitemvalue("Desc")

    frm = "ItemDialog"
    flag = wksp.dialogbox(frm,True,True,False,False,False,False,_
"Select the Bill of Materials")

If flag = False Then
        Exit Sub
    End If

'Get the new values
        nPart = doc.getitemvalue("Part")
        nList = doc.getitemvalue("List")
        nCost = doc.getitemvalue("Cast")
        nQty = doc.getitemvalue("Qty")
        ndesc = doc.getitemvalue("Desc")
        nupper = Ubound(nPart)

        up = oupper + nupper + 1
        num = 0
        Redim Alist(up)
        Redim Acost(up)
        Redim ANum(up)
        Redim Aqty(up)
        thenum = num + 1

    'create the combined list
        Forall y In oPart
            AList(num) = oList(num)
            ACost(num) = oCost(num)
            Anum(num) = thenum
            Aqty(num) = oqty(num)
            thenum = thenum + 1
            num = num + 1
        End Forall
        Snum = oupper + 1
        num = 0
        Redim Preserve odesc(up)
        Redim Preserve oPart(up)
        Forall y In nPart
```

```
            oPart(Snum) = nPart(num)
            AList(Snum) = nList(num)
            ACost(Snum) = nCost(num)
            Aqty(Snum) =  nQty(num)
            odesc(Snum) = ndesc(num)
            Snum = Snum + 1
            num = num + 1
        End Forall


    'Write the new field values to the document
        Set fld1 = doc.replaceitemvalue("Part",oPart)
        Set fld1 = doc.replaceitemvalue("List",AList)
        Set fld1 = doc.replaceitemvalue("Cost",ACost)
        Set fld1 = doc.replaceitemvalue("Qty",Aqty)
        Set fld1 = doc.replaceitemvalue("desc",odesc)
```

LISTING 24.18   Does Current Document Already Have Parts Entered? If So, Get These Values – 5.0 Code

```
uidoc.autoreload = False
oPart = doc.getitemvalue("Part")
    oList = doc.getitemvalue("List")
    oCost = doc.getitemvalue("Cost")
    oQty = doc.getitemvalue("Qty")
    odesc = doc.getitemvalue("Desc")

    frm = "ItemDialog"
    flag = wksp.dialogbox(frm,True,True,False,False,False,False,_
"Select the Bill of Materials")

If flag = False Then
        Exit Sub
    End If

'Get the new values
nPart = doc.getitemvalue("Part")
    nList = doc.getitemvalue("List")
    nCost = doc.getitemvalue("Cost")
    nQty = doc.getitemvalue("Qty")
    ndesc = doc.getitemvalue("Desc")

    'create the combined list
Arrayappend(oList, nlist, Alist)
ArrayAppend(oCost, nCost, Acost)
ArrayAppend(oQty, nQty, Aqty)
ArrayAppend(oDesc, nDesc, Adesc)
ArrayAppend(oPart, nPart, Apart)
```

continues

LISTING 24.18 continued

```
    'Write the new field values to the document
Set fld1 = doc.replaceitemvalue("P",oPart)
Set fld1 = doc.replaceitemvalue("L",AList)
Set fld1 = doc.replaceitemvalue("C",ACost)
Set fld1 = doc.replaceitemvalue("Q",Aqty)
Set fld1 = doc.replaceitemvalue("desc",odesc)
```

Next, let's explore the modifications made to existing classes as well as the new classes that are available in LotusScript 4.

Additions to the `NotesACL` Class

The `NotesACL` class has one new property available—the `InternetLevel`. This new property returns the value of the highest access an Internet client can have. It is a read-write property, so you can also set the level. This information can be found in the Advanced tab of the ACL and is set as Editor by default.

Additions to the `NotesACLEntry` Class

The `NotesACLEntry` has seven new properties. These properties provide information about the other options available for an entry. In other words, the checkboxes to the right of the ACL list and the `UserType` properties are now available through LotusScript. See Figure 24.4.

- `CanCreateLSOrJavaAgent`—Returns the value of Create LotusScript/Java Agent for an entry with Reader access. This is a read-write property so it can also be set through the property.

- `CanCreateSharedFolder`—Returns the value of the Create Shared Folders/Views entry for a user with Editor Access.

- `IsAdminReaderAuthor`—Returns a value indicating whether the Administration Server for this database can modify the Reader and Author fields.

- `IsAdminServer`—Checks the ACL to see whether the name is indicated to the Administration server for the database.

- `IsGroup`—Checks an ACL entry's user type to see whether it is a group name or sets an entry as a group.

- `IsPerson`—Checks an ACL entry's user type to see whether it is a person or sets an entry as a person.

- `IsServer`—Checks an ACL entry's user type to see whether it is a server name or sets an entry as a server.

FIGURE 24.4

The UserType *properties can now be set through LotusScript.*

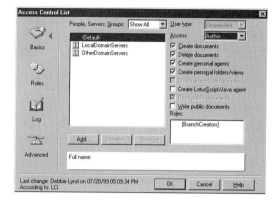

Additions to the NotesAgent Class

There are four new properties for agents that provide helpful information regarding when an agent should run and what causes it to run as well as whether the agent can run from a Web client or Notes client:

- IsNotesAgent—Returns a Boolean value that indicates whether the agent is a Notes agent that can be run by a Notes client.

- IsWebAgent—Returns a Boolean value that indicates whether the agent can be run by a Web client.

- Target—Returns a Boolean value or an integer, depending on syntax. The target of an agent is determined in the Which Documents Should This Act On? entry for the agent.

- Trigger—Returns a Boolean or an integer, depending on syntax. The target of an agent is determined in the When Should This Agent Run? entry for the agent.

Additions to the NotesDatabase Class

There are four new properties available for the NotesDatabase class that return information about things such as the maximum size of a database and the replication information for a database:

- FolderReferencesEnabled—Returns a Boolean value that indicates whether folder references are enabled for a database. This is to be used prior to looking up the folder references for a document. Folder references provide information about all the folders a document is in. Not all databases use folder references and in order to use folder references, the database must contain two views. They are the $FolderInfo and $FolderRefInfo views, and they can be copied from the Notes mail template.

24

WRITING LOTUSSCRIPT

- IsDirectoryCatalog—Returns a Boolean value indicating whether the database is a Directory Catalog database. In order for this property to return the appropriate value, the database must be explicitly opened through the address book property of the session class.

- MaxSize—Returns the maximum size property for a database.

- ReplicationInfo—Returns the replication info from the database. See the NotesReplication class for more information.

There are three new methods for the database class.

- FTDomainSearch—This new method performs a domain search for the specified string, and returns a document that contains a list of matching documents. This method is used in conjunction with the new R5 Domain Catalog.

- GetFirstProfileDoc—Provides a handle to the first profile document in the database.

- GetNextProfileDoc—Provides a handle to the next profile document in the database.

One method has been enhanced: the GetURLHeaderInfo, which now converts all dashes to underscores.

Additions to the NotesDocument Class

The new properties in the NotesDocument class provides additional information about the state of a document.

- FolderReferences—Returns the universal ID (UNID) for the folders that this document resides in. This will only work if the database contains the $FolderRef and $FolderRefInfo hidden views in it.

- IsDeleted—With the new Soft Delete database property comes the ability to delete and undelete documents. The IsDeleted property is the way to get a handle on the deletion state of the document.

- IsValid—Determines whether a document exists or is a deletion stub.

- FTSearchScore—Provides the percentage value of the full-text search score for a document returned from a Full Text Search Query.

Additions to the `NotesDocumentCollection` Class

The `NotesDocumentCollection` now has the ability to add to and delete documents from the document collection.

- `AddDocument`—Adds a new document to the document collection
- `DeleteDocument`—Removes a document from the document collection
- `GetDocument`—Gets a specific document from the document collection

There is one enhanced method in the Document class. `RemoveAll` has been added as a way to delete all the documents within a collection.

Changes to the `NotesName` Class

The enhancements to the `NotesName` class are all for the `lotus.domino` package in support of IIOP. These enhancements provide for the analysis of Web mail addressing and language requirements.

The New `NotesOutline` Class

The `NotesOutline` Class is new in R5. It contains three properties that enable access to the Alias, Name, and Comment for the Outline. The methods available provide access to existing outline entries as well as the ability to move, create and delete entries.

The New `NotesOutlineEntry` Class

The `NotesOutlineEntry` class is new in R5. It provides access to the individual entries within an outline. The methods provided allow the entries to have the action of the entry changed through script.

Changes to the `NotesRegistration` Class

There is only one change in this class and that is an additional parameter for the `RegisterNewUser` property. It now takes an optional parameter `UserType` that determines the type of Notes Client the user will be registered with.

The New `NotesReplication` Class

This new class in R5 has some great applications. By providing access to modify the replication properties of a database, you can now programmatically turn off replication

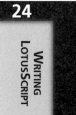

24

WRITING
LOTUSSCRIPT

while performing a particular routine. For instance, say you have a monthly agent that refreshes all the documents in the database and you would prefer that replication not happen until the agent is finished running. You can now use the `Disabled` property to turn off replication at the beginning of the agent and turn it back on at the end of the agent.

Changes to the `NotesRichTextItem` Class

There is one modified property for the `NotesRichTextItem`. `AppendDocLink` includes a new parameter for specifying text for the hotspot link.

There are also two new methods available for a `NotesRichTextItem`. These are

- `AddPageBreak`—Provides a method for placing a page break within the Rich Text Item
- `AppendParagraphStyle`—Provides a method for placing the properties defined in the new `NotesRichText ParagraphStyle` class within a Rich Text Item

The New `NotesRichTextParagraphStyle` Class

The `NotesRichTextParagraphStyle` class provides the ability to set the properties for a paragraph and apply them to a paragraph in a rich-text field.

Changes to the `NotesRichTextStyle` Class

There is one new property for the `NotesRichTextStyle` class: The `PassThruHTML` property provides the ability to set or get the value of this property for manipulating the rich text for a Web or Notes client.

The New `NotesRichTextTab` Class

This new class allows setting of the tabs in a rich-text field.

Additions to the `NotesSession` Class

The `NotesSession` class has two new properties available.

- `NotesBuildVersion`—Returns the number of the Notes build (client)
- `UserNameList`—Returns the primary and alternative names for the current user session

Two new methods are available:

- `CreateName`—Creates a `NotesName` object
- `CreateRichTextParagraphStyle`—Creates a new object that represents a `RichTextParagraphStyle`

Additions to the `NotesUIDatabase` Class

There is one new method and one enhanced method for the `NotsUIDatabase` class:

- `OpenNavigator`—Opens a specific navigator
- `OpenView`—Contains two new parameters that define the keystring and whether it should create a new instance of the view

Two new events are available in R5:

- `PostDragDrop`—This event is triggered after the drag/drop. It can also control whether the drag/drop is completed.
- `QueryDragDrop`—This event is triggered by the occurrence of the drag/drop.

Additions to the `NotesUIDocument` Class

Five new methods are available for the `NotesUIDocument` class:

- `FindFreeTimeDialogEx`—This is the same as the `FindFreeTimeDialog`, but the parameters are all string arrays, which allows multiple entries.
- `FindString`—Allows a test string look up on a field.
- `GetSelectedText`—Provides a way to get the text that has been highlighted on screen.
- `Import`—Imports the associated file into the current field of the UI document.
- `SpellCheck`—Invokes the spell checker and spell-checks the current document.

There is one new event in the `NotesUIDocument` class: The `PostSave` event provides the ability to cause the code to execute after the document has been saved.

Additions to the `NotesUIView` Class

The `NotesUIView` class has one new property and one new method. The new property is the `CaretCategory`, which provides the value of the current category.

The new method is the `Print` method, which invokes the print command for the current document.

Additions to the `NotesUIWorkspace` Class

There are two new properties to the UI Workspace.

- `CurrentDatabase`—Provides access to the current database through the UI
- `CurrentView`—Provides access to the view currently open in the UI

Ten new methods are available in the `NotesUIWorkspace` class:

- `Folder`—Moves the current document to a folder.
- `GetListofTunes`—Provides a list of the available sounds on the workstation.
- `OpenFileDialog`—Displays the Open File dialog box
- `PickListCollection`—Provides the same picklist dialog box that is displayed through the `@picklist` function.
- `PickListStrings`—Provides a picklist that displays names, rooms, resources, or a custom list and returns a string array instead of one entry.
- `PlayTune`—Provides a method to play a tune at an appropriate point in the script.
- `Prompt`—Works like the `@Prompt` command.
- `RefreshParentNote`—Works in conjunction with the values entered in a dialog box. Used in the `QueryClose` event.
- `SaveFileDialog`—Accesses the File Save dialog box and displays the information you provide.
- `SetCurrentLocation`—Provides a method to change the current location for the workstation.

Additions to the `NotesView` Class

The `NotesView` class includes eleven new properties in R5:

- `BackgroundColor`—Returns the background color for a view.
- `ColumnCount`—Returns the number of columns in a view.
- `GetAllEntries`—Creates a `NotesViewEntryCollection`.
- `HeaderLines`—Returns the number of lines that are in the header for the view.
- `IsCategorized`—Returns a Boolean value representing whether the view is categorized.
- `IsConflict`—This is used with calendar views and returns whether the view is enabled for conflict checking.
- `IsHierarchical`—Returns a Boolean value that represents whether the view is set to show response documents in a hierarchy.

- IsModified—Returns a Boolean value that represents whether the view is modified.

- RowLines—Returns the number of lines that are to be displayed for each row in a view.

- Spacing—Returns the spacing value between the rows of a view.

- TopLevelEntryCount—Returns the number of top-level entries in a view.

There are seven new methods available in the NotesView class:

- CreateViewNav—Creates a view navigator that contains all the entries in a view

- CreateViewNavFrom—Creates a view navigator from the designated document on through the rest of the view

- CreateViewNavFromCategory—Creates a view navigator that includes all the documents in the specified category

- CreateViewNavFromChildren—Creates a view navigator that includes all the children for a specific entry

- CreateViewNavFromDescendants—Creates a view navigator that includes all the descendants for a specific entry

- GetAllEntriesByKey—Creates a view navigator that includes all documents that match the specified key within a view column

- GetEntryByKey—Returns the first document that matches the specified key within a view column

Additions to the NotesViewColumn Class

The NotesViewColumn class has many new properties associated with it. These allow you to do such things as set the font for a column, determine whether the contents of the column are the value of a field, and so on.

The New NotesViewEntry Class

This new class provides information about individual rows in a view. The view entry represents the view information, not the document information; therefore, the properties represent things such as ColumnValues, Document, and IndentLevel.

The New NotesViewEntryCollection Class

This new class returns a document collection from a NotesViewNavigator. This collection can be manipulated in the same ways that the NotesDocumentCollection class can.

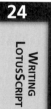

The difference between these two classes is that the NotesViewEntryCollection class is returned in sorted order based on the view sort as shown in Listing 24.19. You can also specify a subset of the view using the GetAllEntriesByKey method. This is a major improvement over a NotesDocumentCollection that does not provide any sort capability.

Listing 24.19   Specifying A ViewEntry Collection

```
Dim session As New NotesSession
Dim db As NotesDatabase
Dim view As NotesView
Dim vc As NotesViewEntryCollection
Set db = session.CurrentDatabase
Set view = db.GetView("By Category")
Set vc = view.GetAllEntriesByKey("Baseball")
Call vc.PutAllInFolder("Sports")
```

The New NotesViewNavigator Class

This is a new class for R5. Although you have had access to the view object through the NotesView class, the NotesViewNavigator class gives you the ability to get information about the view entry as shown in Listing 24.20, as opposed to getting information about the document represented by the view entry returned by the NotesView class. This provides information such as the categories and totals in a view.

Listing 24.20   Creating a ViewNavigator

```
Dim session As New NotesSession
Dim db As NotesDatabase
Dim view As NotesView
Dim Ventry1 As NotesViewEntry
Dim Ventry2 As NotesViewEntry
Dim Vnav As NotesViewNavigator
Dim doc As NotesDocument
Set db = session.CurrentDatabase
Set view = db.GetView("By Category")
Set Vnav = view.CreateViewNav
Set Ventry1 = nav.GetLastDocument
Set Ventry2 = nav.GetPrevDocument(Ventry1)
Set doc = entryB.Document
Call doc.PutInFolder("Y3k Project")
```

Summary

This chapter took the LotusScript fundamentals from Chapter 22, "Introduction to LotusScript," and the Domino classes from Chapter 23, "Basic LotusScript," and tied them into functional examples of LotusScript within Domino. I've also provided coverage of the new and enhanced classes in Release 5. You've learned about using LotusScript in buttons, forms, and fields, and for creating agents to implement significant automation functionality into your applications. You learned how to use ODBC to pull data from and push data to a non-Domino data source and manipulate that data. You also learned what all the new LotusScript classes, properties, and methods are and where you might use them.

With the foundations you built through Chapters 22 and 23, and the examples you've followed along within this chapter, you're well on your way to becoming a LotusScript pro! You'll find it frustrating at times, tedious at others, but always challenging.

Introduction to JavaScript

by Douglas Faulkner

Over the wall of my cubicle, I heard the courseware sales person say, "You will need to take the JavaScript course after taking the LotusScript and Java courses. JavaScript is a combination of the two." I have never been fond or trusting of salesmen but these words were spoken by a misguided co-worker and I might end up with that student in one of my classes!

Why should you read this chapter and the other two JavaScript chapters that follow it? Why should you pay any attention to JavaScript at all? The answer is simple. If you are developing Domino Web applications and you want to make them more efficient, intuitive, and dynamic, you need JavaScript. If you want to develop Domino applications that function the same way with a Web browser as they do with a Notes client, use JavaScript. You can write code once to validate fields on the Web client and Notes client before they are sent back to the server. You can launch a pop-up navigator, simulate dialog boxes, perform local calculations, provide field-level help, or set cookies. To make your Web application shine, you need JavaScript, and in Domino Release 5 your JavaScript code will work with the Notes client.

The Notes client in Release 5 understands JavaScript objects. You should understand these objects as well so that your Notes applications can be coded once and provide the same functions to a Web browser as to your Notes client users. Understanding and using JavaScript objects is the focus of this chapter.

This chapter covers the basics of understanding and using JavaScript. My goal is to get you started with a firm understanding of how the language works, and how it works with Domino. When you have this foundation, you can combine it with many of the detailed reference books on the JavaScript language or check out the Netscape Web site that explains the language and provide a good reference for you. The URL for this site is the following:

```
http://developer.netscape.com/docs/manuals/
```

Understanding JavaScript

Whereas LotusScript works with Domino objects, JavaScript works with Web browser objects. In fact, JavaScript is more closely associated with HTML than either of its namesakes. JavaScript was developed as an extension to HTML to help provide more interactive and dynamic Web applications.

JavaScript is an object-oriented programming language. It enables the developer to create scripts that are interpreted (parsed and run) by a client. As a scripting language, JavaScript works within an existing environment to enable programmed manipulation and automation of the objects in that environment. The Web browser or Notes client provides the environment. JavaScript is the tool to easily change and work with those environments. You need to understand two key concepts: JavaScript is object-oriented and JavaScript code is run by the client. The bonus attached to these two concepts is that your coding controls

- The look and feel of the page
- The results of user actions
- The efficiency of conversation to the server

Because JavaScript works with both the Notes client and a Web browser client, throughout this chapter I will use the term "the client" to refer to both.

JavaScript Versus the Notes Formula Language

JavaScript enables tasks to be performed on the client rather than on the Domino Server. The client performs all JavaScript processing so it does not pass the burden of that processing on to the server. For example, you can use JavaScript to preprocess the values on a form before the document is submitted to the server. A user can enter a value and move the cursor to the next field. Moving the cursor is an event, and it can start your JavaScript code that evaluates what was entered in the field.

In Notes Release 4 you coded field validation with input validation formulas on the Notes form using the macro Formula language. Input validation formulas require the client to submit the document, the Domino server to perform the evaluation, and the Domino server to return an error message to the client. Performing processing on the client gains greater efficiency and a more dynamic Web page. Using JavaScript, the field is evaluated by the client on the spot through your JavaScript code! No response is needed from the server. You get an immediate evaluation on the client because the browser runs the JavaScript code.

Other uses for JavaScript in your application include

- Providing dialog boxes to alert the client that a field entry did not pass validation.
- Displaying a dialog box to prompt for a new entry.
- Performing immediate calculations on the form, such as totals and taxes.
- Setting a cookie containing a value for later retrieval.

> **The History of JavaScript**
>
> JavaScript was developed by Netscape Communications for the release of Netscape Navigator 2.0. It was originally called LiveScript. When Sun Microsystems partnered with Netscape, the name was changed to JavaScript. The goal of the two partners was to enhance the capabilities of HTML. As you will see, JavaScript code is encoded directly within HTML pages. HTML is a static presentation language. When the browser loads the page, there is no facility to perform actions, such as changing colors or evaluating user activity. JavaScript is a dynamic answer to the HTML static limitation.

Browser Variations and Settings Affect JavaScript

Because JavaScript is an interpreted language, a Web browser must interpret it when it is included on a page. Before that can happen, the browser must be able to deal with it.

Most browsers have a property setting to disable or enable JavaScript. However, earlier versions of browsers might not know how to deal with JavaScript at all. You can hide your JavaScript code from browsers that can't deal with it by interrogating the browser version.

JavaScript is evolving. Table 25.1 provides a list of browser versions and the JavaScript levels they support.

TABLE 25.1   JavaScript Support of Various Web Browsers

Browser	*JavaScript Version*
Netscape Navigator 2.0	JavaScript version 1.0
Netscape Navigator 3.0	JavaScript 1.0 and 1.1
Netscape Navigator 4.0	JavaScript 1.0, 1.1, and 1.2
Microsoft Internet Explorer 3.0	JavaScript 1.0
Microsoft Internet Explorer 4.0	JavaScript 1.2 and ECMA-262

Each version release has added new methods and properties to work with. The history of JavaScript versions and browser support might seem confusing, but there are standards and there is a potential for future clarity. ECMA, an organization dedicated to international standards, put JavaScript on its fast track for standards creation. The first set of standards for JavaScript was released in April of 1997 and approved one month later. The most recent standard was released in June of 1998. ECMA has published the following document of JavaScript standards:

Standard ECMA-262 ECMAScript Language Specification for JavaScript

The Microsoft Version of JavaScript

Microsoft developed its own compatible version of JavaScript, called JScript. Version 5.0 is available as of this writing. Microsoft JScript is an implementation of ECMA-262, but it also includes enhancements that only work with Microsoft's Internet Explorer.

As JavaScript evolves, it is becoming more robust. A third edition of the JavaScript standard will probably be released at the end of 1999. It will include improved methods to interface with the user, more ways to work with text entries, and tools for international applications. You can download a copy of the JavaScript specifications document from the ECMA Web site at `http://www.ECMA.ch`.

Domino Release 5.0 supports the ECMA-262 standard as does Internet Explorer 4. Netscape 4.0 is not fully compliant with the standard.

CGI Variables

Common Gateway Interface (CGI) is a standard to interface applications with an HTTP server. CGI programs on an HTTP server provide a limited amount of user interactivity, such as providing capabilities for imagemaps that link to a new URL, and provide the capability to gather information from a submitted page. Although JavaScript was not developed to replace the capabilities of CGI, it does provide an easier way to accomplish the same results and create a more dynamic page. Using CGI alone, nothing happens on the Web page until the user clicks the Submit button. Information is then returned to the server and a response can be created to return to the Web client.

CGI uses a number of variables to pass values back to the server. Some of these variables are available as properties in the JavaScript Location object.

25

INTRODUCTION TO JAVASCRIPT

Integrating JavaScript with Other Tools

JavaScript programs can pass information to Java applets through plug-ins. Plug-ins are software modules that integrate into a browser giving it greater functionality. For example, LiveConnect is a plug-in that enables JavaScript to communicate with Java applets on the same page. When the browser has enabled both JavaScript and LiveConnect, your JavaScript code can access and modify properties and start Java applet components. Similarly, Java code can access JavaScript methods and properties through LiveConnect. For example, after a user makes a field entry, you can use JavaScript and LiveConnect to set a variable or property in an applet and invoke a redraw method in the applet. LiveConnect is supported in Netscape 3.0 and Notes R5 clients. Internet Explorer uses ActiveX scripting to interact with Java applets.

Protecting the Client

Web browsers adhere to the "Same Origin" policy. That policy states that when a browser loads a document from a different origin (some location other than your local PC), the document can't get or set the properties of the browser. In other words, your JavaScript code can't access the client directory, session histories, or other private information. Nor can it delete files, write to files, or set a virus on the client.

JavaScript can write to the browser window, change the properties settings of the window, or spawn other windows. JavaScript can also access from the browser only as much as CGI variables provide information about the type of browser that the client is using or about the IP address of the client. For example, information about the client's email address and password can't be secretly captured and returned to the server without the user's knowledge.

Cookies

Cookies are small amounts of data that are stored by the Web browser and associated with a particular Web page. Cookie data can be transmitted to and from the server via your JavaScript code. Each time a browser connects to your Web page, your JavaScript code can check to see whether a cookie was set on the browser from a previous visit. Functionally, a cookie operates as a kind of environment variable specific to this user at this site. As with other environment variables, you can't always count on the data value being available or stable from one session to another. The user might have deleted the cookie file or might be using different browser software on succeeding visits.

One of the optional settings on a browser allows you to decide to accept cookies and, if you accept them, whether to show an alert before accepting the cookie. Web users might wonder why they ever want to allow cookies set on their machines. Some Web sites use cookies as an intermediate place to store data that must be available to a succeeding page at the site. Other Web-based applications use cookies to store your preferences so that when you return to the site you will receive information based on your needs.

Because JavaScript can work with cookies, you need to be aware of what cookies can and can't do.

- A cookie is not an executable file; it is simply a text string.
- A cookie can't retrieve any information from the client's file system.
- Cookies can only be retrieved by the domain and server URL that originated them.
- Cookies can contain an expiration date. If there is no date, the cookie is deleted at the end of the browser session. If there is an expiration date and the date is passed, the cookie becomes unavailable.

Your JavaScript code can write a cookie, but because the stored data is basically unprotected, a cookie is not a good place to write passwords, login IDs, or any other sensitive information.

JavaScript Code Is Available to All

Most Web browsers enable the user to view the source code of the document delivered to the browser. The view includes HTML as well as any JavaScript code you added to your page. The end result is that any and all of your JavaScript code can be investigated, reviewed, or copied. Of course on the flip side, just as your code can't be hidden, you can investigate and learn from the JavaScript code of other Web pages. This is a great way to find examples of code and learn from Web sites that perform a task you want to apply to your site. While looking at JavaScript code you can see header comments such as the following to deter you from using it:

```
// Written by So and So
// All rights reserved
// Do not copy
```

These lines of comments remind you of the moral dilemma in copying the sweat and toil of other programmers. In the end, though, we all share each other's efforts. All JavaScript is freeware, whether you want it shared or not.

25

INTRODUCTION TO
JAVASCRIPT

Understanding the JavaScript Object Hierarchy

If you have used LotusScript or you have read Chapter 22, "Introduction to LotusScript," in this book, you know about objects and object class structure. You know that a Notes database is an object and that a Notes form, a view, an agent, and all the entities that make up a Domino application are also objects. Some of these objects contain other objects. For example, a Notes form can contain a button object, a field object, or a text object. A rich-text field can contain a spreadsheet object embedded within it.

JavaScript uses objects as well. You can compare the JavaScript structure to real-world physical objects to understand the concept of object properties, which are methods that can be applied to objects.

You can look at objects in the physical world and describe them. For example, suppose that a shoebox is white and rectangular. With a paintbrush, you can change the shoebox color to black. It is still a shoebox, but it is now black. Take the lid off and open the shoebox. It might contain two shoes, which are other objects.

In the shoebox illustration, I listed things that occurred with the shoebox: Its color was changed and it was opened. Looking at the color of the shoebox is looking at the value of the property known as "color". The shoebox color property of "white" has changed to black.

Opening the lid of the box to see what it contains is something you can do with a shoebox. That is the open method. I could continue with this analogy by showing that the shoes have properties (color, size) and methods (put on foot), contain other objects (laces), and so on.

JavaScript Objects

While working in JavaScript you might not be working with physical objects such as shoeboxes, but you are working with an electronically defined object. JavaScript objects can be abstract representations, but as you work with them, if you think of a physical entity, the concept of properties, methods, and containment makes intuitive sense. Add to this understanding the structure of JavaScript objects and syntax rules of the language and you are on your way to coding in JavaScript.

The beginning object for JavaScript is the `Window` object. The `Window` object is the container that forms the base of the hierarchy of objects. Just as a shoebox contains shoes and shoes contain laces, the JavaScript `Window` object can contain a `Document` object and the Document can contain a Link object. The objects-within-objects containment does not go on indefinitely. JavaScript is made up of four layers of containment starting at the Window. Table 25.2 gives you a description of the Window object.

TABLE 25.2 Window Object

Object	Description and Use
Window	The browser window. It is considered the "global object" because all expressions are evaluated in the window context.
	Use the Window object to manipulate the window settings or perform dialog with the user.

As you see in Table 25.3, the Window object contains five objects. Of these, the Document object and Navigator object are containers of other objects.

TABLE 25.3 Objects Contained in the Window

Object	Description and Use
Frame	A frame is a type of Window object. The frames property of Window is an array of frame objects that you can reference.
Location	A reference to the URL of the document.
	Use the Location object to find browser and browser version information.
History	An array of URLs in the browsing history. Security restrictions make these inaccessible.
	Use the History object to move backward or forward in the cache of pages.
Navigator	Information about the Web browser.
	Use the Navigator to determine the browser name, version, and user platform.
Document	A reference to the HTML document displayed in the window.
	Use the Document object to dynamically change the background color or to write information to the page.

In the Document object, the Form is a container of the fourth layer of objects, which you will learn about later in this chapter. Table 25.4 shows the objects contained within a Document.

25

INTRODUCTION TO JAVASCRIPT

TABLE 25.4   Objects Contained in the Document

Object	Description and Use
Layer	Represents an element that is independently positioned, similar to a separate window.
Link	The URL reference to hypertext links on the document.
Image	In the document object, Image is an array of images embedded in a document with the HTML tag <IMG>.
Area	An area of an image, such as an imagemap.
Anchor	An array of objects that reference each named location on the HTML document.
Applet	An array of objects that reference Java programs embedded on the document.
Plugin	An array of MIME-type objects each with an element for each MIME type supported by the plug-in.
Form	An array of HTML form objects.
	Use Form to work with field values, text, selection lists, or buttons.

Capturing User Activity with Events

Events are happenings or actions that you can anticipate will occur in your application as the result of something the user does. Each object has events associated with it. When a Web user moves the mouse over a graphic or clicks a Submit button for example, an event occurs. When the Web user changes the value in a field, an event also occurs.

As a developer, you can write JavaScript instructions that start when an event occurs. Started by an event, JavaScript code can read or modify the properties of the Window objects and any objects contained in the Window object. For instance, notice that Frame is an object contained within the Window object. Because Frame is contained in the Window, JavaScript code can work with any Frame that is currently on the desktop. When an event starts the JavaScript code, you can modify properties such as document background color. You can capture field values and change them. You can also perform any methods available with an object. For instance, the Window object has an alert method that enables you to display a message in a dialog box.

An Example of Coding the Object Hierarchy

Now I will show you some simple examples to help you learn more about JavaScript objects, properties, and methods, and to learn how to access objects contained in objects.

To keep the example simple, JavaScript code is added directly on a Notes form. The code will be marked as Pass-Thru HTML as in Release 4.6. Later in this chapter, I will look at Domino R5 form events and when you use them for JavaScript code.

Look at the Notes form and the JavaScript code in Figure 25.1.

FIGURE 25.1

You can use the Window *object* defaultStatus *property to change the status bar.*

The three lines that start with <SCRIPT and end with </SCRIPT> have the text property "Pass-Thru HTML". When I look at this form in a browser, I see the words "Display this footer on the status bar…" on the browser status bar.

Why is this? One of the properties of the Window object is defaultStatus. Giving defaultStatus a value changes the window and therefore changes what the user sees. Notice that I do not have to set the Window object or declare a variable to hold the Window object. When a Web page with JavaScript is loaded, the Window object is built and available globally. It is already open and becomes the default base object. Because it is the default, I can get the same results with the following code (the object reference is assumed to be the Window):

```
<SCRIPT LANGUAGE="JAVASCRIPT">
defaultStatus = "Display this footer on the status bar..."
</SCRIPT>
```

Rather than leave the defaultStatus property without an object reference, I can also use the JavaScript keyword this. The keyword this refers to itself, the current object, which is the Window object in the following example:

```
<SCRIPT LANGUAGE="JAVASCRIPT">
this.defaultStatus = "Display this footer on the status bar..."
</SCRIPT>
```

> ### Case Sensitive
>
> If you are testing this code yourself, you will quickly see that JavaScript code is case sensitive. `defaultstatus` will not work; it must be typed as `defaultStatus`.

Suppose that you also want to set the background color of the document. As you saw earlier, the `Document` object is contained within the `Window` object. Using dot notation, I can drill down the `Document` object to one of its properties and set its value as in the following example:

```
this.document.bgColor = 'khaki'
```

Or I could write the following code because `Window` is assumed:

```
document.bgColor = 'khaki'
```

Using an Object Method

The previous examples showed how to modify a JavaScript `Window` property. As another example, I use one of the `Window` methods available to us. The `alert` method creates a pop-up message box from the `Window` object. It is coded as follows:

```
window.alert("We make 'em big.")
```

Previous examples show how I use the dot notation to point from the `Window` to a `Document` to a `Document` property. Using a `Document` method, I can capture the current date and time and add it to the form. I can do so with the following code:

```
window.document.write(Date())
```

Exploring Document Objects

The object hierarchy tables (Tables 25.2, 25.3, and 25.4) illustrate the first three tiers of JavaScript objects. To complete the JavaScript object model, Table 25.5 shows the objects contained within the `Form` object. Of all the objects contained in a `Document`, only the `Form` object is a container for other objects.

TABLE 25.5   Objects Contained in the Form

Object	Description and Use
`textarea`	A multiline input test area.
`text`	The input test area on a form.
`fileUpload`	An area that lets the user supply a file as input.

Object	Description and Use
password	A field that hides its value as the user types by displaying asterisks.
hidden	A text object hidden from display.
submit	A Submit button on the form.
reset	A Reset button that set all elements to the default.
radio	A radio button or set of buttons.
checkbox	A toggle button that lets the user select On or Off.
button	A push-button object.
select	A drop-down list that enables the user to choose one or more items.

In the following example, the Form object sets a field value on the form.

```
This.document.forms[0].Comments.value = "Enter your name here"
```

Notice how I move through four JavaScript objects: the Window, Document, Form, and Text objects. In this example, a field name is being referenced as a Text object. The Text object has a value property that is being used to set the field with the words "Enter your name here".

Figures 25.2 and 25.3 show the complete form and the Web page it produces.

FIGURE 25.2

JavaScript code reflects the browser window hierarchy.

FIGURE 25.3

This page is the result of Domino and JavaScript.

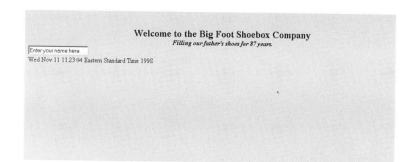

Using HTML Language Tags

JavaScript code is embedded within HTML. HTML is constructed in a series of tags that indicate to a browser what to do with the text between the tags. Consider the following HTML code:

```
<B> State Capitals </B>
```

The HTML tag `<B>` tells the browser to display "State Capitals" in boldfaced type. Similarly, you use an HTML tag to inform the browser that the subsequent lines are JavaScript.

HTML tags that surround JavaScript code are called *language tags*. The HTML language tags `<SCRIPT>` and `</SCRIPT>` tell the browser that a scripting language is declared and code instructions follow the declaration. To use JavaScript in Notes Release 4.0 through 4.5, you needed to enter the HTML language tags directly on the form. Your JavaScript code was contained between the HTML language tags, as in the following example:

```
<SCRIPT LANGUAGE = "JavaScript">
function FieldValidation()
</SCRIPT>
```

All the lines were marked as Pass-Thru HTML.

With Domino Release 4.0 through 4.5, you had to use JavaScript if you wanted more buttons on a form than the single Submit button.

With Release 4.6 each database includes the property "Web access: Use JavaScript when generating pages". Selecting this property told the Domino server to go ahead and create JavaScript code while it turned your Domino document into HTML. Selecting this property enabled you to add multiple buttons to your Domino Web document rather than being limited to a single Submit button. By selecting the Web access property you told the Domino HTTP server to create a `<SCRIPT> LANGUAGE` tag and to generate the necessary JavaScript code to display multiple buttons.

The property "Web access: Use JavaScriptwhen generating pages" remains the same in Domino Release 5. A table in the Release 5 Help database shows which @Functions are translated into JavaScript when this property is selected or not selected.

Domino R5 uses JavaScript natively. Not only does a Notes client understand JavaScript, but the tools for designing applications integrates JavaScript.

Including JavaScript Code in Domino Applications

Domino Release 5 features an Integrated Development Environment (IDE) enabling developers to easily code JavaScript. In Domino 4.x, you included your JavaScript code on the form within HTML tags. In Domino 5, the IDE provides JavaScript events where you can place your code. You do not need to worry about language tags. Because your JavaScript will be recognized by the Notes client as well as Web browsers, you do not have to create separate forms and code for applications used by both Notes clients and Web browsers. Another plus is that you can code for JavaScript events, such as onMouseOver, that were unavailable in previous versions of Notes.

The Domino IDE for Release 5 includes an objects infolist showing the objects on the form. A drop-down list of the available events for each object is provided. The interface is similar to the one included in Release 4.x. What is new is the inclusion of JavaScript events for form objects. When you choose a JavaScript event, the formula window is open to accept your JavaScript code. As you expect, some events can be coded only with the Formula language (window title), some events can be coded only with LotusScript (field exit), some are only JavaScript (onMouseOut), and some events can hold either LotusScript or the Formula language (such as PostOpen). Refer to Chapter 8, "The Integrated Development Environment," for detailed use of the IDE.

The form- and page-level JavaScript events available to the user are listed in Table 25.6.

TABLE 25.6 JavaScript Form and Page Events Available to Notes Designer

Event	When It Occurs
JSHeader	Put code here that will be executed while the HTML document is being displayed. Use this to set properties for the document.
onBlur	The user moves focus from the form.
onClick	The user clicks a link, an element, or any object on the form.
onDblClick	The user double-clicks a link, an element, or any object on the form.
onFocus	The user enters the form.
onHelp	The user presses F1.
onKeyDown	The user presses a key.
onKeyPress	A key is pressed and released by the user, resulting in a combination of onKeyDown and onKeyUp.
onKeyUp	The user releases a key.

continues

TABLE 25.6   continued

Event	When It Occurs
onLoad	A Web page is loaded. (Similar to PostOpen in LotusScript.)
onMouseDown	The user presses the mouse button.
onMouseMove	The cursor is moved.
onMouseOut	The user moves the mouse off the form or page.
onMouseOver	The user moves the mouse over the form or page. This is not a Page event.
onMouseUp	The user releases the mouse button.
onReset	The user uses the reset button. This is not a Page event.
onSubmit	The user submits the form. This event occurs before the form is saved. This is not a Page event.
onUnload	The current Web page is cleared.

Field-level, Action, and button hotspot JavaScript events are shown in Table 25.7.

TABLE 25.7   JavaScript Action Events

Event	When It Occurs
onClick	User clicks on a button.
onDblClick	The user double-clicks a link or element.
onChange	User changes the content of a field, generally, a keyword change.
onBlur	User leaves a field or object.
onFocus	User enters a field or object.
onKeyDown	The user presses a key.
onKeyPress	A key is pressed and released by the user resulting in a combination of onKeyDown and onKeyUp.
onKeyUp	The user releases a key.
onMouseDown	The user presses the mouse button.
onMouseMove	The cursor is moved to the field or object.
onMouseOut	The user moves the mouse off a link or clickable area.
onMouseOver	The user moves the mouse over a field or object.
onMouseUp	The user releases the mouse button.
onSelect	The user selects the field.

Add JavaScript Code to Domino Forms

To demonstrate the logistics of where your code goes, how easy it is, and to review the object hierarchy, I will show you how to enter some JavaScript on an application. The goal of the JavaScript code is to copy the entry from a dialog box and put that value in another field.

Open the form in Domino Designer. In this example, the form will have two fields: a keyword field labeled `Region` and a text field labeled `RegionDisplay`.

In the Designer, select the field `Region`. You can choose Formula language events marked with a diamond icon (such as Default Value), LotusScript events (such as Exiting), and JavaScript events, marked with a circle icon. Notice the choices in Figure 25.4.

FIGURE 25.4

Choose the appropriate field event.

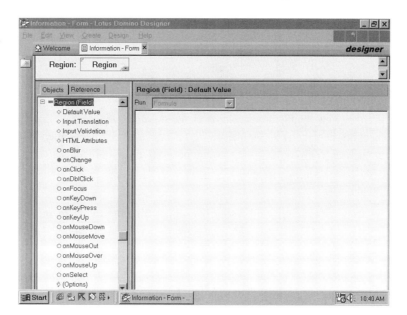

When I choose the event `onChange`, the Design Pane enables entry of JavaScript. Because the Design Pane is expecting JavaScript code, I do not need special formatting or markings around the code.

```
this.form.RegionDisplay.value=this.form.Region.options[this.form.Region.
➥selectedIndex].text;
```

That's all there is to it! If I wanted to send the `Region` value to a second field, I would simply add a second line of JavaScript code. The first line can be ended with an optional semicolon if your habits were formed in the Notes Formula language. Figure 25.5 shows the JavaScript code in place on the form.

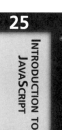

25

INTRODUCTION TO JAVASCRIPT

FIGURE 25.5

The onChange
event with
JavaScript to set
RegionDisplay.

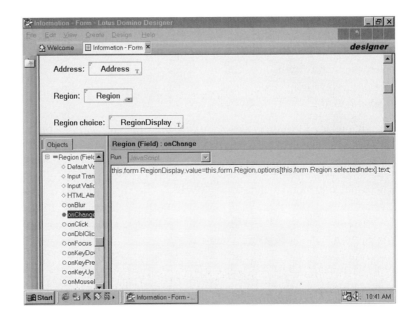

Let me review the hierarchy. The `this` refers to this document. I then point to the form object on the document. On that form, I access a field object called `RegionDisplay` and I am moving a new value into the value property of that object. The new value is taken from the `Region` field on the same form. Do not be concerned about the syntax in the example.

I have shown examples of JavaScript events relating to the form and to fields. In Domino Release 5, JavaScript code can be assigned to events for Actions, button hotspots, and action hotspots as well.

Notes Client Support for JavaScript Events

The Notes client does not support all JavaScript events. The example you saw earlier performs well in Internet Explorer or Netscape, but it does not work for the Notes client. Move the code to the `onBlur` event, and it works for both a Web browser and a Notes Client. The Notes Help database provides a table of what clients support the various JavaScript events.

When writing JavaScript code for objects that are unavailable to the Notes client, add that code to the HTML Body Attributes event. For instance, the event `onResize` isn't available in Domino Designer and doesn't appear on the event lists. It can, however, be used in the HTML Body Attributes event.

Code can continue to be written directly on the form as it was in Release 4.6 by marking it as Pass-Thru HTML. However, in Release 5, you must also hide that code from the Notes client or it will appear as text on the form.

Notes Help Database

The Help database provides some JavaScript help, but it does not include help for all JavaScript objects, events, and methods. Help includes a table of Domino objects showing which coding language is supported for which objects. There is also a table of JavaScript events and a listing of browsers that support those events. The table also includes the Notes client and the Notes browser in the support list.

Throughout the Help database are examples of JavaScript code and references to JavaScript whenever it is applicable.

New Design Synopsis Options

In Domino Release 5, a database design synopsis can include JavaScript code as well as HTML code. When you create a synopsis, checkboxes allow the choice of LotusScript and JavaScript to be included in the design report.

Summary

You have learned some background information about JavaScript, and you should have an overview of the structure and placement of JavaScript code in your Notes applications. You know that JavaScript is now a native language to Notes and can enhance your applications for both Web browsers and Notes clients. JavaScript can

- Reduce send and receive "talk" between the Web client and the Domino server.
- Mimic Notes features, such as dialog boxes or user help.
- Perform calculations for the client so she can visually verify the result before she submits.
- Direct the browser to a different page based on the browser or the user's interest.
- Give immediate verification responses to the user.

Now you are ready to learn the language syntax and rules. You are ready to follow examples of JavaScript code within a Domino application.

25

INTRODUCTION TO JAVASCRIPT

Introduction to Java

by Timothy Falconer

CHAPTER 26

You can do quite a lot with Java, whether or not you're using Notes. Introduced by Sun Microsystems in May 1995, Java quickly attracted widespread attention from both pundits and programmers and has since featured prominently in the strategies of most major software companies, particularly Lotus and IBM.

There's no mistaking it—Lotus likes Java. Nowhere is this more evident than in release 5 of Notes and Domino, which includes these new Java features:

- Improved Java development tools in Domino Designer
- Expanded Java access to the Notes Object Interface (NOI)
- Java server add-ins using the `runjava` task
- Remote access to Domino servers and databases from Web browsers and stand-alone applications using Java and CORBA

Before getting into Domino specifics, I'll present a crash course in Java fundamentals, with tips thrown in from my own experience. Because Java is a huge subject in its own right, with dozens of books devoted to it, this chapter is merely an overview of the vast Java terrain. My aim is to provide a foundation for the next two chapters and to give you a taste of the Java language. For a more in-depth treatment, try *Java 2 Platform Unleashed* by Jamie Jaworski.

Understanding Java

Java is primarily known as a general-purpose programming language, much like C++, Pascal, or Smalltalk. As a language, it borrows from C and C++, so much so that you might mistake Java code for C code until you look more closely. This similarity to these popular programming languages is intentional. Sun is hoping that C and C++ programmers will find the switch to Java a pleasant and painless one.

Were Java just a programming language, though, there'd be fewer programmers making the switch. More important is Java's role as a full-fledged computer platform. Java frees programmers from worrying about which computer or operating system their programs can run on, because Java source code is compiled into an Esperanto-like machine language called *bytecode*, which is independent of any computer or operating system.

Java bytecode is executed by special software known as a *Java Virtual Machine (JVM)*. Each JVM insulates Java programs from the idiosyncrasies of individual operating systems, so the same Java bytecode can execute on Windows PCs, Macintoshes, and UNIX workstations. There's a JVM in every Domino server, Notes client, and Web browser. You can also start up your own JVM from the command-line to run standalone Java programs.

Java's capability to run the same program on almost any computer is particularly useful in networks composed of many computer types, such as the Internet. Much of Java's popularity comes from its unique suitability to developing Internet software.

Because Notes and Domino have always been cross-platform products, you might be unimpressed with Java's "run anywhere" magic. But it's just this aspect of Java that makes it the perfect choice for programming in the Domino environment. Java frees your Domino programs from the need to run on computers with Notes or Domino installed. This can be a big administrative win because there's no need to install and configure Notes on each client machine. Also, Java bytecode can be quickly downloaded from a central location each time it runs, ensuring that everyone will use the most current version of your program.

Like other programming languages and platforms, Java includes an extensive library of core classes for making graphical user interfaces and performing common tasks such as file I/O. As you'd expect, the Java API is platform independent, so you can use it to make dialog boxes and menus without regard to the operating system. Java also includes built-in support for multithreading and network communication.

You will find that time spent learning to program Notes with Java will pay handsome and unexpected dividends, both within and beyond the world of Domino. You can choose from dozens of available third-party components and development tools. The language's increasing popularity means that your skills will remain marketable. Using Java also increases your chances at finding skilled programmers to develop and maintain your software, both now and in the future.

But perhaps the best reason to use Java is the language itself. Java has the power and flexibility of C++ and Smalltalk, but with the ease of use you might expect from Visual Basic or LotusScript. Java's designers were somehow able to blend the best from other languages, avoid many of the more common annoyances, and still create a language with a clear expressive elegance that fosters good design and rapid development.

Writing Java Source Code

As with most programming languages, Java source code consists of a sequence of *tokens* separated by *whitespace* characters. Tokens are basic elements of the language, such as keywords, identifiers, literals, and operators. Whitespace characters include spaces, tabs, carriage returns, line feeds, and form feeds. Java compilers consider any sequence of whitespace characters identical to one single space, so you can add all the spaces, tabs, and blank lines you want without changing the logic of your program.

Comments

Comments are also considered whitespace. Comments are helpful descriptions of your code written for humans to read. Like other whitespace, comments are treated the same as a single space character. There are three forms of comments to choose from:

`// comment text`	Everything from the `//` to the next carriage return or line feed is ignored.
`/* comment text */`	Everything between the `/*` and the `*/` is ignored, even if it spans more than one line.
`/** comment text */`	Indicates a *documentation comment* recognized by the javadoc tool.

The first two forms are the same as in C and C++. Use the first if your comment is confined to a single line of code. Use the second if your comment requires multiple lines or if you want to temporarily "comment out" portions of your code. Be careful when putting comments inside other comments, though. Multiple-line comments don't nest.

The last form, the *doc comment*, is new to the Java language. Doc comments are used to document the purpose and public interface of your source code. Put these comments just before each code element you want to describe. You can then use a tool named javadoc to scan your source, and it will automatically create HTML documentation that can be viewed within a Web browser. You can use special tags within a doc comment to indicate the following kinds of information:

`@author`	Classes only. Indicates the author of a class.
`@version`	Classes only. Indicates the version number of the class.
`@param`	Methods only. Describes each parameter of a method.
`@return`	Methods only. Describes what the method returns.
`@exception`	Methods only. Describes each exception thrown by the method.
`@see`	Used to list other related classes, methods, or fields.
`@since`	Indicates the version in which this class, method, or field appeared.
`@deprecated`	Marks this class, method, or field as unsupported in new versions.

Unicode

Another Java innovation is built-in support for the international 16-bit Unicode character set. *Unicode* contains symbols and alphabets from most of the world's written languages.

Nearly all other programming languages use the ubiquitous 7-bit ASCII character set, which contains only symbols and letters used in English and other Western European languages. Java lets you use the full Unicode character set for all identifiers, strings, and comments, so you can use Cyrillic and Telugu variable names as easily as English ones. To get a look at the characters in Unicode, check out `http://charts.unicode.org`.

Because most text editors still use ASCII, Java converts automatically between ASCII text and Unicode text. This means that you can safely ignore Java's Unicode support if you do not need it. If you're using an ASCII editor and want to use a Unicode character, use the Unicode escape sequence `\u`, followed by the four-digit hexadecimal code for the character. For example, use `\u00F6` to represent ö. Unlike other escape sequences, Unicode escape sequences can be used anywhere in your source code.

Identifiers

Identifiers are the names you choose for programming elements. You can choose any sequence of letters, digits, and underscores, provided that you start with a letter or an underscore. Java identifiers can be any length. Java is a case-sensitive language, so `aHead` and `ahead` refer to different variables. You're also restricted from using the following Java keywords and literals as identifiers:

abstract	default	if	private	throw
boolean	do	implements	protected	throws
break	double	import	public	transient
byte	else	instanceof	return	try
case	extends	int	short	void
catch	final	interface	static	volatile
char	finally	long	super	while
class	float	native	switch	true
const	for	new	synchronized	false
continue	goto	package	this	null

Working with Data Types and Variables

Variables are named storage locations in memory. Every variable has a *data type*, which describes the kind of information the variable can hold. Java data types split into two camps: *primitive* types and *object* types. Primitive types describe "atomic" values such as numbers and characters that cannot be broken into smaller pieces. Object types describe composite data objects made up of primitive values and objects references.

Object types are sometimes called *reference types* because each variable declared with an object type contains a reference to an object and not the object itself. Objects are kept in a separate area of memory known as the *heap*. In contrast, variables declared with primitive types contain actual data values and not references.

This is an important distinction in Java. Primitive values are always used directly, whereas objects are always used indirectly via object references. Because no explicit reference or pointer syntax exists in Java, this may confuse programmers familiar with C or C++. It's really very simple. *There are no pointers in Java*. Instead, objects are always used via implicit object references.

Primitive Types

Table 26.1 contains the eight primitive types in Java.

Table 26.1   Primitive Data Types

Type	Description	Range
byte	8-bit integer value	± 127
short	16-bit integer value	± 32,767
int	32-bit integer value	± 2,147,483,647
long	64-bit integer value	± 9,223,372,036,854,775,807
float	32-bit floating-point value	± 3.4 x 10^{38} with 7-digit precision
double	64-bit floating-point value	± 1.7 x 10^{308} with 15-digit precision
char	16-bit Unicode character	Any of 65,536 characters
boolean	Logical truth value	Either true or false

These data types are the same as used in C and C++, with the exception of byte and boolean. There are two other important differences. First, Java specifies the size and range of each numeric type, whereas size and range in C and C++ vary from machine to machine. This was done to help keep Java platform-independent. Second, all characters in Java use the international 16-bit Unicode character set.

Variables are declared by putting the type name first, then the name of the variable, and then a semicolon:

```
int aCarsInLot;
boolean aIsEmpty;
```

These statements declare an integer variable named `aCarsInLot` and a Boolean variable named `aIsEmpty`. You can declare several variables of the same type on a single line by separating the names with commas:

```
int aGoodOnes, aBadOnes, aTotal;
boolean aIsEmpty, aSheLikesMe;
char aFavoriteLetter, aFavoriteDigit;
```

A variable may also be initialized when it's declared:

```
int aYearToRemember = 1996;
boolean aSheLikesMe = true;
float aPrice = 12.50F, aWalletCash = 3.00F,
ÂaLoanFromHer = aPrice - aWalletCash;
```

The convention in Java is to start nonconstant variable names with lowercase letters and to separate words within the same identifier by using capital letters. Constants are declared with the modifier `final` appearing before the type. By convention, names of constants use only capital letters, with words within the name separated by underscores. Here are some examples:

```
float aTemperatureOutside = 60.5;
final float BOILING_POINT_OF_DISTILLED_WATER = 100.0;
final boolean SHE_LOVES_ME = true;
```

Literals

*Literal*s are constant values such as `1996`, `60.5`, and `true`. A literal can be assigned to a variable if the literal is consistent with the variable's data type. The literal object reference `null` is a special value that indicates "no reference" and can be assigned to any object type. Boolean variables can be assigned the literals `true` and `false`.

Variables with one of the four integer types (`byte`, `short`, `int`, and `long`) can be assigned any number without a fraction, such as `33` and `18015`, provided that the value falls within the ranges specified in Table 26.1.

Integer constants are always considered to be of type `int`, but Java's pretty smart about implicitly converting to the other integer types if it can. If an integer constant is too big to fit in your variable, your code won't compile. You can add an `L` to the end of an integer constant to make it long, as in `35L`. You can also add a lowercase `l` to do this, but because `l` looks like the digit `1`, this is a very bad idea. All integer literals are assumed to be decimal numbers, unless they begin with `0x` (hexadecimal) or `0` (octal). The following integer constants are equivalent:

`22, 0x16, 026.`

Variables with one of the floating-point types, `float` and `double`, can be assigned any number, with or without a fraction, provided that its value falls within the ranges specified. Floating-point constants are numbers with either a decimal point or an E within them and are always assumed to be of type `double`. Unfortunately, Java's not as smart about converting floating-point constants. You cannot assign a double constant to a float variable, even if its value is in range. To give a constant the type `float`, add an F to the end of it. The following constants are valid:

`98.6, .314e1, 22E33, 1.06F.`

Character literals are enclosed by single quotes, as in `'Z'`, `'$'`, and `'3'`. You can use any Unicode character as a character constant, either by typing directly if your editor supports it or by using a Unicode escape sequence, such as `\u2668`. You can also use the following escape sequences to represent the indicated special characters:

`\n`	newline or linefeed (`\u000A`)
`\r`	carriage return (`\u000D`)
`\t`	tab (`\u0009`)
`\\`	backslash (`\u005C`)
`\'`	single quote (`\u0027`)
`\"`	double quote (`\u0022`)
`\b`	backspace (`\u0008`)
`\f`	form feed (`\u000C`)

String literals are enclosed by double quotes, as in `"Show me the money!"`. As with character constants, you can use the special characters in the preceding list in string constants. This is often useful when you want to use a character that might otherwise confuse the compiler, such as a double quote or backslash, as in

```
"He then said, \"Whatever you do, don't turn that thing on!\".
ÂShe didn't listen."
"C:\\Info\\Images\\PromPic.jpg"
```

String constants must always be on the same source line. This constant is illegal:

```
"Walden
by
Henry David Thoreau"
```

Use the newline escape sequence, `\n`, to achieve the same effect:

```
"Walden\nby\nHenry David Thoreau"
```

String literals are actually objects of type `String`, which means that you can use them as you would any `String` variable. The following two expressions are equivalent:

```
"Show me the money!".toUpperCase()
```

```
"SHOW ME THE MONEY!"
```

These two are also the same:

```
"mana" + "tee"
```

```
"manatee"
```

Arrays

Arrays are sequences of data elements that you access by index position. In Java, arrays are considered to be objects, which means that array variables, like other object variables, contain references. The arrays themselves are kept on the heap. An array declaration consists of the data type of its elements, a pair of brackets (`[]`), the name, and a semicolon. The following statement declares an array named `highScoreArray` composed of integers:

```
int[] highScoreArray;
```

C and C++ programmers are accustomed to seeing the brackets after the name, as in

```
int highScoreArray[];
```

Java allows this, but you will almost always see the first form because it's a clearer indication of the type. Another difference from C and C++ is that you cannot specify the array size in the declaration. In Java, the following statement is illegal:

```
char aLine[ 80 ];
```

Instead, you must explicitly create an array object with the keyword `new`:

```
boolean[] ticketsAvailable = new boolean[ 15 ];
```

This declares a Boolean array variable named `ticketsAvailable`. The expression `new boolean[ 15 ]` creates an array on the heap with 15 Boolean elements. A reference to this array is then assigned to `ticketsAvailable`.

To access elements in an array, use brackets and an index number after the variable name. All index values start with `0`, so the first element can be accessed like this:

```
ticketsAvailable[ 0 ] = false;
```

The expression `ticketsAvailable[ 0 ]` is equivalent to a Boolean variable. Array elements behave just like variables of the same type.

To find the length of an array, add a dot and the word `length` to the variable name. To get the last element of an array, use an expression like the following:

```
ticketsAvailable[ ticketsAvailable.length - 1 ]
```

Because array indices begin with `0`, the last index should be one less than the length, which in this case is `14`. The expression `ticketsAvailable.length - 1` evaluates to `14`. If you use an array index that's less than zero or greater than the largest allowable index, Java will throw an `IndexOutOfBounds` exception. Exceptions are essentially runtime errors in Java and are covered later in this chapter.

You can initialize an array all at once with a comma-separated list of literals surrounded by braces. The following statement creates a five-element array:

```
boolean[] ticketsAvailable = { true, false, false, true, false };
```

As in other languages, you can have multidimensional arrays in Java. Simply add a bracket pair for each dimension:

```
int[][] golfScores = new int[ 3 ][ 10 ];
```

This statement creates an array named `golfScores` that has three other arrays in it, each with 10 elements. You can access the elements like this:

```
golfScores[ 1 ][ 5 ] = 85;
```

Unlike other languages, Java lets you have nested arrays of differing lengths. Say that the first dimension (3) represents the golf courses at which you play, and the second dimension is the number of times you play a month. You might want to play at the first course more often than the others, in which case you could use the following statements:

```
int[][] golfScores = new int[ 3 ][];

golfScores[ 0 ] = new int[ 20 ];
golfScores[ 1 ] = new int[ 10 ];
golfScores[ 2 ] = new int[ 10 ];
```

Notice the blank second dimension in `new int[ 3 ][]`. This lets you add arrays at your leisure, with differing lengths if desired. The first dimension must be specified.

To initialize a multidimensional array all at once, nest array initializers as follows:

```
int[][] golfScores =
        {
            { 80, 67, 92, 54 },
            { 60, 70, 75 },
            { 85, 89, 95, 100, 152 }
        };
```

In this example, `golfScores[ 2 ][ 4 ]` evaluates to 152.

Arrays have fixed length in Java. To resize an array, you have to make a new array and copy each element to the new array. Because of this, most people find it more convenient to use the `Vector` class, which allows varying lengths.

Objects and Classes

Objects are created from *classes*, which are essentially templates for making objects. Class declarations consist of the keyword class, the name of the class, and a sequence of *member* declarations surrounded by braces. There are two kinds of class member: *fields* and *methods*. Fields are variables contained within objects. Methods are named blocks of code that operate on objects of a class.

By convention, classnames begin with capital letters. Field and method names begin with lowercase letters. In the examples, I prefix field names with a lowercase m to indicate that they're members of a class. This isn't required of the language; it's just a convention to make life a little easier. For example

```
class WeatherInfo
{
    float    mTemperature;
    float    mBarometricPressure;
    int      mWindMilesPerHour;
    char     mWindDirection;
    boolean mOvercast, mSnowing, mRaining;
}
```

This defines a class named `WeatherInfo` that contains seven fields. As you can see, classes are similar to records and structures of other programming languages. You declare an object variable much like a primitive variable, using the classname as the data type of the variable, as in

```
WeatherInfo aForecast;
```

This declares a variable named `aForecast` that holds a reference to a `WeatherInfo` object. C++ programmers, be careful here! This code will not create a `WeatherInfo` object. To do this, use the new keyword, the name of the class, and a pair of parentheses:

```
WeatherInfo aForecast = new WeatherInfo();
```

The new keyword tells Java to create an object using the given class. The object is first created on the heap; then, a reference to it is stored in `aForecast`.

Now that I have an object, I can access each field by placing a period and a field name after the variable name. For example

```
aForecast.mTemperature = 451.0F;
aForecast.mWindMilesPerHour = 750;
aForecast.mWindDirection = 'N';
aForecast.mSnowing = false;
aForecast.mOvercast = true;
```

This code sets five of the fields of your object to appropriate (if unrealistic) values. But what of the two missing fields, mBarometricPressure and mRaining? Well, whenever an object is created, each of its fields is initialized to the following default values:

byte, short, int, long	0
double and float	0.0
char	The null character (/u0000)
boolean	false
objects and arrays	null

Therefore, by default, mBarometricPressure is set to 0.0, and mRaining is set to false. Array elements are also initialized to the same default values. Unfortunately, variables declared within a method (also called *local variables*) must be initialized before they're used.

Using Expressions and Operators

An *expression* is a sequence of variables, literals, method calls, and operators that evaluates to a single data value. *Operators* determine the manner in which an expression is evaluated and the data type of the result. Here's an example:

```
mWindMilesPerHour > 30
```

This expression contains one variable (mWindilesPerHour), one operator (>), and one literal (30) that together evaluate to a Boolean value. The operator > is the *greater-than* operator, which evaluates to true if the number before it is greater than the number after it. Greater-than is one of the *relational* operators, which are listed here:

>	Greater than
<	Less than
==	Equal to
!=	Not equal to
>=	Greater than or equal to
<=	Less than or equal to

Relational operators are frequently combined with the *logical* operators && (*and*), ¦¦ (*or*), and ! (*not*), as in the following compound expression:

```
mTemperature < 65 ¦¦ mTemperature > 90
```

This expression is read as "mTemperature is less than 65, or mTemperature is greater than 90." Individual operations within a compound expression are performed according to the relative precedence of each operator. Every language has its own operator precedence table, and Java is no different.

postfix	`[]  .  (params)  expr++  expr--`
unary	`++expr  --expr  +expr  -expr  !`
creation or cast	`new  (type)expr`
multiplicative	`*  /  %`
additive	`+  -`
shift	`<<  >>  >>>`
relational	`<  >  >=  <=  instanceof`
equality	`==  !=`
bitwise AND	`&`
bitwise XOR	`^`
bitwise OR	`¦`
logical AND	`&&`
logical OR	`¦¦`
conditional	`expr?expr:expr`
assignment	`=  +=  -=  *=  /=  %=  >>=  <<=  >>>=  &=  ^=  ¦=`

Operators nearer to the top of the table are said to have higher precedence than those below. Operators on the same line have equal precedence. The following expression evaluates to 15, not 30, because multiplication has a higher precedence than addition.

```
3 + 2 * 6
```

You can use parentheses to alter the order of evaluation. This next expression evaluates to 30, not 15:

```
( 3 + 2 ) * 6
```

The data type of the result is usually determined by the last operation performed. The following two expressions (which are equivalent) evaluate to a Boolean value, in this case false:

```
6 + 50 < 5 + 5 * 10
```

```
 ( 6 + 50 ) < ( 5 + ( 5 * 10 ) )
```

Expressions with numeric operands evaluate to the type in the expression with the greatest range. Therefore, an `int` and a `long` result in a `long`, and a `long` and a `float` result in a `float`. You can't implicitly assign a floating-point value to any integer, even if the value is within range. To force Java to do so, you must use an explicit cast, which is a type name within parentheses placed before the value you want to convert, as in

```
int aInteger = ( int ) 123.4;
```

The (`int`) cast converts `123.4` (a floating-point type) to `123` (an integer type). Java simply discards the fractional part in such casts.

The logical operators `&&` and `¦¦` are *short-circuit* operators, which means that evaluation of an expression will quit when the truth value can be determined. This is often useful:

```
boolean aGoodToGo =  aGasTankFull ¦¦ aCar.fillTheTank();
```

If the Boolean variable `aGasTankFull` is `true`, `aCar.fillTheTank()` won't be called.

You have already seen the primary assignment operator `=`, which assigns the value of the expression on the right to the variable on its left, as in

```
aSum = aSum + 24
```

This expression adds 24 to the variable `aSum`. The rest of the assignment operators offer a concise way to write expressions of this form by combining the operator with the equal sign. This next expression also adds 24 to the variable `aSum`:

```
aSum += 24
```

Two other operators can change a variable's value directly: the *increment* (++) operator, which adds one to a variable, and the *decrement* (--) operator, which subtracts one. For example

```
aCount++
```

This adds one to the value of count. (By the way, C++ gets its name from the increment operator. We're meant to think that C++ is "one better" than the C language).

You can place the increment and decrement operators before or after the variable name to achieve different results. Place them before (or prefix) the variable name if you want to use the changed value of the variable in the current expression. Put them after (or postfix) the variable name if you want the increment or decrement to happen after the variable is used in the expression. In the following example, the variable `aEqualsTen` is assigned `true` because `aCount` is incremented after it's used in the comparison:

```
int aCount = 10;
boolean aEqualsTen = ( aCount++ == 10 );
```

In this next one, `aEqualsTen` will be `false` because `aCount` is incremented beforehand:

```
int aCount = 10;
boolean aEqualsTen = ( ++aCount == 10 );
```

Note that the parentheses here aren't strictly necessary. The expression would evaluate the same without them. Parentheses are sometimes used in short Boolean expressions to help the reader spot the logic.

Another place you will often see optional parentheses is with the *conditional* or *ternary* operator, which looks like this:

```
float aPrice = ( aQuantity < 10 ) ? 19.95F : 19.95F * aDiscount;
```

In this expression, `aQuantity < 10` is first evaluated. If it's `true`, `aPrice` is assigned the part between the question mark and the colon, or `19.95F`. Otherwise, `aPrice` is assigned the result of the expression after the colon, or `19.95F * aDiscount`. Again, the parentheses aren't required, but they help make things clearer.

The remaining operators are used less frequently. The shift and bitwise operators manipulate individual binary digits, or *bits*, of an integer. These are sometimes used when setting, clearing, and checking individual *flag* bits within an integer *mask*. The *remainder* operator is used to determine the remainder from an integer division, as in

```
35 % 10
```

This evaluates to 5. The *instanceof* operator determines whether an object was made from a particular class. The following expression evaluates to `true`:

```
aInfo instanceof WeatherInfo
```

Building Methods

A *method* is a named sequence of executable statements. Methods are much like procedures and functions in other programming languages. Like fields, methods are contained within classes and are said to be members of a class.

Method Declarations

A method declaration consists of the return type, the name of the method, a pair of parentheses (which often contain a list of parameters), and a sequence of statements surrounded by braces. The part before the braces is often called the method's *signature*. Here's a method for the `WeatherInfo` class:

```
boolean isGoodBeachDay()
{
   // not good if the temperature is too low or too high
   if ( mTemperature < 60 || mTemperature > 90 ) return false;
```

```
    // not good if the wind is too strong
    if ( mWindMilesPerHour > 30 ) return false;

    // not good if it's overcast, raining, or snowing
    if ( mOvercast || mRaining || mSnowing ) return false;

    // otherwise, let's head to the beach
    return true;
}
```

This method is named `isGoodBeachDay()` and has a return type of Boolean. The return type determines the data type of the result, if any. To indicate that a method returns no result, use the keyword `void`. The return statement tells Java to stop executing the method and return the indicated value. This method returns `false` if any of the three bad-weather conditions are met; otherwise, it returns `true`.

The `main()` Method

A class can have a special method named `main()`, which is the first method to execute in a program. To illustrate, here's the complete `WeatherInfo` class, complete with `main()`:

```java
class WeatherInfo
{
    // fields
    float   mTemperature;
    float   mBarometricPressure;
    int     mWindMilesPerHour;
    char    mWindDirection;
    boolean mOvercast, mSnowing, mRaining;

    // method to determine a good beach day
    boolean isGoodBeachDay()
    {
        // not good if the temperature is too low or too high
        if ( mTemperature < 65 || mTemperature > 90 ) return false;

        // not good if the wind is too strong
        if ( mWindMilesPerHour > 30 ) return false;

        // not good if it's overcast, raining, or snowing
        if ( mOvercast || mRaining || mSnowing ) return false;

        // otherwise, let's head to the beach
        return true;
    }

    // main method
    public static void main( String[] pArgs )
```

```
    {
        // create the weather info object
        WeatherInfo aInfo = new WeatherInfo();

        // initialize some weather stats
        aInfo.mTemperature = 72F;
        aInfo.mWindMilesPerHour = 5;

        // display a message about today's beach day status
        if ( aInfo.isGoodBeachDay() )
        ÂSystem.out.println( "Time to go to the beach!" );
        else System.out.println( "Better rent some movies ..
        Âit's nasty out there." );
    }
}
```

This is a complete Java program. The signature of each `main()` method must appear like this preceding one. I'll explain `public` and `static` later in this chapter. The `pArgs` part is often used to retrieve arguments specified when the program is started, although not in this example. `System.out.println()` writes what you put between the parentheses to the system console. The expression `aInfo.isGoodBeachDay()` is called a method *invocation* or method *call*. It causes the `isGoodBeachDay()` method to execute using fields in the `aInfo` object. In the example, this method returns `true`, so the program will display

```
Time to go to the beach!
```

Local Variables and Parameters

The variable `aInfo` in the `main()`method of the preceding example is a *local variable*. Local variables can be declared anywhere within a method, provided that they're declared before they're used. In the examples, I use the prefix a to indicate a local variable.

When a method ends, the local variables defined within it go *out of scope*, which means that the values and references they contain are lost. Unlike other languages, Java doesn't require that you free or delete your objects. The JVM garbage collects objects on the heap that are no longer referenced. This makes life a lot easier.

Parameters are variables contained within the signature. They're used to pass data to the method when it's called. In the examples, I use the prefix p to indicate parameters.

All parameters in Java are *pass-by-value*, which means that when you change the value of a parameter within a method, the change won't affect the calling method. For example, say that you have a method with the following signature:

```
int getLowTempOnDay( int pDayOfMonth )
```

This method has a single integer parameter. You might call the method like this:

```
int aDayOfMonth = 10;
int aTemp = aInfo.getLowTempOnDay( aDayOfMonth );
```

This initializes the variable aDayOfMonth to 10 and then calls getLowTempOnDay() on the aInfo object, passing the value of aDayOfMonth. The value in aDayOfMonth is then copied (or passed) to the variable pDayOfMonth, which is then available for use within getLowTempOnDay(). Any changes to pDayOfMonth within getLowTempOnDay() are local and will not affect the value of aDayOfMonth in the calling method.

Keep in mind that object variables contain references and not values. References are passed by value, but the objects to which they point can be accessed from both the calling method and the called method. Say that your method has this signature:

```
int getLowTempOnDay( Date pSecondDate )
```

You could then use the method like this:

```
Date aFirstDate = new Date();  // defaults to right now!
int aTemp = aInfo.getLowTempOnDay( aFirstDate );
```

If you make a change to the object referenced by pSecondDate in getLowTempOnDay(), it will affect aFirstDate because both reference the same object.

Every primitive type has a corresponding *wrapper* class that can be used in places where an object is more useful than a primitive value. The classname in each case is the full descriptive name of the type, but with a capital letter:

```
Character aInitial = new Character( 'Z' );
```

This statement creates a Character object that contains the letter z. Wrapper classes can be used to pass primitive values by reference, as with the previous Date example.

You can have more than one method in a class with the same name, provided that each takes a different set of parameters. This technique, called *overloading*, enables you to have both versions of getLowTempOnDay() in your class. Java chooses which to use depending on whether you passed an integer or a Date.

Constructors

Classes can have a special kind of method known as a *constructor* that's called whenever an object of the class is created with new. Constructors are used to initialize an object when default values aren't enough. Constructor declarations use the same name as the class, and they leave out the return type. For example

```
WeatherInfo()
{
```

```
   mTemperature = 72F;
   mWindMilesPerHour = 30;
}
```

This initializes `mTemperature` and `mWindMilesPerHour` to the indicated values when you create a `WeatherInfo` object like this:

```
WeatherInfo aInfo = new WeatherInfo();
```

Constructors can have parameters, just like other methods. You can also overload constructors to provide more than one way to initialize an object:

```
public WeatherInfo( float pTemperature, int pWindMilesPerHour )
{
   mTemperature = pTemperature;
   mWindMilesPerHour = pWindMilesPerHour;
}
```

This constructor lets you specify the initial temperature and wind speed, as in

```
WeatherInfo aInfo = new WeatherInfo( 65.5, 10 );
```

Modifiers

Notice the word `public` in the preceding declaration. This is an *access control modifier*. Such modifiers are placed in front of any member (field or method) to indicate whether and how the member can be used outside the class. Members declared public can be accessed from any class. Members declared private can be used only within their own class. Methods declared without an access modifier can be used only by classes in the same package. Members declared protected can be used only by subclasses and classes in the same package.

It's a great programming practice to hide fields by declaring them private. This enables you to make internal changes to a class without affecting other code that uses the class. You should refrain from using fields directly, as in

```
aInfo.mTemperature = 65F;
```

Instead, use *accessor methods* to *encapsulate* your object's data. By convention, use the prefix `get` for methods that retrieve a field's value, and `set` for methods that change a value. Fields accessed in this way are called *properties*. The part after the `get` or `set` is the property name. Boolean properties may use `is` instead of `get`. For example

```
class WeatherInfo
{
   private float   mTemperature;
   private boolean mOvercast;
```

```
    public float getTemperature()   { return mTemperature; }
    public void setTemperature( float pVal )  { mTemperature = pVal; }

    public boolean isOverCast()  { return mOvercast; }
    public void setOvercast( boolean pVal )  { mOvercast = pVal; }
}
```

The modifier static can be used to indicate that a field or method belongs to the class
itself and not individual objects of the class. Static fields are similar to global variables in
other languages. In the examples, I use the prefix s to indicate static fields.

```
class WeatherInfo
{
    public static int sRecordLowTemp = -30;

    ...

    public static boolean isRecordLow( int pTemp )
    {
        return ( pTemp < sRecordLowTemp )
    }
}
```

Here, the field sRecordLowTemp is shared by all objects of type WeatherInfo. The static
method isRecordLow() uses sRecordLowTemp directly. Static fields and methods can be
used outside the class by using the classname instead of a variable name:

```
if ( WeatherInfo.isRecordLow( aTemp ) )
ÂWeatherInfo.sRecordLowTemp = aTemp;
```

They can also be used with object variables or within methods, just like normal fields:

```
aTampaInfo.sRecordLowTemp = 25;
aBuffaloInfo.sRecordLowTemp = -50;
```

Both these statements change the same shared field. Therefore, the first assignment has
no effect because the value 25 is immediately replaced by the value 50. Were
sRecordLowTemp a normal field, both objects would have their own internal copy.

Making Statements

A *statement* is a single action in a program. Statements always end with a semicolon.
The most common kinds of statement are *declaration, expression,* and *compound* statements. Declaration statements declare and optionally initialize variables:

```
char aMiddleInitial = 'Q';
```

Expression statements are essentially expressions with a semicolon at the end. The expression types that make sense as statements are assignment, increment, decrement, and method invocation, such as the following:

```
aSum += aDelta;  // assignment
aSum++;   // increment
aDelta--;  // decrement
aInfo.setTemperature( aSum );  // invocation
```

Compound statements, also called *blocks*, consist of a sequence of statements contained within braces. Compound statements can be used wherever a normal statement is allowed. Variables declared within a block are local to that block and cannot be used outside it. Blocks are often used with loops and conditional statements:

```
if ( aTempNow < aLowestTemp )
{
   aLowestTemp = aTempNow;
   aInfo.setLowestTemp( aTempNow );
}
```

The remaining statement types are named for the keywords they use. Most of these are identical in form and function to their C and C++ counterparts.

return

The `return` statement is used to end execution of a method and possibly return a value. The returned value must be consistent with the return type in the method's signature:

```
int getTheAnswerToLifeTheUniverseAndEverything()
{
   return 42;
}
```

Methods with a return type of `void` cannot return a value, although you can still use `return` to exit a method prematurely—simply omit the value:

```
return;
```

`return` statements contained within a `try` block that has a `finally` clause will always execute the `finally` clause before returning. This enables you to simplify your method by putting all the cleanup code in the `finally` clause.

while

The `while` statement is one of three looping constructs in Java. It consists of the keyword `while`, a Boolean expression contained within parentheses, and a statement to execute repeatedly as long as the expression evaluates to `true`, if ever. For example

```
while( aInfo.isRaining() ) aInfo.getNewestWeatherStats();
```

If `aInfo.isRaining()` evaluates to `false` the first time, the statement `aInfo.getNewestWeatherStats()` is never executed. Otherwise, it is called repeatedly, presumably updating the rain status, until `isRaining()` returns `false`.

Compound statements are often used with `while` statements:

```
int aCount = 1;
while( aCount < 10 )
{
    System.out.println( "Count is " + aCount );
    aCount++;
}
```

for

The `for` loop is the most concise. The preceding example can be written as

```
for( int aCount = 1; aCount < 10; aCount++ )
    System.out.println( "Count is " + aCount );
```

The meat of the loop is in the three expressions in parentheses. The first expression is the initialization expression. It is executed before the loop begins. As you can see, variables can be declared here. The second expression is the loop conditional. Like the `while` loop, this is checked before each iteration of the loop. If the conditional is `false` to start with, the loop will never execute. The third expression is the iteration expression. This is executed after each iteration of the loop.

You can leave out any of the three expressions, but you still have to put in each semi-colon. The most extreme case is the "forever" loop:

```
for( ;; ) doSomething();
```

There must be a way to break out of this, like a break, return, or thrown exception, or it will keep looping until the user kills the program.

do...while

The `do...while` loop is the same as the `while` loop, except that the conditional is evaluated *after* each iteration. This means that `do...while` loops always execute their statement at least once. This loop is nearly equivalent to the earlier `isRaining()` example:

```
do
{
    aInfo.getNewestWeatherStats();
}
while( aInfo.isRaining() );
```

The only difference is that getNewestWeatherStats() will be called whether or not it's raining. The braces aren't strictly necessary here because there's only one statement in the block, but they help clarify the logic.

break and continue

The break statement is used to exit a block, usually contained within a loop:

```
for( ;; )
{
   aInfo.getNewestWeatherStats();
   if( !aInfo.isRaining() ) break;
}
```

This code keeps getting weather stats until it's not raining; it then exits this otherwise infinite loop. The break statement is also used in switch statements.

The continue statement behaves like break, but instead of breaking entirely out of a loop, it skips the rest of the current iteration and starts a new one. For example, you might want a loop that calculates the prime numbers to one hundred:

```
for( int aCount = 3; aCount < 100; aCount++ )
{
   if ( aCount % 2 == 0 ) continue;

   // prime number test
}
```

The expression aCount % 2 == 0 tests whether aCount is even. Because even numbers greater than 2 are never prime, there's no point in testing them, so continue skips to the next iteration. (A better way to do this is use aCount += 2 as an iteration expression.)

Both break and continue can specify a *label* to skip to. Labels are names given to statements or blocks that are sometimes helpful when using nested loops. For example

```
outer:
   for( int aOuterCount = 0; aOuterCount < 10; aOuterCount++ )
   {
      for( int aInnerCount = 10; aInnerCount > 0; aInnerCount-- )
      {
         if ( aInnerCount == 2 ) continue outer;

         // some processing

         if ( aOuterCount == aInnerCount ) break outer;
      }
   }
```

The label outer is used to indicate the outer loop. When aOuterCount and aInnerCount are equal, both loops end because of the break outer statement. Using break by itself would end only the inner loop. Likewise, the continue outer statement starts another iteration of the outer loop, not the inner loop.

if...else

The if statement is very straightforward. It's used to test a Boolean expression before executing another statement:

```
if( thisIsTrue ) doThis();
```

The doThis() method will execute only if the expression between the parentheses evaluates to true. You can also add an else clause:

```
if( thisIsTrue ) doThis();
else doThat();
```

The doThat() method executes if the conditional evaluates to false. You can nest if...else statements as much as you like, but keep in mind that each else matches the preceding if. Blocks are used to execute groups of statements conditionally:

```
if( getRoomTemp() < mGaugeTemp )
{
   turnOnHeat();
   while( getRoomTemp() < mGaugeTemp ) blinkHeatLight();
   turnOffHeat();
}
```

switch

The switch statement uses an integer expression to choose between a sequence of statement groups. Each group begins with a *case label*, which consists of the keyword case, an integer expression, and a colon. Java executes the first statement group with a case label that matches the initial integer expression. For example

```
switch( aLotionSPF )
{
   case 0:
      System.out.println( "Better have a good base." );

   case 4:
      System.out.println( "Don't get burned!" );
      break;

   case 30:
      System.out.println( "Why bother!" );
      break;
```

```
   default:
      System.out.println( "Never heard of SPF " + aLotionSPF );
}
```

If aLotionSPF is equal to 0, 4, or 30, the first statement following the corresponding case label is executed. If no matching case label is found, the default case is used. The default case is optional. If no default exists, the entire switch statement is skipped.

Two things worth noting about switch statements. First, it's unnecessary to place statement groups within braces. Second, if you don't have a break statement at the end of each statement group, it will keep executing until it reaches a break or the end of the switch statement. So, if aLotionSPF equals 0, the program displays

```
Better have a good base.
Don't get burned!
```

try...catch...finally and throw

Java has built-in support for exception handling. Exceptions are objects that represent exceptional events, usually errors. Exceptions are *thrown* with the throw statement:

```
throw new IOException( "The hard drive's on fire!" );
```

Code where an exception might occur is enclosed within try blocks. Should an exception happen within a block, it's passed as a kind of parameter to the catch clause that follows the block:

```
void doSomething()
{
   try
   {
      // dividing by zero is a no-no
      System.out.println( 441 / 0 );
   }
   catch( ArithmeticException e )
   {
      System.out.println( "My goodness!
      ÂSomething went wrong: " + e.getMessage() );
   }
}
```

This example causes an ArithmeticException to be thrown, which is then caught in the catch clause and passed as the parameter e. The method getMessage() is then used to retrieve a text message explaining the exception. This example will display

```
My goodness!  Something went wrong: / by zero
```

There are many kinds of exceptions, each represented by its own class. You can have more than one catch clause after a try block to handle different exception types. You can also tack on a `finally` clause, which encloses code that will always be executed whether an exception occurs. This is a great place to put cleanup code.

```
void doSomething()
{
    try
    {
        // open files to process
    }
    catch( IOException e )
    {
        System.out.println( "Hey, something went wrong
                            Âreading the file!" );
    }
    catch( ArithmeticException e )
    {
        System.out.println( "Okay, so math's not my subject!" );
    }
    finally
    {
        // close files and say goodnight
    }
}
```

Java's a stickler about exception handling. Your code won't compile unless you handle all *checked* exceptions, such as `IOException`. If you'd like to pass the buck in a given method, you can add a `throws` clause in the method's signature:

```
public void passTheBuck() throws IOException
{
    // open some files
}
```

It then becomes the calling method's responsibility to handle the exception. You can pass the buck all the way back to `main()` if you want, but it stops there. Exceptions that are thrown several methods deep cause each calling method to abort until a `catch` clause is found. This is called *stack unwinding*, and it's a wonderful thing. Error checks need only appear where errors happen and where they're handled, not every step in between.

Understanding Inheritance

Inheritance is a fundamental feature of Java and is critical to the design of any nontrivial software system. Because Notes makes little use of it, though, I'll just cover the bases here.

A class can inherit fields and methods from another class. You do this by adding the keyword extends and the name of the class from which you want to inherit:

```
class ExtremeWeatherInfo extends WeatherInfo
{
    int mTornadoClass;
    int mSnowInches;
    float mEarthquakeRichterValue;

    public boolean isHurricane()  { return ( mWindMilesPerHour > 75 ); }
    public boolean isBlizzard()   { return ( mSnowInches > 10 ); }
}
```

The ExtremeWeatherInfo class is said to *extend* the WeatherInfo class. The original class is called the *superclass*, and the extending class is called the *subclass*. Although this might seem backward, it makes sense when looking at a *class hierarchy diagram*, which almost always has superclasses near the top of the page and subclasses down below.

Objects created from a subclass contain the fields of its superclasses along with its own. Methods of a subclass can use superclass fields, as in the isHurricane() method, which uses the mWindMilesPerHour field of WeatherInfo. This arrangement enables you to put common attributes and behavior in superclasses and share functionality between subclasses. This helps cut down on cut-and-paste duplication, a practice usually leading to buggy code that's very hard to maintain and extend.

Object Casting

Subclass objects can be assigned to variables with a superclass type. This is called *implicit* casting. Such variables can use members of the superclass, but not the subclass:

```
ExtremeWeatherInfo aExtremeInfo = new ExtremeWeatherInfo();
WeatherInfo aInfo = aExtremeInfo;

if ( aInfo.isRaining() )
    ÂSystem.out.println( "Is it in Spain? On a plain?" );
if ( aExtremeInfo.isHurricane() )
    ÂSystem.out.println( "Batten down the hatches!" );
if ( aInfo.isHurricane() )
    ÂSystem.out.println( "This won't compile. It's ILLEGAL!" );
```

You can also pass a subclass object to a superclass parameter. For example, you can invoke the following method with an ExtremeWeatherInfo parameter:

```
public void recordStats( WeatherInfo pInfo )
{
    // ...
}
```

The reverse isn't true, though. Assigning variables of a superclass type to variables of a subclass type is called *downcasting* and can be dangerous. If you really want to force the issue, you can use an *explicit* cast. To do this, put the subclass in parentheses, like this:

```
aExtremeInfo = ( ExtremeInfo ) aInfo;
```

Be prepared for a `ClassCastException` if the class doesn't match the object.

The `Object` Class

All classes inherit from the `Object` class. Classes that don't have an `extends` clause implicitly inherit from `Object`, as do arrays. The `Object` class defines many useful methods, such as `equals()`, which is used to determine whether an object is equal to another object, and `clone()`, which creates a copy of an object. The `equals()` method in `Object` returns `true` if the variables being tested refer to the same object:

```
if ( aInfo.equals( aExtremeInfo ) )
    ÂSystem.out.println( "They're the same thing!" );
```

You will often want to *override* this default `equals()` method so that you can use it to see whether two different objects have the same field values. For example, the following method could be added to the `WeatherInfo` class:

```
public boolean equals( Object pObj )
{
    // downcast the passed-in Object to the appropriate class
    WeatherInfo aInfo = ( WeatherInfo ) pObj;

    if ( aInfo.mTemperature != mTemperature ) return false;
    if ( aInfo.mBarometricPressure != mBarometricPressure ) return false;
    if ( aInfo.mWindMilesPerHour != mWindMilesPerHour ) return false;
    if ( aInfo.mWindDirection != mWindDirection ) return false;
    if ( aInfo.mOvercast != mOvercast ) return false;
    if ( aInfo.mSnowing != mSnowing ) return false;
    if ( aInfo.mRaining != mRaining ) return false;

    return true;
}
```

This method compares each field in both objects. It can be used like this:

```
if ( aSeattleInfo.equals( aNaplesInfo ) )
    ÂSystem.println( "Don't see this every day!" );
```

Objects of type `ExtremeWeatherInfo` can use this method, but it won't test subclass fields such as `mSnowInches`. Because of this, you will also want to override `equals()` in `ExtremeWeatherInfo`:

```
public boolean equals( Object pObj )
{
    // check equality of superclass fields
    if ( !super.equals( pObj ) ) return false;

    // downcast the passed-in Object to the appropriate class
    ExtremeWeatherInfo aExtremeInfo = ( ExtremeWeatherInfo ) pObj;

    if( aExtremeInfo.mTornadoClass != mTornadoClass ) return false;
    if( aExtremeInfo.mSnowInches != mSnowInches ) return false;
    if( aExtremeInfo.mEarthquakeRichterValue != mEarthQuakeRichterValue )
        Âreturn false;

    return true;
}
```

The keyword `super` is used as a special kind of variable. Use it to call the superclass version of a method. In the example, `super.equals()` calls the `WeatherInfo` version of `equals()`. Another special variable name is `this`, which contains a reference to the object on which the method was called. All fields in an object have an implicit `this` reference in front of them, as in `this.mSnowInches`. You will sometimes find this useful when passing a reference to the current object, as in

```
recordStats( this );
```

You cannot use `super` or `this` in static methods because static methods operate on the class fields and not fields within objects. Static methods have no `this`!

Interfaces

Interfaces are used to define a common set of attributes and behaviors that many classes share. Classes can *implement* many interfaces, but they can only *extend* one class. This means that Java does not support *multiple inheritance.* Instead, interfaces are used to determine functionality beyond that provided by the superclass.

Interface declarations look like class declarations, but with two differences. First, they're declared with the keyword `interface` instead of the word `class`. Second, their methods contain only signatures, not bodies:

```
public interface Thermostat
{
    int MAX_TEMP = 100;
    int MIN_TEMP = 60;

    int getRoomTemp();
    void turnOnHeat();
    void turnOffHeat();
    void blinkHeatLight();
    void checkTemp();
}
```

This interface declares two fields and five methods. To implement this interface in a class, use the keyword `implements` after the classname or `extends` clause. You can implement more than one interface by separating the names with commas:

```
class PortableHeater extends Heater implements Thermostat, HomingDevice
{
    // ...
}
```

Fields of an interface are implicitly `static` and `final`, which makes interfaces a good place to put constants. Methods in an interface must be defined in every class that implements the interface. This might seem like a pain, but it's not so bad in practice. One common approach is to create a helper class that implements the interface and then include a helper object in your class. You can then provide quick "patch" methods like this:

```
class Heater implements Thermostat
{
    ThermostatHelper mHelper = new ThermostatHelper();

    int getRoomTemp()     { return mHelper.getRoomTemp(); }
    void turnOnHeat()     { mHelper.turnOnHeat();  }
    void turnOffHeat()    { mHelper.turnOffHeat(); }
    void blinkHeatLight() { mHelper.blinkHeatLight(); }
    void checkTemp()      { mHelper.checkTemp(); }
}
```

Interfaces are a kind of data type, just like classes. Objects made from a class that implements an interface can be assigned to variables with the interface type. You can also call methods with these variables, provided that the method belongs to the interface:

```
Heater aHeater = new Heater();
Thermostat aThermostat = aHeater;
aThermostat.checkTemp();
```

Summary

As I said earlier, Java deserves a book of its own. I've covered a lot of ground in this chapter, but there's still much to learn about the Java language and environment. There are strings, streams, threads, packages, JAR files, serialization, abstract classes, nested classes, inner classes, anonymous classes, `clone()`, `finalize()`, adapters, listeners, and resources, to say nothing of the 504 classes and interfaces in the Java 1.1 class library. More is revealed in the next chapter, where I describe the many ways to use Java with the Notes and Domino environment.

Basic Java

by Timothy Falconer

Java first showed its face in release 4.5 of Notes, which allows developers to add preexisting applets to documents. Although these applets can run in both the Notes client and Web browsers, they can't access Notes information. Therefore, their use is limited.

Release 4.6 added support for Java agents and servlets that can access back-end Notes information using a new Java binding of the Notes Object Interface (NOI). This new Java API can also be used by standalone applications, provided that they run on machines with Notes or Domino installed. Although this was a step forward, release 4.6 lacks any real tools for Java development. You have to build your classes outside Notes and import them manually. There is also no easy way to debug your agents.

In release 5, Domino Designer lets you edit and compile Java source in the Programmer's pane. You can also use it to easily browse through the Notes API. Although Designer still lacks any direct debugging support, you can use the AgentRunner database to help debug agents with another Java IDE such as Borland JBuilder or IBM's VisualAge for Java. Release 5 also lets you write programs that can access Notes information remotely, using a special CORBA version of the Java API.

In this chapter, I present each of the ways you can use Java in Notes and why you'd choose one approach over another. I also explore the Java binding of the NOI, which lets you create and manipulate Notes objects, just as you can with LotusScript. In fact, if you've used LotusScript to program Notes, you will have an easy time with the Java interface because it's nearly identical. The rest of the chapter focuses specifically on agents and includes two examples that help QA teams keep track of bugs.

Choosing a Java Solution in Domino

You have about a dozen ways to deploy and run Java code in a Notes/Domino network, making it the most flexible programming option available. You can use Java to make agents, applets, servlets, and applications. Your code can run from Notes clients, Domino servers, Web browsers, and remote computers without Notes or Domino installed. Choosing between the many options might seem mystifying at first, but fear not, there's a lot of overlap in what you must learn.

Which option you choose depends primarily on three factors: where you want to put your code, how you want to start it, and where you want it to run, as shown in Table 27.1.

TABLE 27.1 Java Usage in Domino

Type	*Code Kept*	*Starts From*	*Runs On*
Agent	Notes database	Notes, event, or URL	Notes client, Domino server
Applet	Notes DB or file system	URL	Notes client, browser
Servlet	Domino or Web server	URL	Domino or Web server
Application	File system	Command line	Any JRE

Agents

Java agents work just like their LotusScript counterparts. They're kept in Notes databases, so they can be replicated like any other design element. Agents also have the most flexible start options of the four program types. They can be started manually from either the Notes client or a Web browser. They can be run on a schedule or in response to an event such as email arriving or a document changing. Agents started manually from a Notes client run within the client's JVM. Agents that start automatically can execute on any Domino server you choose.

A primary benefit to using agents is security. Each agent is digitally signed by the author each time it's modified, which prevents unscrupulous tampering. The signature is also used to determine access rights. Agents running on a Domino server assume the identity and access rights of their author. Agents executing within a Notes client use the access rights of the current Notes user.

There are two drawbacks to using Java agents. First, they can't interact with users. The Java binding lacks the "front-end" classes of the NOI, such as LotusScript's `NotesUIDocument`. This essentially cuts you off from being able to display information or gather new information from users while your agent is running. The second drawback is that agents must execute on machines with Notes or Domino installed. The other three program types can execute remotely using CORBA.

Applets

Applets are small Java programs that run within larger applications such as a Web browser or a Notes client. You've probably seen them while browsing the Web. The big thing about applets is that they're downloaded on the spot and run within the JVM contained within your application. This enables you to deploy your Java code in one common location, which ensures that all users will run the most current version. Because of their "download on demand" nature, applets are the best way to access Domino servers remotely via CORBA.

Downloading someone else's code and running it on your machine can be a scary thing, which is why Java applets are usually forbidden from accessing your hard disk or printing a file. Applets that are subject to such restrictions are called *untrusted* applets. If your applet needs special access, it can be digitally signed to indicate its origin, although each user must still approve its use before it becomes a *trusted* applet.

The best time to use applets in a Notes/Domino environment is when you want to make a custom user interface and have it be equally accessible from both Notes clients and Web browsers. If you've ever accessed a Notes database from a Web browser, you know that the HTML "Web-ized" Domino interface isn't quite as useful or responsive as the Notes client interface. Applets let you present a consistent, customized interface to both sets of users. You also gain the benefit of Java's extensive windowing environment, as well as access to numerous third-party tools and components.

Applets let you present a secure, professional, and universally accessible Domino client that sidesteps the administrative hassles of installation, upgrading, and maintenance. So why use anything else? The main drawback is that large applets can take a long time to download to a browser, particularly over a slow modem connection. Newer browsers will cache your code after it's downloaded, which helps speed up things the second time, but for many, it's that first impression that sells the show. As such, applets are usually best kept small if users will be connecting at slow speeds.

Servlets

Servlets are the server-side equivalent of applets: small Java programs that run within a Domino server or a Web server. They're executed as a result of a Web browser request, such as when a user fills out a form and clicks Submit. The information in the form is passed to the servlet, which then generates a response page and returns it to the browser.

Servlets perform roughly the same function as traditional CGI programs, which are typically written in languages such as Perl or C. Although Domino lets you use CGI programs, I wouldn't advise it unless you're using something off-the-shelf or have to access some low-level system resources. Servlets offer much better performance. They're loaded once and start a new thread for each request, whereas CGI programs start and stop a new process each time. This can be costly, particularly if dozens of people hit the same page at the same time.

Domino agents can also be used to serve up dynamic pages. This is useful if you have limited access to the file system on your Domino server. Although agents can be developed and replicated from any Notes client, servlets require that you put Java code in the server's data/domino/servlet directory. If this isn't a problem, I suggest that you use servlets instead. Like CGI programs, agents start up and shut down with each request, so they're less efficient. Another drawback is that agents lack the capability to remember session state from page to page. Servlets use cookies to keep track of user sessions, so your servlets can process multipage interactions, as found in shopping cart applications.

You can also put servlets on a regular Web server and have them use CORBA to remotely access information on separate Domino servers. This can be useful when your corporate Web site is outside your firewall and you want to better control access to internal servers.

Applications

Java applications are full-fledged standalone programs that run in their own JVM. They're usually started from the command line, but can easily be associated with a desktop icon or menu shortcut in your operating system.

The benefit to using Java applications is that you can create larger programs that make full use of Java without worrying about download time or UI restrictions. Because they can use CORBA to remotely access Domino servers, Java applications are great for enhancing your Domino network with full-featured standalone GUI clients or quick command-line tools.

The drawback to Java applications is deployment. Like most programs, they have to be installed on individual machines. This makes administration more difficult. You must also find and use an existing JVM on each machine during installation or install a platform-specific one. Sun Microsystems allows free distribution of its Java Runtime Environment (JRE) for Windows and Solaris. Check out `http://java.sun.com`. Even better, use a product like InstallAnywhere, which creates platform-specific installers for your program that will first check for an existing JVM and install one if necessary.

Understanding the Notes Object Interface

The Notes Object Interface is a class library first introduced in Notes 4.0 with LotusScript. Under the hood, the NOI is really a bunch of C++ classes contained in dynamic link libraries. Both LotusScript and Java use the LSX (LotusScript eXtensions) architecture to bind to the same underlying C++ code.

When I worked at Lotus on R5, I had the good fortune to study and extend the source code for NOTES.JAR, the Java API library. I was surprised to find that most classes in NOTES.JAR are simple wrapper classes that use JNI (Java Native Interface) to patch each Java method to corresponding C++ code in NLSXBE, the Notes LSX back-end library. This is why you must install Notes or Domino before using the Java API. No Notes, then no NLSXBE, which means that NOTES.JAR is useless.

There are other implications of the underlying "native nature" of Java NOI objects. First, you can't use the new operator to create Domino objects in Java. Instead, you will use methods like `NotesFactory.createSession()` and `Session.getDatabase()` that create native Notes objects and return them wrapped as Java objects. Second, you will have to make sure that the Notes system is initialized for each thread of your program. This is done automatically for the first thread in agents and applets, but you will have to use the `NotesThread` class to initialize servlets, applications, and extra threads in agents or applets. Details of `NotesThread` are presented in the next chapter.

The NOI describes a containment hierarchy. At the top of the hierarchy is the `Session` object, which contains all other objects. The `Session` object contains `DbDirectory` objects, which contain `Database` objects, which contain `DocumentCollection` objects, which contain `Document` objects, and so forth. You will usually have to start from the top and work your way through the hierarchy to find objects you want to use.

Keep in mind that an object can't exist without its containing parent object. When a parent object is destroyed in memory, its children are also destroyed. Because Java objects are automatically garbage-collected when they go out of scope, you might run into problems with code like this:

```
public Document getBugEntry() throws NotesException
{
    Session aSession = NotesFactory.createSession();
    DbDirectory aDbDir = aSession.getDbDirectory( "" );
    Database aDb = aDbDir.openDatabase( "BugBase.nsf" );
    DocumentCollection aDocList = aDb.getAllDocuments();

    return aDocList.getFirstDocument();
}
```

This method first creates a `Session` object and then wends its way through the containment hierarchy to get the first document in the BugBase.nsf database. The problem lies in the fact that these variables are local to the method and go out of scope when it's over. Java will eventually garbage-collect these objects, so they might be destroyed before you're done with your document. Because children objects are destroyed with their parents, this is a problem. One solution is to reference container objects as fields of your class rather than as local variables. You can then use them throughout your class without worrying about the garbage collector ruining your day.

Chapter 23, "Basic LotusScript," contains more information on the concepts and classes in the NOI. Although written from a LotusScript standpoint, the classes discussed are nearly identical to those in the Java API. Simply omit the `Notes` prefix in the classname, so `NotesDocument` in LotusScript becomes `Document` in Java. Also, take a look at Appendix B, "Java and CORBA Classes," which gives a brief description of each class in the Java binding of the NOI.

Unfortunately, the Java API lacks the front-end UI classes in the LotusScript API, such as `NotesUIWorkspace`. These NOI classes haven't yet been "exposed" in the Java binding. Likewise, both Java and LotusScript lack functionality found in the C++ API, such as the capability to use tables and other composite data objects. If you really have to get at this hidden NOI functionality, you can write C++ code and wire it to your Java classes using JNI. This is a tricky business, though, and beyond the scope of this book.

Writing Java Agents

To use Domino Designer to create a Java agent, do the following:

1. Open the database that will contain the agent.
2. Select the Create/Agent menu item.
3. Name your agent something like `Filter Junk Mail` or `Reschedule Appointments`.
4. Choose whether it's a *shared agent*, that is, one that other people will be able to use.
5. Select the way you want your agent to start.
6. Determine which documents you want your agent to process, or choose Run Once.
7. Select Java from the Run list box in the Programmer's pane.

You will then see something like Figure 27.1.

As you can see, Domino Designer starts you off with some sample Java source code. Here's a slightly reformatted version of this simple template:

```java
import lotus.domino.*;

public class JavaAgent extends AgentBase
{
    public void NotesMain()
    {
        try
        {
            Session session = getSession();
            AgentContext agentContext = session.getAgentContext();
```

```
        // (Your code goes here)
    }
    catch( Exception e )
    {
        e.printStackTrace();
    }
  }
}
```

This is a complete class definition that declares an agent named JavaAgent. Although it doesn't really do anything, all the elements of an agent are here. I'll discuss each in turn.

FIGURE 27.1

Domino Designer starts your agent off with a simple code template.

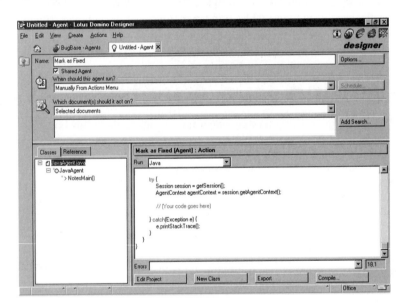

Packages

The first line is an import statement that tells the Java compiler that this class makes use of the lotus.domino package. You will want to put this statement in every source file that uses classes in the Notes API, such as Session and AgentContext.

A *package* is a named group of related classes. Packages use a hierarchical naming system to prevent name clashes with other code. The widespread convention is to start package names with your domain name reversed, as in com.immuexa and org.apache. As you can see, Lotus opted to leave off the com. Each level in the hierarchy is then separated by periods, so you can have lotus.domino (the Notes Java API package) or lotus.notes.apps.reports (the package I wrote for R5).

Package names are essentially paths to your source and class files. Each name in the hierarchy maps to a directory or subdirectory. For example, the `RepChart` class in the `lotus.notes.apps.reports` package is found in the lotus/notes/apps/reports directory. To see this for yourself, use a tool like WinZip to open the NOTES.JAR file and look at the class files and directories. JAR files are a handy way to collect class files together into one big compressed file. NOTES.JAR contains most of the Java files used by Notes and Domino, including some by IBM and others by a company called Acme.

Most of the `lotus.domino` classes are duplicated in `lotus.notes`, which was the package name of the Notes Java API in previous releases. The old classes are still around for backward compatibility. Use `lotus.notes` if you need your code to work with older installations. Use `lotus.domino` if you want to use the new features of R5.

Just as files can be specified with a pathname, classes can be specified with their package name, as in `lotus.domino.Session`. If you want, you could prefix all the classnames in your code with their package name, but this quickly becomes cumbersome. Import statements are easier. These tell the compiler which packages to search in order to find the classes in your code. For example

```
import lotus.notes.*;
```

This statement tells the compiler to search the `lotus.notes` package, although it won't search subpackages like `lotus.notes.apps.reports`. Import statements can also specify a particular class in a package:

```
import com.mcp.naddu.AssignAgent;
```

This is useful when you're importing separate packages that contain classes with the same name. Using an import statement to explicitly specify the desired class helps clear up any ambiguity.

Many people confuse import statements with `#include` directives in other languages. Import statements don't actually import anything. They're more like `PATH` statements that inform the operating system where to look for programs on your hard disk.

AgentBase and NotesMain()

To make a Java agent, you create a class that extends Domino's `AgentBase` class. This will ensure that your agent initializes the Notes system because `AgentBase` extends the `NotesThread` class. `NotesThread` is discussed next chapter.

AgentBase then creates a `Session` object and an `AgentContext` object. Both are used to get runtime information about the agent's environment. `AgentBase` also takes care of things such as wiring the standard Java input and output streams to the Notes Java console and setting up a timer thread that can limit agent execution time according to administrator settings. After everything's been set up, `AgentBase` calls `NotesMain()`.

The `NotesMain()` method, like the `main()` method in Java applications, is where your program begins and ends. Simple agents often consist of just this method, although it's usually a good idea to split up larger amounts of code into several methods and classes.

`NotesMain()` is one of the few Java methods names I've seen that starts with a capital letter. Unfortunately, the folks at Lotus choose to ignore the lowercase method name convention. Perhaps they thought Notes deserved to be capitalized!

The `Session` Object

Every Java program thatNotes and Domino needs a `Session` object. `Session`s are your program's connection to the underlying Notes system. You can use the `Session` object to do a variety of things. For the most part, you will use it to access existing data, such as `DbDirectory` objects and `Database` objects. You will also use it to create "independent" objects such as `DateTime`, `DateRange`, `Name`, and `NewsLetter`. Use the `Session` object to access system properties like the Notes version, current username, and platform. `Session` is also used to call "global" methods like `evaluate()` and `freeTimeSearch()` that don't seem to fit anywhere else.

Each agent starts with its own `Session` object, which you can access from any method in your agent's class by using the `getSession()` method, as in

```
Session aSession = getSession();
```

You can then use the variable `aSession` to call methods like this:

```
If ( aSession.isOnServer() ) System.out.println( "Hey, this is
➥ running on the server!" );
```

API Help

To learn the full story about `Session` or any other class in the NOI, do the following:

1. In Domino Designer, choose Help/Context Help or press F1.
2. Open the Java Classes section.
3. Open the Java Classes A–Z section.
4. Scroll down and click on the classname, such as `Session`.

When the help system refers to the *properties* of a class, it means fields that can be accessed with get methods, as in getServerName(). The property is ServerName. Things aren't always so clear-cut, though. Methods like getDatabase() are listed separately, presumably because they retrieve data outside the class in question.

You can also use the Info pane to bring up help on a class or method (see Figure 27.2):

1. Click on the Reference tab in the Info pane.

2. Choose Notes Java from the pull-down list.

3. Open lotus.domino and then Interfaces.

4. Open Session or another class.

5. Open Methods if you want to see the methods in the class.

6. Click on a class or method and press F1 (or click Help) to view its help page.

FIGURE 27.2

Use the Info pane to browse the classes and methods of the Notes Java API.

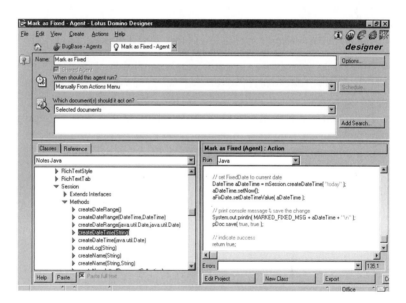

Most of the Notes classes are listed as *interfaces* in the Info pane, even though they're not really interfaces in the strict Java sense. From what I can tell, the folks who wired up the Info pane consider a class an interface when it wraps a C++ object and cannot be directly instantiated or extended. Classes that can be used like normal Java classes, such as AgentBase and NotesThread, are considered *classes* in the Info pane.

The `AgentContext` Object

Before `NotesMain()` is called, `AgentBase` creates an `AgentContext` object and initializes it with information specific to the current agent's execution environment. You access the `AgentContext` object using the `Session` object like this:

```
Session aSession = getSession();
AgentContext aAgentContext = aSession.getAgentContext();
```

`AgentContext` is most often used to get a list of documents in the current database that must be processed. The documents that are considered unprocessed depend on the Which Documents(s) Should It Act On setting in the Programmer's pane. You can choose to process unread documents, selected documents, modified documents, all documents in the view, or all documents in the database. To further narrow the list, add search criteria with the Add Search button. To access the list in your code, use the `getUnprocessedDocuments()` method to retrieve a `DocumentCollection` object. Use this object to cycle through the list, processing each document as you see fit. Take a look at the `processDocuments()` method in Listing 27.1 for an example.

`AgentContext` can also be used to access a handful of other agent-specific properties. Use `getCurrentDatabase()` to retrieve the agent's database. Use `getLastRun()` to learn when the agent last ran and `getLastExitStatus()` to find out how things turned out. The `getSavedData()` method returns a `Document` object you can use to save data between runs of the agent. This special document won't appear in any view. Keep in mind, though, that this document is cleared every time you make changes to your agent.

Exception Handling

The last part of the sample code template is an exception handler:

```
catch( Exception e )
{
    e.printStackTrace();
}
```

Any errors that happen in the preceding `try` block cause an immediate transfer to this handler. The variable e contains an `Exception` object that's been passed, or *thrown*, from the spot where the error occurs, whether it's in the same method or several methods deep in your code.

The `printStackTrace()` method writes a snapshot of the event to the Java console, which in Domino Designer can be found in File, Tools, Show Java Debug Console. For example, this method makes an illegal call to `Session.createDateTime()`:

```
public void makeEntry() throws NotesException
{
    Session aSession = getSession();
```

```
    DateTime aDateTime = aSession.createDateTime( "two weeks from now" );

    // .. more processing
}
```

The throws NotesException clause in the signature tells Java to send NotesException errors back to the calling method. If you don't use a throws clause, your method *must* handle all possible Notes exceptions.

Calling this method from NotesMain() results in this console output:

```
lotus.domino.NotesException
    at lotus.domino.local.Session.createDateTime(Session.java:736)
    at JavaAgent.makeEntry(JavaAgent.java:21)
    at JavaAgent.NotesMain(JavaAgent.java:11)
    at lotus.domino.AgentBase.runNotes(AgentBase.java:160)
    at lotus.domino.NotesThread.run(NotesThread.java:202)
```

The indented lines are the stack trace in reverse order. Parentheses contain the source files and line numbers of each method call. Reading from bottom to top, you can see that NotesThread.run() called AgentBase.runNotes(), which in turn called the agent's NotesMain() method. These lines will appear in any agent stack trace.

The good stuff is in the next three calls. First, the makeEntry() method was called from NotesMain() on line 11 of the JavaAgent source file. Then, the createDateTime() method was called from makeEntry() on line 21. The exception occurred within createDateTime() because it's the first method listed. The very top line is the exception message, which usually contains more information. This one isn't very helpful.

Unfortunately, exceptions are another area where Notes strays from the Java way. Most exceptions describe themselves when you call getMessage(), which is what printStackTrace() uses to get the exception message. The NotesException class simply returns lotus.domino.NotesException, which tells you nothing.

Also, most non-Notes exceptions use class inheritance to organize exceptions into hierarchies. For example, Java's FileNotFoundException inherits from IOException, which in turn inherits from Exception. This is useful because handlers can be crafted to catch exceptions at any level in the tree. Notes, on the other hand, uses the sole NotesException class for its several hundred possible errors. Because NotesException uses error numbers instead of class types to distinguish exceptions, you must use if statements or switch statements within catch clauses, like this:

```
try
{
    makeEntry();
}
catch( NotesException e )
{
```

```
switch( e.id )
{
    case NotesError.NOTES_ERR_NOTAFILE:
        System.err.println( "Couldn't make the newsletter!" );
        break;

    case NotesError.NOTES_ERR_FILEOPEN_FAILED:
        System.err.println( "Couldn't open file!" );
        break;

    default:
        System.err.println( "Notes Exception " + e.id +
                        ➥" -- " + e.text );
}
}
catch( Exception e )
{
    e.printStackTrace();
}
```

Running this example displays

```
Notes Exception 4468 -- Invalid date
```

Each `NotesException` object has an `id` field, which contains the Notes error number, and a `text` field, which contains the text description. The `NotesError` class holds all the error number constants, such as `NOTES_ERR_NOTAFILE`.

Also, note that `catch` clauses can be listed one after another. The first clause that matches the exception gets to handle it. Therefore, if a `FileNotFoundException` occurs in the preceding example, it will skip the `NotesException` handler to the more general `Exception` handler.

Making BugBase

For the rest of this chapter and the next, you will be shown several examples that center around BugBase.nsf, a database located in the bugbase directory on the CD. The code examples are located a few layers deeper in bugbase\com\mcp\naddu\bugbase because each example uses the package name `com.mcp.naddu.bugbase`.

BugBase is used to track software errors in a programming project. Each document in the database contains data on a single bug: when it was found, when it was fixed, who should fix it, a description, and its priority (see Figure 27.3). Documents are added by people with depositor access to the database, presumably members of a quality assurance team (see Figure 27.4). Managers can then review bugs, assign them, change their priority, or mark them as fixed.

FIGURE 27.3

BugBase can be used to keep track of bugs in a programming project.

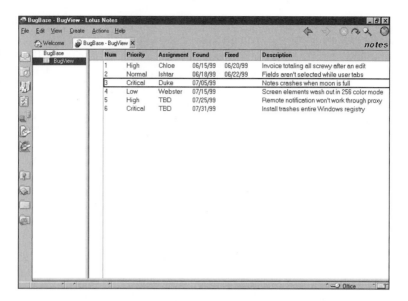

FIGURE 27.4

A sample bug document shown in edit mode.

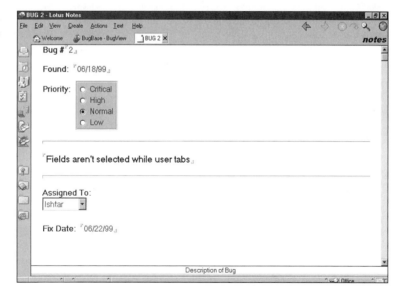

The first example, Listing 27.1, is an agent that marks selected bugs as fixed by assigning them a fix date equal to the current date. It consists of only three methods. The first, NotesMain(), simply sets up things and calls the second, processDocuments(), which cycles through each document to process, handing each to the third, markAsFixed(), which performs the actual work. The first two methods can be used with little modification in any agent you write that processes a batch of documents. The third method illustrates how to access and change items in a document with the Java API.

I'll let the code speak for itself.

LISTING 27.1 The Java Agent That Marks Selected Bug Documents as Fixed

```java
// BugBase, version 1.0 alpha 1 -- MarkAsFixedAgent.java
// Copyright (c) 1999 by Macmillan Computer Publishing

package com.mcp.naddu.bugbase;

import lotus.domino.*;

/////////////////////////////////////////////////////////
/**
 ** Notes Java agent for the BugBase database      <BR>
 ** that marks selected bug documents in the       <BR>
 ** current view as fixed by filling in the        <BR>
 ** FixDate item with the current date.            <BR>
 ** Selected bug documents that are already        <BR>
 ** marked as fixed are ignored. Must run in       <BR>
 ** the Notes client.                              <BR>
 **
 ** @author  Timothy Falconer
 ** @version 1.0 alpha 1
 */

public class MarkAsFixedAgent extends AgentBase
{
    // message constants
    static final String PROCESSING_BUG_MSG = "Processing Bug ";
    static final String TOTAL_CHANGED_MSG = "Total marked as fixed: ";
    static final String ALREADY_FIXED_MSG = "Bug already fixed on ";
    static final String MARKED_FIXED_MSG = "Marked bug as fixed on ";

    // item name constants
    static final String BUG_NUM_ITEM = "BugNum";
    static final String FIX_DATE_ITEM = "FixDate";

    /** the session object */
    protected Session mSession;

    /** the agent context object */
    protected AgentContext mAgentContext;

    //-----------------------------------------------
    /** Main agent processing routine --
     ** handles initialization and error handling.
```

```
      */

  public void NotesMain()
  {
    try
    {
        // set session and context members for quick classwide access
        mSession = getSession();
        mAgentContext = mSession.getAgentContext();

        // perform agent tasks
        processDocuments();
    }
    catch( NotesException e )
    {
        // print informative error message and stack trace
        System.err.println( "Notes Exception " + e.id +
        ③" -- " + e.text );
        e.printStackTrace();
    }
    catch( Exception e )
    {
        // non-Notes exceptions already have informative message
        e.printStackTrace();
    }
  }


  //-----------------------------------------------------------------
  /** Cycle through list of documents to be processed          <BR>
   ** and process each. Count successful changes and           <BR>
   ** display total to user at end.                            <BR>
   **
   ** @exception NotesException Pass the buck back to NotesMain()
   */

  public void processDocuments() throws NotesException
  {
    // tally of successful changes
    int aChangeCount = 0;

    // get document list & first document (or null if list is empty)
    DocumentCollection aDocs = mAgentContext.getUnprocessedDocuments();
    Document aDoc = aDocs.getFirstDocument();

    // cycle through documents until none are left
    while ( aDoc != null )
    {
        // process the document and increment count if successful
        boolean aSuccess = markAsFixed( aDoc );
        if ( aSuccess ) aChangeCount++;
```

continues

27

BASIC JAVA

LISTING 27.1 Continued

```java
            // mark doc as processed & get next document (or null if done)
            mAgentContext.updateProcessedDoc( aDoc );
            aDoc = aDocs.getNextDocument();
        }

        // print changes tally & separator
        System.out.println( TOTAL_CHANGED_MSG + aChangeCount );
        System.out.println( "---------------------------------------\n" );
    }

    //-------------------------------------------------------
    /** Mark bug document as fixed if it isn't fixed already.
     **
     ** @param pDoc Bug document to test and possibly mark as fixed
     ** @return boolean Return true if change was made,
     ** false if bug was fixed
     ** @exception NotesException Pass the buck back to NotesMain()
     */

    public boolean markAsFixed( Document pDoc ) throws NotesException
    {
        // get bug number and write message to console
        int aBugNum = pDoc.getItemValueInteger( BUG_NUM_ITEM );
        System.out.println( PROCESSING_BUG_MSG + aBugNum );

        // get fix date item & its text representation
        Item aItem = pDoc.getFirstItem( FIX_DATE_ITEM );
        String aItemText = aItem.getText();

        // if fix date has a value, print a message and return as failure
        if ( aItemText.length() > 0 )
        {
            System.out.println( ALREADY_FIXED_MSG + aItemText + "\n" );
            return false;
        }

        // set fix date to current date
        DateTime aDateTime = mSession.createDateTime( "today" );
        aDateTime.setNow();
        aItem.setDateTimeValue( aDateTime );

        // save the change
        pDoc.save( true, true );

        // print console message and return a success
        System.out.println( MARKED_FIXED_MSG + aDateTime + "\n" );
        return true;
    }
}
```

Running this agent with several documents selected will result in console output similar to that in Figure 27.5. Any text you pass to `System.out.println()` will be sent to this console. It's a good place to put messages to yourself about the progress of your agent.

FIGURE 27.5

BugBase displays result messages to the Java Debug console.

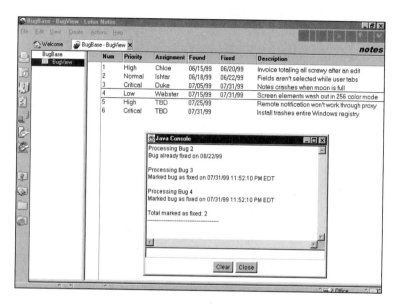

As you can see, I've followed good programming etiquette and placed all text messages and item names in constants that are conveniently located at the top of the class. This practice pays handsomely if you have to internationalize your software because your text is grouped together and easy to change. You can later put your message constants into language-specific Java resource bundles, which are used automatically according to the system preferences of each user. This is a real benefit for multinational Notes applications.

Another discipline I've adhered to is thorough commenting. Take a close look at the "doc comments" that precede each method. Each fully describes the purpose of the method; each contains a `@param` tag for each parameter, a `@return` tag for the return type, and an `@exception` tag for each exception thrown. I can't recommend this practice enough. Consistent use of doc comments will make your life much easier. You can use HTML tags such as `<BR>` for line breaks or `<B>` for bold to add extra formatting. To use the javadoc tool to create HTML documentation like that in Figure 27.6, make sure that you have installed a copy of Sun's free Java Development Kit (JDK), open up a DOS window or command shell, and type this:

```
javadoc com.mcp.naddu.bugbase
```

FIGURE 27.6

The javadoc tool creates HTML docs from your source that can be viewed in a browser.

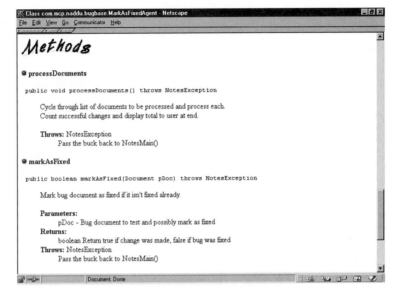

Using Other Java IDEs

You will want to use an external Java development environment for all but the most basic agents. Domino Designer lacks many features that exist in other Java IDEs, not the least of which is debugging support. Designer won't allow you to watch variables, set breakpoints, or step through code. This means that you're stuck with System.out.println() as your sole debugging tool unless you use a Java IDE like Borland JBuilder or IBM's VisualAge for Java. Luckily, Designer makes it relatively easy for your agents to coexist with other environments.

Agent Files

Agents can contain numerous source files, class files, JAR files, data files, and image files. You can add new source files to your agent by clicking the New Class button in the Programmer's pane. You can switch between source files with the Classes tab or by scrolling in the editor window. Source for each class is separated in the editor by thin, gray title bars. You can double-click these title bars to hide and show their source text. After editing your source, be sure to click the Compile button to make Designer compile your class files. If any errors are found, you will be brought to the first, and you will see a brief error message. Simply fix each error and recompile till none are left.

You can also use the organizer window, as shown in Figure 27.7, to add preexisting files to your agent. Open it by clicking the Edit Project button; then, locate your files by choosing the appropriate base directory and file type. Click the archive check box to show JAR files and ZIP files. Click the resource check box to show image files. To add files to your agent, select them on the left and click the Add/Replace File(s) button. To remove files from your agent, select them on the right and click Delete.

FIGURE 27.7

The organizer window helps you manage the files in your agent.

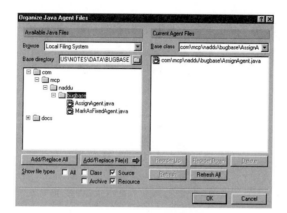

Copies of each file are kept in the database with the agent. Domino uses these copies when it runs the agent, never the originals on disk. Although this allows for easy replication of the agent, it makes working with external IDEs a bit more difficult because the files in your agent and the files on the disk can easily get out of sync with each other.

To copy your agent files to disk so that they can be used outside Designer, click the Export button and choose a directory to serve as base. It's a good idea to put the files in a directory specific to your project, such as c:\lotus\notes\data\bugbase.

You can then edit and debug your files with external tools such as JBuilder, but the changes you make won't affect your agent until you refresh the files back in the organizer window. To do this, click Refresh All, or select individual files in the right pane and click Refresh. Designer will ask whether you want to replace your existing files. Clicking Yes and saving your agent will again bring it in sync with the outside world.

AgentRunner

In the past, externally debugging your agents was problematic because you needed Notes to set up the agent's context. In R5, you can use a class named `AgentRunner` to initialize the context and start your agent. `AgentRunner` obtains the context information from documents stored in AgentRunner.nsf, a database that comes with Designer.

To use `AgentRunner`, simply change the superclass of your agent from `AgentBase` to `DebugAgentBaseand` and then run your agent as usual. Rather than execute `NotesMain()` as usual, agents derived from `DebugAgentBase` create a context document like the one in Figure 27.8, then display the following message, and quit:

```
AgentContext dumped to file AgentRunner.nsf
```

FIGURE 27.8

The AgentRunner database contains documents with simulated AgentContext information.

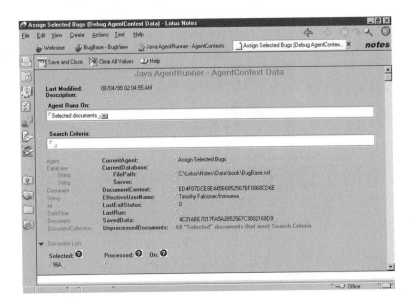

To illustrate AgentRunner, I've created another example that's complex enough to warrant the need for a real debugger. Listing 27.2 shows a class named `AssignAgent` that automatically assigns and emails bugs to a pool of developers on a rotating basis. I've also created two agents in BugBase.nsf, both of which use this class. The first is `Assign Selected Bugs`, which runs from the Notes client on selected documents. The second, `Assign New Bugs`, runs automatically on Domino servers when new bugs are added to the database. The only difference between the two is how they start.

This example is very similar to the last one. The class begins much the same, although this one extends `DebugAgentBase` instead of `AgentBase`. The `NotesMain()` method is exactly the same as before. The `processDocuments()` method has only one change—it calls `assignBug()` on each document, instead of `markAsFixed()`. Like its earlier counterpart, `assignBug()` first obtains the item in question (this time, `AssignedTo`) and then checks whether it's already been processed, in which case it returns unsuccessfully. Otherwise, it calls `chooseDeveloper()`, assigns the choice, and saves the change. It then uses the `mailBug()` method to send the document to the chosen developer.

Here's the code.

LISTING 27.2   The Java Agent That Assigns Bug Documents to Developers

```java
// BugBase, version 1.0 alpha 1 -- AssignAgent.java
// Copyright (c) 1999 by Macmillan Computer Publishing

package com.mcp.naddu.bugbase;

import lotus.domino.*;

////////////////////////////////////////////////////////////////////
/**
 **   Notes Java agent for the BugBase database that assigns each    <BR>
 **   pending bug to the next developer in a rotation. After         <BR>
 **   being assigned bugs, developers are notified of this           <BR>
 **   by e-mail.                                                     <BR>
 **                                                                  <BR>
 **   Can be started manually in the Notes client, or                <BR>
 **   automatically from either the Notes client or Domino
 **   server when new bugs arrive.
 **
 **   @author  Timothy Falconer
 **   @version 1.0 alpha 1
 */

public class AssignAgent extends DebugAgentBase
{
    // message constants
    static final String PROCESSING_BUG_MSG = "Processing Bug ";
    static final String TOTAL_CHANGED_MSG = "Total assigned: ";
    static final String ASSIGNED_AND_MAILED_MSG = "Bug assigned
    ③and mailed to ";
    static final String ALREADY_ASSIGNED_MSG = "Bug already assigned to ";
    static final String BUG_HEADER_MSG = "BUG ";

    // item name constants
    static final String BUG_NUM_ITEM = "BugNum";
    static final String ASSIGNED_TO_ITEM = "AssignedTo";
    static final String DESCRIPTION_ITEM = "Description";
    static final String SUBJECT_ITEM = "Subject";

    // value constants
    static final String TBD_VALUE = "TBD";

    /** the session object */
    protected Session mSession;

    /** the agent context object */
```

continues

27

BASIC JAVA

LISTING 27.2   Continued

```java
   protected AgentContext mAgentContext;

   /** array of developer names (don't hard code this at home) */
   protected String[] mDevelopers = { "Webster", "Chloe",
                                      ③"Ishtar", "Duke" };

   //------------------------------------------------------------
   /** Main agent processing routine -- handles initialization
    ** and error handling.
    */

   public void NotesMain()
   {
      try
      {
         // set session and context members for quick classwide access
         mSession = getSession();
         mAgentContext = mSession.getAgentContext();

         // perform agent tasks
         processDocuments();
      }
      catch( NotesException e )
      {
         // print informative error message and stack trace
         System.err.println( "Notes Exception " + e.id + " -- "
         ③+ e.text );
         e.printStackTrace();
      }
      catch( Exception e )
      {
         // non-Notes exceptions already have informative message
         e.printStackTrace();
      }
   }

   //------------------------------------------------------------
   /** Cycle through list of documents to be processed       <BR>
    ** and process each.                                      <BR>
    ** Count successful changes and display total to user at end.
    **
    ** @exception NotesException Pass the buck back to NotesMain()
    */

   public void processDocuments() throws NotesException
   {
      // tally of successful changes
      int aChangeCount = 0;
```

```
    // get document list & first document (or null if list is empty)
    DocumentCollection aDocs = mAgentContext.getUnprocessedDocuments();
    Document aDoc = aDocs.getFirstDocument();

    // cycle through documents until none are left
    while ( aDoc != null )
    {
        // process the document and increment count if successful
        boolean aSuccess = assignBug( aDoc );
        if ( aSuccess ) aChangeCount++;

        // mark doc as processed and get next document (or null if done)
        mAgentContext.updateProcessedDoc( aDoc );
        aDoc = aDocs.getNextDocument();
    }

    // print changes tally and separator
    System.out.println( TOTAL_CHANGED_MSG + aChangeCount );
    System.out.println( "-------------------------------------\n" );
}

//------------------------------------------------------
/** Assign bug document to next developer in the rotation
 **
 ** @param pDoc Bug document to assign
 ** @return boolean Return true if change was made,
 ** false if bug was fixed
 ** @exception NotesException Pass the buck back to NotesMain()
 */

public boolean assignBug( Document pDoc ) throws NotesException
{
    // get bug number and write message to console
    int aBugNum = pDoc.getItemValueInteger( BUG_NUM_ITEM );
    System.out.println( PROCESSING_BUG_MSG + aBugNum );

    // get assigned-to item and its text representation
    Item aItem = pDoc.getFirstItem( ASSIGNED_TO_ITEM );
    String aItemText = aItem.getValueString();

    // make sure that the bug's assignment is yet To-Be-Determined
    if ( !aItemText.equals( TBD_VALUE ) )
    {
        System.out.println( ALREADY_ASSIGNED_MSG + aItemText + "\n" );
        return false;
    }

    // choose the developer and set the item
    String aDeveloper = chooseDeveloper( aBugNum );
    aItem.setValueString( aDeveloper );
```

continues

27

BASIC JAVA

LISTING 27.2 Continued

```java
        // save and mail the document
        pDoc.save( true, true );
        mailBug( pDoc, aDeveloper );

        // print console message and return a success
        System.out.println( ASSIGNED_AND_MAILED_MSG + aDeveloper + "\n" );
        return true;
    }

    //------------------------------------------------------------
    /** Choose the next developer in the rotation that gets a bug
     **
     ** @param pBugNum The bug number determines the developer
     ** @return String Return Common name of developer
     ** @exception NotesException Pass the buck back to NotesMain()
     */

    public String chooseDeveloper( int pBugNum ) throws NotesException
    {
        // take remainder of the bug number divided by number of developers
        int aDeveloperNum = pBugNum % mDevelopers.length;

        // return corresponding developer
        return mDevelopers[ aDeveloperNum ];
    }

    //------------------------------------------------------------
    /** E-mail bug document to developer
     **
     ** @param pDeveloper String containing common name of developer
     ** @exception NotesException Pass the buck back to NotesMain()
     */

    public void mailBug( Document pDoc, String pDeveloper )
    ③throws NotesException
    {
        // make appropriate subject of form "BUG 2 - bug description"
        int aBugNum = pDoc.getItemValueInteger( BUG_NUM_ITEM );
        String aDescription = pDoc.getItemValueString( DESCRIPTION_ITEM );
        String aSubject = BUG_HEADER_MSG + aBugNum + " - " + aDescription;

        // set the subject and send
        pDoc.replaceItemValue( SUBJECT_ITEM, aSubject );
        pDoc.send( true, pDeveloper );
    }
```

```
//-----------------------------------------------------------
/** Agent debug main method, used with AgentRunner database
 **
 ** @param pArgs Command-line parameters
 */

public static void main( String[] pArgs )
{
    // specify information as appears in AgentContext document
    String aAgent  = "Assign Selected Bugs";
    String aDb     = "C:\\Lotus\\Notes\\Data\\book\\BugBase.nsf";
    String aServer = "Local";

    // construct hard-wired parameters array
    String[] aParams = { aAgent, aDb, aServer };

    try
    {
        // replace aParams with pArgs to use command-line parameters
        AgentRunner.main( aParams );
    }
    catch( Exception e )
    {
        e.printStackTrace();
    }
}
}
}
```

The main() method in AssignAgent makes it easier to start AgentRunner from your external IDE. AgentRunner uses the agent name, the database, and the server as parameters, although only the agent name is strictly required. The text in aAgent, aDb, and aServer should be identical to that found in the agent context document in AgentRunner.nsf, although you will have to double up your backslashes if you have any.

To get things going, load the file in your IDE and compile it. Then, set a breakpoint on the first line of NotesMain() and run the program. When the debugger stops in NotesMain(), you should be able to step through code, line by line, watching variables as they change. Figure 27.9 shows a debugging session in JBuilder with it stopped just before the call to mailBug(). On the left, you can see the current stack trace. Below that, you can see the value for each local variable.

FIGURE 27.9

Using JBuilder to debug your agent enables you to step through code, watch variables, and view real-time stack traces belonging to multiple threads.

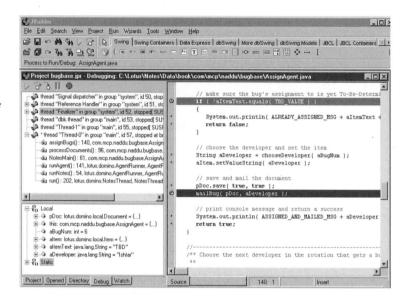

Before this example will work, you must replace the names in the mDevelopers array with some valid names from your own network. You can add as many developers as you like. When you're done playing with it in your IDE, change the superclass back to AgentBase and refresh both AssignBug agents in BugBase.nsf with Domino Designer.

Summary

This chapter begins by outlining the many ways you can use Java with Notes and Domino. It then focuses on the most common type of Notes program—Java agents—by developing and discussing BugBase, a working QA database that makes it easy to manage and assign pending bugs from a Notes client.

In the Chapter, I'll discuss the remaining Java program Types by developing three new examples that will allow your team to use BugBase on machines without Notes or Domino installed.

Using Java in Domino Applications

by Timothy Falconer

IN THIS CHAPTER

While agents are the most common type of Notes program, they're not the only game in town, especially given the advances in Notes and Domino R5. It's now possible to write applications, servlets, and applets that interact with Domino servers from just about anywhere. This chapter discusses how to do just that with three new programs that allow users to interact with BugBase in different ways.

The first program is a console app that lets programmers list bugs from the command line and mark them fixed when they're finished. The second is a servlet that lets you view your bug list in a browser. The last is an applet that lets you add bugs from afar.

While you can do any of these things easily with Notes, these programs can run on machines with or without Notes and Domino installed. This magic is made possible by a technology called CORBA (Common Object Request Broker Architecture), which lets you easily interact with remote Domino servers. I think you'll be pleasantly surprised at how easy it is to use CORBA with Domino.

Using Multithreading and NotesThread

Java makes it easy to use multiple threads in your programs. A *thread* is a single path of execution. Having multiple threads allows your program to do more than one thing at a time. For example, you can have one thread transmitting data over a network while another thread interacts with the user.

Every Java program starts with a single thread. You can then create and start new threads using the Thread class, usually by creating a class that extends it. Your class will then inherit the capabilities of Thread, such as the `start()` method that gets things going. You also need to define a `run()` method to define the thread's actions. Here's an example:

```
class MyThread extends Thread
{
   public void run()
   {
      for( int i = 0; i < 10; i++ )
         System.out.println( "This happens in its own thread" );
   }

   public static void main( String[] pArgs )
   {
      MyThread aThread = new MyThread();
      aThread.start();
   }
}
```

Here, the `main()` method creates an instance of `MyThread` called `aThread`, and then starts it by calling the `start()` method. Every thread starts and ends with the `run()` method, which in this case prints a message 10 times. When the `run()` method finishes, the thread ends. When all threads in a program have ended, the program ends.

You can also implement the Runnable interface instead of extending Thread. This is useful when your class needs to extend a different superclass. To do this, create an instance of your class, wrap it with a new Thread object, and call `start()` as before:

```
class MyRunner extends AnotherClass implements Runnable
{
   public void run()
   {
      for( int i = 0; i < 10; i++ )
         System.out.println( "This happens in its own thread" );
   }

   public static void main( String[] pArgs )
   {
      MyRunner aRunner = new MyRunner();
      Thread aThread = new Thread( aRunner );
      aThread.start();
   }
}
```

Each thread that uses the Notes Java API needs to initialize the Notes system with the `NotesThread` class. NotesThread acts just like Thread, with the one difference being that its subclasses must implement a `runNotes()` method instead of a `run()` method. In its own `run()`, NotesThread initializes the Notes system and calls `runNotes()`, which acts just like `run()`. Here's an example:

```
import lotus.domino.*;

class MyNotesThread extends NotesThread
{
   public void runNotes()
   {
      try
      {
         Session aSession = NotesFactory.createSession();
         Database aDb = aSession.getDatabase( "", "BugBase.NSF" );
         System.out.println( aDb.getTitle() );
      }
      catch( NotesException e )
      {
      }
   }
```

```
   public static void main( String[] pArgs )
   {
      MyNotesThread aThread = new MyNotesThread();
      aThread.start();
   }
}
```

As with Thread, your class can implement Runnable instead of extending NotesThread. You can then use a regular old run() method, since NotesThread is simply a wrapper:

```
import lotus.domino.*;

class MyRunner implements Runnable
{
   public void run()
   {
      // same code as in previous runNotes() method
   }

   public static void main( String[] pArgs )
   {
      MyRunner aRunner = new MyRunner();
      Thread aThread = new NotesThread( aRunner );
      aThread.start();
   }
}
```

Because often it's inconvenient to create a new class just to use Notes, you can initialize the Notes system yourself with the static sinitThread() method of NotesThread. Make sure you also use the stermThread() method when you're finished:

```
import lotus.domino.*;

class MyApp
{
   public static void main( String[] pArgs )
   {
      NotesThread.sinitThread();

      // same code is in previous runNotes() method

      NotesThread.stermThread();
   }
}
```

As you've already learned, Notes agents are created by extending AgentBase, which itself extends NotesThread. As you'll soon learn, Notes applets are created by extending AppletBase, which uses NotesThread automatically. This means that if you're making agents or applets and you stick to one thread, you're all set. With local applications and servlets, you need to use NotesThread or your program can't use the Notes API.

Using CORBA

CORBA is a technology created by a multi-company consortium called the Object Management Group (www.omg.org). CORBA allows you to use software objects located on another machine halfway around the world as easily as objects on your own machine.

To do this, you create "proxy" objects on your machine that can communicate with remote objects via the Internet Inter-ORB protocol (IIOP). Every time you call a method on a proxy object, the call and its parameters get automatically transmitted to an object request broker (ORB) on the remote machine. The ORB then passes the call to the real object, which executes the call and returns the results back to the proxy object. While this may sound complicated, it's really simple. If you have an ORB and a way to make proxy objects, just use the proxy objects as though they were the real ones.

Domino R5 comes with its own ORB, a server task named DIIOP, which loads by default when you specify "Web Server" during the Domino install. The DIIOP task requires the HTTP Web server task. To see if these are running, use the "show tasks" command at your Domino console, or use Domino Administrator. If they're not running, edit the ServerTasks line in your server's NOTES.INI file to include HTTP and DIIOP.

```
ServerTasks=Router,Replica, ... ,HTTP,DIIOP
```

You'll also need to change some settings in that machine's Server document to allow remote users to access that server via IIOP. Open the Server document with Notes or Domino Administrator, and then click on the Security tab (see Figure 28.1). Under IIOP Restrictions, you'll see two fields, one for restricted Java and another for unrestricted Java. Specify users and groups with appropriate access, or use an asterisk to indicate all users. The only difference between the two kinds of access is that restricted users can't use several "sensitive" methods in the Java API, such as sign() and openFileLog(). After you've added these tasks and changed the settings, restart your Domino server and you'll have a working ORB that can serve up Domino objects almost automatically.

Getting the ORB going is only half the battle. You also need a file called NCSO.JAR, which contains a special CORBA version of the Notes Java API. Each class in NCSO.JAR is a special proxy version of the corresponding class in NOTES.JAR. The file NCSO.JAR comes with the Domino Toolkit for Java/CORBA, which you can download for free from http://www.lotus-developer.com/lotusdominotj. The toolkit also contains NCSOC.JAR, which is a compressed version of the library, and NSCO.CAB, which is the library in Microsoft's CAB format instead of Java's JAR format.

Once you have NCSO.JAR, add it to your Java CLASSPATH and use a special version of NotesFactory.createSession(), which specifies the server address, Domino user name, and password. For example

FIGURE 28.1

To use CORBA, you must give users access by setting the IIOP restrictions in the Server document's Security tab.

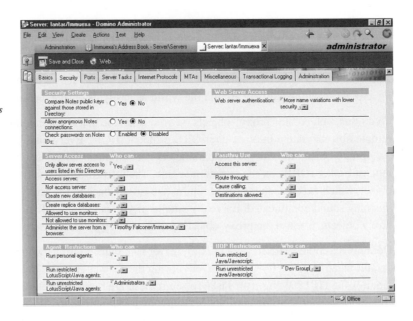

```
Session aSession = NotesFactory.createSession( "waveplace.com", "Crissi
➥Corbin", "secret" );
```

You can then use Session and all the other classes in the Notes Object Interface just as you normally would. The CORBA proxies communicate automatically with their real equivalents on the remote Domino server without any help from you. It's really that easy.

By the way, you shouldn't use NotesThread with the CORBA library because NotesThread loads the native Notes system. Use Thread instead.

Writing Java Applications

To make standalone Java applications that use Notes, you'll need to download and install the Java Development Kit (JDK) from http://java.sun.com. The Gold release of Notes and Domino R5 supports version 1.1.6 of the JDK, although this may change with each maintenance release. As of this writing, the latest JDK is version 1.2.2, but until Notes explicitly supports JDK 1.2 and later (a.k.a. "Java 2"), I suggest you download the latest 1.1 version, which is currently JDK 1.1.8.

After you've installed the JDK, you need to make sure your PATH statement includes the JDK bin directory. Also, if you're using Notes locally and not CORBA, you need to add the Notes directory to your path. Here's an example:

```
set PATH=%PATH%;c:\lotus\notes;c:\jdk1.1.8\bin
```

You also need to append your Java CLASSPATH to include NOTES.JAR if you're using Notes locally and NCSO.JAR if you're using CORBA. Also add the base directory for the BugBase examples (the one that contains com\mcp\naddu\bugbase). For example

```
set CLASSPATH=%CLASSPATH%;c:\lotus\notes\notes.jar;c:\lotus\notes\data\bugbase
```

Be sure to restart your machine or log back in to make these changes effective.

Using BugApp

Programmers like command-line tools because they're usually faster and more flexible than their GUI equivalents. The next example lets programmers working in the command-line trenches perform the two BugBase tasks that matter most: listing the bugs that need fixing and marking them fixed when they're finished.

Because Java applications need to run in their own JVM, we'll be using Sun's java.exe, which is located in the JDK's bin directory. Type java followed by the name of the class and any parameters you want passed. A class must have a main() method in order to execute as an application. With your PATH and CLASSPATH set correctly, you can run your app from any directory in the system.

To run BugApp on a system with Notes installed, use a command-line like this:

```
java com.mcp.naddu.bugbase.BugApp list all
```

Here, I'm executing the BugApp class, which is in the com.mcp.naddu.bugbase package. Java will search each directory and JAR file in the CLASSPATH until it finds this package and class. It then loads the class and calls the main() method, passing it the arguments "list" and "all". If you make a mistake in your typing, BugApp prints an error and a syntax message. Otherwise, it lists all the bugs in your BugBase (see Figure 28.2). Make sure BugBase.NSF is located in the Notes data directory before running.

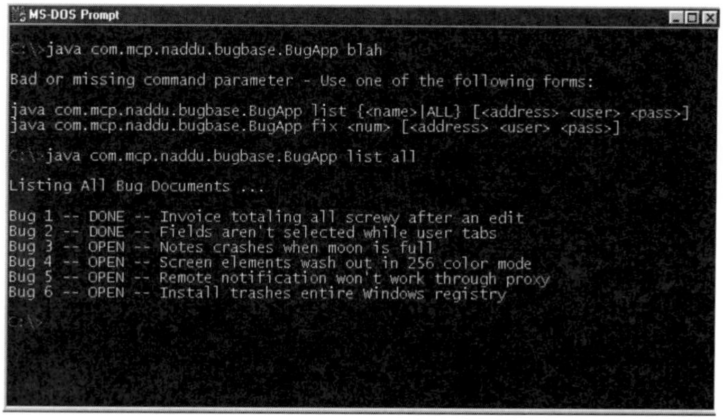

28

USING JAVA IN DOMINO APPLICATIONS

FIGURE 28.2

You can use BugApp on a machine with Notes installed to interact with BugBase from the command line.

As you can see from the syntax message, BugApp takes two commands: LIST and FIX. The LIST command can be followed with either the parameter ALL or the name of a particular developer. In the latter case, BugApp will only list the bugs assigned to that developer. If the developer's name includes a space, you need to enclose it in quotes or Java will think the last name is the next parameter. The FIX command takes only one kind of parameter: the number of the bug you want to fix.

To use BugApp on machines without Notes, you need to specify three additional parameters: the domain name or IP address of your Domino server, a user name, and a password. Make sure that the user has access to the server and that you've granted him or her IIOP permission as discussed earlier. Also make sure that a copy of BugBase.NSF is located in the data directory of your Domino server.

Figure 28.3 lists three CORBA runs. The first connects to the Domino server with IP address 90.0.0.2 as the user Chloe (with password meow) to list bugs assigned to Duke. The next connects as Timothy Falconer to lantar, the TCP/IP machine name of my server, to fix bug 3. Note the use of quotes around the username. The last run connects as Chloe to lantar. As you can see, bug 3 is now marked DONE.

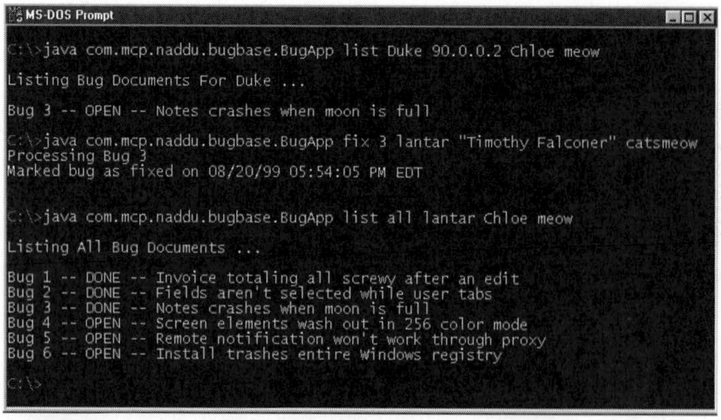

FIGURE 28.3

If you specify a host address, username, and password, BugApp will use CORBA to interact with a remote Domino server.

```
MS-DOS Prompt

C:\>java com.mcp.naddu.bugbase.BugApp list Duke 90.0.0.2 Chloe meow

Listing Bug Documents For Duke ...

Bug 3 -- OPEN -- Notes crashes when moon is full

C:\>java com.mcp.naddu.bugbase.BugApp fix 3 lantar "Timothy Falconer" catsmeow
Processing Bug 3
Marked bug as fixed on 08/20/99 05:54:05 PM EDT

C:\>java com.mcp.naddu.bugbase.BugApp list all lantar Chloe meow

Listing All Bug Documents ...

Bug 1 -- DONE -- Invoice totaling all screwy after an edit
Bug 2 -- DONE -- Fields aren't selected while user tabs
Bug 3 -- DONE -- Notes crashes when moon is full
Bug 4 -- OPEN -- Screen elements wash out in 256 color mode
Bug 5 -- OPEN -- Remote notification won't work through proxy
Bug 6 -- OPEN -- Install trashes entire Windows registry

C:\>
```

BugApp Source

Listing 28.1 contains the source for the BugApp class, which contains quite a few constants, a few member fields, and several methods. The last method is identical to the markAsFixed() method in Listing 27.1. In a production system, I'd move this method into a common class that is used by both BugApp and MarkAsFixedAgent, but for our purposes, cut-and-paste will suffice.

Execution starts with the `main()` method, which like all `main()` methods is static, meaning it's not associated with any particular object instance. First off, `main()` tries to create a `BugApp` instance by passing the command-line arguments in `pArgs` to the `BugApp` constructor. This constructor, listed next, parses the arguments and checks for errors. If any are found, the constructor throws an `IllegalArgumentException`. This exception is caught back in `main()`, where an error message and syntax reminder is printed before quitting. If no errors are found, the arguments are tucked away in the appropriate member fields and the app object is created.

What happens next depends on the address parameter. If none was supplied, this is a local run, so the app object is passed to a `NotesThread` constructor. Otherwise it's a CORBA run and the app object is passed to a normal `Thread` constructor. Note that the `BugApp` class implements `Runnable`, so either is allowed. The new thread is then started, which results in `run()` being called.

In `run()`, the address field is again checked to determine whether to create a CORBA session or a normal one. The BugBase database is then opened and either `listBugs()` or `fixBug()` is called depending on the command supplied. The rest of the code is fairly straightforward. Notice how the `search()` method is used to find documents that match a given Notes formula. This can be quite handy.

LISTING 28.1   Java App that Allows Developers to Interact with BugBase from the Command Line

```
// BugBase, version 1.0 alpha 1 -- BugApp.java
// Copyright (c) 1999 by Macmillan Computer Publishing

package com.mcp.naddu.bugbase;

import lotus.domino.*;

/////////////////////////////////////////////////////////////////////////////
/**                                                                     <BR>
 **   Command-line tool which lets developers list bugs & mark them fixed.  <BR>
 **   Run it with either of the following sets of parameters:          <BR>
 **                                                                     <BR>
 **       LIST name [address user password]                            <BR>
 **       FIX num [address user password]                              <BR>
 **                                                                     <BR>
 **   where "address", "user", and "password" are optional CORBA arguments.  <BR>
 **   The parameter "name" can be a developer name to list bugs assigned   <BR>
 **   to a particular developer, or "all" to list all bugs. Put individual  <BR>
 **   parameters in quotes if they contain a space.                    <BR>
 **                                                                     <BR>
```

continues

LISTING 28.1 Continued

```java
**   Note: production apps need a more secure way to input the password.    <BR>
**
**   @author  Timothy Falconer
**   @version 1.0 alpha 1
*/

public class BugApp implements Runnable
{
    // message constants
    static final String NOTES_EXCEPTION_MSG = "Notes Exception ";
    static final String CONNECTED_LOCALLY_MSG = "Connected locally";
    static final String CONNECTED_TO_SERVER_MSG = "Connected to server ";
    static final String AS_USER_MSG = " as user ";
    static final String PROCESSING_BUG_MSG = "Processing Bug ";
    static final String MARKED_FIXED_MSG = "Marked bug as fixed on ";
    static final String ALREADY_FIXED_MSG = "Bug already fixed on ";
    static final String OPENED_DB_MSG = "Opened database: ";
    static final String NO_DOC_FOUND_MSG = "No matching document found.";
    static final String BUG_MSG = "Bug ";
    static final String LISTING_ALL_DOCS_MSG = "Listing All Bug Documents";
    static final String LISTING_DOCS_FOR_MSG = "Listing Bug Documents For ";
    static final String FIXED_MSG = "DONE";
    static final String OPEN_MSG = "OPEN";
    static final String BAD_CMD_MSG = "Bad or missing command";
    static final String BAD_CMD_PARAM_MSG = "Bad or missing command parameter";
    static final String MISSING_USER_PASS_MSG = "Missing user or password";
    static final String CMD_LINE = "java com.mcp.naddu.bugbase.BugApp ";
    static final String SYNTAX_MSG = "Use one of the following forms:\n\n" +
        CMD_LINE + "list {<name>|ALL} [<address> <user> <pass>]\n" +
        CMD_LINE + "fix <num> [<address> <user> <pass>]";

    // commands
    static final String FIX_CMD = "FIX";
    static final String LIST_CMD = "LIST";

    // item name constants
    static final String BUG_NUM_ITEM = "BugNum";
    static final String ASSIGNED_TO_ITEM = "AssignedTo";
    static final String FIX_DATE_ITEM = "FixDate";
    static final String DESCRIPTION_ITEM = "Description";

    // value constants
    static final String BUGBASE_NSF = "BugBase.NSF";
    static final String ALL_PARAM = "ALL";
    static final String QUOTE = "\"";

    /** the session object */
    protected Session mSession;
```

```
   /** BugBase database object */
   protected Database mDb;

   /** command */
   protected String mCmd;

   /** command param */
   protected String mCmdParam;

   /** Domino host domain name or IP address */
   protected String mAddress;

   /** Domino user name */
   protected String mUser;

   /** Domino user password */
   protected String mPassword;

   //------------------------------------------------------------------------
   /** Main method - initializes BugApp object with pArgs and starts thread.
    **
    ** @param pArgs Command-line parameters
    */

   public static void main( String[] pArgs )
   {
      Thread aThread;

      try
      {
         // initialize runnable bug application object with command-line args
         BugApp aApp = new BugApp( pArgs );

         // create local or remote thread for runnable app object
         if ( aApp.mAddress != null ) aThread = new Thread( aApp );
         else aThread = new NotesThread( aApp );

         // start execution thread
            aThread.start();
      }
      catch( IllegalArgumentException e )
      {
         // print exception message & syntax reminder
         System.out.println();
         System.out.print( e.getMessage() + " - " );
         System.out.println( SYNTAX_MSG );
      }
   }
```

continues

LISTING 28.1   Continued

```java
//-----------------------------------------------------------------
/** Constructor that parses command-line arguments, checking for errors
 **
 ** @param pArgs Command-line parameters
 ** @exception IllegalArgumentException Argument errors cause syntax printout
& abort
 */

public BugApp( String[] pArgs ) throws IllegalArgumentException
{
    // parse command-line arguments in reverse order.
    // use fallthrough to parse each in turn (note lack of breaks)
    switch( pArgs.length )
    {
        case 5: mPassword = pArgs[ 4 ];
        case 4: mUser     = pArgs[ 3 ];
        case 3: mAddress  = pArgs[ 2 ];
        case 2: mCmdParam = pArgs[ 1 ];
        case 1: mCmd      = pArgs[ 0 ];
    }

    // if no command was specified, throw exception
    if ( mCmd == null ) throw new IllegalArgumentException( BAD_CMD_MSG );

    // if no command param was specified, throw exception
    if ( mCmdParam == null )
        throw new IllegalArgumentException( BAD_CMD_PARAM_MSG );

    // if command doesn't equal "FIX" or "LIST" throw exception
    if ( !( mCmd.equalsIgnoreCase( FIX_CMD ) ||
            mCmd.equalsIgnoreCase( LIST_CMD ) ) )
        throw new IllegalArgumentException( BAD_CMD_MSG );

    // if there's an address and there's no user or password, throw exception
    if ( mAddress != null && ( mUser == null || mPassword == null ) )
        throw new IllegalArgumentException( MISSING_USER_PASS_MSG );
}

//-----------------------------------------------------------------
/**  First method of thread - creates session, opens database, and    <BR>
 **  dispatches control to appropriate command handler.                <BR>
 */

public void run()
{
    try
    {
        // if no address, create a normal session, otherwise create a CORBA
one.
```

```
            if ( mAddress == null ) mSession = NotesFactory.createSession();
            else mSession = NotesFactory.createSession( mAddress, mUser, mPassword
);

            // open the bugbase database
            mDb = mSession.getDatabase( mSession.getServerName(), BUGBASE_NSF );

            // pass control to command-specific handler
            if ( mCmd.equalsIgnoreCase( LIST_CMD ) ) listBugs();
            if ( mCmd.equalsIgnoreCase( FIX_CMD ) ) fixBug();
        }
        catch( NotesException e )
        {
            // print informative error message
            System.err.println( NOTES_EXCEPTION_MSG + e.id + " -- " + e.text );
        }
    }


    //----------------------------------------------------------------------------
    /** List either all bugs or bugs specific to a developer.            <BR>
     ** Value of command parameter determines scope of list.
     **
     ** @exception NotesException Pass the buck back to run()
     */

    public void listBugs() throws NotesException
    {
        DocumentCollection aList;

        // start with blank line
        System.out.println();

        // if command param is "ALL" then get all documents
        if ( mCmdParam.equalsIgnoreCase( ALL_PARAM ) )
        {
            aList = mDb.getAllDocuments();
            System.out.println( LISTING_ALL_DOCS_MSG + " ... \n" );
        }
        else
        {
            // otherwise, search with formula of form: AssignedTo = "Duke"
            String aFormula = ASSIGNED_TO_ITEM + " = " + QUOTE + mCmdParam + QUOTE;

            aList = mDb.search( aFormula );
            System.out.println( LISTING_DOCS_FOR_MSG + mCmdParam + " ... \n" );
        }

        // cycle through the list
        Document aDoc = aList.getFirstDocument();
```

28

continues

LISTING 28.1 Continued

```
    while( aDoc != null )
    {
        // print information on the bug
        printBugLine( aDoc );

        // get next document in list (if any)
        aDoc = aList.getNextDocument();
    }
}

//------------------------------------------------------------------
/** Prints information for a single bug on a single line
 **
 ** @param pDoc Bug document to display
 ** @exception NotesException Pass the buck back to run()
 */

public void printBugLine( Document pDoc ) throws NotesException
{
    // check fix date for value & set display indicator
    Item aFixDateItem = pDoc.getFirstItem( FIX_DATE_ITEM );
    String aFixDateText = aFixDateItem.getText();
    String aFixFlag = ( aFixDateText.length() < 1 ) ? OPEN_MSG : FIXED_MSG;

    // print info on each document on a single line
    System.out.print( BUG_MSG + pDoc.getItemValueInteger( BUG_NUM_ITEM ) );
    System.out.print( " -- " + aFixFlag + " -- " );
    System.out.print( pDoc.getItemValueString( DESCRIPTION_ITEM ) );
    System.out.println();
}

//------------------------------------------------------------------
/** Mark the bug indicated by the parameter as fixed if it isn't.      <BR>
 ** This method uses the same exact markAsFixed() method as in          <BR>
 ** MarkAsFixedAgent. As such, some refactoring could be done.          <BR>
 **
 ** @exception NotesException Pass the buck back to run()
 */

public void fixBug() throws NotesException
{
    // get list of documents with indicated bug num
    String aFormula = BUG_NUM_ITEM + " = " + mCmdParam;
    DocumentCollection aList = mDb.search( aFormula );

    // if found, mark first (and only) as fixed, otherwise print message
    if ( aList.getCount() > 0 ) markAsFixed( aList.getFirstDocument() );
    else System.out.println( NO_DOC_FOUND_MSG );
}
```

```
//--------------------------------------------------------------------
/** Mark bug document as fixed if it isn't fixed already.
 **
 ** @param pDoc Bug document to test and possibly mark as fixed
 ** @return boolean Return true if change was made, false if bug was fixed
 ** @exception NotesException Pass the buck back to NotesMain()
 */

public boolean markAsFixed( Document pDoc ) throws NotesException
{
   // get bug number & write message to console
   int aBugNum = pDoc.getItemValueInteger( BUG_NUM_ITEM );
   System.out.println( PROCESSING_BUG_MSG + aBugNum );

   // get fix date item & its text representation
   Item aItem = pDoc.getFirstItem( FIX_DATE_ITEM );
   String aItemText = aItem.getText();

   // if fix date has a value, print a message & return as failure
   if ( aItemText.length() > 0 )
   {
      System.out.println( ALREADY_FIXED_MSG + aItemText + "\n" );
      return false;
   }

   // set fix date to current date
   DateTime aDateTime = mSession.createDateTime( "today" );
   aDateTime.setNow();
   aItem.setDateTimeValue( aDateTime );

   // save the change
   pDoc.save( true, true );

   // print console message and return a success
   System.out.println( MARKED_FIXED_MSG + aDateTime + "\n" );
   return true;
   }
}
```

If you'd like to experiment with this example, switch to the directory that contains BugApp.java and use your favorite text editor to make changes. You then need to run javac, the Java compiler, to build your source into a new class file:

```
javac BugApp.java
```

Keep in mind that you're not limited to developing command-line apps like this one. You can use Java's Abstract Windowing Toolkit (AWT) to make full-featured GUI apps that interact with Notes. Even better, use the new and nifty Swing class library to make professional user interfaces that rival those found on Windows or Macintosh.

Writing Java Servlets

The next example, BugServlet, allows anyone with a Web browser to review the contents of the BugBase. By specifying a name as a request parameter, it can list bugs assigned to a particular developer, such as the LIST command. BugServlet could be used by customers to monitor the progress of a beta product, or it could be used by managers when they're on machines without Notes.

"But wait," you might say. "Doesn't Domino already do this?" Yes, Domino lets you review databases with a Web browser by generating HTML code on-the-fly with its Domino Web Engine. While this is often useful, it's not always the most presentable or flexible solution (see Figure 28.4). With very little work, you can write a custom servlet that produces results like those in Figure 28.5.

FIGURE 28.4

The Domino Web Engine can generate HTML on-the-fly from any Notes database, but it's not always what you want.

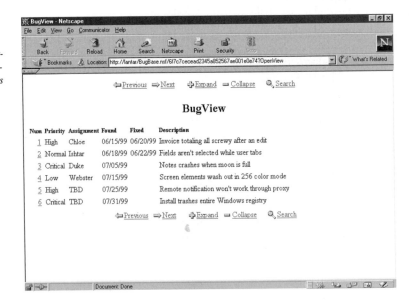

Understanding Servlets

To run servlets you need a Web server and servlet engine. Domino has both, but it's often a good idea to use CORBA to connect to Domino from an external Web server, such as Apache, running with a separate servlet engine, such as JRun or IBM's WebSphere.

FIGURE 28.5

BugServlet displays information in a presentable table that you can easily customize.

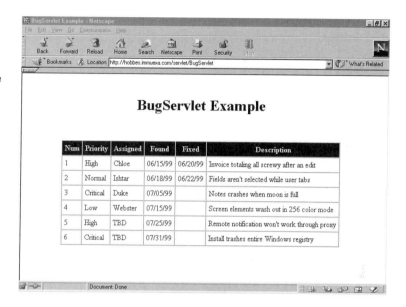

Servlets themselves are pretty easy to understand. To kick things off, point your browser to a Web address like the following:

```
http://www.mcp.com/servlet/BugServlet?who=Ishtar
```

This request gets sent to the Web server at www.mcp.com, which recognizes the /servlet/ part, and sends the request off to its servlet engine. If BugServlet hasn't been loaded, the servlet engine does so and then calls the servlet's init() method to do some initialization. The engine then creates a request object that contains the context and parameters of the browser request, such as the parameter who with the value Ishtar. It also creates a response object, which is used later to generate the result.

Both objects are then passed to the service() method which determines whether it's a GET request or a POST request. GET requests are more common, though many Web forms use POST when you click Submit. The main difference is that GET requests pass parameters in the address, whereas POST parameters are hidden from view. Once the service() method has determined the type, the request, and the response, objects are passed to either the doGet() method or the doPost() method. Most servlets use one or the other as their main processing routine for generating response pages.

Because each request is handled in its own thread, you'll have to be careful with shared member fields. Servlet engines can handle dozens of requests at a time. Serious problems can occur if one thread causes a change to a shared object while another thread is still using it. Most Notes objects are *thread-safe*, meaning separate threads won't step on each other's toes, but other fields need to be declared with the synchronized modifier.

```
public synchronized Item mItem;
```

This declaration assures that only one thread can use mItem at a time. You can also declare methods synchronized, but this can seriously affect performance, particularly in a servlet, so I wouldn't advise it unless you know what you're doing. The best bet is to stick to local variables, because these are always unique to each thread.

Using Servlets in Domino

To use servlets in Domino, you first need to make sure that the HTTP task is set to load. You also need to enable the Domino Servlet Manager by changing the Java Servlet Support option in your Server document (see Figure 28.6).

FIGURE 28.6

To use servlets in Domino, you must turn on Java Servlet Support in the Server document in the Internet Protocols and Domino Web Engine tabs.

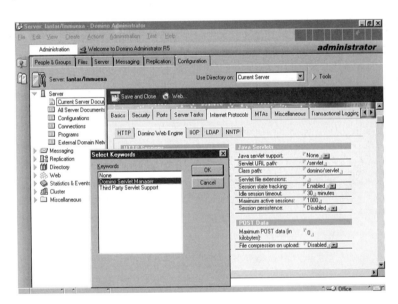

Next, create a subdirectory called servlet in your server's data\domino directory. This is the base directory for all servlet files. Since BugServlet uses the package com.mcp.naddu.bugbase, it'll go in the data\domino\servlet\com\mcp\naddu\bugbase directory. Ordinarily, you'd have to type requests that contain the full package path. For example

```
http://www.mcp.com/servlet/com.mcp.naddu.bugbase.BugServlet
```

For security reasons, Domino won't allow fully qualified class names like this one. Instead, you'll need to put a text file called `servlets.properties` in the data directory. This file can define any number of servlet aliases that map short names to their corresponding full class names. For example

```
servlet.BugServlet.code=com.mcp.naddu.bugbase.BugServlet
```

This definition maps the alias `BugServlet` to `com.mcp.naddu.bugbase.BugServlet`. You can then make like this:

```
http://www.mcp.com/servlet/BugServlet
```

Domino will then use the alias to find the class file. The `servlets.properties` file can also be used to define `init` parameters, which can be used in the `init()` method when the servlet is first loaded. BugServlet uses `init` parameters to define the three CORBA parameters from the last example: host address, username, and password. If these are found, the servlet will connect to the specified Domino server instead the local one. This is useful if the Domino server that's used for Web access is located outside a firewall and needs to connect to a server inside. To specify `init` parameters in the `servlets.properties` file, use a definition like this:

```
servlet.BugServlet.initArgs=address=90.0.0.2,user="Rosie Brady",password=bonita
```

You can also specify `init` parameters in an external servlet engine like JRun (see Figure 28.7), which can then connect via CORBA to your Domino server.

FIGURE 28.7

BugServlet can run with a remote Web server and servlet engine by specifying the Domino host address, user-name, and password as servlet init parameters.

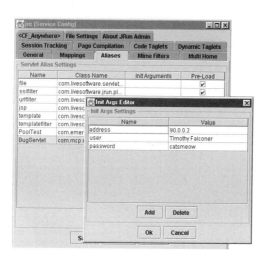

BugServlet Source

Listing 28.2 shows the source for `BugServlet`, which like most servlets is derived from the `HttpServlet` class. The first three methods are ones that are often appear in servlets. The `getServletInfo()` method returns a simple description of the servlet. The `init()` method checks for the presence of the CORBA `init` parameters using the `getInitParameter()` method, which returns `null` if the parameter isn't found. The `doGet()` method is called for each request. Note the `pReq` and `pResp` parameters.

Because creating a new thread each time would be overkill, I choose to use the `sinitThread()` approach to initialize the Notes system for local runs. Notice the corresponding `stermThread()` call in the `finally` clause. The session and database objects are then created in a manner identical to the `run()` method in BugApp. The `who` parameter is then checked using the `getParameter()` method on the request object. Like `getInitParameter()`, this method returns `null` if the parameter isn't found. The MIME type of the response page is then set to `text/html`, which is appropriate for Web pages. I then secure the output stream from the request object and pass the stream, the database, and the `who` parameter to the `writeResponse()` method.

The rest of the example should be straightforward, providing you understand basic HTML syntax. The mechanics of listing the bugs is similar to BugApp. The primary difference is that each line is surrounded by `<TR>` tags that define table rows. Feel free to experiment with this example, but make sure you remember to copy the class file to your servlet directory each time you compile it.

LISTING 28.2 Java Servlet that Displays BugBase Data in a Formatted HTML Table

```
// BugBase, version 1.0 alpha 1 -- BugServlet.java
// Copyright (c) 1999 by Macmillan Computer Publishing

package com.mcp.naddu.bugbase;

import lotus.domino.*;
import java.io.*;
import javax.servlet.*;
import javax.servlet.http.*;

///////////////////////////////////////////////////////////////////////////
/**                                                              <BR>
 **   Servlet which displays a list of bugs.  Use a URL like:    <BR>
 **                                                              <BR>
 **      http://www.immuexa.com/servlet/BugServlet              <BR>
 **                                                              <BR>
 **   Use "who" as a parameter to limit the list to a single developer.  <BR>
 **   Names with a space should use '%20' instead of the space, as in:   <BR>
 **                                                              <BR>
```

```
**      http://www.immuexa.com/servlet/BugServlet?who=Paula%20Zerkle         <BR>
**
**  @author  Timothy Falconer
**  @version 1.0 alpha 1
*/

public class BugServlet extends HttpServlet
{
    // message constants
    static final String NOTES_EXCEPTION_MSG = "Notes Exception ";
    static final String SERVLET_TITLE = "BugServlet Example";
    static final String BOOK_TITLE = "Notes and Domino Development Unleashed";
    static final String COPYRIGHT_MSG = "(c) 1999 by Macmillan Computer
Publishing";

    // item name constants
    static final String BUG_NUM_ITEM = "BugNum";
    static final String PRIORITY_ITEM = "Priority";
    static final String ASSIGNED_TO_ITEM = "AssignedTo";
    static final String FIND_DATE_ITEM = "FindDate";
    static final String FIX_DATE_ITEM = "FixDate";
    static final String DESCRIPTION_ITEM = "Description";

    // parameter name constants
    static final String ADDRESS_PARAM = "address";
    static final String USER_PARAM = "user";
    static final String PASSWORD_PARAM = "password";
    static final String WHO_PARAM = "who";

    // web page constants
    static final String LABEL_START = "<DIV ALIGN=CENTER><FONT
COLOR=#FFFF33><B>";
    static final String LABEL_STOP = "</B></FONT></DIV>";
    static final String COL1_LABEL = "Num";
    static final String COL2_LABEL = "Priority";
    static final String COL3_LABEL = "Assigned";
    static final String COL4_LABEL = "Found";
    static final String COL5_LABEL = "Fixed";
    static final String COL6_LABEL = "Description";

    // value constants
    static final String BUGBASE_NSF = "BugBase.NSF";
    static final String QUOTE = "\"";

    /** Domino host domain name or IP address */
    protected String mAddress;

    /** Domino user name */
    protected String mUser;
```

28

USING JAVA IN
DOMINO
APPLICATIONS

continues

Listing 28.2   Continued

```
/** Domino user password */
protected String mPassword;

//--------------------------------------------------------------------------
/** Over-ridden method which returns general information about servlet.
 **
 ** @return Informational message about servlet
 */

public String getServletInfo()
{
   return SERVLET_TITLE + " - " + BOOK_TITLE + "\n" + COPYRIGHT_MSG;
}

//--------------------------------------------------------------------------
/** Initialization method called by servlet engine when servlet loads.   <BR>
 ** The servlet stays loaded until the servlet engine is restarted.       <BR>
 **
 ** @param pConfig Configuration object that contains init params & context
 */

public void init( ServletConfig pConfig ) throws ServletException
{
   // must call superclass init() with pConfig
   super.init( pConfig );

   // initialize CORBA connection params if found, otherwise null
   mAddress = getInitParameter( ADDRESS_PARAM );
   mUser = getInitParameter( USER_PARAM );
   mPassword = getInitParameter( PASSWORD_PARAM );
}

//--------------------------------------------------------------------------
/** Called by servlet engine for each web browser request. Each request  <BR>
 ** occurs in its own thread, which lasts the length of the call.         <BR>
 **
 ** @param pReq Request object that contains request parameters & context
 ** @param pResp Response object used to return a response page to browser
 ** @exception IOException Handled by servlet engine
 ** @exception ServletException Handled by servlet engine
 */

protected void doGet( HttpServletRequest pReq, HttpServletResponse pResp )
   throws ServletException, IOException
{
   // make session and database local variables because of multi-threading
   Session aSession;
   Database aDb;
```

```
        try
        {
          // Notes system must be initialized for each thread if not using CORBA
          if ( mAddress == null ) NotesThread.sinitThread();

          // if no address, create a normal session, otherwise create a CORBA
one.
          if ( mAddress == null ) aSession = NotesFactory.createSession();
          else aSession = NotesFactory.createSession( mAddress, mUser, mPassword
);

          // open the bugbase database
          aDb = aSession.getDatabase( aSession.getServerName(), BUGBASE_NSF );

          // get "who" request parameter, if any
          String aWhoParam = pReq.getParameter( WHO_PARAM );

          // set MIME content type to HTML and acquire output stream for response
          pResp.setContentType( "text/html" );
          ServletOutputStream aOut = pResp.getOutputStream();

          // write the response page to the output stream
          writeResponse( aOut, aDb, aWhoParam );
        }
        catch( NotesException e )
        {
          // print informative error message & stack trace
          System.err.println( NOTES_EXCEPTION_MSG + e.id + " -- " + e.text );
          e.printStackTrace();
        }
        finally
        {
          // For every sinitThread, there must be an stermThread.
          // Putting it in the finally clause assures it will be called.
          if ( mAddress == null ) NotesThread.stermThread();
        }
      }


  //-------------------------------------------------------------------------
  /** Writes HTML tags and page content to response output stream.
  **
  ** @param pOut Servlet output stream used to create response page
  ** @param pDb Database object used to create page contents
  ** @param pWho String containing developer name to focus on
  ** @exception IOException Handled by servlet engine
  ** @exception NotesException Pass buck back to doGet()
  */
```

continues

LISTING 28.2   Continued

```java
    public void writeResponse( ServletOutputStream pOut, Database pDb, String
pWho )
        throws IOException, NotesException
    {
        // write start tags and window title
        pOut.println( "<HTML>" );
        pOut.println( "<HEAD>" );
        pOut.println( "<TITLE>" + SERVLET_TITLE + "</TITLE>" );
        pOut.println( "</HEAD>" );
        pOut.println( "<BODY>" );
        pOut.println( "<CENTER>" );

        // write title on page surrounded by line breaks
        pOut.println( "<BR><BR>" );
        pOut.println( "<H1>" + SERVLET_TITLE + "</H1>" );
        pOut.println( "<BR><BR>" );

        // write table start and a row of six column labels
        pOut.println( "<TABLE BORDER=1 CELLSPACING=0 CELLPADDING=5>" );
        pOut.println( "<TR BGCOLOR=#000000>" );
        pOut.println( "<TD>" + LABEL_START + COL1_LABEL + LABEL_STOP + "</TD>" );
        pOut.println( "<TD>" + LABEL_START + COL2_LABEL + LABEL_STOP + "</TD>" );
        pOut.println( "<TD>" + LABEL_START + COL3_LABEL + LABEL_STOP + "</TD>" );
        pOut.println( "<TD>" + LABEL_START + COL4_LABEL + LABEL_STOP + "</TD>" );
        pOut.println( "<TD>" + LABEL_START + COL5_LABEL + LABEL_STOP + "</TD>" );
        pOut.println( "<TD>" + LABEL_START + COL6_LABEL + LABEL_STOP + "</TD>" );
        pOut.println( "</TR>" );

        // write a row for each bug in database
        listBugs( pOut, pDb, pWho );

        // write end tags for page
        pOut.println( "</TABLE>" );
        pOut.println( "</CENTER>" );
        pOut.println( "</BODY>" );
        pOut.println( "</HTML>" );
    }

    //-------------------------------------------------------------------------
    /** List either all bugs or bugs specific to a developer.          <BR>
     ** Presence of "who" request parameter determines scope of list.  <BR>
     **
     ** @param pOut Servlet output stream used to create response page
     ** @param pDb Database object used to create page contents
     ** @param pWho String containing developer name to focus on
     ** @exception IOException Handled by servlet engine
     ** @exception NotesException Pass buck back to doGet()
     */
```

```java
    public void listBugs( ServletOutputStream pOut, Database pDb, String pWho )
       throws NotesException, IOException
    {
       DocumentCollection aList;

       // if no request parameter was given, list all bugs
       if ( pWho == null ) aList = pDb.getAllDocuments();
       else
       {
          // otherwise, search with formula of the form: AssignedTo = "Duke"
          String aFormula = ASSIGNED_TO_ITEM + " = " + QUOTE + pWho + QUOTE;
          aList = pDb.search( aFormula );
       }

       // cycle through the list
       Document aDoc = aList.getFirstDocument();
       while( aDoc != null )
       {
          // print information on the bug
          writeBugRow( pOut, aDoc );

          // get next document in list (if any)
          aDoc = aList.getNextDocument();
       }
    }

    //--------------------------------------------------------------------------
    /** Prints information for a single bug on a table row
     **
     ** @param pDoc Bug document to display
     ** @exception IOException Handled by servlet engine
     ** @exception NotesException Pass the buck back to run()
     */

    public void writeBugRow( ServletOutputStream pOut, Document pDoc )
       throws IOException, NotesException
    {
       // get date items
       Item aFindDateItem = pDoc.getFirstItem( FIND_DATE_ITEM );
       Item aFixDateItem = pDoc.getFirstItem( FIX_DATE_ITEM );

       // get date time values, checking first for empty fix date
       DateTime aFindDateTime = aFindDateItem.getDateTimeValue();
       boolean aIsFixed = ( aFixDateItem.getText().length() > 0 );
       DateTime aFixDateTime = ( aIsFixed ) ? aFixDateItem.getDateTimeValue() :
null;
       // get date-only text or HTML non-breaking-space for unfixed bugs
       String aFindDateText = aFindDateTime.getDateOnly();
       String aFixDateText = ( aIsFixed ) ? aFixDateTime.getDateOnly() :
" ";
```

continues

LISTING 28.2   Continued

```
        // print info on each document in a single table row
        pOut.println( "<TR>" );
        pOut.println( "<TD>" + pDoc.getItemValueInteger( BUG_NUM_ITEM ) + "</TD>"
);
        pOut.println( "<TD>" + pDoc.getItemValueString( PRIORITY_ITEM ) + "</TD>"
);
        pOut.println( "<TD>" + pDoc.getItemValueString( ASSIGNED_TO_ITEM ) +
"</TD>" );
        pOut.println( "<TD>" + aFindDateText + "</TD>" );
        pOut.println( "<TD>" + aFixDateText + "</TD>" );
        pOut.println( "<TD>" + pDoc.getItemValueString( DESCRIPTION_ITEM ) +
"</TD>" );
        pOut.println( "</TR>" );
    }
}
```

Writing Java Applets

With R5, you can write Java applets that access Domino databases from either a Web
browser or a Notes client. Better yet, the same applet can run in either environment without any source code or configuration changes. As such, applets are terrific in Notes
because they allow you to provide a single professional UI for all your users. Applets use
Java's AWT windowing library, which contains most of the components found in other
GUI environments, such as text fields, drop-down lists, and buttons.

The next example is an applet called BugApplet, which is used to add new bugs to the
BugBase. As you can see in Figures 28.8 and 28.9, the user interface is identical in both
Notes clients and Web browsers. To add a bug, click New, fill in the appropriate fields,
and click Save. Messages are displayed in the box next to the buttons.

Using Applets in Domino

In Domino, applets need to be added to a page, form, or document. For BugApplet, I created a page in `BugBase.NSF` and clicked the Create/Java applet menu item. I then chose
my base directory, added the three BugApplet class files, and picked `BugApplet.class`
as the base class (see Figure 28.10).

To allow your applet to use CORBA, you need to open the Java Applet properties box
(see Figure 28.11) by right-clicking on the applet and choosing Java Applet Properties.
Put a check mark next to Applet Uses Notes CORBA Classes. While you're there, type in
the height and width of your applet, which you can usually get from the source code.

FIGURE 28.8

BugApplet allows you to add bug documents from a Web browser.

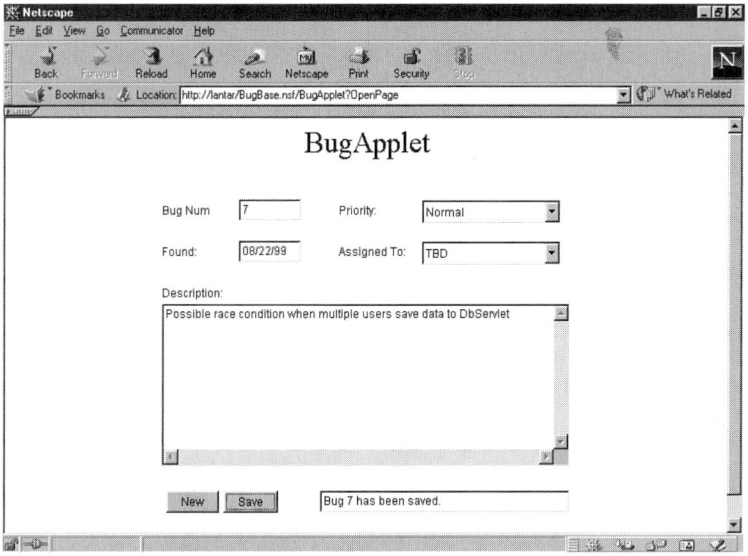

FIGURE 28.9

BugApplet looks identical when running in the Notes client.

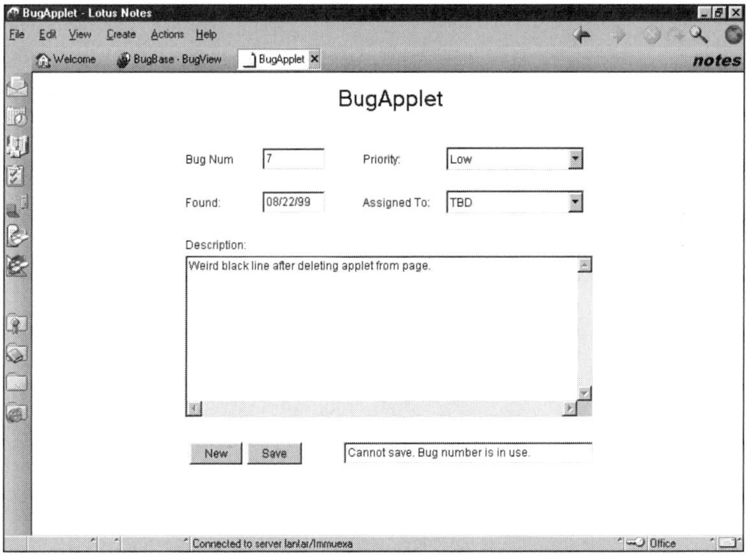

The last step is changing your Notes client security settings so you can run applets. Open your User Preferences and make sure Enable Java Applets is checked. Then click the Security Options button and choose Default or a specific applet author, such as yourself.

When you click Java Applet Security, you'll see a list of activities that are considered security risks (see Figure 28.12). You need to enable Access to Notes Java Classes for your applets to use the Java API. If you forget to do this, it causes an Execution Security Alert box to pop up when you try to run the applet in Notes. You can then click Trust Signer to grant permission to use the applet.

FIGURE 28.10

Use Domino Designer to add an applet to a page or form.

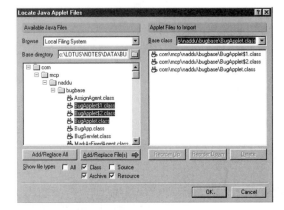

FIGURE 28.11

Use the Java applet properties box to enable CORBA and change the dimensions.

FIGURE 28.12

Make sure Enable Java Applets has a check mark in User Preferences and select the first three Java applet security items in Security Options.

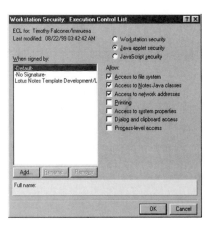

Applets usually extend the `Applet` class, but Notes applets should instead extend the special `AppletBase` class, which, like `AgentBase`, initializes the Notes system if needed. In normal applets, you'd usually override these methods: `init()` (called when the applet first loads), `start()` (called when the applet begins), `stop()` (called when the user navigates off the page), and `destroy()` (called when the browser closes). Because Notes needs to do its own behind-the-scenes processing, you should instead use the equivalent `AppletBase` versions of these methods: `notesAppletInit()`, `notesAppletStart()`, `notesAppletStop`, and `notesAppletDestroy()`. As you can see, the designers of `AppletBase` choose to stick with Java convention and use an initial lowercase letter, unlike the designersof the `NotesMain()` method.

BugApplet Source

Listing 28.3 shows the source for the `BugApplet` class. As with the other examples, it starts with a series of constant definitions and field declarations. Execution starts with `notesAppletInit()`, which first calls `initLayout()` and `initHandlers()`, and then establishes the Notes session and opens the database. Unlike the other CORBA program types, you don't need to distinguish between local and CORBA connections when creating the session. Notes figures it out behind the scenes. Notice that the server name, user, and password are hard-coded into the example. You'll have to change these values and recompile to get BugApplet to work with your system.

The `initLayout()` method creates the applet's user interface. Designing Java UIs is well beyond the scope of this book, so I won't explain this long and complex method. Keep in mind that you can use visual authoring tools in products like JBuilder to create user interfaces without writing code.

The `initHandlers()` method creates two event handlers (Java calls them listeners) that respond to button clicks in the applet. Each handler is defined as an "anonymous" class, which is a special syntax used in cases when a separate class definition is overkill. Anonymous classes compile into their own class files, as in `BugApplet$1.class`.

Once the applet is loaded, the `notesAppletStart()` method is called. This calls `doNew()` and prints an instructional message to the user.

The heart of the applet is the `doNew()` and `doSave()` event-handler methods, which are called whenever the user clicks the New or Save buttons. Keep in mind that handlers are started in their own thread, so unless the applet is using CORBA, you need to initialize and shut down the Notes system at the beginning and end of each handler. Both `doNew()` and `doSave()` check for a local run with `isNotesLocal()`, and then use `sinitThread()` and `stermThread()` as needed.

LISTING 28.3   Continued

```java
/** array of developer names (don't hard code this either) */
protected String[] mDevelopers = { "TBD", "Webster", "Chloe", "Ishtar",
"Duke" };

//-------------------------------------------------------------------
/** Over-ridden method which returns general information about the applet.
 **
 ** @return Informational message about applet
 */

public String getAppletInfo()
{
    return APPLET_TITLE + " - " + BOOK_TITLE + "\n" + COPYRIGHT_MSG;
}

//-------------------------------------------------------------------
/** Notes version of the init() method .. called when the applet loads.  <BR>
 ** This one initializes the GUI and event handlers, then creates the    <BR>
 ** session and opens the database.
 */

public void notesAppletInit()
{
    // initialize applet GUI and event handlers
    initLayout();
    initHandlers();

    try
    {
        // open session (this works for both local and CORBA connections)
        mSession = getSession( USER, PASSWORD );

        // if session is null, print message and return
        if ( mSession == null )
        {
            mMsgField.setText( CANNOT_CONNECT_MSG );
            return;
        }

        // otherwise open database
        mDb = mSession.getDatabase( SERVER, BUGBASE_NSF );
    }
    catch( NotesException e )
    {
        mMsgField.setText( NOTES_EXCEPTION_MSG + e.id + " -- " + e.text );
    }
}
```

```
//---------------------------------------------------------------------
/** Initializes the layout of the applet GUI components using the       <BR>
 ** GridBagLayout manager. Also initializes the drop-down lists.        <BR>
 */

public void initLayout()
{
   // set up layout manager & data panel
   GridBagLayout aGB = new GridBagLayout();
   GridBagConstraints aC = new GridBagConstraints();
   mDataPanel.setLayout( aGB );
   add( mDataPanel );

   // bug num & find date labels
   aC.insets = new Insets( 20, 10, 0, 10 );
   aC.anchor = GridBagConstraints.WEST;
   aC.gridx = 0; aC.gridy = 0; mDataPanel.add( mBugNumLabel, aC );
   aC.gridx = 0; aC.gridy = 1; mDataPanel.add( mFindDateLabel, aC );

   // bug num & find date fields
   aC.insets = new Insets( 20, 0, 0, 10 );
   aC.fill = GridBagConstraints.HORIZONTAL;
   aC.gridx = 1; aC.gridy = 0; mDataPanel.add( mBugNumField, aC );
   aC.gridx = 1; aC.gridy = 1; mDataPanel.add( mFindDateField, aC );

   // priority & assigned-to labels
   aC.insets = new Insets( 20, 30, 0, 0 );
   aC.gridx = 2; aC.gridy = 0; mDataPanel.add( mPriorityLabel, aC );
   aC.gridx = 2; aC.gridy = 1; mDataPanel.add( mAssignedToLabel, aC );

   // priority & assigned-to drop down fields
   aC.insets = new Insets( 20, 0, 0, 20 );
   aC.fill = GridBagConstraints.HORIZONTAL;
   aC.gridx = 3; aC.gridy = 0; mDataPanel.add( mPriorityChoice, aC );
   aC.gridx = 3; aC.gridy = 1; mDataPanel.add( mAssignedToChoice, aC );

   // description label
   aC.insets = new Insets( 20, 10, 0, 0 );
   aC.fill = GridBagConstraints.NONE;
   aC.gridx = 0; aC.gridy = 3; mDataPanel.add( mDescriptionLabel, aC );
// description area
   aC.insets = new Insets( 0, 10, 0, 10 );
   aC.gridx = 0; aC.gridy = 4; aC.gridwidth = 4;
   mDataPanel.add( mDescriptionText, aC );

   // buttons
   mButtonPanel.add( mNewButton );
   mButtonPanel.add( mSaveButton );
   aC.gridx = 0; aC.gridy = 5;  aC.gridwidth = 2;
```

28

USING JAVA IN
DOMINO
APPLICATIONS

continues

LISTING 28.3   Continued

```java
    aC.insets = new Insets( 20, 10, 20, 30 );
    mDataPanel.add( mButtonPanel, aC );

    // message area
    aC.gridx = 2; aC.gridy = 5; aC.gridwidth = 2;
    aC.fill = GridBagConstraints.HORIZONTAL;
    aC.insets = new Insets( 20, 10, 20, 10 );
    mDataPanel.add( mMsgField, aC );

    // disallow editing of message field
    mMsgField.setEditable( false );

    // add priorities to choice object
    for( int aCount = 0; aCount < mPriorities.length; aCount++ )
      mPriorityChoice.add( mPriorities[ aCount ] );

    // add developers to choice object
    for( int aCount = 0; aCount < mDevelopers.length; aCount++ )
      mAssignedToChoice.add( mDevelopers[ aCount ] );
}

//----------------------------------------------------------------------
/** Creates event handlers, or listeners, and ties them to the buttons.  <BR>
 ** Note the special syntax with the new keyword followed by a class      <BR>
 ** definition. These are "anonymous" classes, and show up after          <BR>
 ** compilation as BugApplet$1.class & BugApplet$2.class.  The net         <BR>
 ** effect is that every time you click "New", the doNew() method is       <BR>
 ** called in its own thread.  Same for Save.                             <BR>
 */

public void initHandlers()
{
   // add new button event handler
   mNewButton.addActionListener(
     new ActionListener()
     {
        public void actionPerformed( ActionEvent e )
        {
           doNew();
        }
     }
   );

   // add save button event handler
   mSaveButton.addActionListener(
     new ActionListener()
     {
        public void actionPerformed( ActionEvent e )
        {
```

```
            doSave();
        }
    }
    );
}

//------------------------------------------------------------------
/** Notes version of an applet's start() method - starts a new bug and   <BR>
 ** prints a message informing the user to type a bug and click save.     <BR>
 */

public void notesAppletStart()
{
    doNew();
    mMsgField.setText( TYPE_BUG_AND_SAVE_MSG );
}

//------------------------------------------------------------------
/** Clears the applet's fields and initializes them to starting values.  <BR>
 ** The bug number is derived by simply adding one to the number of       <BR>
 ** documents in the database, which can sometimes be misleading if       <BR>
 ** there isn't a strict linear progression of bug numbers.               <BR>
 */

public void doNew()
{
    try
    {
        // since this can be called by a new handler thread,
        // we need to initialize the Notes system for local runs
        if ( isNotesLocal() ) NotesThread.sinitThread();

        // get current number of bug documents
        DocumentCollection aList = mDb.getAllDocuments();
        int aCount = aList.getCount();

        // set bug num to count plus one (note trick to convert to a string)
        mBugNumField.setText( "" + ( aCount + 1 ) );

        // get current date & set find date field
        DateTime aDateTime = mSession.createDateTime( "today" );
        mFindDateField.setText( aDateTime.getDateOnly() );

        // set both drop-downs to default values
        mPriorityChoice.select( 0 );
        mAssignedToChoice.select( 0 );

        // clear the description & message field
        mDescriptionText.setText( "" );
        mMsgField.setText( "" );
```

continues

LISTING 28.3   Continued

```java
        }
        catch( NotesException e )
        {
           mMsgField.setText( NOTES_EXCEPTION_MSG + e.id + " -- " + e.text );
        }
        finally
        {
           // shut down the Notes system if it's a local run
           if ( isNotesLocal() )  NotesThread.stermThread();
        }
    }

    //--------------------------------------------------------------------------
    /** Creates a Notes document from the current field values and saves it, <BR>
     ** first making sure the bug number doesn't already exist.            <BR>
     */

    public void doSave()
    {
       try
       {
          // since this can be called by a new handler thread,
          // we need to initialize the Notes system for local runs
          if ( isNotesLocal() ) NotesThread.sinitThread();

          // check for existing bug with the same number
          String aFormula = BUG_NUM_ITEM + " = " + mBugNumField.getText();
          DocumentCollection aList = mDb.search( aFormula );

          // if found, print message and return
          if ( aList.getCount() > 0 )
          {
             mMsgField.setText( BUG_NUM_IN_USE_MSG );
             return;
          }

          // convert bug num & date to appropriate values
          int aBugNum = Integer.parseInt( mBugNumField.getText() );
          DateTime aFindDateTime = mSession.createDateTime(
mFindDateField.getText() );

          // make document and fill items
          Document aDoc = mDb.createDocument();
          aDoc.replaceItemValue( BUG_NUM_ITEM, new Integer( aBugNum ) );
          aDoc.replaceItemValue( FIND_DATE_ITEM, aFindDateTime );
          aDoc.replaceItemValue( PRIORITY_ITEM, mPriorityChoice.getSelectedItem()
    );
```

```
        aDoc.replaceItemValue( ASSIGNED_TO_ITEM,
mAssignedToChoice.getSelectedItem() );
        aDoc.replaceItemValue( DESCRIPTION_ITEM, mDescriptionText.getText() );

        // save item & print message
        aDoc.save();
        mMsgField.setText( BUG_MSG + aBugNum + HAS_BEEN_SAVED_MSG );
    }
    catch( NotesException e )
    {
        mMsgField.setText( NOTES_EXCEPTION_MSG + e.id + " -- " + e.text );
    }
    catch( NumberFormatException e )
    {
        // this exception is called when a number has more than digits
        mMsgField.setText( BAD_BUG_NUM_MSG );
    }
    finally
    {
        // shut down the Notes system if it's a local run
        if ( isNotesLocal() )  NotesThread.stermThread();
    }
  }
}
```

28

USING JAVA IN
DOMINO
APPLICATIONS

Summary

Feel free to expand on these examples. One idea for improving BugApplet is to add a loadBug() method that could retrieve data for an existing bug so you could edit it. You might even pass the bug number in an applet parameter, which could be generated on-the-fly from BugServlet when the user clicked the number in the list. BugApp could also be improved with additional commands for adding or editing bugs. The best way to explore the new Java capabilities of Notes and Domino R5 is to dive right in and code what comes to mind. I'm sure you'll agree: the new possibilities are endless.

Advanced Design Topics

PART

IV

IN THIS PART

Adding Framesets to Domino Applications

by Steve Kern

Framesets originated on the Web as a way to present content from more than one HTML page at a time. Framed Web sites have become quite common lately because you can link one frame within the frameset to the contents of another frame. This technique provides a nice way to navigate a Web site. Framesets are a new design element in R5.

A frameset splits the client window into two or more frames similar to a multipaned window on a house. Frames are sections of a window that can present content independently of each other and can optionally display borders or scroll. Each frame can display a different page or design element. Used properly, framesets can enhance your applications considerably. There are several distinct advantages.

Framesets grew out of HTML tables, and to a certain extent, you could simulate a frameset with a table. Like a table, framesets improve the interface by adding structure to your application, including navigational elements that can remain in the same location. In other words, you can combine static content (a set of links) with dynamic content (the pages that the links point to). In R4.x, you could create a view template for use with a Web client by creating a form and naming it $$ViewTemplate for *view name* or $$ViewTemplateDefault. You could use a table in the form to add structure to the view and provide navigation through the use of the reserved field $$ViewList, an embedded Navigator or an embedded Folder Pane in one cell of the table. In another cell, you could place navigation icons, and in still another cell, you could place the reserved field $$ViewBody or an embedded view element to display the actual view. If this sounds like a lot of work, it is (see Figure 29.1).

FIGURE 29.1

The Web Mail default view template from R4.6 uses a table, an embedded navigator, hotspots, and the reserved fields $$ViewList *and* $$ViewBody *to display mail.*

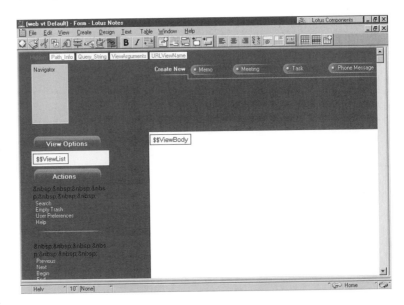

In R4.6, the developers of Notes and Domino also added a frameset tool in the form of a database template titled Frameset (R4.6). Although this was indeed a step in the right direction, it pales in comparison to the ease of use in the R5 Domino Designer. What the Frameset template essentially did was create the HTML necessary to produce the frameset. It was somewhat difficult to work with this template, but it was better than coding the HTML by hand (see Figure 29.2).

FIGURE 29.2

The R4.6 frameset designer is primitive compared to R5. Note the dialog window used to specify dimensions for a frame.

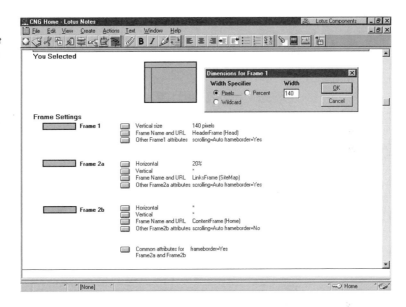

The disadvantage of both these examples from R4 is that you had to write separate code for Web clients and for Notes clients. For example, a Web client couldn't directly interact with a standard Notes mail database. In R4.6, there were actually three separate mail templates: one for Notes clients only (`mail46.ntf`), one for Notes and Web clients (`mailc46.ntf`), and one for Web clients only (`mailw46.ntf`). Although some elements were common to all the templates, essentially, the designers had to write three completely separate applications to handle mail. Applications based on the R4.6 frameset needed Notes clients to add content, but neither the content nor the frameset was usable by a Notes client. It only worked for Web browsers. You could use the frameset template to create a homepage for your Web clients, but a completely separate application would have to be designed to provide the same functions for your Notes clients. As you can imagine, this made for a lot of extra work. In addition, if you didn't know HTML, you would be hard pressed to get a frameset to function well "out of the box."

29

ADDING FRAMESETS TO DOMINO

One of the biggest advantages in R5 is that framesets are usable by both Web and Notes clients.

In case you missed that point, framesets work for both Web and Notes clients! In R5, there is only one mail template (compared to three in R4.6), and it launches directly into a frameset called MailFS (see Figure 29.3). The frames within a frameset can contain documents, folders, pages, navigators, outlines, views, and so forth. Frames can even contain other framesets. You can create hotspots on pages or entries in outlines that create forms, run agents, and open other applications or URLs. A frameset is a very powerful design element that is a welcome addition to R5. Best of all, it is surprisingly simple to use.

FIGURE 29.3

The R5 MailFS frameset is launched on the opening of a database for both Notes and Web clients. Displaying the content of the frames is a nice feature of the Frameset Designer.

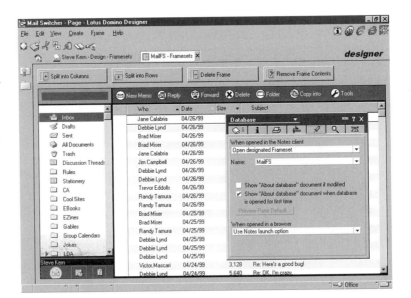

Creating a Frameset

As always, it is a good idea to plan the frameset first, before designing it. You might consider several common layouts for framesets. The Frameset designer window has twelve such layouts; a drop-down list selects the number of frames from 2 to 4, and each selection has four arrangements from which to choose (see Figure 29.4). The following list describes common uses for the frames in these framesets:

- **Two-paned**—Split into columns, theleft pane provides navigation and the right pane the content.

- **Three-paned**—Split into two rows, with a narrow row at the top. The bottom pane is split into two columns. The topmost row contains a banner which usually consists of a logo, site name, links, and so on. The left pane again provides navigation, and the right pane displays content.

- **Four-paned**—Similar to the three-paned, except that there is a narrow row at the bottom as well containing site links. The top pane contains a banner and logo; the left pane contains navigation links, the bottom pane contains other site links, and the middle or right frame contains content.

FIGURE 29.4

Choices for arrangements are available in the Create New Frameset dialog box. Each numbered selection from 2 to 4 has four prebuilt arrangements, for a total of 12 different styles.

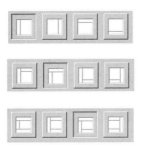

Rather than take up space with layouts based on all the previous arrangements, you'll see how to put together a frameset starting with three panes. To create a new frameset, choose Framesets from the database design list. Click the New Frameset button, and the Create New Frameset dialog box opens (see Figure 29.5). Choose 3 for the Number of frames and click the second arrangement from the right.

FIGURE 29.5

Choosing a frameset style is easy with the Create New Frameset window.

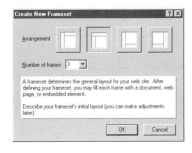

29

ADDING FRAMESETS TO DOMINO

You've now got a nice neat three-paned frameset right in front of you!

Using the Frameset Designer

The Frameset Designer is pretty straightforward; after all, most of the action happens in the frames themselves. However, there is a Properties box and some menu choices you should be aware of before moving on to designing the frames. Figure 29.6 shows the Frameset Designer with the Properties box open to the Basics tab.

FIGURE 29.6

The Frameset Designer has four buttons to alter the appearance of the frames and frameset.

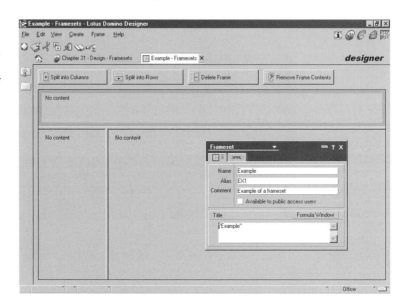

You'll notice that the Properties box tab has information already filled in. As always, you should name the frameset and provide an alias. You can also provide a title for the frameset. The title can be plain text, as in this example, or you can write a formula to calculate the title. It is a good idea to add a title formula; if you don't, the frameset shows as "Untitled." For you HTML fans, this becomes the document title, enclosed in the container tag <TITLE>. Titles are displayed in the window title of the Notes client, as shown in Figure 29.7.

Figure 29.8 shows the HTML tab, on which you can place settings for cascading style sheets.

FIGURE 29.7

This illustrates a typical frameset with navigator, banner, and content frames. Note the name of the frameset in the window title bar.

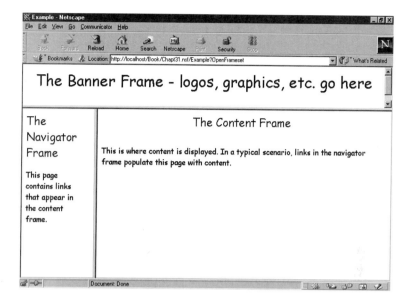

FIGURE 29.8

All settings except for the Other field on the HTML tab are used for cascading style sheets. Note that the Name field is disabled.

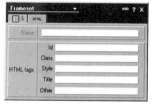

Using the View and Frame Menus

Whenever you work in a frameset, a new choice appears in the View menu and a new menu appears, the Frame menu. The View menu consists of a Refresh All option and a new setting, Show Frame Content. Show Frame Content is a toggle that turns the display of the frame contents in the Frame Designer on and off. When it's turned on, you can see the pages and other objects you are displaying in a frame "live." When it's turned off, frames display a gray background with text indicating the content type and value of each frame. With Frame content turned on, you can more easily adjust the sizes of the frames to fit the contents.

29

ADDING
FRAMESETS TO
DOMINO

> **Caution**
>
> If you have Show Frame Content turned on and the contents of a frame consist of an Internet URL, that link is displayed in the frame during design. This is not a problem as long as you have a constant connection to the Internet, but if you have a dial-up connection, Domino dials your Internet service provider!

The Frame menu has the following choices:

> Frameset Properties
>
> Frame Properties
>
> Split into Columns
>
> Split into Rows
>
> Delete Frame
>
> Refresh Frame Content
>
> Remove Frame Content
>
> Preview in Notes
>
> Preview in Web Browser

Four of the choices on the Frame menu have corresponding buttons in the Frameset Designer: Split into Columns, Split into Rows, Delete Frame, and Remove Frame Contents. Refresh Frame Content does not have a corresponding button. Refreshing the Frame Content is useful if you work on a page or other design element that you've linked in a frame while the Frameset Designer is open. To see the changes to the element, choose Refresh Frame Content.

> **Right Click to Access the Frames Menu**
>
> You can right click a frame in the Frameset Designer. A context menu is displayed with the same menu choices.

Splitting Frames in a Frameset

You are by no means limited to the twelve basic layouts, nor are you limited to the number of frames in the Create New Frameset window. When you've created a basic frameset, you can split any frame into new frames either vertically (Split into Columns) or horizontally (Split into Rows). For example, you could start with the basic three-paned layout shown in Figure 29.6 and add a frame to the upper-right corner for a logo. To do this, click in the topmost frame, the "banner" frame. You should notice that the frame has a thick gray border when selected, so you can always tell which frame you're working with. Click the Split into Columns button, and a new frame is added to the right of the existing frame (see Figure 29.9).

FIGURE 29.9

The top frame has been split vertically into two frames. Note the thick gray bar in the frame at the upper right, indicating that it is selected.

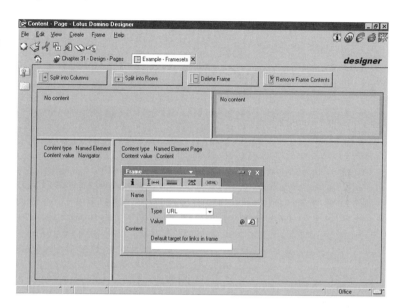

Framesets Within Framesets!

You can also use another frameset in a frame to give additional flexibility and additional frames.

The sizes of each frame can be easily changed as well. Simply grab the frame border with the mouse and click and drag it to the desired position. You can also alter the size of frames using the Frame Properties box, which is discussed later in the section titled "Working with Frames."

You can easily test the frameset at any time during development. The Frame menu contains Preview selections, or you can simply click one of the four preview buttons in the upper-right part of the Domino Designer window: Notes Preview, Domino Preview, IE Preview, or Netscape Preview.

Now that you've learned how to create a basic frameset, add new frames, and resize the existing frames, you're ready to begin working with the contents of the frames themselves.

29

ADDING FRAMESETS TO DOMINO

Working with Frames

Most of the work done with a frame is through the Frame Properties box. The Properties box has five tabs: Basics, Frame Size, Frame Border, Advanced, and HTML. On the Basics tab, you name the frame, define the contents, and set the target frame if appropriate. The Frame Size tab lets you control the size of the frame and the type of scrolling. The Frame Border tab has settings for the style and color of the frame borders. In the advanced tab, you can set frame spacing and margins. The HTML tab has settings for Style sheets.

Use Unique Names!

You should use a name that is unique across all framesets in a database for each frame. Because elements such as pages can launch into named frames, having two frames with the same name in two separate framesets could cause unpredictable results. It is important to avoid the use of the reserved frame names: _top, _self, _parent, and _blank. One naming technique is to use a reference to the frameset name, perhaps the alias, as a prefix to the frame name.

Following this technique, the names of the frames in the Example frameset in the database on the CD accompanying this book for this chapter (Chapt29.nsf) are

> EX1Logo
>
> EX1Banner
>
> EX1Nav
>
> EX1Content

EX1 is the alias of the Example frameset. Figure 29.10 shows the Basics tab of the Properties box for the EX1Logo frame.

FIGURE 29.10

The Basics tab of the Frame Properties box has two sections: Name and Content.

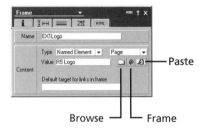

Browse ⎯⎯ Frame

Paste

Adding Content to Frames

The contents of a frame can come from a Link, a Named element, or an URL. To add content, you can click the Type drop-down box, and choose one of the three types. When you change types, the Browse, Formula, and Paste buttons are conditionally displayed. For example, for a Link, only the Paste button appears; for URLs, only the Formula and Paste buttons appear. When you've specified the contents for the frame, a text description of the contents appears next to Content value in the frame when Show Frame Content is turned off. If you use a formula, Computed appears next to Content value.

Pasting Links and URLs

If you have a link or URL copied to the clipboard, you can click the Paste button from any setting for Type. The Type setting changes to the appropriate one, and the value field is set for you.

Links can be view links, document links, or anchor links and must first be copied to the clipboard and then pasted into the Content section using the Paste button. Note that you cannot copy a database link into a frame.

Using a Named element gives designers access to Pages, Forms, Framesets, Views, Folders, and Navigators. To select a Named element from the list of available objects, click the Browse button. When you do so, the Locate Object dialog box opens. This dialog box has three fields: Kind of Object, Database, and Object. The name of the last field changes to the type of object selected in the first field. Figure 29.11 shows the Locate Object dialog box.

FIGURE 29.11

The Locate Object dialog box is easy to use and gives you access to a wide variety of objects.

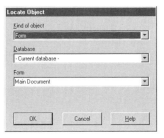

Pages are frequently used in framesets because you can embed other elements in them and combine those elements with text and graphics. For example, you can add a view to a frame, and it would display properly. You can also add a view to a page; include graphics, text, and additional objects on the page; and then place the page into a frame. As you can see, using a page to display design elements is often better than simply using the object itself. You can conceivably construct a complete application using pages and framesets, as long as you don't need to input any data! You can read more about Pages in Chapter 14, "Using the Page Designer."

When you enter a URL by pasting it into the Content area, by typing it in directly, or by using a formula, you must use the full URL syntax starting with `http://`. If you paste it using the Paste button, the Type field automatically changes to URL and the URL appears in the Value field.

For both URLs and Named Elements, you can determine the contents of a frame with a formula. To enter a formula, click the Formula button; the Formula window opens. The formula must evaluate to an URL or the name or alias of a Named Element. In addition, you must select the appropriate type of Named Element. For more information on writing formulas, see Chapters 18, "The Formula Language," 19, "Formula Language Basics," and 20, "Writing Formulas."

The last field on the Basics tab of the Frame Properties box is the Default Target for Links in This Frame. This is useful when you have a frame containing an element that provides navigation, such as a page of links, a navigator, an outline, a view, or a folder pane. A navigational pane often occupies a smaller frame and, when the links are clicked, the linked content appears in a larger pane. In the example used in this chapter, the navigation frame is on the left and the content frame is on the right. This is where the naming of frames is important! In this example, the navigational frame is named EX1Nav, and the Default target for links in this frame is the content frame, EX1Content.

As an example, return to the four-paned frameset and add content and navigational capability. First of all, you need to create several pages to populate the frames. The database for this chapter on the accompanying CD has several ready-made pages:

- **R5Logo**—Contains the shared image resource, `R5Logo.gif`.
- **Banner**—Contains a page for the Banner frame.
- **View Navigator**—Contains an embedded outline.

The R5Logo page goes in the EX1Logo frame in the upper-right corner as a Named Element. The Banner page goes in the EX1Banner frame in the top right. The View Navigator page goes in the EX1Nav frame on the left underneath the EX1Logo frame. The links in the EX1Nav frame need to point to the EX1Content frame, so in the Properties box for the EX1Nav frame, specify EX1Content as the Default target for links in this frame (see Figure 29.12).

FIGURE 29.12

Adding content to the Example frameset using the Properties box. Note the target for the EX1Nav frame is the Content frame.

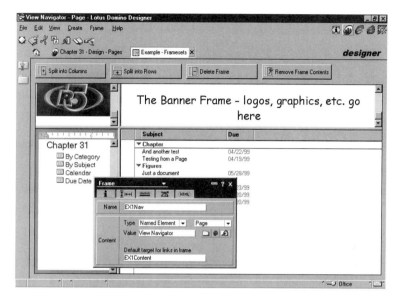

In Figure 29.12 you might have noticed that the target frame EX1Content already has a value. Normally, you specify a "default" link so that the user doesn't see a blank area when the frameset is initially displayed. In this case, the view displayed is the By Category view. See Figure 29.13, which shows the Properties box for the EX1Content frame.

FIGURE 29.13

The Properties box for the Content frame is set to a default view.

When you use a view as a Named Element, a Simple Appearance checkbox appears in the Properties box. When checked, the view displays without the column headers. This is similar to deselecting the Show column headings checkbox on the Style tab of the View properties box.

You might recall that you can specify a target for some design elements, such as pages and forms. When you do this and you open the element, it opens to the frameset in which the frame exists. In other words, the target frame for the element takes precedence over the target frames in a frameset. If you experience unexpected results in your framesets, check the target frames of the elements.

Controlling Frame Size, Scrolling, and Resizing

When you've mastered setting content and links for frames, you can move on to setting the properties for frame size and scrolling. You can do a lot by dragging the borders of frames in the Frameset Designer, but for really precise control, you can turn to the Frame Size tab of the Frame Properties box (see Figure 29.14).

FIGURE 29.14

The Frame Size tab of the Properties box has settings for Width, Height, Scrolling, and Resizing for the frame.

For Width and Height, you can choose from Relative, Percent, or Pixels. When you initially set up a frameset, Domino Designer uses Percent to split the frameset into frames. For example, in the original three-paned frameset, the leftmost frame had a width of 20% and the frame on the right had a width of 80%. Similarly, the top frame had a height of 20% and the lower frames had a height of 80%. This is handy because you can't control the display resolution of clients. Sometimes you need more control, however. In that case, you can switch to pixels.

You can use Relative to set either the width or the height relative to an adjacent frame. For example, if you set the left and top frames to a specific width and height using pixels, you can set the width and height of the lower-right frame to Relative. As a case in point, R5Logo.gif, which is used in the EX1Logo frame via a page, doesn't fit into the 80%/20% scheme very well. Scrollbars appear and white space shows up around the image. If you open the GIF itself in a good graphics program, you can find the dimensions of the image. In this case, it's 159 pixels wide by 81 pixels high. You can set the width and height to these dimensions in the Frame Size tab. Notice that when you do this, the other frames don't exactly line up. First, go to the EX1Nav frame and set the width to 159 pixels. Set the height to Relative. Next, go to the EX1Banner frame and set the height to 81 pixels and set the width to Relative. In EX1Content, set both width and height to Relative. When you're finished, you'll notice that the borders of all four frames once again line up. However, when you preview the frameset, you'll see scrollbars, both vertical and horizontal in the Logo frame. This is not quite what you want, and you can remove them easily. Set Scrolling to Off and Allow Resizing to No, as shown in Figure 29.15.

FIGURE 29.15

The Frame Size tab for the Logo frame has scrolling and resizing turned off.

The finished product is visible in Figure 29.16. Scrollbars can be set to On, Off, Automatic, or Default. Auto is the default and, when set, the client determines whether scrollbars should be displayed or not. On sets the scrollbars permanently on and Off sets them permanently off. Resizing can be turned Off or On. The default is On. When you set Allow Resizing to On, either a Web or a Notes user can resize the frames by clicking and dragging the borders.

FIGURE 29.16

The completed Example frameset neatly displays the R5 Logo without scrollbars or white space.

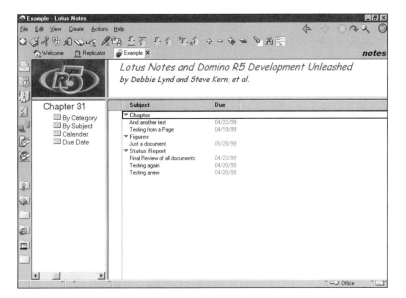

Working with Borders and Margins

The Frame Borders tab lets you manipulate the border style for individual frames or the entire frameset. You can turn 3D borders on and off; if you want to apply the change to all frames in the frameset, click the Apply to All Frames button. The remaining settings in the bottom half of the Tab apply to the entire frameset (see Figure 29.17).

FIGURE 29.17

Settings in the Frame Border tab control the border style, color, and width.

If you uncheck Default, you can change the width of the border by clicking the spinner to the desired number of pixels. You can even turn the border off by reducing the number of pixels to 0. You can also choose a border color.

Reset System Colors

If you change colors from the system color and want to return to the system color, open the color picker. Look just to the left of the RGB color button (a colored circle in the upper-right), and you'll see another button which looks like a monitor. This button returns you to the system color.

The Advanced tab has settings for Frame Spacing, Margin Height, and Margin Width. These are all checked Default. To access the spinner, uncheck the Default setting, and you can then change the property (see Figure 29.18). Frame Spacing affects all frames in the Frameset and has the same effect as setting the Border Width on the Frame Borders tab. The Margin Height and Width affect specific frames.

FIGURE 29.18

The Advanced tab lets you change the Frame Spacing, the Margin Height, and the Margin Width.

Viewing the HTML Source of your Frameset

If you want to see what kind of HTML Domino produces, you can do so in two ways. First, you can preview it in a Web browser and view the source. You can also get at the HTML for the frameset itself through the Design Synopsis. To use the Design Synopsis, choose File, Database, Design Synopsis from the menu. This opens the Design Synopsis dialog box. Choose Framesets in the Design Elements tab and select your frameset. Switch to the Content tab and select Frameset from the Line Item list. Make sure that Include JavaScript and HTML is checked. Click OK, and the HTML for the frameset is produced. See Chapter 16, "Analyzing Your Applications," for more information on how to use the Design Synopsis. See Figure 29.19 for an example of the HTML of a frameset.

FIGURE 29.19

The HTML code for the Example frameset doesn't include all the code necessary to produce the frameset.

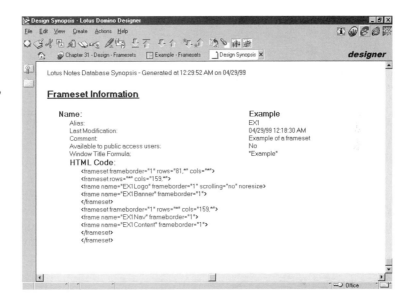

You've probably already noticed that it's pretty sparse. It's certainly not enough HTML to actually launch a frameset. In fact, all that it really contains is the settings for the <FRAMESET> and <FRAME> tags. As such, you can get a look at the frames to see whether they are set the way you want, but that's about it.

Launching the Frameset

It's very easy to launch a frameset. You've already read about launching specific design elements such as pages and forms directly into a frame in a frameset, but what if you want to use the frameset to be the front door to your application? Simply open the Database Properties box to the Launch tab and in one or both of the When Opened lists, specify Open Designated Frameset. Select your frameset and now, whenever users open the database, the frameset opens. Note that you can create a single frameset that works both for Notes and Web clients (see Figure 29.20).

FIGURE **29.20**

Launching a database into a frameset is done through settings in the Launch tab of the Database Properties box.

Note that you can also have different framesets for the Web and for Notes clients, or open a frameset for Web clients, but not for Notes clients.

Summary

Framesets are a great way to pull all the various elements in your application into one pleasing front end. As pointed out earlier, for the most part, Framesets function equally well for both Web and Notes clients. This is without doubt one of the most significant enhancements to R5 of Notes and Domino. You can build a few pages, include an outline on one page, perhaps, and wrap it all into a Frameset very quickly. What used to be nearly impossible in R4.6 has suddenly become quite easy in R5!

Automating Your Application with Agents

by Debbie Lynd

IN THIS CHAPTER

Agents automate tasks in a Domino database. Along with mail-enabling forms, agents are at the heart of the power of Domino Applications. In Release 3, agents were called macros. In Release 4, the name was changed to *agent*, and provided a dramatic improvement over macros. The design interface was significantly improved, and the power of agents was greatly expanded with the addition of Simple Actions, LotusScript, and, in Release 4.6, the ability to import Java. Release 5 continues to improve Agents, by providing expanded functionality, such as enabling the creation of Java Agents in the IDE.

Working with Agents

Agents are the workhorses of a Domino database. They are similar to programs in other application design systems, but agents have some significant differences. First, agents are event-driven. A number of different events can trigger the execution of an agent, such as the following:

- Agents can be scheduled to run at any time of the day or night.
- Agents can be executed based on the addition or modification of a document.
- Agents can be invoked by a user.
- Agents can be triggered by a mail message being delivered.

Agents are used throughout Lotus Notes. You might not have noticed that you use agents in Notes daily. All the Actions that appear in the Actions menu are agents. For example, in the Mail database, the mail calendar tools on the Actions menu are agents. To see this for yourself, open your mail database and click the Agents folder in the view navigator. Using the slash character (\) causes the agent to cascade on the Actions menu, just as it does for views and forms. There are actually more agents listed in the Agents folder, shown in Figure 30.1, than appear in the Actions menu. That's because you can choose which actions appear on the Actions menu.

Working in the Agent ViewPane

When you select agents from the Design menu, the list of agents for the database is displayed in a view as shown in Figure 30.1. The columns displayed in this view describe the properties shown in Table 30.1.

FIGURE 30.1

The Agents folder of the Mail template displays all agent types.

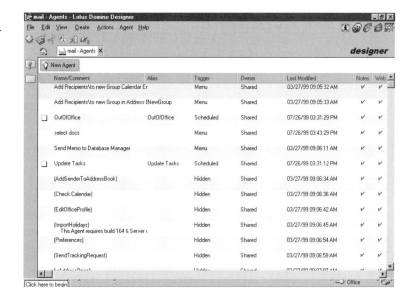

TABLE 30.1 Agent View Columns

Property	Description
Name/Comment	The name of the agent and any comment
Alias	The alias of the viewname if one is defined
Trigger	The value from When Should This Agent Run
Owner	Shared if this is a shared agent; the name of the user if it is a private view
Last Modified	Date the agent was last modified
Notes	If checked, the agent runs in Notes
Web	If checked, the agent runs on the Web

Agents have a multitude of possible uses. After you understand how agents function, more and more uses will become apparent. Some agents merely automate tasks that are routine. Others are highly complex and sophisticated, performing multiple actions that would not otherwise be possible.

30

AUTOMATING YOUR APPLICATION

Examples of the simple agents are those that move documents into archive databases, such as the Archive agent in the mail database. Agents can also search a database for documents that meet certain criteria and then move or copy them into a folder. For example, the Page Minder agent in the Notes Personal Web Navigator checks for updates to Web pages that you select, and refreshes them on a schedule. This agent can save a lot of time because it can execute in the wee hours, without human intervention. Another example, is the Web Ahead agent in the same database that automatically retrieves Web pages to the "depth" that you specify. The combination of these two agents makes a very powerful research tool.

In typical applications, such as a workflow application, an agent might send notifications to reviewers that the allotted time for the review has passed. Other agents might add or modify information in newly created or modified documents. For a mail-in database, an agent could be created to modify the Form field of a document mailed in to the database. That way, the new document could be displayed using a form appropriate to the database. For example, a rejected change request mailed to an archive database could be displayed with a special Rejected form. The agent would change the form field, and the document would then be displayed using the Rejected form.

Discussion databases often have newsletter agents that email participants in the discussion when documents have been modified or added to the database. These can be scheduled on the server to run on a daily, weekly, or hourly basis.

More complex agents might handle the movement of data from external databases into a Domino database. An agent such as this might use LotusScript and ODBC, and be scheduled to execute during nonpeak times. Or, this agent might execute when a user accesses a Domino Web site and query a SQL database. Agents can also call other agents to accomplish complex multistep processes.

Still more agents can be created to process only in Web applications. These agents could be written in Java and extend the capabilities of the agent to the Web browser.

As you can see, there are many possible uses for agents, and they are valuable and powerful tools.

Comparing Personal and Shared Agents

There are two general categories of agents: shared and personal. A personal agent can be used only by the person who created the agent. When an agent is created and saved, the signature of the active User ID is saved with the agent. This is what is used to determine whether or not a personal agent is one you can run. Anyone with reader access can create a personal agent stored in a shared database if they have been given access when the

ACL option Create Personal Agents is checked. This means that they can create an agent using Simple Actions or the Formula language. For someone with reader access to create an agent with LotusScript, Create Personal Agents and Create LotusScript/Java Agent must both be checked as indicated in Figure 30.2.

FIGURE 30.2

Whether a user can create an agent depends on the ACL Options set for that user.

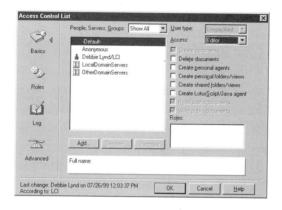

To be able to run a personal agent stored on the server, you must be listed in the Run Personal Agents field of the Agent Manager section of the Server document or be in a group listed in that field. If you are not listed in this field, you cannot store a personal agent in a shared database, no matter what the setting in the ACL is.

A shared agent can be used by anyone who has Reader access to the database. To create a shared agent, you must have at least Designer access in the ACL of a database. This enables you to create an agent using Simple Actions and the Formula language. In order to create a LotusScript or Java agent as a Designer, you must still check the Create LotusScript/Java agent selection in the ACL. By default it is unchecked.

Two other fields control the execution of agents on a server: Run Restricted LotusScript/Java Agents and Run Unrestricted LotusScript/Java Agents. Granting access to unrestricted LotusScript and Java agents is potentially dangerous because these agents can manipulate file I/0, operating system commands, and system time on the server. Most administrators limit access to unrestricted agents.

Note

You must be listed or in a group that is listed in the Run Restricted LotusScript/Java Agents field in the server document for the Out of Office agent to run in the mail database.

Restricting Agents

There are quite a few restrictions that an Administrator can place on running agents. You should review the restrictions that are set on your server before attempting to schedule an agent. These restrictions are in the Agent Manager tab of the Server Tasks tab in the directory of the Server document as displayed in Figure 30.3.

FIGURE 30.3

The Agent Manager section of the Server document provides settings for who can execute agents on the server.

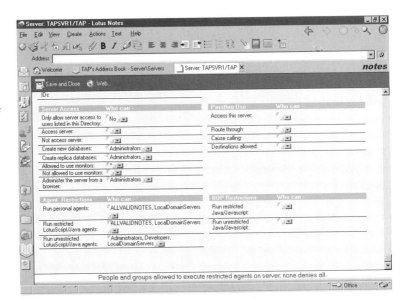

Limiting Agent Processing

One setting that an Administrator can set for limiting agents is the length of time that an agent can run. By default this is set to 10 minutes during the day and 15 minutes at night. I have had agents scheduled to run at night that require at least an hour to complete. With a 15-minute default, my agent would quit before completing.

Always time your agents during testing to ensure they have the time they need to run to completion.

Triggering Agents

There are specific ways that Agents can be triggered. Agents can be

- Scheduled on either a server or a client
- Run manually from a hotspot, form or view action, the Action menu, or the Agent list
- Executed based on an action, such as a new document being created, or a document being modified, mailed into the database, and so on

These triggers determine whether the agent is run without user intervention and what kicks the agent off.

Each of these triggers can take action on all documents or a subset of documents. There are three questions to answer when writing an agent:

- When should the agent run? This is the trigger.
- Which documents should it run on? This is the set of documents the agent will act on.
- What actions should it take? This is the code that you will write.

Each of these questions are answered in the Agent Builder window. The section "Working in the Agent Builder Design Window" describes this window in detail. The Agent Builder window is where agents are written or coded. Let's take a look at some possible uses for agents.

Creating an Agent

Before creating an agent, you must determine what the agent is supposed to accomplish. Essentially, this analysis answers the questions in the Agent Builder design window. The analysis should also include a general description of the agent.

There are several ways to create an agent. If you are in one of the design folders, you can click the Create Agent SmartIcon. You can also choose Create, Agent or Create, Design, Agent from the menu. You can also copy agents from other databases or even the current database, paste them, and then modify the agent to suit your purposes. Figure 30.4 shows a new, untitled agent.

FIGURE 30.4

The Agent Builder window.

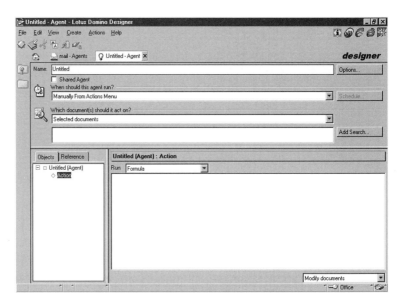

Developers create shared agents to handle tasks that are common to all users or the database itself. End users usually create personal agents; however, developers usually have one or two personal agents in an application for clean up and corrections. Unlike views or folders, there is no way to create an agent that is shared and personal on first use. To make the agent shared, simply click the Shared Agent checkbox. Keep in mind that if the agent is to be run manually by a user, the agent will be limited by the user's ACL restrictions. For example, if an agent creates a new copy of a document, it will not work for a user who has reader access to the database.

Caution

By default, an agent is private. Make sure you choose the Shared checkbox before saving a new agent if it is to be a shared agent. When an agent is saved, you cannot change it from private to shared or shared to private.

Working in the Agent Builder Design Window

Each of the sections of the Agent Builder control different aspects of the agent. The design window contains a three-pane interface as shown in Figure 30.5.

FIGURE 30.5

Agents are created in the agent builder. The Out of Office agent used in the Mail database operates on new documents.

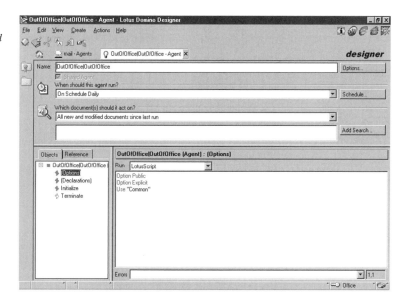

The top portion of the window is where the agent is named and scheduled and where selection criteria can be specified. Because agents do not have actions, there is no action pane. The bottom portion, which should be familiar by now, is the Design pane on the right and the Browser pane on the left.

> **Note**
>
> Although a special section for selecting documents is in the top half of the Agent Builder, selection criteria can still be entered into the Programmer's Pane. This can be done using the Formula language, LotusScript, or Java.

Naming Agents

Naming an agent is similar to naming forms and views. If an agent appears on the Action menu, it can be cascaded in submenus, as illustrated in Figure 30.6. If the number of agents that are run manually from the Actions menu is large, consider collecting them into submenus by cascading. Agents are sorted alphabetically, just as forms and views are. You can include an accelerator key by prepending an underscore to a character. This causes the letter to be underlined in the menu. Users can then type the letter when they are in the Action menu and have the agent execute.

FIGURE 30.6

Agent names can be cascaded just as form and view names can.

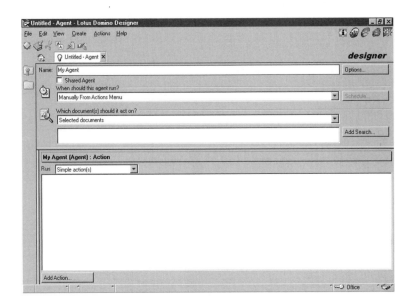

Next to the agent name, is a button called Options. After clicking on Options you will find three checkboxes on the Options dialog box and an area for a comment. See Figure 30.7. The comment window is fairly small and is not expandable, although it is scrollable. It is a good idea to keep the comment succinct, so that as much of the comment as possible will fit into the visible area. The comment can briefly describe the purpose of the agent.

FIGURE 30.7

The Options window for an agent includes an area for comments.

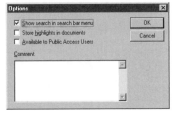

The first two checkboxes relate to search agents. Search Agents are agents that can be stored and used from the SearchBar of a database that is full-text indexed.

Determining When the Agent Should Run

The When Should This Agent Run? section of the Agent Builder is used to choose which event triggers the agent. Table 30.1 lists the choices. The Schedule column indicates whether the agent can be scheduled.

TABLE 30.2   When Should This Agent Run?

Event Trigger	*Schedule*
Manually from Actions Menu	No
Manually from Agent List	No
If New Mail Has Arrived	No
Before New Mail Arrives	No
After New Mail Has Arrived	No
If Documents Have Been Created or Modified	Yes
If Documents Have Been Pasted	No
On Schedule More Than Once a Day	Yes
On Schedule Daily	Yes
On Schedule Weekly	Yes
On Schedule Monthly	Yes
On Schedule Never	No

The two manual options are listed first. The first lists the agent in the Actions menu. The second hides it from the menu. Both can be run from the Agent folder (also referred to as the Agent list) by double-clicking the agent or by highlighting the agent and choosing Action, Run from the menu. Because these events are manual, they cannot be scheduled. On the other hand, a scheduled agent can be run manually from the Agent list. The next four events relate to the addition and modification of documents. Only the If Documents Have Been Created or Modified event can be scheduled. Clicking the Schedule button allows the developer to choose on which server the agent runs, as well as start and stop dates. The Schedule window is shown in Figure 30.8.

Running an Agent if New Mail Has Arrived

A caveat with running New Mail agents is that the server the agent is run on must be the home server for the signer of the agent. There is a workaround for this in R4.5 or higher. A modification to the Notes.INI to include the parameter `AMgr_DisableMailLookup=1` disables the lookup of the signer's mail file location in the directory.

The trigger Before New Mail Arrives is new to Release 5. This could be helpful if you need to initiate changes prior to a mail message being sent. There can only be one of

30

AUTOMATING
YOUR
APPLICATION

these agents active at a time in the database. The Router is responsible for executing the agent; therefore, an agent of this type could delay mail delivery if it takes a long time to execute.

FIGURE 30.8

The If Documents Have Been Created or Modified Schedule window sets the server the agent should run on.

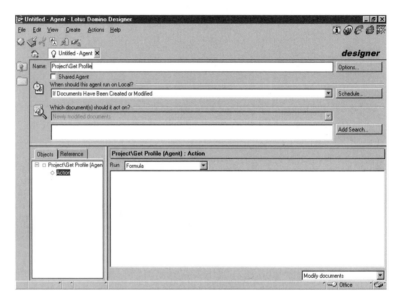

Each of the remaining events are scheduled, with the exception of On Schedule Never.

Scheduling Agents

Figure 30.9 shows the Schedule window for On Schedule More Than Once a Day. There are three portions to the Schedule window. The top two sections deal with *when* and the bottom section with *where*. The daily, weekly, and monthly schedule windows are essentially the same as this window.

Take Care When Running Agents on Servers

If you schedule an agent to run on a server and that agent will modify documents, be sure to specify which server the agent should run on. If you run the agent on multiple replicas of the database, you will encounter replication conflicts!

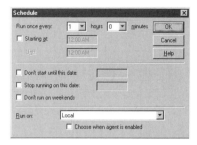

FIGURE 30.9

The Hourly sched-ule window defaults to run every hour.

An agent scheduled hourly is actually a misnomer, because the minimum repeat time for an agent is 5 minutes. The drop-down list Run Once Every: has 12 choices for hours (0 through 11 hours) and 12 choices for minutes (0 through 55 incremented by fives). If you check Starting At, you can specify a range of time during which the agent should run. This is useful because some agents can take significant server resources.

Schedule Agents to Run When They Are Needed

If you choose to have an hourly agent notify users when documents are added to a database, there is no sense having it run when there are no users present. Click Starting At and choose a range when users are at work, say from 8:00 a.m. to 5:00 p.m. Check Don't Run on Weekends if you are lucky enough to work somewhere that people actually don't work on the weekends.

Each of the other scheduled agents have a similar section. The weekly schedule window allows you to choose the day of the week and time of day. The monthly schedule lets you choose the day number (1–31) and the time of day.

The middle portion of the Schedule window has three options: Don't Start Until This Date, Stop Running on This Date, and Don't Run on Weekends.

The bottom part of the window, the *where* part, is also common to all variations of the Schedule window. The Run Only On drop-down menu lists all available servers as well as local. Developers can either choose the server on which the agent runs when the agent is designed or click the Choose When Agent Is Enabled. Clicking the checkbox allows you to choose the server to run on when the agent is enabled if it is not to be enabled now. Figure 30.10 shows the result of this choice. When the server name is chosen, a small square checkbox appears in the margin of the Agent folder to indicate that the agent is enabled.

30

AUTOMATING YOUR APPLICATION

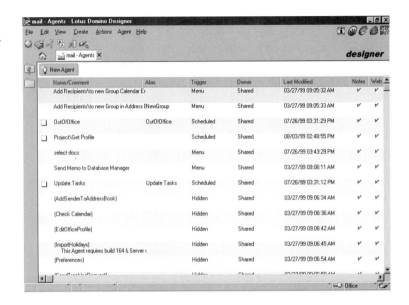

To activate an agent to run on a specific server, click the checkbox. The Choose Server To Run On window is displayed with a drop-down list of available servers. Figure 30.11 shows this window.

FIGURE 30.11

The Choose Server To Run On window presents a drop-down list of available servers.

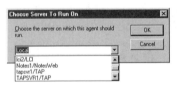

On Schedule Never is included for backward compatibility with Release 3 macros that have Never as the schedule option. An agent called by other agents can also have this trigger.

Selecting Documents

After you determine when an agent should run, it is time to determine which documents it should act on. Document selection is available for all events except those listed in Table 30.3.

TABLE 30.3   Triggers with Automatic Document Selection

Trigger	*Selected Documents*
If New Mail Has Arrived	Newly received mail documents
Before New Mail Arrives	Each incoming mail document
If Documents Have Been	Newly modified documents Created or Modified
If Documents Have Been Pasted	Pasted Documents

The choices available are the following:

- All documents in database
- All new and modified documents since last run
- All unread documents in view
- All documents in view
- Selected documents
- Run Once (@Commands can be used)

The On Schedule events have only the first two options available, but all the options are available for the two manual events, which makes them far more flexible.

Test Agents Manually Before Scheduling Them

When you write new agents, it is a good idea to test them against a small subset of documents in the database. One way to test an agent—even one that will be scheduled to run in the background—is to choose Selected Documents and Manually From Actions Menu. Select a few documents and run the agent. When the agent is running properly, switch to the appropriate schedule.

Creating an agent to run against selected documents is useful for allowing users to change fields in multiple documents.

Using @Commands in Agents

The @Commands are not available for any agent except the Run Once agent. A Run Once agent is the only type of agent that can be executed by a Web browser. This is because a Web browser has no concept of the other options.

30

AUTOMATING YOUR APPLICATION

Documents can also be selected by using the Search Builder. Clicking the Add Search button displays the Search Builder window. Using this feature is useful for search agents. Figure 30.12 shows the choices available: By Author, By Date, By Field, By Form, By Form Used, In Folder, and Words and Phrases. This is the same window used in a full-text search and functions in exactly the same manner. A search agent can run on a database selecting documents that meet certain criteria, as shown in Figure 30.12. A newsletter can then be composed and emailed containing doclinks to the selected documents. Similarly, the agent can move the documents into a folder. The Search Builder can create very sophisticated selection criteria.

FIGURE 30.12

The search builder window allows you to build a search with multiple conditions.

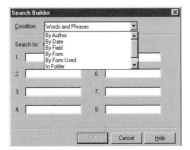

> **Note**
>
> You can add multiple search conditions to the same agent by successively clicking the Add Search button. These conditions are connected by default with a Boolean AND, but OR and NOT can also be used. Using parentheses to change order of execution is also supported so complex search conditions can be created.

Putting Your Agent to Work

As always, the Design or Programmer's Pane occupies the bottom-right portion of the Design window. Agents can perform Simple Actions, formulas, LotusScript, or Java. Many common tasks can be accomplished using Simple Actions; Simple Actions can be combined with each other and with @Functions. The Formula language can handle more sophisticated agents. However, neither Simple Actions nor formulas can be combined with LotusScript or Java. As you learned in Chapters 22, "Introduction to LotusScript," 23, "Basic LotusScript," and 24, "Writing LotusScript," LotusScript is particularly suited to agents because it can iteratively process documents. Neither Simple Actions nor the Formula language can do that because they are limited to a single pass through the documents. Java agents provide portability of agents to Web browsers.

Defining Simple Actions in Agents

Simple Actions are options that you can choose to have a set of commands executed automatically. The name of the action defines the task that is executed when the agent is run. Following is a list of Simple Actions:

- Copy to Database
- Copy to Folder
- Delete from Database
- Mark Document Read
- Mark Document Unread
- Modify Field
- Modify Fields by Form
- Move to Folder
- Remove from Folder
- Reply to Sender
- Run Agent
- Send Document
- Send Mail Message
- Send Newsletter Summary
- @Function Formula

Simple Actions can be added together in the same manner as search criteria. These actions are then performed in sequence, with the following exception: the Delete from Database action is always executed last, regardless of its position in the Simple Action window. To use a Simple Action in an agent, click the Run Simple Action radio button. Click the Add Action button to add an Action. After the action is programmed and saved, you can add additional actions to the agent by clicking the Add Action button again. You can edit actions by double-clicking the text with the gray background in the Design Pane that symbolizes the action. Although Simple Actions are limited, they can be useful. They are particularly useful for end users because of the ease with which they can be programmed.

In a mail-in database, an agent using the Reply to Sender Simple Action can send a confirmation of receipt to the person emailing a document to the database. Creating an Action such as this is easy because it requires no knowledge of the Formula language or of LotusScript. Simple Action agents can also be used to chain together more than one agent by using the Run Agent action. To be able to run, this agent must already exist in the database.

30

AUTOMATING
YOUR
APPLICATION

An example of a limitation of Simple Actions is the Modify Field action. This allows you to add only a text, numeric, or time value. You cannot store the value of another field in the field to be modified with this action. To do that, you must either choose the Run @Function Simple Action or use an agent based on the Formula language or LotusScript.

Using Formulas in Agents

Formula-based agents, or agents based on the Domino Formula language, are significantly more powerful than Simple Action agents. Formulas for agents can be added to a Simple Action by clicking the Run Formula button. Formula-based agents have a special listbox that appears in the lower-right corner of the Design Pane. This is illustrated in Figure 30.13. The listbox has the following three selections:

- Modify documents (the default)
- Create new documents
- Select documents in view

FIGURE 30.13

There are many actions that a formula-based agent can use.

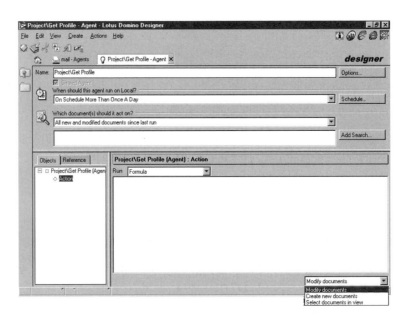

Most often, you will write agents that modify documents. The agent in Listing 30.1 is an example of one that modifies documents. You might occasionally create an agent that creates a new document and perhaps archives the original. Search agents can be used to select documents in view and will place a checkmark in the view margin next to the documents that meet the selection criteria.

Creating a formula-based agent requires a SELECT statement. If one is not present, Domino appends SELECT @All to the end of the formula. If you want to change the SELECT statement to restrict the documents, the statement must be placed at the beginning of the formula or it will not function. The SELECT statement can be used to further refine the selection criteria. If an agent includes a SELECT statement that specifies a condition, as opposed to selecting all documents, you should test the agent using Select Documents in View to ensure that you are selecting the appropriate documents before choosing to modify documents.

Formulas for agents can easily manipulate field values using the FIELD keyword or the @SetField() function. Using one of these two options allows the value of the field to be set to that of another field, a combination of fields and text, and so on. You can also create and delete fields in documents. None of this is possible with a Simple Action.

You will find that through the course of developing an application, you might want to change field names. However, if documents already exist in the database, the new field name will not be updated in the existing documents. Listing 30.1 displays an agent to make the changes.

LISTING 30.1 Moving Data from an Old Field to a New Field in Existing Documents

```
SELECT Form = "Name of Form"
FIELD NewField := OldField
Field OldField := @DeleteField
```

Another agent that is frequently used by developers is one to recalculate all the fields in existing documents based on design changes made to the forms. This can be accomplished through a formula agent as listed in Listing 30.2.

LISTING 30.2 Recalculating Fields in Documents

```
@Command([ToolsRefreshAllDocs])
```

Flagging a Document Can Be Useful

Setting a flag when an agent processes a certain document is often useful. This flag can be used to limit further actions by the agent or can be used simply for informational purposes.

The following code fragment illustrates setting flags in a document:

```
REM "Mark document macro run time and set flags";

FIELD ChkResponse := @Now;
FIELD ReviewersNotified := "No";
FIELD CheckFlag := "On";
```

These fields did not originally exist in the document but were added using the Formula language. The value of fields set by the agent can be checked in subsequent runs. For example, in the preceding code fragment is a flag field called `ReviewersNotified`. If certain conditions were met, the reviewers would be notified by email and the value of this field would be set to `Yes`. When the agent executes in the future, the `SELECT` statement could be used to prevent the agent from executing on this document. Otherwise, reviewers would be notified on all subsequent runs of the agent. Such a selection statement might look like the following:

```
SELECT (FORM = "ECR" & ECRStatus = "Released for Review" &
➥ReviewersNotified != "Yes")
```

Creating a Complex Agent

In this section I will explain a simple utility to enable users to mail a document to a database. This agent includes an attached graphic with the document that is mailed. The document will be mailed to a central repository for graphics elements within a company that can be later used in Domino applications. This provides you with a practical application for learning how to use agents for mailing purposes and for storing attachments.

This database consists of a form named `NewGraphic¦NG` that contains the information we are interested in displaying from the mail message that is received. For the database to receive mail, a mail-in database record must be created. When the database receives mail, the form is the Mail Memo form. This must be changed to the form name `NewGraphic¦NG`, and the unnecessary fields must be stripped from the document. The name of the person mailing the document must be appended to the subject of the memo and stored in the comment field. A message must be sent on receipt of the mail to the Graphics database manager (GMan) because he must approve the graphic before it can be made available to the users of the database for inclusion into any of the company's applications. A confirmation message to the sender of the graphic indicating that the graphic was received and is under consideration also needs to be sent. To illustrate a couple of techniques, I made the architecture of this agent a bit more complex than is probably necessary.

First, I created a Reply to Sender Simple Action agent with a New Mail trigger. Figure 30.14 shows the Reply to Sender action being defined. The reply message is simple and straightforward. Because this is a Simple Action, it executes with the New Mail trigger.

FIGURE 30.14

The Confirmation agent during design displays the Add Action dialog box for creating the Reply to Sender Simple Action.

Next, I created a formula-based agent to convert the form name, modify fields, and delete unnecessary fields. This is the Convert Mail Memo agent, which has a trigger of If Documents Have Been Created or Modified. This is the formula in Listing 30.3.

LISTING 30.3 Formula Agent for the Submission of a New Graphics File

```
REM "Make sure this runs only on Memo forms. This effectively limits
➥the execution of the agent" ;
REM "because the form is changed from Memo to NG" ;

SELECT  Form = "Memo"  ;

REM "Change Form to Mail Convert form" ;
FIELD Form := "NG" ;

REM "Initialize fields" ;

FIELD cComment := Subject  + ", submitted by " +@Name([CN];From) ;
FIELD NGReaders :="GMan" ;

REM "Delete fields" ;

FIELD Subject := @DeleteField ;
FIELD From := @DeleteField;
FIELD Categories := @DeleteField ;
FIELD CopyTo := @DeleteField;
FIELD DefaultMailSaveOptions := @DeleteField;
FIELD DeliveredDate := @DeleteField;
FIELD Encrypt := @DeleteField;
FIELD LayoutField := @DeleteField;
```

continues

LISTING 30.3 continued

```
FIELD Logo := @DeleteField;
FIELD MailSaveOptions := @DeleteField;
FIELD PostedDate := @DeleteField;
FIELD PRINCIPAL := @DeleteField;
FIELD RouteServers := @DeleteField;
FIELD RouteTimes := @DeleteField;
FIELD SECURE-MAIL := @DeleteField;
FIELD SenderTag := @DeleteField;
FIELD SendTo := @DeleteField;
FIELD Sign := @DeleteField;

REM "The AuthorList field gets added by Domino and will allow access
➥because it is a read/edit " ;
REM "access field. Delete it to prevent accidental access to the
➥documents." ;

FIELD AuthorList := @DeleteField;
REM " A mail message should now go to the database administrator notifying
➥him/her that the graphic has been submitted for approval";

@MailSend(NGReaders;"";"";"New Graphic Submission";"";"The attached
➥document has been submitted for review";[IncludeDocLink])
```

Notice that I have the agent automatically send a message with a doclink to the database administrator, to review and approve the graphic. I could have sent mail confirmation to the sender directly from this formula agent, but I wanted to illustrate how it can be done with a Simple Action agent. Another possible technique is to combine the Reply to Sender Simple Action with the Run Agent Simple Action. This is illustrated in Figure 30.15. Because this is a formula-based agent, you cannot use the New Mail trigger and instead must use the If Documents Have Been Created or Modified trigger.

There is one more problem to solve. When the NGReaders field is created in a document, even though it is a Reader Names field on the Newgraphics/NG form, it ends up being a text field until the document is refreshed. It is too bad that the field type cannot be enforced. Unfortunately, there is no easy way to refresh a document via an automatic agent. The only technique available with traditional coding methods is to use a Run Once agent with @Command([ToolsRefreshAllDocs]) or @Command([ToolsRefreshSelectedDocs]). Run Once agents are manual agents, and because this @Command relates to the UI, it will not execute when called from another agent. Therefore, the agent must be run by an administrator after the database is opened.

Next, let's see how this agent can be handled using LotusScript.

FIGURE 30.15

The Process Mail agent replies to the sender and runs the Convert Mail Memo agent.

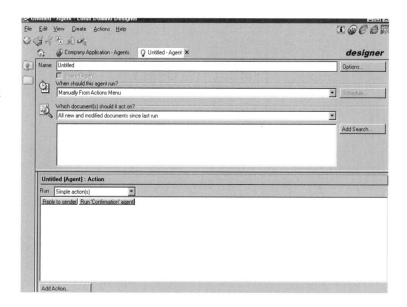

Using LotusScript in Agents

Accomplishing the same actions in LotusScript requires a slightly different approach—not different in that you have to do different things, just that you have to get more into the details of what it is you're trying to do. Using the Formula language, many of the back-end details are taken care for you by the commands and functions. For example, consider the agent just discussed. The agent "knows" that if I change a field value, the document is to be saved when the agent has finished processing that document. This isn't true when using LotusScript. LotusScript does exactly what you tell it to do, nothing more or less, which is not always what you want it to do! In my LotusScript agent, after changing a field value, I have to specifically tell the agent to save the document or my changes are lost. Although this might seem cumbersome at first, it's not unreasonable. With the added power and flexibility from having the LotusScript access to Domino objects at a lower level than what's available through the Formula language comes the responsibility to control exactly what it does.

Now take a look at how the example agent can be written in LotusScript. I'll describe each line of the script in some detail.

Following is the code for our LotusScript agent—all this code is entered into the
Initialize event for the agent:

```
'Process Archive Mail-In - LotusScript Version:
Sub Initialize

'Section I
%REM
 Processing Flow:
 1. Find the mail memo that was just received
 2. Send a reply message to the sender
 3. Change the form from Memo to NG
 4. Add the cComment field
 5. Add the NGReaders field
 6. Delete all the mail and other fields that are not required for the
    ➥NG form
 7. Delete the AuthorList field
 8. Send a mail message to the database manager notifying him/her of need
    ➥to review
 9. Save the changes we've made
%END REM

'Section II
 'declare the variables used for this procedure
 Dim s As NotesSession
 Dim db As NotesDatabase
 Dim note As NotesDocument
 Dim reply As NotesDocument
 Dim collection As NotesDocumentCollection
 Dim dbmgr As NotesName
 Dim item As NotesItem
 Dim rtitem as NotesRichTextItem

'Section III
 'create the object reference variable for the Notes Session
 Set s = New NotesSession

 'create the object reference for the current database
 Set db = s.CurrentDatabase

'Section IV
 'create the object reference for the Unprocessed documents collection.
 'For Agents, the UnprocessedDocument list is a document collection of all
 '    documents that meet the "Which documents should it act on?" criteria
 '    for the agent
 Set collection = db.UnprocessedDocuments

 '1. Find the mail memo which was just mailed in
 ' Because the trigger for this agent is "When documents are
 ' created or modified"
```

```
'     we have to verify that the documents we get in the collection are
'➥actually
'     mail memos. If they're not, then this is a modified, already existing
'➥document,
'     and we don't want to do anything with it.
Set note = collection.GetFirstDocument

'Section V
' This is our main processing loop. As long as there are any documents
' to process in our collection, we'll keep repeating this loop
Do Until note is Nothing

'Section VI
    If note.Form( 0 ) = "Memo" Then
        ' This is a mail memo, so we'll process it
        ' 2. Send a message to the dbmgr as indicated in the NGReaders field
            ➥of the document
        Set reply = New NotesDocument( db )
        reply.Form = "Memo"
        reply.SendTo = "GMan"
        reply.Subject = "New Graphic Request"
        reply.Desc = "Please review the newly submitted graphic."
         Set rtitem = reply.body
         call rtitem.appenddoclink(doc,doc.Subject)
         Call reply.Send( False )

'Section VII
        '3. Change the form from Memo to NG
        note.Form = "NG"

        '4. Add the cComment field
        Set sender = New NotesName( note.From( 0 ) )
        note.cComment = note.Subject( 0 ) & ", submitted by " &
        ➥sender.Abbreviated

'Section VIII
        '5. Add the NGReaders field
        Set item = note.AppendItemValue( "NGReaders" , "GMan" )
        item.IsReaders = True

'Section IX
        '6. Delete all the mail and other fields that are not
        'required for the MI form
        Call note.RemoveItem( "Subject" )
        Call note.RemoveItem( "From" )
        Call note.RemoveItem( "Categories" )
        Call note.RemoveItem( "CopyTo" )
        Call note.RemoveItem( "DefaultMailSaveOptions" )
        Call note.RemoveItem( "DeliveredDate" )
        Call note.RemoveItem( "Encrypt" )
```

```
    Call note.RemoveItem( "LayoutField" )
    Call note.RemoveItem( "Logo" )
    Call note.RemoveItem( "MailSaveOptions" )
    Call note.RemoveItem( "PostedDate" )
    Call note.RemoveItem( "Principal" )
    Call note.RemoveItem( "RouteServers" )
    Call note.RemoveItem( "RouteTimes" )
    Call note.RemoveItem( "Secure-mail" )
    Call note.RemoveItem( "SenderTag" )
    Call note.RemoveItem( "SendTo" )
    Call note.RemoveItem( "Sign" )

    '7. Delete the AuthorList field
    Call note.RemoveItem( "AuthorList" )

    '8. Save the changes we've made
    Call note.Save( True, True )
  End If

'Section X
  Set note = collection.GetNextDocument( note )

Loop

'Section XI
'Set these documents marked as processed by this agent
Call collection.UpdateAll

End Sub
```

Now run through the code and see what it does.

Section I

Notice that the first thing I do is put in a comment block that describes what this agent is supposed to do and the general flow of processing. I do this, as you should, to help whomever might come along in a year and make modifications to this agent (it could even be you!). As an active developer, you'll crank out a lot of code in a year and it's hard to remember all the formulas you've written, what they were supposed to do, and why you wrote them the way you did.

Section II

In section II, all the object reference variables for the objects that will be used in the script are declared. Note that at this time none of the object references have a value; they all equate to NOTHING (an internal LotusScript constant).

Section III

Here, the s and the db object references are set to their respective objects. s becomes the pointer to everything Notes knows about the current user session—the known universe, as it were. db becomes the pointer to the current database. Now that I've given Notes a reference to the database I want to work with, db, I can get to objects within the database.

Section IV

The object reference collection is set to what is actually a property of the database, the UnprocessedDocuments property. An explanation of a couple of terms is in order here. A *collection* is a view of documents. The view doesn't necessarily have to be a user view; it might be an internally generated and manipulated view. The UnprocessedDocuments property is a collection of all the documents in the database that are considered unprocessed for the current view action or agent—an agent in this case. The UnprocessedDocuments returned for a particular agent could change depending on what the agent does.

The last line of the section sets the note object reference equal to the first document in the document collection. Note here that I don't test to see whether there are actually any documents in the document collection. Why not? The answer lies in the trigger for the agent. This agent is set to run if documents have been created or modified. Therefore, if there were no unprocessed documents, the agent would not have been invoked. So now, the note object points to the first unprocessed document.

Section V

Although not very exciting, this Do...While loop is the heart of the script. As long as the note object points to a document—in other words, if it's not NOTHING—the loop will continue.

Section VI

Remember that the trigger for this agent is If Documents Have Been Added or Modified. Remember, too, that the purpose of this agent is to take mailed-in documents and convert them to New Graphics¦NG documents. However, because someone could conceivably modify a document that already exists in the database, I have to test for that condition, because I do not want to process anything except new mail memos.

The IF statement begins a block of code that will be executed only if I decide to process this document. To test whether I want to process the current document, I check the contents of the Form field. If the Form field is set to Memo, I know that it just got here and that I should process it. So, process it I do. The first thing I want to do is send a message to the database manager that there is a new graphic and that it needs to be processed.

To send a mail message, I first have to create a new Notes document, which I do with the Set reply = statement. This creates a new, blank Notes document with no fields; it's literally a blank piece of paper. I have to tell Domino everything about this new document. I set the Form field, the SendTo field, the Subject field, and the Body field. Look at how I set the SendTo field. Right now, the reply object reference points to my brand new reply document, and the note object reference points to the group name for the database managers. The following line says to take the contents of the group GMan and make the SendTo field on the reply object the same value:

```
reply.SendTo = "GMan"
```

The last line of Section VI invokes the Send method of the reply object. Back in section II of the agent, reply was declared as an instance of the NotesDocument class and in section IV was set to point to an actual object. The NotesDocument class has a method called Send that takes the NotesDocument object and mails it to the recipients named in the SendTo field (which I set previously). The False parameter to the Send method tells Notes to not send the form with the document.

Section VII

I've finished sending the reply message, so now I can concentrate on processing the current message, still pointed to by note. First, I change the form field from Memo to NG. Next, I fill in the cComment field with some text that includes the name of the sender of this memo. However, because Domino stores names fully canonicalized (such as CN=Debbie Lynd/O=TAP), which isn't very user-friendly, I need to manipulate the sender's name to get it into the abbreviated format (for example, Debbie Lynd/TAP).

To do this, I first instantiate an object reference of the NotesName class. The NotesName class allows me to manipulate Notes names with a great deal of detail. Note the argument I pass to the NotesName declaration note.From(0). Knowing now that this is dot notation, you've already deduced that I'm using the From field of the document pointed to by note. But what's with the (0)?

In LotusScript, every field is actually stored as an array, even if there's only one element in the field. Therefore, in order to get to the field contents, I have to reference the field as though it were an array (which it is!). So, to get the one and only element from the From field on the note document, I need to reference note.From(0).

Missing Index

I can guarantee you that when you start writing LotusScript code on your own, you'll forget to use an index when trying to reference a field's contents. But don't worry! The compiler will give you notice in the form of a `Type Mismatch` error. So when you've looked at your declaration statements and the data types all match, and you're still getting that `Type Mismatch` error, look for the missing (`0`) index.

Section VIII

The two lines of section VIII create the `NGReaders` field and set it to be a readers field. Had I not needed to set a field property, in this case the `IsReaders` property, I could have created the `NGReaders` field the same way I created the fields on the reply document or the `cComment` field created in section VII. In order to manipulate the properties of a field, I have to declare and use an object reference to a `NotesItem` object. Then I can use the dot notation to set the `IsReaders` property of the `item` object.

Section IX

In section IX, I invoke the `NotesDocument` method `RemoveItem`, which deletes the named field from the document. Finally, the `Save` method is called, which saves the document— which brings us to the end of the `IF` block.

Section X

At this point, all processing for the current document, the one pointed to by the `note` object reference variable, is complete. Now I need to continue and process any other remaining documents in the list of unprocessed documents contained in the `collection` object. So, I set the `note` variable to the next document in the collection with the `GetNextDocument` method. What if there were no other documents in the collection? In that case, the `note` variable will be equal to `NOTHING`.

The `LOOP` statement sends us back up to the top of the `Do...While` loop, where our condition, `Not (note is nothing)` is checked again. If there is another document to process, the entire loop is repeated. If, at this point, the `note` object is equal to `NOTHING`, the loop condition is no longer true and the next statement after the `LOOP` line is executed.

30

AUTOMATING
YOUR
APPLICATION

Section XI

This brings us to the last line of executable code in the agent. Remember that the list of documents the agent was to take care of came from the UnprocessedDocuments property of the database. If the agent exited after processing documents, those same documents would be listed in the UnprocessedDocuments collection the next time the agent was invoked. Why, you might ask, is this so? Each agent tracks which documents it has acted on previously. This should be obvious, because how else would an agent know whether or not a particular document was modified since the last time the agent ran? With a simple agent or a formula agent, the process is automatically taken care of for you. However, with a LotusScript agent, you must do it yourself. So, conveniently, there's a NotesDocumentCollection method, UpdateAll, which flags all the documents in a collection as having been processed by this agent. Then, the next time the agent is invoked, these documents won't be processed again unless they've been changed by some other process.

That completes the discussion of the LotusScript agent. It took a few more lines of code to do the same thing that the formula agent did. With this particular agent, the compelling reason to write it in Script is due to the Reader Names field. Only in LotusScript or Java could the field property IsReaders be set. Using the traditional approach discussed earlier, the Refresh agent had to be run manually to permanently hide the new documents from any ID other than the GMan group. Although it could be argued that this is taken care of via the ACL, because the users indicated in the GMan group are the only user IDs that can access the database, it is still a nice touch and one fewer step for the administrator.

Most of us would probably have chosen to do this particular agent in the Formula language, primarily because we *could,* and in some respects it's easier. There will be times when you'll have no choice but to write LotusScript agents simply because you'll need the additional control and object manipulation capability that LotusScript provides you.

Creating Web Agents Using Formulas and LotusScript

Creating formula or LotusScript agents for use on the Web requires that the agent be placed in the WebQueryOpen or WebQuerySave event of a form, or that it be accessed via the URL for that agent such as http://www.domserver.com/agentdb.nsf/ agentname/?openAgent.

This is due to the fact that the agents must be run on the server because a Web client does not know what to do with the formulas and the LotusScript in the agent.

What kinds of things can you do from an agent run from one of these events? Following are some examples:

- Populate the value of a field, just before the document is displayed
- Display information to a user after the document has been saved
- Collect information from a user through the use of CGI variables and store them for statistical analysis

Using Java in Agents

Writing Java agents within the IDE is new to Release 5. However, using Java agents in Domino began in Release 4.6. In Release 4.6, Java agents could be created in another editor and imported into an agent. This continues to be true in Release 5, with the additional option of writing a Java agent in the IDE, which enables you to use the full functionality the IDE provides. Java agents can be written from scratch in the IDE or imported. I will not cover Java agents here as they are covered in detail in Chapter 28, "Using Java in Domino Applications." Because there are a few differences between a formula or LotusScript agent and in what needs to be completed when importing a Java agent, an explanation of the screens is provided later in this chapter.

When you select Imported Java from the run option in the design pane, a button is available at the bottom of the design pane for Importing the class files. When you click that button, the Define Java Agent Files dialog box appears as shown in Figure 30.16. From the dialog box, you can select the class files that must be imported for your agent, and reorder them as needed.

FIGURE 30.16

Importing class files for a Java agent allows you to select them from any directory.

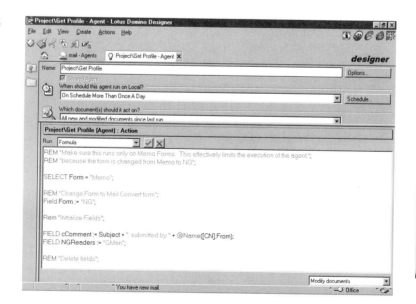

Testing Agents, the Agent Log, and Agent Properties

Just as you can test views and forms, you can test agents by highlighting the agent in the Agent folder and then choosing Actions, Test from the menu. Figure 30.17 shows the menu. Figure 30.18 shows the Agent Log window with the results of the test run of an agent that selects documents meeting a specific criteria. This agent doesn't actually perform any actions; it merely selects the documents. The Agent Log window reports on statistics such as the number of documents meeting the criteria, the number of documents modified, and start and stop times.

FIGURE 30.17

Testing agents is done from the Actions menu.

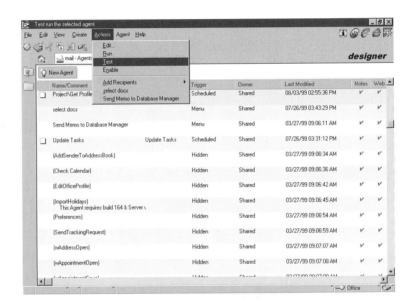

FIGURE 30.18

The results of a test run of an agent to select documents based on a condition shows that the agent ran with no problems.

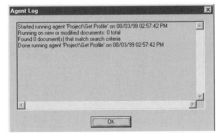

The log is also available from the Agent menu that appears when you are in the Agent folder. From this menu, there are two options: Agent Properties and Log. Choosing Log presents the Agent Log window containing statistics for the last time the agent ran. If the agent has never run before, a Prompt window appears stating that fact.

The Agent Properties window is really the Design Properties InfoBox and is just like those for forms and views. There are three tabs: Information, Fields, and Design. The Information tab shows when the agent was created, modified, and accessed, and also shows the ID for the design element. The Fields tab contains fields related to the agent itself, such as $TITLE, which is the name of the agent and alias if you have given it an alias. $MachineName, which is the name of the machine on which the agent is scheduled to run if it is a scheduled agent. $MachineName contains the fully distinguished name of a server or user, or an asterisk (*) to indicate any server or user. $Signature is the cryptographic signature for the agent. This is the signature that causes the message for cross-certification, if it has been signed by an entity outside of your organization. The $UpdatedBy field displays the list of IDs used to edit this agent as it does for all other design elements, including documents.

The Design tab is shown in Figure 30.19. On this tab appears the name of the last editor, which is also the last name stored in the $UpdatedBy field, the size of the agent in bytes, any design inheritance, and multiple checkboxes. The first checkbox to not allow design refresh/replace to modify keeps the design process from modifying or deleting the agent when it updates the design of the database with its template. The second checkbox hides the agent from the menu bar if the Notes client is above Release 3. Some agents are intended for use with R3 clients only and might not be appropriate or have unpredictable results when executed from an R4 client. Hiding them prevents accidental execution of the agent.

FIGURE 30.19

Whether or not to propagate the agent is defined in the Design tab of the Agent Properties dialog box.

The next two checkboxes are also related to hiding the agent. The first hides the agent from Web browsers, and the second from Notes 4.6 or later clients. The last provides the Notes client with the ability to run the agent as a Web client.

Tracking the execution of an agent can be done in the Notes log. To activate agent logging, a Notes administrator must create or modify a Configuration document in the Public Directory and set the configuration LOG_AGENTMANAGER=1. This setting logs agent execution events in the Miscellaneous view of the Server log. This is somewhat limited, but when testing a scheduled agent, at least the times of execution will be listed in the log.

Figure 30.20 shows the Configuration document being edited.

FIGURE 30.20

The administrator usually sets the parameters for logging agents in the log database.

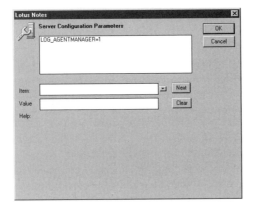

It is also possible to create an agent log database to log agent information when using LotusScript. The LotusScript class is NotesLog. With this class, you can log the agent information not only to a database, but also to a mail message or any Domino database.

Listing 30.4 shows how to create a log entry in an existing log to show completion of an agent.

LISTING 30.4 Logging Agent Information

```
Sub Initialize
  Dim s As New NotesSession
  Dim db As NotesDatabase
  Dim coll As NotesDocumentCollection
  Dim cLog As NotesLog
  Dim doc As NotesDocument
  Dim j As Integer
  Set db = s.CurrentDatabase
  Set coll = db.FTSearch( "Buttons", 0 )
  Call cLog.OpenNotesLog("","Alog.nsf")
  For j = 1 To coll.Count
    Set doc = coll.GetNthDocument( j )
    Call doc.PutInFolder( "Buttons" )
  Next
Call cLog.LogAction( "Buttons Agent Processed " & j & "buttons found" )

Call currentLog.Close
End Sub
```

Summary

This chapter presented techniques of automating Domino applications using agents. This chapter discussed the available types of agents and provided ways to create useful agents. This chapter also covered the triggers for agents and illustrated a complex agent combined Simple Actions and the Formula language; this chapter also presented a LotusScript version. Finally, you were shown how to test agents and view the Agent log.

Security and Domino Applications

by Debbie Lynd

IN THIS CHAPTER

The power of Domino security is almost legendary. The encryption technology that Domino employs, RSA, is classified and under export control. For this reason, there are two versions of Domino encryption: the North American version available only in Canada and the U.S. and the International version. The encryption technology in the International version is not as powerful as that in the North American version. Never have I worked with an application with such rich and powerful security features. Best of all, I didn't have to write one line of code! Of course, as a developer of Domino applications, you need to understand how security functions and how to work with it, which this chapter covers.

This chapter is not intended to present an in-depth treatment of Notes security because this is a book about application development and not a book on system administration. In this chapter you will learn about security and how it applies to application design.

How Does Notes Security Work?

Notes Security is based on the dual-key RSA Cryptosystem encryption technology. RSA is a company formed by three mathematicians: Rivest, Shamir, and Adelman. When an ID file is created using this system, a public and a private key are assigned. The public and private keys are stored with the ID file, and the public key is also stored in the Domino Directory. A mathematical relationship exists between the two keys and is used in a process called *authentication,* which is discussed in a moment. There is more to security than a powerful encryption scheme, however. Encryption is only one part of the overall security of a Notes system.

The levels of security available to a Domino server are

- Physical
- Server
- Database
- Agent
- Form
- View
- Document
- Field

Enabling Physical Security

Security begins with the physical layer; access to servers should be limited to authorized personnel, such as Notes and network administrators. Servers should be in a physically

secure location, such as a locked server room. In large organizations, this is usually not a problem because the servers are kept in the computer room with minicomputers or mainframe computers, and access to this room is restricted to the appropriate personnel. However, in many small companies, the server is sitting in a cubical or a closet that is accessible by virtually anyone.

Obviously, all the protection in the world will do no good if a would-be robber or vandal can walk right in and access the server itself. Stealing data is a simple matter of copying files.

Setting Server Access

Servers can be accessed from the Internet, a network, or a dial-up modem connection. This is where the first layer of Domino security exists. Servers can communicate with other servers, and users can communicate with servers. Servers never initiate communication with users. Users can never initiate a dialog directly with another user; users must go through a server. Accessing a server means that the server is letting you in the door—nothing more. When inside, there is plenty of security to keep you from wandering into the wrong place. Before communication takes place, the parties involved must be assured that each are who they say they are.

Whether a Domino server lets you talk to it depends first on whether or not you are on the list of people who are allowed to access the server. If your name does not appear on the list, you can't get in. This is even before authentication takes place. There are five ways in which you can be given access to a server:

- Notes client or server ID
- Anonymous
- Username and Internet password
- X.509 certificate
- Anonymous Notes client or server

On the Internet, I can represent myself as just about anyone. To a Domino server, anyone is represented as Anonymous. An anonymous user is anyone coming in with a browser who has not identified themselves with a name that is in the list. But being anonymous does not mean I automatically have access. Actually, it's the opposite. If the server administrator does not do anything, I won't have access from a browser. I can get in only if a Domino server is set up with Internet access and the server administrator allows anonymous access. The only other way to represent yourself as someone else is to know that person's name and Internet password. If that happens, the thief has all the access privileges of the ID's owner. The ID file, therefore, plays a pivotal role in controlling access to servers and should be protected and secured from possible theft.

Identifying Types of Notes IDs

There are three basic types of Notes ID files: server IDs, client IDs, and certifier IDs. Certifier IDs are used to create all the other IDs and can also create other certifiers. The first certifier ID that is created for a company is the Organization certifier. This ID file creates Organizational Unit certifiers, or in a small company, it directly creates the user IDs and server IDs. In large companies, many OU certifiers are created, so that multiple administrators can certify their users and servers. This produces a hierarchical tree that frequently resembles the organizational chart of the company. Although the Organization certifier ID can be created at any time from a Notes client, it is usually created when the first server in an organization is created, along with server ID and administrator ID. A certifier ID that issues another certifier ID is known as an *ancestral certifier*. Each ID contains certificates from all the certifiers in its lineage.

Figure 31.1 shows a hierarchical diagram of the infamous Acme Sales organization. The sales organization has three territories: Northwest, Southwest, and Great Plains. The certifiers for the organization match the actual corporate organization. The Northwest sales territory has a certifier called NWest, for example. User and server ID files have names listing all the certificates. The top certifier is listed last. This way, it is easy to find where users are located, and it is also a way for a large organization to differentiate among the groups of users. Sometimes, organizations are split up geographically, sometimes functionally. A functional organizational chart might have certifiers for Human Resources, Engineering, Sales, Shipping, and so forth. Examples of usernames and their certificates are listed at the bottom of the figure.

FIGURE 31.1

An organizational chart is often used to create OU certifiers.

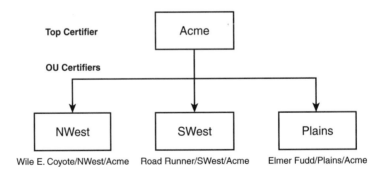

Understanding Authentication

To gain access to a server, there is a process called authentication that occurs between one certified entity and another. This is true for both Notes IDs and x.509 certificates. Authentication is based on a challenge/response protocol. To explain how authentication

Security and Domino Applications

CHAPTER 31

911

31

SECURITY AND
DOMINO
APPLICATIONS

works in its simplest terms, one certified entity (either client or server), which I'll call (A), attempts to establish communication with a server, which I'll call (B). (B) sends a list of its certificates to (A) and asks the entity to compare the list with its own list for a certificate that they share in common. (A) sends back a message indicating the certificate they share. (B) then sends (A) an encrypted message using the shared certificate to create the message. (A) then decrypts the message and sends it back to (B). (B) then reads the successfully decrypted message and says, "Come on in!". But (A) at this point says, "Not so fast!". Because (A) is now not sure if (B) is really who he says he is, (A) then performs the same process with (B). Not until both are satisfied that each is who he says he is will authentication be successful.

There is also password-enhanced authentication, which requires that the user's password be checked against the password stored in the person document for that person in the Domino Directory. This password corresponds with the password stored in the user's ID file.

Authentication does not take place between an Internet user with a password and a Domino server. Instead the user is asked for his name and password, and if the name and password given match the name and password stored in a person document in the Domino directory, that person will be given access to the server. An Internet client, however, can be authenticated through SSL with an x.509 client certificate. This authentication process is similar to the Notes authentication process. With client authentication, the client holds an X.509 certificate that contains a public and private key, and a person document for that user must exist and contain the same public key.

After access to the server is granted, the server checks the Restriction settings in the Access Server and Not Access Server fields in the Server document. If the user or server is allowed access, the next layer of security is at the database level. Each database has an Access Control List, or ACL. If the user or server is not listed in the ACL for a particular database, access is refused or granted at the Default level. It is the role of the database manager to determine the ACL—in other words, to allow or deny access to users, servers, and groups of users. It is the role of the database developer to understand and work with the ACL. To do that effectively, the designer needs to understand how the ACL, Notes security levels, view security, form security, field-level security, and encryption work together to provide data security.

Setting Security Levels in Notes

As a database designer, it is your responsibility to work closely with the owners and users of the application to determine the access privileges for users of the application. By "owner," I mean the person or persons who have authority over the design of the application. This is often the person who had the vision for the application or someone assigned by that person to manage the development effort. Project owners settle disputes over design issues and direction. Whether you work for a consulting firm or directly for a company, there should always be someone in this role. By "user," I mean not only those who enter data, but also those who use the information in the application. There are often multiple types or classes of users with different access needs—even different access needs at different stages in the life cycle of a document. Access to applications can range from the very simple to the very complex and very tightly controlled. The first step to understanding this subject is to learn about the security levels.

There are seven database access levels as shown in Figure 31.2. The definitions for these levels are listed in Table 31.1. Access privileges can be granted to individuals or to groups in the ACL of a database.

FIGURE 31.2

Each database has its own Access Control List.

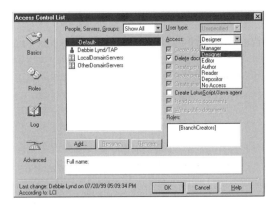

Additional granularity can be provided through the use of roles and special fields. Roles are discussed in the section titled "Restricting Use of Forms and Views with Roles," and reader and author fields are discussed later in this section as well as in the section titled "Implementing Document-Level Security." If the application has multiple databases, the ACLs for each of the databases must be considered.

TABLE 31.1 Domino Database Security Levels

Level	User Privileges
No Access	None.
Depositor	Allowed to create a document and save it, but cannot edit that document, or read any documents—not even one they authored.
Reader	Able to read documents but not create or edit.

Level	User Privileges
Author	Allowed to create and edit their own documents. Can also read other documents, and can delete their own documents.
Editor	Can create new documents and edit documents, even those created by others. Can also delete.
Designer	All privileges listed previously, but also can design databases.
Manager	All privileges listed previously, and in addition, can change the Access Control List.

Access Levels Are Not Always Enough

Even with an access level of Author, unless the Create Documents box is also checked, the Author will *not* be able to create a document but will only be able to edit a document that contains his or her name in a field of Authors data type.

An Author cannot edit his or her own document unless the form contains a field of Authors data type that contains the Authors name.

No one at any level of the ACL can delete a document from the database if the Delete Documents checkbox is not checked.

A Note from the Author

Being a developer who likes having control, I of course believe that I should be the manager of every database that I place on a server. However, most Domino administrators take exception to this, which I can fully appreciate. The administrator is the only person who should actually be given manager access to a database because he is ultimately responsible for all security on their servers.

Applying No Access

At first glance, you might think that the No Access level would not be involved in the design of a database, but that is not the case. Each database has a -Default- entry in the ACL. This entry represents everyone who is not otherwise entered in the list and provides the default access level in the ACL. If the database is not available for public access, the manager of the database would set the default to No Access. This determination needs to be made by the designer in conjunction with the owners and users of the system.

Setting Depositor Access

Although not frequently used, depositor access is useful for some databases. Depositor access allows users to create documents but not to see any documents, even those that they've created. This can be useful for suggestion box databases, surveys, and evaluations. For example, when I teach Notes/Domino certification classes, an evaluation form is filled out by the students at the end of the class. This evaluation is deposited in the database, and because the students only have depositor access to the database, the database appears to be completely empty. I of course have manager access because in the classroom I am the developer and the administrator. Chances are, you will not come across many applications where this is necessary.

Setting Reader Access

Reader access allows users to read documents but not to edit or create any documents. Reader access can be refined by using a Reader Names field. If the document has a Reader Names field and the user is not in the field or in a group listed in the field, he or she will not be able to read the document. In fact, the user will not even know that the document exists. Reader Names fields are discussed in more detail in the section titled "Implementing Document-Level Security," later in this chapter. Although you might not always grant author or editor access to a database, reader access is often used as the default. An example would be a company policy database. Obviously, only certain individuals are capable of authorizing company policy, but everyone needs to know and understand the policies. Granting read access to the entire company, and author or editor access to a select group of individuals would handle this situation. This is a very common usage of reader access.

> **Categories Can Show in Views, but the Document Cannot**
>
> If a document containing Reader Names fields has been categorized and a user previously had access, the categories will show up in views, but the user will be unable to open the document.

Setting Author Access

Author access usually allows the user to create a document and, typically, to edit the documents he or she has created. Authors fields can refine this further by specifying a list of users or groups who can edit the document. Authors fields are discussed in more detail in the section titled "Implementing Document-Level Security," later in this chapter. You might wonder why create access could be turned off for an Author. A perfect example of

Security and Domino Applications

CHAPTER 31

915

31

SECURITY AND
DOMINO
APPLICATIONS

how this is used is the person documents in the Domino Directory. I can edit my person document, but I cannot create one. The reason I can edit the document is because I am listed as Author in the ACL, and my name is in the Owner field, which is an Authors data type. Authors can also be given rights to create personal folders and views. This is not automatic and applies only to Notes clients. There are very good reasons not to give someone the ability to create personal views. A user with this ability can very easily mimic a view that contains documents that they would otherwise not have access to.

Setting Editor Access

Editor access is usually restricted to a few individuals. Editor access allows users to edit documents, regardless of who authored them. Editors can also create documents, but the capability to delete documents can be turned off in the ACL. Editors can also be allowed to create shared folders and views. If you allow editors to create views, you should be sure that they understand how to do this. Users with this privilege should also understand that it is not a good idea to create a large number of views. Over time, as users request new ways of looking at data, views tend to proliferate. Too many views can make the database slow and difficult to navigate. Be selective when you assign this role to users of the database.

Setting Designer Access

Designer access—this is you, the developer—provides all the capabilities of an Editor, and also allows the user to create and modify all the design elements in a database. The only optional capabilities are creating LotusScript and Java agents and deleting documents. In fact, a user with design access can be given rights to do anything to a database except modify the ACL. That is reserved for the manager level. If you do not have manager access to the database, you must work with the database manager to determine the access levels of users and to create any roles necessary. Roles are discussed later in this chapter in the section titled "Restricting Use of Forms and Views with Roles."

Setting Manager Access

The primary function of manager access is to manage the ACL of a database. Anyone with manager access has all the privileges of all the other levels. In addition, the manager can change the Access Control List and can delete the database. The only restrictions that can be set for the manager are delete privileges. The person who is assigned manager access is referred to as the database manager and is usually also the Domino administrator.

Setting the ACL for Servers

Servers also have access privileges to a database that roughly correspond to those of a user. If there is only one server in the company, this will not be a concern. If there are multiple servers or the database is shared with servers outside the company, ACL entries for servers must be considered. Typically, the lowest setting assigned to a server is editor. This allows all documents to be exchanged, deleted, and modified. You have to be careful to assign designer access to the servers that will be responsible for propagating any design changes to the other servers. Designers must work closely with database managers and Domino administrators, especially in large companies with multiple servers, to ensure that all the changes to documents and designs are made successfully.

I've talked about the -Default- entry in the ACL and how it determines the access level of anyone not otherwise listed. This includes unknown users accessing the database through a Web browser, unless an entry named Anonymous is included in the list. The entry Anonymous will take precedence over -Default- for Web access, as shown in Figure 31.3.

FIGURE 31.3

An ACL listing with an Anonymous entry.

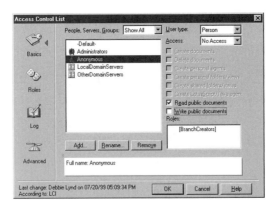

I can use the Anonymous entry in an ACL to set access from the Web for anyone who does not have a name and password (Anonymous) set to None. And, if I now set the -Default- access to Reader, anyone who attempts to access this database will be challenged for a name and password, as indicated in Figure 31.4. If they do not enter a name that is on the ACL or is contained within a group that is named in the ACL, or if they cannot produce the correct password that corresponds with the password entered in the Internet password field for their person document, they cannot access the database.

FIGURE 31.4

The Challenge/ Response screen is displayed when a user attempts to access a restricted database from the Web.

Understanding Security in the Domino Directory

Each Domino domain is defined by a Domino Directory. This directory contains many documents that relate to the servers and users in the domain. It is far more than simply a listing of users and servers, however. It controls access to the servers and databases in the domain, establishes and defines connections between servers for mail routing and replication, controls access to outside or "foreign" domains, controls which outside organizations and domains can access the domain, and so on. Most of the capabilities of the Directory are beyond the scope of this book. This subsection focuses on what you, as a developer, need to know concerning the part the Domino Directory plays in security. In large organizations, the roles of Domino administrators, developers, and database managers are often discrete and distributed. In smaller organizations, these roles are often combined; a few individuals are responsible for all roles. To create new databases and replicas on a server, your name must be explicitly listed or you must be a member of a group that is listed in the Security tab of the Server document. Figure 31.5 shows this section.

If you are unable to create databases or replica copies of databases on the server, you are not listed in the appropriate fields in the Security tab of the Server document. To create databases, you must be specifically listed in the Create New Databases field or in a group listed in the Create New Databases field; similarly, to create replicas, you must be in the Create Replica Databases field. Any time that changes are made to these fields, the server must be restarted. To make it easy to grant this privilege to individual users, most administrators create groups such as Domino administrators and Domino developers and place the group names in these two fields. Granting a privilege to an individual is then a simple matter of adding the individual to the appropriate group, and thus avoiding the need to restart the server.

FIGURE 31.5

*The Security tab
of a Domino
Server document
controls access to
the server.*

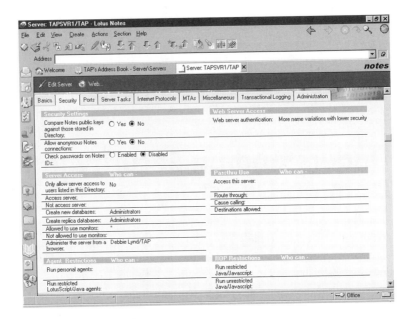

You Need Appropriate Access to Create Databases on a Server

You must be a member of the `GroupCreator` role in the Public NAB to create groups and in the `GroupModifier` role to modify the groups. Typically, administrators reserve this for a select group of individuals, especially in large organizations.

The next important document is the person document. The person document is created every time a new user is registered. The public key is stored with this document and is accessible by other users and the server whenever encryption of a mail message to that user is requested. The public key is a lengthy series of hexadecimal numbers listed near the bottom of the person document. This number is created when the ID is created, as mentioned earlier in this chapter. To register new users, you must be assigned the `UserCreator` and `UserModifier` roles in the Domino Directory and you must use the Domino Administration client.

Figure 31.6 shows the Basic tab of a person document, and Figure 31.7 shows the certified public key in the Certificates tab of the same document. The *certified public key* is the key issued to a Notes ID. A quick look at the public key gives some indication of why it would take so long to crack the RSA Cryptosystem technology used by Notes. Person documents can also be created for any type of user that needs to be known within your domain. This allows those users to be accessed easily from the Mail Address dialog boxes, and allows those users to be added to Groups and to the ACLs of databases, if appropriate. The person document is analogous to a personal listing in a phonebook. Person documents are listed in the People view of the Domino Directory.

FIGURE 31.6

The Basic tab of a person document contains all the possible names used to identify a user in the `FullNames` *field.*

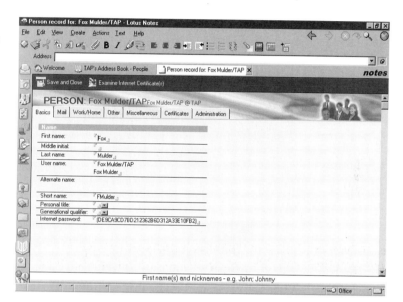

FIGURE 31.7

The certificates tab of a person document, showing simply a small portion of the certified public key.

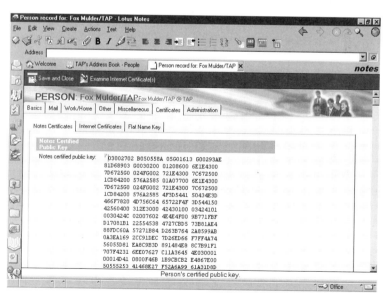

This chapter has mentioned groups several times. Groups are listed in the Groups view of the Domino Directory. Figure 31.8 shows a Group document. Groups are the preferred way to grant access to databases. The only individual name that I generally leave in any ACL is the developer's name. Whenever a new database is created, Notes automatically adds the name of the user who creates it to the ACL at the manager level. I just change that name to have Designer access (after it is placed on the server). To create groups, you must be assigned the `GroupCreator` and `GroupModifier` roles in the Domino Directory.

FIGURE 31.8

This Group document is used for Domino developers in my domain.

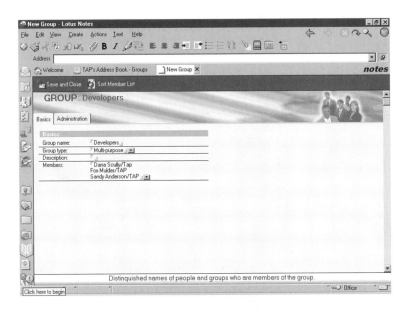

Granting Manager Access to Appropriate People

As a Domino administrator, it is my role to make sure the appropriate people have access at appropriate levels to the databases. With few exceptions, databases that go on my server always have an entry in the ACL for an administrator group at manager level. An entry is also there for a developer group. And if a database is preproduction, I generally grant the developers manager access because they will often need to test different access levels and might want to change the ACL. They might also work with roles. To create a role in the ACL, they need manager access. It is easier to grant manager access to the developers during development than it is to have them hounding me for changes. Of course, it's always better if there is a test server rather than a production server available for testing databases, but in a small organization, that is not always a possibility.

Working with the ACL

Each level of access in the ACL has different settings that can be changed. Rather than show screen shots of all seven levels, I will omit no access and depositor. Figures 31.9 through 31.13 show the ACL settings for each remaining access level. Grayed-out checkboxes are disabled and cannot be changed. Note that by default, Author access does not include Create access.

FIGURE 31.9

The ACL for a reader does not allow creation or deletion of documents.

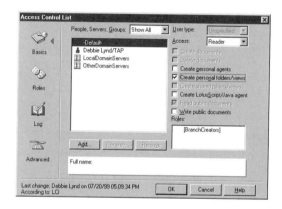

Having Author access does not mean that I will be able to modify the documents that I create. In order to modify a document that I create, my name must also appear in a field of Author data type.

FIGURE 31.10

The ACL settings for an author does not include create or delete options by default.

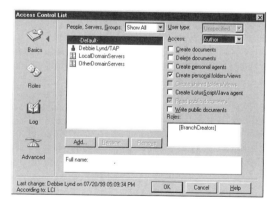

By giving someone editor access, I am stating that they are allowed to edit any document in the database. This should be considered carefully. For instance, if I am putting out a discussion database, do I want anyone to be able to modify the comments of another person?

FIGURE 31.11

The ACL settings for an editor do not include deleting documents by default.

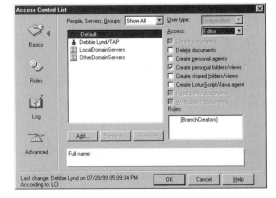

Having designer access inherits all the capabilities of an Editor. Notice that the designer does not automatically have the right to create LotusScript and Java agents.

FIGURE 31.12

The ACL settings for a designer will still not allow deletion of documents by default.

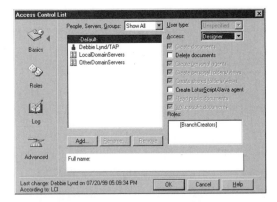

FIGURE 31.13

The ACL settings for a manager. Only a manager can change the ACL for a database.

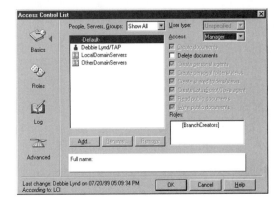

Security and Domino Applications

CHAPTER 31

923

31

SECURITY AND
DOMINO
APPLICATIONS

It is the role of the database manager or Domino administrator to manage all the levels with input from the database designers.

Choosing the Checkboxes to Set in the ACL

Under the Access level in the ACL screen, there are eight checkboxes as presented in Figure 31.14. I have covered all these except the last two. These are Read Public Documents and Write Public Documents.

FIGURE 31.14

Checkboxes in the ACL provide additional access to specific tasks.

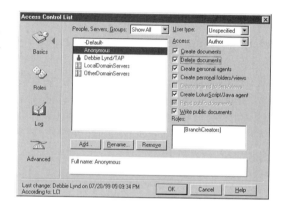

The read and write public access documents checkboxes can expand the access level of users with No Access, Depositer, or Reader access to include reading or writing forms and views that have been created for public access without giving access to all the forms, documents, and views in a database. To enable public access to specific documents, an entry in the ACL should be set to Depositer or No Access. In addition, a form must be enabled with the Available to Public Access Users security setting turned on, and those views that the users should be able to access must also have the same setting on. This will enable the Depositer and No Access user to be able to access those views and documents displayed with the specified form. Users with Reader access can already read all the documents by default. If a user with no access or Reader access is given the Write public documents right, they will be able to create documents using a form that has been designed with the Available to Public Access users security setting on.

Understanding User Types

The four tabs in the Access Control List are Basics, Roles, Log, and Advanced. In the Basics tab, I have covered everything except User Type. The use of this field prevents someone from "spoofing" the system by pretending to be a name in the ACL that he is not.

Any name listed in the ACL can be assigned an appropriate user type. For instance, if my name is listed in the ACL as a Person Group, I will not be able to access the database because I am a person not a group. The valid `UserTypes` are

- Person
- Server
- Mixed group
- Person group
- Server group
- Unspecified

Setting Editor Access for Web Browsers

An additional ACL setting affects the level of access that all Web browsers have to a database. This setting is found in the Advanced tab of the ACL as shown in Figure 31.15. The Maximum Internet Name & Password field defaults to Editor, which is actually the highest level of access that a non-Notes client can have because the Designer and Manager features are not available from a Web browser.

FIGURE 31.15

Maximum Internet access in the Advanced tab defaults to Editor access.

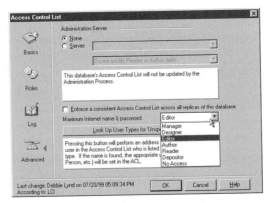

Enforcing a Consistent Access Control List

Enforcing a consistent access control list is helpful for maintaining an access control list that will not be changed by a user with a replica copy or another server administrator. This option is found on the Advanced tab along with the Maximum Internet option as indicated in Figure 31.15. This is useful when administration is decentralized, but the database manager needs to have central control over access to the database. This does not ensure, however, that a user cannot change the ACL on his or her local replica of the database. It does ensure that if the ACL is changed locally, replication will no longer take place with the local replica. This option should not be considered a security feature because a locally accessed database ignores the ACL settings.

Enabling Database Encryption

An entire database can be encrypted when creating a new database or a new replica of an existing database. When a database is encrypted locally, it can only be opened by the Notes User ID that was used to encrypt the database. It is inadvisable to encrypt a database that is on a server because it's too easy to lock everyone out of it that way. Locally encrypting a database is useful for databases that contain sensitive information and are carried on a laptop. As shown in Figure 31.16, if you encrypt the database and the laptop is stolen, the database cannot be accessed unless the password for the Notes User ID is known.

FIGURE 31.16

Encrypting a new local replica of a database provides additional security for laptop users.

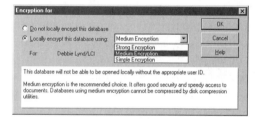

As indicated in Figure 31.16, three levels of encryption can be applied. The first is simple encryption, which provides the fastest access to documents but also is the least secure. Medium encryption is recommended as the best choice in that it provides decent access to documents while providing a good level of security. With strong encryption, the documents take longer to open, but it is the most secure.

Take Care with Encrypted Databases

When using Medium or Strong encryption, the databases should not be compressed by a compression utility.

Restricting Use of Forms and Views with Roles

Roles are used to further refine restrictions in a database. They are created in the ACL but are used the same way that you would use a username for restrictions in forms and views. If I want a group of people to be able to access a Controlled Access Section in a form, I have three ways to specify access:

- Explicit naming
- Group name
- Role name

Just like groups, people are assigned to roles. What's different about roles is that groups can also be assigned to a role. In fact, anyone listed in the ACL can be assigned to a role. However, this is also the major flaw in using Roles. Only those entities listed in the ACL can be assigned to a role. Therefore, if I use group names in the ACL and I want only some of the people in that group specified in a particular role, I can't do it unless I explicitly place those users' names in the ACL.

Version History

Release 2 and 3 of Notes included privileges that could be set for further restrictions. Roles were new in Release 4 and can be added to the ACL of a database by anyone with manager access. The ACL dialog box has four buttons, or tabs, on the left side of the window: Basics, Roles, Log, and Advanced. To add roles to the database, click the Roles button. Figure 31.17 shows the Roles tab of the ACL. Roles are quite powerful and can be very useful in further restricting access.

FIGURE 31.17

The Roles tab of the ACL is where database managers can add and delete roles.

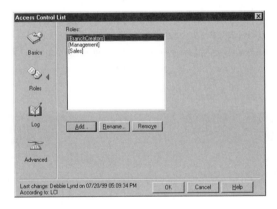

To create a new role in a database, follow these steps:

1. Open the ACL for the database.
2. Click the Roles button.

3. Click the Add button.

4. Type the name of the new role and click OK.

5. Click OK to close the ACL window.

Clicking the Add button brings up a simple window to add a new role. Type the name of the role and click OK. Figure 31.18 shows the available roles in the Domino Directory and the Add Role dialog box. The role appears in brackets in the Role window. Roles also appear in the Roles window in the lower-right corner of the Basics tab of the ACL. Up to 75 roles can be added to a database. Role names can contain numbers, characters, and spaces. By convention, I follow suit with the designers at Lotus and omit spaces.

FIGURE 31.18

Roles that determine who can create or modify documents in the Domino Directory are listed in the Roles tab.

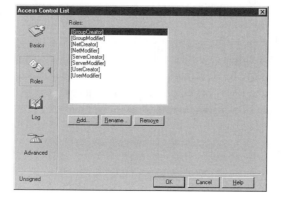

After a role is added to the database, it can be used to limit access to design features of the database. Both forms and views have a Security tab on the Properties box where roles can be used. This is useful if you have certain documents that store values that only specific groups of people should update, such as lists that are used in keyword fields. You can limit create access to the form that stores the lists and read access to the view that displays the form to that group of individuals. The values in the forms can still be accessed by using @DbColumn or @DbLookup against a hidden view. The list returned can then be used in a keyword field. Roles can also be used to limit access to documents. To limit access to a form using a role, follow these steps:

1. Open the form in design mode.

2. Open the form's Properties box and click the Security tab (the tab with the key).

3. Deselect All Authors and Above from the Who Can Create Documents with This Form section in the middle of the Properties box. See Figure 31.19.

4. Click the role in the list box.

FIGURE 31.19

The Security tab of a form determines who can read and create documents using the form. Only users assigned the BranchCreators role can create documents with this form.

Similarly, read access to documents created by the form can be limited by deselecting All Readers and Above at the top of the Properties box under Default Read Access for Documents Created with This Form. Choose the appropriate role. In both cases, make sure that groups and individuals have the role selected in the Basics tab of the ACL. This is accomplished very easily by selecting the group or individual in the ACL and clicking the appropriate role in the Roles list box. A checkmark appears beside the role. Figure 31.20 shows an example of assigning a role to an individual.

FIGURE 31.20

The BranchCreators role is assigned to individuals and groups by placing a checkmark beside the role.

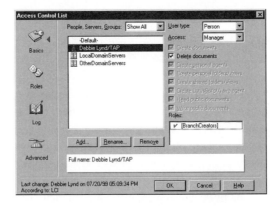

Using roles in View security is similar, as you can see in Figure 31.21. To use a role to limit access to views:

1. Open the view in design mode.
2. Open the View Properties box and switch to the Security tab.
3. Deselect All Readers and Above under May Be Used By.
4. Click the role and save the view.

FIGURE 31.21

The Branch Setup view is available only to those users and groups assigned the BranchCreators *role.*

Roles are not the only means of limiting access to forms and views. Access can also be assigned to groups and individuals in the same manner. Furthermore, this technique will not override the ACL. If a user has Reader access to a database, he can only read documents in that database. Even assigning that user Create access for a form will not allow the user to create a document with a form. You can think of this technique as a refinement of the ACL.

Roles can also be used to limit read and edit access to specific documents. Adding a role to a Reader or Author Names field will accomplish this. The role must be enclosed within quotes and square brackets as in the following example: "[BranchCreator]".

Implementing View-Level Security

Using a read access list is a way in which view access can be restricted. This can only be considered security, however, if the user that cannot access the view is also restricted from creating views of his or her own. Keep in mind that any user with design capabilities and the ability to create a view in your database can mimic any view that you restrict.

The read access list is contained in the Security tab of the View properties as seen in Figure 31.22. The Security tab is represented by a key in all design elements that contain security.

To restrict access to the view, uncheck the All Readers and Above checkbox and check the individual and group names in the name list for those names that should have access to the view. The names that appear in the list will be all the names in the ACL including Roles. You can also select individual names from the Domino Directory by clicking on the person icon next to the names list. Remember, this is a security refinement and does not supercede the ACL.

Notice the checkbox for Available to Public Access Users in Figure 31.22. Checking this box is all that is required to make a view available to Public Access users.

FIGURE 31.22

The read access list for a view can be used to restrict access to data.

Implementing Form-Level Security

Create and read access lists are the basis of security at the form level. These are both maintained in the security tab of the Form Properties box. These two options operate in the same way as the read access list for a view.

Notice the Available to Public Access Users box in Figure 31.22. I covered the settings for Public Access in the ACL, but not how to create a public access form. There are two steps to creating a public access form for create access.

1. Select Available to Public Access Users from the Security tab of the Form Properties box.

2. Create a field in the form with a name of `$PublicAccess`. Make the data type `text` and field type `computed` when composed. Put the number 1 in the formula field. All these settings are shown in Figure 31.23.

FIGURE 31.23

The `$PublicAccess` field in a form controls whether a document can be created.

Implementing Document-Level Security

Other techniques can secure the data in documents—down to the field level, if necessary. Within the realm of Documents, quite a few restrictions can be set. Three data types store names: Names, Authors, and Readers, all of which are described in Table 31.2. The field data types of Reader and Author Names fields can limit who can read or edit documents.

Security and Domino Applications

CHAPTER 31

931

31

SECURITY AND
DOMINO
APPLICATIONS

These fields can be manipulated programmatically or a designer can allow the user to edit the fields and determine the read and edit lists. Access Controlled sections were discussed in Chapter 10, "Advanced Form Design," but are not true security measures because the fields within the section can be accessed by other means such as views, other documents, and the field list in a document Properties box. The tools available in Domino provide a sophisticated, highly refined system to secure information. New to Release 5 is the Password field, which allows a user to enter a password into a field on a form while displaying only asterisks in the field.

The only problem with the password field is that if the contents are stored in the document, the actual value can be seen by anyone who can look at the fields in the Document Properties box. The only real way to make a password field secure is to blank out the filed prior to saving the document, so that the contents are not saved.

The three types of names fields are listed in Table 31.2.

TABLE 31.2   Names Fields

Field Type	Usage
Names	Displays names as they appear on IDs. Not useful for securing data.
Author	Allows anyone listed in the field who also has Author access to edit the document.
Reader	Restricts Read access to the document for users and groups with reader access or greater.

Groups, users, and roles can be added to author and reader names fields. These fields can be multivalue or single value depending on the needs of the application.

Using Readers Fields

In some ways, a reader data type is more powerful than the Author data type. If a user, group, or server is not in the reader field of a document, to the user or server, it is as though the document doesn't even exist. It will not be replicated, not even server to server. This is very powerful! Imagine creating an application for salespeople who are on the road so they can access a database on their laptops. The database provides the Main office with information about all the customers that the salesperson calls on, statistical information about that person's sales figures, and so on. Do you think each of the salespeople would want their information shared with other salespeople? None of the salespeople I know would want that! The good news is that by using Readers data types, I can create a field on each of the forms that will allow the Management group and all servers to have reader access to all the documents, but at the same time, the salespeople would only be listed in the authors field as the author of their individual documents. When a salesperson replicates with the server at the main office, all her information is sent to the server, but she will not replicate any of the documents that does not contain my name as the author or a reader.

End users accessing a database with a Notes client can actually apply reader restrictions all by themselves. The good news is that most of them do not know how. The bad news is that if they apply a reader restriction, the only people who will be able to access the document will be the people named in the readers list. In order to restrict access to a document as an end user, highlight the document in a view, right-click and choose Document Properties. Figure 31.24 displays the Security tab for setting reader access. Setting this restriction will cause a reserved field $Readers to be created in the document.

Removing the $Readers Field

As a developer, you need to be able to remove unwanted reader restrictions. If you can't access the document with the restrictions from your ID and the document resides on the server, run a local agent on the server to delete the $Readers field. Because the server is accessing the document locally, it will be able to see it. If the document only resides in a user's local copy of the database, you will have to run the agent on that user's machine, which means that you must ensure that they have sufficient access to do so.

FIGURE 31.24

Setting the reader's restriction in the Document Properties box can be hard to troubleshoot by an administrator.

Caution

Be sure to add all server names to a reader's field so that the documents can be replicated.

Using Authors Fields

As a developer, a field of Authors data type should appear on every form that you create!

Without the existence of an authors field, the person who creates a document cannot edit that document.

In a workflow application, it is useful to manipulate the values of an author field programmatically based on the status of a document. To do this, set up a computed authors field and use an @If() statement to change the value. The following formula for an authors field called ECRDocAccess is an example:

```
@If(ECRStatus = "Accept"; "ECRAdmin";
        ECRStatus = "New"; ECRDocOwner;
        ECRDocAccess)
```

In this formula, ECRAdmin is a group, and ECRDocOwner is a field that stores the name of an user. ECRStatus is a field that stores the status of the document.

If the authors or readers field is left editable, the users can enter the values. Most often, the values of both reader and author fields are handled programmatically.

Applying Field-Level Security

The security techniques discussed so far have been at the document level or higher. The field-level security options can all be found in the Security Options drop-down box in the Field Properties box. Three security options are available for fields:

- Sign If Mailed or Saved in Section
- Enable Encryption for This Field
- Must Have at Least Editor Access to Use

Using Signed Fields

Notes documents can be signed if certain conditions are met. First, a field must have the property Sign If Mailed or Saved in Section set in the Security Options section of the Advanced tab of the Field Properties box. Figure 31.25 shows this setting.

FIGURE 31.25

The Security Options of a field are on the Advanced tab of the Properties box.

As the option implies, the field must be in either an Access Controlled section or a mail-enabled form. Access Controlled sections are discussed in Chapter 10. Mail-enabled forms are discussed in Chapter 32, "Creating Workflow Applications." Unfortunately, this option is rather restrictive in that the entire document is signed only when it is mailed or saved in a section. Therefore, I can't have a field on a form that is signed based solely on an entry in that field. I can, however, have multiple signatures if I create a signed field in multiple controlled access sections. When a document is signed, Domino creates an unique electronic signature from the user's private key. The user's public key and list of certificates is also stored in the document in a field called $Signature if the document is being mailed, or Sig_SectionName, (where SectionName is the name of the section field), if the signature is signed in a section.

Using Encryption

The lowest level of security that can be applied is field-level encryption. Encryption is based on the dual-key system. A designer can allow a field or fields to be encryptable on a form by taking the following steps:

1. Choose or create a field.
2. Open the Field Properties box and click the Options tab.
3. Click Enable Encryption for This Field under Security Options.

On color monitors, encryptable fields are distinguishable from other fields by their red brackets.

When the document is encrypted, each field in the document that has the encryption attribute set is encrypted with the encryption keys contained in the Notes user ID file as specified in the form Default Encryption Keys field. If the user does not have an encryption key as listed in the form, the fields are not encrypted. If the user ID does not contain all the keys in the default encryption keys field, the fields are not encrypted. All keys that are used are contained as a list in a field in the document, which then tells Domino which keys can decrypt the document when a user requests access.

Any user opening a document that contains encrypted fields must hold only one of the encryption keys that was used to encrypt the fields in his Notes user ID file.

Caution

In order for encryption to work, you must hold a Notes ID with the necessary encryption keys. Without the encryption keys, the fields remains unencrypted.

A default encryption key can be assigned to the form on the Security tab of the Form Properties box. In order to assign an encryption key to a form, you must first hold a key in your ID. To save a document with encrypted fields, the user must possess the key. An encryption key can be created and distributed from a user ID. To create a new encryption key, follow these steps:

1. Select File, Tools, User ID from the menu and enter your password at the prompt.

2. Click the Encryption tab in the User ID dialog box. See Figure 31.26.

3. Click the New button.

4. Select the type of key, and add a name and a comment. See Figure 31.27.

FIGURE 31.26

The Encryption tab of the User ID window has options for working with encryption keys.

FIGURE 31.27

The New Encryption Key dialog box is where the key is named and the type chosen.

> **Caution**
>
> Two types of Notes keys can be created with an ID: North American and International. Documents or fields encrypted with North American keys will not be readable by international users. If there are international users of your application, you must create international keys.

After you create the key, distribute it to those who will need to use it to enter data in the encrypted fields. Do this by clicking the Mail button or by exporting the key to a file. Then, you can mail the file, electronically or physically. The recipient then merges or imports the key into her ID. After a field has been encrypted, the document will still be readable by those who do not possess the key. The encrypted fields will simply be blank. Users who possess the key will be able to view, enter, and edit data in the field.

Applying Must Have at Least Editor Access to Use Restriction

This is a security feature that is hardly ever used. There are actually a couple of very good reasons for this. The first reason is that there are plenty of other security measures to use in order to achieve the same effect. Second, it is rare to want an editor to be able to do more than an Author. Third, when a document is first created (by an Author), the person creating the document can access this field because he is assumed to be the editor. So, although this restriction exists, I would venture to say you will never use it.

Hiding the Design of Your Application

When an application will be rolled out to the users, you might want the design of that application to be hidden. This will inhibit tampering of the design by dubious developers or end users who think they are developers. Or maybe you are packing and selling your application and do not want to give away the source code. In any case, it's quite easy to hide the design of the database.

When the design is hidden, no one will be able to make design changes or even display the design by making a copy of the database.

Security and Domino Applications

CHAPTER 31

937

31

SECURITY AND
DOMINO
APPLICATIONS

> **Caution**
>
> Hiding the design disables all the design capabilities for the database. Before doing this, make sure you have a template or a copy of the database where the design isn't hidden or you will not be able to make any changes!

To hide the design of a database, follow these steps:

1. Create a database template.
2. Create a new database using the template.
3. With the new database selected, choose File, Database, Replace Design from the Notes menu.
4. Select the template you used to create the database and choose Hide Formulas and LotusScript, as shown in Figure 31.28.
5. Make sure Inherit Future Design Changes is also selected.
6. Choose Replace and Yes to confirm the replacement.

FIGURE 31.28

The database design can be hidden by choosing the Hide Formulas and LotusScript from the Replace Database Design dialog box.

Summary

This chapter has given you information about Notes security that is essential to developing effective Notes applications. You were shown how the seven access levels worked with the ACL of databases and how to extend and refine Notes security by using roles, reader names, and author names fields. This chapter also covered various aspects of form security, such as encryption and signed fields. You will find that a thorough understanding of Notes Security as it applies to application design will be a great ally when designing effective applications.

Creating Workflow Applications

by Steve Kern

By now, you have seen just how powerful Lotus Notes and Domino are as an applications development system. Perhaps the most powerful feature—mail-enabling an application—is described in this chapter. Chapter 1, "Introducing Lotus Notes and Domino?" discussed the difficulties with the share and send models, and how Notes and Domino overcame those difficulties by combining the two. Merging the mail engine with a database means that the database is no longer static as it was in the share model. In effect, the database is now "alive" because it can take actions based on internal conditions. Because the application is still a database, the difficulties of the send model are no longer a factor. At any point in time, anyone who is authorized may open the database and view the documents. This capability has enabled Lotus Notes and Domino to become the premier groupware applications development system.

Introducing Workflow

Workflow generally refers to the way a business process functions, such as approval for payment of expenses. What is workflow in the context of applications development? Simply put, it is the means by which a business process is automated. In a paper-based office, approval for payment of expenses usually starts with a form filled out by the employee listing the expenses—dates, amounts, and justifications. This paper is then routed to the employee's manager, who signs it and sends it to accounts payable for reimbursement to the employee. Of course, this example is a very simplistic process and, in practice, there can be several levels of approval. Why automate such a process? There are a number of good reasons.

Understanding the Problem

First, take a look at a more complex business process. One with which you are most likely to be familiar is software development. With any significant software application, many changes can accumulate over time. As you know, managing those changes can be more challenging than making the changes themselves! Requests for changes can come from many sources: from the users of the application to senior management. The reasons for change requests are just as varied; a request for a change might be as simple as a new view or report, or it could be a result of a strategic change in the company's business strategy. Likewise, the scope of the change could potentially affect many people across many departments. To manage such changes, an approval process is often put in place that will enable all those affected to review and approve or deny the request. This can result in a multitiered approval process which can be cumbersome to manage.

Using a paper-based process can break down in multiple ways. Perhaps a change can affect five departments, and in each of the five departments, one or more individuals are appointed to review change requests for impacts on their department. The individual who creates the change request has to distribute the paper change request form to all reviewers—after determining who those reviewers are. When the reviewers have a chance to look at the request, they can forward their comments to yet another group of individuals. Perhaps a meeting is scheduled, and a discussion of the change request takes place before it is forwarded on to the next level of review. There is really no easy way to keep tabs on this process because it is entirely manual, and if a reviewer isn't timely in her review, the whole process can drag on indefinitely. The length of time from the initiation of the change request to its final disposition is referred to as *cycle time*. Ultimately, each request and its associated documents wind up in filing cabinets, necessitating a physical search if it needs to be reviewed sometime in the future.

This example illustrates two fundamental problems with paper-based processes. First, it is anybody's guess just how long the cycle time might be for any given request. Second, there is no easy way to keep track of the status of the request, which is similar to the problems outlined with the Send model in Chapter 1. Automating this process can help solve these two difficulties. First, the cycle time can be compressed by electronically routing the documents via email notifications. Second, because the requests are documents in a database, the status of the document can be displayed and accessed by anyone who is interested and has access to the database. No longer will you have to rifle through folders in file cabinets to research a request because there is an electronic record in a fully searchable database. These are some of the principal arguments for automating business processes with database applications.

Solving the Problem with Automation

The methods by which business processes are automated using Notes and Domino typically involve the use of email notifications. Occasionally, a document can be routed in its entirety, but most often, a link to the document is emailed. Notifications are of two general types: either a newsletter that broadcasts a list of documents or a notification of a single document that needs to be acted on. Very often, these two techniques are combined in an application. In the change request example described in the previous paragraphs, email notifications containing a document link to a single new change request can be created and emailed to the reviewers after the document is saved. The process administrator can receive a newsletter containing a list of document links to requests that have past-due reviews. Email notifications can be created using all the languages available to you as a developer: the Formula language, LotusScript, JavaScript, and Java. The remainder of this chapter covers the methods of sending mail notifications, from simple mail-enabling at the form level, to using the Scripting languages to mail-enable an application.

Automating a Business Process

A high-tech engineering firm had a process that was paper-based and quite tedious, involving what were called engineering change requests. These requests could be originated by anyone in the company and could involve a better part design or a better manufacturing process. After the change request was approved, it became a change order, and new engineering drawings and specifications were made.

The problem with the paper-based solution revolved around the approval process. First, the administrator had to determine who owned the process that was affected and then determine who was assigned to review the process. The change request was then photocopied and stuffed into the process owner's mailbox. The process owner would then review it, and release it for review, but first it went back to the administrator, who had to photocopy the document with the process owner's comments and distribute it to all the reviewers' mailboxes. Technically, the reviewers had 24 hours to respond, and the administrator had the responsibility of ensuring that they did indeed respond. This often involved multiple phone calls; the actual cycle time of this process was usually quite lengthy. When all reviewers had responded, a meeting was optionally scheduled. If the change request met everyone's approval, it was turned into a change order, which necessitated—you guessed it—more photocopies.

Using Notes and Domino

How does Domino handle this process? The Domino application determines who the process owner and reviewers are. Domino automatically emails the process owner with a notification of the new change request. The message includes a link to the actual document, which can then be opened. The process owner can assess the change request and approve it on the spot, releasing it to the reviewers. Releasing it generates email to the reviewers, again including a link to the change request. Rather than having the administrator be responsible for ensuring a timely response, a Notes agent runs nightly on the server sending tardy reviewers email notices. After a certain number of tardy notifications go out to reviewers, the administrator receives a notification of which reviewers are tardy for each outstanding request. After all reviewers respond, an agent generates a notification to the process owner and administrator. Because all the notifications are automatic, the cycle time is reduced from weeks to a matter of days. Because the administrator no longer has to photocopy and distribute the change requests and supporting documents, a significant amount of time is recovered.

This paragraph has only touched the surface of the Engineering Change Request application. Even so, it is quite apparent that this workflow solution solves a lot of administrative headaches and significantly reduces the cycle time of a change request. Were this

32

simply a shared database, none of the email notifications or the agents would be present. A send model would not enable the originator or the administrator to determine the status of a change request. There would be no automatic monitoring of reviewers.

Another very important point is that not only does the process work better, the company now has a history of change requests and change orders that can be easily researched. In other words, they now have a knowledge base! Prior to this, the only research involved a large file cabinet wherein copies of the old change requests were supposed to be stored. With the full-text search capabilities of Notes, this application became a very sophisticated tool for the engineering firm. The application was completed, tested, and debugged in about 300 hours of development.

The combination of the two technologies—shared databases and messaging—very obviously had a significant effect on this application. This is a classic example of a Notes application and how Notes can benefit an organization in a short period of time. User acceptance was very positive, and a tremendous burden was lifted from the administrator's shoulders.

Simple Mail-Enabling at the Form Level

The simplest method of mail-enabling an application is to create a form that is mail-enabled from the Form Properties box. Follow these steps to mail-enable a form:

1. Open a form in design mode or create a new one.
2. Open the Form Properties box and click the Defaults tab.
3. In the On Close section, click Present Mail Send Dialog (see Figure 32.1).

FIGURE 32.1

The Form Properties box Defaults tab is where a form can be mail-enabled.

> **Caution**
>
> Mail-enabling a form does not work for Web clients. A Notes client can route mail, because that function is built into the client. However, a browser only interacts with HTML documents and does not have a way to send mail.

For this to function properly, at minimum, a field called `SendTo` must be included on the form with a valid email address—either a username or a group. `SendTo` is one of several reserved fields. A full list of reserved fields for mailing is listed later in this chapter in Table 32.3. At this point, the document is mailed optionally; that is, the user is presented with the Mail Send options window, which is called Close Window and is illustrated in Figure 32.2. This window has more options on it than the window presented from a New Mail memo when the Escape key is pressed. That window is shown in Figure 32.3.

> **Using Reserved Fields to Set Options**
>
> If the `Sign`, `Encrypt`, or `SaveOptions` reserved fields are included on the form and assigned a value, they override any choices made by the user in the Close window. They also do not affect what is displayed in the dialog box, so the user is unaware of the effects of these fields. For the document to be mailed automatically, include the `MailOptions` reserved field as a computed field with a value of 1.

FIGURE 32.2

The Mail Send window for a mail-enabled form enables the user to choose how the document is mailed.

FIGURE 32.3

The simpler Close window is used in the Mail database.

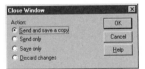

Understanding the Disadvantages

There are some disadvantages to this approach. When the document is mailed, it does not display properly unless it has the same fields as the Memo form in the Mail database. This is because Domino attempts to locate the form used to compose the document, and when that fails, Domino displays the document with the default form of the database. In the Mail database, that form is the Memo form. There are several ways to work around this limitation.

Working Around the Limitations

First, and easiest, is to click the Store Form in Document property on the Defaults tab of the Form Properties box. Unfortunately, if the source form changes, none of the documents mailed with the earlier versions reflect the changes. This has an additional drawback of significantly increasing the disk storage space of the database. Even a small form with a few fields can be 5KB or 6KB. A larger form can be 50KB or 60KB. Embedded graphics, such as might be found in a layout region, can increase the size significantly. You can do some quick math and see how much additional storage space a stored form can add to the database. Nonetheless, this technique does have the advantage of displaying the document with the original form.

Design Document Size

You can find out how many bytes the form itself consumes by looking at the Design tab of the Design Document Properties box. Open the database and go to a design folder. Highlight a form and click Design, Design Properties. This is new to Release 4.

A second way around this is to add the form itself to the Mail database. This enables the form to be displayed in its native format. However, unless you make a corresponding change to the Mail template or disable the template for the Mail database, your change is overwritten when the Design task runs on the server at night. Any changes can also be lost when Domino is upgraded to a new version. To prevent this from happening, all customizations to the Domino mail template or databases must be archived to a temporary database and then restored after the mail databases are converted to the new version.

The third way around this is to use some of the fields that are in the Memo form. If you include Subject and Body fields, the form, in effect, duplicates the Mail Memo form. When Domino is unable to find the form the document was created in, it displays successfully using the default Memo form. An easy way to do this is to open the Memo form in design mode, copy the fields you want to use to the clipboard, and then paste them into the new form.

Although this is certainly simple and convenient, there is a price to pay. In most mail-enabled applications, you should retain greater control over who gets mail routed and when. Users most often won't be able to override or initiate mail. Mail is usually sent automatically based on the status of the document. Mail-enabling at the form level is a rather crude technique and is not suitable for most applications.

Working with Mail @Functions, @Commands, and Reserved Fields

As you can imagine, there are many useful @Functions, @Commands, and reserved fields specially designed for mail-enabling a database. These are listed in Tables 32.1–32.4.

TABLE 32.1 Useful @Functions

Function	Usage
`@MailSend` without parameters	Sends the document to the recipient in the `SendTo` field.
`@MailSend` with parameters	Creates a new memo based on parameters. See Table 32.4 for a list of the parameters.
`@IsDocBeingMailed`	Returns 1 (Boolean true) if the document is being mailed.
`@Optimize-mailAddress`	Removes unnecessary domains from the address.
`@MailEncryptSavedPreference`	Returns 1 (Boolean true) if Encrypt Saved Mail is selected in User Preferences.
`@MailEncryptSentPreference`	Returns 1 (Boolean true) if Encrypt Sent Mail is selected in User Preferences.
`@MailSavePreference`	Indicates the option the user has selected in User Preferences for saving mail. Returns 0 for Don't Keep a Copy, returns 1 for Always Keep a Copy, and returns 2 for Always Prompt.
`@MailSignPreference`	Returns 1 (Boolean true) if Sign Sent Mail is selected in User Preferences.
`@MailDBName`	Returns the server and mail filename of the current user.

TABLE 32.2   Some Useful Mail @Commands

Function	Usage
@Command([MailAddress])	Presents the Address Book dialog box and stores the To in the SendTo field of the document, cc in the CopyTo, and so on.
@Command([MailComposeMemo)	Composes a mail memo.
@Command([MailForward])	Forwards the current or selected document.
@Command([MailSend])	Displays the Mail Send dialog box before sending the current document with two options: sign and encrypt.

@Command([MailAddress]) is quite useful. It is intelligent enough to populate the dialog box with To, cc, and bcc only if SendTo, CopyTo, and BlindCopyTo fields are present on the form! In other words, if you place only the SendTo and CopyTo fields on the form, @Command([MailAddress]) displays only those fields in the dialog box. Chapt32.nsf has a form titled "Mail Send Form" that illustrates the use of this @Command. To see how it works, remove one of the Address fields such as CopyTo or BlindCopyTo.

TABLE 32.3   Reserved Fields

Field Name	Purpose
SendTo	Multivalue text list of primary mail recipients.
CopyTo	Multivalue text list of other mail recipients.
BlindCopyTo	Multivalue text list of Mail recipients unknown to other recipients of the document or memo.
Subject	Subject of memo.
Body	Rich-text field containing message.
Sign	A value of 1 signs the document; 0 doesn't.
Encrypt	A value of 1 encrypts the document; 0 doesn't.
DeliveryPriority	A value of L is low priority, N is normal priority, and H is high priority.
DeliveryReport	A value of B is basic and creates only a delivery failure report, C confirms delivery, T traces failures, and N never generates a report.
ReturnReceipt	A value of 1 sends a receipt when the document is opened by the recipient, and a value of 0 sends no receipt.
SaveOptions	A value of 1 always saves; 0 never saves.
MailOptions	A value of 1 overrides the Present Mail Send Dialog in the Form Properties box On Close section of the Defaults tab.

> **Caution**
>
> The `Sign`, `Encrypt`, `ReturnReceipt`, `SaveOptions`, and `MailOptions` are text or keyword fields and not numeric, although the values of 1 and 0 might lead you to think they were numeric.

Using `@MailSend` with Parameters

Of all the functions listed, `@MailSend` is the most often used and the most powerful. It is with this function that a database becomes mail-enabled. `@MailSend` without parameters can be used to send the document itself, as long as there is a `SendTo` field available. `@MailSend` is discussed in the "Working with Mail @Functions" section. The `@MailSend` function with parameters is the most useful and interesting of the @Functions listed. The syntax of the `@MailSend` function is

```
@MailSend( sendTo; copyTo; blindCopyTo; subject; remark;
➥ bodyFields; [flags] )
```

The `SendTo`, `CopyTo`, `BlindCopyTo`, and `Subject` fields are described in Table 32.3. These parameters are exactly the same as the descriptions for the reserved fields. The only required parameter is `SendTo`. The remaining parameters are listed next in Table 32.4.

TABLE 32.4 `@MailSend` Parameters

Parameter	*Comment*
`Remark`	Optional text; included at the beginning of the Body field of the memo.
`BodyFields`	Adds fields to the memo in the order listed. One or more fields from the document can be included. To include fields, put the field name in quotes; to include multiple fields, use a colon to create a list, as in `"Field1":"Field2":"Field3"`. The fields can be any data type.
`[flags]`	One or more flags can be included and are described next. To include more than one flag, use the colon to separate the flags, as in `[Sign]:{IncludeDocLink]`.
`[Sign]`	Signs the memo.
`[Encrypt]`	Encrypts the memo using the recipient's public key.
`[PriorityLow]`	Sends the memo at low priority.
`[PriorityNormal]`	Sends the memo at normal priority.

Parameter	Comment
[PriorityHigh]	Sends the memo at high priority.
[ReturnReceipt]	Sends a receipt when recipient opens memo.
[DeliveryReportConfirmed]	Sends confirmation of delivery failure or success.
[IncludeDocLink]	Sends a doclink to the document that generated the mail memo.

@MailSend, with parameters, is discussed in the next section.

Caution

These Notes Mail functions do not work directly in Web clients. However, you can work around that limitation by using an Agent, and including @MailSend in the agent.

Sending Document Links

The previous examples used the @MailSend @Function with parameters to generate an email message. Including a doclink is done with the [IncludeDocLink] flag. A doclink is a small icon that contains a pointer to a document. If the user has access to both the document and the database, the document is opened when double-clicked. This means that a user can work on documents in the database without switching from the mail file.

@MailSend(SendTo; ""; ""; Subject; Remark; ""; [IncludeDoclink])

Using Variables

You might have noticed the use of variables rather than literals in the @Function. This makes the formula easier to read, easier to code, and easier to debug. You should avoid hard-coded values if possible. An additional benefit is that the values to SendTo, Subject, Remark, and so on can be assigned through a formula.

FIGURE 32.4

*This email mes-
sage has a doclink
embedded in the
message body.*

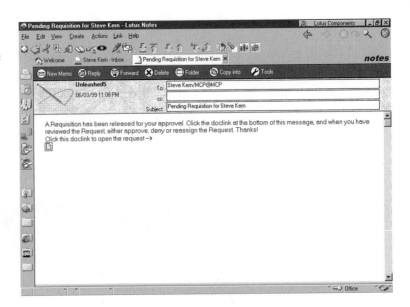

Sending doclinks is by far the most flexible way to mail-enable an application and is used by the vast majority of the mail-enabled applications I've worked on or seen. Most, if not all, of the mail-enabled templates that come with Notes and Domino also use doclinks. Using @MailSend and including a doclink is a very effective technique.

Using @MailSend Without Parameters

@MailSend without parameters is in many ways very similar to enabling a form to send mail from the Form Properties box. If the form is sent to a user's mail database using @MailSend, the same display problems exist. If the database doesn't contain the form for the document, Domino attempts to display it with the default form. @MailSend sends the document automatically. @MailSend can also be combined with reserved fields such as DeliveryPriority and DeliveryReport.

The form property "On Close: Present mail send dialog" takes care of mailing the document when it is saved. When using @Command([MailSend]) or the @Function @MailSend, you have to ensure that the document is mailed at the appropriate time and that the SendTo field at minimum has a legitimate value. One way to ensure that the SendTo field has a valid username is to make the field a keyword field and select "Use Address dialog for choices." In the Input Validation for the field, include the following line of code:

```
@If(SendTo = "" ;@Failure("You must choose an addressee!"); @Success)
```

If the SendTo field is blank, a message box displays with the message "You must choose an addressee!" in it. The Input Validation formula executes only when the document is being saved or refreshed.

You must also take steps to ensure that @MailSend executes when the document is being saved. There are a variety of @Functions that return the state of a document. @IsDocBeingSaved returns True when the document is being saved, so the following formula works:

```
@If(@IsDocBeingSaved; @MailSend; "")
```

As discussed previously, there are some inherent drawbacks to using this technique. Principally, it involves the display of the form. However, @MailSend can be useful when mailing documents to a mail-in database. @MailSend executes without presenting the Mail Send dialog box and therefore requires no user intervention.

Sending Mail with Simple Actions

There are a few simple actions that can be used in both Action Bar buttons and agents to send mail. They are listed in Table 32.5.

TABLE 32.5 Simple Actions for Mailing Documents

Action	What Happens
Send Newsletter Summary	Sends a mail message listing documents with doclinks that fit the criteria.
Send Document	Sends the document, such as @MailSend. Needs a SendTo field at minimum. This is a default system command in views and forms.
Reply to Sender	Sends reply. Useful in mail-in databases.
Send Mail Message	Sends a document or doclink. A dialog box allows choices from an address book for recipients.

Simple actions are available for use in both agents and Action Bar buttons. In this respect, they are not context-sensitive. For instance, it doesn't make much sense to send a newsletter summary from a form action. Simple actions are not supported on the Web. Figure 32.5 shows a Newsletter agent under construction in a database. This Newsletter agent notifies all participants in a particular database of new and modified documents, using the Send Newsletter Simple Action.

FIGURE 32.5

*The Send
Newsletter
Summary simple
action in design.*

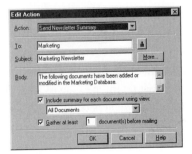

This agent is useful because it helps to keep a database alive. As the name implies, it is very simple to set up:

1. Choose Create, Agent from the menu.

2. Change the name to `Newsletter` or a name of your choosing. Click the Shared Agent box.

3. Under When Should This Agent Run? choose On Schedule Daily.

4. Click the Schedule button and in the Schedule window, choose the server on which the agent is to run.

5. Under Which Document(s) Should It Act On? choose All New and Modified Documents Since Last Run.

6. Under What Should This Agent Run? click Simple Actions and then click the Add Action button at the bottom of the Design pane.

7. Choose Send Newsletter Summary, pick the appropriate addressees and enter a subject and a brief text message.

8. Click Include Summary for Each Document Using View and choose the view.

9. Click Gather at Least # Document(s) Before Mailing and either leave the default of 1 or enter a new value.

10. Save the agent.

This is not the only way to create a mail agent. You can also use @Functions, LotusScript, or Java. You can run agents under many different conditions, as you will see in Chapter 32, "Automating Your Applications with Agents." Search conditions can also be included that can create truly powerful focused agents that only act on documents that match the criteria.

Using Mail-In Databases

Your Domino mailbox is simply a Domino database. As such, the router can deposit mail directly into the database.

The Mail Router

The Router is a task that runs on the Domino server. This task is responsible for delivering mail to databases on the local Domino server and for forwarding mail on to other servers. The Router task also takes care of sending mail destined for cc:Mail or the Internet and other foreign mail domains.

A mail-in database is an extension of this concept; documents can be emailed directly to a mail-in database. Furthermore, any forms you want to email to this database can be included in the design of the database, eliminating the need to store the form with the document. This technique is used for statistics—reporting databases on servers, for instance. To create a mail-in database, complete the following steps:

1. Open the Domino Directory.
2. Go to the Servers\Mail-In Databases and Resources view.
3. Click the Add Mail-In Database button in the Action Bar.
4. Fill out the Mail-In Database document.
5. Close and save the document.

Creating Mail-In Database Documents

You must be a member of the NetCreator role in the Domino Directory to create a Mail-In Database document. If you do not have this access to the Domino directory, you have to ask an administrator to create the document for you or give you the appropriate access.

Figure 32.6 shows a mail-in database for Technical Tips. To send mail (such as documents) to a mail-in database, include the mail-in name of the database as it appears in the Domino Directory in the memo's address. A mail-in database appears in the Domino Directory with all other users and is therefore available for mail addressing. You can access the mail-in database in an address field in the same manner that you would a user or group, using type-ahead or the Directory dialog box. The mail router treats the mail-in database entry just as it would a person document and deposits messages into the database file specified in the `Filename` field.

FIGURE 32.6

Mail-in database documents have fields identifying the name that appears in the directory (not shown), the domain, the server on which the database exists, and its filename.

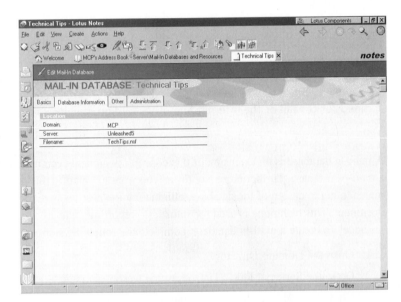

> **Internet Mail Name!**
>
> In R5, you can now specify the Internet name for a mail-in database.

Using Triggers to Send Email

Most documents have a *lifecycle* or a series of stages that they go through before they are considered complete. At each step of the way, there is usually a field that identifies the status of the document. Often, when the status of the document changes, certain actions are required from specific individuals. Email is the means of notifying those individuals of the need for action on their part. A change in a document's status is the event that triggers the email.

Identification of these triggers should take place during the analysis phase, and is usually refined during prototyping and testing. The process flow is often diagrammed on paper using a flowchart. It is also useful to create a table listing the triggers, any significant fields and document conditions, and the recipients and the messages. Combined with the process flowchart, it is an excellent means of communicating with the client as well as a good testing tool. As the application is tested, you can check the behavior with the table and flowchart for accuracy. Table 32.6 is a sample table for a Change Request application. The message text in this table is abbreviated to save space in the illustration, but this should give you the general idea. The actual mechanism of getting triggers to work is simple.

TABLE 32.6   Email Triggers for the Change Request Form

Trigger	*Form Logic*	*Recipients*	*Part of the Message Text*
New	`cStatus = "New"`	Doc. Owner	A new change request has been submitted. Please review.
In Review	`cStatus = "In Review"`	Reviewers	The document owner has released a change request for review.
Accepted	`cStatus = "Accepted"`	All	The change request has been accepted and will be processed as a change order.
Rejected	`cStatus = "Rejected"`	All	The change request has been rejected for the following reasons.

There are two principal means of sending mail notifications when the triggers have been established. First, you can include a field on the form that executes @MailSend (usually with parameters) when the document is saved. Second, you can create agents that send the mail notifications.

There is a distinct disadvantage to using a field on a form to send mail notifications. @MailSend doesn't work for Web clients, and neither does LotusScript. If you have Web clients participating in a workflow application, using a field on the form to generate email notifications will fail.

You can easily work around this limitation by moving the code to send mail notifications out of the form and into an agent. Because an agent runs on the server, it does not depend on the type of client accessing the application. It can execute whenever a document is created or modified, and test for the trigger. If the conditions for the trigger are met, it can then send email notifications to the appropriate person(s). For obvious reasons, this is the preferred method of mail enabling an application.

32

CREATING WORKFLOW APPLICATIONS

Using a Field to Send Mail

Typically, @MailSend with parameters is used to send email notifications based on the triggers established. For example, @IsNewDoc returns a Boolean true at the time the document is composed. Used in a computed field to send mail with @MailSend(), @IsNewDoc sends mail out unexpectedly when the document is first created, not when it is saved:

```
REM "This sends mail when the document is new" ;

@If(@IsNewDoc; @Success; @Return(""));

@MailSend("Steve Kern/MCP";"";"";"Change Request";

        "A new change request has been added. Please review!";
        ""; [IncludeDocLink])
```

Adding @IsDocBeingSaved to the formula solves that problem. A typical formula for sending email when a document is first composed and saved is

```
REM "Test for a new doc and if the doc is being saved" ;
REM "and send e-mail. @Return stops the execution of the ";
REM "formula if either of the two conditions is not true" ;

@If(@IsNewDoc & @IsDocBeingSaved ; @Success; @Return("")) ;

REM +"Send a doclink to this document" ;

@MailSend("Steve Kern/MCP";"";"";"Change Request";
        "A new change request has been added. Please review!" ;"";
        [IncludeDocLink])
```

To use a field to trigger the routing, take advantage of the order in which formulas are evaluated: from left to right and from top to bottom. Email triggers cannot rely on the value of the status field to send mail but must instead detect whether the status has changed. To accomplish this, you can use hidden fields at the bottom of the form. One stores the value of the status field. This field is usually named something such as cOldStatus and has a formula of

```
@If(@IsNewDoc; "New"; cStatus)
```

Another field actually sends the mail. If this field is positioned before the cOldStatus field, the value of cStatus can be compared to cOldStatus. If they are not the same, an appropriate email can be sent. How does this work? It's simple. The cStatus and the Mail Send fields are above cOldStatus in the form and are evaluated before cOldStatus. Therefore, if a user changes cStatus, the value of cOldStatus is computed after the Mail Send field. cOldStatus retains the value of the status field before the user changed it.

```
REM "Compare the values of cStatus and cOldStatus" ;
REM "If they are different, send e-mail" ;

@If(cStatus = "New"; @Return(""); @Success);

SendTo := "Steve Kern/MCP";
Subject := "Status Change";
Remark := "The Approval Status of your Change Request # " + cCRNumber +
          " has changed from " + cOldStatus + " to " + cStatus +
          ". Double-Click this document link to review ==> ";

@If(@IsDocBeingSaved & cOldStatus != cStatus;
        @MailSend(SendTo; ""; ""; Subject; Remark; "";
        [IncludeDoclink]); "")
```

Figure 32.7 shows a very rudimentary Change Request form. This is available on the CD-ROM in the database file Chapt34.nsf. Figure 32.7 shows the resulting mail message including the document link.

FIGURE 32.7

*Fields on the
Change Request
form must be in a
specific order.*

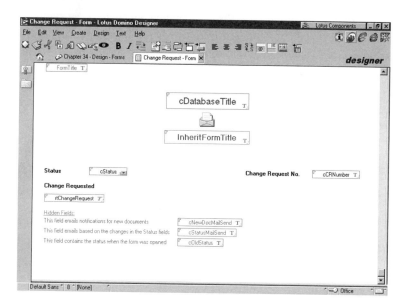

Caution

Please note that although using fields to route mail works, it is not the preferred method. The preferred method is to use Agents, which are discussed next.

Using Agents in Workflow

With the advent of Web browsers as an alternative client for Domino Applications, the use of Agents to mail-enable an application has become very important. A Web client does not have the capability to send mail, whereas the Notes client does. For this reason, you should consider avoiding the use of mail functions in forms.

Agents are discussed in more detail in Chapter 32.

One of the goals of a workflow application is to reduce the amount of time it takes to complete a given task. This is also known as *cycle time*. Often, a set period is allotted to process a document, after which it is considered past due. After an initial notification, reminders are sent on a daily basis to reviewers. When a document is past due, the application logic might then route it to the database administrator or the reviewer's supervisor for further action. Agents are used to send notifications at appropriate times, thereby compressing the cycle time.

You can implement this workflow by creating agents for each status trigger. For example, you create an agent to send notifications when a document is created, and the status is "New." Create another agent to send reminders on a daily basis. When the number of reminders reaches a certain level, another agent can be used to escalate the request to the next person. Of course, you'll want to create an agent to notify the appropriate persons whenever the document is approved or denied—some sort of final notification. Other agents can be created to meet the needs of your application.

> **Caution**
>
> You could always create a single agent to handle all possible status conditions for a document. However, it is much simpler to create a single agent for each notification trigger. The logic is less complex, and therefore it's easier to debug any problems that might arise.

It is a good idea to log the activity of both users and agents. You can track the activity in multivalued fields. Here is a list of typical tracking fields:

- cDocHistory—This field keeps a history of all activities associated with the document, including agent activities.
- cLastAgent—This field tracks each agent which runs on the document. Agents populate this field with their names.

- `dNotified`—This field tracks the date and time the agents ran.

- `nReminders`—This field is used as a counter for the number of reminders sent. It is incremented by a Reminder agent. The maximum value can be stored in a profile document, where an application manager can modify the setting.

The Agent in Listing 32.1 is used to remind reviewers that a document is past due for their approvals. It incorporates the techniques discussed, and the fields listed previously:

LISTING 32.1   Reminder Agent

```
REM "Send reminder of new requests to the Approver";
REM "Schedule is daily, not on weekends";

SELECT Form = "OSR2" & cDocStatus = "New";

REM "Initialize and increment Reminder counter";
jnReminders := @If(@IsAvailable(nReminders); nReminders + 1; 1) ;
FIELD nReminders := jnReminders ;

REM "Write doc history";
jcDocHistory := "Reminder #" + @Trim(@Text(jnReminders)) +
     " of Office Supply Requisition emailed to " +
      @Name([Abbreviate];cApprover) +
      " on " + @Text(@Now;"S2") ;
@SetField("cDocHistory"; cDocHistory : jcDocHistory) ;

REM "Add agent tracking fields." ;
FIELD dNotified := dNotified ;
@SetField("dNotified";
            @If(dNotified = ""; @Now; dNotified  : @Now));
FIELD cLastAgent := cLastAgent ;
jcLastAgent := "Remind Approver" ;
@SetField("cLastAgent"; @If(cLastAgent = ""; jcLastAgent;
   cLastAgent  : jcLastAgent));

REM "Email reminder";
jcSendTo :=@Name([Abbreviate]; cApprover);
jcCC := "" ;
REM "For testing, add a blind carbon copy" ;
jcBCC := "";
jcSubject := "Reminder: Requisition for " + cAssociate ;
jcBody := "You have not responded to the Requisition for "  +
  cAssociate + ". Click the doclink at the bottom of this message!" ;

@MailSend(jcSendTo; jcCC; jcBCC; jcSubject; jcBody;
            ""; [IncludeDoclink])
```

Listing 32.2 is of an escalation agent. This agent uses a value stored in a profile document as a "late" trigger. It compares that value with the value in the nReminders field and sends notification to the supervisor.

LISTING 32.2   Escalation Agent

```
REM "Escalate new Requests that have a value in nReminders";
REM "that is greater than the late trigger." ;
REM "Schedule is daily, not on weekends";

jnLateTrigger := @GetProfileField("GPF"; "nLateTrigger") ;
SELECT Form = "OSR2" & cDocStatus = "New" &
       nReminders > jnLateTrigger;

REM "Add agent tracking fields." ;
FIELD dNotified := dNotified ;
@SetField("dNotified";
          @If(dNotified = ""; @Now; dNotified  : @Now));
FIELD cLastAgent := cLastAgent ;
jcLastAgent := "Escalate Approval" ;
@SetField("cLastAgent";
          @If(cLastAgent = ""; jcLastAgent; cLastAgent  : jcLastAgent));

jcAdmin := @GetProfileField("GPF"; "cAppManager") ;
jcSendTo := @Name([Abbreviate];jcAdmin) ;

REM "Set up the Body message" ;
jcRemark := @Name([CN];cApprover) + " has not responded to this request.
➥ Please review this request, and take appropriate action. Thanks!"
        + @NewLine +  "Click this doclink to open the request —> " ;

REM "Set up the Subject field" ;
jcSubject :=  "Request approval past due!" ;

REM "Use @MailSend with parameters to notify recipients";
@MailSend( jcSendTo ; "" ; "" ; jcSubject ; jcRemark ;
             "" ; [IncludeDoclink] ) ;

REM "Add a line to the document history field." ;
jcDocHistory :=  "Approval escalation notice emailed to " + jcSendTo +
     " on " + @Text(@Now; "S2") ;
@SetField("cDocHistory" ; cDocHistory : jcDocHistory)
```

You can use the techniques in these two examples to build applications with a complex workflow. Using the Formula language is entirely appropriate for this kind of mail notification. It is far simpler to create an agent such as this using the Formula language than it is using LotusScript. LotusScript requires many more lines of code to accomplish the same result. However, LotusScript should be considered when the logic is more complex.

An example of an agent with more complex logic involved in notifications can be found in the next section.

Sending Mail with LotusScript

To send mail with LotusScript, you can use the `NotesNewsletter` class or the `Send` method of the `NotesDocument` class. Of the two, the `Send` method of the `NotesDocument` class is perhaps the most useful. Without getting into an elaborate discussion of the various properties and methods of each class, this section shows you how to use LotusScript to your advantage.

LotusScript and Web Clients

Remember when you use LotusScript that it functions in a Notes client or in an agent running on a server, but it is not available directly to a Web client. If you want to run LotusScript from a Web client, you can create a LotusScript agent and run the agent.

The `NotesNewsletter` class has a limited number of properties and methods. You can send an image of the document with the `FormatDocument` method, or you can send a collection of document links with the `FormatMsgWithDoclinks` method. This class is used to create a newsletter containing a collection of documents created from the `NotesDocumentCollection` class. You can customize the newsletter's using the three properties: `DoScore`, `DoSubject`, and `SubjectItemName`. If set to `True`, `DoScore` shows the relevance ranking as a percent. This is useful for document collections obtained using a full text search. `DoSubject` and `SubjectItemName` work together to set and display a field (item) as the subject line. The subject would appear next to the doclink in a newsletter composed using the `FormatMsgWithDoclinks` method. Because this class is somewhat limited in features, you might find it more useful to work with the `Send` method of the `NotesDocument` class.

With the `Send` method of the `NotesDocument` class, you can use the properties and methods of this rich class, and related classes such as `NotesRichTextItem` and `NotesRichTextStyle` to create attractively formatted messages. You can also produce a newsletter by successively appending document links to the body of the message. Whether you are sending a single document or a collection of documents, the technique to create the actual message is the same. First, you create a new `NotesDocument`, and assign `Memo` to the `Form` field. Next, you create a Rich Text field called `Body` and add doclinks and text to it. Send accepts two parameters, `attachForm` and `recipients`. The first stores the form of the document in the memo, and the second is the list of recipients for the memo.

Listing 32.3 is an Agent that runs on a database containing documents with information about new hires for the company. This information needs to be sent to the supervisors to whom the new hires report. First, the agent instantiates the objects needed. The view is set to a hidden view that orders the documents by the supervisor's name. Next, a memo is created using the `NotesDocument` class and the `Form` is set to `Memo` in preparation for sending the mail memo. The Subject field is set to `New Hire Newsletter` and the `Body` field is created. The `Body` field will contain the doclinks. The `NotesRichTextStyle` is used to format the text in the `Body` field. When the memo is created, the `Send` method is used to email the message.

Technically Speaking...

Two sections in the Agent listing set up the body of the memo. These could be moved into a function, and the function could then be called to set up the body of the memo. However, it is included here in "long form" so that you can see how the agent functions in its entirety.

After the body of the memo is set up and the initial text is inserted, the code loops through the documents in the view, building a line consisting of the doclink and column values from the view. When the supervisor changes, code at the beginning of the `Do Until` loop sends the memo and creates a new blank memo.

LISTING 32.3   Sending a Newsletter Using the `NotesDocument` Send Method

```
Sub Initialize
    ' Instantiate the objects used in this agent
    Dim session As New NotesSession
    Dim db As NotesDatabase
    Dim dc As NotesDocumentCollection
    Dim doc As NotesDocument
    Dim vw As NotesView
    Dim memo As NotesDocument
    Dim RTStyle As NotesRichTextStyle

    Dim rtItem As NotesRichTextItem
    Dim jcDate As Variant
    Dim jcFullName As String
```

```
Dim jcSendTo As String
Dim jbSendFlag As Variant

    ' Set up a smaller font than the default of 10
Set RTStyle = session.CreateRichTextStyle
RTStyle.NotesFont = FONT_COURIER
RTStyle.FontSize = 8
RTStyle.Bold = False


Set db = session.CurrentDatabase
Set vw = db.GetView("(rptBySuper)")
' Set up the first doc
Set doc = vw.GetFirstDocument

    ' Set up a new memo
Set memo = New NotesDocument( db )
memo.Form = "Memo"
memo.Subject = "New Hire Newsletter"

    ' Set up the Rich Text item and set the style
Set rtitem = New NotesRichTextItem( memo, "Body" )
Call rtItem.AppendStyle(RTStyle)
Call rtItem.AppendText("The following associates have been
    ➥ scheduled to start recently:")
' Add column headers
RTStyle.Bold = True
Call rtItem.AppendStyle(RTStyle)
Call rtItem.AddNewLine( 2 )
Call rtItem.AddTab( 1 )
Call rtItem.AppendText("Start") ' Column 1
Call rtItem.AddTab( 2 )
Call rtItem.AppendText("Location") ' Column 2
Call rtItem.AddTab( 2 )
Call rtItem.AppendText("Shift") ' Column 3
Call rtItem.AddTab( 2 )
Call rtItem.AppendText("Cost Ctr") ' Column 4
Call rtItem.AddTab( 1 )
Call rtItem.AppendText("Name") ' Column 5
RTStyle.Bold = False
Call rtItem.AppendStyle(RTStyle)

    ' group by the supervisors - set up the first one.
    ' If the Notified flag is Yes then set
    ' jcSendTo to blank
If doc.cSprNotified(0) = "No" Then
    jcSendTo = doc.cSuperAddr(0)
Else
    jcSendTo = ""
```

continues

32

CREATING
WORKFLOW
APPLICATIONS

LISTING 32.3   continued

```
End If
    ' Step through the view
jbSendFlag = False
Do Until (doc Is Nothing)
    If doc.cSprNotified(0) = "No" Then
        If jcSendTo = "" Then jcSendTo = doc.cSuperAddr(0)
        If jcSendTo <> doc.cSuperAddr(0) Then
                ' Send the memo
            Call memo.Send(False, jcSendTo)
            jcSendTo = doc.cSuperAddr(0)
            ' Set up a new memo
            Set memo = New NotesDocument( db )
            memo.Form = "Memo"
            memo.Subject = "New Hire Newsletter"

            ' Set up the Rich Text item and set the style
            Set rtitem = New NotesRichTextItem( memo, "Body" )
            Call rtItem.AppendStyle(RTStyle)
            Call rtItem.AppendText("The following associates
➥ have been scheduled to start:")
                ' Add column headers
            RTStyle.Bold = True
            Call rtItem.AppendStyle(RTStyle)
            Call rtItem.AddNewLine( 2 )
            Call rtItem.AddTab( 1 )
            Call rtItem.AppendText("Start") ' Column 1
            Call rtItem.AddTab( 2 )
            Call rtItem.AppendText("Location") ' Column 2
            Call rtItem.AddTab( 2 )
            Call rtItem.AppendText("Shift") ' Column 3
            Call rtItem.AddTab( 2 )
            Call rtItem.AppendText("Cost Ctr") ' Column 4
            Call rtItem.AddTab( 1 )
            Call rtItem.AppendText("Name") ' Column 5
            RTStyle.Bold = False
            Call rtItem.AppendStyle(RTStyle)

        End If ' jcSendTo <> doc.cSuperAddr(0)

        ' Add the doclinks
        Call rtItem.AddNewLine( 1 )
        Call rtitem.AppendDocLink( doc, "" )
        ' Add information from the document
        Call rtItem.AddTab( 1 )

        ' Start Column
        jcDate = Evaluate("@Text(dStart; 'D0S0')", doc )
```

```
        Call rtItem.AppendText( jcDate (0))
        Call rtItem.AddTab( 1 )

        ' Location Column
        Call rtItem.AppendText(doc.ColumnValues( 2 ))
        ' Adjust tabs for length of the location
        If Len(doc.ColumnValues( 2 )) < 13 Then
            Call rtItem.AddTab( 2 )
        Else
            Call rtItem.AddTab( 1 )
        End If
        ' Shift Column
        Call rtItem.AppendText(doc.ColumnValues( 3 ))
        ' Adjust tabs for length of the shift
        If Len(doc.ColumnValues( 3 )) < 6 Then
            Call rtItem.AddTab( 2 )
        Else
            Call rtItem.AddTab( 1 )
        End If

        ' Cost Center Column
        Call rtItem.AppendText(doc.ColumnValues( 4 ))
        ' Adjust tabs for length of the shift
        If Len(doc.ColumnValues( 4 )) < 6 Then
            Call rtItem.AddTab( 2 )
        Else
            Call rtItem.AddTab( 1 )
        End If

        ' Name Column
        Call rtItem.AppendText(doc.ColumnValues(5))
        ' Mark the agent run time and set the notified flag
        doc.dSprNotified = Now
        doc.cSprNotified = "Yes"
        Call doc.Save(True, False)
        jbSendFlag = True
      End If ' doc.cSprNotified = "No"
      Set doc = vw.GetNextDocument( doc )
  Loop
  ' Send the last memo
  If jbSendFlag Then
      Call memo.Send(False, jcSendTo)
  End If ' jbSendFlag

End Sub
```

32

CREATING WORKFLOW APPLICATIONS

Summary

This chapter introduced perhaps the single most powerful feature of Lotus Notes and Domino, the combination of the mail engine and a Domino database. Techniques of mail-enabling applications were discussed that ranged from the very simple mail-enabled forms to highly sophisticated LotusScript code. You were also shown how to use the mail @Functions, @Commands, and simple actions in both forms and agents. Last, you saw some more powerful methods of sending notifications using the scripting languages.

CHAPTER 33

Tracking Design Changes and Using Templates

When a database is in production and changes need to be made to the design, a template is used to store the design and update the production database. Templates are defined in the dictionary as a pattern or guide used in shaping something. In Domino, that is exactly how a template is used. Templates are design copies of databases and are distinguished by the extension .ntf, which stands for Notes Template Facility. The extension for a Domino database is .nsf, which is short for Notes Storage Facility.

What Is a Template?

Domino database files are unlike database files in most application development systems. They store not only the data but the code for the application as well. In most other development systems, a database file holds only the data for the application. Applications are written and stored in separate files, which are usually compiled into an executable application. The application then opens the data files allowing users to interact with the data.

In the simplest terms, a *template* is a copy of a database's design without data. A template is much more than a copy, however. Databases can be created from templates, as you'll see later in this chapter. Databases can also be linked to templates and inherit any design changes from them. A database can inherit its entire design from a single template file, and various design elements can inherit their designs from different templates. For instance, a database can inherit its entire design from a template and also be set to inherit the design of one form from another template. A process called *Design* runs on the server at 1 a.m. by default, although an administrator can change the time. This process checks all the databases on the server and refreshes the designs of those databases or database elements that inherit their designs from templates. Inheriting designs from database templates is a powerful feature of Lotus Domino.

Domino ships with many templates. There are basically two different groups of templates: system templates, such as the public directory and personal name and address books, and application templates. There are many useful application templates. For example, in a new Domino installation, I always create one or more discussion databases for user groups. This takes only a few minutes, and the database is completely functional and ready for the end users. The reason I can create them so quickly is that they are based on the template Discsw50.ntf, which comes complete with forms, views, and agents thoroughly tested and debugged. There are many more useful templates. When designing an application, take a look at the templates to determine whether there are any close matches or whether design elements can be taken from a template to leverage your time.

Note

In earlier releases of Notes, there are some limitations to templates. Not all templates can be used by all types of Notes licenses. Notes Mail licenses in Release 4 and earlier have a restricted set of templates that they can use. In Release 5 there are no longer different Notes licenses; therefore, all templates can be used by all Release 5 Notes clients.

Creating a Template

You can create your own templates based on a database that you have designed or modified. Creating a template is a relatively simple process that involves making a copy of the design elements of a database minus the data and modifying the copy's database properties to enable the template and name it. Here are the steps to take:

1. Choose the database that you will make the template from.

2. Choose File, Database, New Copy from the menu.

3. Leave the server at Local for now.

4. Change the title of the database if necessary.

5. Change the filename if necessary and change the extension to .ntf.

6. Click Database Design Only.

7. Click OK. See Figure 33.1.

FIGURE 33.1

A template being created should not include documents.

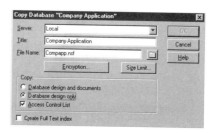

Caution

When you are creating a database template, it should always be placed in the default data directory so that it can be chosen from the list of available template databases in the new database dialog box. If it is placed in a subdirectory, it will not be available in this list.

33

TRACKING DESIGN CHANGES AND USING TEMPLATES

What you have now is a design copy of the database with an extension of .ntf; it is not yet a full-fledged template. To make it a template, you have to change the database properties to give the template a name:

1. Open the Database Properties box to the Design tab.

2. Click the Database Is a Template checkbox.

3. Enter a name in the Template Name field (see Figure 33.2).

4. Close the Properties box.

FIGURE 33.2

The Design tab of the Database Properties box specifies whether the database is a template or inherits from a template. Note that Database Is a Template is checked and a name has been entered.

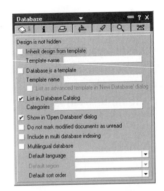

Template File Extension Is Important

Templates do not actually have to be saved with an .ntf extension, but it is a good pattern to follow. You can turn a database file with an .nsf extension into a template by changing the database properties using the previous steps. However, the file will not be listed in the template listing when creating a new database unless it has the .ntf extension.

Caution

The template name, title, and categories assigned in the Properties box cannot exceed 99 characters.

New databases can now be created from this template and can inherit design changes if the database and template both reside on a server because refreshing the design is accomplished through the server task. If a database and its template reside on a workstation, the design can be refreshed manually. Manually refreshing the design is covered later in this chapter.

When a new database is created, the Default entry in the Access Control list is set to Designer, and you are set as the Manager. You can set a default ACL that is stored in the template by placing square brackets around the entries that you want to inherit to the new database. If you choose to do this, make sure you are listed as the Manager or Designer. Using the ACL of a template, you can change the Default entry and add users, servers, or groups to the ACL. To do this, create another default entry with brackets, [-Default-], in the ACL and set the access to No Access. Follow that with whatever additional groups, servers, and users you want to add. A sample template's ACL is shown in Figure 33.3.

FIGURE 33.3

The ACL of a template can be set for future databases created with the template. The entries enclosed in square brackets will appear in a new database created from this template.

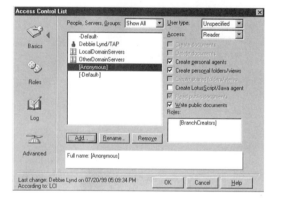

Inheriting Designs from Templates

Basing the design of a database on a template is generally done when the database is created and a design template is used to create the database.

> **Caution**
>
> When creating a database from a template, you can choose any of the checkboxes in the Advanced tab to set whatever properties you want to. The new database will not inherit the selections from the template regardless of the selections you have made there. These settings must be made after the database is created.

33

TRACKING DESIGN CHANGES AND USING TEMPLATES

Breaking the Relationship Between a Database and Its Template

You can continue to inherit the design elements from the template or break the relationship. You might find a database template that is very close to what you need but want to change certain design elements. By breaking the relationship between the template and the new database, you can modify the design of the database safely. The design process on the server will not overwrite the new design if you have broken the relationship. To break the relationship between the template and the new database, deselect the Inherit Future Design Changes checkbox in the New Database dialog box, as shown in Figure 33.4.

FIGURE 33.4

Deselecting Inherit Future Design Changes breaks the relationship between a template and the new database.

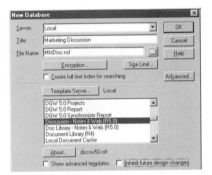

Another way to break this relationship is from the Database Properties box. Select the Design tab and deselect Inherit Design from Template. The contents of the Template Name field will disappear. Figure 33.5 shows the Design tab of the Properties box with the Inherit Design property checked to illustrate the location and content of the fields.

FIGURE 33.5

The Design tab of the Properties box controls design inheritance.

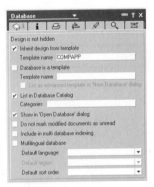

There is yet another way for a database to base its design on a template: by replacing the database's design. To replace a database design,

1. Highlight the database on the workspace.

2. Choose File, Database, Replace Design.

3. Choose the desired template, as shown in Figure 33.6.

4. Change the other options as appropriate and click Replace.

FIGURE 33.6

The Replace Database Design window.

If you want to inherit future designs, make sure that Inherit Future Design Changes remains checked (the default).

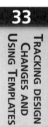

> **Caution**
>
> The Hide Formulas and LotusScript checkbox is intended for final release of a database. When you select this option, you will no longer be able to edit the design of the database that you are creating. Hiding the design of a database removes all design access to the database formulas and LotusScript, even if you have designer or manager access to the database. Before choosing this option, be sure you have a master design copy somewhere that does not have the design hidden and make sure the template you are using does not have the design hidden.

Inheriting Individual Design Elements From Templates

As indicated earlier, individual design elements can inherit designs from templates. A single database can have elements from different templates; the design process keeps track of them all.

To copy individual design elements:

1. Open the database template in the designer and switch to the design folder for the design elements you want to copy.

2. Highlight the design element. You can select multiple elements by holding down the Control key and clicking once on each element. See Figure 33.7.

3. Copy the design elements to the Clipboard by pressing Ctrl+C or choosing Edit, Copy from the menu.

4. Open the database into which you want to copy the design elements in the Designer.

5. Open the appropriate design folder and press Ctrl+V or choose Edit, Paste from the menu. Domino asks whether you want to have the forms automatically updated when the design of the template changes. To preserve the inheritance, choose Yes. See Figure 33.8.

FIGURE 33.7

Multiple forms can be selected to copy in a design template.

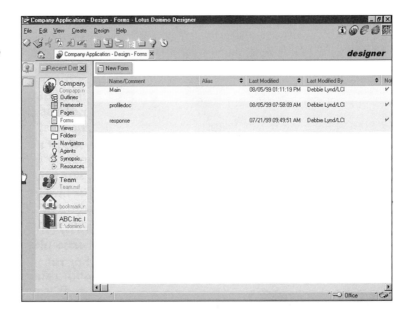

Copying Design Elements

When Domino copies design elements to the Clipboard, they are not copied to the Windows Clipboard. Instead, they are copied to a special file named ~clip-brd.ncf. These can then be pasted into other Domino databases or templates.

FIGURE 33.8

Domino will ask whether you want to maintain the link to the template when you copy design elements into a database.

Take Care When Copying Design Elements That Contain Shared Elements

When a form contains a subform, shared field, shared action, or any other shared element, the subform or shared element must be copied and pasted independently. If you fail to do so, the form will not be able to find the subform or shared element and will not function properly.

What happens if I inadvertently attempt to change a design element in my database that inherits its design from a template? I get a warning message, such as the one shown in Figure 33.9.

FIGURE 33.9

Modifying a form that inherits its design from a template causes a warning to display.

This message indicates that any changes you make to the design element will be lost when the Design task runs on the server and updates the design of my database. Can you break the association between my design element and the template without breaking the association for all other design elements in the database? Of course you can. In order to break the association between a design element and the template that replaces the database design you must do the following:

1. Highlight the design element in the design folder
2. Choose Design, Design Properties from the menu, or right-click and choose Design Properties from the menu pop-up

3. Choose the Design tab from the Properties box

4. Choose the checkbox for Do Not Allow Design Refresh or Replace to Modify

These options are displayed in Figure 33.10. Notice also the database property for Inherit from the Design Template, which is where a template name would be entered if the design element were inheriting its design from a different template than the rest of the database.

FIGURE 33.10

The Form Design Element Properties box is where the design template is specified.

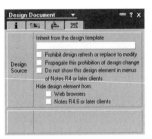

These examples have shown you how easily design elements can be copied from a template into your own database. Design changes to the template can be inherited or not, depending on your needs. Agents can be copied in the same way. This technique also works from database to database; in other words, copying design elements can take place from both Domino templates and Domino databases. This is a fast and easy way to avoid reinventing the wheel.

Refreshing Other Design Elements

There are some design considerations to be aware of when creating templates. In Release 4, the database icon, About document, and Using document were not automatically refreshed by the template. However, in Release 5, this is not the case. The default is to refresh everything. If you do not want these design elements to be refreshed, you must check Prohibit Design Refresh or Replace to Modify for that design element, as shown in Figure 33.11.

The elements that are not refreshed by default are as follows:

- The ACL is not refreshed by the template. This is a good thing because you will probably make changes to the ACL that you would not want overwritten

- The database title and category are not automatically refreshed

- Any design elements that you have set with the design property of Prohibit Design Refresh or Replace to Modify is not refreshed

- All the properties in the Advanced tab are not refreshed

FIGURE 33.11

Prohibit Design Refresh or Replace to Modify causes the design element to be ignored by the design task.

Using Templates to Replicate Design Changes

Although it is relatively easy to make changes to a database's design, propagating those changes can be problematic if the database is distributed among many servers. You can use the design process to make changes to a database that is already in production as long as the design is stored in a template file (or files) on the server and the production database or its elements are set to inherit the design. As pointed out earlier, this can be done for all design elements in the database or for individual design elements.

For obvious reasons, you would not typically make design changes to a database that is in production unless the changes have been thoroughly tested. Mistakes could have far-reaching and potentially disastrous consequences. It is therefore much better to make a copy of the production database and make the changes to the copy. After the changes are tested and working in the test copy, the design of the production database can be updated.

Updating a production database should always be done using a template. Almost every Domino developer will tell you that they have made design changes directly to production databases while they are up and people are in them. These same developers will tell you that this is foolish and quite dangerous and that all changes should be made through a template. You now know that a database will automatically be replaced by its template at night, but what if you have a crisis and your design changes can't wait overnight?

There are two ways of applying the changes manually. After a template is created, you can

- Replace the design of the production database by choosing File, Database, Replace Design from the menu. Choose the appropriate template from the list presented.

- Refresh the design of the production database by choosing File, Database, Refresh Design from the menu.

Caution

Replacing the design of the database will cause all the design elements to be replaced with the template even if there have been no changes. This could cause the next replication of the database with other servers or mobile users to take considerably longer than usual because all the design elements will be replaced when they replicate. Refreshing the design is a better way to go whenever possible.

Using a template is not the only way to propagate design changes. A replica copy of the production database can be created and modified locally. When the changes have been tested thoroughly, replication can be used to change the design of the production copy. This is not the best way to work however, and there might be design elements—especially server-based scheduled or new mail agents and mail-enabled features—that cannot be tested properly unless the database is on a server. In this case, a database copy (not a replica) must be placed on the server for testing. Never make a second replica of a database on a server. The two databases will attempt to replicate and this can have a disastrous effect. A template is also the only way to upgrade the design of a database when the design is hidden, as described earlier in this chapter.

Consider the following scenario: You have created a copy—not a replica copy—of a production database to make some rather extensive changes. The database is mail-enabled and has several scheduled and new mail agents. The changes were made locally, and a replica was placed on a server for testing. Testing is now complete, and the database is functioning as expected. The production database has replicas on many servers spread across the United States and Europe. How will you change the design of all these databases?

In a large organization, servers are typically set up in a hub-and-spoke configuration. One of the benefits of this arrangement is that the hub server usually has manager access, and the spoke servers have only editor access to a database. Therefore, any changes made to the hub server's copy of the database will eventually be replicated to copies on each of the spokes. Very large organizations might have several hub-and-spoke server arrangements. In that case, the hubs usually communicate with each other. The changes are then replicated between hubs and from there to the spoke servers.

To answer the question posed, the design could be replaced on a single hub server, and it would eventually replicate throughout the entire organization. Now let's complicate things a little. This database design serves as a template for many similar databases in your organization. Each server could have its own local database created from the same template, but not replicas of each other. You've made a significant improvement in the design of this database, and now you want to distribute the change to all the local databases on all the servers. How will you accomplish this?

Templates can be replicated just like any other database. If each server has a replica of the template, changes to the template can be replicated throughout an organization as changes to a database. The design process that runs nightly on the server can take care of making the changes to all the different copies of the database. regardless of whether they are replica copies. All the developer would have to do in this case would be to replace the design of the template on a hub server.

> **Caution**
>
> Be careful with multiple replicas of a template database on servers. If you are making changes to a copy of a database and creating a new template database from the fully tested copy, the new template database has a new replica ID, and the copies on the other servers will never receive the changes from the new template. In this scenario new replicas of the template would have to be distributed to the other servers.

Using Templates as Design Libraries

Using the power of replication and the design process, you can create and maintain libraries of design elements. Using the copy-and-paste technique described earlier in this chapter, you can copy elements from a library into new or existing databases. Inheritance can be preserved or not depending on the database or design element. To inherit design changes, both the database inheriting the design and the template must be on a server.

Because the design elements in this database can be used in many databases, great care must be taken when elements are modified. When a design element is changed, it must not break any databases that use earlier versions of the element. Therefore, rigorous testing must take place before the modification is made. Similarly, testing should take place before a new element is added to the design library. Large organizations with developers distributed in different geographic locations should have a review process in place before making any changes or additions to a commonly shared design library.

Many organizations use design libraries to provide consistency in design elements such as headers and footers in subforms that must be applied to every form in a database and include such things as company logo and required fields such as an author's name and readers' restrictions. Other shared design elements that are useful to store in a design library are shared fields that are commonly used in applications to provide a "data dictionary" of sorts.

Using a design library such as this can leverage the efforts of the entire Domino developer community. A design library not only enables databases to be developed faster, but also can enforce standards across an organization, giving a common look and feel to databases.

Archiving Versions with Templates

Domino does not have a built-in facility for archiving design changes. Some third-party tools offer an automated archive facility. Although not entirely automatic, there is a way to archive designs using standard Domino procedures. When changes are made to a database, unless they are minor, it is good programming practice to make a copy of the database design before and after the changes. There have been times when I have changed the design of a database, put it into production, and found that I needed to go back to the previous design due to some glitch. I have found that, for me, the answer is to keep a database that tracks my templates and the versions.

There are two forms in the database. The first is used to provide the initial information about the database template. The second is a response form that records the changes and the attached template.

The way the database works is this. A document is created in the database that describes the template. I then attach the original template file to this document. This can be done manually or through the Auto Fill action. Every time I make design changes to the template, I create a response document in my template database that includes a list of the design changes, as well as an attachment of the modified design. I also include a revision number in both the title of the template and the response document. Revision numbers are typically incremented using numbers or numbers plus letters. It is not important how you number the versions; it is important that you pick a standard and stick with it.

Reviewing the Release 5 Database Templates

Many of the database templates that come with Release 5 are a good place to start in developing your applications. However, there are many templates that are used for administrative purposes and are not something a developer would use as the basis for a new application. In the tables that follow, the last column defines whether the template is used for administrative databases or something a developer would use to create an application for end users.

Standard Templates

Table 33.1 lists the standard templates for R5.

TABLE 33.1   Standard Templates

Database Title	Template Filename	Template Name	Administrative or Developer
User Registration Queue	userreg.ntf	This template can be used to create a database but does not have a template name for refreshing the design	Administrative
Agent Log	Alog4.ntf	StdR4AgentLog	Both
Bookmarks	Bookmark.ntf	Bookmarks	Administrative
Cluster Analysis	Clusta4.ntf	StdR4ClusterAnalysis	Administrative
Database Analysis	Dba4.ntf	StdR4DBAnalysis	Both
Database Library	Dblib4.ntf	StdR4DatabaseLib	Developer
Design Synopsis	Dsgnsyn.ntf	DesignSynopsis	Both
Discussion	Discsw50.ntf	StdR50Disc	Developer
Doc Library	Doclbw50.ntf	StdR50WebDocLib	Developer
Local Document Cache	Cache.ntf	NotesDocCache	Administrative
Mail Router Mailbox	Mailbox.ntf	StdNotesMailbox	Administrative
Mail (R5.0)	Mail50.ntf	StdR50Mail	Administrative
Microsoft Office Library	Doclbm50.ntf	StdR50DocLibMS	Developer

33

TRACKING DESIGN CHANGES AND USING TEMPLATES

continues

TABLE 33.1 continued

Database Title	Template Filename	Template Name	Administrative or Developer
NNTP Discussion	Nntpdi50.ntf	StdR5NNTPDisc	Developer
Notes Log	Log.ntf	StdNotesLog	Administrative
Notes Log Analysis	Loga4.ntf	StdR4LogAnalysis	Administrative
Personal Address Book	Pernames.ntf	StdR4PersonalAddressBook	Administrative
Personal Journal	Journal4.ntf	StdR4Journal	Administrative
Personal Web Navigator	Perweb50.ntf	StdR50PersonalWebNavigator	Administrative
Site Registration	Siregw50.ntf	StdSite50Reg	Administrative
Statistics and Events	Events4.ntf	StdR4Events	Administrative
Statistics Reporting	Statrep5.ntf	StdR5StatReport	Administrative
Subscriptions	Headline.ntf	StdNotesHeadlines5.0	Administrative
Team Room	Teamrm50.ntf	StdR50TeamRoom	Developer

Advanced Templates

The advanced templates, as shown in Table 33.2, are available only by selecting the Show Advanced Templates checkbox when creating a new database.

TABLE 33.2 Advanced Templates

Database Title	Template Filename	Template Name	Administrative or Developer
Archive Log	Archlg50.ntf	StdR50ArchiveLog	Both
Bookmarks	Bookmark.ntf	Bookmarks	Administrative
Decommission Server Reports	Decomsrv.ntf	StdNotesDecommissionServer	Administrative

Database Title	Template Filename	Template Name	Administrative or Developer
Domino Administrator	Domadmin.ntf	StdAdminDatabase	Administrative
Domino R5 Certificate Authority	Cca50.ntf	StdNotes50SSLAuth	Administrative
Local Free Time Info	Busytime.ntf	BusyTime	Administrative
Mail (IMAP)	Imapcl5.ntf	StdR50Mail	Administrative
MIME Conversion Forms	Cmcforms.ntf	MimeConvForms	Administrative
News Articles (NNTP)	Nntpcl5.ntf	StdR50NNTPClient	Administrative
NT/Migrating Users' Passwords	Ntsync45.ntf	StdNotesNewUserPasswords	Administrative
Server Certificate Admin	Csrv50.ntf	StdNotes50SSLAdmin	Administrative

Summary

Templates are useful for many reasons. They can serve as design repositories that can leverage the developer's time and enforce consistency and standards. They can also propagate design changes of an entire class of databases or a single database throughout an organization. This chapter showed various techniques of inheriting designs from templates, both of an entire database and of individual design elements. This chapter also illustrated a technique of archiving versions of a database design. Templates are versatile, and it is worth your time to learn how to work with them.

33

TRACKING DESIGN CHANGES AND USING TEMPLATES

Other Development Tools

PART

V

IN THIS PART

CHAPTER 34

Using Domino Global WorkBench 5.0

by Debbie Lynd

Understanding Domino Global WorkBench

In many companies, it is necessary to provide applications in multiple languages. Release 4.6 introduced a new tool, called Notes Global Designer. This tool was designed to enable the conversion of the design of an application to multiple languages. Domino Global WorkBench (DGW) grew out of that tool and has become a great application for translating the design of a Domino database into multiple languages, as well as providing a tool for synchronizing the content of the database across those languages. This is beneficial for multinational corporations that need to provide applications in the local language, as well as those who want to deploy Web applications in local languages. DGW is a set of tools that comes with Release 5; however, it has a separate installation process and a good part of it is actually a separate application.

In this chapter, I will explore the process of using this tool to convert a database to an additional language. The goal here is to provide you with the information you need to determine if this is a tool you will want to use to help you to build multilingual applications.

Understanding Localization

DGW translates a Domino database through a process called "localization." This process is accomplished by specifying the elements of the design that are to be translated and providing the translated text. The end result is a localized database that contains all the tagged text translated into the appropriate local language.

When creating a database that will be localized, you should consider the roles that you play as you walk through the process. The first role is you as the developer. This is the role you normally play when developing an application, so nothing more needs to be said about it. Next is the tagger who determines which terms should or should not be translated. After the terms are defined for translation, the next person to step in is the translator, who provides the translation of terms from the source language into the new language. The last role is played by the builder, who actually creates the language databases from the defined terms and keeps the database changes current.

Specifying the Type of Localization

When using DGW to produce an application in multiple languages, you either create separate databases for each language you choose or you create one database that contains all the chosen languages. Each separate database is called a *unilingual database*; one database with multiple languages is called a *multilingual database*.

A multilingual database has some advantages over creating several unilingual databases. In a multilingual database, the design is translated into multiple languages within one database; the language preference of the user automatically determines the language displayed to the user. This is useful on a Web site where you have less control over the language of the user accessing the database.

Defining the Tools in Domino Global WorkBench

I have already explained a few of the pieces of the DGW. You should understand, however, what each piece does in relationship to the others. The tools include the WorkBench, the Tagger, the Synchronizer, and the Glossary.

Identifying the WorkBench Program

The WorkBench is a separate application that creates tagged databases from source databases; builds the language databases from the tagged databases and the associated glossaries; updates the tagged databases, the glossaries, and the language databases based on changes made to the design of the source database; and logs messages about the process as shown in Figure 34.1.

FIGURE 34.1

The WorkBench program provides an organized view of databases and options for a specific project.

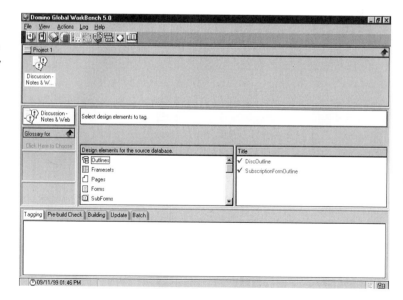

In the WorkBench is also a Project Manager that organizes the databases included in an application and appears as shown in Figure 34.2. These database groupings then become known as a project. The information displayed in the Project Manager is contained in a Domino database called Project.nsf.

FIGURE 34.2

*The Projects that
you define are all
listed within the
Projects database.*

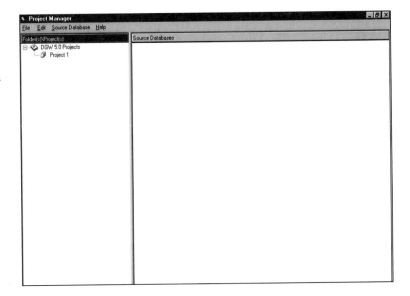

Identifying the Tagged Database

From each source database, a tagged database is created that links the text that is to be translated from the source database to text specified in the glossary database. So for every piece of text that is tagged as translatable in the tagged database there is also a term created for that text in the glossary database. The result of this is that all text to be converted is tagged and specified in the glossary where a translator can then provide the translated text for each of the tagged terms.

Creating a tagged database takes the source database and creates a new database from it that defines which terms are to be tagged for translation. This is part of the process that is done within the WorkBench; however, there is also a separate Tagger program that is used to make manual adjustments to a tagged database. Tags are automatically created by the WorkBench, but you might occasionally need to create or manually adjust a tag using the Tagger program. In Domino Global Designer the Tagger program was known as the Populator. The Tagger program screen is shown in Figure 34.3.

FIGURE 34.3

You can manually adjust tags in the Tagger program screen.

Identifying the Glossary Database

Glossaries are a big part of the process. These Domino databases contain the terms from the source database that are to be translated and translation documents that provide the translated terms in the additional languages. The translated terms will be added by a translator. The role of translator will be played by someone who is fluent in the languages that the database will be converted to.

Glossaries are created from the glossary template, DGWGLOSS.NTF. Each glossary contains information that defines which languages will be supported in the glossary and each term in the database that will be translated. In addition, the glossary contains translation documents that contain the translated text for each term in the supported languages. This translated text is provided by the translator. You might have multiple glossary databases for a project or use one glossary database for multiple projects. Often a company has a global glossary for terms common to all its applications, just as it might have a database template defining the global design elements for all its applications. In that case, an additional glossary is created for each localized application. This new glossary, then, contains only the terms that are specific to the application and not already defined in the global glossary.

Identifying the Synchronizer Agent

The synchronizer is an agent that is run from one of the language databases handling requests for synchronization of documents. The synchronizer then translates the data contained in that document. Synchronization occurs for documents created with forms that have been marked as translatable. Forms can be marked as translatable in three ways, as indicated in Table 34.1.

34

USING DOMINO GLOBAL WORKBENCH 5.0

Table 34.1 Translatable Forms

Translation Type	Definition
Translatable	Any document created is copied to other language databases and marked for translation.
Global	Any document created is copied to other language databases but isn't translated.
Local	Any document created isn't copied to other language databases.

For unilingual databases, a Language Switchbar can be included to provide a way for users to switch languages when viewing synchronized documents.

Preparing the Application for Translation

Prior to creating a new project in the WorkBench, you need to do a few things in the Domino database that will be translated. Certain design considerations need to be addressed that will make it easier to translate the application. In developing the application, you need to consider the language that you are using to develop the database as well as the languages that the database will be translated into. Some languages use longer words and phrases to say the same things that other languages say in one or two words. Therefore, it is important to consider how the forms, actions, and other text will be displayed within the database to ensure that the user will be able to see all the design elements and text easily.

Reviewing the Database Design

The first thing to do is check the source database to ensure that there are aliases for all your design elements. It is important to use aliases for design elements because they will not be translated terms. The aliases should always be used to refer to design elements in code. All aliases should start with the same prefix; this way, it's easier to identify the text in formulas that you don't want to tag and translate. The elements that you want to make sure you have aliases for are the following:

- Agent names
- View names

- Folder names
- Form names
- Pages
- Outlines
- Navigators
- Keyword field values

Create Aliases for Design Elements That Won't Be Translated[sh box]

It is a good idea to create a unique prefix for your aliases. You should be able to easily define the text that is not to be translated. By using aliases, you can quickly determine where the alias occurs in formulas and specify that the term will not be translated.

Creating a Glossary

As stated earlier, the glossary is an integral part of the localization process. The process for creating the database and setting it up to be used for testing is defined in this section.

You create a glossary database from the DGWGLOS.NTF template as shown in Figure 34.4.

FIGURE 34.4

Use the glossary template to create a new glossary database.

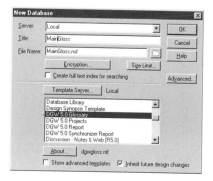

After you create the glossary database, open it in Notes and enter the project description and the language of the source database—in other words, the language the database was originally developed in. Next, select the Pseudo Language as the language that you will translate to. The Pseudo Language will provide you a way to convert the database and ensure that your design elements still appear properly to the end user before converting to an actual language. When these steps are complete, you are ready to launch Global WorkBench.

Setting Up the Project in WorkBench

When you first open the WorkBench, a new project is created for you. The WorkBench screen appears as shown in Figure 34.5. The next step is to open the Project Manager window by clicking the blue bar at the top of the screen and choosing the option Open Project Manager. The Project Manager window is where you can arrange projects in folders. You can minimize the Project Manager window at any time and return to the WorkBench screen.

FIGURE 34.5

The WorkBench screen is where the databases are defined and set up for translation.

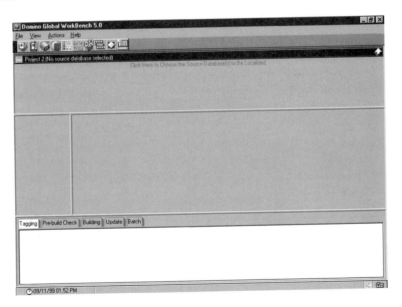

From the WorkBench screen, you must first select the Source Databases that you will work with for this project. In Figure 34.5 you will see text that says "Click Here to Choose the Source Database(s) to be Localized." If you click anywhere on that text, a dialog box appears from which you can choose the databases that will be part of the project as indicated in Figure 34.6. You can select databases from a server or from your local machine. The list that appears will include both NSF and NTF files.

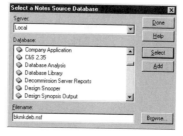

FIGURE 34.6

You must select each source database that you'll include in the translation of an application.

The next step is to define which glossary you will use for the translation. You will notice that in the pane on the left of the WorkBench there is text that says "Click here to choose the Glossaries for Universal Discussion." By clicking the text, you can choose the glossary database that was created earlier. The Select a Glossary Database dialog box, shown in Figure 34.7, allows you to determine wheater this glossary is to be used for the source database only, all databases in this glossary is to be used for the source database only, all databases in this project, or all new projects that are created.

FIGURE 34.7

The Select a Glossary Database dialog box displays all the glossaries you have defined.

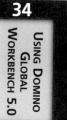

Creating the Tagged Database

After you select a source database and a glossary database, you can then create a tagged database. This is where it becomes critical that you have created aliases for the design elements. When the database is tagged, the aliases are ignored for each design element, thus ensuring that your references will be intact. When the tagged database is created, all the text in the source database is referenced in the glossary database. If there is not a matching glossary entry for an item, you will be asked if you would like to have one created in the glossary.

To set up the source database for tagging, highlight the database in the WorkBench, so that the design elements are displayed in the Design Elements and Title panes. Click the title pane for any design elements that you don't want to tag. By default, all items are tagged as shown in Figure 34.8.

FIGURE 34.8

All design elements are tagged by default in the WorkBench.

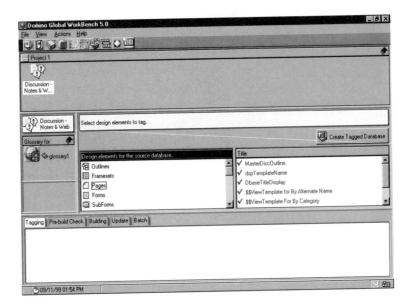

Next, click the Create Tagged Database button to define the tagged database and the tagging properties. The dialog box, as shown in Figure 34.9, provides five sections on the left-hand side that you will select to complete the information for each section. Enter the filename you want to use for the tagged database in the New Database section of the dialog box.

FIGURE 34.9

The filename for the tagged database must be entered in the New Database section of the Tagged Database Creation dialog box.

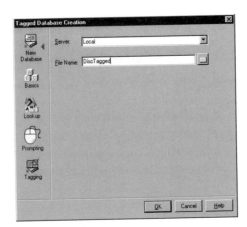

Understanding the Basics Section

In the Basics section, you select the language that the source is written in, the term type (a way of categorizing terms), and the name of the glossary database that will contain the terms for translation as shown in Figure 34.10. Select the glossary that you will use to specify new terms, in our case the only glossary you have. You should also select a report database to which to write all errors. The Reports database will not exist by default, but it is a Notes database that you can create using the DGW Report template.

FIGURE 34.10

The Basics section of the Tagged Database Creation dialog box must be completed before moving on.

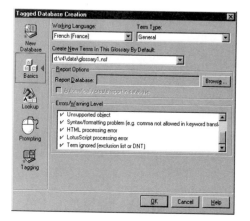

The Errors and Warning level for reporting purposes are all selected in the Errors/Warning Level checkbox. If there are errors or warnings that you do not want to log, you can deselect the option.

Understanding the Lookup Section

The lookup section is where you will define how the terms are matched between the database and the glossary as seen in Figure 34.11. The options are described in Table 34.2.

TABLE 34.2   Glossary Lookup Options

Option	Definition
Match Exactly	The term in the design element must be an exact match with the term in the glossary.
Match from Beginning	The term in the design element must begin with the same text as is defined in the glossary.

continues

TABLE 34.2   continued

Option	Definition
Case Sensitive	If the term is defined differently for uppercase and lowercase, check this option.
Accent Sensitive	If differently accented terms are handled differently, choose this option.
Combine Broken Terms	Attribute changes in text are stored as separate terms by default. Choose this option if the attributes do not have an effect on the term.
Rich Text Sensitive	This treats attributed text as rich-text glossary entries.
Limit of Terms to Lookup	Limits the lookup in the glossary to the number of terms indicated.

FIGURE 34.11

Matching is defined in the Lookup Section of the tagging options dialog box with defaults selected.

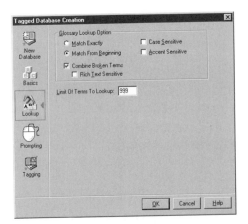

Understanding the Prompting Section

The Prompting section is where you will determine the settings for handling terms that do not already exist in the glossary and determine the level of prompting that will happen during the tagging process. The default selections are displayed in Figure 34.12. The options and their definitions are included in Table 34.3.

TABLE 34.3   The Prompting Options

Option	Definition
Never Prompt (Automatic)	Does not prompt as the tagged database is created, unless the "Always Prompt When Tagging Formulas" is checked.

Option	Definition
Create New Terms	If this is unchecked and the glossary contains a match, a tagged term is created in the tagged database from that match. If there are multiple matches, it uses the first.
Automatically for Each New Term	If checked, a new entry is created in the new terms glossary whenever the text does not yet exist. The tagged term is then created based on the new glossary entry.
As Needed	If checked and a match exists in the glossary, the term is tagged based on that glossary entry. If there are multiple matches, the first one is used. If there is not a match in the glossary, a new entry is created in the new terms glossary and a tagged entry is placed in the tagged database based on that entry.
Prompt When (Semi Automatic)	Allows you to select whether to prompt when a term is not found or if more than one term is found.
A Term Is Not Found	If a match is not found in any of the selected glossaries, you are then prompted to decide whether to create a new entry for the term in the glossary or to skip it.
More Than One Term Is Found	If more than one match is found in the selected glossaries, you are prompted to decide which term should be associated.
For Each Term (Manual)	For every term in the database, you will be prompted to either choose the match found in the glossary or create a new entry in the glossary.
Always Prompt When Tagging Formulas	For every formula in the database, you will be prompted before the text is tagged.

FIGURE 34.12

The Prompting section of the Tagged Database Creation dialog box provides options for tagging text.

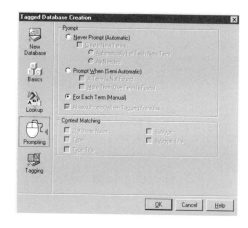

Understanding the Tagging Section

The Tagging section includes options for excluding types of text or certain words from the tagging process, as well as setting the delimiters that are to be used at the beginning and end of each tag as seen in Figure 34.13. Make sure that you choose a delimiter character that you are not using anywhere in the design of the database.

FIGURE 34.13

Selection of elements to tag and excluded terms is defined in the Tagging section of the Tagged Database Creation dialog box.

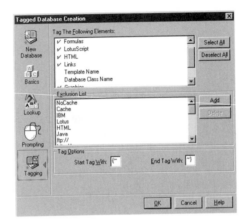

The Tagged Database Creation dialog box is where you can take one last stab at choosing the design elements that will or will not be tagged. The initial determination of what is to be tagged is made from the WorkBench main screen when the source database is selected.

The exclusion list contains terms that are not to be tagged. There are default terms provided such as Lotus, IBM, Notes, NoCache, and so on. You can also add your own terms to the list. Note that the text is case sensitive. When specifying aliases that you do not want tagged, specify the prefix you used to define your aliases and an asterisk to easily identify all the aliases. For instance, if you choose to name all your aliases with the *xx* prefix, you would add the entry *xx** to the exclusion list.

The tag options specify the delimiters to use that determine how tagged text appears in the tagged database. The delimiters are placed around each piece of tagged text. You should specify a delimiter character that you are not using in any other way within your application.

After the tagging section is completed, click OK to begin creating the tagged database.

Using the Tagging Window

Because you indicated that you want to be prompted when tagging, the Tagging Window will now appear as shown in Figure 34.14.

FIGURE 34.14

The Tagging Window prompts you when text does not appear in the glossary.

From this window, you will decide how the displayed term will be represented or tagged in the tagged database, as well as the glossary. The Tagging Window has three display panes, one of which, the Lookup panel, is displayed in Figure 34.14.

The content of the Lookup panel provides the Source term within context as the current term being considered for translation. The context section directly below this specifies where within the design of the database this term is found. The Terms Found in Glossary section displays any occurrences of the term already entered in the glossary along with the Context of the occurrence in the section immediately following the terms. The buttons along the bottom of the panel are described in Table 34.4.

TABLE 34.4   Buttons in Lookup Panel

Button Caption	Description
Tag	Creates a tag entry for the current source term using the selected glossary term
Create	Opens the Create Terms panel where a new term can be defined in the glossary

continues

TABLE 34.4 continued

Button Caption	Description
Options	Opens the tagged options dialog box, where the default tagging options are set
Skip	Skips the current source term and leaves it untagged
Stop	Returns to the WorkBench main display without completing the tagging process

The Create Terms panel provides a place to specify a new term in a glossary database as shown in Figure 34.15. If you are using more than one glossary database, the database that you want the term defined in can be chosen from the Create Term in Glossary drop-down box. A term type can be selected or a new term type added under the Term Type heading, and a new description for the term can be added at the bottom of the panel.

FIGURE 34.15

New terms are defined in the New Term Type dialog box.

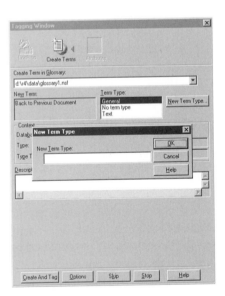

The Attributes panel will display any rich text found with the associated rich-text attributes, such as fonts, size, color, and so on as shown in Figure 34.16.

Now that I have described the tagging process, you should be able to step through the terms and create the appropriate entries in the tagged database and glossary.

FIGURE 34.16

The Attributes panel display rich text with its associated attributes.

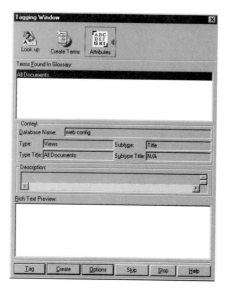

Working with a Pseudo Language

The next step is to check to see what the translated database will look like by converting it to a Pseudo Language. A Pseudo Language is not really a language at all, but a way of testing the conversion to determine whether the final layout and the terms will all be converted properly. The method used to convert to the Pseudo Language is the same as you will use to do a final conversion to the languages that you specify. When converting to the Pseudo Language, you have two options: You can choose to reverse terms or expand terms as described in Table 34.5.

TABLE 34.5 Options for Pseudo-Translation

Option	Description
Reverse Terms	Identifies those terms that would not be translated in the application
Expand Terms	Identifies what within the application screens would look out of proportion due to text conversion

You will run the Pseudo-Translation twice in order to test for both the untranslated terms and the final layout. When converting from English to another language, the converted

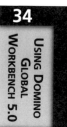

terms could take up to 30% more room on-screen. To perform the Pseudo-Translation to reverse the terms, follow these steps:

1. From the WorkBench, open the Glossary.

2. From the Main Navigator, choose Glossary Management and then choose Select/Deselect languages.

3. Next, highlight the Pseudo Language and click the Select action.

4. From the navigator on the left, choose Pseudo-Translate.

5. In the Pseudo-Translate dialog box, choose Reverse Text and then choose OK.

After the translation is complete, it's time to review what has been translated and determine where adjustments should be made.

This is done from the Glossary database, using the entries in the Terms with Translations view as shown in Figure 34.17. Go through each of the terms in the view and check the translation into pseudocode. Look for any terms that were not translated.

FIGURE 34.17

The terms converted into pseudocode can now be checked for accuracy.

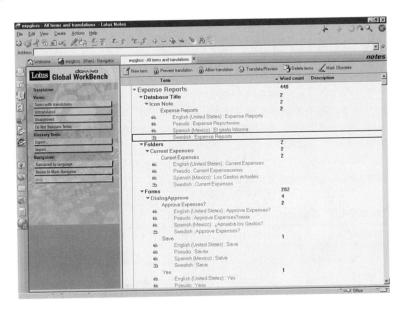

Next, you will build the application using the Pseudo Language.

When that process is completed, the translation to pseudocode must again take place with the Expand Terms option in order to see how the UI will appear in another language that might take up more screen real estate.

Working with the Glossary

The first step to an actual translation is to prepare the glossary for the translator. The translator is a person who actually creates the translated terms for the language databases. This person might not have access to the application being translated and might not understand the technical terms that can be used in an application. The translator will need to have information about the terms you are using in order to understand the context of your text. By adding comments to the terms and marking terms that should not be translated, the translator will be better prepared to perform the translation.

When the glossary database is opened in the Notes client, the main navigator provides two options. The first, Translation and Review, is provided as a way to help the translator to view those terms that are and are not translated. This is discussed in the following section, "Translating the Terms." The second option, Glossary Management, is what you will be working on now.

When the Glossary Management option is selected from the main navigator, the view of terms will be displayed with a navigator to the left of available views and tools to help with the management of the glossary entries as shown in Figure 34.18.

FIGURE 34.18

Glossary Management includes a navigator that provides views and tools for working with glossary entries.

I will not cover all the options in the Navigator in detail; however, Table 34.6 provides a description of each option.

TABLE 34.6 Glossary Management Options

Option	Description
Terms with Translations	Displays a view of all terms and their translations
Select/Deselect Languages	Displays a view of all available languages along with actions to create new languages and select or deselect a language
View Glossary Information	Displays the information about the glossary database in the glossary information document
Do Not Translate Terms	Displays a view of the terms that are not to be translated
Obsolete Terms	Displays a view of the terms that are now obsolete
Export	Displays a dialog box for exporting terms to a structured text file
Import	Displays a dialog box for importing terms from a structured text file
Retrieve	Displays a dialog box for adding translations from another glossary
Pseudo-Translate	Displays a dialog box for initiating a pseudo-translation
Delete Duplicates	Displays a dialog box for deleting duplicate terms in a glossary
Delete Orphan Translations	Displays a dialog box for deleting terms that no longer have a term definition document
Delete Non-Linguistic Conflicts	If there are multiple translation documents for a specific term, the unapproved can be deleted from this action

In order to ensure that the glossary is ready to be translated, comments should be added to terms that might be misinterpreted and terms that should not be translated need to be specified. There might also be some text strings that are never displayed to a user but provide clarity that should not be translated.

In order to prepare the discussion database for this process, choose the Terms with Translations view from the Glossary Management Navigator. From this view, go through the terms that are specified and pick and edit the documents pertaining to any of the terms that need clarification or should not be translated.

After this task is completed, you can then select the languages that you want to enable for the glossary. This is done from the Select/Deselect Languages view. First, select the languages in the view and then choose the Select action from the Action Bar. This will create new language documents for each of the languages that you have selected.

This then completes the process of preparing the glossary for the translator.

Translating the Terms

This is where you need to get a language expert involved. The terms in the glossary must now be translated by that expert into the selected languages. This can be done in the glossary itself, or the terms can be exported and translated using some other tool.

You will look at translating the terms from within the glossary. In order to do the translation from within the glossary, the ACL roles need to be applied to the translators and the reviewers of the glossary entries. These roles are defined in Table 34.7.

TABLE 34.7   ACL Roles in the Glossary

Role Name	Description
rTranslator	Provides edit capabilities to the translation documents only
rApprover	Provides same capabilities as the translator but an additional option to mark a translation as approved

The Translation and Review Navigator in the glossary database offers views to help a translator through the translation process. The available views and their descriptions are shown in Table 34.8.

TABLE 34.8   Translation Views in the Glossary Database

View Name	Description
Terms with Translations	Displays all the terms in the database, categorized by database name, design type, and design type name
Untranslated	Displays all terms that are not yet translated along with the language they are to be translated into
Unapproved	Displays all the translation documents that are translated but have not been approved
Do Not Translate Terms	Displays all terms that are in the glossary with Translation Allowed set to No
Translated by Language	This choice provides a new navigator with a list of available language views

To enter the translations, choose the Terms with Translations View and begin by highlighting one of the terms to be translated. Then choose the translate/review action from the Action Bar. This will bring up the dialog box for translation as shown in Figure 34.19.

FIGURE 34.19

The translator must enter a translation for each term in the glossary.

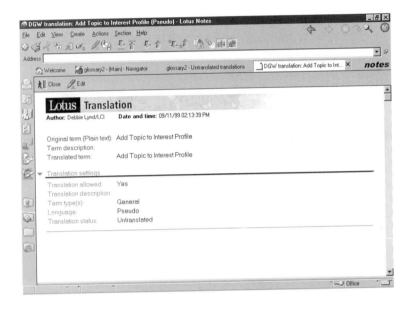

When the translation of the terms is completed, the database can then be translated into the language version of the database. Creating a language version of the database is done using the same steps you used in creating the Pseudo Language database. The only difference is that you can choose multiple languages.

Synchronizing the Data

When content providers create new documents in an application, those documents can be converted to the local languages through the synchronizer. The synchronizer is an agent that runs at a predetermined interval on all the new and modified documents within the database that have been flagged as translatable. The method for setting the documents as translatable is accomplished by defining at the form level which forms are used to create translatable documents. Synchronization can occur between unilingual or multilingual databases.

Fields Added to a Synchronized Database

When you create a localized database, the agents to synchronize the data are also added. There is also a hidden subform that is added to all the forms that have been translated as well as a profile document that is added to the database. The subform provides the necessary fields for tracking the documents that will need to be synchronized (as described in Table 34.9), whereas the fields in the profile document specify the language information for the database (as described in Table 34.10).

TABLE 34.9 Fields in the Subform for Synchronized Databases

Field Name	Description
$Language	The language the document is in
$Lng_UNID	An ID assigned to the document for synchronization with the other language versions
$Lng_SynchType	Setting that determines whether the document type is local, global, or translatable
$Lng_Original	Flag that determines whether this is the original of the document or a translated version
$Lng_State	Setting that determines the translation state of the document
$Lng_LastSynchronised	The date and time of the last synchronization
$Lng_LastModified	The date and time the document was last modified
$Lng_WorkflowState	This will be used in the future
$Lng_Switchbar	Contains doclinks to all the language versions of the document for the switchbar
$Lng_SwitchbarText	Setting to determine which languages to display in the switchbar
$Lng_Switchbar_*xxx*	Multiple files where *xxx* is the language and the content is language-specific information for the language switchbar
$Lng_SwitchbarUpdate	Switch to force updating of the language switchbar for a document

TABLE 34.10 Fields in the Profile Document for Synchronization

Field Name	Description
$Language	The language or languages represented in the database
$Lng_Databases	The databases being synchronized
$Lnd_Id	The abbreviations for the languages being synchronized
$Lng_Names	The full names of the languages being synchronized
$Lng_Switchbar	Switch to determine whether the switchbar is being used

Defining the Document Types for Synchronization

For each form that will be used to create a document that should be synchronized, the type of synchronization must be selected. By selecting the type, you set the appropriate synchronization fields for the underlying documents that will be created. Setting the type is done from the WorkBench by selecting a language database and then highlighting the forms selection in the Design Elements pane as shown in Figure 34.20.

FIGURE 34.20

The Anonymous Response form is selected and set for Local translation.

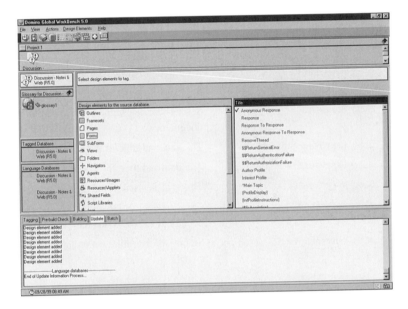

From this point each form should be set for the appropriate document type as specified in Table 34.11. In Figure 34.20 the Anonymous Response form has been set to Local as indicated by the icon to the left. The Response form has been set to Global, and the Response to Response form has been set to Translatable.

TABLE 34.11 Document Type

Type	Description
Local	Documents created with a form that has a document type of local will only be stored in the native language and not copied to the other language databases.

Type	Description
Global	Documents created with a form that has a document type of global are not translated to other languages, but they are copied to the other language databases.
Translatable	Documents created with a form that has a document type of translatable are copied to the other languages and marked as untranslated.

Setting individual forms is done by clicking to the left of the form name once for Local, twice for Global, and three times for Translatable. An optional way of setting each form is to right-click the form name and choose Properties, as shown in Figure 34.21; then choose the Synchronizer tab and click the appropriate radio button.

FIGURE 34.21

The document type can be set from the form properties box in the WorkBench.

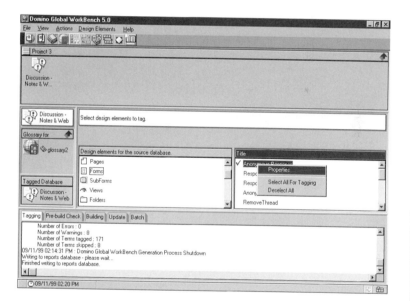

To set all the forms to the same value, right-click a form name and choose one of the available options, as shown in Figure 34.22.

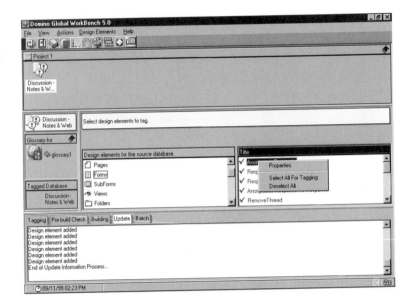

Setting Up the Synchronization Process

When the forms are set, the next step is to set up synchronization in all the language databases and designate which database the synchronizer agent will be set to run in. You can do this by choosing the Action Synchronize Language databases as shown in Figure 34.23. This is also where you will define whether to include a language switchbar for the documents.

FIGURE 34.23

The database that will run the synchronizer agent is selected from the Synchronize Language databases action.

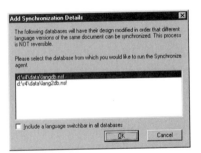

After you choose OK, the information for synchronization is added to the database as can be seen from the Building tab of the WorkBench in Figure 34.24. The last step to enabling synchronization is to set the agent in the database to run at a scheduled interval.

FIGURE 34.24

The Building tab of the WorkBench displays the log information for the addition of synchronizer information to the database.

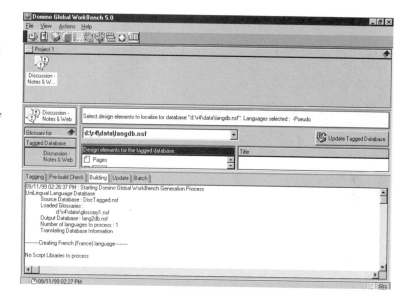

Summary

This chapter introduced the conversion of databases to multiple languages through the Domino Global WorkBench tools. The tools that make up the WorkBench and the process for converting to additional languages should help you to understand how powerful this product is and the capabilities it provides for you to build multilingual Internet applications and Web sites.

Real-Time Access to Enterprise Data

by Debbie Lynd

IN THIS CHAPTER

What Is DECS?

DECS stands for Domino Enterprise Connection Services. This product was introduced in Release 4.63 of Notes and grew out of a need for real-time access to external data sources on a field-by-field basis. Due to the fact that many applications and data reside in databases that are not Domino based, it is important to most companies to be able to gain access to this data in their Domino applications. The real-time access to this data was first made available in Notes Pump, which is mainly used for exchanging large quantities of information between Domino and back-end systems. Lotus Enterprise Integrator is the new name for Notes Pump and in its current version it contains the capabilities for moving large quantities of data as opposed to the real-time feature of DECS. The purpose of DECS is to provide a Notes application with the ability to access, create, update and delete data from an external database. The major restriction of DECS is its inability to provide a Notes application with the ongoing synchronization of data that has been added to or deleted from the back-end database through processes other than the Notes application. For this, you need to provide an external method of synchronizing the data, using Lotus Enterprise Integrator, a third-party tool, or the LotusScript: DataObject (LS:DO).

The engine for DECS is a separate server task. This process runs on a Domino server, intercepting requests for the external data and fulfilling those requests. The client can be either a Notes client or a Web browser and the client does not need a local connection to the data source that contains the back-end information that is being retrieved. However, because this is a server task, the requests cannot be fulfilled if the client is a Notes client and the user is running the application from a local replica, unless the client has access to the back-end data from the server through a defined data source. This is an important fact to consider when developing applications that could potentially run on a standalone client or for a disconnected user.

Notes Documents Can Be Added Remotely

You can create a document and replicate it to the server running with a DECS connection. The DECS server task then sends any changes that you make to the back end (including the addition of new documents). So, one-way data flow *is* possible, even if disconnected. Additionally, if you select the option "Leave Real-Time Fields in Document" then you *can* do full data exchange when you replicate, but you'll encounter replication and synchronization issues.

DECS is not only a server process, but it contains a Domino database for setting up and administering the connections and retrieval of data. This database is known as the DECS Administration database, and is created when you install DECS.

Prior to running DECS, your Domino administrator must set it up to run on the server. Installation of DECS is an option when installing the server or upgrading the server. If done at this time, it automatically creates the DECS Administrators database and start the DECS task on the server. If it has not been installed at the time of the server install, or upgrade, it can be easily started by the server administrator adding the DECS task to the Notes.ini file in the `ServerTasks=` line, or it can be manually started using the Load DECS server command. If it's installed separately, you have to create the DECS Administrators database manually from the template.

> **Note**
>
> In order for DECS to operate, the DECS task must be running on the server. There must also be a DECS administrator database on the server with a valid connection document and an activity document that the DECS task is running in order to test DECS.

When installed, the process for using DECS is fairly easy, with wizards that guide you through the process. Three basic steps are involved:

- Creating a connection to the external data source
- Creating the Notes application that accesses the external data source
- Creating a RealTime activity that defines the relationship between the Notes application and the external data source

There are a few things to consider when deciding to run an application with DECS: Will the application be installed on multiple servers? will clients store a replica locally? and will the back-end data change and need to be refreshed within the Notes application? I'll look at each of these separately.

If the application is installed on multiple servers, you need to either have DECS installed on each server or store the data from the external data source in the document. By default, all data other than the key fields is retrieved by DECS each time the document is opened and is not stored with the document. Therefore, it would be unavailable from a server that is not running DECS and the appropriate activity. However, if you store the data in the document, it also means that the data would not be changed in the document if it is accessed from a server that does not run DECS and have a connection to the back-end data source.

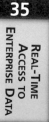

Also, if mobile users keep a local copy of the data, you have to store the data in the document.

When you have initiated the keys for an activity, the data that is in the Notes database is never refreshed by the back-end database if the keys change or are deleted, or there are new keys added through a method on the back end. Therefore, you need to provide a method for propagating the changes. Lotus Enterprise Integrator can be used for this purpose, although this is an add-on product that you have to pay for, or you could write your own routine using the LS:DO as described in Chapter 24, "Writing LotusScript."

The External Data Source

Prior to attaching to a data source, the appropriate network connectivity must be in place and defined. There is a separate Notes database to help you through this because the requirements for each data type is different. The database is the "Domino Connectors Setup Guide" and is stored under the filename of LCCON.NSF. This database is installed on the server in the Help directory by default.

At the time of this writing, DECS can connect to 90 data sources. There are 5 native connections as shown in the following list:

- SAP
- Sybase
- Oracle
- DB2
- File system

Standard connections can be made through ODBC and JDBC. Legacy and transaction-based systems available include MQ/Series, CICS, and EDA/SQL. The data sources available to DECS will continue to be expanded and you should check the Web site for Enterprise Integration for new releases at `http://www.lotus.com/home.nsf/welcome/ei`.

DECS is very similar to Enterprise Integrator (the new name for Notes Pump) in the way that the requests are defined and stored. The DECS Administrator database is at the heart of the process and is where all relationships and activities are defined.

What DECS means to you is that you can provide real-time access to back-end data through the data mapping functionality provided in DECS. After fields are defined in a form, DECS is used to create a map from the fields linked to fields in an external data source.

DECS Administrator

The DECS Administration database stores all the information necessary to connect an external data source with a Notes database. It is managed from the Notes client or from the Notes Administrator client, and it is stored on the server running the DECS task. On opening the database, you are presented with a View pane and a Navigator pane as displayed in Figure 35.1. The Navigator pane is all you need to build and view the connection and activity information for all the applications that use DECS.

FIGURE 35.1

The DECS Administrator database defines all the data connections and activities that the DECS task can run.

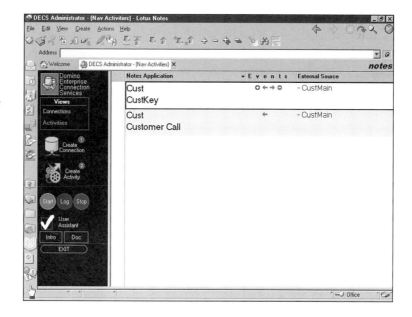

The DECS Administrator database consists of two major types of information: Connections and Activities. There are views for each of these types as indicated in Figure 35.1. Connections defines how connections are made between the Notes database and the external data source. Activities describes which fields should be exchanged and the trigger that causes the exchange to happen. The Administrator database is responsible for providing all the information that the DECS server task needs to execute an activity and provide the appropriate responses.

Because it would be impossible to cover all the possibilities of DECS in this chapter, I will instead guide you through the creation of a Notes database to access data stored in a dBASE format table and you will access the data through an ODBC connection. In doing so, I should cover the basics and a few helpful hints besides. The actual steps that I will cover in this chapter are

35

REAL-TIME
ACCESS TO
ENTERPRISE DATA

- Creating the application
- Defining the external data source to ODBC
- Creating a connection to the data source in the DECS Administrator database
- Setting up an activity for the connection in the DECS Administrator database
- Accessing the application

Creating the Application

The application you will work with is a very simple application that provides you a way to access customer information stored externally in a Notes database that tracks customer calls. I am purposely not making this a full application, only enough to show how this works, and to give you ideas for implementing your own applications.

First, I've created a Domino Database that contains a form called CustKey with the Customer information that both Domino and the external database have in common. The fields with an asterisk (*) are the fields you retrieve from the external database. The Cname field is the key field used to compare the documents with the table. The dBASE field names are the same as the Notes field names. This is always a good idea to provide consistency between applications and standardized naming conventions throughout an organization. A second form contains all the fields in Table 35.1. And then a third form contains the Cname field and a Form field.

TABLE 35.1 Fields Created for Domino and dBASE Files. Fields Without Asterisk Appear Only in Domino Database

Field Name	Field Type	Field Description
Cname	Text *	Customer name
Cadd1	Text *	Address line 1
Cadd2	Text *	Address line 2
Ccity	Text *	City
Cstate	Text *	State
Czip	Text *	Zip code
CallDate	Date	Date the call was received
CallSubject	Text	Short description of call
CallDetail	Rich Text	Full description of call
Author	Text	Person entering the information

The CustKey form defines the customer information. This is the form you will use to populate the Domino database with the initial data from the external database. You will use the Customer Call form to log customer calls and the third form, CustLog, to select the customer for a new customer call.

Defining the External Data Source to ODBC

Prior to setting up a connection to a data source, you must have a way to access the data. In the case of an ODBC connection, ODBC must be set up to provide a link to the data source. The ODBC data source is set up from the ODBC administrator program in Windows 95 and Windows NT. The only tip I will give you about ODBC connections is that you should create a System DSN, not the User DSN. This is necessary for clients to be able to make the connection. If the User DSN is used, the only computer that can see the connection is the server because a User DSN is available only to the local machine. The system DSN that you have created for this connection is displayed in Figure 35.2. Lotus also recommends using Intersolv's ODBC drivers unless a driver is provided by the vendor of the data source.

FIGURE 35.2

An ODBC Connection should be set up as a System DSN.

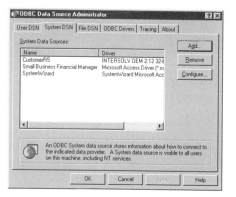

Creating the Connection

Connections define the external data that is to be captured or manipulated. Based on the data source chosen, the appropriate form opens and the fields that are required for an appropriate connection are displayed. Common to all connections are the data source, the table or view to access, and the username and password that should be used for the connection. In the case of your connection, Figure 35.3 displays the document that is created to support the ODBC connection that you created.

FIGURE 35.3

The DECS Connection document for the ODBC connection defines which external data source and Notes database are connected.

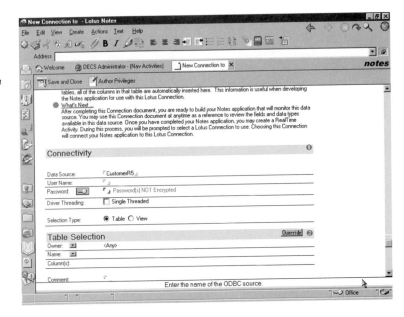

The first field is the data source that defines the name for the ODBC connection that was created in ODBC administration. If the application you are accessing requires a user-name and password, these are entered in the next two fields. They must be entered here because you will not have a way for the user of the Notes application to be able to enter them.

There is a button to enable encryption on the password field by using an encryption key. Setting up an encryption key is not covered in this chapter.

Next, you need to select the type of data, either table or view, from the external data source. You are using a table.

The section for table selection is next. If you want to use this connection to access multiple tables, nothing needs to be entered in this section, you specify the table you want to use when creating the Activity. However, if this connection is only available for one table, you can specify that table here. You leave this blank, so that I can demonstrate selecting the table within the Activity itself. When you select the table you want to use, the column names appear in the column fields. You can see how this works in Figure 35.4, which shows the `Custmain` table.

FIGURE 35.4

The columns available from the Custmain *table are automatically added to the connection document when the table is chosen.*

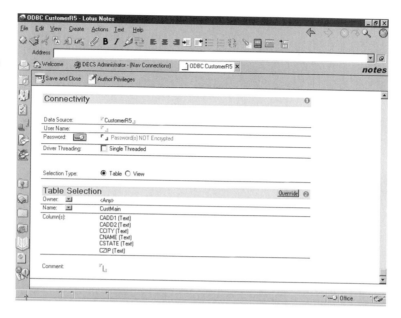

Creating the Activity

Activities define what happens when the connection is made to the external data source. Activities can be created to retrieve information from a data source and populate a field in a Domino Database or can take the data in a Domino database field and update the back-end data source. In other words, an activity defines the relationship between the Domino application and the data source.

So, now you are ready to create an activity. When Create Activity is chosen from the Navigator pane, the activity form appears, as shown in Figure 35.5. The dialog box that pops up appears every time you create a new activity, unless you turn off the User Assistant from the Navigator pane. To turn it off, click the check mark next to the User Assistant label. If you want to turn it back on, simply click in the same spot where the check mark used to be.

After closing the dialog box, another one pops with a list of Notes databases to choose. Select the Cust.nsf database as shown in Figure 35.6.

After you select the Customer database, you get another dialog box that prompts you for the form, or "metadata," that you want to use from the Customer database. Select the CustKey form as shown in Figure 35.7.

FIGURE 35.5

The Creating a RealTime Activity dialog box appears as long as the User Assistant is turned on.

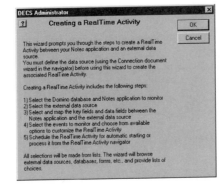

FIGURE 35.6

The Select Domino Database dialog box provides a list of available databases to choose from.

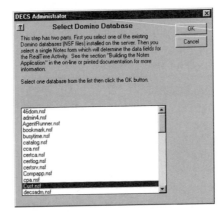

FIGURE 35.7

The Notes Selection dialog box is where you select the form to use in mapping the data.

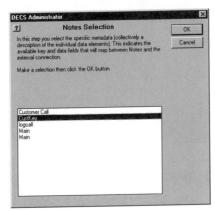

When you select the form, you then get another dialog box that prompts you for the ODBC connection that you will use to connect to the external data source. Select the ODBC Customer R5 data source (or whatever you have named your ODBC connection), as shown in Figure 35.8.

FIGURE 35.8

The Select Connection dialog box lists all the connections that have been created in the DECS Administration database.

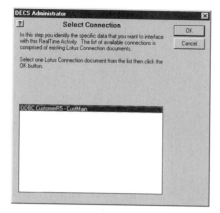

The `Custdata` table is selected as it was defined in the Connection document, so now you're ready to begin mapping fields. From the Key and Data Field Mapping section of the form, select the appropriate fields as indicated in Figure 35.9.

FIGURE 35.9

The Key and Data Field Mapping section shows the fields in each of the data sources and allows you to define how they are mapped.

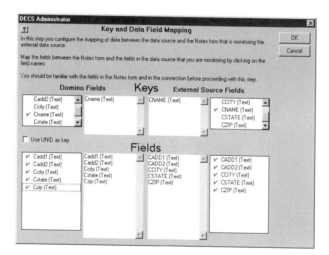

To map the fields, you simply check the field names that you want to use as the key fields, and the fields that you want to be able to access.

Next, there are a few key decisions that you need to make for this activity. The first decision is which events you want to invoke for the application. The available events are listed in Table 35.2. You are going to invoke all the events because you want to be able to both access the external data in the documents and add new and modified data back to the external data source as it is added and changed in Notes.

TABLE 35.2   Events

Event Name	Description
Create	Creates a new record in the external data source when a new document is created in Notes
Open	Populates the Notes document with the data from the external data source
Update	Modifies the data for the record in the external data source when the Notes document changes
Delete	Deletes the record in the external data source when the Notes document is deleted

Next, you have to set up any options that you need to use. By expanding the Options section, as shown in Figure 35.10, you can set the general options and then determine which options to choose for each of the events that you have invoked. You will not change any of the defaults for the available options.

FIGURE 35.10

The expanded options section of the Activity document provides a place to define additional processing that should take place when an event is invoked.

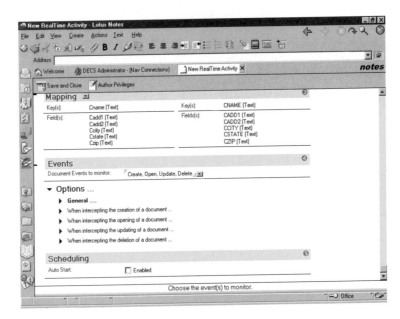

General Options

The general options apply to all the events that have been enabled for the activity. These options are shown in Figure 35.11.

FIGURE 35.11

The general options for an activity are applied to all events.

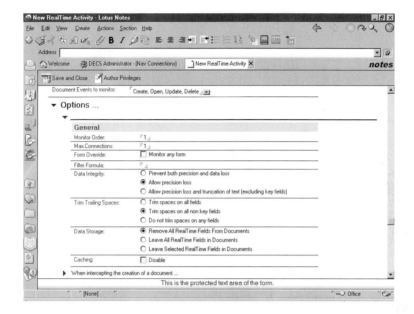

The first option is Monitor Order. This is useful if there are multiple activities running against the same form that have to occur in a specific order to be successful. That is, if you had an activity called B that would need data that was the result of another activity called A, you would set the Monitor Order for activity A to 1 and the Monitor Order for activity B to 2.

The second option is Max. Connections. This determines how many concurrent connections can be made to this data source at one time. A connection transaction occurs very quickly, so you should not have to set this to more than 2 or 3. Many ODBC connections accept only one connection at a time, and with a setting higher than 1, additional users connecting could encounter an error message if there is already a connection established. The third option is Form Override. You specified the form you will use earlier in the Notes Application section of the activity document, and by choosing to override the form you are saying that for all events indicated here, you want to monitor all documents in the database that have the same key field data. For this application, you do not use this option but instead have two separate activities, one for the Customer data that monitors all events and one for the Customer Calls that monitor only the Open event.

The fourth option is Filter Formula, which provides the ability to set a formula to determine a subset of documents in the database to be monitored with this activity. This is useful if there are multiple external databases that should be accessed based on things such as region or business segment, and so on.

The Data Integrity options define what to do in the case of information entered into the application that does not conform to the requirements for the external data source, such as field lengths. Allow Precision Loss is the default.

The Trim Trailing Spaces options define how trailing spaces in the data in the external data source should be handled when it comes into Notes.

The Data Storage options determine whether or not the data that is retrieved from the external data source is actually saved with the document. By default, the data is not saved. The other options are to store all the fields in documents or to select specific fields. So, when do you want to save the data? Save it if you have remote users accessing the application locally, or if the application is on multiple servers and not all servers have DECS running, or if you want to create views that include any of the Realtime fields. The Error Logging option determines where DECS errors are logged and the choices are to log in to a document or to the Notes Log and the Activity log.

The Caching option should be used when there are a lot of changes written back to the external data source.

Document Creation Options

The document creation options a re available only when creating a new document that is written back to the external data source. These options are displayed in Figure 35.12.

FIGURE 35.12

The document creation options in the activity document provide a means for running a stored procedure when the event occurs.

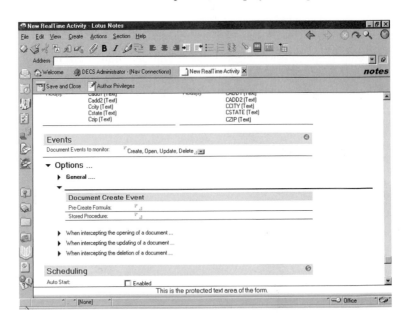

The Pre-Create Formula option provides an opportunity to have a formula run against the document before it is saved in the external data source.

The Stored Procedure option provides an opportunity to run a program that can manipulate the data for the external data source as the data is saved.

Document Open Options

The document open options are available only when opening an existing document and are displayed in Figure 35.13.

FIGURE 35.13

The document open options of the activity document include additional options.

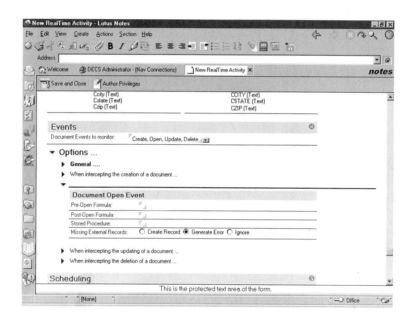

The Post-Open Formula option provides an opportunity to manipulate the data being read into the document from the external data source. This is helpful particularly when you want to parse the data coming in from a specific field to place it in multiple fields in the document.

The Stored Procedure option provides an opportunity to execute a procedure that determines what data is retrieved based on the query.

The Missing External Records option provides an opportunity to have a new record written in the external data source if the key is not found when opening an existing document.

Document Update Options

The document update options are available only when editing an existing document that is written back to the external data source and are displayed in Figure 35.14.

FIGURE 35.14

Document updates can be furthered defined in the Options section of the activity document.

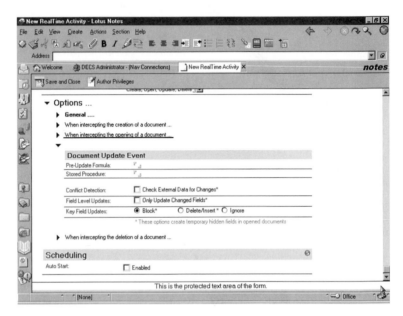

The Pre-Update Formula option runs a formula as specified against the data prior to updating it in the external data source.

The Stored Procedure option provides an opportunity to run a procedure that can manipulate the data for the external data source as the data is saved.

The Conflict Detection option checks to see whether the matching record in the external data source has changed since it was opened. If it has, the update fails.

The Field Level Updates option updates fields in the external data source only if the fields have been edited in the Notes document.

The Key Field Updates option determines how changes to key fields made in the Notes document are handled in the external data source. The first option is to block all key field changes, which means that a key field cannot be changed in Notes or the external data source. The second option is to delete the existing record in the external data source and then insert a new record with the new values, and the last option is to ignore the changes in Notes and do nothing to the record in the external data source.

Document Deletion Options

The document deletion options are available only when deleting an existing document in the external data source and are displayed in Figure 35.15.

FIGURE 35.15

The document deletion options for the activity document only provides additional options for running a stored procedure or formula.

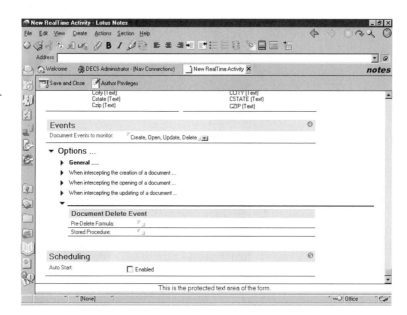

The Pre-Delete Formula option provides an opportunity to specify a formula that is to run prior to deleting the document.

The Stored Procedure option runs a named procedure on the external data source when deleting the record.

Setting Up an Activity Without the User Assistant

In your application, you can retrieve the customer data in the customer documents, and you can also create documents to log calls from customers. In order to create customer calls that also display the customer information that is stored in the external data source, you need to have another activity to support the open activity for the custcall form. So, create this activity without the aid of the User Assistant. First, turn off the User Assistant by clicking on the check mark next to the label in the Navigator pane. The check mark disappears, as shown in Figure 35.16.

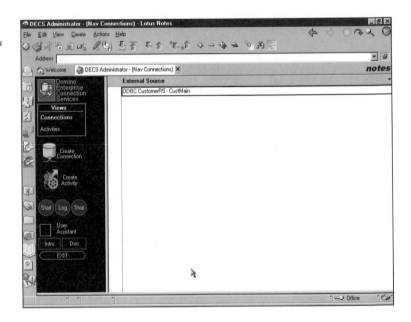

Next, create a new activity and name it CallTrack.

Then choose the button next to the Notes Application label. This brings up the dialog box to select the database to monitor. Choose the Cust.NSF file and click OK. This then invokes the dialog box to select the form to monitor. Choose the Customer Call form and click OK. Your selections should look like the selections in Figure 35.17.

Next, choose the button next to the Lotus Connection. This brings up the dialog box to select the ODBC connection. Choose the ODBC Customer R5 connection (or whatever it is that you have named the connection), and choose OK. This then brings up the dialog box to select the table. Choose the CustMain table. Check Figure 35.17 to be sure you choose the appropriate options.

Next choose the button next to Mapping, and map the fields as shown in Figure 35.17.

Lastly, choose just the Open event to monitor as shown in Figure 35.17.

That's it, you are now ready to set up and test DECS in the application.

Accessing the Application

There are three steps to make the application work after you have the connection and the activities in place.

FIGURE 35.17

The completed Customer Call Activity shows both data sources selected.

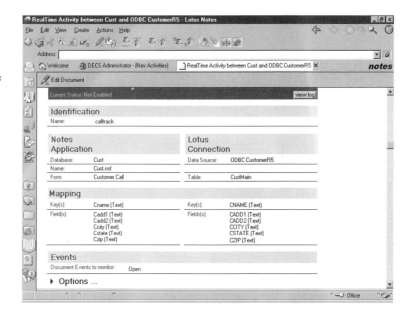

Initializing the Keys

Prior to running the application, the Notes database must be populated with documents that contain the key fields from the back-end database. You do this through the action "Initialize Keys." This action creates a new document (called a "stub" in the DECS documentation) from each of the records in the back-end database. The documents that are created contain the key and the form name by default. If you have specified that you want to monitor all forms in the database, the form name for the documents that are created is the default form for the database.

> ### New Data from the Back-End Source Is Not Refreshed
>
> Keep in mind that new records added to the external database after you have initialized the keys are not added to the Domino database after you have initialized the keys. You have to find another method to do this either through LS:DO or LEI.

Starting the Activity

After the keys are initialized, you can start the activity by selecting the activity in the view and clicking the Start button in the navigator. As long as DECS is running on the server, the activity starts. You can tell that it has started by looking at the activity in the view. The column next to the external source displays an icon indicating that the activity is running, as shown in Figure 35.18.

FIGURE 35.18

The Activity view shows the status of the activities that have been created.

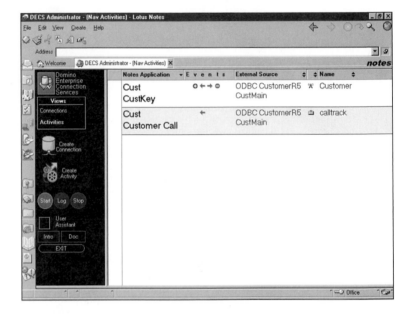

When testing has been completed and the application is ready to deploy, you want the activities associated with the application to be automatically invoked. You can do this by choosing the Auto Start option in the Scheduling section of the Activity document.

Testing the Application

To begin testing the application, you test the Open Event for the activity by opening one of the Customer documents from the view. The address fields should be filled in with the appropriate information. This information is not stored with the document, but it is accessed each time the document is opened. In fact, you can see that the address fields are blank: Select a document in the Customers view, select the Document Properties (by right-clicking on the document and selecting Document Properties), and select the second tab, which is the fields tab, as shown in Figure 35.19.

FIGURE 35.19

If the data from the external data source is not stored in the Notes document, the field contents are blank in the Document Properties.

Next you can test the Create event. In order to do this, choose the New Customer action from the Customers view. Enter a new customer and then save the document. The data is written to the external database.

Now test the Update event. Open one of the existing customers in edit mode and change the address. Save the document and the modifications are saved in the external database.

Last, test the Delete event by deleting one of the existing customers.

When everything is working fine with the customer records, you can test the call records. Here you are merely monitoring the Open event. So, you need to create a new call record, but there is a caveat. Because you are monitoring the open event, it means that when you open a document, the information for the address fields is located in the external database and must be accessed by DECS to populate the document fields. This means that when you create a new document, you have not yet identified the customer name, and, therefore, the address information is not available. In order to get the address information, you have to save the document and reopen it in edit mode when the customer name is chosen. In your application, you have a separate frame that opens the LOGCALL form as a new document. This then allows the user to select a name from the available list of names. From there, the user selects the New Call button which saves the document with a form name of CUSTCALL and then reopens that document in the frame on the right, as shown in Figure 35.20.

After the user enters the call information, she can then choose the Save button, which resaves the document, and at the same time issue a compose command for a new LOGCALL document in the frame on the bottom left of the screen. You do this to avoid overwriting the document you have just created when the user selects a new name.

35

REAL-TIME ACCESS TO ENTERPRISE DATA

FIGURE 35.20

A new customer call document includes the customer information from the back-end data source.

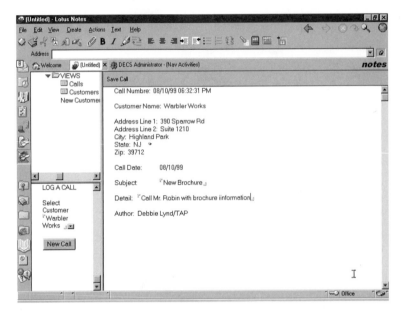

Summary

This chapter provided an overview of DECS and a walk through a sample application of its capabilities. This is a powerful addition to Domino and provides many ways in which integrated applications can be created. The capabilities within DECS coupled with the ability to provide Web based applications in Domino should prove to be a great combination for broadcasting information about company products and legacy information to the Web, without re-creating the data in a secondary application. This chapter should provide a great start to using DECS with your own applications.

NetObjects BeanBuilder

Debbie Lynd

Understanding NetObjects BeanBuilder

NetObjects BeanBuilder started life as Lotus Bean Machine. It was recently acquired by NetObjects and rebranded as BeanBuilder. So, although this is Version 1.0 of Bean Builder, it could really be considered version 2 of Bean Machine. You can download a trial version of Bean Machine from the NetObjects Web site. Bean Machine 1.0 and 1.5 are still available and can be downloaded from Lotus' Web site. Check out the Products category; you'll find it there.

BeanBuilder is a visual authoring tool for creating Java applets without having to write any code. Instead of writing the code, you combine Java Beans into applets. This means that anyone can create an applet for use in a Domino application, or as a stand-alone application. Yes, I said anyone. As long as you can click a mouse, you can connect a button to a video clip, or an URL link, thereby creating an applet that would allow a user to click on your button and run a video or go to another Web page. BeanBuilder takes advantage of JavaBeans, which are Java components that are built by using a specification that was partially defined by Sun Microsystems.

By following the specification, JavaBeans—or, *parts*, as they are known by BeanBuilder—can be assembled by BeanBuilder into a Java applet. BeanBuilder will also use other Java applets or JavaBeans as parts. NetObjects provides a library of these parts, which include animation, buttons, images, sounds, and database connections. In addition, you can import your own parts, or download and import parts from many Java sites on the Web. For some interesting applets (some of which are free), try Java Boutique at `javaboutique.internet.com`.

One of the most powerful aspects of BeanBuilder is its capability to connect to any ODBC-compliant database in order to access data in your applet even from the Web. In addition, BeanBuilder provides wizards to walk you through the process of creating an applet, adding your own parts to BeanBuilder, and publishing your applet.

The applets created by BeanBuilder require a 1.1.4 Java Virtual Machine, so the browser must be IE 4.x, Netscape Navigator 4.x, or Notes 4.6 or better. New features and new beans also are included in this version. The new beans are listed here:

- Math
- Email
- Text Source
- HTML Parameter
- Enhanced database bean that includes a query wizard

This chapter cannot possibly cover everything you can do with BeanBuilder, but it will give you a good idea of how it can be used to spice up a Web page.

Four simple steps are involved in creating an applet using BeanBuilder:

- Select and place parts in the Composer window.
- Define the properties for the parts.
- Define the actions and events that connect the parts.
- Test and publish the applet.

Before we get into creating an applet, you'll need to know how to work with BeanBuilder. First you should know the components of BeanBuilder—in other words, the pieces of the product that you will be using to develop applets.

Working in BeanBuilder

When you create an applet in BeanBuilder, understanding the components of the product is very important to knowing how it works. Five windows that comprise the major areas of developing an applet with BeanBuilder:

- Composer
- Palette
- Details
- Log
- Gallery

Three wizards aid in developing, publishing, and adding new parts to BeanBuilder:

- Applet Wizard
- Publish Wizard
- Bean Wizard

And then there are the parts themselves, which are the reason for everything else!

Understanding Parts

Parts are JavaBeans. You can also think of parts as objects that have properties, actions, and events associated with them. Even the applet itself is considered a part because it is an object that you can manipulate. The properties, actions, and events are different for each of the part types (see Tables 36.1–36.4). For instance, Animation has a loop count property, which specifies how many times the animation should play; the Image Type has a transition property that determines the special effect used in transitioning the image. This is not unlike the different properties, actions, and events in Notes objects.

TABLE 36.1 Parts in the Multimedia Category

Part Icon	Part Name	Part Description
anim.pcx	Animation	Displays sequential .GIF or .JPEG files
audio.pcx	Audio	Provides sound from .AU files
clock.pcx	Clock	Displays a digital or analog clock
image.pcx	Image	Displays a .GIF or .JPEG file
motion.pcx	Motion	Provides a screen in which the motion of an object may be defined
nervous.pcx	Nervous Text	Displays text with the capability to move on the screen
rollover.pcx	Rollover	Displays an image with changes when the mouse is moved across the image
shadowtext.pcx	Shadow Text	Creates a rollover effect on text
Teletype.pcx	Teletype	Displays text one letter at a time, and also provides sound.
Text.pcx	Text	Displays formatted text
Tickertape.pcx	Ticker Tape	Displays scrolling text
timer.pcx	Timer	Is used as a signal, to set the beginning, duration, and/or end of an event

TABLE 36.2 Parts in the Controls Category

Part Icon	Part Name	Part Description
button.pcx	Button	Displays a button that can be clicked by the user
checkbox.pcx	Checkbox	Displays a list of options that can be selected or deselected
choice.pcx	Choice	Provides a drop-down box of choices
label.pcx	Label	Displays a single line of text
list.pcx	List	Displays a list of items that can be selected or deselected

Part Icon	Part Name	Part Description
panel.pcx	Panel	Creates a panel or new display area that can hold other parts
textA.pcx	Text Area	Displays or edits multiple lines of text
text.pcx	Text Field	Displays or edits one line of text

TABLE 36.3 Parts in Networking Category

Part Icon	Part Name	Part Description
db.pcx	Database	Provides JDBC access to a back-end database
email.pcx	Email	Provides a way to send an email message
head.pcx	Headline	Displays a scrolling set of text with URL links associated with each line of text in the set
html.pcx	HTML Parameter	Provides access to the HTML properties of the bean
mail.pcx	Mail Link	Displays the browser's email window
url.pcx	URL Link	Displays a new page in the browser

TABLE 36.4 Parts in Accessories Category

Part Icon	Part Name	Part Description
Bool.pcx	Boolean Evaluation	Test for true/false conditions
Math.pcx	Math	Provides the capability to perform mathematical calculations
Num.pcx	Numeric Evaluation	Performs analysis of numeric values
Text Source	Text Source	Provides access to the text in a file

Parts are selected through the Palette window. The properties, actions, and events for parts are controlled through the Details window.

Using the Composer

The Composer is the main window that is displayed when you launch BeanBuilder. Within the Composer window is the area that displays the layout of the parts chosen to run in the applet being composed, as shown in Figure 36.1.

FIGURE 36.1

*The Applet Layout
Region, where all
parts are placed
within the
Composer
Window.*

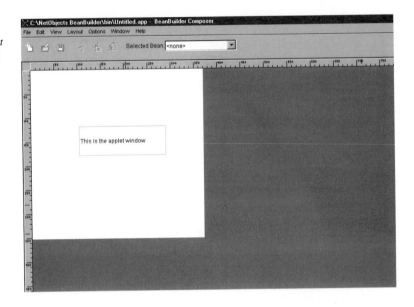

The available parts are grouped into one of four categories. The first category is multimedia, which includes animation, images, and generally anything that moves. The second category, controls, includes those parts that would cause another action or that would provide user input such as buttons, checkboxes, text, and fields. The third category, networking, handles database access and links to URLs and headlines that provide access to multiple URLs. The fourth category is accessories. This category covers Boolean and numeric evaluations, math, and text sources. You can add your own categories when you add parts to the palette. (Adding parts to the palette is covered later in this chapter.) If you choose to add the parts that Lotus has placed on its Web site, you will find that the category Enhanced Parts has been added to your palette. Work in the Composer can be automated through the use of the Applet Wizard, or you can place parts in the Composer manually. Before you can place parts, however, you need to understand what they are.

Understanding the Palette Window

From the palette, you select the parts that you want to put in the Composer window. After you place the parts, you can move them around in the palette, as shown in Figure 36.2. You will also be able to size most parts after they are placed. The drop-down box enables you to pick the category of parts.

FIGURE 36.2

Parts are listed under Categories.

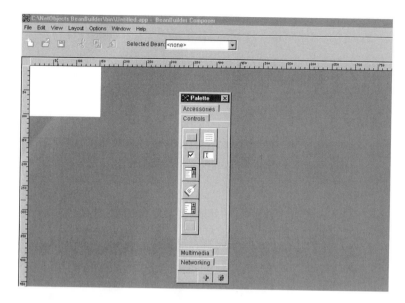

After you select a category, choose one of the parts in that category by clicking on the part icon. The icon will appear to be indented, with a thick border around it, as shown in Figure 36.3.

FIGURE 36.3

The palette with the Audio part selected appears to be indented.

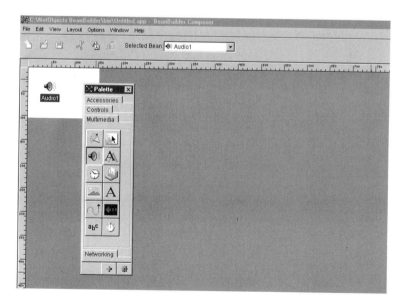

To place the part, click in the Composer window, and the part will appear. The size of the part is set to the default size for the part you have chosen.

Sizing a Part

If the part is resizable, you will see handles on the part that you can then click and drag to size the part in your applet, as shown in Figure 36.4.

FIGURE 36.4

An image part with handles in the Composer window.

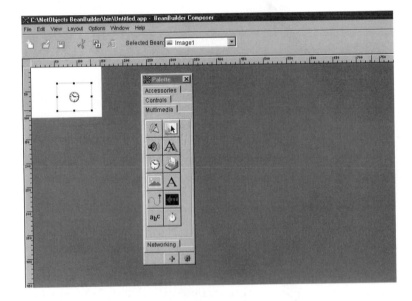

You can also return to the default size (which is called the preferred size in BeanBuilder), by choosing the Preferred Size from the layout option in the menu. This is shown in Figure 36.5.

> **Set the Size of a Part in the Details Window**
>
> You can also set the size, or return to the preferred size of a part, in the size and position property of the Properties tab in the Detail window.

After you have placed some parts in the Composer, you will want to adjust the layout of those parts by moving them around the Composer screen, sizing them, and setting the layout property of the applet. We have already discussed sizing, so now it's on to selecting and adjusting the layout.

36

NETOBJECTS
BEANBUILDER

FIGURE 36.5

Layout menu option.

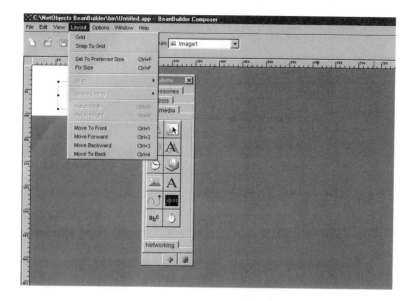

Selecting and Moving Parts

To move the part, just click inside the part to select it and drag it to the new location. You can move multiple parts by clicking on a part and then holding the Shift key while clicking on the next part that you wish to select. This is depicted in Figure 36.6.

FIGURE 36.6

Selecting multiple parts.

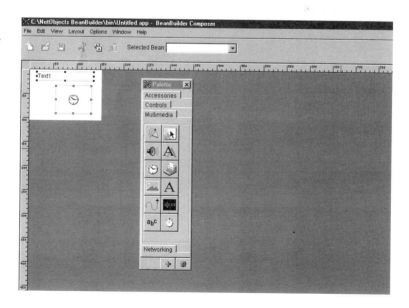

Select a Part from the Main Menu

You can also select a part by choosing the part name from the Selected Part drop-down list on the main toolbar.

Setting the Layout Property for the Applet

The Layout property of the applet provides four ways in which the applet can be displayed from a browser, as shown in Figure 36.7.

- Position
- Flow
- Gridbag
- Border

FIGURE 36.7

Layout properties for an applet are set in the Details window.

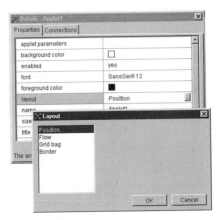

The default is Position, which means that the parts will be displayed exactly where you place them. The border layout partitions the applet canvas into distinct sections consisting of four quadrants and a center section. When you select the border layout, the applet canvas displays drop guides to indicate the various sections, as shown in Figure 36.8.

The flowed layout aligns the parts horizontally or vertically. In doing so, it prevents a part from being cut off in a browser that does not provide the necessary screen width, by causing the parts to flow from row to row, filling the space. See Figure 36.9.

FIGURE 36.8

The border layout displays guides for the sections.

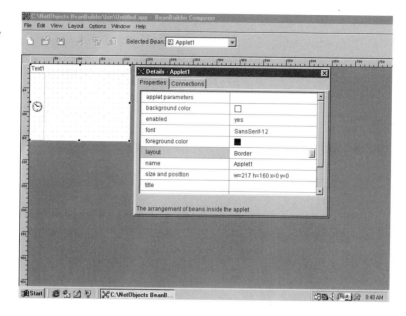

FIGURE 36.9

The flow layout options are either horizontal or vertical.

The default size of the drop guides for the border and flow layouts is 40 pixels. You can change the default size in the Composer tab of the Preferences dialog box, which is chosen from the Options menu, Preferences option.

Setting the Details

The Details window is where the properties and connections are set for a defined part, as shown in Figure 36.10. The properties are the attributes for the part, while the connections are the events and actions triggered by those events. A part must be selected in the Composer window to use the Details window. After an applet is created, the Details window is instrumental in defining the properties and the actions that will run based on the events.

FIGURE **36.10**

*Properties for a
part are set in the
Details window.*

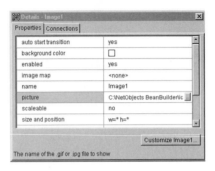

Using the Other Windows

Besides the Composer palette and the Details windows, you will use three additional
windows when creating an applet. These are the Gallery, Log, and Java windows. The
Gallery is where you can select images to place in the Composer. The Log window displays errors that are logged during testing, and the Java window is where you can import
or write Java code.

Working in the Gallery Window

The Gallery window displays thumbnails of available .GIFS and .JPEGs that are contained in a selected directory, as shown in Figure 36.11. The directory can be on any
available drive, including a network drive. Thumbnails in the Gallery can be selected and
dropped onto the Composer to create a part in an applet.

FIGURE **36.11**

*Images, both ani-
mated and single,
can be previewed
from the Gallery
by clicking on
the bottom-right
corner of the
thumbnail.*

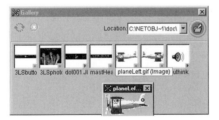

Viewing the Log Window

In the Log window, errors are recorded. The types of errors that you will find here are
compile errors for Java methods you may write, as well as general errors that may occur
when running an applet from BeanBuilder. These errors can occur by having the wrong
settings for a part that then causes the applet to malfunction.

Coding in the Java Window

The Java window is where you write Java methods that you can include in the applet, as shown in Figure 36.12. The methods that you write are available through connections as actions. You can also modify Java that you have imported from within this window.

FIGURE 36.12

The Java window is where you can write Java to add to the applet.

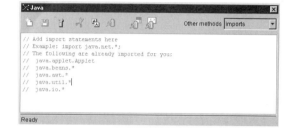

Creating an Applet with the Applet Wizard

The Applet Wizard is a great way to start using BeanBuilder by walking you through the steps necessary to create an applet in a matter of minutes (see Figure 36.13). You can also define an external database to be displayed in either free form or tabular style. After you have begun to work with the Palette and Details windows, you will find that you will no longer need the wizard.

FIGURE 36.13

When working with the Applet Wizard, only one part can be chosen for each of the tabs in the wizard. Other parts can be added manually after the wizard is finished.

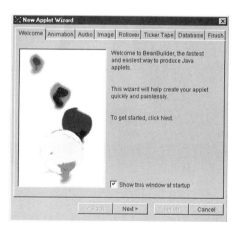

Creating a New Applet with the Wizard

By default, the wizard automatically appears when you start BeanBuilder. By following the directions and moving through tabbed pages, you define which parts you will use and how they should behave. With the exception of the Database tab, all the parts that you add with the wizard are multimedia parts.

Working in the Animation Tab

In this tab, you select the beginning file of the .GIF or .JPEG series you wish to use. You then define how fast the animation should run, as shown in Figure 36.14. The choices are slow, medium, or fast, which identifies the number of frames per second (slow being 1 frame per second, medium being 5 frames per second, and fast being 15 frames per second). These can be adjusted manually through the Details window after the wizard has finished. The speed of the animation is only one of the many properties that can be manually set in the Details window. Animations also have events that can be set to cause actions to happen when the event is triggered. The Details window, events, and properties will all be covered later in this chapter.

FIGURE 36.14

After selecting the speed, it is a good idea to preview the animation.

Working in the Audio Tab

The Audio tab enables you to select an .AU file that should play in the applet, as shown in Figure 36.15. By default, the audio part will be placed outside the applet space in the Composer and will be set to start automatically, but not to loop. Where the audio part is placed does not matter because it is not seen, only heard. No events are associated with audio parts, and the only properties they have are the filename, the title of the part, whether it is auto-started, and whether it loops. If you don't want the audio to start when the applet is invoked, you will have to set a connection through the Details window.

FIGURE 36.15

You can also preview the sound from the Audio tab.

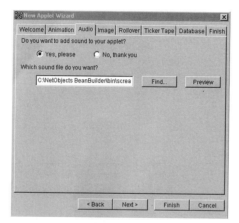

Working in the Image Tab

From the Image tab, you select a file to use for the image, and you also select a transitional effect for the image, much like you would set in a Freelance or PowerPoint presentation (see Figure 36.16). By default, the transition will start automatically, and the speed will be set to fast.

FIGURE 36.16

You can choose from the available transitional effects or create your own effects.

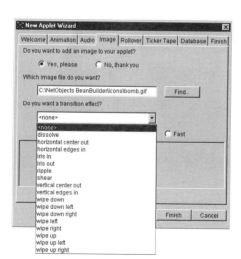

Creating your own transitional effects can be done with any image editing tool that has the capability to apply gradients to the image.

Working in the Rollover Tab

The Rollover tab is where you can select an image to display as a button, and then select alternative images to display when the mouse is moved over the button and when the button is pressed (see Figure 36.17). Of course, you will probably want to initiate more than an image change when the button is pressed, but you'll have to wait to do that after the wizard is finished.

FIGURE 36.17

Rollover buttons are easy to create by selecting different images in the wizard.

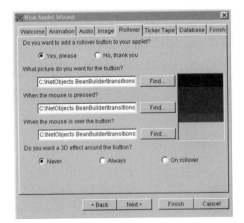

Working in the Tickertape Tab

The Tickertape text that you choose can be typed into the wizard, or you can select a text file. Selecting a text file gives you the flexibility of changing the text that is displayed by changing the text in the text file. All you have to do is tell the wizard how often to check the file. It's important to note that you can also use an URL to point to the file, instead of the file path of the text file.

Defining a Database to Use

In the Database tab, you can define what information you would like displayed from a database and how it is displayed. To access the data, you need to create an ODBC, DB2, or other supported connection so that the applet will know how to find the data.

Modifying an Applet

After you have created an applet with the wizard, you will probably want to add parts or modify properties, and set actions to correspond with events. The properties, actions, and events that are available for a part will depend on the purpose of that part. For instance, all parts that move will have an auto-start property that determines whether the movement occurs when the applet is first run. Not all parts have events associated with them; most events occur when there is mouse movement around the part. Some events, however, occur because of the nature of the part, as in the transition-ended event for the Image part. This list notes which parts do not have events associated with them:

- Audio
- Label
- Mail Link
- URL Link
- HTML Parameters

Most events are caused by the movement of the mouse, but a few events occur outside the user's control.

The wizard does not give you the opportunity to choose any of the Control parts. However, you will probably want to use them in your applets because they enable user input and provide the capability to create multiple display screens that can be hidden or shown at the click of a mouse.

Working with the Palette

The Palette window is used to add parts to the composer, as shown in Figure 36.18. If the Palette window is not already open, open it by choosing Palette from the Tools menu.

The parts available in the Controls category can be used to elicit a response from the user.

Changing the Properties Through the Details Window

With the Details window open and a part selected, all the properties for that part are exposed. The properties can be changed directly from the Details screen.

FIGURE 36.18

*The Controls cate-
gory contains
parts to elicit
response.*

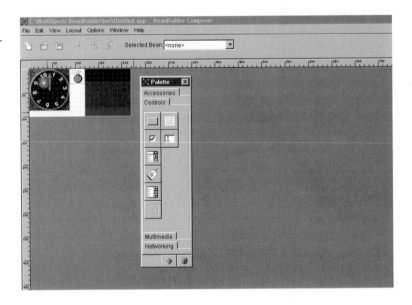

The Connections Wizard

When setting up connections, we are talking about connections between beans, triggered by events. Any part that has events associated with it can have connections to other parts or to itself. The connection that is made can be to an action or to a property in that part. For my application, I want to set connections from a button to the Animation bean I placed earlier. If you haven't been following along but would like to set this up, make sure that you have the following beans in the applet window.

Place the following beans in the Applet area.

TickerTape

For this bean, set the following properties:

Text: `The pressure is building.....Too Slowly!!!.....Speed it up!!!!!`

Button

For this bean, set the following properties:

Label: `SPEED UP`

Name: `Speedbutton`

NervousText

For this bean, set the following properties:

Text: `Too Fast! You must stop it!!!`

Visible: `No`

Button

For this bean, set the following properties:

Label: `PANIC`

Name: `Panicbutton`

Visible: `No`

Animation

For this bean, set the following properties:

First picture: `C:\NetObjects BeanBuilder\samples\animation\gauge01.gif`

The way these beans are set in my application, the Speed Up button will display while the gauge runs on slow and the tickertape displays the text. Next, I'll create connections from the `Speedbutton` to the Animation speed property to make the gauge run faster, and then we'll create another connection to hide the `Speedbutton` and make the Panic button and the NervousText visible. Then I'll create a connection from the Panicbutton to the Animation to stop the animation.

Now, I'll open the Connections Wizard and set up the first connection. After one connection is made, the rest are pretty obvious, so I'll step through only the first one.

1. Open the Details window.
2. Select the Connection tab.
3. Choose the button on the right of the Connections window to invoke the Connections Wizard.
4. For the Source bean, choose the Speedbutton.
5. In the What Happens tab, choose Clicked.
6. For the target bean, choose Automation.
7. In the Do This tab, choose Set Frames per Second.
8. In the Property Parameters tab, choose the Set Value button, and set the value to 10.
9. Set the rest of the connection for the Speed button.

That's it! Now it's time to test the applet.

Testing the Applet

Testing is actually quite simple. Just choose File Run from the menu (or press Ctrl+R, if you prefer the keyboard), and your applet will be compiled and displayed in the applet viewer, as shown in Figure 36.19.

FIGURE 36.19

The applet viewer enables you to test the applet.

You may have an applet that you are working on but not ready to publish. Saving it and coming back to it later would be a good thing. So, if I want to save my Pressuregauge applet prior to publishing, I can choose File, Save As from the menu, choose the directory I wish to save it in, and give it a name. That's all there is to it. The file is saved with an extension of APP, which is the file type of an applet prior to publishing.

Now, what if somebody gives me a cool bean and I want to incorporate that into my applet? Actually, I can use a tool called the Bean Wizard to add the class or the .JAR file to the beans available to me in BeanBuilder.

Using the Bean Wizard

The Bean Wizard provides a way to customize the palette, by adding new categories and parts to the palette. In this section, we walk through the addition of a part to the palette, and then I'll address making changes to a part. Figure 36.20 displays the Welcome tab of the Bean Wizard

FIGURE 36.20

The Welcome tab of the Bean Wizard.

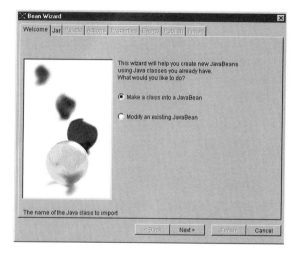

Adding Parts to the Palette

You can add your own JavaBeans and applets to the Palette. The question is, are you adding a bean (which is just a Java class), or do you want to add a .jar (which is all the files required to run an applet packed into one file)? If you are adding a class, the class needs to be stored in a folder that is in your classpath, or the wizard will not be capable of finding it. When BeanBuilder is installed, your classpath is modified to include the Bean folder under the BeanBuilder folder; the easiest way to handle the class files that you want to add is to place them in the Beans folder.

Starting the Wizard and Choosing a Class File

To begin working with the Bean Wizard, choose Options from the menu, followed by Bean Wizard. This displays the Bean Wizard tabbed dialog boxes, as shown in Figure 36.21. There are nine tabs in the wizard, some of which will be grayed out.

As you make choices, additional tabs may become available. Any tabs that are grayed out means that they are unavailable for use due to the choices that you have made.

BeanBuilder includes a few Java class files for you to play with. One of these is Fireworks, which is automatically stored in your Beans folder (see Figure 36.22). On the Welcome screen of the Bean Wizard, select the Add a Java Class radio button, and type in Fireworks for the class filename; then choose the Next button at the bottom of the screen.

BeanBuilder will read the file before moving on and will let you know if it can't find the filename you have given. After the file is read, you will then go to the Palette tab.

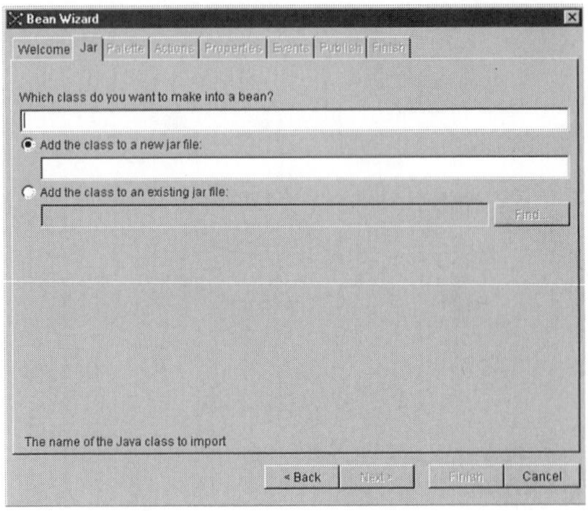

FIGURE 36.21

The tabs in Bean Wizard may not all be available.

FIGURE 36.22

Fireworks is the name of the class we will add to the palette.

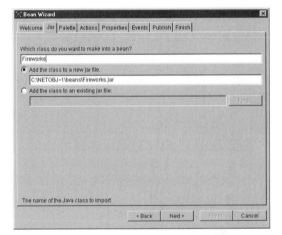

Class Files Become .JARs

When you add a new part from a class file, BeanBuilder automatically creates a .JAR file for that class.

Choosing Settings in the Palette Tab

In the Palette tab, I've selected the name I want displayed on the palette for this part, a description of the part, and which category I want the part listed under, as shown in Figure 36.23. On the left, I have chosen the icon I would like to display for this part in the palette.

The last option on the Palette tab is a checkbox labeled Part Accepts Children. This determines whether this part can have other parts placed inside it. For instance, the panel is a part that accepts children. If I am using a Panel part, I might put a button, some text, and a headline on that panel. The next tab that I will work with is the Applet tab.

FIGURE 36.23

The Palette tab is where you define the part for the palette.

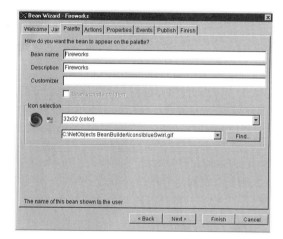

The Applet Tab

The Applet tab enables you to enter applet parameters. This modifies the applet parameter property and works the same way that it does in the Details window.

The Actions, Properties, and Events tabs enable you to define the actions, properties, and events to use in this applet. The choices made will make the selections available to the details window in BeanBuilder. These are covered more fully later in this chapter. The Actions tab is shown in Figure 36.24. For now, we'll skip the options.

FIGURE 36.24

The Actions tab.

The Publish Tab

When the Publish tab is selected, all the files currently in the .JAR file that is to be publish are displayed. At this point, I can modify the contents of the .JAR file by adding, renaming, or removing classes and files. All files that are required to run an applet must be checked before publishing your .JAR, or your bean may not run properly.

The Finish Tab

This is the last stop before your part is converted to a .JAR file, as shown in Figure 36.25. When you select Finish, the .JAR file is created in the Beans folder, and the new part will be available the next time you start BeanBuilder.

FIGURE 36.25

The Finish tab is the last stop in creating a new part.

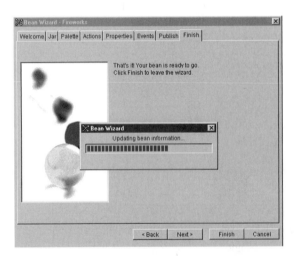

Making a Part Available in the Palette

You must restart BeanBuilder after adding a part for the part to appear in the palette.

Adding a Bean from a .JAR

If I already have a .JAR file, I can add it to the parts in the palette. Adding a part from a .JAR is a quick two-step process:

1. Select the name of the .JAR file from the drop-down list in the Welcome screen.
2. Choose Finish from the Finish tab.

Try this on your own, using the BlinkingText.JAR that comes with BeanBuilder.

Modifying Parts

Any part that has been added to the palette, or any of BeanBuilder's base parts, can be modified. From the Welcome screen of the Bean Wizard, if you choose Modify an Existing JavaBean, you can then choose from the list of available parts. After you've chosen the part you want to change, it's time to move on to the Palette tab. Based on the type of part you modify, you will either see the Applet tab grayed out or the Actions, Properties, and Events tab grayed out. So, if the part is not an applet, the Applet tab will be grayed out. However, even if the part is an applet, you can still set the Actions, Properties, and Events by selecting the Enable Advanced Applet settings from the Applet tab.

For demonstration purposes, I will modify the Fireworks part that we added in the last section.

All the settings in the Palette tab can be modified. If you want to change the category or the icon for the part, you can do so on this screen.

> **Caution**
>
> Before modifying any part, make a copy of it so that you can return to the original if you completely mess up the modification.

The Actions Tab

The Actions tab contains a list of all the available actions or methods on the left side of the page in a scrollable window. Any action that you want to use when making a connection in the Details window should be checked. Those actions that are not checked will not be available.

In Figure 36.26, I have set the actions for use in connections.

The Name and Description fields displayed in Figure 36.26 are where you can give the action a name other than the name displayed in the methods list. The name in this field will override the given name of the action in the Connections tab of the Detail window. The Description field provides a place to define the description that should display in the status line of the Actions tab when the action is highlighted.

If the action accepts parameters, they can be entered in the Parameters field and can be assigned a name in the Name field under the Parameters field.

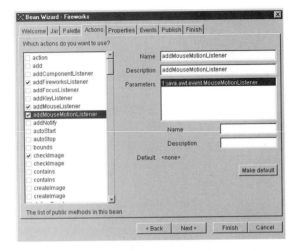

FIGURE 36.26

Actions are selected in the Actions tab by checking them.

Defining a Default Action

The Make Default button defines a selected action as the default action that is displayed in the Connections window for this part. If you select an action in the list and click the Make Default button, the action will display in bold type.

The Properties Tab

The Properties tab looks very similar to the Actions tab and provides a similar function, in that all properties checked in the properties list are available in the Properties tab of the Details window in BeanBuilder. This is shown in Figure 36.27.

The Name and Description fields also provide the same functionality for properties as they do for Actions.

For each of the properties selected, the Get and Set methods should be selected. These can be selected from their associated drop-down lists, as shown in Figure 36.28.

The description field and the Make Default button provide the same functionality for properties as they do for actions. The Properties tab also contains two additional checkboxes. The Visible in the Properties tab and Visible in the Connections tab determine whether the property is available in the respective tabs. Some properties should not have connections associated with them because they do not have the capability to change state. These properties should not be visible in the Connections tab. The Font property is an example of one of these properties.

FIGURE 36.27

*The Properties tab
governs selection
of properties that
will be used.*

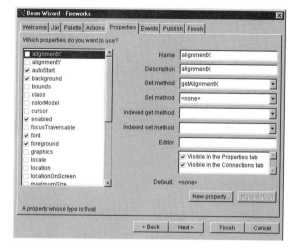

FIGURE 36.28

*Select the Get
Method from the
drop-down list.*

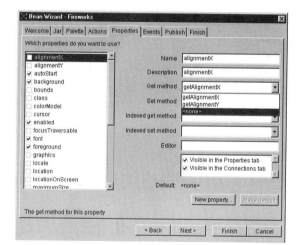

The Events Tab

The Events tab provides the same functionality as both the Action tab and the Properties tab. For each of the events that are checked, a name and description can be entered and a default event can be selected, as shown in Figure 36.29.

Saving and Testing the Changes

When the part is completely modified, choose the Finish button from the Finish menu. The modifications will be saved, and the modified part will be available.

Before using the part in an actual applet, it is a good idea to test it to be sure it works.

FIGURE 36.29

*The Events tab
is where the
events that you
want to use can be
selected.*

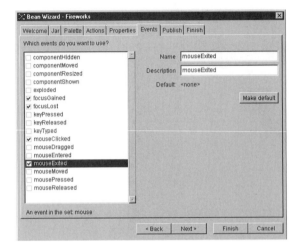

> **Using a Modified Part in an Existing Applet[sh box]**
>
> Modifying a part will not apply that part to any existing applications that you
> may have published. To modify an existing application so that it will accept the
> changed part, you will have to open the application for editing in BeanBuilder,
> make any necessary changes to the properties and connections for that part,
> and republish the applet.

Publishing an Applet for Use with Domino

Right now, our applet can be run only in BeanBuilder. To make it available to a Web
page, we will have to compile, or publish, the applet. To publish an applet, you will use
the Publish Wizard in BeanBuilder. This process puts all the .class files and media files
in a .jar file, creates an HTML file with the code necessary to call your applet, and places
it all in a directory on the local machine or a Web server.

When you publish the applet, you can put it on your local hard drive and move it later to
another machine if you wish, or you can choose to publish it as a NetObjects Fusion
component (nfx) and later add it to the Fusion palette.

After it's published, the applet can be added to your application.

Using the Publish Wizard

To publish, choose the File Publish option from the menu. This brings up the Publish Wizard, which walks you through publishing your applet (see Figure 36.30).

FIGURE 36.30

The Publish Wizard Welcome screen walks you through publishing an applet.

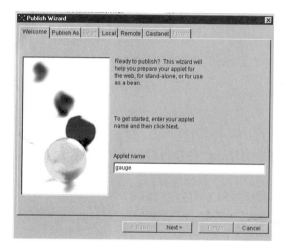

After naming the applet on the first screen and choosing Next, the Local, Remote, and Castanet screens provide the place to choose where your applet will be published.

Castanet Is an ADM Product

Castanet is a software product that falls under the Application Distribution and Management (ADM) category. This software controls the distribution of applications and services over corporate intranets, extranets, and the Internet. The company that makes Castanet is Marimba (www.marimba.com).

When you choose to publish locally, you also have the option of publishing a NetObjects Fusion component. NetObjects Fusion is a Web development tool that provides a consistent look and feel for a site. More information about this product can be found at the Web site www.netobjects.com.

In any case, when you publish your applet, there are two steps:

1. Naming the applet
2. Specifying where to publish the applet (see Figure 36.31).

FIGURE 36.31

The Local tab of the Publish Wizard is where the location of the applet is specified.

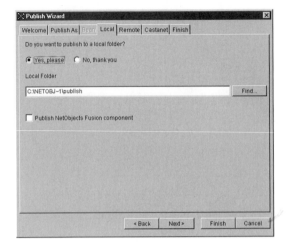

Using the Applet in Domino

Okay, so now we have an applet that resides on the file system somewhere. Now we want to run that applet in a Domino application. To do so, we need a database, and we need a form to put the applet on. Because I do not have a database to work with, I will create a new database using the Notes & Web Discussion template for Release 5. The form that I will use to hold my applet will be the Main Topic form. There is a spot to place the applet right below the header area and above the content area, as you can see in Figure 36.32.

FIGURE 36.32

The MainTopic form in the discussion database will reference the applet created.

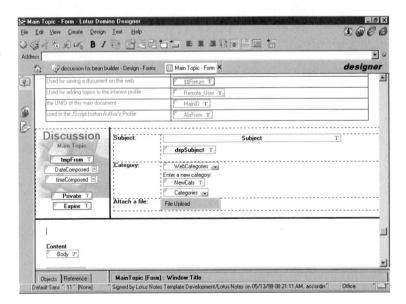

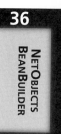
Position the cursor on the form above this text, and choose CreateJava Applet from the menu (see Figure 36.33).

FIGURE 36.33

The Create Java Applet dialog box is where applets are defined.

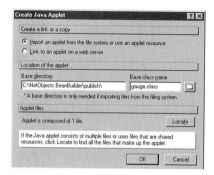

Because a Java applet may consist of multiple files, you should use the Locate button to find all the files associated with your applet.

The applet is then added to the form, and the Applet Parameters screen appears in the design pane. We will come back to this screen in the next section. If you select the Java Applet Properties for the Java Applet menu options, you can then set all the properties for your applet.

Maintaining the Applet

If I'm going to use an applet in a Domino application, I expect to be able to pass parameters to my applet from Domino. And, of course, I need to pass parameters back to my Domino application from my applet.

Passing parameters to my applet will require a line of code in Java, but it's not a big deal.

Two steps are involved in enabling the parameter passing from Domino to the applet:

1. Set up the applet to accept the parameters to pass.
2. Set the values for those parameters in Domino.

Set Up the Applet

This is where we need to write code to let the applet know what parameters it should be looking for. The Java window in BeanBuilder is where we need to write the code, as indicated in Figure 36.34.

FIGURE 36.34

The Java window is used to write methods for use in your applet.

This is not a tutorial on Java—that is covered later in this book. This is just a set of steps to provide you with the information you need to pass parameters without having to learn Java. We will write a method that contains the code to tell the applet the name of the parameter to pass from the Domino application and what part to put it in when it gets to the applet. I am going to use the Nervous text part of my applet as the part to accept the text. Then I will be able to change the text that displays in the Nervous Text part, by changing the contents of a field in the form that contains the part.

To create the Java method for passing the text and posting it to the Notes document, use the following steps:

1. Open the Java Window.

2. Click on New Method.

3. Replace the words New Method with `getdomparms`.

4. Type the next line exactly as you see it in Figure 36.35. Java is case-sensitive.

    What the `nervous_text1.settext(getParameter("parm1"))` code tells the applet is to pass the HTML value called "parm1" to the setText property of the text part.

5. Save the method.

6. Next, make a connection from the applet to the method just created so that it will actually get the text. This means that when the applet begins running, we want to invoke the method.

7. In the Details window, choose the applet part and set a connection to the `getdomparms` method when the applet is started. The code for this method is shown in Figure 36.35.

Setting Up the Parameters in Domino

To send the appropriate text, we will have to create a place to store the text. In this case, we'll just create an editable field on the same Main Topic form on which we placed the applet. This field will then contain the text that we would like displayed, and we can change it whenever we wish (see Figure 36.36).

FIGURE 36.35

The code that is needed for the getdomparms method.

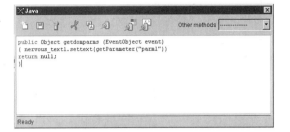

```
public Object getdomparms (EventObject event)
{ nervous_text1.settext(getParameter("parm1"))
return null;
}
```

FIGURE 36.36

The way the Main Topic form appears with Ntext field added.

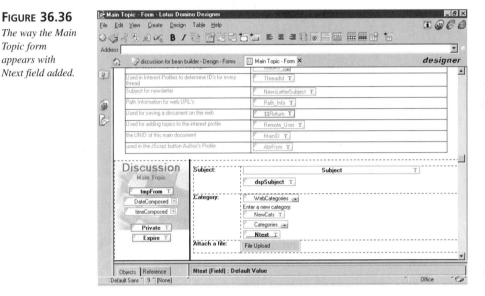

Then we will have to inform the applet that we have a parameter to pass, and we'll give it the name of the field as the parameter. The following list explains the steps to do this:

1. Open the Main Topic form in design mode, and place the cursor at the bottom of the form.

2. Create a text field, and name it Ntext.

3. Highlight the applet placed on the form earlier, and open the Programmers pane to expose the applet parameters.

4. Choose the Add button, and type in the parameter name we chose in the applet, TapeTest.

5. In the parameter value, type in the name of the field you just placed, Ntext.

Applet Parameters Can Be Set in Multiple Places

The applet parameters can be set from the Design pane in Domino or from the Applet Parameters property in the Details window within BeanBuilder, as shown in Figure 36.37.

FIGURE 36.37

Changes can be made to the Applet parameters dialog box within the Details window in BeanBuilder

That's it! You should now test this by previewing the form in a browser. Make sure you have the ACL set for browser access.

From what we've done, you can probably see many ways in which parameter passing can be a way to make some really cool applets do interesting things. For instance, I could create a form that stores a daily phrase and populate a view with a document for each day of the week using the daily phrase form. I could then set up a formula as the parameter value that selects the daily phrase from the view based on the day of the month.

Because we could use a Notes formula as the parameter value and in that way send information from a column in a view, or information based on a condition, this now gives you the ability to set up an applet that has information fed to it by the user or based on the user's responses.

Summary

BeanBuilder can be used quite effectively by anyone who would like to build an applet without having to learn Java. To create an applet, parts must be placed in the Composer window, and properties and connections between parts must be set in the Details window.

The parts that are used to compose an applet can be another applet, a Java class file, or a .JAR file. These parts can be modified to include or exclude the actions, properties, and events available for the part in the Details window of BeanBuilder.

Lotus Components

by Steve Kern

CHAPTER 37

This chapter presents a survey of Lotus Components, which are reusable software applets that can be embedded in your Domino applications and documents. These applets can be customized, and the custom versions distributed to users. This chapter also covers the distribution application, the Product Warehouse that ships with version 1.3 of Lotus Components.

Introducing Lotus Components

As mentioned in Chapter 1, "Introducing Lotus Notes and Domino," Lotus Components are small, fast, reusable software applets based on ActiveX technology. Because they run only on 32-bit Windows platforms, they are not available for older versions of Windows or other operating systems. Components also do not run in Web browsers. The release of eSuite, a suite of production applets which is basically Components written in Java, has supplanted Lotus Components. Because eSuite is written in Java, it does run in Web browsers. Version 1.3 of Components, due out in the first half of 1999, will be the last version of Components.

> **Caution**
>
> Earlier versions of Components, including version 1.2, are incompatible with Notes R5. If you use Components and upgrade to R5, you must upgrade to Components 1.3. As of this writing, if you use Components 1.2, the entire Components Palette menu is grayed out in R5, and many of the components either do not work at all or behave unpredictably.

Although Components only works in the 32-bit Windows world, Components has some great features, and is still worth exploring and using. Today, most corporate Intranets are based on Windows 32-bit technology, so this is not a significant limitation. You can consider using Components under the following conditions:

- The users' workstations are NT, Windows 95, or Windows 98.
- You need to quickly create small, fast, reusable applets.
- You want to go beyond the functionality of a standard Notes and Domino application.
- You don't need to support Web clients.

Most people probably use less than 25 percent of the power of a typical office suite application. Realistically, they don't need all the power and sophistication. Lotus Components answers this need by replacing full-blown applications with scaled down applets. For example, the spreadsheet applet in Components is not as full-featured as Lotus 1-2-3 or Excel, but it also doesn't require anywhere near the amount of disk space. It also provides all the functionality that a typical user requires.

The entire suite of six applets requires less than 15MB. Compare that to the 120+ MB of disk space that a typical office suite uses. What you're seeing is a migration away from the huge and ever-growing office application suites. This migration has continued with the introduction of eSuite in the spring of 1998.

Another significant advantage of Lotus Components is that you don't have to launch another application to complete your work. You can do it all in Notes! Lotus Components provides a pull-down menu that can be used to insert an applet into a document, or you can use the Create, Object menu choice. Application developers can add a component to a form in a Domino database.

Don't Have Components?

Don't worry; other users can view your work without installing Components. They won't be able to interact with the object without installing Components, but they can read and print a document containing a Component.

Components are purchased and licensed separately from Lotus Notes, and are installed on each user's workstation as a separate product. Components has an application that can be used to track licensing (this is discussed later in this chapter in the section titled "The Product Warehouse"). There is also a set of demo applets in the Product Manager database, which are not covered in this chapter.

What's New in Lotus Components 1.3?

The principal focus of release 1.3 is to ensure Year 2000 compliance and compatibility with Notes and Domino R5. In order to achieve Year 2000 compliance, any component saved in 1.3 format will not be readable by earlier versions. Users can still view the component, but cannot edit it.

Although this is the last release of Components, there are some additions and changes:

- An Uninstaller has been added that enables you to uninstall Components or Templates separately through the Windows Settings applet, Add/Remove Programs.

continues

37

LOTUS COMPONENTS

- Because R5 switched viewing technologies from Inso Outside-In to Verity Key View, the File Viewer supports both.
- A new LotusScript method was added to the Draw/Diagram component that supports polyline objects.

Understanding the Six Component Types

Lotus Components consists of the following six applets, in order of appearance on the Lotus Components menu:

- **Chart**—Usually used in conjunction with the Spreadsheet component to produce charts of your data.
- **Comment**—Like an electronic sticky note, but with some interesting twists.
- **Draw/Diagram**—Used to create drawings, flow charts, and so on.
- **File Viewer**—Allows a wide variety of different file types to be viewed.
- **Project Scheduler**—Provides the capability to schedule tasks and set up dependencies, milestones, and so on. The display is a standard Gantt chart.
- **Spreadsheet**—A scaled-down version of the familiar Lotus 1-2-3.

Each component is customizable and supports Notes FX/2.0 data-exchange technology. Components are also accessible to developers via LotusScript.

Components can be added to forms when they are designed, or added to rich-text fields in a document. Components can also be added programmatically through LotusScript.

Each component has its own toolbar, menus, and Properties boxes. Each component also has extensive built-in help for end users and programmers.

When a Component is added to a rich-text field, a new set of SmartIcons, a component-specific menu, and an Applet menu appear. A new Help menu replaces the Notes client Help menu for the Component.

The Chart Component

The Chart Component (see Figure 37.1) can display many different styles of charts. Charts can be based on data entered specifically for the chart or it can display data in a linked Spreadsheet component. To enter data manually for a chart, either choose Chart, Edit Data from the menu or right-click the Chart Component and choose Edit Data from the floating menu that appears. The Chart Properties box has a lot of detail that enables users to set many different properties, including Chart Type, Footnote, Title Position, font, and many more. This component does nearly everything its more sophisticated cousins in 1-2-3 and other spreadsheets do.

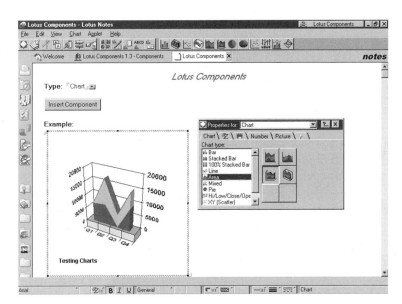

The Chart component is most useful when linked to a Spreadsheet component. Creating a link to a Spreadsheet component is very easy, as the following steps reveal:

1. Create the Spreadsheet component and add some data. Add a Chart component.

2. Highlight the data range you want to chart. Rest the pointer on the border of the selected data range.

3. When the pointer changes to a hand, drag it to the chart. The Chart component does the rest!

As easy as 1-2-3!

Sorry, couldn't resist. Figure 37.2 shows the Edit window for the Chart component's data.

The Comment Component

The Comment component (see Figure 37.3) is unique because it has security properties built into it. Authors of a Comment component can control who has access to the compo-nent and at what level. Comments can also be printed without printing the entire document in which they live. At first, I didn't see much practical use to these electronic sticky notes, but they can be useful in some circumstances. In a project notebook, they can be used to identify changes to a version or to attach a commentary to a document. Using the Comment component like this keeps the comment discrete from the underlying document. Comments can be minimized so that they appear as a small icon of the same size and a similar appearance to a doclink.

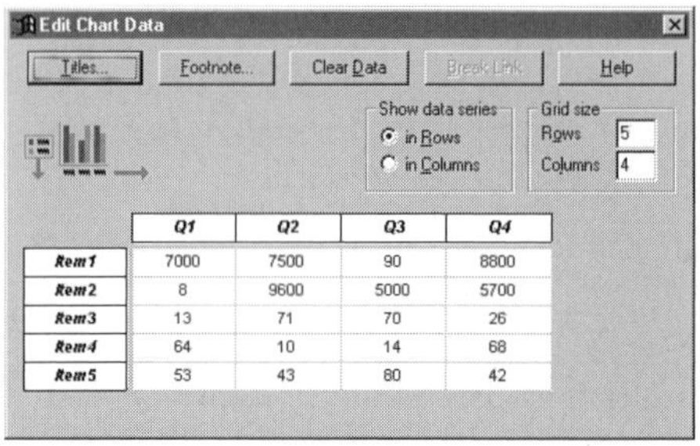

FIGURE 37.2

Editing the Chart component's data is done through the Edit Chart Data window.

FIGURE 37.3

The Comment component Properties box is open to the Security tab.

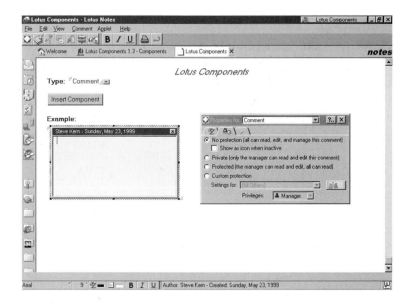

Comments have the same security levels as Notes except for a designer access level; in effect, these applets have built-in ACLs. A comment cannot be copied from one document and opened in another, which also protects the contents of comments. You can set security for a comment as long as you have manager access to the comment.

To set the security for a comment, open the Comment Properties box and switch to the Security tab. Choose the option you want to set from the following options:

- **No Protection**—Everyone can read, edit, and manage the comment.
- **Private**—Only the manager can read and edit the comment.
- **Protected**—The manager can read and edit the comment; all others can read it.
- **Custom Protection**—Enables you to specify individuals and access levels (see Figure 37.4).

FIGURE 37.4

The Comment Security tab has its own security list.

Adding Users to the Comment Component

You can add a user to the Comment component by clicking the button to the right of the Settings For drop-down list. The dialog box does not access the Domino Directory, unfortunately, so you have to enter names manually.

The Draw/Diagram Component

Creating a drawing or diagram with the Draw/Diagram component is somewhat clumsy compared with a more sophisticated drawing tool, such as Visio (see Figure 37.5). When you get used to it, however, it does its job reasonably well. You can choose from a set of canned diagrams and artwork or create your own. The Draw/Diagram Component comes with drawing tools, flowchart connectors, shapes with text, and so on.

When you add a Draw/Diagram component, you can choose from a predefined set of images. You can add clip art and diagrams. The clip art is somewhat limited in quantity as shipped. However, additional clip art files (`.SYM`) can be added to the `C:\Lotus Components\draw` folder. They are then accessible from the Clip Art dialog box.

The drawing pallet shown in Figure 37.5 enables you to draw objects such as rectangles and decision diamonds, and connect them with a wide variety of different connectors. Text can be added to the objects just as in any standard art package, such as Freelance Graphics or Visio.

FIGURE 37.5

This Draw/Diagram component uses a hub-and-spoke diagram—note the floating drawing pallet.

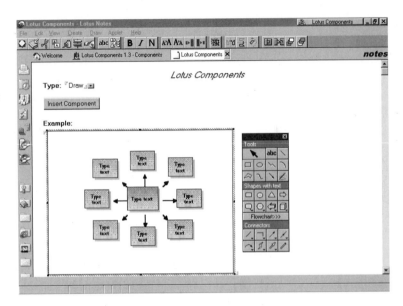

The File Viewer

When you create an object with the File Viewer component, you are prompted to locate a file to insert (see Figure 37.6). The file viewer displays files of virtually any popular type, ranging from plain-text files to graphics, spreadsheets, word processing files, and many more. This is an enhancement from a simple file attachment.

FIGURE 37.6

The File Viewer Component prompts you to add a file with a standard Windows file dialog box.

With a standard Notes file attachment, you have to either launch the application or view the attachment. If the user doesn't have the application associated with the file and the file can't be viewed, he is out of luck. With the File Viewer component, the document is displayed more or less in its native format within your document. Figure 37.7 shows a graphic presentation file containing clip art for the Draw/Diagram Component.

FIGURE 37.7

This clip art file is displayed with the File Viewer component.

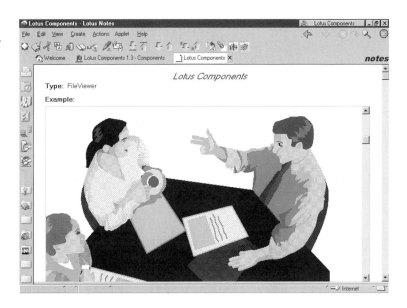

The Project Scheduler Component

The Project Scheduler component is a very versatile and useful component (see Figure 37.8). It has most of the features needed to manage projects, although it is not as sophisticated as some full-version project schedulers. Adding tasks, creating dependencies, configuring resources, and so on are all available and reasonably easy to use. If you have ever used a project-scheduling package, you will no doubt pick this one up quickly. Many users find its simplicity very appealing, having sweated through some of the more "sophisticated" full versions. The project scheduler can import Microsoft Project files.

Entering Tasks into the Project Scheduler is very easy:

1. Position the cursor on a row in the Tasks column.

2. Enter the name of the task and press the Tab key to move to the start date column. A button appears that produces a calendar display when clicked. Choose a date or accept the default date.

3. Enter the duration of the task. The default is in days, but it can be changed to hours in Preferences. (Project Scheduler, Preferences from the menu. See Figure 37.9.)

4. To demote task, which inserts it underneath the task immediately above, click the Demote Task SmartIcon or choose Project Scheduler, Demote Task.

FIGURE 37.8

The Project Scheduler component is easy to use.

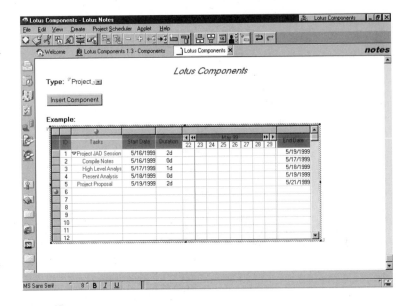

FIGURE 37.9

To change global settings, use the Preferences dialog box.

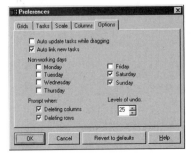

The Project Scheduler presents a standard project Gantt Chart. The Gantt chart is customizable in several ways. You can customize global settings in the Preferences window (see Figure 37.9). You can also customize the appearance of each column through the Properties box.

New columns can be added to the component. The default scheduler contains columns for the row ID, Task, Start Date, Duration, Timeline scale, and End Date. In addition to the default columns, you can add the following column types:

- Planned Start
- Actual Start
- Actual End
- Task Notes

- Percent Complete
- Actual Duration

As a developer, you can customize this small, powerful applet so that it matches your company's approach to project management. You can add columns such as Percent Complete and Actual Duration to a template and distribute the template or embed it in a database form. If your company uses a specific project methodology with a series of ordered steps, you can add them to the template as tasks. This enables you to enforce a degree of standardization to project management. When a user creates a project based on your template, they will see the standard project outline, to which they can add tasks specific to their project.

Cool Tool!

Marin Research (www.marinres.com) has an application that uses the Project Scheduler Component called Project Gateway. The Scheduler is used to create an initial outline for a project, which is then "published." When a project is published, LotusScript is used to extract the tasks and create Notes documents. The tasks are then assigned, and the status of each task is tracked. Notifications of pending tasks, overdue tasks, and soon can be sent automatically.

The Spreadsheet Component

I don't think much needs to be said about creating and using spreadsheets. I doubt you'd be reading a book about application development without having used 1-2-3, Excel, or another spreadsheet application. Figure 37.10 shows a Spreadsheet Component embedded in a form. This component can be used to create very sophisticated spreadsheets with relative ease. As with the other components, Properties boxes are available for nearly every conceivable aspect of a spreadsheet. The menu and SmartIcons provide access to many powerful functions, and help is extensive for both users and application developers. Figure 37.11 shows the help available for the Spreadsheet Component. It is standard Windows help, with Contents, Index, and Find tabs.

Developers can easily customize the Spreadsheet Component for many different uses. As you undoubtedly know, a spreadsheet is ideal for summing columns of numbers. You can create templates for entering expenses, mileage, order forms, sales summaries, forecasts, and so on.

FIGURE 37.10

You can customize the presentation of the spreadsheet applet using the Show tab of the Lotus Spreadsheet Properties box.

FIGURE 37.11

Extensive help is available for Lotus Components in a standard Windows Modal help window.

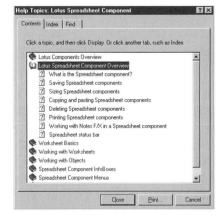

Subtables in Notes?

One source of frustration for many developers who have migrated from the relational world into Notes is the lack of subtables. Well, here they are! Add a Spreadsheet component, and you have a mini-table within a document that can be accessed programmatically—even down to the cell level with Notes/FX.

Using traditional Domino development techniques to create an order form, you're limited in what you can do. Sure, you can create a table on a form and populate it with fields such as `nQuantity1` and `nCost1`—or better yet, to ease typing, `nQty3` and `nQty4`. That gets old, and isn't very flexible. Plus, summing and extending all those fields is very tedious programmatically. A spreadsheet is certainly a better solution. Create a customized Spreadsheet template, embed it in a form, and then create the Notes/FX links to fields in the underlying document.

Using Notes FX

Notes/FX (Notes Field Exchange) technology enables you to exchange information between a Component and fields in the underlying document. For example, if you create a spreadsheet template for mileage reporting, you can use Notes/FX to capture the total mileage and amount due in the underlying document. Exchanging field information is done on the Notes/FX tab, identifiable by the lightning bolt, and is available for each Component (see Figure 37.12).

FIGURE 37.12

The Notes/FX tab allows easy exchange of information between the Spreadsheet Component and the underlying document.

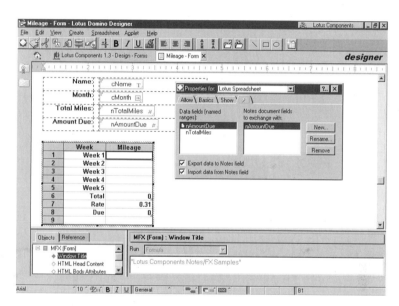

On the CD

A simple application called Lotus Components 1.3 (chapt41.nsf) is included on the CD-ROM that you can use to experiment with components. Of course, you'll need to have Components first; you can find out about getting them from the Lotus Web site: http://www.lotus.com. This application enables you to choose the component type from a keyword field and adds the component to the rich-text field when you click the Insert Component button. There is also a form titled Mileage that uses a Spreadsheet Component to exchange information with a Notes document.

It is very easy to exchange information between documents and components with the Properties box. In the database for this chapter is a form titled Mileage. This form includes a spreadsheet that totals the mileage entered for each week, and calculates the dollar amount due to the user. The Spreadsheet Component has two named cells, nTotalMiles and nAmountDue, for the total miles traveled and the dollar amount due. Fields of the same name exist on the form. You don't have to use the same names to exchange information, but it is easier than trying to guess which field belongs to which named range.

Exchanging Information with a Spreadsheet

To create a form with an embedded spreadsheet, as in this example, take the following steps:

1. Create a new database, if necessary, and create a new form.

2. Title the form, and add fields to capture any information necessary, such as user-name and date.

3. Add the fields you will use to exchange information with the spreadsheet. Name them appropriately, set them to the correct data type (most likely, numeric for this example), and set them to Computed.

4. From the Components menu, select Spreadsheet.

5. In the embedded spreadsheet, enter the rows and columns necessary for your application.

Adding Column Headers

You can quickly enter titles for columns or rows by double-clicking the column or row header. In the dialog box, enter the text for the header. This replaces the column letters and row numbers.

Now that you have a spreadsheet created in a form, you are ready to set up Field Exchange. First, you have to choose and name the cells with which you will exchange the information, and then link them to the document fields. To use Field Exchange with the spreadsheet, use the following steps:

1. Select a cell that will exchange information with the form, and open the Range Properties box. Name the cell appropriately in the Range Name field on the Basics tab (see Figure 37.13).

2. Name any other cells that will exchange information with the underlying document.

3. Switch to the Properties box for the Spreadsheet Component, and select the Field Exchange tab (the one with the lightning bolt).

4. Select one of the Data fields (named ranges). Click the New button, and enter the name of a form field (see Figure 37.14).

5. Deselect Import data from Notes field, if appropriate (for this application, it is not appropriate to import data from Notes, so you should deselect it).

6. Repeat the process for any other fields you want to exchange.

7. Save and close the form.

Figure 37.13

You name a cell by first selecting it in the Spreadsheet Component and then naming it in the Range Name field.

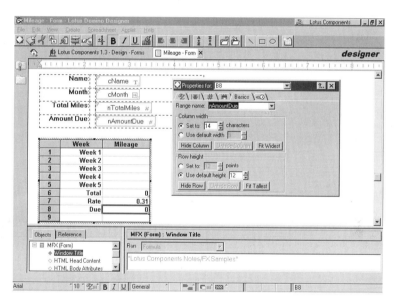

After you've set up field exchange between the spreadsheet and the form, you can test it to see how it functions. As you enter mileage into the spreadsheet, the cells that total the mileage and calculate the amount due change. At the same time, the fields in the document will reflect the changes (see Figure 37.15). Cells that are named and are set up for Notes/FX have a small square box in the lower right corner of the cell.

FIGURE 37.14

To set up Field Exchange, enter the field name into the Notes FX Field Name dialog box.

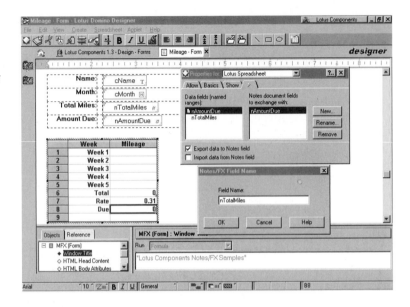

FIGURE 37.15

Information flows from the spreadsheet directly to the underlying Notes document as it is entered into the cells of the spreadsheet.

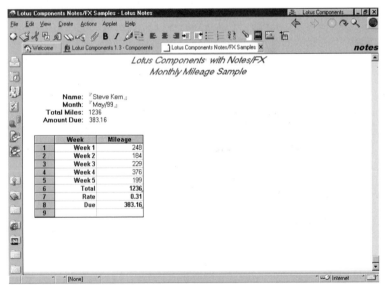

Importing Data from Notes Fields

You can also set up a field exchange to flow from a document to a Component. Perhaps your company only pays you the difference between the miles you travel selling products, and the miles to the company offices. In other words, if you travel 100 miles in a day, and it is 10 miles to the office, you are paid for 90 miles. You first add a field to capture the number of office miles. Next, add a second field to capture the number of days traveled. You then capture this information in the spreadsheet and use it to calculate the total mileage.

To set up this exchange, you follow the same basic procedure that you used for the `nAmountDue` and `nTotalMiles` fields. However, you want this exchange to occur in the opposite direction—from the document to the component. On the Notes/FX tab, deselect Export data to Notes field and make sure that Import data from Notes field is selected (see Figure 37.16).

Figure 37.16

You set information to flow from the Notes document to the spreadsheet by selecting Import data from Notes field.

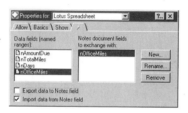

The database contains a form titled Mileage 2, which has a spreadsheet with field exchange set up so that the information entered by the user for office miles and days traveled flows into the spreadsheet (see Figure 37.17).

Figure 37.17

This revision of the mileage spreadsheet correctly calculates the amount due, taking office mileage and days traveled into account.

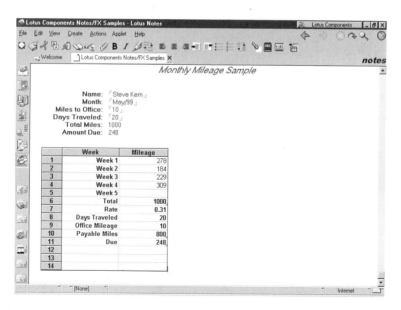

> **Caution**
>
> Spreadsheet Components can only import information from text fields. When information is sent from a spreadsheet to a document, it is always exported as text.

Exchanging Information Bidirectionally

As you may have guessed, you can also set up Notes/FX to exchange information in both directions. To do this, simply leave both the Export data to Notes field and Import data to Notes field checked. This is the default behavior.

Using Notes/FX with Other Components

This is impressive technology! The field exchange technology incorporated into this release of Components is very powerful and has great potential, as long as you can develop for 32-bit Windows clients only. The example here described its use with a spreadsheet, but each type of Component can exchange information with a Notes document:

- **Chart**—You can exchange chart data fields with Notes document fields.
- **Comment**—You can exchange data with four fixed fields: Editor, Edited Date, Created Date, and Contents.
- **Draw/Diagram**—You can exchange text data on a Notes form with text blocks and text shapes in the Draw/Diagram Component.
- **File Viewer**—You can exchange information only from the File Viewer object to Notes. You can export three fields: File Name, File Size, and File Type.
- **Project Scheduler**—There is extensive support for Notes/FX in this Component. The Project Scheduler even has its own Notes/FX Setup window. Information can be exchanged between specific tasks, task data fields, and fields in the Notes document.
- **Spreadsheet**—You can set up the exchange of data between fields in a Notes document and named ranges in a Spreadsheet Component.

Integrating Components into Your Applications

You can insert components into your applications in the following three ways:

- Directly in a form when the form is in design
- Into a rich-text field in a Notes document
- Programmatically inserted into a rich-text field using LotusScript

Adding Components to Forms

The two Mileage forms discussed previously illustrated the technique you use to add a Spreadsheet Component. You use the same technique to add the other Components. To add a Component to a form, simply position the cursor where you want the Component to live and choose the appropriate Component from the Components menu. Figure 37.18 shows a form in design with a Project Scheduler component.

FIGURE 37.18

This form has a Project Scheduler embedded in it; note the Notes/FX set up dialog box.

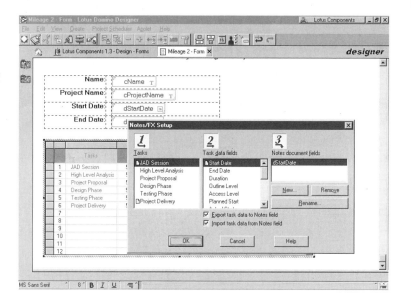

Adding Components to Rich-Text Fields

Enabling users to add a component to your applications is also easy. Simply include a rich-text field and give Components to the users. Users can then add Components to documents to their hearts' content. Have no fear that users will try to add a Component to the wrong sort of field, because the Components menu is disabled unless the cursor is positioned in a rich-text field.

Although this method certainly works—and you cannot prevent users from adding components in this manner—most likely you will want to exercise some control over the process. This leads us to programmatically inserting components.

Using LotusScript to Insert Components

You can use LotusScript to insert and control components. In the sample application discussed in this chapter, LotusScript is used to dynamically insert a component based on the choice made in a keyword field.

To insert a component using LotusScript, use the `CreateObject` method of the `NotesUIDocument` class. Figure 37.19 shows the Components form in design; the following LotusScript is attached to the button:

```
Sub Click(Source As Button)
        Dim ws As New NotesUIWorkspace
        Dim uidoc As NotesUIDocument
        Dim doc As NotesDocument
        Dim jcComp As String
        Dim jcExecute As String

        Set uidoc = ws.CurrentDocument
        Set doc = uidoc.Document


        'Set jcComp equal to the keyword field value
        jcComp = doc.cComponentType(0)

        'Build the string to insert the component
        jcExecute = "Lotus." + jcComp + ".1"
        uidoc.GotoField("rtExample")
        Set rtExample = uidoc.CreateObject("rtExample", jcExecute)


End Sub
```

If you don't understand the preceding script, don't worry; there are three chapters in Part III, "Domino Programming Languages," about programming with LotusScript. Table 37.1 contains the arguments for the `CreateObject` method.

The syntax for this method is the following:

```
CreateObject("<rich text field>"; ComponentObject).
```

FIGURE 37.19

The Components form uses LotusScript in the click event of the Insert Component button.

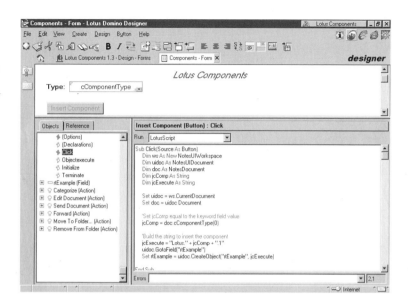

37

TABLE 37.1 Creating Components with Script

Component	CreateObject *Argument*
Chart	Lotus.Chart.1
Comment	Lotus.Comment.1
Draw/Diagram	Lotus.Draw.1
File Viewer	Lotus.FileViewer.1
Project Scheduler	Lotus.Project.1
Spreadsheet	Lotus.Spreadsheet.1

Each Component has its own classes built into LotusScript. Table 37.2 lists the LotusScript classes for the components.

TABLE 37.2 LotusScript Classes for Components

Component	*Class*
Chart	Ltschart
Comment	Ltscomment
Draw/Diagram	Ltsdraw
File Viewer	Ltsfileviewer
Project Scheduler	Ltsproject
Spreadsheet	Ltssheet

Each class has numerous methods and properties, in fact, too numerous to elaborate on here. As an example of the extensive amount of support for LotusScript, see Figure 37.20.

FIGURE 37.20

The Reference tab in the Programmer's pane lists the methods for the Ltssheet *class.*

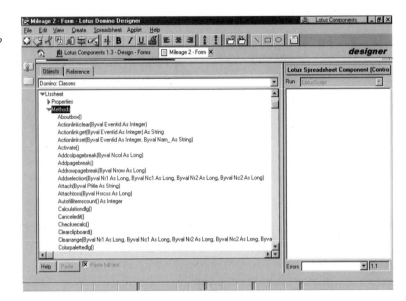

Customizing Components with the Template Builder

The Template Builder comes with Lotus Components. You use the Template Builder to create customized versions of applets. When you choose Template Builder from the Components menu, you are presented with a blank sheet from which you can open an existing template or create a new one.

Opening an existing template requires that you have one installed. Components 1.3 ships with a database called Product Warehouse that contains the six component applets plus three customized templates. To install one of the templates from the Product Warehouse, follow these steps:

1. Open the Product Warehouse.

2. Choose a template to install—for example, the Marketing Plan template (see Figure 37.21).

3. Click the Install Now button. You will see a progress bar as the template is installed, and then a confirmation box is displayed.

FIGURE 37.21

Installing a Template Component from the Product Warehouse Template form is done with a simple click of a button.

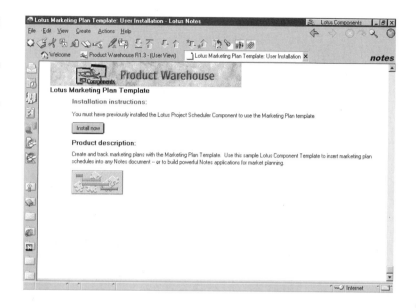

To open the template in the Template Builder, choose Template Builder from the Components menu. Next, click the Open an Existing Component template SmartIcon or choose File, Open Template from the menu. From the dialog box, choose a template (see Figure 37.22).

FIGURE 37.22

The Expense Report template is based on the Spreadsheet component—note the Quick Help window.

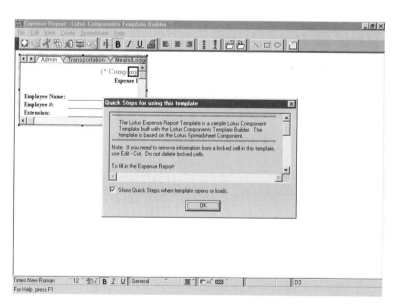

A template can be treated just like a component. End users can embed it in a rich-text field or it can be included in forms you design. You can even access it programmatically via LotusScript. Existing templates can be modified and saved under a new name.

To create a new template, follow these steps:

1. Click the Create a Component template SmartIcon or choose File, New Template.

2. In the dialog box, choose a component to use as a basis for the new template. Click OK.

3. Modify the component to suit your purposes. See Figure 37.23, which shows a Project Management template being designed.

FIGURE 37.23

This Project Management template is intended for software design.

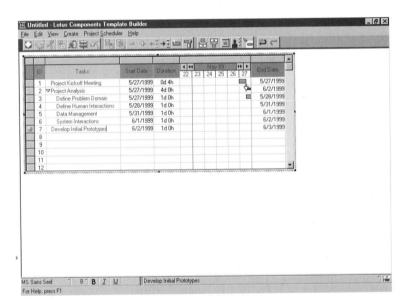

4. Choose File, Save from the menu. The Save As Template window shown in Figure 37.24 appears.

5. Enter a name in the Descriptive Name field. The Template Builder enters the same characters in the LotusScript name field but without spaces.

6. Enter any help text you want to have displayed in the Enter Quick Steps dialog box. If you want this text to be displayed when the component is opened, click the Show Quick Steps field.

7. If you want to lock the template to keep users from changing its properties, click the Lock Template checkbox. If you click the Lock Template checkbox, you must supply a password.

8. Choose File, Close from the menu, and the new template is available.

FIGURE 37.24

The Save as Template dialog box enables you to name the template and add help text.

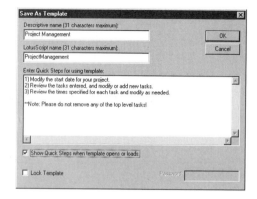

Distributing Templates

The act of creating a template makes it available on your local machine; in fact, it is even stored in the Windows Registry. However, it is not yet available to others and, you might want to distribute it. If it is necessary to make it available to other users, you can do so by creating a distribution pack for the template.

Templates cannot be distributed like a Domino database or Domino design template. You cannot copy a template to another machine and make it available. The way to distribute your templates to others is to use a distribution pack, which is an executable file that can then be sent to other users. When you create a distribution pack, you can choose which templates are included. Note that the user must have Components installed ; at a minimum she must have the component on which the template is based. To create a distribution pack, follow these steps:

1. Choose Create Distribution Pack from the File menu.
2. Choose the template(s) you want to distribute and either confirm or change the name in the dialog box (see Figure 37.25).
3. Click OK.

FIGURE 37.25

The Create Distribution Pack window enables you to choose the templates to include in the installation file.

When the Distribution Pack is completed, a confirmation window is displayed. You can then send this to other Notes users. After installation, you can use and install the template just as you would any other component. To use the new template, you must add it to the Component menu. To do so, use the following steps:

1. Choose Customize Palette from the Components menu.

2. You can add submenus and separators by clicking the Add Submenu and Add Separator buttons, respectively.

3. Add the new template to the Components menu by clicking the template and dragging it to the desired location (see Figure 37.26).

4. Click OK to close the Customize Component Palette window.

FIGURE 37.26

Customizing the Component Menu enables you to add newly installed templates to the Component menu.

Caution

The Components menu is a not something an administrator or a developer can control. Customizing the menu is solely in the hands of the end users.

Using the Product Warehouse

The Product Warehouse ships with Lotus Components (versions 1.1 and above), and it provides a method of cataloging and distributing components and custom templates. The Product Warehouse has three custom templates included: the Lotus Expense Report Template, the Lotus Marketing Plan Template, and the Lotus Time Sheet Template. You can add and distribute additional templates as well.

Setting up the Product Warehouse is relatively simple: Replicate the Product Warehouse from the CD to a local drive, modify the ACL to suit your organization, and replicate it to a server. Instructions on how to modify the ACL are included in the "About this database" document.

When you open the Warehouse, it opens to a User view (see Figure 37.27). This view lists the available templates and Lotus Components. Each is stored in its own document. Users can install them on their local workstation by opening the document and clicking the Install Now button (see Figure 37.21). Installation of a template from the Warehouse was described earlier in this section.

FIGURE 37.27

The User view of the Product Warehouse contains documents that enable users to install Components and Templates.

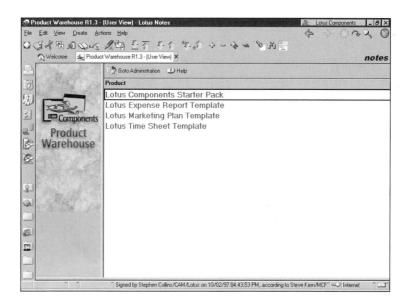

Administration views are also available. Click the Goto Administration button. Figure 37.28 shows the available Administration views. These views track products and licenses. To add a new template, such as the one created earlier in this chapter, use the following steps:

1. Click the Product Administration button.

2. In the Product Administration\By Product view, click the Add New Product button. In the form that appears, enter the name of the template and a brief description.

3. If you have a picture file, embed it in the Picture field. Click Template in the Product Type field.

4. Attach the distribution file (in this case, `Project Management.exe`) using File, Attach from the menu. The distribution file is stored in the `c:\Lotus Components\Runtime` folder (see Figure 37.29).

FIGURE **37.28**

*The
Administration
views navigator
provides access to
the Administration
views.*

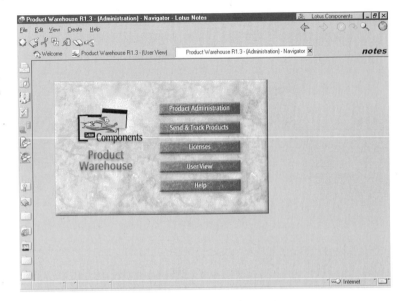

FIGURE **37.29**

*The top portion of
the New Product
form has fields to
describe the tem-
plate, attach a
related image,
and embed the
distribution pack.*

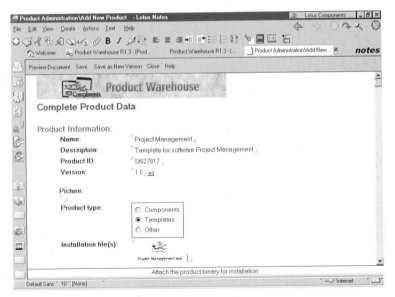

5. Under Installation Information, you can limit who can install the template from the
   Product Access keyword field. Clicking the Entry Helper button brings up the
   Address Book dialog box from which you can choose users or groups.

6. Enter installation instructions in the Instructions field and the name of the template in the Command Line field. You can leave the licensing information as is or modify it to suit your needs (see Figure 37.30).

FIGURE 37.30

The bottom half of the New Product form contains installation and licensing information.

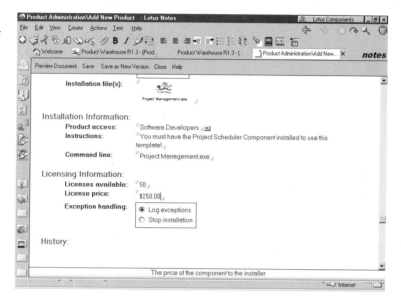

7. Click Save. If you want to preview your document, click the Preview button. When you are finished, click Close. Figure 37.31 shows the finished document.

FIGURE 37.31

The completed Project Management template document is ready for installation.

37

LOTUS
COMPONENTS

The new template now appears in the User view. As you can see from this very short tour of the Product Warehouse, it is an extremely useful application. If you are going to use components, you should definitely consider using the Product Warehouse. It is more than a convenient way of delivering both Components and templates to your users. It also lets you specify a number of licenses for each component, and tracks the number licenses in use. You might have noticed the Send & Track Products button in Figure 37.28. Clicking this button opens a view with actions that enable an administrator to send a specific template or all templates to a user or group of users. Several tracking views are available for administrators to see how many licenses were distributed and when and to whom they were distributed.

Summary

Despite requiring the 32-bit Windows OS, Components are indeed a useful tool. Components are very small, powerful, and easily customizable. Plus, you can access virtually anything about a component with LotusScript and exchange data between Components and Domino database fields with Notes/FX. These features make components worth a very close look if your site supports the technology, and you don't need to support Web clients. Components can literally save hundreds of hours of programming and often provide much more flexible solutions to business problems than traditional Notes application design. Using the Product Warehouse application makes it easy to distribute customized solutions.

Creating Reports for Domino Applications

by Steve Kern

IN THIS CHAPTER

Virtually every system that collects data needs to turn that data into useful information somehow. Obviously, data is of minimal value if it can't be presented in a fashion that is understandable to the user. In its rawest form, data is a collection of 1s and 0s. Not too many people can read binary! Even though the binary data storage is presented in letters, numbers, images, and symbols, it is still relatively meaningless unless presented in an understandable format. Developers spend a good deal of time developing programs that report on the information contained in database applications. Notes and Domino present some unique opportunities as well as some unique challenges to developers. This chapter covers some of the ways reports can be designed for Domino Databases.

Understanding the Issues

To gain a better understanding of what's involved in creating reports for Notes and Domino, a review of some basic elements and concepts is in order. First and foremost, remember that Domino database applications have their origin in a distributed document management system. Domino databases contain documents. Documents are the primary containers of data and are roughly analogous to records in a relational database system. Like a relational database record, a document contains fields that hold the actual data. In technical terms, a field in Domino is actually called an *item*, but by convention and in practice, items are referred to as *fields*.

By their very nature, many types of documents tend to be unstructured. Some items are present in all documents, such as creation date, date of last modification, authors, and so forth, but the content that the user deals with is often unstructured. For example, a discussion database would be severely limited if a user could enter only 256 characters in the body of a topic. Similarly, if the subject field contains only 10 characters, it isn't very indicative of what's in the document. The length of the fields contained in a document— and, consequently, the length of the document itself—is variable, or unstructured.

When adding a text field to a form in Domino Designer, you just pick text. To add a text field to a table in a relational database system, you must also choose a width. Granted, you can set widths fairly large these days, but there are limits to the record size in systems such as SQL Server. With the exception of Memo type fields and some fields that have a predefined width in a relational table, all fields must have a width specified when they are defined in the table. Data contained in a relational database is referred to as structured data.

In addition, no new fields can be added to a record in a relational table without first modifying the table. This is not the case with documents in a Domino database, where fields can be added and deleted from specific documents at will. The point here is that in Domino, the documents, the data items, and the data are unstructured. This presents some very special challenges to creating reports.

As you may already know, technically speaking, a relational database is a collection of related tables. Developers who work with relational database systems create separate applications that permit users to enter, delete, and modify the data contained in the database. The term *database* is not always used that precisely, as is the case with a Domino database. For Domino databases, the definition does not apply for two primary reasons. First, application code is contained within the database along with the data and is not separate as it is with applications written to work with Oracle, Sybase, or other relational databases. Second, the concept of a table does not truly apply. In fact, there is really only one table in a Domino database: the Universal Relation table. This single supertable contains all data and all fields in a Domino database.

What Is ODBC and SQL?

NotesSQL, an ODBC driver, can be used to access data in a Domino database using SQL statements. *Open Database Connectivity (ODBC)*, is a standard for accessing information in databases. *Structured Query Language (SQL)*, was created to retrieve data from a relational database system. Using SQL, you select a list of fields from a list of related tables in which certain conditions apply. SQL returns rows in a result set, similar to a view in a Domino database. These topics are covered later in this chapter.

By now, you should know how to construct views and should know that views are the primary means of presenting data contained in documents. In a relational database system, SQL is used to retrieve rows of data. In Domino, a view performs the same function. When a view is created, a selection formula can be written to restrict the documents that appear in the view, and columns are defined to present the actual data items contained within the documents. This is the only built-in report writer in Domino.

To an extent, a form can be used to retrieve and present data, but neither views nor forms are true report writers when compared to what's available in Lotus Approach, the Notes Reporter, or Crystal Reports. Views are fine for searching for and looking at the data onscreen. While it is true that view columns can be totaled and averaged, and that views can have headers and footers defined when printed, views simply lack the polish and sophistication of a true report writer.

Views also have some technical limitations. First, the data displayed in view columns must be contained in the documents displayed in the view. Neither @DbColumn() nor DbLookup() work in views, so you cannot retrieve information in other databases or other documents and then display it in a view column.

Second, information contained in different documents cannot be mixed in the same row, although they can be presented in the same view. Although you can use a selection formula such as SELECT Form = "OFSR" ¦ Form = "SR", which retrieves documents created by two different forms, each document will occupy a different row in the view.

In many database applications, neither of these issues will be a problem. However, in large data-tracking applications, there are frequent situations in which you need to present information in different related documents created with different forms. Executives frequently request summaries of information in a single row. Using SQL with a *Relational Database Management System (RDBMS),* this is not a problem—but in Notes it is.

Domino does have a facility that provides a way to relate documents in a parent/child fashion. This is the relationship that exists among documents, response documents, and response-to-response documents. The linkage is maintained through the use of the parent document's UNID (Unique ID), a 32-character unique hexadecimal number. The children all have a reserved field containing the parent UNID, called $Ref. In hierarchical views, the children are all indented underneath the parent, and Domino maintains the relationship between them.

Some limitations exist in this arrangement as well. First, response documents contained in a hierarchical view can't be totaled. As a workaround, response documents can be placed in a view of their own and then totaled. Unfortunately, the link to the parent is lost, as is any information contained in the parent document. Second, information from different documents still can't be combined in the same row.

So what do you do? If you need information in a document that originated in another document, use inheritance to retrieve the information when the new documents are composed, and store the information in both documents. This would make any self-respecting relational database designer roll his eyes, if not laugh outright, but that's the only way to make it work directly in Notes and Domino. Unfortunately, there's a drawback to this approach as well—what do you do when the information held in common among multiple documents changes in one of the documents? Code must be written to update the values in all the other documents. Depending on the number of documents involved, that can be a rather daunting task.

Updating Parents When the Children Change

If you find yourself in this situation, use @SetDocField() and @GetDocField() to set and get information in fields in other documents. Both use the UNID to locate the documents and retrieve or write information to the fields. Between documents and response-type documents, $Ref can be used in the argument. If you need to store information in multiple documents that are related, assign the parent UNID to a field using @DocumentUniqueID. Use inheritance to store that value to a field in any related documents. Then, use that field as the argument for @GetDocField() and @SetDocField().

Views in Domino are not like browses or views in other databases. Domino views occupy physical space in a database file. The more information included in a view, the larger the view. The more complex the formulas are in view columns, the longer the view takes to refresh. Views can conceivably occupy more space than the data stored in documents themselves. For applications that require a significant number of reports, using views can add significantly to the size of a database. This can adversely affect the performance of the database.

To a certain extent, you can reduce the amount of work the server must perform by changing the view refresh rate from one of the automatic settings to manual. While this saves server resources, this just transfers the pain from the server to the user, who now needs to refresh the views whenever he needs to see current information. In very large databases, having a large number of views can significantly reduce performance to the point where users are frustrated and the server is adversely affected as well. In this situation, turning to another means of reporting on the data is preferable.

38

CREATING
REPORTS

How Big Is Too Big?

Several years ago, the rule of thumb was that a database of 100MB was pushing the boundaries of usability. This was a well-publicized standard. Since then, Notes and Domino have improved considerably, and the power of both servers and workstations has increased dramatically. R5 has added significant performance enhancements and has increased the maximum size from 4GB for R4 to 64GB for Windows and Unix, and 32GB for OS/2. Therefore, it is difficult to state

continues

a specific size limit for databases at which performance and usability begins to break down. Despite these impressive gains in performance and size limits, the lowest common denominator will determine database usability. A Pentium 166 with 32MB of RAM will probably have a difficult time dealing with a database exceeding 500MB, whereas the newer Pentium III 500 with 128MB RAM would probably have little difficulty. There is no easy answer to this question, but users of the application will certainly let you know!

Finding the Sizes of Views

You can find the sizes of views on a server by opening the servers log and looking in the view Database\Sizes. Each database on the server has its own document in which the view sizes are listed.

One last limitation to cover with regard to views involves printing headers and footers. Both forms and databases have headers and footers for printing. Designers specify the headers and footers for forms, and these are stored with the database design. Database headers and footers, on the other hand, apply to the entire database, although a form's headers and footers take precedence over the database settings. This means that each view will print the headers and footers that are specified for the entire database. The inability to customize the printed appearance of individual views can be a real problem. Printer settings for a database are not sticky and are a part of individual users' desktop files. Each user can maintain individual settings, but if the desktop icon is deleted, the settings go away.

In R5, this is not readily apparent. For example, if a database is removed from the bookmark folder and then restored, the settings remain. However, if the database icon is removed from the workspace, the settings vanish. While users enjoy the flexibility of customizing their own printer settings for each database, this approach presents two distinct problems. First, database developers cannot specify a setting. Second, if the user's workstation needs to be rebuilt, or if the workspace becomes corrupted for some reason, or if the icon is removed from the workspace, the printer settings vanish and have to be reconstructed. Using database printer settings is not always a particularly good solution for printing reports from Notes and Domino.

As is plainly evident, there are some serious limitations to reporting on data in Domino applications using the tools available in Notes and Domino. Sometimes, especially in data collection applications, you will find requirements for executive summaries of data for presentation to vice presidents, CEOs, and board members. With these requirements, you will have to go beyond what is available in Domino. On the other hand, many applications are fairly simple in scope and content; if there are no extensive reporting requirements, you may not run into these limitations. Views may work just fine for these sorts of applications. If more extensive and sophisticated reports are required, developers must look outside Notes and Domino.

Perhaps the most obvious choice for reports is Lotus Approach and its cousin, the Notes Reporter. Both of these interpret Domino data natively and respect database ACLs. Other choices are worthy of consideration as well. If you set up NotesSQL (covered later in this chapter), other applications can access Domino data through ODBC. Examples include Crystal Reports and Microsoft Access. Crystal Reports is a commonly used universal report generator that works with almost any type of database. It is most often used with RDBMS databases, but it will work with Domino databases as well. Microsoft Access is also designed primarily with RDBMS databases in mind, but it, too, will work with Domino databases. You can also export data from views in one of three formats: Lotus 1-2-3 Worksheet, Structured Text, or Tabular Text. Files produced by exporting data can then be imported into other applications from which reports can be generated. Each of these options is covered in the remainder of this chapter.

Creating Statistical Reports with Views

The facility for generating statistical reports with views is somewhat limited. Still, it can be done. The database for this chapter, Chapt44.nsf, has some views representing a rudimentary purchase order system. The application tracks the Purchase Order Number, Type, Department, Ship to, Amount, Order Date, Ship Date, Justification, and so forth. As you know from reading Chapter 11, "View Design," constructing views is generally pretty simple. The Purchasing department would probably like to see views sorted by Purchase Order Number, Type, Department, and Order Date. In addition, Purchasing might like to see a count of POs for each sort as well as total expenditures.

Counting and Totaling Columns

Creating a count is very simple: Create a column with a numeric value of 1, and on the Sorting tab of the Column Properties box, set the Totals Field to Total; then click the Hide Detail Rows checkbox. Totaling an amount column is also simple and is done the same way. However, you may not want to hide the detail rows for the amounts. Doing so would hide the purchase amount for each PO (see Figure 38.1).

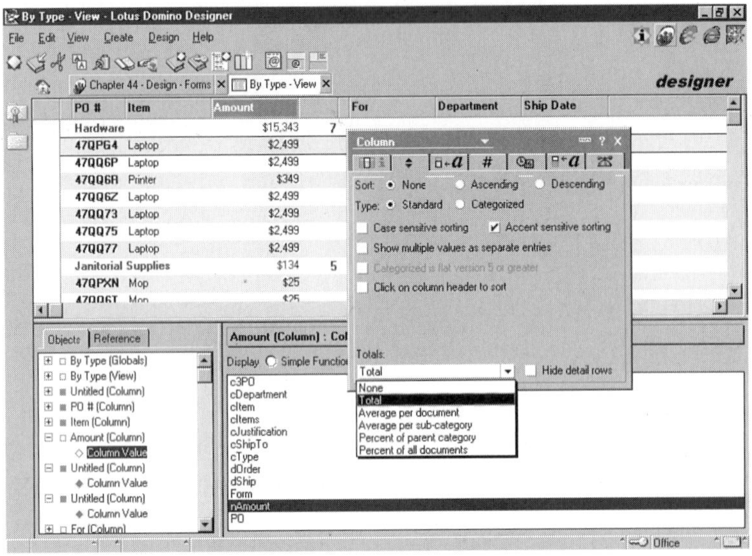

FIGURE 38.1

Setting a view column to total is done on the Sorting tab of the Column Properties box—note the list of choices for totaling.

View columns can be totaled with the following settings:

- *None*—The default.
- *Total*—Creates totals for each category in the view.
- *Average per document*—Creates averages based on the total divided by the number of documents.
- *Average per subcategory*—Creates an average for each category based on the total for all documents divided by the number of subcategories within the category.
- *Percent of parent category*—Calculates the percentage of a subcategory by comparing the total for the subcategory with the total for the parent category.
- *Percent of all documents*—Calculates the percentage of a subcategory by comparing the total for the subcategory with the total of all documents.

Figure 38.2 illustrates the effects of each totaling type. Columns that total using any of the previously described methods have a side effect. The category text is chopped off at the beginning of the total column. To work around this, add some extra space to the column just before the total column.

As is evident in Figure 38.2, Domino differs from conventional reports, which place totals at the end of the category, because it places totals at the top of the category, with a grand total at the bottom of the row. Many people find this confusing at first, and many executives request reports with more conventional displays showing the subtotals and totals at the bottom of a column of numbers. This necessitates creation of reports with something other than Notes and Domino.

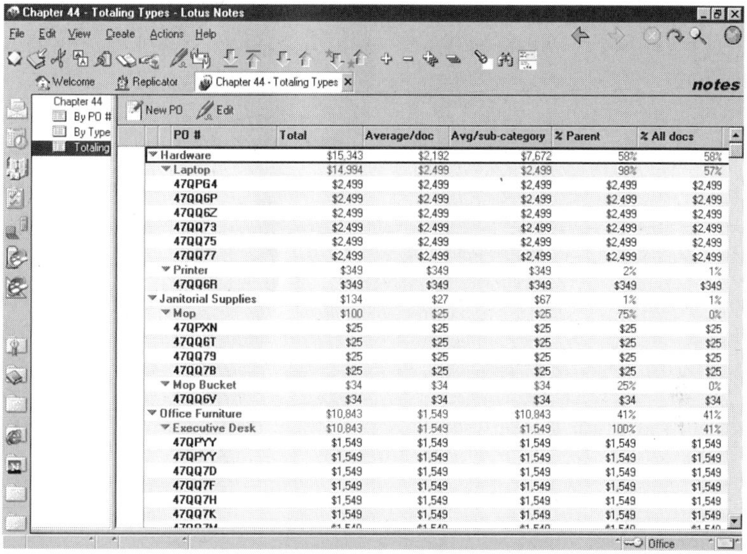

FIGURE 38.2

Totaling columns is the only statistical reporting available in views.

The example in Figure 38.2 is very straightforward and simple because each column uses values stored in the document itself. Sometimes, you will be asked to compute the counts of documents that meet certain criteria. These criteria can range from the extremely complex to the relatively simple. A simple example is the following view column formula:

```
nAmount > 1000
```

If the amount stored in the field nAmount is greater than 1000, then the number 1 is returned in the column. If not, a 0 is returned. This takes advantage of the fact that, in the Formula language, 1 is true and 0 is false. A formula such as this could be used to count the number of purchases for each department that are greater than $1,000.

More complex formulas can certainly be constructed to count documents in a column. For example, the following formula uses Boolean ANDs (the ampersand—&) and ORs (the pipe—¦) to determine whether a document is counted:

```
@Left(cApproved;1) = "Y" & @Left(cUsed;1) = "N") ¦
@Left(cSuitable; 3) = "123" ¦
@Left(cSuitable; 3) = "456" ¦
@Left(cSuitable; 3) = "789"
```

Using formulas to determine whether a document should be counted in a column can be combined with sorted and categorized views to produce statistical reports.

38

CREATING
REPORTS

Working with Advanced Date Columns

Notes and Domino handle dates better than many other applications, so it is easy to construct sorts by year, month, and quarter. This enables the presentation of statistics in various date sorts. Date sorts such as this are very useful for applications that are work-flow-related or that have time-sensitive information. For example, help desk or call center applications benefit from seeing the number of calls per month, quarter, and year. The Purchasing application example in this chapter has a view titled By Ship Date, which sorts the purchases by year, quarter, and month (see Figure 38.3).

FIGURE 38.3

This view has columns sorted and categorized by year, quarter, and month—note the formula for the quarter.

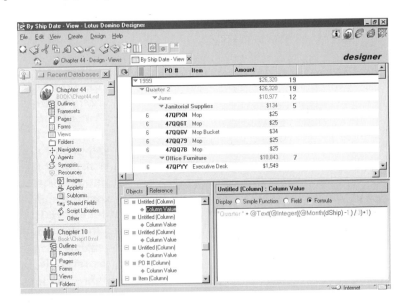

The first column's formula is simple: @Year(dShip), which returns the year of the ship date. The second column's formula returns the quarter using the following formula:

```
"Quarter " + @Text(@Integer((@Month(dShip) -1 ) / 3)+1)
```

The third column is hidden, and uses @Month(dShip) that is sorted but not categorized. This column ensures that the fourth column, which has the names of the months, is sorted properly. To obtain the month, use the following formula:

```
@Select(@Month(dShip); "January"; "February"; "March"; "April";
        "May"; "June"; "July"; "August"; "September"; "October";
        "November"; "December")
```

If you have multiple documents per day, you can also sort and categorize by date in a column. If the date contains both a date and a time value, you can strip off the time portion by using @Date(*date-time value*).

Users can drill down from the year to the quarter, month, and day. Columns can be designed to count and summarize information by each grouping, placing totals and averages per date category. If you combine columns that use formulas to determine which documents to count with categories based on dates, you can create reasonably sophisticated reports.

Ad Hoc Reporting with Views

Views lend themselves nicely to creating ad hoc reports because they can be constructed by anyone with Author access or above. Users with Author access can create only private views, but users with Editor access can create shared as well as private views. Of course, Designers and Managers can create both. The ability of Authors and Editors to create shared and/or private views is controlled with entries in the ACL of the database. With this in mind, a database manager can effectively distribute the responsibility of creating reports with views to a select few trained individuals throughout the organization.

Using Private Views

Because they are relatively easy to construct, views tend to proliferate over time in a heavily used database. An excessive number of views can lead to clutter and can consume server resources and disk space, so it is important to manage the number and type of views. As you learned in Chapter 11, there are two broad classifications of views: shared and private. If you need to conserve space on the server or keep the size of the database to a minimum, consider using one of the private types of views. As a database designer, you can create views that are shared, private on first use, or shared, desktop private on first use. Private views do not occupy disk space on the server.

> **Caution**
>
> When a user opens a shared-to-private view, the design is fixed. If a designer modifies the source view, changes will not appear automatically in the private copies of the view. To see the design changes, the user must delete the private instance of the view and then open it again, recreating the view with the changes.

A shared, private on first use view can occupy space either on the server or in the user's desktop file, depending on the user's rights in the database ACL. If your goal is to reduce disk space usage on the server, choose Shared, Desktop Private on First Use. This choice forces the view to appear only in the user's desktop file. Similarly, if you have distributed the responsibility for creating views to specific users, make sure that they create private views when appropriate.

Caution

After a view type has been defined, there is no way to change it. You cannot convert a shared view to any of the shared-to-private views or to a private view.

Using Lotus Approach

By far, Lotus Approach is the easiest-to-use and the most powerful reporting tool available for Domino databases. Approach is a part of Lotus SmartSuite and supports accessing many different types of databases in addition to Domino databases. This section covers the basics of creating reports.

Approach can be used to design simple reports, complex reports, reports that join non-Notes and Notes data, and so forth. Approach can even be used to create a polished front end for applications, such as an executive information system. Naturally, Approach respects the ACL of each database opened. All in all, Approach is well worth investigating.

The Notes Reporter

A few years ago, Lotus split the reporting functionality from Approach and created a product called the Notes Reporter. This product is still available, but because it is virtually identical to Approach, it will not be covered in this chapter.

Two methods exist for accessing Domino databases with Approach. The first and easiest method is to open the databases natively; the second is through an ODBC driver. Setting up an ODBC driver requires NotesSQL and is discussed later in this chapter.

Opening Domino Databases

Opening a Domino database from Approach can be done as soon as Approach is launched by clicking the Browse for More Files button in the Welcome to Lotus Approach screen, or by choosing File, Open from the menu. In both cases, the Open window appears (see Figure 38.4).

FIGURE 38.4

The Open dialog box offers many different file formats, including three choices for Notes.

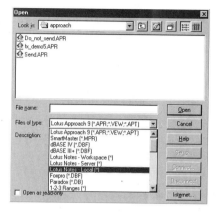

As you can see from Figure 38.4, there are three methods of opening Domino databases directly in Approach:

- **Lotus Notes—Workspace**—This choice lets you choose from databases stored on your workspace.

- **Lotus Notes—Server**—You can specify a server and choose from databases on that server with this choice.

- **Lotus Notes—Local**—This choice lets you open databases stored on your local hard drive.

Caution

As of this writing, the Workspace choice does not work when using R5.0 dated March 30, 1999 and SmartSuite Millennium Edition version 9.1. It's possible that Approach doesn't recognize the new desktop file, Desktop5.dsk.

Experience will best show you whether to use a server database or a local database. Depending on how powerful your workstation is, it can be better to use a local replica for better performance. On small databases, this is not a factor; on large databases, however, it can become one. For example, opening a view in the Notes KnowledgeBase—a nearly 500MB database—on the server took a few minutes, whereas it took less than half a minute to open a local copy of the same database. However, there are simply too many factors to predict the impact of local versus server-based reporting. Factors that affect performance include the speed of the network, the power of your workstation, the power of the server, how much traffic there is on the network, and how busy the server is.

38

CREATING REPORTS

You must also consider how the report will be used. If the reports are to be distributed to other users, using a server database will make it easier for an end user to use the new report. If you do choose to use a local copy of a database, steps must be taken to ensure that the data is up to date.

Replicate Databases from Approach!

If you do use a local replica of a database, you can include a menu choice in an Approach file that enables you to replicate with the server. Switch to Design, and choose Create, Custom Menu, New from the menu. Name the menu, and create a prompt that specifies Replicate with Notes server. Save the new menu, and attach it to the Approach view.

Using the Open Dialog Window

From the Open dialog window, you can make several settings that affect the way Domino databases are opened. In the lower-left corner is the Open as Read-Only checkbox, clicking this setting prevents Approach from updating documents in a Domino database. This is generally a good idea unless you are going to write an application in Approach that enables users to update a Notes database from Approach.

The other settings can be found by clicking the Setup button options. This opens the Notes Powerkey Setup window (see Figure 38.5). In this window, you can create a list of servers to access by typing the server name into the User Server List field and then clicking Add.

You can also set two preferences—Show Hidden Views and Never Create Views (indices)—in main NSF; both of these settings remain in force even after the current session. When you choose to show hidden views, all views in a database will be displayed, including those hidden by enclosing the view name in parentheses. Setting Never Create Views in Main NSF can impact performance because Approach creates views in a Domino database to increase performance. However, as you know by now, adding views increases disk space usage for the database.

FIGURE 38.5

Clicking the Setup button opens the Notes Powerkey Setup window, which enables you to specify servers and set options.

Opening Views or Forms

After you've located the database you are opening in the Open dialog window, you can double-click it to expose the available design elements. You can choose from views or forms. If you aren't sure of the type, you can click the element once, and Approach will display text such as Notes Form or Notes View, followed by the last modification date.

If you open a view, Approach displays a browser titled Worksheet1 that mirrors the view. Only the visible columns appear; the hidden columns are not opened in Approach. Opening a view is a handy way to get a jump-start on creating a report. Your data is already preselected by the view's selection formula, and it is already ordered. This is also an easy way to get documents created by more than one form into a report.

You can also open a form. When you do so, Approach opens both a form (Form1) and a browse (Worksheet 1). All fields up to the first 26 are included in the form and in the worksheet. Hidden fields are excluded from both the form and the worksheet, just as they are when opening a view.

Adding and Creating Fields

Additional fields can be added to forms and worksheets manually. Choose Worksheet (or Form), Add Field from the menu while in Design mode, and the Add Field window will open. You can then select a field and drag it to the worksheet or form (see Figure 38.6).

FIGURE 38.6

Adding new fields to worksheets is easy—just click a field in the Add Field window and drag it to the worksheet.

You can also create new fields by choosing Create, Field Definition from the menu (see Figure 38.7). If you choose Calculated as a Field Type, you can create a new field based on a calculation. The calculation can combine fields and statements to produce a new value.

FIGURE 38.7

When you create a new calculated field, you enter the calculation into the formula window at the bottom of the Field Definition window.

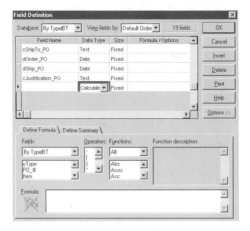

Creating Reports with Approach

When you have a worksheet ready, you can create reports based on the data in the work-sheet. To create a new report, choose Create, Report from the menu. The Report Assistant window opens (see Figure 38.8).

FIGURE 38.8

The Report Assistant has two tabs to help you define the characteristics of your report and the data it will contain.

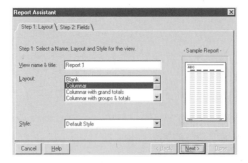

The first tab, labeled Step 1, enables you to name and select a format for the report. You can choose from several layouts and styles. As you change your selections, a graphic rep-resentation of the report changes in the Sample Report area of the dialog window. Additional tabs are added to reflect your selection. Table 38.1 lists the available report layouts.

TABLE 38.1　Layouts for Reports in Approach

Item	Description
Blank	Creates a blank page with no additional tabs.
Columnar	Provides a columnar listing of data, with no totals (the default). Adds a second tab, Step 2: Fields.
Columnar with grand totals	Sums columns with a grand total at the end of the report. Adds a second tab, Step 2: Fields; and a third tab, Step 3: Grand Totals.
Columnar with groups and totals	Includes totals for groups, plus a grand total. Adds a second tab, Step 2: Fields; a third tab, Step 3: Groups; and a fourth tab, Step 4: Totals.
Standard	Has a similar appearance to a form, and contains rows of fields. Adds a second tab, Step 2: Fields.
Summary only	Creates summaries with no detail rows. Adds a second tab, Step 2: Groups; and a third tab, Step 3: Summary.

Numerous styles are available. Styles affect the graphic presentation of the report, modifying the formatting of the title, column headers, rows, and totals. When you select different styles, the Sample Reports image changes, just as when you chose different layouts.

After you have chosen a report layout and style, you can either click a tab or click the Next button to move through the tabs for all report layouts except Blank.

Selecting Fields

To select fields, move to the Fields tab (see Figure 38.9). Select the fields in the list, and click the Add button. If you add a field that you don't need, you can select it in the Fields to Place On view, and then click the Remove button.

> **Caution**
>
> When you click the Add button, the field is fixed in the Fields to Place On view list. You can't click and drag or otherwise adjust the position in the list. If you get a field out of order, you must remove all fields until you reach the correct location for the field in the sequence; then add the remaining fields again.

38

CREATING REPORTS

FIGURE 38.9

Selecting fields for the report is done in the tab labeled Step 2: Fields.

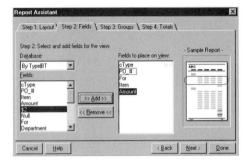

Grouping and Totaling Your Report

If you create a report that uses groups, you must select the field or fields to group the data. Click the Groups tab, and select the field or fields in the Fields list; then click the Add button (see Figure 38.10).

FIGURE 38.10

You add fields to group your data by selecting fields from the list and clicking the Add button.

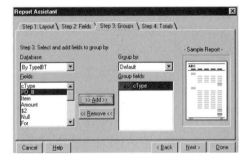

You are not restricted to the fields that you selected on the Fields tab; you can choose any available fields. You can also select more than one field to group your data. This has the same effect as using more than one sorted and categorized column in a view. The second grouping is nested beneath the first, the third is nested under the second, and so on.

The Group By field is a drop-down list that consists of Default, 1st character, 1st 2 characters, 1st 3 characters, 1st 4 characters, and 1st 5 characters. Default is the entire contents of the field.

You are now ready to choose the fields to total. Again, you are presented with a list of fields, Add and Remove buttons, and a list of Summary fields (see Figure 38.11). You can choose multiple fields to sum, and you have a number of statistical operations available in the Calculate list.

38

CREATING
REPORTS

FIGURE 38.11

To create summaries of columns, select the field, click Add, and choose Sum in the Calculate list—note the icons next to the field names.

You can choose from the following operations in the Calculate list. Each option displays a different symbol next to the field in the Summary Fields list.

- Average
- Count
- Maximum
- Minimum
- Standard Deviation
- Sum
- Variance

Finishing Your Report

When you are satisfied with your choices, click the Done button to complete your report. A new tab is added that uses the report title that you supplied (see Figure 38.12).

Depending on your choices, you'll see several panels, a header, leading and trailing summaries, and the body of the report. You can see this more easily by turning off the display of data on the report. You can do this by choosing View, Show Data from the menu. This menu selection acts like a toggle switch, turning on and off the display of data (see Figure 38.13). With data turned off, you can modify the fields and text in the report, and then turn data back on to see the results of your changes.

Using the Tools Palette

When you create a new worksheet or a report, the Tools palette invariably appears (see Figure 38.14). This is a set of buttons that floats on the design surface. You can toggle it on and off by choosing View, Show Tools Palette from the menu. From this palette, you can add text and fields, or you can draw shapes and lines. Although it is not useful for a report, you can also use the Tools palette to add buttons and checkboxes and to create fields that accept images and drawing.

FIGURE 38.12

*You can change
the title of the
report by
double-clicking
the Report tab and
entering a new
title.*

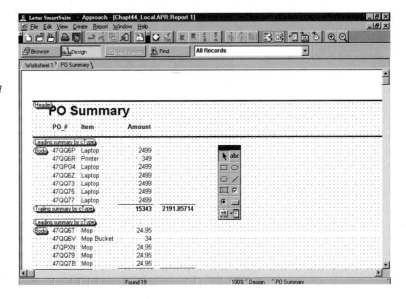

FIGURE 38.13

*When Show Data
is off, you can see
the report panels
and fields more
easily.*

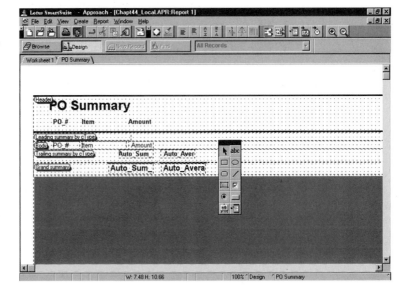

FIGURE 38.14

The Tools Palette enables you to quickly create objects to reports, forms, and worksheets.

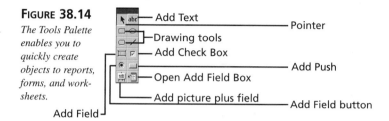

Creating Finds

If your view doesn't restrict the data set for your report, or if you need to further restrict the data, you can create a find to narrow the record set. Even better, you can name the find and save it for use later. Creating a find is pretty simple—just click the Find button. This displays the worksheet with a single empty row into which you can type the conditions for each field. You can use the buttons in the SmartIcon toolbar to help you build conditions (see Figure 38.15).

FIGURE 38.15

You can build a Find by entering values in the fields.

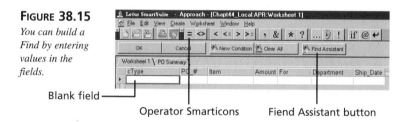

38

CREATING
REPORTS

It is far easier to use the Find Assistant, available when you click the Find Assistant button. The Find Assistant enables you to quickly build queries without much effort on your part. The Find Type tab lets you create the following types:

- **Basic**—Searches for values contained in fields. Tabs for Condition, Sort, and Name are present.

- **Find Duplicate Records**—Searches for duplicate records. Tabs for Find Duplicates, Sort, and Name are present.

- **Find Distinct Records**—Is similar to a SELECT DISTINCT in SQL. Tabs for Find Distinct, Sort, and Name are present.

- **Find the top or lowest**—Searches for maximum or minimum values. Tabs for Find Top/Lowest, Sort, and Name are present.

- **Query by Box**—Enables you to quickly build complex queries using fields, values, and operators. The query is displayed as a graphical representation in a box. Tabs for Query by Box, Sort, and Name are present.

To begin building a Find, simply choose the type of Find you want to create in the first tab, and fill in the remaining tabs (see Figures 38.16 through 38.18).

FIGURE 38.16

When you enter conditions in a Basic Find, the description box displays a text version of the Find.

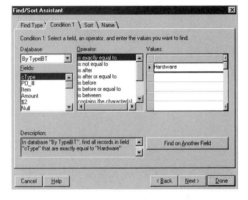

FIGURE 38.17

The Query by Box Find provides a visual representa-tion of the query you construct.

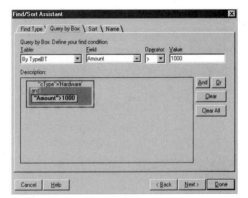

FIGURE 38.18

With the Sort tab, you can choose from a list of fields to sort by; you can sort in either ascending or descending order.

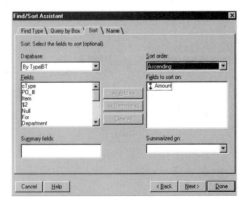

When you have completed the Find, you can name it and save it by clicking the Name tab and entering a name. When ready, click Done. The named Find appears in the Find drop-down list (see Figure 38.19), and the Find is executed. The result set reflects the conditions defined in the named Find.

FIGURE 38.19

This result set contains hardware requisitions greater than $1,000, as defined in the Hardware Named Find.

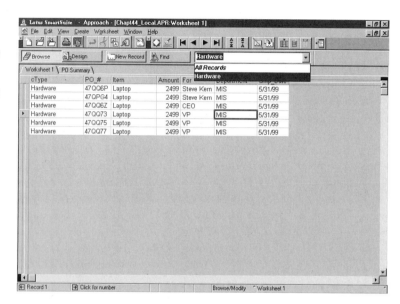

Adding a Front End

You can easily and quickly create a front end or menu system for a collection of reports. Simply create a blank form, and then add text and buttons to open the reports (see Figure 38.20).

After you have created the blank form and added the text, you can add buttons by choosing the Button tool from the Toolbar palette. Click the location on the form where you want the button. The default text label for a button is Button, and the size is roughly a half-inch wide by one-third inch high. Drag handles appear at each corner that you can use to resize the button. The Button Properties box has tabs for font size and attributes, button size, button name, macros, and style (see Figure 38.21).

FIGURE 38.20

This simple menu was created in a few minutes using macros attached to the buttons.

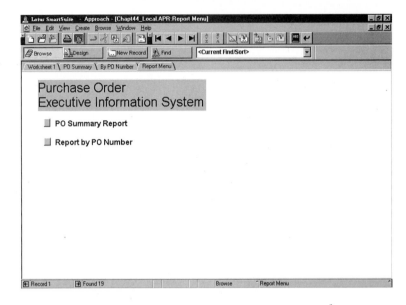

FIGURE 38.21

Buttons are programmed on the Macros tab of the Button Properties box.

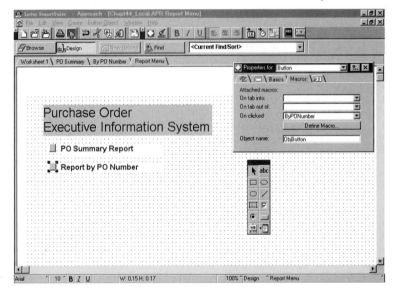

The Macros tab enables you to define and attach macros. Approach macros are fairly simple to create: Simply click the Define Macro button on the Macros tab, and build the macro. For example, to create a macro that opens a report from a button, do the following steps:

1. Click the Define Macro button on the Macros tab of the Button Properties box.

2. In the Macros window that opens, click New.

3. Name the Macro in the Define Macro window.

4. In the Command column, select View. Choose the report you want to display in the Views list at the bottom of the Define Macro window (see Figure 38.22).

FIGURE 38.22

The Define Macro window enables you to build sophisticated links to reports (views).

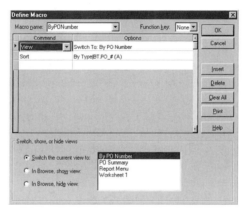

5. If you need to add a sort or create a new command, choose Sort in the Command column and pick the sort from the list.

6. Click OK to close the Define Macro window.

7. Click Done in the Macros window.

8. To attach the macro to the button, choose the name of the newly create macro in the drop-down list for the button On Clicked Event.

9. You can test your new menu by clicking the Browse button and testing the buttons.

After you have linked the menu to the reports, you'll want to create a way back from the report to the menu. To do this, simply create another macro, naming the Report form as the view. You can attach a function key to the macro (such as F10) so that the user doesn't have to click a button.

38

CREATING REPORTS

To execute this macro from a Report, you can include text such as "F10 for Menu" or a button with a label such as Return to Menu. By default, buttons are nonprinting, but text prints. You can set a text object to be nonprinting from the Basics tab of the Text Object Properties box. When you click Nonprinting, the text object vanishes, and a second checkbox, named Show in Print Preview, appears. Clicking this causes the text object to appear once again. If you've attached F10 to the macro as suggested, the user can return to the Report menu either by using the function key or by clicking the text object.

Going Beyond Reports

Approach is capable of much more functionality. The following list summarizes a few of the other capabilities of Approach:

- **Charts**—You can quickly create charts of your data with a number of different styles and colors.

- **Form letters**—If your data contains contact information, you can quickly create form letters, inserting fields in the appropriate locations within the text of your letter.

- **Envelopes**—You can choose from a variety of standard envelopes and can add addressing information from your data.

- **Mailing labels**—Mailing labels can be generated from a contact list. You can choose from the standard label sizes.

- **Crosstabs**—Crosstabs enable you to report on three data items. One data item becomes the row, the other becomes the column, and the third summarizes the data at the intersection of the row and column.

- **Joins**—You can use Approach to join related databases. You can even join Notes and non-Notes databases.

Setting Up ODBC with NotesSQL

Open Database Connectivity (ODBC) is a standard for accessing data stored in a wide variety of databases. ODBC requires a *driver* to provide access to the data source. Lotus provides a driver called NotesSQL that grants access to Notes data via ODBC.

After you set up ODBC access with NotesSQL, you can use or *Structured Query Language (SQL)* to retrieve Notes data. You can then use applications such as Microsoft Access, Crystal Reports, or even Approach to create reports on Notes data. This chapter uses Access 2000 to demonstrate ODBC.

Installing NotesSQL

Setting up NotesSQL is pretty straightforward. You can find NotesSQL on Lotus' Web site at http://www.lotus.com. After you download it, place the file (Nsqlw32.exe) in its own folder, and run it to extract the setup files. Next, run Setup.exe in the folder you've created for NotesSQL. Answer the Install Shield prompts, choosing Typical or Custom. When installation is complete, you are prompted to configure a data source for NotesSQL. You can also configure a data source at any time by following these steps:

1. Choose Start, Settings, Control Panel.
2. Open the 32-bit ODBC manager.
3. Click the System DSN tab, and click the Add button.
4. Click Lotus Notes SQL 2.0 (32-bit) ODBC Driver (.nsf), as shown in Figure 38.23.

FIGURE 38.23

It is usually best to configure a System DSN, especially if you are working on a network.

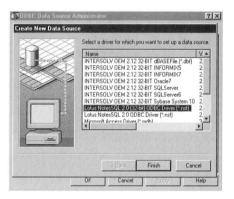

38

CREATING
REPORTS

5. Click Finish, and fill in the fields in the Lotus Notes ODBC 2.0 Setup dialog box (see Figure 38.24).

FIGURE 38.24

Leaving the Server field blank means that you must have a local replica of the database on your hard drive; you can also open a database on a server.

6. Specify a name for the data source, the server, and the filename, including the path. Leave the rest of the settings alone for now.

7. Click OK to return to the System DSN tab.

8. Click OK to close the ODBC manager.

Caution

The ODBC driver treats all Notes fields as text, regardless of how Notes itself registers them. Furthermore, all fields will be the width that you specified in the Lotus Notes ODBC 2.0 Setup dialog box, which defaults to 254. If you are having difficulty with your queries, open the dialog box and change the default from 254 to a smaller value. You must keep this in mind when working with numbers because you will have to convert them from text to perform calculations.

NotesSQL Documentation

The NotesSQL documentation is in a database, which by default is placed in the `c:\Windows\System` directory. For easier reference, move it from that directory to the default Notes data directory.

Querying Notes Data with SQL

When you open the Domino data source, it will not look much like a relational database. Design elements such as forms and views are treated as tables. Rather than using a form to retrieve data items, it is often best to use a view, but this means that the information on which you want to report must be in a view column.

In Microsoft Access, when you open an external data source through NotesSQL, you can either import the data or link to the tables. If you are going to report on Notes data that will be changing, it is a good idea to use the link option. To open the data source in Access, you take these steps:

1. Create a new blank database in Access.

2. Choose File, Get External Data, Link Tables.

3. In the Link dialog box, choose ODBC Databases from the Files of Type drop-down box (see Figure 38.25).

FIGURE 38.25

The Link dialog box enables you to specify the file type as ODBC.

4. Click the Machine Data Sources tab in the Select Data Source dialog box, and choose the Notes ODBC source you defined (see Figure 38.26).

FIGURE 38.26

Click the Machine Data Source tab to select your Notes ODBC data source.

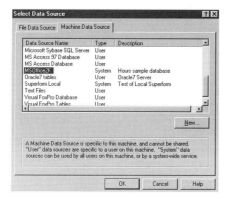

5. Click OK.

After you choose the Notes ODBC data source, the Link Tables dialog box appears with what may be a bewildering array of elements (see Figure 38.27). Here you must have some knowledge of the internal design of the database to determine which element to choose.

FIGURE 38.27

Knowledge of the database's design will help you choose the correct design element for your report.

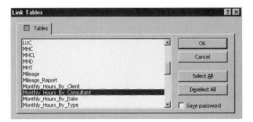

After you choose an element, Access prompts you to choose a field or fields to uniquely describe each record—again, you need to have some knowledge of the design of the Notes database. After this is completed, you can query the table (see Figure 38.28).

FIGURE 38.28

The Simple Query Wizard after several fields have been selected.

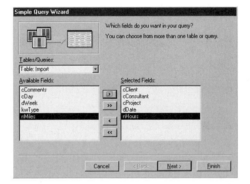

Now that you have a query, you can apply the selection criteria you need, and you can use any of the sophisticated reporting tools available in Access to present a polished report.

Exporting Data to Other Formats

If none of the described options for creating reports provide the functionality you need, you can always export the data to a different format. Because you will most often be reporting on data in rows, you'll be exporting from a view. You have the following three choices for formatting your data when you export from a view:

- **Lotus 1-2-3 Worksheet**—This exports files in the standard WK1 format, which is recognized by many database and spreadsheet applications.

- **Structured text**—Structured text files include both field names and field contents.

- **Tabular text**—Tabular text files arrange data in rows and columns. The separator between the fields is the tab character.

Exporting to a Lotus 1-2-3 worksheet is one of the most reliable methods of getting data from Notes into other applications. Using a WK1 file is a great way of getting data from Notes into a spreadsheet program such as Lotus 1-2-3 itself or Excel. From there, you can create column summaries and otherwise work with the data in a spreadsheet format.

Structured text files can be used in mail merges and can be imported into other applications such as Approach or a RDBMS. Approach does not have a built-in import filter for structured text files, but you can treat them as text files. Use the tilde (~) as a field separator and CRLF (Carriage Return, Line Feed) as the record delimiter.

Tabular text files are used frequently to move data from Notes to other applications. However, some applications will not recognize a tabular text file generated from Notes as a tab-delimited file. If this happens, there are two ways to work around the problem. First, you can open the file in a spreadsheet such as Microsoft Excel, and then save it in another format. Second, you can embed a column in between each column in the view that contains another delimiting character such as a semicolon. A column such as this has a width of 1 with a value of ":" (including the quotes).

You can also produce a comma-delimited text file, which many applications recognize. To do so, create a view with a single column. In the column, include all the fields separated by quotes. Make sure to convert nontext fields to text. For example, to export all the users in your public directory, you can use the following formula:

```
REM "Use the slash character to embed the quotes";
"\"" + LastName + "\",\"" + FirstName + "\",\"" +
@Name([Abbreviate]; @Subset(FullName;1)) + "\""
```

This formula produces the following as output:

```
"Kern","Steve","Steve Kern/MCP"
```

Make sure that you make the column wide enough to accommodate all the text, or that you select the view property Extend Last Column to Window Width.

When the view is constructed to your satisfaction, you simply export it using tabular text format. You can then import the comma-delimited file into other applications.

Summary

The techniques in this chapter can be used to remove one of the major inadequacies of Lotus Notes and Domino itself—the lack of a true report generator. Lotus Approach provides the greatest flexibility and power because it integrates so well with Notes. However, many companies that use Notes do not use Lotus SmartSuite, opting instead for Microsoft Office. The sections on NotesSQL and Exporting Notes data provide you with a means of reporting on Notes data using Microsoft Office applications. The capability to provide reports beyond views can add sophistication and polish to your Notes applications.

Appendixes

PART VI

Domino Objects for LotusScript Classes

by Debbie Lynd

This appendix contains a descriptive list of the classes available in LotusScript. It also covers the available list of LSXes and ODBC classes.

Front-End Classes

Button

> Provides access to the click event for buttons, actions, and hotspots on forms, subforms, and pages
>
> Does not contain any properties or methods

Field

> Provides access to the entering and exiting events for fields found on forms and subforms
>
> Does not contain any properties or methods

Navigator

> Provides access to a navigator object
>
> Does not contain any properties or methods

NotesUIDatabase

> Provides access to the database open in the Notes Workspace
>
> Contains `NotesDatabase` and `NotesDocumentCollection`

NotesUIDocument

> Contained within `NotesUIWorkspace`. Provides access to the current document opened in the workspace
>
> Contains `NotesUIDocument`

NotesUIView

> Provides access to the view currently open in the Notes Workspace
>
> Contains the `NotesDocumentCollection` and the `NotesView` objects

NotesUIWorkspace

> Provides access to the current workspace
>
> Contains the `NotesUIDocument` object

Back-End Classes

The back-end classes provide access to the database from behind the scenes. Use these classes whenever you want access to objects outside of the UI.

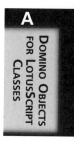

NotesACL

> Provides access to the Access Control List of a database
>
> Contained within the NotesDatabase object
>
> Contains the NotesACLEntry object

NotesACLEntry

> Provides access to an individual entry in the ACL
>
> Contained within the NotesACL object

NotesAgent

> Provides access to an agent
>
> Contained within the NotesSession or NotesDatabase objects

NotesDatabase

> Provides access to a Notes database and its properties and methods
>
> Contained within a NotesSession, NotesDbDirectory, or a NotesUIDatabase object
>
> Contains the NotesACL, NotesAgent, NotesDocument, NotesDocumentCollection, NotesForm, NotesOutline, NotesReplication, and NotesView classes

NotesDateRange

> Provides access to a range of dates and times
>
> Contained within the NotesSession class
>
> Contains the NotesDateTime class

NotesDateTime

> Provides access to a date and time for the purpose of translating between the Domino date/time format and the LotusScript date/time format
>
> Contained within the NotesDateRange or the NotesSession classes

NotesDbDirectory

> Provides access to the databases contained within a directory on a specific server or the local machine
>
> Contained within the NotesSession object
>
> Contains the NotesDatabase object

`NotesDocument`

> Provides access to a document within a database and its associated properties and methods
>
> Contained within the `NotesDatabase`, `NotesDocumentCollection`, `NotesNewsletter`, `NotesUIDocument`, `NotesView`, and `NotesViewEntry` objects
>
> Contains the `NotesEmbeddedObject`, `NotesItem`, and `NotesRichTextItem` objects

`NotesDocumentCollection`

> Provides access to a set of documents selected based on a specified criteria
>
> Contained within the `NotesDatabase`, `NotesSession`, `NotesUIDatabase`, or `NotesUIView` objects
>
> Contains the `NotesDocument` object

`NotesEmbeddedObject`

> Provides access to any embedded object, linked object, or file attachment
>
> Contained within the `NotesDocument` or `NotesRichTextItem` objects

`NotesForm`

> Provides access to a form in a database
>
> Contained within the `NotesDatabase` object

`NotesInternational`

> Provides access to the operating system's international settings
>
> Contained within the `NotesSession` object

`NotesItem`

> Provides access to a data item within a document
>
> Contained within the `NotesDocument` object
>
> Base class for the `NotesRichTextItem` class

`NotesLog`

> Provides the ability to record information about the execution of a script and place that information in a database, mail memo, or file
>
> Contained within the `NotesSession` class

`NotesName`

> Provides access to a user or server name and its associated properties and methods
>
> Contained within the `NotesSession` class

NotesNewsletter

Provides access to a document that contains links to a set of documents that meet a specified criteria

Contained within the NotesSession class

Contains the NotesDocument class

NotesOutline

Provides access to an outline and its properties and methods

Contained within the NotesDatabase class

Contains the NotesOutlineEntry class

NotesOutlineEntry

Provides access to one of the entries within an outline

Contained within the NotesOutline class

NotesRegistration

Provides access to an ID file for registration or administration of that file

Contained within the NotesSession class

NotesReplication

Provides access to the replication settings for a database

Contained within the NotesDatabase class

NotesRichTextItem

Provides access to a Notes item of the rich text data type

Contained within the NotesDocument class

Contains a NotesEmbeddedObject class

Derives its properties and methods from the Item class

NotesRichTextParagraphStyle

Provides access to the text paragraph attributes of a rich text item

Contained within the NotesSession class

Contains the NotesRichTextTab

NotesRichTextStyle

Provides access to the style attributes of a rich text item

Contained within the NotesSession class

NotesSession

> Provides access to the current environment
>
> Contains the NotesAgent, NotesDatabase, NotesDateRange, NotesDateTime, NotesDbDirectory, NotesDocumentCollection, NotesInternational, NotesLog, NotesNewsletter, NotesRichTextParagraphStyle, or NotesTimer class

NotesTimer

> Provides access to an object to trigger an event on a timed basis
>
> Contained within the NotesSession class

NotesView

> Provides access to a view or folder
>
> Contained within the NotesDatabase or NotesUIView classes
>
> Contains the NotesDocument, NotesViewColumn, NotesViewEntry, NotesViewEntryCollection and NotesViewNavigator classes

NotesViewColumn

> Provides access to a column in a view
>
> Contained within the NotesView class

NotesViewEntry

> Provides access to a specified row in a view
>
> Contained within the NotesView, NotesViewEntryCollection, or the NotesViewNavigator class
>
> Contains the NotesDocument class

NotesViewEntryCollection

> Provides access to subset of view entries, sorted in view order, the results of which are defined by a defined criteria
>
> Contained within the NotesView or NotesViewEntry class

NotesViewNavigator

> Provides access to a subset of the entries in a view
>
> Contained within the NotesView or NotesViewEntry class

ODBC Classes

The ODBC classes provide access to back-end data from any ODBC-compliant application. In order to use the ODBC classes, the ODBC LSX must be defined in the Options event of the Globals for the object as UseLSX "*LSXODBC".

ODBCConnection

Provides access to an ODBC connection object

Not contained in any other class

ODBCQuery

Provides access to an ODBC query object to define the SQL query that will be used to return the appropriate data

Not contained in any other class

ODBCResultSet

Provides access to the data returned from the ODBC query of the ODBC connection

LSS Files

Constants are available for use with LotusScript, instead of using the numeric equivalent. Constants are used to return error messages and as arguments within LotusScript statements. These constants are defined in files that contain an extension of LSS. These files must be defined in the Declarations event of the object that you want to use them in.

LSCONST.LSS

The LotusScript global constants; also includes the file LSPRCVAL.LSS

LSERR.LSS

Error message constants for API and Client

LSPRCVAL.LSS

Constants used for LSITHREADINFO

LSXBEERR.LSS

Error messages for the back-end methods

LSXUIERR.LSS

Error messages for the user interface or front-end methods

Java and CORBA Classes

by Debbie Lynd

The `lotus.domino` classes available for Java access to Domino objects are described in this appendix.

ACL

>   Provides access to the Access Control List of a database

>   Contained within the `Database` object

>   Contains the `ACLEntry` object

ACLEntry

>   Provides access to an individual entry in the ACL

>   Contained within the `ACL` object

Agent

>   Provides access to an agent

>   Contained within the `AgentContext` or `Database` object

>   Contains `Database` and `DateTime`

AgentContext

>   Provides access to the environment that the agent is running in

>   Contained within the `Session` object

>   Contains `Agent`, `Database`, `DateTime`, `Document`, `DocumentCollection`, and `Name`

Database

>   Provides access to a Notes database, its properties, and methods

>   Contained within a `Session`, `DbDirectory`, or `AgenContext` object

>   Contains the `ACL`, `Agent`, `Document`, `DocumentCollection`, `Form`, `DateTime`, `Replication`, and `View` classes

DateRange

>   Provides access to a range of dates and times

>   Contained within the `Session` class

>   Contains the `DateTime` class

DateTime

>   Provides access to a date and time value

>   Contained within the `DateRange`, `Session`, `AgentContext`, `Database`, `Document`, and `View` classes

DbDirectory

> Provides access to the databases contained within a directory on a specific server or the local machine
>
> Contained within the `Session` class
>
> Contains the `Database` and `DateTime` class

Document

> Provides access to a document within a database and its associated properties and methods
>
> Contained within the `Database`, `DocumentCollection`, `Newsletter`, and `View` classes
>
> Contains the `EmbeddedObject`, `Item`, `RichTextItem`, and `DateTime` classes

DocumentCollection

> Provides access to a set of documents selected based on a specified criteria
>
> Contained within the `Database`, `AgentContext`, and `View` classes
>
> Contains the `Document` object

EmbeddedObject

> Provides access to any embedded object, linked object, or file attachment
>
> Contained within the `Document` or `RichTextItem` classes

Form

> Provides access to a form in adatabase
>
> Contained within the `Database` object

International

> Provides access to the operating system's international settings
>
> Contained within the `Session` class

Item

> Provides access to a data item within a document
>
> Contained within the `Document` object
>
> Contains the `DateTime` class
>
> Base class for the `RichTextItem` class

B

JAVA AND CORBA CLASSES

Log

> Provides ability to record information about the execution of a script and place that information in a database, mail memo, or file
>
> Contained within the Session class

Name

> Provides access to a username or server name and its associated properties and methods
>
> Contained within the AgentContext or Session class

Newsletter

> Provides access to a document that contains links to a set of documents that meet a specified criteria
>
> Contained within the Session class
>
> Contains the Document class

Outline

> Provides access to an outline, its properties, and methods
>
> Contained within the Database class
>
> Contains the OutlineEntry class

OutlineEntry

> Provides access to one of the entries within an outline
>
> Contained within the Outline class

Registration

> Provides access to an ID file for registration or administration of that file
>
> Contained within the Session class

Replication

> Provides access to the replication settings for a database
>
> Contained within the Database class

RichTextItem

> Provides access to a Notes item of the rich-text data type
>
> Contained within the Document class
>
> Contains the EmbeddedObject and RichTextStyle class
>
> Derives its properties and methods from the Item class

RichTextParagraphStyle

> Provides access to the text paragraph attributes of a rich-text item
>
> Contained within the `Session` class
>
> Contains the `RichTextTab` class

RichTextStyle

> Provides access to the style attributes of a rich-text item
>
> Contained within the `Session` and `RichTextItem` class

RichTextTab

> Contained within the `RichTextParagraphStyle` class

Session

> Provides access to all other objects and the Domino environment
>
> Contained within the `AgentBase` and `NotesFactory` classes
>
> Contains the `AgentContext`, `Database`, `DateRange`, `DateTime`, `DbDirectory`, `International`, `Log`, `Name`, `Newsletter`, `Registration`, `RichTextParagraphStyle`, or `RichTextStyle` classes

View

> Provides access to a view or folder
>
> Contained within the `Database` class
>
> Contains the `Document`, `DateTime`, `ViewColumn`, `ViewEntry`, `ViewEntryCollection`, and `ViewNavigator` classes

ViewColumn

> Provides access to a column in a view
>
> Contained within the `View` class

ViewEntry

> Provides access to a specified row in a view
>
> Contained within the `View`, `ViewEntryCollection`, or `ViewNavigator` class
>
> Contains the `Document` class

ViewEntryCollection

> Provides access to a subset of view entries, sorted in view order, the results of which are defined by a criterion
>
> Contained within the `View` class
>
> Contains the `ViewEntry` class

ViewNavigator

Provides access to a subset of the entries in a view

Contained within the View class

Contains the ViewEntry class

JavaScript Classes

by Steve Kern

Notes and Domino R5 supports JavaScript 1.3, although not all properties or methods are available. And, as of this writing, there is no documentation available for the methods and properties that are available. You can see which JavaScript methods and properties are available in the Object Reference tab of objects that are scriptable with JavaScript. However, although context help is available for the Formula language and LotusScript, no context help is available for JavaScript. Therefore, there are no examples, and there is no way to tell which JavaScript reference listed is a method or a property.

Each object reference includes a brief description, followed by the Document Object Models (DOMs) in which the object is available, and then the properties, methods, and event handlers. Because the implementation of JavaScript is not well documented in Domino Designer, all properties and methods are included for each object that is available.

Two DOMs are available: Web and Notes. Not all objects are available in both DOMs. Each object reference listed below includes the DOMs for which it is available.

The event handlers are a part of the JavaScript language definition and are included here for the sake of completeness. As you know, each scriptable JavaScript event is plainly identified in the Domino Designer IDE.

Area Object

Defines a clickable region or an area of an image used in an imagemap, and creates a link to a hypertext reference that is loaded into its target window. Area objects work like Link objects.

DOM: Web

Properties

hash: The anchor name in the URL.

host: The host and domain name; or the IP address of a server.

hostname: The host:port part of the URL.

href: As in HTML, the full URL.

pathname: The path part of the URL.

port: The communications port of the server.

protocol: The beginning of the URL (including the colon) such as http:.

search: A search string.

target: The TARGET attribute.

text: A string containing the content of the A tag.

Methods

handleEvent

eventHandler: Invokes the event handler.

This object inherits the watch and unwatch methods from Object.

Event Handlers

onDblClick, onMouseOut, onMouseOver

Array Object

Enables you to work with arrays.

DOM: Web, Notes

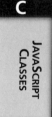

Properties

constructor: The function that creates the object's prototype.

index: The zero-based index of the match in the string for an array created by a regular expression match.

input: The original string against which the expression was matched for an array created by a regular expression match.

length: The number of elements in the array.

prototype: Adds properties to objects.

Methods

concat: Joins two arrays, creating a new array.

join: Creates a string by joining all elements of an array.

pop: Returns and removes the last element in the array.

push: Adds elements to the end of an array. Returns the array's new length.

reverse: Switches the first and last array elements. The first element becomes the last, and the last element becomes the first.

shift: Returns and removes the first element from an array.

slice: Returns a new array from a section of the array.

splice: Removes or adds array elements.

sort: Sorts array elements.

toSource: Creates a literal representation of an array that can be used to create a new array.

toString: Creates a string representation of the array elements.

unshift: Adds elements to the start of an array and returns the array's new length.

valueOf: The primitive value of the array.

Inherits the watch and unwatch methods from Object.

Boolean Object

The object wrapper for a Boolean value.

DOM: Web, Notes

Properties

constructor: The function that creates an object's prototype.

prototype: A property that is shared by all Boolean objects.

Methods

toSource: Creates an object literal representing the Boolean object. This value can create a new object.

toString: Creates a string representing the specified Boolean object.

valueOf: The primitive value of a Boolean object.

Inherits the watch and unwatch methods from Object.

Button Object

Works withpushbuttons.

DOM: Web

Properties

form: The form containing the Button object.

name: The NAME attribute of the Button object.

type: The TYPE attribute of the Button object.

value: The VALUE attribute of the Button object.

Methods

blur: Removes focus.

click: Simulates a mouse click.

focus: Gives focus.

handleEvent: Invokes the event handler.

Inherits the watch and unwatch methods from Object.

Event Handlers

onBlur, onClick, onFocus, onMouseDown, onMouseUp

C

JAVASCRIPT
CLASSES

Checkbox Object

Works with checkboxes in JavaScript.

DOM: Web

Properties

checked: A Boolean property reflecting the current state of the checkbox.

defaultChecked: A Boolean property reflecting the CHECKED attribute of the checkbox.

form: The form that contains the checkbox.

name: The NAME attribute of the checkbox.

type: The TYPE attribute of the checkbox.

value: The VALUE attribute of the checkbox.

Methods

blur: Removes focus.

click: Simulates a mouse click.

focus: Gives focus.

handleEvent: Invokes the event handler.

Inherits the watch and unwatch methods from Object.

Event Handlers

onBlur, onClick, onFocus

Date Object

Handles date objects.

DOM: Web, Notes

Properties

constructor: The function that creates the date object prototype.

prototype: Adds properties to a date object.

Methods

getDate: The day of the month in local time.

getDay: The day of the week in local time.

getFullYear: The year in local time.

getHours: The hour in local time.

getMilliseconds: The milliseconds in local time.

getMinutes: The minutes in local time.

getMonth: The month in local time.

getSeconds: The seconds in local time.

getTime: The numeric value representing the time in local time.

getTimezoneOffset: The time-zone offset in minutes for the current locale.

getUTCDate: The day (date) of the month in universal time.

getUTCDay: The day of the week in universal time.

getUTCFullYear: The year in universal time.

getUTCHours: The hours in universal time.

getUTCMilliseconds: The milliseconds in universal time.

getUTCMinutes: The minutes in universal time.

getUTCMonth: The month in universal time.

getUTCSeconds: The seconds in universal time.

getYear: The year in local time.

parse: The milliseconds in a date string since January 1, 1970 00:00:00 in local time.

setDate: Sets the day of the month for a date in local time.

setFullYear: Sets the full year for a date in local time.

setHours: Sets the hours for a date in local time.

setMilliseconds: Sets the milliseconds for a date in local time.

setMinutes: Sets the minutes for a date in local time.

setMonth: Sets the month for a date in local time.

setSeconds: Sets the seconds for a date in local time.

setTime: Sets the value of a date object in local time.

setUTCDate: Sets the day of the month in universal time.

setUTCFullYear: Sets the full year in universal time.

setUTCHours: Sets the hour in universal time.

setUTCMilliseconds: Sets the milliseconds in universal time.

setUTCMinutes: Sets the minutes in universal time.

setUTCMonth: Sets the month in universal time.

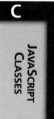

setUTCSeconds: Sets the seconds in universal time.

setYear: Sets the year in local time.

toGMTString: Converts a date object to a string value using the Internet GMT conventions.

toLocaleString: Converts a date object to a string value using the current locale's conventions.

toSource: Returns an object literal representing the date object.

toString: Returns a string representation of the date object.

toUTCString: Converts a date to a string value using the universal time convention.

UTC: The milliseconds in a date object since January 1, 1970 00:00:00 in universal time.

valueOf: Primitive value of the date object.

Inherits the watch and unwatch methods from Object.

Document Object

Contains information about the current document, and provides methods for displaying HTML output to the user.

DOM: Web, Notes

Properties

alinkColor: A string specifying the color for the ALINK attribute (active link color).

anchors: The array containing entries for the document's anchors.

applets: The array containing entries for the document's applets.

bgColor: A string specifying the color for the BGCOLOR attribute (background color).

cookie: Refers to a cookie.

domain: The document server's domain name.

embeds: The array containing entries for the document's plug-ins.

fgColor: A string representing the document's TEXT attribute (foreground color).

formName: A separate property for each named form in the document.

forms: The array containing entries for the document's forms.

images: The array containing entries for the document's images.

lastModified: A string specifying the last modification date.

layers: The array containing entries for the document's layers.

linkColor: A string that specifies the LINK attribute (link color).

links: The array containing entries for the document's links.

plugins: The array containing entries for the document's plug-ins.

referrer: The URL of the document that called the current document.

title: The contents of the TITLE tag.

URL: The full document URL.

vlinkColor: A string specifying the VLINK attribute (visited link color).

Methods

captureEvents: Tells the document to capture all specified event types.

close: Closes output and displays data.

getSelection: A string that contains the current selection.

handleEvent: Invokes the event handler.

open: Collects the output of the write method or the writeln method.

releaseEvents: Releases events captured in the window or document, sending the objects further down the event hierarchy.

routeEvent: Sends a captured event down the normal event hierarchy.

write: Writes HTML expressions to a document in the window you specify.

writeln: Writes HTML expressions to a document in a window, followed by a newline character.

Inherits the watch and unwatch methods from Object.

Event Handlers

onClick, onDblClick, onKeyDown, onKeyPress, onKeyUp, onMouseDown, onMouseUp

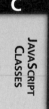

C

JAVASCRIPT
CLASSES

Form Object

Enables users to input information and post data to a server.

DOM: Web, Notes

Properties

action: The ACTION attribute of the form object.

elements: An array representing all form elements.

encoding: The ENCTYPE attribute of the form object.

length: The number of elements on a form.

method: The METHOD attribute of the form object.

name: The NAME attribute of the form object.

target: The TARGET attribute of the form object.

Methods

handleEvent: Invokes the event handler.

reset: Resets the form.

submit: Submits the form.

Inherits the watch and unwatch methods from Object.

Event Handlers

onReset, onSubmit

FileUpload Object

A file upload element.

DOM: Web

Properties

form: The form that contains the FileUpload object.

name: The NAME attribute of the FileUpload object.

type: The TYPE attribute of the FileUpload object.

value: The current value of the file upload element—that is, the name of the file to upload.

Methods

blur: Removes focus.

focus: Gives focus.

handleEvent: Invokes the event handler.

select: Selects the input area.

Inherits the watch and unwatch methods from Object.

Event Handlers

onBlur, onChange, onFocus

Frame Object

Manipulates a frame within a window.

DOM: Web

Properties

closed: Indicates that a window has been closed.

defaultStatus: The window's default status bar message.

document: Information on the current document; also, methods for displaying HTML output.

frames: The array of a window's frames.

history: History of the URLs the client has visited in a window.

innerHeight: The vertical dimension of a window's content area in pixels.

innerWidth: The horizontal dimension of a window's content area in pixels.

length: The number of frames that are in a window.

location: A string representing the current URL.

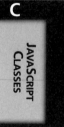

C

JAVASCRIPT
CLASSES

locationbar: The browser window's location bar.

menubar: The browser window's menu bar.

name: The window's unique name.

opener: The calling document's window name.

outerHeight: The vertical dimension of the window's outside boundary in pixels.

outerWidth: The horizontal dimension of the window's outside boundary in pixels.

pageXOffset: The current x-position of a window's viewed page in pixels.

pageYOffset: The current y-position of a window's viewed page in pixels.

parent: The name of the window or frame containing the current frame.

personalbar: The personal bar of the browser window.

scrollbars: The scrollbars of the browser window.

self: Refers to the current window.

status: A message in the status bar of the window.

statusbar: The status bar of the browser window.

toolbar: The toolbar of the browser window.

top: Refers to the top window.

window: Refers to the current window.

Methods

alert: Shows an Alert dialog box with an OK button and a message you specify.

back: Goes back one step in the history list of a frame in the top window.

blur: Removes focus.

captureEvents: Tells the window or document to capture specific events.

clearInterval: Clears a timeout interval created by setInterval.

clearTimeout: Clears a timeout created by setTimeout.

close: Closes the window you specify.

confirm: Shows a Confirm dialog box with OK and Cancel buttons and a message you specify.

disableExternalCapture: Stops external event capturing.

enableExternalCapture: Enables a window with frames to capture events in pages loaded from other locations.

find: Searches for a text string in the specified window's contents.

focus: Gives focus.

forward: Navigates to the next item in the URL history.

handleEvent: Invokes the event handler.

home: Navigates to the user's home page URL as set in the browser's preferences.

moveBy: Moves the window using amounts you specify.

moveTo: Moves the upper-left corner of the window using coordinates you specify.

open: Opens a new browser window.

print: Prints the window or frame contents.

prompt: Shows a Prompt dialog box with a field for input and a message.

releaseEvents: Releases captured events of the type you specify, and sends the event down the event hierarchy.

resizeBy: Resizes the window by an amount you specify, moving the window's bottom-right corner.

resizeTo: Resizes the window using amounts you specify for height and width.

routeEvent: Sends an event that was captured down the normal event hierarchy.

scroll: Scrolls a window to a coordinate you specify.

scrollBy: Scrolls a window's viewing area by an amount you specify.

scrollTo: Scrolls a window's viewing area to the coordinates you specify.

setInterval: After the number of milliseconds you specify elapses, calls a function or evaluates an expression.

setTimeout: After the number of milliseconds you specify elapses, calls a function or evaluates an expression once.

stop: Stops the download currently in progress.

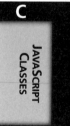

Event Handlers

onBlur, onDragDrop, onError, onFocus, onLoad, onMove, onResize, onUnload

Function Object

Defines JavaScript code to be compiled into a function.

DOM: Web

Properties

arguments: Array corresponding to the arguments passed to a function.

arguments.callee: The currently executing function's body.

arguments.caller: The name of the function that called the function currently executing.

arguments.length: The number of arguments passed.

arity: The number of arguments expected.

constructor: The function that creates a prototype.

length: The number of arguments expected.

prototype: Adds properties to a Function object.

Methods

apply: Applies a method from another object in the context of the calling object.

call: Lets you execute a method from another object in the context of the calling object.

toSource: A string representing the source code.

toString: A string representing the source code.

valueOf: A string representing the source code.

Hidden Object

Lets you to work with hidden fields. Also, a hidden Text object on an HTML form.

DOM: Web

Properties

form: The form containing the Hidden object.

name: The NAME attribute.

type: The TYPE attribute.

value: The current value of the Hidden object.

Methods

Inherits the watch and unwatch methods from Object.

History Object

An array, or list, of the URLs that the client has visited while in a window.

DOM: Web, Notes

Properties

current: The URL of the current entry.

length: The number of entries in the history array.

next: The URL of the next entry.

previous: The URL of the previous entry.

Methods

back: Loads the previous URL.

forward: Loads the next URL.

go: Loads an URL in the list.

Inherits the watch and unwatch methods from Object.

Image Object

An image on an HTML form.

DOM: Web, Notes

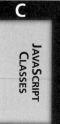

C

JAVASCRIPT
CLASSES

Properties

border: The BORDER attribute.

complete: A Boolean value indicating whether the Web browser has finished loading the image.

height: The image's HEIGHT attribute.

hspace: The image's HSPACE attribute.

lowsrc: The image's LOWSRC attribute.

name: The image's NAME attribute.

src: The image's SRC attribute.

vspace: The image's VSPACE attribute.

width: The image's WIDTH attribute.

Methods

handleEvent: Invokes the event handler.

Inherits the watch and unwatch methods from Object.

Event Handlers

onAbort, onError, onKeyDown, onKeyPress, onKeyUp, onLoad

Layer Object

Describes and manipulates a layer in an HTML page.

DOM: Web

Properties

above: The window object, if the layer is at the top; otherwise, the layer above the current one in z-order.

background: The background image for the layer's canvas.

bgColor: The background color for the layer's canvas.

below: Null if the layer is at the bottom; otherwise, the layer object below the current one in z-order.

`clip.bottom`: The clipping rectangle's bottom edge (the part of the layer that is visible).

`clip.height`: The clipping rectangle's height (the part of the layer that is visible).

`clip.left`: The clipping rectangle's left edge (the part of the layer that is visible).

`clip.right`: The clipping rectangle's right edge (the part of the layer that is visible).

`clip.top`: The clipping rectangle's top edge (the part of the layer that is visible).

`clip.width`: The clipping rectangle's width (the part of the layer that is visible).

`document`: The document associated with the layer.

`left`: Horizontal position of the left edge in pixels relative to the origin of its parent layer.

`name`: The name of the layer as specified in the ID attribute of the `LAYER` tag.

`pageX`: Horizontal position of the layer in pixels relative to the page.

`pageY`: Vertical position of the layer in pixels relative to the page.

`parentLayer`: The enclosing window object if the current layer is not nested in another layer; otherwise, the layer object that contains the current layer.

`siblingAbove`: Returns null if the layer has no sibling above; otherwise, the layer object above the current one in z-order.

`siblingBelow`: Returns null if the layer is at the bottom; otherwise, the layer object below the current one in z-order.

`src`: The URL of the content for the layer.

`top`: Vertical position of the top edge of the layer in pixels relative to the origin of its parent layer.

`visibility`: Boolean; true if the layer is visible.

`zIndex`: The relative z-order of the current layer.

Methods

`captureEvents`: Captures all events of the type specified in the window or document.

`handleEvent`: Invokes the event handler.

`load`: Loads the contents of the specified file, discards the original source, and changes the wrapping width of the layer.

`moveAbove`: Moves the current layer above the layer specified. Does not affect the positions of either layer.

`moveBelow`: Moves the current layer below the layer specified. Does not affect the positions of either layer.

`moveBy`: Moves the layer position by the pixels specified.

`moveTo`: Moves the top-left corner of the layer to screen coordinates that you specify.

`moveToAbsolute`: Moves the current layer to coordinates you specify in pixels in the same page.

`releaseEvents`: Releases captured events from the layer and sends the events down the hierarchy.

`resizeBy`: Resizes the layer by the values you specify in pixels for height and width.

`resizeTo`: Resizes the layer to the values you specify in pixels for height and width.

`routeEvent`: Moves a captured event down the event hierarchy.

Inherits the `watch` and `unwatch` methods from `Object`.

Event Handlers

`onMouseOver, onMouseOut, onLoad, onFocus, onBlur`

Input Object

No description available.

Link Object

Text, image, or an image area that contains a hypertext link reference. Clicking the link launches and opens the URL.

DOM: Web, Notes

Properties

`hash`: The anchor name in the URL.

`host`: The IP address or host and domain name of a server.

`hostname`: The host:port part of the URL.

`href`: The entire URL referenced.

pathname: The path part of the URL.

port: The communications port the server uses.

protocol: The first part of the URL, identifying the protocol to be used, including the colon. Example: http: or ftp:

search: A search string.

target: The TARGET attribute.

text: The content of the corresponding A tag.

Methods

handleEvent: Invokes the event handler.

Inherits the watch and unwatch methods from Object.

Event Handlers

onClick, onDblClick, onKeyDown, onKeyPress, onKeyUp, onMouseDown, onMouseOut, onMouseUp, onMouseOver

Location Object

Contains information on the current URL.

DOM: Web, Notes

Properties

hash: The anchor name in the URL.

host: The IP address or host and domain name of a server.

hostname: The host:port part of the URL.

href: The entire URL referenced.

pathname: The path part of the URL.

port: The communications port the server uses.

protocol: The first part of the URL, identifying the protocol to be used, including the colon. Example: http: or ftp:

search: A search string.

Methods

`reload`: Reloads the current document.

`replace`: Loads the URL.

Inherits the `watch` and `unwatch` methods from `Object`.

Math Object

A built-in object that has properties and methods for mathematical constants and functions. For example, the Math object's `PI` property has the value of pi.

DOM: Web, Notes

Properties

`E`: The base of natural logarithms known as Euler's Constant. Approximately 2.718.

`LN10`: The natural logarithm of 10. Approximately 2.302.

`LN2`: The natural logarithm of 2. Approximately 0.693.

`LOG10E`: The Base 10 logarithm of E. Approximately 0.434.

`LOG2E`: The Base 2 logarithm of E. Approximately 1.442.

`PI`: Ratio of the circumference of a circle to its diameter. Approximately 3.14159.

`SQRT1_2`: The square root of 1/2. Approximately 0.707.

`SQRT2`: The square root of 2. Approximately 1.414.

Methods

`abs`: The absolute value of a number.

`acos`: The arccosine in radians of a number.

`asin`: The arcsine in radians of a number.

`atan`: The arctangent in radians of a number.

`atan2`: The arctangent of the quotient of its arguments.

`ceil`: The smallest integer greater than or equal to a number.

`cos`: The cosine of a number.

`exp`: Returns E *n*, where *n* is the argument and E is Euler's constant.

floor: The largest integer less than or equal to a number.

log: The natural logarithm of a number.

max: The greater of two numbers.

min: The lesser of two numbers.

pow: Base to the exponent power.

random: Returns a pseudorandom number between 0 and 1.

round: The value of a number rounded to the nearest integer.

sin: The sine of a number.

sqrt: The square root of a number.

tan: The tangent of a number.

Inherits the watch and unwatch methods from Object.

MimeType Object

A multipurpose Internet mail extensions (MIME) type supported by the client.

DOM: Web, Notes

Properties

The MIME type's description.

enabledPlugin: The Plugin object that is configured for the MIME type.

suffixes: A list of filename extensions for the MIME type.

type: The MIME type's name.

Methods

Inherits the watch and unwatch methods from Object.

Navigator Object

Contains information about the version of Navigator in use.

DOM: Web, Notes

Properties

appCodeName: The code name of the browser.

appName: The name of the browser.

appVersion: The version of the browser.

language: The language (translation) used by the browser.

mimeTypes: A list (array) of all MIME types available to the browser.

platform: The platform of the browser.

plugins: A list (array) of all plug-ins currently available to the browser.

userAgent: The header of the user-agent.

Methods

javaEnabled: Indicates that Java is enabled.

plugins.refresh: Makes newly installed plug-ins available and optionally reloads open documents that contain plug-ins.

preference: Gets and sets preferences.

taintEnabled: Indicates that data tainting is enabled.

Inherits the watch and unwatch methods from Object.

Number Object

This object is a wrapper for primitive numeric values; it lets you work with numbers.

DOM: Web, Notes

Properties

constructor: The function that creates a prototype.

MAX_VALUE: The largest number representable.

MIN_VALUE: The smallest number representable.

NaN: Represents a value that is not a number.

NEGATIVE_INFINITY: This value represents "negative infinity" and is returned on overflow.

POSITIVE_INFINITY: This value represents infinity and is returned on overflow.

prototype: Adds properties to the object.

Methods

toSource: Sets an object literal to represent the Number object that can be used to create a new Number object.

toString: Sets a string that represents the object.

valueOf: Returns the primitive value of the object.

Inherits the watch and unwatch methods from Object.

Object Object

This is the primitive JavaScript object type from which all JavaScript objects are descended (the base object). All JavaScript objects have the methods defined for Object.

DOM: Web, Notes

Properties

constructor: The function that creates an object prototype.

prototype: Adds properties to all objects.

Methods

eval: Evaluates a string of JavaScript in the object's context. This method has been deprecated.

toSource: Returns an object literal representing the object that can be used to create a new object.

toString: Returns a string that represents the object.

unwatch: Removes a watchpoint from an object's property.

valueOf: Returns the primitive value of the object.

watch: Adds a watchpoint to an object's property.

Option Object

An option (choice) in a selection list. Usually used in conjunction with a Select object.

DOM: Web, Notes

Properties

defaultSelected: The initial selection state of the option (the default choice).

selected: The current selection state of the option.

text: The text for the option.

value: The selected value returned to the server when the form is submitted.

Methods

Inherits the watch and unwatch methods from Object.

Password Object

Similar to a field in Domino, this object hides text entered by users with asterisks.

DOM: Web

Properties

defaultValue: The VALUE attribute of the password object.

form: The form that contains the password object.

name: The NAME attribute of the password object.

type: The TYPE attribute of the password object.

value: The current value of the password object.

Methods

blur: Removes focus from the password object.

focus: Adds focus to the password object.

handleEvent: Invokes the event handler.

select: Selects the password object's input area.

Event Handlers

onBlur, onFocus

Plugin Object

A software module installed on the client that the browser can invoke to display certain kinds of data.

DOM: Web, Notes

Properties

description: The plug-in description.

filename: The filename of the plug-in.

length: The number of elements in the array of MimeType objects for the plug-in.

name: The plug-in's name.

Methods

Inherits the watch and unwatch methods from Object.

PluginArray Object

This object is part of Notes, but not a part of JavaScript 1.3. Please see information for the Plugin object.

DOM: Notes

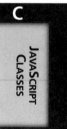

Radio Object

A radio button in a radio button set on an HTML form.

DOM: Web

Properties

checked: This selects an individual radio button programmatically.

defaultChecked: This represents the CHECKED property of an individual radio button.

form: The form containing the Radio object.

name: The NAME attribute of the array of buttons.

type: The TYPE attribute of the array of buttons.

value: The VALUE attribute of the array of buttons.

Methods

blur: Removes focus.

click: Simulates a mouse click.

focus: Gives focus.

handleEvent: Invokes the event handler.

Inherits the watch and unwatch methods from Object.

Event Handlers

onBlur, onClick, onFocus

RegExp Object

The pattern of a regular expression. Used to find and replace matches in strings.

DOM: Web, Notes

Properties

$1, ..., $9: Parenthesized substring matches.

constructor: The function that creates an object prototype.

global: If set to true, tests the regular expression against all possible matches in a string. If false, tests only against the first.

ignoreCase: Ignore case while matching a string.

input: Also $_. String against which a regular expression is matched.

lastIndex: The starting index for the next match.

lastMatch: Also $&. The characters last matched.

lastParen: Also $+. The last parenthesized substring match.

leftContext: Also $`. Substring before the most recent match.

`multiline`: Also $*. Search strings across multiple lines.

`prototype`: Adds properties to all objects.

`rightContext`: Also $'. Substring after the most recent match.

`source`: The pattern's text.

Methods

`compile`: Compiles the object.

`exec`: Executes the search.

`test`: Tests for a match.

`toSource`: Returns an object literal that represents the object, which can be used to create a new object.

`toString`: Returns a string that represents the object.

`valueOf`: The primitive value of the object.

Inherits the `watch` and `unwatch` methods from `Object`.

Reset Object

Represents a button that resets all form elements to their initial values.

DOM: Web

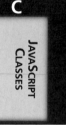

Properties

`form`: The form containing the `Reset` object.

`name`: The `NAME` attribute.

`type`: The `TYPE` attribute.

`value`: The `VALUE` attribute.

Methods

`blur`: Removes focus.

`click`: Simulates a mouse click.

`focus`: Gives focus.

`handleEvent`: Invokes the event handler for the specified event.

Inherits the `watch` and `unwatch` methods from `Object`.

Event Handlers

`onBlur, onClick, onFocus`

Screen Object

Describes the display screen.

DOM: Notes

Properties

`availHeight`: The height of the screen in pixels. Does not include permanent or semipermanent UI features, such as the Windows Taskbar.

`availWidth`: The width of the screen in pixels. Does not include permanent or semipermanent UI features, such as the Windows Taskbar.

`colorDepth`: The bit depth of the color palette. If no color palette is in use, this value comes from the property `screen.pixelDepth`.

`height`: The height of the display screen.

`pixelDepth`: The screen color resolution in bits per pixel.

`width`: The width of the display screen.

Methods

Inherits the `watch` and `unwatch` methods from `Object`.

Select Object

A list of choices, or selections, on an HTML form.

DOM: Web

Properties

`form`: The form containing the selection object.

`length`: The number of options in the list.

name: The NAME attribute.

options: The OPTION tags.

selectedIndex: The index of the selected option. If more than one option is chosen, the first selected option.

type: Returns either select-multiple, indicating that multiple choices are possible, or select-one, indicating that only a single choice is possible.

Methods

blur: Removes focus.

focus: Gives focus.

handleEvent: Invokesthe event handler.

Event Handlers

onBlur, onChange, onFocus

String Object

Represents a series of characters.

DOM: Web, Notes

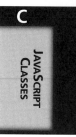

Properties

constructor: The function that creates an object's prototype.

length: The length of the string.

prototype: Adds properties to a String object.

Methods

anchor: Creates an HTML anchor. Anchors are used as the target of a hypertext link.

big: Displays the string in a big font, as if it were inside a <BIG> tag.

blink: Displays a blinking string, as if it were inside a <BLINK> tag.

bold: Displays the string in bold, as if it were inside a <B> tag.

charAt: Returns the character at a specified location in the string.

`charCodeAt`: Returns the Unicode value of the character at the specified location in the string.

`concat`: Concatenates two strings and creates a new string.

`fixed`: Displays the string in fixed-pitch font, as if it were inside a `<TT>` tag.

`fontcolor`: Displays the string in the color specified, as if it were inside a `<FONT COLOR=color>` tag.

`fontsize`: Displays the string in the font size specified, as if it were inside a `<FONT SIZE=size>` tag.

`fromCharCode`: Creates a string from a sequence of Unicode values.

`indexOf`: Returns the position of the first occurrence of the value within the String, or a -1 if not found.

`italics`: Displays the string in italic, as if it were inside an `<I>` tag.

`lastIndexOf`: Returns the position of the last occurrence of the value within the String, or a -1 if not found.

`link`: Creates a hypertext link.

`match`: Matches a regular expression against a string.

`replace`: Replaces the matched substring from a regular expression with a new substring.

`search`: Searches the string for a match with a regular expression.

`slice`: Returns a new string from a section of a string.

`small`: Displays the string in a small font, as if it were inside a `<SMALL>` tag.

`split`: Creates an array of strings by splitting the string into substrings.

`strike`: Displays the string in strikethrough, as if it were inside a `<STRIKE>` tag.

`sub`: Displays the string in subscript, as if it were inside a `<SUB>` tag.

`substr`: Returns the number of characters specified from a starting position in a string.

`substring`: Returns the characters in a string between a starting and ending position in the string.

`sup`: Displays the string in superscript, as if it were inside a `<SUP>` tag.

`toLowerCase`: Converts the string to lowercase.

`toSource`: Returns an object literal that represents the object and that can be used to create a new object.

`toString`: Returns a string that represents the object.

`toUpperCase`: Converts the string to uppercase.

`valueOf`: The primitive value of the object.

Submit Object

A button that submits an HTML form.

DOM: Web

Properties

`form`: The form containing the Submit object.

`name`: The NAME attribute.

`type`: The TYPE attribute.

`value`: The VALUE attribute.

Methods

`blur`: Removes focus.

`click`: Simulates a mouse click.

`focus`: Gives focus.

`handleEvent`: Invokes the event handler.

Event Handlers

`onBlur`, `onClick`, `onFocus`

Text Object

Represents a text input field.

DOM: Web

C

JavaScript
Classes

Properties

defaultValue: The VALUE attribute.

form: The form containing the Text object.

name: The NAME attribute.

type: The TYPE attribute.

value: The current value of the field.

Methods

blur: Removes focus.

focus: Gives focus.

handleEvent: Invokes the event handler.

select: Selects the object's input area.

Event Handlers

onBlur, onChange, onFocus, onSelect

Textarea Object

Represents a multiline field on an HTML form.

DOM: Web

Properties

defaultValue: The VALUE attribute.

form: The form containing the Textarea object.

name: The NAME attribute.

type: Defines the object as a Textarea object.

value: The current value of the object.

Methods

blur: Removes focus.

focus: Gives focus.

handleEvent: Invokes the event handler.

select: Selects the object's input area.

Event Handlers

onBlur, onChange, onFocus, onKeyDown, onKeyPress, onKeyUp, onSelect

Window Object

Represents a browser window or frame. This is the top-level object for each document, location, and history object group.

DOM: Web, Notes

Properties

closed: Indicates that a window has been closed.

defaultStatus: The window's default status bar message.

document: Information on the current document; also, methods for displaying HTML output.

frames: The array of a window's frames.

history: History of the URLs the client has visited in a window.

innerHeight: The vertical dimension of a window's content area in pixels.

innerWidth: The horizontal dimension of a window's content area in pixels.

length: The number of frames that are in a window.

location: A string representing the current URL.

locationbar: The browser window's location bar.

menubar: The browser window's menu bar.

name: The window's unique name.

opener: The calling document's window name.

outerHeight: The vertical dimension of the window's outside boundary in pixels.

outerWidth: The horizontal dimension of the window's outside boundary in pixels.

pageXOffset: The current x-position of a window's viewed page in pixels.

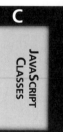

C

JAVASCRIPT
CLASSES

pageYOffset: The current y-position of a window's viewed page in pixels.

parent: The name of the window or frame containing the current frame.

personalbar: The personal bar of the browser window.

scrollbars: The scrollbars of the browser window.

self: Refers to the current window.

status: A message in the status bar of the window.

statusbar: The status bar of the browser window.

toolbar: The toolbar of the browser window.

top: Refers to the top window.

window: Refers to the current window.

Methods

alert: Shows an Alert dialog box with an OK button and a message you specify.

back: Goes back one step in the history list of a frame in the top window.

blur: Removes focus.

captureEvents: Tells the window or document to capture specific events.

clearInterval: Clears a timeout interval reated by setInterval.

clearTimeout: Clears a timeout created by setTimeout.

close: Closes the window you specify.

confirm: Shows a Confirm dialog box with OK and Cancel buttons and a message you specify.

disableExternalCapture: Stops external event capturing.

enableExternalCapture: Enables a window with frames to capture events in pages loaded from other locations.

find: Searches for a text string in the specified window's contents.

focus: Gives focus.

forward: Navigates to the next item in the URL history.

handleEvent: Invokes the event handler.

`home`: Navigates to the user's home page URL as set in the browser's preferences.

`moveBy`: Moves the window using amounts you specify.

`moveTo`: Moves the upper-left corner of the window using coordinates you specify.

`open`: Opens a new browser window.

`print`: Prints the window or frame contents.

`prompt`: Shows a Prompt dialog box with a field for input and a message.

`releaseEvents`: Releases captured events of the type you specify and sends the event down the event hierarchy.

`resizeBy`: Resizes the window by an amount you specify, moving the window's bottom-right corner.

`resizeTo`: Resizes the window using amounts you specify for height and width.

`routeEvent`: Sends an event that was captured down the normal event hierarchy.

`scroll`: Scrolls a window to a coordinate you specify.

`scrollBy`: Scrolls a window's viewing area by an amount you specify.

`scrollTo`: Scrolls a window's viewing area to the coordinates you specify.

`setInterval`: After the number of milliseconds you specify elapses, calls a function or evaluates an expression.

`setTimeout`: After the number of milliseconds you specify elapses, calls a function or evaluates an expression once.

`stop`: Stops the download currently in progress.

Event Handlers

`onBlur, onDragDrop, onError, onFocus, onLoad, onMove, onResize, onUnload`

HTML Reference

by Steve Kern

This reference is not meant to be a complete listing of HTML tags, but is intended to cover tags you may frequently use or that are otherwise interesting. For example, although you may have little need to use the Applet or Frameset tags, they are included for informational purposes. Tags such as those related to Input and Form are not listed at all because the Domino Designer handles those tags and because you are not likely to create a Form from scratch with Input tags. Similarly, there is no reason to cover tables because tables are handled easily in Notes. You can always find the latest specifications at http://www.w3.org. This is the URL for the World Wide Web Consortium (WC3), which is the group responsible for formalizing and standardizing the HTML language.

HTML tags are grouped in this appendix by their usage: Applet, Document, Formatting, Frames, and Hyperlink. A tag's type (standalone or container), its syntax, and a brief description follow each tag name. My intention is to provide you with a quick, handy reference to locate tags you may want to use. You can then research them further, as needed, on the Web.

On the Book CD

A database titled HTML reference (HTMLRef.nsf) is on the CD accompanying this book.

Applet Tags

Applet tags provide a way to place executable objects on Web pates. <APPLET> is used for Java applets, and <OBJECT> is used for other types of executable objects.

<APPLET>

Type: Container

Syntax:

```
<APPLET WIDTH="pixels" HEIGHT="pixels" CODEBASE="applet url"
CODE="class file" OBJECT="applet file" NAME="applet name" ARCHIVE="archive"
ALT="alternate text" ALIGN="TOP ¦ MIDDLE ¦ BOTTOM ¦ LEFT ¦ RIGHT"
HSPACE="pixels" VSPACE="pixels"
```

Description: Used to place a Java applet on a page that can be run by the browser. Note that you can use Domino Designer to embed applets.

\<OBJECT>

Type: Container

Syntax:

```
<OBJECT CLASSID="object information" CODEBASE="object url"
CODETYPE="MIME type" TYPE="MIME type of data" STANDBY="message"
USEMAP="name" ALIGN="TEXTTOP ¦ MIDDLE¦ TEXTMIDDLE ¦ BASELINE ¦
TEXTBOTTOM ¦ LEFT ¦ CENTER ¦ RIGHT" WIDTH="pixels or percent"
NAME="name of object" HEIGHT="pixels or percent" HSPACE="pixels"
VSPACE="pixels" BORDER="pixels"> </OBJECT>
```

Description: Used to add an executable object to a page. For example, you could launch an ActiveX module or a plug-in such as Acrobat.

\<PARAM>

Type: Standalone

Syntax:

```
<PARAM NAME="name" VALUE="value" VALUETYPE="DATA ¦ REF ¦ OBJECT"
TYPE="MIME type"
```

Description: Used with the \<APPLET> tag to pass a parameter to the Java applet.

Document Tags

Document tags are used in HTML to define the HTML document. There are three parts to a document: the HTML declaration, the document head, and the document body.

\<BASE>

Type: Standalone

Syntax:

```
<BASE HREF="url"> or <BASE TARGET="frame">
```

Description: Accepts values for HREF and TARGET.

\<BODY\>

Type: Container

Syntax:

```
<BODY BGCOLOR ¦ BACKGROUND ¦ LINK ¦ ALINK ¦ VLINK ¦ TEXT "color">
body of the document </BODY>
```

Description: Follows the \<HTML\> tag. All content and tags for a document go in the \<BODY\> container tag.

\<HEAD\>

Type: Container

Syntax:

```
<HEAD> head tags </HEAD>
```

Description: Follows the \<HTML\> tag and can contain other tags, such as \<BASE\>, \<ISINDEX\>, \<META\>, \<SCRIPT\>, \<STYLE\>, \<TITLE\>. Other HTML content follows this tag.

\<HTML\>

Type: Container

Syntax:

```
<HTML> document content </HTML>
```

Description: Indicates that the document is HTML.

\<LINK\>

Type: Standalone

Syntax:

```
<LINK HREF ¦ TITLE ¦ REL ¦ REV value>
```

Description: Declares the relationship between two linked files, as defined by an URL and a TITLE. REL and REV describe the relationship between the files.

<META>

Type: Standalone

Syntax:

```
<META NAME="value" CONTENT="value">
```

or

```
<META HTTP-EQUIV="value" CONTENT="value">
```

Description: Takes several different attributes used to identify meta-level information about a document. These attributes can be author, software used to create the document, keywords used in searches, and so forth.

<SCRIPT>

Type: Container

Syntax:

```
<SCRIPT LANGUAGE ¦ DEFER ¦ SRC ¦ TYPE></SCRIPT>
```

Description: Usually used with LANGUAGE; defines the type of scripting language, such as JavaScript.

<STYLE>

Type: Container

Syntax:

```
<STYLE TYPE ¦ MEDIA ¦ TITLE> </STYLE>
```

Description: Used to define the specifications for the document style. TYPE is required. Often used with cascading style sheets.

<TITLE>

Type: Container

Syntax:

```
<TITLE> text </TITLE>
```

Description: The title for the document, as presented to the browser.

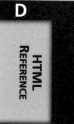

D

HTML REFERENCE

Formatting Tags

Formatting tags are used to modify the presentation of text in HTML. Some of these tags modify the font and style of the text, and others create line feeds, quotes, and horizontal rules.

<BASEFONT>

Type: Standalone

Syntax:

```
<BASEFONT SIZE="size" COLOR="color" FACE="typefaces">
```

Description: Sets size, color, and font face of fonts for a document.

<BIG>

Type: Container

Syntax:

```
<BIG> text </BIG>
```

Description: Sets text to a size larger than the default font.

<BLOCKQUOTE>

Type: Container

Syntax:

```
<BLOCKQUOTE> text </BLOCKQUOTE>
```

Description: Indents a block of text.

Type: Standalone

Syntax:

```
<BR CLEAR ¦ LEFT ¦ RIGHT ¦ ALL>
```

Description: Creates a linefeed in the text. The attributes are all optional and determine where the line break falls.

\<B\>

Type: Container

Syntax:

`<B> text </B>`

Description: Sets text to bold.

\<CENTER\>

Type: Container

Syntax:

`<CENTER> text </CENTER>`

Description: Centers text.

\<FONT\>

Type: Container

Syntax:

`<FONT SIZE="size" COLOR="color" FACE="typeface"> text </FONT>`

Description: Used for formatting. Sets size, color, and font face of fonts for text. Can be used to offset the `<BASEFONT>` tag.

\<H*n*\>

Type: Container

Syntax:

`<Hn ALIGN="value"> text </Hn>`

where "*n*" is a number between 1 and 6, such as `<H1> text </H1>`.

Description: Sets the size of the text inside the container to one of six font sizes: 1 is the largest, and 6 is the smallest. `ALIGN` can be set to LEFT, RIGHT, CENTER, or JUSTIFY.

\<HR>

Type: Standalone

Syntax:

```
<HR ALIGN="value" NOSHADE SIZE=value WIDTH=value
```

Description: Creates a horizontal line. Using `ALIGN`, you can specify LEFT, RIGHT, or CENTER. `NOSHADE` turns off the shadow effect. `SIZE` controls the thickness of the line in pixels. `WIDTH` can be set to a percentage (preferable) such as 50%, or to a number of pixels. Note: You can insert a horizontal rule through the Domino Designer.

\<I>

Type: Container

Syntax:

```
<I> text </I>
```

Description: Sets text to italics.

\<PRE>

Type: Container

Syntax:

```
<PRE> text </PRE>
```

Description: Sets the text in the container to a fixed-width font, which preserves spaces, tabs, and similar elements. Note: Typically, HTML ignores tabs, extra spaces, and carriage returns.

\<P>

Type: Container

Syntax:

```
<P ALIGN="value"> text </P>
```

Description: Creates a paragraph. `ALIGN` can be set to LEFT, RIGHT, CENTER, or JUSTIFY.

<SMALL>

Type: Container

Syntax:

`<SMALL> text </SMALL>`

Description: Sets text to a size smaller than the default font.

<SPAN>

Type: Container

Syntax:

`<SPAN STYLE="style"> text </SPAN>`

Description: Used to apply styles in the STYLE list. Styles are set as they are in Cascading Style Sheet Level 1.

<SUB>

Type: Container

Syntax:

`<SUB> text </SUB>`

Description: Sets text to subscript.

<SUP>

Type: Container

Syntax:

`<SUP> text </SUP>`

Description: Sets text to superscript.

<S>

Type: Container

Syntax:

`<S> text </S>`

Description: Sets text to strikethrough.

<TT>

Type: Container

Syntax:

```
<TT> text </TT>
```

Description: Sets text to a fixed-width font, such as Courier.

<U>

Type: Container

Syntax:

```
<U> text </U>
```

Description: Sets text to underline.

Frameset Tags

Frameset tags are included here largely for informational purposes because a Frameset is a Domino design object. These are the tags used to split the browser window into frames, displaying different pages in each frame.

<FRAMESET>

Type: Container

Syntax:

```
<FRAMESET ROWS="size list" COLS="size list"></FRAMESET>
```

Description: Creates a frameset. Framesets can be defined by rows (ROWS) or by columns (COLS), but not by both. ROWS and COLS can be specified in pixels or percents.

<FRAME>

Type: Standalone

Syntax:

```
<FRAME SRC="document url" NAME="name" FRAMEBORDER="0¦1"
MARGINWIDTH="pixels" MARGINHEIGHT="pixels" NORESIZE
SCROLLING="YES¦ NO ¦ AUTO">
```

Description: Used with <FRAMESET> to create a frame with content.

<IFRAME>

Type: Container

Syntax:

```
<IFRAME SRC="document url" NAME="name" FRAMEBORDER="0¦1" WIDTH="value"
HEIGHT="value" MARGINWIDTH="pixels" MARGINHEIGHT="pixels" NORESIZE
SCROLLING="YES¦ NO ¦ AUTO"> alternate text or image </IFRAME>
```

Description: Produces a frame that floats on the page. Width and height can be specified in pixels or percentages.

<NOFRAME>

Type: Container

Syntax:

```
<NOFRAME> content </NOFRAME>
```

Description: Used as an alternative for browsers that cannot display frames. The content between the beginning and ending tags frequently is an URL pointing to an alternate site.

Hyperlink Tags

Hyperlink tags are used in HTML to link to other pages or Web sites. These tags are extremely powerful; although you can accomplish similar effects with the Domino Designer, it is good to understand what actually makes a link function.

<A>

Type: Container

Syntax:

```
<A HREF="URL" TARGET="frame" REL="forward link" REV="reverse link"
ACCESSKEY="letter" TABINDEX="tab position"> hyperlink content </A>
or <A NAME="value"> text </A>
```

Description: Used with HREF; sets up a hyperlink from the content to the specified URL. Used with NAME, <A> sets an anchor link in the document.

<IMG>

Type: Standalone

Syntax:

```
<IMG SRC="path to file (url)" HEIGHT="pixels" WIDTH="pixels"
ALT="alternate text" ALIGN="alignment" HSPACE="pixels" VSPACE="pixels"
ISMAP USEMAP="name">
```

Description: Used to Display images. Frequently used to create clickable images that launch URLs.

Using NotesPeek

by Steve Kern

In This Appendix

NotesPeek gives you a way to browse Domino objects and data in what amounts to its raw form. NotesPeek has been around for quite a while, and it has been updated to include the new design objects in R5. This free application is available from Lotus' Web site and, at less than 500K, is a relatively small download.

Installing NotesPeek

The version of NotesPeek this appendix discusses is available only for Intel Windows 32-bit platforms. Different versions of NotesPeek are also available for R4 and R3; the R3 version is even available on the Windows 3.1 platform.

Installing NotesPeek is very easy. The zip file contains just three files: the executable (`Ntspk32.exe`), a help file (`Notespk.hlp`), and a readme file (`Readme.txt`). The readme file contains the installation instructions. Using WinZip or similar software, you can extract these files to any directory, but it is best to unzip them to the directory that contains the Notes executables (by default, that is `c:\Lotus\Notes` for R5). You don't need to extract the readme file unless you want to.

> **Caution**
>
> It is very important that the Notes dll's and the `Notes.ini` file be on your computer's path. To verify this, open a command window and type "Path" without the quotes. You should see the Notes directories for the dll's and `Notes.ini` in the output from Path.

You can now run NotesPeek by double-clicking `Ntspk32.dll` in the Windows Explorer, but you might find it easier to create a shortcut either on the desktop or in the menu. NotesPeek comes with its own set of icons (see Figure E.1).

FIGURE E.1

The NotesPeek Icons are pretty humorous!

Understanding NotesPeek

NotesPeek works with the object containment hierarchy of Notes and Domino, starting with servers at the highest level and drilling down to items at the document level. Servers contain databases, which in turn contain views, forms, and documents, which contain items. Figure E.2 shows the NotesPeek window, which has three panes.

What's an Object?

In NotesPeek, things are not always what you think. For example, in the Domino Designer, you refer to "design objects," such as forms and views. In NotesPeek, objects are "large chunks of data that are associated with notes but do not need to be displayed by the Notes client…. The most common use of objects is to store the contents of file attachments." To many people, *PAB* is shorthand for the Public Address Book, but in NotesPeek, it is the Paragraph Attribute Block. As you can see, NotesPeek deals with elements of Notes and Domino differently and at a much lower level than you may be used to.

FIGURE E.2

The three panes of a NotesPeek window graphically show the containment hierarchy of a database.

Collapsed node

Expanded node

Tree pane

Context pane

Info pane

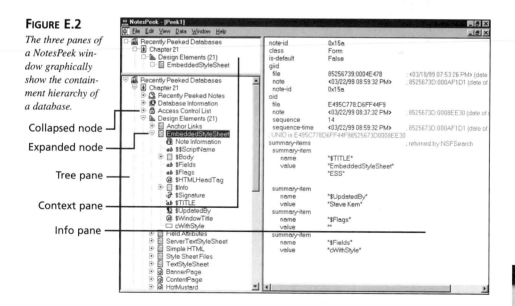

The pane in the upper-right corner is the Context pane, which shows the context of the currently expanded node. You can't do anything with this window—and, by default, you don't even see it. To see the Context pane, drag the splitter bar down to expose the pane.

E

USING
NOTESPEEK

The pane at the lower left is called the Tree pane, which displays the hierarchy of the objects. You will notice that the Tree pane contains objects that act like twisties, called boxed-plus and boxed-minus in NotesPeek Help. To expand a node, click the boxed-plus symbol. When expanded, the plus changes to a minus; clicking the boxed-minus symbol collapses the node. The Tree pane contains a large number of different icons, which are described in NotesPeek Help (see the section titled, "Using NotesPeek Help").

For Keyboard Fans!

NotesPeek Help contains a list of keyboard shortcuts that can be used in place of the mouse.

Opening Multiple Peek Windows

If you want to look at two databases at the same time, perhaps to compare objects, you can do so because NotesPeek is a Multiple Document Interface (MDI) application. Simply click the menu or desktop shortcut again, and a new NotesPeek window will open.

Information about the current selection in the Tree pane is displayed in the Info pane on the right. In Figure E.2, the Info pane is open to the EmbeddedStyleSheet form. With Release 1.5 of NotesPeek, you can now navigate the Info pane with cursor keys and highlight and copy text to the Clipboard. You can change what's displayed in the Info pane by choosing View, Options from the menu. At the bottom of the list on the left side of the dialog box is Info Pane. Click that, and the dialog window shown in Figure E.3 is displayed.

FIGURE E.3

You can control what is displayed in different parts of NotesPeek by using the View Options dialog box.

Using the NotesPeek Menu

The NotesPeek menu is patterned in the classic Windows style. The main menu consists of the standard File, Edit, View, Data, Window, and Help menu prompts. Table E.1 lists the menu choices, followed by a brief description of their use.

TABLE E.1 Using the NotesPeek Menu Items

Command or Menu	*Description*
	File
New	Opens a new window containing a local and a server node.
Open File	Opens a database file in a new window.
Open Server	Opens a server in a new window.
Exit	Exits NotesPeek.
	Edit
Copy	Copies text highlighted in the Info pane to the Clipboard.
Delete	Deletes the current Note Selector node from the tree.
Find	Searches the current node and all descendants for a string.
	View
Set Font	Changes the font in all three panes.
Options	Opens the View Options dialog box, enabling you to specify settings for the following tabs: Databases, Notes, Open, Items, and Info Pane. See the section "Setting Options for NotesPeek," later in this appendix.
Hide All	Hides all nodes of the same type as the current node. This prompt changes with the node selected, as in `Hide All: Databases`.
Show All	Removes placeholders of the current node type. This prompt changes with the node type, as in `Show All: Databases`.
Show All Data	Displays all data.

continues

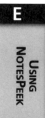

E

USING
NOTESPEEK

TABLE E.1 Using the NotesPeek Menu Items

Command or Menu	*Description*
Placeholders for Hidden Data	Toggles the display of placeholders (see Figure E.4). If selected, placeholder icons appear where hidden data nodes exist. If not, the data is simply hidden.
Save Options as Default	Saves current settings for the font, node types to hide, the Placeholders setting, and setting made in the View Options dialog box as the default.
Data	
Expand	Expands the current node in the tree pane.
Collapse	Collapses the current node in the tree pane.
Expand Lots	Expands several nodes at once.
Select Notes	Creates a Note Selector node from the current node.
Open Note	For a database node, locates a note by the UNID or NoteID.
Dump to File	Creates a text file from the Tree pane and the Info pane.
Window	
Cascade	Cascades NotesPeek windows.
Tile Left-Right	Tiles NotesPeek windows left to right.
Tile Top-Bottom	Tiles NotesPeek windows top to bottom.
Arrange Icons	Arranges minimized NotesPeek windows.
Help	
Contents	Opens the Help database, `Notespk.hlp`.
Tell Me About	Changes the cursor to an arrow plus a question mark. Click anywhere in NotesPeek and get help on that item.
License Agreement	Displays the End User License Agreement.
About NotesPeek	Displays the splash screen for NotesPeek.

As you can see from this lengthy table describing the commands available on the menu, NotesPeek is a fairly extensive product. Fortunately, there is a very good help file available with the product to help you find your way through all these choices.

Using NotesPeek Help

NotesPeek Help can be used in two ways. Choosing Help, Contents from the menu opens standard Windows-style rich-text help as a separate application. The Help file is adequately cross-referenced and provides you with plenty of information on what the product is and how to use it. For example, more than 100 different icons appear in Tree view. If you open NotesPeek Help, click Common Questions, and then choose "What do all these icons mean?" from the list of questions, you'll get a document listing all the icons. Each icon has hot-linked text next to it leading to a document describing the icon (see Figure E.4).

FIGURE E.4

This NotesPeek Help window lists the icons available in the Tree pane.

For such a small program, NotesPeek is very well documented. And there is yet another way to get help: From the menu, choose Help, Tell Me About, and click an object. NotesPeek help will launch open to a document describing the object you clicked.

Working with Nodes

Nodes are found in the Tree pane. A *node* is a line of information about an object that contains an icon, followed by descriptive text. Nodes can contain other nodes as well. For example, a server node contains database nodes, and a database node contains form nodes, and so on.

You can work with nodes in a lot of ways. Choices in the View and Data menus enable you to hide, display, expand, and collapse nodes. You can also click the boxed-plus and boxed-minus symbols to expand and collapse nodes. Right-clicking a node produces a floating contextual menu from which you can make choices.

Most likely, you are already used to expanding and collapsing views in Notes, so expanding and collapsing nodes in NotesPeek shouldn't be anything new to you. A similar feature is Expand Lots, which is available from the Data menu. If you happen to expand a server with a multitude of databases, performance may suffer. If this happens, as in Notes, you can press Ctrl+Break to stop the execution of the command.

You may have noticed some nodes titled Recently Peeked Servers, Recently Peeked Databases, and (under a database node) Recently Peeked Notes. NotesPeek keeps track of the 10 most recently peeked servers and databases, and the five most recently peeked Notes for each database. This handy feature enables you to pick up where you left off very easily.

One of the most powerful features of NotesPeek is the capability to hide an entire object class. For example, you might not want to see pages; you can hide them by right-clicking the object and choosing Hide All: Pages from the context menu. What happens next depends on the setting for Placeholders. If you refer to Table E.1, you'll see that Placeholders for Hidden Data is a toggle. If this is checked, a placeholder icon and text indicating the hidden objects appear next to the object when you hide an object class. If this is not checked, the object class disappears completely. Hiding an object class and turning off placeholders removes extraneous items from the Tree pane, enabling you to concentrate on the objects in which you are interested (see Figure E.5).

FIGURE E.5

The contextual menu offers an easy way to access menu choices, such as Hide All, for an object class.

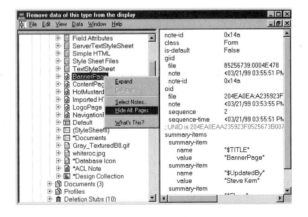

Another very powerful feature is the capability to select Notes. From the menu, choose Data, Select Notes; the Select Notes window shown in Figure E.6 opens.

FIGURE E.6

The Select Notes dialog box offers an extremely powerful means of entering selection criteria.

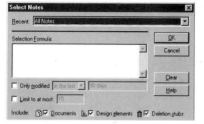

As you can see from Figure E.6, a wide variety of options are available. Recently used criteria can be chosen from the recent drop-down list at the top of the window. You can even enter a selection formula using the Formula language to retrieve documents. The default is all documents, but you can include design elements and even deletion stubs. When you have set up the selection criteria, you can click OK, and a new node appears in the tree containing the selected Notes with descriptive text indicating the selection criteria (see Figure E.7).

FIGURE E.7

The Note Selector node shows the Design Elements that were modified within the last 90 days.

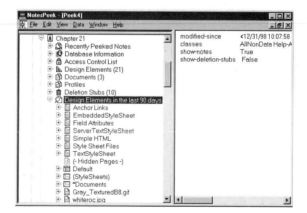

The Note Selector node is the only item in NotesPeek that you can delete. To delete it, highlight the node and either hit the delete key or choose Edit, Delete Selector. Creating Selector Nodes is a quick way of gathering documents and design elements and conveniently collecting them in a single location.

E

USING NOTESPEEK

Creating a Text File from NotesPeek

You can create a text file from the information in the Tree and Info panes. However, this file may not be of much value to you, outside of a certain amount of intellectual curiosity: According to the documentation, the text file is not meant to be human-readable. To dump the contents of a node and displayed descendents, highlight the node and choose Data, Dump to File from the menu. To display descendents that are collapsed, check Include Collapsed Data. Listing E.1 shows a portion of the file dump.

LISTING E.1   NOTESPEEK—A Text-File Dump from NotesPeek

```
(recently-peeked-notes )
    (database-information
        (creation-class NoteFile)
        (database-id 85256739:0004E478) ; <03/18/99 07:53:26 PM>
    ➡ (date of creation)
        (replica-info
            (replica-id 85256739:0004E478) ; <03/18/99 07:53:26 PM>
        ➡ (date of creation of original db)
            (flags 0)
            (priority Medium)
            (cutoff-interval 90)    ; days
            (cutoff-date <>))    ; 0
        (version
            (major 41)
            (minor 0))
        (data-modification <03/27/99 09:15:42 PM>)    ; 85256742:000C6C8F
        (nondata-modification <03/28/99 07:46:07 AM>)   ; 85256742:00462404
        (options NoBgAgent)
        (db-quota
            (warning-threshold 0)    ; kilobytes
            (size-limit 0)    ; kilobytes
            (current-db-size 384)    ; kilobytes
            (max-db-size 4294967295))    ; kilobytes
        (max-password-access Editor)
        (item-def-table    ; 53 items
            (item    ; #0
                (name "$DesignVersion")
                (type Text))
            (item    ; #1
                (name "$Version")
                (type Text))
```

```
(item      ; #2
    (name "$Formula")
    (type Formula))
(item      ; #3
    (name "$FormulaClass")
    (type Text))
(item      ; #4
    (name "$Collation")
    (type Collation))
(item      ; #5
    (name "$UpdatedBy")
    (type TextList))
```

As you can see, this is rather lengthy and makes for laborious reading.

Setting Options for NotesPeek

You open the Options dialog window by choosing View, Options from the menu. Five tabs are available. The Databases tab lets you specify what appears in the title of a database node. The default is the database title, but you can also display the filename and the title and template.

The Notes tab enables you to control what appears in the Info pane. You can choose Simple or Formula. When you choose Simple, three check boxes are available: Note ID, Is-Default Flag, and Title. Formula is intended to be used with documents, not with design notes. When you specify a formula, the result of the formula is displayed in the Info pane.

Settings on the Open tab enable you to determine how a Note is opened. Note that this doesn't affect Notes that are already opened.

The Items tab enables you to make two choices: Include value in text, and sort by name. These settings control the way a node appears in the Tree pane. If you choose Include Value in Text, then the node's text will display both the name and the value. Sort by Name causes the items in a note to be displayed in alphabetical order. Otherwise, the items are listed in the order in which they are stored. Remember that an item corresponds to a field in the designer.

Settings for the Info pane are numerous and enable you to control the display of strings and dates. These settings also include some general settings.

When you get everything set up the way you like, simply choose View, Save Options as Default.

Summary

This short appendix has shown you how to use NotesPeek to get a good look at your databases and to get at information that is otherwise unavailable. For example, one of the book's technical editors used NotesPeek to track down a problem in a client's application. One of the database's designs mysteriously and inexplicably grew in size. With NotesPeek, the editor was able to quickly track down the specific elements and remove them with a custom-written C++ program (the elements were unavailable from the designer). Getting to know this powerful application is well worth your time!

Domino URL Reference

Domino URLs can be embedded in documents as HTML and enable access to various Domino features. Domino URLs follow a fairly straightforward syntax, as in the following example:

```
http://Host/DominoObject?Action&Arguments
```

`Host` can be an IP address or a DNS entry. `DominoObjects` consist of documents, views, databases, agents, framesets, and so forth. `Actions` are taken against `DominoObjects`, and `Arguments` are passed to the `Action`. `Actions` are prefixed with the question mark (?) and all `Arguments` are prefixed with the ampersand (&). For example, the following code opens the database `myhome.nsf` on the Domino server `www.myserver.com` and requires the user to log in:

```
http://www.myserver.com/myhome.nsf?OpenDatabase&Login
```

Because spaces are not permitted in URLs, in general, you can replace them with the plus sign (+) as in the following URL that opens the Main Topic view:

```
http://www.myserver.com/myhome.nsf/Main+Topics?OpenView
```

A database titled Domino URL Reference (`DomURLRef.nsf`) is on the CD accompanying this book.

Domino URL Identifiers

Table F.1 lists the object references (identifiers) that can be used to open the default view, form, and so on of a Domino database.

TABLE F.1   Domino Identifiers

Identifier	*Reference*
$defaultView	The default view
$defaultForm	The default form
$defaultNav	The default navigator
$searchForm	A form used to search databases
$file	Used to access a file attachment in a document
$icon	The database icon
$help	The Using this database document
$about	The About this database document
$first	The first document in a view

Alphabetical List of Domino URLs

CreateDocument

Syntax: `http://host/database/form?CreateDocument`

Description: Creates a new document based on the specified form. Form can be specified with the name, UNID, NoteID, or by `$defaultForm`.

DeleteDocument

Syntax: `http://host/database/view/document?DeleteDocument`

Description: Deletes the specified document.

EditDocument

Syntax: `http://host/database/view/document?EditDocument`

Description: Edits the specified document.

OpenAbout

Syntax: `http://host/database/$about?OpenAbout`

Description: Opens the About this database document.

OpenAgent

Syntax: `http://host/database/agent?OpenAgent`

Description: Opens (runs) an agent. The agent can only be referred to by its name. You cannot use the UNID or NotesID.

OpenDatabase

Syntax: `http://host/database/?OpenDatabase`

Description: Opens a specific database. Database can be the filename, as in `mydatabase.nsf` or a replica ID followed by `.nsf` as in `__85256736:0008FEE9.nsf`. Note the required double underscore before the Replica ID.

OpenDocument

Syntax: `http://host/database/view/document?OpenDocument`

Arguments: `CollapseOutline=n ExpandOutline=n StartOutline=n`

Description: Opens the document specified. The document can be specified using a key, the UNID, the NoteID, or using `$first`, the first document in the view. All three arguments are optional and work with outline controls on the page. n in each case can be listed in dotted hierarchical fashion, as in 1.3.1, which opens the first document under the third category under the top level category.

OpenElement

Syntax:

For file attachments:

`http://host/database/document/$File/filename?OpenElement`

For images:

`http://host/database/document/FieldName/FieldOffset?OpenElement`

For OLE objects:

`http://host/database/document/FieldName/FieldOffset/$OLEOBJINFO/Field Offset/obj.ods?OpenElement`

Arguments: `FieldElemFormat=imagetype`

Description: Opens file attachments, images and OLE objects. `FieldElemFormat` is optional for use with images, and can be set to `gif` or `jpeg`. `gif` is the default.

OpenForm

Syntax: `http://host/database/form?OpenForm`

Arguments: `ParentUNID=DocumentUniqueID SpecialAction=FieldName`

Description: Opens a form in the database. `Form` can be specified by its name, UNID, or NoteID, or the default form can be opened with `$defaultForm`. The `ParentUNID` is an optional argument that can be used when opening a response document. `SpecialAction` is an optional argument that automates SSL. It is set to the name of a text field on the form that must contain one of three values: `"SubmitCert"`, `"ServerRequest"`, or `"ServerPickup"`.

OpenFrameset

Syntax: `http://host/database/frameset?OpenFrameset`

Description: Opens the frameset specified by "frameset."

OpenHelp

Syntax: `http://host/database/$help?OpenHelp`

Description: Opens the Using this database document.

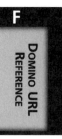

OpenIcon

Syntax: `http://host/database/$icon?OpenIcon`

Description: Opens the database icon.

OpenNavigator

Syntax: `http://host/database/navigator?OpenNavigator`

Description: Displays the specified navigator to the browser. Navigator can be specified by name, UNID, or NotesID, or the default can be opened with $defaultNav.

OpenPage

Syntax: `http://host/database/page?OpenPage`

Arguments: `CollapseOutline=n ExpandOutline=n StartOutline=n`

Description: Opens the page specified. Pages can be identified by the page name, UNID, or NoteID. All three arguments are optional and work with outline controls on the page. n in each case can be listed in dotted hierarchical fashion, as in 1.3.1.

OpenServer

Syntax: `http://host/?OpenServer`

Description: Opens the databases on a server, as long as browsing the server is not restricted.

OpenView

Syntax: `http://host/database/view?OpenView`

Arguments: `Collapse=n CollapseView Count=n Expand=n ExpandView Start=n StartKey=document key`

Description: Opens a view in a Domino database. `view` can be the name of the view, the universal ID of the view, the Note ID of the view, or the default view using $defaultview. The arguments bear some description: `CollapseView` and `ExpandView` do exactly what they sound like they do: collapse and expand the view when opened by the user. `Collapse` specifies the collapsed row number to display. `Expand` specifies the expanded row number to display. `Count` determines the number of rows to display in the browser. `Start` defines the row number to start the display. `StartKey` is a string value that is a key to a document in the view. The view starts the display at that document.

ReadForm

Syntax: `http://host/database/form?ReadForm`

Description: Displays the form without any fields open for editing. Form can be specified by name, UNID, NoteID, or $defaultForm can be used to open the database default form.

Redirect

Syntax: `http://MyServer/MyHome.nsf?Redirect`

Arguments: `Name=server Id=replica id To=url`

Description: Redirects the browser to another URL.

RequestCert

Syntax:

For users: `http://host/database/ResultForm?RequestCert`

Arguments:

For users:

`&Command=SubmitCert&TranslateForm=TranslationForm`

For servers:

`&Command=ServerRequest&TranslateForm=TranslationForm`

Description: Creates requests for user and server SSL certificates. The form specified must contain specific fields in order to be processed correctly.

SaveDocument

Syntax: `http://host/database/view/document?SaveDocument`

Description: Saves the document; equivalent to the HTML <POST> tag.

SearchDomain

Syntax: `http://host/database/[templateForm]?SearchDomain[Arguments]`

Description: Searches a Domino domain. You can first open a search form to gather input, and then display the results in a results form. The `templateForm` and `Arguments` are optional. If you don't specify a results form (`templateForm`), then Domino uses `$$SearchDomainTemplate`. An error will be generated if a results form or the `$$SearchDomainTemplate` doesn't exist. Note to reviewer: there is no documentation on what the arguments could be. It is possible that the arguments are the same as the SearchSite and SearchView Domino URLs.

SearchSite

Syntax: http://host/database/[$SearchForm]?SearchSite[Arguments]

Arguments:

Query= search string

Count=n

SearchEntry = form name

SearchFuzzy=[TRUE,FALSE]

SearchOrder=[1,2,3] 1 = "Sort by relevance", 2 = "Sort by date ascending", 3 ="Sort by date descending."

SearchMax=n

SearchWV=[TRUE, FALSE] TRUE = include word variants.

Start=n

Description: Allows multidatabase site searches. You must have a Site Search database created before using this command. $SearchForm and Arguments are optional.

SearchView

Syntax: http://host/database/view/[$SearchForm]?SearchView[Arguments]

Arguments:

Query= search string

Count=n

SearchEntry = form name

SearchFuzzy=[TRUE,FALSE]

SearchOrder=[1,2,3] 1 = "Sort by relevance", 2 = "Sort by date ascending", 3 ="Sort by date descending."

SearchMax=n

SearchWV=[TRUE, FALSE] TRUE = include word variants.

Start=n

Description: Searches documents in a specific view. The $SearchForm identifier and Arguments are optional.

Glossary

.nsf A file extension for a Domino Database (as in Mail.nsf). The letters are short for *Notes Storage Facility*.

.ntf A file extension for a Domino Database design template (as in perweb.ntf). The letters are short for *Notes Template Facility*.

@Function A commonly used or complex formula that is built into Notes.

About This Database document A special document that describes the purpose of a Domino database. The document can be viewed from the Help menu.

Accelerator key See *Hotkey*.

Access control See *Access Control List*.

Access Control List (ACL) A list of users, groups, and servers and their rights and access privileges to a Domino database.

Access control section Within a Notes form, a section where the capability to edit can be restricted to specific individuals. An individual must already have the right to edit the document in the ACL before she can be granted the privilege to edit an access-controlled section. Other users can still read the section.

Access level A security feature that defines the degree of access to a database granted to a user, group, or server. There are seven levels of access: No Access, Depositor, Reader, Author, Editor, Designer, and Manager.

ACL See *Access Control List*.

Action Bar   Also called a *button bar*, this nonscrolling region at the top of a view or form contains predefined Actions for that view or form.

Action Buttons and Hotspots   Preprogrammed areas of a view or form that users click to automate.

Address bar   The area of a window that shows the current file path or Web page address (URL). New file or address requests are entered here.

Address Books   See *Personal Address Book* and *Enterprise Directory.*

Agent (also called macro)   A program that consists of and performs a series of automated tasks. Agents can be initiated by the user or can run on a scheduled basis. An Agent is composed of three parts: when it acts (the Trigger), what it acts on (the Search), and what it does (the Action). Agents are written in the Lotus Formula language, LotusScript, JavaScript, or Java.

Alarm   In Domino, an automated notification that a triggering event has occurred. For example, a calendar event can notify a user that he has a meeting in 30 minutes, or a server event can trigger an alarm to the Domino administrator that a performance threshold has been reached.

Attachment   A file attached to a document or form.

Authenticate   In Domino, to exchange identifying information in such a way that the identity of both parties is established.

Authentication   In Domino security, the process by which clients or servers establish their identities to each other. Authentication can use certificates or in the case of a Notes client, a name and password, to establish identity.

Author access   A level of security (defined in the Access Control List) that permits a user or server to create and edit his own documents.

Authors field   A field that contains the name of the author of a document. When combined with author access to the database, an Authors field can be used to grant editor access to users who are not authors of the document.

Autolaunch   Automatically launches an attachment or embedded object in its native format when a Notes document is opened.

Bookmark folder   A folder on the bookmark bar that holds bookmarks linking to Domino databases, Notes views or documents, or Web pages.

Bookmark(s)   In Domino, a link that references a document or a location in a document on the Web or in a Domino database.

Broadcast meeting   A type of calendar entry that invites people to a meeting, but no response is required.

Browser   A graphical interface that lets users interact with the World Wide Web on the Internet.

Button bar   See *Action Bar*.

Button Hotspot   Also known as a *pushbutton*, a Button Hotspot contains actions that appear in the form of a clickable button which can be added to forms, subforms, pages, and documents. See also *Action*.

Calendar   In Domino, the calendaring views, forms, and documents built in to the Notes mail template, used to make and track events such as appointments, meetings, and anniversaries. The Calendar function also includes the scheduling of shared resources and tracking freetime for meeting scheduling and group calendaring.

Canonical format   The format in which Notes stores hierarchical names internally, with each hierarchical component identified by a one- or two-character code. For example, CN=John Smith/OU=East/O=Acme/C=US.

Cascading   Falling from. In Cascading *menu*, a collection of menu items that fall under a single prompt in a parent menu. The File, Database menu prompt is an example. In Cascading *actions*, a collection of actions that appear under a single action button in the Action Bar.

Category   In Domino, a word, number, or phrase used to group Notes documents in a view.

Certificate   A file that verifies the identity of a computer when two computers communicate. Certificates are used to verify the identity of an email sender and to exchange and authenticate identities with an Internet server.

Channel   A Web site to which one can subscribe to receive information from the Internet, which uses Web pages that update themselves using *push technology*.

Checkbox   A small area on a form in which the user makes selections by clicking that area. When clicked, a checkmark or X appears in the checkbox. Checkboxes are toggle keys: Click once to place a checkmark; click a checkmark to remove it.

Checkbox fields   In Domino, a keyword field type that presents a list of choices to the user in a checkbox format. Users make a choice by clicking the checkbox, which places an *x* in the box. This keyword field is used where multiple choices can be made, as in a checklist.

Child document   A Notes document created using a Response-type form. The child document inherits data from its parent document and is permanently associated with that parent. If the parent document is deleted, the child document will be orphaned unless it is also deleted.

Collapse   In Domino, to condense a view so that it displays only categories or only main documents (with the responses hidden). The term is also used when sections within documents are condensed so that only the section header is displayed.

Combobox field   A keyword field type that presents a list of choices to the user in a drop-down list format.

Command key   A keyboard shortcut for performing an immediate action. For example, to print a document, you can use Ctrl+P in Windows (Command+P on a Macintosh).

Common Name   The first element in the X.500 naming convention. Each name requires at a minimum the Common Name element (CN) and the Organization element (O). This field contains the user's full first and last names.

Compact   (in Domino) Compress a database by removing any white space created when documents are deleted.

Connection document   A Domino document that defines the connection properties between two servers. In order for two servers in separate domains to communicate, a connection document must exist in the PAB. It is required to transfer mail between adjacent domains.

Context Pane   The area of the Notes Window in which a document (such as a Mail Memo) is displayed while creating a response to that document, or a Mail Memo.

Context-sensitive   A term used to describe menus and help screens which change depending on the task or function being performed in the program.

Data directory   The top-level directory in which local Domino databases and templates are stored, along with DESKTOP.DSK files and CLS files. UNIX and OS/2 also store the NOTES.INI file in the data directory. By default, the directory is called DATA and is directly under the Notes or Domino directory.

Data type   The type of data a specific field on a Notes form can contain—for example, text, rich text, numbers, or names.

Database Catalog   A database that lists information about databases on a Domino server, in a group of Domino servers, or in a Domain.

Database library   A database that lists information about selected databases on a workstation or shared databases on a server.

Database Manager In Domino, a person who has been granted Manager access in the database ACL. The manager can edit the ACL and delete the database, as well as perform all database design and edit functions.

Database replica A database created using replication. A database replica has the same ID as the database from which it was created and can exchange information with the original database through replication.

Date/Time field A field defined with the date/time data type. The field can only store data that is entered using date/time formats via user input or formulas.

DDE See *Dynamic Data Exchange*.

Default The setting, direction, or choice made by a program unless intervention is made by the user. Built into an application or program when values or options are necessary for the program to function.

Default Value (for fields) The value displayed in an editable field when a document is first created.

Default value formula A formula that computes a value for a field, requiring no intervention by the user. For example, a default value formula can insert today's date into a field that the user has the option of changing.

Default view The view that is displayed when a database is first opened.

Depositer access Level of security (defined in the Access Control List) that allows users or servers to create documents but not see or edit any documents.

Designer access Level of security (defined in the Access Control List) that allows users or servers to modify the design of a database. Designer Access does not permit changes to the database Access Control List.

Desktop.dsk A file that stores the options selected for the Notes client desktop.

Detach In Domino, to save to a disk drive a copy of a file that appears as an attachment in a Notes document.

Dialog box A box that is displayed on the screen so the user can provide further information when it is required before the system can continue.

Dialog list field A keyword field type that presents a list of choices to the user in the Notes client. This field appears with the entry helper button by default. In a Web client this is presented as a combobox. See also *Combobox field*.

Dial-up A type of connection in which you connect to a server or network using a modem over a telephone line.

Digital speech synthesizer   A device that translates what is on the screen into voice output, used as a way for the blind to get information from the computer screen.

Document   A type of form independent of all other forms. It stands alone. It does not respond to other forms. It is sometimes referred to as a *main document*.

Document ID   See *Notes identification number.*

Domain   In relation to the Internet, the last part of an Internet address (for example, .gov and .com). In networks, a group of connected computers that share the same security system, so a user has to use only one ID and password to access resources within the Domain. In Domino, an Address Book. See also *Domino Directory.*

Domino (also Domino server)   The server component in a Lotus Notes environment.

Domino application server   A Domino server used primarily to provide access to Domino databases for Lotus Notes clients.

Domino database   A container for both data and program code. (Note that this does not match the definition used for Relational Databases, which is a collection of related tables.)

Domino Designer   The software program used by application developers and programmers to create Domino databases.

Domino Directory   The Public Address Book stored on the Domino server containing names and addresses of people and servers in that Domino Domain. This Address Book is accessible to all individuals in the Domain.

Domino Enterprise Server   A Domino Server license type that provides the tools for scaling the Domino Application Server to a wider enterprise, with clustering, load balancing, and failover.

Domino Mail Server   A Domino server license type for a server whose primary use is for mail routing and hosting Notes mail databases.

Dual key encryption   An encryption using two sets of keys: one set for creating and reading digital signatures, and another set for encrypting and decrypting messages.

Dynamic Data Exchange (DDE)   A method of displaying data created in another application so that there is a link to the live data. When the data is displayed in Notes, the information is dynamically updated to reflect what is currently stored in the original application.

ECL   See *Execution Control List.*

Edit mode   The condition in which a document can be modified or created.

Editable field   A field in which the user can enter or change values. The database designer can manipulate user input with formulas such as default value formulas, input translation formulas, or input validation formulas.

Editor access   Level of security (defined in the Access Control List) that allows users or servers to create, read, and edit documents in a database, whether or not they created the original document.

Electronic signature   See *Signature, electronic.*

Email signature   See *Signature, email.*

Embedded element   Design or other objects embedded in forms and pages.

Encryption   The scrambling or encoding of data to make it unreadable. Encrypted data must be decrypted to read it. Encryption and decryption involve the use of keys associated with or assigned by the software. Domino uses both public and private encryption keys and both single and dual key encryption methods.

Enterprise Directory   A highly compressed directory containing entries from multiple Domino Domains. Used in large corporations to facilitate username lookups across Domains. Also used to allow mobile users to maintain a local copy of a corporate-wide address book using minimal disk space.

Execution Control List (ECL)   A list of settings that users control and maintain to enhance the security of workstation data. Accessed through the User Preferences dialog box.

Export   To save a Lotus Notes document or view in a file format other than Notes (.nsf).

Extended accelerator key   Keys used to access bookmarks and task buttons. To view the extended accelerator keys, press and hold down the Alt key.

Extranet   A group of interconnected intranets with extended access usually protected by a firewall. For example, companies in business with each other can form extranets in order to share certain types of information as in the case of a manufacturer and a parts supplier. See also *Intranet.*

Field   An area of a form which can contain a single data type of information, such as numbers, graphics, and rich text.

Field data type   The classification of data a field is designed to accept. Examples of field data types are text, date/time, numbers, rich text, and names.

Field value   The value stored in a field in a saved document.

File Transfer Protocol (FTP)   A protocol designed for transferring large messages (files) between two points on the Internet, providing error-checking functions so that the entire data file arrives intact.

Folder   A container similar to a view into which the user can place documents for later reference. The user can move documents into and out of a folder, whereas a view depends on a formula to determine which documents are displayed.

Folder pane   The workspace area that shows the folders and views available in the opened database.

Form   An item used for collecting and displaying information in a Domino application. Forms can contain subforms, graphics, fields, links, embedded elements, and so forth. Forms are used to create and display documents. There are three types of forms: Document, Response, and Response-to-Response.

Formula   A collection of commands and variables to effect a result. Formulas can be written for numerous events in Domino such as view formulas, input validation, default value, and so forth.

Formula field   Used to populate a subscription list. Subscription lists are used by the Headlines database.

Formula Pop-up Hotspot   The collection of commands and variables (*formula*) that computes the text which appears on screen (*Pop-up*) when a mouse is held over an area of the screen (*Hotspot*).

Frames   One of the panes of a frameset which can contain pages, documents, forms, links, views, and so forth.

Framesets   A collection of frames. Each frame within the frameset can work independently of the other frames.

FTP   See *File Transfer Protocol*.

Full-text index   A series of files containing the indexes to text in a database, allowing Notes to process user search queries.

Full-text search   Search option supporting word and phrase searches of Domino databases as well as advanced searches, such as logical expressions.

GIF   See *Graphical Interchange Format*.

Graphical Interchange Format (GIF)   A graphics file format with widespread use on the Internet. GIF files are compressed graphic files that can be animated and have transparent backgrounds. See also *Joint Photographic Experts Group.*

Graphics   Graphics placed on a form appear in every document that uses that form. Graphics can be converted to imagemaps by adding hotspots.

Group   In Domino, a list of users or servers used for addressing, access control lists, and address books.

Groupware   A loosely defined term which refers to applications that allow groups of people to work together in a collaborative environment. Discussion databases are considered a Groupware application.

Hierarchical   Having a structure with gradations. See also *Hierarchical naming.*

Hierarchical naming   A naming system in which an entity's name includes the names of the entity's antecedents. As used in Notes, your hierarchical name includes at least the name of the organization to which you belong, and can also include the names of subunits within the organization and the country in which you reside. For example: Bob Dobbs/Sales/Stillwater/US. The benefit of hierarchical naming is that it increases security by providing a standard way of distinguishing between people who might otherwise have the same name. Thus Bob Dobbs/Sales/Stillwater is not the same person as Bob Dobbs/Acctg/Stillwater.

Hierarchical view   A view that displays response documents indented   and directly beneath the documents to which they respond.

Home page   The first page that displays when a user visits an Internet or intranet site. The home page of a site usually contains a company logo, a welcome message, and links to the other pages within the site.

Home server   The term used for the Domino server on which your mail database resides.

Hop   A mail stop along the delivery path of routed mail when the recipient's and sender's servers are not directly connected.

Hotkey   The underlined letter in a menu used to select a menu command. Also referred to as *accelerator key.*

Hotspot   An object or specific area on an object that has programming or a link attached to it. Hotspots can be attached to text or graphics. See also *Text Pop-up Hotspot, Action Buttons and Hotspots, Formula Pop-up Hotspot, Button Hotspot,* and *Link Hotspot.*

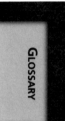

GLOSSARY

HTML   See *Hypertext Markup Language.*

HTTP   See *Hypertext Transfer Protocol.*

Hyperlink   A block of text (usually colored and underlined) or a graphic that represents a connection to another place in a document or a separate document. Clicking the hyperlink opens the document to which it is linked.

Hypertext   Special text contained in a Web page that, when clicked, takes the user to a related Web page. Hypertext often appears as blue underlined text, changing to purple text when clicked.

Hypertext Markup Language (HTML)   A collection of instructions or tags that tell a browser program how to display a document—as in when to bold or italicize. HTML tags typically appear embedded within a document, set apart from the document text by angle brackets.

Hypertext Transfer Protocol (HTTP)   Protocol that defines how HTML files are sent and received via the Internet.

Imagemap   A special kind of graphics object that can contain multiple hotspots linking to other objects or URLs.

IMAP, IMAP4   See *Internet Message Access Protocol.*

Internet Message Access Protocol (IMAP, IMAP4)   A protocol allowing mail clients to access their mail over the Internet or intranet.

Internet Protocol (IP)   The system which defines the "location," or IP address, of the networks that comprise the Internet. See also *Transmission Control Protocol/Internet Protocol.*

Internet Service Provider (ISP)   A company that provides access to the Internet.

Internotes Server   A Domino Server process that retrieves Web pages and stores them in a Server Web Browser database so that users can retrieve the pages to their Personal Web Browser database without having to connect to the Internet.

Intranet   A restricted-access network that shares information intended for internal use within a company, although intranets can span the globe. Similar to the Web, intranet software allows the routing of HTML documents which are read using a Web browser. A major distinction between an intranet and the Web is access control. See also *Extranet.*

ISP   See *Internet Service Provider.*

Java   An interpreted programming language developed by Sun Microsystems. A Java program is delivered in textual, compressed, or tokenized form from an Internet server to a computer. The Java interpreter or *Java virtual machine* (such as the one that comes with Internet Explorer) interprets and executes the program, just as though it were stored on the receiving computer's hard drive. Java makes possible the transmission of logical and often user-tailored content (such as a desktop stock ticker), whereas HTML by contrast is merely a system for the format and display of text and graphics.

Java applets   Small, self-contained applications that can be embedded into forms.

JavaScript   A scripting language that permits access to the Document Object Model (DOM) and runs on both Notes and Web clients.

Joint Photographic Experts Group (JPG, JPEG)   One of two graphics files formats in use on the Internet. See also *GIF*.

JPG, JPEG   See *Joint Photographic Experts Group*.

Keyboard shortcut   A combination of keys that performs a command in lieu of selecting an item from the menu. For example, Ctrl+P is the keyboard shortcut for printing.

Keyword field   A multiple choice field which presents users a list of choices in checkbox, combobox, dialog list, listbox, and radio button format.

Labels   In database design, text accompanying a field which indicates the use or intended contents of the field. By convention field labels are usually positioned to the left or above the field.

LAN   See *Local area network*.

Letterhead   The manner (style) in which your name, date, and time at the top of a mail message.

Library   See *Database library*.

Link   A pointer to a block of data, graphic, or page in an external file or document. On the Web, a link can reference another Web page, a file, or a program, such as a Java program. In Domino, links can open other views, databases, or documents without closing the object containing the link.

Link Hotspot   In Domino, an area which, when clicked, links to other Domino objects or URLs. Link hotspots can be text, graphics, or regions on a graphic object.

Local area network (LAN)   A network that connects a group of computers located within an immediate area, such as the same building. Computers are connected to each other by network cable.

Location document   A document, stored in the Personal Address Book, that contains settings that determine how Notes communicates with Domino servers from a specific location. Useful for working in Notes at a specific location.

Lotus Notes   A groupware product by Lotus Development Corporation consisting of server products and client products. Previous to Release 5 of Lotus Notes, all server and client products were referred to as Notes products. In Release 4.5 of Notes, Lotus Development Corporation renamed the server products *Domino* and the client products maintained the name *Lotus Notes*.

Macro   See *Agent*.

Mail database   A Lotus Notes database in which you send and receive mail. Your mail database is stored on your home server. See also *Outgoing mail database*.

Manager access   A level of security (defined in the Access Control List) that gives all rights to a database, including the right to modify a database Access Control List and delete a database. All other access levels (Designer, Editor, Reader, and so forth) fall under the level of Manager; the Manager has the rights defined in all those other access levels.

MIME   See *Multipurpose Internet Mail Extensions*.

Modem   A piece of hardware, either internal or external, that allows a user to send data via telephone lines.

Multipurpose Internet Mail Extensions (MIME)   An Internet standard that permits data transfer. An Internet browser or Internet mail viewer associates a MIME type with a file type, which gives information about which program should run when the file is opened over the Internet.

Names field   A field of Names data type. It can hold the names of people, servers, and groups.

Navigation buttons   In Notes, browser-like buttons that enable navigation among open database documents or Web pages. Functions include Back, Forward, Stop, Refresh, Search, and Go.

Navigation pane   The left pane of a Notes screen that displays either icons for all views, folders, and agents in a database, or the currently selected navigator.

Navigator   In Notes, a menu made up of hyperlinked rich text, or hotspots. When clicked, the links or hotspots perform certain actions or access other documents. Netscape has a Web browser called Netscape Navigator.

Nested table   Tables that reside within (or inside) other tables.

Network News Transfer Protocol   The protocol of Usenet Newsgroups. Defines how newsgroup lists and articles will be transferred between NNTP servers and between NNTP servers and newsreaders.

Newsgroups   Online discussion groups on the Internet. Messages posted to the newsgroup can be read and responded to by others.

Newsreader   An NNTP client program that allows a user to browse, subscribe to, and unsubscribe from newsgroups, also to read, create, and print newsgroup articles.

NNTP   See *Network News Transfer Protocol.*

No access   In Notes, a database access level. Entities having no access to a database cannot, in general, see or add to the contents of a database or, for that matter, even add a shortcut for the database to their desktops. An exception to this rule is "public" documents. Users assigned "No Access" can still be permitted either to create or to read "public" documents in the database.

Notes client   Software designed for use by Lotus Notes users. Allows the user to access a Domino server, send mail, and browse the Web.

Notes Identification Number   Every element in a Notes database has two unique identification numbers: a universal ID (UNID) and a Notes ID. The UNID is unique across all replicas of a database. The Notes ID is unique within a single copy of the database. An element retains its UNID when it is replicated to another copy of the database but gets a new Note ID in each copy of the database.

NOTES.INI   A text file that consists of a list of variables and their values, each recorded on a separate line in the form *variable=value*. Notes and Domino refer to the settings in NOTES.INI when loading into memory and periodically while they are running to determine how to do various things.

Number field   In Notes, a field designated to hold a numerical value.

Operands   In programming, the data that will be "operated on" by the operator.

Operators   The "verbs" in a formula. In programming, operators manipulate data or perform certain operations (add, subtract, multiply, and so on) on operands. In "2 + 2" the + is the operator, the 2s are the operands.

Outgoing mail database   A Notes database that temporarily stores mail while it is en route to its final destination. Unlike most Notes databases, it does not use the NSF file extension. Rather, its filename is mail.box or, if in a Domino server uses multiple outgoing mail databases, mail*n*.box (where *n* is an integer).

Pages   In Web browsers, individual HTML documents that can display text, links to other documents, forms, and graphics.

Pane   A portion of a window, usually divided from the remainder of the window by a movable border.

Parent document   In Domino, a document from which information is derived or inherited by another document, such as a response document. All response and response-to-response documents have a parent document.

Passthru server   A Domino server used to receive incoming calls from mobile Notes users, authenticate those users, and allow them to access and authenticate with target servers to which they are not directly connected.

Permanent pen   A toggle feature of the Lotus Notes client software that allows users to enter text in rich text fields using a font or font color different from the default font, without affecting the default font settings.

Personal Address Book   A database designed for each Notes user which contains contact information entered by that user and which is protected by the user's password and Notes ID.

POP3   See *Post Office Protocol Version 3.*

Post Office Protocol Version 3 (POP3)   An Internet protocol that defines a standard method for post office servers and mail users to communicate with each other so that the users can retrieve from the servers any mail waiting for them there.

Preview Pane   A window in which you view documents selected in the view pane without opening those documents. This pane is sizable (adjustable).

Private folder   A folder that users can create for their own, exclusive use.

Private key   The secret half of the public/private key pair that every Notes certifier, user, and server has. It is stored in the Notes ID file. Because it is private and unique to its owner, the private key makes possible Notes authentication, electronic signature, and mail encryption. See also *public key.*

Private view   In Notes, a password protected view of Notes documents that is accessible only to the user who created it. Sometimes also known as a *personal view.*

Properties   Settings that control the behavior or appearance of Notes elements, documents, or databases.

Protocol   In networking, the established rules that servers and applications follow in order to communicate across networks. For example, the Internet Protocol (IP) describes how two computers will connect and exchange information over the Internet. FTP and HTTP are also examples of protocols.

Proxy server   Intermediary servers, providing controlled access through a firewall. Instead of allowing direct connections, proxy servers connect to the intended destination and handle data transfers.

Public key   The public half of the public/private key pair that every Notes certifier, server, and user has. Your public key is unique to you and the certificates in your ID file attest to that fact. You publish your public key in the Domino Directory so that others can use it to encrypt documents that they want to send you and to decrypt your signature on documents you send them.

Pull-down menu   A list of related commands or actions that expand when activated by the mouse or keyboard.

Radio button   Small round checkboxes that allow users to indicate their choice of items in a list.

Read access list   A list of authorized readers of a document or of documents created using a given form. Reader access lists can be defined in two places, either on the Security pane of Form and Document Properties boxes or in fields of Readers data type in forms and documents.

Read marks   See *Unread marks*.

Reader access   In the Access Control List of a database, the access level that allows users to read the contents of the database.

Readers field   In Notes, the readers field contains a list of individuals and groups who will be allowed to read the document in question.

Replicator   A Domino server task that replicates databases between servers.

Replicator page   The page in Notes where the user manages the replication process.

Role   Database-specific group or variable created to simplify the maintenance of a database. Roles allow a database manager to define who has access to restricted fields, documents, forms, and views without having to change the design of the database.

Screen reader   A device that reads what is displayed on the computer screen. See *Digital speech synthesizer*.

Search engine   A special program that allows users to find information on the Internet by typing in a keyword or phrase. The search engine searches the Internet for pages containing the keyword or phrase. The search engine then returns a list of Web addresses to the browser which are active links to pages on which the keyword or phrase was found.

Sections   Collapsible areas of a document that are helpful in managing large documents. When collapsed, sections display one line of information when expanded sections reveal their entire contents.

Serif/sans serif   Serifs are the short, horizontal bars at the tops and bottoms of text characters. If a typeface has serifs, it is known as a serif typeface or *serif font*. If it does not have serifs, it's known as a *sans serif font*.

Server   A computer whose purpose is to store files or programs and provide file, program, and resource access to clients.

Shared Field   A special kind of Notes field that exists independently of any form and can be reused on multiple Notes forms. Shared fields streamline the Notes application development process by eliminating the need to re-create the same field in multiple forms.

Shared views   Views that are public and accessible to multiple users.

Shared, Private on First Use View   A view that is shared or private on the First Use, but reverts to another behavior (private or shared) on subsequent uses.

Shortcut keystroke   A keystroke or combination of keystrokes that allow a task to be performed without using a mouse.

Sibling document   In a hierarchical view or folder, all documents at a given level under a parent document are "siblings" of each other.

Sign   The act of attaching an electronic signature to a document. The signature assures that the document originated with the signing party and that the signed document is unaltered since signed.

Signature, electronic   An encryption method that allows Notes users to verify the identity of the author of a document or of a section in a document. At times, Domino automatically applies signatures to documents; other times, users can manually apply signatures.

Signature, email   Text or object appended to the end of a mail message used in the way you would close a letter with your handwritten signature. Signatures can contain a name, email address, phone number, postal address, and other pertinent information.

Simple Mail Transfer Protocol (SMTP)   The Internet's mail transfer protocol.

SmartIcons   Lotus' name for icons located on the Notes client and Designer software toolbars.

SMTP   See *Simple Mail Transfer Protocol.*

Stacked icon   In releases of Notes prior to R5, a database icon that represents more than one replica of a database. A stacked database icon has a small button in its upper-right corner that, when clicked, displays a list of the represented replicas.

Static text   The unchanging text on a form. The title, field labels, and so on.

Subform   A form fragment, stored as a separate design element, that becomes part of another form when the other form is called into use. Subforms can appear in forms based on conditions (formulas). For example, if a user places an *X* in a field indicating she is a first-time visitor to your site, a subform opens in the current form asking her to supply registration information.

Subscription   A Web page, channel, or Active Desktop item whose information is updated on a computer at preset intervals determined by the user. Subscriptions also apply to newsgroups.

Surfing   Browsing the Internet, similar to browsing or "surfing" channels on cable TV.

System Administrator   The person who oversees and manages a network. The administrator can grant a user permission to access certain files and resources, troubleshoot problems with the network, and control each computer on the network. The administrator has the ability to track each user's activities on the network.

TCP/IP   See *Transmission Control Protocol/Internet Protocol.*

Template   A Notes database that usually contains only design elements and is intended to provide the starting design of a production database.

Text constants   A fixed value (text) that does not change.

Text field   In a Notes form, a field that can hold and display text. Rich text fields in Notes can hold attachments, graphics, and code in addition to plain text.

Text Pop-up Hotspot   Text that appears when a user holds their mouse over or clicks on a specially marked or highlighted object. Text pop-ups are used to provide additional information to the user about the object. Text pop-ups are popular for parenthetical or extraneous information. See also *Link Hotspot, Button Hotspot, Formula Pop-up Hotspot,* and *Action Buttons and Hotspots.*

Transmission Control Protocol/Internet Protocol (TCP/IP) The protocol that defines how data should be sent from point to point over the Internet. Following TCP protocol, data is broken into packets which are flushed through the Internet in the general direction of their recipient. There, they are collected and reorganized into their original sequence. Because TCP and IP protocols work hand-in-hand, people refer to them together as TCP/IP.

Twistie The name of icon which, when clicked, expands and collapses a Domino document section.

UI See *User interface.*

Uniform resource locator (URL) A pointer to the location of an object, usually the address of an Internet resource. URLs conform to a standard syntax which generally looks as follows:

```
http://www.lotus.com
```

Unread marks Characters (stars) in a Domino database that indicate when a document has not been read. Unread documents also appear in red text in a view. When documents have been read, the unread marks disappear and the document text appears in black in a view.

URL See *Uniform resource locator.*

User ID A file that uniquely identifies every user and server to Lotus Notes and Domino.

User interface (UI) The onscreen environment that gives the user the ability to control and view the actions of an application.

Using This Database document A special document that describes how a database works. The document can be viewed from the Help menu and it provides users with instructions on using the database.

View In Notes, the method for grouping and sorting documents for display in table format, like a table of contents. Documents are selected for views based on their characteristics (for example, Field contents, Subject, Name, Date, and so on).

WAN See *Wide area network.*

Web See *World Wide Web.*

Welcome page The opening screen in the Lotus Notes client. This page is customizable, contains a search bar, and links to major tasks such as sending mail and using the calendar.

Wide area network (WAN)   A network (usually private to a single company) that connects users and network components spread over a large geographical region.

Window tab   A tabbed page that represents an open window in Notes. Used to switch back and forth between open windows.

Workgroup   A group of people working together and sharing computer data, often over a company intranet.

Workstation   A computer used for work by an individual. Workstations can be stand-alone computers or networked computers.

World Wide Web (or Web)   A component of the Internet. It is a collection of HTML documents accessible through the Internet.

GLOSSARY

INDEX

O